Cultural Anthropology

Cultural Anthropology

Tribes, States, and the Global System

Fifth Edition

JOHN H. BODLEY

ALTAMIRA
PRESS

A Division of

ROWMAN & LITTLEFIELD PUBLISHERS, INC.

Lanham • New York • Toronto • Plymouth, UK

Published by AltaMira Press
A division of Rowman & Littlefield Publishers, Inc.
A wholly owned subsidiary of The Rowman & Littlefield Publishing Group, Inc.
4501 Forbes Boulevard, Suite 200, Lanham, Maryland 20706
http://www.altamirapress.com

Estover Road, Plymouth PL6 7PY, United Kingdom

British Library Cataloguing in Publication Information Available

Library of Congress Cataloging-in-Publication Data

Bodley, John H.
  Cultural anthropology : tribes, states, and the global system / John H. Bodley. — 5th ed.
    p. cm.
  ISBN 978-0-7591-1865-2 (cloth : alk. paper) — ISBN 978-0-7591-1866-9 (pbk. : alk.
paper) — ISBN 978-0-7591-1867-6 (electronic)
  1. Ethnology. I. Title.
  GN316.B63 2011
  305.8—dc22

                                                                              2010048588

♾™ The paper used in this publication meets the minimum requirements of
American National Standard for Information Sciences—Permanence of Paper for
Printed Library Materials, ANSI/NISO Z39.48-1992.

Printed in the United States of America

Contents

Preface

Given the interconnections among cultural groups on the current world stage (and the rapidity with which those dynamics change), it is imperative that we learn as much as we can about world culture, history, and geography in order to lead informed, productive lives. What better way to start than by applying the traditional methods of anthropology to a modern view of the world? With this as my underlying goal, I've presented the basic concepts of cultural anthropology in this introductory text by comparing cultures of increasing scale and focusing on universal human concerns. The end result, I hope, is a stimulating, culturally integrated approach to the discipline.

Throughout the text, I've challenged students to consider the big questions about the nature of cultural systems: How are cultures structured to satisfy basic human needs? What is it like to be human under different cultural conditions? Are race, language, and environment determinants of culture? Are materialist explanations more useful than ideological ones? What are the major turning points in human history?

The culture-scale perspective highlights the unique problems of the present world system. Roughly one-third of the text is devoted to issues of current concern, especially the problem of inequality and how to make our world sustainable. A wide range of global humanitarian issues such as ethnocide, genocide, and ecocide also are considered, along with a variety of more narrow theoretical and methodological issues. My hope is that understanding how tribes, states, and global systems work and how they differ might help citizens design a more secure and equitable world.

PERSONAL PROLOGUE:
A CHALLENGE TO THE READER

I intend this book to be a provocative alternative to bland, topically arranged, encyclopedic texts. Anthropology is a subversive science. This book provides students with anthropological tools to question the status quo and its representation of the world. Readers are invited to ask what's going on and who's in charge in the world and in their own culture. This book has a viewpoint. It offers a radical anthropological critique of firmly held cultural beliefs and practices about growth and progress that threaten the well-being and continued survival of humanity in the twenty-first century. I invite students to explore the relationship between growth, scale, and power throughout human history and prehistory. I suggest that our most serious human problems are caused by a collective social failure to restrain the natural individual drive to increase personal social power at the expense of others. Given the opportunity, unrestrained aggrandizing individuals will use culture to transform society to benefit themselves and their direct descendants. Elites will alter people's perceptions of reality. They will manipulate cosmologies and technologies to create the belief that elite-directed growth is natural and inevitable, even though it disproportionately concentrates social power and makes everyone else pay the costs.

Throughout history, growth has intensified human problems. These are problems of growth in scale, power, and complexity. Growth first became a problem 7,000 years ago when a few aggrandizing individuals took advantage of local crises created by global climate change at the end of the Ice Age and were able to centralize social power in the first chiefdoms. Power elites then promoted growth to increase their power, setting off cycles of growth, cultural transformation, and crises, culminating in the creation of a global commercial world dominated by U.S. elites. It is possible that further growth beyond the present threshold may prove unsustainable. The global evidence of cultural crisis is overwhelming: billions of people are impoverished, malnourished, and unhealthy; economic and political systems are in turmoil; nature is under siege; and human activities are changing global climate in ways that could be catastrophic. Millions of people are immigrants and refugees fleeing intolerable conditions. Even the richest and most powerful nation is unable to guarantee employment, education, basic health care, and keep the lights on. We all need to question how this state of human affairs came to be and to concentrate our efforts on creating a better future.

ORGANIZATION OF THE BOOK

To demonstrate the vitality of fieldwork and to generate enthusiasm for the discipline, chapter 1 begins with a personal account of my fieldwork with the Asháninka of Amazonia. Not only does it explain why I was inspired to approach anthropology from a humanistic, culture-scale perspective, but it also introduces the field methods employed by cultural anthropologists. Ensuing chapters examine a representative sample of cultures in sufficient depth to maintain cultural context and to provide students with a sound understanding of the world's major cultural areas and dominant civilizations.

The book is designed to provide balanced coverage of three dramatically different cultural worlds. After its introduction to doing fieldwork, part I examines domestic-scale, autonomous cultures in the tribal world. Part II presents politically organized, class-based civilizations and ancient empires in the imperial world, and part III surveys global, industrial, market-based civilizations in the commercial world. Scale is used as an organizing principle to provide a basis for comparison; however, I've avoided the implicit value judgments that are part of popular ideas about evolutionary progress. The following universal issues about the human conditions are explored from a comparative, anthropological perspective: What is "natural" about humans? What is "cultural" about humans? Which human inequalities are natural? Which are cultural? Is population growth natural or cultural? Is economic growth natural or cultural? What are the human costs and benefits of socioeconomic growth? The ethnographic material will focus on the influence of culture scale and the distribution of social power on such basic matters as quality of life, domestic organization, intergroup relations, and relationship to the environment. The causes and consequences of changes in culture scale and the role of elite decision makers are central themes.

Ethnographic case studies are used to describe the functional interconnections between the material bases and the social and ideological systems of representative cultures in each of the three cultural worlds. The cultures selected as case studies are those that are best described in ethnographic films and monographs, and they are the subject of abundant analytical materials. Australian Aborigines, Amazonian villagers, and East African pastoralists represent tribal cultures and are treated in separate chapters. Politically centralized cultures are represented by Pacific Island chiefdoms and the ancient and modern great civilizations of Mesopotamia, the Inca, China, Islam, and Hindu India. The commercial cultures of the United States, the British empire, contemporary indigenous peoples, and the rural peasantry are examined as part of the global commercial system. The text shows cultures in depth—as adapting, integrated systems—and as part of regional, continental, and global systems, as appropriate.

Acknowledgments

THE FIFTH EDITION OF THIS BOOK WAS A TWO-YEAR PROJECT that began in spring 2008 at the suggestion of the late Alan McClare, who was then executive editor of Rowman & Littlefield. I was pleased to move to AltaMira Press because it is in line with my preferences for smaller publishers, and I regret that Alan was not able to see the project through to completion. I am grateful to executive editor Wendi Schnaufer and Marissa Parks for taking over with this project. Special thanks also to those who kindly provided illustrations for this edition, especially Victor Bloomfield at the University of Minnesota, Christopher B. Donnan at the University of California at Los Angeles, Gregory A. Keoleian at the University of Michigan, and my brother Thomas M. Bodley in Singapore.

This book began as a one-page outline in the spring of 1981, and over the years it has benefited greatly from discussions with my colleagues and suggestions from numerous readers. I'm very grateful to all who offered me advice and support.

I'd like to thank especially Jan Beatty, Gerald Berreman, Geoffrey Gamble, and Thomas Headland, who wrote in support of my sabbatical leave from Washington State University in 1990, which enabled me to complete much of the primary research and writing in one concentrated effort. In July 1991, I made the first public presentation of the culture-scale approach in a paper titled "Indigenous Peoples vs. the State: A Culture Scale Approach," which I gave at a conference called "Indigenous People in Remote Regions: A Global Perspective," organized by historian Ken Coates at the University of Victoria, British Columbia.

My students and colleagues at Washington State University who listened to my ideas and offered suggestions and materials were particularly helpful; I'd like to thank Robert Ackerman, Diana Ames-Marshall, Michael Blair, Brenda Bowser, Mark Collard, Ben Colombi, Mark Fleisher, Lee Freese, Chris Harris, Fekri Hassan, Christa Herrygers, Barry Hewlett, Barry Hicks, Michael Kemery, Tim Kohler, Grover Krantz, William Lipe, Robert Littlewood, William Lyons, Jeannette Mageo, Nancy McKee, Peter J. Mehringer Jr., Frank Myka, John Patton, Mark Pubols, Margaret Reed, Vanessa Ross, Allan Smith, Linda Stone, Matt Wanamaker, Brad Wazaney, and Troy Wilson. Special thanks also to Shila Baksi for help with Sanskrit pronunciation and Xianghong Feng for help with Chinese pronunciation.

At the risk of omitting someone, I also want to thank those who provided me with materials that found their way into the book: Mary Abascal-Hildebrand, Clifford Behrens, Diane Bell, Gerald D. Berreman, Jean-Pierre Bocquet-Appel, Cecil H. Brown, Stephen B. Brush, John W. Burton, Gudren Dahl, Shelton H. Davis, Paul L. Doughty, Nancy M. Flowers, Richard A. Gould, Brian Hayden, Thomas Headland, Howard M. Hecker, L. R. Hiatt, Arthur Hippler, Betty Meehan, Peter G. Roe, Nicholas Thomas, Norman B. Tindale, and Gerald Weiss.

For the second edition, I owe special thanks to Bill Lipe and Linda Stone in my department for directing me to new material on the global culture. Also thanks to Barry Hicks of the Health Research and Education Center, Washington State University, Spokane, for assistance with my state- and county-level research. Kevin Norris in the Information Systems Department of Spokane County, Washington, provided me with data on Spokane County land ownership. Zoltan Porga, system analyst, and Gilbert A. Pierson, Information Technology, at Washington State University, guided me through the intricacies of SAS. The staff in my department, especially LeAnn Couch and Joan Pubols, provided important support as I served as department chair while preparing this revision.

Special thanks to Kevin Witt, sponsoring editor for anthropology at McGraw-Hill Higher Education, for directing the fourth edition, and to my development editor, Gabrielle Goodman White, for her painstaking help in making the text more useful for students. Thanks also to the rest of the book team at McGraw-Hill who contributed to this edition: marketing manager Dan Loch, editorial coordinator Kathleen Cowan, project manager Roger Geissler, designer Susan Breitbard, cover designer Violeta Diaz, media producer Shannon Gattens, and supplements producer Marc Mattson.

I am grateful to the reviewers of the all editions of this book whose thoughtful comments contributed much:

FOURTH EDITION REVIEWERS

Scott E. Antes, Northern Arizona University; Jeffrey Cohen, Pennsylvania State Univesity; Rebecca Cramer, Johnson County Community College; Jerry Hanson, College of Lake County; Sandra L. Orellana, California State University.

THIRD EDITION REVIEWERS

Jeffrey H. Cohen, Texas A&M University; Robert Dirks, Illinois State University; Michael P. Freedman, Syracuse University; Susan A. Johnston, University of Rhode Island; Adrian S. Novotny, Long Beach City College; and Lars Rodseth, University of Utah.

SECOND EDITION REVIEWERS

James Armstrong, State University of New York, Plattsburgh; Diane Baxter, George Washington University; Michael P. Freedman, Syracuse University; Josiah M. Heyman, Michigan Technological University; David T. Hughes, Wichita State University; Ronald R. McIrvin, University of North Carolina, Greensboro; David McMahon, Saint Francis College; Richard K. Reed, Trinity University; and William Stuart, University of Maryland, College Park.

FIRST EDITION REVIEWERS

Gerald D. Berreman, University of California, Berkeley; Peter J. Bertocci, Oakland University; Daniel L. Boxberger, Western Washington University; Jill Brody, Louisiana State University; Thomas E. Durbin, California State University, Stanislaus; James E. Eder, Arizona State University; James F. Garber, Southwest Texas State University; James W. Hamilton, University of Missouri, Columbia; Patricia Lyons Johnson, Pennsylvania State University; Arthur C. Lehmann, California State University, Chico; Fran Markowitz, DePaul University; David McCurdy, Macalester College; Michael D. Olien, University of Georgia; Mary Kay Gilliland Olsen, Pima Community College and University of Arizona; Aaron Podolefsky, University of Northern Iowa; Scott Rushforth, New Mexico State University; and Daniel J. Yakes, Muskegon Community College.

Finally, I'd especially like to thank Kathi, Brett, and Antonie for their encouragement and patience. Kathi helped create the index and offered her support throughout the entire project. We walked together through every edition.

Part One

THE TRIBAL WORLD:
THE WORLD BEFORE THE STATE

MOST OF HUMAN EXISTENCE HAS BEEN IN THE TRIBAL WORLD. With small societies living in an uncrowded world and a minimum of social inequality except for natural differences of age and gender, tribal people could enjoy a maximum of human freedom. People living in the tribal world were able to make their first priority the satisfaction of their individual self-interest in maintaining and reproducing successful households. Self-interest was easily compatible with the interests of society. Because tribal societies typically contained fewer than 2,000 persons, there was no need for government. At birth all tribal people received a personal estate that guaranteed them access to all the natural, social, and cultural wealth needed to make a successful living. Everyone shared natural resources and the goods that they produced, while at the same time maintaining clear property rights. Global population remained below 100 million and because there was little incentive to increase production, tribal societies could generally maintain a sustainable relationship with their natural resources and ecosystems. Tribal lifestyles promoted good health, and generally low population densities minimized the occurrence of communicable disease. Conflict certainly occurred, both within and between groups, and feuds were sometimes difficult to contain, but on balance life in the tribal world was probably good.

The following two chapters describe three culture areas that are representative of the tribal world: aboriginal Australia, Amazonia, and the East African pastoral zone. Each area includes a brief description of the natural ecosystem, how people came to be living there, and some of the details of making a living. There are descriptions of daily life in tribal households, kinship relations, relations between men and women, and beliefs and practices related to the supernatural. Chapter 5 examines how outsiders have evaluated the quality of life in the tribal world and offers an objective assessment of its human benefits.

CHAPTER 1

Culture: A Scale and Power Perspective

Figure 1.0. Kathleen Bodley showing Asháninka women how to use a fingernail file.

PRONUNCIATION GUIDE

Peruvian place names and Asháninka words are written using Spanish orthography. Their approximate pronunciations for English speakers are as follows:

Key
 a = *a* in f*a*ther
 o = *o* in g*o*
 ay = *ay* in d*ay*
 ee = *ee* in b*ee*t
 oo = *oo* in f*oo*d
 h = *h* in *h*at
 • = Syllable division / = Stress
 Asháninka = [a • sha / neen • ka]
 Chonkiri = [Chon / kee • ree]
 cushma = [coosh / ma]
 Gran Pajonal = [Gran • pa / ho • nal]
 Obenteni = [O • bayn • tay / nee]

LEARNING OBJECTIVES

After studying this chapter you should be able to do the following:

1. Describe what cultural anthropologists do, what their goals are, and what their principal methods of field research are. Explain why anthropology is useful.
2. Describe the different aspects, features, and functions of culture.
3. Differentiate between the biological and cultural aspects of human beings, explaining how individual self-interest shapes culture.
4. Compare and contrast inside and outside views of culture and explain how each relates to the problem of observer bias. Explain why ethnocentrism is a problem.
5. Distinguish among the three functionally interconnected aspects of all cultural systems:

3

superstructure, structure, and infrastructure, in relation to the mental, behavioral, and material aspects of culture. Explain why these distinctions are useful.

6. Distinguish among the three cultural worlds: tribal, imperial, and commercial, identifying the most important cultural processes at work in each.

7. Discuss the relationship between scale of society and organization of social power.

8. Explain how the concept of the "good life" can be used to evaluate cultures.

Cultural anthropology can help you understand culture's contribution to the security and well-being of individual humans and to humanity as a whole. To facilitate that objective this book sorts the world's historically known and contemporary sociocultural systems into three "worlds" of increasing scale and complexity: (1) tribal, (2) imperial, and (3) commercial. The following chapters examine representative cultures from each world in depth to illustrate and analyze the diverse ways people living in sociocultural systems of different scale relate to one another and to the natural environment. The cultural world is now so complex and people are so interconnected and interdependent that cultural understanding has become an essential survival skill. Cultural understanding matters because culture is a tool that people use to exercise power over other people and solve human problems. Anthropological description and analysis can reveal the internal meanings and practical utility of cultural beliefs and practices that might seem irrational to an outsider. An anthropological view of culture can also help people understand their own culture in new ways that can reveal new possibilities for improvement. Many small sociocultural systems successfully foster human well-being but are little known to outsiders. Such ways of life certainly deserve our respect and tolerance, but they may also contain crucial human lessons that we can learn from. Anthropological analysis can also identify cultural practices that people might choose to modify because they cause war, poverty, disease, and environmental degradation.

Anthropology is the most holistic academic discipline. Cultural anthropologists need to be both scientists and humanists, because they examine any and all aspects of what people think, make, and do everywhere in the world, from the beginning of time into the future. Anthropologists must consider both the material and the symbolic meanings that people use to maintain and reproduce themselves and their culture. At the same time anthropologists need the insights

about nature that come from the physical and biological sciences.

The first part of this chapter draws on my field experiences in South America to show what it is like to actually do anthropology and to explain why I use culture scale as an organizing principle. The chapter then introduces the key concepts of culture and ethnocentrism and illustrates how culture scale, growth, and process will be used throughout the book. Here, we review some major turning points in human history and demonstrate that anthropology has enormous practical significance and is directly concerned with the great public issues of our time.

DOING ANTHROPOLOGY

Adventures in the Field

Doing cultural anthropology is a continuous adventure. It means exploring the unknown to gain a better understanding of other peoples and cultures. Such understanding can be obtained indirectly from books and class work, but it is most exciting and vivid when it comes directly from real-life experiences—sometimes in unexpected ways. For example, my richest understanding of native Amazonian political leadership was gained during a two-day encounter with Chonkiri, a proud and independent Asháninka **bigman,**[*] who lived with his small band in the rugged foothills of the Andes along the headwaters of the Peruvian Amazon (see figure 1.1). Bigman leadership is based entirely on force of personality, and Chonkiri displayed this quality admirably (see figure 1.2).

In 1969, my wife, Kathleen, and I were exploring the remote interior of the Asháninka homeland to assess the living conditions of those Asháninka still maintaining a self-sufficient way of life. A bush pilot flew us to Obenteni, a tiny frontier outpost in the Gran Pajonal, five days by mule trail from the nearest truck road and fifty air miles from the nearest town. At that time the Gran Pajonal was an unmapped maze of savanna-covered ridges and deep forested canyons. It was a vast wilderness, inhabited by fiercely independent Asháninka.

After a hard day's walk from Obenteni, we spotted a column of four Asháninka men on the skyline of an intersecting ridge. Carrying bows and arrows and shotguns, they were an awe-inspiring sight in their long brown cotton robes (*cushmas*) and bright red face paint. They approached briskly and then halted astride

---

[*] Key terms are set in bold type and are defined at the end of the chapter.

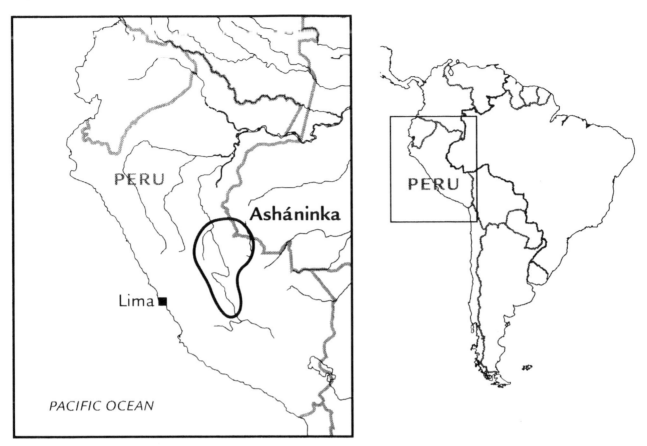

Figure 1.1. Map of the territory of the Asháninka in the Peruvian Amazon.

Figure 1.2. Chonkiri, the Asháninka bigman, at home—on the left, sitting on a beer trough.

the trail a few paces in front of us. With potentially hostile strangers meeting, there was fear and uncertainty on both sides. But the Asháninka were armed and on their home ground, so they controlled the situation. Their leader Chonkiri, obviously a traditional bigman, stepped forward, struck a defiant pose, and shouted a tirade of angry questions at me. The same scene might have greeted the first European explorers to enter Asháninka territory in 1673.

Chonkiri demanded to know where we were going, why we had come, and whether we were bringing sickness. These were legitimate questions, and although I knew his hostile manner was a formal ritual, I was still uneasy because the Pajonal Asháninka had every reason to resent outsiders. Recent measles epidemics had killed many Asháninka, and colonists and missionaries were appearing in ever greater numbers. In isolated areas such as this, Asháninka often fled at the approach of strangers. However, Chonkiri betrayed no fear. He was playing the role of a powerful and supremely self-confident bigman.

Satisfied with my answers, Chonkiri became a generous host (see figure 1.3). He led us to his house and offered his hospitality—cooked manioc and taro tubers along with handfuls of live ants, which he and his sons had just collected. (I knew that insects were an important food throughout the Pajonal, because game was scarce, but I was amazed to see children sorting through heaps of corn husks to extract fat, inch-long white grubs and pop them, still wiggling, into their mouths.)

After dinner, Chonkiri and his well-armed men followed us back to our camp. They were eager to see what we had brought, and Chonkiri insisted that we unload our backpacks for his inspection (see figure 1.4). Smiling broadly, he immediately took possession of the box of shotgun shells that I had tucked into my pack for trading purposes.

"These are mine!" he announced, handing the shells out one at a time to his men. I nodded my approval, hoping that he would be satisfied with such a lavish gift but feeling more and more uneasy at his brashness.

Figure 1.3. Women and children in Chonkiri's group.

Figure 1.4. Chonkiri, the Asháninka bigman, seated, investigating the contents of my backpack. The ears of corn in the left foreground are his reciprocal gift. The boy in shirt and pants is the son of my Asháninka field assistant.

The next morning, Chonkiri returned with a gift basket of corn and bananas. This was simple sharing, giving and receiving, with no monetary scorekeeping. Intellectually, I recognized his gesture as a textbook example of **generalized reciprocity** in a **nonmarket economy**. His generosity reminded me that yesterday Chonkiri had behaved like a tribal bigman by giving away things, even if they were my things.

My instinctive distrust of Chonkiri's real motives was immediately justified. With no further preliminaries, he began to root through our possessions, snatching up whatever he wanted—clothing, trade goods, medical supplies, food, and utensils. In my culture, this was armed robbery, and we were outnumbered, unarmed, and virtually defenseless. An earlier warning that some Pajonal bigmen were killers suddenly flashed to mind, and I graciously allowed Chonkiri's followers, including his sons, to share my entire assortment of little mirrors and all the rest of my trade goods, even though this would leave me in an awkward position (see figure 1.5).

Chonkiri betrayed his own nervousness when he ripped open a box of unexposed film and started to unreel it, but dropped it with a start when Kathleen blurted, "Stop!" He quickly regained his composure, and his boisterous demands soon became so outra-geous that we were forced to call his bluff. He was turning our encounter into a test of will. First, he demanded the hunting knife that Kathleen wore in a sheath on her belt. She refused, insisting that it belonged to her father. Becoming frustrated, Chonkiri picked up my *cushma*, which I used as my only blanket, announcing loudly that it was newer than his and that he intended to take it. When I said "No!" he flung it to the ground, angrily stomping his feet in a display of temper befitting a true bigman. I cautiously assumed that this outburst was for show and would not escalate to violence.

I had a general understanding of the rules. Normally, one was expected to show generosity by giving away anything that was asked for, but now, clearly, Chonkiri was asking for too much. He was showing his bigman status by pushing the limits. I was obliged to refuse his request with no show of fear, although I had no idea how the game would end. The final test came when Chonkiri appropriated the fat roll of cash (fifty *Sole* bills worth approximately two dollars each) hidden in my pack. He triumphantly peeled off the bills and handed them out to his men. Using unmistakable gestures, I responded with my most emphatic "No!" If I had not shown personal strength at that moment, it would have been a humiliating, perhaps

Figure 1.5. Chonkiri's sons eagerly snatching up all of my trade goods.

even dangerous, defeat. To my considerable relief, he promptly collected the money and restored it to my pack. Chonkiri and I had reached an understanding based on mutual respect. In this situation, familiarity with the culture was as important as courage. I realized that Chonkiri's bravado and bluster betrayed his personal vulnerability as a bigman. If he failed to command the respect of his followers, they could simply walk away. A bigman had no means of coercing loyalty in a culture in which every household could be economically self-sufficient.

After our standoff, Chonkiri became the generous host again. He gave us a grand tour of his house and garden and provided one of his sons to serve as a trail guide. However, he continued to emphasize his dominance by firmly kicking aside Kathleen when she sat on the overturned beer trough that he wanted to occupy. I chose not to consider that gesture a personal affront, but it helped me decide that we would cut short our visit. We parted on friendly terms.

This episode gives a brief glimpse into the daily politics in an autonomous *tribal culture* beyond the reach of government control. However, the apparent isolation was illusory, for Chonkiri and his band were part of the global market economy, even though its direct influence was slight. Several of Chonkiri's men were wearing factory-made pants under their *cushmas*. There were steel axes and metal pots lying about. Obenteni had been a Franciscan mission since the 1930s, and the entire region had been briefly missionized in the eighteenth century. Chonkiri's house was located near an abandoned cattle ranch that three years earlier had served as a temporary base for Marxist guerrillas. Nevertheless, we were inspired to witness the vitality and autonomy of Asháninka culture after three centuries of European pressure.

Anthropological Research in Amazonia

During my first visit to the Peruvian Amazon in 1964, my experience with the Asháninka led me to question many fundamental assumptions about the place of tribal cultures in the contemporary world. I developed a profound respect for the Asháninka and their ability to live so well and so self-sufficiently in their rain forest environment. I also recognized that even though the Asháninka were one of the largest indigenous groups in the entire Amazon basin, outsiders seeking to exploit Asháninka resources were threatening their independence and their culture. I learned that although some Asháninka were avoiding all contacts with the colonists who were invading their

territory, others were attempting to adjust to their changing circumstances by establishing economic relationships with the intruders.

According to conventional anthropological theory, the Asháninka were undergoing rapid **acculturation**, and their culture would soon disappear as Asháninka society was absorbed into the dominant Peruvian national society. I was disturbed by the obvious negative aspects of this process and wanted to learn how their increasing involvement with the global system was affecting the Asháninka and Asháninka culture. My knowledge of the long history of Asháninka resistance to foreign intrusion convinced me that, contrary to popular wisdom, there was nothing inevitable about acculturation. Furthermore, the neutral term *acculturation* seemed to disguise the harsh fact that the Asháninka were being forcibly conquered and dispossessed. This did not seem to be a natural process and was perhaps neither fair nor beneficial. But no one had gone to the trouble of asking the questions that would illuminate the process. I hoped that my research findings would lead to new government policies that would allow the Asháninka and similar peoples to maintain their independent lifestyle.

Altogether I spent some fifteen months working on this problem on three separate visits to Peru over a five-year period. I wanted to understand how specific changes in Asháninka economic adaptation were reflected in changes in their society. I collected most of my data by directly observing and participating in the daily life of Asháninka settlements. This basic anthropological field method, called **participant observation**, involves total immersion in the alien culture and a suspension of one's own cultural judgments about appropriate behavior. However, the participant observer never loses his or her own cultural identity and can never become a full member of the other culture. I never pretended to be an Asháninka, although I lived in their houses, studied their language, shared their food and drink, accompanied them to their gardens and on foraging expeditions, and listened to their nightly stories and songs. This allowed me to *see* Asháninka economy and society in ways that would never have been possible if I had remained a complete outsider. Participant observation also generates empathy and respect for the other culture, especially when it is used as a method of learning rather than as a means to induce others to change their way of life.

Effective participant observation is combined with the **ethnographic method**. That is, the anthropologist observes everyday activities and asks informal questions, often working closely with a few **key informants** rather than relying entirely on formal interviews or impersonal survey questionnaires. The key informant may be one's host in the community or a hired guide, translator, or teacher. Because cultures are integrated in complex, often unexpected ways, at first I could not be sure which Asháninka activities had economic or social implications. Thus, it was critical that I observe with an open mind and record as much as possible. I kept a daily journal in which I recorded all my observations and interviews with informants. Even the most obscure observations might have eventually proved useful. For example, it turned out that knowing the native names of the palm trees used for roof thatch became a clue to the intensity with which forest resources were being used in a given area.

Anthropologists often work intensively in a single village, with one or two key informants, but my research required a broader approach. Relying on aerial photos to locate isolated settlements, I worked in four different regions, collecting detailed census data on more than four hundred Asháninka households living in some forty local groups and speaking four closely related languages. Altogether, six men, one twelve year old boy, and one woman were my primary Asháninka assistants.

The key to much of my work was the **genealogical method**. This involved sitting down with the senior man in a group or household and asking him to name his wife or wives and all his children by relative age. I would ask where everyone was born and determine where they were living or where and how they had died. If possible, I would compile similar information on more distant kin. Then I would draw a sketch map of the village, numbering each house and identifying the occupants by name (see figure 1.6). I also worked intensively with many individuals to outline their life histories in greater detail. All this material allowed me to begin recognizing culturally meaningful social patterns. Without knowing who people were by name, where they lived, and who their relatives were, I would have remained an outsider. This information allowed me to analyze settlement and household structures, migration patterns, marriage and kinship terms, and fertility and mortality rates, and it proved indispensable for understanding the impact of changing economic patterns.

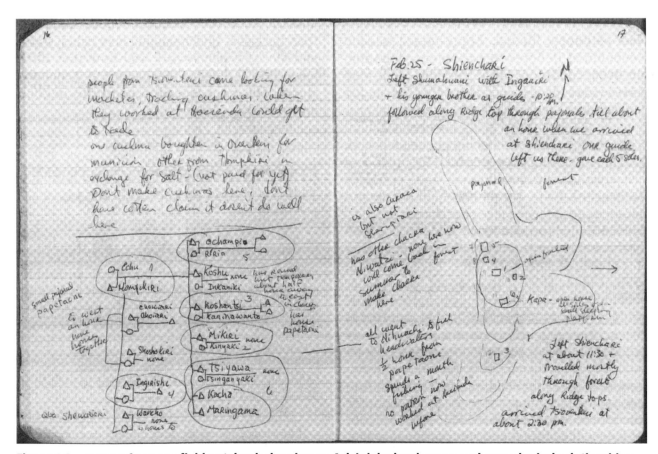

Figure 1.6.   A page from my field notebook showing an Asháninka local group and genealogical relationships.

What emerged from these data was a shocking pattern of Asháninka depopulation and exploitation. For example, I found that diseases spread by uncontrolled contact with colonists had dramatically elevated Asháninka mortality. In some areas, the Asháninka were indeed disappearing. Many had died violently or been taken captive to work for colonists. Local groups and families were fragmented and scattered, and subsistence activities suffered as people were drawn into virtual debt slavery. Opportunities for individual Asháninka to participate successfully in the market economy were extremely limited. Many joined mission communities in hopes of escaping exploitation, but living conditions at the missions often were poor because the concentrated population quickly depleted local resources. Furthermore, the missionaries disapproved of many Asháninka cultural practices. It was a discouraging picture; however, Asháninka culture was extremely resilient, and vast areas of their traditional lands remained undisturbed. I was certain that both people and culture could survive if given the chance.

Eventually I presented my findings in a doctoral dissertation and in a series of articles.[1] Some of my Asháninka ethnographic material illustrates important aspects of independent, tribal societies as they existed in the **ethnographic present** before they were seriously disrupted by intruders from politically centralized, politically organized **cultures** (see chapter 2). Of course, anthropology involves much more than ethnographic description. It can also provide insights on critical issues of national and international policy. For example, my research led me to advocate for the political and economic autonomy of the Asháninka on the lands that they traditionally occupied.

My research on the Asháninka also forced me to ask questions about my own culture. I was impressed by the contrast between the precariousness and inequality of our market-based, industrial way of life and the ability of the Asháninka to provide for all of their material needs—food, clothing, and shelter—while maintaining a high-quality environment and high levels of social equality. In this respect, their culture seems to be more effective than our own, and its integrity deserves to be safeguarded from uninvited intrusion. This realization launched me into a much larger research project to systematically compare tribal cultures, like the Asháninka, with the larger-scale cultures in politically organized states of the imperial world and modern, industrial cultures whose influences span the globe in the contemporary commercial world. Understanding how tribes, states,

and the global system work and how they differ might help us design a more secure and equitable world. This book is a product of this ongoing investigation.

CULTURE: A POWERFUL HUMAN TOOL

People are unique animals in our almost total reliance on **culture** as our primary means of survival.[2] Culture is socially transmitted information that shapes human behavior. Socially transmitted behavior is also important for many other animals, but only humans use speech to accelerate the production and transmission of culture and thereby vastly expand its utility. Speech facilitates our ability to symbol,[3] or assign arbitrary meanings to phenomena, giving people an enormously powerful tool to manipulate other people and the physical world.

The Humanization Process: Producing People and Culture

Culture is part of a biocultural evolutionary process that produced and sustained *Homo sapiens*, the human species. Our genes and our culture are interdependent and have coevolved as a dual inheritance over millennia.[4] Genes and culture must be reproduced and transmitted to the next generation. However, there is a crucial difference between natural selection operating on genes and cultural selection operating on culture. People often quite deliberately guide cultural selection, although cultural choices may have unintended consequences. Genes and culture are connected because genes give us our biological capacity for culture, and culturally directed behavior shapes the frequency of particular genes in a population. People are likely to adopt and transmit cultural patterns that seem to meet their needs, and these patterns may also improve an individual's *genetic fitness,* or the degree to which one's genes are reproduced.

Cultural ideas constitute the templates for a series of human actions that produce outcomes chosen by individual human actors. These actions can be called *cultural processes*. The most important cultural process is **humanization**—the production and maintenance of people, societies, and cultures. Humanization involves a tightly integrated series of subprocesses that collectively define a uniquely human way of life centered on marriage, the nuclear family, and the household (see table 1.1). The most crucial humanization subprocess is the human ability to conceptualize and thereby produce the abstract concepts and symbols, such as father, mother, son, and daughter that define the family as the primary social unit and the founda-

Table 1.1. Cultural Processes and Subprocesses by Cultural World

Tribal World

Humanization: the production, maintenance, and reproduction of human beings and culture.
- Conceptualization: producing abstract concepts and symbols that shape behavior
- Materialization: giving physical form to concepts
- Verbalization: producing speech
- Socialization: producing human societies by exogamy
- Cultural Transmission: reproducing culture

Imperial World

Politicization: the production and maintenance of centralized political power by co-opting the humanization process.
- Taxation: extracting surplus production to support government
- Conquest: extracting booty, slaves, and tribute
- Specialization: government employment
- Militarization: development of professional military
- Bureaucratization: hierarchical command structures
- Urbanization: development of cities

Commercial World

Commercialization: the production and maintenance of private profit-making business enterprise as a means of accumulating capital, by co-opting the humanization and politicization processes.
- Commodification: market for land, labor, money, basic goods and services
- Industrialization: mass production, distribution, and consumption of goods and services
- Capitalization: ownership of means of production separated from labor
- Corporatization: business enterprise becomes suprahuman
- Externalization: costs of commercial growth are socialized
- Supralocalization: business enterprise is detached from community
- Financialization: finance institutionalized, separated from production

tion of human society. Speech, or the ability to verbalize concepts, makes it possible for people to store and efficiently transmit vast quantities of cultural information. Cultural concepts also are frequently given physical form, or materialized, when people build shelters and make tools and ornaments or art objects, or when they act out, and thereby help to maintain their beliefs, in rituals or stories. For culture to exist, it must be stored and transmitted, or reproduced in the next generation. Cultural transmission can occur in many ways, including by observation and borrowing, but vertical transmission from parents to children within the household is the most basic transmission process.

Machiavellian Intelligence,
Self-Interest, and Human Society

The humanization process requires complex cognitive abilities linked to **social intelligence**, which is based in the frontal lobes of the brain (the neocortex). Individuals use social intelligence to monitor and manipulate others in order to maintain support and to keep their group together. We humans have highly developed abilities to monitor what others do, to persuade others to believe they will benefit by doing what we want, even when they don't, and to detect similar deceits on the part of others. This mental ability seems

based on the realization that everyone has similar minds and perceptions that can be advantageously manipulated. Our closest primate relatives seem to have made this intellectual breakthrough, but their smaller neocortex limits their ability to use their social intelligence to form larger social groups. The average number of individuals that can form a stable group among primates is called Dunbar's number, after its discoverer, and seems to reflect relative size of the neocortex and level of social intelligence.[5] For humans this seems to be about 150 individuals. Chimpanzees, with their relatively small neocortex, have only rudimentary culture and can sustain social groups of only about sixty-five individuals. Like all nonhuman primates they must use direct, "hands-on" social grooming to remain integrated. Under controlled conditions chimpanzees have been taught to use up to 150 signs based on American Sign Language,[6] but they do not construct new signs, and gestures seem to have only limited use among free-ranging chimpanzees. Humans can use their richly productive speech to process more social information, and our more elaborate culture allows us to "groom" and manipulate others at a distance. Pioneer British anthropologist Edward B. Tylor recognized the importance of speech in his 1875 *Encylopaedia Britannica* article on "Anthropology."

He declared that the ability to speak and the powerful symbolism of language was what distinguished humans from the great apes:

> To use words in themselves unmeaning, as symbols by which to conduct and convey the complex intellectual processes in which mental conceptions are suggested, compared, combined, and even analyzed, and new ones created—this is a faculty which is scarcely to be traced in any lower animal.[7]

The larger neocortex and greater social intelligence of humans in comparison with chimpanzees corresponds to our Dunbar's number of about 150 people, which closely approximates the average size of tribal clans, Neolithic villages, church congregations, small military units, and the social network of individuals. This is apparently the number of people that we are biologically and culturally most suited to interact with on a regular, face-to-face basis and seems to be a genuine human universal. It is difficult for people to remember more than about 150 unique individuals unless we sort them into impersonal subcategories. Larger social groupings also require the formation of more difficult and costly coalitions based on cultural institutions, perceptions, and conceptions that work around our "natural" cognitive limitations and selfish inclinations. This is an important reason why social scale is such a crucial variable for understanding human sociocultural systems.

Culture is the primary tool that individuals use to pursue actions that they perceive to be in their self-interest, but culture, language, and social organization must be shared. These human realities pose special problems. Biological evolution operating through natural selection programs us to propagate our individual genetic material through our descendants and closest relatives. Like our "selfish genes,"[8] we are naturally selfish individuals, but we also must cooperate and form social groups to survive. Altruism, or self-sacrifice (helping others at one's own expense), is rare because we are naturally driven to do things that favor the well-being of ourselves and our children above everyone else. It is physically easy for small groups of closely related people to extract a living from the natural environment, but the real challenge is how to live socially with enough other groups of people to maintain and reproduce culture. Learning how to successfully relate to other human groups is perhaps the most critical human problem, because intergroup conflict can be so costly. This is not easy, especially in a dynamic physical world, and this is why sociocultural systems are in constant motion, continually merging, splitting, diversifying, and moving apart.

Culture: What People Think, Make, and Do

Chimpanzees have culture, but there are obvious qualitative and quantitative differences between them and us.[9] Human cultural behavior is readily transmitted and highly uniform, whereas chimp learned behavior is more likely to be idiosyncratic and may not be easily or widely shared.[10] Only a few chimp groups use stick tools to extract termites. A particular chimp may learn a very efficient way to crack open a nut, but it might never be copied by any other chimp. Human culture always involves numerous behaviors that are uniform and universally shared by all members of a given cultural tradition.

Culture is the most basic concept in anthropology, yet there is remarkable variation in how anthropologists define culture and what aspects of culture they think are important. The most widely cited technical definition of culture as socially patterned human thought and behavior was originally proposed by Edward B. Tylor in his now-classic book *Primitive Culture*: "Culture ... is that complex whole which includes knowledge, belief, art, law, morals, custom, and any other capabilities and habits acquired by man as a member of society."[11]

Virtually all anthropologists take Tylor's definition as a starting point. Tylor assumed that culture was a uniquely human trait, and he distinguished between biologically inherited and socially transmitted human traits. As a learned inheritance, culture can be unlearned and modified to help solve human problems. If all aspects of culture were biologically inherited, we would need to resort to genetic engineering to solve certain human problems.

Human culture includes all the social things that people think, make, and do that are *not* in themselves biologically inherited. Human biology provides us with the physical abilities and psychological propensities that make culture possible, such as the ability to speak and to manipulate symbols with our minds and objects with our hands. Culture and nature are so closely intertwined that it would be misleading to speak of an essential, unchanging human nature, given the dynamics of change. Our biology allows us to respond in novel ways to novel situations, such that the outcome of cultural development is neither preordained nor inevitable. Culture is a humanly directed response to historical events. We use culture to change our behavior and the behavior of others for personal benefit, but the conscious choices that we make are aimed at immediate outcomes, which may be poorly related to the long-term goal of the survival of human beings as a species. Personal survival, high social status, and access to resources are short-term goals of self-interested individuals that might not also benefit humanity.

Social Power: How People Get What They Want

This book emphasizes one of the most important and interesting functions of culture: the way people use culture to produce social power to achieve their goals in relation to other people and the natural environment. **Social power** is not easily defined or measured, but it is a familiar feature of daily life. Broadly, it is a measure of a person's ability to influence others for personal advantage, even when others might object. Following the lead of historical sociologist Michael Mann,[12] in this book we will distinguish among four types of social power: ideological, economic, military, and political (see table 1.2).

Ideological power refers to control over what people know. Ideological power is arguably the most important form of social power, because it may be the most effective and efficient way to secure one's self-interest. Ideological power includes control over how people know, the methods of knowing, or epistemology; control over what people know by sight and sound, or phenomena known through the senses; and pure ideas, or **noumenal** subjective things that we know only as conceptions in the mind. Rulers demonstrate the power of ideas when they materialize them, or make them physical objects. For example, they may transform noumenal deities into stone monuments to make them phenomena that their followers can see. It may be less costly to build monuments to persuade people to accept the legitimacy of the social establishment, rather than to threaten them with physical violence.

Economic power is the ability to direct the labor of other people to one's own advantage and to control and accumulate wealth, income, and material resources. Political power is personal power over the institutions of government and is typically linked to military power, which is the use of, or threats to use, organized physical violence.

Individuals construct self-centered personal networks of power, or **imperia**, incorporating the individuals and institutionally organized groups of people they can personally command or influence to do things for their personal advantage. The imperium describes how individuals organize their personal power to realize their self-interest. Personal power networks are based on kinship, marriage, friendship, and patronage, and they can crosscut otherwise functionally separate ideological, economic, military, and political institutional sources of social power. This means that a single person, or a small oligarchy, can command an entire society. The larger and more diverse the personal imperium, the more people one can command, the larger and more successful one's household can be, and the more numerous and successful one's children and grandchildren might become.

Cultural Illusions, Delusions, and Reality

Culture is an imperfect tool that needs continuous verification and revision. It is a structure in our minds. What matters is what people actually do, and we know that people do not always follow their cultural rules. The difference between cultural structure and actual practice is crucial because deviant behavior may have serious social consequences. Even when our culturally directed behavior follows the rules it might not produce the outcomes that we imagine, and may therefore not be sustainable.

Culture creates an imagined physical world that may not correspond to the reality that objectively exists, and this can be both beneficial and problematic. It is helpful to distinguish between our *perceptions* of the physical world gained directly through our senses of touch, sight, and sound and our cultural *conceptions* of the world, which may be formed in our minds independently of direct perceptions of physical reality. We may be deceived by natural illusions, such as mirages. For example, the planet Earth looks solid, but at the atomic level reality is mostly empty space. Even the constellation Ursa Major, the Great Bear, or Big Dipper is an illusion created by our earthbound perception of unrelated stars scattered across vast distances. We may also be intentionally misled or deluded by

Table 1.2. Types and Cultural Organization of Social Power

Types of Social Power	
Ideological	Military
Economic	Political
Cultural Organization of Social Power	

By kin in the tribal world
By rulers in the imperial world
By business owners, managers, and financiers in the commercial world

false beliefs and misconceptions that are deliberately propagated by those who benefit from them. A certain amount of illusion and delusion may be necessary to maintain happiness, and too much reality testing may be unhealthy, but the human problem is that our perceptions and conceptions may sometimes both be dangerously wrong.

People may be objectively wrong when they imagine their subjective constructions of spirits and demons to have a physical reality, but "mistaken" beliefs can prove beneficial. Using the illusory Big Dipper to find the North Star may be a life-saving skill. A scientific way of knowing reality can also be wrong, even when it produces beneficial outcomes. Both subjective and objective ways of knowing have consequences in reality, and both may need revision when they prove unsustainable. People may even be wrong about what they perceive to be in their self-interest and may be unaware of their long-term interests. It is not always easy to correctly identify the short-term actions that will best meet our long-term objectives in an uncertain world.

OUT OF AFRICA: HUMAN BIOLOGICAL AND CULTURAL DIVERSITY

The Descendants of Eve: The DNA Family Tree

Ancestral humans and our bipedal relatives including *Australopithecus* are placed in the subtribe *Hominina* that separated from our common ancestors with chimpanzees about 6 million years ago. Humans and chimpanzees are now classified in different subtribes of the primate tribe *Hominini*, because we share 98 percent of the genetic information in our genomes.[13] The DNA molecule is a chain of 3 billion base pairs each linking an adenine (A) or thymine (T) with a guanine (G) or cytosine (C) amino acid to compose our genetic code. The DNA evidence shows that all contemporary people are descendants of fully modern human ancestral *Homo sapiens* living in Africa about 150,000 years ago. A single genetic mutation occurring perhaps 100,000 years ago may have made human speech possible.[14] Shortly thereafter, culturally distinct human groups spread beyond Africa to Europe and Asia about 50,000 years ago and quickly replaced closely related Neandertal and *Homo erectus* populations.

Because *Homo sapiens* is a relatively new species that spread quickly from small ancestral African populations, we are genetically all Africans. Only about 0.1 percent of our 3 billion base pairs (one in 1,000) differ between individuals. There is about as much genetic diversity within a population as between populations anywhere in the world.[15]

Researchers associated with National Geographic's Genographic Project[16] designed to trace the history of human population movement have distinguished 116 genetic lines called haplogroups among contemporary indigenous people worldwide based on clustered variations in mitochondrial DNA (MtDNA), which is transmitted only in the female line. Ninety lines have also been distinguished based on the Y chromosome, which is present only in males.[17] Other geneticists have detailed the genetic relationships among fifty-one indigenous groups worldwide using variations in paired chromosomes shared by males and females.[18] This data shows that geographic proximity is a better predictor of shared genetic variation, rather than ethnicity.[19] Theoretically, all people are descendants of a single African woman, our mitochondrial Eve. Geneticist Bryan Sykes has given names to the founders of some thirty-two "World Clans" descended from "Eve" including seven "daughters of Eve" whose descendants presumably populated Europe beginning some 45,000 years ago.[20]

The International HapMap Project[21] is exploring sample populations worldwide for medically significant genetic diversity in order to improve human health care. Even though we are all Africans by ancestry, as individuals we can still vary on 10 million polymorphic traits, sometimes in ways that affect our health.

Cultural Construction of Race

The genetic data demonstrates that the popular concept of "race" is a cultural construction, not a biological realty. For example, the five racial categories—black, white, American Indian–Alaskan Native, Asian–Pacific Islander, and Hispanic—used by the U.S. Census in 1980 and 1990 are biological fictions that have no scientific validity. Culturally defined racial categories confuse legal citizenship and ethnicity with naïve assumptions about skin color and "blood" that ignore the facts of life. Such confusion helps to perpetuate the implicit assumption that some peoples are biologically inferior to others, even though there is absolutely no scientific basis for such racist beliefs. Racial stereotyping is not only unscientific, but it can also be medically dangerous for particular individuals because disease susceptibility and response to medication can have a large genetic component quite unrelated to culturally defined "race." After consulting with the American Anthropological Association the U S Census Bureau declared that for the 2000 Census "race" was not a biological or anthropological definition, but nevertheless they continued to use the race concept. Census respondents were offered six major race categories, including "other," and had the choice of self-identifying as multiracial, but the process continued to confuse genetics, ethnicity, and nationality. Race continues to have social, political, and economic significance in the United States.

The cultural definition of race matters because it may be used to support discrimination and social inequalities. Anthropologists have made educating the public on the misuse of race a professional responsibility. In 2007 the American Anthropological Association launched a website and traveling exhibit on race and racism in the United States called "Race: Are We So Different?"[22] This project reviews the cultural history of race in the United States, showing graphically the way visible physical differences in people such as skin color are genetically complex features related to climate. They exist as gradients rather than discrete units, and different features overlap in ways that are not expressed by culturally constructed racial categories.

Ethnologue: Cataloging World Languages

In addition to their shared genes, human populations are also distinguished by shared culture including language, other cultural features, and their ethnic identities. Language is the most fundamental and readily distinguishable form of cultural diversity, and the number of known languages is truly remarkable. Languages are speech communities and are broadly related to genetic populations. SIL International, (the Summer Institute of Linguistics), a Christian organization that for many years has conducted linguistic research and development with over 2,500 languages worldwide, has cataloged nearly 7,000 living languages, including 516 that are considered nearly extinct.[23] Two-thirds of these languages originated in Africa and Asia and are now spoken as first languages by nearly 75 percent of the world's people. Fewer than 4 percent of the world's existing languages originated in Europe, but because of recent colonial expansion, European languages now count as first languages for more than a fourth of the world's people. The vast Pacific region has more than 1,300 languages, but most are small, averaging only 800 speakers. There are more than 1,000 indigenous languages in the Americas, averaging about 2,000 speakers each. SIL catalogs 94

families of related languages, most of which have been grouped into about a dozen larger families or macrofamilies by historical linguists following American linguist Joseph Greenberg.[24] These larger groupings reflect large-scale population movements over millennia and correspond fairly closely with similar genetic groupings of populations, as would be expected of speech communities. A language is a culture, but is not always the basis of a particular ethnic group. A single ethnic group may speak multiple languages, and multiple ethnic groups may share the same language.

Linguistic Relativity and the Sapir-Whorf Hypothesis

Every known language appears to be fully functional and equally capable of conveying cultural meanings, and each language represents a unique way of viewing the world that is at the heart of cultural diversity. This perspective is known as the **Sapir-Whorf hypothesis**, after anthropological linguists Edward Sapir and Benjamin Whorf. As Whorf expressed it, "...the world is presented in a kaleidoscopic flux of impressions which have to be organized in our minds. This means, largely, by the linguistic system in our minds."[25] In effect, the speakers of different languages live in different perceptual worlds. This is a profound insight that helps explain why different people can view the same reality yet see it in totally different ways.

Other researchers have shown that linguistic categories are not completely arbitrary. In a classic study, Berlin and Kay presented speakers of 98 different languages with the same chart of 329 standard color chips arranged by hue and brightness (see figure 1.7).[26] Each speaker was asked to identify the focal point of every basic color term in their language. Berlin and Kay found no language had more than eleven basic color terms, and they usually were added in the same order in different languages. No language had fewer than two terms, and these two were always black and white. Languages of tribal societies had fewer color terms than those spoken by commercial societies, but fewer terms does not suggest any physical inability to perceive color differences. When a language had three terms, red would be added to black and white, next green or yellow, then blue and brown, and so on (see figure 1.8). The sequence of color terms could not be explained beyond the possibility that they represented levels of distinctive physical contrast, which were perceptual universals. Similar sequences of perceptual categories have been found in plant and animal taxonomies.[27] These findings remind us that physical reality does impose limits that people must accommodate

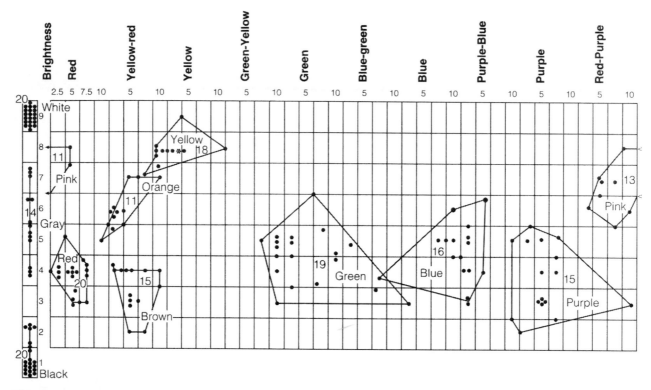

Figure 1.7. Normalized foci of basic color terms in twenty languages. Numerals appearing along the borders of the chart refer to the Munsell system of color notation, distinguishing hue, brightness, and color strength. Numerals appearing in the body of the chart refer to the number of languages in the sample of twenty that encode the corresponding color category. The smallest possible number of lines are used to enclose each color area (Berlin and Kay 1969).

culturally, although we may be allowed considerable flexibility according to the demands that we make on our natural environment.

UNDERSTANDING SOCIOCULTURAL SYSTEMS

Ethnocentrism: The Problem of Observer Bias

One of anthropology's most important contributions toward cross-cultural understanding is its recognition of the problem of ethnocentrism—the tendency to evaluate other cultures in reference to one's own (presumably superior) culture. Ethnocentrism contributes to internal social solidarity, but it can seriously distort one's perception of others and hinders understanding.

Insiders and Outsiders: Emics and Etics

It is impossible to really know any culture except from the inside, as a native member. Even the most skilled anthropologist will always be an outsider when viewing a different culture. The problem for anthropologists is how to overcome, or at least become aware of, their own cultural biases, while attempting to understand other cultures from the inside. Translation of symbols from a given culture into categories that will be meaningful to outsiders will often be imprecise. The problem is compounded by the fact that cultural insiders may be quite unconscious of the underlying meanings of their own cultural categories.

One way to move beyond ethnocentric bias is to self-consciously try to view another culture through

$$\begin{bmatrix} \text{White} \\ \text{Black} \end{bmatrix} \rightarrow [\text{Red}] \begin{matrix} \nearrow [\text{Green}] \rightarrow [\text{Yellow}] \searrow \\ \searrow [\text{Yellow}] \rightarrow [\text{Green}] \nearrow \end{matrix} [\text{Blue}] \rightarrow [\text{Brown}] \rightarrow \begin{bmatrix} \text{Purple} \\ \text{Pink} \\ \text{Orange} \\ \text{Gray} \end{bmatrix}$$

Figure 1.8. Development sequence for the acquisition of basic color terms (Berlin and Kay 1969:4).

the eyes of a cultural insider. This requires the use of insider cultural categories. Anthropologists use the terms **emic** and **etic** to refer to the inside and outside perspective on a culture.[28] For example, an insider emic understanding of Asháninka leadership would start with the Asháninka term *pinkatsari*, literally, "big man." I learned that a *pinkatsari* was a prominent person with a forceful personality. If I had applied the outsider etic category "chief" to Chonkiri, I would have completely misunderstood his cultural role. As a *pinkatsari*, Chonkiri could harangue and persuade, but he held no coercive authority over his followers. He did not inherit his position and could not automatically pass it on to his sons. In fact, the Asháninka reject the kind of central political authority implied by the outsider word *chief*.

This distinction between emic and etic is based on the use of these terms in linguistics to refer to phonemic and phonetic transcription.[29] **Phonemes** are the unique sounds recognized as significant by speakers of a given language. For example, the words *pray* and *play* are distinguished by speakers of English because *r* and *l* are different phonemes and are thus heard as different sounds. Speakers of another language might not hear any difference between *pray* and *play*. A phonetic transcription records the sounds as heard by a nonspeaker of the language who does not know which sound distinctions are meaningful. Phonetic transcriptions may be clumsy approximations of the "real" sounds of a language. Similarly, the meanings of unique words, symbols, rituals, and institutions may be difficult to translate cross-culturally. Even a trained observer can only watch what people do and record native explanations. Observations must be selectively screened through the observer's own cultural categories; then, in effect, an interpretation of the culture must be created.

Three Cultural Worlds

Over the past 2 million years of cultural development people like us and our hominid ancestors have created three distinct cultural worlds: tribal, imperial, and commercial (see table 1.1). Each world is distinguished by differences in sociocultural scale and complexity, and these differences are reflected in the ways people organize their lives. Each cultural world produces measurably different human outcomes that affect the sustainability of societies and the life chances of individuals.

All ethnographic cultures organized as chiefdoms and states, and with local communities averaging 5,000

people or more are assigned to the imperial world. The term *imperial* refers to the presence of a political ruler who commands with supreme authority over subject people within a territory. The tribal world, in contrast, has leaders and followers. Some imperial societies are also incorporated by the commercial world as will be explained below. The increased social scale of the imperial world is supported by the **politicization** process: the production and maintenance of political power. Politicization is an elite-directed process that co-opts the humanization process, reducing the freedom of most people by means of various culturally complex subprocesses including taxation, conquest, specialization, militarization, bureaucratization, and urbanization.

The commercial world is distinguished by modern nation-state government organization and the predominance of the **commercialization** process: the production and maintenance of commercial business based on financial capital and financial markets. Commercialization co-opts both humanization and politicization processes to promote economic growth and the accumulation of financial capital. Economic elites have been constructing the commercial world since 1500 and have largely extinguished or incorporated tribal and imperial world sociocultural systems, turning tribal societies into ethnic groups and imperial world societies into dependent states. Many of the twentieth-century state-level cultures in the *Ethnographic Atlas*[30] belong in the commercial rather than imperial world, but the necessary financial variables have not been coded in the atlas.

The Functional Organization
of Sociocultural Systems

In addition to the ideological, economic, military, and political sources of social power; personal imperia; and the three cultural worlds discussed above, it will be helpful to distinguish three functionally interconnected aspects of all cultural systems: superstructure, structure, and infrastructure (see table 1.3), following an analytic framework introduced by anthropologist Marvin Harris.[31] These categories crosscut in illuminating ways the mental, behavioral, and material aspects of culture that individual human beings experience. They help us understand how the different parts of societies and cultures work together to produce distinctive cultural worlds. Superstructure, structure, and infrastructure are functional categories describing components of the sociocultural system viewed as a whole. They connect empirical

Table 1.3. Infrastructure, Structure, and Superstructure in Three Cultural Worlds

	Tribal World	Imperial World	Commercial World
Infrastructure: Material Basis of Society & Culture			
Human Population	6-84 million	100s of millions	Billions
Nature, Energy, and Materials	Natural resources & services	Natural resources & services	Natural resources & services, fossil fuels
Technology	Tools of foraging, gardening, herding	Tools of intensive agriculture, irrigation, plows, metal, writing	Industrial tools, factory farming, mechanized transport, electronic information systems
Structure: Organization of Society			
Economy	Domestic subsistence, feasting, reciprocal exchange	Tribute, tax, plunder, conquest, slavery, specialization, coins, unequal exchange, limited markets, long-distance luxury trade	Global markets, commodities, money, factories, financial institutions, public debt, corporations, capital accumulation, unequal exchange
Society	Low density rural, bands of 50, tribes and villages of 500, family, kin, affines, young, old, male, female, language	High density rural, cities of 100,000, social class: royalty, nobles, commoners, slaves, castes, ethnicity	High density rural, cities of millions, capitalists, laborers, consumers, race, ethnicity, nationality, social classes, community, commonwealth
Polity/Government	Autonomous bands and villages of 500, descent groups	Chiefdoms of 5,000, city-states of 50,000, kingdoms of 5 million, empires of 50 million, armies, tyranny, bureaucracy	Constitutional nation states of 100s of millions, courts, police, professional military, democracy, universities
Superstructure: Empirical Knowledge, Noumenal Beliefs & Practice			
Ideology	Animism, shamanism, ancestor cults, spirits, myth, ritual, taboo, magic, divination, animal sacrifice	Mana, high gods, polytheism, divine kings, priests, sacred texts, human sacrifice	Nationalism, patriotism, monotheism, knowledge, advertising, economic growth, progress, free market

knowledge and noumenal beliefs and practice in the superstructure, with the institutional forms that direct human behavior and interaction in the structure. The superstructure is what people collectively know about their society, culture, and natural environment, both the things that they can verify empirically by observation and experiment and the things that they only imagine and believe to be true. Superstructure is information encoded in language and other symbols. Structure is primarily behavior. It is how people organize their activities within visible social groups and institutions such as households, families, villages, political units, and economic structures and practices. Contained within the structure is the organization of social power, whether by domestic households in the tribal world, by political rulers in the imperial world, or by economic elites and their political allies in the commercial world. The infrastructure is the physical

basis of society. It includes flows of energy and raw materials; all the natural resources and services that support human life and culture; and physical tools, animals, plants, and machines that people employ. Human beings themselves are included in the infrastructure as biological organisms. Without this physical infrastructure there could be no human society and no culture. Particular details of infrastructure are functionally connected with but do not cause structure and superstructure.

EVALUATING SOCIOCULTURAL SYSTEMS
Cultural relativity and their ethical standards do not prevent anthropologists from pursuing what may be our most important function: evaluating sociocultural systems to judge how best to maximize human well-being, social justice, and social sustainability. Anthropological work must be "truthful" or accurate,

culturally relative, objective, and nonethnocentric, but it can also be used for national and international public policy development and for advocacy on behalf of particular peoples. Anthropology codes of ethics specify our responsibility to "avoid harm or wrong" and respect the well-being of the peoples and communities we study, even as they stress the practical utility of our work. The Society for Applied Anthropology Code of Ethics (1983) declares: "To the communities ultimately affected by our activities we owe respect for their dignity, integrity, and worth. We recognize that human survival is contingent upon the continued existence of a diversity of human communities...We will avoid taking or recommending action on behalf of a sponsor which is harmful to the interests of the community."[32] Likewise, the American Anthropological Association Code of Ethics (1998) urges anthropologists to ". . . consider carefully the social and political implications of the information they disseminate."[33] This has not always been the case.

In the nineteenth century much anthropological work supported racism and colonialism. For example, Edward B. Tylor and Lewis Henry Morgan[34] ranked cultures by stages from savagery and barbarism to civilization in a sequence that made European civilization the pinnacle of evolutionary progress. Lacking a scientifically rigorous theory of cultural change, they defined savagery by foraging subsistence practices; barbarism by the use of pottery; and civilization by writing, although they included many other variables in characterizing savagery, barbarism, and civilization. They viewed these stages as levels of intellectual development that produced natural and inevitable material and moral improvement for humanity as a whole. Many people continue to believe that technological developments in themselves drive changes in society and culture. Certainly technology has multiplied our ability to shape the physical world, but technologies are tools that are directed and controlled by human agents. Technology does not dictate the distribution of social power and thereby determine the form of our societies and the quality of our daily lives. There is much empirical evidence that in the absence of countervailing public policy measures, elite-directed increases in social scale and cultural complexity have amplified social inequality, making it more difficult for most people to meet their basic human needs. In order to understand how this seemingly paradoxical outcome could have occurred, we must rethink the meaning of progress and existing explanations for its origin.

The Delusion of Progress

In his book *Guns, Germs, and Steel*, geographer Jared Diamond poses the question "How did European societies, but not other societies, first conquer and now still dominate the world?"[35] Diamond focuses on whole societies and technologies, not individuals, and he argues that prior geographical advantages put some societies on upward trajectories and are the ultimate explanation for present inequalities of global wealth and power. Diamond appropriately rejects racist explanations and disavows ethnocentric comparisons between tribes and industrial civilization, acknowledging that "progress" may not always be "good." He also disavows historical inevitability; nevertheless, his answer is incomplete and deceptively misleading.

The combined effects of guns, germs, and steel certainly helped Europeans conquer the world, but it would be a mistake to see biological circumstances and technology as sufficient explanations for the historical rise of Europeans to global dominance. The power and scale perspective offered in *Cultural Anthropology* argues that the fate of humanity is determined by three variables rooted in human nature and culture: (1) the scale at which people organize their sociocultural systems, (2) how people control social power, and (3) their deceptive use of culture to control perception. Over the past 10,000 years human decision making regarding these crucial variables, especially elite decision making, has produced decisive differences among societies that have nothing to do with genetics. Tribal peoples are unlikely to become imperialists, because they actively limit the power of their leaders and they implicitly understand enough about realities of the physical world to maintain sustainable systems of production and consumption. The imperial world was produced by peoples who allowed their leaders to become rulers and who allowed themselves to be deceived into believing that elite direction was natural and inevitable, and that imperialism would benefit everyone. They were also so deceived about the realities of the physical world that they believed that their material systems could grow continuously.

Diamond imagines humanity lined up at a 13,000 BP "starting line" in a race to see which society could become the most imperialistic. This is a deceptive view, because in reality, throughout history the big winners in imperialism are not whole societies, but only the top 0.5 percent of households who direct and most benefit from conquest and the expansion of large polities. The losers, including many individuals in winning societies, are exterminated, enslaved, and impoverished. This makes imperialism fundamentally inhuman, especially given how frequently great empires rise and fall. It is equally plausible and much more useful to see the goal of human development to be a continuous humanization process, in which people use open and overlapping sociocultural networks as tools to maintain and reproduce humanity and culture. This is sustainable development, the opposite of imperialism. Taking care of people humanely is a tough challenge, but by 13,000 BP humanity had already won the humanization race by successfully peopling the world. The imperialism race was started some 7,000 years ago by aggrandizing individuals who, in times of crisis, convinced their followers to accept them as rulers, rather than leaders, and to pay them tribute.

The Summum Bonum: Human Well-Being, Freedom, and Happiness

In assessing how well different cultures function to meet human needs, it will be helpful to use a working definition of the universal good life, the **summum bonum**, or supreme good. Following political scientist Leopold Kohr, it can be assumed that in addition to household well-being, individuals also need sociability, material prosperity, security, and the opportunity to enjoy expressive culture.[36] These conditions are also included in the 1948 United Nations *Universal Declaration of Human Rights*,[37] and they are similar to Malinowski's "individual needs,"[38] and psychologist Abraham Maslow's "hierarchy of human needs."[39] In this regard the "best" culture would maximize human freedom, happiness, and the general welfare and would sustain a just and moral society. Individual freedom can be defined positively as the realization of self-interest and negatively as freedom from interference.

The inherent tension between individual freedom and the necessity for social cooperation is the basis of morality. Moral philosophers debate whether the "right" is a transcendent value or simply a culturally relative social construction. The problem is that morality defined as a shared understanding of what is "right" might conflict with individual freedom. Social norms might also violate universal summum bonum values, sometimes making cultural relativity difficult to either defend or challenge. From this perspective, there are bad and even pathological cultures, just as there are bad individuals.

This book assumes that a just society would promote the universal good life, but this might not be the "good life" recognized by the culture of a particular community. It is inadequate to either remain neutral on community cultural conventions or to simply accept them all as "good" by definition. Rather, we can judge cultural definitions of the "right" in reference to what political philosopher Michael Sandel calls "the moral importance of the ends they serve."[40] Aristotle made the same point when he said, "If we wish to investigate the best constitution appropriately, we must first decide what is the most desirable life."[41] We can not avoid talking about "moral worth," but at the same time what is moral can not be culturally relative.

Any culture's moral worth could be its effectiveness in providing the universal good life measured by individual human health and well-being, human freedom, social stability, and the sustainability of the sociocultural system's material base. These measures are also incorporated in the *U.N. Millennium Development Goals*[42] and in the *U.N. Human Development Index*.[43] To the extent that all members of any culture are able to secure these benefits, that culture could be considered successful and morally worthy, even though individuals and communities may vary in how the "goods" of the "good life" are defined in detail. All cultures produce both "bads" and "goods," or costs and benefits. What matters is how these are distributed in society, and that the goods truly outweigh the bads. The accounting is not always easy, because culture itself often obscures reality. However, the ethnographic material presented in the following chapters suggests that most people were best able to enjoy the good life in the tribal world, where individual freedom was the highest, and everyone was assured an **irreducible minimum**[44] of material benefits and opportunities (see figure 1.9). The imperial world gave a few people a very good life, while exploiting and pushing down the majority. The commercial world accepts extreme levels of inequality, poverty, sickness, conflict, and environmental degradation, even as large numbers of people enjoy high levels of material prosperity.

Social cohesion is closely related to equitable distribution of social power: Societies that are more equitable are likely to be more cohesive, and they may generate fewer incentives for destabilizing growth. Conspicuous concentrations of wealth can create a maladaptive, runaway growth process when people support and emulate elite cultural patterns, because they believe that by copying the elite, they will improve their own life chances. Significantly, health and well-being in the commercial world, as measured by life expectancy, have now been found to be improved

Figure 1.9. An Asháninka woman relaxing on a beer trough. In the tribal world everyone has access to an irreducible minimum to satisfy their material needs.

more by social equality and social cohesion than by absolute increases in wealth. The distribution of wealth and power thus may be the most important cultural pattern determining the success of the humanization process. The following chapters will explore these issues in depth.

SUMMARY

Culture, the most important concept of cultural anthropology, refers to the socially transmitted, often symbolic information that shapes human behavior. Culture has mental, behavioral, and material aspects. Culture is what people think, make, and do as members of society. It is patterned and provides a model for proper behavior, and it regulates human society so that people can successfully maintain themselves and reproduce. The goal of cultural anthropology is to increase cultural understanding. Cultural anthropology's most important research technique, the ethnographic method, relies on participant observation and key informants and strives to achieve a sympathetic,

nonethnocentric view of other cultures from an inside, or emic, perspective.

A major objective of cultural analysis is to sort out the different ways people use culture as a source of social power to achieve their goals in relation to other people and the natural environment. Understanding other cultures and how they work can help us construct sustainable sociocultural systems that will maximize our ability to achieve the good life. Although not all aspects of culture are unique to humans, humans are unique in their emphasis on linguistically patterned symbolic meanings. All people have the same potential to create culture, and all cultures share many universal features. The most important cultural differences concern the three distinctive ways that people can organize social power: 1) domestically by households, 2) politically by rulers, or 3) commercially by business enterprises. Each method of organization involves its own dominant cultural process, whether humanization, politicization, or commercialization, and each requires distinctive ideologies and progressively larger-scale societies, more complex polities, and more intensive technologies. Humanization is the most crucial cultural process, because it is centered on the household and involves the maintenance and reproduction of individual humans, human society, and human culture. Sociocultural systems can be grouped into different cultural worlds according to their dominant mode of organizing social power: 1) domestically organized tribal world systems; 2) politically organized chiefdoms, kingdoms, states, and empires in the imperial world; and (3) commercially organized businesses, markets, and governments in the commercial world.

SUGGESTED READING

DeVita, Philip R. 1990. *The Humbled Anthropologist: Tales from the Pacific.* Belmont, CA: Wadsworth. A collection of personal accounts of fieldwork experiences in the Pacific written by twenty anthropologists.

Fagan, Brian. 2009. *People of the Earth: An Introduction to World Prehistory.* Upper Saddle River, NJ: Pearson Prentice Hall. An overview of world prehistory.

Gamst, Frederick C., and Edward Norbeck. 1976. *Ideas of Culture: Sources and Uses.* New York: Holt, Rinehart and Winston. An extensive examination of the culture concept.

GLOSSARY TERMS

Bigman A self-made leader in a tribal society. His position is temporary, depending on personal ability and the consent of his followers.

Generalized reciprocity The distribution of goods and services by direct sharing. It is assumed that in the long run giving and receiving balances out, but no accounts are maintained.

Nonmarket economy Goods and services distributed by direct exchange or reciprocity in the absence of markets and money.

Acculturation Culture change brought about by contact between peoples with different cultures. Usually refers to the loss of traditional culture when the members of tribal societies adopt cultural elements of commercial-scale societies.

Participant observation Field method in which the observer shares in community activities.

Ethnographic method Reliance on direct participant observation, key informants, and informal interviews as a data-collecting technique.

Key informant A member of the host culture who helps the anthropologist learn about the culture.

Genealogical method Method used to trace the marriage and family relationships among people as a basis for identifying cultural patterns in a community.

Ethnographic present An arbitrary time period when the process of culture change is ignored in order to describe a given culture as if it were a stable system.

Culture What people think, make, and do. Socially transmitted, often-symbolic information that shapes human behavior and that regulates human society so that people can successfully maintain themselves and reproduce. Culture has mental, behavioral, and material aspects; it is patterned and provides a model for proper behavior.

Humanization The production and maintenance of human beings, human societies, and human cultures, based on social power organized at the household or domestic level.

Social intelligence The cognitive ability to imagine what others are thinking.

Dunbar's number The number of individuals that can interact in a face-to-face social group, as limited by cognitive ability. Approximately 150 individuals for humans.

Social power An individual's ability to get what he or she wants, even when others might object.

Noumenal Relating to mental constructs, concepts, things that people know through the mind, rather than phenomena observed or perceived through the senses.

Imperia, imperium (singular) An individual's personal power network, including everyone that one might command or call on for assistance, as well as the institutional structures that one might direct.

Sapir-Whorf hypothesis Suggests that one's view of the world is shaped by language, such that the speakers of different languages may live in different perceptual worlds.

Emic Relating to cultural meanings derived from inside a given culture and presumed to be unique to that culture.

Etic Relating to cultural meaning as translated for cross-cultural comparison.

Phoneme The minimal unit of sound that carries meaning and is recognized as distinctive by the speakers of a given language.

Politicization The cultural process of producing and maintaining centralized political power by co-opting the humanization process.

Commercialization The cultural process of producing and maintaining private profit-making business enterprise as a means of accumulating capital, by co-opting the humanization and politicization processes.

Summum bonum The maximum human good, or the "good life" as culturally defined.

Irreducible minimum The culturally defined standard of material needs for food, clothing, and shelter. In the tribal world this material standard is available to everyone.

NOTES

1. John H. Bodley (1970, 1972a, 1972b, 1973, 1981a, 1992, 1993). See bibliography.
2. Slurink, Pouwell. 1994. "Causes of Our Complete Dependence on Culture." In *The Ethological Roots of Culture*, edited by R. A. Gardner et al., pp. 461–474. Dordrecht, Boston, and London: Kluwer Academic Press.
3. White, Leslie A. 1949. *The Science of Culture*. New York: Grove Press.
4. Boyd, Robert, and Peter J. Richerson. 1985. *Culture and the Evolutionary Process*. Chicago and London: University of Chicago Press; Durham, William H. 1991. *Coevolution: Genes, Culture, and Human Diversity*. Stanford, CA: Stanford University Press.
5. Dunbar, Robin I. 1993. "Neocortex Size as a Constraint on Group Size in Primates." *Journal of Human Evolution* 20:469–93.
6. Gardner, R. Allen, and Beatrix T. Gardner. 1994a. "Development of Phrases in the Utterances of Children and Cross-Fostered Chimpanzees." In *The Ethological Roots of Culture*, edited by R. A. Gardner et al., pp. 223–55. Dordrecht, Boston, and London: Kluwer

Academic Press. Gardner, R. Allen, and Beatrix T. Gardner. 1994b. "Ethological Roots of Language." In *The Ethological Roots of Culture*, edited by R. A. Gardner et al., pp. 199–222. Dordrecht, Boston, and London: Kluwer Academic Press; Fouts, Roger S. 1994. "Transmission of a Human Gestural Language in a Chimpanzee Mother-Infant Relationship." In *The Ethological Roots of Culture*, edited by R. A. Gardner et al., pp. 257–70. Dordrecht, Boston, and London: Kluwer Academic.

7. Tylor, Edward B. 1875. "Anthropology." *Encyclopaedia Britannica*, vol. 1.

8. Dawkins, Richard. 1989. *The Selfish Gene*. New York: Oxford University Press.

9. Waal, Frans de. 1982. *Chimpanzee Politics: Power and Sex Among Apes*. London: Jonathan Cape. Goodall, J. 1986. *The Chimpanzees of Gombe*. Cambridge, MA: Belknap Press; McGrew, W. C. 1992. *Chimpanzee Material Culture*. Cambridge, Eng.: Cambridge University Press.

10. Tomasello, Michael. 1994. "The Question of Chimpanzee Culture." In *Chimpanzee Culture*, edited by Richard W. Wrangham, Frans B. M. de Waal, and W. C. McGrew, pp. 301–17. Cambridge, MA: Harvard University Press.

11. Tylor, Edward B. 1871. *Primitive Culture*. London: Murray.

12. Mann, Michael. 1986. *The Sources of Social Power*, vol. 1, *A History of Power from the Beginning to AD 1760*. Cambridge: Cambridge University Press.

13. Gunter, Chris, Ritu Dhand, Tanguy Chouard, Henry Gee, Jane Rees, and John Spiro. 2005. "The Chimpanzee Genome." *Nature* 4371 (September): p. 47.

14. Enard, Wolfgang, et al. 2002. "Molecular Evolution of FOXP2, a Gene Involved in Speech and Language." Author's *Nature* advance online publication, 14 August 2002 (doi:10.1038/nature01025).

15. Rosenberg, Noah A. 2002. "Genetic Structure of Human Populations." *Science* 298:2381–85.

16. https://genographic.nationalgeographic.com/genographic/index.html; Spencer Wells. 2002. *The Journey of Man: A Genetic Odyssey*. Princeton and Oxford: Princeton University Press.

17. Underhill, Peter A., and Toomas Kivisild. 2007. "Use of Y Chromosome and Mitochondrial DNA Population Structure in Tracing Human Migrations." *Annual Review of Genetics* 41:539–64.

18. Li, Jun Z. 2008. "Worldwide Human Relationships Inferred from Genome-Wide Patterns of Variation." *Science* 319:1100–1104; Cavalli-Sforza, Luigi Luca. 1991. "Genes, Peoples, and Languages." *Scientific American* 265(5):104–10.

19. Manica, Andrea, Franck Prugnolle, and François Balloux. 2005. "Geography Is a Better Determinant of Human Genetic Differentiation than Ethnicity." *Human Genetics* 118:366–71.

20. Sykes, Bryan. 2001. *The Seven Daughters of Eve*. New York: W. W. Norton. Sykes established Oxford Ancestors to supply the public with DNA-based genetic ancestries www.oxfordancestors.com/component/option, com_frontpage/Itemid,1/.

21. International HapMap Consortium. 2003. "The International HapMap Project." *Nature* 426:789–96.

22. American Anthropological Association. Race: Are We So Different? www.understandingrace.org/humvar/index.html.

23. Gordon, Raymond G. 2005. *Ethnologue: Languages of the World*. 15th ed. Dallas: SIL International. Web version: www.ethnologue.com/home.asp.

24. Ruhlen, Merritt. 1987. *A Guide to the World's Languages*, vol. 1, *Classification*. Stanford, CA: Stanford University Press.

25. Whorf, Benjamin Lee. 1956. "Science and Linguistics." In *Language, Thought and Reality*, John B. Carroll, ed. Cambridge, MA: MIT. See also: Kay, Paul, and Willett Kempton. 1984. "What is the Sapir-Whorf Hypothesis?" *American Anthropologist* 86(1):65–79.

26. Berlin, Brent, and Paul Kay. 1969. *Basic Color Terms: Their Universality and Evolution*. Berkeley and Los Angeles: University of California Press.

27. Berlin, Brent. 1972. "Speculations on the Growth of Ethnobotanical Nomenclature." *Language in Society*. 1:51–86; Berlin, Brent, Dennis E. Breedlove, and Peter H. Raven. 1973. "General Principles of Classification and Nomenclature in Folk Biology." *American Anthropologist* 75(1):214–42.

28. Headland, Thomas N., Kenneth L. Pike, and Marvin Harris. 1990. *Emics and Etics: The Insider/Outsider Debate*. Newbury Park, CA: Sage.

29. Pike, Kenneth. 1954. *Language in Relation to a Unified Theory of the Structure of Human Behavior*, vol. 1. The Hague: Mouton.

30. Murdock, George P. 1967. *Ethnographic Atlas*. Pittsburgh: University of Pittsburgh Press.

31. Harris, Marvin. 1980. *Cultural Materialism: The Struggle for a Science of Culture*. New York: Random House/Vintage Books.

32. Society for Applied Anthropology. "Ethical and Professional Responsibilities." www.sfaa.net/sfaaethic.html (accessed April 26, 2009).

33. American Anthropological Association. 1998. *Code of Ethics of the American Anthropological Association*. www.aaanet.org/committees/ethics/ethcode.htm (accessed April 25, 2009).

34. Morgan, Lewis Henry. 1877. *Ancient Society*. New York: Holt.

35. Diamond, Jared. 1997. *Guns, Germs, and Steel: The Fates of Human Societies*. New York and London: W. W. Norton & Co.

36. Kohr, Leopold. 1978. *The Breakdown of Nations*. New York: Dutton.

37. United Nations. 1948. Universal Declaration of Human Rights. www.un.org/Overview/rights.html (accessed April 26, 2009).

38. Malinowski, B. 1944. *A Scientific Theory of Culture.* Chapel Hill: University of North Carolina Press.

39. Maslow, Abraham H. 1954. *Motivation and Personality.* New York: Harper.

40. Sandel, Michael J. 1998. *Liberalism and the Limits of Justice.* Cambridge, U.K., and New York: Cambridge University Press, xi.

41. Aristotle, *The Politics.* 1323al4.

42. United Nations Millennium Development Goals. www.un.org/millenniumgoals/ (accessed April 26, 2009).

43. United Nations Human Development Reports. http://hdr.undp.org/en/ (accessed April 26, 2009).

44. Radin, Paul. 1953. *The World of Primitive Man.* New York: Dutton.

CHAPTER 2

Native Amazonians: Villagers of the Rain Forest

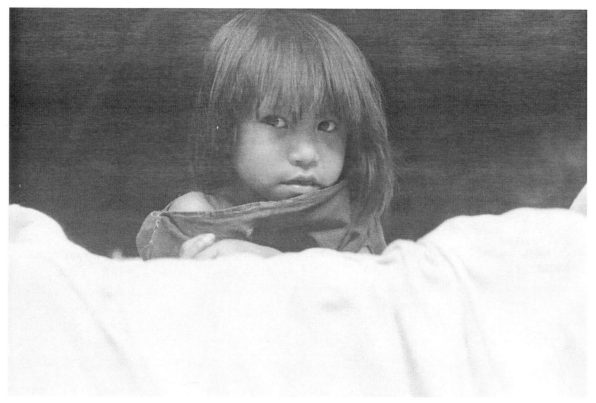

Figure 2.0. Asháninka girl.

PRONUNCIATION GUIDE

AMAZONIAN PLACE-NAMES AND TERMS ARE VARIOUSLY DE-rived from Spanish, Portuguese, Quechua, and numerous tribal languages. Their most common pronunciation can be approximated by English speakers using the following orthography and sounds:

Key
  a = *a* in f*a*ther
  o = *o* in g*o*
  ay = *ay* in d*ay*
  ee = *ee* in b*ee*t
  oo = *oo* in f*oo*d
  ng = *ng* in si*ng*
  • = Syllable division
  / = Stress
  Kuikuru = [koo • ee • koo / roo]

Matsigenka = [ma • tsi • gen / ka]
Mundurucú = [moon • doo • roo • koo /]
Waiwai = [wai / wai]
Xingu = [shing • goo /]
Yanomami = [ya • no • ma / mee]

LEARNING OBJECTIVES

After studying this chapter you should be able to do the following:

1. Describe the main climatological and biological features of the Amazon environment that distinguish this region from temperate environments.
2. Explain why the Amazon rain forest has global importance for humanity.
3. Assess the traditional ecological knowledge of indigenous Amazonian peoples.

4. Define tropical forest village culture and explain how the process of subsistence intensification is related to cultural development in Amazonia.

5. Describe shifting cultivation in Amazonia and explain why manioc is so important.

6. Describe the environmental and cultural factors that shape settlement patterns and population density in Amazonia and evaluate the relative importance of each factor.

7. Evaluate the evidence for affluence and environmental sustainability in tribal Amazonia and explain the cultural conditions that make affluence possible.

8. Compare the social organization and belief systems of Amazon villagers with Australian Aborigines, identifying and explaining the most important similarities and differences.

9. Distinguish between raiding and feuding in the tribal world, and war in the imperial and commercial worlds.

10. Compare river peoples and forest peoples, citing specific points of contrast and account for the differences.

11. Outline and interpret the main features of Amazon cosmologies.

12. Discuss the significance of gender roles and sex in Amazon village life.

In the twenty-first century indigenous Amazonians exemplify small-scale, domestically focused, highly self-sufficient peoples who rely on local resources and ecosystems. Beginning some 7,000 years ago, their ancestors developed a highly successful cultural system suited to South American tropical forest and riverine environments using manioc cultivation, ceramics, bow and arrow, and canoes.[1] Today these peoples are organizing to protect their distinct cultures and communities, their territories, and the natural resources that sustain them. Amazonia is one of the last large areas of the world where until recently many tribal societies existed with minimal direct influences from the commercial world. In 2009 it was known that fifty to one hundred independent tribal groups were still living in voluntary isolation from the outside world in forested areas throughout the Amazon.[2] Today most Amazonian peoples are engaged with the commercial world but continue to make a living from the rain forest, while conducting various commercial activities as citizens of modern nation-states.

LIVING IN THE TROPICAL RAIN FOREST: WHY AMAZONIA MATTERS

For our purposes *Amazonia* is a biocultural region centered on the drainage of the Amazon and Orinoco Rivers and adjacent forests and savannas covering most of the tropical half of South America east of the high Andes. There has been considerable scholarly debate about how these peoples and their ancestors used this environment and how they organized their societies. One issue is the extent to which Amazonia was "wilderness" at European "discovery" in 1500 and how much it was a humanly produced landscape.[3] Another major issue is whether Amazonian societies were predominantly organized as families and independent small villages, and thus were tribal world following the framework used in this book, or were primarily large, centralized chiefdoms characteristic of the imperial world. The ultimate question today is how Amazonian peoples can sustain their distinctive sociocultural systems and the natural environments that they depend on while still interacting with the larger, globally organized commercial world that is itself proving to be unsustainable. These issues matter to indigenous peoples and others who want to both protect and sustainably develop the rain forest and its inhabitants and will be examined in this chapter in some detail.

The Fragile Abundance of the Rain Forest

Amazonia is home to the world's largest tropical rain forest and is now receiving international attention from environmentalists and humanitarians because of the global implications of deforestation, loss of biodiversity, climate change, and threats to its indigenous peoples. Conservation biologists have characterized Amazonia as "the greatest tropical wilderness area on the planet," stressing its strategic benefits for the entire world. It is "the world's most important biological asset" because of its immense productivity and biodiversity.[4] The biological productivity of tropical rain forest is three to five times that of most temperate forests, and the total biomass (weight of plants and animals per hectare) is among the highest of any terrestrial ecosystem. Worldwide, tropical forests potentially cover only 6 percent of the earth's land surface yet contain half of all species. The Amazon is also the world's largest river system, and it accounts for nearly 20 percent of the world's freshwater flowing into the oceans. The forest and river constitute a single system in which the forest sustains the water and the Amazon's wealth of fish, because many species feed on fallen fruit in seasonally flooded forests.[5]

Much of the Amazon is also recognized to be wilderness. *Conservation International,* one of the world's largest and most influential conservation organizations, officially defines "wilderness" as areas of 10,000 square kilometers or more, where at least 70 percent of the original vegetation remains and population density is under five persons per square kilometer.[6] By this definition most of Amazonia is wilderness and probably has been throughout prehistory, but it has also been extensively shaped by human activities. Classifications of *anthropogenic biomes* mapping human impacts on the global landscape show that most of Amazonia is still either "remote forests" with fewer than one person per square kilometer or "wild forests" with so few people that their presence is barely visible.[7] Only more-settled areas along the Andean foothills, major rivers, or new highways are currently "populated forests" with more than one person per square kilometer, but this is an incomplete picture of the indigenous record, as will be shown.

Unfortunately, the Amazon is now virtually under siege by large-scale development projects that could dramatically change its character in this century. This matters because tropical forests contain more than 20,000 terrestrial vertebrate species (mammals and birds, amphibians and reptiles), many found nowhere else in the world.[8] This is more than double the biodiversity of any other biome in the world. Biodiversity helps maintain healthy ecosystems, and ecosystems provide us with food, water, fuel, and materials essential for the good life. Healthy ecosystems also create soil; they regulate climate, disease, and water flow; and they provide aesthetic, spiritual, educational, recreational, and cultural services.

The importance of Amazonian biodiversity is exemplified by Conservation International's designation of three Biodiversity Hotspots in the greater Amazonian biocultural region: the Tropical Andes; the Cerrado; and Brazil's Atlantic Forest. These are three of just thirty-four exceptionally rich biogeographic areas in the world that are especially threatened by human activities.[9] The Peruvian section of the Tropical Andes, which is also home to the Asháninka people, is now blanketed by newly created national parks, protected areas, communal reserves, and titled indigenous community lands. It is also threatened by inadequate management, uncontrolled logging, colonization, gold mining, the drug trade, antigovernment militants, and contradictory support from the World Bank, the Inter-American Bank, and governments for oil and gas development, large-scale timber concessions, and highway and dam construction.[10]

The most ominous large-scale threat to Amazonia is the Initiative for the Integration of the Regional Infrastructure of South America, begun in 2000 with support from major international development banks. By 2008 $69 billion had already been invested. This massive intergovernmental project is designed to connect all twelve South American countries in a vast transportation, energy, and telecommunications network to promote economic growth.[11] This will intensify all of the current problems of deforestation, colonization, oil and gas development, soy bean production, and cattle ranching. The most extreme longer-term threat to Amazonia is that drought caused by global climate change could further devastate much of the rain forest by 2100, but climate effects combined with clearing and burning could produce the same effect even sooner.[12]

Tropical Forest Cultural Diversity:
Tribes and Chiefdoms

The diversity of ethnographically known Amazonian cultures mirrors the biological diversity of the region, but it is only a small sample of the cultural diversity that must have existed when Europeans discovered the Amazon in 1500. Some six hundred indigenous languages have been identified in Amazonia, most belonging to three major subfamilies (Chibchan-Paezan, Equatorial-Tucanoan, and Ge-Pano-Carib) of the greater Amerind Family.[13] More than a hundred of these languages are already extinct. About 150 indigenous cultures appear as names in the *Outline of World Cultures*, but only about sixty were well enough described to be included in the 1967 *Ethnographic Atlas*.

There is considerable uncertainty over how many indigenous people were living in the tropical lowlands of South America in 1500. Estimates range from about 2 to 8 million, but the European invasion caused a massive dying off from exotic disease and violence. In 2005 fewer than a million indigenous people remained, but they were swamped by some 240 million nonnative colonists, the modern descendants of relative newcomers who can now only be supported by global trade systems and imported fossil fuels, food, and materials.

The archaeological evidence shows that native peoples have lived in Amazonia for at least 11,000 years.[14] Until about 10,000 years ago everyone in South America apparently lived by hunting, fishing, and collecting wild foods in a continent-wide tribal world (see table 2.1). Over several millennia people gradually developed and borrowed a variety of cultivated plants in the Andean and Amazonian regions, making it possible for population to increase overall and for settlements to become larger and more permanent. The earliest

Table 2.1. Prehistory of Amazonia, 12,000 BP–AD 1542

AD 1542	European invasion begins
2000 BP	Chiefdoms on central Amazon floodplain
5000–2000 BP	Spread of tropical forest tribal villagers
7000–5000 BP	Domestication of manioc and maiz, forest expands
12,000-7000 BP	First settlers, hunters, and foragers Post-glacial climate changes, forest retreats

evidence for the shift from hunting to food crops is from the Andean region, where preservation is the best, but archaeologists assume that cultivated crops such as manioc and maize were probably well established in Amazonia by 5,000 years ago. By about 4,000 years ago people were making ceramics in the Peruvian Amazon and living in villages much like those described ethnohistorically, and elites in coastal Peru had begun constructing chiefdoms with elaborate masonry ceremonial centers and commanded large enough populations for these societies to be considered imperial world.

By about 3,000 years ago elites were building small tribal chiefdoms on the northern fringe of Amazonia, and people along the main rivers were participating in a continental-scale trade network linking Amazonia with the Caribbean and Andean regions. Archaeological, historical, and ethnographic sources show that important trade goods included blowguns, curare poison, arrows, baskets, dye materials, shells, shell beads, gold, and salt. It is likely that these trade networks helped define and maintain ethnic identities throughout Amazonia in a process involving interplay among ethnicity, environment, and material culture.[15]

Anthropologists first speculated that Amazonia was a relatively uniform environment with limited potential for cultural development that could only support small tribal villages of shifting cultivators (see figure 2.1).[16] Although Amazonia is mostly tropical rain forest, it contains many diverse ecoregions including two main regions: the aquatic riverine environment *varzea* of the Amazon river system itself and the interfluvial *terra firma* zones between the major rivers, as well as large areas of savanna or shrublands. These environmental differences have important consequences for people. In the *varzea* people lived in fairly dense settlements on bluffs that remained above the floodplain, whereas density was lower in the interfluvial areas before Europeans brought metal axes.

Tribal chiefdoms became widespread in the *varzea* by 2,000 years ago and were then carried by Tupi-speaking peoples along the Brazilian coast by about a thousand years ago. About 750 years ago Arawak-speaking peoples in the upper Xingu River of central Brazil built large, circular villages that housed perhaps 1,000 people and were enclosed by palisades and ditches or earthen berms. As many as 2,500 people may have shared ceremonial activities and intensively managed their natural resources and interacted within a regional society of perhaps 50,000 people.[17]

The first Europeans to descend the Amazon in 1542 described large, almost continuous villages lining sections of the main river, and they were resisted by thousands of warriors. They called these societies kingdoms and they spoke of provinces, but there is no certain evidence of social class, rulers, or government institutions. Some interpretations of the historical accounts suggest the existence on the central Amazon of large towns of up to 10,000 people with hundreds of multifamily houses.[18] Most anthropologists consider these societies to have been either tribes or chiefdoms, but it is unknown how they were actually organized. Chiefdom organization means that a leader has control over more than one village, but the level of control might be quite variable. Many ethnographically known Amazonian groups do show hierarchical features including leadership ranks, inherited rank or chiefly titles, status rank by birth order, asymmetry between wife-giving and wife-receiving groups, rank endogamy, and formalized relations with other communities or groups.[19] These traits do create inequalities between people but do not create social classes that exclude disadvantaged groups from the basic necessities of life.

It seems likely that the interior forests of Amazonia were occupied by tribal peoples living in small, autonomous extended-family villages like the contemporary and historical Asháninka, or sometimes in large multifamily houses (*malocas*), as was recently the case for the Shipibo. These small societies were organized by kinship, age, and gender and were highly egalitarian in allowing everyone access to material resources, and leadership was usually not coercive. Thus, most people were likely to enjoy high levels of freedom and opportunity for success. The most prominent people were shamans and village headmen who were informal leaders, rather than rulers and priests.

ASHÁNINKA AND MATSIGENKA ETHNOECOLOGICAL KNOWLEDGE

Anthropologists may dispute whether or not indigenous Amazonian peoples were "ecologically noble savages" living "in harmony with nature" as intentional

Figure 2.1. Map of the Amazonian culture area showing the culture groups discussed. Note that the Amazon basin proper covers only part of the culture area.

conservationists, but they did not degrade their regional environment. The Tropical Andes Biodiversity Hotspot, which includes the homeland of the Matsigenka and Asháninka peoples, contains 20,000 plant species found nowhere else, and some 1,500 unique vertebrates. Living successfully in this region is no simple task; it requires an impressive array of very specific environmental knowledge that must be produced, continuously verified, stored, and transmitted to each generation. I was introduced to a small sample of this knowledge one evening when I loaned my portable audio recorder to a small group of Asháninka who were visiting my camp. They immediately created a word game in which they excitedly passed the microphone back and forth, recording a steady stream of Asháninka words. They were spontaneously reciting a seemingly endless list of animal names, playing with their working knowledge of rain forest biodiversity. Biodiversity is the foundation of their way of life, and they treat it as "natural capital." It is their investment in the future. The Asháninka not only know the names of the animals but understand many details of their natural history and imbue many species with rich cultural significance. I later found that the Asháninka's knowledge of rain forest animals is matched by their knowledge of useful cultivated plants. I found dozens of named varieties of manioc and bananas in Asháninka gardens. People experimented with new varieties and were eager to discuss their different qualities. It is not surprising that rain forest peoples are interested in biological diversity, because it is the very source of their existence. Isolated Asháninka groups that I visited in the 1960s were entirely self-sufficient. With the exception of a few metal pots, knives, and axes, they found materials for everything they needed in their forest and gardens. They made their own houses, implements, food, medicine, and clothing directly from the raw materials that they extracted from their local environment.

The biological diversity of the Amazon forest presents an enormous information management problem for people living in the forest. For example, within Matsigenka territory along the Manu River in the Peruvian Amazon, researchers have identified more than 825 tree species in study plots covering only 36 hectares of forest scattered over a 400-square-kilometer area.[20] Many species were uncommon, or restricted to particular habitats. There were 310 bird species within a single square kilometer.[21] More ant species (43) were found on a single tree than are found in all of Great Britain.[22] The Matsigenka must not only name

the species, but they must know where to find them. For example, they knew precisely where to locate a specific bamboo containing an anticoagulant that was ideal for making arrow points. Ethnobotanist Glen Shephard Jr. found that the Matsigenka could name and distinguish at least 77 distinct habitat types, sorting by topography, hydrology, succession patterns, soil, indicator species, and aspects of vegetation. The Panoan-speaking Matses Indians in the northeast Peruvian Amazon use an even finer classification, distinguishing 178 habitat types, many of which help them locate specific palm trees and small mammals in particular seasons.[23] This kind of knowledge proved to be more precise than what researchers could extract from satellite images.

In my own research with the Shipibo I found they had names for 22 different palms, which corresponded closely with the formal botanical classifications. They made extensive use of many of these palms for housing materials, artifacts, and food. Figure 2.2 shows silhouettes of the most important species occurring in the Ucayali Moist Forest ecozone together with their Shipibo and botanical names and uses.[24]

Rain Forest Gardening and Manioc

Manioc production, the key to successful human occupation of Amazonia, depends on a specialized system of **shifting cultivation** that minimally disrupts the forest ecosystem. It is the forest that ultimately maintains soil quality, regulates the local climate, recycles nutrients and water, and sustains fish and game resources. With shifting cultivation food is harvested from small, temporary forest clearings containing mixed gardens. In comparison with the large monocrop farms and plantations that have recently been introduced in Amazonia for commercial purposes, native gardens, or *swiddens*, rely on a diverse mix of crops. The overlapping layers of different plant species minimize erosion and losses to insects and disease while making efficient use of the space. Sweet potato vines and beans quickly cover the ground and then are shaded by maize and manioc, which in turn are shaded by bananas and various fruit trees.

This gardening system is sometimes called **slash and burn** because it is based on an apparently simple technology of cutting the forest and then burning the dry slash (see figure 2.3). The burn is usually incomplete, and many trees survive and quickly regrow. Some wild plants may even be deliberately protected. The burning concentrates nutrients in the ash, thus eliminating

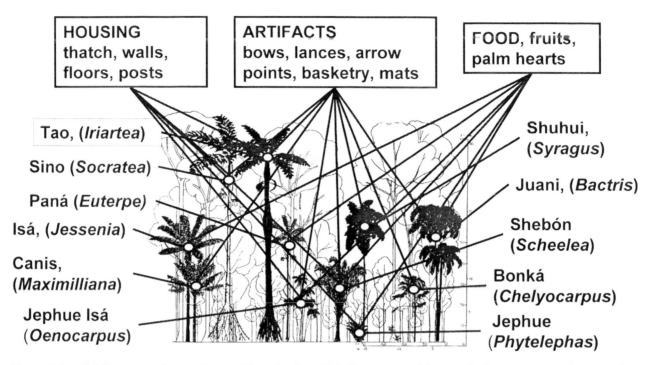

HOUSING
thatch, walls,
floors, posts

ARTIFACTS
bows, lances, arrow
points, basketry, mats

FOOD, fruits,
palm hearts

Tao, (*Iriartea*)

Sino (*Socratea*)

Paná (*Euterpe*)

Isá, (*Jessenia*)

Canis,
(*Maximilliana*)

Jephue Isá
(*Oenocarpus*)

Shuhui,
(*Syragus*)

Juani, (*Bactris*)

Shebón
(*Scheelea*)

Bonká
(*Chelyocarpus*)

Jephue
(*Phytelephas*)

Figure 2.2. Shipibo uses of ucayali moist forest palms (Shipibo names with botanical genus names in parentheses).

Figure 2.3. Shifting cultivation in Amazonia: (a) an Asháninka mother and child rest in the shade in a newly cleared swidden; (b) an Asháninka man carrying a bundle of manioc cuttings to be planted.

the need for additional fertilizer. Unburned logs provide an easy source of wood for cooking fires.

Shifting cultivation requires specialized knowledge and vocabulary. For example, the Matsigenka distinguish ten different soil types and five stages in the garden cycle.[25] Because many varieties of manioc require more than six months to produce large edible roots, or tubers, manioc must be grown on land that is not seasonally flooded; thus, manioc gardens cannot take advantage of the annually renewed alluvial soils along the major rivers. Gardens typically are about a hectare (2.5 acres) or less in size. Although they are seldom carefully tended for more than a year, they may yield manioc for up to three years. New gardens might be made each year, so that at a given time every **household** has gardens at different stages of production. In this **forest fallow** system, a plot usually would not be replanted for at least twenty-five years to allow ample time for forest regrowth. Full forest regrowth might require fifty to one hundred years or more, but as long as gardens remain small and widely scattered, a twenty-five-year cycle can adequately protect the forest. Shifting cultivation works well until commercial agriculture invades tribal areas. Large-scale corporate business owners may displace subsistence cultivators, pushing them into marginal areas where they are forced to shorten the fallow cycle. Under these conditions shifting cultivation cannot be sustained, and people and lands are impoverished.

The Asháninka prefer the forest fallow system to more intensive cultivation for several reasons. Gardens are abandoned in part because rapid forest regrowth makes weeding a burdensome task. In most forest soils, continuous replanting would soon lead to a decline in fertility and yield. Reclearing of old garden sites is avoided because during the early stages of forest succession the vegetation is very dense and difficult to clear with hand tools. Village sites themselves may be shifted every few years to reduce conflict or to find better hunting ground.

The productivity of manioc is truly impressive and readily explains its importance in the subsistence system. I found that a single garden belonging to an Asháninka household could produce some 30,000 kilograms of manioc in a year. This is five times the household's normal consumption even disregarding replanting. Such apparent overproduction provides an important security margin. Other researchers found that the Matsigenka obtained more than two-thirds of their food by weight from manioc, which was produced at roughly 10 percent of the labor cost by weight

of food produced by hunting, foraging, and fishing (see table 2.2). The historically recent use of metal axes has no doubt increased the relative advantage of manioc by making tree felling easier, but even with stone tools, manioc cultivation would have been very attractive. The Matsigenka allocated just over half of their total subsistence effort to gardening, which produced over 90 percent of their total food by weight.[26] But manioc alone does not provide a balanced diet, so the Matsigenka raise a dozen other important crops and cultivate some eighty named plant varieties for various purposes.[27]

Manioc is an amazingly useful plant. Most Amazonians grow a dozen or more varieties and some recognize over one hundred varieties, carefully distinguishing them based on characteristics of tuber and leaf.[28] Manioc grows from clones rather than seeds, and genetic variations are produced slowly by natural mutations. In order to maintain the vigor of their plants, people must constantly introduce new varieties obtained from distant growers. The Matsigenka attribute the strength of new varieties to the powers of the shamans, who are thought to use their supernatural powers to find them.[29]

All manioc tubers contain potentially toxic substances. In "sweet" varieties, they can be eliminated merely by peeling and cooking, but the "bitter" varieties require more elaborate processing. The quality of the starch in bitter manioc is especially suitable for flour, which is made by an elaborate, labor-intensive process of squeezing, sifting, and roasting the grated pulp. Some Amazonian peoples produce more than two dozen types of bread and beverages from bitter manioc and its by-products.[30] The flour may be sifted in various ways, baked in bread, toasted, or used in soups and stews. The juice is used directly in soups, and there are several uses for the tapioca starch extracted from the juice (see figure 2.4). Manioc may be stored in the ground until it is used, or it may be stored as processed flour or bread as long as it is kept dry. Potentially, it could provide an important **surplus** that could help support a political-scale society, but as will be shown, a variety of other factors—both cultural and ecological—keep this surplus only potential. Manioc's only downside is that it is not a source of protein.

Village Size Limits: Gardens, Game, or Autonomy?

Amazonia was primarily a world of small local communities and societies of tribes and small chiefdoms, in which people were connected by overlapping

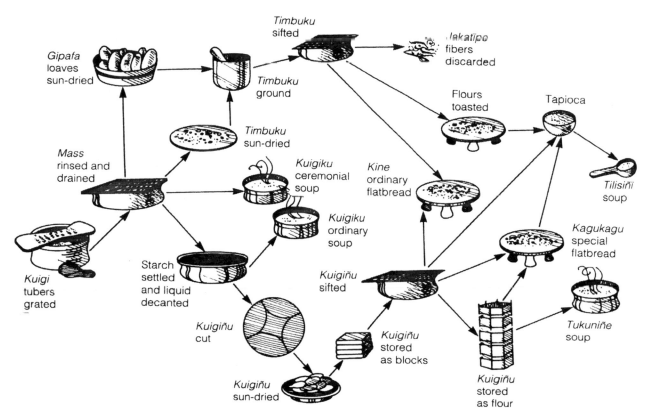

Figure 2.4. Steps in the preparation of manioc among the Kuikuru (redrafted from Dole 1978).

networks of kinship and exchange relationships. There were no rulers, no government, and no bureaucracies. Size and permanence of settlements and subsistence patterns are important dimensions of social scale and complexity, but it is not always obvious what factors shape these variables. The Asháninka and Matsigenka have very small, relatively impermanent settlements and very low-density populations, and represent the extreme small end of the size scale. These scale features maximize individual freedom, access to natural resources, community autonomy, security, and overall sustainability, but it is uncertain how long these conditions have existed for particular peoples, or how and why they produced and maintained them.

The record suggests that small-scale tribal societies have been the most successful ethnographically known societies in South America. Tribal societies were found throughout South America in 1500. They displayed a wide range of **subsistence intensification** from extensive foraging and shifting cultivation, to semi-intensive horticulture, whereas imperial world societies have farming systems based on intensive irrigation, terracing, and pastoralism that are very productive in arid and high-altitude environments. The

cross-cultural dimensions of South American societies are explored in more detail in chapter 5.

The case for at least some environmental limits on cultural development in the Amazon is strong, because the biological wealth of the rain forest hides some curious paradoxes. High biological productivity does not automatically mean high human carrying capacity, because the forest puts much energy into what for people is inedible wood and leaves. Except along the main rivers, soil fertility is often naturally very low and easily depleted by intensive cultivation. There is little easily harvested carbohydrate in the natural vegetation, and 90 percent of the animal biomass is composed of ants, termites, and other small invertebrates that can eat leaves and wood.[31] Large vertebrates are relatively scarce, and animal protein is difficult for hunters to secure because game is often nocturnal or hidden in the forest canopy. Natural food resources for people are so scarce that some authorities have argued that no one could live in the rain forest without access to garden produce.[32]

The infertility of Amazonian soils is due to the combination of heavy humidity and warm temperature, which fosters both luxuriant growth and the rapid breakdown of forest litter. The top humus layer of the soil is actually very shallow, and most tree roots are near the surface, where they can quickly take in the nutrients liberated by decomposition. Trees are so efficient that more nutrients are held in the forest itself than in the soil. The forest vegetation pumps moisture through transpiration into the atmosphere to be returned in daily thundershowers, even as the leaves reduce erosion by cushioning and dispersing the heavy downpours.

There is considerable disagreement among archaeologists over how large and how permanent settlements were in pre-Columbian Amazonia, and over the importance of the river versus forest distinction. It is possible that many archaeological sites in the *varzea* that look very large and permanent may have been produced by periodic reoccupation by small, impermanent settlements.[33] Away from the major rivers people combined foraging with small shifting gardens that took advantage of natural tree-fall clearings and areas with soft vegetation that could be more easily cleared with stone axes.[34] Larger, more permanent gardens that supported chiefdoms were intensively cultivated in floodable savannas using raised fields, or with composting and mulching and household waste, which about 2,200 to 2,300 years ago produced the rich *terra preta* soil that is now found in many areas. Use of maize and beans with their complementary proteins would have made the relatively low availability of fish and game in the interior forests less important as a factor limiting human population, but nevertheless forest peoples apparently preferred to hunt and fish.

It is striking that interfluvial terra firma villages usually remain small, averaging fewer than one hundred and seldom exceeding four hundred people. These villages are relatively impermanent, as villagers relocate every few years. Anthropologists have often assumed that the low productivity of forest soils and the limited availability of animal protein must set upper limits on village size. However, the abundant carbohydrate from manioc gardening could easily support villages of five hundred people, as long as people could get the dietary minimum of fifty grams of protein needed per capita daily from fish and game[35] (see box 2.1). In fact, the protein intake of tribal Amazonians typically exceeds this minimum.[36] Furthermore, it appears that wild game might theoretically support human densities as high as one person per square kilometer, and even more if fish and edible insects are included. However, actual tribal densities were much lower than this. The Asháninka averaged only 0.4 persons per square kilometer, suggesting that the size, density, and permanence of human settlements in the Amazon were also determined by cultural factors such as beliefs about what constituted the good life.

Apparently, villages could be larger throughout Amazonia if people were willing to either hunt or fish more intensively, rely more on plant protein, maintain domestic animals, or accept a nutritionally lower standard of living and/or the higher levels of political authority or social inequality that such changes might require. It seems likely that cultural factors connected with the human advantages of domestic-scale society encourage people to halt gardening, hunting, and fishing production at levels well below what would be theoretically sustainable. Cultural preferences for large game animals, maximum leisure, and household-level autonomy seem to be more important objectives than supporting the largest possible villages. It seems that the tropical forest village way of life offers Amazonian peoples sufficient personal satisfactions that they choose to maintain and reproduce it as long as they have enough personal freedom to make that choice. This suggests that the transformation of the tribal world first into the imperial and then into the commercial world involved a loss of human freedom in the sense that the range of lifestyle choices became much narrower. In the Asháninka case village size is related to village politics and the structure of leadership, as well as the availability of game, as will be discussed in another section.

BOX 2.1. CARRYING CAPACITY CALCULATIONS: MANIOC STARCH VERSUS WILD GAME

Robert Carneiro[37] devised a formula to specify the critical variables that determine the maximum size of a village as limited by the productivity of manioc under shifting cultivation (se figure 2.5). The amount of arable land is set by the maximum distance women choose to carry produce from the garden—usually about 3 miles (5 km), yielding 18,000 acres (7,290 hectares). Assuming Carneiro's modest figure of 13,350 acres (5,468 hectares) of arable land, gardens cultivated for 3 years, and a 25-year fallow, a village of 2,043 people could meet its manioc needs without ever moving. This is more than six times the observed upper limit for Amazonian villages. Extending the fallow to 100 years would reduce the potential size of the village to 561 people, still well above average for Amazonia. These figures demonstrate that manioc shortages do not limit village size.

Village size limits based on the productivity of rain forest hunting are more difficult to estimate because we do not have accurate figures for game populations. Figure 2.6 lists some of the variables that must be taken into account, along with a formula for calculating the number of people who theoretically could obtain 2 ounces (50 g) of protein from game per year per square kilometer (0.4 mile^2) on a sustained basis. The most critical value is the biomass (the total weight of biological organisms living in a given area) of the game, but this can be estimated based on zoological surveys of rain forest mammals,[38] allowing for cultural definitions of edibility, technology, and sustainability. These calculations predict a potential village size remarkably close to that seen ethnographically. The high estimate for biomass suggests that up to 300 people could supply their protein needs within a 6 mile (10 km) hunting radius of a permanent village.

Basic Formula:

$$P = \frac{[T/(R+Y)]Y}{A}$$

Where P = village population, T = arable land, R = years in forest fallow, Y = years garden cultivated, and A = garden area per person.

If T = 13,350 acres, R = 25 yr, Y = 3 yr, and A = .7 acres, then P = 2043 people.

If R = 100 yr, then P = 561 people.

Figure 2.5. A formula for environmental limits on gardening on Amazonian villagers (text from Carneiro 1960).

Basic Formula:

$$P = \frac{BHSCN}{R}$$

Where P = people/km^2, B = mammal biomass, H = mammals hunted, S = sustainable harvest, C = carcass weight, N = protein content, R = protein required per person per year.

If B = 5300 kg/km^2, H = .43, S = .10, C = .50, N = .16, and R = 50 g × 365 days = 18 kg, then P = 1 person/km^2.

Therefore, a 10-km hunting radius covering an area of 314 km^2 supports 314 people.

Figure 2.6. A formula for estimating the number of people who could be supported by hunting within a 6-mile (10-km) radius of a rainforest village.

Asháninka Wealth, Affluence, and Ecological Footprint

Amazonian villages clearly demonstrate some striking advantages of life in tribal societies. The villagers have developed an equitably balanced subsistence system. Men do the heavy work of garden clearing in seasonally concentrated bursts of effort, and women carry out the bulk of routine cultivation, harvesting, and food processing. Men, women, and children forage for wild plant food, insects, and small animals. Everyone may join large-scale fishing expeditions, but men provide most of the daily animal protein by hunting and fishing. Meat and fish are pooled and distributed to each household in the village to smooth out the variation in productivity between households. All of these activities are individually directed, and everyone controls the necessary tools. There are no major inequalities here.

This production system guarantees that each household can meet its nutritional needs with relatively moderate workloads while maintaining a reasonable labor balance between the sexes. It also provides strong incentives for maintaining low population densities because as densities increase, workloads quickly accelerate due to game depletion and the increasing distances that women must walk to their gardens. Workloads also would be increased dramatically if people needed to produce food to support the nonfood-producing specialists who often accompany increases in societal scale and complexity. Thus, an incentive to maintain social equality is also the foundation of tribal societies.

Subsistence workloads in Amazonia are not significantly different from those reported for Australian Aborigines. In both cases, there is abundant leisure time. On average, all food production needs can be met with just two to three hours of work a day.[39] Men average about three hours and women about two hours. Total workloads are gender balanced. All work, including everything that must be done around the house, requires only five to seven hours daily and would be unlikely to exceed eight hours. This means that if the workday begins with the equatorial sunrise at 6 a.m., one could quite possibly spend the whole afternoon lounging in a hammock.

These figures must be interpreted with caution because they were collected by different researchers who did not always classify activities in the same way. Some researchers did not regard child care as work. There is also the basic problem of the cross-cultural validity of the concept of "work." For example, should hunting, which is often an exciting and enjoyable activity, be considered work? Researchers also used different techniques for recording time expenditures.

Allen Johnson[40] (1985) made a useful comparison of the workload of the Matsigenka, which is heavy by Amazonian standards, with the way modern urban French people spend their time (considering women working both in and outside the home). He showed that although both the Matsigenka and the French get about eight hours of sleep a night, the Matsigenka work about two hours less a day than the French to satisfy their basic needs. The Matsigenka have fewer other demands on their time than the French and enjoy five hours more free time a day, which they spend resting and visiting. Data such as these tend to confirm the idea of affluence in tribal societies, lending credibility to the early reports from frustrated colonial plantation owners that tribals were "lazy" and hated to work. In fact, they do work, but only until their basic needs are satisfied, and their society is structured so that no one works for an overlord.

It would be a mistake to view these systems as underdeveloped technological stages that will inevitably evolve into something more productive. These are already highly developed systems that elegantly solve the problems posed for them. They would be difficult to improve upon, given their culturally defined objective of equitably meeting everyone's physical needs in small communities.

Workloads are kept low in village Amazonia both by the limited demand on food production in a system where each household is basically self-sufficient in food, but also by the limited range of material culture that people produce, own, and maintain. The Asháninka can fit their most valuable personal effects into a cane box with a volume of less than one cubic foot, whereas many Americans must rent additional storage space for their goods. The material differences are vast. According to moving companies, the average weight of American household goods is 7,200 pounds, and the contents of an average three-bedroom home fills a standard twenty-foot long storage container with a volume of 1,172 cubic feet.

The Asháninka make only about 120 separately named material items apart from food products.[41] This list includes a full range of domestic articles such as the house (see figure 2.7) and tools for hunting, gardening, fishing, and trapping; food processing implements such as grinders; ceramic pots; baskets; strainers; trays; gourd containers; pounders; stirrers; grills; looms and spindles; clothing and adornments such as robes, headdresses, necklaces, bandoliers, and pendants; face paint; combs; depilators; toys; and musical instruments such as drums, flutes, and panpipes. Only about a dozen additional industrially manufactured items are imported, such as metal knives; axes; needles; and pots, but these things can usually be obtained by trade. This is all the material culture needed to maintain the Asháninka good life on the fringes of the commercial world. This is a substantially richer list of things than possessed by Australian Aborigines and reflects the more sedentary lifestyle of the Amazon villagers, but it is far less than the thousands of material items possessed by households fully dependent on the commercial world and its products.

Many Asháninka men maintain a formal exchange relationship with trading partners called *ayompari*, who often live far away. Goods such as arrows, *cushmas*, and resin are exchanged on a deferred basis, such that on a given visit a man might give his partner a dog, expecting a return gift on another visit maybe a year later. What is remarkable about such exchanges is that they typically involve objects that everyone has available and could make themselves. The larger function of such exchanges is that they allowed non-kin to safely interact, while providing a justification for long-distance travel, and they create a chain of connections that also make it possible for imported manufactured goods to reach remote areas in exchange for traditionally manufactured items.

Perhaps even more important than the details of their material culture is how it is distributed. Every Asháninka adult owns all the basic tools needed for daily life and has free access to all necessary natural resources. Because they pay no taxes and do not need money to buy anything, the Asháninka are free to devote 88 percent of their productive time to producing and maintaining the members of their households by hunting, foraging, gardening, cleaning, bathing, food preparation, child care, and eating. Society and nonmaterial culture take 8 percent of their effort, which is devoted to maintaining their social networks and reproducing their culture through visiting, feasting, singing, dancing, and storytelling. The rest of their material culture takes only 4 percent of their effort.[42]

Asháninka affluence depends on wealth as well as income, and a careful accounting for comparative purposes shows that they are well endowed in both respects. If we assign an arbitrary dollar value of $9.08 per hour (the lowest average wage of service workers in the retail sector of the American economy in 1999) to the time the Asháninka expend in their productive

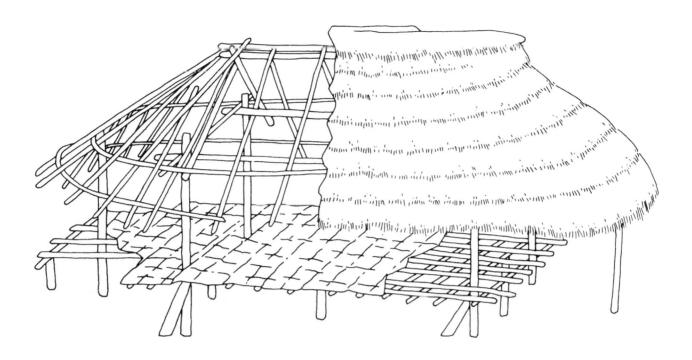

Figure 2.7. An Asháninka house. Each household usually occupies a single palm leaf-thatched house constructed of posts and beams, with slats peeled from palm trunks as flooring: (a) construction details, (b) Asháninka house with platform bed.

activities, we can estimate an imputed annual household income of $70,924 and a corresponding gross domestic product of $14,185 per capita. This would be comparable to the gross domestic product (GDP) of a modestly high-income country. It allows everyone to be well fed, comfortably housed, and maintained according to the standards of their culture. The commercial world does not normally count nature, people, society, and culture in national accounts and does not relate them to GDP, but if we treat our estimated Asháninka household income as a modest 5 percent return on the natural, human, social, and cultural capital that made this income possible, then each household draws on wealth of $1,032,873. This represents the value of all the human effort invested in their households, their individually owned stock of material culture, and the shared value of their society and culture.

The Asháninka are millionaires based on the capital value of their income, but a wealth calculation based on income alone does not account for the full value of their natural capital. Given the richness of the tropical forest ecosystem, it would be reasonable to estimate that most of Asháninka wealth is in nature, because as with Australian Aborigines, nature's services provide most of their material needs. Ecological economists estimated in 1997 that the ecosystem services provided to the world by tropical forests recycling materials, forming soil, and producing food, freshwater, and biodiversity and so on, were worth $2,007 per hectare per year.[43] Since then the market value of forests for carbon storage to reduce global warming has risen substantially. In 2008 the European Climate Exchange valued a ton of stored carbon dioxide at $26. This makes the 455 tons of carbon dioxide stored in an average hectare of tropical forest worth $11,823 as directly tradable capital and represents nearly $15 million per Asháninka household, estimating 21,000 people and 52,000 square kilometers of forest. The annual $2,007 per hectare value of nature's services would represent a per-household value of nearly $50 million as a 5 percent return on capital if the entire territory is counted as a forest and game conservation area.

I estimate that the Asháninka make direct use of the equivalent of 1.15 global hectares of average biological product per capita per year, or approximately 65 million kilocalories per person. More than 90 percent of this represents their gardens, firewood, plant materials, and the food chain supporting the game, fish, and foraged food that they consume. The forest biomass removed for the house site represents the balance. This is their **ecological footprint**,[44] and it is substantially higher than my estimates for foragers such as Australian Aborigines, African pastoralists, and south Asian Indians. The American footprint of 9.5 global hectares was nearly an order of magnitude higher than the Asháninka footprint, but the critical difference was that the American population was more than tenfold greater. Americans used nearly 200 percent of the biocapacity of their territory, whereas the Asháninka were using only 0.24 percent of their biocapacity. The American ecological footprint could only be sustained from year to year by burning massive amounts of fossil fuels and by importing energy and materials from all over the world. In contrast, the Asháninka were virtually self-sufficient, and the archaeological record demonstrates the long-term sustainability of their way of life.

VILLAGE LIFE IN AMAZONIA

This section describes and compares two culturally distinct contemporary peoples living today in the Peruvian Amazon, the upland forest-dwelling Asháninka-Matsigenka and the Shipibo-Conibo who occupy the upper Ucayali River floodplain and tributaries. The objective is to illustrate the cultural diversity of tribal Amazonian sociocultural systems, showing how closely attuned these peoples are to their environments and the way in which seemingly small differences in scale and complexity affect the details

Table 2.2. Matsigenka Subsistence per Household per Year

	Production		Energy Cost	Subsistence Effort
	(kg)	(%)	(kcal/kg)	(%)
Gardening*	6755	93	80	55
Fishing	298	4	740	22
Hunting/gathering	194	3	1151	22
Total	7247	100	1971	99

Source: Johnson and Behrens (1982).

*Manioc alone = 4887 kg, or 67 percent of total production weight.

of their daily life. These two tribal peoples live side by side yet speak very different languages, occupy different ecological zones, and show remarkable differences in settlement patterns, family life, and material culture. This account first situates both peoples within their prehistoric, historic, and contemporary settings.

The primary material distinction between these peoples is that much of the territory of the Asháninka and their relatives is in the hilly and rugged tropical Andes and the headwaters of the main Amazon and its tributaries including extensive lowland forests,[45] whereas the Shipibo primarily occupy the floodplain zones in the central Peruvian Amazon. The Shipibo pride themselves on their fishing, canoe building, fine textiles, and ceramics. Life is more intense and more ritualized in Shipibo villages than in the often more isolated Asháninka hamlets, but historically neither group were formal chiefdoms.

Arawak-speaking peoples like the Asháninka may have been central to the Amazonian interaction trading system, judging by the wide distribution of Arawak languages. In the Peruvian Amazon today the various Arawak speakers see themselves as similar to Panoan speakers like the Shipibo, and both groups define themselves as similar peoples distinguished by their woven cotton clothing in contrast to "naked wild peoples" like the Panoan-speaking Matses, Amahuaca, and Cashibo-Cacataibo who live in remote headwaters. The Asháninka still trade baskets for finely made painted Shipibo pottery. Trade helped maintain peace and defined a broader cultural system. Asháninka salt was traded throughout Amazonia, and the Asháninka peoples had previously obtained metal goods from the Inca. I found that the Asháninka retained a memory of their trade with the Inca, and I saw indigenous Amazonian trade goods still displayed in Andean markets.

The Asháninka: A Forest People

The Asháninka consider themselves to be expert hunters and skilled gardeners, and until recently their settlements were widely scattered and impermanent. Their ancestors can be traced back thousands of years to a probable origin in the northwest or central Amazon. The archaeological record suggests that over time many cultural changes occurred, but the broad pattern of tribal village life based on manioc cultivation remained the same. Excavating beneath a modern Shipibo village on oxbow lake Yarinacocha near the city of Pucallpa, Peru, in the 1960s, archaeologist Donald Lathrap discovered 4,000-year-old decorated pottery and indications of an ancient village that would

have been occupied by hundreds of people. A different, slightly younger ceramics tradition was found in Asháninka territory to the south on the upper Pachitea River. These sites all contained large ceramic urns of the kind used for brewing manioc beer, and Lathrap believed they were all occupied by Arawak-speaking peoples. By at least 3,000 years ago these peoples were trading with people in coastal Peru and Ecuador, and by 2,500 years ago they were in contact with the nearby Andean peoples who created the Chavin chiefdom temple cult that became the foundation of Andean imperial societies. Twenty-two hundred years ago a new ceramics tradition originating in the central Amazon appeared in the Peruvian Amazon lowlands. These newcomers lived along the river in large villages that may have contained 500 to 1,000 people, and at one site houses were arranged in a circle around a large open ceremonial plaza similar to the layout of modern villages in the upper Xingu of Brazil. These peoples were apparently the immediate ancestors of the ethnographically known Asháninka and their relatives. The dispersed settlements and minimal ceremonial life of the ethnohistoric and modern Asháninka suggest that they experienced a gradual simplification of their sociocultural system over 1,500 years.[46]

The Basics of Asháninka Family and Society

Asháninka society is a very simple system based on the family. Only a few cultural rules and terms need to be understood to master the system. Asháninka villages consist of a few individual houses—often only two and usually located in the same ridgetop clearing—occupied by closely related individual **nuclear families** (husband, wife, and dependent children). A village, or household group, is either an **extended family** or households connected by sibling ties. Extended families are formed when married children reside near their parents, either matrilocally or patrilocally (see box 2.2 and figure 2.8). Each married couple constitutes an independent domestic unit with its own kitchen hearth and garden, but there is daily economic cooperation between households, and fish and game are pooled. Household groups might be an hour's walk from any neighboring groups, but such groups might periodically socialize over manioc beer and sing and dance. They also might combine to form raiding parties.

The Asháninka recognize three categories of people: kin, formal trading partners, and strangers who are potential enemies. If friendly interaction is to take place, strangers are immediately placed in a kinship

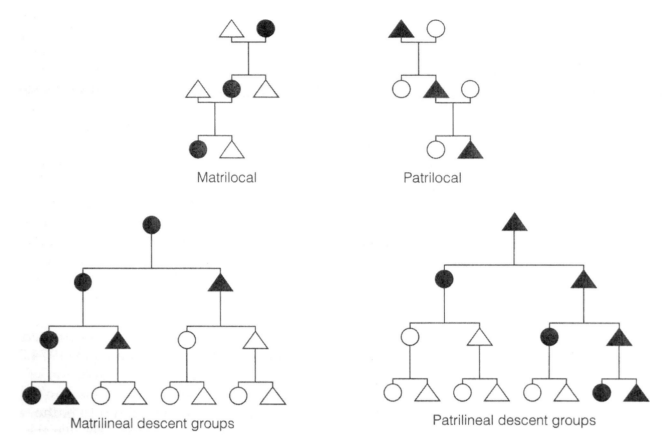

Figure 2.8. Residence patterns and descent groups.

Matrilocal

Patrilocal

Matrilineal descent groups

Patrilineal descent groups

category and treated appropriately. For example, men who wanted to request a favor from me would address me as "brother." When they wanted to show deference, they would call me "father-in-law."

The distinctive feature of the Asháninka kinship terminological system is that one's immediate kin are sorted into just two groups: (1) parents and siblings, and stepparents and stepsiblings, who are close family and thus not marriageable; and (2) those who are potential in-laws and spouses (see figure 2.9). As is common in Australian aboriginal society, one marries someone in the category of **cross-cousin**, and the

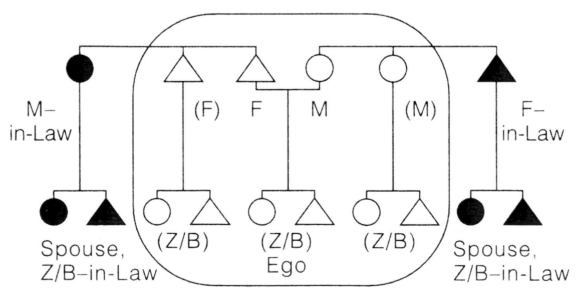

M–in-Law (F) F M (M) F–in-Law

Spouse, Z/B–in-Law (Z/B) (Z/B) Ego (Z/B) Spouse, Z/B–in-Law

Figure 2.9. Asháninka kinship system.

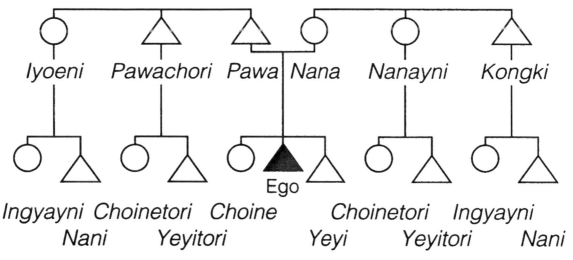

Figure 2.10. Asháninka kinship terminology.

parents of cross-cousins are called in-laws. Parallel cousins, the children of one's father's brother and mother's sister, are often treated as siblings, and their parents are treated like one's own parents.

Figure 2.10 illustrates some of the actual terms that are used in one Asháninka language. Father is called *Pawa*, and one's father's brother is called *Pawachori*, which might be translated as "step" or "potential" father. *Pawachori* might, in fact, marry one's mother if one's father died (a practice known as the levirate marriage), and his spouse would be called *Nanayni*, or mother's sister.

When an Asháninka man seeks a spouse, he must find someone whom he can call *Ingyayni*, or cross-cousin. The terms need not refer to actual biological relationships. Any unrelated woman might be placed in that category if everyone agrees, but this is an important decision because it has obvious sexual implications. A man will almost certainly call his lover *Ingyayni*. The parents of someone called *Ingyayni* would be called *Kongki* and *Iyoeni* (in-laws). A husband would show respect for his in-laws and would be expected to work for them during the initial, often **matrilocal residence**, phase of his marriage.

Although the Asháninka kin system reflects cross-cousin marriage, it can also be characterized as a sibling-exchange marriage system in which a brother and sister marry a brother and sister. Figure 2.11 illustrates how the Asháninka terms accommodate both forms of marriage. Cross-cousin marriage could be conceptualized as the continuation of sibling exchanges in consecutive generations, and with the Asháninka, sibling-exchange marriages are more common than

marriages of "biological" cousins. Using a genealogy generated by the 100-person model of Asháninka society described in box 2.3, figure 2.12 illustrates the geographic distribution of personal kin networks applying the appropriate kin terms. The ego #47 in this example is a forty-year-old man living in household #19 in hamlet A, which is a local group consisting of nine people living in three households. This man is living patrilocally adjacent to his father, who is sixty-five years old, alongside his twenty-year-old son, who is also residing patrilocally. Man #47 is linked by kinship and marriage to five other hamlets in the region. The outcome of these cultural patterns is that Asháninka territory is blanketed by a web of interpersonal connections that supports the humanization

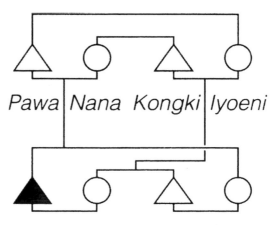

Figure 2.11. Sibling-exchange marriages Asháninka and cross-cousin marriages as reflected in kinship terminology.

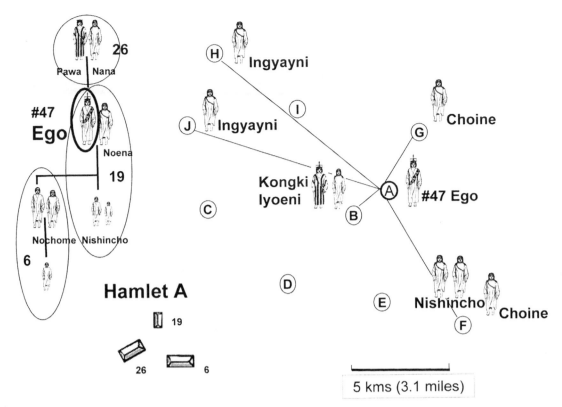

Figure 2.12. Close kin of 40 years old Asháninka man #47, hamlet A.

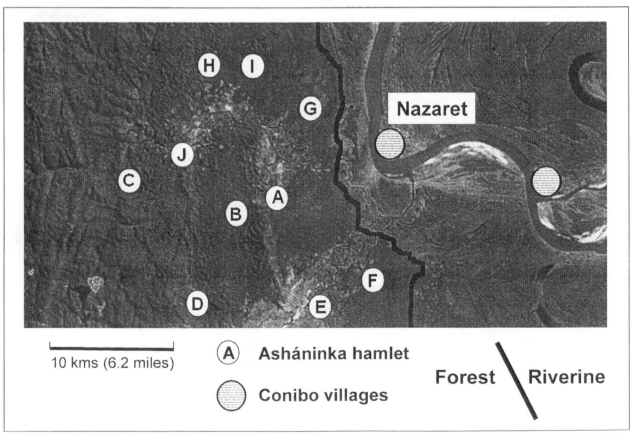

Figure 2.13. Asháninka hamlets in model 100 person society in forest zone at 0.2 persons/km2 compared with 100 Conibo in two villages in riverine zone.

process. Figure 2.13 places the Model Asháninka Society on a forest zone landscape at a density of 0.2 persons per square kilometer next to the riverine environment of the Upper Ucayali River, which is occupied by two Conibo villages at a density of five to twenty-five persons per square kilometer. This geographic and demographic comparison helps explain the dramatic differences in these two Amazonian tribal societies.

BOX 2.2. DOMESTIC RESIDENCE AND DESCENT GROUPS

When descent groups in the form of clans or lineages are advantageous, people can construct them out of the spatial alignments produced when a newly married couple chooses to live near the husband's or wife's parents, either patrilocal or matrilocal, respectively. Figure 2.8 illustrates the domestic groupings that are created by patrilocality and matrilocality. Patrilocality and matrilocality create de facto patrilineages and matrilineages, respectively. There are also interesting cases, such as the Mundurucú, in which residence matrilocality occurs with patrilineal descent groups.

In Amazonia, the emphasis on manioc gardening seems to encourage matrilocal residence patterns, in which a husband lives with or near his wife's family. This may be because mothers, daughters, and sisters often form cooperative work groups when gardening, processing manioc, or making ceramics. More than 80 percent (31) of a sample of 37 Amazonian societies either are listed as matrilocal (17) or show matrilocality as a temporary or alternative pattern (14). With temporary matrilocality a newly married couple will remain near the wife's mother until after their first child is born so that the new mother has help from her mother and the new husband can perform bride service. The high frequency of patrilocality may be related to the occurrence of revenge raiding in Amazonia, which makes it advantageous for closely related men to remain close together.

BOX 2.3. BUILDING A MODEL ASHÁNINKA SOCIETY

In order to better understand how Asháninka Society worked as a system I constructed a model society of one hundred individuals sorted by age and gender following a computer-generated demographic table that assumed a stationary population with stable fertility and mortality rates that approximated tribal

world conditions.[47] I started with the biological facts that the population was half male, half female, and in five-year age grades with approximately half over age fifteen. Women were randomly assigned children based on their age. Initially, the only social facts were that people would know their mother and their siblings. I then created twenty-six households by following Asháninka cultural rules specifying (1) everyone belongs to a household; (2) everyone marries and has children; (3) brothers and sisters marry another brother and sister or a mother's brother's child (MZD, MBD); (4) polygyny is permitted; (5) wives move to their husband's hamlet. As soon as a few marriages were arranged following these rules, it became possible to arrange bilateral cross-cousin marriage (MBD, MBS, FZD, FZS) because fathers could now be identified.

Constructing households following these simple rules produced twenty-six households in ten hamlet clusters of genealogically related people that closely approximated the kinship composition of the Asháninka settlements that I actually observed (see figures 2.14 and 2.15). The model helped explain why both brother-sister exchange and cross-cousin marriages occur so commonly, and why the kinship terms reflect this pattern. Network analysis also revealed that the cultural rules produced a basically egalitarian society with little basis for anyone to concentrate significant social power. Most households were no larger than two to five persons, and the largest had only eight. Of the ten hamlets composed of closely related households most had only five to eleven persons and the largest only sixteen. These small social differences were generated by random demographic events.

Asháninka Bigmen: Leaders Not Rulers

One of the most distinctive features of tribal cultures is the way they resist any concentration of political power that might threaten the autonomy of households and communities. Village leaders serve the people and are granted no undue power. The largest local settlement in Amazonia is a politically autonomous unit, even if it contains only twenty-five people. Political autonomy means that people can relocate their village whenever they choose, can kill intruders in self-defense, and can control their natural resources. Given exogamy, there cannot be complete village autonomy, because spouses must be drawn from other settlements. A leader, or **headman**, often is recognized and may even be called a "chief" by outsiders, but his authority is extremely limited. A headman's responsibilities increase with the size of

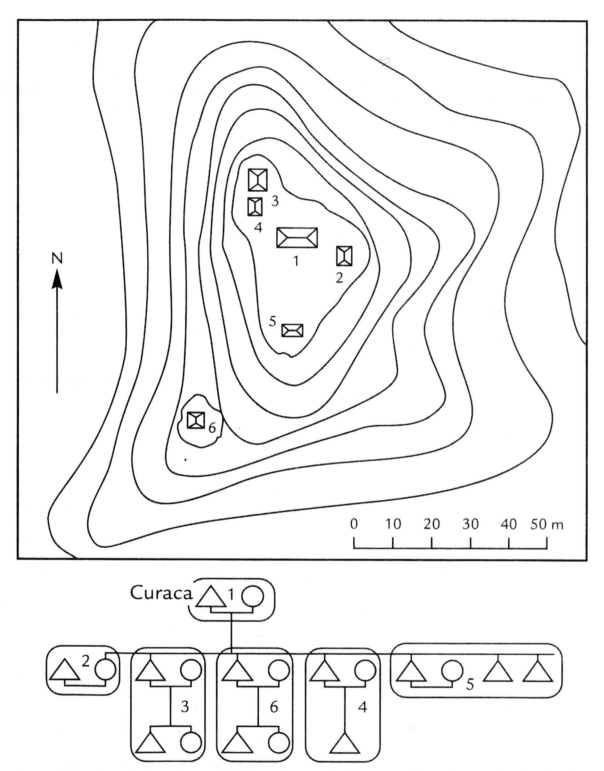

Figure 2.14. Ground plan of an Asháninka extended family group situated on a ridgetop clearing. Curaca is the Quechua (Inca) term for headman. House numbers correspond to the circled household members in the genealogical diagram.

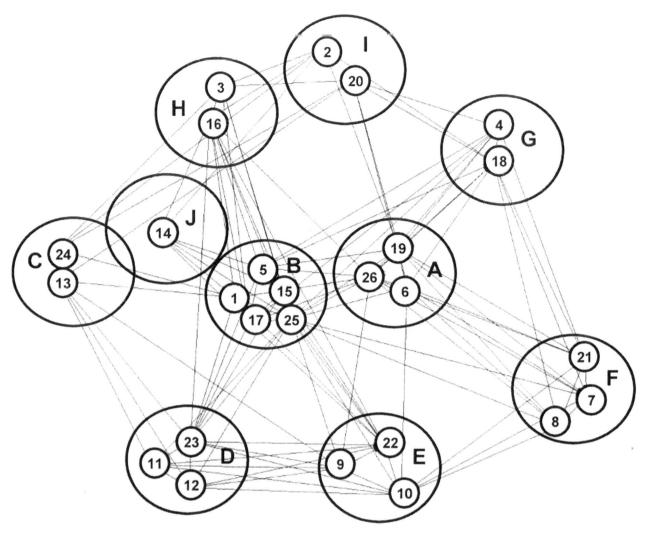

Figure 2.15. Ashaninka household network, 100 persons, 26 households, 10 household groups.

the village, but normally he is a powerless coordinator who formally announces what everyone had already decided to do, such as clean the village plaza or begin a group fishing expedition. Such a headman cannot force anyone to do anything against his or her will.

As French ethnologist Pierre Clastres[48] observed, an Amazon village is essentially a "society against the state" in that it is designed to prevent the concentration of political power that would allow anyone to gain control of the economy for his own benefit. In some respects, the headman is held hostage by the community. He is granted a certain degree of privileged status, often indicated by polygyny, which is more likely to be practiced by a headman. But he also frequently works harder than everyone else and is denied coercive power. Polygyny is not an exclusive prerogative of headmen and should not be construed as payment for the headman's leadership services. Rather,

it is a requirement of the job because more wives are needed to help brew the extra manioc beer expected from a generous headman. Society is not paying for the leader's services, but he can hold his position only as long as he serves the community. Leadership in this system is its own reward, and only a few would take on the responsibility.[49]

A good headman must be a good public speaker and be especially generous, giving things away on request, but he is not distinguished by special dress or insignias of office. The importance of the headman's oratorical skills further shows that he cannot use coercive violence. He must be verbally persuasive at settling intravillage conflicts; but if he fails as a peacemaker, the village simply breaks apart. Society's refusal to grant political power to the headman may be the most critical limit on the size of villages in Amazonia. Amazonian political organization relates to game resources because disputes over meat distribution increase as villages become larger. When a headman's powers are limited to verbal persuasion, he may be unable to keep the peace in a community larger than two hundred to three hundred people.

The Ashaninka headman's position is temporary because it is based on his personality and the number of his sons and sons-in-law that he can persuade to remain in his hamlet to form a local group. His status is enhanced by his ability to give good feasts with plenty of manioc beer. This is an incentive for polygyny, because women make beer, and I recorded two cases of especially powerful bigmen with five wives, but seven wives was apparently the maximum.

The underlying source of village conflict is the shortage of game and the related competition between village men for access to women, which in the absence of a powerful headman can lead to village fragmentation.[50] Sexual competition is intensified by the relative scarcity of women created by exogamy and by even a limited practice of polygyny. Throughout Amazonia, hunting success is equated with virility, and the successful hunter can support extra wives and lovers through gifts of meat. Successful hunters also have free

time to engage in infidelities while less-skilled hunters are still in the forest. This leads to conflict, and villages break apart before potentially irreversible game depletion sets in. When game is really abundant, individual differences in hunting abilities are less prominent, and men may turn to raiding other villages to capture women. Successful raiding would increase village size, raise the pressure on hunters, and result in village fragmentation. The crucial underlying variable is settlement size, because population growth would intensify all of the sources of conflict between men. Village fissioning, ritualized combat, external raiding, and feuding could all occur. In the riverine environment where protein resources are more abundant, villages may become larger, the authority of the headman may be greater, and people might allow chiefdoms to form (see figure 2.16).

The Shipibo-Conibo: Matrilocal River People

In 1966 I carried out a household and genealogical survey of the Conibo village of Nazaret located on the east bank of the Ucayali River across from the mouth of the Shahuaya. This was an opportunity to make a careful comparison of the remarkable differences

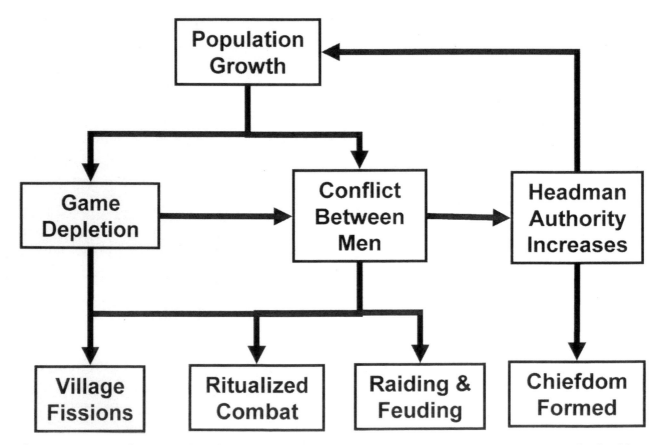

Figure 2.16. Excessive internal conflict leads to either village fissioning, ritual combat, or stronger leadership.

in the kinship and social organization between the Conibo and the Asháninka who lived virtually next door to each other in this region. River people and forest people have very different lives. Nazaret was a small Shipibo-Conibo village, but it was larger and more compact than most Asháninka hamlets. There were sixteen households and forty-seven people in Nazaret, with their houses in a line facing the river (see figure 2.17). Each household had ready access to its own canoe landing, which was very important because these are fishing people. It was immediately apparent that closely related women—mothers, daughters, and sisters—formed the core of this small Conibo community. This was very unlike Asháninka settlements, where fathers, sons, and brothers often formed the core.

Shipibo-Conibo occupy the protein-rich floodplain environment. The men are fishermen, and they provide the crucial protein in the diet, but the women manage the gardens and the household, do the food preparation, and manufacture the distinctive ceramics and textiles that constitute the primary cultural identity of the Shipibo-Conibo people (see figure 2.18). Residence in Nazaret was predominantly matrilocal, with men marrying in, but there were no recognized matrilineages, or named matriclans, because with shifting cultivation and plenty of forest available, garden plots were not inherited. Conibo households are formed by a man moving into his wife's mother's household. One matrilocally extended family in Nazaret had three generations of adult women; another family had five in-marrying men. The only polygynous marriage was by a man who married two sisters, which allowed him to accommodate the expectation of matrilocality. This ideal residence practice is closely adhered to. Clifford Behrens found nearly 95 percent of households in the Shipibo village of Nuevo Eden on the upper Pisqui River were formed this way.[51] In the recent past matrilocally extended families occupied one long house structure, but now most households

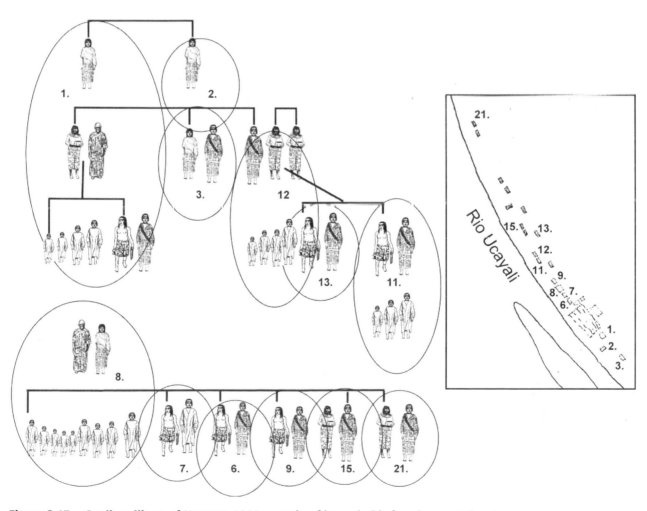

Figure 2.17. Conibo village of Nazaret, 1966, sample of households forming matrilocal core.

Figure 2.18. Conibo woman with large ceramic cooking pot.

occupy adjacent individual houses, often sharing the same kitchen. The advantage of matrilocally extended Conibo families is that they facilitate the transfer between mothers and daughters of the skills involved in ceramic and textile manufacturing, including the elaborate decorative designs that are applied to them.

I found that Conibo men were scrupulously careful to avoid looking at or talking to their mothers- and fathers-in-law. A man called his wife's parents, uncles, and aunts *rayoos* (avoided ones) (see figure 2.19). Formal avoidance has the practical effect of minimizing conflict between the in-marrying men and their affines in crowded villages, but conflict among in-marrying men continued to be a problem. A man called all of his brothers and male cousins *huetsa* (same) and his sisters and female cousins *poe* (other) (see figure 2.20). In the opposite way, a woman called her sisters and female cousins *huetsa* and her brothers and male cousins *poe*. Conibo kinship is a Hawaiian, or generational, system, reflecting the social fact that

cousins can not marry each other, and that there is no reason to bias one side of the family in the absence of lineages or clans.

The Asháninka and Conibo have stereotypes about each other that reflect their cultural differences and that have some validity. For example, the Asháninka say the Conibo don't know how to hunt and make gardens, whereas the Conibo say the Asháninka don't know how to fish and make pottery. Today, the Asháninka don't in fact make pottery, and they trade baskets to the Conibo for their very fine pottery. Both groups hunt, fish, and make gardens very well, but there are important differences in practice (see figure 2.21). In one study of the Shipibo at the mouth of the Aguaytia River men were found spending an average of about an hour a day fishing to supply about 60 percent of their total protein. [52] Fish are netted, speared, and shot with arrows, and harpoon-headed arrows are even used. An average Shipibo fisherman might bring home nearly 900 pounds (406 kg) of fish

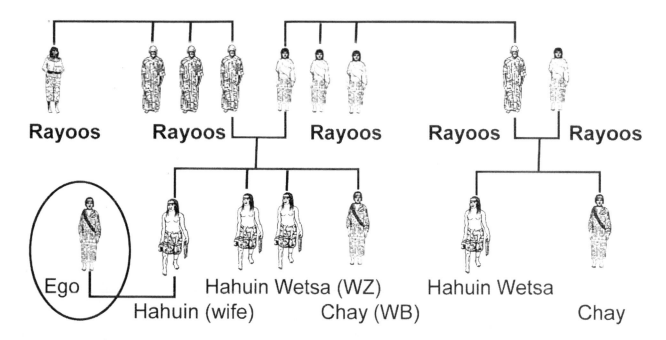

Poe = "opposite"
Wetsa = "another"

Figure 2.19. Conibo affinal kinship terms.

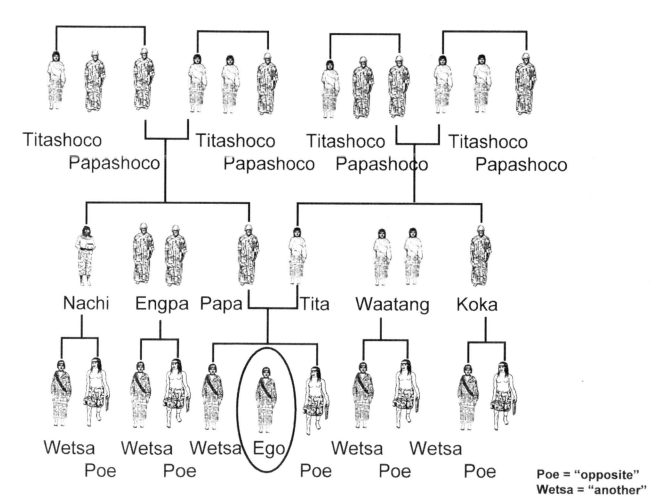

Poe = "opposite"
Wetsa = "another"

Figure 2.20. Conibo consanguine kinship terms.

Figure 2.21. The Asháninka are skilled fishermen like the Conibo, but have fewer opportunities to fish in the forested uplands.

per year, whereas the Asháninka bring in 655 pounds (298 kg) of fish.[53] The prize fish for the Shipibo is the paiche (*Arapaima gigas*), which can weigh over 200 pounds and grow to more than 6 feet in length. Hunting is much less important for the Shipibo, and men averaged less than 15 minutes a day hunting, which provided only 14 percent of their protein. The balance of their protein came from the garden. Matsigenka men divide their time about equally between hunting and fishing, spending about an hour and a half total per day, which is somewhat more than the Shipibo. For their efforts the Matsigenka produced about 25 percent of their protein from fish, but only 5 percent from hunting. This means that nearly 70 percent of their protein must come from the garden. Clearly, the Shipibo are in an animal protein–rich environment.

Total subsistence workloads, and the relatively equal balance of work and the complementarity of economic functions between men and women, seem to be about the same for the Shipibo-Conibo and the Asháninka-Matsigenka, although the particular mix of tasks will vary. For example, Shipibo women may spend considerably more time at food preparation, perhaps because their kitchen groups are larger and Shipibo feasting and ritual life is more intense.

Matsigenka women may spend more time spinning and weaving than Shipibo women spend at all of their household manufacturing and cleaning tasks, but this has to do with the nature of these technologies.

Shipibo material culture is richly elaborated to support their intensive social life. Heavy ceramic cooking pots come in several sizes and are unpainted, but jars, beer mugs, and food bowls are finely made and decorated. Many elaborately designed ceramic pots are dedicated to beer from the high-capacity two-foot-tall (60 cm) fiesta beer pots to the small animal effigy pots that are used to dip beer from the large beer pots into communal drinking mugs. Each type of pot has its own mix of clays, temper, slip coating, glazing, and painting. Pots are constructed from clay coils that are welded and smoothed with special scrapers made from pieces of gourds. Potters design their pots from the bottom up, choosing among ten different shapes of bottoms, base, bodies, necks, and rims. This is a labor-intensive process carried out individually by each woman potter. With all the materials at hand, a large pot might take some fifteen hours of work, spread over a week. A typical household might have some fourteen ceramic pots available.[54] Three kinds of clay and pigments are used for slip coating and painting ceramics. Clays are usually obtained locally within one to five kilometers of the village, but some women might travel hundreds of kilometers throughout the Ucayali drainage to gather raw materials.

The Shipibo are well-known for the geometric art style that appears prominently on their pottery, textiles, beadwork, wooden artifacts, and faces, virtually defining the Shipibo as an ethnic group.[55] This distinctive style is controlled by the women and requires high levels of artistic and technical skill and attention to detail. Specific designs are owned by individuals and taught to their daughters and granddaughters when they repaint the lines. Women highly value artistic quality and stylistic innovation within accepted limits and critically compare and judge each others' work, keeping especially valuable articles as heirlooms. There is a linguistic proliferation of technical terms to describe the style and the production process. Ceramics judged to be of inferior quality may reinforce negative ethnic stereotypes between Shipibo-Conibo subgroups, as between upriver and downriver groups, or those living off the main Ucayali River.[56] The Shipibo also generally see their linguistic relatives such as the Cashibo, Amahuaca, and Isconahua who live in small widely dispersed settlements in the interior headwater areas as culturally "backward."

The Shipibo Big Drinking Ceremony

The more intense social life of the Shipibo-Conibo is expressed in the elaborate series of girls' puberty rituals culminating in the Ani Ŝhrëati, "big drinking," clitoridectomy ceremony.[57] The operation itself is conducted by women. It is the female counterpart to the male circumcision-subincision genital mutilation rituals practiced by some Australian Aborigines as discussed in chapter 3, but the cultural context is different. Genital mutilation is also widespread in Africa, and female genital mutilation as practiced by the Maasai is mentioned in chapter 4, but any form of genital mutilation is exceedingly rare in North and South America. The Shipibo Ani Ŝhrëati highlights the stresses between the sexes in a society where gender roles are strongly differentiated and complementary. This complementary opposition is also on display and symbolically reinforced in Amazonian mythology generally, and there are many ways that it can be expressed. Peter Roe interprets the Ani Ŝhrëati as a symbolic conversion of "natural" women, who are superior to men, to a cultural state through marriage that makes them subordinate to men. After the ceremony, women are vulnerable to supernatural attack

by water spirits and demons and must be protected by men. This is a public denial of the sociological reality that women are in fact dominant in Shipibo society, but it may somehow help men deal with their actual subordination. The ceremony also, of course, makes the girl the center of public attention and allows her to wear beaded articles and monkey-teeth bracelets that are ordinarily worn only by men.

The Ani Ŝhrëati ceremony is also about "big drinking." It is an opportunity for considerable feasting, public drunkenness, and club and knife fighting between men. In relatively large Shipibo communities persistent marital infidelity may cause stress and conflict between men who, given matrilocality, may be strangers to each other. I came to appreciate the importance in village life of the drinking and fighting complex when a Conibo man at Shahuaya presented me with a small, curiously curved knife and a large, flat, wooden paddle-shaped decorated club with a V-shaped end. He made these very special objects as reciprocity to me for transporting his brother downriver to find medical assistance after he was bitten by a snake. I learned later that the club was designed for knocking a man down and pinning him to the ground by the neck, in order to slash the back of his neck with the knife. This would produce a lot of blood and leave scars as payback for philandering. Such fighting is one of the costs that river people pay for their larger, denser villages, but it is worth noting that the richer material culture does not become a basis for formal rank differences or the construction of social class. Shipibo culture is measurably more complex than Asháninka culture, but both societies are fundamentally egalitarian and remain focused on the humanization process that remains dominant in the tribal world.

The archaeological evidence shows direct continuity in Shipibo ceramic designs and ritual activities, including the Ani Ŝhrëati, in their present territory along the main Ucayali River for the past twelve hundred years.[58] More recently, clitoridectomy is being abandoned and is now likely to be found only in the more remote areas, but I knew Shipibo women who had gone through the ceremony on the Ucayali. What remain strong are the textile and ceramic arts and the basic matricentered social structure. Before Europeans arrived in 1542, the banks of the Amazon River were annually enriched by deposits of waterborne (alluvial) soil, and there were abundant fish, manatees, caimans, and turtles. Prehistorically, the main Amazon floodplain supported dense permanent villages that often exceeded five hundred people and were organized into politically centralized chiefdoms. These societies were quickly destroyed by European colonists, whereas the tribal villagers hidden in the interior upland forests survived.

Men and Women in the Mundurucú Village

Gender roles are critical for understanding how rain forest cultures work because age and sex, not wealth and class, are the primary differences between people in these tribal cultures. The Tupi-speaking Mundurucú illustrate how the antagonisms between men and women are played out in the daily life of village cultures in Brazilian Amazonia. In 1953, anthropologists Yolanda and Robert Murphy spent a year with 350 Mundurucú, who lived in small villages of fifty to a hundred people in the savannas and forests of the upper tributaries of the Tapajos River.[59] As a husband and wife team the Murphys could observe Mundurucú culture from both sexes' viewpoints. The world of Mundurucú men and women is sharply divided. Men are primarily hunters, although they also do the heavy work of garden clearing. Women cultivate, harvest, and process bitter manioc. Mundurucú men assume public roles, which are symbolically reflected in the physical structure of the village. Adult males and older boys sleep communally and spend much of their time in the *eksa*, an open-walled men's house, whereas all females and young boys sleep in individual, close-walled domestic houses.

As is common in Australian aboriginal society, the Mundurucú are divided into exogamous moieties. Mundurucú moieties are color-coded "red" and "white," and membership in them is allocated through males. People marry their cross-cousins, who belong to opposite moieties. The moieties are subdivided into thirty-eight patrilineal clans (sixteen red, twenty-two white), each with an animal founder, like the Australian Dreaming ancestors. Clan loyalties are strong, and ancestral spirits are symbolically present in sacred flutes, which are hidden in the men's house. The potential for intervillage conflict is reduced by the Mundurucú practice of matrilocality, which contrasts significantly with the patrilocality of Australian Aborigines. Matrilocality requires that a young man, who must marry outside of his clan and moiety, leave his own village and move into the men's house in his new wife's village. The result is that village residence crosscuts clan loyalties such that the men of a given village, who cooperate daily, are unlikely to fight their fellow clansmen in another village.

According to the Murphys, men consider themselves to be the superior sex, and they frequently draw on symbolic support for this position, but the women reject this male understanding. The entire mythic charter for the male view is enshrined in the central myth of the phallic sacred flutes. The myth tells how women originally possessed mysterious flutes that reversed normal gender roles. As long as women had the flutes, they occupied the men's house, relegating the men to the domestic houses to cook, carry water and firewood, and be seduced by aggressive women. The downfall for the women was that the flutes demanded meat, but only men could hunt. Eventually, the men grew impatient with this arrangement and threatened to stop hunting, thereby forcing the women to surrender the flutes and restoring normal gender roles. The myth explains why men are both sexually and publicly dominant. Men are "superior" to women—not because they are inherently superior, but because gender roles differ and male hunting is culturally the most important gender role. Hunting and meat are thus crucially important for understanding Amazonian cultures.

The sacred flute myth highlights a central human problem: Men are sexually attracted to women and physically dependent on them, but they fear their power. Patrilineality gives men rights over the status of children, but only women can produce children. The **myth** suggests that men know their vulnerability and must constantly assert themselves, or women will overcome them. The mythic flutes are symbolically embodied in four-foot-long hollow wooden tubes, which are stored and regularly played in the men's house. Sometimes the flutes are paraded about the village, but the women are never supposed to view them; women who do see them can expect to be gang raped. The flutes reinforce the male role in patrilineality and hunting because they contain the spirits of the patriclan (a named **descent group** with membership assigned through male lines), and they must be offered meat. The phallic symbolism of the flutes is explicitly recognized by the Mundurucú, and men openly joke about penis power and vaginas with teeth.

Mundurucú male dominance is a male ideology of gender roles. Publicly, women remain in the background, actively maintaining their separation from men, but in practical terms, they have real power in their daily lives. Regardless of male ideology, Mundurucú women are in charge of their households. Each house contains a single cooking hearth to serve an extended family, with twenty to twenty-five people in four to five nuclear families. Senior women direct household activities and control food distribution, handing out both manioc and meat. Given matrilocality, households are centered predominantly on sisters, mothers, and daughters. Kin ties between women are very strong and are expressed in the question "How would a girl manage without her mother to help her?"[60] Thus, women are likely to be supported by close kin in any domestic struggle. Women also gain solidarity by routinely working together in the manioc-processing shed. Women carry out all their daily activities in groups, because a woman alone is assumed to be sexually available. Thus, women are effectively united in their resistance to male ideological domination.

The Mundurucú women questioned Yolanda Murphy about her daily home life. Recognizing the apparent social isolation of American women, they asked, "But if you don't go with the other women to get water and to bathe, aren't you lonely?" Yolanda responded, "Yes, we are."[61]

Although in Mundurucú society the nuclear family is not the primary domestic unit, marriage and nuclear families perpetuate moieties, clans, and the kinship roles that structure everything. The Asháninka of the Peruvian Amazon provide an example of the specific kinship categories that are functionally connected to simple moiety systems and cross-cousin marriage, which are so common in domestic-scale cultures.

Raiding and Feuding in the Tribal World

The downside of the apparent harmony and tranquility of Amazon village life is that personal conflicts between individual men can sometimes escalate to violence and homicide. This is, of course, true in any society, but in the tribal world there are no central political authorities or institutions with police, courts, and judges that could curb offenders, settle disputes, and prevent endless cycles of revenge and killing. People fear internal conflict and might simply move out of a village if violence threatens, although sometimes angry people are allowed to come to blows with fists or clubs and inflict minor injuries in a public setting. Tribal people often clearly distinguish the use of episodes of dueling to dissipate anger from intergroup violence with lethal weapons, or "war," intended to kill. When a man participates in a successful attack on another community he may be rewarded with increased status and perhaps an additional wife. This means that the world outside of one's immediate circle of kin and family is a dangerous place where one must

constantly be on guard. I experienced this directly when my Asháninka guide reacted with immediate alarm at our discovery of strange footprints on a faint trail deep in the forest. In this case, the possibility of an unexpected encounter with a potential enemy produced an exhilarating sense of danger rather than immobilizing fear, because the Asháninka are generally confident in their capability for self-defense.

Violence in the tribal world is best called raiding and **feuding** rather than war, because the objective is not conquest, and actions are small-scale and brief. Tribal fighting typically involves at most a few dozen warriors, fighting sporadic raids in hit-and-run fashion. Although any conflict directed at another group can technically be considered war, there are enormous qualitative differences between tribal intergroup conflict and wars fought between governments. Typically, tribal raids are neither sustained nor coordinated, and their objective is to kill someone in revenge for previous killings or to capture women and children, but not ordinarily to kill everyone or to take territory or property. In contrast, political rulers in the imperial and commercial worlds use organized violence as instruments of state policy to conquer other societies; take property, territory, and resources; and collect tribute. Conflicts between states may properly be called war, and the scale and scope of destruction in such war is vastly greater than the raids and feuds in the tribal world.

Many tribal groups are relatively peaceful, but when violence does occur it is too horrible to forget and is likely to generate outrage and desire for revenge. Although the total casualties from tribal conflict are tiny compared with the hundreds of millions killed in the politically directed wars that were fought by governments in the twentieth century,[62] mortality rates in the tribal world can sometimes be extremely high in particular villages.[63] Furthermore, the possibility of low-level, sometimes devastating violence of this sort encourages people to maintain a hostile stance toward outsiders.

In the absence of any legal authority such as a police force, people must resort to self-help in the event of serious trouble. A single homicide can set off a chain of revenge killings, which can go on for years because there are few mechanisms for making peace. This is a situation of political anarchy in the sense of an absence of formal government, but it does not mean that total chaos reigns. There is great variability in the frequency and intensity of such conflict, but normally the loss of life is not great. Exogamy works to reduce the potential for conflict by creating in-law/kinship relationships between people in different villages. Formal trading partnerships and feasting can prepare the way for marriage ties. Everyday objects such as arrows may be traded on the basis of **deferred exchanges** in which the initial gift giving will not be reciprocated for several months or even years as in the example of the Asháninka *ayompari* partnerships. In this way, a continuing relationship is maintained, and there is always an excuse for further visits.

Whatever its extent, even the possibility that such conflict might occur has consequences for the pattern of life in Amazonia before the intervention of governments. For example, villages may be located on easily defended ridgetops, or they may be encircled by stout log palisades. There may also be pressures to maintain larger villages for defense. Where raiding is especially common, extensive "no-man's lands" may develop between hostile groups and can serve as de facto game reserves to replenish adjacent hunting territories.

Anthropologists have variously explained Amazonian raiding and feuding as examples of individual men striving consciously or unconsciously for reproductive success, measured as **inclusive fitness**[64]; as a cultural adaptation centered on a **male supremacy complex**[65]; or more broadly in reference to the perceived benefits that warriors and their families apparently derive from successful combat.[66] Clearly, in the tribal world warfare is a complex, multidetermined activity. If men have a biologically driven propensity to use violence to advance their self-interest, culture and society regulate this propensity to promote domestic tranquility even in tribal societies that maximize individual freedom and autonomy.

Amazonia is an especially fertile area for theorists interested in understanding armed conflict in the tribal world, because many groups have remained beyond the effective reach of government control until very recent times. Nevertheless, it must be understood that using ethnographic data to describe war in the "tribal world" necessarily refers to an imaginary ethnographic present for academic purposes. All of the peoples referred to in this chapter are encompassed by the commercial world and have been influenced by it in varying degrees for centuries. Anthropologists have sometimes conducted fieldwork with people where raids and feuds were either ongoing or had occurred within recent memory. For example, I interviewed several Asháninka who remembered being kidnapped and seeing their family members killed by raiders a few years earlier. I assumed that raiding continued in the most remote Asháninka areas, and was warned not to go into some areas because people there were "killers." On one occasion I saw an armed group attempt to barter a captive woman in exchange for a shotgun. Today, outsiders and many Asháninka might consider such activities to be either expressions of political autonomy or examples of criminality.

Certainly armed conflict in any society merits scientific explanation, but it is impossible for an anthropologist to be totally objective and dispassionate about tribal warfare, because, except in self-defense, armed conflict in any society is a violation of basic human rights, and assaults on women and children and noncombatants are a violation of the civilized rules of war and offend our sense of humanity. Furthermore, it would be difficult for a field researcher to remain neutral or have no influence in a tribal combat zone if their material wealth and power as an outsider were conspicuous. Even more problematic, any published descriptions or analysis of tribal warfare could have a negative impact on the people described if it made them appear excessively savage, nasty, or animal-like.

AMAZONIAN COSMOLOGY

The Amazonian equivalent of the Australian Dreaming is found in a rich body of myth, beliefs, and ritual practices that, like the Dreaming, help people answer basic questions about the meaning of life and death, the origin of things, how people should behave, and the relationship between nature and culture. Amazonian cosmology also helps people deal with their reasonable fears that uncontrolled self-seeking, lust, anger, and jealousy will destroy society. Their myths are conveyed in the colorful and entertaining stories that people share in the evening. These stories describe exciting encounters between people and supernatural beings, spirits, and demons in which thoughtless or greedy individuals do bad things and as a consequence, are killed and eaten, transformed into monsters, or meet some other equally unpleasant fate. Amazon myths are not everywhere acted out in dramatic rituals as in Australia, but nevertheless they help sustain the moral order by demonstrating the horrible consequences of bad behavior. The cosmology also explains why people get sick, offers therapy, and provides routine procedures that help hunters, gardeners, and warriors feel more confident and have more success in relating to others in society. Supernatural beliefs do function to integrate society, and they serve important psychological functions that benefit individuals.[67]

In tribal societies there are no priests, no full-time professionals to formalize the belief system, and nothing codified in writing. And despite considerable fluidity in individual beliefs, there are underlying uniformities. E. B. Tylor[68] called the unifying ideological theme **animism**, a belief in spirits. The spirit world is animated with human, animal, and plant souls and a wide variety of anthropomorphic beings with superhuman characteristics. These beings can intrude directly in the affairs of humans and control natural resources. Individuals may have personal spirit helpers, but **shamans** are the religious specialists who by training and self-selection are particularly adept at communicating with the spirit world. Shamans may have especially powerful spirit helpers that allow them to perform remarkable supernatural feats, diagnose and cure illness, and harm enemies through sorcery. In the absence of centralized political authority, shamans often play a key role in the politics of village life by using their spirit power to enforce social control. Shamans can also use their supernatural powers to counterbalance the political power of village headmen.

The Amazonian soul concept calls attention to striking contrasts between tribal world and commercial world ways of knowing the physical and metaphysical worlds (Table 2.3). Considering the invisible, or metaphysical aspects of people and animals from the academic perspective of the humanities, we assume that only people have souls, and make that the major difference between people and animals. Natural scientists assume that people are physically animals, and don't consider the existence of souls. As animists, Amazonian peoples see the physical differences between people and animals, but they are what Brazilian anthropologist Viveiros de Castro[69] calls *perspectivists* in that they imagine how other animals also see the world, assuming they have minds and souls like us. This leads to some interesting and useful ways of relating to nature.

According to Asháninka cosmogony the Asháninka were the original life form. All life forms, animals and plants, or their spirit masters, as well as spirit beings are transformed Asháninka, or human persons, and still have human-like spirits or souls. Animals are spiritually humans on the inside with animal exteriors, or "clothing" on the outside. The modern scientific view of course is the opposite, that humans were originally animals, and in effect are now animals wearing cultural clothing.

Thinking of animals as having souls with a point of view makes them philosophically subjects, capable of intention or agency. This makes other life forms anthropomorphic for the Asháninka, human-like, but the Asháninka are not anthropocentric like the scientific view of human evolution which typically makes humans the "highest" form. This means that human people can relate socially to animals and spirits in similar ways to how they relate to other human people.

The idea that animals were formerly human helps account for the many food taboos in Amazonia. People don't want to be cannibals. Eating a taboo animal can cause the spirit of the animal to become a counter-cannibal eating the violator, and thereby in the least causing illness. Tabooed animals must be desubjectified, made into objects that can be eaten, rather than subjects with human souls, in order to be safely eaten.

Viveiros de Castro calls the Amazonian cosmology "multi-naturalist" and ours "multi-culturalist." In contrast, we assume that nature is the universal condition and culture the variable particular. For Amazonians other life forms have a human-like consciousness and a point of view, and all have culture. The Asháninka also assume that among life forms appearances change depending on the observer, such that jaguars see themselves as humans, but jaguars may see humans as tasty wild pigs, whereas humans see jaguars as animals. In the Amazonian view, all life forms perceive the world in the same way, but they are seeing different worlds. All souls (animal and human) perceive the same things. Different species have different affects, or dispositions, that is they eat different things, move differently, live in different places, have different social habits, and differently shaped bodies.

Table 2.3. Amazonian and Commercial World Cosmologies Compared

Physics		Metaphysics	
		Animism: Both people and animals have souls	Humanities: Only people have souls
	Natural Science: People are animals		Commercial world perspective
	Perspectivism: People are physically different	Amazonian perspective	

For us the "natural sciences" can study people, because we are animals, but the humanities and social sciences study only people, because animals are not human beings. Amazonians consider animals to be physically different, but their souls or their cultures are the same as humans.

Human people can relate socially to animals and spirits in similar ways to how they relate to other human people. This perspective is also seen in the common stories of people who marry animals and the problems that they experience. This makes it reasonable to think of particular animal as in-laws, and to apply kinship terms to them. Given that marriage is a form of exchange, this draws attention to the fact that marriage also is likely to involve an exchange of perspectives between two families. This helps explain why in-laws don't always get along.

Sexual Symbols and Forest Demons

Amazonian ideology is part of a highly elaborate, logical, and consistent philosophy of life. Spirit beings normally are invisible, but they can assume visible form and freely transform from human to animal form and back again. In Asháninka thought, any unusual animal or otherwise unexplained event may be attributed to a spirit.[70] The Asháninka recognize and name scores of specific spiritual entities; some include the souls of their own ancestors, which are ordinarily considered harmless. Malevolent spirit beings may appear as blue butterflies, tapirs, jaguars, hairy red humanoid dwarfs, or hoof-footed human impersonators. They are found in the deep forest, and they frequent whirlpools and rocky cliffs. Human contact with or even sight of malevolent spirit beings may cause illness or death.

Anthropologists have struggled with how best to understand beliefs in spirits and the supernatural generally. Some have considered belief in the spirit world to be childlike thought, crude science, or even a psychopathology (see chapter 5).[71] It is important to recognize that beliefs in the supernatural must be both memorable and useful because they are so universal. They are memorable because supernatural entities violate our normal expectations about the physical world. They are also useful for dealing with other people.[72]

A central feature in Amazonian cosmology is the theme that women in animal form were originally the possessors of culture, which was wrested from them by men who humanized them and took control of culture in the form of fire and cultivated plants. This theme is present in widespread myths of phallic sacred flutes and in related rituals. The entire cosmology is permeated by sexual antagonism; it is primarily a male construction, relegating women to a negative role, as in their symbolic association with sickness and death. The principal actors in the myths and their spirit representatives in the forest and rivers invariably are oversexed demons seeking to seduce people, especially vulnerable women. In their sexual natures people are also most like animals, so it is not surprising that sexual themes are projected onto animal-like supernatural beings. The sexual content of myths and symbols, of course, also makes them memorable, entertaining, and readily reproduced. Uncontrolled sex, incest, and adultery are perpetual threats to the integrity of any society, and they both attract and repel people. Adultery is a common source of conflict in village life, but fear of supernatural sexual encounters must act as a powerful deterrent to such misbehavior.[73]

The utility of supernatural understandings is illustrated by the account that the Asháninka related to me of the death of a prominent local man caused by a strange woman who appeared in his hunting blind in the forest. As he described it, she seduced him, then turned into a tapir and ran away. He realized that she was a demonic spirit and the encounter would almost certainly kill him. He came home, immediately fell ill, vomited up green stuff, and died. This tragic event was still so fresh in people's memories when I arrived that several recalled it in precisely the same detail. After I learned more about the culture I realized that this event fit a predictable pattern and was thus quite understandable. Eventually in its retelling the story would become an entertaining mythic object lesson about the dangers of indiscriminate sex.

Amazonian myths consistently focus on the cosmic issues of reproduction and fertility, the relationship between the sexes, the origin of culture, and illness and death. The dominant characters are drawn from especially powerful **natural symbols** found in the rain forest, such as the anaconda, jaguar, tapir, caiman, and harpy eagle (see box 2.4 and figure 2.22). To introduce novelty, Amazonian storytellers might explore classic themes using a complex series of character transformations based on logical chains of association that may depend on specific knowledge of the animal in question. For example, the anaconda, caiman, tapir, king vulture, and frog may all be associated as feminine symbols. The ana-

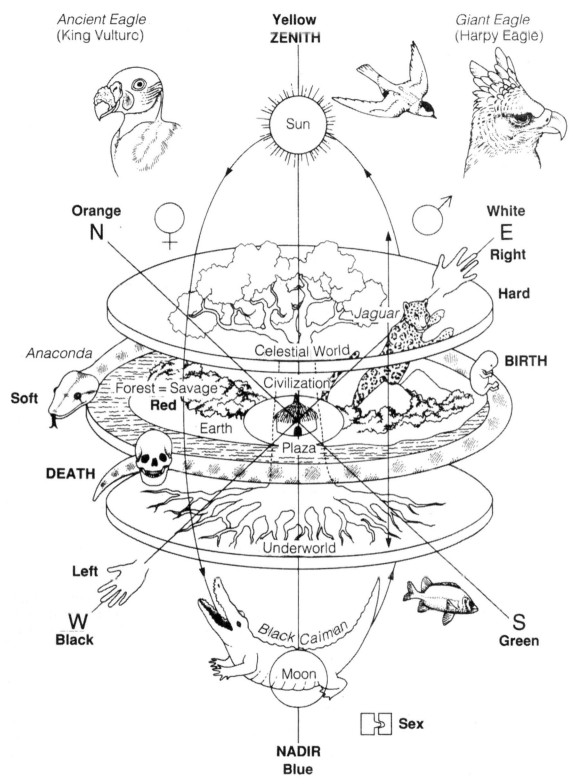

Figure 2.22. Schematic view of Roe's model of the Amazonian metacosmology (redrafted from Roe 1982).

conda has multiple associations and may be seen as both masculine and feminine. Hollow beehives may replace gourds as a feminine symbol, whereas the giant anteater may replace the anaconda as a masculine symbol because he introduces a long, phallic tongue into the hive (see box 2.5). Roe[74] relates this sexual antagonism in the cosmology to the striking gender division in Amazonian society, which often physically separates men and women, as demonstrated by the Mundurucú. The vivid sexual imagery also can be attributed to the fact that sex is one of the only activities that men and women engage in together and thus is a major preoccupation. Furthermore, men seem to be jealous of women's role in reproduction, and in the myths masculine characters sometimes assume important creative roles. This jealousy is reflected in the special vulnerability of women to assaults by demons when their biological role is especially evident at puberty, menstruation, and pregnancy. During these times, women may be secluded and may observe specific food taboos.

Gerardo Reichel-Dolmatoff,[75] who analyzed the cosmology of the Tukano of the Colombian Amazon, has called attention to the similarity between Tukano cosmology and basic ecological principles. He notes that the Tukano believe in a circuit of solar sexual energy that fertilizes the earth and flows through both people and animals. They assume that a balance must be maintained between a finite supply of fish and game and the human population that depends on them. People threaten that balance through overhunting and through uncontrolled sexual behavior, which leads to overpopulation. Sexual repression through observation of the rules of exogamy and basic restraint helps maintain the energy cycle. The game animals are protected by a spirit being, the Keeper of the Game, who is identified with the jaguar in Roe's model but who can exist in many forms. The Keeper of the Game regulates the supply of animals and may release them to be hunted at the request of the shaman, who communicates with him while in a hallucinogenic, drug-induced trance or with the aid of tobacco smoke. This explains the obsessive concern of the Keeper of the Game with the sex life of humans. He may withhold game or send sickness if he feels that people are being irresponsible. Hunting itself is replete with sexual imagery: It is literally seen as making love to the animals and, in preparation for hunting, people must practice sexual abstinence and observe other specific requirements.

There is no doubt a connection between the belief systems of native Amazonians, as seen in their cosmologies, and sexual behavior, food taboos, and hunting patterns—all of which can have important adaptive significance. Hornborg[76] emphasizes that a significant part of the culture of Amazonian peoples involves subtle feelings and observations about the environment such as signs and sounds associated with particular animals that might be transmitted mimetically, rather than linguistically, for example, by hunters watching and copying each other. From a semiotic or symbolic perspective, particular animals may be eaten or avoided because of metaphorical, idiosyncratic associations that people draw, contingent on specific circumstances. For example, a particular fish prone to rot quickly might be avoided at planting time, on the theory that the fish and the garden might *affect* each other.

BOX 2.4. AN ANACONDA MYTH

The following myth was recounted to archaeologist Peter Roe by my Shipibo assistant Manuel Rengifo in 1971. It portrays the anaconda as a source of noxious pests and illustrates how spirit beings take on human form and can influence hunter success.

"One day a man who was a very bad hunter set out once more to pursue the game of the forest with his blowgun. He had had no luck, as usual, until he approached the shores of a lake. There he noticed a man wearing a decorated *cushma* [woven cotton robe]. The man greeted him and asked him if he would like to accompany him so that the strange man could show the hunter his 'real *cushma*.' The hunter agreed, and they set off, only to finally encounter a huge coiled 'Mother of All Boas,' the anaconda. This, the man informed the hunter, was his real *cushma*. The hunter was very frightened, but the man reassured him and said that he would show him how to be a good hunter. The anaconda man first blew through his blowgun, but out came only a horde of stinging, poisonous animals like mosquitoes, black biting flies, stingrays, scorpions, and spiders. When the stranger blew again, hosts of deadly vipers as well as all the other evil snakes of the jungle poured forth from the tip of his blowgun. He then handed his blowgun to the hunter, whom he instructed to do as he had done. The hunter blew through the instrument and immediately killed a monkey. From that day on the hunter, thanks to his friendship with the anaconda man, always enjoyed success as a great hunter."[77]

BOX 2.5. MYTHIC JAGUARS AND ANACONDA RAINBOWS

French anthropologist Claude Levi-Strauss[78] demonstrated that Amazonian people construct their myths logically from very simple binary oppositions that metaphorically restate the central contrast between nature and culture. He believed that myths help people cope with life's basic contradictions by allowing them to manipulate them symbolically and intellectually. For example, in the myths the everyday conflicts and contradictions between nature and culture and male and female are explained metaphorically and symbolically in the A:B::C:D formula: Male is to Female as Culture is to Nature. This makes the claim that men have culture and that in their biological natures women are like animals, and may help men deal with their inferior role in reproductive biology.

Following Levi-Strauss's lead, Peter Roe[79] sifted through hundreds of myths in order to understand the internal logic linking the symbols. He selected the relationships between the most prominent symbols and constructed a simplified model of Amazonian cosmology that would be generally recognizable by most tribal Amazonian people (see figure 2.2). Roe's basic model depicts a three-tiered cosmos of earth, celestial world, and underworld, centered on the communal house and joined together by a world tree rooted in the underworld. Three cosmic layers account for the daily cycle of sun and moon. The house is surrounded by a cleared plaza that represents culture in opposition to the surrounding forest, which is savage nature inhabited by demons. The underworld is a source of death and disease and has many feminine associations, whereas the celestial world is dominated by male symbols. The underworld is represented in the night sky as the Milky Way galaxy, which is also associated with the rainbow and the multicolored anaconda.

The dominant symbol in the cosmology is the world tree represented by the kapok or silk cotton tree (*Ceiba*) and its relatives. This tree has predominantly feminine associations because it is soft, hollow, and filled with water. It is considered to be a source of life and culture and may appear in myths in varied form, sometimes as a dragon tree, a fish woman, a tree with fish and frogs inside, and so on.

Two primary opposing associations center on the dragon and the jaguar. The dragon, usually represented by the caiman, is a sinister underworld being. The jaguar has both male and female associations and is an ambiguous figure, mediating between oppositions. The most striking natural features of real jaguars are that they are active day and night, they are at home in the water and on land—in trees and on the ground—and they are dangerous to humans. It is not surprising, then, that powerful shamans may transform themselves into jaguars.

The Asháninka Jaguar Shaman

I was impressed by the cultural reality of Amazonian shamanism while conducting a routine residence pattern survey in an Asháninka village. I was surprised to find that Inkiteniro, a man I was interviewing, maintained a separate house from his wife. It is common for young unmarried Asháninka men to build separate houses, but this case was unusual enough for me to question further. Inkiteniro told me that he was a jaguar shaman who could cure people and transform himself into a jaguar. Jaguar shamans are widely respected and feared by the Asháninka, and their supernatural exploits are well known. I had heard accounts of someone shooting an intruding jaguar at night only to discover that he had killed a shaman. Inkiteniro explained to me matter-of-factly that it sometimes upset his wife when he became a jaguar in his dreams at night, so he often slept in his own house, but this did not account for the underlying cultural meaning of jaguar-human transformations.

There are many reasons for the association between shamans, tobacco, and jaguars, but the key element involves the soul concept. Asháninka shamans are called *sheripiári*, or "tobacco shamans" (*shéri* is "tobacco"). The word *shéri* also sounds like *ishíre*, "soul," and "my tobacco" has the double meaning of "my soul." Tobacco has a guardian spirit jaguar woman and may also be embodied as a swallow-tailed kite, or hummingbird, but if a shaman's soul is tobacco, and the tobacco spirit is a jaguar, then the shaman is also a jaguar. The Asháninka smoke tobacco, take it as snuff, and drink it as an infusion, but only shamans process tobacco into a thick, tarlike tobacco paste or syrup, store it in a bamboo tube (also called *shéri*), and lick it from a stick. Tobacco paste is a powerful preparation that produces visions and a state of intoxication that alters perceptions and emotions and allows the shaman to enter the otherwise invisible spirit world. A fully experienced shaman may gain heightened perceptions, including acute night vision, and wakefulness, which would convey the feeling of being transformed into a jaguar.[80]

Inkiteniro said his tobacco tube was a jaguar, and it took him four years of training to learn how to use it. A shaman may also refer to his tobacco tube as "my wife" and his shaman mentor as *kongki*, "my father-in-law." When I offered fifty *Soles* to buy his tobacco tube, Inkiteniro refused, warning me that his jaguar would be displeased and it would be dangerous for me, but he did accept 150 *Soles* (about $15 in 2008 dollars) for his *shéri*, whereas he gave me a tube of red face paint for ten *Soles*, and a bird call for one *Sole*.

Jaguars, like humans, are at the top of the food chain in the Amazon, and a viable jaguar population requires as much territory as a tribal population of five hundred people. Jaguars have superhuman abilities in reality, and they carry important symbolic associations. A regurgitated jaguar fur ball is equated with the magical objects that shamans extract during curing sessions. Jaguars eat people, they are active in the daytime and at night, they live on land and they swim, and they climb trees. They can be yellow or black. Troublesome jaguars are assumed to embody the souls of living jaguar shamans, and when their particular jaguar dies, the jaguar shaman will also die. Likewise if the shaman dies first, he will be embodied as his jaguar.

SUMMARY

Amazonia provides a background for discussing a variety of theories on the causes and consequences of sedentary village life based on domesticated plants. Sedentary living is certainly a great divide, and it undermines many of the mechanisms that promote social equality and stability among mobile foragers. Major issues for villagers include resolving conflict, limiting individual acquisition of political power, and maintaining access to resources as density increases. Ecological factors, in combination with cultural preferences for wild game and a desire to maintain light workloads, help keep villages small and population densities low. The Asháninka kinship system shows how kin terms are used to define social relationships and are related to marriage and family patterns.

Structuralist interpretations of Amazonian life use examples of Amazonian myth and symbolism and related ritual practices, which express an underlying pan-Amazonian cosmology. This cosmology illustrates symbolic patterns that are virtually universal, but it also distinctly reflects tribal culture in the rain forest environment and provides an important point of comparison and contrast with the cosmology underlying the Inca empire to be described in chapter 7. In functional terms, Amazonian cosmology works to resolve important logical contradictions while contributing to the basic adaptation of the culture.

Important cultural-ecological issues in Amazonia include the contrasts between the river and the forest environments, the success of shifting cultivation, and the controversy over the cultural importance of animal protein. Conflicting sociobiology and cultural materialist interpretations of infanticide and raiding in Amazonia have been advanced.

Revenge killing, homicide in general, and raiding for women can be a chronic problem of tribal life in the Amazon, but the small scale of Amazonian societies, their low population density, and the ease with which households change residence minimize the frequency of violence. Under some conditions violence can advance both individual and group interests; however, such benefits are an inadequate explanation for the occurrence of violence in tribal societies, because peace and cooperation are also beneficial. Any explanation of tribal warfare needs to take into account the overall cultural context and history of particular cultures, as well as the impact of influences from the imperial and commercial worlds. At the present time anthropologists dealing with tribal violence also need to consider the ethical aspects of their research, especially when the existence of many tribal groups is at risk due to the intrusion of outsiders.

STUDY QUESTIONS

1. Why might protein be considered a population control factor in Amazonia? What other factors also influence village size?
2. How is shifting cultivation adapted to the special conditions of the tropical rain forest environment?
3. Describe the kinship terminology system of the Asháninka and show how it is related to marriage practices.
4. Describe the kinship terminology system of the Shipibo and show how it is related to marriage practices.
5. In what ways do the religious beliefs and practices of Native Amazonians relate to social and ecological conditions?
6. Why do the Shipibo practice matrilocal residence and what other aspects of the culture is it related to?

SUGGESTED READING

Chagnon, Napoleon. 1997. *Yanomamo.* 5th ed. Fort Worth, TX: Harcourt Brace College Publishers. Well-rounded ethnography, but focused on the issue of conflict.

Johnson, Allen W. 2003. *Families of the Forest: The Matsigenka Indians of the Peruvian Amazon.* Berkeley: University of California Press. Full ethnography of people who are closely related and whose culture is very similar to the Asháninka. Family life, kinship, and ideology are highlighted.

Reichel-Dolmatoff, Gerado. 1971. *Amazonian Cosmos: The Sexual and Religious Symbolism of the Tukano Indians.* Chicago: University of Chicago Press. Very detailed analysis of an Amazonian belief system covering ritual and myth and relating it to rain forest adaptation.

Sponsel, Leslie E. 1995. *Indigenous Peoples and the Future of Amazonia: An Ecological Anthropology of an Endangered World.* Tucson and London: The University of Arizona Press. A collection of articles examining key issues focused on native peoples and environment in Amazonia, emphasizing changing rather than static elements in Amazonian human ecology.

GLOSSARY TERMS

Slash and burn A gardening technique in which forest is cleared and burned to enrich the soil for planting; a forest fallow system depending on forest regrowth. Also called swidden cultivation.

Household A social unit that shares domestic activities such as food production, cooking, eating, and sleeping, often under one roof, and is usually based on the nuclear or extended family.

Forest fallow A system of cultivation in which soil nutrients are restored by allowing the forest to regrow.

Surplus Subsistence production that exceeds the needs of the producer households and that is extracted by political leaders to support nonfood-producing specialists.

Subsistence intensification Technological innovations that produce more food from the same land area but often require increased effort.

Ecological footprint The amount of the biological product that people consume measured as the equivalent of the global average biological product per hectare.

Nuclear family The primary family unit of mother, father, and dependent children.

Extended family A joint household based on a parent family and one or more families of its married children.

Cross-cousin The son or daughter of someone in the category of mother's brother or father's sister.

Matrilocal residence Residence near the wife's kin, normally near her parents.

Headman A political leader who coordinates group activities and is a village spokesman but who serves only with the consent of the community and has no coercive power.

Myth A narrative that recounts the activities of supernatural beings. Often acted out in ritual, myths encapsulate a culture's cosmology and cosmogony and provide justification for culturally prescribed behavior.

Descent group A social group based on genealogical connections to a common ancestor.

Feuding Chronic intergroup conflict that exists between communities in the absence of centralized political authority. It may involve a cycle of revenge raids and killing that is difficult to break.

Deferred exchange A form of trade in which gift giving is reciprocated with a return gift at a later time, thus providing an excuse for maintaining contacts and establishing alliances between potentially hostile groups.

Inclusive fitness A biological concept referring to the degree to which individuals are successful in passing on a higher proportion of their genes to succeeding generations.

Male supremacy complex A functionally interrelated series of presumably male-centered traits, including patrilocality, polygyny, inequitable sexual division of labor, male domination of headmanship and shamanism, and ritual subordination of women.

Animism A belief in spirits that occupy plants, animals, and people. Spirits are supernatural and normally invisible but may transform into different forms. Animism is considered by cultural evolutionists to be the simplest and earliest form of religion.

Shaman A part-time religious specialist with special skills for dealing with the spirit world; may help his community by healing, by divination, and by directing supernatural powers against enemies.

Natural symbols Inherent qualities of specific plants and animals used as signs or metaphors for issues that concern people.

NOTES

1. The general outlines of Amazonian prehistory are based on Donald W. Lathrap, 1970. *The Upper Amazon.* London: Thames & Hudson.
2. RAISG, Red Amazónica de Información Socioambiental Georeferenciada. 2009. *Amazonia 2009 Áreas Protegidas Territorios Indígenas.* www.raisg.socioambiental.org. (accessed April 14, 2009).
3. Heckenberger, Michael, et al. 2003. "Amazonia 1492: Pristine Forest or Cultural Parkland?" *Science* 301:1710–14.
4. Killeen, Timothy J. 2007. *A Perfect Storm in the Amazon Wilderness: Development and Conservation in the Context*

of the Initiative for the Integration of the Regional Infrastructure of South America (IIRSA), 8, 12. AABS, Advances in Applied Biodiversity Science, No. 7. Arlington, VA: Conservation International. www .conservation.org/publications/Pages/perfect_storm.aspx (accessed April 27, 2009).

5. Goulding, Michael. 1980. *The Fishes and the Forest: Explorations in Amazonian Natural History.* Berkeley: University of California Press.

6. Mittermeier, Russell, Cristina Goettsch Mittermeier, Patricio Robles Gil, Gustavo Fonseca, Thomas Brooks, John Pilgrim, and William R. Konstant. 2003. *Wilderness: Earth's Last Wild Places.* Chicago: University of Chicago Place; Mittermeier, Russell, Norman Myers, Cristina Goettsch Mittermeier. 2000. *Hotspots: Earth's Biologically Richest and Most Endangered Terrestrial Ecoregions.* Arlington, VA: Conservation International; Mittermeier, Russell, Patricio Robles Gil, Michael Hoffman, John Pilgrim, Thomas Brooks, Cristina Goettsch Mittermeier, John Lamoreux, Gustavo A. B. da Fonseca, Peter A. Seligmann, Harrison Ford. 2005. *Hotspots Revisited: Earth's Biologically Richest and Most Endangered Terrestrial Ecoregions.* Arlington, VA: Conservation International; Myers, Normal, Russell A. Mittermeier, Christina G. Mittermeier, Gustavo A. B. da Fonseca, and Jennifer Kent. 2000. "Biodiversity Hotspots for Conservation Priorities." *Nature* 403, 24 February, 853–58.

7. Ellis, Erle C., and Navin Ramankutty. 2008. "Putting People in the Map: Anthropogenic Biomes of the World." *Frontiers in Ecology and the Environment* 6(8):439–47. www.ecotope.org/people/ellis/papers/ellis_2008.pdf (accessed May 18, 2009).

8. Millennium Ecosystem Assessment. 2005. *Ecosystems and Human Well-Being: Biodiversity Synthesis.* Washington, DC: World Resources Institute, Figure 1.2, p. 23.

9. To qualify as a "hotspot" an area must contain at least 1,500 endemic vascular plant species (0.5 percent of the world's 300,000 known plants found nowhere else in the world), and it must have lost at least 70 percent of its original area. The originally designated 24 Hotspots now cover less than 1.4 percent of the terrestrial earth, but they contain 60 percent of the world's plants and animal species.

10. Critical Ecosystem Partnership Fund. 2005. *Tropical Andes Hotspot: Vilcabamba-Amoró Conservation Corridor: Peru and Bolivia Briefing Book. www.cepf.net/ Documents/final.tropicalandes.vilcabambaamboro.briefingbook.pdf. (accessed May 12, 2008).*

11. Initiative for the Integration of Regional Infrastructure in South America (IIRSA). http://iirsa.org/index_ENG.asp?CodIdioma=ENG (accessed May 7, 2009).

12. Bush, M. B., M. R. Silman, C. McMichael, and S. Saatchi. 2008. "Fire, Climate Change, and Biodiversity in Amazonia: A Late-Holocene Perspective." *Philosophical Transactions of the Royal Society*, B 363:1795–1802.

13. Greenberg, Joseph H., and Merritt Ruhlen. 1992. "Linguistic Origins of Native Americans." *Scientific American* (November):94–99; Cavalli-Sforza, Paola Menozzi, Alberto Piazza. 1994. *The History and Geography of Human Genes.* Princeton, NJ: Princeton University Press, 302–42. Although Greenberg's language groupings have been widely used, many linguistics do not accept them. See: Bolnick, Deborah A. (Weiss), Beth A. (Schultz) Shook, Lyle Campbell, and Ives Goddard. 2004. "Problematic Use of Greenberg's Linguistic Classification of Native American Genetic Variation." *American Journal of Human Genetics* 75:519–23.

14. Peregrine, Peter N. 2003. "Atlas of Cultural Evolution." *World Cultures* 14(1):2–75, p. 39, Figure 5.A.9.

15. Hornborg, Alf. 2005. "Ethnogenesis, Regional Integration, and Ecology and Prehistoric Amazonia." *Current Anthropology* 46(4):589–620.

16. This early view is best exemplified by Meggers, Betty J. 1954. "Environmental Limitation on the Development of Culture." *American Anthropologist* 56:801–24.

17. Heckenberger, Michael, et al. 2003. "Amazonia 1492: Pristine Forest or Cultural Parkland?" *Science* 301:1710–14.

18. Myers, Thomas P., William M. Denevan, Antoinette Winklerprins, Antonio Porro. 2003. "Historical Perspectives on Amazonian Dark Earths." In J. Lehmann, et al, eds. *Amazonian Dark Earths: Origin, Properties, Management,* pp. 15–24. Netherlands: Kluwer Academic Publishers.

19. Hornborg, Alf. 1988. "Dualism and Hierarchy in Lowland South America: Trajectories of Indigenous Social Organization." *Acta Universitatis Upsaliensis, Uppsala Studies in Cultural Anthropology* 9. Uppsala University, Uppsala, Sweden.

20. Pitman, Nigel C. A., John Terborgh, Miles R. Silman, and Percy Nuñez V.1999. "Tree Species Distribution in an Upper Amazonian Forest." *Ecology* 80(8):2651–61.

21. Terborgh, John 1990. "An Overview of Research at Cocha Cashu Biological Station." In A.H. Gentry, ed., *Four Tropical Rainforests,* pp. 48–59. New Haven, CT: Yale University Press.

22. Wilson, E. P. 1987. "The Arboreal Ant Fauna of Peruvian Amazon Forests: A First Assessment." *Biotropica* 19(3):245–51.

23. Fleck, David W., and John D. Harder. 2000. "Matses Indian Rainforest Habitat Classification and Mammalian Diversity in Amazonian Peru." *Journal of Ethnobiology* 20(1):1–36.

24. Bodley, John H., and Folecy C. Benson. 1979. *Cultural Ecology of Amazonian Palms.* Reports of Investigations, No. 56. Pullman, Washington: Washington State University Laboratory of Anthropology.

25. Shepard Jr., Glenn H., Douglas W. Yu, Manuel Lizarralde, Mateo Italiano. 2001. "Rain Forest Habitat Classification Among the Matsigenka of the Peruvian Amazon." *Journal of Ethnobiology* 21(1):1–38.

26. Johnson, Allen, and Clifford A. Behrens. 1982. "Nutritional Criteria in Machiguenga Food Production Decisions: A Linear-Programming Analysis." *Human Ecology* 10(2):167–89.

27. Johnson, Allen. 1983. "Machiguenga Gardens." In *Adaptive Responses of Native Amazonians*, edited by Raymond Hames and William Vickers, pp. 29–63. New York: Academic Press.

28. Boster, J. 1983. "A Comparison of the Diversity of Jivaroan Gardens with that of the Tropical Forest." *Human Ecology* 11(1):47-68; Carneiro, Robert L. 1983. "The Cultivation of Manioc among the Kuikuru of the Upper Xingu." In *Adaptive Responses of Native Amazonians*, edited by Raymond Hames and William Vickers, pp. 65–111. New York: Academic Press.

29. Shepard Jr., Glenn. 1999. "Shamanism and Diversity: a Machiguenga Perspective." In Daryl Posey, ed., *Cultural and Spiritual Values of Biodiversity*, pp. 93–95. United Nations Nairobi, Kenya: Environment Programme.

30. Yde, Jens. 1965. *Material Culture of the Waiwai*. Nationalmuseets Skrifter. Ethnografisk Roekke 1. Copenhagen: National Museum.

31. Fittkau, E., and H. Klinge. 1973. "On Biomass and Trophic Structure of the Central Amazonian Rain Forest Ecosystem." *Biotropica* 5(1):2–14.

32. Bailey, Robert C., G. Head, M. Jenike, B. Own, R. Rechtman, and E. Zechenter. 1989 "Hunting and Gathering in Tropical Rain Forest: Is It Possible?" *American Anthropologist* 91(1):59–82.

33. Meggers, Betty J. 2007. "Sustainable Intensive Exploitation of Amazonia: Cultural, Environmental, and Geopolitical Perspectives." In Alf Hornborg and Carole L. Crumley, eds. *The World System and the Earth System: Global Socioenvironmental Change and Sustainability Since the Neolithic*, pp. 195–209. Walnut Creek, CA: Left Coast Press.

34. Denevan, William M. 2002. *Cultivated Landscapes of Native Amazonia and the Andes*. Oxford, NY: Oxford University Press.

35. Carneiro, Robert L. 1960. "Slash-and-Burn Agriculture: A Closer Look at Its Implications for Settlement Patterns." In *Men and Cultures: Selected Papers of the International Congress of Anthropological and Ethnological Sciences*, edited by A. Wallace, pp. 229–34. Philadelphia: University of Pennsylvania Press.

36. Gross, Daniel R. 1975. "Protein Capture and Cultural Development in the Amazon Basin." *American Anthropologist* 77(3):526–49.

37. Carneiro, Robert L. 1960. "Slash-and-Burn Agriculture: A Closer Look at Its Implications for Settlement Patterns." In *Men and Cultures: Selected Papers of the International Congress of Anthropological and Ethnological Sciences*, edited by A. Wallace, pp. 229–34. Philadelphia: University of Pennsylvania Press.

38. Eisenburg, J., and R. Thorington, Jr. 1973. "A Preliminary Analysis of a Neotropical Mammal Fauna." *Biotropica* 5(3):150–61; Walsh, J., and R. Gannon. 1967. *Time Is Short and the Water Rises*. Camden, NJ: Nelson.

39. Bergman, Roland W. 1980. *Amazon Economics: The Simplicity of Shipibo Indian Wealth*. Dellplain Latin American Studies, 6. Ann Arbor, MI: University Microfilms, Department of Geography, Syracuse University; Flowers, Nancy M. 1983. Seasonal Factors in Subsistence, Nutrition, and Child Growth in a Central Brazilian Indian Community." In *Adaptive Responses of Native Amazonians*, edited by Raymond Hames and William Vickers, pp. 357–90. New York: Academic Press; Johnson, Allen. 1975. "Time Allocation in a Machiguenga Community." *Ethnology* 14(3):301–10; Lizot, Jacques. 1977. "Population, Resources and Warfare Among the Yanomami." *Man* 12(3/4):497–517; Werner, Dennis. 1983. "Why Do the Mekranoti Trek?" In *Adaptive Responses of Native Amazonians*, edited by Raymond Hames and William Vickers, pp. 225–38. New York: Academic Press.

40. Johnson, Allen. 1985. "In Search of the Affluent Society." In *Anthropology: Contemporary Perspectives*, edited by David Hunter and Phillip Whitten, pp. 201–06. Boston: Little, Brown (Reprinted from *Human Nature*, September 1978.)

41. Weiss, Gerald. 1975. *Campa Cosmology: The World of a Forest Tribe in South America*. Anthropological Papers no. 52(5). New York: American Museum of Natural History.

42. This discussion uses time data for the Matsigenka from Johnson, Allen. 1975. "Time Allocation in a Machiguenga Community." *Ethnology* 14(3):301–10; and estimates for monetary value based on Bodley, John H. 2005. "The Rich Tribal World: Scale and Power Perspectives on Cultural Valuation," paper presented at the Annual Meeting of the Society for Applied Anthropology, Santa Fe, NM; and Bodley, John H. 2008. *Anthropology and Contemporary Human Problems*, 5th ed. Lanham, NY: AltaMira Press, pp. 67–70.

43. Costanza, Robert, et al. 1997. "The Value of the World's Ecosystem Services and Natural Capital." *Nature* 387(6630): 253–9.

44. Loh, Jonathan, and Mathis Wackernagel. 2004. *Living Planet Report*. Gland, Switzerland: WWF-World Wide Fund for Nature.

45. For ease of reference when general comparisons are being made, the designation "Asháninka" covers all closely related Asháninka peoples, including the Matsigenka (Machigenga); and "Shipibo" will refer to the Shipibo, Conibo, and Pisquibo.

46. Lathrap, Donald. 1970. *The Upper Amazon*, p. 123.

47. Weiss, Kemmeth M. 1973. *Demographic Models for Anthropology*. Memoirs of the Society for American Archaeology No. 27. *American Antiquity* 38(2).

48. Clastres, Pierre. 1977. *Society Against the State: The Leader as Servant and the Humane Uses of Power Among the Indians of the Americas.* New York: Urizen Books.

49. Levi-Strauss, Claude. 1944. "The Social and Psychological Aspects of Chieftainship in a Primitive Tribe: The Nambikuara of Northwestern Matto Grosso." *Transactions of the New York Academy of Sciences* 7:16–32.

50. Siskind, Janet. 1973. *To Hunt in the Morning.* London: Oxford University Press.

51. Behrens, Clifford A. 1984. *Shipibo Ecology and Economy: A Mathematical Approach to Understanding Human Adaptation.* Doctoral Dissertation. Los Angeles: University of California, 155.

52. Bergman, Roland W. 1974. *Shipibo Subsistence in the Upper Amazon Rainforest.* Ph.D. dissertation, Department of Geography, University of Wisconsin-Madison. Ann Arbor, MI: University Microfilms, Figures 14 and 23.

53. Bergman, 1974. *Shipibo Subsistence,* 237, Johnson, 2003. *Families of the Forest,* Table 16, p. 71.

54. DeBoer, Warren R. 1974. "Ceramic Longevity and Archaeological Interpretation: An Example from the Upper Ucayali, Peru." *American Antiquity* 39(2):335–43; DeBoer, Warren R., and Donald W. Lathrap. 1979. "The Making and Breaking of Shipibo-Conibo Ceramics." In Carol Kramer, ed., *Ethnoarchaeology: Implications of Ethnography for Archaeology,* pp. 102–38. New York: Columbia University Press.

55. Roe, Peter G. 1980. "Art and Residence among the Shipibo Indians of Peru: A Study in Microacculturation." *American Anthropologist* 82(1):42–71.

56. Roe, Peter G. 1981. "Aboriginal Tourists and Artistic Exchange Between the Pisquibo and the Shipibo: 'Trade Ware in an Ethnographic Setting.'" In *Networks of the Past: Regional Interaction in Archaeology,* edited by Peter D. Francis, F. L. J. Kense, and P. G. Duke, pp. 61–84.

57. Roe, Peter G. 1982. *The Cosmic Zygote: Cosmology in the Amazon Basin.* New Brunswick, NJ: Rutgers University Press, 93–112.

58. Raymond, J. Scott, Warren R. DeBoer, and Peter G. Roe. 1975. *Cumancaya: A Peruvian Ceramic Tradition.* Occasional Papers No. 2. Calgary, Alberta: Department of Archaeology, The University of Calgary.

59. Murphy, Yolanda, and Robert F. Murphy. 1974. *Women of the Forest.* New York and London: Columbia University Press.

60. Murphy and Murphy, 1974, *Women of the Forest,* 122.

61. Murphy and Murphy, 1974, *Women of the Forest,* 219.

62. Rummel, R. J. 1997. *Death by Government.* New Brunswick, NJ: Transaction.

63. Keeley, Lawrence H. 1996. *War Before Civilization.* New York and Oxford: Oxford University Press.

64. Chagnon, Napoleon A. 1968b. "Yanomamo Social Organization and Warfare." In *War: The Anthropology of Armed Conflict and Aggression,* edited by Morton Fried, Marvin Harris, and Robert Murphy, pp. 109–59. Garden City, NY: Doubleday; 1979. "Is Reproductive Success Equal in Egalitarian Societies?" In *Evolutionary Biology and Human Social Behavior: An Anthropological Perspective,* edited by Napoleon Chagnon and William Irons, pp. 374–401. North Scituate, MA: Duxbury Press; 1983. *Yanomamo: The Fierce People,* 3rd ed. New York: Holt, Rinehart and Winston; 1988. "Life Histories, Blood Revenge, and Warfare in a Tribal Population." *Science* 239(4843): 985–92.

65. Divale, William, and Marvin Harris. 1976. "Population, Warfare and the Male Supremacist Complex." *American Anthropologist* 78(3):521–38; Harris, Marvin. 1971b. *Culture, Man, and Nature: An Introduction to General Anthropology.* New York: Crowell; 1974. *Cows, Pigs, Wars, and Witches: The Riddles of Culture.* New York: Random House; 1984. "A Cultural Materialist Theory of Band and Village Warfare: The Yanomamo Test." In *Warfare, Culture, and Environment,* edited by R. Brian Ferguson, pp. 111–40. New York: Academic Press.

66. Durham, William H. 1991. *Coevolution: Genes, Culture, and Human Diversity.* Stanford, CA: Stanford University Press.

67. Malinowski, Bronislaw. 1948. *Magic, Science, and Religion.* Boston: Beacon Press Radcliffe-Brown, A.R. 1952. *Structure and Function in Primitive Society.* London: Oxford University Press.

68. Tylor, Edward B. 1871. *Primitive Culture.* London: Murray.

69. Viveiros de Castro, Eduardo. 2004. "Exchanging Perspectives: the Transformation of Objects into Subjects in Amerindian Ontologies. *Common Knowledge* 10(3):463-484.

70. Weiss, Gerald. 1975. *Campa Cosmology: The World of a Forest Tribe in South America.* Anthropological Papers, no. 52(5). New York: American Museum of Natural History.

71. Hallpike, C. R. 1979. *The Foundations of Primitive Thought.* Oxford, Eng.: Clarendon Press; Frazer, Sir James 1990 [1890] 1900. *The Golden Bough.* 3 vols. London: Macmillan; Kroeber, Alfred L. 1948. *Anthropology.* New York: Harcourt, Brace and World, p. 298.

72. Boyer, Pascal. 2000. "Functional Origins of Religious Concepts: Ontological and Strategic Selection in Evolved Minds." *Journal of the Royal Anthropological Institute* 6:195–214.

73. Johnson, Allen. 2003. *Families of the Forest: The Matsigenka Indians of the Peruvian Amazon.* Berkeley: University of California Press, p. 98.

74. Roe, Peter G. 1982. *The Cosmic Zygote: Cosmology in the Amazon Basin.* New Brunswick, NJ: Rutgers University Press.

75. Reichel-Dolmatoff, Gerardo. 1971. *Amazonian Cosmos: The Sexual and Religious Symbolism of the Tukano Indians.*

Chicago: University of Chicago Press.; Reichel-Dolmatoff, Gerardo, 1976. "Cosmology as Ecological Analysis: A View from the Rain Forest." *Man* 11(3): 307–18.

76. Hornborg, Alf. 2002. *Beyond Universalism and Relativism.* Presented at the Ninth International Conference on Hunting and Gathering Societies, Heriot-Watt University, Edinburgh, Scotland.

77. Roe, 1982, *The Cosmic Zygote*, 52.

78. Levi-Strauss, Claude. 1969. *The Raw and the Cooked: Introduction to a Science of Mythology 1.* New York: Harper & Row; 1973. *From Honey to Ashes: Introduction to a Science of Mythology 2.* New York: Harper & Row; 1978. *The Origin of Table Manners: Introduction to a Science of Mythology 3.* New York: Harper & Row.

79. Roe, 1982, *The Cosmic Zygote*.

80. Wilbert, Johannes. 1987. *Tobacco and Shamanism in South America.* New Haven & London: Yale University Press, pp. 192–200; Shepard Jr., Glenn H. 1998. "Psychoactive Plants and Ethnopsychiatric Medicines of the Matsigenka." *Journal of Psychoactive Drugs* 30(4):321–32. For an extended discussion of Amazonian shamanism see Whitehead, Neil L. 2002. *Dark Shamans: Kanaimà and the Poetics of Violent Death.* Durham and London: Duke University Press.

CHAPTER 3

Australian Aborigines: Mobile Foragers for 50,000 Years

Figure 3.0. Aboriginal woman of New South Wales (Ratzel 1896:99).

ay = *ay* in d*ay*
ng − *ng* in si*ng*
e = *e* in b*e*d
i = *i* in b*i*t
ee = *ee* in b*ee*t
• = Syllable division
/ = Stress
Anbarra = [an • ba / rra]
borrmunga = [borr • moo / nga]
Gidjingarli = [gij • ing • ar / li]
gurrurta = [goorr • oor / ta]
Kakadu = [ka / ka • doo]
Manggalili = [mang • ga • lee / lee]
molamola = [mo / la • mo / la]
Murrumbur = [moorr • oom / boor]
Nourlangie = [nor • layng / ee]
Oenpelli = [o • en • pel / lee]

PRONUNCIATION GUIDE

THERE ARE MANY VARIANT SPELLINGS OF ABORIGINAL WORDS. For example, Kakadu of Kakadu National Park has also been written Gagadu and Gagudju and is also the name of a resident aboriginal language. Nourlangie Rock, a major rock art site within the park, is known to the Aborigines as Burrungguy, or Nawulandja. The following pronunciations are recommended by the Australian Nature Conservation Agency as English equivalents for aboriginal terms:[1]

Key
   a = *a* in father
   oo = *oo* in f*oo*d
   o = *o* in g*o*
   rr = *rr* in ca*rr*y, with trill

LEARNING OBJECTIVES

After studying this chapter you should be able to do the following:

1. Describe the physical challenges that faced the first aboriginal peoples who settled Australia.
2. Explain how both empirical and nonempirical knowledge operate in aboriginal culture, discussing the role of each.
3. Explain the central contribution of the Dreaming and totemism to the long-term success of the aboriginal way of life.
4. Describe the basic structure of aboriginal society, distinguishing band, clan, and tribe by composition and function.
5. Explain why size of social units was such an important feature of aboriginal society and how size contributed to the long-term success of the aboriginal way of life.
6. Explain how Aborigines made a living and why they may be considered "the original affluent society," drawing specific comparisons with contemporary commercial societies.
7. Explain why aboriginal society can be considered egalitarian, even though aboriginal social status differs significantly by age and gender, with old men apparently having the most social power.

8. Describe aboriginal marriage practices, including rules of marriageability, who arranges marriages, and the function of polygyny.

The Australians have been the historical, evolutionary and sociological prototype for the study of hunter-gatherers and for the relations between man and nature. From the onset of modern anthropology they have inspired, challenged or provided the limiting case for nearly every view of man's behavior. —N. Peterson (1986)[2]

Australia, the only continent in the modern world to have been occupied exclusively by tribal foragers, has always been central to anthropological theories about tribal cultures. The 50,000-year prehistory of aboriginal culture raises major questions about cultural stability and change, carrying capacity and population regulation, quality of life, and the inevitability of cultural evolution. Furthermore, Australian Aborigines are justly famous for their elegant kinship systems and elaborate ritual life, supported by one of the world's simplest known material technologies. The Australian aboriginal culture also raises important questions about the function of initiation rituals and the meaning of equality in a tribal society in which the old men appear to control much of the ideological system. The extent to which such cultures can be considered affluent, egalitarian, and "in balance with nature" is also an issue for debate. All of these issues are discussed in this chapter.

The discovery and successful colonization of the Australian continent by foraging peoples and its continuous occupation for at least 50,000 years is surely one of the most remarkable events in human history. It clearly demonstrates the tremendous potential of mobile foraging technology and egalitarian social systems, which allowed people to live in diverse, and often unpredictable, environments and adjust to long-term climatic change. The foraging way of life is certainly one of the most successful sociocultural systems people have ever developed.

Aboriginal people maintained and transmitted the broad features of their culture for millennia because it allowed them to enjoy the good life. The culture was sustainable because it worked for people. It helped people meet their needs fairly, reliably, and easily, and therefore they willingly reproduced the system with only minimal, fine-tuning changes to suit changing conditions. Aborigines designed and reproduced a cultural system that rewarded people for keeping their families small and their material requirements low.

They correctly understood that nature would generously provide all of their material needs in return for minimal human effort. They also believed that everyone was family. As members of the same family everyone was entitled at birth to an estate that gave them access to the natural, cultural, and human resources needed to make a living and form a successful household. There was no conflict between individual self-interest and the needs of society, or between the needs of nature and the needs of culture. The genius of the system was that it treated individual and society, nature and culture, male and female, young and old as complementary oppositions that worked together for mutual benefit. Mobile foraging set a low threshold for total population and density and made nature itself the primary form of material wealth. Under these conditions it was difficult for anyone to concentrate enough social power to promote destabilizing growth in society or economy.

It is estimated that at the time of European contact in 1788, Australia was occupied by at least 300,000 people and perhaps a million or more, representing some 600 culturally distinct groups and speaking some 268 languages.[3] Throughout the millennia, the Aborigines intensified their subsistence techniques and managed and shaped their natural resources, but they never resorted to farming or sedentary village life. Australia was, in fact, the largest world area to avoid domestication and social stratification and the associated burdens of agriculture. The aboriginal "mode of thought" represented by the "Dreaming" seems to be the central integrative key to the entire culture. The Dreaming was an interconnected set of ideas, stories, rituals, objects, and practices that explained the origin and meaning of nature and culture and told people how to live harmoniously.

CONSTRUCTING A SUSTAINABLE DESERT CULTURE

Imagine yourself with five hundred other people of all ages—men, women, and children—naked and empty-handed on the shore of an uninhabited desert continent. You are all participants in a great human experiment. Your collective challenge is more than mere survival. The experiment requires you to design a fully self-sufficient culture that will satisfy everyone's human needs while guaranteeing the same security for all future generations. Without machines, metal tools, or libraries, you need to find food and shelter in your strange surroundings. This task requires extensive, highly specialized knowledge and skills, which need to be acquired, stored, and reproduced without the aid of electronic devices. Perhaps even more difficult, you need to establish rules to regulate marriage, prevent conflict, and reproduce the culture. Whatever culture you create will need to provide enough human satisfaction that the people will maintain and reproduce it. There will be no chance to start over. This *was* the challenge that faced the first Australians, and they solved it brilliantly.

The great achievement and continuity of aboriginal culture took on a personal meaning for me in 1988 when I visited Nourlangie Rock and the rock shelter of Ubirr in Kakadu National Park on the edge of the great Arnhem Land escarpment. Both of these sites contain richly painted galleries with pictures of people, mythological figures, fish, and animals, many in the unique x-ray style of contemporary Arnhem Land bark painting. Some of the most recent paintings date to the 1960s, but there are multiple layers of increasingly faded red ochre and white line drawings that shade into the remote past. There are also stenciled hand prints, hauntingly reminiscent of those seen in Ice Age cave paintings in France. Archaeological excavations show that people lived in the Kakadu more than 20,000 years ago. Aborigines living in the Kakadu today assert their traditional ownership over these sites and are extremely protective of these direct links to their land and culture. Later I went on a foraging expedition on the floodplain of the South Alligator River escorted by members of the Murrumbur clan. I saw wallabies, saltwater crocodiles, goannas (lizards), and cockatoos in this game-rich country and watched my guides gather wild tomatoes and edible waterlilies. They made fire by twirling a stick, and we dined on roast magpie geese and long-necked turtles that the women extracted from the muddy bottom of a shallow lake.

The Earliest Australians

The first major event in Australian prehistory was the original settlement of the continent (see table 3.1). Archaeologists have obtained absolute dates—ages of objects given in years rather than less precisely—of 50,000 to 60,000 BP for human occupation in northern Australia using thermoluminescence, a technique for directly calculating the age of certain minerals.[4] Genetic evidence suggests that the ancestors of Australian Aborigines must have come from Southeast Asia, but it will never be known precisely how they crossed the 44-mile (70-km) stretch of open water that separated the closest Asian islands from Australia. Because this must have occurred during the Ice Age when Australia and New Guinea were connected by the dry land Sahul Shelf, any evidence of these earliest pioneers would have been obliterated by rising sea levels (see figure 3.1).

The suitability of Australia for occupation by foraging peoples, those who use no domesticated plants or herd animals, is determined by the availability of wild plants and animals, which in turn is shaped by the complex interaction of geological history and geography. Remarkably, the Australian continent, which has the same land area as the lower forty-eight United States, is almost totally lacking in major rivers and mountains and has been called the driest continent in the world. This is because Australia is situated in the southern hemisphere astride the Tropic of Capricorn so that much of the rain that comes from the east across the south Pacific is stopped by the Great Dividing Range that fringes the east coast. This mountain barrier creates a vast rain shadow and makes the interior a desert. Aridity is the principal factor limiting the density and diversity of organisms, including foraging humans, throughout the continent.

Table 3.1. Australian Preshistory, 60,000 BP–AD 1788

AD 1500-1788	1788	European colonization
	1500	Indonesian fisherman visit
5000–6000 BP	5000	Small Tool Tradition; spear points, backed-blade microliths, spear-thrower; dingo; subsistence intensification
8000-15,000 BP	8000	Cape York separated from New Guinea
	10,000	Earliest dated wooden implements: spear, digging stick, firestick, boomerang
	12,000	Tasmania cut off from mainland
	15,000	Sea levels begin to rise
20,000-60,000 BP	20,000	Widespread occupation
	12,000–50,000	Pleistocene extinctions of megafauna
	40,000–60,000	Initial settlement

Sources: Flood (1983), Lourandos (1987), and White and O'Connell (1982).

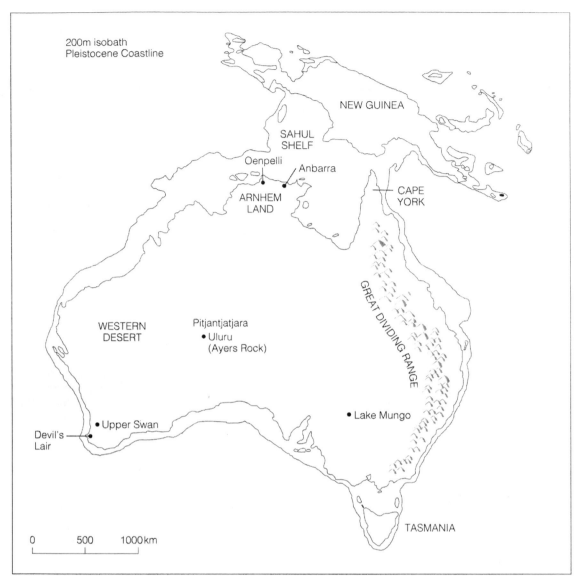

Figure 3.1. Map of Australia showing principal geographic features and locations of groups and sites (redrafted from Lourandos 1987, Figure 2).

Biologically, Australia is famous for its unique flora and fauna, especially the numerous gum trees (eucalyptus), the marsupials (the pouch-bearing kangaroos and opossums), and the world's only egg-laying mammals (the platypus and echidna).

Because the Aborigines did not raise domestic crops or animals, they were totally dependent on the natural productivity of the environment, as measured by the biomass available for human consumption. Human population density was thus largely determined by rainfall and was highest in the biologically rich coastal regions, especially in the tropical north and east. Population densities remained extremely low in the dry interior. Conditions are most extreme in the Western Desert, where there is no real seasonality or predictability in rainfall, and drought conditions may continue for years. In the open country, distant rainstorms can be observed for up to 50 miles (80 km), and people watch the clouds and rely on their detailed knowledge of the locations of specific rock holes and soaks to plan their movements. Population densities there were among the lowest for foragers in the world, averaging less than 0.01 person per square kilometer.[5]

Aboriginal Sociocultural System Resilience

Given the vast time period that people have lived in Australia and the relatively low total population when Europeans arrived, many anthropologists have wondered whether Aborigines achieved a balance between population and resources. Joseph Birdsell believed that Aborigines rapidly reached the maximum potential population that could be supported by their foraging technology throughout Australia and then maintained a constant balance between population and resources.[6] Others suggest that Aborigines very gradually expanded their population and elaborated their technology over many thousands of years.[7] In either case, the aboriginal achievement is impressive.

During the Pleistocene geological epoch, which ended some 10,000 years ago, glaciation caused global sea levels to drop to 328 to 492 feet (100 to 150 m) below present levels. As the ice retreated at the end of the Pleistocene, sea levels began to rise, inundating the Sahul Shelf and cutting New Guinea and Tasmania off from the mainland. It is estimated that the sea advanced across the Sahul by as much as 3 miles (5 km) in a single year and 62 miles (100 km) in a generation.[8] These events have been enshrined in aboriginal myths. It is a tribute to the success of the forager mode of thought and the Dreaming that Aborigines were able to resist environmental pressures to intensify their forager subsistence production system. We can only assume that aboriginal culture was so well integrated and resilient Aborigines could use it to adjust to major environmental perturbations with minimal change. This also suggests that social power was so evenly distributed that no one was able to take advantage of circumstances to promote their self-interest over the interests of society in stability.

Australian aboriginal society offers an interesting test case for the proposition that foraging peoples were more resilient than village farmers or large-scale societies. Resilience means avoiding collapse yet retaining overall system structure, or recovering quickly in the face of stress.[9] The archaeological record shows that the foraging way of life has existed vastly longer than any other, and there is no evidence that foraging peoples experienced periodic population crashes or depleted their resources (except in the most extreme cases, as in the Arctic). The implication is that stationary populations, in which births exactly replace deaths, must have been the norm. Some culturally regulated population controls must have operated, because even the smallest deviation from balanced fertility and mortality rates operating over thousands of years would have led either to extinction, overpopulation, and hardship or to drastic cultural change. Aboriginal societies had optimum sizes, but it is not certain how population actually was regulated.

Carrying capacity is the term anthropologists use to describe the number of people who could, in theory, be supported indefinitely in a given environment with a given technology and culture. Birdsell estimated that tribal territories were optimally populated at 60 percent of their carrying capacity to allow for random fluctuation in resources.[10] He assumed that intentional infanticide involving up to 50 percent of births was the primary mechanism limiting population. It is known that babies were sometimes killed at birth, but there is little direct evidence for the actual rate. Infanticide was most likely carried out by women because they could carry and nurse only one child under three or four years of age. This kind of family planning increased the likelihood that a given child could be raised to maturity, and in combination with a high "natural" infant mortality rate, could produce a stationary population.

Infanticide was related to foraging conditions because both mobility and the burden of carrying children increase when resources are scarce. Similarly, given existing food sources and preparation techniques, there was no baby food other than mothers' milk; thus, nursing would be prolonged, often for four years or more. Infanticide reflected the autonomy that women maintained in reproductive decision making, and it also gave them some covert political leverage in a society that was publicly dominated by men.[11] The balance between population and resources was also under unconscious biological control because extended lactation and nutritional deficiencies can lower fertility by causing hormonal changes in a woman's reproductive cycle.

It has sometimes been suggested, on the basis of census data showing sex ratios skewed in favor of boys, that girls were more likely to be killed than boys, thereby making infanticide a more powerful means of population control. However, these data are suspect because girls may have been hidden from census takers, and a careful review of completed families in Australia shows no evidence that girls were selectively killed.[12] Computer simulation studies also suggest that, if systematically applied, even very low rates of selective female infanticide would have led to population extinction.

The Dreaming and Aboriginal Social Structure

It is impossible to discuss Australian culture without confronting the metaphysical aspects of aboriginal understandings about the invisible world of the Dreaming and associated totems, souls, and spirits, and their representation in nature, myth, ritual, and society.

The key element of aboriginal culture is the complex, multidimensional concept Aborigines call the Dreaming, which recognizes the interdependence and vitality of all parts of the cosmos. Humans are actors along with other species in a balanced living system whose goal is the continuity of life and the maintenance of the cosmos itself. Aborigines believe their culture to be fundamentally changeless and in balance with nature.

The emic term *Dreaming* refers variously to creation; the moral order; an ancestral being; people; a spirit; the origin point of a spirit, a specific topographic feature; and a **totem** species, object, or phenomenon. Furthermore, all of these can be thought of as the same, whereas in Western thought they would be sharply distinguished. Outsiders have treated the Dreaming as aboriginal religion, but it is a profound concept that permeates all aspects of the culture and defies easy categorization. Aborigines identify themselves completely with their culture and their land through the Dreaming in a way that non-Aborigines have difficulty comprehending. For an Aborigine to say "I am a kangaroo" might sound like nonsense, but within the Dreaming context such a statement carries important meaning.

Generations of anthropologists have called these aboriginal beliefs "totemism," or "animism," and often deprecated them as childish, unscientific, and false, even though they served obvious individual and social functions. However, it is more helpful to view totemism and the Dreaming as a particular way of knowing the world, an aboriginal epistemology. What qualifies these beliefs as "supernatural" is that they are based on the *noumenal,* a nonempirical way of knowing. They are ideas, or concepts in the mind, of beings whose physical existence may not be verified by observation and experiment. What matters is not their physical reality, but the social reality that they facilitate.

Spirits are not directly visible to the senses, although they may be embodied in physical objects. Totemism is a way of understanding the world that can be as useful and therefore is as "true" as a scientific empirical epistemology. Beliefs about the supernatural can also be considered religious when they connect with morality, and this is certainly the case with Australian totemism.

In aboriginal culture the nonempirical way of knowing exists alongside of, and does not conflict with, a scientific observational epistemology that ab-

original people use to create, store, and reproduce detailed information about the *phenomenal* world that appears to their senses. This empirical knowledge tells people what plants and animals are good to eat, where they live, when to collect them, and how to prepare them. Aborigines know that it is both logical and useful to view things in different ways. They recognize that things can, in effect, be two things at once, just as Amazonian peoples who conceptualize human-jaguar transformations.

Totemism is based on beliefs in the supernatural that are virtually universal in all societies. Souls and spirits fit normal expectations about natural beings, but what makes them *supernatural* beings is that they may behave in ways that violate the intuitive understandings that people have about how persons, animals, plants, and objects behave in the natural world.[13] For example, spirits are named, and people may attribute humanlike personalities to them, giving them beliefs and intentions, and physical form, but when people think of spirits as invisible or as passing through other objects they are supernatural, and they may have supernatural effects on people. These supernatural qualities make spirit beings memorable, and this makes them useful vehicles for storing and transmitting information, for building moral systems, and for manipulating other people. Supernatural beliefs and practices are tools that people use in their daily lives.

The early British anthropologist A. R. Radcliffe-Brown[14] thought that Aborigines first ritualized species because they were "good to eat," and then adopted them as totemic emblems for their social groups (see figure 3.2). In this view totems functioned to support group identity and maintain social integration, but this was not a fully satisfactory explanation of their origin. Later, French structuralist Levi-Strauss[15] added a new dimension to the functionalist interpretation when he suggested that totemism resulted from a universal tendency of people to create mental sets of paired opposites, such as day and night, male and female, nature and culture. Such complementary oppositions were "good to think" because they were intellectually satisfying and because they created memorable chains of meaning, analogies, and metaphor from which social solidarity could be constructed. Totems helped make aboriginal society seem natural and permanent. It was useful to imagine that the members of clan A and clan B were culturally different, just as their respective ritual namesakes, the emu and the kangaroo, were naturally different. Each member of the pair existed only in relation to the other, and this mutual interdependence

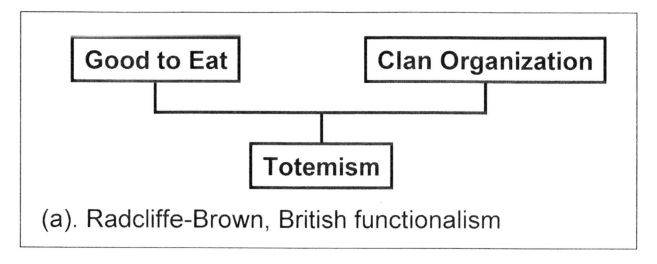

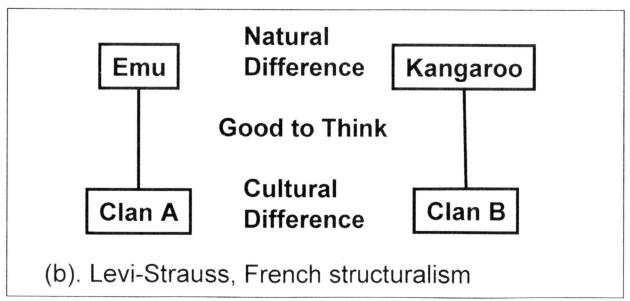

Figure 3.2. Theories of totemism: (a). British functionalism, (b). French structuralism.

created an alliance. Recognizing such complementarity was the basis of exogamy, or marriage exchanges between social groups, which in turn was the very basis of human society.

As a philosophy of life, the Dreaming provides both a **cosmogony** to account for the origin of everything and a **cosmology** to explain the fundamental order of the universe. The Dreaming thus answers the basic meaning-of-life questions; offers a detailed charter for day-to-day living, including basic social categories and ritual activities; and ascribes cultural meanings to the natural environment (see figure 3.3). Supernatural beliefs and practices are tools that people use in their daily lives.

When regarded as a mythic cosmogony, the Dreaming is sometimes imprecisely called the Dreamtime, referring to the creation time when a series of heroic ancestor beings crisscrossed the landscape and transformed specific topographic features as a permanent record of their activities. The problem with referring to creation as the Dreamtime is that Aborigines are not really concerned with origins as historical events; instead, origin myths are timeless explanations. Time, culture, and nature are viewed as cyclical and changeless. The Dreamtime ancestors followed the same cultural rules that are practiced today, and their influence is still so vital that it is more reasonable to refer to the Dreaming as the Every-when, or the Eternal

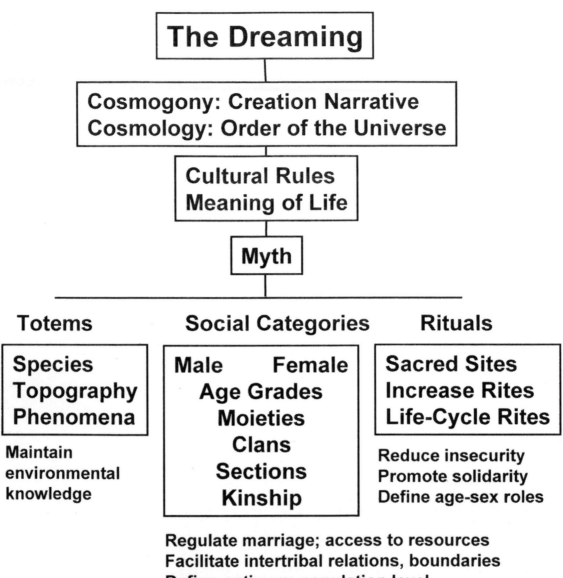

The Dreaming

Cosmogony: Creation Narrative
Cosmology: Order of the Universe

Cultural Rules
Meaning of Life

Myth

Totems

Species
Topography
Phenomena

Maintain
environmental
knowledge

Social Categories

Male   Female
Age Grades
Moieties
Clans
Sections
Kinship

Regulate marriage; access to resources
Facilitate intertribal relations, boundaries
Define optimum population level

Rituals

Sacred Sites
Increase Rites
Life-Cycle Rites

Reduce insecurity
Promote solidarity
Define age-sex roles

Figure 3.3.   A functional model of Aboriginal culture.

Dreamtime, than to place it in the Dreamtime past (see box 3.1).

When the Dreaming is referred to as the moral authority for behavior, it may be called simply the *Law,* or the *Dreaming Law,* and in this respect it is beyond question. Stability is thus a fundamental feature of the culture.

The aboriginal cosmos differs in striking ways from the religions of larger-scale cultures. There is no all-powerful god and no rank order in the Dreaming. Similarly, there is no heaven or hell, and the distinctions between sacred and profane, natural and supernatural, are blurred. Aborigines experience the mystical as a perpetual unity with the cosmos as they follow the Dreaming Law in their daily life. For example, a seemingly mundane activity, such as seasonally burning grass, can be considered a religious act because it perpetuates life and the cosmic balance between sun and rain, people, plants, and animals.

BOX 3.1. AN ABORIGINAL WOMAN TALKS ABOUT THE DREAMING

During an Australia-wide conference of aboriginal women held in Adelaide in 1980, Nganyintja Ilyatjari, a Pitjantjatjara woman from central Australia, interpreted the Dreaming and related it to the land. Ilyatjari drew a series of small circles on a map of Australia and explained in Pitjantjatjara:

I am drawing the places all over Australia where our Dreamtime started a long, long time ago—Listen! . . . This is Dreaming, Dreaming of the kangaroo, the goanna, the wild fig, and lots of other different ones— a long time ago the Dreaming was there, a very long time ago.

This is what all people have always listened to, this Dreaming is ours . . . In all these different places all over Australia lots of aboriginal people have always lived since the beginning. If I could speak English well I would tell you in English.

Our country, the country out there near Mt. Davies, is full of sacred places. The kangaroo Dreaming has been there since the beginning, the wild fig Dreaming has been there since the beginning, many other women's Dreamings are also there. In other places men and women's Dreaming were together from a long time ago. . . .

These places have been part of the sacred Dreamtime since the beginning of time. They were made then by our Dreamtime ancestors—like the kangaroo. Our country is sacred, this country is sacred."[16]

Sacred Sites and Dreamtime Pathways at Uluru

Misunderstanding of aboriginal culture began with the British colonization of Australia in 1788. Because they saw no aboriginal farms or permanent houses, British authorities mistakenly concluded that the Aborigines had no fixed relationship to the land. Australia was declared *terra nullius,* an empty wasteland, free for the taking, and so aboriginal land was appropriated. Nineteenth-century evolutionary anthropologists did little to help the situation. Lewis Henry Morgan,[17] one of the founding fathers of cultural anthropology, considered Aborigines to be living representatives of his evolutionary stage of "middle savagery." This would make Aborigines roughly equivalent to archaic *Homo sapiens,* with little if any symbolic culture or ritual. Only over the past hundred years have anthropologists begun to appreciate the subtle complexities of the Aborigines' enduring ties to their land.

The Dreamtime ancestors, or totemic beings, make a direct link between people and their land by means of the sacred sites, which are the physical remains of ancestral beings or their activities. The role of these beings is dramatically illustrated at Uluru, or Ayers Rock, a giant monolith in central Australia. Uluru is a weathered dome, some 5 miles (8 km) around and rising more than 1,100 feet (335 m) above the desert floor. As the largest such monolith in the world, it was designated as a national park and biosphere reserve in 1985 and is administered jointly by the aboriginal owners and the Australian National Park and Wildlife Service. Since 1994[18] Uluru has been designated by UNESCO as both a natural and cultural World Heritage site. More importantly for the Anangu people, the local Western Desert speakers who are the aboriginal owners of Uluru, it is a cultural landscape monument. They care for it according to *Tjukurpa,* their term for the "law."

The north side of the rock belongs to the clan of hare wallabies, rabbit-size kangaroos, while the south side belongs to the carpet boa clan. A series of stories recounts the activities of ten totemic ancestors and their relatives, including various snakes, reptiles, birds, and mammals, who created the existing landscape and established the clan boundaries, leaving specific rock outcrops, stains, caves, and pockmarks that represent their bodies, camps, and physical signs.[19]

The same totemic beings who created sites at Uluru traveled widely across the country, leaving permanent Dreaming paths. During their travels, they interacted with other beings and created similar sites elsewhere. Specific Dreaming pathways can stretch for hundreds of miles, crossing the territory of different clans and tribes.

Dreaming locations, or sacred sites, such as those at Uluru, are centers for ritual activity and help define territorial boundaries and regulate use of resources. Some sites contain the spirit essence of their creators and are the places where special "increase ceremonies" are conducted to perpetuate particular species. For example, control of a kangaroo increase site means ritual control over the supply of kangaroos. Entry to or even knowledge of such sites often is restricted, and unauthorized intrusion may be severely punished. Other sites are believed to contain especially dangerous supernatural substances that can kill, or make people violently ill, and must be avoided by everyone. To avoid the risks of trespassing, people must seek permission before entering unfamiliar areas. Since

1976, many of these sacred sites have been officially protected by federal legislation, and fines can be levied for trespass.

The spirit essence localized at certain sites also completes the direct link between people and their individual Dreamings, because this animating power is believed to be an essential but not an exclusive element in human conception and reproduction. Pregnancy is identified with the totemic "soul stuff" emanating from a specific Dreaming site, and this soul stuff returns to the site at death. Thus, in a real sense, an individual is a physical part of the Dreaming, and this spiritual connection is a more important cultural fact than biological paternity. Some early anthropologists misinterpreted aboriginal beliefs in totemic conception and assumed that they did not understand the "facts of life," but this was clearly not the case.

An added value of the Dreaming tracks is that they serve as mnemonic devices to help fix in memory the location of permanent waterholes, which are critically important. The Dreaming myths and related rituals are dramatic reminders of specific geographic details and preserve them in people's minds as accurately as would any large-scale printed map. The Dreaming also takes on visible form in body paint, sand drawings, rock art, and paintings or carvings on ritual objects, all of which may incorporate an elaborate iconography (figure 3.4).[20]

Aboriginal Band, Clan, and Tribe: Equality and Flexibility

Australian society is based on highly flexible, multi-family foraging groups or bands and a ritual estate, or religious property, which is tied to the land. **Band** and **estate** are functionally interconnected in the territory defined by Dreaming sacred sites and occupied by the band. The band-estate system serves a resource management function and helps space out and define the optimum limits for local populations, thus contributing directly to long-term stability.

Because Aborigines tend to form their bands around a core of male members and their in-marrying wives, anthropologists often speak of **patrilocal bands** and call the estate-owning groups patriclans. The underlying cultural rules are **clan exogamy**, the requirement to marry outside of the clan, and **patrilocality**, the expectation that a woman will join her husband's band. However, for Aborigines the band is a group of households that live on and use the resources of the estate. The band's core group is a clan estate group of men and their sons and daughters who reside on the clan territory. The women who are members of the clan are also owners of the clan estate, but they may be resident on their husbands' clan territories. Members of the band, including the core group and in-marrying women, have use rights in the clan estate (see figure 3.5). Aborigines may speak of the camp, the

Figure 3.4. Contemporary Aboriginal painting depicting women sitting around a waterhole to collect water which runs down the slopes. Artist George Bush Tjungula, Walpiri and Luritja from Mount Wedge, 1988.

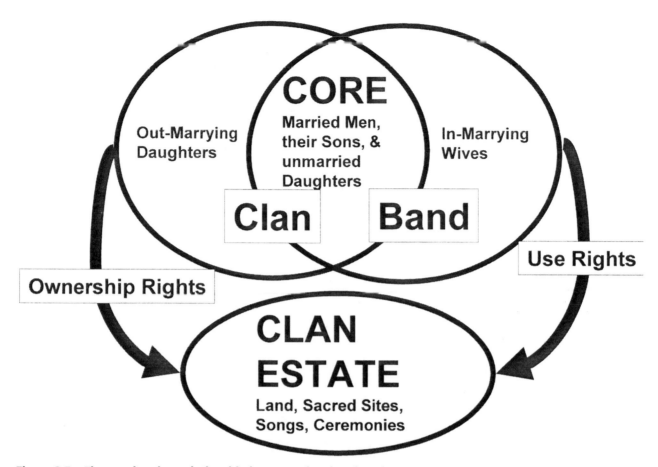

Figure 3.5. The overlapping relationship between clan, band, and estate.

residents of the camp, and the country they occupy, but these terms may have multiple meanings for them. For example, depending on the context, *country* may refer to land as a spiritual landscape or as a foraging territory. Band members may be referred to as "people of" a particular place, but they may claim affiliation with several countries. In practice, the band is not exclusively patrilocal and may change composition frequently as individual families visit relatives in other areas. Nevertheless, the band is an important social group, and individual bands retain their unity during temporary multiband encampments.

Likewise, the clan is not a sharply defined unit in a fixed hierarchical structure. This gives people numerous possibilities for making claims on other people and resources and makes the entire system more flexible. Flexibility seems not to generate conflict, because in a small face-to-face society where everyone is family and resources are not really scarce, the human problem is how best to allocate people to resources.

Clan members control a diverse bundle of supernatural property as well as social connections with other people and places. The same ancestral beings may belong to multiple clans, and they may even extend to different tribes speaking different languages. The important point is that there are cultural rules and structures, but they may sometimes be intentionally vague to give people more advantages in daily life. It should not be surprising that aboriginal clans do not constitute sharply distinguished groups, because they are shaped by dynamic historic processes in which clans die out and new ones are created, and their constitutive elements get resorted. Different people belonging to the same clan do not always agree on either its components or membership. The Yolngu in Arnhem Land conceive of their social groups as yam plants, or trees with branches, where the ancestors are roots. They use the phrase "same but a little bit different" in describing their social identities, which they also characterize as "bundled together, just like a bundle of sticks."[21]

The band forages over a discrete territory containing the critical resources that sustain the band during normal years. Band territorial boundaries are recognized but not directly defended. Visitors must observe special entry rites upon arrival at a camp. They also must ask permission before they can forage within band territory. Under this system, the "owners" of the country operate as resource managers. Permission to forage would rarely be denied, but knowing who is foraging where makes resource exploitation much more efficient and minimizes potential conflicts.

It is important to distinguish between use rights to band territory and ownership rights to the land as a spiritual estate. All band members and those asking permission can use the natural resources of the territory, but only those qualified to be estate owners can give permission and act as managers. The legal nature of the aboriginal landholding system was formally recognized by an Australian judge who presided over a court hearing in 1970 in which the Yolngu people tried to prove their traditional ownership of their land. The three weeks of direct testimony about clans, spirit beings, and the land included the following exchange between the court and a man from the Manggalili clan about permission to use clan land:

Q: Before you went hunting kangaroos, did you talk to anyone?

A: Yes, we would talk together.

Q: Who would you talk to?

A: If I was living with the Rirratjingu [clan], I would talk to those Rirratjingu people.

Q: And what did you say to them?

A: I am going to get animals—kangaroos.[22]

The judge found that the Yolngu land tenure system was "highly adapted to the country" and "remarkably free from the vagaries of personal whim or influence."[23]

Many sorts of overlapping claims are recognized, both to the right to ask to use a territory and to the right to estate ownership. Patrilineal descent from an owner invariably provides the strongest claim, but a person also has special claims on a mother's estate and use rights in a spouse's country. Extended residence also can provide a claim, as can one's place of conception and birth and the burial place of kin. Under this system, ownership and use are distributed in a way that discourages any concentration of social power. Households always have many places to go during droughts or famines. An owner can also be sure that visitors will return to their own countries where their Dreaming connections are strongest. The ease with which people can move among bands helps reduce

conflict because people who are not getting along can simply move apart.

The size and density of the band is in part determined by environmental, demographic, and cultural factors. Worldwide, forager bands average twenty-five to fifty people. Because food, especially game, is pooled among families within the band, the minimum average of twenty-five is probably determined by the number required to maintain foraging security by ensuring that enough adult food producers are available. There are strong reasons for people to hold down the upper limits of band size. Given fixed territories, increased numbers above minimum levels would soon result in a reduction in leisure and more frequent moves as resources became depleted.

The minimum size of bands also may be shaped by the need to maintain marriage alliances that would reduce the likelihood of interband conflict. Bands tend to space themselves uniformly across the landscape in roughly hexagonal territories, such that each band is surrounded by five or six neighboring bands. The cultural requirement of band exogamy is a good excuse for marrying otherwise potentially hostile neighbors.

Like all domestic-scale, tribal societies, Australian Aborigines recognize no political leaders beyond their local residential communities. Band leaders are coordinators with little coercive power. Decision making is by consensus. Aboriginal bands are politically autonomous, but the requirements of exogamy mean that they are not totally self-sufficient. Aboriginal people are members of a broader social network linking people in neighboring bands through common language and culture, marriage alliances, joint ceremonies, feasting, and frequent visits. This larger decentralized society can be called a **tribe**. Its members typically consider themselves to be kin and self-identify with a group designation that often means "the people." The tribe must be large enough to support a demographically viable population through intermarriage (**endogamy**) and to reproduce a distinct language and culture. Australian tribes apparently averaged about 500 people, men, women, and children.[24] If tribes dropped below 200 people, tribal members would have difficulty finding mates, whereas tribes of more than 1,000 people would split up because of internal conflicts and the infrequency of social interaction. The demographics of aboriginal society were so predictable that the optimum sizes of 50 for Australian bands and 500 for tribes have been called "magic numbers." Thus, if the aboriginal population was 300,000 when Europeans arrived in 1788, there may have been some 600 tribes, potentially speaking as many languages.

Australian tribes were normally food self-sufficient, although they maintained sporadic social interaction with the members of neighboring tribes. As with band territories, tribal territories varied in size according to the richness of natural resources. In areas where rainfall was sufficient to increase natural biological productivity, food supplies improved and tribal territories became smaller than in drier zones. In the driest interior deserts territories were vast and population densities very low. People had to move frequently to find food and water.

Aborigines are multilingual, and intermarriage and joint ceremonies between people speaking different languages and dialects are common. Language groups often are associated with territories, but such territories are probably de facto artifacts of the aggregated territorial estates when viewed from the outside. There are few, if any, occasions when the members of a tribe would act as a unit, and joint defense of tribal territory must have been a rare event. However, there is often a strong sense of "tribal" identity reflecting shared language, territory, and culture.

Aboriginal Australia comprises overlapping networks of social interaction that span the entire continent. Aboriginal material culture is the simplest of any ethnographically known people. In the next section, we examine how they remain well fed and comfortable in the desert, with nothing more than fire and a few implements of wood and stone.

Aboriginal Cognitive and Perceptual Systems

The European invaders of Australia were convinced of the intellectual inferiority of Aborigines, often considering them to be mental children, and deprecated their cultural beliefs as "obsolete" and obviously erroneous. Later, culturally sensitive assessments of the cognitive abilities of Aborigines showed them to be superior to Europeans in many practical situations. Aborigines excelled on visual memory and spatial tests, skills that served them well in route finding, tracking, hunting, and gathering.[25] Early anthropological observers were also impressed by the superior visual acuity and observational abilities of Aborigines; but in line with their racist and evolutionary biases, they devalued these abilities as instinctive survival skills and "lower" mental functions. A less ethnocentric assessment of cognitive abilities recognizes that different "cultural environments" produce different patterns of abilities.[26] The complex of cultural concepts associated with the Dreaming help explain the remarkable abilities of Aborigines to orient for vast distances across seemingly empty landscapes. Researchers found that Aborigines routinely kept detailed mental track of the topographic features that they passed when traveling across country that seemed virtually featureless to outsiders.[27] In random tests with a compass, Aborigines could point with great precision in the direction of sacred sites that were seventy-seven or more miles (200 km) away. Such accuracy required them to constantly update a mental map of their movements, and they were able to do this even in unfamiliar country.

One aboriginal color-term system has been found to distinguish just two colors, but this does not suggest any cognitive or perceptual shortcomings. Color terms are presumably added in response to cultural requirements, but just two terms could work perfectly well when very specific color differences can be described in reference to specific natural objects (see box 3.2). Two color terms are used for simple dualistic symbolic oppositions, such as between life and death, male and female, or sacred and profane.[28] The addition of red creates a mediated opposition in which red can variously be opposed to either dark or light, like the ambiguous Amazonian jaguar mediating between the complementary opposites of male and female described in chapter 2. The further addition of either green or yellow creates a pair of analogous oppositions, as in the *a:b::c:d* pattern.

BOX 3.2. AN ABORIGINAL COLOR SYSTEM

That any culture could function with no more than two basic color terms is difficult to imagine, but an Australian aboriginal example of such a system shows how feasible it is.[29] The Anbarra Aborigines of Arnhem Land use two basic color terms as adjectives: *-gungaltfa* (light) and *-gungundfa* (dark). Only a few of the very lightest colors, including bright red, are called *-gungaltja*. All objects can be described using these two terms. For example, storm clouds, the sky, granite, and Aborigines are "dark," while other clouds, the sea, sandstone, newborn babies, Europeans, and sunsets are "light." Four mineral pigments are used as paints and are distinctively named: white clay, black charcoal, red ochre, and yellow ochre. These pigments are very ancient in Australia and have great symbolic significance. Objects painted with these pigments or resembling their color could be described in reference to the pigment. Thus, a sunset might be described as "light, red ochre present within it," but such restricted use would seem to disqualify such pigment terms for recognition as basic color terms as defined by Berlin and Kay.[30] A gray-green–colored, waterborne algal scum is also treated as a paint pigment term. The restricted nature of pigment terms was apparent as well from the fact that each belonged to a specific **moiety**, whereas the basic color terms, *light* and *dark,* had no moiety affiliation. Many plant dyes were in use, and dyed objects were described by reference to the specific plant used, but such terms were not generalized further. In recent years, the Anbarra have readily applied English color terms to the brightly colored European objects that have entered their region.

MAKING A LIVING WITH FORAGING TECHNOLOGY

Foraging technology is a brilliant human achievement based on mobility and the productivity of natural ecosystems. Foraging allows an appropriately organized and culturally outfitted regional population of a mere five hundred people to maintain itself indefinitely in virtually any environment with no outside assistance. Human survival under such conditions is an impressive achievement. It is unlikely that a contemporary urban population of five hundred people, including families with dependent children and elderly, could survive if placed empty-handed in a wilderness. Foraging requires a vast store of knowledge about plants and animals, specialized manufacturing and food-processing techniques, and hunting-and-gathering skills, as well as assorted material implements and facilities.

Foragers ultimately are constrained by the level of food resources produced by the natural ecosystems they occupy, but many options exist for adjusting subsistence output to meet basic human needs, including the tools used, the species eaten, and the organization of labor. Most important is the ability to move as local resources are consumed.

For optimum efficiency and sociability, foragers in temperate and tropical areas typically organize themselves into camps of twenty-five to fifty people, based on a flexible division of labor by gender: women collect plant food and small animals within a 3-mile (5-km) radius of camp, and men hunt within a 6-mile (10-km) range. These distances allow people to return easily to camp each day. Except as compensation for severe seasonal shortages, food storage is rare, and camps are moved as soon as food yields decline. The degree of mobility is directly related to the size of camps and resource availability. As long as the human population density remains low, there is little danger of serious resource depletion.

Lizards and Grass Seeds: Aboriginal Food Resources

Virtually every edible plant and animal has been part of the aboriginal diet somewhere in Australia. The list would include insects, lizards, whales, birds, mammals, turtles, fish and shellfish, nuts, fruits, greens, and grass seeds. Aborigines commonly distinguish between plant and animal foods, with the latter usually ranked higher. Animal fat, rather than meat as such, is often the food most desired by foragers.

Although animal food might be preferred, there is great variation throughout Australia in actual consumption patterns (see figure 3.6). The Anbarra and Oenpelli Aborigines, who live in the tropical monsoon north, have enjoyed the greatest abundance of animals, especially when they have had access to marine ecosystems (see figure 3.7). Foragers have considerable difficulty maintaining a high intake of meat in the desert, where species diversity and abundance are low, and they rely heavily on lizards as a staple, supplemented with insects.

The importance of lizard meat in the Western Desert is striking (see figure 3.8). Lizards made up nearly half, by weight, of the total meat animals brought in by a group of ten Aborigines observed in the 1960s.[31] Lizards represent one of the most efficient desert resources, considering the time and energy needed to collect and process them in relation to their food value.[32] It takes only 15 minutes to capture and cook 2.2 pounds (1 kg) of lizard, which yields more than 1,000 kilocalories of food energy. Kangaroos, though highly desired, are not so easy to secure and contributed only 16 percent to the total meat supply. The famous witchetty grub, actually the larva of a wood-boring moth that is extracted from the roots of certain desert trees, is also quite energy efficient. The grubs, which weigh a little over 1 ounce (30 g) each, are almost pure fat and protein. Aborigines can extract 1 kilogram of grubs in 30 minutes.[33]

Desert Aborigines have relatively few plant foods available to them, but they use them intensively. In the Central Desert, more than one hundred plant species are consumed, especially grasses and seeds, which are among the most costly food resources. Seed collecting and grinding requires up to six hours of work per kilogram produced.[34] The use of seeds is a testimony to the skill and resourcefulness of the desert foragers.

Throughout Australia, the primary concern traditionally was to maintain long-term food security,

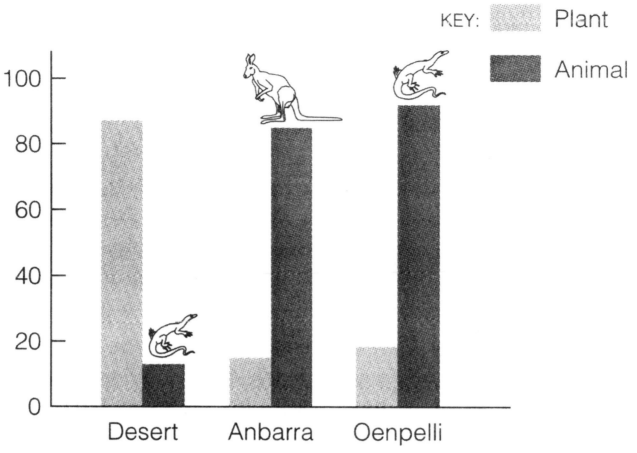

Figure 3.6. Food consumption patterns in percentage by weight of plants and animals by three Aboriginal groups (data from Gould 1980 for Western Desert; Meehan 1982 for Anbarra, and McArthur 1960 for Oenpelli).

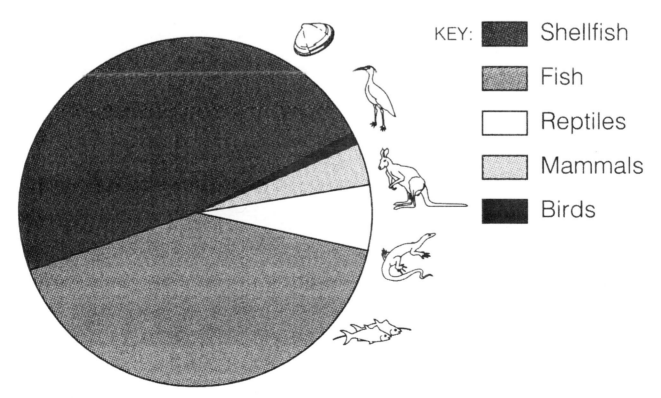

Figure 3.7. Meat consumption pattern, in percentage by weight of shellfish, fish, reptiles, mammals, and birds by Anbarra (coastal) Aborigines (data from Meehan 1982).

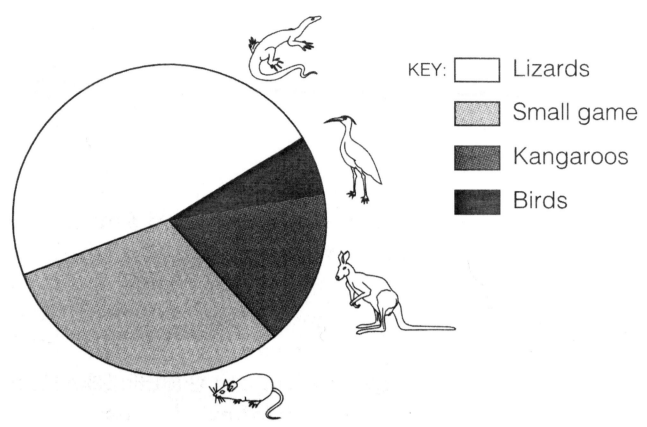

Figure 3.8. Meat consumption pattern in percentage by weight of lizards, small game, kangaroos, and birds by desert Aborigines (data from Gould 1980).

because unpredictable fluctuations and shortages of key staples could occur even in the richest areas. Techniques of food storage were known, but they were used only to address short-term emergencies or to sustain temporary aggregations of people. Rather than stockpiling food, the basic strategy was to maintain access to resources over a wide area through kinship ties and social networks. In the desert, a combination of rain and an unusual abundance of kangaroos might provide the occasion for a joint encampment of a hundred or more people for feasting, performing rituals, and arranging marriages. The most remarkable food bonuses were the great masses of moths that congregated in the summer on the rock walls of the Great Dividing Range.[35] A rich source of fat, the moths could be eaten immediately or ground to a paste and shaped into cakes. The moth feast supported temporary aggregations of up to seven hundred Aborigines at specific campgrounds.

Aboriginal Tools: Digging Stick, Firestick, and Spear

The diverse foraging activities of the Aborigines have been supported for 50,000 years by a remarkably sparse tool kit of simple stone, bone, and wood implements, which was expanded only about 4,000 to 5,000 years ago. The oldest and most universal food-getting tools in Australia are the digging sticks used by women to collect roots and small animals, the men's wooden hunting spear, and the firestick.

This division of tools by gender is symbolically valid, but in practice the Aborigines are much more pragmatic than anthropological stereotypes suggest. For example, a group of women from Borroloola, on the Gulf of Carpentaria, declared: "We are Aboriginal women. We talk for our hunting business, ceremony business. We used to go hunting. We can't wait for the men. We are ladies, we go hunting and feed the men too. . . . Sometimes we use that shovel spear—kangaroo, emu and fish, all that with the spears. . . . Sometimes camping out, leave husbands, just the women go hunting."[36]

The tools themselves are simple, but they can be manufactured, maintained, and used only in combination with a vast store of specialized environmental knowledge. Aborigines on the move always carry glowing firesticks and in the dry season intentionally set fire to large areas of brush and grassland. This is a resource management tool that Aborigines use to drive game, facilitate growth of wild food plants, and keep the country open for easier travel. Many plants will not reproduce without periodic burning, and frequent burning prevents the accumulation of plant litter that might fuel destructive fires. Signal fires also help widely scattered groups keep track of one another.

About 5,000 years ago, a technological change known as the Small Tool Tradition spread throughout Australia. It was distinguished by the mounting of small stone flakes on spear shafts, the use of the spear-thrower, and the appearance of the dingo, a semidomesticated dog. These new developments may have increased hunting efficiency and made possible increased ritual activities and the expansion of social networks.

The *woomera*, or spear-thrower, increases the power and accuracy of the spear. It is a long, thin, curved piece of wood with a hook on one end and a chipped-stone blade, or adze, mounted on the other end (see figure 3.9). This multipurpose tool also can be used as a shovel, fire starter, or percussion musical instrument.[37]

In much of Australia, very simple stone-flaked tools satisfied all aboriginal cutting needs. However, where boomerangs and throwing clubs were frequently used it made sense to use edge-ground rather than chipped-stone tools.[38] Grinding an edge is more work than chipping, but a ground tool can be resharpened many times. Furthermore, because they are so durable, edge-ground tools can be mounted on handles to make a stone ax with twice the striking force of a handheld tool.[39] The edge must be carefully aligned and painstakingly ground on sandstone with water. Crafting the head shape is not easy, and the hafting technique requires much skill. The haft must be rigid enough to keep the head in place while maintaining enough handle flexibility to cushion the shock

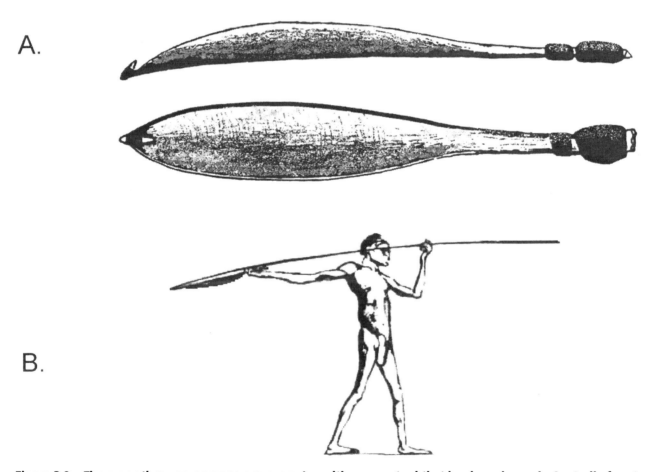

A.

B.

Figure 3.9.   The spear-thrower, or woomera, a man's multi-purpose tool that has been in use in Australia for at least 5000 years. (a). Side and top views—note the gum-mounted chipped stone blade and bone hook on the ends (redrafted from Gould 1979); (b) an Aboriginal man launching a spear using a spear-thrower (redrafted from Mc-Carthy and McArthur 1960, fig. 2, page 154).

of chopping blows. The head usually is grooved to receive a wraparound, heat-treated, wooden handle, which is glued with vegetable gum and tied in place. Stone axes can be very sharp and efficient tools, but they take longer for a given cutting task than steel axes because the stone blade is thicker and more wood must be removed to cut to a given depth.

The Forager Way of Life: Aboriginal Affluence As Mode of Thought

For centuries social theorists have had difficulty imagining what life was like before the creation of politically organized societies and before agriculture. English philosopher Thomas Hobbes (1588–1679) in a famous passage in his classic book on the state, *Leviathan*, imagined that life for all pre-state peoples was "poor, nasty, brutish, and short."[40] This resembles archaeologist Robert Braidwood's (1907–2003) description of pre-Neolithic life as: "... a savage's existence, and a very tough one. A man who spends his whole life following animals just to kill them to eat, or moving from one berry patch to another, is really living just like an animal himself."[41] Europeans readily applied this negative view of the tribal world to Australian Aborigines because they raised no crops and had no permanent villages and no government to protect private property. These were important points of contrast, but in reality tribal life was rich, satisfying, and sustainable. The obvious simplicity of aboriginal material culture created an illusion of poverty that misled generations of superficial European observers.

The illusion of aboriginal poverty was intensified by the material impoverishment, sickness, and death that followed the disruption of aboriginal social networks, the displacement of aboriginal food sources by sheep and cattle, and the deliberate destruction of aboriginal culture following the European conquest of aboriginal territory after 1788. The descriptions of aboriginal life offered in this chapter refer primarily to pre-European conditions, or contemporary Aborigines living independently in rural communities. In 2001 about 20,000 Aborigines were living in local, bandlike communities, or outstations averaging about 25 people.[42] "Bush foods" were an important part of the diet for many of these peoples, and their daily lives were directly shaped by the Dreaming. The official Australian census estimated a total population of 517,000 indigenous Australians including both Aborigines and Torres Strait Islanders in 2006. Approximately one-fourth of indigenous Australians were living in aboriginal communities in remote or very remote areas of the country.[43]

Modern anthropologists have variously identified details of subsistence, society, or ideology as the most remarkable features of foragers in comparison with other types of society. These dimensions of culture are so interconnected that they are all equally important. However, in the analysis offered in this book, the small size of forager bands and tribes is treated as perhaps the most important physical feature shaping the forager way of life. The scale or small size of aboriginal society is such a significant factor that it can help explain other details of forager subsistence, society, and beliefs.

Surprisingly, when twentieth-century anthropologists began to scientifically examine the material aspects of foraging systems, they soon discovered that Aborigines were actually quite healthy and were comfortably meeting their material needs. Marshall Sahlins concluded that foragers in fact represented "the original affluent society,"[44] citing Arnhem Land Aborigines who were able to keep themselves well nourished with only four to five hours a day of foraging and processing food (see figure 3.10). Significantly, this was a weekly average (see box 3.3). Actual time expenditures were quite variable, and there was plenty of time for daytime relaxing. Likewise, in the harsh Western Desert the Pitjantjatjara Aborigines spent five to seven hours a day on subsistence, even under drought conditions, and still managed to thrive.[45] Sahlins noted that outsiders thought that tribal people refused to accumulate wealth because they were lazy and improvident, but tribal nonaccumulation was actually a measure of tribal affluence. The key point of misunderstanding was that aboriginal wealth did not consist of stored food, structures, or other familiar forms of tangible wealth in the commercial world. Paradoxically, even though Aborigines had the absolute minimum of material culture, they were very wealthy. Their wealth was in nature and the land, people, and intangible culture. Nature provided most of the goods and services that they required, and this made it reasonable to credit nature's services as forager income, and to count nature as wealth, even though Aborigines did not buy and sell anything. Aboriginal income, or tribal product, was primarily food production, and it was consumed daily, but their primary investment effort was in raising children, maintaining social relations, and reproducing the ideas and information stored in their culture. Aborigines worked at subsistence only until their material needs were satisfied, and they did

Figure 3.10. Aboriginal man in north Australia, with spears, axe, and club (Ratzell 1896:359).

not store food because they could gather what they needed every day. As long as foraging bands remained small and moved frequently, there was no scarcity of food. Forager subsistence workloads varied considerably under different conditions, but the logic of their system, which emphasized sharing and abundance, always remained the same. Sahlins suggested that the key to aboriginal affluence was their cultural ability to limit their material needs to levels that could be easily satisfied. This means that the aboriginal definition of what constituted the good life determined their choice of technology and mode of production. Perhaps most importantly, the tribal good life depended on social units maintaining a small-scale optimum size, but this was easy because when bands grew too large, workloads increased, quarrels might occur, and the group would split.

Aboriginal foragers represent what Sahlins called a **domestic mode of production**, where production decisions are made at the household level with minimal outside pressure.[46] Aborigines did not use labor, technology, and resources to their maximum productive potential, choosing instead to maximize their leisure, sharing, and ceremonial activities above purely material concerns. The relative uniformity and durability of their forager system suggests that Aborigines had designed a sustainable no-growth culture, whether intentionally or not. Aborigines did not "invest" surplus production in either supporting larger populations or expanding economic production; instead they directed it into activities that helped individuals build their social and cultural capital in ways that also benefited society as a whole and contributed to the reproduction of the culture. Food sharing, ceremonial feasting, and leisure provided growth-dampening effects and helped Aborigines avoid the Malthusian dilemma of endless cycles of population growth and subsistence intensification.[47] When people shared food, there was little incentive to produce beyond their immediate needs. The absence of wealth accumulation also left little basis for individuals to build large personal command structures, and this made it easier for everyone's needs to be met.

Limited material production by Aborigines can be partially understood as the outcome of cost-benefit decisions given forager technology. The more hours per day foragers work, the less efficient their efforts become, because their prey becomes scarcer relative to the number of people to be fed. Computer simulations show that relatively low work effort actually produces the largest sustainable human population and the best return for forager effort.[48] It may seem counterintuitive, but increased effort in the form of longer hours spent foraging appears to only reduce efficiency because of resource depletion. Of course, Aborigines could have intensified their food production by becoming farmers, but they chose not to, unlike their New Guinea neighbors who became gardeners.

It is not always obvious what constitutes production.[49] What some observers consider leisure may be social investment or may indirectly support food production. Discussing the day's events over the evening fire may be an exchange of economic information rather than leisure,[50] and applying body paint to a kinsman or preparing a dance ground is providing a service.[51]

Sharing among kin can also be considered the extraction of social surplus. The continuous pressure of **demand sharing** may push people to produce more than they would need for their own consumption, especially when they can gain benefits from sharing viewed as social investment. Demand sharing is when people ask for things based on kinship obligations.[52] In Australia giving away meat helped men build support networks to gain access to social capital such as wives, hunting territory, and sacred property. The important point is that in small-scale societies there were severe limits on how much social capital anyone could accumulate, because there were very few people to command and the ideology was emphatically antigrowth and antiaccumulation.

In comparison with people in the imperial and commercial worlds, Australian Aborigines and other foraging peoples exemplify a distinctive mode of thought that is shared by tribal peoples generally and that persists even when modes of production change.[53] The forager mode of thought is part of forager self-identity and includes beliefs related to many social power issues involving production, consumption, politics, and society. Foragers expect people to readily share things for immediate consumption by everyone. Accumulation is antisocial. In contrast, the "accumulation mode of thought" characteristic of people in the commercial world generally treats sharing and consumption only within one's own household as proper and considers not saving and not accumulating to be antisocial. In political affairs, foragers are suspicious of anyone who takes a leadership position, and they prefer to follow the group consensus. Tribal leaders are deferred to out of respect for their special skills that come with age and experience. In contrast, in the commercial world, leadership is seen as a positive trait, and to be a follower suggests weakness.

Under the forager mode of thought, society is based on what has been called "universal kinship."[54] This means that all members of a forager society are placed in a kinship category and treated as "family." This is also called the "cosmic economy of sharing."[55] Foragers recognize a direct kinship with spirit beings who socialize and share food with people as part of the natural order of existence. This is the essence of Dreamtime symbolism. Thus, Australian Aborigines call everyone kin, and they do not consider themselves to be members of any centrally controlled, territorially based political unit, although they do recognize common language and culture. Foragers treat their territory as an inviolable possession, a common property that is too sacred to be sold or alienated, although individuals do own their scant moveable possessions. Foragers consider individuals to be free and autonomous and reject the constraints imposed by government. In contrast, in commercial societies land is bought and sold by individuals, and private property must be protected by government authority.

The foraging technological subsystem provides the energy, nutrients, and raw materials needed by the population, but the technology depends on a much more complex social and ideological system. Tribal cultures generate social status and power only through marriage and the family. In the following section, we look at how these social networks are organized and how power is obtained.

BOX 3.3. A DAY IN THE LIFE OF THE FISH CREEK BAND

It is impossible to know in exact detail what daily life was like for prehistoric aboriginal peoples, but modern ethnographies can give a reasonable picture of the ease of making a living by foraging. From October 7 to 20, 1948, anthropologists Frederick McCarthy and Margaret McArthur[56] kept a careful diary of the daily activities of a small group of Aborigines foraging in the monsoon forest in Arnhem Land a few miles from Oenpelli Mission. This research was part of a larger study of the health, nutrition, and food consumption of Aborigines who relied heavily on bush foods. The Fish Creek band included three older men with three of their wives, and three younger, unmarried, initiated adolescents, all led by Wilira, a thirty-five- to forty-year-old man. The group used wooden digging sticks, dip-nets, spears, and spear-throwers as well as a metal ax, metal spear points, a hunting dog, and iron rods for digging. This was late in the dry season, and wild plants were in short supply, but even so, during 11 days the group consumed 390 pounds of kangaroo and wallaby, 116 pounds of fish, 7 pounds of honey, and 35 pounds of plant food, including 28 pounds of wild yams. This exceeded their per-capita caloric requirements and provided 300 grams of protein per person per day, which was more than 5 times their recommended daily requirements. October 7 unfolded as follows:

8:00 am	Breakfast of yams.
8:00–9:30	Men work on their hunting equipment.
9:30 AM–2:00 PM	Five men stalk kangaroo and wallaby, killing one kangaroo.
8:30 AM–12:45 PM	The women walk through the forest, dig out a bandicoot, extract a honey hive from an anthill, catch a few fish by hand from a pool, dig roots, and catch a goanna lizard.
12:45–2:00	Women rest, then prepare and cook food.
2:00–3:45	Men rest, women gather firewood, men eat kangaroo innards, roast the carcass in earth oven, divide and eat it.
3:45–6:30	Everyone rests.
6:30–10:00	Everyone sings and dances.

DAILY LIFE IN FORAGER SOCIETY: KINSHIP, AGE, AND GENDER

Australian aboriginal society, although rooted in antiquity and sustained by simple technology, is a fully developed and dynamic system. It is not a fragile relic of the Paleolithic or a step on the way to political centralization. The basic challenge for Aborigines is the circular problem of maintaining a tribal system that will perpetuate their population and, in turn, reproduce the culture. Understanding how Aborigines solve this problem has preoccupied anthropologists for more than a century.

Anthropological interpretations of aboriginal culture have shifted dramatically over time as theoretical perspectives have changed and new data have become available. This debate has helped establish many of the most basic concepts of cultural anthropology while gradually revealing the genius of aboriginal culture. The broadest theoretical issues concern how the culture actually works: the role of the belief system and the way the culture relates to environmental and demographic factors. Important humanistic issues concern how much equality there is in aboriginal society and whether women and young men are being exploited by old men.

A Kinship-Based Society

Aboriginal society is highly decentralized and egalitarian, with people in overlapping and interdependent roles that minimize the possibility that divisive interest groups will come into serious conflict. Under this social system, an individual might encounter as many as five hundred or so people and be able to sort them into a workable number of social categories that specify appropriate interpersonal behavior, especially in the critical areas of marriage and access to spiritual property. The totemic estate groups are among the most important social categories. In a given aboriginal society, there might be dozens of totemic estate groups, or clans that regulate rights in spiritual property and indirectly provide access to natural resources. Who one marries is partly determined in reference to the totemic groups of one's parents, and marriage establishes access to territory associated with one's spouse's totemic estates.

All social interaction takes place between people who can place themselves in specific kinship categories. Kinship terms simplify social relations by categorizing people. Terms such as *mother, father, uncle,* and *sister* define an individual's personal network of culturally significant categories that are conceptually based on the relationships arising from the nuclear family of mother, father, and children. Aboriginal **kinship terminology** systems typically distinguish some fifteen to twenty relationship pairs such as father/daughter, brother/sister, and so on. Kin terms may distinguish gender and relative age or generation, and whether one is a **consanguine** (related by a common ancestor) or an **affine** (related by marriage). Aboriginal kin terms also indicate whether someone is a potential marriage partner and relative totemic estate group affiliation. Because everyone must be fitted into a "kinship" category, most people are not necessarily what nonaboriginals would consider "real kin," but Aborigines *do* treat them as kin. The terms reflect shared understandings of social status, and they are basic guides for expected behavior.

Kinship terms are cultural categories, and their specific application varies considerably cross-culturally. For example, in a given system, someone might refer to several women using the same term applied to biological *mother.* The term *mother* might then mean "woman of mother's generation who belongs to mother's totemic estate group (clan)." The biological facts of motherhood might be irrelevant in this context. When the biological relationship needs to be designated, a modifier such as *true* or *real* might be attached to the term. Similarly, a man might refer to several women as "wife's mother," yet not be married to any of their daughters. From an aboriginal viewpoint, what is most important is potential marriageability and relationship to totemic estate groups.

The kinship terminologies and estate groups are further simplified by another system of categories in aboriginal society known as moieties and sections. **Moieties** sort people in each tribe into two sides by

estate groups, or from the viewpoint of a specific individual, they may divide the entire society into "own group" and "other group." In some aboriginal societies, all people, totems, and natural phenomena are assigned to a specific moiety. For example, one-half of a society might be associated with the color black, kangaroos, acacia trees, and goanna lizard Dreaming sites, whereas the other half is white, emus, gum trees, and rainbow serpent Dreaming sites. Membership may be assigned through mother (matrimoiety) or father (patrimoiety) or by generation level.

Moiety groupings help organize ritual activities and can be used to specify roles in initiation ceremonies, marriages, and funerals. For example, one moiety may "own" a particular ritual, while the other moiety actually carries out the ritual. This is a form of **complementary opposition**, because the ceremony could not be performed without the cooperation of both groups.

The **section system** simply extends the number of summary social categories from two moieties to four sections and sometimes eight subsections. Because a given society may be crosscut by overlapping moiety systems, sections can significantly simplify social status and help determine whom people can marry (see box 3.4). People belong to the same section category in relation to everyone, unlike the case of kinship terms that depend on each person's unique network of kin. Thus, sections serve as convenient identifying labels, especially because Aborigines often consider it rude to use personal names in public. Knowing someone's section would allow one to make reasonable inferences about more specific social categories. Furthermore, because sections are recognized intertribally, strangers can quickly fit into a local social network.

Moieties, sections, totems, and kinship terms all work together in a neatly integrated system to guide people in their daily interaction with one another and in their relationships to their countries and spiritual properties. It is a remarkably successful system that significantly reduces the potential for conflict and makes authoritarian rule unnecessary.

The emphasis that Aborigines place on following social rules makes it clear that the early anthropologists who thought that Aborigines epitomized selfish immorality were mistaken. The Gidjingarli people of Arnhem Land in northern Australia make altruism a central value, and this is strongly reflected in their language.[57] The Gidjingarli have terms for "good" (*molamola*) and "bad" (*werra*). These terms may be used for moral judgments about individuals, such that a *molamola* person cares for others and shares, whereas a *werra* person is unkind and perhaps harmful. The value of benevolence and mutual support are expressed in terms for kin or countrymen *(borrmunga)*, for kin responsibilities *(gurrurta)*, and kin reciprocity *(gurrurta-gurrurta)*. Marriage and trading partnerships are important reciprocal obligations that are contractual agreements involving trust. Such contracts are moral concerns and may be expressed in kinship terms, but the partners may not be "real" kin. Thus, a good person is someone who behaves like close kin, who are assumed to be good. Extending the sentiments of kinship to society at large converts potential enemies into friends. There are many Gidjingarli customs based on the Dreaming that specify polite speech and overall proper behavior covering all aspects of interaction with kin, especially with universal life-cycle events such as initiation, betrothal, marriage, childbearing, and death. People who repeatedly threaten the well-being of the community may be killed by mutual agreement.

In contrast to the simplicity and functionality of aboriginal society, in commercial societies it is impossible for any individual to be acquainted with more than a tiny sample of the many individuals, social statuses, and corporate groups that exist. For example, in the United States there were 272 million people, some 20,000 occupational titles, and nearly 5 million for-profit business corporations in 1999.

BOX 3.4. CROSS-COUSINS AND MARRIAGE SECTIONS

Aboriginal marriage practices provide an important key to understanding many aspects of the social system. Marriages, normally arranged by the elders, fit within precisely defined cultural categories, which vary in detail from group to group. Frequently, the ideal mate for a man (Ego in figure 3.11) would be the daughter of someone he would refer to as "wife's mother" (WM). WM might also be a woman of the father's totemic clan and in the "father's sister" (FZ) category. WM might be married to a man whom ego would place in the "mother's brother" (MB) category. MB could be any man who was a member of the same totemic clan to which ego's actual mother belonged. Of course, several men could be in this category, and they would not need to be the actual brother of ego's actual mother. Also, an appropriate spouse often will be someone in the kinship category of *cross-cousin* (the daughter of mother's brother or father's sister— MBD or FZD) because these women could not belong to ego's descent group (see figure 3.12).

A person would be expected to marry within a certain range of ego-based kin and in reference to specific clan, moiety, and section categories. One would always marry outside of one's own clan and might even refer to one's own-generation fellow clan members as brother and sister, emphasizing the incestuous nature of clan *endogamy*—marriage within a culturally defined group. Where society-wide moieties exist, spouses would be drawn from opposite moieties, and the moiety groups could be called exogamous. This is a two-section system (see figure 3.13).

Appropriate marriages also can be described in relation to the section system. With a four-section system, there are four named sections, and an individual can marry into only one specific section (see figure 3.14). Siblings always belong to the same section but belong to different sections from their parents, reflecting the fact that marriage within parent-child and sibling categories would be incestuous. Sections only indirectly regulate marriage because not all women in the appropriate section will be in the marriageable MBD category. Knowing someone's section identity simply narrows the search.

BOX 3.5. KINSHIP AND MOTHER-IN-LAW AVOIDANCE

One striking form of aboriginal kinship behavior is the extreme avoidance operating between a man and any woman whom he calls wife's mother (WM). In some aboriginal groups, a man cannot look at, remain near, or speak directly to his WM. She is considered to be a source of "shame," and he must avoid any sexual references in her presence and may even use a special form of avoidance speech full of circumlocutions to avoid embarrassment. Early observers thought such customs were absurd, but in cultural context, they make a great deal of sense.

L. R. Hiatt[58] points out that in Australia, a man often may live close to his WM and may provide her with meat as a form of bride-service, even before marrying his WMD. Given the often great age differential at marriage, a man may be nearly the same age as his WM and could find her attractive, while the WM might find a young daughter's husband more attractive than the old man who would be her husband. Meat giving also has sexual implications and takes place between husband and wife. Under these circumstances, extreme avoidance would certainly reduce the possibility of conflict between a man and his wife's father (WF). Avoidance also would prevent the possibility of father-daughter incest because if a man did have an affair with his WM, he could be his own WF.

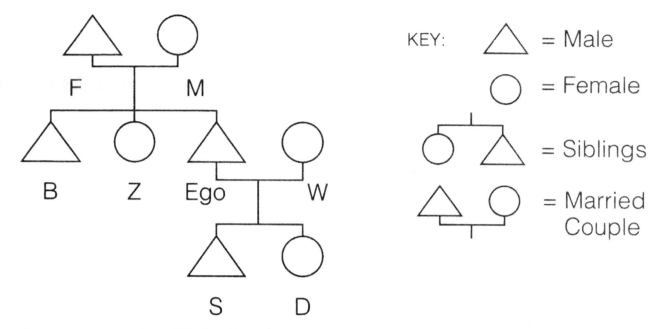

Figure 3.11.   Conventions of kinship diagramming. Anthropologists describe all kinship relationships using a set of eight primary terms with standard abbreviations (shown in key). These terms are then combined to describe additional relationships. Thus, FB = father's brother, MB = mother's brother, FF = father's father, FBD = father's brother's daughter, MBD = mother's brother's daughter, and so on. Ego, always the reference point in any kinship diagram, is the person who applies the terms shown. These designations are culturally specific social categories; they need not represent actual biological relationships. Even primary terms such as mother can be applied to several people who are not one's biological mother.

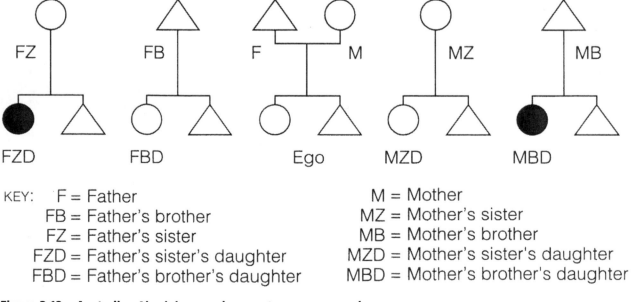

Figure 3.12.   Australian Aborigine marriage systems: cross-cousins.

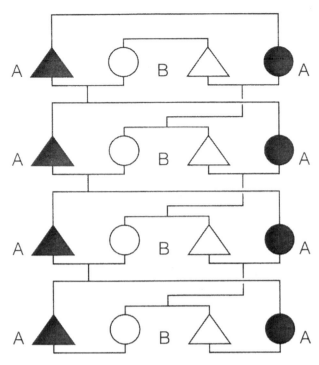

Figure 3.13. A simple two-section moiety system.

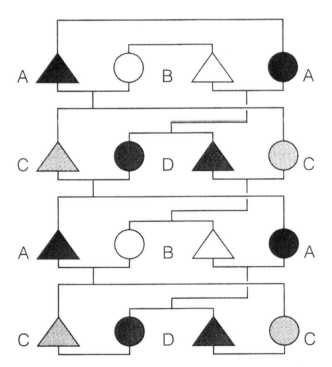

Figure 3.14. A four-section system in which there are four named sections (A, B, C, D distinguished by shade). Each person marries into only one section, and section membership alternates by generation (each person is in the same section as a grandparent).

Many aspects of aboriginal society are related to the widespread practice of **polygyny** (plural wives). Polygyny automatically creates a scarcity of potential wives, which is partially alleviated by the large age difference between men and women at marriage. Girls may be promised in marriage long before they are born, and men might be well beyond thirty years of age before their first marriage, perhaps to a much older widow, while a fifteen-year-old girl might marry a fifty-year-old man. If one assumes an even sex ratio, then the only way in which some men could have more than one wife would be for women to marry at a younger age than men. The wider the age differential at marriage, the more polygynous marriages can take place. Research in Arnhem Land in the 1960s found that nearly one-half of the men over forty years of age had more than one wife, and one-third had three or more.[59] More than one-third of the men aged twenty to forty were still unmarried.

In some respects aboriginal society is a polygynous **gerontocracy** in which the old men use polygyny and Dreamtime ideology to control women and the labor supply. The young men are deprived of wives and kept subservient by the male initiation system (see box 3.6). This interpretation may reflect the perceptions of some of the old men, particularly when they are describing the system to male anthropologists, but it is a misleading generalization. Emphasis on male gerontocracy ignores the important role of women both in the ritual system and in domestic life, and it obscures the essentially egalitarian nature of aboriginal society.

Although the marriage age differential facilitates polygyny, the existence of polygyny itself remains to be explained. It may appear to be the direct result of manipulation by self-interested and influential older men, but this is a narrow view. Polygyny also offers important benefits for the entire society. Polygynous households may provide childbearing women with greater security. An older man is more likely than a young man to be knowledgeable and have a wide kinship network, which will benefit his entire household, especially in times of resource shortage. Similarly, delaying marriage provides the young men with an opportunity to learn the intricacies of the cultural landscape and the locations of critical waterholes while they remain free of domestic responsibilities.

The way in which aboriginal marriage customs are discussed by anthropologists, as with the terms *wife-givers* and *wife-receivers*, often implies male domination where it is not present. The terms *wife bestowal* and even *mother-in-law bestowal* are sometimes applied to the spouse selection process. Mother-in-law bestowal refers to a ceremony in which a young girl is publicly designated as wife's mother to a young man. The term *bestowal*, rather than the more neutral term *betrothal*, may suggest that a father is "giving away" a daughter, when in fact the girl's mother or mother's brother is more likely to make the arrangements. Furthermore, the term suggests that the marriage might never take place. Given a man's age at marriage, he might not even be around when his daughter actually marries, although he might have had some involvement in her prenatal betrothal.

The place of women in aboriginal culture has been interpreted in many different ways. Ethnocentric European travelers mistakenly described these women as degraded and passive servants of the men. The seemingly sharp gender divisions in the activity spheres of aboriginal society made it difficult for anthropologists to obtain a balanced picture. Early anthropologists were mostly men who necessarily observed male culture and talked to male informants. These male anthropologists were also quite comfortable with the male superiority view because it corresponded closely to their own Victorian biases. Victorian anthropologists considered women in general to be spiritually inferior and even described them as "profane," whereas men were seen as "sacred." More recent fieldwork by female anthropologists working with aboriginal women broadened the picture by showing that these women have a very active secret ritual life and exercise considerable autonomy in domestic affairs.

Australian anthropologist Diane Bell[60] spent many months living in aboriginal communities in northern Australia. As a divorced woman with children, she was treated as an adult widow, given a kinship status, and included in public ceremonies. When her female hosts were satisfied that she would respect their secrecy, she was allowed to participate in women's secret rituals. From this perspective, she discovered that aboriginal women share joint and complementary responsibility with men for maintaining their spiritual heritage. Whereas men's rituals emphasize creative power, women's rituals focus on the nurturing role of women, health, social harmony, and connections with the land.

Women also play a major role in subsistence, may arrange marriages, control family size by means of infanticide, and can influence the choice of conception totems. Some anthropologists still consider aboriginal men "superior" but would grant women the

status of "junior partners." However, the notion of rank by sex is probably not a culturally significant issue for Aborigines. Throughout the world, foraging peoples that are characterized by high mobility and low population density are the most egalitarian societies known. Equality is reflected in the conspicuous absence of differences in material wealth among individuals, in the availability to each household of the resources needed to secure its existence, and in the absence of permanent political leaders with coercive power over others. However, social equality does not mean that everyone is alike. Obvious differences exist between men and women, between young and old, and between individuals with different personalities and physical characteristics.

Foragers like the Aborigines, who operate with immediate-return systems, provide little basis for people or corporate groups to maintain coercive power over others.[61] With immediate-return systems, there is no investment of labor in fixed structures, gardens, or herds that will produce a delayed return and that might require long-term storage. Thus, there is no particular advantage in long-term control of a labor force. When basic production is left to nature and food is harvested and consumed on a daily basis, population densities must remain low, and social groups must be highly flexible and mobile to respond to natural fluctuations in supply. Reciprocity, especially pooling and sharing of food, levels out individual variation in production, reduces individual risk, and operates among all households in a camp. In immediate-return production systems, every household has freely available the productive tools and natural resources that it requires. Mobility reduces the potential for social domination and exploitation by discouraging wealth accumulation and making it easy for people to walk away from adverse interpersonal situations.

Social equality also is closely related to the "openness" of aboriginal society. Open societies derive their special characteristics from their mobility and the absence of permanent houses, tombs, temples, and institutionalized leadership. Domestic life takes place in the open, where people can pay close attention to one another.[62] Under these conditions, there are few secrets and few sources of conflict. Furthermore, with weapons always at hand, the use of force is available to everyone and is less likely to become a means for domination.

Outsiders may be struck by the apparent frequency of conflict in aboriginal society, the violence of domestic quarrels, and the charges of infidelity or failure to share. Conflicts of this sort apparently are more common under the crowded conditions of modern settlements. Furthermore, any conflict is a public event in an open society and cannot be hidden behind walls as may be the case in other societies. Anthropologist Victoria Burbank, who specifically studied domestic conflict, recorded hundreds of incidents of verbal and physical aggression between individuals during eighteen months of research in an aboriginal community in Arnhem Land.[63] Contrary to the way Americans view domestic conflict in their own culture, she found that aboriginal women were not passive victims of male aggression. Women initiated fights nearly as often as men, sometimes physically assaulting men. Burbank emphasizes that for Aborigines, aggression is culturally constructed as an often-legitimate expression of anger. Its openness means that kin may intervene to prevent serious injuries. The social support for aboriginal women taking an aggressive stance toward men is a way of balancing the otherwise unequal physical differences between men and women that could be expressed as unequal social power.

The religious life in open societies is primarily concerned with healing, love magic, and natural fertility rather than with witchcraft. Individual souls are recycled and may exist briefly as ghosts, but they are not permanently commemorated in ancestor cults. Groups, even those based on kinship, are not rigidly bounded corporate entities. Both individual friendships and kinship categories define social relationships; they are not exclusively determined by genealogical criteria.

Paradoxically, aboriginal society is at the same time intensely egalitarian and religiously authoritarian.[64] Although aboriginal society is sometimes described as a society without politics because of the absence of formal chiefs, elders do have moral authority, based on the Dreaming, over their juniors, both men and women. Relationships among individuals at different generation levels are hierarchical and may be expressed as a kinship responsibility to "hold" or "look after" or "raise" the junior.[65] This is considered nurturing and guiding behavior, not domination or exploitation. In aboriginal English, one's elder may be referred to as a "boss" who has control over one's marriage and ritual advancement. Such an elder-junior system extends throughout the society so that everyone but the youngest child would be responsible for a junior, but the context is always specific. No one has generalized power over all others.

An age hierarchy is different from a government bureaucracy because, in the age system, status is al-ways relative, everyone at a given level is equivalent, and everyone moves up. No one is permanently excluded from access to basic resources or political power by membership in a lower social class. As they mature, everyone—men and women alike—moves to positions of greater decision-making ability in society. People in commercial societies often imagine their societies as ladders that people ascend. This is certainly the hope, but in class-based societies there is never room at the top for everyone who aspires to "rise." However, everyone does move up the ladder of aboriginal society.

For Aborigines, the ideological foundation of their society is the Dreaming, which defines and is perpetuated by the generational hierarchy. Knowledge of the Dreaming is concentrated in the elders, who are obligated to transmit it to the juniors. Holding and transmitting such knowledge can be considered an exercise of political power, but it is a very special kind of power that cannot be directly compared with the political power in large-scale, nonegalitarian societies.

There often are aboriginal "bigmen" or "men of high renown" who stand out because of their vast ritual knowledge or oratorical skills, but their range of action is limited. They may have considerable influence in the ceremonial life and may be able to manipulate certain social relationships to their advantage with threats of supernatural punishment. However, in the larger society, even such powerful individuals can take little political action without broad popular consensus.

BOX 3.6. MALE INITIATION: THE TERRIBLE RITE

The physical ordeals of scarification (see figure 3.15), nose piercing, bloodletting, tooth evulsion, genital mutilation, and fingernail extraction associated with aboriginal male initiation rituals have been a continuing source of amazement for outsiders and have generated endless speculation about their origins and persistence. These rites occur throughout Australia, but not all groups share the same specific forms. For males, the rituals mark different age grades in social maturity and acquisition of ritual knowledge. Women and girls pass through similar maturation grades but with few physical ordeals.

The obvious functionalist interpretation of these rituals is that they are **rites of passage** publicly marking an individual's change of status. For example, a boy must be circumcised before he can marry. The pain makes the new status more valuable and increases one's pride of membership, thus contributing to social solidarity. The value of body mutilation, especially where little clothing is worn, is that the change in status is permanently visible and unlikely to be faked; genital mutilation is performed only on males. These rituals are part of the formal instruction in ritual lore and make the ritual more valuable and more memorable. The initiates must accept the discipline of the older men, and they owe respect and gifts of meat to their tutors.

The most dramatic male ordeal is subincision, which follows circumcision and involves slitting the underside of the penis lengthwise to open the urethra. The operation is performed by the initiate's MB or WF, who uses a very sharp stone knife. The initiate must remain passive and show no signs of experiencing pain. After healing, the incision remains open, but infection or reproductive impairment does not normally occur.

Subincision appears to have been a recent invention and was actively spreading from tribe to tribe when Europeans arrived. Young men willingly submit to the ordeal because it admits them to the privileges of manhood in a society in which other tests of strength and courage such as warfare are of little importance. As psychologist S. D. Porteus explained, "It is the price that must be paid for tribal membership, and all must pay. . . . that the price is high puts an enhanced value on these bonds of tribal union."[66]

From the aboriginal viewpoint, subincision requires no special explanation beyond the fact that it originated in the Dreaming. Aborigines may point to the physical resemblance between the subincised penis and the genitals of kangaroos and emus as confirmation of the Dreaming connection.[67]

Psychoanalysts have suggested that subincision is a subconscious way for aboriginal men to deal with Oedipal fears, castration anxiety, or their supposed envy of female reproductive powers. In opposition to the aboriginal interpretation, the subincision would represent a woman's vagina, not a totemic kangaroo penis. The best support for the psychoanalytic view is that the initiates are symbolically killed in the ritual and reborn as men. However, because men already have a culturally acknowledged role in fertility through totemic increase ceremonies, vagina envy seems unnecessary. A conflicting psychological argument is that boys who grow up too closely associated with their mothers need a painful initiation to affirm their identity as males.

None of these explanations are completely satisfactory. We may never know how rituals such as subincision originated in the first place. But they play an important role in the culture and are best understood as expressions of the overwhelming importance of the Dreaming.

Figure 3.15. Aboriginal men showing chest scarification, New South Wales, nineteenth-century (Ratzel 1896:354).

SUMMARY

Australian Aborigines demonstrate that domestic-scale sociocultural system can remain egalitarian and in balance with their resource base indefinitely as long as they are not invaded by larger-scale neighbors. For over 50,000 years, gradual adjustments in aboriginal technology occurred as environmental conditions changed, and the ritual system and social organization underwent continuous elaboration; aboriginal culture, however, retained its fundamental character as a domestic-scale system. This is clearly a dynamic, responsive, and highly creative system, but it appears to have changed in such a way that the most fundamental cultural elements remain in place. The Dreaming itself, and all its associated features, seems to be the key element in understanding this remarkable cultural stability.

STUDY QUESTIONS

1. In what sense could the aboriginal subsistence system be considered an affluent economy?
2. Discuss the role of women in aboriginal society. Are they really oppressed and exploited by the old men as some suggest?
3. Demonstrate the connections between religion and society *or* between religion and adaptation to the natural environment in aboriginal Australia.
4. Discuss explanations for the remarkable initiation practices of the aboriginals, distinguishing between how Aborigines view these practices and how anthropologists and other outsiders see them.
5. Describe the significance of cross-cousin marriage in aboriginal society.
6. In what sense can aboriginal society be considered egalitarian? What cultural mechanisms contribute to equality?
7. Evaluate the relative importance of mode of thought and mode of production as the most crucial cultural elements in aboriginal culture.
8. What factors helped regulate the size of aboriginal social units?

SUGGESTED READING

Flood, Josephine. 1983. *Archaeology of the Dreamtime.* Honolulu: University of Hawaii Press. A comprehensive overview of the prehistory of Australia.

Gould, Richard A. 1980. *Living Archaeology.* Cambridge, Eng.: Cambridge University Press. An engaging work by an archaeologist who studied contemporary Aborigines in the Western Desert to help understand the prehistoric remains.

Sahlins, Marshall. 1968. "Notes on the Original Affluent Society." In *Man the Hunter,* edited by Lee, Richard B., and Irven DeVore, pp. 85–89. Chicago: Aldine. A short section that compares foraging and market economies.

Tonkinson, Robert. 1991. *The Mardudjara Aborigines: Living the Dream in Australia's Desert,* 2nd ed. New York: Holt, Rinehart and Winston. A well-rounded ethnography of aboriginal culture in the Western Desert.

GLOSSARY TERMS

Carrying capacity The number of people who could, in theory, be supported indefinitely in a given environment with a given technology and culture.

Totem In Australia, specific animals, plants, natural phenomena, or other objects that originate in the Dreaming and are the spiritual progenitors of aboriginal descent groups. Elsewhere, it refers to any cultural association between specific natural objects and human social groups.

Cosmogony An ideological system that seeks to explain the origin of everything: people, nature, and the universe.

Cosmology An ideological system that explains the order and meaning of the universe and people's places within it.

Band A group of twenty-five to fifty people who camp and forage together.

Estate Property held in common by a descent group, perhaps including territory, sacred sites, and ceremonies.

Patrilocal band A theoretical form of band organization based on exogamy and patrilocal residence.

Clan A named group claiming descent from a common but often remote ancestor and sharing a joint estate.

Exogamy Marriage outside a culturally defined group.

Patrilocality A cultural preference for a newly married couple to live near the husband's parents or patrilineal relatives.

Tribe A politically autonomous, economically self-sufficient, territorially based society that can reproduce a distinct culture and language and form an in-marrying (endogamous) society.

Endogamy Marriage within a specified group.

Domestic mode of production Material production organized at the household level with distribution between households based on reciprocal sharing.

Demand sharing Requesting food or other things from kin who are obligated to give.

Kinship terminology An ego-centered system of terms that specifies genealogical relationships of consanguinity and affinity in reference to a given individual.

Consanguine A relative by culturally recognized descent from a common ancestor; sometimes called a "blood" relative.

Affine A relative by marriage.

Moiety One part of a two-part social division.

Complementary opposition A structural principle in which pairs of opposites, such as males and females, form a logical larger whole.

Section system A social division into four (sections) or eight (subsections) intermarrying, named groups, which summarize social relationships. Members of each group must marry only members of one other specific group.

Polygyny A form of marriage in which a man may have more than one wife.

Gerontocracy An age hierarchy that is controlled or dominated by the oldest age groups.

Rite of passage A ritual marking culturally significant changes in an individual's life cycle, such as birth, puberty, marriage, old age, and death.

NOTES

1. Adapted from Morris, Ian. 1996. *Kakadu National Park Australia.* Steve Parish Natural History Guide. Fortitude Valley, Queensland: Steve Parish Publishing.

2. Peterson, Nicolas. 1986. *Australian Territorial Organization.* Oceania Monograph, no. 30. Sydney: University of Sydney.

3. Lewis, M. Paul, ed. 2009. *Ethnologue: Languages of the World.* 16th ed. Dallas, TX: SIL International; Tindale, Norman B. 1974. *Aboriginal Tribes of Australia: Their Terrain, Environmental Controls, Distribution, Limits, and Proper Names.* Berkeley: University of California Press.

4. Roberts, Richard G., Rhys Jones, and M. A. Smith. 1990. "Thermoluminescence Dating of a 50,000-Year-Old Human Occupation Site in Northern Australia." *Nature* 345:153–56.

5. Gould, Richard A. 1980. *Living Archaeology.* Cambridge, Eng.: Cambridge University Press.

6. Birdsell, Joseph B. 1957. "Some Population Problems Involving Pleistocene Man." *Cold Spring Harbor Symposium on Quantitative Biology* 22:47–70.

7. Bowdler, S. 1977. "The Coastal Colonisation of Australia" In *Sunda and Sahul: Prehistoric Studies in Southeast Asia, Melanesia and Australia,* edited by J. Allen, J. Golson, and R. Jones, pp. 205–46. London: Academic Press; Louandos, Harry. 1985. "Intensification and Australian Prehistory." In *Prehistoric Hunter-Gatherers: The Emergence of Cultural Complexity,* edited by Douglas Price and James A. Brown, pp. 385–423. New York: Academic Press; Louandos, Harry. 1987. "Pleistocene Australia: Peopling a Continent." In *The Pleistocene Old World: Regional Perspectives,* edited by Olga Soffer, pp. 147–65. New York: Plenum.

8. Flood, Josephine. 1983. *Archaeology of the Dreamtime.* Honolulu: University of Hawaii Press.

9. Gunderson, Lance H., and C. S. Hilling, eds. 2002. *Panarchy: Understanding Transformations in Human and Natural Systems.* Washington, DC: Island Press.

10. Birdsell, Joseph B. 1973. "A Basic Demographic Unit." *Current Anthropology* 14(4):337–50.

11. Cowlishaw, Gillian. 1978. "Infanticide in Aboriginal Australia." *Oceania* 48(4):262–83.

12. Yengoyan, Aram A. 1981. "Infanticide and Birth Order: An Empirical Analysis of Preferential Female Infanticide Among Australian Aboriginal Populations." In *The Perception of Evolution: Essays Honoring Joseph B. Birdsell,* edited by Larry Mai, Eugenia Shanklin, and Robert Sussman, pp. 255–73. *Anthropology UCLA,* vol. 7, nos. 1 and 2. Los Angeles: Department of Anthropology, University of California.

13. Boyer, Pascal. 2000. "Functional Origins of Religious Concepts: Ontological and Strategic Selection in Evolved Minds." *Journal of the Royal Anthropological Institute* 6:195–214.

14. Radcliffe-Brown, A. R. 1929. "The Sociological Theory of Totemism." *Proceedings of the Fourth Pacific Science Congress.* (Reprinted in *Structure and Function in Primitive Society,* edited by A. R. Radcliffe-Brown, pp. 117–32. New York: Free Press, 1965.)

15. Levi-Strauss, Claude. 1963. *Totemism.* Boston: Beacon Press; Levi-Strauss, Claude. 1966. *The Savage Mind.* Chicago: University of Chicago Press.

16. Ilyatjari, Nganyintja. 1983. "Women and Land Rights: The Pitjantjatjara Land Claims." In *We Are Bosses Ourselves: The Status and Role of Aboriginal Women Today,* edited by Fay Gale, pp. 55–61. Canberra: Australian Institute of Aboriginal Studies, 55–57.

17. Morgan, Lewis Henry. 1877. *Ancient Society.* New York: Holt.

18. Australia, Director of National Parks. 2009. Uluru-Kata Tjuta National Park. Draft Management Plan 2009–2019. Canberra: Department of the Environment, Water, Heritage and the Arts. www.environment.gov.au/parks/publications/uluru/draft-plan.html (accessed July 13, 2009).

19. Australia, Director of National Parks. 2005. *Welcome to Aboriginal Land: Uluru-Kata Tjuta National Park Visitor Guide and Maps.* Canberra: Department of the Environment, Water, Heritage and the Arts. www.environment.gov.au/parks/publications/uluru/visitor-guide.html (accessed July 13, 2009); Mountford, Charles P. 1965. *Ayers Rock: Its People, Their Beliefs, and Their Art.* Honolulu: East-West Center Press.

20. Munn, Nancy D. 1973. *Walbiri Iconography: Graphic Representation and Cultural Symbolism in a Central Australian Society.* Ithaca, NY, and London: Cornell University Press.

21. Keen, Ian. 2000. "A Bundle of Sticks: The Debate over Yolngu Clans." *Journal of the Royal Anthropological Institute* 6(3):419–36, 429.

22. Williams, Nancy M. 1986. *The Yolngu and Their Land: A System of Land Tenure and the Fight for Its Recognition.* Stanford, CA: Stanford University Press, 171.

23. Justice Blackburn, cited in Williams, 1986, *The Yolngu and Their Land,* 158.

24. Birdsell, Joseph B. 1973. "A Basic Demographic Unit." *Current Anthropology* 14(4):337–50.

25. Klich, L. Z. 1988. "Aboriginal Cognition and Psychological Nescience." In *Human Abilities in Cultural Context,* edited by S. H. Irvine and J. W. Berry, pp. 427–52. Cambridge, Eng.: Cambridge University Press.

26. Irvine, S. H., and J. W. Berry, eds. 1988. *Human Abilities in Cultural Context.* Cambridge, Eng.: Cambridge University Press, 4.

27. Lewis, D. 1976. "Observations on Route-Finding and Spatial Orientation among the Aboriginal Peoples of the Western Desert Region of Central Australia." *Oceania* 46(4):249–82.

28. Sahlins, Marshall. 1976a. "Colors and Cultures." *Semiotica* 16:1–22.

29. Jones, Rhys, and Betty Meehan. 1978. "Anbarra Concept of Colour." In *Australian Aboriginal Concepts,* edited by L. R. Hiatt, pp. 20–39. Canberra: Australian Institute of Aboriginal Studies.

30. Berlin, Brent, and Paul Kay. 1969. *Basic Color Terms: Their Universality and Evolution.* Berkeley and Los Angeles: University of California Press.

31. Gould, Richard A. 1980. *Living Archaeology.* Cambridge, Eng.: Cambridge University Press.

32. O'Connell, James F., and Kristen Hawkes. 1981. "Alyawara Plant Use and Optimal Foraging Theory." In *Hunter-Gatherer Foraging Strategies,* edited by B. Winterhalder and E. A. Smith, pp. 99–125. Chicago: University of Chicago Press.

33. O'Connell, James F., and Kristen Hawkes. 1981. "Alyawara Plant Use"; Tindale, Norman B. 1981. "Desert Aborigines and the Southern Coastal Peoples: Some Comparisons." In *Ecological Bio-geography of Australia,* vol. 3, pt. 6, edited by Allen Keast, pp. 1853–84. *Monographiae Biologicae,* vol. 41. The Hague: Dr. W. Junk.

34. O'Connell, James F., and Kristen Hawkes. 1981. "Alyawara Plant Use," 123.

35. Flood, Josephine. 1980. *The Moth Eaters.* Atlantic Highlands, NJ: Humanities Press; Flood, Josephine. 1983. *Archaeology of the Dreamtime*; Gould, 1980. *Living Archaeology.*

36. Gale, Fay, ed. 1983. *We Are Bosses Ourselves: The Status and Role of Aboriginal Women Today.* Canberra: Australian Institute of Aboriginal Studies, 70–71.

37. Gould, 1980. *Living Archaeology.*

38. Hayden, Brian. 1977. "Stone Tool Functions in the Western Desert." In *Stone Tools as Cultural Markers: Change, Evolution and Complexity,* edited by R. V. S. Wright, pp. 178–88. Prehistory and Material Culture Series, no. 12. Canberra: Australian Institute of Aboriginal Studies.

39. Dickson, F. P. 1981. *Australian Stone Hatchets: A Study in Design and Dynamics.* Sydney: Academic Press.

40. Hobbes, Thomas. 1907 [1651]. *Leviathan; or, The Matter, Form and Power of a Commonwealth, Ecclesiastical and Civil.* London: Routledge and Sons; New York: Dutton and Co., chapter 13, paragraph 9.

41. Braidwood, Robert J. 1964. *Prehistoric Men,* 6th ed. Chicago: Chicago Natural History Museum, 122, cited in Winterhalder, Bruce. 1993. "Work, Resources and Population in Foraging Societies." *Man* 28(2):321–40.

42. Altman, J. C. 2006. *In Search of an Outstations Policy for Indigenous Australians.* Working Paper No. 34. Centre for Aboriginal Economic Policy Research, 3, Tables 1 and 2.

43. Australian Bureau of Statistics. 2007. *Population Distribution, Aboriginal and Torres Strait Islander Australians, 2006.* Cat no. 4705.0, page 5. www.abs.gov.au/AUSSTATS/abs@.nsf/DetailsPage/4705.02006?OpenDocument.

44. Sahlins, Marshall. 1968. "Notes on the Original Affluent Society" In *Man the Hunter,* edited by Richard Lee and Irven DeVore, pp. 85–89. Chicago: Aldine.

45. Gould, Richard A. 1969. "Subsistence Behavior among the Western Desert Aborigines of Australia." *Oceania* 39(4): 253–73; Gould, Richard A. 1980. *Living Archaeology.* Cambridge, Eng.: Cambridge University Press.

46. Sahlins, Marshall. 1972. *Stone Age Economics.* Chicago: Aldine.

47. Sahlins, 1972, *Stone Age Economics*; Peterson, Nicolas. 1997. "Demand Sharing: Sociobiology and the Pressure for Generosity among Foragers." In *Scholar and Sceptic: Australian Aboriginal Studies in Honour of L. R. Hiatt,* edited by F. Merlan, J. Morton, and A. Rumsey, pp. 171–90. Aboriginal Studies Press, Canberra.

48. Winterhalder, Bruce. 1993. "Work, Resources and Population in Foraging Societies." *Man* 28(2):321–40.

49. Allen, Harry. 2002. *The Hunter Gatherer Mode of Thought and Change in Aboriginal Northern Australia.* Presented at the Ninth International Conference on Hunting and Gathering Societies, Heriot-Watt University Edinburgh, Scotland.

50. Smith, E. A. 1988. "Risk and Uncertainty in the 'Original Affluent Society'. Evolutionary Ecology of Resource-Sharing and Land Tenure." In *Hunters and Gatherers, vol. 1, History, Evolution, and Social Change,* edited by T. Ingold, D. Riches, and J. Woodburn, pp. 222–51. Berg, Oxford.

51. Altman, J. C. 1987. *Hunter-Gatherers Today: An Aboriginal Economy in North Australia.* Canberra: Australian Institute of Aboriginal Studies, 221–22, 228–30.

52. Peterson 1997. *Demand Sharing.*

53. Barnard, Alan. 2002. "The Foraging Mode of Thought." In *Self and Other-Images of Hunter-Gatherers,* edited by Henry Stewart, Alan Barnard, and Keiichi Omura, pp. 1–24. Senri Ethnological Studies No. 60. Osaka: National Museum of Ethnology.

54. Barnard, 2002. "The Foraging Mode of Thought."

55. Bird-David, Nurit. 1992. "Beyond 'The Original Affluent Society': A Culturalist Reformulation." *Current Anthropology* 33(1):25–47.

56. McArthur, Margaret. 1960. "Food Consumption and Dietary Levels of Groups of Aborigines Living on Naturally Occurring Foods." In *Records of the American-Australian Scientific Expedition to Arnhem Land.* Vol. 2 of *Anthropology and Nutrition,* edited by Charles Mountford, pp. 90–135. Melbourne: Melbourne University Press.

57. Hiatt, L. R. 2002. *Edward Westermarck and the Origin of Moral Ideas.* Presented at the Ninth International Conference on Hunting and Gathering Societies, Heriot-Watt University, Edinburgh, Scotland.

58. Hiatt, L. R. 1984b. "Your Mother-in-Law Is Poison." *Man* 19(2):183–98.

59. Shapiro, Warren. 1981. *Miwuyt Marriage: The Cultural Anthropology of Affinity in Northeast Arnhem Land.* Philadelphia: Institute for the Study of Human Issues.

60. Bell, Diane. 1983. *Daughters of the Dreaming.* Sydney: McPhee Gribble/Allen & Unwin. Bell, Diane. 1987. "Aboriginal Women and the Religious Experience." In *Traditional Aboriginal Society: A Reader,* edited by W. H. Edwards, pp. 237–56. South Melbourne: Macmillan.

61. Lee, Richard B. 1981. "Is There a Foraging Mode of Production?" *Canadian Journal of Anthropology* 2(1):13–19; Woodburn, James. 1982. "Egalitarian Societies." *Man* 17(3): 431–51.

62. Wilson, Peter J. 1988. *The Domestication of the Human Species.* New Haven, CT, and London: Yale University Press.

63. Burbank, Victoria Katherine. 1994. *Fighting Women: Anger and Aggression in Aboriginal Australia.* Berkeley: University of California Press.

64. Hiatt, L. R. 1987. "Aboriginal Political Life." In *Traditional Aboriginal Society,* edited by W. H. Edwards, pp. 174–188. South Melbourne: Macmillan.

65. Myers, Fred R.. 1980. "The Cultural Basis of Politics in Pintupi Life." *Mankind* 12(3):197–214.

66. Porteus, S. D. 1931. *The Psychology of a Primitive People.* London: E. Arnold, 280–81.

67. Cawte, John. 1974. *Medicine Is the Law. Studies in Psychiatric Anthropology of Australian Tribal Societies.* Honolulu: University Press of Hawaii.

CHAPTER 4

African Cattle Peoples: Tribal Pastoralists

Figure 4.0. Maasai woman (Ratzel 1897:484).

PRONUNCIATION GUIDE

TRIBAL NAMES AND VOCABULARY IN NILOTIC LANGUAGES ARE usually pronounced by English speakers according to the following orthography and sounds:

Key
a = *a* in f*a*ther
o = *o* in g*o*
ay = *ay* in d*ay*
ai = *i* in *i*ce
e = *e* in b*e*d
oo = *oo* in f*oo*d
• = Syllable division
/ = Stress
Nuer = [noo • ayr/]
Maasai = [ma / sai]
eunoto = [ay • oo • no / to]
moran = [mo • ran/]

LEARNING OBJECTIVES

After studying this chapter you should be able to do the following:

1. Describe the physical features of the East African environment that make pastoralism an attractive form of subsistence.
2. Explain the strategies that cattle peoples use to maximize their return from cattle and minimize the risk of material shortages in an unpredictable environment.
3. Define "cattle complex" and explain the central importance of cattle in the material, social, and ideological aspects of African pastoral life.
4. Describe how cattle peoples structure their intergroup relations in the absence of centralized political authority.
5. Evaluate the status of women in herding societies in comparison with that of men, judging the extent of gender equality or inequality.
6. Explain how men use cattle to extend their personal imperia beyond their immediate kin in ways that prevent the creation of permanent concentrations of social power and hierarchy.
7. Compare the ideological systems and cosmologies of African herders, Australian foragers, and Amazonian villagers.
8. Describe how the Maasai age class system organizes the life cycle of Maasai and explain how it contributes to social stability.

The Nuer, Karamojong, Maasai, and other Nilotic-speaking peoples in East Africa have fascinated casual European observers and anthropologists for more than a century. The pride and arrogant self-confidence of these peoples were so striking, and their warriors were so brave and numerous, that they commanded the immediate respect of the first European colonialists. The Maasai were viewed with special awe, because their warriors made a contest out of killing lions with spears and wore their manes as a badge of courage. It was even more impressive that these peoples could support themselves almost entirely from their cattle in an environment that Europeans considered a wilderness paradise for big game. In fact, cattle dominated all aspects of their culture, to a degree that outsiders thought irrational and obsessive. However, these East Africans, who may be respectfully called cattle peoples, have survived droughts and epidemics, and some have retained much of their autonomy despite many government-imposed changes.

After the Ice Age ended, animals were domesticated in many parts of the world. This opened up new possibilities for people while creating many new problems. In the absence of animal domesticates the population density of farming peoples was limited by the availability of fish and game, as in Amazonia. However, African herders used domesticated cattle as a special form of tangible, reproducible, and mobile wealth that made social equality possible in spite of increases in population density and growth in the scale of society. East African peoples clearly demonstrate that people can live in settled villages, control and accumulate wealth within limits, and still enjoy the human advantages of life in small-scale domestically organized societies focused on the well-being of households. Tribal herders have designed sustainable cultures that maximize personal autonomy for men and women, while meeting the needs of society without producing extreme inequities in the distribution of social power. Even though their food production systems are very different from those that sustain Australian foragers and Amazon villagers, African herders also reject any form of centralized political power. The archaeological and historic record shows that tribal people lived successfully as herders in East Africa for nearly 5,000 years, while making detailed changes in their lifestyle in response to changing circumstances over the centuries. Significantly, by keeping the politically independent unit no larger than small villages, relying on age-grade organization to maintain social solidarity, and distributing cattle in a way that maximized household equality, African herders achieved overall sustainability at higher population densities and with larger societies than either Australian Aborigines or the Amazon forest villagers. The fact that these people continue to maintain, modify, and reproduce these sociocultural systems shows that they serve individual self-interest very effectively. The key to their success was perhaps the inability of even the most aggrandizing power seekers to force people into supporting them against their will, because they could never gain monopoly control over crucial resources.

MAKING A LIVING WITH COWS

Cattle Herding and Tropical Grasslands

East Africa is part of the Tropical and Subtropical Grasslands, Savannas, and Shrublands Ecoregion of the Afrotropic Biome and is topographically a highly diverse region (see figure 4.1). Much of the area occupied by the Nilotic pastoralists in Kenya and Tanzania straddles the equator along a zone lying 3,000 to 7,000 feet (914 to 2,134 m) in elevation and consisting of arid plains and wetter, grassy uplands. Today this region includes some of the most famous game parks in the world, such as the Amboseli and Serengeti national parks in Kenya and Tanzania, respectively. It is also home to many tribal groups involved in a wide range of subsistence economies. The tropical savanna ecosystem is a grassland zone, which may have a few trees and shrubs, separating tropical rain forests from arid deserts (see figure 4.2). Fire and grazing play an important role in maintaining and extending savannas, but savannas result primarily from climate, soil, and topographic conditions, especially a pronounced wet and dry season. In striking contrast to the diversity and stability of tropical rain forests, savannas are dominated by very few species and exist in an unstable, dynamic equilibrium. Drought cycles or changes in grazing pressure caused by livestock disease can rapidly change the inventory of plant species and shift the balance between trees and grasses. Biological productivity in the savanna is high in relation to biomass, but plants are short-lived in comparison to rain forest species. Nutrients are turned over, or cycled, much more rapidly in the savanna. There are proportionately more leaves and grass and less wood in the savanna, and the foliage is more palatable because it contains fewer resins and other chemical defenses. Extreme seasonal variations in rainfall create periodic pulses of biological productivity resulting in brief food surpluses that are best exploited by nomadic grazers.[1]

Pastoralism in East Africa, like the savanna itself, exists along a rainfall continuum from wet to dry, showing greater dependence on animals and greater nomadism as rainfall declines. In areas where the average annual rainfall exceeds approximately 25 inches (650 mm) per year, people are likely to be village farmers, relying on grains such as millet, with livestock raising a minor subsistence activity. Where rainfall drops lower than 25 inches, pastoralism becomes increasingly attractive, nomadism increases, and people become more and more dependent on their animals, while farming becomes supplemental. In extreme cases, as with some Maasai groups, people may subsist

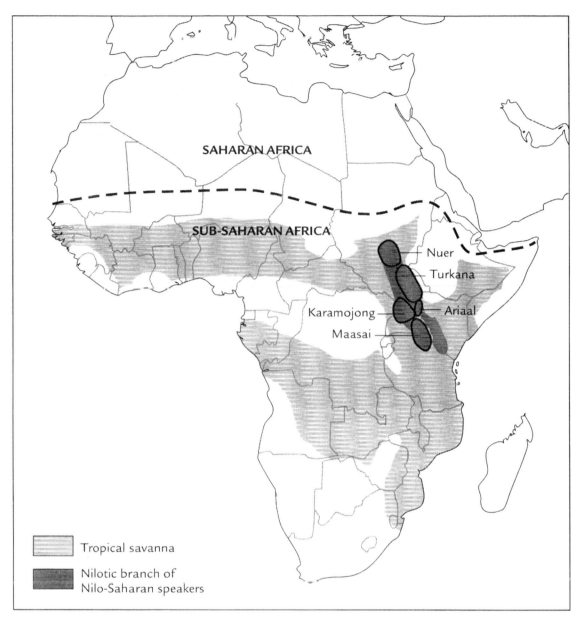

Figure 4.1. Map of savanna regions of Africa showing the Nilotic-speaking East African cattle cultures discussed.

Tropical savanna

Nilotic branch of
Nilo-Saharan speakers

almost entirely on animal products, although some may exchange animal products for grains from their settled neighbors.

The great advantage of domestic livestock is that they convert otherwise inedible plant material into meat, blood, and milk for human consumption, in areas where farming would be at best a marginal activity. The use of domestic animals also permits dramatic increases in human population density over that supported in the same environment by foraging. East Africa can support up to 22,076 pounds (10,000 kg) of wildlife biomass per square kilometer with some fifty species of large grazing mammals. This is easily double

the biomass of game mammals in the Amazon. The Hadza of Tanzania, who forage in this hunter's paradise, take only a small fraction of the game and maintain themselves at typically low population densities of just 0.4 persons per square kilometer. The Maasai, their pastoral neighbors, support 2 to 6 people per square kilometer. Pastoralism permits precise control over reproduction and harvesting of the animals and leads to large increases in food production per unit of land. However, successful pastoralism is a complex, delicately balanced system that poses many difficult problems and requires major adjustments in the organization of society and labor.

Figure 4.2. Dinka village, upper Nile (Ratzel 1898: 42).

East African cattle peoples, operating within domestic-scale cultures, manage their cattle and relate to their grassland ecosystem in radically different ways from market-oriented ranchers operating within the commercial culture. The first objective of subsistence pastoralists is to extract the maximum food value from their animals for direct consumption as efficiently as possible, while emphasizing self-reliance and long-term security.[2] African cattle may appear scrawny in comparison with the hefty beef cattle of North American rangelands and feedlots, but range-fed African cattle do not require an enormous input of fossil fuel energy, and they are well adapted to survive seasonal drought and disease (see box 4.1). American cattle are raised with the least human labor possible. They must gain weight quickly so they can be sold for the maximum financial profit. They thrive on water pumped from deep wells; special food that is planted, processed, stored, and trucked to their feeding troughs and feedlots; and expensive antibiotics, growth hormones, and appetite stimulants (see chapter 11). Furthermore, American beef goes through a chain of processors, wholesalers, and retailers to be processed, packaged, advertised, stored, and marketed before being consumed. By contrast, no remote

shareholders who did not participate in raising them profit from African cattle. African cattle are ritually sacrificed, butchered, and eaten by the same people who care for them.

BOX 4.1. CATTLE CARRYING CAPACITY

Comparative analysis of subsistence herders requires several types of data and concepts. Calculating the carrying capacity for herd animals and the number of people who could be supported by pastoralism is a deceptively simple theoretical problem. One need only know the amount of plant biomass that animals can consume in a given area each year on a sustained basis and the amount of human food that the herds can produce. The basic formula for estimating carrying capacity (CC) for African cattle is $CC = (AGNPP/.5)/C$, where AGNPP = above-ground net primary productivity in kilograms of dry plant matter, the new plant biomass produced each year, and C = kilograms of cattle biomass, measured in TLUs, tropical livestock units of 250 kilograms, which is the equivalent of one cow. The number of people that can be supported by the cattle is (P), calculated as $P = CC/R$, where R = the TLUs required for human subsistence per person per year.

In practice, none of these figures can be precise, and the formula is not so easily applied. This explains why there is so much professional disagreement over whether pastoralists are managing their herds rationally and maintaining the quality of their pastures. The primary problem is that AGNPP, the most critical value, varies dramatically in time and space in the pastoral zones. Successful pastoralists must plan for long-term, minimum carrying-capacity values, taking into account the frequency of droughts. Actual productivity rates of human food will depend on the particular mix of animals in use and the specific pattern of herd management.

The Prehistory and History of African Pastoralism

Pastoralism, as a full-time specialization in domestic animals, probably has been practiced in Africa as long as anywhere in the world. Sheep and goats likely were brought into North Africa from the Middle East, whereas wild cattle may have been locally domesticated by 7000 BP or earlier.[3] The Zebu, or humpbacked cattle, apparently reached Africa from India about 4000 BP. Because the cattle, sheep, or goats have no known wild ancestors in sub-Saharan Africa, it is assumed that they were introduced to East Africa from elsewhere as domesticates. Pastoralism first became established in East Africa in the central Sudan by 5400 BP and then in the arid zone of northeast Kenya by 5200 BP, where it was presumably introduced by early Cushitic-speaking peoples from Ethiopia (see table 4.1). Because of tsetse flies, the higher savannas of East Africa apparently were not occupied by pastoralists until 3300 BP, when changes in climate and vegetation made conditions more favorable. Shortly thereafter, by 2500 BP, Nilotic-speaking ancestors of the modern Maasai and Turkana peoples arrived.[4] Therefore, African pastoralism was a well-established human adaptation and can reasonably be considered a basic component of the savanna ecosystem. This interpretation of the prehistory is also supported by recent genetic research in East Africa showing that African pastoralists evolved the ability for adults to digest milk (lactase persistence).[5]

Anthropologists often group the cattle peoples of East Africa into a single culture area stretching from Sudan to South Africa, but they are a diverse group of cultures organized at different scales of social complexity and united only by their common interest in cattle. The most famous cattle peoples, such as the Nuer, Dinka, Karimojong, Turkana, and Maasai, all belong to the Nilotic branch of the Nilo-Saharan language family. *Nilotic* also refers to the very tall physical type of Nilotic speakers (see figure 4.3.).

Outsiders recognized the Maasai as a distinct cultural group since at least the early 1600s, and they were actively expanding their territories into what is now Tanzania by 1800.[6] Arab Muslim traders established themselves off the coast on the island of Zanzibar at about the same time, trading into the interior for slaves and ivory. The Arabs were followed in the mid-nineteenth century by European explorers and missionaries.

European colonial governments were moving into place by the 1880s, followed by national independence in the 1960s.

Table 4.1. Prehistory of East Africa, 200,000–1000 BP

2000–1000 BP	Expansion of Bantu-speaking, iron-using village farmers
Pastoral Neolithic in Kenya (5200–2500 BP)	
2500	Southern Nilotic speakers from southern Sudan enter highlands as mixed farmer/pastoralists with livestock, millet, and sorghum
3300	Modern climate and vegetation established Savanna pastoral Neolithic in highlands
5200	Savanna pastoral Neolithic introduced in lowlands by Cushitic speakers bringing domestic livestock and ceramics
Saharan Pastoralism (8000–4000 BP)	
4000–5400	Domestic livestock and ceramics in central Sudan
7000–8000	Local domestication of cattle in Sahara Domestic sheep and goats reach North Africa from Near East
***Homo Sapiens* Foragers (200,000–40,000 BP)**	
200,000	Middle Stone Age; core tools, flake points, scrapers

Sources: Ambrose (1984), Clark (1984), Phillipson (1985), Smith (1984), and Wendorf and Schild (1984).

Figure 4.3.   Shillook warrior and girl, Nilotic cattle peoples, upper Nile, nineteenth century (Ratzal 1898:21).

The Cattle Complex:
Obsession or Resilient Adaptation?

Historically, East African pastoralists have been seriously misunderstood by anthropologists, development planners, and conservationists. Many observers concluded that they irrationally overemphasized cattle in culturally determined ways, leading to overgrazing and poor-quality animals. American anthropologist Melville Herskovits[7] apparently was the first to refer to the East African cattle area and to describe the Cattle Complex as an irrational cultural value on cattle for nonutilitarian purposes. According to Herskovits, Cattle Complex peoples used cattle more for social and ritual purposes than for subsistence. Cattle were treated as wealth objects and sources of prestige. People rarely ate cattle; instead, they exchanged cattle at marriage, used them to settle disputes, and sacrificed them on ritual occasions. Besides these noneconomical uses, East Africans seemed to have an exaggerated and personal attachment to their animals. When range management professionals later found that pastoral cattle were underweight and less productive than their counterparts in the American West, they unfairly accused the pastoralists of overgrazing and blamed them for desertification, the process by which a savanna is converted to arid desert by overgrazing.

British anthropologist E. E. Evans-Pritchard conducted one of the first and most detailed studies of a cattle culture among the Nuer of Sudan between 1930 and 1936.[8] This study, which became a classic in ethnographic literature, showed the social, ritual, and emotional value of cattle but also demonstrated their utilitarian function.

Evans-Pritchard called the Nuer "pre-eminently pastoral." He reported that they considered themselves herdsmen above all else and only grudgingly resorted to farming when they didn't have enough animals. They looked contemptuously on people without cattle, as he discovered on his arrival in Nuerland, when the Nuer refused to carry his baggage. He found that they had "the herdsman's outlook on the world" and considered cattle "their dearest possessions." Cattle were ornamented and named, and their genealogies were remembered. Boys received an "ox-name" at birth, men were addressed using names that referred to their favorite oxen, and women were named after the cows they milked. And, to Evans-Pritchard's dismay, they always talked about their animals: "I used sometimes to despair that I never discussed anything with the young men but livestock and girls, and even the subject of girls led inevitably to that of cattle. Start on whatever subject I would, and approach it from whatever angle, we would soon be speaking of cows and oxen, heifers and steers."[9]

For Evans-Pritchard, this "pastoral mentality" took on the appearance of an "over-emphasis," a "hypertrophy of a single interest." As further indication of Nuer obsession with cattle, he pointed to the "linguistic profusion" of cattle terminology. He found ten terms for describing cows of one solid color and hundreds of possible permutations of terms based on combinations of white with various patterns and associations with natural objects. Further Nuer terminological distinctions are based on horn shape, ear cropping, and age and sex categories. In all, the Nuer had thousands of ways of describing cattle and composed poetry and songs using their names. The Luo, Nilotic neighbors of the Nuer, apply 125 terms to cattle anatomy, both internal and external, covering bones and internal organs in great detail[10] (see figure 4.4).

Evans-Pritchard recognized that this extreme interest in cattle had a utilitarian basis. He noted that the Nuers' flat, clay-soiled, seasonally flooded environment was deficient in such basic raw materials as stone and wood and was a difficult area to grow crops, but it provided excellent pasturage. The Nuer therefore lavished seemingly extravagant care on their animals, such that the cattle enjoyed a "gentle, indolent, sluggish life."[11] He described the virtually symbiotic relationship between the Nuer and their cattle, in which each depended on the other. The Nuer extract an impressive array of material resources from cattle. Milk is the primary product, and it may be consumed fresh or sour, or processed as cheese. Blood is drawn from veins in the neck and then boiled or allowed to coagulate and roasted in a block. An animal is ordinarily slaughtered only for ritual purposes, but then it is butchered and the parts distributed. Dung is a critical fuel for cooking, and dung fires help drive off biting insects. Dung is also used as a construction plaster, as well as for medicinal and cosmetic purposes. Cattle urine is used in cheese making and tanning, while skin and bones have many uses in the manufacture of various artifacts such as containers and ornaments. Without cattle and their products, life would be very difficult in Nuerland.

Pastoralists have been widely accused of irrationality for supposedly raising far more poor-quality animals than they need for mere subsistence in order to achieve the prestige and social value of large numbers of cattle. They have been accused of overstocking their ranges and degrading their environments,

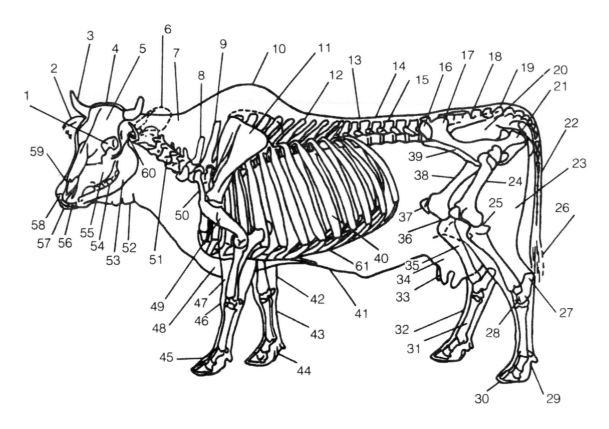

1. Chokndorro
2. It
3. Tuṅ
4. Tatwich
5. Sihanga or patwich
6. It (omwot it)
7. Ṅgut
8. Chok ṅgutmachiek
9. Chok ṅgutmabor
10. Kuom
11. Opal
12. Ariedi lihumblu
13. Giko nyakmeru
14. Dierṅgech
15. Giko nyakmeru
16. Wichok oguro
17. Chokoguro
18. Choktie ip
19. Oguch dhiang
20. Ringsarara
21. Dhokisonga

22. Ip
23. Ring em maoko
24. Odiere machien
25. Fuond odire gi ogwala
26. Orengo
27. Fuond ogwala
28. Nyapoṅg tielo
29. Odofuny tielo
30. Okak tielo
31. Chok oluko
32. Ogwala
33. Thuno
34. Dagthuno
35. Chok em
36. Fundodiere
37. Nyapoṅg odiere
38. Odiere
39. Chokbam
40. Ṅgede
41. Pinyich
42. Bat korachich

43. Ogwala
44. Ofunjtielo or ṅguttielo
45. Witielo
46. Choṅg
47. Bat korjachien
48. Agoko
49. Chokbat mar oriere
50. Chokrangach (colar bone)
51. Choke ṅgudi
52. Jund dhiaṅg
53. Choklem mapiny
54. Nyiponge
55. Choklem mamalo
56. Lep
57. Leke mamon
58. Um
59. Chok um
60. Tiend it
61. Chokagoko

Figure 4.4. A sample of the 125 anatomical terms applied to cattle by the Nilotic-speaking Luo (Ocholla-Ayayo 1979, reprinted with permission).

thus contributing to desertification. This is sometimes seen as a classic tragedy of the commons situation, a destruction of a communal resource by self-interested individuals as described by biologist Garrett Hardin.[12] East African grazing lands are common properties, but they are not the kind of unregulated open-access system that Hardin imagined. The tragedy of the com-

mons interpretation overlooked the fact that African herders act as a community to regulate grazing by individual herders.[13] Herders practice seasonal conservation in an adaptive way that minimizes overgrazing.[14]

Development planners often recommend that pastoralists would do better to raise beef for the market as private ranchers. Actually, little firm evidence supports the view that domestic-scale pastoralism is inherently prone to overstocking, while abundant evidence suggests that outside development pressures do contribute to overgrazing.[15] Domestic-scale subsistence pastoralists operating outside of the market economy are unlikely to find any conflict between individual self-interest and their social responsibility to maintain range quality.[16] Rainfall, which is highly irregular, not the total number of animals, appears to be the primary determinant of range condition over the long run.[17] Herd size appears to fluctuate up and down, maintaining an average level in response to droughts and disease.

Whether or not African pastoralists are self-conscious conservationists, their traditional subsistence practices include important limiting factors that reduce the likelihood of overgrazing and producing a highly resilient system. First, the subsistence needs of a household determine herd size, and the labor supply and the declining feeding efficiencies that arise as herds grow set its upper limits. Second, in the absence of trucks, pumps, and deep wells, the frequency that animals must be watered and the distance they can travel between grazing areas and water severely limit grazing during the dry season. More recently, the more extreme drought conditions associated with global warming are creating a more difficult challenge for pastoralists who must operate under more restricted conditions imposed by government policies.[18]

African cattle under traditional nomadic pastoralism do appear to be of lower quality when compared with U.S. beef and dairy cattle. African animals convert less of their forage into human food and produce less body weight because the frequent droughts cause animals to channel more of their energy into biological maintenance than into meat production. They must adjust their metabolisms to cycles of periodic thirst and starvation followed by recovery.[19] Low production is thus a long-range adaptation to severe environmental constraints. As mentioned previously, U.S. cattle achieve their high biological output thanks to a significant fossil fuel energy subsidy, which is not counted in these calculations but which is required to produce and distribute tractors, farm chemicals, feed, and agricultural research.

Pastoral Subsistence: Meat, Blood, and Milk

To design a reliable food system based on domestic animals, a subsistence herder must solve several problems: which animals to use, what food products to produce, how many animals to herd, what age and sex categories to maintain in the herds, when to slaughter, when to time breeding, how to feed and water the herd, and how to protect the herd from disease and predators. Whereas hunters let nature take care of most of these matters, herders must constantly attend to the needs of their animals.

Most East African pastoralists are considered, and consider themselves, to be cattle peoples because of the dominant cultural role they assign to cattle, but they actually depend on several functionally distinct domesticates, including cattle, camels, sheep, and goats. Cattle play major social, ritual, and subsistence roles while providing important material products. Camels become increasingly important as rainfall declines or pastures become overgrazed. The small stock (sheep and goats) may provide more of a household's meat requirements than cattle and can be a significant source of milk. Cattle are not as efficient as goats at meat production, so cattle are rarely slaughtered except ritually, although they are eaten when they die naturally. Small stock also are useful to speed recovery after a serious drought because they reproduce more quickly than cattle. Reliance on animal domesticates makes for a situation that is the reverse of the protein limitation situation in Amazonia. East African pastoralists have an abundance of protein but have some difficulty producing adequate carbohydrates and calories except where they can grow grain or obtain it by barter with neighboring farmers.

Complementarity between domesticates is a striking aspect of pastoral systems. Maintaining mixed herds of large and small grazers and browsers makes for more efficient utilization of available forage and, like Amazonian gardens, makes maximum use of the diversity of the natural ecosystem. As grazers, cattle and sheep feed primarily on grasses and herbaceous vegetation; as browsers, goats and camels rely on woody shrubs and trees. Utilization of diverse domesticates also helps level out seasonal fluctuation in food production: Camels often produce milk year-round, cows produce only during the wet season, and sheep and goats produce most milk during the dry season.

The diverse animal products that pastoralists consume also have the advantage of complementarity, and they maximize sustainable subsistence yield. Rather than emphasizing meat production, which obviously represents a onetime use of an animal, herders are concerned primarily with milk production. Milk maximizes biological efficiency because the calories in milk can be produced four times more efficiently in terms of energy costs than the calories in meat.

Blood and milk can be produced without harm to the animal, and they complement each other in that blood is a major source of iron and can be drawn from animals that are not producing milk. This is especially important for cows when their milk production drops during the dry season. The importance of milk production in herder diets is shown by the remarkable fact that the Karimojong derive one-third of their total caloric requirements from their cattle, 88 percent of which is in the form of milk, with meat representing only 8 percent, and blood 4 percent of cattle dietary component.[20] These figures show that cattle peoples are really dairy farmers.

Traditional herding is a labor-intensive activity. Individual herds may be subdivided to better reflect the abilities and requirements of different types of animals. Herds are moved seasonally to take advantage of the best pasture. In some areas this may involve **transhumance**, or herd movement into higher or lower environments. Pastoralists manage their herds to maximize the number of female animals to keep milk yields and growth potential high. Given the natural mortality rates of cattle and their reproductive biology, a herd is unlikely to contain more than about 30 percent fertile cows, and only half of these will be producing milk.

Although the production of milk per animal under pastoral nomadism is lower than on American dairy farms, pastoral milk is more concentrated, and its nutritional value is 30 percent higher than that of commercially produced milk. Given the archaeological record of pastoralism in East Africa and the incredible resilience of the system under the impact of colonial invasion and recent forces for change, traditional herders seem to be operating quite rationally. Their herding strategies contribute to the long-range survival of their families in a challenging environment.

Herding continues to be an important way of life, even as population growth, shrinking grazing lands, development programs, and restrictive government policies force herders to raise food crops and engage in the commercial economy to save their cattle. The Maasai described the situation in the 1990s: "I cultivate to avoid selling my cattle." "Life is now expensive, there is a demand in the family for food, education, and medical care, and the livestock are not enough to fulfill these life requirements."[21]

DAILY LIFE IN EAST AFRICA

East African cattle cultures are an ideal place to examine the relations between men and women in the tribal world, and the degree of personal freedom and social equality that tribal life makes possible. Just as there was an anthropological myth of irrational herders obsessively attached to their cattle, until recently many anthropologists mistakenly believed that African pastoralism, and indeed pastoralism generally, was naturally and totally male dominated. Male domination meant that men were the owner-managers of the cattle, that pastoral societies were gerontocracies directed by the old men, that men controlled patrilineages that structured the entire social system and defined the pastoral identity of their cultures. The implication was that women were totally subordinate in "status" to men and culturally inferior, if not completely irrelevant.

These misleading interpretations should not be surprising, because just as outsider men have had difficulty fully understanding Australian aboriginal society; it has been difficult for male anthropologists to view African societies from a woman's perspective. The existence of male bias in fieldwork is clearly demonstrated in the following comment by a leading ethnographer of the Samburu Maasai who declared, "Samburu is essentially a man's society and *from the male point of view* women are inferior and politically uninfluential" [italics added].[22] Although Australian foragers, Amazon villagers, and African herders all appear to fit the model of a tribal male supremacy complex, this interpretation is at best incomplete. We may suspect that how men describe their societies is likely to reflect male ideology rather than the realities of domestic life. A further difficulty, just as we saw with the problem of understanding violence in Amazonia, is the historical influence of the commercial world and colonialism, which disrupted domestically organized systems of social power in ways that consistently disadvantaged women. Nevertheless, there is an apparent contradiction between tribal cosmologies that portray men as culturally superior and the ideals of complementary opposition between men and women that also seems to characterize these societies. Gender equality can exist in the tribal world in spite of contrary ideologies because the household is the primary social institution, and the household is created and maintained by an age- and gender-based division of labor.

The following sections describing the Nuer and Maasai will demonstrate that, just as in tribal Australia and Amazonia, in African herding societies men and women play complementary, but not totally equitable, roles within the household, where they share a common interest in producing children who will become successful adults. Both men and women shape the direction of their society and culture, but this does not mean that they share equal social status. The reality of gender relations in any society is seldom easily understood or explained. As will be shown, in African herding societies even women repeat myths that describe, and offer explanations for, the subordination of women to men. Women also practice and perpetuate rituals such as female circumcision that outsiders, as well as some members of the culture, may consider oppressive.

Age and gender inequities show that preexisting cultural patterns are not always totally consistent and may not always benefit everyone equally. We may assume that the apparent injustices that an individual experiences will tend to balance out through the life cycle. However, culture may constrain individuals to accept inequity and personal pain and suffering as natural and unavoidable. Unjust cultural practices can be difficult for individuals acting alone to successfully challenge and change, even when alternative ways of life are almost always possible.

Nuer Society: Bride-Wealth, Lovers, and Ghosts

Apart from the obvious utilitarian value of their cattle, the Nuer say that the "supreme value" of cattle came from their use as **bride-wealth**, which is the basic requirement for establishing a fully legitimate household.[23] (We will avoid the use of the term *legal* to refer to marriage or household in this context because it implies formal law, supported by courts and an enforcement structure that does not exist in Nuer society.) Nuer marriage involves rights over cattle and women and their children and is an agreement between the families of the bride and groom (see box 4.2). It requires a lengthy series of negotiations, public and private ceremonies, and transactions, which are not complete until children are born to the couple. Because Nuer marriage is so complex and involves so many different rights, it is an ideal case from which to examine the meaning of marriage, family, gender relations, and household as cross-cultural concepts.

The process of Nuer marriage is initiated by preliminary talks between the two families to specify the animals that can be transferred. The bride's family can demand cattle for six different categories of claimants by order of precedence: the bride's grandparents or their ghosts, the bride's parents, her uncles, her aunts, the spirits of her father and mother, and her brothers and half-brothers (see figure 4.5). Ideally, some forty head of cattle ultimately are transferred to the bride's father, who is then obligated to distribute them to each of the claimants on his side of the family and to the bride's mother's family. In a typical distribution, twenty animals would go to the bride's immediate family, with her father getting the largest share, and ten animals would go to each set of uncles and aunts. Each category of claimant receives a specific number and type of animal. For example, the bride's full

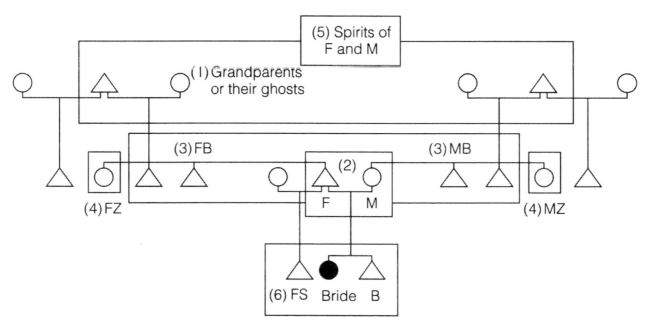

Figure 4.5. Order of precedence of claimants on Nuer bride-wealth cattle: (1) grandparents or their ghosts; (2) father (F) and mother (M); (3) father's brother(s) (FB) and mother's brother(s) (MB); (4) father's sister(s) (FZ) and mother's sister(s) (MZ); (5) spirits of father (F) and mother (M); (6) brother(s)(B) and half-brother(s) (FS) (data from Evans-Pritchard 1951).

brother can receive three cows, two oxen, and one cow with its calf, seven animals in all. In the negotiations, animals are promised by name to specific people.

The preliminary negotiations are formalized in the betrothal ceremony, which is the first public marriage ritual. Betrothal is marked by the sacrifice and distribution of an ox by the bride's father to the groom's family. The first installment of bride-wealth cattle also is transferred to the bride's father. Several weeks later, at the wedding ceremony, negotiations are finalized and more cattle transferred, but the transfer and the marriage are not considered official until a later consummation ceremony with its own series of rituals. After this, the groom's family can demand compensation in the event of his wife's infidelity, but the couple does not establish a joint homestead until after their

first child is weaned. Until then, the wife remains in her parents' homestead, and her husband is a visitor who must maintain a ritual distance from his in-laws.

Once completed, the "ordinary" Nuer marriage creates a simple nuclear family household based on husband, wife, and child. Such a household draws its subsistence from his herd and from the wife's garden. The homestead contains a *byre* (a cattle barn) and its *kraal* (corral), a cooking hearth, and a small sleeping house for the wife. In a polygynous marriage, each wife has her own house. Several such homesteads belonging to a group of brothers or a father and his sons might cluster around a common *kraal* as a composite homestead.

Many other domestic arrangements are possible (see figure 4.6). For example, a woman, especially if

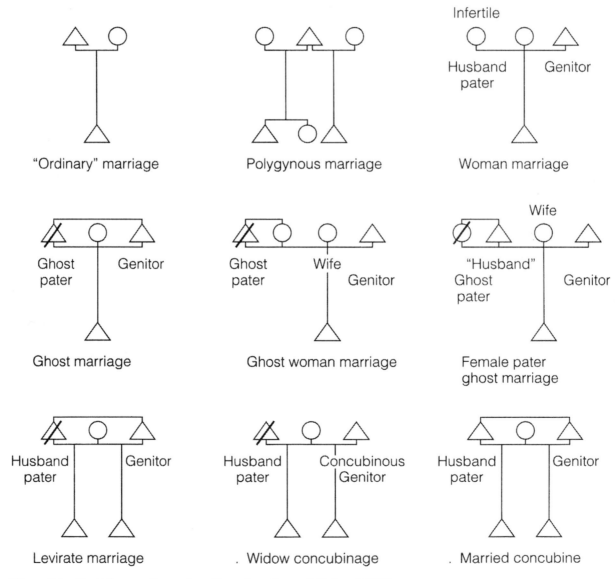

Figure 4.6. Nuer forms of marriage (based on Evans-Pritchard 1951).

she were infertile, might become a "husband" and have children by marrying another woman who then takes a male lover who becomes the biological father, or **genitor**, of the female husband's children. In this case, the female husband is the legitimate father, or **pater**, of the children, as well as the husband, and her family transfers cattle as bride-wealth to the family of her wife. In a "ghost marriage," someone marries in the name of a sibling or other relative who has died without having completed a marriage and who thus has left no descendants. In all such cases, cattle are transferred to the bride's family, while the deceased, male or female, becomes the pater; the stand-in relative lives with the wife as "husband" and genitor but has no rights over the children. **Levirate** marriage, in which a man marries his deceased brother's wife, resembles ghost marriage except that the dead husband was already married and the bride-wealth had been transferred. The original, now dead, husband is still considered the husband, and the brother who stands in his place has less control over his wife's children than the "husband" in a ghost marriage. Women have considerable freedom in Nuer domestic arrangements, even though all marriages are officially arranged by the families involved. Instead of remarrying, widows sometimes live with lovers, who may father children by them. However, the original legitimate family, established by bride-wealth, remains intact, and her children will be filiated to her original husband, who is always their pater. Evans-Pritchard[24] called such arrangements "widow concubinage." In some cases, a woman may move in with a lover while she is still married. She will be a "married concubine," and again her children will all be filiated to her husband because of the bride-wealth.

For the Nuer, the concept of paternity, or "belonging to," is far more important than biological parentage or the details of domestic arrangements. Paternity is established by bride-wealth cattle, thereby providing one with claims to cattle that may, in turn, be used for bride-wealth. Marriage also links one to a set of ancestor ghosts and spirits that must be ritually acknowledged. Maintaining such claims is more important than whether a "father" is living or dead, male or female, or with whom one's mother cohabits.

The use of bride-wealth, such as cattle, to formalize marriage has so many ramifications throughout the culture that some anthropologists recognize societies based on bride-wealth and those based on **bride-service** as distinctive societal types.[25] These two marriage systems create different culturally defined systems of domestic relations, organizing the inequalities of age and sex in different ways. Young men in bride-service societies, such as in aboriginal Australia and Amazonia, do not incur long-term debt obligations when they marry and need only hunt or provide other services to their in-laws during the early stages in their marriage. In bride-wealth societies, the exchange of bride-wealth valuables between male "heads" of families sharply defines the social statuses of husband, wife, parent, and child. The social importance of bride-wealth cattle also gives a man more of a vested interest in the marriages of his brothers and sisters than he might have in a bride-service society.

Bride-wealth was sometimes called *bride-price* by anthropologists, who sometimes even referred to wife markets, but these terms are better avoided because they imply purchase and incorrectly suggest that women are chattels in cattle societies. With the Nuer, this is certainly *not* the case because women have the final say over whom they marry. It would be foolish for a father to force his daughter into a marriage against her wishes, because bride-wealth cattle would have to be returned in the event of a divorce before children were born to the marriage. There are, however, inequalities of age and gender built into the system. The marriage transaction gives a man, or a woman acting as a man, the right to establish paternity, to demand cattle as an indemnity for adultery, and to claim cattle when his wife's daughters marry. Men in this system sometimes explicitly equate women with cattle because, when women are "given" in marriage, they bring cattle in exchange (see box 4.3).

BOX 4.2. HOW DO NUER MEN VIEW WOMEN?

Anthropologist John Burton[26] asked several Atuot (Nuer) men and women to respond to this question: "What are the relations of a wife and husband, and how do they come to quarrel?" He felt that their answers closely matched what he observed. Mayan Akuot, a father of six children, answered as follows:

> In our land, it is for a woman to give birth to children. Women are not good or bad—they are in between. Their badness is that even if you are married with one hundred cows, she may still leave. Even if you cultivate much grain, she may still leave you. This is because some women have no heart. If it is a good woman she will bear many children. If there were no women, how would all the people be here? She is the one

who created the land. There is the wife of the black people, of the animals, of the cows, of the fish—all of them have this land. If it were not for women, how would people be so many? Women are good—they make children and food and beer. The woman has the land. If a man stays in this land without a woman, he will not go ahead [that is, his progeny will never be realized].[27]

These comments show that men are well aware of their dependence on women for the essentials of food, beer, and descendants. A man must be married, or he cannot be successful.

BOX 4.3. CATTLE AND MAASAI KINSHIP TERMINOLOGY

The importance of cattle in marriage exchanges is also reflected in kinship terminology. For example, the Maasai kinship system places kin from different generations into the same category (see figure 4.7), because as a group they all have an interest in the bride-wealth cattle they received from Ego's father's kin when Ego's mother married. From Ego's perspective, this makes the members of mother's patrilineage a single group. They are all like mothers or mother's brothers.[28] Note that in the Nuer example the bride's father and her brother (MB to her son) are the major recipients of the bride-wealth cattle.

The Status of Women in East African Pastoral Society: Ideology versus Reality

In describing East African cattle peoples, ethnographers who followed Evans-Pritchard repeatedly described patrilineages as the essential organizational basis of society, yet they also knew that the most important social connections were actualized through women and that it was primarily women who managed and reproduced the daily affairs of the household and were principally responsible for nurturing children. Patriarchy as an ideal social structure implies that men are naturally the exclusive "heads" of "their" households, whereas the reality of life in the tribal world is that there is no single ruler. Husbands and wives are partners in the cooperative project of producing and socializing children and transmitting culture to the next generation. The routine division of labor gives men and women complementary rights and responsibilities in their respective spheres of action, but this is not a hierarchy with a single authority. Extraordinary decisions are typically made jointly. The organization of domestic life maximizes the autonomy and independence of men and women, giving both control over the conditions of their daily life.

The difference between the ideology of how the social system is designed and how it actually operates is a paradox that anthropologists have long recognized. For example, Evans-Pritchard[29] suggested that even when the Nuer traced descent through women, this

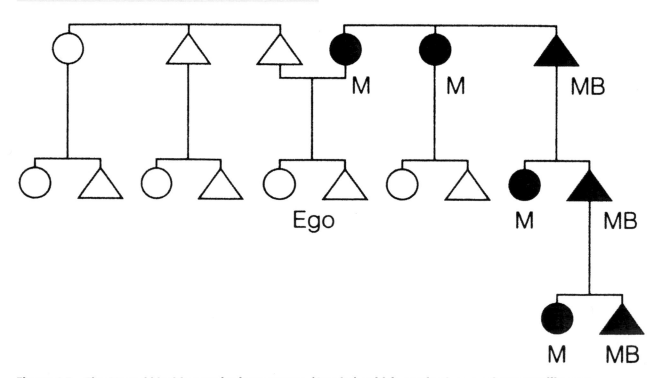

Figure 4.7. The Maasai kinship terminology system (Omaha), which emphasizes mother's patrilineage.

did not challenge the validity of the patrilineal model. The patrilineal Turkana were said to have patrilineages composed of the descendants of a grandmother.[30] In reality, sons inherit movable wealth in the form of cattle from their mothers. Each of a man's wives holds and manages property for her respective sons. Schneider[31] is explicit about this, stating "paradoxically, the wealth a man inherits comes from his mother's household, the product of her labor and management. In a sense, a man really inherits from his mother...."

The misleading emphasis on men gaining rights over women through the transfer of cattle obscures other important dimensions of gender relations in these societies. For example, when Nuer boys are initiated into manhood by receiving deep scars across the forehead known as *gaar,* they are no longer allowed to milk cows or cook food. These prohibitions signify the complete dependence of adult men on women for their food. Initiated men also can no longer drink milk directly from a cow, and instead are expected to nurture cattle by herding.[32] Nuer women can withhold food and beer to punish their husbands. This is a sensitive issue for men (see box 4.2). Women might also influence their husband's political status by not cooking for his guests, or they might use food to influence whether or not men go on raids, or make peace.

The ideology of male owner-managers of cattle obscures the reality that the primary economic purpose of cattle raising is milk production, and this process is entirely controlled by women. Women also produce and control numerous other cattle by-products such as clothing and bedding made from cow hides, and fuel and mortar from dung. In reality, both men and women hold diverse, overlapping rights over animals, and to say that men exclusively own cattle would be misleading. Furthermore, women own and control their houses, hearths, and all domestic household articles, as well as all cooked food. The term *hearth-hold* calls attention to the centrality of the domestic space that women control and the crucial role that women play in maintaining and reproducing African pastoral households.[33] Where seasonal nomadism is important, the matrifocal hearth-hold is the family's fixed center. A woman manages the animals that her husband allocates to her sons. Women also may contribute to the household economy by gardening, foraging, trading, and by their services as healers and midwives.

In approaching gender relations, anthropologists often describe two separate realms of social action, the political sector controlled by men and the domestic sector controlled by women. The Nuer example shows that domestic and political realms are closely interconnected in the tribal world. Some authorities have suggested that women's domestic roles are "encompassed" by men's presumably more powerful public and political activities,[34] whereas women manipulate in the background using their perhaps not fully legitimate power.[35] However this is conceptualized, the Nuer case shows that women's control over the domestic sphere gives them influence over the entire society. From this perspective, tribal politics are really about men negotiating among themselves over the distribution of the goods and services that only women can provide, or that women actually control.[36]

In addition to questions of differences between men and women in ownership and use of livestock, there are also age and gender differences in labor expenditures. Time allocation studies of the Ariaal, a Maasai-related people in Kenya, show that men and women work seven to ten hours daily, respectively, at household, livestock, and manufacturing tasks.[37] This is a higher and less equitable workload than enjoyed by Aborigines and Amazonian peoples and reflects the extra burden of livestock as well as the age and gender division of labor. Because they take the largest share in livestock tasks, unmarried males from age twelve to thirty-four rest less than three hours a day, whereas women rest nearly six hours and married men more than eight hours. Furthermore, workloads are lighter in richer households with more cattle, because caring for small stock is more labor intensive. Women also welcome co-wives who share the work.

Understanding Nuer Descent Groups

Evans-Pritchard devised an ingenious model to describe the political organization of Nuer society. The Nuer, with a population of some 300,000 in the 1930s, were said to be organized by clans, lineages, and territorial groups into an **acephalous**, or headless, political system, which operated in the absence of formal political offices.[38] The clans and lineages were descent groups that recruited members exclusively through males by means of patrilineal descent, or **filiation**. In Evans-Pritchard's scheme, the highest descent-based unit was the clan, which was composed of maximal, major, minor, and minimal lineages. These units corresponded to the territorial units, with the tribe at the top and primary, secondary, and tertiary tribal sections down to the village community at the lowest territorial level (see figure 4.8a).

As the figure shows, this system can be represented in a tidy diagram, but the Nuer themselves may well

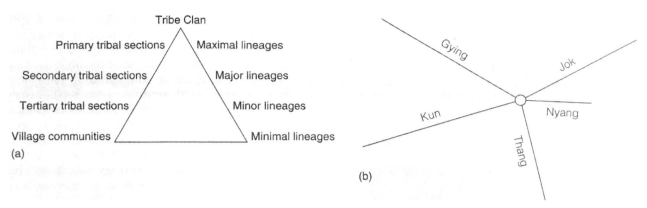

Figure 4.8. The segmentary lineage system of Nuer society as seen by (a) Evans-Pritchard (1940), and (b) the Nuer themselves (Evans-Pritchard 1940, reprinted with permission).

understand it differently.[39] The Nuer apparently have no term in their own language for clan or lineage; when Evans-Pritchard pressed them for lineage affiliations, they did not understand what he wanted to know. He was able to obtain names for lineage segments, but these were merely the names of particular ancestors. When he asked the Nuer to draw their lineages, they came up with lines radiating from a center, not the branching trees and pyramids that he preferred (see figure 4.8b). He also observed that "lineages" did not, in fact, form discrete localized groups. That is, the members of a lineage often did not live in the same village, nor were they strictly patrilineal. He found that lineages often incorporated children filiated through women or through adoption.

Despite the inconsistencies, Evans-Pritchard declared that clans and lineages appeared on ritual occasions when people made sacrifices to their ancestors, when groups mobilized to settle disputes, or when groups conducted raids. Such ephemeral descent groups acquired their own reality in the anthropological literature—especially in the work of British functionalists in Africa, where they became standard descriptive devices, and in major comparative studies. However, regardless of whether the Nuer linguistically identify clans and lineages, they do divide their society into nested levels of inclusiveness, based on their assumptions about relations to ancestors and territory. Perhaps most importantly, they successfully organize large numbers of people without central political authority.

When it became obvious that the natives were not very concerned with the purity or even the existence of their descent groups, some argued that descent was simply "ideology." Sahlins[40] observed that differ-

ent ideological models of descent organization could be projected onto the same arrangement of people. A given group might, for example, consider themselves to be patrilineal, matrilineal, or even bilateral, without making any changes in individuals. Descent thus became a cultural fiction that people adopted for whatever purpose.

The anthropological conception of lineages and clans grew out of nineteenth-century evolutionary theories that viewed them as stages on the way to statehood.[41] A clan-based society was thought to represent an evolutionary advance over societies organized only by families, but because they were still based on kinship or biological descent, clan societies were considered to be more "primitive" than territorially organized states. Lineages and clans were seen as equivalent to corporate legal entities that, like business corporations, existed in perpetuity apart from their individual members. However, in case after case critical examination showed that clans and lineages did not form consistent, culturally recognized units. East African pastoralists do remember ancestors, and they marry outside of specific categories of kin; but like Australian Aborigines, they seem not to organize themselves into descent groups. Instead their lives are organized around politically autonomous villages, households, and overlapping networks of kinship. The Nuer categories that Evans-Pritchard called **patrilineages** have also been described as interest groups of individuals sharing claims in cattle.[42] Ranked descent lines may be traced to elite persons in hierarchically organized societies; in such cases, "royal" or "noble" clans and lineages may be culturally significant, but such is not the case with the Nuer, or the other African pastoralists considered here.

Politics in Headless Societies: Leopard-Skin Chiefs and Stock Associates

Although the Nuer do not distinguish descent groups, many other peoples, such as the Maasai, do have named clans, and all East African tribal peoples use genealogical and residential proximity to structure their intergroup relations without resorting to political hierarchy. All of these societies face important organizational problems in the world beyond the village, because cattle raiding is a constant threat and temptation, and the total social universe is much larger, denser, and potentially more dangerous than in Australia, or much of Amazonia. For example, government census figures for 1955–1956 listed some 460,000 Nuer living in an area of some 25,000 square miles (65,000 km²).[43] This was more people than the entire population of aboriginal Australia and in a much smaller area. People who live closer together are also likely to believe themselves more closely related, and Nuer men mobilize their kinship connections to conduct raids or organize defense. Kinship connections, whether real or fictive, make possible a form of order without permanent, formal leaders and without government. This is ordered anarchy, organized by what anthropologists have called a **segmentary lineage system**,[44] the familiar situation where geographic distance corresponds to social distance. In the tribal world, people living close together believe themselves to be related by common descent, and they align themselves as segments in opposition to more distant segments.

These are acephalous societies that maximize individual freedom. East African cattle peoples do distinguish regional ethnic groups, but in practice individual ethnic identity is flexible (see box 4.4). It was Nuer rejection of central authority that most impressed Evans-Pritchard about the Nuer. He called them "proud and individualistic" and declared: "Their attitude towards any authority that would coerce them is one of touchiness, pride, and reckless disobedience. Each determines to go his own way as much as possible, has a hatred of submission, and is ready to defend himself and property from the inroads of others. They are thus self-reliant, brave fighters, turbulent and aggressive, and are extremely conservative in their aversion from innovation and interference."[45]

This picture of Nuer individualism and autonomy is historically accurate. They resist "innovation" because their social system serves their interests. The key feature of the Nuer segmentary system is that political alliances form according to the affiliation of individual combatants. Thus, for example, if a conflict developed between two villages, members of other villages would not join in; but if someone stole a cow from another district, then neighboring villages might form a temporary alliance against the perceived common enemy. The Nuer resisted repeated punitive raids by the British colonial government in the Sudan and engaged the independent Sudanese government in a civil war from 1956 to 1972, and 1983 to 2005.

Evans-Pritchard[46] described a political system with increasing levels of violence as social distance increased. Within a village, men might fight with clubs, but serious disputes would be settled quickly. Between villages, men might fight with spears, and blood feuds were possible, but cattle could be accepted as compensation for homicide. Raiding for cattle routinely occurred between more distant groups of Nuer villages, which Evans-Pritchard designated as tribes but which were probably shifting alliances of adjacent villages. Women and children and granaries were spared in "intertribal" raiding, but they might not be spared in raids against non-Nuer groups such as the Dinka, even though they developed from a common culture. Conflicts seemed to arise primarily over cattle, either from cattle raiding or from disputes over unpaid bride-wealth transfers. Homicides could lead to feuds between kin groups, which could lead to further vengeance killings as in Amazonia, but among the Nuer there was a mechanism for mediation. Specific individuals, whom Evans-Pritchard called leopard-skin chiefs, served as mediators and attempted to persuade the conflicting parties to settle the dispute by means of compensation in the form of cattle transfer. Leopard-skin chiefs were respected as ritual practitioners and as mediators, but they were not chiefs with political authority. In his mediator role, the chief was expected to threaten to curse a reluctant party with supernatural sanctions but, in fact, had no coercive power.

Although cattle are a major cause of conflict, they also provide an incentive for reducing conflict. Inter-village feuding would disrupt bride-wealth transfers because wide extension of incest restrictions, which reduces confusion in bride-wealth transfers, means that villages are usually exogamous. This divides the loyalties of people who might feel obligated to support one another in blood feuds as covillagers, as close kin, or as claimants to bride-wealth cattle. It is thus in virtually everyone's self-interest to keep feuding to an absolute minimum. By crosscutting village membership in this way, domestic-scale societies create what has been called the peace in the feud.[47]

BOX 4.4. TRIBAL ETHNIC IDENTITY: WHO ARE THE NUER AND THE MAASAI?

A careful reader of Evans-Pritchard's *The Nuer*[48] might be surprised to learn that the Nuer do not call themselves "Nuer." They are "Nath" or "Naath." In a footnote, we find that "the word 'Nuer' is sanctioned by a century of usage" and is what the Naath are called by the Dinka, and by all other outsiders, we might add. The Dinka, in turn, call themselves "Jieng." In both cases, just as with the Asháninka and Matsigenka, the words *Naath* and *Jieng* mean "people."[49] Because there is no permanent Nuer political entity, it follows that there is no Nuer "tribe." Indeed, anthropologist John Burton declared, "Such ethnic designations as 'Nuer' and 'Dinka' . . . are at best marginally indicative of observable interethnic relations and associations."[50] The only consensus, apparently shared by the Nuer and the Dinka and their observers, is that the Nuer raid cattle from the Dinka.

The absence of fixed boundaries between Nuer and Dinka frustrated British colonial administrators for years. The Nuer and Dinka freely intermarry, and cattle move between them as booty and as bridewealth. Someone might grow up as a Dinka and be initiated into adulthood as a Nuer. There are other rituals that convert adult Dinka into Nuer. Indeed, the two apparent ethnic categories share so many cultural traits that in mixed camps, they may tell each other apart most easily by referring to physical differences in their cattle. As Burton observes, "They are first of all pastoralists rather than antagonistic representatives of supposedly pure ethnic groups. . . . Ethnicity therefore moves on the hoof."[51]

John Galaty[52] examined the problem of ethnic identity from the viewpoint of another Nilotic people, the Maasai of Kenya and Tanzania. According to Maasai ethnosociology (how a society views its own cultural identity), the Maasai are speakers of the Maa language who belong to any of a number of named tribal sections of a single Maasai "nation," which has no formal political organization. The term *Maasai* literally means "I will not beg" and is a frequently used polite expression associated with the dominant Maasai values of bravery and arrogance. In their self-designation, Maasai also call attention to the beads that are featured in their dress and, most prominently, to their association with cattle. In their own eyes, the Maasai are "people of cattle." However, as the term *Maasai* is used, it has multiple meanings that shift depending on context. Galaty has represented this as a series of three nested triangles of three sets of contrasting identities, based on distance from a central Maasai identity. In the widest context Maasai speakers see themselves as pastoralists distinguished from other people who emphasize hunting or farming for their subsistence. Non-Maasai-speaking pastoral peoples, such as the Somali, may be considered "Maasai" in deference to their herding and are treated with special respect. At a second level, encompassing all Maasai speakers, there are specific categories based on dominant economy, such that Maasai who hunt are called *Torrobo*, those who farm are *Ilkurr-man*, and "other Maasai" herders are *Iloikop*. Thus, at this level, common descent from mythical Maasai ancestors is invoked to verify one's Maasai identity even when herding is not practiced. Closest to the center, Maasai blacksmiths are *Ilkunono*, diviners are *Iloibonok*, and ordinary herders are called *Ilomet* by the blacksmiths and diviners. Because the specific meaning of Maasai and the nine related social categories are so dependent on the context in which the terms are used, the confusion experienced by colonial-era Europeans when they attempted to elicit East African "tribal" names is understandable. They were looking for discrete, territorially based, politically organized "tribes," led by "chiefs" with whom they could sign treaties, and that they could "administer" as colonial dependencies.

Bigman Wealth and Power in Herding Societies

The crucial economic condition that makes herding societies egalitarian is that cattle, the principal economic resource, are mobile and reproducible. Whereas in Australia and Amazonia natural wealth exists as wild game and plants, in herding systems it is found in the form of movable, reproducible wealth in animals, whose care and reproduction humans control directly. Beyond their immediate subsistence uses, men and women who are acting as men use cattle as currency to store social credits and debt obligations, and in this way can expand their personal imperia, but only within limits. The striking contrast with hierarchical societies that have chiefs, governments, and social class is that tribal herders seldom exchange labor service with non-kin and do not pay tribute. Instead all production is organized within households. Men make balanced exchanges of cattle, and in this respect treat each other as equals. Herders maintain relative equality between households by "setting up wideranging, crosscutting, balancing bonds between people which keep anyone from obtaining a monopoly of wealth which can be turned to creating hierarchy."[53] Moving cattle between households also makes them available to people who need them for household consumption and thereby minimizes material poverty.

The nature of cattle in a tribal setting makes it difficult for any one person to control either the means of production (all the cattle) or to create unequal exchanges with dependent clients to concentrate coercive power within a personal imperium. Cattle are tangible wealth, or capital, and although they have the ability to multiply, they can only do so within natural, biological limits. Cattle are also mobile, which makes them vulnerable to theft and other hazards. For these and other reasons, herd size fluctuates unpredictably. This contrasts with intangible financial capital, such as dollars in account books in the commercial world that individuals can accumulate and concentrate seemingly without limit.

Individual men use cattle to establish exchange relationships with other men that extend and supersede kinship relations. Every man extends his personal imperia beyond his close circle of kin by loaning cattle to more distant kin, to affines, and to friends to whom he is otherwise unrelated. These exchanges effectively distribute cattle for people to use, so that even poor households can subsist and cattleless men can borrow bride-wealth. Anthropologists have called people who share cattle in this way "stock associates."[54] Loans of cattle are long-term deferred exchanges that carry the expectation of continuous repayment, and in this respect resemble Amazonian trading systems. Significantly, a Turkana man referred to his stock associates as "my people."[55] One particularly powerful man had 28 stock associates (3 agnates, 12 affines, and 13 friends) scattered over an area of some 4,800 square miles (12,480 km^2).

African herders are ideal capitalists in the sense that they can maximize their economic freedom, having no political rulers to regulate their economic activities. Herders enjoy an equality of opportunity that allows for wide variation in outcome but produces little extreme poverty. For example, detailed livestock figures for an Ariaal village of 38 households and 187 people in 1976 show that half (19) of the households were "rich," one-third (12) had sufficient animals, and only 18 percent (7) were "poor."[56] This reverses the social hierarchy found in the politically centralized imperial world, where there was typically only a very small wealthy elite, a small maintenance level, and the majority were poor. Calculated in TLUs (tropical livestock units) per person (see box 4.1), rich households had the equivalent of more than 9 cattle per person, and the poor had fewer than 4.5. The richest household had the equivalent of 205 cattle (22 per person) and the poorest only 2 (0.8 per person). The

richest households were often polygynous. They were also better able to survive and recover from droughts. A poor man might work as a herder for a richer man in exchange for cattle, or he might seek wage labor in towns. In the past those who were unable to herd became foragers or farmers. Men with the largest herds may be widely respected as "bigmen." Herd size is determined by a combination of a man's age, his personality, his network of kin and associates, as well as the number of fertile cows in his herd and the vagaries of fortune. A particularly successful Maasai man might have 12 wives and 60 children, suggesting a local herd of 300 cattle, but this is probably an upper limit for any man's domestic establishment.

Nuer Spirits, Symbolism, and Sacrifice

The religious beliefs of African pastoralists such as the Nuer and Maasai are primarily expressed in life cycle rituals or during crisis events, such as drought and disease, and often feature the sacrifice of animals. The cosmologies of African herders often deal with gender issues and show striking similarities with Amazonian cosmologies (see box 4.5).

The most basic distinctions in Nuer cosmology are made between Spirit and Creation, or between the immaterial and material worlds, which exist in complementary opposition.[57] When people show proper respect (thek) for these distinctions, their lives can normally be expected to go smoothly; misfortune occurs, however, when these categories intrude on each other, either in natural events or due to immoral human actions involving natural categories or human society. Failure to observe incest restrictions, for example, can bring illness. Confusion of categories causes ritual pollution, or contamination by "dirt," as "matter out of place."[58] Sacrifice and ritual can restore the previous order by mediating between the opposing principles of Spirit and Creation.

In Evans-Pritchard's[59] analysis of the Nuer concept of Spirit (his translation for the Nuer word Kwoth), he described a hierarchy of spirit manifestations ranked from high to low and with distinctions based on their location and social associations (see table 4.2). He thought that all of these different spirits were simply different "refractions" of a single unitary Spirit concept. The highest level is called God and is considered to be a pure spirit who is located in the sky and is associated with humanity in general. Genealogically, he may be referred to as father, but his involvement with human affairs is indirect. The air spirits occur at a lower level, in the atmosphere, and are represented

Table 4.2. The Nuer Concept of Spirit (Kwoth)

Spirit Type	Location	Social Association	Manifestation	Genealogy	Rank
God	Sky	Humanity	Pure spirit	Father	Aristocratic
Air spirits	Air, clouds, breezes	Political movements, raiding	Prophets	Upper: God's children Lower: God's grandchildren	
Totemic spirits	Earth	Kinship groups	Animals	Children of God's daughters	Dinka-like
Nature spirits, fetishes	Earth, underworld	Individuals	Things	Children of daughters of air spirit	Foreigners

Source: Evans-Pritchard (1953).

by charismatic religious specialists known as prophets who are thought to communicate directly with these spirits. They may help warriors prepare themselves spiritually for cattle raiding and may be instrumental in organizing relatively large-scale military expeditions. Lower-level spirits may be manifest in animals and objects and are associated with kin groups and individuals. There are many ritual specialists including earth priests, cattle priests, and grass priests, to name a few, and a wide range of curers and diviners, all of whom maintain special relationships with these spirits. According to T. O. Beidelman's[60] analysis, Nuer religious specialists demonstrate their association with Spirit by assuming the ambiguous characteristics of confused categories. Prophets have long hair and beards, wear clothing, and appear unkempt, when ordinary Nuer would be unclothed, clean-shaven, and neat. They accomplish their role as mediators between Spirit and Creation because they partake of both categories and thus are in a position to realign them. When anyone performs a ritual sacrifice, he in effect helps restore the cosmic order.

The preferred sacrificial animal is an ox (a bull, castrated at maturity), and every sacrifice is called an ox even when a sheep or goat is used. Because cattle are slaughtered only on ritual occasions and because herds are managed for maximum growth potential and milk production, it is reasonable on strictly utilitarian grounds that male animals would be sacrificed. However, oxen may be chosen for sacrifice because of their close symbolic association with men and because oxen are male animals but sterile—thus, in an ambiguous category, making them ideal mediators between Spirit and Creation. Nuer cows are equated with women. Nuer women are allocated cows from bride-wealth, and women may be named after the cows that they milk. Men have ox names and a favorite ox, which is "initiated" with cuts on its horns that duplicate the scars that young men receive at their ini-

tiations. Young men marry after their initiation, but their oxen (technically bulls until that point) are then castrated. There is a close parallel between marriage and restrained sexual morality for men and castration as moral domestication of the animal. When men are called bulls, it means that they are seen as aggressive and troublesome. Even with the ethnographic reports of high gods, priests, and prophets for cattle pastoralists, these ideological systems are essentially egalitarian. There is no codified religious system and no fraternity of religious specialists. Spirit possession is available to anyone. Individuals retain a brief identity after death in relation to cattle and children, but there is no ancestor cult. Any man can perform sacrifices, and the political roles that prophets and leopard-skin chiefs play are strictly limited. These roles do not give them control over strategic resources or allow them to extract labor or tribute. At least one especially charismatic nineteenth-century Nuer prophet gained enough influence to convince people to erect a dirt-mound pyramid shrine, but he was unable to convert it into permanent political power or an enduring ancestor cult.

BOX 4.5. TURKANA HOUSEHOLD SYMBOLISM AND COSMOLOGY

The Maasai myth of women originally owning cattle in the form of wild animals is the African equivalent of the Amazonian myth in which, in the beginning, women have culture and lose control to men. In the Maasai myth women allow their children to neglect their herds, and men take over the animals so they can claim to be the main providers for the household. This story combines the cultural ideology that men are said to "own" the cattle with the reality that women care for children and manage the household. Terms used by the Turkana to describe different aspects of the household and related symbolic associations outlined by Vigdis Broch Due[61] (2000) help to demonstrate the primacy of domestic processes and the prominent role of women in African pastoral societies. The Turkana term *ekol*, "umbilicus," conceptually denotes the household as a space belonging to a woman within the extended family compound. *Awi*, both "belly" and "paternal family," refers to the containing space of the domestic compound and represents the early phase of the domestic cycle, based on an old husband and his young wife. As the household matures and children marry, the founder's widow will become the senior household member. Each *ekol* within the compound is fenced off by a brush windbreak and contains a woman's private cooking hearth and structures for shade and sleeping. Conceptually, *ekol* also refers to her children and the animals that she cares for, as well as her descendants, or house-line.

Drinking milk, both mother's milk and cow's milk, and eating butter, blood, and meat together make people related as kin, because kinship is based on shared substance. The Turkana emphasis on maternal functions is made explicit by their reference to a cow and calf as mother and child, and a mother as a "milking cow." Like a woman, a cow founds an *ekol*, or house-line. Turkana society is biologically constructed by common blood and milk from matrifiliation, and socially by livestock, from patrifiliation, or agnatic connections. Patrilineages require the flow of livestock between men to establish paternity.

In herder cosmology, nature is wet and soft, as in Amazonia, and culture is hard and dry. Children are born soft and wet, and they dry and harden as they mature. Old people are hard and dry. The four directions—east, west, and up (north) and down (south)—also have life cycle and sexual associations as in many cultures. A woman's cow's-milk container is a prominent sexual symbol of her fertility, with its round, womblike base and phallic neck. Sexual imagery is seen in other comparisons between people and livestock. Cattle are creations of grass and water, as people are creations of semen and blood. Cooking in ceramic pots is a cultural act that makes people human, and a woman's round clay cooking pot is another prominent sexual symbol.

The Maasai Age-Class System

The Maasai pastoral system has remained viable even after years of colonial rule, cycles of drought and disease, persistent penetration by the market economy, and political control by the modern independent states of Kenya and Tanzania. African pastoralism has proved to have remarkable resilience, not only to the natural environment but also to the wider political economy surrounding it. The Maasai demonstrate that a domestic-scale culture based on subsistence herding organized at a family level can maintain a high degree of social equality and autonomy while coexisting with larger-scale social systems (see figure 4.9). The principal reason for the success of Maasai pastoralism may be the personal rewards offered by the **age-class system** common to many East African cattle peoples rather than the pervasiveness of "cattle complex values."[62]

In its ideal form Maasai pastoralism represents the extreme in subsistence dependence on herding by African cattle peoples. As described by anthropologist Paul Spencer,[63] the Maasai system depends on three critical social roles: 1) the elders, who control normal herding activities; 2) the wives, who do the milking and take care of the animals within the domestic compound; and 3) the *moran,* unmarried warriors who until recently raided for cattle. The Maasai settlement pattern resembles the Nuer pattern described previously. Family herds are managed by the male heads of households, which are ideally polygynous. A man's married sons live in the same homestead compound, with their individual corrals grouped around a common corral (see figure 4.10).

As is frequently the case with polygynous societies, women marry at a very young age, whereas men marry significantly later. This arrangement makes polygyny possible and makes it the prerogative of the older men, as in aboriginal Australia. With the Maasai surveyed by Spencer, only 16 percent of the young men ages eighteen to twenty-five years were married, and none polygynously, whereas 60 percent of the men over forty (ages forty-one to seventy years) had more than one wife. Polygyny offers direct advantages to the herd manager because it increases his labor force and allows him to subdivide responsibility for his animals.

The age-class system, with its associated rituals, helps balance the social stresses created by polygyny and patriarchy. Life stages and generation levels are marked by a series of rituals that occur throughout an individual's lifetime (see table 4.3). Step by step, pre-pubescent children are named, their heads are shaved, their lower incisors are removed, and their ears are pierced and stretched. Each ceremony indicates increasing maturity. Removal of the lower incisors, for example, means that a young boy is old enough to herd livestock near the homestead, but he does not go far afield with the animals until he is old enough to

Figure 4.9. Maasai man and woman, nineteenth century (Ratzel 1897:484).

tolerate large incisions in his ear lobes. A calf is ritually slaughtered at the first stage of adulthood, but this must occur after the father has been ritually inducted into his status as a full elder by having an ox slaughtered and after the mother has ritually completed the process of her marriage. The spacing of these two ceremonies thus marks a generation. Ceremonies surrounding initiation make the initiation process a ritual rebirth, and the initiate symbolically becomes a dependent child. Initiation itself is marked by genital mutilation—clitoridectomy for girls and circumcision for boys. Shortly after the operation, girls are led to

Table 4.3. Maasai Age Grades

Grade	Age*	Features
Senior Elder	50+	Religious and ritual power, charisma of old age assumed
Great Ox Ceremony—Precedes Son's Initiation		
Junior elders	35-50	Incest avoidance of daughters of the age class, not expected to fight, have power to curse, sponsor new age class
Olngesher Ceremony—_Moran_ Become Elders, Age Class United and Named		
Senior moran	20-35	Preparation of elderhood, may marry, meat and milk avoidance lifted
Eunoto Ceremony		
Junior moran	15-20	Wear red ochre, braid hair, dance with girls, have distinctive spears, perform ritual rebellion, form manyata warrior village, avoid meat and milk
Initiates	12-15	Age mates begin to associate, distinctive regalia
Circumcision Ceremony		
Boyhood	10-12	Earlobes cut and stretched, work as herdboys
Childhood	0-10	Naming, lower incisors removed

Source: Spencer (1965, 1988).

*Age intervals overlap because the actual age of specific individuals in a particular grade will vary widely.

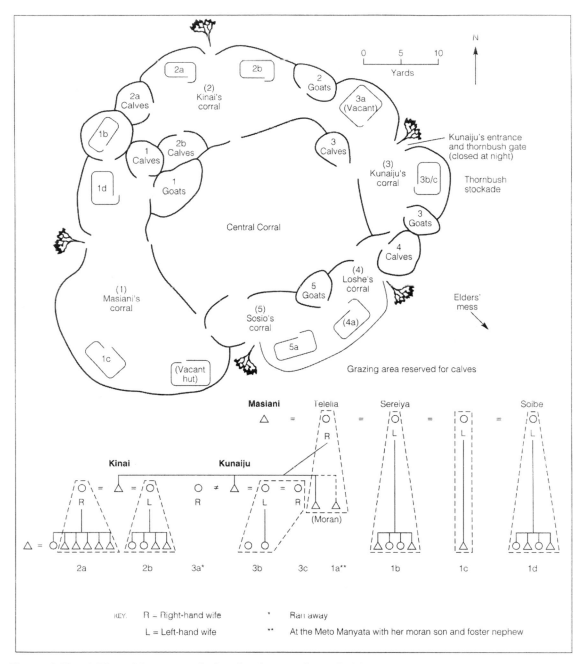

Figure 4.10. A Maasai homestead, showing houses, household composition, and livestock corals (redrafted from Spencer 1988).

their new husband's homesteads as brides, and boys move through other ceremonies that ritually separate them from their status as children and prepare them for *moran-hood*. Only males participate in the age-class system.

Age class refers to the group of people who are promoted together through the same sequence of **age grades**, or culturally designated stages.[64] Thus, for example, males of roughly the same age move as a

group sequentially through a series of subgrades from boyhood, to warriorhood (or the *moran* grade), to elderhood, and finally to retirement. Age classes are named, and the members of each class carry a distinct style of hand-forged iron spear and form a fraternity.[65]

Each tribal section independently operates its own age-class system. A new class is formed roughly every fifteen years under the sponsorship of the elders, who are two classes ahead of them, or approximately thirty years their senior, and who will serve as patrons of the new class. The recruitment period for each class is ritually closed by the elders in the class immediately senior to it. Each class is, in effect, forced up the age-grade ladder by the demands of the youths below who do not want to be the last to join a class that is about to advance. Late recruits experience a foreshortened time period in the favored warrior grade. The extended time during which a given age class can recruit means that there will be a relatively wide spread of ages within a given class; some Maasai set up junior and senior subsets within a single class, granting each different privileges and moving each subset through their own ritual stages of maturation. When the youngest subset of a class enters the grade of elderhood, the entire class assumes a single name.

The highlight of the entire age sequence is the *moran* grade, which young men enter after going through ceremonies that ritually separate them from their natal families. As *moran,* they become the warrior protectors of their communities; at the same time, however, these young men form their own egalitarian communities of age mates united by special bonds of loyalty and shared experience. Freed from domestic routines and still unmarried, the novice *moran* are expected to dress in special finery, wear their hair in braids, dance and display, and carry on with young girls. Traditionally they conducted raids to capture cattle and defended the local herds against raiders and lions. The most important privilege of the *moran* is the few years they spend in segregated warrior villages, known as *manyat* (singular, *manyata),* which are set up to defend individual districts. The *moran* flaunt their independence and live the communalistic ideals of *moran* brotherhood in their *manyat.* The supreme ideal of the *manyata* is represented by individual warriors, known as "diehards," who pledge themselves to die in combat rather than retreat (see figure 4.11).

To establish a *manyata,* the *moran* conduct raids on their parental homes and carry off their mothers and small herds of cattle, sometimes against the protests of their fathers. This is clearly a ritual rebellion against the fathers. The *manyat* villages of the *moran* are organized around egalitarian and communalistic principles in direct opposition to the age hierarchy and individualism of the domestic homestead.

The midpoint of *moran-hood* is ritually marked by an extended ceremony known as *eunoto,* which begins five years into the grade and initiates a ten-year series of steps leading to elderhood. After this ceremony, a *moran* may be expected to marry. In the *eunoto,* the *manyat* villages are disbanded, and the combined age class is formally launched. This ceremony involves a spectacular display of massed warriors that even attracts fee-paying European tourists and film crews.

Although many ceremonial phases of the Maasai age-class system incorporate ritualized rebellions against parental authority, the excesses of the *moran* are held in check, and they are guided through the maturation process by their elder patrons, who maintain ultimate control by their power to curse their charges. It could certainly be argued that the age-class system constructively channels the otherwise potentially disruptive energies of young men who grow up as subservient herdboys and must wait at least ten years before they can marry. The age system may divert the stresses that are inherent in the family system away from the senior male household heads to elders in general. In some respects, the *manyata* phase places the *moran* in a transition, or **liminal** phase.[66] It is a rite of transition in which the *moran* are ritually suspended in the space between being herdboys and elders.

The age-class system is functionally related to incest avoidance and marriage practices in a mutually reinforcing way. Spencer points out that Maasai incest restrictions are more elaborated toward daughters and mothers-in-law than mothers and sisters. This is apparently because a system of age-class exogamy operates in which the men of one age class marry the daughters of the men in the class senior to them, rather than marrying the daughters of their own age mates. The age classes thus are linked by marriage alliances, such as might operate between exogamous clans. This reinforces the respect that must be obtained between junior and senior classes if the age-class system is to survive, because the junior class members will find their fathers-in-law in the senior class. Their wives would be the daughters of forty-five- to fifty-year-old senior men, who might have married at thirty and could have fifteen- to twenty-year-old marriageable daughters. Age-class exogamy thus means that men will tend to marry much younger women, thereby creating the age differential that makes frequent polygyny possible.

The persistence of the Maasai as a society up to the present day is evidence of the importance of their age-class system. It is significant that while the population of Kenya as a whole has recently experienced extremely high increases that threaten the economic viability of the entire country, settled farming groups were growing much faster than the Maasai and other

Figure 4.11.   Maasai warriors, nineteenth century (left, Ratzel 1897:527; right, Ratzel 1897:408).

pastoralists. It is possible that the traditional Maasai practices of polygyny, postpartum taboos on sexual intercourse, and prolonged lactation, which are all linked to patriarchy and the age-class system, are significant child-spacing and fertility-dampening factors.[67]

Women do not become elders, but they clearly do have a stake in their society and work to maintain the system, especially as they grow older. Senior wives may welcome polygyny because it lightens their domestic routine (see box 4.6). Women themselves perform the clitoridectomy, and they accept it as a precondition of

marriage. Divorce is an option, especially early in an unhappy marriage. After women have children, they gain more autonomy, and because they marry young, they usually outlive their husbands. Abused wives may appeal to the elders for help; men who commit serious offenses against women may be perceived as a threat to all women; they may be assaulted and beaten and have their cattle slaughtered by a large group of enraged women acting in a publicly sanctioned role as enforcers of community morality. Women also conduct their own rituals of rebellion against male authority.

The underlying principle of male age classes is that every male enjoys the same potential to be a warrior, marry, raise a family, officiate at rituals, and so on, and these potentials are realized in orderly sequence by virtue of his membership in an age class in which these rights are jointly shared. Conflicts do arise in the system, but they occur primarily over the timing of promotions. Political struggle takes place between groups, not individuals. Political power thus is widely distributed and strictly regulated. The system is not simply a gerontocracy with power concentrated at the top.

BOX 4.6. MAASAI WOMEN

In the film *Masai Women*[68] anthropologist Melissa Llewellyn-Davies, who speaks the Maasai language and has years of research experience with the Maasai, engages several Maasai women in a free-ranging discussion about their experiences as women. In their own words, these Maasai women define and accept as a given the gender roles of their culture. Women milk cows, bear children, and build their own houses. A woman "has nothing." Women care for animals and have milking rights but no ownership rights over them. Men make the decisions about herds. Yet in this discussion with a sympathetic and knowledgeable nonnative woman, the Maasai women are quick to place their own cultural roles in a positive light. Clitoridectomy (female circumcision), which is strongly condemned by international feminists, is defended as something "we've always done." One woman explains, "It is something God began long ago. A girl wants to hurry up and be circumcised. It is a very good thing." When Llewellyn-Davies asks if the initiate is happy about the experience, she is told emphatically that she is "very happy" because the girl will then be thought of as a woman and will be able to marry soon.

Female circumcision may not be fully supported by all Maasai women, regardless of what they say about it. It may not even be a functionally irreplaceable part of their culture. In this case, women themselves may feel compelled to perpetuate customs that may not be in their best interests.

In the film, the women tell Llewellyn-Davies that although they accept arranged marriages to old men, they are not always happy about it and may select young warriors as lovers even though their husbands would be angry if they found out. When Llewellyn-Davies raises the possibility of women being jealous over young co-wives in this polygynous society, a Maasai woman declares:

We're not jealous like you Europeans. . . . To us a co-wife is something very good because there is much work to do. When it rains, the village gets mucky and it's you who clears it out. It's you who looks after the cows. You do the milking, and your husband may have very many cows. That's a lot of work. You have to milk and smear the roof and see to the calves. . . . So when you give birth and it rains, who will smear the roof if you have no co-wife? No one. Who will clear the muck from the village? No one. So Maasai aren't jealous because of all this work.

However, the film also shows women greeting new co-wives with open, "ritualized" hostility.

It is a hard life, but there are rewards. After a girl's initiation, a group of women in the film sing, "Listen God to what suits women. It suits us to prepare charms for the initiates, to be busy with our children's circumcisions, to have celebrations, which are lavish in honey beer and milk and meat and butter. It suits us when our sons go out herding. It suits us to sit resting in the shade. It suits us when we suckle children. God, nursing mother, remember what suits us."

SUMMARY

East African cattle peoples have developed a highly successful cultural system that makes effective use of a difficult environment. They have created a society in which men and women and young and old share different responsibilities for supporting and reproducing households, society, and culture. The presence of cattle and other domesticated animals makes it possible for African pastoralists to support much higher population densities and larger societies than the Australian Aborigines and Amazonian forest peoples. However, this is not always an advantage, because workloads increase and people's personal lives are more highly regulated. Like all tribal societies, there are no formal political leaders or governmental structure, and kinship remains the primary organizing principle. There are permanent villages, but herds and young men are mobile. Raiding is focused on capturing cattle rather than revenge killing of men and capturing women as in Amazonia, and young men must spend ten or more years with age mates in the status of warrior herdsmen before they can marry. The social roles of married men and women are less equitable than in aboriginal Australia and Amazonia. Women work harder than men and cannot ordinarily own and manage livestock or engage in politics, although they do have use rights to animals for subsistence purposes. Ideologically, women are in the contradictory position of being socially marginalized yet highly valued. However, women control domestic life, because they own their houses, beds, and hearths. Most importantly, women give men descendants to maintain their patrilines, and in polygynous households a man's mother is the source of his cattle inheritance.

Cattle are central to household subsistence and the primary means for men to pursue their individual self-interest beyond the household. However, their use of cattle as individually owned, movable, reproducible wealth makes it possible for more wealth differences to emerge than in other tribal societies. There are practical upper and lower limits on the size of household herds, but most households are wealthy enough in livestock to enjoy a comfortable margin to protect them from the effects of droughts, epidemics, and raids.

STUDY QUESTIONS

1. Describe the subsistence uses East African pastoralists make of their cattle.
2. What are the most critical limiting factors to which African pastoralists must adapt?
3. Why is it difficult to determine how many cattle African pastoralists actually need and to establish the carrying capacity of the range?
4. Describe the marriage process for the Nuer, including the concepts of bride-wealth, household, husband, wife, pater, and genitor.
5. How does the Maasai age-class system relate to gerontocracy and patriarchy, and how does it contribute to the resilience of Maasai society?
6. Describe the social and ritual uses of cattle in East Africa.
7. Describe the social power available to women in herding societies.
8. What conditions work to maintain social and economic equality between households in herding societies?

SUGGESTED READING

Evans-Pritchard, E. E. 1940. *The Nuer: A Description of the Modes of Livelihood and Political Institutions of a Nilotic People.* New York and Oxford, Eng.: Oxford University Press. The most famous early ethnography of East African cattle people; vividly describes their dependence on cattle, emphasizing ecological relationships.

Spencer, Paul, and Fratkin, Elliot. 1998. *Ariaal Pastoralists of Kenya: Surviving Drought and Development in Africa's Arid Lands.* Needham Heights, Massachusetts: Allyn & Bacon.

Spencer, Paul. 1988. *The Maasai of Matapato: A Study of Rituals of Rebellion.* Bloomington and Indianapolis: Indiana University Press. An excellent modern ethnography that focuses on social organization, life cycle, and ritual.

GLOSSARY TERMS

Transhumance Seasonal movements of livestock to different environmental zones often at different elevation, or latitudes.

Bride-wealth Goods, often livestock, transferred from the family of the groom to the family of the bride to legitimize the marriage and the children of the couple.

Genitor The biological father of a child.

Pater The culturally legitimate, or sociological, father of a child.

Levirate A cultural pattern in which a woman marries a brother of her deceased husband.

Bride-service The cultural expectation that a newly married husband will perform certain tasks for his in-laws.

Acephalous A political system without central authority or permanent leaders.

Filiation A parent-child relationship link used as a basis for descent-group membership.

Patrilineage A lineage based on descent traced through a line of men to a common male ancestor and sharing a joint estate.

Segmentary lineage system A tribal political system in which there are no permanent leaders, and instead individuals align with groups according to their assumed genealogical distance.

Age-class system A system in which individuals of similar age are placed in a named group and moved as a unit through the culturally defined stages of life. Specific rituals mark each change in age status.

Age grade A culturally defined stage of an age-class system such as childhood, adolescence, parenthood, and old age.

Liminal phase An ambiguous phase of ritual transition in which one is on the threshold between two states.

NOTES

1. Bourliere, François, and M. Hadley. 1983. "Present-Day Savannas: An Overview." In *Ecosystems of the World 13: Tropical Savannas,* edited by François Bourliere, pp. 1–17. New York: Elsevier.
2. Dyson-Hudson, Rada, and Neville Dyson-Hudson. 1969. "Subsistence Herding in Uganda." *Scientific American* 220(2):76–89.

3. Smith, Andrew B. 1984. "Origins of the Neolithic in the Sahara." In *From Hunters to Farmers: The Causes and Consequences of Food Production in Africa,* edited by J. Desmond Clark and Steven Brandt, pp. 84–92. Berkeley: University of California Press.

4. Ambrose, Stanley H. 1984. "The Introduction of Pastoral Adaptations to the Highlands of East Africa." In *From Hunters to Farmers: The Causes and Consequences of Food Production in Africa,* edited by J. Desmond Clark and Steven Brandt, pp. 212–39. Berkeley: University of California Press.

5. Tishkoff, Sarah A., et al. 2007. "Convergent Adaptation of Human Lactase Persistence in Africa and Europe." *Nature Genetics* 39(1):31–40.

6. McCabe, J. Terrence. 2003. "Sustainability and Livelihood Diversification among the Maasai of Northern Tanzania." *Human Organization* 62(2):100–111, 203.

7. Herskovits, Melville J. 1926. "The Cattle Complex in East Africa." *American Anthropologist* 28(l):230–72, 28(2): 361–88, 28(3):494–528, 28(4):633–64.

8. Evans-Pritchard, E. E. 1940. *The Nuer: A Description of the Modes of Livelihood and Political Institutions of a Nilotic People.* New York and Oxford, Eng.: Oxford University Press.

9. Evans-Pritchard 1940, *The Nuer,* 18–19.

10. Ocholla-Ayayo, A. B. C. 1979. "Marriage and Cattle Exchange Among the Nilotic Luo." *Paideuma* 25:173–93.

11. Evans-Pritchard 1940, *The Nuer,* 36.

12. Hardin, Garrett. 1968. "The Tragedy of the Commons." *Science* 162(3859):1243–48.

13. McCabe, J. Terrence. 1990. "Turkana Pastoralism: A Case Against the Tragedy of the Commons." *Human Ecology* 18:81–103.

14. Ruttan, Lore M., and Monique Borgerhoff Mulder. 1999. "Are East African Pastoralists Truly Conservationists?" *Current Anthropology* 40(5):621–52.

15. Homewood, K. M., and W. A. Rodgers. 1984. "Pastoralism and Conservation." *Human Ecology* 12(4):431–41.

16. McCay, Bonnie J., and James M. Acheson, eds. 1987. *The Question of the Commons: The Culture and Ecology of Communal Resources.* Tucson: University of Arizona Press.

17. McCabe, J. Terrence. 2003. "Sustainability and Livelihood Diversification among the Maasai of Northern Tanzania." *Human Organization* 62(2):100–111.

18. Kirkbride, Mary, and Richard Grahn. 2008. "Survival of the Fittest: Pastoralism and Climate Change in East Africa." Oxfam Briefing Paper 116, Oxfam International.

19. Coughenour, M. B., et al. 1985. "Energy Extraction and Use in a Nomadic Pastoral Ecosystem." *Science* 230(4726):619–25; Western, David, and Virginia Finch. 1986. "Cattle and Pastoralism: Survival and Production in Arid Lands." *Human Ecology* 14(l):77–94.

20. Little, Michael A., and George E. B. Morren Jr. 1976. *Ecology, Energetics, and Human Variability.* Dubuque, IA: Brown.

21. McCabe, J. Terrence. 2003. "Sustainability and Livelihood," 106.

22. Spencer, Paul. 1965. *The Samburu: A Study of Gerontocracy in a Nomadic Tribe.* Berkeley: University of California Press, 3.

23. Evans-Pritchard, E. E. 1951. *Kinship and Marriage Among the Nuer.* Oxford, Eng.: Oxford University Press, 96.

24. Evans-Pritchard, E. E. 1951. *Kinship and Marriage.*

25. Collier, Jane Fishburne. 1988. *Marriage and Inequality in Classless Societies.* Stanford, CA: Stanford University Press.

26. Burton, John W. 1980. "Women and Men in Marriage: Some Atuot Texts (Southern Sudan)." *Anthropos* 75:710–20.

27. Burton, John W. 1980. "Women and Men in Marriage." 717.

28. Radcliffe-Brown, A. R. 1941. "The Study of Kinship Systems." *Journal of the Royal Anthropological Institute.* (Reprinted in *Structure and Function in Primitive Society,* edited by A. R. Radcliffe-Brown, pp. 49–89. New York: Free Press, 1965.)

29. Evans-Pritchard, E. E. 1940. *The Nuer,* 139–40.

30. Gulliver, P. H. 1955. *The Family Herds: A Study of Two Pastoral Tribes in East Africa, the Jie and Turkana.* London: Routledge & Kegan Paul, 151.

31. Schneider, Harold K. 1979. *Livestock and Equality in East Africa: The Economic Basis for Social Structure.* Bloomington and London: Indiana University Press, 111.

32. Holtzman, Jon. 2002. "Politics and Gastropolitics: Gender and the Power of Food in Two African Pastoralist Societies." *JRAI* 8(2):259–78.

33. Hodgson, Dorothy L., ed. 2000. "Introduction" In Hodgson, Dorothy L., ed., *Rethinking Pastoralism in Africa: Gender, Culture and the Myth of the Patriarchal Pastoralist,* pp. 1–28. Oxford: James Currey; Athens, OH: Ohio University Press.

34. Rosaldo, Michelle Zimbalist, and Louise Lamphere, eds. 1974. *Woman, Culture, and Society.* Stanford, CA: Stanford University Press.

35. Ortner, Sherry B. 1996. *Making Gender: The Politics and Erotics of Culture.* Boston: Beacon Press, 142.

36. Collier, Jane Fishburne. *Marriage and Inequality in Classless Societies.* Stanford, CA: Stanford University Press.

37. Fratkin, Elliot. 1989. "Household Variation and Gender Inequality in Ariaal Pastoral Production: Results of a Stratified Time-Allocation Survey." *American Anthropologist* 91(2): 430–40.

38. Evans-Pritchard. 1940, *The Nuer.*

39. Verdon, Michel. 1982. "Where Have All Their Lineages Gone? Cattle and Descent Among the Nuer." *American Anthropologist* 84(3):566–79.

40. Sahlins, Marshall. 1965. "On the Ideology and Composition of Descent Groups." *Man* 65 (July/August):104–7.

41. Kuper, Adam. 1982. "Lineage Theory: A Critical Retrospect." *Annual Review of Anthropology* 11:71–95.

42. Verdon, Michel. 1982. "Where Have All Their Lineages Gone?"

43. Southall, Aidan. 1976. "Nuer and Dinka Are People: Ecology, Ethnicity and Logical Possibility." *Man* 11:463–91.

44. Sahlins, Marshall. 1961. "The Segmentary Lineage: An Organization of Predatory Expansion." *American Anthropologist* 63(2, pt. l):322–45.

45. Evans-Pritchard. 1940, *The Nuer*, 41.

46. Evans-Pritchard. 1940, *The Nuer*.

47. Gluckman, Max. 1956. *Custom and Conflict in Africa*. New York: Barnes & Noble.

48. Evans-Pritchard 1940. *The Nuer*.

49. Southall, Aidan. 1976. "Nuer and Dinka Are People."

50. Burton, John W. 1981. "Ethnicity on the Hoof: On the Economics of Nuer Identity." *Ethnology* 20(2):157–62, 157.

51. Burton, John W. 1981. "Ethnicity on the Hoof." 160, 161.

52. Galaty, John G. 1982. "Being 'Maasai'; Being 'People-of-Cattle': Ethnic Shifters in East Africa." *American Ethnologist* 9(1):1–20.

53. Schneider, Harold K. 1979. *Livestock and Equality*, 193.

54. Gulliver, P. H. 1955. *The Family Herds*; Schneider, Harold K. 1979. *Livestock and Equality*, 192–203.

55. Gulliver, P. H. 1955. *The Family Herds*, 198.

56. Fratkin, Elliot, and Eric Abella Roth. 1990. "Drought and Economic Differentiation Among Ariaal Pastoralists of Kenya." *Human Ecology* 18(4):385 402.

57. Beidelman, T. O. 1966. "The Ox and Nuer Sacrifice: Some Freudian Hypotheses About Nuer Symbolism." *Man* 1(4): 453–67; Beidelman, T. O. 1971. "Nuer Priest and Prophets: Charisma, Authority, and Power Among the Nuer." In T. O. Beidelman, ed., *The Translation of Culture: Essays to E. E. Evans-Pritchard*, pp. 375–415. London: Tavistock.

58. Douglas, Mary. 1966. *Purity and Danger: An Analysis of Concepts of Pollution and Taboo*. New York: Praeger, 35.

59. Evans-Pritchard, E. E. 1953. "The Nuer Conception of Spirit in Its Relation to the Social Order." *American Anthropologist* 55(2, pt. 1):201–14.

60. Beidelman, T. O. 1966. "The Ox and Nuer Sacrifice"; "Nuer Priest and Prophets."

61. Broch-Due, Vigdis. 2000. "The Fertility of Houses and Herds: Producing Kinship and Gender among Turkana Pastoralists." In Hodgson, Dorothy L., ed., *Rethinking Pastoralism in Africa: Gender, Culture and the Myth of the Patriarchal Pastoralist*, pp. 165–85. Oxford: James Currey; Athens, OH: Ohio University Press.

62. Spencer, Paul. 1988. *The Maasai of Matapato: A Study of Rituals of Rebellion*. Bloomington and Indianapolis: Indiana University Press.

63. This section is based largely on Spencer, Paul. 1988. *The Maasai of Matapato*.

64. Bernardi, Bernardo. 1985. *Age Class Systems: Social Institutions and Polities Based on Age*. Cambridge, Eng.: Cambridge University Press.

65. Larick, Roy. 1986. "Age Grading and Ethnicity in the Style of Loikop (Samburu) Spears." *World Archaeology* 18(2):269–83.

66. Gennep, Arnold L. van. 1909. *Les Rites de Passage*. Paris: E. Nourry.

67. Sindiga, Isaac. 1987. "Fertility Control and Population Growth Among the Maasai." *Human Ecology* 15(l):53–66.

68. *Masai* [sic] *Women—the Masai of Kenya*. 1974. Researcher and anthropologist Melissa Llewellyn-Davies; producer and director, Chris Curling. Disappearing World Series. Granada Television International. Chicago: Films Incorporated.

CHAPTER 5

Cross-Cultural Perspectives on the Tribal World

Figure 5.0. Tribal world culture trait distribution map.

LEARNING OBJECTIVES

AFTER STUDYING THIS CHAPTER YOU SHOULD BE ABLE TO DO the following:

1. Explain the difficulties involved in determining whether or not there are differences in the cognitive abilities of peoples in different cultures.

2. Describe the range of cultural diversity in subsistence, social organization, and religious belief and practice in the tribal world, drawing contrasts with imperial and commercial worlds.

3. Evaluate the hypothesis that tribal peoples live in a different and unique perceptual world.

4. Explain how shamanism and other beliefs and practices related to the supernatural may benefit individuals.
5. Evaluate the quality of life experienced by people in the tribal world, making specific comparisons with people in the commercial world.

Perhaps the most striking reality about the tribal world in comparison with other cultural worlds is that the tribal sociocultural system functioned in a way that reduced the potential for growth in scale by minimizing the possibility that aggrandizing individuals could transform themselves from leaders into rulers. Given this general pattern, the tribal world was characterized by tremendous cultural diversity in social, ideological, and material features. There are especially conspicuous differences in cultural beliefs and practices related to the supernatural.

SOCIOCULTURAL GROWTH AND THE SCALE OF CULTURE

The enormous differences in the distribution of social power in each of the three cultural worlds suggest that the great transformations of the tribal world into the imperial world, and the imperial world into the commercial world, were **elite-directed growth** processes in which particular individuals intentionally made self-interested decisions that changed the scale of society, wealth, and power. These transformations can be called elite-directed because the outcome was so inequitable. Growth in scale concentrated social power in a few hands, whereas the majority paid the costs, effectively subsidizing the growth process. The significance of this interpretation is that these great cultural transformations were neither natural nor inevitable. They were humanly directed. Elites apparently took advantage of crisis events to persuade people that it would be in their best interests to give them more power. It is possible that if the majority had a clearer understanding of the cultural and physical realities of their world, they could take democratic control over cultural development and create a world that distributed costs and benefits more equitably, more humanely, and more sustainably, especially in times of crisis. The crucial problem is thus what people know, and that is why control over the cultural superstructure is so important.

Social Power and Growth Trajectories

Each cultural system of social power produces a different growth trajectory and scale of culture and a distinctive distribution of social power and household living standards. When any sociocultural system grows larger, it can be expected to undergo organizational and technological changes simply because it is larger. The quality of everyday life and human relationships will necessarily change. Most people will have less control over their daily affairs; new, more powerful leaders will emerge; and the familiarity characteristic of village life in the tribal world will disappear. Direct participatory democracy is impossible in a large nation. Likewise, when every household cannot be self-sufficient, production systems must become larger, more energy intensive, and more centralized. When households lose control over production, they may have more difficulty meeting their basic material needs, and poverty may emerge.

Ethnographic analysis reveals that as societies adopt larger-scale power systems, order-of-magnitude differences appear in the quantity and concentration of social power as measured on various socioeconomic dimensions. As the case studies in the previous chapters demonstrated for the tribal world, when social power is organized exclusively at the domestic level, the largest politically autonomous social unit seldom exceeds five hundred people. But when power is centralized and politically organized as in imperial world societies, power becomes dominant and millions of people can be politically integrated into a single system. Likewise, maximum household wealth, measured by the number of people the richest household could support in a year, can be millions of times greater in commercially organized societies than in domestically organized tribal societies, where wealth is not typically accumulated. Differences of this magnitude, and the cultural changes that make them possible, are so striking that cultures that organize power differently have come to constitute distinctly different worlds.

Scale differences have such an important effect on the distribution of social power that it is helpful to refer to cultures in the tribal world as **domestic scale**, in the imperial world as **political scale**, and in the commercial world as **commercial scale**. Recognizing the scale distinctions highlights the reality that growth concentrates power.

Sociocultural growth, and accompanying changes in the scale of culture, has been neither a steady nor a totally predictable process. The anthropological record shows a very long, relatively stable era, from approximately 100,000 to 8,000 years ago, when all societies were organized as domestic-scale, tribal cultures. During this phase of cultural development, humanity spread in great migrations around the globe and diversified into thousands of ethnolinguistic groups adapted to innumerable local ecosystems. They lived exclusively in small-scale, self-sufficient local and regional societies based initially on mobile foraging and later on sedentary village life (see figure 5.1). All the major domestic technologies, including ceramics, textiles, farming, and herding, were invented and disseminated during this time. These technologies uniformly improved the quality of daily life, because they were equally available to every household. Regional populations remained small, and densities were low. Limits were established by the optimum size of households and kinship groups and by the population density that local ecosystems and domestic technologies could sustain, as will be discussed in the following chapters.

Politicization and Commercialization versus the Tribal World

Under the influence of the politicization process, which began perhaps 8,000 years ago, chiefdoms, small agrarian kingdoms, and then larger political empires emerged wherever more energy-intensive production systems could be developed and populations enlarged (see figure 5.2). Global population peaked and then receded as various empires proved unsustainable. Tribal sociocultural systems remained the dominant societies in more than half of the world until after 1500, when major European colonial expansion began.

Cultural changes associated with the commercialization process, beginning about AD 1400, led to increased economic activity culminating in a new wave of technological development that permitted faster and larger-scale production and distribution systems. World population rapidly soared, but this growth and cultural change caused enormous social upheaval and widespread impoverishment. Resource consumption rates grew rapidly, but dramatic improvements in living standards did not become widespread in the industrialized nations until the 1950s. Influenced by the bustling money economy and the use of cheap fossil fuels, growth accelerated exponentially, unfettered by cultural limits.

The emergence of commercial-scale cultures is a challenging anthropological problem, because it creates a world that is so different from both tribal and imperial worlds. In comparison with the relatively static conditions in the tribal world, socioeconomic growth in both imperial and commercial worlds is difficult to explain because the immediate benefits are so unevenly distributed and growth creates obvious new burdens such as taxes, wars, insecurity, and dependency. It is thus not surprising that tribal peoples have consistently resisted imperial and commercial intrusions. Significantly, even in the twenty-first-century autonomous tribal peoples still choose to live in "voluntary isolation" from the commercial world.

Throughout this book, we will examine the possibility that cultural developments, as measured by population growth and increased economic indicators, are caused not by popular demand but by individual power seekers striving to increase their immediate personal power. Elites can attain more power only by having more people to control and more economic resources to exploit, and this necessarily requires growth. Elites may gain the power to direct culture change in their own short-term interests. However, they cannot predict the long-term consequences of their actions, nor can they necessarily control the events that they set in motion, including the counterforces of popular social movements led by disaffected people.

The diverse selection of world cultures presented in the following chapters will allow us to test the hypothesis that socioeconomic growth is an elite-directed process that concentrates social power in direct proportion to increases in culture scale. This hypothesis runs counter to the conventional understanding of how economic growth works in the contemporary world: Everyone supposedly benefits from growth, and growth supposedly is natural and inevitable. If the power-elite hypothesis proves correct, then larger-scale cultural systems should have more concentrated social power, and people may be disproportionately impoverished and disempowered by certain growth processes. This analysis raises important questions about the relative benefits of different cultural systems, and it can provide an informed basis for the argument that growth itself may be the biggest human problem and that development without growth may be a solution.

TRIBAL CULTURAL DIVERSITY

The sociocultural systems of the tribal world exhibit perhaps the greatest cultural diversity in human experience. Eight thousand years ago during the Neolithic period and before the imperially organized societies became important regional influences, there may have been as many as 16,000 languages and ethnic groups in the world. This assumes a global population in 8000 BP of 8 million people and language tribes of five hundred people, as in aboriginal Australia. We have defined "culture" in the singular as what people think, make,

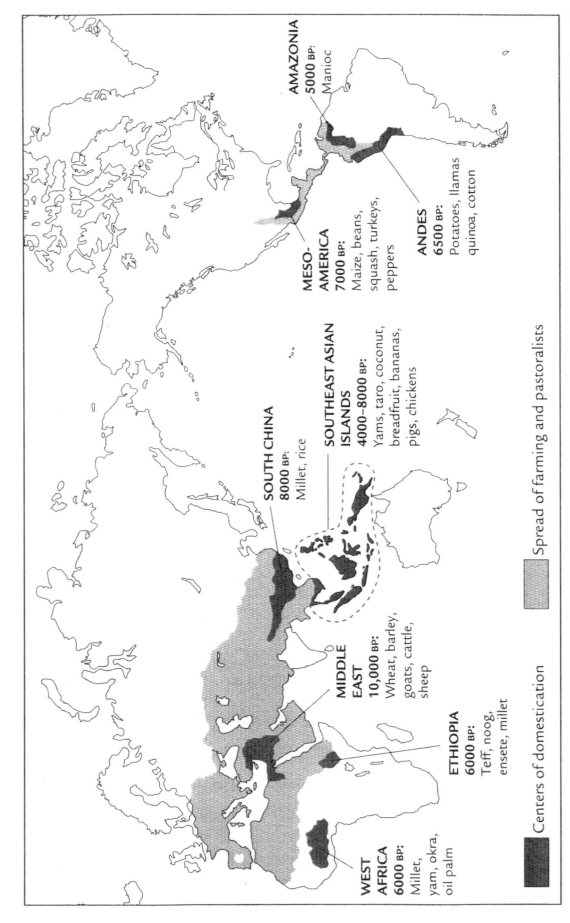

Figure 5.1. The world of tribal villagers, showing independent centers of plant and animal domestication and the areas where farming or pastoralism had spread by approximately 5000 BP.

AMAZONIA
5000 BP:
Manioc

MESO-
AMERICA
7000 BP:
Maize, beans,
squash, turkeys,
peppers

ANDES
6500 BP:
Potatoes, llamas
quinoa, cotton

SOUTH CHINA
8000 BP:
Millet, rice

SOUTHEAST ASIAN
ISLANDS
4000–8000 BP:
Yams, taro, coconut,
breadfruit, bananas,
pigs, chickens

MIDDLE
EAST
10,000 BP:
Wheat, barley,
goats, cattle,
sheep

ETHIOPIA
6000 BP:
Teff, noog,
ensete, millet

WEST
AFRICA
6000 BP:
Millet,
yam, okra,
oil palm

Centers of domestication

Spread of farming and pastoralists

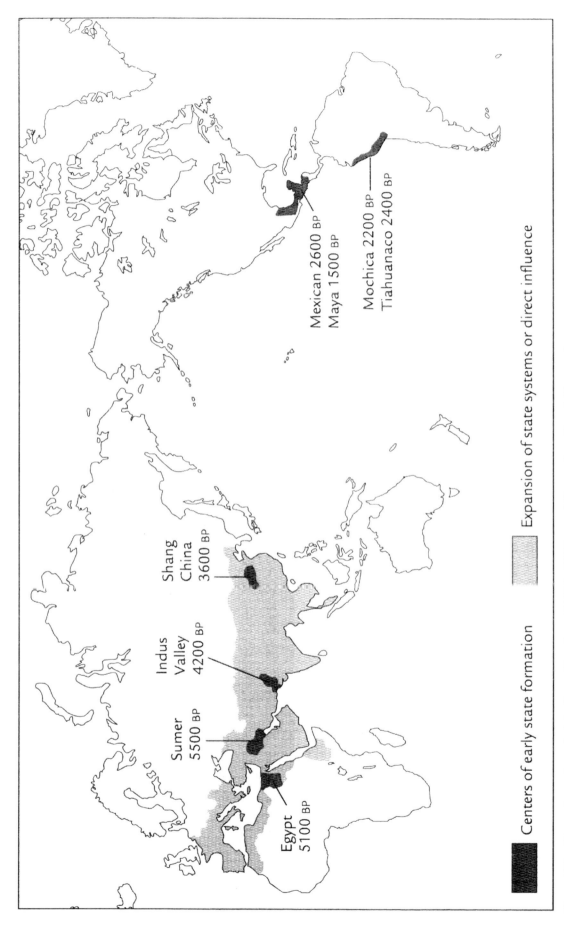

Figure 5.2. **Six early centers of state formation from 5500 to 1500 BP and the regions they influenced.**

Centers of early state formation

Expansion of state systems or direct influence

Sumer 5500 BP

Egypt 5100 BP

Indus Valley 4200 BP

Shang China 3600 BP

Mexican 2600 BP
Maya 1500 BP

Mochica 2200 BP
Tiahuanaco 2400 BP

and do as members of society, but "cultures" and "societies" are notoriously slippery concepts because as entities they are fictions that people imagine. A *culture* as an object of anthropological research can be defined to include the group of people who produce and maintain the culture, speak a common language, and occupy a common territory.

HRAF and the Ethnographic Atlas

The definitive list of reasonably well-known world cultures was published by distinguished ethnographer George Peter Murdock in his 1962 *Ethnographic Atlas*, which originally cataloged 862 cultures and has now been expanded to include 1,276 societies, or cultures (see figure 5.3).[1] This is, of course, still only a partial sample of all the world's historically known cultures, which may be nearly 4,000.[2] Known cultures are only a tiny fraction of all the cultures that may have ever existed, considering that even at the end of the Neolithic period the global population of 85 million people could have had as many as 170,000 tribes of 500 people, and recognizing that cultures evolve over time.

British ethnographers began listing cultural features, or variables, in 1871 in work pioneered by Edward B. Tylor.[3] The *Atlas* was an outgrowth of Murdock's earlier work on the *Human Relations Area Files* (HRAF), a compilation of source materials on the world's best-known cultures selected from the hundreds in the *Outline of World Cultures*.[4] Cultures included in HRAF are indexed according to the *Outline of Cultural Materials*, a numbered list of some 88 cultural categories and 700 subcategories. For example, nine subcategories are listed under the major category Kinship (which is coded as number 600): 601, Kinship terminology; 602, Kin relationships; 603 Grandparents and grandchildren; 604 Avuncular and nepotic relatives; 605 Cousins; 606 Parents-in-law and children-in-law; 607 Siblings-in-law; 608 Artificial kin relationships; and 609 Behavior toward nonrelatives. Finer distinctions in cultural categories can, of course, be made. For example, in the 1930s American ethnographers cataloged the distribution of 1,094 cultural "elements" among California Indians.[5]

Many cultural anthropologists use the term *seme* to describe shared cultural units, practices, or *schemas* as the basic units of culture for cross-cultural comparison and for studying cultural evolution. Zoologist Richard Dawkins introduced the term *memes* as a minimal cultural unit to emphasize the analogy between genes and culture. As of 2007, the HRAF files contained well-documented ethnographic material on 344 cultures,

and 165 of these were available online to students of member institutions.[6] The *Atlas* is a more complete summary in tabular form of a sample of about a hundred cultural variables for each of 1,276 cultures. Murdock selected a Standard Cross-Cultural Sample (SCCS) of 186 cultures to be statistically representative of the universe of known cultures, and this sample has been used widely for cross-cultural research.[7] In designing his SCCS, Murdock distinguished 412 clusters of cultures presumed to be linguistically related within at least 1,000 years, and he arbitrarily grouped cultures into six world regions: Sub-Saharan Africa, Circum-Mediterranean, East Eurasia, Insular Pacific, North America, and South and Central America. Over the years various cultural areas have been identified for different parts of the world to take into account historical relationships between peoples, cultures, and the environment.

There is also an *Outline of Archaeological Traditions* (OAT) incorporated in Peter Peregrine's *Atlas of Cultural Evolution*,[8] in which cultures are viewed in a much larger archaeoethnological framework. An archaeological tradition is defined as "*a group of populations sharing similar subsistence practices, technology, and forms of socio-political organization, which are spatially contiguous over a relatively large area and which endure temporally for a relatively long period* [italics original]."[9] Archaeological traditions typically last for many centuries. The OAT listed 289 *traditions* in 2001 and included all prehistoric traditions known worldwide. These archaeological traditions would in theory be the precursors of the culture clusters that Murdock identified and form a bridge between prehistoric archaeology and historic ethnography. The ten cultural variables currently listed for each tradition in the OAT include subsistence, settlement, technological patterns, and sociopolitical organization, which are useful measures of social scale and cultural complexity. Preliminary analysis of these data arranged in time series shows that overall cultural complexity, social scale, and technology have generally increased over millennia. Understanding the causes of these long-term cultural trends, how they affect people, and what the future might hold is a primary goal of cultural anthropology.

Explanatory Models:
Diffusion, Adaptation, and Migration

One of the most important insights of early-twentieth-century anthropology was Radcliffe-Brown (1881–1955) and Malinowski's (1884–1942) conclusion

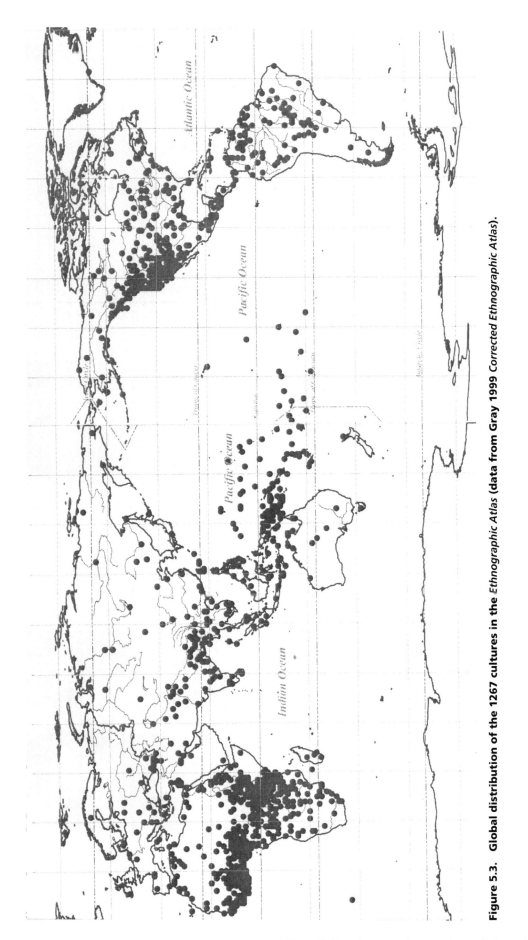

Figure 5.3. Global distribution of the 1267 cultures in the *Ethnographic Atlas* (data from Gray 1999 *Corrected Ethnographic Atlas*).

that human societies and cultures could be viewed metaphorically as biological organisms with organs or structures with their corresponding functions.[10] This means that cultures are not random collections of beliefs and behaviors, but that the parts of culture are likely to fit together to form a sociocultural system that functions to satisfy the needs of individuals for subsistence and reproduction, as well as the secondary needs of maintaining and reproducing culture itself.[11] It is very helpful to understand how cultural things fit together, but explanation of how particular traits originated and how they came to fit together remains problematic because there are often many different ways that particular needs can be satisfied. Functionalist analysis can not by itself explain where the pieces of culture came from originally.

Cultural anthropologists have long disputed whether the material conditions of a society or the ideas in people's heads have been primary in shaping culture. Prominent materialists such as Leslie White (1900–1975) and Marvin Harris (1927–2001) ranked the components of sociocultural systems into three levels that Harris labeled material infrastructure, social structure, and ideological superstructure (see table 1.3). They proposed that material conditions produced the social structure, which in turn shaped ideology. This perspective makes adaptation to the physical environment the most important cultural process, and it is similar to a biocultural evolutionary perspective that links cultural patterns to individual reproductive success, or inclusive fitness. Others, such as Claude Levi-Strauss, Marshall Sahlins, and Clifford Geertz (1926–2006) have focused on the cultural meanings encoded in symbols, myth, and ritual that exist in people's minds as the primary influences on culture. We will necessarily draw on all of these perspectives in this book. However, several cross-cultural studies have shown that kinship and social organization seem to be the most conservative, least diffused, and least adaptive of cultural traits and are most likely to show internal functional connections.

The most promising approaches to cultural explanation are those that take material, social organizational, and ideological features fully into account. Near the end of his career, which had focused on political economy (Harris's structure) as the most important dimension of culture, anthropologist Eric Wolf compared three cultures—the Kwakiutl, small tribal chiefdoms of the Pacific Northwest; the imperial world Aztecs of Mesoamerica; and Nazi Germany in the commercial world—to examine how political

elites used culture and ideology to legitimize their power.[12] He showed how elites shape and use worldviews embedded in culture for their own purposes. Given the propensity of individuals to use deception to influence the perception of other people to achieve their personal objectives, it is reasonable to assume that power is decisively situated in the cultural beliefs, myths, rituals, and symbols people use as tools to influence the behavior of others.

In addition to the cultural processes of humanization, politicization, and commercialization that are the focus of the scale and power perspective used in this book, anthropologists use three cultural processes to explain the development of cultural diversity, or the origin of particular cultural elements: (1) diffusion or borrowing from other cultures; (2) adaptation to local environment; and (3) migration of people and culture.[13] These processes are interrelated and not always mutually exclusive, but all involve human decision making and may be subject to elite direction.

It seems useful to speak of cultural evolution as changes in the frequency of *semes* in particular ethnic populations, just as in biological evolution caused by changes in gene frequencies in biological populations due to natural selection, genetic drift, and mutation. Cultural ideas and practices necessarily change over time and space like biological species and genes, but unlike genes, culture can be transmitted by various means, including most routinely by vertical transmission from parents to children or by social pressure on group members. Language is also often vertically transmitted together with genes, because people are most likely to marry people who speak the same language. Family and kinship patterns also reflect vertical transmission, are less shaped by environment or diffusion from neighboring peoples, and are likely to be carried by peoples as they migrate.[14] Vertical transmission is conservative and inhibits culture change, whereas horizontal transmission between unrelated persons or from an elite person to many others can produce rapid cultural change.[15] Horizontal and elite-directed cultural transmission give people the ability to adapt quickly to changes in the social and natural environment and must have greatly facilitated the spread of humans across the world.

The Tribal World in Prehistory and the Ethnographic Atlas

There is complete enough information on 289 archaeological traditions in the *Atlas of Cultural Evolution* and the 926 cultures in the *Ethnographic Atlas* to unambiguously sort each tradition and culture into tribal and imperial worlds using just two unambiguous social scale measures: (1) level of political centralization beyond the local community, local autonomy, chiefdoms, or states; and (2) population size of the local community to distinguish small tribal world chiefdoms from large imperial world chiefdoms. Combined, these two measures identify the scale of the largest politically autonomous society in each prehistoric tradition or ethnographic culture. Archaeological traditions composed of politically autonomous local communities, or small chiefdoms with the largest community having fewer than four hundred people, are assigned to the tribal world. All other prehistoric traditions are placed in the imperial world. All ethnographically known cultures with local community autonomy and any organized as small chiefdoms with mean community size under 5,000 are in the tribal world.[16] Figure 5.4 shows where the 852 tribal world societies described in the *Ethnographic Atlas* are distributed in the world, disregarding distinctions between fully egalitarian tribal societies from tribal chiefdoms that show some social rank distinctions.

What is most interesting is that both prehistoric and ethnographic cultures show almost totally nonoverlapping profiles on several important measures of social inequality. Tribal world prehistoric traditions and ethnographic cultures are highly egalitarian and are unlikely to have money, metal, wealth distinctions, economic elites, social classes, or hereditary aristocrats. Imperial world societies are by definition all elite-directed, whereas tribal world societies are more likely to be directed by consensus decision making. Expanding imperial societies sometimes invaded tribal territories and turned tribal peoples into ethnic peasants or landless serfs, but few tribal societies opted to centralize power except in self-defense.

When the 289 prehistoric archaeological traditions in the *Atlas of Cultural Evolution* are ranked by political complexity and sorted into tribal and imperial worlds, the two cultural worlds show strikingly different social class profiles. In this sorting the 115 traditions classified as politically autonomous and the 102 organized as small chiefdoms, with the largest settlement under 400 persons, are placed in the tribal world (see table 5.1). This leaves fifteen large chiefdoms and fifty-seven states that are assigned to the imperial world. These 289 traditions are then sorted by three variables measuring the degree of their social class distinctions as they appear in the archaeological record: (1) egalitarian traditions with no apparent rank distinctions; (2) two social classes; (3) three or more social classes; and by two additional indirect indicators of class distinctions reflecting intensified exchange systems and technological specialization: (4) money; and (5) metal. When all the occurrences of each of these five variables in the 289 traditions are graphed by percentage for each cultural world, it is apparent that tribal and imperial world archaeological traditions are largely nonoverlapping (see figure 5.5). Tribal world traditions are conspicuously egalitarian, and the few that show class distinctions are small chiefdoms recognizing only two social ranks, typically nobles and commoners. Three levels are rare in tribal world archaeological traditions, as are money and metalworking.

The distribution of important social rank and stratification variables among Tribal and Imperial ethnographic societies described in the *Ethnographic Atlas* likewise shows that Tribal and Imperial worlds are indeed sharply distinct sociocultural worlds. They are different worlds on cultural dimensions that have major impacts on people's daily lives. The *Atlas* has full information on 891 societies according to five social rank and class variables: (1) egalitarian societies with no class distinctions; (2) wealth distinctions between individuals based on property, but no distinct social classes; (3) elite stratification into two superior and inferior classes based on unequal access to property; (4) aristocracy based on inherited rank, title, and property; and (5) complex social classes, with occupational statuses, wealth, and rank distinctions. When these societies are sorted into tribal and imperial worlds (see table 5.2) and they are graphed by the percent of societies with each type of social distinction (see figure 5.6), it is apparent that just as in the prehistoric traditions in the ethnographic record, there is little overlap between the two worlds. The occurrence of slavery among 864 societies sorted by cultural world also shows a distinctly different social profile for the two worlds. Slavery is completely absent in more than 60 percent of tribal societies, but it is a significant presence in nearly 40 percent of imperial world societies (see figure 5.7).

Measuring Complexity

The utility of the Tribal-Imperial distinction is further demonstrated by the distinct cultural complexity profiles that emerge when the 289 prehistoric traditions are sorted by tribal and imperial worlds to display their average rankings on ten complexity dimensions.[17] Imperial world traditions average sig-

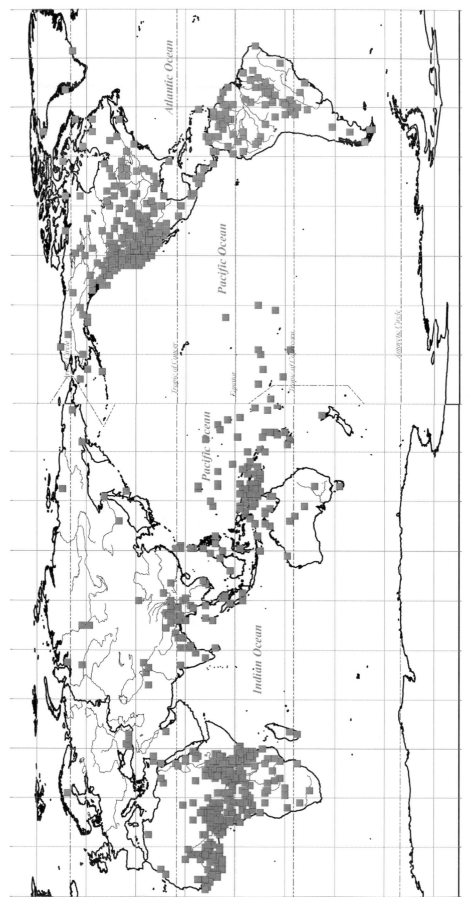

Figure 5.4. Global distribution of the 852 tribal world societies in the *Ethnographic Atlas* (data from Gray 1999 *Corrected Ethnographic Atlas*).

Table 5.1.   Social Class Distinctions in 289 Archaeological Traditions by Political Complexity and Cultural World

	Political Complexity	Direct Measures of Social Class			Additional Indicators		Total for Direct Measures
		Egalitarian	Two Classes	Three + Classes	Money	Metal	
Tribal World	Autonomous	115	0	0	0	2	115
	Small Chiefdoms	21	68	13	16	16	102
	Tribal Totals	*136*	*68*	*13*	*16*	*18*	*217*
Imperial World	Large Chiefdoms	0	14	1	1	6	15
	States	0	0	57	25	53	57
	Imperial Totals	*0*	*14*	*58*	*26*	*59*	*72*
Grand Totals		*136*	*82*	*71*	*42*	*77*	*289*

nificantly higher than tribal world traditions on all complexity measures: use of writing; fixity and compactness of settlement; dependence on agriculture; degree of urbanization; technological specialization; form of transportation; use of money; population density; political integration; and social stratification. Likewise, the 926 best-known ethnographic cultures can be ranked by five complexity measures used in the *Ethnographic Atlas* (settlement pattern; social class; metallurgy; agricultural intensity; and importance of high gods), where the rankings range from 0 to 9 and the higher score represented higher complexity. This ranking also reveals distinct profiles for each cultural world (see figure 5.8).

Complexity rankings provide a general measure of the scale differences between societies and cultures. We can expect more complex societies to have more concentrated social power as well as more possibilities for elite direction, but they may not be "better" societies in regard to the humanization process, hu-

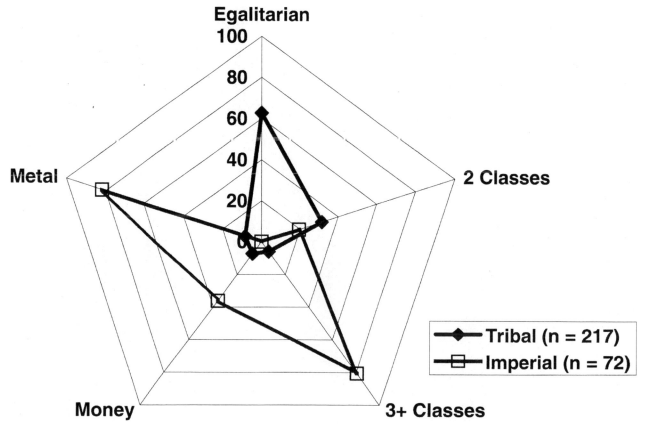

Figure 5.5.   Social class distinctions in 289 archaeological traditions by cultural world, by percentage of societies (data from Peregrine 2003 *Atlas of Cultural Evolution*).

Table 5.2. Social Class Distinctions in 891 Ethnographic Societies by Political Complexity and Cultural World

	Political Complexity	Egalitarian	Wealth Distinctions	Economic Elite	Hereditary Aristocracy	Economic Classes	Totals
Tribal World	Autonomous Tribal	359	119	4	34	0	516
	Tribal Chiefdoms	54	36	3	26	4	123
	Tribal Totals	*413*	*155*	*7*	*60*	*4*	*639*
Imperial World	Chiefdoms	20	20	14	79	12	145
	Small States	3	4	5	32	36	80
	Large States	0	1	1	4	21	27
	Imperial Totals	*23*	*25*	*20*	*115*	*69*	*252*
Grand Total		**436**	**180**	**27**	**175**	**73**	**891**

man well-being generally, or sociocultural system sustainability. Complexity rankings are not the same as the evolutionary stages of Savagery, Barbarism, and Civilization proposed by nineteenth-century anthropologists such as Lewis Henry Morgan and Edward B. Tylor, because complexity need not mean "progress" in the sense of human good, and increasing complexity is not assumed to be inevitable.

South American Cultural Complexity: Asháninka, Shipibo, and Inca

It will be helpful to look more closely at complexity using a few specific cultures in one part of the world. For example, there is a very strong relationship between the size of local community, jurisdictional hierarchy, and cultural world for all eighty-two South American societies in the *Ethnographic Atlas*. Where complete information is available, most South American societies (fifty-one of fifty-three) are tribal world, including all societies with average local communities smaller than four hundred people, and three that ranged in size from four hundred to 1,000 (see table 5.3). There were only two tribal chiefdoms in the sample. What is remarkable is that even these three societies with somewhat larger local communities were still tribally organized. The Andean Chibcha

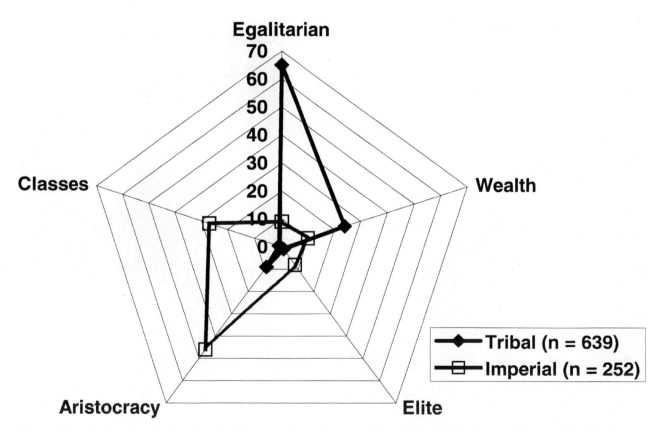

Figure 5.6. Social class distinctions in tribal and imperial worlds for 891 societies in the *Ethnographic Atlas*, by percentage of societies (data from Gray 1999 *Corrected Ethnographic Atlas* and Peregrine 2003 *Atlas of Cultural Evolution*).

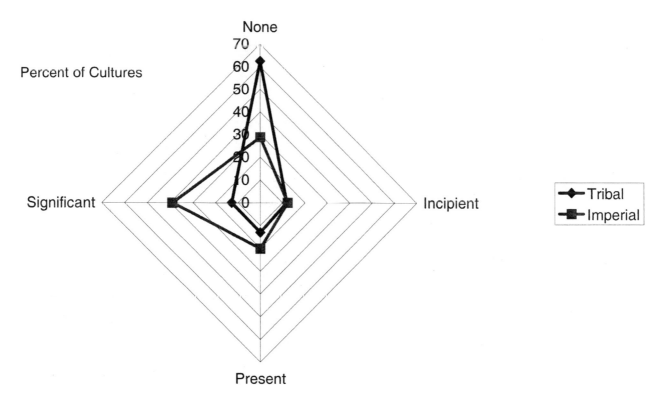

Figure 5.7. The occurrence of slavery among 864 societies in the *Ethnographic Atlas* by cultural world (data from Gray 1999 *Corrected Ethnographic Atlas*).

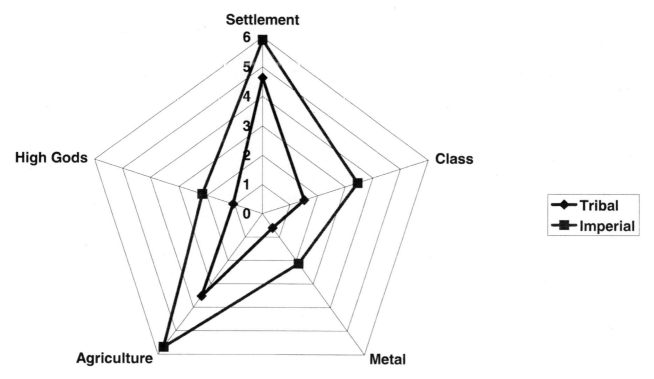

Figure 5.8. Average complexity rankings for 926 ethnographic societies.

Table 5.3. Mean Size of Local Community and Jurisdictional Hierarchy for 82 South American Societies

Mean Community Size	Jurisdictional Hierarchy				
	Tribal World		Imperial World		
	Tribal	Tribal Chief	Large Chief	State	**Totals**
Under 400	46	2	0	0	**48**
400+	3	0	1	1	**5**
Totals	49	2	1	1	**53**

large imperial world chiefdom and Inca state societies had one or more settlement in the 5,000 to 50,000 size range. Tribal societies in South America show a wide range of subsistence intensification, whereas imperial world societies are exclusively the most intensive irrigated farming systems that maximize production in arid environments. The correlation between irrigated agriculture and the imperial world societies in South America suggests a causal connection, implying that irrigation increases scale and complexity. However, this does not explain the origin of irrigation, and there are examples from other parts of the world of tribal societies with irrigation. What matters is not the technology by itself, but how it is organized and how the benefits are distributed.

It is also important to add an archaeological perspective to our view of South American cultural complexity. Approximately the first 6,000 years of South American prehistory was entirely in the tribal world, and the first 5,000 years was predominantly hunting, gathering, shellfish collecting, and foraging. Imperial world large chiefdoms and states only gained a foothold in a narrow Andean coastal band about 6,000 years ago. Large states expanded into the Andean highlands, but lasted barely 2,000 years, whereas tribal

societies remained and persisted everywhere on the continent until Europeans arrived in about AD 1500. Fully self-sufficient tribal societies are still found in wilderness refuges where the commercial world has barely penetrated.

Cultural complexity differences can be more meaningfully understood by comparing just three adjacent South American cultures that are treated in detail in chapters 2 and 7—the Asháninka, the Shipibo, and the Inca. This analysis follows the somewhat more elaborate methods that Murdock used for measuring cultural complexity for one of his research projects.[18] Rather than five, Murdock used ten variables that he assumed to be related to complexity: writing and records; fixity of residence; agriculture; urbanization; technological specialization; land transport; money; population density; level of political integration; and social stratification. He examined a sample of 186 cultures from all over the world, assigning each a complexity rating of 0 to 4, from simplest to most complex. Rankings on each variable were then totaled to produce a final complexity level for each culture. This analysis showed 116 societies ranked as low and lower middle with values of 19 or below and corresponding in general to tribal world. The remaining

Table 5.4. Asháninka Cultural Complexity Rating 8

Scale	0	1	2	3	4
Writing	**None**	Tallies	Quipus	Writing	Written records
Residence	Nomadic	Semi-nomadic	Semi-sedentary	**Sedentary, impermanent**	Sedentary, permanent
Agriculture	None	<10% of food	>10%, but not dominant	**Dominant, but extensive**	Dominant, intensive
Urbanization	**<100 persons**	100–199	200–399	400–999	1,000+
Specialization	None	Pottery	**Weaving**	Smiths	Smiths, weavers, potters
Transport	**Human**	Pack animals	Draft animals	Wheeled	Mechanized
Money	**Barter**	Exchange Media	Imported money	Tokens	Currency
Density/Miles2	**<1 Persons**	1–5	5.1–25	26–100	100+
Political	**No central authority**	Local Political communities	1 supra-local level	2 levels	3+ levels
Stratification	**Classless**	Wealth-based status, slavery	Nobles and commoners	2 Classes, +slaves or castes	3+ Classes

Note: Boldface type represents complexity rating for each scale trait.

Table 5.5. Shipibo-Conibo Cultural Complexity Rating 15

Scale	0	1	2	3	4
Writing	**None**	Tallies	Quipus	Writing	Written records
Residence	Nomadic	Semi-nomadic	Semi-sedentary	Sedentary, impermanent	**Sedentary, permanent**
Agriculture	None	<10% of food	>10%, but not dominant	**Dominant, but extensive**	Dominant, intensive
Urbanization	<100 persons	100–199	200–399	400–999	1,000+
Specialization	None	Pottery	**Weaving**	Smiths	Smiths, weavers, potters
Transport	**Human**	Pack animals	Draft animals	Wheeled	Mechanized
Money	**Barter**	Exchange Media	Imported money	Tokens	Currency
Density/Miles2	<1 Persons	1–5	5.1–25	26–100	100+
Political	No central authority	**Local Political communities**	1 supra-local level	2 levels	3+ levels
Stratification	**Classless**	Wealth-based status, slavery	Nobles and commoners	2 Classes, +slaves or castes	3+ Classes

Note: Boldface type represents complexity rating for each scale trait.

70 cultures were upper middle and high complexity. Individual cultures that may rank at the same overall level of complexity may vary widely in their rankings on specific variables, but the general rankings correspond fairly closely with Robert Carneiro's evolutionary sequence of cultural development, which is discussed in chapter 7.

Using Murdock's method, the Asháninka, Shipibo, and Inca ranked 8, 15, and 26 respectively (see tables 5.4–5.6). The Asháninka are in the low complexity ranking of zero on seven of the ten categories. They lacked writing; had settlements of fewer than one hundred persons; had no pack animals, draft animals, or wheeled or mechanized vehicles; their population density was low; and they had barter exchange, no central political authority, and no social stratification. They received a 2 for loom weaving and 3 for sedentary but impermanent settlements, and for the importance

of extensive agriculture, or gardening. The Shipibo are lower middle complexity, showing greater complexity because their villages are larger and more permanent, their population density is higher, and they have local political communities. These differences are reflected in their more intense village life and rituals. The Inca are Upper Middle complexity, ranking at the top in five categories: residence, agriculture, specialization, political complexity, and social stratification. They also had the quipu, bundles of knotted yarn, as a writing equivalent and pack animals for transportation. They do not rank in the highest complexity category overall, where a maximum score of 40 is possible, because they had neither markets nor a formal media of exchange, and most of their population lived in villages rather than cities. This is why the Inca Empire can be considered to be an elite-constructed imperial state imposed on top of a vast territory occupied

Table 5.6. Inca Cultural Complexity Rating 20

Scale	0	1	2	3	4
Writing	None	Tallies	Quipus	Writing	Written records
Residence	Nomadic	Semi-nomadic	Semi-sedentary	Sedentary, impermanent	**Sedentary, permanent**
Agriculture	None	<10% of food	>10%, but not dominant	Dominant, but extensive	**Dominant, intensive**
Urbanization	<100 persons	**100–199**	200–399	400–999	1,000+
Specialization	None	Pottery	Weaving	Smiths	**Smiths, weavers, potters**
Transport	Human	**Pack animals**	Draft animals	Wheeled	Mechanized
Money	**Barter**	Exchange Media	Imported money	Tokens	Currency
Density/Miles2	<1 Persons	1–5	5.1–25	26–100	100+
Political	No central authority	Local Political communities	1 supra-local level	2 levels	**3+ levels**
Stratification	Classless	Wealth-based status, slavery	Nobles and commoners	2 Classes, +slaves or castes	**3+ Classes**

Note: Boldface type represents complexity rating for each scale trait.

by basically self-sufficient "tribal" communities. The archaeological and the historical ethnographic material on Andean cultures in chapter 7 will show how the greater complexity of the Inca had a significant impact on daily lives of ordinary people. The benefits of this added complexity were especially visible in the ostentatious and luxurious lifestyles of the Inca elite.

Rank and Hierarchy in Amazonia: Comparing Forty-Eight Tribes

Cultural complexity is primarily about the construction of hierarchy by power-seeking individuals. To increase their personal power leaders must lead larger and culturally more complex societies. A comparative look at Amazonian societies shows a wide variation in cultural variables that relate to the potential for constructing hierarchy. Data compiled by Swedish anthropologist Alf Hornborg[19] on twelve variables related to hierarchy and external relations for forty-eight Amazonian societies show the great diversity of these tribal societies, as well as the ability of the majority in these societies to prevent their leaders from becoming rulers by transforming any of these tribal societies into imperial world societies. These societies are scattered throughout the Amazon Basin and surrounding areas as shown in the map in figure 5.9, which includes the Shipibo-Conibo and Asháninka. The key identifies the language family and the commonly used name for each culture.

Statistical analysis for seven rank-related variables and four external relations variables for a subsample of forty societies where full data was available revealed that only a few hierarchy variables were strongly interconnected and could potentially become the basis for a village headman leader to turn himself into a chiefly ruler. For example, the presence of special great names, a birth order hierarchy, and rank endogamy, in which person only married within their rank, were closely interconnected. Achieved status was associated with trade. A hierarchy of leaders was associated with societies that were integrated with neighboring societies, rather than isolated or hostile. A wife-taker hierarchy was strongly associated with aggressive external relations. The Asháninka-Matsigenka had three rank variables: rank endogamy, achieved status, and a hierarchy of leaders, and their external relations were integrated by trade and marriage with neighbors (see figure 5.10). In comparison, the most hierarchical society, the Tukano-speaking Cubeo of the Vaupes region of the Colombian Amazon, had six of the seven rank and hierarchy variables but were still not even

considered to be a small chiefdom. Three-fourths of these societies had fewer than four hierarchy traits. Amazonian peoples seemed firmly opposed to allowing their leaders to become rulers.

Tribal World Subsistence Systems

The cross-cultural data on tribal world societies in the *Ethnographic Atlas* show how representative the Asháninka-Matsigenka, Australian Aborigines, and the East African cattle peoples that we have examined are of tribal peoples generally (see figure 5.11). The most striking aspect of tribal world subsistence is that it is most likely to be on the lower end of the intensification scale. Subsistence intensification is the amount of energy that people must put into their food production per unit of territory, either in human labor, the energy of domestic animals, or other forms of energy such as wind, water power, or fuels. For most tribal societies only human energy is applied in food production, and relatively high levels of leisure can be enjoyed. This works because tribal societies are all domestically organized production systems in which each household produces primarily for itself and for sharing with immediate kin. As the detailed ethnographic material in previous chapters demonstrated, there was no incentive in the tribal world for increasing food production beyond basic needs, and no "surplus" production was extracted by political rulers. Any surplus production was normally not harvested, and thus it was available as a strategic reserve in the event of any unforeseen emergency.

About a third of the tribal societies in the *Atlas* depended primarily on gathering, hunting, and fishing. This is a powerful reminder of the direct importance of nature in the tribal world and demonstrates the viability of allowing nature to maintain the primary job of food production. The *Atlas* lists 272 "forager" or "hunter-gatherer" societies that were neither cultivators nor pastoralists, but of course many more nonagriculturalists were ethnographically described. A recent exhaustive survey lists 339 well-documented hunter-gatherer societies in the world, most of which are either no longer existing or living traditionally.[20] Western and northern North America and Australia are where ethnographically described foragers were concentrated, and where foraging continues to be an important cultural activity for many indigenous peoples. Foraging is typically a very land-extensive production system, often with a relatively low average return in kilocalories for each kilocalorie of human effort expended. This works as long as population

No.	Language	Culture	No.	Language	Culture
1	Ge	Kraho	26	Tupi	Tupinamba
2	Ge	Ramkokamekra	27	Tupi	Siriono
3	Ge	Krikati	28	Pano	Amahuaca
4	Ge	Apinaye	29	Pano	Mayoruna
5	Ge	Kayapo	30	Pano	Sharanahua
6	Ge	Suya	31	Pano	Cashinahua
7	Ge	Shavante	32	Tukano	Cubeo
8	Ge	Sherente	33	Tukano	Barasana
9	Ge	Caingang	34	Tukano	Bara
10	Ge	Bororo	35	Tukano	Makuna
11	Ge	Karaja	36	Yanoama	Yanomamo
12	Ge	Nambikwara	37	Yanoama	Yanomamo
13	Arawak	Matsigenka	38	Yanoama	Sanuma
14	Arawak	Mehinacu	39	Jivaroan	Jivaro
15	Carib	Trio	40	Jivaroan	Achua
16	Carib	Kalapalo	41	Jivaroan	Aguaruna
17	Carib	Kuikuru	42	Other	Piaroa
18	Carib	Karinya	43	Other	Witoto
19	Carib	Barama River	44	Other	Bora
20	Carib	Pemon	45	Other	Trumai
21	Carib	Waiwai	46	Other	Warao
22	Carib	Txicao	47	Other	Kadiweu
23	Tupi	Tapirape	48	Other	Cuiva
24	Tupi	Mundurucu	49	Pano	Shipibo-Conibo
25	Tupi	Tupi-Cawahib	50	Arawak	Asháninka

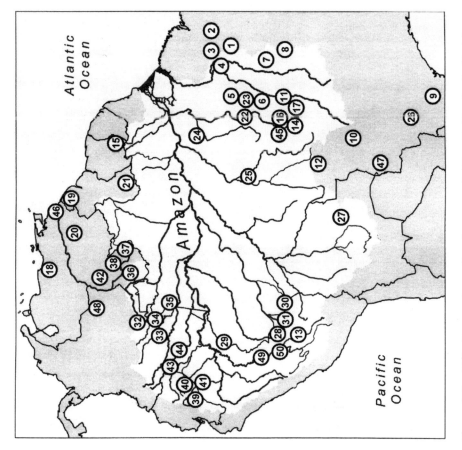

Figure 5.9. Fifty Amazonian cultural groups. A. Map; B. Key (redrafted from Hornborg 1988).

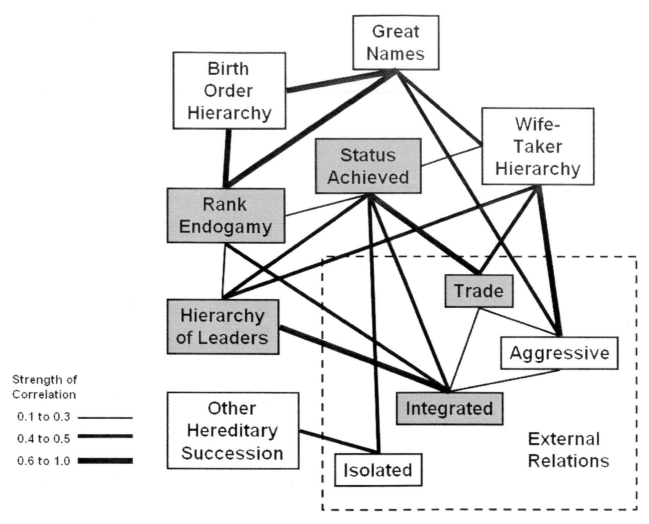

Figure 5.10. Asháninka-Matsigenka hierarchy and external relations traits (data from Hornborg 1988).

remains low and demand is limited to the family. Foragers typically take very little of the total biological product within their territories. For example, my estimates for central desert Aborigines suggests that a tribe of 560 people living as traditional foragers at a density of 0.01 persons per square kilometer would take only about 0.01 percent of the natural biological product of their desert environment. Because each desert Aborigine would draw subsistence from more than 80 square kilometers of territory, the energy input per hectare remains very low. Their ecological footprint would be only about 0.08 global equivalent hectares per capita. Foragers living in richer environments would have higher population density, but their impact on the environment would likely remain small.

Shifting cultivation is the most common subsistence activity in the tribal world and is represented by more than 40 percent of the tribal societies in the *Atlas.* This suggests that it is a sustainable production system. Tribal shifting cultivators are most common in sub-Saharan Africa, Southeast Asia, Melanesia, and Amazonia. They are gardeners who rely on root crops, seed crops, and tree crops as a source of carbohydrates. They use axes and fire to clear the forest and plant with digging sticks and machetes. They obtain their protein from fish and game, or from domestic poultry, or from small livestock such as pigs. Shifting cultivators are typically low-density village peoples living in extensive forested areas. Taking the Asháninka as representative shifting cultivators using a 25-year forest fallow rotation, their energy input per hectare in their gardening is more than 1,000 kilocalories per hectare, compared with only 24 for Aborigines. This is obviously a more intensive form of subsistence. It also supports a denser population and more permanent settlement. However, as noted in chapter 2, the

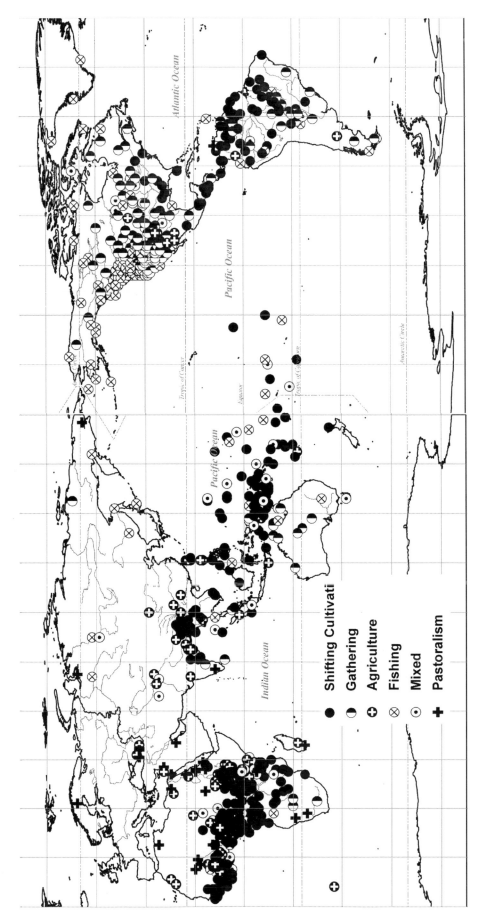

Figure 5.11. Tribal world subsistence (data from Gray 1999 *Corrected Ethnographic Atlas*).

ecological footprint of the Asháninka exceeds 1 global hectare per capita, which is much higher than for desert Aborigines, but because their population density is still low, the Asháninka use only 0.24 percent of the natural biological product of their territory.

The crucial point is that most tribes, whether foragers or shifting cultivators, are on the low end of the subsistence intensification continuum. This helps to keep their ecological footprints small. The adoption of food production techniques more intensive than shifting cultivation means that more energy must be applied per unit of land. Hoes, rather than digging sticks, must be used to work the soil when fallow periods are shortened and the cultivated area is allowed to regrow only as weedy bush or grass rather than forest. Many African tribal cultivators and Melanesians use hoes and short fallow periods. Energy input/output efficiencies may be lower with hoe cultivation, meaning more work is required, but less land is needed, so productivity per hectare rises significantly. At the same time the impact on the local ecosystem increases and local and regional anthropogenically modified ecosystems may be produced. Only about 14 percent of tribal societies are more intensive agriculturalists who combine livestock with their crop production and who may use intensive cropping techniques such as plows, irrigation, or fertilizer. In contrast, about half of imperial world societies base their subsistence on intensive agriculture.

Relatively few tribal pastoralists are included in the *Atlas*, only 36 out of 842. This is because pastoralists are likely to become politically centralized societies and would thus be considered to be in the imperial world. Nearly half of the 69 pastoral societies in the *Atlas* are imperial world societies. As discussed in chapter 4, large livestock such as cattle are a form of movable and reproducible property that seems to make social inequality more difficult to maintain. Many tribal societies have either cattle (235) or sheep and goats (130) as their primary animal domesticate, but most of these societies are not full-time pastoralists (see figure 5.12). Pigs are the next most frequent domesticate (99). Livestock support higher population densities than foragers in similar arid environments. They also require extra labor, and that is an incentive for raising larger families. The higher pastoral populations and their domestic animals mean that pastoralists take a significantly higher proportion of the biological product of their territories than either aboriginal foragers or Amazonian shifting cultivators.

Diversity of Marriage, Family, and Kinship

Somewhat fewer than half (45 percent) of tribal societies, especially in Africa, Asia, and Melanesia, are organized by patrilineal kinship groups, whereas somewhat more than a third, like the Asháninka, most Amazonian societies, and many North American tribals, are bilateral. Patrilineal societies can be expected to recognize clans and lineages as corporate groups (see figure 5.13). Patrilineal societies are more likely to occur where men want to transmit property such as rights to land or territory, titles, cultural knowledge, or movable property such as livestock to their sons. This means that foragers or shifting cultivators often do not have clans or lineages, because they do not need them. Matrilineal tribal societies are relatively rare (14 percent) and are most likely to occur with societies where women are gardeners and control access to land or where mother-daughter women's task groups are especially important.

In the imperial world about two-thirds of societies are patrilineal, fewer than one-fourth are bilateral, and only 12 percent are matrilineal. The priority of patrilineal kinship in the imperial world reflects the importance of inherited wealth and property, political positions, ranks, and titles. There is also an obvious association between these variables and intensive agriculture, which in turn sustains the higher densities and larger total populations that are defining features of imperial world societies.

Most tribal societies (88 percent) allow polygyny (see figure 5.14), and nearly two-thirds allow cousin marriage, which is normally between individuals categorized as cross-cousins (see figure 5.15). The Asháninka are fairly typical tribal societies in these respects. Polygyny is allowed in 85 percent of the 1,231 societies combining tribal and imperial world societies in the *Ethnographic Atlas* where form of marriage is known. This means people in most societies find polygyny acceptable, but it is rarely the dominant form of marriage in any society, because it is hard and sometimes costly to arrange, depending on what constitutes wealth and how it is distributed in particular societies. The most striking difference in how marriage exchanges are arranged between tribal and imperial world societies is that dowry exchanges, in which goods move from the bride's to her new husband's family, are very rare in the tribal world but fairly common (13 percent) in imperial world societies (see figure 5.16). Bride-wealth exchanges, where the husband's family gives property to the wife's family, occurs in more than half of tribal marriages and is

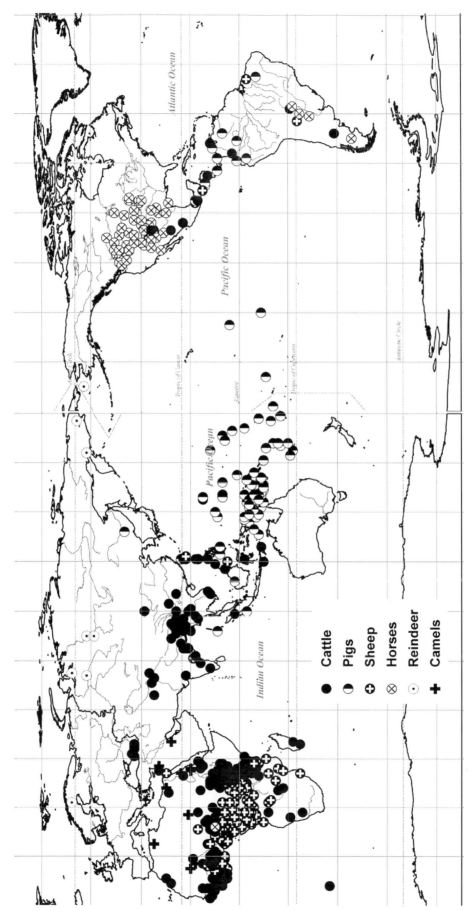

Figure 5.12. Domestic animals in tribal world societies (data from Gray 1999 *Corrected Ethnographic Atlas*).

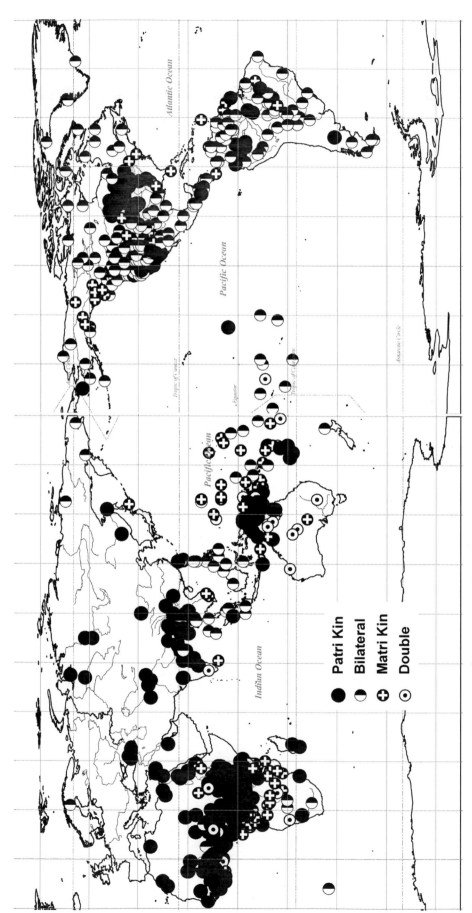

Figure 5.13. Kinship groups in tribal societies (data from Gray 1999 *Corrected Ethnographic Atlas*).

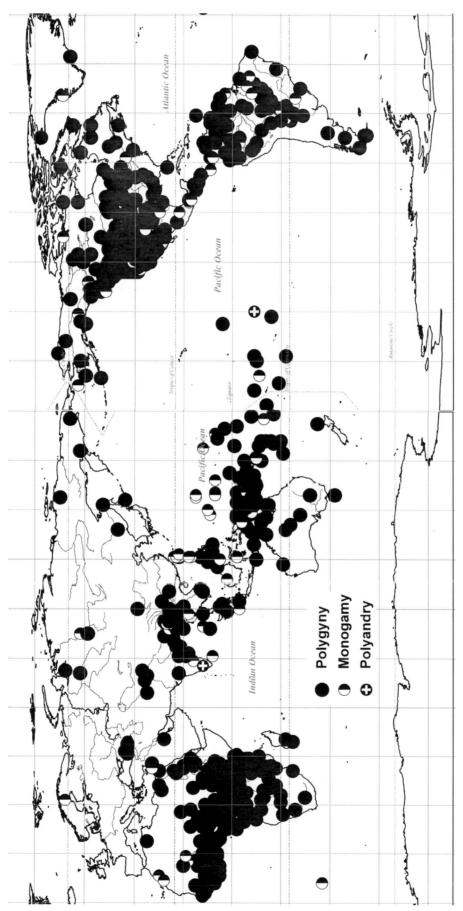

Figure 5.14. Forms of marriage in tribal societies (data from Gray 1999 *Corrected Ethnographic Atlas*).

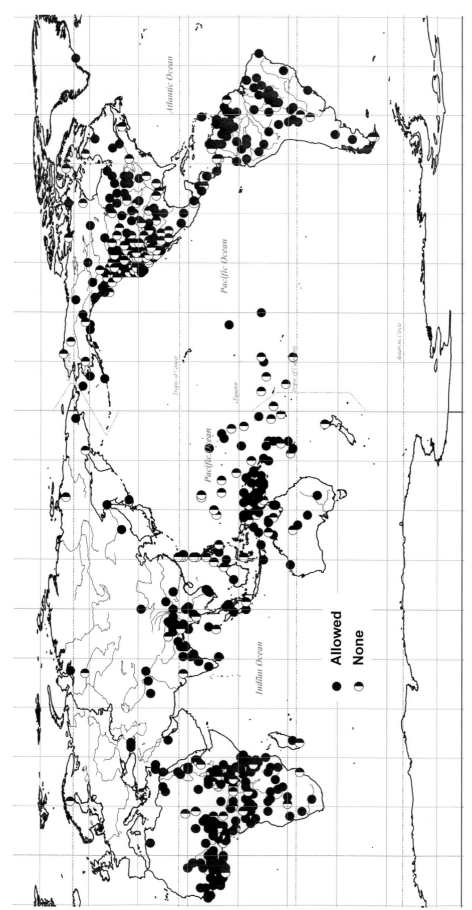

Figure 5.15. Cousin marriage in tribal societies (data from Gray 1999 *Corrected Ethnographic Atlas*).

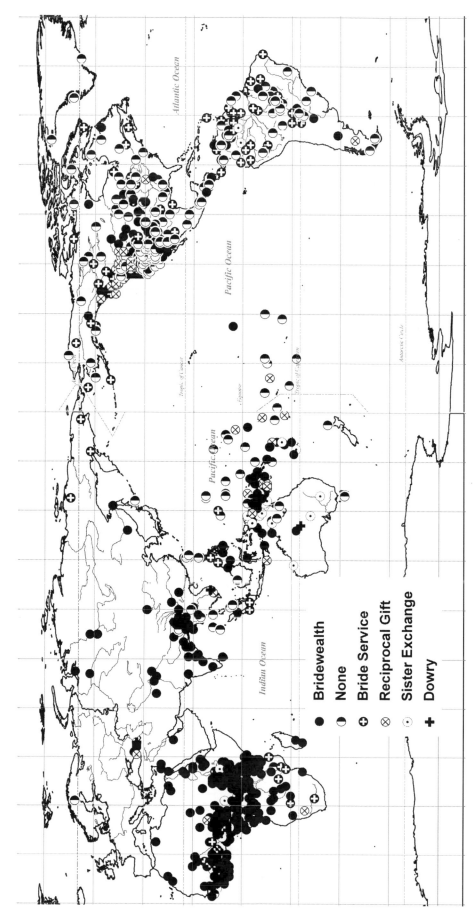

Figure 5.16. Forms of marriage exchange in tribal societies (data from Gray 1999 Corrected *Ethnographic Atlas*).

Bridewealth

None

Bride Service

Reciprocal Gift

Sister Exchange

Dowry

almost as common in the imperial world (46 percent). Bride-service, where a young man works for his wife's family, and sister-exchange marriages, where two men marry each other's sisters—both of which occur with the Asháninka—are more common in the tribal world (16 percent) than in the imperial world (11 percent). This difference can again be attributed to the relative unimportance of movable property in the tribal world.

The Shipibo kinship terminological system, Hawaiian, in which all cousins and siblings are placed in the same category, is the most common system in both the tribal (40 percent) and imperial worlds (28 percent) (see figure 5.17). The Asháninka system, Iroquois, which makes siblings and parallel cousins family and parallel cousins affines, is the second most common system in both tribal (29 percent) and imperial (25 percent) worlds. The Maasai system, called Omaha, places ego's mother's patrilineal kin in a special category because of the importance of patrilineages in bride-wealth exchanges. Omaha is the third most common system in the tribal world (9 percent), followed by Crow and Eskimo systems (7 percent each). Crow systems, which distinguish ego's father's matrilineal kin, are the mirror opposite of Crow, reflecting the importance of matrilineages. Eskimo terminologies are similar to the system used by English speakers and separate all cousins from siblings.

Where a newly married couple resides relative to their parents after they marry is an important clue to the overall social organization, because it reflects the importance of the parents as well as the relative importance of side of the family. In both tribal and imperial worlds residence is predominantly patrilocal (71 percent) (see figure 5.18). In the tribal world patrilocality may be preferred when men want to remain within familiar hunting territories, or when it is important for fathers, sons, and brothers to cooperate in defense. The greater importance of family and close kin in the tribal world is seen in the virtual nonexistence of **neolocal residence** (1 percent), where a newly married couple resides independently of either set of parents. Neolocality occurs in 12 percent of imperial world societies and is very common in the commercial world, were employment often takes a new couple away from family. Other kin-related residence patterns are common in the tribal world, such as matrilocality (15 percent), which is practiced by the Shipibo; **ambilocality** (10 percent), where a couple resides near one set of parents or the other depending on circumstances; and **avunculocality** (5 percent), where a new

couple resides with the husband's mother's brother in matrilineal societies.

There is a clear trend for economic considerations to be associated with particular residence patterns and for residence patterns to in turn be associated with descent group organization, which correlates with marriage practices and kinship terminologies.[21] These cultural practices are all functionally interconnected in predictable ways, but the societies also change, and at any particular moment the different kinship and social organization elements may not be in perfect harmony. Nevertheless, patterns can be discerned, and the system usually makes sense.

The Trobriand Islanders:
Threshold of the Imperial World

The Trobriand Islanders of Papua New Guinea are one of the best-known tribal societies in the anthropological world thanks to the ethnographies of Bronislaw Malinowski[22] based on his extensive fieldwork from 1914 to 1920 and the work of many ethnographers who came later.[23] Following my scale and power classification, the Trobrianders are a tribal chiefdom, but they are perched on the threshold of the imperial world. The *Ethnographic Atlas* categorizes the Trobrianders as petty chiefdoms, with "compact and relatively permanent settlements" averaging only 100 to 199 people, or even as a "minimal state," because the total population of the society is in the 1,500 to 10,000 range and there is a paramount chief. There is one level of jurisdictional hierarchy beyond the local community, and the class structure is described as "Elite stratification, in which an elite class derives its superior status from, and perpetuates it through, control over scarce resources, particularly land, and is thereby differentiated from a property-less proletariat or serf class."[24] When the Trobrianders are fitted into Murdock's complexity ranking, their score of 17 is only slightly more complex than the Shipibo's 15, placing them well within the lower middle tribal world level (see table 5.7).

Trobriand is an interesting case in several respects. It is a good example of a matrilineal society where subsistence is based on gardening supported by fishing, much as in Micronesia. In this case matriliny follows from gardening, where both men and women work together, and no large livestock, plows, or irrigation works are involved. Residence is avunculocal. Upon marriage a man leaves his natal household and moves to the community where his mother's brother lives.

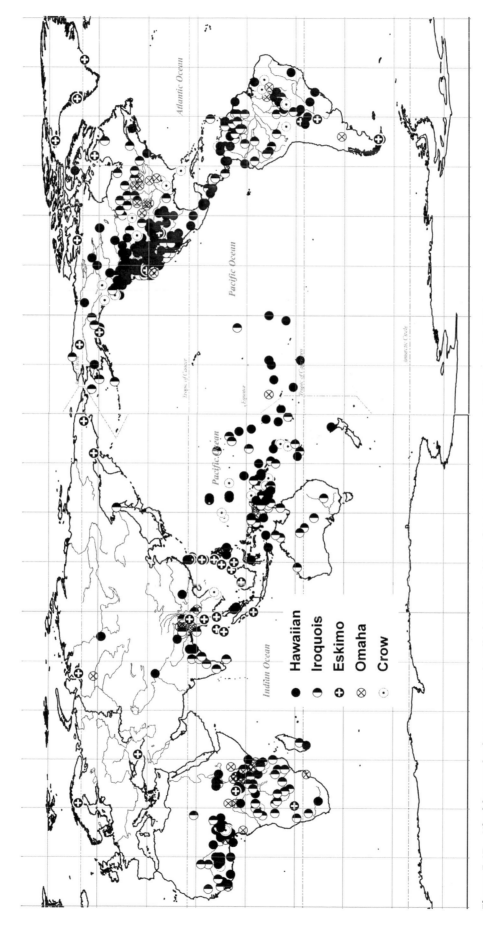

Figure 5.17. Kinship terminology systems in tribal societies (data from Gray 1999 *Corrected Ethnographic Atlas*).

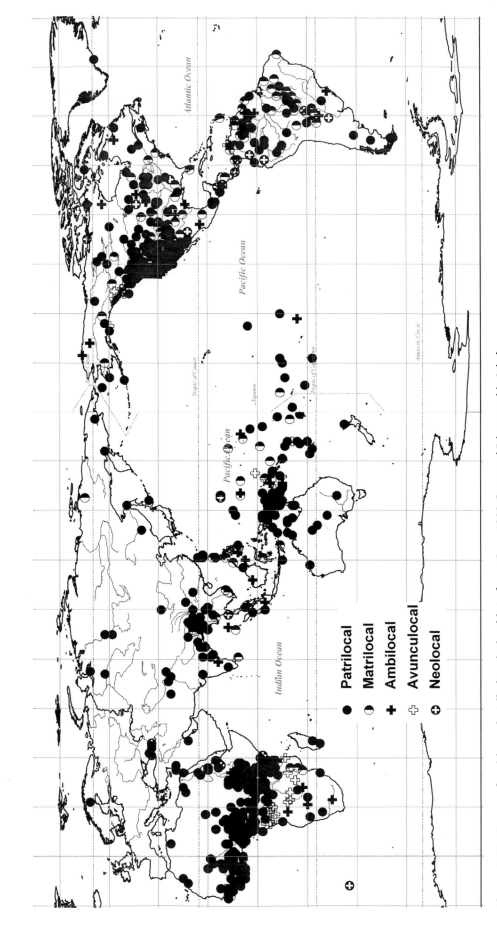

Figure 5.18. Forms of residence in tribal societies (data from Gray 1999 *Corrected Ethnographic Atlas*).

Patrilocal

Matrilocal

Ambilocal

Avunculocal

Neolocal

Table 5.7. Trobriand Cultural Complexity Rating 17

Scale	0	1	2	3	4
Writing	**None**	Tallies	Quipus	Writing	Written records
Residence	Nomadic	Semi-nomadic	Semi-sedentary	Sedentary, impermanent	**Sedentary, permanent**
Agriculture	None	<10% of food	>10%, but not dominant	Dominant, but extensive	**Dominant, intensive**
Urbanization	<100 persons	100–199	**200–399**	400–999	1,000+
Specialization	**None**	Pottery	Weaving	Smiths	Smiths, weavers, potters
Transport	**Human**	Pack animals	Draft animals	Wheeled	Mechanized
Money	**Barter**	Exchange Media	Imported money	Tokens	Currency
Density/Miles2	<1 Person	1–5	5.1–25	**26–100**	100+
Political	No central authority	Local Political communities	**1 supra-local level**	2 levels	3+ levels
Stratification	Classless	Wealth-based status, slavery	**Nobles and commoners**	2 Classes, +slaves or castes	3+ Classes

Note: Boldface type represents complexity rating for each scale trait.

The kinship terminology is Crow, which fits well with the matrilineal descent system, as discussed above.

A close look at Malinowski's data shows that the Trobrianders are indeed more complex than the Asháninka and Shipibo, but the power of their chiefs seems limited, and in spite of the importance of rank their society remains remarkably egalitarian and focused on the humanization process. Trobriand subsistence is based on shifting cultivation, but it is a bush fallow system with rotation of only six or seven years, rather than twenty-five or more years in Amazonian forest fallow systems. There are no full-time craft specialists, and population densities are in the 26 to 100 per square mile range, which is only one level higher than the Shipibo. The primary difference between the Shipibo and the Trobrianders is that the Trobrianders have chiefs whose authority extends beyond their local villages. The Trobriand ranking system and associated elite wealth and privilege is elaborated enough that it was possible to describe the society in Malinowski's time as being stratified into a two-class system of elites and commoners. There were four totemic clans—pig, dog, lizard, and crocodile—ranked by their mythic order of emergence from their sacred places. Villages were ranked by the status of their highest-ranked subclan, which was considered to be the owner of the village and the village garden land. However, even though chiefs and high-ranked village headmen were called "owners" of the land, everyone gained access to land through their kinship relationships and no one was denied access.

A chief could make demands on people from other villages for their labor, but it was always assumed that he would feed anyone who helped him. Malinowski

described chiefs as having "tributary" districts but clarified by explaining that the "tribute" was actually annual marriage gifts, which he called dowry, *urigubu*, or "harvest gifts" that came from the labor of the chief's wife's matrilineal relatives. Such gifts are from wife's brother to sister's husband but are also from a brother to his sister's yam house. They are about kinship and marriage relations, not political tribute. They are better understood as a variation of many types of exchanges that occur between Trobriand families at marriage, at funerals, at competitions, and to acknowledge descent group ownership of garden lands. Women accumulate large quantities of woven banana leaf skirts and bundles of dried banana leaves to distribute to mourners who attend the funerals of their matrilineal kin. Exchanges go all directions and involve different goods or services, connecting people in complex overlapping networks. Between two men yams may go in one direction and axes in the other. Men's valuables include imported stone ax blades, ceramic pots, and articles of shell.

The most famous exchange objects are those involved in the Kula Ring, which refers to a ring of islands connecting the Trobriands with Woodlark Island 150 kilometers to the east and other islands some 300 kilometers south of the Trobriands, including Dobu and Ferguson and Normanby Islands. The Kula exchange system resembles the Asháninka system of *ayompari* exchanges and likely had similar functions. In the Kula, a man would give his partner (*karayta'u*) a shell necklace (*soulava* or *vaiguwa*) for which he later expected to receive a shell armband (*mwali*). The necklaces moved around the ring of islands in a clockwise direction, and the armbands went counterclockwise. These valuables had no intrinsic utility, but they could be sorted into several subcategories and were distinguished by individual names, exchange histories, color, and other ranked features. Men gained prestige from participating in the exchange and competed with each other to obtain the most famous, highest-ranked objects, which of course they could not retain, because their value was in giving them away. These exchanges were occasions for the exchange of other, more utilitarian objects, as well as feasting and partying. The larger function may well have been that the Kula maintained an interpersonal network that integrated some twenty-eight widely dispersed island communities of culturally diverse people speaking some five different language groups. The Kula operated in the absence of centralized political authority and without money or markets and was a distinctly tribal world cultural activity. The system is still in operation; in the 1970s nearly 3,000 men participated, and it integrated a total Kula community of some 25,000 people.[25]

Polygyny was an exclusive prerogative of chiefs, and it was the annual contributions in yams that wives brought that gave the chief the means to support lavish rituals and maintain his supporters. The larger and denser Trobriand population meant that chiefs could accumulate more wives and influence than Asháninka bigmen. For example, Malinowski reported that at the peak of his career To'uluwa, village headman of Omarakana (see figure 5.19) and chief of the island of Kiriwina (see figure 5.20), had as many as sixty wives extending his influence over dozens of villages and hamlets across the northern half of the island. There were three ranks of chiefs readily distinguishable by the number of their wives. Second-rank chiefs averaged ten wives, although in the past all chiefs may have had more. To'uluwa was still chief when Malinowski was in the Trobriands, but by then To'uluwa had only sixteen wives (see figures 5.21 and 5.22), because the British colonial authorities disapproved of polygyny and would not allow him to replace his wives. Nevertheless, To'uluwa received urigubu yams from sixty-one men from some twenty villages scattered across the five districts of the northern part of the island (see figure 5.23). Men from eight villages contributed areca palm nuts to him for special feasts of merit. The numbers of yam baskets given annually to chiefs provided a measure of donor rank as well as the status of the chiefly recipient. For example, a commoner might give 50 baskets, whereas higher-ranked individuals might give from 100 to 500, and chiefs would give 1,000 or more baskets. Baskets average about 15 pounds, so these gifts represent a vast quantity of yams. According to Malinowski's count of To'uluwa's harvest gifts in 1918, he received more than 20,000 baskets, which might have contained 136 metric tons of yams.[26]

The chief's person is protected by strict taboos. For example, commoners must keep their heads below his, and Malinowski often photographed Chief To'uluwa seated on an elevated platform. His actual powers were strictly limited, but he could protect his privileges. It was considered justifiable if he had someone speared who touched him improperly, stole his possessions, or interfered with his wives. However, normally he would use sorcery to punish offenders and could not act arbitrarily, but Malinowski acknowledged that chiefs sometimes were capable of "actual oppression and crass injustice," although such cases were rare.[27] In most cases the Trobriand chief operated like an Asháninka bigman. At least one authority on Trobriand competitive leadership describes the system as a variant of the Melanesian bigman system because the political hierarchies that particular chiefs create are not durable; they break down when the chief dies or loses his power, just like an Asháninka bigman's group of followers.[28] A Trobriand chief's son could not inherit his position, because the matrilineal descent system means that the chief's sister's son might inherit his position, not his own son. The chief's sister's son would need to work at building his support and might not succeed. Trobriand chiefs are leaders, not rulers, and this keeps Trobriand society in the tribal world. This fits with the limited powers of the chief as Malinowski described it: "When he wants to declare war, organize an expedition, or celebrate a festivity, he must issue formal summons, publicly announce his will, deliberate with the notables, receive the tribute, services and assistance of his subjects in a ceremonial manner, and finally repay them according to a definite scale."[29]

In comparison with the Asháninka and the Shipibo, community life is much more intensive in the Trobriands. Political leaders are more powerful, there are more wealth objects to accumulate, more dramatic rituals for marriage and death, and more elaborate exchange networks. All of these differences are closely related to the greater scale and density of population.

TRIBAL RELIGIOUS BELIEFS AND PRACTICES

Just as any attempt to understand another culture is colored by the biases of one's own culture, the way anthropologists have historically understood the cultural

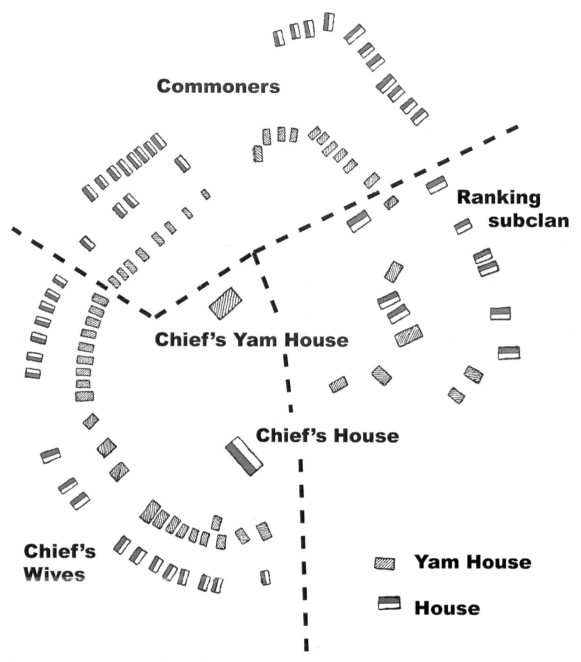

Figure 5.19. Omarakana village, 1920 Trobriand Islands, based on Malinowski.

beliefs and religious practices of tribal peoples was shaped by their theoretical preconceptions about human biology and how human cultures are constructed and how they work. Modes of anthropological explanation have changed over time like fashions, often reflecting changes in national politics and changes within the global culture itself. Historically, the most misleading and damaging anthropological theories were those that assumed that biological differences made some human groups inferior. Equally damaging were theories that assumed not only that cultural

evolutionary progress was inevitable, but that it was always progress in the sense of human improvement. This left little room for evaluating the achievements of small-scale tribal culture in a positive light.

The Mental Abilities of Tribal Peoples

Prior to 1945, when the modern colonial era ended, biological explanations of cultural difference were still closely linked with European notions of cultural superiority. This was racist because it equated cultural differences with racial differences and always

Figure 5.20. Trobriand Chief To'uluwa seated on a platform before his decorated house (source: LSE Library, Malinowski Collection 1915-1918 #684).

Figure 5.21. Trobriand chief To'uluwa during a canoe launching festivity on the beach of Omarakana seated on a platform specially erected for the occasion. He is surrounded by some of his wives and his children, with his son, Gilayviyaka on his right (source: LSE Library, Malinowski Collection 1915-1918 #680).

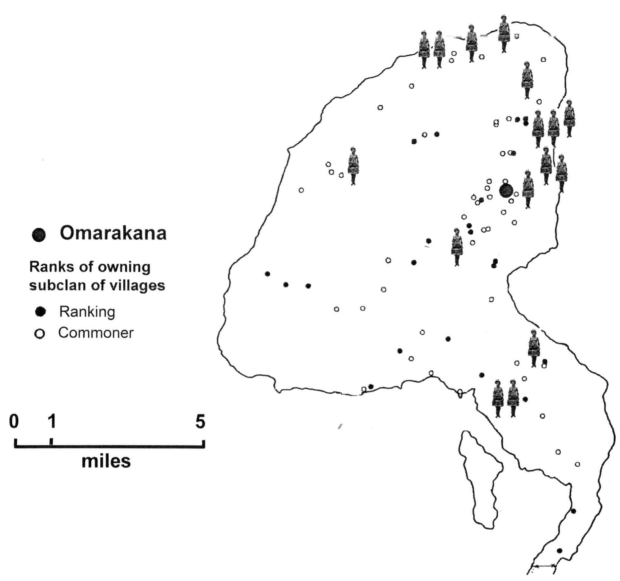

Omarakana

Ranks of owning subclan of villages

● Ranking

○ Commoner

0   1   5

miles

Figure 5.22.   Home villages of 16 of Trobriand Chief To'uluwa's wives (data from Malinowski 1965, map based on Powell 1960).

judged tribal peoples to be inferior. In extreme cases, such biological determinism took the form of **social Darwinism**, applying competitive natural selection and survival-of-the-fittest theories of biological evolution to entire cultures. Social Darwinists concluded that the peoples and cultures that European colonists were destroying were culturally and biologically "unfit" and therefore doomed to disappear. They viewed small-scale cultures as living fossils representing the earlier stages of evolutionary development beyond which Europeans had presumably advanced. This ethnocentric approach is illustrated in Staniland Wake's 1890s description of Aborigines as backward children (see box 5.1). Such extremely derogatory

representations of tribal peoples led to insensitive colonial policies that accelerated the disintegration of tribal societies under the pressure of European conquest. Ethnocentric ethnography was rejected as unscientific by British functionalist anthropologists such as Radcliffe-Brown, Malinowski, and Evans-Pritchard, who by the 1930s began to assist colonial administrators by describing tribal societies and cultures as organism-like systems. Functionalists warned that even tribal cultural beliefs and practices that seemed disgusting or bizarre to Europeans could be shown to have "functions," or social purposes, and that indiscriminate colonial interference could have unintended negative consequences.

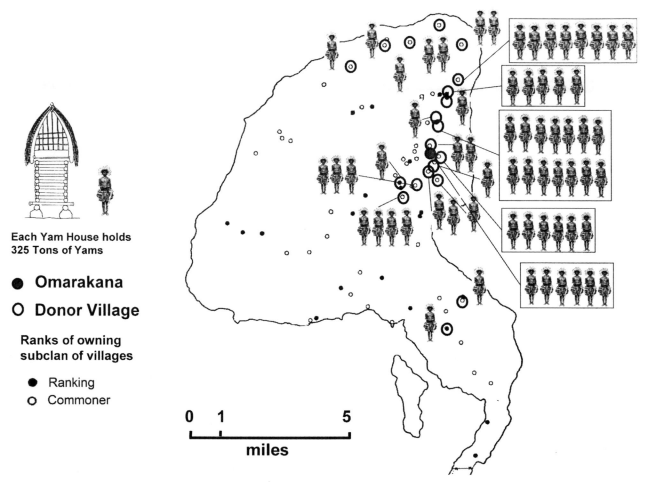

Each Yam House holds
325 Tons of Yams

● **Omarakana**

○ **Donor Village**

**Ranks of owning
subclan of villages**

● Ranking

○ Commoner

0   1   5
miles

Figure 5.23. Villages of 61 men giving *Urigubu* yams to Chief Mitakata (data from Malinowski 1965, map based on Powell 1960).

BOX 5.1. AN ETHNOCENTRIC LOOK AT AUSTRALIAN ABORIGINES

Ethnocentric distortion is well illustrated by an outrageous paper on Australian Aborigines read before the Anthropological Institute in London in 1871 by the institute's director, Charles Staniland Wake.[30] (Chapter 3, which is entirely devoted to Australian aboriginal culture, will demonstrate how misleading Wake's views were.) The language of Wake's paper is so offensive that it is difficult to imagine that it was presented as objective science. Wake's ethnocentrism is readily betrayed by his derogatory references to "moral defects" and the "barbarity" and "absurdity" of aboriginal customs, which he claimed were founded on "unmitigated selfishness." Such astonishing ethnocentrism had its origins in the assumptions of racial and cultural superiority that supported European colonialism.

In Wake's view, Aborigines, with their simple material culture, were living examples of the earliest stage of human evolution. He sought to describe their mental characteristics but felt that it was inaccurate to speak of their "intellectual" abilities, because Aborigines operated almost by instinct, barely above the animal level. They had "no aim in life but the continuance of their existence and the gratifications of their passions, with the least possible trouble to themselves."

Their technological achievements, such as the boomerang, were derided as accidental discoveries, while their art was likened to "the productions of children." Even aboriginal languages and complex marriage systems were treated as mere unconscious developments, reflecting no particular intellectual ability.

Morally, Aborigines were described as children, who enjoyed song and dance and became "extremely indolent" when food was abundant. The aboriginal mind was "saturated with superstition," but the Aborigines had no religion. In Wake's view, they also had no abstract concept of morality, could not form any idea of death, and routinely mistreated women, the young, and the weak. They cannibalized their children and beat, speared, and enslaved their wives. Wake even had doubts about whether aboriginal mothers had "natural affection" for their children, although he also accused them of being overindulgent parents.

In regard to their relations with Europeans, Wake found the Aborigines to be haughty, insolent, cunning, and treacherous thieves and liars who unpredictably killed strangers. He made no connection between these negative personality traits and the obvious facts of colonial invasion, yet he did attribute their "treachery" to suspicion. Wake's interpretation of aboriginal culture did not go beyond his original assumption that Aborigines represented the very "childhood of humanity." They were moral and intellectual children, not degenerates from a higher state. Given Wake's assumptions that European culture was the most highly evolved and that Europeans would inevitably dominate the world, his ethnocentrism is hardly surprising for that time. Wake never actually saw an Aborigine, and his knowledge of the culture apparently did not go beyond the superficial stereotypes of unsympathetic European explorers and settlers.

Collective Representations, Primitive Mentality, and Structuralism

The rapid European colonial domination of Africa, which was in full swing by the late nineteenth century, made it imperative for the new European administrators and petty colonial officials to understand the peoples that they were attempting to control. Because it was so difficult for foreigners to predict the behavior of natives, it was widely believed that native thought processes were inferior to those of Europeans. And because explicitly racist evolutionary theories were used to justify colonialism, Europeans readily assumed that people living in tribal societies must be physically and culturally underdeveloped and therefore childlike in their thinking.

The approach of American anthropologists to the understanding of cultural differences was profoundly influenced by Franz Boas, who, during his years at Columbia University from 1899 to 1937, trained many of the researchers who became the most prominent anthropologists of the twentieth century. Boas was a German immigrant with a Jewish heritage, and he emphatically opposed any theories of racial superiority or that attributed cultural differences to racial

type. Boas rated Euro-American civilization as the highest human cultural achievement, but in a dramatic departure from the ethnocentric views of tribal peoples that prevailed at the time, he believed that there were no significant differences in basic mental faculties between "uncivilized primitives" and "civilized" peoples. In his book *The Mind of Primitive Man* (1911),[31] he easily refuted a list of presumably inferior mental features that were widely attributed to tribal people, including their supposed inability to inhibit their emotions, their shortened attention spans, and their limited powers of original thought. Boas found that natives were impulsive and improvident when it was culturally appropriate but showed remarkable restraint when necessary. He noted that the supposed inability of natives to focus their attention was most likely to be reported by frustrated ethnographers who found it difficult to get reluctant informants to answer a long series of irrelevant questions. Likewise, within their own cultural context, natives showed plenty of creativity. Boas certainly acknowledged differences in forms of thought between tribal and civilized peoples, but these he attributed to social or cultural differences, not racial factors. He concluded that tribal peoples simply classified experiences differently and merged concepts in ways that appeared peculiar to us.

British anthropologist E. B. Tylor[32] argued in *Primitive Culture* that seemingly bizarre tribal religious beliefs and rituals developed out of what he called **animistic thinking**, in which intellectually curious people attempted to explain dream experiences and death by attributing a detachable animating soul to people, animals, plants, and "inanimate" objects. Tylor felt that the soul concept was the basis of all religion, shamanism, and witchcraft and that tribal people arrived at it by logical mental processes, which were basically like our own. Sir James Frazer elaborated this intellectualist approach in *The Golden Bough*[33] when he identified the laws that he thought underlay magical practices. His **law of sympathy** held that things such as hair that were once part of someone could still influence that person even after they were separated. Therefore, a man's hair clippings might be used by shamans to harm him. Tribal people may not recognize Frazer's "law of sympathy," but they do see a metaphorical relationship between substance and person. In this case the shaman can use the shared belief in invisible connections between biological substance and an individual to influence that person, just as in our society, where DNA analysis of a detached bodily substance can be used as legal evidence. DNA is invisible to most of us, yet we believe in its existence and use this belief to influence people. Like Tylor, Frazer argued that primitives were crude logicians who thought like Englishmen but simply made mistakes.

French positivist philosopher Lucien Levy-Bruhl was one of the first scholars to systematically examine the thought processes of tribal peoples with the practical purpose of showing how they differed from those of "civilized" peoples. He applied the concept of **collective representations**, or group ideas, developed by French sociologist Emile Durkheim. According to Levy-Bruhl[34] collective representations, like culture in general, are emotion-laden thoughts, or ideas, that are shared by the members of a specific society and transmitted across generations. These thoughts are collective in that they are not the unique property of specific individuals, and therefore they cannot be understood according to the principles of individual psychology. He insisted throughout that primitive mentality was not inferior and that natives were not childlike; their thinking was simply different. Levy-Bruhl agreed with Boas that thought was culturally conditioned, but he emphatically departed from Boas, as well as from Tylor and Frazer, by declaring that the mental processes of "primitives" are distinctively different and can be understood only by their own "laws." He rejected animist, intellectualist explanations because they were based on individual, not collective, thought.

The most critical aspect of primitive thought, Levy-Bruhl argued, was that it assumed a "mystic" reality based on a socially conditioned belief in imperceptible forces. Such thought was based on a **law of participation**, under which contradictions were ignored and something could be two things at once. Thus, tribal people saw nothing contradictory in a shaman being a man and a tiger at the same time. Of course, all peoples have this ability.

Levy-Bruhl declared, "Primitives perceive nothing in the same way as we do,"[35] even though their brains and their senses are the same as ours. They formed concrete impressions that they felt and lived emotionally, whereas civilized people worked with abstract, conceptual thought. In his own contradictory terms, Levy-Bruhl suggested that primitive thought was thus "concrete," whereas civilized thinking was abstract and conceptual. Despite the difficulties Levy-Bruhl experienced in grappling with cross-cultural understanding, he correctly observed that barriers to emic understanding (meanings internal to a given culture) were in a sense insurmountable. Translation problems are critical because categories are seldom precisely the same even when superficial resemblances exist. For example, traditional exchange objects, which often are called "money," are not actually money as it exists in a market economy. Although the difference in meaning may not be accurately characterized as that between concrete and abstract, Levy-Bruhl was correct in calling for in-depth linguistic knowledge because it is perfectly possible to have a minimal speaking knowledge without really being able to think in another language.

After Levy-Bruhl, anthropologists largely abandoned efforts to examine the mental world of tribal peoples until the 1960s, when another French anthropologist, Claude Levi-Strauss,[36] elaborated his structuralist approach to the mental processes underlying tribal culture. **Structuralism** and the method of analysis that Levi-Strauss pioneered remained a dominant theoretical perspective in cultural anthropology and the humanities for decades. Levi-Strauss questioned the entire distinction between abstract and concrete words by relating it to differences in level of attention and interest, not to differences in method of thought. Levi-Strauss argued that tribal people, like civilized people, use many abstract words and pursue objective knowledge about the environment for its own sake. People name things not simply because these are objects of immediate utilitarian interest, but because they find it aesthetically pleasing to impose order on the world through careful observation and cataloging. Such attention to detail was well illustrated in our previous discussion of the ethnoecological knowledge of native Amazonians and the Dreaming maps of Australian Aborigines. According to Levi-Strauss, it is this common drive for order that underlies all human thought and that makes unfamiliar thought patterns understandable.

Levi-Strauss did not find it particularly mystical that people identify with totemic animals. Natives are not confused by a law of participation into thinking that they are their totems. There is no contradiction in holding empirical and emotional knowledge about a single object. Levi-Strauss maintained that magical thought, or what he preferred to call mythical thought, differs from formal scientific thought in method and purpose, but not in logic. **Mythical thought** is scientific in that it produced the important technological developments of the Neolithic, such as domestication, pottery, and weaving. However, the **Neolithic paradox** for Levi-Strauss is the difficulty in explaining why technological development seemingly stagnated after the scientific achievements of the Neolithic until the establishment of formal science. To resolve the paradox, Levi-Strauss argued that there are two distinct but opposite types of scientific thought, each equally valid and neither a stage in the development of the other: the **science of the concrete**, which is based on perceptions and signs, and formal science, which works with concepts. Here he uses the term *science* in the sense of a systematic ordering of observations and ideas to help people define and understand reality. The science of the concrete as applied in the tribal world is not directed toward creating new technology to change the physical world directly; it is concerned with shaping perception. In that respect, it resembles the use of visual images in the contemporary film and video media.

Mythical thought works with a culturally limited set of signs, including significant images and events, which it orders into structured relationships that provide aesthetic satisfaction while helping people understand reality. Levi-Strauss is here referring to the structured sets of logical associations and complementary oppositions that are so characteristic of myths and the ritual beliefs and practices that are related to them. These were discussed in some detail in the Amazonian cosmology examined in chapter 2. Formal scientific concepts remain as close to natural reality as possible. They are derived from structured theories and hypotheses and are used to expand the total cultural inventory and to make changes, or create events, in the external world.

Shamanism and Psychopathology

Shamans are part-time religious specialists and healers who personify the most extreme elements of so-called primitive mentalities and magical thinking in tribal societies. Early missionaries often called shamans witch doctors, attributing their supernatural powers to the devil, and confronted them as enemies of Christianity. Government authorities often disapproved of shamans because they sometimes used their powers within the community to organize resistance to government programs and because shamanistic curing practices frequently were considered contrary to modern medical science, if not actually dangerous. Even anthropologists have had difficulty being objective about shamans. For example, Alfred Kroeber, a prominent Boas-trained anthropologist, suggested in the 1948 edition of *Anthropology*, long a standard textbook, that modern civilization's rejection of shamanism and related beliefs was a measure of scientific progress. He observed that people in our own society recognize as abnormal or insane anyone who talks to the dead or who thinks they can turn into a bear, whereas "backward people" consider such behavior socially acceptable and even admirable. Kroeber regarded shamanism as a psychopathology and emphatically declared: "When the sane and well in one culture believe what only the most ignorant, warped, and insane believe in another, there would seem to be some warrant for rating the first culture lower and the second higher. Or are our discards, insane, and hypersuggestibles perhaps right and the rest of us wrong?"[37]

It is important to recognize, however, that shamanism is based on concepts about the supernatural that are useful, not irrational. Psychological anthropologist Pascal Boyer suggests that people remember and pass on supernatural concepts that are important to them socially.[38] The mental skills that people apply to the supernatural are the same skills they use in dealing with each other, and they involve close attention to human perceptions, beliefs, and desires. Shamans use shared beliefs about the supernatural to reinforce the moral dimensions of human behavior, thereby helping people be more confident that others will cooperate with them. Using, or "believing in," supernatural concepts does not mean that people accept the supernatural as natural, but they do find belief in the supernatural to be useful. The supernatural beliefs that people universally recognize as "religious" are related to morality, commitment, group identity, ritual, and individual experience. Such concepts generally involve supernatural "persons," or objects believed to have humanlike minds but that behave in extraordinary ways.

Shamanism does involve a striking collection of phenomena, including various trance states, magical flight, and spirit possession,[39] all of which may be difficult to understand outside of the cultural context in which they occur. Shamans induce trances using rhythmical chanting, dancing, deprivation, and psychoactive drugs. Anthropologist Michael Harner,[40] who conducted popular workshops and seminars on shamanism, demonstrated that under the proper conditions, virtually anyone can induce such trance states. Shamanism may well be tens of thousands of years old, judging from parallels between the distinctive lines and grid patterns scratched on European cave walls during the Ice Age and similar designs characteristic of rock art associated with shamans in many parts of the world. Some researchers infer that these are images that tribal shamans see with their mind's eye during trance states. In ecstatic trance, shamans contact the otherwise invisible spirit world and perform amazing feats, including the magical killing of enemies and transformations into animals. Using their spirit helpers to cure, shamans massage their patients and dramatically suck out intrusive objects thought to be the causes of illness; or they shoot invisible darts into the bodies of enemies to harm them. Australian aboriginal shamans reportedly have killed people simply by pointing a bone in their direction. The "dark side" of Amazonian shamanism is well documented in a recent ethnography from Guyana.[41]

Many observers have questioned the authenticity of shamanistic performances, pointing to incidences in which the shaman does not seem to be in a genuine trance or when a curer has hidden in his mouth the object that he intends to suck from his patient. Deliberately hidden objects of this sort simply add drama to the curing performance. Some shamans may indeed pretend to be in trance, but most suspicions of fraud may be due to a misunderstanding of the nature of shamanism, especially the fact that shamanistic trances often differ from other forms of spirit possession. A shaman typically is in a "lucid trance" or a "waking dream" in which he communicates with both the spirits and his audience, and he will usually be able to remember the events later. This is not the same as pathological hysteria, and it does not mean that the shaman becomes totally dissociated. The shaman trance is a temporary reduction of normal reality testing in which dream images are treated as if real within a specific cultural context and are then used for social purposes.[42] The psychopathological view of shamanism by anthropologists was in favor for a long time. For example, Julian Silverman[43] emphasized the parallels between acute schizophrenics who behave in bizarre fashion and shamans who experience cognitive disturbances, or altered states of consciousness, as an apparent reaction to a major personal crisis involving guilt or failure. In Silverman's view, like Kroeber's, the most significant difference between schizophrenics in our society and shamans in tribal societies is that schizophrenics find no social support for their behavior, and it is consequently maladaptive, whereas shamans are culturally accepted. Thus, in this view, shamanism can be considered a therapeutic psychological adjustment to a psychopathology.

The connection between schizophrenia and shamanism is also implied in the authoritative *Diagnostic and Statistical Manual of Mental Disorders* (DSM-III), the guidebook published by the American Psychiatric Association for use by clinicians. According to DSM-III, "magical thinking" is seen "in children, in people

in primitive cultures, and in Schizotypal Personality Disorder, Schizophrenia, and Obsessive Compulsive Disorder."[44] The belief that the members of domestic-scale cultures are sick and childlike dies hard!

The clinical concept of schizophrenia has been refined considerably since Silverman's analysis was published in the 1960s, and even using the definition of schizophrenic disorders contained within DSM-III, striking differences between schizophrenics and shamans now seem evident. The DSM-IV[45] Glossary of Technical Terms (Appendix C) defines "magical thinking" as "the erroneous belief that one's thoughts, words, or actions will cause or prevent a specific outcome in some way that defies commonly understood laws of cause and effect." The definition adds: "Magical thinking may be a part of normal child development." However, the revised DSM-IV entry for "Schizophrenia" advises clinicians to take cultural differences into account, because even "bizarre delusions" are not always easy to identify. In fact, "In some cultures, visual or auditory hallucinations with a religious content may be a normal part of religious experience (e.g., seeing the Virgin Mary or hearing God's voice)." Attributing shamanistic experiences to an altered state of consciousness implies out-of-control hallucinations and other paranoid delusions that we tend to view negatively but that, in fact, are not characteristic of shamanism.[46] A shamanic state of consciousness can be distinguished from an altered state of consciousness as it is usually recognized. The altered state of the schizophrenic is obviously maladaptive. It comes unbidden, and the schizophrenic hears uncontrollable mocking voices, whereas the shaman can enter the shamanic state virtually at will, remains aware of his state, sees visions, uses them for socially beneficial purposes, and then freely returns to his normal consciousness. A successful shaman achieves a balance between his spiritual experiences and the demands of everyday life, but there is no reason to view the shamanic state as a psychopathology.

Aboriginal Voodoo Death and Culture-Bound Syndromes

Anthropologists and medical researchers have been fascinated by reports of mysterious deaths and illnesses in tribal societies that are culturally attributed to supernatural causes and that have not always been readily explainable in purely physical terms. A prime example from aboriginal Australia are cases of so-called voodoo death, such as the bone pointing referred to previously, in which people are killed by sorcery. The long-established anthropological interpretation of such incidents was that the victim died from shock, caused by intense fear of death combined with an absolute belief in the reality of sorcery.[47] More extensive observations by medically trained individuals clarified both the physical and cultural basis of such deaths. Harry Eastwell,[48] who conducted periodic psychiatric clinics in aboriginal communities in Arnhem Land between 1969 and 1980, treated thirty-nine patients for a variety of physical and emotional symptoms that he called "fear of sorcery syndrome." In nearly all cases, some specific event—such as the death or illness of close kin, interpersonal conflicts, or a ritual violation—led to suspicions of supernatural danger. Patients showed the typical symptoms of extreme fear: bulging eyes, dilated pupils, sweating, agitation, and sleeplessness. Two of the patients died, one with an abnormality of the adrenal glands, which may have made him more vulnerable to stress, and the other from kidney and heart failure.

Because so few deaths actually occurred in these cases, Eastwell began to suspect that more than merely fear was involved in voodoo death. This suspicion was further supported when two patients thought to be dying from sorcery were found to be severely dehydrated and were saved by prompt medical intervention. Additional analyses of the process of dying experienced by elderly Aborigines revealed a regular cultural pattern in which both dying person and kin decide that death is imminent and mutually facilitate the process—the dying person refuses to drink and the kin withhold water so that death by dehydration occurs within twenty-four to forty-eight hours.

The parallels between aboriginal patient-assisted euthanasia and voodoo death are striking. In both cases, the actual mechanism of death is probably dehydration, but it occurs because the patient and the community agree that the patient is dying. Water is withheld at the same time that wailing and formal funeral rituals are begun. It is believed that only the totemic spirit animates the dying person, and it does not need to drink. At death, this spirit returns to the ancestral well.

Psychiatrist John Cawte[49] describes another Australian culture-bound syndrome, Malgri, from the Wellesley Island Aborigines in the Gulf of Carpentaria. In this case, violation of ritual restrictions on keeping land foods and seafoods separate causes local totemic spirits to afflict a person with severe abdominal swelling and pain. The condition apparently is not fatal, and sufferers usually respond to specific ritual treatment. To observers trained in psychoanalysis, Malgri suggested hysterical "displacement" of Oedipal conflicts, but Cawte felt that it was more understandable as part of the totemically regulated system of territoriality based on the Dreaming. He noted that Malgri was most likely to affect people outside of their own estate territories, and the most dangerous spirits were those controlling the richest resource zones, where foraging pressure was the greatest. Furthermore, Malgri did not occur on the nearby mainland, where population densities were lower and resources thus less critical.

The Healing Power of Myth and Symbols

Medically trained observers generally agree that shamanistic healers can successfully treat people suffering from a variety of psychiatric complaints, such as Malgri, using ritual techniques. Native curers may also be adept at treating injuries and illnesses with herbal remedies that have empirically identifiable chemical properties. Researchers further concede that shamanistic rituals may involve important psychotherapeutic techniques including the power of suggestion, the restructuring of social relations, catharsis, and the stimulation of neurochemicals.[50]

Whatever the specific healing mechanism might be, shamanistic ritual may work because culturally defined symbols are manipulated to influence the body-mind relationship by helping people to alter their self-perceptions. Symbols, whether they involve totemic spirits or psychoanalytic concepts such as guilt and repression, are drawn from cultural myths that condense important truths about the human experience in society. For psychotherapy to succeed, the patient and practitioner must establish a working relationship, and the shaman may facilitate this through what anthropologist James Dow calls the "shamanic paradox."[51] That is, the patient must suspend any disbelief about the validity of the empirically unbelievable supernatural powers claimed by the shaman—he must implicitly believe in the authenticity of the therapeutic process before it can be effective. When the patient fully participates in the curing process, through belief or the suspension of disbelief, he may be able to reevaluate his own experiences and gain control over his feelings. These therapeutic principles help explain the persistence and apparent success of many ritual symbols.

Australian material (again from Arnhem Land) illustrates the effectiveness of symbols. In this area, the central Dreamtime myth, which is reenacted in a major series of rituals including circumcision ceremonies, concerns the Wawilak sisters, two Dreaming ancestors who created the local cultural landscape during their Dreamtime travels. The myth details the creative activities of the Wawilak sisters and recounts how they lose ritual power to men when they are swallowed by the Rainbow Serpent, who is attracted when the sisters' menstrual blood contaminates the snake's pool. The Wawilak sisters, and women in general, are associated with the fertile dry season. The Rainbow Serpent rising up to eat the Wawilak sisters has obvious male associations and creates the widespread flooding of the lowlands during the Arnhem Land wet season.

The Wawilak myth parallels the sacred flute myths found in Amazonia and deals with the same classic issues of life and death, reproduction, and gender roles. Although the Wawilak ritual complex does not directly involve shamanistic curing, according to the analysis of anthropologist Nancy Munn,[52] participants in the rituals consciously identify with the characters in the myth, and as they enact it they convert their personal fears of death into more positive outcomes and satisfying images of health and community well-being. For example, circumcision of a boy is metaphorically compared to the swallowing of the sisters, only in this case he is ritually reborn. In other ceremonial reenactments, women happily avoid being eaten by the serpent. Bloodletting conducted in connection with circumcision ceremonies is equated with the menstrual blood of the Wawilak sisters and is converted to ritual use as body paint, thus transferring symbolic strength and actual positive feelings to the participant. As one aboriginal man explained, "It makes us feel easy and comfortable and it makes us strong. It makes us good. . . .We have that . . . strength from that blood. It goes inside when we put that blood on."[53]

Interpreting the meaning of many other specific practices that we identify as "magical" because we assume they have no empirical basis is equally challenging. Michael Brown[54] has examined ritual songs that the Aguaruna of the Peruvian Amazon use to improve their hunting, especially when they go after spider monkeys with blowguns. The songs may be sung before a man goes hunting or sung silently as the hunt is in progress, and they contain complex allusions to myths and images of hunting success. Brown argues that the Aguaruna consider these songs to be as instrumental for their hunting success as the technical quality of their blowguns and stalking skills. In his view, the Aguaruna are right because these "magical" songs help them focus their energy on the hunting task. They alter their internal mental states, giving them confidence, in the same way that ritual symbols can have a psychotherapeutic effect. This line of argument is similar to Bronislaw Malinowski's functionalist theory that magic helps people deal with the uncertainties that lie beyond the limits of their technical capabilities.[55]

Diverse Beliefs about God, Morality, and Sex

Virtually all societies have beliefs about the soul and spirits, and spiritual entities with supernatural powers. What does vary significantly between tribal and imperial worlds is what people believe about a superior, or high god, who is a creator, or ultimately in charge of the world. Nearly 90 percent of tribal societies either do not recognize the existence of such a high god, or do not believe that he is actively concerned with the world, or with morality. In contrast, only about half of imperial world societies have such lack of concern for a high god; the other half believe in the existence of a high god who is concerned with morality. There is an obvious correlation between belief in an active high god, concerned with proper behavior, and political rulers, who legitimize their authority as gods themselves or as God's representative. This connection will be clear in the following chapters.

Tribal societies generally do not put a high god in charge of morality, but they use beliefs about spirit beings or supernatural dangers to regulate their sexual lives. This is clearly seen in the high frequency with which tribal women observe a taboo on sexual intercourse following the birth of a child. More than 98 percent of tribal societies where information about these practices are recorded observe the postpartum sex taboo, and nearly half (47 percent) do so for six months or more. Such practices help space births and have an obvious fertility-dampening effect. They may also help explain why polygyny is so commonly permitted.

HEALTH AND NUTRITION IN TRIBAL SOCIETIES

Many well-meaning people who are neither racist nor unusually ethnocentric may mistakenly assume that tribal peoples must have a low quality of life because their sanitation standards seem lower and they lack the advantages of modern medicine. This is not a simple issue, because public health programs and modern medicine associated with the commercial world have improved life expectancy for many people; nevertheless, independent tribal societies typically enjoy a high quality of life as long as they are not negatively affected by outsiders. Perhaps what tribal peoples have, and what we have lost, is an equitable distribution of social power, giving everyone the feeling of control over their daily lives. Tribal peoples living in autonomous, tribal cultures seldom experience material impoverishment. In this section, we consider specific evidence on tribal health and well-being bearing on these important questions.

Myth and Reality of the "Noble Savage"

Most early visitors to undisturbed tribal societies were impressed with the health and vigor of the peoples they saw. These first impressions likely were basically accurate, but they were confused and embellished with unnecessary pronouncements about morality and human perfection that became the myth of the "noble savage." For example, some of the first Europeans to visit Brazil reported that the Indians "naturally follow goodness" and "live together in harmony, with no dissension."[56] From such glowing descriptions, it was easy to conclude that "savages" were superior human beings living idyllic lives in Eden-like innocence. The comfortable nudity of most Native Amazonians that astonished Europeans certainly contributed to this noble savage image.

Most anthropologists have been careful to disassociate themselves from such noble savage romanticism. Members of tribal societies clearly are no more superior or inferior as individual human beings than any other group of humans. Tribal peoples can be selfish and cruel. They quarrel and kill one another, just like people who live in cities. Tribal culture is also not perfect. Tribal societies are not perfectly egalitarian, nor are they perfectly balanced with nature. And dietary and medical practices, as well as many aspects of tribal culture, may sometimes be harmful.[57] It is not unusual for tribal therapy to conflict with accepted practices in the medical community. For example, I witnessed a snake-bite victim being treated with herbal hot compresses, which would have accelerated the spread of the venom. Individuals must sometimes pay high personal costs for tribal membership, as people must to live in any human society. Nevertheless, generally good health and vigor seem to be two advantages of life in tribal cultures for those who reach adulthood.

Evidence for the overall high quality of life in relatively independent tribal societies appears in a report by geneticist James Neel.[58] This is the same James Neel who was falsely accused of crimes against humanity by journalist Patrick Tierney (2000),[59] but Neel's record of humanistic concern for the Yanomami is clear. Neel summarized the findings of eight years of biochemical and health research among Native Amazonians, carried out by an interdisciplinary team of more than a dozen researchers using sophisticated techniques. Neel reported that, in general, they found the Xavante, Yanomami, and Makiritare, whom they examined in Brazil and Venezuela, to be in "excellent physical condition" (see box 5.2). Infant and childhood mortality rates were higher than in fully industrialized countries, but the general pattern of life expectancy was better than in colonial India at the end of the nineteenth century.

Neel concluded that these tribal peoples were well adjusted to the viruses, bacterial diseases, and internal parasites naturally occurring in their territory. The Yanomami and Xavante were found to have twice the levels of gamma globulin, the blood protein containing infection-fighting antibodies, found in civilized populations. Yanomami babies are born with a high degree of natural immunity acquired from their mothers and maintained by prolonged breast-feeding. Yanomami infants then quickly develop additional immunities because they are continuously exposed to all the local pathogens. The most significant diseases, including malaria and measles, were assumed to be post-Columbian introductions to which people were not yet well adjusted. Neel inoculated a group of Yanomami to protect them from an ongoing measles epidemic, but Tierney questioned his motives and suggested incorrectly that he used an improper vaccine.

The Yanomami could be classified as malnourished by international standards because by age their heights and weights are too low.[60] However, the obvious vitality of the Yanomami suggests that such measures are inappropriate in their case. Small stature actually may be an adaptive genetic response, allowing people to be well nourished as tribal villagers in the rain forest. The implication is that outside intervention that changed their lifestyles to improve their health might be counterproductive.

Theoretically, there are many reasons the quality of life should be high in tribal societies. The most important are their generally low population densities and relative social equality, which help ensure equal access to basic subsistence resources so that everyone enjoys good nutrition. Furthermore, low densities and frequent mobility significantly reduce the occurrence of epidemic diseases, and natural selection—in the absence of antibiotics, immunizations, surgery, and other forms of medical intervention—results in a population with high levels of disease resistance.

Healthy people are those who survive. Tribal societies, in effect, maintain public health by emphasizing prevention of morbidity rather than treatment. The healthiest conditions likely exist under mobile foraging and pastoralism, whereas there might be some health costs associated with the increased densities and reduced mobility of settled farming villages.

BOX 5.2. HEALTH REPORT ON THE WAORANI

A detailed assessment of the health status of the Waorani of Ecuador, a Native Amazonian group, was conducted in the field by a seven-person medical team in 1976. At that time, the Waorani were living independently as manioc gardeners and hunters and maintained only limited contacts with outsiders. In all, 293 people received thorough medical exams. On the positive side, more than 95 percent of the sample appeared to be "very robust" and in "excellent health."[61] There was no malnutrition, no obesity, no high blood pressure, and no cardiovascular disease. Everyone had excellent eyesight, with no color blindness, and no one was deaf.

There were some negatives: Many children had scalp infections, but these were attributed to contacts with outsiders; some two-thirds out of a sample of sixty-three people showed evidence of light intestinal parasite infestation; two old women had pneumonia; three people were blind in one eye due to accidents; and there were many scars from spears and jaguar and peccary bites. Six people were described by the Waorani themselves as mentally deficient, and most of these cases were readily attributed to head injuries, fevers, or genetic defects. Surprisingly, the Waorani of all ages had high rates of dental decay. Only 5 out of the 230 people checked by the dentist were found to be completely free of cavities. It was suggested that such exceptionally high cavity rates were due to the unusual fact that the Waorani, unlike most Amazonians, consumed their manioc drink unfermented, while it still had a high sugar content. Although no estimate of mortality rates was given, it appears that many adults died in violent conflicts. Like James Neel's Yanomami report, the Waorani study attributed much of the excellent health of the Indians to the high quality of their diet, low population density, and relative isolation from outside diseases.

Dental Health and Tribal Diets

Health researchers have increasingly recognized that the typical diet found among tribal subsistence foragers and farmers, which is low in fat, salt, and refined sugars and high in fiber and various beneficial nutrients, is actually an ideal human diet. Skeletal evidence suggests that archaeologically, the shift from foraging to farming frequently was accompanied by a decline in overall health and human nutrition.[62] Significant epidemiological evidence suggests that many forms of cancer are associated with relatively recent dietary changes related to food marketing, processing, and storage, such as salting, pickling, and refining, and to dramatic increases in consumption of fat and simple carbohydrates or refined sugars. Of course, foods eaten by self-supporting subsistence peoples are also free of the contaminants and additives that are introduced into industrially produced foods by the chemicals used in agriculture and in processing.

Perhaps the first scientific evidence that tribal peoples could be shown to be physically superior to "civilized" peoples appeared in an article published in 1894 in the *Journal of the Royal Anthropological Institute* by Wilberforce Smith, who compared the teeth of Sioux Indians with those of typical Londoners. Smith became interested in this problem while conducting a survey of the teeth of his fellow Englishmen, which he found to be disastrously decayed. He knew that the skulls of prehistoric European "savages" invariably contained healthier teeth than contemporary peoples and decided to find out if modern "savages" also had healthy teeth. Taking advantage of the appearance of Buffalo Bill's Wild West Show in London, he obtained permission to examine the teeth of ten Sioux men, roughly ages fifteen to fifty. He found that all had "massive admirably formed teeth, evenly ranged." They were well worn, but none were decayed, and no molars were missing. He concluded, "Their teeth alone proved them to have led the life of genuine savages."[63] By comparison, the younger portion of the three hundred Londoners whom he also examined had half as many usable pairs of opposed molars as the Sioux of the same age category, while Londoners ages thirty-five to forty-five had some 80 percent fewer paired molars than the older Sioux.

When Smith presented his findings in a lecture before the Royal Anthropological Institute, he displayed a dental cast made from a member of his own family, which showed the terrible condition of a typical Londoner's teeth alongside the skull of an average "savage" showing beautifully preserved teeth. To test the possibility that the remarkable health of the Sioux's teeth was because they were exceptionally robust and healthy people, Smith did a comparison check of the teeth of twelve men of the regiment of Horse Guards from the Royal Household Cavalry, who would have been in superb physical condition. He found that the cavalrymen had teeth that were only a "trifling degree better preserved" than the average Londoner's. Smith correctly concluded that the lack of dental decay and tooth loss observed in tribal peoples was due to increased tooth wear, which kept the teeth clean and polished. He attributed the increased wear to the consumption of less cooked and less refined food, to the absence of knives and forks, which meant that more chewing was required, and to the presence of grit or "dirt" in the food. It was later learned that the absence of refined carbohydrates also contributed to healthy tribal teeth. The reduced tooth wear of contemporary peoples who eat industrially processed foods is also likely related to the common problem of impacted molars.[64] People eating coarse foods wear down not only the grinding surfaces of their teeth but also the sides of their teeth, which creates enough jaw space to accommodate the third molars when they erupt. When there is no significant wear, these "wisdom teeth" often must be extracted.

The association between traditional dietary patterns and healthy teeth was documented more systematically in a series of field studies conducted by American dentist Weston Price between 1931 and 1936.[65] Price visited some of the most traditional peoples in Amazonia, East Africa, Australia, and the Pacific and found that tooth decay and periodontal disease were virtually absent among self-sufficient peoples but steadily increased as these same peoples adopted the food patterns of industrial societies.

In 1956, shortly after Price's dental research, T. L. Cleave, a doctor in the British Royal Navy, used medical data on tribal peoples to isolate a single feature in the diets of industrialized peoples that caused what he called the "saccharine disease," a wide-ranging complex of conditions including tooth decay, ulcers, appendicitis, obesity, diabetes, constipation, and varicose veins. Like both Smith and Price before him, Cleave[66] was impressed by the fact that tribal peoples did not suffer from many of the common ailments of civilization. Thus, he attempted to find the special conditions that made tribal peoples healthier. His primary finding was that the traditional foods of tribal groups were consistently much higher in dietary fiber than the highly refined complex carbohydrates consumed by industrialized peoples. High-fiber diets speed the transit time of food through the digestive system, thereby reducing many common diseases of civilization. It took many years for his findings to be incorporated into popular nutritional wisdom in the industrial world, but now high fiber, along with low fat and low salt, is widely accepted as an important component of a healthy diet.

Anthropologist Clifford Behrens[67] provides some insights into how traditional classification systems are related to the maintenance of a high level of nutrition in tribal diets. Behrens found that the Shipibo of the Peruvian Amazon grouped their most preferred foods into two main emic categories, which he called "not-wild and cooked" and "wild and cooked." The Shipibo placed garden products such as plantains, maize, and manioc, which are high in carbohydrates, in the first category, and fish and game, which are high in protein and fat, in the second. The Shipibo considered their diet adequate only when it contained a balance of foods drawn from both categories. They accurately identified garden foods as the source of the energy needed for daily activities, while they felt that fish and game were needed for long-term health and growth.

Tribal Life Expectancy and Quality of Life

At a special symposium on the health of tribal peoples, held at the CIBA Foundation in London in 1976 and attended by more than two dozen specialists, it was concluded that self-sufficient tribal groups were generally healthy, and it was recognized that intervention by outsiders, even when well intended, could seriously undermine existing balances.[68] However, researchers found that some important tribal health "paradoxes" remained unanswered: (1) How is population growth regulated? (2) If foragers are well nourished, why are they physically small? and (3) If disease rates are low, why is tribal mortality high?[69] These studies may seem out of date, but these issues may never be fully resolved, because only small, refugee-like tribal groups had escaped the negative impacts of the commercial world by the late twentieth century. The invasion and destruction of the tribal world is discussed in more detail in chapter 13.

We still cannot fully answer these apparent paradoxes. Population regulation is a critical issue because maintaining a stationary population seems to be a key to relative balance between resources and quality of life. Population stability at constant, low-density levels also seems to be a general, but not invariable, characteristic of tribal groups. More recent interpretations suggest that fertility-limiting cultural mechanisms, such as prolonged lactation and postpartum sex taboos, were probably more important population regulators than raiding and infanticide, but the evidence is incomplete. High mortality due to raiding and infanticide would imply a reduced quality of life because it would lower average life expectancy. Yet from a functionalist perspective, it might arguably increase life quality for the survivors by promoting stability between people and resources.

There are some troubling and probably unanswerable philosophical issues involved in the preceding paradoxes. Although tribal peoples in general are often smaller and slighter than Europeans and appear to have shorter life expectancies, how does one decide that a given stature or life expectancy should be an appropriate cross-cultural measure of well-being? Some evidence suggests that very low birth weights or relatively low infant weight gain or growth rates may be associated with higher infant mortality rates. Some researchers also argue that small stature may indicate poor nutrition, especially in densely populated tribal areas.[70] However, taller and longer may not always be better, especially if taller or longer-lived people experience a reduced quality of life within their particular cultural and environmental setting.

Estimating the life expectancy of tribal populations is an inherently difficult task because there are few reliable data that unambiguously represent fully independent populations. Many widely cited demographic profiles of tribal peoples are actually inferences based on paleodemographic techniques of questionable validity. Life tables, such as those used by insurance companies to show the probability of someone surviving to a given age, have been drawn up for various tribal and prehistoric populations and generally show a significantly lower life expectancy for tribal peoples than for contemporary industrial populations (see table 5.8). Demographers often calculate life expectancy at age fifteen for populations where infant and childhood mortality may be high. This means, for example, that Northern Territory Aborigines with a life expectancy of thirty-four years at age fifteen could expect to live on the average to forty-nine. Of course, a few might live significantly longer. The figures presented in table 5.1 yield an estimated average life expectancy at age fifteen for seven ethnographically known foraging groups, including three from Australia, of only 26.4 years. By comparison, the figure for European Americans in 1986 was 61.3 years at age fifteen; however, 26.4 years was higher than the figures estimated for several archaeological populations and was higher than in fourteenth-century England.

Although tribal life expectancy appears to be lower than that of modern industrial populations, this should not be surprising, because life expectancy

Table 5.8. Estimate of Average Life Expectancy at Age 15 of Prehistoric and Tribal Populations

Population	Life Expectancy at Age 15
Upper Paleolithic	16.9
Catal Huyuk (Neolithic)	17.0
Neandertals	17.5
Natufians (Mesolithic)	17.5
Angamgssalik Eskimo*	19.2
Aborigines (Groote Eylandt)*	23.3
East Greenland Eskimo*	23.5
Birhor (foragers, India)*	24.0
England (fourteenth century)	25.8
Baker Lake Eskimo*	27.7
Aborigines (Tiwi)*	33.1
Aborigines (northern territory)*	34.0
European American (1986)†	61.3

Source: Hassan (1981:118).

*Ethnographicall described foragers; average life expectancy = 26.4 years

† Data from Wright (1990:225)

has made dramatic increases only within the past two centuries. Tribal peoples compare favorably with many preindustrial groups. However, all demographic estimates for tribal peoples must be used cautiously. Only figures based on reliable census records can be accepted at face value. There are significant sources of bias and uncertainty in demographic research on tribal populations.[71]

Anthropologists have long known that tribal lifestyles were conducive to good health, but that conclusion, and its corollary that the commercial world promoted unhealthy lifestyles, was confirmed by an international panel of health experts convened by the United Nations World Health Organization and Food and Agriculture Organization in 2002 to make recommendations on the prevention of chronic noncommunicable diseases such as obesity, diabetes, cardiovascular disease, cancer, dental disease, and osteoporosis. These are precisely the diseases that are either nonexistent or occur at very low rates among independent tribal peoples, yet they accounted for 60 percent of global mortality in 2001. The infrequency of these diseases in the independent tribal world is partly because they become more frequent with advancing age, and tribals may not live long enough to develop these conditions. However, tribals show lower rates of these diseases than other populations at the same age. Furthermore, many of these conditions now occur in children and are becoming more frequent in middle-aged adults in the commercial world. The panel produced a major technical report that directly linked "the growing epidemic of chronic disease" to specific unhealthy dietary and lifestyle changes associated with "industrialization, urbanization, economic develop ment and market globalization."[72] The market-driven "nutrition transition" from healthy traditional diets to unhealthy diets based on high "value added" processed food commodities was clearly the central problem.[73] According to the WHO report, commercial diets high in salt, sugars, and saturated fats, including processed vegetable fats with trans-fatty acids, all of which are now known to promote chronic disease, have "swept the entire world," swiftly replacing "traditional" diets that were high in fiber, complex carbohydrates, and natural fats known to be beneficial. The panel stressed that the harmful effects of these diet changes were amplified by the reductions in physical activity promoted by mechanization, motorized transport, and sedentary lifestyles. Significantly, the report concluded that traditional diets based on whole grains and unprocessed fruits, nuts, and vegetables were "particularly protective of health, and clearly environmentally sustainable. Much can be learned from these."[74]

SUMMARY

This chapter introduces some of the formal methods of cross-cultural analysis that cultural anthropologists use to better describe and compare sociocultural systems, and to make sense out of the cultural diversity. In keeping with our overall focus on scale and power, we make careful comparisons of South American and Amazonian societies, looking specifically at how they deal with individual differences in social rank and status. This chapter also demonstrates the difficulties of making meaningful cross-cultural quality-of-life comparisons of mental ability and health. It should make anyone cautious of simple stereotypes about tribal peoples as "underdeveloped." Although tribal individuals have the same basic intellectual and perceptual abilities as people in larger-scale cultures, their collective view of the world as reflected in myth, religion, and linguistic classification differs in significant ways that may be related to cultural scale and the absence of writing. However, when viewed from a relativistic and culturally sensitive position, tribal peoples are no more irrational, ignorant, or childish than people anywhere.

Tribal peoples have tremendous stores of culturally transmitted knowledge about the world around them, and their religious beliefs are perpetuated because they work effectively and because their validity is reinforced by the experience of daily life. This position must be spelled out clearly because some anthropologists have suggested that developmentally, tribal peoples are children who do not use adult logic and have difficulty separating fantasy from reality. Others have argued that tribal religious practices such as shamanism are the product of psychopathology. Formal schooling and institutionalized medicine clearly are not the only route to understanding and health. Not only are there inherent problems in data collection on these issues, but there are dangers in generalizing from individuals to groups and major problems in deciding what standard of comparison can be used. The evidence suggests that although infant mortality rates appear to be high and life expectancy low relative to those of urban industrial populations, tribal peoples are generally free of infectious disease and nutritional deficiencies and avoid many of the dental problems and degenerative diseases that are so common in other populations. The most conservative conclusion is that tribal peoples show no basic differences in their mental abilities, even though they lack writing. The average tribal person would appear to enjoy a healthy vigorous life, relatively free of disease.

STUDY QUESTIONS

1. What is elite-directed growth and how is it limited in the tribal world?
2. What are the relative merits of diffusion, adaptation, and migration as explanations of cultural differences?
3. How can cultural complexity, social rank, and hierarchy be measured?
4. Explain the views that each of the following took on the nature of "primitive" mentality: Boas, Tylor, Frazer, Levy-Bruhl, and Levi-Strauss.
5. Explain the cultural context of Malgri.
6. Use the Wawilak myth to illustrate the effectiveness of symbols.
7. Are there any important differences in the way that peoples in tribal and imperial worlds conceptualize reality?
8. Critique the psychopathological explanation of shamanism.
9. What conditions of tribal cultures contribute to health?

SUGGESTED READING

Boyd, Robert, and Peter J. Richerson. 2005. *The Origin and Evolution of Cultures*. Oxford: Oxford University Press. A bioevolutionary perspective of cultural development.

Cavalli-Sforza, Luigi Luca, and Francesco Cavalli-Sforza. 1995. *The Great Human Diasporas: The History of Diversity and Evolution*. Reading, MA.: Addison-Wesley. A useful overview of the migrations of peoples and their effects on genetic diversity.

Cohen, Mark, and George Armelegos (eds.). 1984. *Paleopathology and the Origins of Agriculture*. Orlando, FL.: Academic Press. A collection of essays on the health consequences of the transition to agriculture.

Eaton, S. B. Boyd, Melvin Konner, and Marjorie Shostak. 1988. *The Paleolithic Prescription*. New York: Harper & Row. An examination of the health aspects of forager dietary patterns that applies them to contemporary society.

Harner, M. J. 1980. *The Way of the Shaman*. New York: Harper & Row. A "how-to" manual that can be used by anyone interested in experimenting with the shamanistic experience.

GLOSSARY

Elite-directed growth When less than a majority, often a tiny percent of people, promote growth that concentrates benefits and socializes costs, or disperses costs to society at large.

Domestic scale Characterized by small, kinship-based societies, often with only five hundred people, in which households organize production and distribution.

Political scale Characterized by centrally organized societies with thousands or millions of members and energy-intensive production directed by political rulers.

Commercial scale Organized by impersonal market exchanges, commercial enterprises, contracts, and money, and potentially encompassing the entire world.

Neolocal residence Where a newly married couple resides independently of either set of parents.

Ambilocality (avunculocal residence) Where a couple resides near one set of parents or the other depending on circumstances.

avunculocality In matrilineal societies where a new couple resides with the husband's mother's brother, who is a member of his own matrilineage.

Social Darwinism A political "philosophy" that treats other societies as biologically and culturally inferior and therefore "unfit" for survival.

Animistic thinking The soul concept used by tribal individuals as an intellectual explanation of life, death, and dream experiences, part of Edward B. Tylor's theory of animism as the origin of religion.

Law of sympathy Sir James Frazer's explanation for the logic underlying magic, sorcery, and shamanism. He thought that tribal peoples believed that anything ever connected with a person, such as hair or blood, could be manipulated to influence that person.

Collective representations Ideas or thoughts and emotions common to a society as a whole, especially in reference to the supernatural.

Law of participation The assumption that a thing can participate in or be part of two or more things at once.

Structuralism A theoretical approach that examines how people construct meaning by using contrasting relationships between symbols, much as languages create meaning by contrasting sounds (phonemes).

Mythical thought Claude Levi-Strauss's term for the thinking underlying myth and magic; logically similar to scientific thought but based on the science of the concrete and used to serve aesthetic purposes and to solve existential problems,

Neolithic paradox Claude Levi-Strauss's term for the fact that tribal peoples invented all the major domestic technologies, such as cooking, textiles, and ceramics, that satisfied household needs, but did not go on to invent metallurgy and writing, which served political ends.

Science of the concrete Claude Levi-Strauss's term for thought based on perceptions and signs, images, and events, as opposed to formal science based on concepts.

NOTES

1. Murdock, George Peter. 1962. *Ethnographic Atlas*. Pittsburgh: University of Pittsburgh Press; Gray, J. Patrick. 1999. "A Corrected Ethnographic Atlas." *World Cultures* 10(1):24–85, http://worldcultures.org/.

2. Murdock, George Peter. 1972. *Outline of World Cultures*. 4th ed. New Haven, CT.: Human Relations Area Files.

3. Royal Anthropological Institute of Great Britain and Ireland. 1951. *Notes and Queries on Anthropology*. 6th ed. London: Routledge and K. Paul.

4. Murdock, George Peter. 1983. *Outline of World Cultures*. 6th ed. New Haven, CT: Human Relations Area Files; Murdock, George Peter, et al. 2000. *Outline of Cultural Materials*. 5th ed. New Haven, CT: Human Relations Area Files.

5. Gifford, E. W., and A. L. Kroeber. 1937. "Culture Element Distributions: IV. Pomo." *University of California Publications in American Archaeology and Ethnology* 37(4):117–254.

6. eHRAF www.yale.edu/hraf/collections.htm; Much related material is also available online at the World Cultures website which includes interactive mapping: http://worldcultures.org/.

7. Murdock, George P., and Douglas R. White. 1969. "Standard Cross-Cultural Sample." *Ethnology* 8(4):329–69.

8. Peregrine, Peter N. 2001. *Outline of Archaeological Traditions*. Human Relations Area Files.

Peregrine, Peter N. 2003. "Atlas of Cultural Evolution." *World Cultures* 14(1):2–75.

9. Peregrine, Peter N. 2003. "Atlas of Cultural Evolution." *World Cultures* 14(1):2–28, p. 3; Peregrine, Peter N. 2001. *Outline of Archaeological Traditions.* Human Relations Area Files.

10. Radcliffe-Brown, A. R. 1935. "On the Concept of Function in Social Science." *American Anthropologist* 37(3):394–402.

11. Malinowski, B. 1944. *A Scientific Theory of Culture.* Chapel Hill: University of North Carolina Press.

12. Wolf, Eric R. 1999. *Envisioning Power: Ideologies of Dominance and Crisis.* Berkeley: University of California Press.

13. Hewlett, Barry S., Annalisa De Silvestri, and C. Rosalba Guglielmino. 2002. "Semes and Genes in Africa." *Current Anthropology* 43(2):313–21.

14. Burton, Michael L., Carmella C. Moore, John W. M. Whiting, and A. Kimball Romney. 1996. "Regions Based on Social Structure." *Current Anthropology* 37(1):87–123; Hewlett, Barry S., Annalisa De Silvestri, and C. Rosalba Guglielmino. 2002. "Semes and Genes in Africa"; Jones, Doug. 2003. "Kinship and Deep History: Exploring Connections between Culture Areas, Genes, and Languages." *American Anthropologist* 105(3):501–14.

15. Guglielmino, C. Viganotti, B. Hewlett, and L. L. Cavalli-Sforza. 1995. "Cultural Variation in Africa: Role of Mechanisms of Transmission and Adaptation." *Proceedings of the National Academy of Sciences* 92:7585–89.

16. It is necessary to use largest settlements of 400 people for archaeological traditions and average settlements of 5,000 for ethnographic cultures to distinguish small from large chiefdoms, because of the categories used respectively in the *Atlas of Cultural Evolution* and the *Ethnographic Atlas.*

17. Complexity measures were developed for archaeological cultures by Peregrine (2003) and are adapted from Murdock, George P., and Suzanne F. Wilson. 1972. "Settlement Patterns and Community Organization: Cross-Cultural Codes 3." *Ethnology* 11(3): 254–95, and Murdock, George P., and Caterina Provost. 1973. "Measurement of Cultural Complexity." *Ethnology* 12(4):379–92.

18. Murdock, George P. 1973. "Measurement of Cultural Complexity." *American Anthropologist* 12(4):379–92.

19. Hornborg, Alf. 1988. "Dualism and Hierarchy in Lowland South America: Trajectories of Indigenous Social Organization." *Acta Universitatis Upsaliensis, Uppsala Studies in Cultural Anthropology* 9. Uppsala University, Uppsala, Sweden.

20. Binford, Lewis R. 2001. *Constructing Frames of Reference: An Analytic Method for Archaeological Theory Building Using Hunter-Gatherer and Environmental Data Sets.* Berkeley: University of California Press.

21. Murdock, George P. 1949. *Social Structure.* New York: Macmillan; Driver, H. E. 1956. *An Integration of Functional Evolutionary, and Historical Theory by Means of Correlations.* Indiana University Publications in Anthropology and Linguistics. Memoir 12.

22. Malinowski, Bronislaw. 1922. *Argonauts of the Western Pacific: An Account of Native Enterprise and Adventure in the Archipelagoes.* London: G. Routledge; 1926. *Crime and Custom in Savage Society.* New York: The Humanities Press; 1941. *The Sexual Life of Savages in North-Western Melanesia: an ethnographic account of courtship, marriage and family life among the natives of Trobriand Islands, British New Guinea.* New York: Halcyon House; 1965. *Coral Gardens and Their Magic.* 2 vols. Bloomington, IN: Indiana University Press.

23. Weiner, Annette B. 1988. *The Trobrianders of Papua New Guinea.* New York: Harcourt Brace Jovanovich.

24. Murdock, George P. 1967. *Ethnographic Atlas.* Pittsburgh: University of Pittsburgh Press; Gray, J. Patrick. 1999. "Ethnographic Atlas Codebook. *World Cultures* 10(1):86–136. 1999. "A Corrected Ethnographic Atlas." *World Cultures* 10(1):24–28.

25. Leach, Jerry W. 1983. "Introduction." In Leach, Jerry W., and Edmund Leach, eds. *The Kula: New Perspectives on Massim Exchange,* pp. 1–26. Cambridge: Cambridge University Press.

26. Malinowski, 1965. "Computation of the Harvest Gift Presented after the *Kayasa* in Omarakana in 1918," *Coral Gardens,* vol. 1, Document 2, 392–405.

27. Malinowski, 1926. *Crime and Custom,* 92.

28. Powell, H. A. 1969. "Competitive Leadership in Trobriand Political Organization." *Journal of the Royal Anthropological Institute of Great Britain and Ireland* 90(1): 118–45.

29. Malinowski, 1926. *Crime and Custom,* 46–47.

30. Wake, Charles Staniland. 1872. "The Mental Conditions of Primitive Man as Exemplified by the Australian Aborigine." *Journal of the Royal Anthropological Institute* 1:78–84.

31. Boas, Franz. 1911. *The Mind of Primitive Man.* New York: Macmillan.

32. Tylor, Edward B. 1871. *Primitive Culture.* London: Murray.

33. Frazer, Sir James 1990 [1890] 1900. *The Golden Bough,* 3 vols. London: Macmillan.

34. Levy-Bruhl, Lucien [1922] 1923. *Primitive Mentality.* New York: Macmillan. Levy-Bruhl, Lucien. 1926. *How Natives Think [Les Fonctions Mentales dans les Societes Inferieures].* New York: Knopf.

35. Levy-Bruhl, Lucien. 1926. *How Natives Think,* 43.

36. Levi-Strauss, Claude. 1966. *The Savage Mind.* Chicago: University of Chicago Press.

37. Kroeber, Alfred L. 1948. *Anthropology.* New York: Harcourt, Brace and World, 298.

38. Boyer, Pascal. 2000. "Functional Origins of Religious Concepts: Ontological and Strategic Selection in Evolved Minds." *Journal of the Royal Anthropological Institute* 6:195–214, 196.

39. Peters, Larry G., and Douglass Price-Williams. 1980. "Towards an Experiential Analysis of Shamanism." *American Ethnologist* 7(3):397–418.

40. Harner, M. J. 1980. *The Way of the Shaman.* New York: Harper & Row.

41. Whitehead, Neil L. 2002. *Dark Shamans: Kanaimà and the Poetics of Violent Death.* Durham & London: Duke University Press.

42. Peters, Larry G., and Douglass Price-Williams. 1980. "Analysis of Shamanism."

43. Silverman, Julian. 1967. "Shamans and Acute Schizophrenia." *American Anthropologist* 69(1):21–31.

44. American Psychiatric Association (APA). 1980. *Diagnostic and Statistical Manual of Mental Disorders,* 3rd ed. Washington, DC: American Psychiatric Association, 363.

45. American Psychiatric Association (APA). 2000. *Diagnostic and Statistical Manual IV.* Text Revision (DSM-IV-TR).

46. Noll, Richard. 1984. "The Context of Schizophrenia and Shamanism." *American Ethnologist* 11(1):191–92.

47. Cannon, Walter B. 1942. "'Voodoo' Death." *American Anthropologist* 44(2):169–81.

48. Eastwell, Harry D. 1982. "Voodoo Death and the Mechanisms for Dispatch of the Dying in East Arnhem, Australia." *American Anthropologist* 84(1):5–18.

49. Cawte, John E. 1976. "Malgri: A Culture-Bound Syndrome." *Culture-Bound Syndromes, Ethnopsychiatry, and Alternate Therapies.* Vol. 4 of *Mental Health Research in Asia and the Pacific,* edited by William Lebra, pp. 22–31. Honolulu: University Press of Hawaii.

50. Dow, James. 1986. "Universal Aspects of Symbolic Healing: A Theoretical Synthesis." *American Anthropologist* 88(l):56–69.

51. Dow. 1986. Symbolic Healing.

52. Munn, Nancy D. 1969. "The Effectiveness of Symbols in Murngin Rite and Ritual." In *Forms of Symbolic Action: Proceedings of the 1969 Annual Spring Meeting of the American Ethnological Society,* edited by Robert Spencer, pp. 178–207. Seattle and London: American Ethnological Society.

53. Munn, 1969. "Effectiveness of Symbols," 195, citing Warner, W. L. 1958. *A Black Civilization.* New York: Harper.

54. Brown, Michael F. 1984. "The Role of Words in Aguaruna Hunting Magic." *American Ethnologist* 11(3):545–58.

55. Malinowski, Bronislaw. 1948. *Magic, Science, and Religion.* Boston: Beacon Press.

56. Hemming, John. 1978. *Red Gold: The Conquest of the Brazilian Indians.* Cambridge, MA: Harvard University Press, 15.

57. Edgerton, Robert B. 1992. *Sick Societies: Challenging the Myth of Primitive Harmony.* New York: Free Press; Krech, Shepard, III. 1999. *The Ecological Indian: Myth and History.* New York: W. W. Norton and Co.

58. Neel, James V. 1970. "Lessons from a 'Primitive' People." *Science* 170(3960):815–22.

59. Tierney, Patrick. 2000. *Darkness in El Dorado: How Scientists and Journalists Devastated the Amazon.* New York: Norton.

60. Holmes, Rebecca. 1995. "Small Is Adaptive: Nutritional Anthropometry of Native Amazonians." In *Indigenous Peoples and the Future of Amazonia,* edited by Leslie E. Sponsel, pp. 121–48. Tucson and London: The University of Arizona Press.

61. Larrick, James W., James A. Yost, Jon Kaplan, Garland King, and John Mayhall. 1979. "Patterns of Health and Disease Among the Waorani Indians of Eastern Ecuador." *Medical Anthropology* 3(2):147–89.

62. Cohen, Mark Nathan. 1989. *Health and the Rise of Civilization.* New Haven, CT, and London: Yale University Press.

63. Smith, Wilberforce. 1894. "The Teeth of Ten Sioux Indians." *Journal of the Royal Anthropological Institute* 24:109–16, 110.

64. Krantz, Grover S. 1978. *Interproximal Attrition and Modern Dental Crowding.* Occasional Papers in Method and Theory in California Archaeology, no. 2, pp. 35–41. Society for California Archaeology.

65. Price, Weston Andrew. 1945. *Nutrition and Physical Degeneration: A Comparison of Primitive and Modern Diets and Their Effects.* Redlands, CA: Weston Price.

66. Cleave, T. L. 1974. *The Saccharine Disease.* Bristol, Eng.: John Wright.

67. Behrens, Clifford A. 1986. "Shipibo Food Categorization and Preference: Relationships Between Indigenous and Western Dietary Concepts." *American Anthropologist* 88(3):647–58.

68. CIBA Foundation. 1977. *Health and Disease in Tribal Societies.* CIBA Foundation Symposium 49, pp. 49–67. Amsterdam: Elsevier/Excerpta Medica/North-Holland.

69. Lozoff, Bettsy, and Gary M. Brittenham. 1977. "Field Methods for the Assessment of Health and Disease in Pre-Agricultural Societies." In *Health and Disease in Tribal Societies,* pp. 49–67. CIBA Foundation Symposium, no. 49. Amsterdam: Elsevier/Excerpta Medica/North-Holland.

70. Dennett, Glenn, and John Connell. 1988. "Acculturation and Health in the Highlands of Papua New Guinea." *Current Anthropology* 29(2):273–99.

71. Bocquet-Appel, Jean-Pierre, and Claude Masset. 1981. "Farewell to Paleodemography." *Journal of Human Evolution* 11:321–33.

72. United Nations, WHO/FAO. United Nations, World Health Organization / Food and Agriculture Organization. 2003. *Joint WHO/FAO Expert Consultation on*

Diet, Nutrition and the Prevention of Chronic Diseases. WHO Technical Report Series 916. Geneva, 1.

73. Drewnoski, Adam, and Barry M. Popkin. 1997. "The Nutrition Transition: New Trends in the Global Diet." *Nutrition Review* 55(2):31–43; Popkin, Barry M. 1998. "The Nutrition Transition and its Health Implications in Lower-Income Countries." *Public Health Nutrition* 1(1):5–21.

74. UN, WHO/FAO, 2003. *Prevention of Chronic Diseases*, 101.

Part Two

THE IMPERIAL WORLD: THE END OF EQUALITY

THE TRIBAL WORLD WAS THE ONLY WORLD UNTIL PERHAPS 7,500 years ago, when the first aggrandizing individuals succeeded in concentrating political power to form chiefdoms. This was the beginning of a global cultural transformation in which very quickly a handful of ruling elites successively constructed large, complex chiefdoms, kingdoms, city-states, and empires in favorable locations worldwide. These were large societies, numbering up to 100 million people, and they created totally different living conditions from the tribal world. The most important difference was that most people in the imperial world were subjects, not rulers. In contrast, tribal people enjoyed maximum freedom and personal autonomy. Tribals were in charge of the conditions of their daily lives. Imperial subjects were dependents. They were forced to pay taxes and tribute, and their lives might be expended at the whim of the emperor. Many subjects were literally slaves. The living conditions of most subjects were probably significantly lower than in the tribal world. Imperial societies are totalitarian systems, ruled by the head of a single family, who typically assumes supernatural powers. Imperial societies are large, complex, and expensive to maintain. They also degrade ecosystems and collapse frequently. It is difficult to explain how such societies were ever developed.

The following four chapters first describe Pacific Islander societies as representative chiefdoms and then explore the problem of state origins with a case study on Mesopotamia in the ancient Near East. The Inca Empire represents a New World civilization. Imperial China, Hindu kingdoms, and the Mughal Empire represent Old World Great Tradition Civilizations.

Pacific Islanders: From Leaders to Rulers

Figure 6.0. Woman from Paumoto Islands, French Polynesia, nineteenth century (Ratzel 1896:200).

PRONUNCIATION GUIDE

THE PRONUNCIATION OF HAWAIIAN AND OTHER PACIFIC Islander words in this chapter can be approximated by English speakers using the following orthography and sounds:[1]

KEY

a = *a* in f*a*ther
o = *o* in g*o*
ai = *i* in *i*ce
e = *e* in b*e*d
i = *i* in b*i*t
ee = *ee* in b*ee*t
oo = *oo* in f*oo*d
h = *h* in *h*at
y = *y* in *y*ou
• = Syllable division
/ = Stress

' = glottal stop ; resembles the stop in English between *oh-oh*
ahupua'a = [a • hoo • pu / a a]
ali'i = [a • lee /' ee]
kahuna = [ka • hoo / na]
Kamehameha = [ka» me / ha • me / ha]
kanaka = [ka • na / ka]
kapu = [ka • poo /]
konohiki = [ko • no • hee / kee]
Kumulipo = [koo • moo • lee / po]
Lapita = [la • pee / ta]
Makahiki = [ma • ka • hee / kee]
maka'ainana = [ma • ka '/ ai • na • na]
mana = [ma / na]
moku = [mo / koo]
ohua = [o • hua]

The vast Pacific region, known as Oceania, was successfully explored and colonized by Austronesian-speaking voyagers, who spread out from their earlier footholds in the western Pacific beginning about 3,500 years ago. By 1000 BP, virtually every habitable Pacific island supported thriving societies. When Europeans began to arrive in significant numbers in the nineteenth century, they found the Pacific Islanders, except for those in New Guinea, organized into chiefdoms, or small kingdoms. Pacific cultures were perched on the "great divide" between tribes and states, displaying much of the social equality and equilibrium of tribal societies yet maintaining a pervasive concern with **rank**. Larger Pacific Island societies have simple forms of social stratification and are important examples of the way politicization divides people based on differing access to wealth and power. From a human perspective, pervasive social stratification is perhaps the most important feature of the imperial and commercial worlds.

Remote from the centers of power in the industrializing world and offering relatively few resources to attract outsiders, many Pacific islands maintain much of their traditional cultural system today. They also offer ideal material for examining the contrasts between tribes and states and for understanding the development of political-scale cultures. Given the severe environmental constraints of small islands, Oceania also offers an important place to examine the relationships between population, culture, and resources. The archaeological evidence suggests that Pacific Island societies were already chiefdoms when they began their migration into the Pacific from Island Southeast Asia. Therefore, this chapter will highlight the scale-related contrasts between tribal and chiefdom societies and focus on how chiefdom societies were organized and how they developed on different Pacific islands, but not on how chiefdoms originated. Chapter 7 will examine the origins of Mesopotamian chiefdoms from tribal societies and their further development into city-states and empires.

LEARNING OBJECTIVES

After studying this chapter you should be able to do the following:

1. Explain the physical challenges facing the first people to explore and settle the Pacific Islands and describe the cultural solutions that they used.
2. Define and distinguish between the three ethnogeographic regions of the Pacific: Melanesia, Polynesia, and Micronesia.
3. Explain how we can be certain that the ancestors of the Pacific Islanders originated in Asia, not South America.
4. Describe the main components of Pacific Islander subsistence and compare with Amazonian systems.
5. Explain the ways in which life in the Pacific Islands makes demands on people that conflict with the moral systems that characterize the tribal world.
6. Evaluate the Pacific Islander evidence for the theory that growth is an elite-directed process that concentrates social power and diffuses the costs.
7. Using Pacific Islander examples, describe the conditions that facilitated the construction of complex chiefdoms and weigh the evidence for alternative causal explanations.
8. Describe the distribution of social power in Hawaii under King Kamehameha in 1819.
9. Describe the main features of Pacific Islander religious belief and practice in comparison with those of the tribal world.
10. Describe how absolute size of island societies is related to cultural organization and the distribution of social power.
11. Compare gender relations in island societies with gender relations in the tribal world.

OCEANIA: LIVING IN THE ISLAND WORLD

Searching for Paradise:
From High Islands to Low Coral Atolls

In the popular imagination, the reef-fringed, palm-shaded islands of the Pacific are paradises. In reality, many Pacific islands have no drinking water, no soil, and virtually no native plants or animals, and they may be subject to devastating typhoons. Furthermore, without a chart, they are difficult to find in the first place. Exploring and successfully colonizing the Pacific world was one of the greatest human adventures, and it is surely a tribute to the courage and ingenuity of generations of Austronesian-speaking peoples who accomplished this feat roughly a thousand years ago.

The Pacific Ocean covers roughly one-third of the earth's surface. Excluding Hawaii and New Zealand, most Pacific islands are very small, and many are uninhabitable. There are some 10,000 islands scattered across a vast area of ocean, with a total land area of only 4,500 square miles (12,000 km²). The average island is barely more than a square mile of land, and island groups are separated by immense ocean distances. It is 8,000 miles (12,800 km) from Easter Island at the eastern end of Polynesia to Palau in Western Micronesia. There are 2,000 Micronesian islands averaging a third of a square mile spread over an area the size of the continental United States.

Following the original distinctions drawn in 1832 by French geographer Dumont d'Urville (1790–1842), Oceania customarily is divided into three ethnogeographic regions: Melanesia, Polynesia, and Micronesia (see figure 6.1). Melanesia ("black islands") originally was distinguished from Polynesia on ethnocentric and racist grounds. The early European explorers were more comfortable with the Polynesians because they were lighter skinned and more hierarchically organized and were seen as attractive, friendly, and almost civilized.[2] By contrast, the relatively dark-skinned Melanesians were associated with Africans and were viewed as savage, tribal, and hostile, and even as cannibals and headhunters. In reality, however, the boundaries between Melanesia, Micronesia, and Polynesia were not that sharp, either biologically or culturally, as we will see.

Melanesian islands are predominantly large, mountainous islands formed on the Indian continental plate. They derive their rich and varied terrestrial ecosystems from their proximity to the Southeast Asian mainland and Australia. The true oceanic islands, which make up most of Polynesia and Micronesia, are either the above-water tops of volcanoes or coral that was

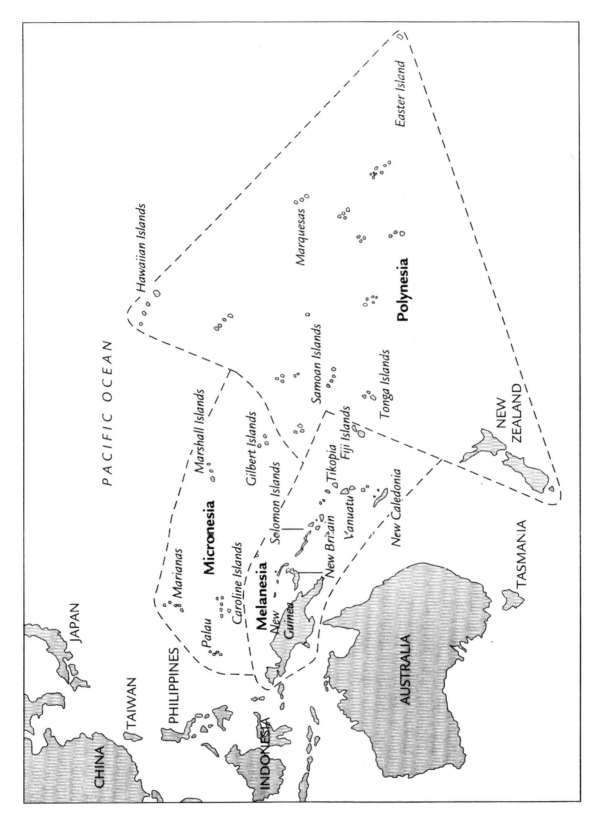

Figure 6.1. Three Pacific island culture areas, Melanesia, Polynesia, and Micronesia, with the principal island groups and cultures discussed in the text.

formed in the shallow waters on undersea volcanic slopes. Hawaii, New Zealand, and Easter Island form the corners of the vast Polynesian triangle. Polynesia ("many islands") contains many high volcanic islands, most of which lie south of the equator. The islands of Micronesia ("tiny islands") are primarily very small islets of coral sand that form on the reefs that fringed ancient, now submerged volcanoes. Before the arrival of Europeans, the two largest cultural areas, Polynesia and Micronesia (see figure 6.1), which will be the focus of this chapter, together contained a population estimated at 700,000 people.[3]

Many factors affect the habitability of islands. Generally, large, high, volcanic islands, such as those found in Melanesia and Polynesia, contain relatively more land resources than the small coral islands of Micronesia. High islands will support a larger human population and are likely to have several zones of natural vegetation, rich soils, and flowing freshwater. However, there may be significant environmental dif-

ferences between the moist windward side of these islands and the dry leeward side, which is sheltered from the rain by the mountains. There is also a general decline in biological diversity with increasing distance from the Asian mainland and Australia. For example, only a few reptiles, rats, and bats are native to the oceanic islands, and the most remote islands have only a few seabirds. Unless human colonists brought animal domesticates with them, animal protein could only be obtained from marine life. Similarly, few if any edible plants occurred naturally on the smaller islands, and a reliable source of carbohydrates in the form of domesticated plants had to be introduced.

Perhaps the most critical limiting factors are related to climate and the absolute size of an island. The tiny coral islets might be no more than 6 to 8 feet (2–3 m) above sea level and lack flowing freshwater. But if they are at least 350 feet (107 m) in diameter, they might support an underground layer of freshwater, which forms when rainwater percolates through the porous coral and sand and mixes only gradually with the denser seawater beneath. Many islets support a small freshwater or brackish swamp in the center, but they depend on rainfall that is regionally variable and erratic, so that in some places serious droughts can occur. The freshwater supply of small atolls may also be temporarily destroyed by typhoons, which can wash saltwater completely over low islets. Despite all these limitations, an islet as small as 0.25 square miles might sustain 200 people, given the appropriate technical skills, as long as they maintain contacts with neighboring groups who can be relied on for support.

Speculation on the origin of the Pacific Islanders began as soon as outsiders encountered them. But in the absence of solid linguistic, archaeological, and biological data, many fanciful and mutually exclusive theories were devised.[4] Some theorists deprecated the navigational skills and cultural creativity of Pacific Islanders, believing that only ancient Egyptians could have settled the Pacific.[5] In 1947, Norwegian adventurer Thor Heyerdahl drifted on a balsa-log raft westward with the winds and currents across the Pacific from South America to prove his theory that Pacific Islanders were Native Americans. Contrary to these theorists, however, the overwhelming evidence of physical anthropology, linguistics, and archaeology shows that the Pacific Islanders came from Southeast Asia and were sufficiently skilled as navigators to sail against the prevailing winds and currents (see box 6.1). Table 6.1 outlines the prehistory of the Pacific Islands and adjacent Island Southeast Asia.

Figure 6.2. Man from Truk, Micronesia, nineteenth-century (Ratzel 1896:202).

Table 6.1. Prehistory of the Pacific Islands

AD 1778	Captain James Cook lands in the Hawaiian Islands
AD 1522	Ferdinand Magellan expedition crosses the Pacific
Polynesian Expansion (3600 BP—AD 800)	
AD 800	New Zealand settled
AD 400	Easter Island settled
AD 300	Hawaii settled
2000 BP	Marquesas settled
3250 BP	Lapita pottery in Fiji
Proto-Oceanic Expansion (5000 BP—3600 BP)	
5000 BP	Outrigger canoes enter Oceania
Proto-Oceanic maritime specialization	
Proto-Austronesians (15,000 BP—5000 BP)	
7000 BP	Domestication of banana, sugarcane, breadfruit, coconut, sago, rice; fishing technology
9000 BP	Taro and yams horticulture in New Guinea
***Homo sapiens* Foragers (60,000 BP—15,000 BP)**	
60,000	Ancestral Australian and Papuan foragers in Sundaland
***Homo erectus* in Java (1.5 million BP—250,000 BP)**	

Sources: Bellwood (1980), Kirch (1985, 2000), Oliver (1989).

The basic cultural requirements for the successful colonization of the Pacific Islands include the appropriate boat-building, sailing, and navigating skills to get to the islands in the first place; domesticated plants and gardening skills suited to often-marginal conditions; and a varied inventory of fishing implements and techniques. It is now generally believed that these prerequisites originated with peoples speaking Austronesian languages and began to emerge in Southeast Asia by about 7000 BP. The Proto-Austronesian culture of that time, based on archaeology and linguistic reconstruction, presumably had a broad inventory of cultivated plants including taro, yams, banana, sugarcane, breadfruit, coconut, sago, and rice. Just as important, the culture possessed the basic foundation for an effective maritime adaptation, including outrigger canoes and a variety of fishing techniques effective for overseas voyaging.

Contrary to the arguments of some that much of the Pacific was settled by Polynesians accidentally marooned after being lost and adrift at sea, it seems reasonable that this feat was accomplished by deliberate colonization expeditions that set out fully stocked with food and domesticated plants and animals. Detailed studies of the winds and currents using computer simulations suggest that drifting canoes would have been a most unlikely means of colonizing the Pacific.[6] These expeditions likely were driven by population growth and political dynamics on the home islands, as well as the challenge and excitement of exploring unknown waters. Because all Polynesians and Micronesians and many Melanesians speak Austronesian languages and grow crops derived from Southeast Asia, all these peoples most certainly derived from that region, and not the New World or elsewhere.

BOX 6.1. THE ORIGIN OF THE PACIFIC ISLANDERS

By about 5000 BP, Austronesian-speaking peoples began to expand toward the Pacific Islands, first into Taiwan and the Philippines and then along coastal New Guinea. By 3000 BP virtually all of Melanesia and much of Micronesia were occupied, and the Proto-Polynesians had established a firm foothold in Fiji, Tonga, and Samoa on the western edge of what would become Polynesia.

Some of the best archaeological evidence for the sequence of colonization in the Pacific is based on the discovery of a distinctive red, stamped, and incised pottery style, known as Lapita (see figure 6.3), and associated domesticated plants and fishing technology. Lapita peoples ultimately were derived from the Proto-Austronesians of Island Southeast Asia. But they appear to have developed their distinctive style in the New Britain area off eastern New Guinea about 3,600 years ago before spreading through the closely spaced chain of Melanesian islands to New Caledonia.[7] The crossing of the 528 miles (850 km) of open ocean between Vanuatu and Fiji, which took place about 3250 BP judging by the appearance of Lapita pottery in Fiji at that time, was a major achievement that set the stage for expansion into the rest of the

Glottochronology: Word Tracks across the Pacific

The general picture of the settlement of Oceania seems to conform well with linguistic reconstructions based on **glottochronology**, which suggests that most modern Austronesian languages emerged within the past 50,000 years (see figure 6.4). Glottochronology assumes that all languages lose words from a common core vocabulary at a constant rate historically documented for Indo-European languages.[8] The core vocabulary is a list of 100 to 200 words for cultural universals such as body parts and geographic features. The years since two languages separated from a common ancestor are calculated from the percentage of cognates identified in the core vocabulary. **Cognates** are words that are recognizably derived from a common source in a parent language, and thus their frequency is assumed to be a measure of their separation time. To cite a Polynesian example, table 6.2 lists the words for *deity*, *chief*, and *taboo* in Tikopian, a member of the Samoic branch of Nuclear Polynesian, and Hawaiian, an Eastern Polynesian language. The words in both languages obviously are similar enough to be considered cognates, implying a common ancestry, even though their speakers live more than 3,000 miles apart.

Languages sharing more than 80 percent cognates are considered to be dialects of the same language and are assumed to be separated by no more than 500 years. In theory, relationships as remote as 10,000

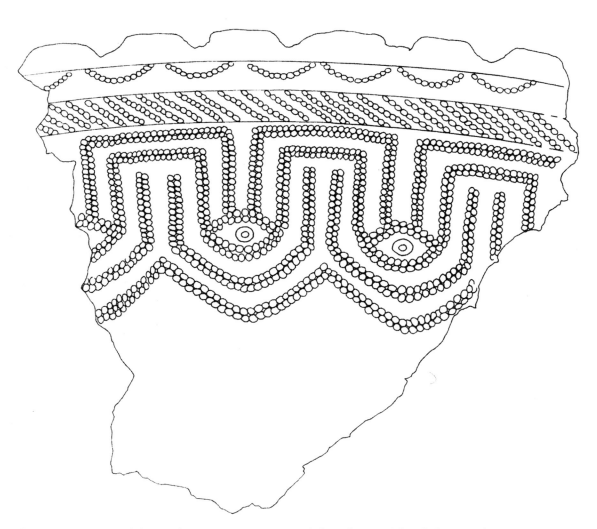

Figure 6.3. Stamped decorations on Lapita pottery (after Figure 4.3 in Kirch 200:90).

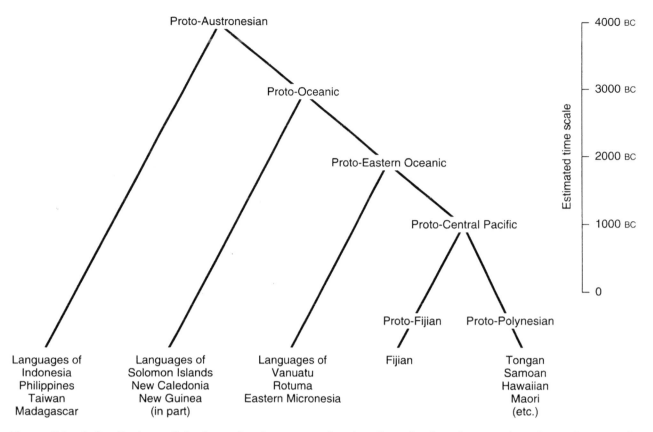

Figure 6.4. A family tree of Austronesian languages showing time depths of separations from the Oceanic branches (source: Kirch 1985:62).

years might be suggested on the basis of extremely low percentages of shared cognates.

Islander Survival Skills:
Outrigger Canoes and Navigation

Canoes and navigation were a vital part of Pacific Island culture. Not only did they make discovery and colonization possible, but they were necessary for making a living and maintaining communication between islands. Seagoing Micronesian outriggers, which were routinely used to cross more than 300 miles (483 km) of open ocean, were only 25 feet (8 m) long, whereas the huge double-hulled Polynesian canoes used in overseas colonization were nearly 100 feet (30 m) long and could easily accommodate supplies for an extended voyage. Canoes were designed to be extremely seaworthy and, unlike rafts, were highly maneuverable and could be propelled by both sail and paddles. The most widely distributed canoe type was the outrigger, which in Micronesia was usually constructed from a carved breadfruit-log hull with wooden planks lashed on the side. The outrigger was a wooden float suspended approximately half a hull length off the windward side of the canoe

and counterbalanced by a platform suspended off the lee side. The outrigger was oriented so that the float would be lifted by the wind on the sail. When the float dipped into the water, it pulled the canoe back into the wind. The great advantage of the outrigger was that it maximized speed and stability without a deep keel (to counterbalance the sail), which would impede passage over the reefs surrounding most Pacific islands.

The addition of an outrigger posed many design problems that traditional canoe builders solved in very sophisticated ways. The hull had to be asymmetrical in cross section, and its overall contours were shaped within very narrow tolerances to achieve a balance between seaworthiness, speed, and maneuverability.[9] Only a few specialists had the necessary skills for direct

Table 6.2. Cognates between Tikopian and Hawaiian Languages of Nuclear Polynesian

Word	Tikopian (Samoic Outlier)	Hawaiian (Eastern Polynesian)
Deity	Atua	Akua
Chief	Ariki	Ali'i
Taboo	Tapu	Kapu

Sources: Firth ([1936] 1957), Malo (1951), and Ruhlen (1987).

construction of such a complex craft. The bow and stern of the outrigger were reversible, and when a major change in direction was made, the sail was shifted from end to end to keep the float facing the wind.

The navigational techniques that allowed Polynesian explorers to maintain a steady course across vast distances in search of islands are still being practiced by a few skilled navigators on some of the most isolated Micronesian atolls (see figure 6.5). Thomas Gladwin's[10] research on the atoll of Puluwat revealed the main features of the system. Gladwin found that Micronesian navigation was based on an elaborate body of formal knowledge, both empirical and mythical. A few titled specialists, known as master navigators, controlled the system and offered formal instruction to aspiring navigators. Out of the island population of four hundred people, only six men were considered master navigators. Successful navigation depended on the ability to sail a steady course on a specific bearing while keeping a mental record of the distance traveled, for days or weeks at a time, at night, during storms, across changing currents, and in unfamiliar waters. The key to the system was a star chart with thirty-two named bearing points based on the rising and setting points of specific stars. For each route traveled, a navigator had to commit to memory a unique sequence of bearing stars.

The navigators on Puluwat routinely sailed between twenty-six islands using 110 different routes. To follow a given bearing, the navigators needed to know what stars would be observed en route, and they kept careful track of wave patterns and weather conditions. There was little margin for error on a long voyage because small atolls were only visible for 10 miles (16 km) at sea and so might easily be missed in passing. And even upon arrival, the navigator had to find narrow passes through treacherous reefs.

Navigators were greatly respected, high-status individuals. Canoes were treated with great care. They were stored in special canoe houses to prevent waterlogging, and the lashings and caulking might be replaced every two years.

Long-distance voyages also depended on a reliable system of food storage. Whole coconuts were a ready, storable source of food and drinking water, but there were elaborate ways of processing other important staples such as breadfruit, pandanus palm fruits, and taros so that they could be stored indefinitely without

Figure 6.5. Panopeans, Micronesia, nineteenth-century: a. man (Ratzel 1896:198); b. women (Ratzel 1896:273).

canning or refrigeration.[11] Micronesians had at least four different ways of preserving breadfruit, involving grating, pounding, soaking, fermenting, cooking, and sun drying. In one method, peeled slices of raw ripe breadfruit were soaked for one and a half days in the lagoon, fermented for two days on the ground, then squeezed and stirred with fresh water for three more days to convert them to dough. When the dough was shaped into slabs and sun-dried, it could be stored for up to two years before being reconstituted by soaking again in water.[12]

Breadfruit is more nutritious than potatoes and is rich enough in calories and vitamins to supply virtually all daily food requirements when supplemented with fish and coconut. Because many of the cultivated plants in the Pacific are grown from cuttings, special techniques were developed for transporting them. The root-balls of delicate young breadfruit trees were wrapped in rotted coconut husks, bound with dried leaves, and bundled in woven baskets to protect them from saltwater.[13]

Fishing and Gardening:
The Island Technological Base

Pacific Island subsistence is similar to that of Amazonia in that it is based on two rather distinct systems: 1) fishing and gathering of marine animals to provide protein and 2) gardening to produce the bulk of dietary calories. According to the usual gender division of labor, men do the fishing and heavy gardening work while women gather marine animals and do the daily garden cultivating and harvesting. Three crop zones, which on small islands are often arranged in concentric zones according to altitude and proximity to the ocean, include orchard crops, dry crops, and wet crops. The orchard crops are the breadfruit trees and the relatively salt-tolerant coconuts and pandanus palms that can grow near the beach (see figure 6.6a). All of these trees provide food as well as raw materials for canoe building, house construction, and basketry. On the smaller islands, they are the only significant sources of wood and fiber. The subsistence importance of coconuts is indicated by the fact that Polynesians name seventeen different stages of nuts according to their edibility.[14] Micronesians specialize in producing a fermented drink from the sap tapped from the unopened flower stem.

The dry gardens produce sweet potatoes, yams, and bananas, but the extent of such gardens is severely limited by soil conditions and rainfall, especially on the smaller coral islands and atolls. On many of these islands, soil other than coral sand is virtually absent, and humus must be created and maintained by a continuous process of mulching. Throughout much of the Pacific, the most important food plants are the taros, members of the arum family (*Araceae*), known as aroids (see box 6.2 and figure 6.6b).

The productivity of taro and its subsistence importance are indicated by data obtained by William Alkire[15] on the Micronesian atoll of Lamotrek in the central Caroline Islands. In Lamotrek, approximately 200 people live on a 0.25-square-mile (158-acre or 64-hectare) islet. Alkire estimated that taro supplied approximately three-fourths of the average 2 pounds (0.9 kg) of plant food consumed daily by adults on the island. An estimated 500,000 taro plants grew on the island, with some 15,000 per acre in the 58 acres of the island's swampy interior. Annual consumption was only about 20 percent of the total crop, but even if most of the plants were slow-growing swamp taro, the consumption rate still would have been well below potential production. However, if typhoons swept saltwater into the swamp and destroyed the crop, recovery would take at least three years.

Taro-based subsistence was a time-consuming female task on Lamotrek. During the half of the year when breadfruit was not being harvested, Lamotrek women worked more than two hours a day in the taro swamp, cultivating and harvesting. Taro processing took nearly an additional three hours a day. Breadfruit harvesting and processing required about three hours a day in season.

Fishing was a primary male activity throughout the Pacific. On an average day, nearly one fourth of the male population of Lamotrek would be out fishing. Men typically spent more than five hours fishing at a time and brought back about 9 pounds (4 kg) of fish. Virtually every major fishing technique was used, including traps, nets, spears, and hook and line. Fish were also raised in fish farms—rock-lined pools in tidal shallows—where they were fed and allowed to reproduce.

Coral reef ecosystems cover less than 0.1 percent of the globe, but they produce some 10 percent of the world's fish and support many other traditionally important food animals, such as sea turtles, and edible marine invertebrates, such as shellfish. Estimates for sustained productivity of these rich coral reef zones range as high as 22 tons (20 metric tons) of fish per square kilometer of reef per year.[16] This would be enough for 110 people. The availability of animal protein is clearly not a limiting factor for most

Figure 6.6. Primary Pacific island subsistence crops. (a) orchard crops: (1) coconut palm; (2) breadfruit; (3) banana; and (4) pandanus palm. (b) root crops: (1) yam; (2) sweet potato; and (3) taro.

Pacific Islanders. In comparison, the mammal protein produced in a square kilometer of tropical rain forest would support only one person per year.

The amount of specialized knowledge that successful fishing required was most impressive. Many important marine ecozones were exploited in different ways. Atolls, for example, included at least five broad marine zones: the lagoon in the center of the atoll, shallow waters, deep waters along reef edges and coral heads, intertidal reefs and flats, and the open ocean.[17] Pacific Islanders themselves recognized many finer distinctions. The shallow waters, reef edges, and lagoons generally were the most intensively exploited zones, where nets, traps, and weirs could be used most

effectively (see figure 6.7). The people of Fais, in the Carolines, named four broad marine zones and thirteen subzones ringing their 1-square-mile (2.6-km^2) raised coral island.[18] They located specific fishing areas by reference to some sixty submerged coral heads, which were individually named, and they identified eleven lines radiating from the island and aligned with named features on shore and at sea. The Gilbertese Islanders in Kiribati have names for 254 fish species, 95 marine invertebrates, and 25 fish anatomical features.[19]

Marine biologist Robert Johannes[20] has documented the knowledge employed by native fishermen on Palau in Micronesia. A critical element in organiz-

Figure 6.7. In Micronesia fish are frequently taken in traps.

ing Palauan fishing activities was keeping careful track of the seasons. For this purpose, the Palauans utilized a twelve-month lunar calendar that allowed them to predict with considerable precision changes in wind, weather, and waves and the movements and breeding patterns of many pelagic fish, turtles, and seabirds. Palauans understood how ocean currents were deflected by islands and reefs, and they knew where specific fish would concentrate seasonally in relation to the eddies and calm places (see figure 6.8).

A profusion of fishing gear and techniques reflected an understanding of the specific feeding habits, life history, and anatomy of many different fish species. The curiously incurved shell fishhook, so widely used in the Pacific, works more effectively than the standard barbed steel hook, which Europeans assumed to be superior (see figure 6.9). The traditional shell hook is designed to slide to the corner of the fish's mouth after a light tug and then to rotate, penetrating and locking securely in the fish's jaw.[21]

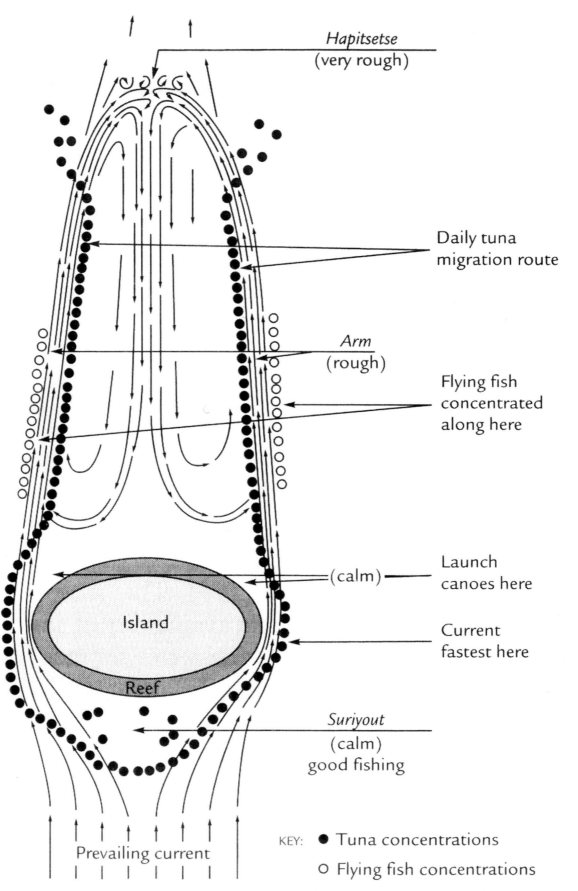

Figure 6.8. Micronesians in Palau use their knowledge of ocean currents to locate fish (source: based on Johannes 1981, Figure 3).

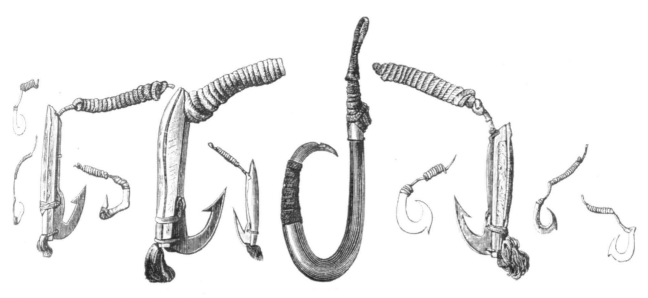

Figure 6.9. A selection of fish hooks from Oceania, nineteenth century (Ratzel 1896:83).

BOX 6.2. TARO

The arum family includes many familiar leafy tropical ornamentals, such as the philodendron. The edible aroids grow large heart-shaped ears and are sprouted from cuttings. They produce starchy corms and bulbous underground stems and are highly productive, but they require large amounts of relatively fresh water. The true taro, *Colocasia esculenta*, is sometimes grown in terraced, irrigated ponds on high islands. It can be planted at any time and is harvested within a year, but it does not store well, either in the ground or after harvest. Another important aroid, *Cyrtosperma*, the swamp taro, produces a more fibrous corm. It takes three years to reach full maturity, but it can be harvested over a longer period, allowing it to be stored in the ground, and it keeps for about two weeks after harvest. It is the preferred taro in much of Micronesia, where it is grown in the swampy center of small coral islands where freshwater reaches the surface. Another aroid, *Alocasia macrorrhiza*, or giant taro (elephant ear), grows under drier conditions, but its corms require special processing to remove irritating crystals.

PACIFIC ISLAND SOCIETIES: LIVING WITH INEQUALITY

Understanding Pacific Island chiefdoms requires a brief review of the evolutionary background of human society that was introduced in chapter 1. Early hominids shared ancient primate social instincts with their chimpanzee relatives that made it possible for both chimps and humans to live in very small, intimate family groups of twenty-five to fifty individuals. Such small societies depended on direct physical contact, interpersonal cooperation, mating, grooming, and simple dominance hierarchies. The evolution of fully modern humans living in tribal societies of five hundred or more people required new, culturally transmitted, social instincts for morality and ethnocentrism, and the cultural construction of social identity based on kinship, marriage, and exchange.[22]

Prototribes developed by means of a coevolutionary process of natural selection operating on the genetics of individuals and cultural selection operating on the shared beliefs and practices of organized human groups. Individuals most likely to reproduce would have been those who could live cooperatively in a successful group. The cultural meanings and behaviors that people transmitted to their children and to society at large were those that favored individual survival and reproduction, and that also favored group survival in competition with other human groups. People were morally compelled to seek group approval, and they had to believe that their own society was superior to all others. For this kind of evolution to work, all individuals and the tribe as a whole had to succeed.[23]

Thus, morality and ethnocentrism became powerful forces for social equality, and they made it difficult for any individuals to concentrate social power in personal imperia that were conspicuously larger than average. In view of the apparent success of tribal constraints against concentrated social power, the evolution of larger, less egalitarian chiefdoms and states has been called a "grand series of experiments at the expense of the social instincts."[24]

Elite-Directed Cultural Transformation in Polynesia

Pacific Island societies were strikingly different from any of the tribal groups we have examined thus far. Before the invasion of the commercial world, Pacific Islanders lived in politically centralized chiefdoms that were often orders of magnitude larger than tribes, and they were ruled by elites who enjoyed special privileges. The size difference matters enormously. Chiefdoms were not simply tribes grown larger. Chiefdoms required social transformations that conflicted with the human predilections for personal freedom and equality that defined the tribal way of life. The natural laws of scale meant that when tribal societies grew larger, unless they segmented, rulers had to radically transform the culture in order to prevent social disintegration. Why this was so is explained in box 6.3. These larger chiefdom societies so restricted human freedom and apportioned benefits so unequally and were so out of step with the lifestyles and personalities familiar to tribal people that they could only have been sustained with coercive institutions directed by the principal beneficiaries of this enormous cultural transformation.

Elites constructed the world's earliest known chiefdoms in Mesopotamia 7,500 years ago (see chapter 7). Their appearance was so sudden and so recent that they had to have been the product of cultural rather than biological change. It seems likely that chiefdoms required a combination of circumstances that made it possible for power-seeking individuals to enlarge their personal imperia beyond the constraints typically imposed by tribal societies. Chiefdom organization did not originate independently in Polynesia. The Proto-Austronesian peoples who settled the Pacific brought simple chiefdoms with them from Southeast Asia. However, the processes involved in the transformation of tribes into chiefdoms, and chiefdoms into larger-scale, more complex states, which are explored in chapter 7, are similar to the transformation from simple to complex chiefdoms that occurred in the Pacific. Any culture must be reproduced by people in a continuous process, but this is more difficult in chiefdoms where the benefits are not equally shared. Less-privileged members of chiefdom societies must be forced to make the best of their inferior positions, or they are persuaded by elite-manipulated symbols to imagine that they are not actually disadvantaged.

The central organizational problem that rulers must repeatedly solve is that people naturally don't like to be commanded by others, and they don't like social inequality unless they are at the top.

The discovery and settlement of the Pacific Islands by Polynesians involved a dynamic process of population growth and subsistence intensification. On several of the largest islands, elites used cycles of competitive feasting and warfare to construct complex chiefdoms with highly unequal social classes.[25] This was an elite-directed politicization process, in which a handful of people successfully manipulated the legitimizing power of cosmology to create political economies that compelled the majority of society to support elite self-interested growth projects. When the scale of Polynesian societies increased, social power became more concentrated in the hands of the chiefs, and most people lost control over the natural and cultural resources they needed to meet their basic needs.

The colonization of unoccupied Polynesian islands would have favored very rapid initial population growth, with founder populations potentially doubling within a single generation up to natural and cultural limits. However, cultural forms of population regulation were as important as natural limits, and continuous growth was not inevitable. Even at a modest 2 percent annual growth, a doubling time of thirty-six years, a founder population of twenty-five would have grown to more than a trillion people within 1,234 years. Polynesians settled the Pacific over 3,500 years, and island populations did not regularly crash. On some islands it took a long time for limits to be reached. For example, the archaeological record shows that over 1,400 years Hawaii's population may have reached 800,000 before Europeans arrived in 1778.[26] By then they were probably approaching overall carrying capacity for their intensive, hand-powered subsistence technology. It took global commercial trade and an enormous input of fossil fuels to push Hawaii's population to 1.2 million people by the year 2000.

As island populations grew larger, people modified and sometimes degraded the natural ecosystems by creating artificial plant communities. Many unique native birds were exterminated in the process.[27] Growth also meant that people had to work harder, steadily intensifying their subsistence activities by developing irrigation systems and fish ponds to produce more food from a very limited space. Similar subsistence intensification growth trends also characterized the Neolithic and were familiar to tribal peoples, but in the islands the human outcome was different, because power-seeking chiefs took advantage of the stresses of population growth to expand their personal imperia. Tribal peoples were apparently able to maintain lower limits on the size of their societies and seldom felt compelled to transform the internal structure of their societies. Generally, when growing tribal populations segmented, they did so simply by dividing into two or more identical, small-scale groups. Rather than segmenting and remaining the same, Polynesians apparently felt compelled to accept greater inequality, hierarchy, technological change, and specialization in order to meet chiefly demands for greater production and organizational complexity to integrate society at a higher scale. The underlying constraint was that islands filled up quickly and were so small that it was difficult for people to separate and move apart to maintain their independence. People had invested too much effort to easily move away. The power and authority of the chiefs was the most remarkable feature of Polynesian societies. Most significantly, much of production was stimulated by the demands of chiefs who had a vested self-interest in promoting technological intensification so that more commoners could supply more tribute. In the tribal world every household controlled their own productive resources and stopped production when their needs were met. However, in Polynesia the chiefs controlled access to productive land, and many people performed specialized economic activities, such as canoe making or craft production, or became full-time chiefs, or priests. Specialists had to be supported by the common people who actually worked the land. The chiefs used the supporting ideological concepts of ranked descent lines, *mana, tabu*, and sacrifice to the gods as the key organizing principles of Polynesian societies. These elements were present at least on a small scale from the very beginning of the colonization of the Pacific.[28] The religious basis of Pacific Island status systems appeared most conspicuously in the related concepts of *mana* and *tabu* (taboo), or *tapu*. *Mana* has been variously defined as an impersonal supernatural force, or power, that could manifest itself in people, objects, and spirits. Cognate terms occur throughout the Pacific, and the *mana* concept has close parallels in many parts of the world. It is sometimes referred to as animatism to distinguish it from the more elementary belief in souls, or animism.

Mana was inherited with chiefly rank, and its presence was demonstrated in the chief's objective ability to control his followers. A chief with powerful *mana* could give goods to his subjects in exchange for their labor services, and he could influence nature as an agent of the gods. Thus, in a circular fashion, the hereditary elite demanded respect because they had *mana*, and the presence of *mana* was expressed in the respect that they received. The elite could possess various degrees of *mana*, while commoners might have none. The Polynesian term *tabu*, usually translated as "forbidden actions," refers to a wide range of ritual avoidances that lower-ranked individuals must observe as an acknowledgment of the sanctity of elite status. Deference toward chiefs included such things as bowing, keeping one's head below the chief's head, using special "respect language," and making special offerings.

Chiefly prerogatives might also be marked by special forms of dress, badges, housing, and foods, which accrued to the chief by birth to the status; but perhaps more important were the claims that a chief could make over land, labor, and goods, as an expression of his personal power. Polynesian status inequality also appeared in honorific titles that were applied to outstanding warriors and to a variety of individuals, including priests and craftsmen, who displayed special skills. These individuals, especially if they were already elites with *mana*, were important challenges to chiefly authority.

BOX 6.3. A MATTER OF SCALE: THE TRANSFORMATION OF TRIBES INTO CHIEFDOMS

In the tribal world most human interaction, as we have seen, took place between the members of households and between the members of nearby households in a village or band. A five-person household forms a very small network in which there are only ten possible interactions between all the individual members, and these can be handled easily by the institutionalized distinctions of age and gender. In a village of fifty people there are suddenly more than 1,000 possible human interactions, according to the mathematics of network law $I = P*[P-1]/2$, where I = interaction and P = population). Thus, when the population increases by 1 power of 10, possible human interactions multiply by 2 powers of 10. This growth creates significant new sources of interpersonal stress and conflict, but the problem is vastly greater at the tribal level, where with 500 people there are more than 100,000 human interactions possible. A typical Polynesian chiefdom of 5,000 people would have more than 12 million possible interactions, and a small kingdom encompassing 300,000 people in all of the Hawaii islands, nearly 20 billion. The solution to the intensified stress of tribal society was the addition of organizational complexity in the form of new cultural institutions, such as moieties, lineages, clans, myths, and rituals but not powerful rulers. Robert Carneiro[29] examined 100 small-scale societies and found that as societies grew, the number of organizational traits approximated the square root of the population. By these calculations we would expect the Hawaii kingdom of 300,000 people to be an order of magnitude (tenfold) more complex than a tribal society. The additional complexity was primarily in the addition of specialists to manage the political economy and new ideological institutions to persuade people of the legitimacy of the king's authority.

Population size is an important variable because size constrains decision-making processes. In a social group of 150 or fewer people, virtually everyone can participate in decisions; but in a society of 500 or more, public decision making is likely to be controlled by the adult men. A consensual village head might be able to informally coordinate up to 500 household heads within a local group of 2,500 people, but a formal political elite is necessarily required to manage larger settlements. Five hundred is a crucial number because the limits of human memory and information-processing ability make it difficult for people—including chiefs—to keep track of more than that number of items in any information domain.[30]

Chiefdoms and the Politicization Process

Chiefdoms were a radical transformation of life in the tribal world, where local bands and villages were politically autonomous and economically self-sufficient. This "first transcending of local autonomy in human history" was the great social divide between egalitarian and nonegalitarian societies, and it occurred only within the past 7,500 years when the first villagers surrendered their political autonomy to chiefs from other villages.[31] The defining feature of chiefdoms was that chiefs styled themselves as superior human beings and were able to establish dynasties and transmit their advantageous position to their descendants. Chiefdoms were the first step in the politicization process that ultimately allowed power-seeking rulers to build kingdoms, city-states, states, and empires. A chief directing a simple chiefdom might have political authority over ten local village heads and bigmen and perhaps command 5,000 people (see figure 6.10). A more enterprising chief might

use military force to gain another tenfold increase in social power by pulling several district chiefs under his leadership, creating a complex chiefdom of 50,000 people or more. From there it would be a short step for a power-driven ruler to conquer his neighbors and bring several complex chiefdoms together to form a simple kingdom that could draw tribute from hundreds of thousands of commoners.

It is not easy to explain the successes of political power seekers, because the benefits of the politicization process are enjoyed by only a very small proportion of society, whereas most people are burdened by reduced social status, higher taxes, warfare, and insecurity. Concentrated power disproportionately improves the chief's quality of life and genetic fitness while diminishing the fitness of others. Power also can be used coercively to threaten or otherwise manipulate cultural choices so that people are persuaded to lend their support to the chief. As William Durham notes, "cultural evolution is an intrinsically political process."[32] The emergence and persistence of chiefdoms is an example of the imposition of cultural patterns by a power elite, rather than free choice by the population at large. Chiefdoms are produced by biased cultural transmission that is likely to work against the humanization process for most households. Politicization is the first step in an evolutionary process that rewards a powerful, self-interested minority for promoting cultural ideas that support runaway growth harmful to others.

Politicization requires growth. Power seekers must mobilize household labor, warriors, technology, trade, and religion in their growth projects. Politicization works because as growth occurs, political leaders become a mathematically smaller proportion of society and their power steadily increases. Elites are thus naturally rewarded for developing cultural ideas that remove the barriers to growth. The power of Polynesian chiefs increased simultaneously with economic productivity as measured by the size of the networks in which food was redistributed, the frequency of redistribution, and the number of specialists who were not directly involved in primary food production and who were therefore supported by "surplus" production.[33]

The concept of environmental or social **circumscription** offers the most attractive explanation for understanding why people accepted chiefly rule.[34] Here the argument is that in times of stress or crisis, living with even oppressive rulers may sometimes not seem as bad an alternative as the risks of immigration. Circumscription, or "social caging,"[35] occurs when

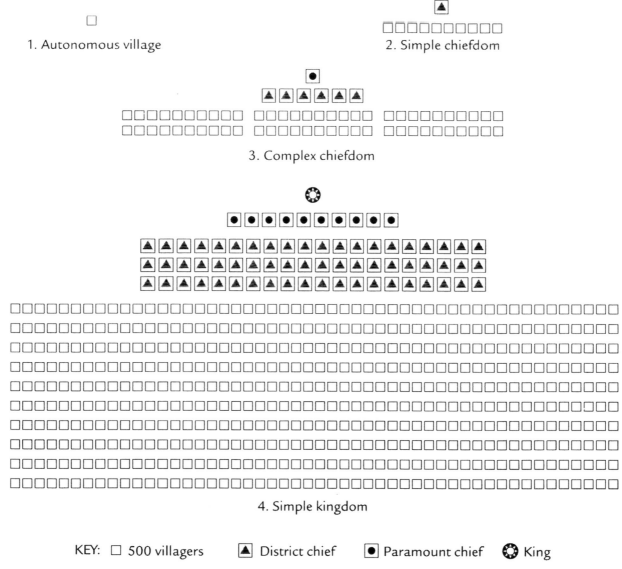

1. Autonomous village

2. Simple chiefdom

3. Complex chiefdom

4. Simple kingdom

KEY: □ 500 villagers   ▲ District chief   ▣ Paramount chief   ✪ King

Figure 6.10. Levels of political complexity from autonomous village to kingdom.

geographic or environmental barriers in combination with social circumstances and historical contingencies prevent villagers from easily escaping threats of political domination. Often the crucial contingency is armed conflict driven by status rivalry, or power struggles between chiefs fighting to control narrowly circumscribed intensive food production zones and productive populations. Villagers in conquered territories would have little choice but to pay tribute to a high chief unless flight were possible. The exploration and settlement of Polynesia was probably driven by people escaping political crises, but not everyone could leave, and the risks of failure were high.

The Polynesian Chiefdoms: Elementary Aristocracies

Polynesian chiefdoms were **aristocracies** in which a small elite directed the activities of people living in more than a single village. In Polynesian cosmology, as presented in origin myths and ritual, a Polynesian high chief symbolized the entire society before the gods. The chief was treated like a god, often called a god, and sometimes claimed to be a god. In a real sense the chief was the principal human agent in society.[36] This was reflected in a chief's use of the pronouns "I" and "my" to refer collectively to everyone on the island, and in the fact that Polynesian mythic histories invariably recounted the actions of chiefs and detailed their lengthy genealogies. As Sahlins expressed it, "The king encompasses the people in his own person, as projection of his own being."[37] This would be unimaginable in the tribal world and literally made the well-being of one person and one family line more important than the well-being of everyone else.

As chiefdoms, many Polynesian societies were organized into segmentary or "conical" descent groups based on an ideology of a patrilineal descent system resembling Nuer segmentary lineages but centered on the chief. Like the Nuer system, the segments or branches of Polynesian conical descent groups were associated with territorial units, but unlike Nuer tribal segments, in Polynesia the segments were ranked and under the control of a titled leader, who directed production and collected tribute for higher authorities. The striking difference in Polynesia was that everyone and every line of descent were ranked by social status relative to everyone else by their genealogical distance from the founding chiefly ancestor. The underlying principle was a belief in the "inherent superiority of a line of descent."[38] The top chief was the senior member of the senior descent line.

Typically there were five ranks in the Polynesian social hierarchy, from bottom to top as follows: (1) the household, (2) local kin group under a senior head, (3) subdistrict under a lesser chief, (4) district under a paramount chief, and (5) an island-wide high chief. A few Polynesian societies such as Hawaii and Tonga were exceptionally large, multi-island polities, representing a sixth level of social complexity. They were small kingdoms ruled by especially powerful chiefs who could be called kings. All social levels were connected into a single command structure that was effectively headed by one person's imperium. In comparison, a tribal society had only a very weak authority structure at the local kin group level.

The Polynesian ranking system was based on the hierarchy between ancestor and descendent, and on **primogeniture**, order of birth within a family, with firstborn ranking highest. This was reflected symbolically in the familiar logical equation father : son :: older brother : younger brother :: chief : commoner.[39]

Chiefs used this ranking to encompass the entire society. At the bottom, men imagined every household to be a miniature chiefdom, as described by Sahlins: "Like the great chief in his domain, the father is in his own house a sacred figure, a man of superior *mana*, his possessions, even his food, guarded by tabus against defilement by lesser familial kinsmen.

Polynesians know innately how to honor the chief, for chieftainship begins at home: the chief's due is no more than elaborate filial respect."[40]

This was an exaggerated "filial respect," and scale effects enormously magnified its human outcome when chiefs managed to project it to the entire society.

Anthropologists often describe "chief" as an **ascribed status** in contrast with "bigman" in a tribal society, which is said to be an **achieved status**.[41] This suggests that tribal bigmen were self-made leaders, who constantly had to reward their supporters to verify their position, whereas Polynesian chiefs simply received their titles and *mana* (power) at birth. In reality, there was considerable ambiguity in how Polynesian chiefs acquired their "inherited" titles and demonstrated their *mana*. Furthermore, chiefs who misused their authority, or who proved too weak, could be deposed by rivals. Thus, in Polynesian practice the distinction between achieved and ascribed status was often blurred. Ideally, the key to success for both bigmen and chiefs was their ability to organize lavish feasts, give gifts to influential supporters, and provide other chiefs with services such as defense. Chiefs operated on a much grander scale than tribal bigmen.

Chiefdoms are systems of **social status**, a scale of human worth that gives advantages to a few individuals. A status system consists of "the principles that define worth and more specifically honor, that establish the scales of personal and group value, that relate position or role to privileges and obligations, that allocate respect, and that codify respect behavior."[42] In this definition, status is equated with honor. Status systems are found in all societies; but where age, sex, and personal characteristics are the only status criteria, as in most tribal societies, relative equality and balance are likely to prevail.

Chiefs portray themselves in a benevolent public role as the generous feast givers. Anthropologists call this **redistribution**. However, this was not the same as an Asháninka bigman throwing a beer party, because chiefs grew more powerful by converting freely given offerings into forced tribute and diverting public goods to private benefit. Furthermore, commoners did not need chiefs to redistribute resources to them, because subdistrict territorial divisions radiated out from the center of the island like the slices of a pie, crisscrossing all ecozones, so that ideally each subdistrict could be self-sufficient. In larger-scale societies commoners were excluded from feasts, whereas chiefs lived in ostentatious luxury.[43] Chiefs regulated production and maintained the social hierarchy by controlling the ritual calendar, thereby setting everyone's seasonal schedule for all major productive activities such as planting and fishing. Chiefs also used their power to make particular places *tabu* to prevent people from exploiting them. Such *tabus* often directly benefited the chief rather than society as a whole. Commoners benefited from the chief's military defense activities only because the aggressive wars that chiefs waged to expand chiefly imperia made life more dangerous for everyone. The only clear way the entire society benefited from chiefs was when they distributed food from their storehouses in the event of natural disasters. In the event of crisis such redistribution may have been crucial for group survival, but village-level food storage was a reasonable alternative.

Rivalry between older brother and younger brother was an inherent feature of Polynesian ranking systems based on primogeniture, and it was common for younger brothers to usurp the position of their superior. The complexity of the ranking system and the degree of inequality was related to the scale or total population of society. Pukapuka, the smallest Polynesian island with only five hundred people, was the same scale as an Australian tribe and showed only ceremonial distinctions between chief and commoner. However, as societies grew larger, chiefs were able to compel commoners to contribute to chiefly feasts and construction projects. In Hawaii, with the population conservatively estimated at 300,000 people, there were enough chiefs for them to form an in-marrying group that claimed control over all the land and titles. This made the chiefly elite a distinct ruling class, distinguished from the commoners by degree of social power.

Although these societies were often called patrilineal, Polynesians could claim descent from an ancestor through both male and female links, and they are therefore sometimes called ambilateral (Latin *ambo*, "both"). Because it was so important for Polynesians to establish a connection with high-ranking ancestors, it is reasonable to describe their social system as ascent based rather than descent based. As Sahlins describes it, "Hawaiians . . . do not trace descent so much as ascent, selectively choosing their way upward, by a path that notably includes female ancestors, to a connection with some ancient ruling line."[44] In addition to its utility in establishing rank, an ambilateral, ascent-based system is especially useful in island societies where access to land is crucial, because a person could claim land from both his mother's and his father's descent groups.

The extent to which chiefs could elaborate and concentrate their personal command over primary producers differed from island to island with the scale of society and differences in the cultural organization of power.[45] The most powerful chiefs on larger islands emerged from intense struggles with competitors. The victors in these status rivalries organized and directed the construction of increasingly elaborate stone temples, house platforms, and fortifications. With larger-scale populations, chiefs were able to stratify society into distinct **social classes** of nobles and commoners. **Social stratification** is based on differential access to natural resources and cultural capital. Such developments are conspicuously absent in the tribal world and are the foundations from which, under the right historical circumstances and environmental conditions, aggrandizing individuals were able to create ever-larger personal imperia. There were probably only a few places in the world where chiefdoms were originally formed independently and then spread as organized societies into other regions. In only six places were chiefdoms then transformed into states and empires (see figure 5.2). When militant chiefdoms invaded neighboring tribes, tribals sometimes felt compelled to organize their own chiefdoms in self-defense, causing chiefdoms to spread far beyond the few areas where aspiring elites managed to construct them independently. The following ethnographic case studies will examine Tikopia to represent simple chiefdom and Hawaii as an example of a complex chiefdom that was transformed into a small kingdom early in the nineteenth century.

Tikopia: A Traditional Small Polynesian Chiefdom

Tikopia is 3 square miles (4.6 km²) of land, a miniature high island dominated by the jagged rim of an extinct volcano surrounding a crater lake. It is occupied by one of the best-described traditional Polynesian cultures, thanks to the detailed monographs published by Raymond Firth.[46] Tikopia is a Polynesian outlier situated well inside Melanesia, some 1,200 miles (2,000 km) west of Samoa and Tonga in western Polynesia. In 1928, Tikopia was inhabited by 1,200 "healthy and vigorous natives," and Firth considered them "almost untouched by the outside world," although European explorers had landed on the island in 1798.

Archaeological research revealed 3,000 years of continuous occupation of Tikopia, presumably initiated by Austronesian-speaking peoples carrying Lapita-like pottery.[47] In their excavations, archaeologists Kirch and Yen recovered 35,000 bones representing

85 different types of animals, 2,204 pounds of shells, and thousands of artifacts. The record was complete enough to provide a reasonably clear picture of the human impact on Tikopia's ecosystem. The first settlers found a pristine environment teeming with wildlife. The island was covered with rain forest, and the crater lake was then a saltwater bay or lagoon. During the early centuries of settlement, the wild protein resources were decimated. Harvests of fish, shellfish, and sea turtles rapidly declined in volume and diversity and increasingly were augmented by domestic pigs and chickens. At least one wild bird, the megapod, a chickenlike scrub fowl, was locally exterminated, whereas, according to local tradition, sea turtles apparently were protected by *tabu*.

Continuous slash-and-burn cultivation gradually led to severe deforestation that enlarged the land base by some 40 percent at the expense of the reef zone, through infilling by eroded materials from the volcanic slopes. This greatly extended the gardening areas on the west end of the island but also cut off the lagoon, turning it into a lake, thus further reducing marine resources. Over the centuries, the inhabitants gradually abandoned shifting cultivation in favor of a system of permanent gardens and selectively planted domesticated forests. Tikopian arboriculture created a multistoried, multispecies forest orchard of useful trees and shrubs that replaced virtually all of the natural forest on the island. It also stabilized the slopes and dunes and helped buffer the damaging effects of typhoons. At the same time, according to their own accounts, the Tikopians decided to eliminate pigs, thereby reducing demands on their gardens because pigs, although they contributed protein, competed directly for garden produce.

As severely restricted environments, small islands such as Tikopia should be excellent testing grounds for cultural ecological theory. However, it is difficult to discuss carrying capacity and balance with resources on Tikopia because the relationship between people and resources is not simple. Since 1929, the resident population has fluctuated between about 1,000 and 1,700. Population growth historically was regulated by numerous cultural means, including ritual sanctions, abortion, and infanticide, and by emigration. Firth reported that celibacy was required of younger brothers. Traditional history, verified by archaeology, records that bloody intergroup conflicts, exterminations, and expulsions of whole groups occurred a few centuries ago and were attributed to land conflicts. However, this cul-

tural interpretation may have been a rationalization for what was actually a rivalry between competing chiefs. Furthermore, serious food shortages occurred after cyclones hit the island in the 1950s, and in 2002 when Cyclone Zoe struck Tikopia, directly causing massive devastation. Direct and indirect human action has improved the island's agricultural potential, but there has been no effort to intensify agricultural production through terracing or irrigation. The island continues to be highly self-sufficient in subsistence production.

The 1,200 people living on Tikopia in 1928 were organized into two districts, or "sides," divided by the crater rim. Faena was on the (sheltered) lee side and Ravenga on the windward (see figure 6.11). There were some twenty-five named villages concentrated in the lowlands near the western and southern shores. Districts and villages acted as individual units in ritual and economic activities, although they were crosscut by descent-based groups that formed the status hierarchy and organized land tenure.

Each village consisted of a row of named hereditary house sites with attached orchards or garden sites. Houses were accompanied by canoe sheds and ovens. The houses themselves contained the graves of their former owners aligned along the "sacred" inside half of the house, facing the beach. This made each house, in effect, a temple, and long-abandoned houses of important chiefs were marked by upright slabs of stone and were recognized *Marae*. They served as important temples and sites for major rituals. Land was so important that virtually every part of the island was under some form of ownership, which was inherited patrilineally. Boundaries between gardens were carefully demarcated, and every feature of the island was named. Even the lake and reef zones were under chiefly jurisdiction.

The status system was the key to understanding most claims of ownership and explained most personal interaction. Every person was assigned a position in the status hierarchy, which was organized into units at four distinct levels: household; *Paito*, or lineage; *Kainanga*, or clan; and the entire island community (see figure 6.12).

At the highest level, the island-wide ritual community was presided over by a single chief, or *Ariki*, who controlled an elaborate series of rituals founded by the ancestral deity of the chief's descent group. These rituals, known as "the work of the gods," promoted the welfare of the entire island, ensuring productive gardening and fishing.

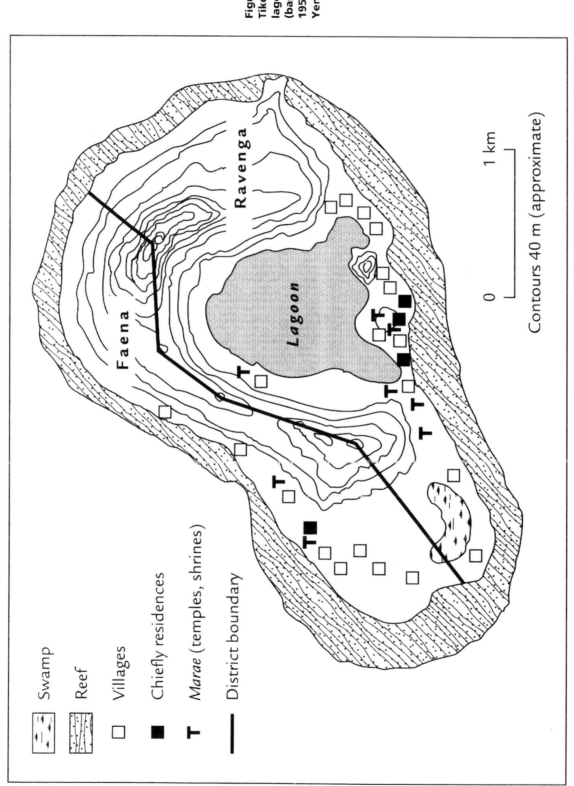

Figure 6.11. Map of Tikopia districts, villages, and temples (based on Firth [1936] 1957 and Kirch and Yen 1982).

Ravenga

Faena

Lagoon

Swamp

Reef

Villages

Chiefly residences

Marae (temples, shrines)

District boundary

0   1 km

Contours 40 m (approximate)

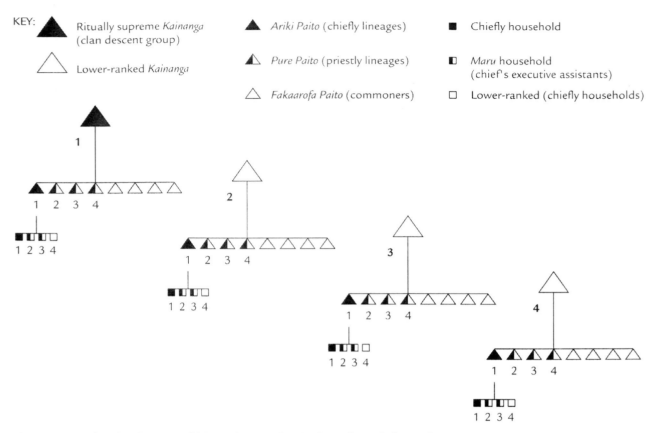

KEY:

▲ Ritually supreme *Kainanga* (clan descent group)

△ Lower-ranked *Kainanga*

▲ *Ariki Paito* (chiefly lineages)

◩ *Pure Paito* (priestly lineages)

◺ *Fakaarofa Paito* (commoners)

■ Chiefly household

◧ *Maru* household (chief's executive assistants)

□ Lower-ranked (chiefly households)

Figure 6.12. The ritual status of hierarchy on Tikopia (based on Firth 1936).

At the second level were four named descent groups, or *Kainanga*, which were ranked by order of ritual precedence and ranged in size from 89 to 443 people (see figure 6.12). Firth called these groups clans, and they claimed patrilineal descent from founding tutelary deities (supernatural entities guarding specific descent groups) enshrined at specific clan "temple" sites. However, the clans were neither localized nor exogamous and only indirectly owned land of their constituent lineages and households. Membership recruitment was usually by patrifiliation, but it was also possible to marry in, as when a stranger would be adopted after marrying the chief's daughter. Each *Kainanga* had its own chief, named for his *Kainanga*, and participated as a unit in the island-wide "work of the gods." The *Kainanga* were linked in pairs for ritual food exchanges, and the chief of each *Kainanga* also had ritual responsibility for the fertility of one of four major food plants: taro, coconut, breadfruit, and yams.

At the third level, the *Kainanga* segmented into individual, named patrilineages called *Paito*, or houses. The primary property-holding unit, these groups averaged about forty persons each. There is no question

about the cultural reality of these clan and lineage groups. Regardless of how the rules of rank or recruitment worked, Tikopian culture had names for these groups, and they had clearly defined functions. The highest-ranked *Paito* (lineage) in a *Kainanga* (clan) supplied the *Ariki* (chief) for that *Kainanga*. Below the *Ariki Paito*, chiefly lineage, were high-ranking lineages, *Pure Paito*, that supplied ritual specialists, or priests, known as *Pure*. Lower-ranked *Paito* were *Fakaarofa Paito*, commoner lineages, whose relative order was irrelevant.

The lowest-level unit was the individual nuclear family household, although polygyny, especially among higher-ranked people, might extend the size of this unit. The husband was the ritual head of the family. The rank of the household was determined by his seniority within the lineage, the seniority of its lineage within the clan, and the ritual precedence of the clan. Relative rank within the *Ariki Paito*, chiefly lineages, was most critical. The households most closely related to the chief supplied the assistants, or *Maru*, who helped carry out his directives.

The authority of the chiefs was derived from their religious position as hereditary representatives of important ancestral deities who were responsible for the welfare of the land. Clan chiefs held titular control over all the lands owned by the members of their clan. Chiefs were sometimes called upon to settle territorial disputes and could impose *tabus* to restrict use of local resources under certain conditions. It was assumed that they worked for the community's benefit, and they seem to have been genuinely respected. They often owned more land than other individuals, but this only helped them fulfill their ritual responsibilities. Chiefs might claim ritual ownership of the freshwater springs near their villages, but they did not deny community access. Wealth in land was generally independent of rank, and even commoners could be richer than chiefs. Land ownership did not mean exclusive use; upon request, individuals were often allowed to plant or harvest resources from land they did not own in return for a token gift of food. There were no landless classes.

A visiting Australian Aborigine would have been overwhelmed by the density and permanence of the population on Tikopia and by the degree to which people manipulated the environment for productive purposes. But the Aborigine also would have understood many features of Tikopian culture. As in any tribal society, kinship was certainly the most important organizing principle of domestic life on Tikopia, and households were largely self-provisioning units that worked cooperatively with kin-related households in the local settlement. Tikopian villages were similar in size to aboriginal bands, but the villages were circumscribed by their neighbors and were much less independent than the mobile bands. The belief that mythical ancestral beings continued to influence human affairs would have been familiar to the Aborigine, but the sanctity of specific descent lines linked to the gods and the pervasive ranking of social units would have seemed strange. Even stranger to the Aborigine would have been the island-wide authority carried by the Tikopian hereditary title *Ariki* and the extreme deferential behavior accorded the person of *Ariki* status. This calls to mind Firth's summary of the chief's politicized role on Tikopia, which has no parallel in tribal societies:

> [T]he chief has been shown to be the most important single human factor in the economic life of the Tikopia. Not only does he play a part as a producer within his immediate household, but by initiative and example he gives direction to the productive work of the community; he is titular owner of the most valuable property of the members of his clan; he imposes far-reaching restrictions on production and consumption and in many important activities he acts as a focal point in the processes of exchange and distribution.[48]

Hawaii: From Kinship to Kingship

The Hawaiian Archipelago is extremely isolated from the rest of Polynesia, and indeed from everywhere else. The major inhabited Hawaiian islands are high, volcanic islands and very large for Polynesia. Hawaii, the largest, contains 6,500 square miles (10,458 km^2) of land, more than all the rest of Micronesia and Polynesia combined, with the exception of New Zealand. Such large, high islands trap considerable rainfall on their windward sides, which are often sharply eroded into steep, narrow valleys, and they support a wide variety of plant communities, from deserts to wet mountain forests with many endemic species.

The reef zones are smaller than might be expected because of the relative youth of the larger islands; furthermore, much of the shoreline is inaccessible because of the steep cliffs. Rainfall and soil are critical variables for crops, yet they are very unevenly distributed. Only restricted windward valleys offer the alluvial soils, abundant rainfall, and flowing streams most favorable for the cultivation of Polynesian crops.[49]

In comparison with Tikopia, the most obvious difference in Hawaiian subsistence patterns is in the elaborate complexes of ditches and terraced and irrigated pond fields for taro cultivation, as well as the extensive area devoted to permanent dry-field cultivation. The Hawaiians also developed true aquaculture, in which fish were raised on a large scale in special fish ponds constructed on reef flats.

The irrigation systems have the most interesting theoretical implications because many theorists have speculated that control of irrigation systems was the primary route to state formation for all the world's great civilizations. Hawaiian irrigation systems were well developed by Polynesian standards. As a significant form of agricultural intensification, they helped produce the surplus that supported the elites, but the construction of these systems seems not to have required either technical specialists or large labor forces.[50]

Hawaiian oral and documentary history and archaeology show that over some 250 years, from approximately AD 1550 to AD 1792, a succession of twenty-five high chiefs, primarily members of a single dynasty, gradually gained political control over the six major districts of the island of Hawaii.[51] This ruling elite steadily expanded the administrative structure, elaborated the religious system, and constructed an intensive production system of fish ponds, terraced garden fields, irrigation systems, stone walls, ditches, trails, and demarcated land parcels. They financed these developments by monopolizing the production of food staples, and wealth objects.[52] This was an intentional project of imperial expansion and infrastructure development that facilitated growth that quadrupled the population and quickly transformed the nature of Hawaiian society. Such growth made it possible for a handful of elites and their families to live luxurious, super-successful lifestyles, while the majority lost control over the conditions of their daily life, were subjected to demeaning restrictions, and were compelled to work harder than ever before. Previously, Hawaiians had lived for more than a thousand years with relatively low-intensity subsistence in relatively small chiefdoms that minimized the human effects of rank and status differences.

In comparison with the small number of people that anyone could command in the tribal world, the scale of Hawaiian chiefly power is astounding. Kamehameha I (1758–1819), twenty-fifth in the dynasty, commanded a personal imperium of 7,000 to 15,000 warriors for his interisland conquests. By 1792, he successfully took full control of Hawaii and the neighboring island of Maui. Then, in 1795 he conquered Lanai, Molokai, and O'ahu. In 1809 he negotiated the takeover of Kaua'i, and was thus able to rule all of the Hawaiian islands, with a total population of some 300,000 people. This became the largest politically centralized society in the Pacific world and roughly equivalent in scale to the entire population of aboriginal Australia.

Hawaii's rulers organized the islands in typical Polynesian structure, but by the time Kamehameha's imperium encompassed all of the islands, he had effectively created a small kingdom, which was an order of magnitude larger than an island-wide chiefdom. Kamehameha was a king. The chiefly rulers divided each island (*moku*) into districts (also *moku*), and

subdistricts (*ahupua'a*) commanded by their respective chiefs (*ali'i*). Each subdistrict chief used land managers (*konohiki*) to allocate land parcels to the commoners and to collect tribute in labor and goods. The largest islands such as Hawaii, Maui, O'ahu, and Kaua'i were subdivided into five or six districts each, and each district was subdivided into an average of thirty subdistricts.[53] This administrative bureaucracy may have supported a total of some 100 high chiefs and priests, 900 subdistrict chiefs, and 1,800 land managers, as well as 32,500 retainers and dependents (see table 6.3).

Chiefs tried to enlarge their personal domestic establishments, or extended households, as much as possible. Hawaiians called this group *ma*, "the people of, or associates of someone," and it was the core of a personal imperium. It included family members (*'ohana*), and retainers (*ohua*), as well as dependent specialists. Chiefs expanded their power network through marriage alliances and gifts to other chiefs. Commoners (*maka'ainana*), "the people of the land," correctly considered the chiefs to be outsiders who "eat the land." This was clearly the case because the paramount chief claimed ownership over all the land and allocated it through the administrative structure to lower-level chiefs and landlords who allocated parcels to commoners to cultivate as tenants.

In viewing growth in the scale of Hawaiian society as an elite-directed process, it is important to consider how social power was distributed. A careful reconstruction of Hawaiian society suggests that there were about 3,000 elite households, about 5 percent of all households. Because the elite had larger families and were closely intermarried, the elite and their close kin may have constituted a subset of some 23,000 people, or just under 8 percent of the total population of 300,000 in AD 1778. Elite households probably included another 32,000 people as retainers. Furthermore, the elite lived lavishly, were feasting constantly, and the highest chiefs were distinguished by their corpulence. In one phase of a temple ritual 1,440 pigs

Table 6.3. The Social Structure of the Hawaiian Kingdom, Estimates for 1809

	Households	Family	Retainers	Average	Persons
King	1	50	950	1,000	1,000
Paramounts	4	25	75	100	400
District Chiefs	30	15	50	65	1,950
High Priests	70	15	50	65	4,550
Ahupua'a Chiefs	900	10	25	35	31,500
Konohikis	1,800	7	2	9	16,200
Commoners	48,880	5	–	5	244,400
	51,685				300,000

were consumed.[54] In contrast to the custom on Tikopia, the Hawaiian elite excluded commoners from their feasts. Elite households with their retainers may have consumed about one-fourth of total production.

Kamehameha's reward for imperial conquest was that he enlarged his domestic establishment to an order of magnitude greater than those of other chiefs. He supported a court of perhaps a thousand people.[55] There were more than a dozen categories of **specialists** who were directly attached to the chief's personal household, including political advisors, military experts, architects, astrologers, food handlers, robe masters, priests, masseurs, keepers of his images and paraphernalia, and servants to whisk away flies and stand over him as he slept, in addition to miscellaneous "hangers-on." As symbolic fertilizing father of the entire society, Kamehameha had sexual access to all commoner women, although he had only eight wives.[56] His primary residence at Kamakahonu on the island of Hawaii was a walled compound of 27,000 square meters containing his sleeping and cooking houses, houses for his wives, storehouses, and his temple, the *Ahuena heiau*, which has been preserved and restored. Chiefly households supported from 30 to 100 people in their imperia including retainers, servants, wives, and family. Polygyny was typically only a prerogative of the nobility, because commoners did not have access to enough land to support a large family. A chief's residential complex of stone platforms covered approximately 1,000 square meters.[57] In comparison, an Asháninka house was only 50 square meters. Hawaiian houses and temples were simple wooden structures on stone platforms. The largest construction was a 300-meter defensive stone wall, which was nearly 4 meters tall with a volume of 5,864 cubic meters.[58] It might have weighed 15 million kilograms. Building it would have required an enormous human effort. Associated with this site was a temple that housed the remains of paramount chiefs, but there were no monumental royal tombs.

The Hawaiian elite were able to support their inflated domestic establishments because they effectively controlled all the natural resources as well as the built infrastructure on the islands. Kamehameha held for his personal use approximately a million acres, a quarter of the land area of all the Hawaiian islands.[59] High chiefs held 10,000 acres, other chiefs 1,500 acres, administrators 75 acres, whereas commoner households were allocated an average of three acres.[60] The elite may have retained nearly 90 percent of the developed land for their own use. The elite drew their daily subsistence from extensive and highly productive irrigated taro pond fields and dryland gardens that they controlled directly. They also consumed food sacrifices offered at temples, as well as tribute collected from the commoners. The chiefs controlled the 449 artificially constructed fish ponds that were capable of producing more than a thousand tons of fish annually.[61] This would have supplied more than 5,000 people with half a kilogram of fish per person, per day, annually.

High Chiefs, Gods, and Sacrifice

The Hawaiian elite created an exclusive religious system that served their interests well. It kept food and goods flowing to them and kept the commoners subservient. For the elite, the most important features of Hawaiian cosmology were the Kumulipo creation myth and the annual ritual drama of the Makahiki in which the divine king (*ali'i akua*) appropriates the gifts of the fertility god Lono and assumes the qualities of the war god Ku. These interconnected cultural elements were the ideological centerpieces of a centrally directed religion based on gods, divine kings, sacrifice, and military conquest. The Kumulipo was a composite of sixteen genealogical chants in 2,102 lines that was recited by a genealogical specialist attached to the royal household. Chanting the Kumulipo affirmed the noble lineage of a new paramount chief and connected him, as a divine king, with the gods at the center of the entire cosmos.[62] Kingship incorporated everything—up and down, land and sea, and everyone in the kingdom.

Like spirit beings in the tribal world, Hawaiian deities (*akua*) were mental constructs given multiple forms. People materialized them as anthropomorphic images, as humans, plants and animals, and as natural phenomena.[63] As in tribal cosmologies, the principal beings were symbolically coded by color, cardinal directions, plants, animals, seasons, and function. For example, the war god Ku was red, up, east, right, mountains, and war. The fertility god Lono was black, leeward, clouds, rainy season, gourds, pigs, dryland farming, and fertility. The deities modeled idealized human types, and they were reproduced in people's minds by the act of ritual sacrifice. Because deities were hierarchically ranked and were identified with particular ranks and individuals, their respective rituals affirmed the structure of society with privileged chiefs at the top and defined proper behavior. These religious beliefs mystified in that they obscured the daily reality of human exploitation, and they legitimized chiefs as naturally superior human beings. The cosmology made extreme social inequality seem perfectly natural, inevitable, and irresistible. The relative ease with which people abandoned the entire system makes it clear that their religion was an elite construction, designed by and for the elite. When circumstances changed, the king abruptly abolished the practice of sacrifice and *tabu* in 1819, shortly after the arrival of Europeans. This was soon followed by the adoption of Christianity, especially by elite women, who thereby increased their social power relative to the chiefs.

The king had virtually all the attributes of divinity. He was a perfect, exemplary human, closest to the gods, and was the only one who, with his high priests, could mediate between society as a whole and the most powerful gods. Kings were descended from the gods and were formally turned into gods by their own funeral rituals. Kings shared with gods the attribute of encompassing the cosmos, and like gods they were defined by incestuous marriage with a full or classificatory sister. Succession was invariably fratricidal and incestuous, with one brother killing the other, sacrificing him to the gods, and marrying his sister.[64] The king kills his rival brother and loves his sister, thereby demonstrated his divinity and producing a divine heir. Only the king could consecrate a human sacrifice, which was another extreme expression of his divine power. Like gods, kings were also represented by transcendent symbols, like rainbows, stars, and the sky. They could be addressed as *kalani* ("heaven") or *kalaninui* ("great heaven"). Kings were assumed to be free of desire because they had everything, and they could not show emotion. Thus they remained immobile and were carried on a litter. Kings also demonstrated their divine powers by remaining out of sight, invisible to commoners, and by their possession of the *kapu moe*, the prostration *tabu*. This *tabu* forced everyone to lie flat on the ground in their presence. Lower-ranked chiefs had the *kapu noho*, which required inferiors to sit in their presence. The highest chiefs were so *tabu* that people had to prostrate themselves on the ground even if only his personal possessions were carried by. Special retainers ran ahead carrying a special staff signaling the *tabu*, and they shouted a warning to people to prostrate themselves. Chiefs sometimes traveled at night to minimize the inconvenience that the *tabus* created. No one could allow his or her shadow to fall across the chief or any of his personal possessions, including his house. No one, other than his immediate retainers, was allowed to approach closer than 12 feet (4 m) to the chief's

back. When the chief ate, everyone in his presence had to remain on their knees.

The paramount chiefs had life-and-death powers over their subjects, including lower-level chiefs. They could kill them or expel them from their land at will. They apparently sometimes did so, although not all chiefs were considered to be abusive and oppressive. Infractions of *tabus* were strictly enforced by burning, strangulation, or stoning. Sometimes, people who violated seemingly minor tabus were put to death. John Papa Ii,[65] who became a personal attendant to high chief Liholiho, described a case in which three men were caught eating coconuts with women while a major ritual for the general welfare was being performed at the paramount chief's temple, or *luakini heiau* (see figure 6.13). Because there was a general *tabu* against men and women eating together and against women eating coconuts, the three men were seized and sacrificed along with pigs on the altar before a row of images of the deities. Human sacrifices of this sort apparently only took place at the temples of paramount chiefs and on special ritual occasions.

On Tikopia, it was understood that the deities might be angered if rituals were neglected or improperly performed and might even take a human life as a sacrifice.[66] But it would have been unthinkable for a chief or any of his priests to carry out such an act themselves. Clearly, the high chiefs of Hawaii enlarged upon an underlying Polynesian belief that chiefs were descended from the gods, and they assumed the role of gods themselves.

The Kumulipo creation myth recognized an explicit interdependence between man and gods. The gods make people, and people make the gods as divine images and in ritual. The Hawaiian gods, like Dreamtime beings and Amazon spirits, were transcendent, nonempirical concepts. They existed in people's minds and in the material objects that embodied them, and they worked because their existence reinforced proper action. Hawaiian cosmology was more highly structured and formalized than tribal cosmologies because Hawaiians had a professional priesthood. Their cosmology assumed that ultimately everyone's well-being was determined by rituals performed by higher-ranking individuals. This supernatural mediation superficially resembled the role of shamans in tribal society, but it was hierarchical and exclusive, and the benefits flowed unequally.

The primary form of Hawaiian ritual was the sacrificial consecration of some offering to a deity. Priests (*kahuna*) performed the sacrifices; guarded, fed, and

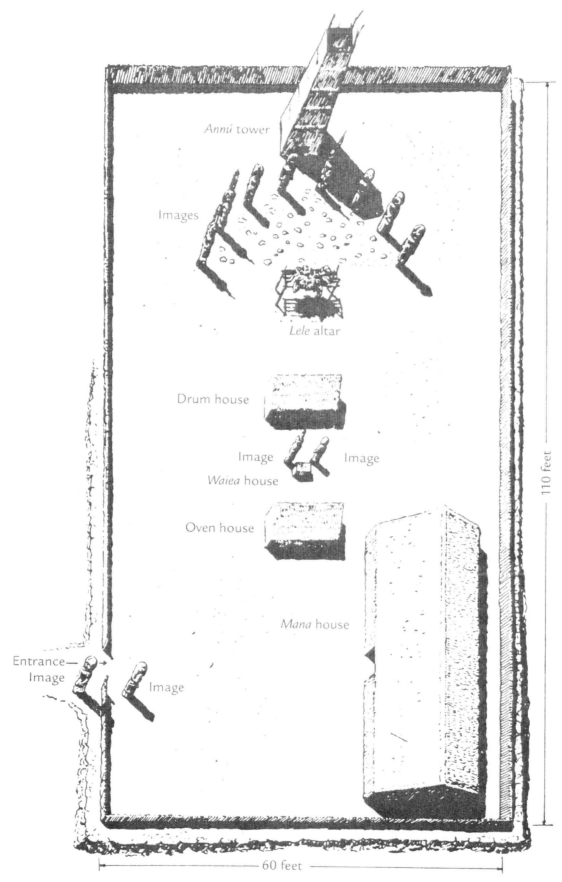

Figure 6.13. The Hawaiian *luakini heiau*, or paramount chief's temple where human sacrifices were performed (from Fig 6.13 David Malo, Hawaiian Antiquities, Bernice P. Bishop Museum, Special Publications 2, Second Edition, reprinted with permission).

cared for the gods; and maintained their temples. Priests were possessed by and effectively belonged to the gods to whom they were sacrificing. High priests who officiated in chiefly temples were themselves chiefs and received land rights in return for their temple services. Sacrifices were accompanied by prayers detailing the intent of the ritual. The god ate the essence, and those attending the ritual ate the remainder. Sacrifice reproduced the social hierarchy because one only sacrificed to the gods that corresponded to one's own social position.

The Makahiki ceremony was a complex ritual cycle that annually renewed both kingship and natural fertility. It involved the king and his entourage making a circuit around the island of Hawaii, collecting tribute, living off the land, and conducting a series of feasts, ritual license, and mock combats. It lasted for months and was coordinated to end with the winter solstice and the end of the rainy season, marking the beginning of the growing season and the return of the Pleiades and the sun. Thus the king was implicitly associated with the sun and fertility. In the final Makahiki rituals, the fertility god Lono is killed in the form of a human sacrifice at the king's personal temple (*luakini heiau*). The king then appropriates the earth's fertility for human benefit and reinstalls himself as the representative of the war god Ku.

Hawaiian Daily Life: Commoner Men and Women

Commoners (*maka'ainana*), who constituted 92 percent of Hawaiian society, were objectively disempowered by their limited access to productive land and by their exclusion from the religious and genealogical sources of status. Land was a portion of divine nature, and the higher one was situated in the land ownership chain, the closer to divinity. Inferior social status made it difficult for most people to make a living. Women were further disadvantaged by their symbolic inferiority. The elite monopoly and extravagance made land a scarce resource. Commoners, who actually worked the land, were at the bottom of a chain of landholders that ran all the way to the king, who held all the land as his divine prerogative. Commoners were marginalized as tenants who cared for land belonging to the chiefs. Use rights had to be legitimized by a gift of the first fruits to the landowner chief. Land rights were held for life, could not be further subdivided, and were normally transmitted to the senior son, or more likely to a senior grandchild. Only couples holding use rights were able to establish households, produce children, and maintain long-term marriages. If juniors were unable to implement claims to land elsewhere, they attached themselves as dependents (*kanaka*) to a chief and/or remained unmarried. Fortunately, Hawaiian society allowed a remarkable degree of sexual freedom, and young and landless commoners readily engaged in informal relationships.[67]

Below the commoners were the *kautva* (sometimes called slaves), a despised category of hereditary outcasts. There were also special terms for vagrants, beggars, and the landless. In comparison, Tikopian commoners did not form a powerless class; Tikopia had no outcasts, beggars, or landless; and Tikopian chiefs remained relatively inconspicuous and unassuming.

The differences in wealth and power between the Hawaiian elites and the commoners were so extreme that it is appropriate to call them social classes. The most conspicuous class markers were the lavish and magnificent feathered short capes, long cloaks, leis, helmets, and whale-tooth necklaces, which only the elite could wear (see figure 6.14). Chiefs were accompanied by bearers of 20-foot (6-m) poles topped with brilliantly feathered banners as insignias of rank.[68] Because as many as 10,000 birds might have been required to produce a single feathered cloak, it had major ostentatious value.[69]

The classic understanding of the relation between men and women in Polynesia was summarized in the structural formula [men : women :: sacred : profane :: pure : impure]. This resembled the negative symbolic position of women in Amazonian cosmology, where women were associated with sickness and death. In Hawaii female symbolic spiritual inferiority was reflected in food taboos and female exclusion from temple sacrifice but was contradicted by the ideology of bilateral descent, in which high rank was inherited through women.[70] The *kapu* system called for a rigid separation of men and women. They could not eat together according to the restrictions of *'ai kapu*, the eating *tabu*. Men did all the cooking, but there were separate earth ovens and separate eating houses for men and women. Women could not enter temples or the men's house. Women were not allowed to eat the most-prized, highest-status foods, including pork, coconut, and bananas, that were also prime articles of tribute to chiefs and sacrifice to gods.

Officially, violations of these taboos were punished by death, with offenders sacrificed to the gods, although such extreme penalties were more likely to be applied to commoner women. This gave men life or death power over women, but the highest-ranking

Figure 6.14. Hawaiian wicker-work helmet (Ratzel 1896:212).

chiefly women were apparently immune from punishment, and they could kill men for breaking *tabus*.

Gender relations in daily life were quite different from how they were symbolically conceptualized. Hawaiian women actively subverted the *tabu* system when they could and clearly viewed it differently than the high-ranking men.[71] Significantly, the entire *kapu* system and the temple cults were overthrown in 1819 at the instigation of high-ranking chiefly women.[72] Even though women in general were symbolically *noa*, "*kapu* free, profane, or common," women chiefs held the highest *kapu* ranks, and profane women made the fine mats and tapa cloth that were used in the sacrificial rituals that high-ranking men needed to confirm their high status. This situation resembles the gender complementarity that was common in the tribal world and suggests that it would be misleading to label the status of Hawaiian women simply as high or low in relation to men.

In Hawaii constructing a personal imperium depended on a person's ability to manipulate kinship networks, real or fictive, to elevate their social rank in an ideologically acceptable manner.[73] Anyone who could trace a genealogical connection to the king within at least ten generations was considered noble, but commoners were forbidden to track their genealogies beyond grandparents. However, in reality, parents could improve the genealogical rank of their children by hypergamy, marrying a higher-status person. Women actively sought high-ranking husbands for their daughters. Men also tried to marry higher-ranking women. Realistically, succession to high rank was always contentious because both men and women often had children by multiple partners. Furthermore, because filiation could be claimed bilaterally, through either male or female links, there were many opportunities for establishing noble links. As soon as a person's claim to high genealogical status was recognized by the king, it became real. In such a competitive society, with power so highly concentrated, it is not surprising that commoners, men or women, did not always endorse the system. When chiefs extracted too much they risked creating open dissatisfaction, and greed and extravagance were often the official justification for a younger brother to usurp power.

Daily life at the village level was not differentiated by hereditary status rankings, and social relations were basically egalitarian.[74] After the *kapu* system and temple cults were abolished in 1819, the core ideology that remained seemed characteristic of the equality of the tribal world. In the 1960s researchers found village Hawaiians more interested in nurturing human relationships than in accumulating material wealth. They measured success by the social relationships that people could construct and maintain, not by material wealth accumulated. People disapproved of public displays of economic success.[75]

Two-Headed Children and Hawaiian Kinship

Hawaiian family structure and the kinship terminology had unusual features that were directly related to the extreme concentration of social power in the noble class. Hawaiians practiced virtually all forms of marriage: polygyny, **sororal polygyny**, **polyandry**, **fraternal polyandry**, levirate, and **sororate**, and they moved in and out of marriage easily.[76] Commoners were not allowed to marry anyone called brother, sister, son, or daughter, but this was the preference among the nobility, because such close marriages preserved their high rank.

Hawaiian kinship terminology was a generational system in which everyone in ego's generation was called brother and sister, everyone in the parents' generation was mother and father, and so on (see figure 6.15). The terms *kaikua'ana* and *kaikaina* mean older and younger sibling of the same sex. This system, which was used by nobles and commoners, reflected the *punalua* co-spouse relationship, in which plural spouses, or spouses and spouses' lovers, treated each other like siblings and their offspring like their own children. Two men married to one woman or a

woman's husband and her lover would call themselves brothers. A child that had two fathers in a punalua relationship was called *po'olua*, a "two-headed child."[77] The advantage of this arrangement was that it made it easier to consolidate kin and reduce land fragmentation. Regardless of the kin terms they used, Hawaiians distinguished "true" kin from classificatory kin. How the system worked in practice is illustrated by the following commentary from a Hawaiian in the 1960s:

> Kealoha is my brother's child. Of course my brother isn't really my brother as both he and I are *hanai* [adopted] children of my father. I guess my father isn't really my father, is he? I know who my real mother is but I don't like her and I never see her. My *hanai* brother is half Hawaiian and I am pure Hawaiian. We aren't really any blood relation I guess, but I always think of him as my brother and I always think of my father as my father. I think maybe Papa is my grandfather's brother ... so I don't know what relationship Kealoha really is though I call her my child.[78]

The reality that chiefs appropriated much of the land forced commoner families to limit their household reproduction to the minimum replacement level. Commoners exchanged children and land to piece together enough usable parcels of otherwise scattered productive land to reproduce the household. This process focused on grandparents (*kupuna*) who adopted their grandchildren, who were favored like chiefs and inherited the ancestral estate. The grandparents were the ancestors, and the term *kupuna* also means ancestor. Their descendants who lived on the land were recognized as consanguines. The descendants of grandparents were considered "true" kin. By adopting grandchildren as their own children, otherwise unrelated people were converted into consanguines, now related through shared grandchildren. This allowed people to hold together pieces of land that might otherwise be dispersed. Noninheriting youths who could not form households enjoyed the "freedom of the dispossessed" by devoting themselves to pleasure seeking.[79] Fertility-limiting practices such as abortion and infanticide were probably common among the landless population. This situation was not a result of "population pressure" on limited material resources. Land existed as a "natural" resource, but because of the existing political economy, it was simply not culturally available to everyone who needed it for household reproduction.[80] The **political economy** controlled by the Hawaiian elite had effectively subordinated the **subsistence economy**.

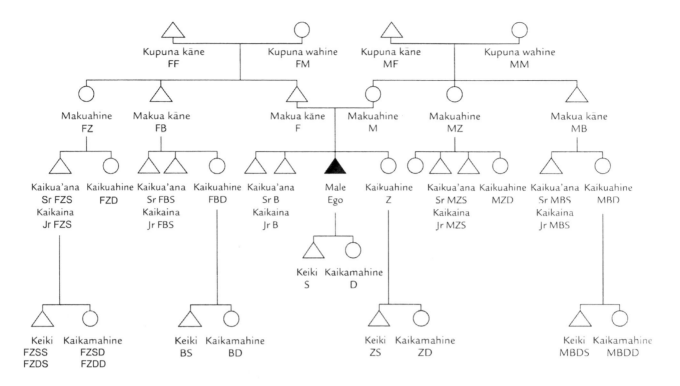

Note: Kāne = "male," Wahine = "female." Kaikua'ana = older same sex sibling;
Kaikaina = younger, same sex sibling. Source: Linnekin 1985:91.

Figure 6.15. Hawaiian kinship terminology.

SUMMARY

The Pacific Islands presented formidable obstacles to successful human occupation because they were so widely scattered and were often very small and resource poor. They were settled by skilled Austronesian-speaking farmers, sailors, and navigators who originated in Southeast Asia about 6,000 years ago. The farthest reaches of Polynesia were settled during a period of approximately 1,000 years ending by 800 AD with the settlement of New Zealand.

The societies of Polynesia and Micronesia represent a major contrast to the domestic-scale societies of Australia, Amazonia, and East Africa examined in earlier chapters. Pacific Island societies were characterized by a great concern with rank, and they developed permanent political and economic structures above the level of local village communities. These island societies were chiefdoms that elevated certain high-ranking individuals to permanent leadership positions as chiefs. The example from the Polynesian island of Tikopia showed that chiefs in small chiefdoms coordinated ritual and economic activities between villages, but they had relatively little power, so there were no social classes. On larger islands, such as Hawaii, political struggles between chiefs led to the formation of powerful chiefdoms. These societies became divided by class into the elites, who extracted tribute from the commoners, who produced food and wealth objects. The highest-ranking chiefs claimed the supernatural power of deities and gained life and death control over lower-ranked people. Some of the Hawaiian chiefdoms were complex enough to be considered proto-states, or small kingdoms.

The ethnographic evidence shows that the larger Polynesian societies were highly inequitable societies in which not everyone could enjoy the sociability, material prosperity, security, and participation in expressive culture that would be the essential elements of the universal "good life." In some cases it was difficult or even impossible for everyone to form successful households. Most people, especially women, were also restricted by various demeaning *tabus*, and their lives could literally be sacrificed by rulers. However, except for the landless, there is little indication that the majority suffered physical poverty. It is possible that most people accepted their inferior social status as natural and did not feel exploited, although in comparison with tribals, Polynesians clearly had much less control over the conditions of their daily life. For the majority, the human cost of supporting a tiny nobility was the increased workload of tribute payments, reduced access to the cultural sources of social power, reduced access to natural resources, and increased insecurity of tenure. It is possible to imagine island cultural systems that could have distributed social power more equitably and maximized human freedom.

STUDY QUESTIONS

1. Characterize and distinguish between each of the following cultural areas: Polynesia, Melanesia, and Micronesia.
2. Discuss the physical constraints limiting settlement on Pacific islands, characterizing the cultural response.
3. Discuss the role of status rivalry, irrigation, redistribution, environmental circumscription, and economic productivity in the development of Pacific Island chiefdoms.
4. How have linguists reconstructed the history of Austronesian migrations by analyzing word lists?
5. What special navigation skills do Pacific Islanders use for long-distance voyaging? What problems are posed by the unusual design of outrigger canoes?
6. What are the most important island crops? What do they contribute to the diet and what makes them especially suited to the island environment? What is the division of subsistence labor? What special skills does fishing require?
7. How are Pacific chiefs different from Amazon headmen? What is the cultural basis of islander ranking systems?
8. How is Tikopian society organized? What is the role of the chief? How would an Australian Aborigine view this society?
9. What is a political economy and how does it contrast with a subsistence economy?
10. How do the power of Hawaiian chiefs and the organization of Hawaiian society compare with the Tikopia? What environmental factors are related to these differences?

SUGGESTED READING

Firth, Raymond. [1936] 1957. *We the Tikopia: A Sociological Study of Kinship in Primitive Polynesia.* 2nd ed. New York: Barnes & Noble. The basic ethnographic description of Tikopia, with an emphasis on social organization.

Firth, Raymond. [1940] 1967. "The Work of the Gods." In *Tikopia*, 2nd ed. London: Athlone Press. Describes in detail the system of ritual feasting on Tikopia.

Firth, Raymond. [1965] 1975. *Primitive Polynesian Economy.* Reprint. New York: Norton. An analysis of the subsistence economy and distribution system on Tikopia.

Kirch, Patrick Vinton. 2000. *On the Road of the Winds: An Archaeological History of the Pacific Islands Before European Contact.* Berkeley: University of California Press. Excellent overview of the prehistory of the Pacific.

Kirch, Patrick Vinton. 2010. *How Chiefs Became Kings: Divine Kinship and the Rise of Archaic States in Ancient Hawai'i.* Berkeley: University of California Press. A synthesis of archaeological theory on Hawaii as an independently developed early state.

GLOSSARY TERMS

Rank Social position in a status hierarchy.

Glottochronology A method of estimating the relative date at which related languages separated from a common ancestral language by calculating the percentage of cognates shared between the related languages.

Cognates Related words that are found in more than one language and that were derived from a common protolanguage.

Mana An impersonal supernatural force thought to reside in particular people and objects. In the Pacific Islands *mana* is the basis of chiefly power.

Tabu Actions that are forbidden under the sanction of supernatural punishment. Tabus may be imposed by chiefs and are supported by chiefly *mana.*

Circumscription Robert Carneiro's explanation for the development of political centralization—that villagers may be forced to surrender their autonomy if they are unable to move away from authorities because of geographic barriers or neighboring societies.

Aristocracy A political system in which a small, privileged elite rule. This is a rule by the "best."

Primogeniture Preferential treatment to a couple's firstborn offspring or oldest surviving child; may be a basis for establishing social rank.

Ascribed status The social status that one is born into; includes sex, birth order, lineage, clan affiliation, and connection with elite ancestors.

Achieved status Social position based on a person's demonstrated personal abilities apart from social status ascribed at birth.

Social status A position that an individual occupies within a social system; defined by age, sex, kinship relationships, or other cultural criteria and involving specific behavioral expectations.

Redistribution A form of exchange in which goods, such as foodstuffs, are concentrated and then distributed under the control of a central political authority.

Social class A group of people in a stratified society, such as elites and commoners who each share a similar level of access to resources, power, and privilege.

Social stratification A ranking of social statuses such that the individuals of a society belong to different groups having differential access to resources, power, and privileges.

Specialist An individual who provides goods and services to elites in hierarchically organized societies. Such a specialist does not produce his or her own food but is supported from the surplus that is politically extracted by central authorities.

Sororal polygyny When a man marries two or more women who are sisters.

Polyandry When a woman marries two or more men.

Fraternal polyandry When a woman marries two or more men who are brothers.

Sororate When a man marries his deceased wife's sister.

Political economy A cultural pattern in which centralized political authority intervenes in the production and distribution of goods and services.

Subsistence economy Production and distribution carried on at the local community and household levels, primarily for local consumption.

NOTES

1. Pukui, Mary Kawena, and Samuel H. Elbert. 1986. *Hawaiian Dictionary.* Honolulu: University of Hawaii Press, xvii–xviii; Lessa, William A. 1986. *Ulithi: A Micronesian Design for Living.* Long Grove, IL: Waveland Press.

2. Thomas, Nicholas. 1989. "The Force of Ethnology." *Current Anthropology* 30(1):27–41.

3. Oliver, Douglas L. 1989. *Oceania: The Native Cultures of Australia and the Pacific Islands.* 2 vols. Honolulu: University of Hawaii Press.

4. Howard, Alan. 1967. "Polynesian Origins and Migrations: A Review of Two Centuries of Speculation and Theory." In *Polynesian Culture History: Essays in Honor of Kenneth P. Emory,* edited by Genevieve Highland, Roland Force, Alan Howard, Marion Kelly, and Yosihiko Sinoto, pp. 45–101. Bernice P. Bishop Museum Special Publication, no. 56. Honolulu: Bishop Museum Press.

5. Perry, W. J. 1923. *The Children of the Sun.* London: Methuen; Smith, G. Elliot. 1928. *In the Beginning: The Origin of Civilization.* New York: Morrow.

6. Levison, M., R. G. Ward, and J. W. Webb. 1973. *The Settlement of Polynesia: A Computer Simulation.* Minneapolis: University of Minnesota Press.

7. Kirch, Patrick Vinton. 1985. *Feathered Gods and Fishhooks: An Introduction to Hawaiian Archaeology and Prehistory.* Honolulu: University of Hawaii Press.

8. Gudschinsky, Sarah C. 1956. "The ABC's of Lexicostatistics (Glottochronology)." *Word* 12:175–210.

9. Gladwin, Thomas. 1970. *East Is a Big Bird.* Cambridge, MA: Harvard University Press.

10. Gladwin, Thomas. 1970. *East Is a Big Bird.*

11. Schattenburg, Patricia. 1976. "Food and Cultivar Preservation in Micronesian Voyaging." Miscellaneous Work Papers. *University of Hawaii Pacific Islands Program* 1:25–51.

12. Murai, Mary, Florence Pen, and Carey D. Miller. 1958. *Some Tropical South Pacific Island Foods: Description, History, Use, Composition, and Nutritive Value.* Hawaii Agricultural Experiment Station, bull. 110. Honolulu: University of Hawaii Press.

13. Schattenburg, Patricia. 1976. "Food and Cultivar Preservation in Micronesian Voyaging."

14. Handy, E. S. C., and E. G. Handy. 1972. *The Native Planters in Old Hawaii: Their Life, Lore, and Environments.* Bernice P. Bishop Museum Bulletin. 233. Honolulu: Bishop Museum Press.

15. Alkire, William H. 1965. "Lamotrek Atoll and Inter-Island Socioeconomic Ties." *Studies in Anthropology,* no. 5. Urbana: University of Illinois Press.

16. Kenchington, Richard. 1985. "Coral-Reef Ecosystems: A Sustainable Resource." *Nature and Resources* 21(2):18–27.

17. Knudson, Kenneth E. 1970. "Resource Fluctuation, Productivity, and Social Organization on Micronesian Coral Islands." Ph.D. dissertation, University of Oregon.

18. Rubinstein, Don. 1978. "Native Place-Names and Geographic Systems of Fais, Caroline Islands." *Micronesica* 14(1):69–82.

19. Lobel, Phil S. 1978. "Gilbertese and Ellice Islander Names for Fishes and Other Organisms." *Micronesica* 14(2):177–97.

20. Johannes, Robert E. *Words of the Lagoon, Fishing and Marine Lore in the Palau District of Micronesia.* Berkeley: University of California Press.

21. Johannes, Robert E. *Words of the Lagoon.*

22. Read, Dwight W. 2002. "A Multitrajectory, Competition Model of Emergent Complexity in Human Social Organization." *Proceedings of the National Academy of Sciences* Vol. 99, Supplement 3, 7251–56; Richerson, Peter J., and Robert Boyd. 1999. "Complex Societies: The Evolutionary Origins of a Crude Superorganism." *Human Nature* 10(3):253–89.

23. Alexander, Richard D. 1987. *The Biology of Moral Systems.* New York: Aldine De Gruyter.

24. Richerson, Peter J. and Robert Boyd. 1999. "Complex Societies," 265.

25. Kirch, Patrick Vinton. 1984. *The Evolution of the Polynesian Chiefdoms.* Cambridge: Cambridge University Press, 13–15.

26. Kirch, Patrick Vinton. 1984. *The Evolution of the Polynesian Chiefdoms* 170; Stannard, David E. 1989. *Before*

the Horror: The Population of Hawai'i on the Eve of Western Contact. Honolulu: Social Science Research Institute, University of Hawaii.

27. Steadman, David W. 1995. "Prehistoric Extinctions of Pacific Island Birds: Biodiversity Meets Zooarchaeology." *Science* (Feb. 24) 267:1123–31.

28. Kirch, Patrick Vinton. 1984. *The Evolution of the Polynesian Chiefdoms.*

29. Carneiro, Robert L. 1967. "On the Relationship Between Size of Population and Complexity of Social Organization." *Southwestern Journal of Anthropology* 23(3):234–43.

30. Kosse, Krisztina. 1990. "Group Size and Societal Complexity: Thresholds in the Long-Term Memory." *Journal of Anthropological Archaeology* 9(3):275–303.

31. Carneiro, Robert L. 1981. "The Chiefdom: Precursor of the State." In *The Transition to Statehood in the New World,* edited by Grant Jones and Robert Kautz, pp. 37–79. Cambridge, Eng.: Cambridge University Press, 37–38.

32. Durham, William H. 1991. *Coevolution: Genes, Culture, and Human Diversity.* Stanford, CA: Stanford University Press, 211.

33. Sahlins, Marshall. 1958. *Social Stratification in Polynesia.* Seattle: University of Washington Press.

34. (Carneiro 1981). Carneiro, Robert L. 1970. "A Theory of the Origin of the State." *Science* 169:733–38; Carneiro, Robert L. 1981. "The Chiefdom: Precursor of the State." In *The Transition to Statehood in the New World,* edited by Grant Jones and Robert Kautz, pp. 37–79. Cambridge, Eng.: Cambridge University Press.

35. Mann, Michael. 1986. *The Sources of Social Power,* vol. 1, *A History of Power from the Beginning to* AD 1760. Cambridge, Eng.: Cambridge University Press.

36. Sahlins, Marshall. 1985a. *Islands of History.* Chicago: University of Chicago Press; Sahlins, Marshall. 1985b. "Hierarchy and Humanity in Polynesia." In *Transformations of Polynesian Culture,* edited by A. Hooper and J. Huntsman. Auckland: The Polynesian Society.

37. Sahlins, Marshall. 1985b. "Hierarchy and Humanity in Polynesia," 214–15.

38. Goldman, Irving. 1970. *Ancient Polynesian Society.* Chicago and London: University of Chicago Press, xvi.

39. Kirch, Patrick Vinton. 1984. *The Evolution of the Polynesian Chiefdoms,* 34.

40. Sahlins. 1968:64.

41. Sahlins, Marshall. 1963. "Poor Man, Rich Man, Big-Man, Chief: Political Types in Melanesia and Polynesia." *Comparative Studies in Society and History* 5:285–303.

42. Goldman, Irving. 1970. *Ancient Polynesian Society,* 7.

43. Kirch, Patrick Vinton. 2001. "Polynesian Feasting in Ethnohistoric, Ethnographic, and Archaeological Contexts: A Comparison of Three Societies." In *Feasts: Archaeological and Ethnographic Perspectives on Food,* *Politics, and Power,* edited by Michael Dietler and Brian Hayden, pp. 168–84. Washington and London: Smithsonian Institution Press.

44. Sahlins, Marshall. 1985a. *Islands of History,* 20.

45. Goldman, Irving. 1970. *Ancient Polynesian Society.*

46. Firth, Raymond. 1957. *We the Tikopia: A Sociological Study of Kinship in Primitive Polynesia,* 2nd ed. New York: Barnes & Noble. Firth, Raymond. 1967. "The Work of the Gods." In *Tikopia,* 2nd ed. London: Athlone Press. Firth, Raymond. 1975. *Primitive Polynesian Economy.* New York: Norton.

47. Kirch, Patrick Vinton, and Douglas E. Yen. 1982. *Tikopia: The Prehistory and Ecology of a Polynesian Outlier.* Bernice P. Bishop Museum, Bulletin 238. Honolulu: Bishop Museum Press.

48. Firth, Raymond. 1975. *Primitive Polynesian Economy.* New York: Norton, 231.

49. Kirch, Patrick Vinton. 1985. *Feathered Gods and Fishhooks.*

50. Earle, Timothy. 1978. *Economic and Social Organization of a Complex Chiefdom: The Halelea District, Kaua'i, Hawaii.* Anthropological Papers, no. 63. Ann Arbor: Museum of Anthropology, University of Michigan.

51. Kirch, Patrick Vinton. 1984. *The Evolution of the Polynesian Chiefdoms,* 253–55.

52. Earle, Timothy K. 2001. "Institutionalization of Chiefdoms: Why Landscapes Are Built." In *From Leaders to Rulers,* edited by Jonathan Haas, pp. 105–24. New York: Kluwer Academic/Plenum.

53. Hommon, Robert J. 1986. "Social Evolution in Ancient Hawai'i." In *Island Societies: Archaeological Approaches to Evolution and Transformation,* edited by Patrick V. Kirch, pp. 55–68. Cambridge: Cambridge University Press.

54. Kirch, Patrick Vinton. 2001. "Polynesian Feasting . . . ," 177.

55. Linnekin, Jocelyn. 1990. *Sacred Queens and Women of Consequence; Rank, Gender, and Colonialism in the Hawaiian Islands.* Ann Arbor: University of Michigan Press, 100.

56. Valeri, Valerio. 1985. *Kingship and Sacrifice: Ritual and Society in Ancient Hawaii.* Chicago: University of Chicago Press, 150.

57. Kirch, Patrick Vinton. 1985. *Feathered Gods and Fishhooks,* 160.

58. Kirch, Patrick Vinton. 1985. *Feathered Gods and Fishhooks,* 164.

59. Linnekin, Jocelyn. 1990. *Sacred Queens,* 8.

60. Linnekin, Jocelyn. 1990. *Sacred Queens,* 204–5.

61. Kirch, Patrick Vinton. 1984. *The Evolution of the Polynesian Chiefdoms,* 180–81, 1985:211–14.

62. Beckwith, Martha Warren. 1951. *The Kumulipo: A Hawaiian Creation Chant.* Chicago: University of Chicago Press.

63. Valeri, Valerio. 1985. *Kingship and Sacrifice.*

64. Valeri, Valerio. 1985. *Kingship and Sacrifice*.

65. Ii, John Papa. 1983. *Fragments of Hawaiian History*. Bernice P. Bishop Museum Special Publication, no. 70. Honolulu: Bishop Museum Press.

66. Firth, Raymond. 1967. "The Work of the Gods."

67. Linnekin, Jocelyn. 1990. *Sacred* Queens.

68. Feher, Joseph. 1969. *Hawaii: A Pictorial History*. Bernice P. Bishop Museum Special Publication, no. 58. Honolulu: Bishop Museum Press.

69. Earle, Timothy. 1987. "Specialization and the Production of Wealth: Hawaiian Chiefdoms and the Inka Empire." In *Specialization, Exchange, and Complex Societies*, edited by Elizabeth Brumfiel and Timothy Earle, pp. 64–75. Cambridge, Eng.: Cambridge University Press.

70. Linnekin, Jocelyn. 1990. *Sacred Queens*.

71. Linnekin, Jocelyn. 1990. *Sacred Queens*, 24.

72. Linnekin, Jocelyn. 1990. *Sacred Queens*, 11.

73. Linnekin, Jocelyn. 1990. *Sacred Queens*.

74. Linnekin, Jocelyn. 1990. *Sacred Queens*, 44.

75. Gallimore, R. and Howard, A. 1968. "The Hawaiian Life Style: Some Qualitative Considerations." In Gallimore, R., and Howard, A., eds. *Studies in a Hawaiian Community. Namakamaka O Nanakuli*, pp. 10–16. Pacific Anthropological Records No. 1. Honolulu: Department of Anthropology, B.P. Bishop Museum, 10.

76. Linnekin, Jocelyn. 1990. *Sacred Queens*, 121–25.

77. Sahlins, Marshall. 1992. "Historical Ethnography." In Kirch, Patrick Vinton, and Marshall Sahlins. *Anahulu: The Anthropology of History in the Kingdom of Hawaii*, vol. 1, pp. 1–243. Chicago: University of Chicago Press, 198.

78. Howard, Alan. 1968. "Adoption and Significance of Children to Hawaiian Families." In Gallimore, R. and A. Howard, eds. *Studies in a Hawaiian Community. Namakamaka O Nanakuli*, pp. 87–101. Pacific Anthropological Records No. 1. Honolulu: Department of Anthropology, B.P. Bishop Museum, 92.

79. Sahlins, Marshall. 1992. "Historical Ethnography," 202.

80. Sahlins, Marshall. 1992. "Historical Ethnography," 200–201.

CHAPTER 7

Ancient Empires in Two Worlds: Mesopotamia and the Andes

Figure 7.0. Mochica Lord (Alva, Walter, and Christopher B. Donnan. 1993. *Royal Tombs of Sipán*. Fowler Museum of Cultural History. University of California, Los Angeles, Figure 245, p. 218, reprinted with permission).

PRONUNCIATION GUIDE

ANDEAN TERMS IN THIS CHAPTER ARE DERIVED FROM SPANISH and Quechua. Their most common pronunciation can be approximated by English speakers using the following orthography and sounds:

KEY

a = *a* in f*a*ther
o = *o* in g*o*
ay = *ay* in d*ay*
ai = *i* in *i*ce
e = *e* in b*e*d
ee = *ee* in b*ee*t
oo = *oo* in f*oo*d
• = Syllable division
/ = Stress
camayo= [ca • mai / o]
ceque = [say / kay]
Chan Chan = [chan / chan]
Chimú = [chee • moo /]
Cuzco = [cooz / co]
huaca = [wa / ka]
llama = [ya / ma]
mita = [mee / ta]
Orejones = [or • ay • ho / nays]
panaqa = [pa • na / ka]
puna = [poo / na]
Quechua = [kaych / wa]
quipu = [kee / poo]
Tawantinsuyu = [ta / wan • teen / soo • yoo]

LEARNING OBJECTIVES

After studying this chapter you should be able to do the following:

1. Compare the ancient Mesopotamian and Andean empires and Pacific Island chiefdoms, highlighting the most important points of contrast related to scale of society.
2. Define the state and civilization in comparison with tribes and chiefdoms and discuss the relationship between size of society, cultural complexity, and the distribution of social power.
3. Evaluate the theory that civilizations originated as an elite-directed process designed to concentrate social power rather than as a natural, inevitable evolutionary process.
4. Use evidence from Mesopotamia and the Andes to assess the interconnections between technology, long-distance trade, population, environment,

and human decision making in the development of large-scale, complex societies.

5. Describe and compare the four social ranks of Ur III and the Inca empire, referring to social function, the distribution of social power, and costs and benefits.

6. Describe and compare the religious system of Ur III and the Inca empire.

7. Evaluate the evidence for tyranny, oppression, and exploitation in Mesopotamian and Andean civilizations.

Although many Pacific Island chiefdoms crossed the "great divide" from the social equality of domestic-scale societies into rank- and class-based social systems, a major gulf separates these island cultures from the larger-scale states and empires to be considered in this chapter. The rulers of early states created monumental temples, pyramids, palaces, and cities that have been hailed as major achievements and attributes of civilization. However, these impressive constructions clearly depended on pervasive social inequality, and these states were characterized by an inherent instability not found in domestic-scale cultures.

The politicization process that rulers used to construct **city-states** and conquest empires represented a major departure from the domestic-scale cultural patterns that had sustained humanity for so long. The rise of centralized state political power is perhaps the greatest anthropological mystery of all. Although no explanation is completely satisfactory, it is clear that states were human constructions, designed by egocentric power seekers who were able to take advantage of unique circumstances that made it difficult for households and communities to escape the influence of elite power and circumstances that could support increases in the scale of the sociocultural system through intensified subsistence production. The existence of civilizations, or societies with cities, governments, and elite-directed institutions and cultural patterns, is difficult to explain because civilizations make such costly demands on people and natural resources. Urban culture and the luxurious lifestyles of elite rulers in the imperial world placed unequal demands on the non-elite majority and required vast and complex bureaucracies and armies as well as enormous expenditures of energy and materials. These developments separated ordinary people from direct control over the daily necessities of life. Because they were such large-scale systems, these urban civilizations also required complex institutional structures that tended naturally to concentrate social power in the hands of a wealthy

aristocratic oligarchy, because the poor majority were either unable or unwilling to demand and implement democratic control and a more equitable distribution of costs and benefits. All of the civilizations examined in this chapter, and in chapters 8 and 9, were despotic political systems that showed remarkable cultural parallels. This suggests that rulers were following similar human solutions to similar problems, but there is no reason to consider these parallel developments to have been the inevitable unfolding of any preordained evolutionary pattern. There are other, more humane and more sustainable, ways that large-scale systems can be organized.

The contrasts between tribal cultures and state civilizations are so extreme, and the comparative disadvantages of state civilizations for all but the elite minority are so obvious, that explaining how states originate and function as cultural systems continues to be a major theoretical challenge for anthropology. Understanding the full implications of urban civilization for the long-term future of humanity is also a critical issue. It is important to remember that urban civilization has existed for only 5,000 years and could be considered a very shaky experiment when its short span and record of chronic collapse are compared with the 50,000-year record of tribal foraging cultures in Australia. In this chapter, we will review the issues surrounding urban civilization within the context of two major civilizations from different parts of the world: the Sumerians of Mesopotamia and the Inca of Peru.

ANCIENT CIVILIZATIONS AND THE TRIUMPH OF ELITE POWER

Civilization is about social power. The cities, writings, monuments, and artwork that identify civilization give certain people massive and historically unprecedented power over others. The principal function of civilization is to organize overlapping social networks of ideological, political, economic, and military power in ways that differentially benefit privileged households.[1] Civilization gives some individuals and their households institutionalized coercive power to permanently control property in ways that reduce the material opportunities of other households. This coercive use of social power would baffle tribal peoples because it overrides the humanization process that equally provided for everyone's material needs in tribal cultures. Simple chiefdoms, such as in Tikopia, introduced differential ranking between individuals, but rank was not used to deny anyone the right to satisfy material needs. Politicization was the cultural process that elites used to institutionalize social inequality in the state, but it is difficult to explain why people allowed this to happen. Civilization is unlikely to develop directly out of tribal cultures because tribal peoples self-consciously refused to grant anyone permanent, coercive social power over other households. Tribal war leaders and village heads are temporary and have no coercive authority; ideological power is open to everyone; and there are no cultural incentives for depriving anyone of life's necessities.

Tribal leaders were community servants who served at the will of the community and did not found dynasties. In the imperial world political elites managed to split society into a tiny elite managerial sector and a commoner working sector where the majority produced the goods and services that the elite disproportionately enjoyed. The elite also organized the structure of society so that their high-status positions could be passed on to their own children, making it possible for them to create dynasties. In effect, the aristocracy transformed the commoner majority into domesticated cattle, forcing them to surrender their freedom and political and economic equality to sustain a hereditary power elite.[2]

The centralization of political power is the most important underlying feature of civilization because it is functionally connected with many other "civilized" traits; this, in turn, suggests that explanatory theories that focus on political power will be most productive. Before treating the issue of the origin of civilization, let us consider in more detail the functionally interconnected organizational features and cultural traits that are most closely related to the concentration of social power in the hands of rulers and that have figured prominently in definitions of civilization.

State Bureaucracy and the Structures of Elite Power

Probably the most useful definitions of the state cite the presence of government institutions, or bureaucratic hierarchies, often characterized as having a monopoly on the legitimate use of force. Thus, kings, courts, and judges, concentrated in an urban center and supported by temples, treasuries, writing systems, police forces, and armies, might be considered the essential features of states. Such formal institutions are uniquely important developments because they have explicit goals, such as the preservation of the social order, and they can legitimately be analyzed in functional terms. Perhaps most importantly, institutionalized state power historically has tended to enclose

people within "social cages"[3] and to make it difficult for them to escape from exploitative relationships. States operate within bounded territories and create fixed societies and ethnic groups where previously there were highly flexible, domestic-scale societies that allowed people to shift allegiances in ways that deprived would-be despots of power.

None of the ancient state societies were democracies in which rule was directly exercised by all of the people. Political societies of 2,500 people are the approximate upper limit for consensus decision making, or direct participatory democracy, which requires face-to-face interaction. It is difficult but not impossible to hold larger communities together, and most known larger societies have formal political leadership, elite rulers, and social classes. German sociologist Max Weber[4] (1864–1920) attributed elite rule to the "law of the small number," pointing out that it is easier for a few to organize against opposition and keep secrets. Elites are likely to act in their self-interest, and they may resort to physical coercion and ideological domination to enforce their decisions. There are exceptional archaeological examples of large villages or towns, or integrated communities that were larger than 2,500 people but show little evidence of government and social classes, such as the Anasazi in the American Southwest,[5] the prehistoric Lillooet in interior British Columbia,[6] Neolithic villages in the Middle East such as Abu Hureya,[7] and Bronze Age Cyprus.[8] These exceptional examples confirm that societies with communities of 5,000 are more are safely considered to be imperial world. It is possible to have social complexity without hierarchy and extreme inequality. These atypical larger societies were probably heterarchies in which individuals were ranked on multiple dimensions, rather than hierarchies with a single dominant ranking system.[9] There are many pathways to social power, not all of which lead inevitably to the state and despotic rulers. The alternative of heterarchy will be examined in part IV.

Deciding who should rule, how rulers should be controlled, and how a society's wealth should be distributed was the persistent problem of social power that plagued all civilizations in the ancient imperial world and is a continuing challenge for all people today. Representative democracy is seen as an ideal government by many in the contemporary world, but it was rare in ancient civilizations. Greek philosopher Aristotle equated democracy, rule by the people, with rule by a poor majority and felt that it was unlikely to endure because popular democratic leaders, or demagogues, would threaten the interests of wealthy elites. Thus, he thought that either tyranny, absolute rule by a king, other forms of monarchy, or some form of oligarchy, rule by the few, would be the most likely political system. Monarchs and oligarchs would constitute an aristocracy and would rule because they were the most virtuous, meritorious, or wealthy.

For rulers to increase the number of people they commanded in their personal imperia, and thereby gain more social power, they needed to increase the scale of society and the complexity of the total cultural system. Initially growth in scale and power occurred together, with positive feedback between the two, but once power becomes firmly established it becomes easier for elites to independently promote growth. Elites created growth by calling into being new organizational forms, new social beliefs and symbols, and in some cases new technologies. These new cultural features were functionally interconnected, and rulers tended to add them in a predictable sequence. Rulers could increase social scale through in-place growth by constructing social hierarchy. This kind of growth in social scale did not require growth in overall population, but it did require that more people become integrated into a larger society. Thus, growth in scale and growth in power occurred simultaneously. When rulers had the institutional structures in place to create and maintain a political economy, they could encourage growth in population by demanding more labor from people. When taxes and tribute replaced kinship reciprocity, it gave people an incentive to increase the size of their families to ease the new burdens. Elite-directed subsistence intensification increased total food production, making it possible to support more people in the same territory.

Figure 7.1 illustrates how increases in cultural complexity allowed aggrandizing individuals to concentrate social power in their personal imperia. This scalogram displays the presence or absence of fifty culture traits among fifteen societies, including three Australian foragers, three Amazon villagers, two African herders, four Pacific Island societies, and three empires (Mesopotamia, the Inca, and China). The fifty traits were sifted out of a list of hundreds of organizational traits because they proved to be generally cumulative and most strongly reflected increasing cultural complexity and culture scale.[10] The scalogram shows, for example, that if a society had a city of 10,000 people or more it would also be likely to have all forty-one traits lower on the list, because these traits were functionally related to urbanization. This means that the presence of large cities is a useful defining feature of civilization.

These rankings demonstrate that the eight societies drawn from the tribal world were very similar in complexity and in the modest scale of the largest personal imperia that they supported. The four Pacific Island chiefdoms and the Hawaiian kingdom were significantly more complex than tribal societies, and they supported personal imperia that were orders of magnitude larger than any in the tribal world. The even more enormous gains made by the Mesopotamian, Inca, and Chinese emperors stand out clearly, but this expansion in elite power required at least seventeen additional traits beyond the Pacific Islanders, including bureaucratic inspectors, census takers, laws, and a hierarchy of urban places.

The scale leap from Pacific Island chiefdoms to empires with millions of tax-paying subjects was costly because of the added expense of cities, information management systems, and social control, as well as the increased need for defense as society's total stock of tangible wealth increased. The big organizational problem was coping with the vast increase in potential social interaction, with inequality magnifying sources of discontent. As discussed in chapter 6, the Hawaiian king had to deal with tens of billions of potential human interactions, but in 1911 the Chinese emperor directed a vast society where 125 quadrillion (12.5 with 15 zeros) social interactions were possible. This required enormous bureaucratic complexity and a corresponding loss of personal freedom for millions of people. The **bureaucracy** that top rulers constructed to administer these vastly larger-scale societies also defined a class structure because rank in the bureaucracy determined access to the benefits that rulers accumulated and distributed.

Weber[11] called bureaucracy an institutionalized form of domination in which rulers with "authoritarian power of command" impose their will on others. Bureaucratic rule is structured by a hierarchy of officials under a top ruler. In the ancient world bureaucratic rule was often based on patronage and nepotism, but ideally a bureaucrat operates like a machine, without regard for human feeling and emotion. Bureaucracy is an advantage for top rulers, but it creates special problems for people. To be effective, bureaucrats must ultimately surrender their will, and their conscience, to dictates of their superiors.[12] There is always a top ruler in a bureaucracy, but lower-level bureaucrats may in turn be despotic rulers in their own spheres of control.

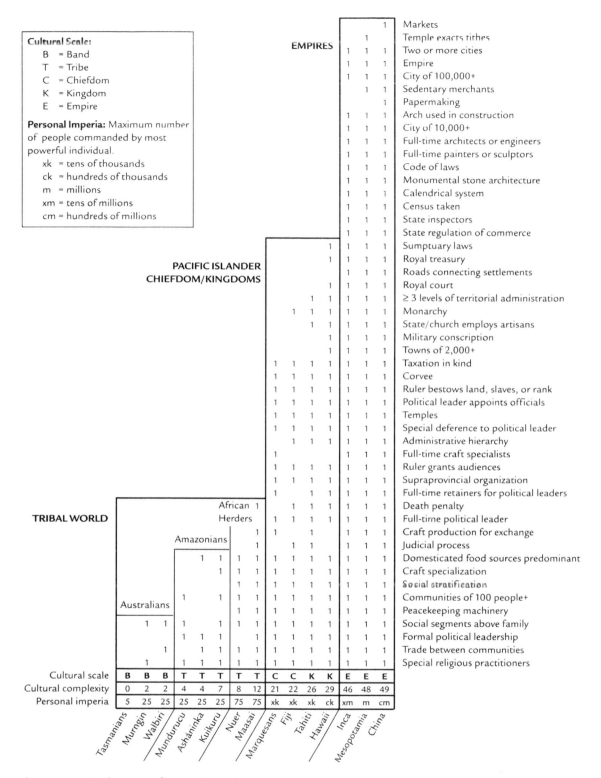

Figure 7.1. Scalogram of 15 societies by cultural scale, cultural complexity, and size of personal imperia (adapted from Carneiro and Tobias 1963, with modification).

Evidence for elite direction of the cultural development process in the imperial world can be seen in the steady concentration of social power in elite hands as rulers increase the scale of society. This is a natural function of the mathematics of scale and bureaucratic hierarchies. To demonstrate how this works, figure 7.2 graphs ruling hierarchies in five hypothetical societies arranged by increasing scale from tribe to empire. The lines show the number of rulers, officials, leaders, or heads by the number of people they command in each society, representing their personal imperia. Each slanted line represents a model society, and each point on the lines is a ranked position in that society's social power hierarchy. Each line extends from self-rule by a single person to a five-person household, and then multiplies each rank by ten to produce the next higher level. For example, a tribe has just four social power ranks, each with its own "ruler": single person, five-person household, fifty-person kin group, and five-hundred-person village. In this simulated tribal society there are only two positions above household head, the kin group head and village head, and only eleven "rulers" (one village head and ten kin group heads). The high degree of human freedom and economic equality in tribal societies meant that tribal "rulers" had very limited coercive power over their personal imperia.

In the typical administrative hierarchies of the chiefdoms, kingdoms, and empires illustrated in figure 7.2, elite power becomes mathematically more concentrated by powers of ten, in direct proportion with increases in social scale. Ruling elite households always represent the top 1.1 percent of society, not counting their retainers. Growth in scale benefits the elite, because it promotes the top ruler and increases the total number of rulers at lower levels in the hierar-

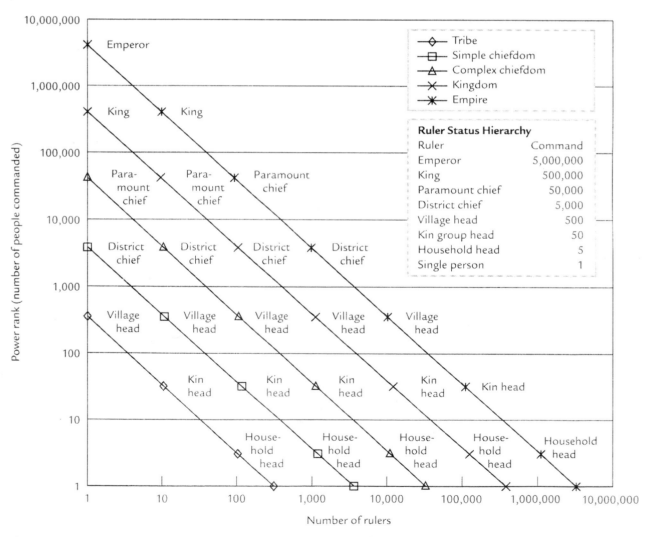

Figure 7.2. Ruler status hierarchies and power ranks for scale of society.

chy. However, the top ruler actually receives a disproportionate increase in power, even when the overall power distribution remains constant. This is because the top ruler's household is always number one, not a fixed percentage of society, and it therefore becomes a declining proportion of all households even as growth magnifies its social power tenfold (see figure 7.3). This power bonus gives the top ruler a powerful incentive to promote more growth.

Figure 7.2 shows that beyond the tribe, when rulers construct a ruling bureaucracy to manage larger-scale societies, they divide society into elite and commoner social classes that comprise increasing numbers of rulers collectively commanding more and more people. More powerful rulers can maintain ever-larger household establishments and can support more and more luxurious lifestyles.

The power of kings and emperors is three and four orders of magnitude greater, respectively, than the power of village heads. Such rulers can be designated "super-elites," because they command hundreds of thousands and millions of people.

These civilizations were all directed by urban-based rulers who produced broadly similar **Great Tradition**

religious ideologies and elite status markers to legitimize their superiority and to help them extract material support from the poor majority. Anthropologists distinguish between city-states and **village-states** to identify two different elite strategies for integrating ancient empires.[13] The rulers of city-states intensively exploited landless commoners who lived in urban and suburban neighborhoods as dependents on urban institutions and urban elites. The rulers of village-states extracted small amounts of labor from vast numbers of self-sufficient peasant villagers, who often lived far from cities. Villagers maintained their own more egalitarian **Little Tradition** cultures that had obvious roots in the tribal world. Mesopotamian city-states and the Inca Empire are ideal examples of a city-state and village-state respectively, whereas the elites who directed imperial China (chapter 8) and Hindu India (chapter 9) drew on a mix of Great Tradition ruling strategies.

Explaining State Origins: Natural Growth or Quest for Power?

Many theorists speak of states as social organisms that simply "emerge," or arise and grow following

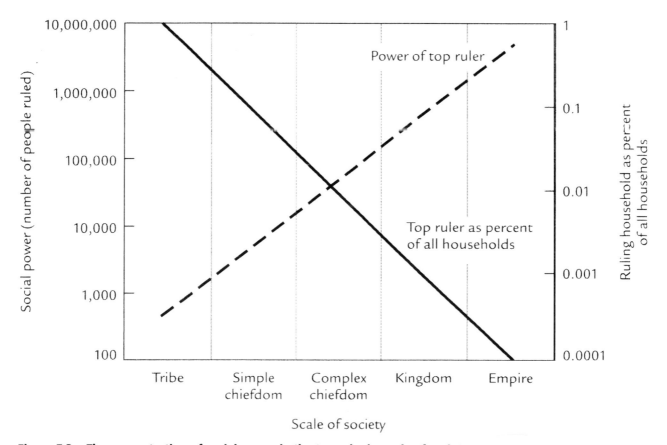

Figure 7.3.   The concentration of social power in the top ruler by scale of society.

a natural evolutionary process in a predetermined sequence. In this view, the process may be set in motion by a prime mover, such as population growth, and then it is fueled by further developments. Often this is described as people solving human problems, and the cultural system that "emerges" is a machine of functionally interconnected parts following its own logic. For example, the invention of farming may have been a response to an environmental crisis. Farming is then said to have "caused" population pressure, which in turn caused irrigation and conquest war, which produced tribute and slaves, which led to greater productivity and more inventions. This treats state development as a progressive, presumably beneficial, process that inevitably unfolded as human creativity increased and populations grew.

Taking an evolutionary approach, anthropologist Julian Steward[14] observed that civilizations in Peru, Mesoamerica, Mesopotamia, Egypt, and China all developed independently along similar **multilinear evolutionary** lines. He stressed the regularities in this process, noting that these early civilizations all developed in arid or semiarid environments, where irrigation could support dense populations. Steward thought that irrigation was the key technology that promoted population growth and that elites were needed to manage the irrigation system. Historian William McNeil[15] simplified this into a sequence in which farmers produced a surplus, thereby "freeing" others to develop specialized skills and new ideas "... until society as a whole became sufficiently complex, wealthy, and powerful to be called 'civilized.'"

There is considerable merit in such explanations, but they are incomplete and misleading. Even when the sequence and the functional interconnections are historically accurate, they do not adequately explain why people actually did these things, because other, perhaps better, solutions to human problems are always possible. Functionalist, evolutionary explanations also obscure the role of elite decision making, minimizing the negative human consequences of social transformation and making the process appear too natural and logical. The problems that ancient civilizations solved were primarily the problems of elites seeking to maintain and expand their powers. Structurally, civilizations are greatly enlarged chiefdoms, and they can best be explained in reference to the politics of circumscription and social caging described in chapter 6. In this view, rulers took advantage of crisis situations to force people to accept the elite's self-interested solutions that precluded alternatives that might have produced better human outcomes.

Explanations that make technology a prime mover disregard who calls technology into being and who directs its use. Inventions don't just happen, and civilization does not need to wait for the right inventive genius to appear. Earlier, equally creative people invented Neolithic technology, which included farming, in a creative process that everyone participated in, because it helped solve everyone's subsistence problems. The Neolithic paradox referred to in chapter 5 questions why Neolithic peoples, who were obviously so creative, failed to invent writing, cities, kingship, and social class. The paradox is resolved by recognizing that as long as tribal societies functioned as their creators intended, they saw no advantage in radical social transformations that would empower rulers and make everyone else pay the taxes and bear the risks.

There are some general benefits to state organization. As with chiefdoms, rulers may collect and store food surpluses, then redistribute them to the population to prevent famine. For example, the Romans used a free grain "dole" to maintain the urban poor, but this sort of welfare disguises the social inequalities that make welfare necessary. Karl Wittfogel,[16] who experienced the "benefits" of life in a Nazi concentration camp, observed that when pirates keep their ship afloat they are not being benevolent to their captives. Despotic rulers can be expected to maximize their own benefits, but too much exploitation would be counterproductive.

The strongest evidence for intentional elite direction of state development, in addition to their mathematical increase in social power as shown above, is the unmistakable material payoff appropriated by the rulers. This is clearly seen in the increasing size of domestic establishments at higher levels in the social hierarchy. For example, in the ancient Egyptian city of el-Amarna, built by King Akenaten in about 1350 BC, the average floor space of 75 percent of houses measured 69 square meters,[17] whereas the houses of the top 25 percent averaged in the hundreds of square meters, and they occupied over half of the total residential space. If King Akenaten's 20,000-square-meter palace is included, the elite share rises to 63 percent. In fourth century AD Rome, a city of a million people, fewer than 2,000 were wealthy enough to live in mansions, whereas 98 percent of the empire of 50 million people remained poor.

A similar picture of wealth concentration appears in ancient Greece, where nearly a third of the population were slaves, and the top 4 percent of free households held more than half of all private wealth.[18] In ancient empires generally larger households meant larger kin networks, larger personal imperia, and improved reproductive fitness for men. The number of a ruler's wives and concubines increased by orders of magnitude from tens in small chiefdoms, to hundreds in larger chiefdoms and small kingdoms, to thousands in empires.[19]

Clearly, there can be no single explanation for such a complex phenomenon as state organization. It will perhaps be most useful to move to specific case studies. The following sections will examine some of the archaeological evidence for the development of Mesopotamian civilization within the larger context of Near Eastern prehistory and environment and will provide a comparative view of Andean civilization.

The Vulnerability of Inequality and Political Hierarchy

Although no culture can claim perfect functional integration, focusing on the issue of collapse makes it clear that large-scale, politically centralized societies are significantly more precarious than small-scale tribal societies. States are more complex systems with more pieces and more things to go wrong. However, this is not just a quantitative matter. Tribes cannot break down because there is no tribal political structure to collapse. Villages and bands undergo continuous reorganization and can be dissolved at any time with no particular impact on the larger society and culture. By contrast, large regional states break down into local kingdoms or city-states, which, in turn, may further split into chiefdoms or autonomous villages and bands.

States are especially vulnerable to collapse because they contain social classes based on major inequities in wealth and power. States create special-interest groups and give them a reason to risk bringing the whole system down in order to improve their own position. A limitation on the number of political offices generates perpetual rivalries. Inequalities of wealth and power may be the most critical defining feature of states and the single most important cause of their breakdown. The creation of wealth requires revenue, but revenue extraction by taxation is a doubly risky state function. State authorities will seek as much revenue as possible, but if they demand too much, the peasantry may rebel. Too high a rate of revenue extraction also forces people to intensify their subsistence activities, which will increase the pressure on natural ecosystems.

Unequal concentrations of wealth—whether in the form of luxury goods, stored food, or labor intensive construction projects—appear to be functional prerequisites for state organization; their presence, however, also causes dangerous instability. Warehoused food is required to support nonfood-producing specialists and to sustain dense populations that might be threatened by fluctuations in production. Luxury goods are necessary status markers and rewards for political service. Storehouses are prime targets for looters from both within and without a particular state, and their defense requires expensive walls and standing armies. The unequal distribution of luxury goods also makes police forces and court systems necessary.

Creating and defending state wealth is a primary reason for costly military campaigns against neighboring states. The maintenance of a full-time officer corps, palace guards, and frontier garrisons is a permanent military expense, and specific campaigns in which large numbers of peasant soldiers are mobilized can be extremely costly. Military expenditures may be the largest category in many state budgets and create constant pressure for potentially destabilizing increases in revenue extraction.

In comparison with a cultural universe occupied exclusively by tribal cultures, states introduced a qualitatively different cultural dynamic into any regional system. Whereas chronic feuding was endemic in tribal systems, territorial conquest was a permanent characteristic of states. Tribal raids and blood feuds did not require permanent leaders or a standing professional army and thus were not incentives for increased production. However, the appearance of states in a nonstate area stimulated trade and raiding by tribal groups against the state. This sometimes pushed tribes into political developments leading to wealth inequality and tribal instability.

THE MESOPOTAMIAN WORLD OF TWO RIVERS

The "fertile crescent" in the Middle East is a remarkable culture area where several of the most significant social transformations in human prehistory and history first took place. This is a 1,500 (2,414 km)-mile-long area curving from the mouth of the Tigris-Euphrates rivers at the head of the Persian Gulf, stretching northwest across modern Iraq, adjacent parts of Iran, and southern Turkey, and through Syria, Lebanon, Jordan, and Israel to the lower Nile Valley in Egypt (see figure 7.4). This environment offered people both unique opportunities and special

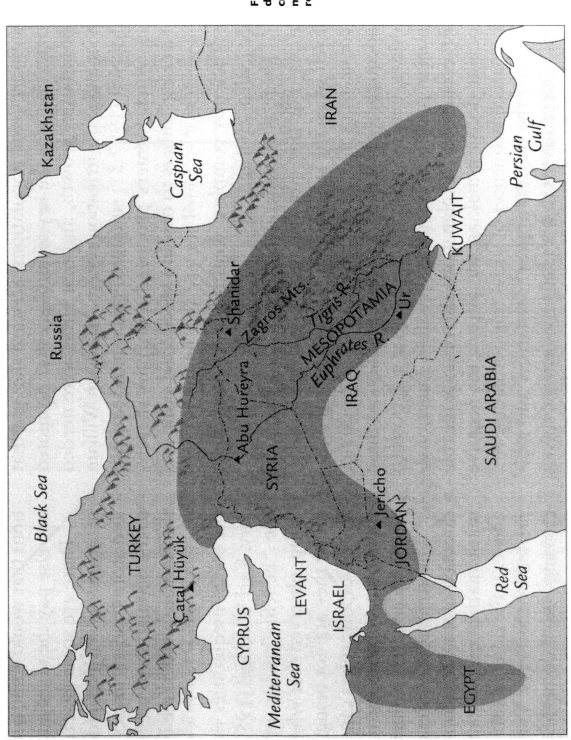

Figure 7.4. Map of the Middle East showing the fertile crescent, Mesopotamia, and major archaeological sites referred to in the text.

challenges. Major rivers traversed arid deserts in Mesopotamia, and elevation changes in the surrounding uplands created diverse belts of steppe vegetation, dry woodland, and upland forests, all rich in diverse plant and game resources. All of these ecosystems were in a dynamic, shifting balance with global and regional climate. People have been repeatedly forced to adjust to unpredictable environmental crises over the millennia since modern humans first lived there at least 100,000 years ago. This was where tribal peoples first domesticated wild plants and animals (11,000 BP) and where elites first constructed chiefdoms (7000 BP), city-states (3500 BC), and empires (2334 BC). Table 7.1 summarizes the chronology of these major cultural events and related environmental changes. The shift in dates from BP (before present) to BC (before the Christian era) marks the beginning of writing and the shift from prehistory to history.

Mesopotamian city-states are especially noteworthy because they were one of a handful of "pristine" civilizations created, presumably independently of any other preexisting states, and they have been heavily researched by specialists from many fields. This makes them an ideal case study for investigating the causes and consequences of the origins of civilization. Before examining life in Mesopotamian city-states, this section reviews the archaeological background and shows how and why a few elite individuals were able to gain control of the urbanization and politicization processes and direct the cultural transformations that created these first civilizations.

The contrast between the consensus response of tribal peoples to environmental changes in the ancient Middle East and the autocratic response of power-seeking elites highlights important differences between the tribal and imperial worlds. These different responses demonstrate that political centralization was not inevitable, but under some circumstances aspiring elites could force the majority to accept their domineering leadership. Village life and farming are often hailed by historians as the first steps toward civilization, but creating the Neolithic was a different

Table 7.1. Mesopotamian Prehistory and Early History

539 BC	Persian Invasion Destroys Mesopotamian Civilization
1000–539 BC	Neo-Babylonia, Neo-Assyrian, Iron Age
	King Nebuchadnezzar II (604–562 BC)
	Metal Coins (650 BC)
1500–1000 BC	Middle Babylonia, Middle Assyrian, Late Bronze Age
2000–1500 BC	Old Babylonian, Old Assyrian, Middle Bronze Age
	City of 100,000 (1600 BC)
	King of Hammurabi (1792–1750)
	Ninlil-zimu family in Nippur (1970–1720 BC)
3000–2000 BC	Early Bronze Age
	City of 30,000 (2250 BC)
	Ur III – King Ur-Nammu, empire (2112–2004)
	Sargon the Great (2334–2279), first empire
	Palaces as Military-Political Centers (2800 BC)
	Semitic-speaking Akkadians arrive (2900 BC)
	Early Dynastic, Sumerian City States (3000–2350)
4000–3000 BC	Uruk
	Writing (3100 BC)
	Temple Centers, Walled Cities (3500 BC)
	Sea level stabilizes (4000 BC)
5000–4000 BC	Ubaid
	Urban Centers of 1000–1500
	Chiefdoms, seals
	Sea level and climatic instability (5500–4000 BC)
11,000–6000 BP	Neolithic (Upper Euphrates River)
	Abu Hureya farmer-herders (8300-7000 BC)
	Abu Hureya forager-farmers (11,000-8300 BP)
	Optimum precipitation (12,000–6000 BP)
	Early Holocene, warmer & drier (10,000–8300 BP)
	Younger Dryas, cooler & drier (11,000–10,000 BP)
20,000–11,000 BP	Epipaleolithic
	Abu Hureya foragers (11,500–11,000 BP)
	Optimum warm, moist climate
100,000 BP	Modern Humans

Note: Dates are rounded and approximate.

process from building cities. The Neolithic resulted from democratic choices that people made freely, and everyone benefited equally. People individually adopted farming and herding, freely opting to gradually intensify their subsistence practices as the best response to changing circumstances. Autonomous Neolithic villages were also enormously successful. People lived in them for millennia without going on to invent civilization (see box 7.1).

Archaeologist Charles Redman[20] offered one of the most comprehensive explanations for the origin of Mesopotamian civilization using an elaborate flow chart and complex systems analysis that expand on and refine Steward's earlier explanation. In Redman's analysis the development process began with an empty, but potentially productive, niche that was colonized by people using irrigated agriculture. Redman then identified five crucial variables: A) population growth, B) specialized food production, C) the "need" to import raw materials, D) warfare, and E) the existence of social stratification and administrative elites, and showed how they were connected to form positive feedback loops that worked together to accelerate state development. The natural dynamic of the evolving system then quickly produced civilization. This interpretation is a helpful starting point, but it makes environment and technology the primary causes and would seem to make human agency irrelevant. It now appears that the development process was not so natural and mechanistic. A different interpretation of Redman's diagram shows that elites actually decided how the system evolved. It was the elite, not society as a whole, who decided to tax people, go to war, monopolize food storage, direct trade, and so on. The elite solution was not the only human alternative. Furthermore, particular technologies such as irrigation did not by themselves cause civilization to "emerge" and were not determined simply by environmental factors.

Redman's analysis and circumscription theory suggest that warring chiefdoms and states were "natural" institutional responses to population growth and resource shortages, but it is striking that this undemocratic solution was the last choice. The Halaf culture of 8000 to 7000 BP in Upper Mesopotamia shows that more than one response to sustainability problems was possible. Village segmentation and migration was the first choice when population growth and environmental conditions made village life difficult. Some villagers began to manage communally stored foodstuffs using seals and tokens made by impressing marks into soft clay. This simple information technology was in public use by 9000 BP. It did not require writing or political centralization, and helped make sure that village leaders could individually identify and fairly distribute stored surpluses in large sedentary communities coping with resource stress. These solutions were clearly designed to help the entire society, whereas many cultural features of chiefdoms and states were self-serving institutions designed by elites to sustain centralized power itself.[21]

Halaf peoples responded to crisis by cooperating to share and reduce the risk among households within communities and among villages within the region. People may have simply extended preexisting forms of cooperative exchange between households to neighboring communities. Villages were probably connected by kinship ties because they developed as population expanded and villages remained small and segmented. Halaf culture supported small, impermanent Neolithic villages showing no indication of status differences in wealth or power in burials, even though elaborate pottery and other luxury objects were common and widely distributed. Archaeologist Marcella Frangipane calls these societies horizontally egalitarian.[22] Villages also had public buildings that were probably used for ceremonies and storage. Subsistence was based on farming, herding, and hunting, but as changing conditions caused insecurity, individual communities apparently began to specialize on what they could produce most reliably, and people developed a cooperative system of storage and egalitarian intervillage exchange.

The first chiefdoms, temples, and small administrative hierarchies didn't just happen. They were constructed incrementally by opportunistic elites during the Ubaid Period (5500–3800 BC). The villages of the early Ubaid have been called chiefdoms, but it seems more appropriate to call them "vertical egalitarian societies" to differentiate them from their horizontally egalitarian Halafian neighbors.[23] Like Amazonian "chiefdoms," early Ubaid communities enjoyed overall economic and political equality, but some households were becoming preeminent. There was simple ranking but not social stratification. Households in these vertically egalitarian villages were individually more self-sufficient than Halafian households, and they tended to compete rather than cooperate. Domestic structures were large and were occupied by extended families, but houses were all of standard form with none particularly differentiated. There may have been small ceremonial structures or proto-temples in these villages but there were no obvious communal spaces or public storehouses and no administrative controls over goods. According to some interpretations, after 5000 BC flooding of the Tigris-Euphrates estuary and shifts in global climate brought on dangerously unpredictable droughts and produced catastrophic crop failures that turned many people into refugees, forcing them to concentrate in a few larger settlements where stored food was still available.[24]

The simple vertical differentiation of early Ubaid households contained a potential for aggrandizement that was avoided by the tribally egalitarian Halafian system. Under the Ubaid system refugees from households experiencing misfortune became dependent laborers for those fortunate few householders whose small irrigation systems didn't fail. The continuous arrival of refugees caused these larger settlements to grow into small towns of 2,000 people surrounded by villages of a few hundred people. These towns became the centers of expanding Ubaid chiefdoms, which may have encompassed 5,000 people, thus becoming imperial world. Town founders became chiefs and developed temples as community grain storehouses that attracted hungry refugees. Temples contained altars and offering tables, and the chiefs used markings on clay proto-tablets to help them collect, store, and manage food surpluses. Managing temples allowed elites to skim off surplus for personal benefit, permitting them to live on a somewhat higher material level than commoners. Chiefs lived in the center of town in houses as big as temples, three to four times larger than commoner houses (see figure 7.5). Elite houses may have been occupied by the same elite family for generations and supported large families and dependent workers. However, material differences between elites and commoners were not yet extreme.

Ubaid chiefs relied on staple finance to maintain their power, in contrast to the Hawaiian chiefs and the Inca emperors who used both staple and wealth finance. The Ubaid elite controlled the water, land, and

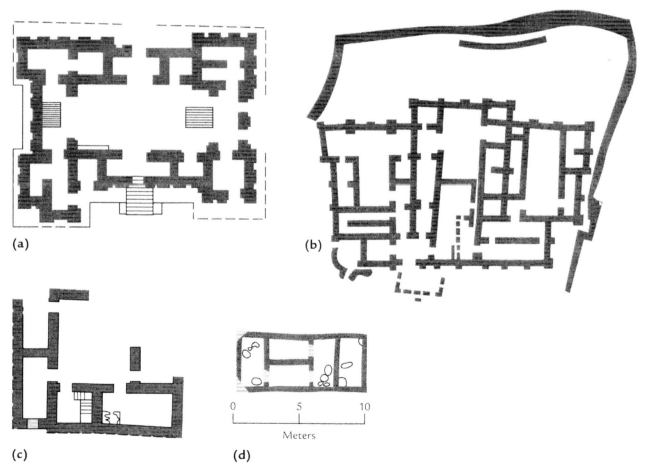

(a)

(b)

(c)

(d)

Figure 7.5. The scale of Mesopotamian structures. (a) Ubaid Temple, (b) Ubaid Great House, (c) Nippur Great House, (d) Neolithic House (Abu Hureyra).

labor needed for irrigation-based food production, but they did not abuse their power. They relied on religious ideology, ritual, and offerings to legitimize their control, and there is no evidence for warfare, political instability, or elite-directed long-distance trade to secure high-status wealth objects.[25] Ubaid chiefdoms seem to have been very peaceful societies focused on temple rituals. The conspicuous absence of status markers made it easier for people to limit elite rivalry and avoid the runaway growth described in Redman's model that later produced the first empires. This made the Ubaid chiefdoms remarkably durable, relatively small-scale societies that lasted virtually unchanged for 1,500 years. They spread by replication, rather than conquest, from Sumer into nonirrigated dry-farming areas in upper Mesopotamia.

When the sea level stabilized by 4000 BC, circumstances abruptly changed. Irrigation became more reliable, and the most successful chiefs moved to create larger-scale societies by further intensifying production, acquiring exotic materials, and waging conquest war to make themselves kings. The first city-states were in place by 3500 BC during the Uruk Period (4000–3000 BC) marking the beginning of Sumerian civilization. The Sumerian elite directed centralized economic systems and distributed rations to workers who produced high-status wealth objects. Scribes were soon keeping administrative records in cuneiform on clay tablets, making Sumerian the world's first written language. By 3000 BC urban centers reached 10,000 people and, including local villagers, may have reached 100,000 people.

Uruk Period elite initiated a fundamental transformation of society. The Sumerian elite not only controlled food production, but they organized the mass production of ceramics and shifted textile production from domestically produced linen to large-scale workshop production of woolen textiles.[26] In Neolithic Mesopotamian villages women controlled textile production, growing their own flax in small domestic plots, making linen, and weaving in the home. In the Uruk city-states, dependent women attached to the temples wove woolens, and men tended large herds of sheep on institutionally owned pastures. The elite then used the woolen goods for long-distance trade. By about 3500 BC there were Uruk colonies on the upper Euphrates in Syria for the acquisition of exotic raw materials such as wood and metals that the elite needed to build cities and to serve as status-marking wealth objects.[27]

Multiple city-states belonged to the same interaction network, sharing a common language and religion, and collectively constituted a single civilization. Private ownership of land by individual households was a key feature of Mesopotamian city-states, and it fostered a class system based on unequal access to landed wealth. City-state governments were in the hands of privileged citizens, who benefited when the system expanded (see box 7.2).

BOX 7.1. BEFORE CIVILIZATION: ABU HUREYRA, 4,000 YEARS OF TRIBAL VILLAGE AUTONOMY

The Neolithic processes of sedentarization and domestication are best documented archaeologically at Abu Hureyra.[28] This settlement mound was situated in an unusually rich and diverse region on the Euphrates River in Syria, some 400 miles upriver from Baghdad. Tribal people founded the village of Abu Hureyra 11,500 years ago, near the end of the Epipaleolithic (Mesolithic) and occupied it virtually continuously for 4,500 years. Abu Hureyra was a remarkable human achievement and a tribute to the resilience of tribal life. It existed as a tribal village for a thousand years longer than the Mesopotamian city-states and empires that followed.

Initially, the area near Abu Hureyra was so rich in wild food plants and game that people were able to construct a small permanent village of semisubterranean houses. Within a few hundred years the village grew to some 300 people who began to build timber and reed houses. They were able to secure a diverse and resilient diet for 500 years by relying entirely on herds of wild gazelles and other wild animals and more than 250 wild plant species, especially wild rye. During the 2,500 years from 11,000 BP to about 8500 BP, people gradually changed their subsistence from wild to cultivated plants, bringing rye and other grains, legumes, and flax under cultivation, while still foraging and hunting part time. They probably took this momentous technological step because cooler and drier conditions pushed favorable vegetation zones out of reach, thereby reducing their supply of plant staples, especially the grains that made sedentary life possible. Domestication was an obvious solution. Wild rye plants that produce tough, easily harvested grain heads that are also easily husked and yield plump, soft grains occur naturally in wild rye populations. By selectively harvesting and cultivating these preferred plants, people could have produced solid stands with these desirable genetic traits within 200 years. Cultivation increased their workload, but it allowed people to produce more food in a given area of land, which meant they could remain in their village as wild foods disappeared. People turned to cultivation because there were no easier resources open to them, and they did not want to abandon their village.

After they adopted farming, the settlement grew to 2,500 people by 9000 BP. Within a few more centuries, people began to live in densely packed mud-brick houses. When the wild gazelle herds declined, they began keeping sheep and goats and quickly domesticated them. By 8000 BP the population had doubled, peaking at an amazing 5,000 people. Remarkably, Abu Hureyra crossed the social scale threshold usually associated with tribal equality yet remained integrated for another 2,000 years without leaving any trace of invidious social ranking. People cooperated in economic activities, made ceramics, used cattle as draft animals, and probably had formal leaders, but they built no temples and apparently refused to construct a centralized chiefdom. A combination of resource depletion and increasing aridity probably forced people to finally abandon the settlement. The Neolithic village of Çatal Hüyük in Turkey also grew large and avoided social stratification.[29]

BOX 7.2. THE MESOPOTAMIAN ELITE AND THE REWARDS OF LEADERSHIP

Because they boasted of their achievements, we have the names of specific rulers and a written record of the cultural changes that they imposed in order to continually increase the scale of Mesopotamian society. Sargon the Great founded the first Mesopotamian empire (2334–2279 BC), and shortly thereafter King Ur-Nammu founded the Ur III dynasty (2112–2004 BC), creating a regional empire of some 5 million people centered on the capital city of Ur.[30] The Ur III rulers started out in command of the small city-state of Ur. King Ur-Nammu and his son Shulgi turned it into a multinational empire and a family dynasty that dominated the entire Mesopotamian plain and neighboring areas for four generations (2112–2004 BC).

Shulgi consolidated his father's territorial conquests by instituting a series of administrative "reforms" according to a "master plan" that he carried out over a ten-year period. Shulgi's reforms involved making himself a god; establishing a standing army and scribal schools; and improving the temple household system, the bureaucracy, the legal code, and the taxation, writing, weights and measures, accounting, and calendar systems. He brought all the temples under government control and created a system of "crown land" as part of his personal royal household and the industrial enterprises operated by the central government.[31] All of the social transformations implemented by this family defined the major institutions of Mesopotamian civilizations for the next twenty-five centuries.

The Ur III kings divided their empire into some 25 provinces, each centered on a formerly independent city-state. They may have incorporated some 25 cities of 10,000 people or more, 48 towns of 2,000, and more than 1,000 villages into their system of tribute and taxation. The largest city probably approached 100,000 people. In an empire of this scale there were positions for more elites, and the emperor could live much more extravagantly than ever before. At 3,000 square meters Shulgi's personal temple palace was 10 times larger than a 300-square-meter Ubaid chief's house. The four main temples in the city of Ur were more than 100 times larger than an Ubaid temple. The elites who directed the temples and the top political leadership were no doubt a few closely interconnected families. The gap between rich and poor in Ur's residential district is shown by the contrast between the "meanest and shoddiest" one-room, nine-square-meter house and a nearby three-story, sixty-room mansion of 1,500 square meters, which was no doubt occupied by a very high-ranking elite person's household.[32] The houses of the poorest in Ur were smaller than standard housing in the tribal world and are an objective indicator of poverty.

The personal payoff for lower-level elites in Mesopotamian empires is demonstrated by the extraordinary success of the Ninlil-zimu family in Nippur (1970–1720 BC). Clay tablets show that this family dominated both the city of Nippur and the family's neighborhood for nearly 200 years.[33] Their carefully constructed family house was more than twice the size of ordinary houses and was occupied by six generations of the Ninlil-zimu family. The family was probably the largest property owner in the city and held several important official titles, including some of the most prestigious temple offices. The family owned at least three houses, as well as fields and orchards on the edge of the city. A single block of undeveloped urban property, twice the size of their residential neighborhood, remained in the family for at least 150 years. The family also received substantial gifts of property from the king, owned slaves, and employed laborers.

MAKING A LIVING IN THE MESOPOTAMIAN CITY-STATE AND EMPIRE

Daily life in Mesopotamian civilization can be reconstructed from the floor plans of excavated houses, inscriptions describing ancient property transfers, and clay tablets containing household inventories.[34] Mesopotamian society was designed to serve elite patrilineal households whose large private landholdings were cultivated by their retinues of dependent laborers. The residential core of the urban centers contained large household compounds, each controlled by a senior household residing in a large central hall. Junior extended-family households and dependent non-kin lived in small, individual household apartments arranged along the side of the main hall and in detached outbuildings. Dependents held reduced titles to land or were totally landless. Household archives show that these compounds were large economic enterprises managing people, land, grain, food, livestock, and craft products. The heads of these private "greathouse" economic units formed the citizens of the Mesopotamian city-state. They also ran the temples and the city government.

Barley Rations, Cylinder Seals, and Social Power in Ur III

The Ur III empire (2112–2004 BC), constructed by the kings of the Ur-Nammu dynasty, consisted of a core area centered on the principal city-states in the Tigris-Euphrates irrigated zone and a peripheral area of tributary provinces. Core and periphery were combined into a single state finance system in which rulers extracted taxes to support the royal family and their corporate establishments.[35] The core economic sectors were the royal domain, the temple domain, and the private sector. The royal domain included vast tracts of farm land, irrigation systems, pastures, and workshops under the emperor's direct control that supported households of his extended family, the military, and the central administrative bureaucracy. The temples were corporate institutions run as great households by governors (ensi) who were connected to the royal family by ties of kinship, marriage, or patronage. The heads of temple establishments also managed workshops and controlled large tracts of land and herds. The poorly documented private sector consisted of private households headed by private individuals operating as independent landholders, farmers, herders, craftsmen, and merchants.

Individuals and households situated in all of these sectors were connected by a flow of materials and services mobilized by the taxation system known as bala, in which individuals of all ranks were required to deliver specific quantities of livestock, grain, craft products, or other materials, and various kinds of

labor service to higher authorities. Various bala taxes were levied according to the products available in particular areas, and in the case of personal income or property taxes, according to an individual's rank and landholdings. Bala goods were transported to distribution centers and passed through the bureaucracy to final consumers.

Initially, there were three broad social ranks in the early Mesopotamian city-states with the city governor, or king (lugal), at the top; administrative officials in the middle; and ordinary people at the bottom. The rank of officials was reflected directly in their salaries, land allotments, and the cylinder seals issued by authorities.[36] Specialists carved designated inscriptions and images into short stone, bone, or metal rods that were then pressed and rolled across wet clay to make impressions. After the clay dried any alterations in the inscriptions could be readily detected. Seals functioned much like identity cards or badges. They attested to one's official authority and responsibility and were used by civil, military, and temple officials and by wealthy private individuals to certify personal business transactions. Each seal carried the personal name of the holder, his family name, and title. For the highest officials, especially ensi (civil governor or temple head), sagina (military general, controlled crown lands), and sukkal-mah (chancellor, the highest civil official under the king), the seal bore standardized images of a presentation scene showing the bearer standing in the presence of a seated king to receive the seal, or being led to the king by a deity (see figure 7.6). Additional inscriptions glorified the king and connected the official with him. The wives of high officials also had personal seals depicting presentations from goddesses, not the king, that were probably used to manage domestic business. The seals of merchants show by the absence of royal presentation images that they were ranked below top administrators.

The Ur III proliferation of seals used by high-ranking bureaucrats corresponds with Ur-Nammu's transformation of city-states into empire, the deification of the king, and the increasing need to use written documents to manage information in a larger-scale society. It is significant that at this time the king appears on seals in a position formerly occupied by a god, reflecting the divine king as emperor ranking over the governors of other formerly independent city-states. The divine king emperor headed a society now expanded into four ranks with parallel political, military, and ideological (temple) power structures (see figure 7.7). Third-level officials such as overseers,

Figure 7.6.   Seal issued by Ur III Emperor Ur-Nammu, seated, to a governor lead by a deity (Mackenzie, Donald A. 1915. *Myths of Babylonia and Assyria*. London: Gresham, figure facing p. 50).

managers, and scribes carried seals presented to them by second-level officials. Merchants were generally third rank because there were apparently no organized markets in Mesopotamian society, although the most important merchants worked directly for the royal household. Long-distance trade was directed by the elite, who also controlled the extraction and distribution of all social surplus production.

Analysis of seal inscriptions and tablets shows that high offices often remained within the same family and were bequeathed from father to son, attesting to the existence of private dynasties that paralleled the royal dynasties. For example, the highest office of the

Temple of Inanna in Nippur remained in the same family for at least five generations.[37] It is likely that the same individuals and families held multiple titles that connected them to different sources of power in palace, temple, the military, and private business. The power elite were a tiny hereditary aristocracy, and there may have been little upward social mobility.

There may have been as many as 500,000 urban nonfood-producing people in the Ur III empire, including elite households and specialists.[38] Given the agricultural production system, it can be estimated that 90 percent of the population lived at the subsistence level and engaged directly in agricultural labor.[39]

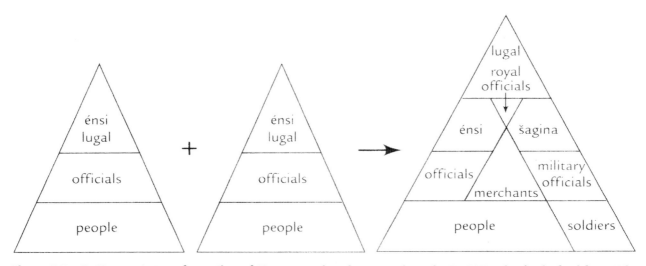

Figure 7.7.   Ur-Nammu's transformation of Mesopotamian city-states into the Ur III Empire (redrafted from Winter 1991:76, Figure 1).

Most other people were nonfood producers working as low-level managers, craft workers, and domestic servants. Ordinary people in the lowest rank faced an insecure existence because they controlled little productive property, and unless they were full-time temple or palace employees or were attached to a large private household, their subsistence was always uncertain. Many employees, especially women, received less than the official annual ration of 720 liters (*sila*) of barley per year for one adult man (see box 7.3).

The Ur III emperors managed a nonmonetary, nonmarket economy. There were no coins, but exchange values were fixed by the ruler. Barley was a universal medium of exchange, and even land was valued according to the amount of barley it could produce. Three hundred liters of barley (one *gur*) was exchanged for eight grams of silver (one *shekel*). One ox was worth ten *shekels*, and a sheep one *shekel*. Low-level managers and administrators received only a few thousand liters of barley a year, which was barely enough to meet the official minimum subsistence level of 1,680 liters of barley per year for a six-person family.[40] This meant that most people survived by putting all family members into wage labor, but at any time misfortune could force householders into indentured servitude, or they might even have to sell themselves or a family member into slavery.

Inequality was pervasive throughout Mesopotamian society. The system was skewed toward the top even for professionals living above the subsistence level. For example, in the largest temples the wage structure shows that 120 managers received an average annual income of 4,775 liters of barley, whereas four upper administrators averaged 30,000. The top official received a regular salary of 60,000, and he was allocated enough land to produce an additional net gain of nearly 18,000 liters of barley, which would have raised his income to the level of 100 minimum wage workers at 720 liters for an adult man.[41]

The Mesopotamian elite constructed a society in which they oppressed and exploited the commoners to enhance their own lifestyles. This was *oppression* because the elite overpowered the majority with cultural institutions, beliefs, and practices that maintained unequal access to productive land and labor. It was exploitation because the labor of those with reduced access to resources sustained the well-being of the elite few who owned or controlled their land and labor.[42] Most people did not own land and were forced to either rent or work as dependents of the landowners.

The four social ranks of imperial Mesopotamia were broadly related to differences in property ownership and employment, which determined an individual's ability to successfully maintain a family. Some people owned property but did not engage in production. Others owned property and worked their land alongside nonowning workers, whereas the majority worked for others and did not own productive property. The latter category included people who were variously called captives, slaves, serfs, or "helots."[43] Slaves were themselves property but were not always readily distinguished from indentured laborers.

Members of the royal household were the largest landowners. The king, his spouse, and their children individually owned crown estates and allocated use rights to others. Members of the royal family hired workers as household domestic labor and as general laborers. Second-rank officials owned property in their own names, held large allotments of crown land in exchange for service, and received large salaries as state officials. This made it possible for them to rent additional property and hire labor. Third-ranked people held smaller allotments and received smaller salaries.

The **social product**, or aggregate income of the empire, was sufficient to securely support the entire Mesopotamian population at a culturally defined decent standard of living, but in reality only the top 1 percent of society was actually prosperous and secure. Measured as grain production, the annual social product must have approached the equivalent of some 1.8 billion liters of barley, assuming 1 million farmer households producing an annual average of 1,882 liters (1,246 kilos). This was net production after deductions for loss in storage, transport, and seed and yielded a 10 percent margin above the official subsistence minimum of 1,680 liters. This margin was not really a "surplus," because in autonomous Neolithic tribal villages where production was approximately at the same level, people themselves would have invested any social product above minimum consumption needs in feasting and alliances, or they stored it as security against misfortune. Under the empire, rulers extracted this "surplus" as a tax; as a sacrifice to the gods, their temples, and the divine king; or as tribute from conquered people. However legitimized, this extraction left producers with virtually no security margin.

A 10 percent tax may seem insignificant. It was less than the 15 percent inevitably lost in production and distribution in ancient agricultural systems. However, this estimate is an average that assumes every household was taxed equally. In reality, the most productive land was taxed most heavily, and in some provinces rulers extracted up to 50 percent of the barley crop for the *bala*.[44] Given the scale of the empire, the tax in the Ur III empire allowed the royal family of perhaps only 500 people to control the social distribution of 188 million liters of grain produced by a million worker households. The cost of extracting, moving, and storing this much grain was a further burden that the tax itself subsidized. This subsidy covered both direct administrative and managerial costs and the costs of the temple and legitimizing temple ritual. There were probably more than 11,000 nonfood-producing administrators and managers, in addition to troops, and other full-time specialists. In addition to the grain, which was produced in irrigated fields near urban centers and transported by boat, more than 30,000 head of livestock were annually driven to a distribution center near the city of Nippur to be allocated to temples, the military, and elite individuals.[45] Many of these activities were unproductive costs, because they were needed to maintain and reproduce the social system itself and did not directly provide consumption goods for most households. The tax system was a **scale subsidy** that supported a social system at a scale that would not otherwise have been sustainable. The rulers also forced nature to subsidize their empire, because intensive floodplain irrigation in the Mesopotamian environment caused an accumulation of salts that steadily degraded the soil.

Table 7.2 offers a provisional sketch of the distribution of social power in the Ur III empire, making reasonable assumptions about agricultural production; numbers of people in different ranks; their income and wealth, based on tax records, land allotments, salaries, and wage or ration rates; the structure of the bureaucracy; and the size of temple establishments.[46] The ranking of personal imperia as super-elite, elite, maintenance, and poor corresponds to the four ranks of Ur III society and represents the relative well-being of households according to their social power. Higher-ranked imperia command more wealth and income, as well as other people. Maintenance-level imperia command enough resources to meet basic needs, whereas poor often must borrow to survive.

Table 7.2. Ur III Imperia by Wealth, Income, and Social Rank, 2000 BC

Rank	Households Population	Wealth	Average Household Income	Imperia
Emperor, Divine King	1 50	Royal Domain 13,000 hectares, Royal Temple-Palace, workshops	9,000,000 (barley liters)	**Super-Elite** 0.01% of population receive 3% of social surplus
Extended Royal Family	100 500	Land, temples, mansions, slaves, livestock, grain, silver	250,000	
Royal Officials, Chancellors, Governors, Generals, Top Administrators	1,000 5,000	Land, mansions, slaves, livestock, grain, silver	60,000	**Elite** 0.1% of population receive 12% of social surplus
Managers, Mayors, Top Specialists, Large Landowners, Merchants	10,000 50,000	Land, mansions, slaves, livestock, grain, silver	5,000	**Maintenance** 0.99% of population receive 14% of social surplus
Independent Farmers, Herders, Low Wage Urban Workers, Low Wage Rural Workers, Indentured Workers, Slaves	1,000,000 5,000,000	Use Rights	1,680	**Poor** 98.9% of population receive 71% of social surplus
Totals	1,011,110 households 5,055,550 persons	2.5 million hectares of irrigated cropland	1.8 billion barley liters social product	188 million barley liters social surplus

Note: The emperor's income represents his command over an estimated 10,000 civil and religious officials and troops, and 5,000 women in royal temples and workshops.

Elites have more than enough to comfortably maintain themselves and can promote growth in their social power. Table 7.2 dramatically demonstrates how growth in scale can disempower and impoverish most of society, even as a tiny elite are disproportionately benefited. Super-elite royal households could have supported an average of nearly 350 extra-household adult laborers at the annual wage ration of 720 barley liters. A thousand top administrator households could have supported eighty laborers and seven extra-household adults. Their larger, more secure household establishments gave the elites and their children improved life chances. At the broad base of the social pyramid, in good times 99 percent of the population would have had a bare minimum to support two adult household members and three children.

BOX 7.3. THE MESOPOTAMIAN RATION SYSTEM

The early Mesopotamian city-state was populated by a large number of full-time urban specialists, who included priests, scribes, overseers, and artisans. All these people were supported by monthly allotments of rations, which in Sumerian were called *Se-ba* (*Se* means "barley"; *ba* means "distribution"). Standard rations included *Se-ba*, *I-ba* (oil), and *Sig-ba* (wool) in standardized units according to a set formula specifying the amounts that people would receive by age and sex.[47] For example, barley was distributed by the *sila*, a volume measurement equivalent to 0.85 liter. Men normally received 60 *sila*; women, 30; boys, 25; girls, 20; and infants, 10. The rations were probably generous, and people no doubt bartered the surplus to fill other basic needs. One liter of barley contained 829 grams, and 100 grams of barley produced 350 calories.[48] The average adult ration of 45 sila would have provided 3,698 calories per day. Barley was the most important subsistence staple, but it probably accounted for only 66 percent of people's average caloric consumption, the balance being supplied by animal products, fruits, and vegetables. Thus, people probably consumed directly only about half of their barley allotments. The oil ration was generally animal fat, although sometimes it might have been sesame oil, and it was used for consumption and in ritual anointings. Besides barley, oil, and wool distributions, there were also irregular distributions of wheat, bread, flour, and cloth. Standard rations were sometimes replaced with equivalent substitutes, such that one *sila* of oil could replace two *sila* of barley. On ritual occasions or to specific categories of people, there were also supplemental distributions of meat, dairy products, beer, wine, fish, dates, fruits, and vegetables.

Cuneiform Writing, Law, and Justice

As the administrative bureaucracy in the Mesopotamian city-states grew, the requirements for information storage increased dramatically. The earliest written inscriptions appeared about 3100 BC in a pictographic script found in the city of Uruk and involved economic control functions such as bookkeeping of receipts, expenses, and goods. By 2400 BC Mesopotamian writing had become a well-developed cuneiform system.[49] The word *cuneiform* (*cunei* means "nails") refers to the distinctive nail shape produced when a stylus with a triangular cross section is pressed into a soft clay tablet at an angle. The early pictographs represented the names of naturalistically portrayed objects, but this limited and cumbersome system was readily improved by simplifying the pictographs into abstract forms and giving some of them phonetic meanings). The basic cuneiform system was used throughout the Near East by the Sumerians, Babylonians, Assyrians, and Persians over a 2,000-year period (see figure 7.8).

A scribal school, the *edubba*, became institutionalized as a formal means to standardize the writing system and to produce the professional body of scribes needed to write and archive the great masses of clay tablets required for routine administration. Students memorized some 2,000 different cuneiform signs by copying standard texts that often consisted of word lists. These academic exercises provide useful insights into the degree of specialization and scale of wage differences at the beginning of civilization. For example, one word list contained a ranking of one hundred professions and titles and is a power-of-ten increase over the level of specialization in Hawaii. The writing system developed rapidly over a period of about 150 years and then became very stable.[50] It was a medium for sacred temple literature, epic poetry, and royal decrees, but the bulk of the material concerned mundane administrative matters and domestic accounts. Numeration was based on a sexagesimal (sixties) system with place values, but it also used a numeral for 10. There was no concept of zero, but complex mathematical calculations—such as multiplication, square roots, and area problems—were still accomplished.

Rulers used writing to publicly endorse the formal structures of society and their concept of official justice. For example, King Hammurabi's (1792–1750 BC) famous "law code," engraved on a stone monument, was a collection of legal cases, or conflict situations, along with his own corresponding "just" decisions.[51] These cases took into account the social positions of

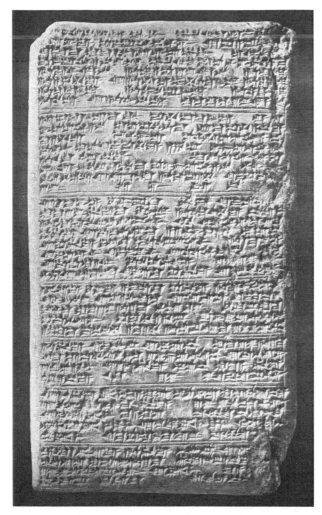

Figure 7.8. Mesopotamian writing. Cuneiform letter from Tushratta, King of Mitanni, to Amenhotep III, King of Egypt. One of the Tell-el-Amarna tables, in the British Museum (Mackenzie, Donald A. 1915. *Myths of Babylonia and Assyria.* **Figure 22.1, p. 308).**

men and women, young and old, aristocrat and commoner, free and slave, and demonstrated the king's awesome life-or-death powers over his subjects. Punishments varied from monetary fines to mutilation and death, but the king's justice always took into account the relative social status of those involved. Personal injuries to servants or the poor were compensated with silver, but if an aristocrat was injured, it was an eye for an eye. If the poor were unable to pay a fine, they could be killed. Punishments could be severe and seemingly arbitrary. Theft might bring death, and a man who struck his father might have his hand chopped off. However, many of the judgments on business disputes would seem reasonable by modern business law, and decisions on divorce and inheritance often protected the rights of women and children.

Mesopotamian Religion in the Service of the Ruler

Like the Hawaiian king, the Mesopotamian king headed a divine cult, built and maintained the temples, appointed officials, and coordinated the ritual calendar. He assumed the role of a fertility god, Dumuzi or Tammuz, in an annual temple ritual in which he ritually married a woman representing the fertility goddess Ishtar, reenacting a divine wedding. This ritual symbolically gave the king power over natural fertility throughout the land, just as it did with the Hawaiian king in the Makahiki ceremony. Rulers were probably exceptionally fertile, producing many children. Although Mesopotamian marriage was typically monogamous for succession to royal titles, matings were polygynous. Rulers had children by their concubines and nourished them with wet nurses in their extended domestic establishments.[52]

Each city belonged to a founding god drawn from the rich Sumerian pantheon and contained temples dedicated to it. The Sumerian word for temple, *ebitum*, meant "house," so the temple was the god's house, and the temple personnel existed as the god's caretakers. The visible focal point of major Sumerian cities was the *ziggurat* (an Akkadian word for "temple tower"), a stepped pyramid of clay bricks built as a shrine to the city's deity.

The Ziggurat of Ur, the best-surviving example, was completed during the third Sumerian dynasty, around 2000 BC. It is one of the best-preserved early ziggurats. The base platform was 200 feet by 150 feet (61 m by 46 m) and 50 feet (15 m) high. Two other levels were built on top of this, and they were topped by a small shrine to the moon god Nanna, so that the total height was at least 70 feet (21 m) (see figure 7.9). Because the ziggurat was built on an elevated terrace, the whole structure must have been an imposing sight rising above the surrounding plain. The ziggurat was part of the *Temenos* (Greek for "sacred ground"), a sacred enclosure containing a major temple to Nanna, other shrines, storehouses, courtyards, and quarters for temple personnel.[53] At this time, Ur was a walled city of some 321 acres (130 hectares) that might have contained 25,000 people.

The spiritual head of the Sumerian temple bore the title *En*, and he or she resided in an elaborate complex within the *Temenos*, called the *Giparu*. The temple administrator was titled *Sanga*, and there were many other named temple or priestly offices. The temple claimed ownership of at least three named categories of land:

1. *Nigenna*, whose produce directly supported the temple

Figure 7.9.   The central ziggurat (temple pyramid) of Ur, built about 2000 BC. U.S. troops are visiting the site near Nasiriya, Iraq in 2003 during the Iraq War (Roseanna Blum).

2. *Kurra*, used to support those who worked *nigenna* land
3. *Urulal*, lands that could be farmed by temple personnel for their own use, in exchange for a share of the produce

Thus, the temple administration, besides conducting major religious activities, managed the farmland, collected and stored grain, and paid out rations to laborers. This arrangement must have reflected the structure of elite private households. The temples also took in dependents, but they were public institutions, and their grain surpluses were probably available in times of shortage.

Secular rulers apparently rose to prominence as military leaders in conflicts with neighboring city-states. As kings (*lugal*, literally "bigman"), they founded dynasties, built palaces and temples, raised armies, maintained the city walls, and were buried in royal tombs. In 1927–1928, Sir Leonard Woolley discovered some of the most spectacular art treasures of the ancient Middle East in the royal tombs of Ur. A series of royal burials dating to the Early Dynastic period were unearthed in a cemetery just beyond the *Tenemos* wall.[54] The burials contained a treasure trove of grave goods, including lyres decorated with golden bull heads, gold and silver weapons, jewelry, and headdresses.

Most remarkable was the discovery that the royal personages were accompanied in death by an entourage of soldiers and retainers, in full regalia, along with wagons and oxen. One tomb contained seventy-four additional people, including four male guards, four female musicians, and sixty-four women of the royal court in ceremonial dress. Many of the sacrificed attendants may have taken poison in a mass suicide ceremony as part of the royal funeral.[55] Human sacrifice on this scale certainly attests to the strength of the religious system, as well as to the despotic power of the rulers of the temple-palace complex. It makes the occasional human sacrifice associated with the Hawaiian temple cults seem almost trivial by comparison.

In Mesopotamian religion, the god Utu was the sun and the sun's numinous power, all at the same time. *Numinous* refers to divine transcendent power that induces emotions of fear and awe. This concept of the supernatural seems qualitatively different from the animism experienced in the tribal world and legitimizes the elite appropriation of the power of nature. The gods represented the indwelling numinous power of specific natural phenomena. Mesopotamian religion was highly polytheistic (**polytheism**) because there were a multitude of situations in which the numinous could be experienced. Rulers could invoke numinous power by building temples and shrines as sacred dwellings for deities, by performing rituals, or by making images.[56]

During the 4,000-year span of Mesopotamian culture, three different metaphors of supernatural power existed. The earliest and most persistent metaphor was of the immanent power of specific nature deities. By the Early Dynastic, gods began to be called "rulers," just as human rulers began to take power in the emerging city-states. By the second millennium BC, during the Old Babylonian period, personal gods began to appear who were concerned with the security of individuals.

The earliest Mesopotamian deities, as revealed in a series of engravings and lyric poems preserved in clay tablets, were nature gods concerned with fertility. Initially, these deities were depicted in the form of the natural objects they represented, but over time they were gradually given more human form. Prominent among them were the gods associated with specific cities and expressing the power of economically important natural resources, such as *Enki* the water god, *Nanshe* the fish goddess, and *Dumuzi*, who was concerned with livestock and the date palm. The most important annual rituals, no doubt performed at the temple, involved a sacred wedding, in which nature deities as bride and groom perpetuated the return of fertility in the spring and mourned the decline and death of fertility in the fall. The temple deity and associated storehouse were direct embodiments of nature's fertility.

By the third millennium BC, deities were referred to as "Lords" or "Masters" and mirrored the actions of human rulers. People were now impressed by the awe-inspiring energy and majesty of the noumenal beings, not simply their life-sustaining powers of fertility. The major city gods assumed new roles as spiritual estate managers, judges, and warriors. This sequence of development shows that religion, as part of a culture's **superstructure**, changes in response to changes in the structure, the social organization and political economy. This functional interconnection is further verified by the statistical association between the presence of high gods and hierarchical political structures found in an extensive sample of world cultures.[57]

The new Mesopotamian deities obviously reflected the rising importance of political rulers in the emerging city-states of the Early Dynastic. For example, *Nin-girsu*, god of life-giving spring thunderstorms and floods and titular deity of the city of Girsu, was head of a twenty-one-deity pantheon of gods who staffed his temple and supervised his estate.[58] Counted as deities were a high constable; a steward; a chamberlain; two musicians; seven handmaidens; a councilor; a secretary; two generals; two herdsmen; a plowman; a fisherman; and a general manager of natural resources. These deities had their human counterparts who directed human laborers in service to *Nin-girsu*. Whereas the original nature deities had no functions beyond their immanent qualities, the new ruler-gods could make demands on people, and their wills were transmitted through dreams and signs that had to be interpreted by diviners.

The entire Mesopotamian cosmos was hierarchically arranged, with deities holding titles and offices. There were seven primary gods, who determined the fate of other gods and humans, and some fifty "great gods," along with a vast multitude of lesser deities, who collectively met as a formal assembly of gods. City deities such as *Nin-girsu* served the higher-ranking deity *Enlil*, Lord of the Wind and primary executive god. The water god *Enki*, Lord of the Soil and Owner of the River, was credited not only with establishing the seasonal regime of the Tigris-Euphrates system but also with placing various deities in charge of a number of recognized occupational specialties such as farming, brickmaking, architecture, and weaving. *Enki* made *Utu*, the sun god and god of justice, responsible for boundary maintenance. Even the creation myths were brought in line with the realities of the political system. By the second millennium BC, the primary Mesopotamian creation epic, known as *Enuma Elish*, was a lengthy account of how the god *Marduk* became the permanent king of the universe, and all the basic elements of the Mesopotamian cosmic politics were in place.

Mesopotamia: The End of a Great Tradition

If state organization began in Mesopotamia with the Uruk Period in 4000 BC and if the Persian conquest of Babylonia in 539 BC marked the end of the distinctively Mesopotamian political system, then the Mesopotamian political system based on the state lasted for approximately 3,500 years, and the Mesopotamian civilization ended some 500 years later in AD 75, when the last cuneiform document is known to have been written.[59] After that time, no recognizable Mesopotamian language, economy, or belief system persisted, although certain specific cultural connections can still be traced in succeeding civilizations.

Mesopotamian civilization was a complex, multiethnic system, incorporating peoples speaking different languages, practicing different subsistence activities, and worshiping different gods. The written tradition and related religious beliefs gave the civilization great continuity. The Mesopotamian political system was based on a network of city-states, which at various times were combined into regional states or empires. There were constant power struggles between the rulers of different cities, and cities were abandoned or relocated after military defeats or changes in the course of major rivers. Dynasties were replaced following foreign invasions or internal conflicts.

The Sumerian King List shows how unstable the political situation was in Mesopotamia. The list names 146 rulers in twenty-six dynasties over the 900-year period between approximately 2900 BC in the Early Dynastic up to 2000 BC. This suggests an average of just 6 years per king and 35 years per dynasty. The dynastic turnover is frequently attributed to military defeat.

Some authors[60] have pointed out that overirrigation under state management may have played a role in the abandonment of southern Mesopotamian cities and the collapse of the third Ur dynasty, which effectively marked the end of the Sumerian period. In this scenario, overuse of irrigation water inadvertently elevated the water table, causing subsurface saltwater to contaminate the soil and damage crops. Identifying such an ecological factor as a sole cause of collapse would be misleading, however, because underlying political factors caused the mismanagement of the irrigation system and created the demand for increased production.

Mesopotamian civilization incorporated different ethnic groups that actually contributed to its persistence. It was only when the Persian invaders from a still-larger empire conquered Mesopotamia that the established political system, and later the entire civilization, was brought down. Previous breakdowns did not prevent the city-states from being regrouped into regional states.

Thus, in the Mesopotamian case, we see a cultural tradition that maintained itself for a very long time despite chronic political instability. In the end, Mesopotamian civilization was superseded by a more powerful regional civilization within what had become a western Asian world system based on extensive tributary empires. Mesopotamian civilization apparently was so weakened when it lost its central position within the local world system that it was unable to recover from a routine dynastic collapse.

THE INCA EMPIRE IN THE LAND OF FOUR QUARTERS

The Inca were situated 3,500 years later in time than the Ur III empire and 8,500 miles away in a different hemisphere, but the two empires were remarkably similar in design and purpose. The Inca rulers commanded an empire of twice as many people as in Ur III, but most importantly, both empires were directed by royal dynastic families and noble aristocracies. Both empires were based on the concept of divine kingship, and both were four-ranked societies where 97 to 99 percent of the population labored at a bare subsistence level to provide luxury and security for a few special people at the top. Temples and rituals in both empires celebrated the cult of the divine king and legitimized totalitarian rule as part of nature.

Andean and Mesopotamian empires were both nonmarket, command political economies designed to extract resources from a subsistence-level commoner majority. Elite rulers directed development projects that intensified agricultural production, which was the basis of their wealth and power. State bureaucrats managed massive food surpluses and directed specialists in the production of wealth objects that were exclusively disposed of by the aristocracy. Royals lived in palaces, surrounded themselves with hundreds and even thousands of military retainers, servants, wives, and concubines, and maintained vast private estates that they transmitted to their children. Like the Ur III emperors, the Inca lords lived luxuriously in a royal capital, but the Inca lived off tribute labor extracted from village commoners scattered over a vast territory, unlike the Mesopotamian nobility who extracted taxes primarily in grain and livestock or other goods. The Inca moved labor about to produce the food staples and wealth objects that they needed to support imperial religious institutions and their administrative bureaucracy. In apparent contrast to the Mesopotamian empire, most Andean villagers held land communally and were highly self-sufficient in basic subsistence. This was a significant difference.

The Inca organized some 9 million people[61] into the following four social ranks according to their differential access to religious power, natural resources, food, wealth objects, status, and control over other people: (1) a tiny super-elite of a few hundred royal households closely related to the emperor; (2) a noble elite of some 6,000 distantly related Inca upper-level administrators and non-Inca local rulers; (3) 60,000 lower-level managers and skilled specialists; and (4) 2 million commoner households from diverse ethnic groups, most working part-time for the state to pay their labor service tax. A few commoners were full-time, low-level state workers supported by surpluses drawn from the Inca warehouses.

The Inca rulers integrated their vast imperial territory and population by appealing to a powerful ideology of common kinship and a shared participation in cults dedicated to the sun and moon, the divine king and queen, and diverse local shrines. Rulers portrayed their empire as a greatly extended, divinely ordained chiefdom where everyone was properly situated in ranked descent groups within a single giant genealogy with the divine monarch at the top. Commoners were offered supernatural rewards and token material gifts in exchange for their labor tribute. This created the illusion of a fair reciprocal exchange, as if the empire was simply a very large egalitarian tribal society. However, the social reality was profoundly unequal.

Andean Environment and Prehistory

The Inca empire, which reached its peak between AD 1476 and 1532, was the last in a series of imperial cultures that developed independently in the Andean region of South America beginning approximately 4,000 years ago (see table 7.3 and box 7.4). This last pre-Columbian empire extended over an area of some 380,000 square miles (984,000 km²), covering the Andean regions of modern Ecuador, Peru, Bolivia, and the northern Andes of Chile and Argentina (see figure 7.10). Estimates of its population range from 6 million to 32 million people. The Inca empire rivaled the Roman empire in scale, yet it was maintained without wheeled vehicles, writing, or draft animals by the effective mobilization of a vast labor force within the framework of an elaborate bureaucracy that was ordered and sustained by a compelling religious system.

The dominant geographic feature of the Andean region is the Andean mountain chain. Because the Andes run north and south, they form a barrier to global weather patterns, blocking westward-flowing moisture from the Atlantic and creating one of the world's driest deserts in the rain shadow along the coast of Peru and Chile. A series of narrow, short valleys descend from the Andes to the Pacific and offer significant irrigation potential not unlike that offered by the Mesopotamian floodplain. An additional advantage of the Andean region is that off the Pacific Coast the cold, upwelling Peru Current lifts rich nutrients toward the ocean surface from the deep offshore trench and thereby supports one of the world's richest marine fisheries. Unfortunately, during an unpredictable phenomenon called El Niño (ENSO, the El Niño Southern Oscillation) the Peru Current is replaced by warmer water that disrupts the ecosystem, destroying marine life and causing rains and flooding.

The bulk of the Andean population occupied the *altiplano*, the high plateau, at elevations from 12,000 feet (3,658 m) to over 16,000 feet (4,877 m). The mountains are an inhospitable place for farmers

Table 7.3. Andean Prehistory, 14,000 BP–AD 1532

AD 1476–1532	Inca empire
AD 1000–1476	Chimu state on north coast
AD 600–1000	Middle Horizon, Moche kingdom, Tiahuanaco, and Huari empires
1400–2200 BP	Mochica and Nazca regional coastal states
2200–2800 BP	Early Horizon; Chavin; metallurgy
2900–3500 BP	Initial Ceramic period, city-states or advanced chiefdoms; ceramics, irrigation, population growth
3500–4000 BP	Late (Cotton) Pre-Ceramic chiefdoms; maize, manioc
5000 BP	Sedentary coastal fishing villages; domestic-scale farming of cotton, gourds, beans, squash
5800 BP	Domesticated potatoes in highlands
6000 BP	Domestic llamas and alpacas
6000–14,000 BP	Mobile foragers and hunters

Sources: Burger and van der Merwe (1990), Lanning (1967), and Wheeler (1984).

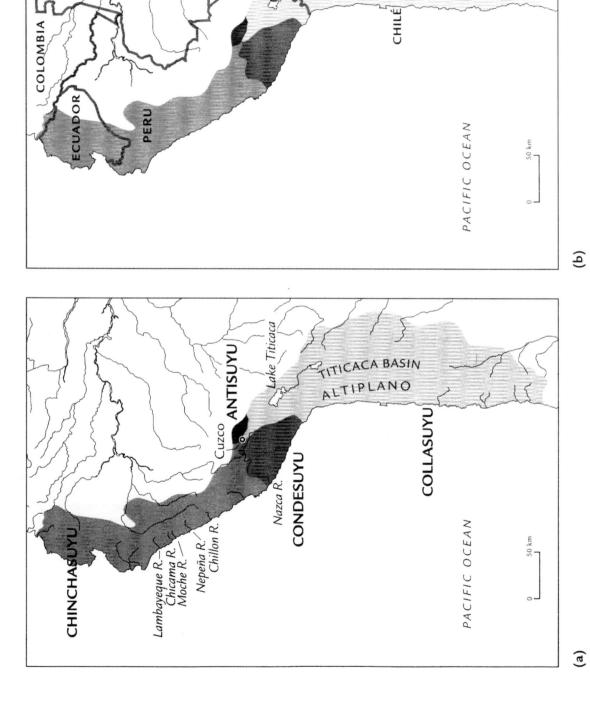

Figure 7.10. (a) Map of the Andean region and the Inca Empire with its division into four quarters: Chinchasuyu, Antisuyu, Condesuyu, and Collasuyu (redrafted from Conrad and Demarest 1984); (b) map of the same region with today's nation's territories.

because soils are thin, freezes can occur at any time, and droughts are frequent. The treeless vegetation, called *puna*, supports only the hardiest grazers such as the native camelids, the guanaco and vicuña. Llamas and alpacas, domesticated members of the camel family, were valued for their meat and wool, and as pack animals they were capable of carrying loads of up to 100 pounds (45 kg). Dried llama dung was an important fuel on the treeless *altiplano*, and as fertilizer, it helped keep thin mountain soils productive. Another important domesticate, the guinea pig, lived on kitchen scraps and was eaten. The potato was the primary highland subsistence crop because it was highly nutritious, tolerated frost, was readily stored, and could be grown at elevations of up to 14,000 feet (4,267 m). Andean farmers developed some 3,000 varieties of potatoes, selecting for differing tuber qualities and environmental tolerances.[62] Another important early highland domesticate was quinoa, *Chenopodium quinoa*, which also grows well under the harsh conditions of the *altiplano* and produces a protein-rich, grainlike seed. Some 200 varieties of quinoa were developed.

Inca cities were administrative centers, populated by bureaucrats and their servants, whose existence depended on sustaining a power network that extended throughout the Andean region. Why independent villagers would support the empire is difficult to explain, because the empire apparently gave them few material benefits. As in Mesopotamia, Andean civilization was an improbable development that depended on certain environmental and cultural circumstances. The Andean cultural tradition was in place 3,000 years ago. The cyclical record of state growth and collapse suggests that tribal agricultural village life, not the state, was the optimal human adaptation for the Andean world. Like their predecessors, the Inca were able briefly to exploit a particular combination of distinctive Andean cultural principles and an agricultural system based on a unique mix of domesticated crops and animals that could thrive in the harsh conditions of the high Andes.

Like the Hawaiian and Mesopotamian kings, Andean rulers expanded their social power by asserting a symbolic connection between themselves, the calendar, the fertility of nature, and the general well-being of society. The crucial symbolic underpinnings combined elements of Amazonian cosmology involving nature and supernatural power, especially the jaguar, caiman, and harpy eagle, together with shamanic practice and hallucinogenic drugs.[63] These features were all in place at the ritual site of Chavín in the northern Peruvian highlands by 900 BC and were appropriated by aspiring aggrandizers to expand their personal imperia, but in the Andean case ordinary people retained significant control over the conditions within their local communities.

Andean rulers claimed to be divine kings with ownership of all the land, resources, and labor within their reach. This was reflected in their control over monumental constructions, irrigation systems, and urban spaces. They also controlled the ritual calendar and the procurement and processing of crucial raw materials such as marine shells, copper, gold, and silver that symbolized their power. Aggrandizing Andean elites were able to construct empires by dominating existing trade routes, taking advantage of regional differences in the value of goods, manipulating cultural traditions of kinship reciprocity and religious belief, and exploiting diverse ethnic groups. The Inca rulers controlled access to raw materials such as gold, silver, and copper from the Andes, marine shells from Ecuador, and tropical plants such as coca from the Amazon. They used these goods to command labor and to convert them into even more valuable wealth objects in a seemingly endless cycle of self-reinforcing accumulation. The Andean elite used imperial military expansion to gain permanent control over the sources of the raw materials needed to produce the prestige goods and gifts that sustained their power. As in Mesopotamia, control over long-distance exchange systems allowed Inca rulers to steadily expand their individual personal imperia by accumulating exotic wealth objects and giving them to their political supporters. Those individuals who gained the most then used their wealth and political power to command large labor forces to build the large-scale terracing and irrigation projects, cities, roads, and temple complexes that allowed them to integrate a large-scale society.

One of the most important sources of Inca power was their monopoly over the exchange of Peruvian copper for shells of *Spondylus*, the thorny oyster, a marine bivalve mollusk from Ecuadorean coastal waters.[64] The Inca called the *Spondylus* shell *mullu* and made them into valuable beads. *Spondylus* shells were considered to be female "daughters of the sea," symbolizing water and fertility, and they were food for the gods. *Spondylus* was also remarkable for its seasonal toxicity and because it appeared off the Peruvian coast only during El Niño events. *Spondylus* was paired in a ritual complex with the gastropod (univalve) conch shell *Strombus*, which was seen as male and when blown was the "voice of god." Both shells had divine qualities and were involved with divination, but *Spondylus* was more difficult to obtain.[65]

Trading Peruvian copper for Ecuadorean *Spondylus* shells was an unequal exchange that disproportionately benefited the Inca, because the shells were symbolically more valuable to the Inca than were copper blades for the Ecuadoreans.[66] Ecuadorean elites used coppers as bride-wealth and funerary valuables, whereas *Spondylus* helped the Inca elite accumulate wealth and command vast supplies of corvée laborers for elite-directed work projects. Those who did the actual work of diving for shells and mining and smelting copper got less than the elites who commanded their labor, because their labor was underpaid relative to the value of the goods to command more labor. Remarkably, many of the new craft goods developed in the Andes were not technical improvements that made life better for ordinary household requirements. Metal goods were wealth and prestige objects, not utilitarian in the ordinary sense. It is thus not surprising that their production was elite directed. The system was based on ritual and symbolic values that obscured the underlying material inequity and was designed by elites primarily to serve their personal needs for legitimizing their power. The Andean elite succeeded by controlling three sources of power: (1) long distance trade of wealth objects, (2) craft production, and (3) ideology.[67]

The immediate beginnings of the Inca dynasty can be traced to a small Quechua-speaking chiefdom in the region of Cuzco in approximately AD 1200. The rapid expansion of the Inca empire, which began in 1438 under Pachacuti, joined together preexisting regional states, chiefdoms, and domestic-scale communities into a centrally managed system. The ultimate ideological foundation of the empire was the religious belief in the supreme divinity of the Inca ruler, who was the sun god personified. The Inca's identity with the sun had a literal reality, given the vast energy resources at the ruler's disposal in the form of enormous quantities of foodstuffs stored in state warehouses scattered throughout the empire. The Inca state also supported large numbers of full-time craft specialists, part-time corvée laborers, and military personnel. Over a sixty-year period, the state financed innumerable monumental building projects, constructed and maintained a vast road network,[68]

and developed large-scale agricultural projects. These impressive activities ultimately depended on maintaining the loyalty of villagers, who cared first and foremost about the day-to-day well-being of their domestic households.

BOX 7.4. BEFORE THE INCA: MOCHICA AND CHIMÚ LORDS

For at least 6,000 years Andean peoples were mobile foragers, hunting wild guanaco and vicunas in the high mountains and gathering plants and seafood on the coast.[69] Probably as an adjustment to postglacial environmental changes by about 5000–6000 BP, foragers began to settle and domesticate potatoes, llamas, and alpacas in the highlands[70] and began living in coastal fishing villages cultivating cotton and gourds. Chiefs may have successfully organized the first large coastal settlements as early as 4,000 BP, even before pottery was in use or maize was cultivated.[71] Rulers may have developed irrigated agriculture in desert river valleys by 3000 BP to protect their power in response to warm El Niño ocean currents that damaged the fisheries (see table 7.4).

The basic elements of the Andean cultural tradition were firmly in place 3,000 years ago. These included centralized political organization, intensive agriculture based on maize and potatoes, high-altitude llama pastoralism, monumental architecture, religious shrines, urban centers, and elaborate ceramics and textiles. Pre-Inca Andean peoples were masters at metallurgy, weaving, and ceramics. Andean peoples worked copper, gold, bronze, and silver, using a variety of techniques, including lost-wax casting, to produce elaborate jewelry and simple implements (see figure 7.11). Textiles, including tapestry and embroidery, were highly developed and, along with jewelry, became important markers of status.

The Inca elite were latecomers who followed cultural patterns, including bureaucratic forms of administration and details of technology and ideology practiced by their immediate predecessors, the rulers of the Moche (AD 100–700) and Chimú kingdoms (AD 700–1465) on the north coast of Peru. Pre-Inca civilizations are less well known than the older Mesopotamian civilizations because they left no writing and their tombs were systematically looted over the centuries. Fortuitously, in 1987–1990 Peruvian archaeologists discovered three Moche royal tombs with their treasures intact at the site of Sipan, near Chiclayo.[72] These burials provide a remarkable glimpse of the material wealth that defined social power in the Andean world before the Inca. Tomb One contained a large wooden casket with the body of a high-ranking Moche warrior priest bundled together with an amazing array of wealth objects, including 1,137 ceramic pots in a single offering cache. There were ten banners and a tunic covered with plates of gilded copper, six shell and copper-beaded pectorals and armbands, numerous gold nose and ear ornaments, finely wrought gold and silver necklaces, gold scepters, gold face masks, several gold and feathered headdress ornaments, ceremonial knives, silver back plates, and silver sandals (see figure 7.12).

The well-preserved Chimú capital city of Chan Chan may have had a population of 30,000 people, making it one of the largest cities in the pre-Columbian New World. The city was dominated by ten walled royal compounds built as residences for successive Chimú kings.[73] Following the Andean custom of split inheritance, when a Chimú king died he retained his divine status and was buried in his own compound with a treasure trove of wealth objects. The deceased king's compound and properties were managed by his close relatives as a religious shrine, and his political successor became the next divine king. Split inheritance kept wealth and power concentrated, but it also gave the new king an incentive to expand the scale of society to build a new estate. This custom was one of the driving forces behind the rapid growth of the Inca empire.

Each Chimú royal compound contained a palace, temples, tombs, courtyards, wells, control posts and audience chambers, and storehouses stocked with wealth objects. These were exclusive places, surrounded by adobe walls nine meters tall and up to five meters thick. Access into their interiors was through one narrow door and labyrinthine halls. The social inequality in Chan Chan resembled conditions in the Mesopotamian city of Ur and is apparent in the relative magnitude of residential structures. The royal compounds were as large as 221,000 square meters—1,785 times larger than commoner houses. Lower-class specialist workers were crowded into small, unwalled compounds of only 125 square meters each, with limited access to water, and containing workshops rather than wealth-filled storehouses.

Potatoes, Maize, and Gold: Foundations of the Empire

The material foundation of the Andean empire was in the hands of the self-sufficient villagers who operated a highly productive, intensive agricultural system based on communal land and complementary labor exchange. Without an effective subsistence sector, there would have been no part-time labor force to sustain the Inca elite. The community-level Andean agricultural system was a major achievement in which egalitarian villagers cooperated to increase agricultural production in an otherwise hostile environment by draining and ridging fields in low areas, terracing steep hillsides, and creating and maintaining irrigation canals. Community leaders managed a technically sophisticated sectoral fallow system in which each sector, or plot of land, was rotated through a five- to fifteen-year production cycle of carefully selected annual crops and grazing fallow periods that maximized yield while maintaining long-term soil fertility. In successive years, specific crops were sequentially planted to take advantage of the particular qualities of a dozen or more distinct environmental zones that were available to the community. This system served everyone. Each household received enough land to sustain itself in exchange for participation in cooperative labor projects that collectively maintained the system.[74]

The highly successful village-level subsistence sector has been characterized as a vertical economy because households and villages exploited resources in different ecological zones at different elevations, rather than depending on trade or market exchanges. The extremely steep Andean topography often meant that several sharply different environments would be within a village's reach. Four major zones, in descending elevation order, produced grazing, potatoes, maize, or tropical crops (see table 7.4).

Andean political centralization is not explained by population pressure or the adaptive advantages of exchange, specialization, or irrigation management because these could be effectively handled by relatively egalitarian local communities without coercive hereditary rulers. Archaeological evidence suggests that ambitious local leaders shrewdly manipulated the power vacuum left by the collapse of the prior Huari and Tiahuanaco empires to increase their personal power, turning local intercommunity rivalries into aggressive conquest warfare. People were forced to move into large, fortified towns for defense, and they accepted increasingly centralized authority as the best of a bad bargain in a threatening world,[75] but in the bargain the villagers managed to maintain control over their own subsistence.

Agricultural work was intensified when large, walled settlements had to be formed, but people resisted inequality. For example, during the century before the

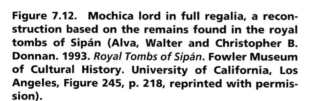

Figure 7.11. Inca copper blades and spondylus shell necklace.

Figure 7.12. Mochica lord in full regalia, a reconstruction based on the remains found in the royal tombs of Sipán (Alva, Walter and Christopher B. Donnan. 1993. *Royal Tombs of Sipán*. Fowler Museum of Cultural History. University of California, Los Angeles, Figure 245, p. 218, reprinted with permission).

Table 7.4. Productive Zones in the Andean Vertical Economy

Zone	Altitude*	Subsistence Production
Puna— alpine	14,000+ feet (4267+ meters)	Grazing of llamas and alpacas on wet and frosty alpine pastures
Puna/Jalka— subalpine	11, 000–14,000 feet (3353–4267 meters)	Potato cultivation in dry, frost-prone zones
Kichwa—temperate	7000–11,000 feet (2134–3353 meters)	Maize and beans
Tropical	Lowest	Tropical crops such as manioc, avocados, coca, and papayas

Sources: Brush (1976) and Murra (1972).

*Elevations of each zone vary from north to south in the Andes and are only approximate.

Inca conquerors arrived, all households in the fortified settlements of the Upper Mantaro valley had access to land and metal goods, and everyone farmed. Community leaders were distinguished only by their larger, wealthier households. For political centralization to emerge, preexisting Andean cultural principles, which fostered community balance, kinship reciprocity, and social equality, had to be subverted to first create and then perpetuate coercive power structures and elite privilege.[76]

The Inca state was a nonmarket political economy based on "supply on command" rather than the "supply and demand" of a market economy.[77] The state economy was functionally divided into a **staple economy** and a **wealth economy**.[78] The staple economy was concerned with the production and storage of potatoes and other primary foodstuffs to provision the army and the vast numbers of full-time state employees. Maize was an important crop used to brew chicha beer, which state officials provided to part-time laborers in ritual feasts in exchange for their labor.[79] The wealth economy involved the state-directed production of luxury goods such as gold and silver jewelry, featherwork, and fine textiles, which were status markers used to reward the ruling class. Gold symbolized the sun god and was a marker of the Inca nobility. Wealth objects also bought the loyalty of local village leaders turned Inca bureaucrats; these bureaucrats, backed by the coercive power of the Inca state and army, facilitated the extraction of the labor tax.

Under the Inca, specialized laborers in full-time service to the state were called camayo (camayoc), with an additional designation to specify their duty. For example, there were llama camayo, who herded llamas; coca camayo, who raised coca; chacara camayo, who farmed; and pukara camayo, who garrisoned frontier fortresses.[80] The mitima (mitmaq) were members of ethnic groups who were relocated as colonists to work on large-scale agricultural projects. Commoner women might also become acllas, or "chosen women," who worked full-time to produce high-status textiles known as kumpi. Acllas might also be married to the yanacona, commoners who served the nobility. Nonspecialist commoners were called suyu runa, "people of the quarter," and were subject to periodic labor service, known as the mita.

Aspiring elites also promoted craft production as a way to support their power-building efforts, to gain control over material resources, and to create material symbols to legitimize their power. The strength of household production systems in tribal societies makes it difficult for leaders to persuade close kin, or extended kin, and non-kin members of their social networks to increase production beyond household needs. However, craft specialization through organized production can gain economies of scale for relatively little increased efforts by individual workers. It is likely that leaders who were able to sponsored large communal work parties supported by feasting and drinking, and that this was a short-term incentive for increased production of craft goods, but making such intensified efforts permanent required changing people's perceptions and beliefs through ideology.[81]

Royal Lineages and Chosen Women

The Inca empire was known as Tawantinsuyu, or the land of four parts. It was directed from the capital of Cuzco, at the center of the named quarters: Antisuyu covered the tropical lowlands; Chinchasuyu, the north coast and highlands; Collasuyu, present-day Bolivia; and Condesuyu, the south coast (see figure 7.10a). Each quarter was directed by a member of the royal family and was subdivided into provinces, also ruled by the nobility. The eighty or so provinces were further subdivided into paired suyus, or moieties, which were ranked as upper and lower, and contained ayllus, or localized kin-based groups. Territorial units were defined in part by the individual huacas, or cult shrines, for which they were responsible, reminiscent of how Australian aboriginal estate groups, or clans, were responsible for Dreamtime sacred sites. In theory, productive lands were owned by the Inca state, temples, and local communities. Much land was centrally administered, but as in Mesopotamia, the line between temple and state was not always clear, and newly elevated local elites administered many locally controlled estates. The empire was apparently not as monolithic in practice as its formal structure might appear.

Much of the rural population was also organized as a labor force into a formalized hierarchy of workers in units that were subdivided alternately into units of two and five. The largest unit was the *hunu*, which contained approximately 10,000 workers. It was divided into two units of 5,000 called *piska* (five) *waranqa*. Each *piska waranqa* contained five *waranqa* units of 1,000 workers. The *waranqa*, in turn, were divided into two units of 500 called *piska pachaka*, which, in turn, contained five *pachaka* units of 100 workers (see figure 7.13).

This bureaucractic system was closely connected with the *quipu* recording system (see box 7.5). Decades after the Spanish conquest, local native leaders were still able to describe the system in detail, and the Spaniards immediately recognized its utility as a census and control mechanism.

Superimposed on the hierarchy of territories and labor units was a hierarchy of offices and social classes and a variety of named occupational specialties and ethnic groups. Social status was defined by a dress code and associated privileges and duties. The Inca god-king was personally sacred in the same way as the Hawaiian rulers. He likewise married a full sister and was the head of the *Capac Ayllu*, or Inca royal family, which consisted of a central patriline and nine ranked **cognatic lines**, or side branches, which were also designated *panaqa*.[82] The members of the royal *ayllu* constituted the nobility, the highest social class, and were the most powerful officials in the bureaucracy. The Spaniards called them *Orejones*, or "big ears," because they were privileged to wear enormous gold earplugs and distinguished headgear. Their social

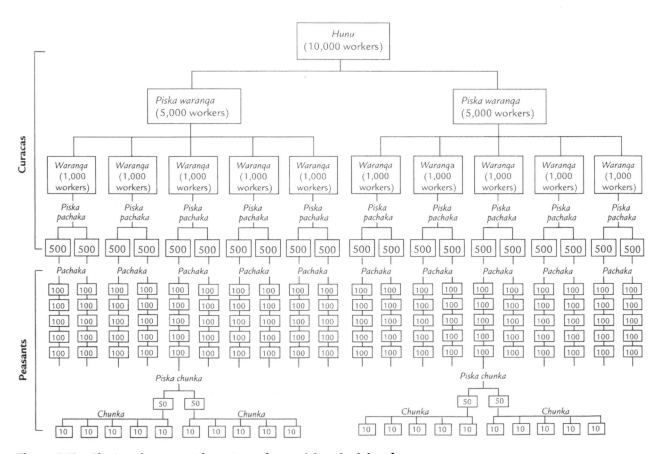

Figure 7.13. The Inca bureaucratic system of organizing the labor force.

status was finely ranked by genealogical distance from the Inca king.

The Inca bureaucracy sustained an amazing concentration of social power that primarily benefited a tiny minority. Figure 7.14 shows the approximate number of individuals who would have occupied the various administrative positions in the system, and the number of taxpayers that they might have commanded at each level. Taxpayers commanded was only an indirect measure of social power, because the product of the *mita* tax was passed up the command chain. However, officials were materially rewarded by the emperor according to their position in the hierarchy. Goods produced by *mita* labor filled the Inca storehouses and were ultimately distributed by the top Inca rulers. Central Andean Inca storehouses had the capacity to store 320,000 cubic yards (244,283 m³) of goods.[83] This is equivalent to more than 7,000 standard 20-foot shipping containers. The Inca used these vast resources to finance their military campaigns and to support their administrators and specialists, but they also diverted much of the surplus into their personal household establishments. The most visible evidence of private use of Inca wealth was the series of great family estates that stretched for 100 kilometers along the upper Urubamba-Vilcanota river valley from Machu Picchu to beyond Cuzco. The "city" of Machu Picchu (see figure 7.15) was actually only one of several private family retreats built by Pachakuti Inca. The primary estate of Inca Huayna Capac (AD 1493–1525) at Yucay is especially well documented.[84] It covered some 27 square kilometers of land and included developed roads, bridges, agricultural terraces, special gardens, private hunting parks and lodge, a palace compound, and towns and housing for some 2,000 support households. This project required construction parties of 150,000 workers and included rerouting the Urubamaba River, filling in swamps, and removing hills. The Inca emperors commanded armies totaling perhaps 200,000 men and used force to expand the empire and to make sure that everyone supported the system.[85] Officials could impose severe punishments for offenders who committed forbidden acts.[86] They were especially concerned with theft,

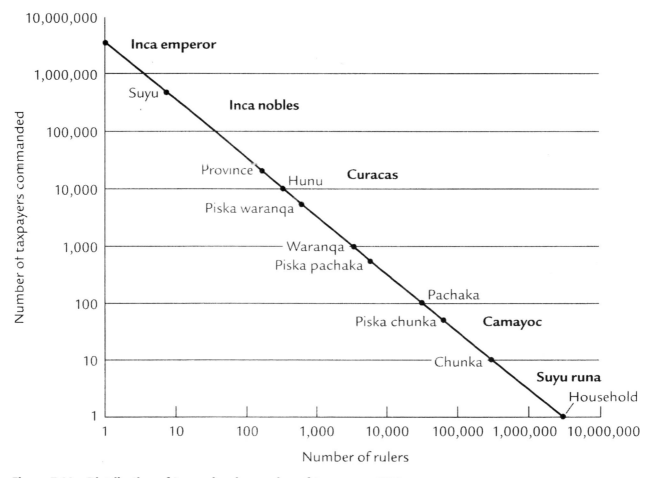

Figure 7.14. Distribution of Inca rulers by number of taxpayers, 1500 AD.

Figure 7.15. View of buildings and stone terraces at Wiñay Wayna, an Inca outpost on the "Inca Trail" near Machu Picchu, a royal family resort built by Pachakuti Inca, emperor from 1438 to 1471 (Victor Bloomfield 2010).

prescribing death for taking even small articles belonging to the Inca or the temples. Hunting in the Inca's game park, moving boundary markers, disobeying a *curaca* rank official, or fleeing from a work assignment were all punishable by death. Poor job performance could bring public whipping or beating with stones. Traveling without permission, changing residence, or hiding from the census taker were all punishable offenses. Clearly, commoners paid a heavy cost in personal freedom for life under Inca rule.

Marriage of the Inca king to his sister was a cultural statement that symbolically used kinship categories and marriage form to dramatize the hierarchical nature of Inca society.[87] All those men within the royal *ayllu* in Cuzco who could claim descent from the Inca king belonged to branch lines that were ranked in several ways. Descent was calculated back five generations to a mythical founding Inca king-ancestor, yielding a six-ranked generational system. The ruling Inca's direct line was considered to be a straight line,

or *ceque*, and its members were most highly ranked, whereas those who belonged to a branch *ceque*, sister's-sons lines, were treated either as high-ranking "sons" with Inca mothers or as low-ranking "nephews" with non-Inca mothers. These categories were also be distinguished as "older" and "younger" sons, with older being superior. Men of the highest genealogical rank, and thus closest to the ruling Inca, were called lords and were associated with eagles; the most distant were called "skunks" and "stinkers," thus emphatically spelling out their relative social worth, even though they all were superior to commoners.

Depending on the genealogical depth of their closest link to the royal *ceque*, these men might be actual grandsons, great-grandsons, and so on of the founding Inca ruler. Those called nephews were the children of the Inca's dozens of secondary non-Inca wives. Sons became administrators over the upper moiety of Cuzco, and nephews were placed in charge of Cuzco's lower moiety. Sons were associated with ruling lords, and younger sons or nephews were servants or priests and sometimes played ritual feminine roles.

Who the men of the royal *ayllu* were permitted to marry revealed their rank along a continuum from extreme endogamy to maximum exogamy, with marriage to the closest kin demonstrating the highest rank. The marriage of the king to his sister represented the highest degree of endogamy and was reserved for the highest-ranking person. Marriage to a full sibling might seem maladaptive because of the possibility of genetic defects in the offspring, but such matings were not common. Furthermore, close inbreeding will also enhance beneficial traits. Individuals ranking immediately below the Inca were permitted to marry half-sisters and parallel cousins. Third-ranking individuals could marry cross-cousins. Finally, people more than five generational ranks removed from the ruling Inca married non-kin, thereby reflecting maximum exogamy.

Women of the royal *ayllu* were placed in six ranked *aclla* (chosen women), categories based on age grades that were associated metaphorically with an invidious ranking based on physical appearance.[88] These age-beauty ranks apparently corresponded to the genealogically based male ranks, such that women of high-ranking genealogical standing relative to the ruling Inca were assigned to high-ranking *aclla* age grades. Those women who, because of their genealogical rank, were assigned to the most prestigious *aclla* group at approximately twenty to twenty-four years of age were considered "most beautiful" and remained in that category for life. They were never supposed to speak to men and performed ritual services in the most sacred shrines. Women of lower genealogical rank were selected for lower-ranked *aclla* age grades as they grew older, and they carried out lower-level ritual duties. For example, the three lowest *aclla* grades were joined at ages thirty-five, forty, and fifty, and these women wove textiles of increasingly lower quality and social worth. At age thirty-five, an *aclla* could make very fine cloth for ritual use in the most important *huacas*, whereas women who became *acllas* at fifty years of age were commoners who made the most ordinary textiles such as belts and bags.[89]

Below the nobility were *curacas*, officials who were in charge of decimal units down to the *pichaka* (100s) level. These Inca appointees held positions that became hereditary offices. Leaders of lower-level units were commoners. The highest non-*curaca* status was that of *yanacona*, who worked as retainers to the nobility. Raised as children in royal households, they were trained to become servants and attendants in the palaces and temples. Sometimes they were rewarded with *Orejon* status.

The decimal-based hierarchy was well suited for labor mobilization, which was a primary and self-serving state function. For example, if a *hunu* (10,000)-level *curaca* needed to draft 1,000 laborers, they could be readily assembled from the bottom up, if one man from the *chunka* (10) level was sent up the hierarchy. A typical labor assignment that was documented for four *waranqas* (4,000 men) showed nearly half the men assigned to permanent assignments as *camayo* craft specialists, in the military service, and as *yanacona*. The other half served on rotating *mita* in the mines, on construction projects, and as soldiers and carriers.[90]

BOX 7.5. THE *QUIPU*: AN ANDEAN INFORMATION STORAGE SYSTEM

A social system as complex as the Inca empire required an effective system of information storage. Instead of writing, the Inca used a highly specialized information system based on bundles of knotted cord known as *quipus* (*quipu* means "knot" in Quechua), which closely paralleled the structure of the Incan bureaucracy as depicted in figure 7.13. The *quipu* was a complex symbolic system of signs for recording statistical information by category of object. The signs were provided by a series of strings or cords, with multiple branches off the top and bottom of a central cord. Besides varying in position, individual pendant cords could vary in color, direction of twist, and ply. Even multicolored cords were used, such that hundreds of color combinations could be produced. Subsidiary cords could be attached at several places to create subcategories. Quantity was recorded using three different knot types and a decimal positional system employing a zero concept. *Quipus* were "written" to and "read" by a class of professionals known as *quipu camayo*, who must have resembled Mesopotamian scribes. The highly specialized knowledge involved in the use of the *quipus* has been described in detail by Marcia and Robert Ascher.[91]

The *quipu* is a good example of the many ways that cultures can be functionally integrated. *Quipus* reflected many aspects of Inca aesthetics and other features of the culture that gave it a uniquely Inca ethos. For example, the Inca were concerned with spatial relationships, symmetry of pattern, portability of objects, methodical and repetitive design, and an overall conservatism, which can be seen in the Inca political system, architecture, ceramics, and textiles.

On a much larger scale, the *ceque* system, which related *ayllu* social groups and *huaca* sacred places within a larger political whole, represented the same cultural reality.

A *quipu* might contain several thousand cords, but each cord occupied a specific place, oriented vertically along a horizontal axis. Like cloth, *quipus* were highly portable and based on spatial relationships. A *quipu* could be designed to represent different levels of the Inca bureaucracy and could record the quantities of goods such as various types of cloth, crops, and animals that were moved and stored, as well as the numbers of soldiers and workers of different types. It was an ideal device for keeping track of *mita* service and goods stockpiled in storehouses. The close parallels between Sumerian writing and the *quipu* suggest that *quipu* makers were, in fact, writing. The *quipu* could be read verbally, and the act of tying knots was tactilely and visually comparable to using a stylus in clay or a pencil on paper. Furthermore, both systems recorded information in the service of the state.

Inca Cosmology: The Universe Is Order and Sharing

The Inca cosmogony was based on an origin myth in which founding heroes emerge from a cave and start descent groups. There are two parallel lines of descent, male and female, respectively from sun and moon, with both ultimately originating with the creator god, *Viracocha*.[92] Inca society is metaphorically a single kin group. Everyone was "family," yet the system remained hierarchical, with distance from the Inca founder determining rank. The Inca bureaucracy was based on traditional Andean cosmology and conceptions of spatial order and reciprocity, of which the Inca rulers were quick to make use. The concept of four quarters still organizes the space around rural Andean villages.[93] Conceptually, the quarters are derived from the great cross in the sky formed by the Milky Way as it shifts its apparent position relative to earth between 6 p.m. and 6 a.m. especially and seasonally during the solstices. This sky cross defines a center and divides the night sky into quarters that people imagine projecting to the ground. Each village contains its own center, called *chawpi* in Quechua, and the individual quarters, or *suyus*, are usually grouped into upper and lower divisions. Imaginary lines, like the descent lines, called *ceques*, radiate from the village center toward sacred points situated on the mountain skyline and along the way align with specific shrines or *huacas*.

There were forty-two *ceques* in Cuzco, radiating as vectors or lines of sight toward the horizon as viewed from the main temple.[94] There were 328 *huacas* located along the *ceque* lines. The *ceques* divided the province of Cuzco into territories, which were assigned to specific *ayllus*, *suyus*, and moieties. This system was integrated with a ritual calendar established by astronomical observations in which special rituals were performed sequentially at specific *huacas* on certain days of the year. The most important of these rituals concerned agricultural activities. The two most basic principles underlying the interaction among households within the village community and among households and nature and the Inca state were *ayni* (reciprocity) and *mita* (a turn or a share).[95] *Ayni* referred to the exchange of services between a variety of entities and was considered essential to the orderly operation of the cosmos. It applied to marriage exchanges, food and drink given for communal labor within the village, gifts of drink to the earth mother at harvest, and water cycling between earth and sky. Labor service to the state was also *ayni* and was rewarded by ritual chicha (maize beer) distributions. *Mita* added temporal order to *ayni*. *Mita* referred to crop rotation, calving seasons, human generations, and an individual's share in labor service to the state. *Ayni* and *mita* were thus ritually sanctioned as part of the natural order.

The divine right of the Inca to rule was supported by the Inca nobility's origin myth, which recounts how the first Incas conquered the indigenous inhabitants of the valley of Cuzco. This event is commemorated in the annual rituals that mark the first planting of maize and the harvest. These elaborate ritual events were presided over by the Inca ruler himself and by the nobility. Because no one in the empire could plant or harvest before these rituals were performed, they gave the Inca effective power over nature, in effect naturalizing their rule.[96]

Figure 7.16 presents a native view of Andean cosmology based on a representation appearing in the temple of the sun in Cuzco, the imperial capital. To provide ideological support for a supreme ruler, the Inca elevated the creator deity, *Viracocha*, and the celestial sun god, *Inti*, to dominant positions above the pantheon of local mountain, earth, and lake deities that connected local communities with their territories. The cosmological model employs the Andean concept of *yanantin*, or balanced oppositions, and presents a parallel hierarchy of divinities, showing male and female aspects. It clearly reflects the central elements of the state hierarchy, even to the detail of depicting *ayni* relationships and showing the state storehouse (*collqa*), terraced agricultural land, and a domestic couple as the foundation. This cosmological system shares some features with the Amazonian tribal cosmology (see figure 2.22) discussed earlier, with which it is no doubt historically connected, but the Inca message is that giving labor to the state is part of the natural order.

Before the Inca took power, ordinary people in local communities had direct, gender-specific access to the supernatural forces of nature. Parallel lines of men and women provided kinship access to the resources households needed to maintain and reproduce themselves.[97] The goddesses and gods gave people their life, and people reciprocated by worship and sacrifice expressed in local shrines and cults. The goddess *Pachamama* was the earth mother, an embodiment of procreative forces equivalent to the Hawaiian god *Lono*, except that *Pachamama* was a female image of earthly regeneration. *Pachamama*'s daughters were also goddesses and included *Saramama* (maize), *Axomama* (potatoes), *Cocamama* (coca), *Coyamama* (metals), and *Sanumama* (clay). For example, *Saramama*, the mother of corn, was embodied in special stalks of corn that produced more ears than normal, or unusually well-formed ears of corn, or kernels of a unique color. Belief in the power of *Saramama* and associated practice was literally true in that venerating and replanting particular plants with outstanding qualities was genetic engineering that produced new varieties.

Gods of sky and mountains embodied masculine political forces. For example, *Illapa*, or *Intillapa* god of thunder and lightning, provided rain, hail, clouds, and storms, and was a god of conquest. As embodied in political conquest, the thunder god, *Illapa*, was seen as the conquering hero ancestor of a dominant local chief and his descent group. Appropriately, male family heads maintained mountaintop shrines dedicated to Thunder. The ancestors of a local *curaca* were sons of *Illapa*. Mountain gods are still recognized in the southern Andes as *Wamanis*, where they accurately embody the natural forces that control springs and glacial meltwater.

Gods and goddesses were always defined in a particular context, or relative to other deities acting in a dialectic. *Pachamama* paired with Thunder, *Illapa*, so that *Illapa*'s rain could combine with *Pachamama*'s fertility. Appropriate seasonal rituals and sacrifice helped fix respect for these supernatural deities in the community culture and symbolized human reciproc-

ity for the powers of nature. The Inca emperor made himself an embodiment of the sun god, *Inti*, redefined as the conquering god, like the Hawaiian war god *Ku*. *Inti* was symbolized by gold, "sweat of the sun." This kept the local chiefs in power but made them subservient. Likewise, the emperor's wife, his sister, became the embodiment of the moon goddess, *Mama-Quilla*, claiming control over water, fertility, and everything feminine. Like the association between *Inti* and gold, *Mama-Quilla* was symbolized by silver, "tears of the moon."

Huanaco Pampa: An Inca City

All elements of Inca society are shown diagrammatically in the layout of Huanaco Pampa, a representative Inca city (see figure 7.17).[98] Huanaco Pampa was a planned city, built about AD 1475 as an administrative center. It covered 0.8 square miles (2 km²) and was situated at an elevation of 12,471 feet (3,801 m) in a prime potato-growing region. The city contained a special platform where the Inca ruler could lead public ceremonies and a residence where he could be accommodated on royal visits. There were elite residences, barracks for rotating *mita* laborers, and great halls where they were entertained at ritual *chichi* beer-drinking feasts. The *aclla*, or chosen women, were securely sequestered within a walled compound. The city's primary function must have been warehousing great quantities of food, judging by the 30,065 cubic yards (23,000 m³) of space in storehouses devoted to potatoes and 18,301 cubic yards (14,000 m³) to maize. The potato storehouses alone could have supplied more than 50,000 workers a year with a pound (0.5 kg) of potatoes a day, which is more than the average daily consumption of potatoes by rural Andean peoples today.[99] Additionally, the stored maize could have been used to brew vast quantities of chicha beer. Some of the stored potatoes and maize would have been grown on state-owned terraced farm land (see figure 7.18).

Some authorities consider food storage to be the most important functional advantage of state organization in the Andean region.[100] The state storehouses could have served to average out environmentally determined fluctuations in food production, which occurred both seasonally and from year to year with El Niño–related events and unpredictable droughts and frosts. Large-scale storage might have raised the overall carrying capacity of the region. This food-energy averaging interpretation tends to support the redistributive social benefits theory of state origins, and many observers have described the Inca system

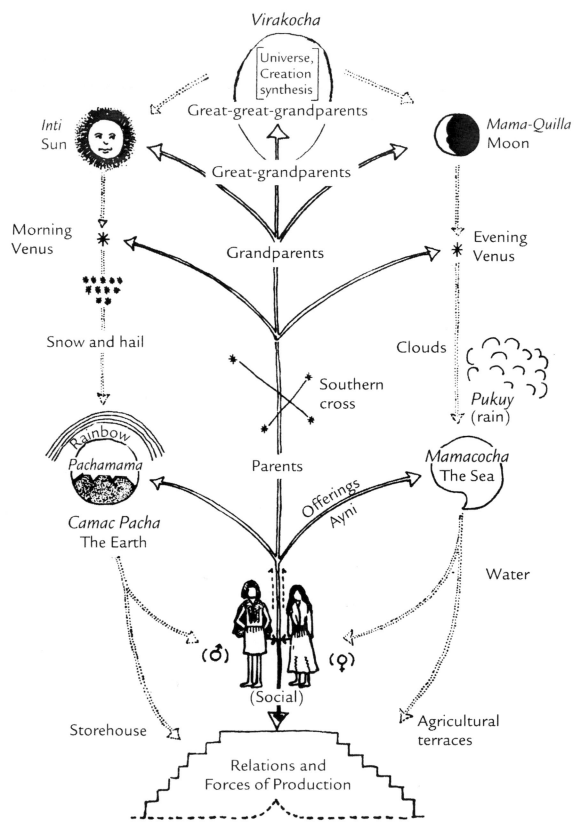

Figure 7.16. An Andean model of the place of people, culture, and the flow of energy in the cosmos, based on a plaque in the Inca temple in Cuzco (redrafted from Earls and Silverblatt 1978).

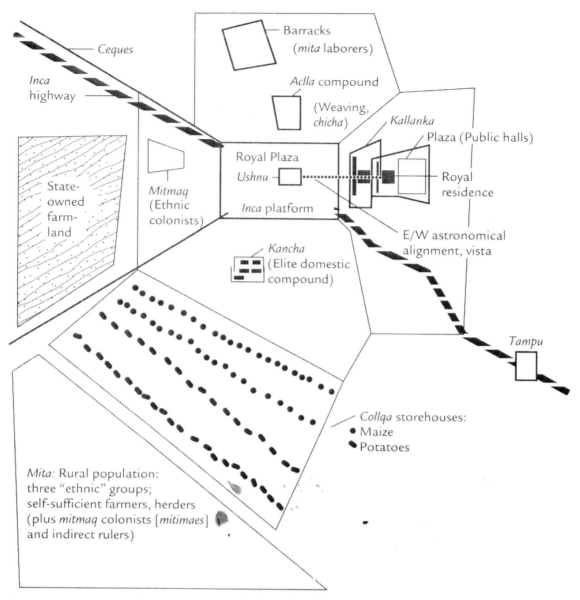

Figure 7.17. Layout of the Inca administrative city of Huanaco Pampa: a 0.8 square mile (2 km²) planned city at 12,471 feet (3801 m), built about 1475. The Spanish took over in 1539. It had 4,000 structures and 10,000–15,000 residents (redrafted from Morris and Thompson 1985).

as a great socialist welfare state. The Inca state could equally well be considered despotic and totalitarian because individual freedom was constrained by how wealth and power were distributed. The state moved whole communities at will and imposed a national language. The real advantage in expanding the scope of national control was that it increased the power of the privileged elite.

SUMMARY

The ancient agrarian civilizations examined in this chapter and in chapters 8 and 9 demonstrate that elite-directed cultural development was neither natural nor

inevitable. They were also not progressive societies, if progress is measured as widely shared improvements in human well-being. These civilizations were the outcome of particular decisions made by a few individuals who were uniquely positioned to take personal advantage of historical circumstances to advance their self-interest.

The most striking parallels between Mesopotamian and Andean civilizations is that both were despotic, four-ranked societies, ruled by divine kings who claimed control over the forces of nature and could demand unquestioned servitude from everyone. These imperial civilizations produced impressive artistic, architectural, and technical achievements, but

Figure 7.18. Inca agricultural terraces at Moray, near Cuzco, Peru (Victor Bloomfield, 2010).

their rulers perpetrated exploitation, oppression, and violence within their societies and waged wars of aggression against neighboring peoples. These imperial cultures had highly productive economies that created tremendous wealth, but their rulers distributed economic benefits in extremely unjust ways that left the majority at or below the margins of subsistence. Social inequality was strongly demonstrated by differences in the size of household establishments. Such unequal outcomes reflect concentrated social power and suggest that these imperial cultures were indeed being directed by their principal beneficiaries. It seems reasonable to consider such cultures to be unjust, even if they were successful as cultures in the sense that people supported and reproduced the system. Rather than marveling at the impressive "achievements" of imperial societies, we might instead ask why they failed to serve human needs more broadly.

STUDY QUESTIONS

1. In what way is centralized political power a fundamental element of "civilization" as it is usually defined?
2. What are the most useful defining features of ancient agrarian civilizations?
3. Discuss the explanations that have been proposed to account for the gradual process of plant and animal domestication in the Near East.
4. What unique environmental circumstances or "crises" were implicated in the adoption of domestication, and the growth of urban centers, chiefdoms, and the state in ancient Mesopotamia?
5. Describe the role of religion in the early Mesopotamian city-state. Make specific comparisons with religion in the Inca state.
6. What was the role of record keeping, and how was it carried out in ancient Mesopotamia and in the Inca empire?
7. Distinguish between wealth economy and staple economy, and show how each operated in the Inca empire.
8. Compare Inca cosmology with the cosmologies of aboriginal Australia and tribal Amazonia and interpret the differences in reference to social structure.

SUGGESTED READING

Alva, Walter, and Christopher B. Donnan. 1993. *Royal Tombs of Sipan*. Los Angeles: Fowler Museum of Cultural History, University of California. Describes the discovery and excavation of the best unlooted tombs known from Peru.

Ascher, Marcia, and Robert A. Ascher. 1981. *Code of the Quipa: Study in Media, Mathematics, and Culture*. Ann Arbor: University of Michigan Press. Explains how the *quipu* was used to encode information.

Bauer, Brian S. 1998. *The Sacred Landscape of the Inca: The Cusco Ceque System*. Austin: University of Texas Press. Monographic treatment of *huacas* and *ceques* and their connection with the Inca royal descent groups.

D'Altroy, Terrence N. 2002. *The Incas*. Oxford: Blackwell. A comprehensive overview of Inca civilization.

Kramer, Samuel Noah. 1967. *Cradle of Civilization*. New York: Time-Life Books. A well illustrated, popular description of Mesopotamian civilization by a respected scholar.

Morris, Craig, and Donald E. Thompson. 1985. *Huanaco Pampa: An Inca City and Its Hinterland*. London: Thames & Hudson. Uses archaeological analysis to describe an Inca city.

Niles, Susan A. 1999. *The Shape of Inca History: Narrative and Architecture in an Andean Empire*. Iowa City: University of Iowa Press. Provides a detailed view of Inca emperor Huayna Capac's estate at Yucay.

Redman, Charles L. 1978. *The Rise of Civilization: From Early Farmers to Urban Society in the Ancient Near East*. San Francisco: Freeman. Presents a complete overview of the origin of Mesopotamian civilization.

Woolley, Sir Leonard. 1982. *Ur "of the Chaldees."* London: Herbert Press. A detailed account of the royal tombs of Ur by the original discoverer.

GLOSSARY TERMS

City-states Politically organized societies based on the intensive exploitation of landless workers in the local area.

Bureaucracy A centralized command and control social structure with officials arranged in an administrative hierarchy.

Great Tradition The culture of the elite in a state-organized society with a tradition that is usually written and not fully shared by nonliterate, village-level commoners.

Village-states Politically centralized societies based on an urban administrative and ceremonial center drawing their support from self-sufficient peasant villagers scattered over a vast region.

Little Tradition Ritual beliefs and practices followed by nonliterate commoners, especially rural villagers who are part of a larger state-level society.

Multilinear evolution Julian Steward's theory that, given similar conditions, cultures can develop independently along similar lines. For example, he argued that irrigation agriculture led to state organization several times.

Social product The value of the aggregate annual production of a society, measured either as production or consumption.

Scale subsidy Social support in the form of taxes or tribute for activities that promote growth in scale, or that maintain a larger-scale society when benefits are inequitably distributed.

Polytheism A religious system based on belief in many gods, or deities.

Superstructure The mental, ideological, or belief systems as expressed in the religion, myths, and rituals of a culture. According to Harris's cultural materialist theory, superstructure is shaped by the structure.

Structure The social, economic, and political organization of a culture, which is shaped by the technological base, or infrastructure, according to Marvin Harris's cultural materialst theory.

Staple economy The state-controlled production, storage, and distribution of subsistence staples, such as potatoes and maize in the Inca case, to support nonfood-producing specialists groups and to provide emergency aid.

Wealth economy The state-controlled production, storage, and distribution of wealth objects that support the status hierarchy.

Cognatic line A descent line that is traced to a common ancestor and that need not rely on exclusively male or female links.

NOTES

1. Mann, Michael. 1986. *The Sources of Social Power*, vol. 1, *A History of Power from the Beginning to AD 1760*. Cambridge, Eng.: Cambridge University Press.
2. Adams, Robert McCormick. 1981. *Heartland of Cities: Surveys of Ancient Settlement and Land Use on the Central Floodplain of the Euphrates*. Chicago and London: University of Chicago Press.
3. Mann, Michael. 1986. *The Sources of Social Power*.
4. Weber, Max. 1968. *Economy and Society: An Outline of Interpretive Sociology*, edited by Guenther Roth and Claus Wittich. 3 vols. New York: Bedminster Press, 942.
5. Plog, Stephen. 1995. "Equality and Hierarchy: Holistic Approaches to Understanding Social Dynamics in the Pueblo Southwest." In *Foundations of Social Inequality*, edited by T. Douglas Price and Gary M. Feinman, pp. 189–206. New York and London: Plenum Press.
6. Hayden, Brian. 1995. "Pathways to Power: Principles for Creating Socioeconomic Inequalities." In *Foundations of Social Inequality*, edited by T. Douglas Price and Gary M. Feinman, pp. 15–86. New York and London: Plenum Press.
7. Moore, A. M. T., G. C. Hillman, and A. J. Legge. 2000. *Village on the Euphrates: From Foraging to Farming at Abu Hureyra*. New York: Oxford University Press.
8. Keswani, Priscilla Schuster. 1996. "Hierarchies, Heterarchies, and Urbanization Processes: The View from Bronze Age Cyprus." *Journal of Mediterranean Archaeology* 9:211–50.
9. Crumley, Carole L. 2001. "Communication, Holism, and the Evolution of Sociopolitical Complexity." In *From Leaders to Rulers*, edited by Jonathan Haas, pp. 19–33. New York: Kluwer Academic.
10. Carneiro, Robert L., and Stephen F. Tobias. 1963. "The Application of Scale Analysis to the Study of Cultural Evolution." *Transaction of the New York Academy of Sciences* (ser. 2) 26:196–207.
11. Weber, Max. 1968. *Economy and Society*, 942.
12. Hummel, Ralph P. 1987. *The Bureaucratic Experience*. New York: St. Martin's Press, 2.
13. Maisels, Charles Keith. 1990. *The Emergence of Civilization: from Hunting and Gathering to Agriculture, Cities, and the State in the Near East*. London and New York: Routledge.
14. Steward, Julian H. 1949. "Cultural Causality and Law: A Trial Formulation of the Development of Early Civilization." *American Anthropologist* 51:1-27.
15. McNeil, William H. 1987. *A History of the Human Community: Prehistory to the Present*. Englewood Cliffs, NJ: Prentice-Hall, 31.
16. Wittfogel, Karl A. 1957. *Oriental Despotism: A Study of Total Power*. New Haven, CT: Yale University Press, 126.
17. Kemp, Barry J. 1989. *Ancient Egypt: Anatomy of a Civilization*. London and New York: Routledge, 298–300.
18. Goldsmith, Raymond. 1987. *Premodern Financial Systems: A Historical Comparative Study*. Cambridge: Cambridge University Press, 16–33.
19. Betzig, Laura L. 1986. *Despotism and Differential Reproduction: A Darwinian View of History*. New York: Aldine; Betzig, Laura L. 1993. "Sex, Succession, and Stratification in the First Six Civilizations: How Powerful Men Reproduced, Passed Power on to Their Sons, and Used Power to Defend Their Wealth, Women, and Children." In *Social Stratification and Socioeconomic Inequality*, edited by Lee Ellis, pp. 37–74. Westport, CT: Praeger.
20. Redman, Charles L. 1978a. "Mesopotamian Urban Ecology: The Systemic Context of the Emergence of Urbanism." In *Social Archaeology: Beyond Subsistence and Dating*, edited by Charles Redman, Mary Jane Berman, Edward Curtin, William Langhorne Jr., Nina Versaggi, and Jeffery Wanser, pp. 329–47. New York: Academic Press; Redman, Charles L. 1978b. *The Rise of Civilization: From Early Farmers to Urban Society in the Ancient Near East*. San Francisco: Freeman.
21. Frangipane, Marcella. 2000. "The Development of Administration from Collective to Centralized Economies in the Mesopotamian World: The Transformation of an Institution from 'System-Serving' to 'Self-Serving.'" In G.

Feinman and L. Manzanilla, eds., *Cultural Evolution: Contemporary Viewpoints*, pp. 215–32. Fundamental Issues in Archaeology. New York: Kluwer Academic/Plenum.

22. Frangipane, Marcella. 2007. "Different Types of Egalitarian Societies and the Development of Inequality in Early Mesopotamia." *World Archaeology* 39(2):151–76.

23. Frangipane, Marcella. 2007. "Different Types of Egalitarian Societies."

24. Hole, Frank. 1994. "Environmental Instabilities and Urban Origins." In *Chiefdoms and Early States in the Near East*, G. Stein and M. S. Rothman, eds., pp. 121–52. Madison: Prehistory Press.

25. Stein, Gil. 1994. "Economy, Ritual, and Power in 'Ubaid Mesopotamia.'" In *Chiefdoms and Early States in the Near East: The Organizational Dynamics of Complexity,* edited by Gil Stein and Mitchell S. Rothman, pp. 35–46. Monographs in World Archaeology No. 18. Madison, WI: Prehistoric Press.

26. McCorriston, Joy. 1997. "The Fiber Revolution: Textile Extensification, Alienation, and Social Stratification in Ancient Mesopotamia." *Current Anthropology* 38(4):517–49.

27. Oates, Joan. 1993. "Trade and Power in the Fifth and Fourth Millennia BC: New Evidence from Northern Mesopotamia." *World Archaeology* 24(3):403–22. Algaze, Guillermo. 2005. *The Uruk World System: The Dynamics of Expansion of Early Mesopotamian Civilization.* 2nd ed. Chicago: University of Chicago Press.

28. Moore, A. M. T., G. C. Hillman, and A. J. Legge. 2000. *Village on the Euphrates.*

29. Mellaart, J. 1967. *Çatal Hüyük: A Neolithic Town in Anatolia.* London: Thames & Hudson; Todd, Ian A. 1976. *Çatal Hüyük in Perspective.* Menlo Park, CA: Cummings.

30. McEvedy, Colin, and Richard Jones. 1978. *Atlas of World Population History.* Middlesex, England, and New York: Penguin Books, 150.

31. Steinkeller, Piotr. 1991. "The Administrative and Economic Organization of the Ur III State: The Core and the Periphery." In *The Organization of Power: Aspects of Bureaucracy in the Ancient Near East,* edited by McGuire Gibson and Robert D. Biggs, pp. 15–33. Studies in Ancient Oriental Civilization, No. 46. The Oriental Institute of the University of Chicago.

32. Woolley, Sir Leonard, and P. R. S. Moorey. 1982. *Ur of the Chaldees,* 204.

33. Stone, Elizabeth C. 1987. *Nippur Neighborhoods.* Studies in Ancient Oriental Civilization No. 44. Oriental Institute of the University of Chicago. Chicago, IL.

34. Maisels, Charles Keith. 1990. *The Emergence of Civilization: From Hunting and Gathering to Agriculture, Cities, and the State in the Near East.* London and New York: Routledge.

35. Steinkeller, Piotr. 1991. "The Administrative and Economic Organization of the Ur III State: The Core and the Periphery." In *The Organization of Power: Aspects of Bureaucracy in the Ancient Near East,* edited by McGuire Gibson and Robert D. Biggs, pp. 15–33. Studies in Ancient Oriental Civilization, No. 46. The Oriental Institute of the University of Chicago.

36. Winter, Irene J. 1991. "Legitimation of Authority through Image and Legend: Seals Belonging to Officials in the Administrative Bureaucracy of the Ur III State." In *The Organization of Power: Aspects of Bureaucracy in the Ancient Near East,* edited by McGuire Gibson and Robert D. Biggs, pp. 59–100. Studies in Ancient Oriental Civilization, No. 46. The Oriental Institute of the University of Chicago.

37. Zettler, Richard L. 1991. "Administration of the Temple of Inanna at Nippur Under the Third Dynasty of Ur: Archaeological and Documentary Evidence." In *The Organization of Power: Aspects of Bureaucracy in the Ancient Near East,* edited by McGuire Gibson and Robert D. Briggs, pp. 101–14. Studies in Ancient Oriental Civilization, No. 46. The Oriental Institute of the University of Chicago, 109.

38. Waetzoldt, Hartmut. 1987. "Compensation of Craft Workers and Officials in the Ur III Period." In *Labor in the Ancient Near East,* edited by Marvin A. Powell, pp. 117–41. American Oriental Series, Vol. 68. New Haven, CT: American Oriental Society.

39. Hunt, R. C. 1991. "The Role of Bureaucracy in the Provisioning of Cities: A Framework for Analysis of the Ancient Near East." In *The Organization of Power: Aspects of Bureaucracy in the Ancient Near East,* edited by McGuire Gibson and Robert D. Biggs, pp. 59–100. Studies in Ancient Oriental Civilization, No. 46. The Oriental Institute of the University of Chicago.

40. Waetzoldt, Hartmut. 1987. "Compensation of Craft Workers and Officials."

41. Waetzoldt, Hartmut. 1987. "Compensation of Craft Workers and Officials."

42. Wright, Erik Olin. 1997. *Class Counts: Comparative Studies in Class Analysis.* Cambridge: Cambridge University Press, 9–13.

43. Diakonoff, I. M. 1987. "Slave-Labour vs. Non-Slave Labour: The Problem of Definition." In *Labor in the Ancient Near East,* edited by Marvin A. Powell, pp. 1–3. American Oriental Series, Vol. 68. New Haven, CT: American Oriental Society; Klengel, Horst. 1987. "Non-Slave Labor in the Old Babylonian Period: The Basic Outlines." In *Labor in the Ancient Near East,* pp. 159–66.

44. Steinkeller, Piotr. 1991. "The Administrative and Economic Organization of the Ur III State: The Core and the Periphery," 23, note 29.

45. Zeder, Melinda A. "Of Kings and Shepherds: Specialized Animal Economy in Ur III Mesopotamia." In *Chiefdoms and Early States in the Near East: the Organizational Dynamics of Complexity,* edited by Gil Stein and

Mitchell S. Rothman, pp. 175–91. Madison: Prehistory Press.

46. Hunt, R. C. 1991. "The Role of Bureaucracy in the Provisioning of Cities; Steinkeller, Piotr. 1991. "The Administrative and Economic Organization of the Ur III State"; Waetzoldt, Hartmut. 1987. "Compensation of Craft Workers and Officials in the Ur III Period"; Winter, Irene J. 1991. "Legitimation of Authority"; Zettler, Richard L. 1991. "Administration of the Temple of Inanna."

47. Gelb, I. J. 1965. "The Ancient Mesopotamian Ration System." *Journal of Near Eastern Studies* 24(3):230–43.

48. Johnson, Gregory Alan. 1973. *Local Exchange and Early State Development in Southwestern Iran.* Anthropological Papers, no. 51. Ann Arbor: Museum of Anthropology, University of Michigan.

49. Nissen, Hans J. 1986. "The Archaic Texts from Uruk." *World Archaeology* 17(3):317–34.

50. Nissen, Hans J. 1986. "The Archaic Texts from Uruk."

51. Johns, C. H. W. 1926. *The Oldest Code of Laws in the World: The Code of Laws Promulgated by Hammurabi, King of Babylon b.c. 2285–2242.* Edinburgh: T. and T. Clark.

52. Betzig, Laura L. 1993. "Sex, Succession, and Stratification in the First Six Civilizations."

53. Woolley, Sir Leonard, and P. R. S. Moorey. 1982. *Ur of the Chaldees.* Ithaca, NY: Cornell University Press.

54. Woolley, Sir Leonard. 1982. *Ur of the Chaldees.* London: Herbert Press.

55. Woolley, Sir Leonard and P. R. S. Moorey. 1982. *Ur of the Chaldees.*

56. Jacobsen, Thorkild. 1976. *The Treasures of Darkness: A History of Mesopotamian Religion.* New Haven, CT, and London: Yale University Press.

57. Swanson, G. E. 1960. *The Birth of the Gods.* Ann Arbor: University of Michigan Press.

58. Jacobsen, Thorkild. 1976. *The Treasures of Darkness.*

59. Yoffee, Norman. 1988a. "The Collapse of Ancient Mesopotamian States and Civilization." In *The Collapse of Ancient States and Civilizations,* edited by Norman Yoffee and George Cowgill, pp. 44–68. Tucson: University of Arizona Press.

60. Jacobsen, Thorkild, and Robert McAdams. 1958. "Salt and Silt in Ancient Mesopotamian Agriculture." *Science* 128 (3334):1251–58.

61. Cook, Noble David. 1981. *Demographic Collapse: Indian Peru, 1520–1620.* Cambridge: Cambridge University Press, 114.

62. Brush, Stephen B., Heath J. Carney, and Zosimo Huaman. 1981. "Dynamics of Andean Potato Agriculture." *Economic Botany* 35(l):70–88.

63. Burger, Richard L. 1992. *Chavin and the Origins of Andean Civilization.* London: Thames and Hudson; Rowe, John H. 1962. *Chavin Art: An Inquiry into Its Form and Meaning.* New York: The Museum of Primitive Art.

64. Hornborg, Alf. 2001. *The Power of the Machine: Global Inequalities of Economy, Technology, and Environment.* Walnut Creek, CA: Alta Mira Press, 65–87; Paulsen, Allison C. 1974. "The Thorny Oyster and the Voice of God: Spondylus and Strombus in Andean Prehistory." *American Antiquity* 39(4):597–607.

65. Cordy-Collins, Alana 1978. "The Dual Divinity Concept in Chavin Art." *El Dorado* 3(2):1–31.

66. Hornborg, Alf. 2001. *The Power of the Machine,* 65–87.

67. Vaughn, Kevin J. 2006. "Craft Production, Exchange, and Political Power in the Pre-Incaic Andes." *Journal of Archaeological Research* 14: 313–44.

68. Hyslop, John. 1984. *The Inka Road System.* New York: Academic Press.

69. Lanning, Edward P. 1967. *Peru Before the Incas.* Englewood Cliffs, NJ: Prentice-Hall.

70. Wheeler, Jane C. 1984. "On the Origin and Early Development of Camelid Pastoralism in the Andes." In *Animals and Archaeology*, vol. 3, edited by Juliet Clatton-Brock and Caroline Grigson, pp. 395–410. BAR International Series, no 202. Oxford, Eng.: BAR.

71. Moseley, Michael Edward. 1975. *The Maritime Foundations of Andean Civilization.* Menlo Park, CA: Cummings; Quilter, Jeffrey and Terry Stocker. 1983. "Subsistence Economies and the Origins of Andean Complex Societies." *American Anthropologist* 85(3):545–62.

72. Alva, Walter, and Christopher B. Donnan. 1993. *Royal Tombs of Spain.* Los Angeles: Fowler Museum of Cultural History, University of California.

73. Day, Kent C. 1982. "Ciudedelas: Their Form and Function." In *Chan Chan: Andean Desert City,* edited by Michael Moseley and Kent C. Dean, pp. 55–66. Albuquerque: University of New Mexico Press; Moore, Jerry D. 2004. "The Social Basis of Sacred Spaces."

74. Hastorf, Christine A. 1993. *Agriculture and the Onset of Political Inequality before the Inka.* Cambridge, Eng.: Cambridge University Press.

75. Hastorf, Christine A. 1993. *Agriculture and the Onset of Political Inequality.*

76. Hastorf, Christine A. 1993. *Agriculture and the Onset of Political Inequality.*

77. La Lone, Darrell E. 1982. "The Inca as a Nonmarket Economy: Supply on Command Versus Supply and Demand." In *Contexts for Prehistoric Exchange,* edited by Jonathon Ericson and Timothy K. Earle, pp. 291–316. New York: Academic Press.

78. D'Altroy, Terrence N. and Timothy K. Earle. 1985. "Staple Finance, Wealth Finance, and Storage in the Inka Political Economy." *Current Anthropology* 26(2):187–206.

79. Murra, John V. 1960. "Rite and Crop in the Inca State." In *Culture in History: Essays in Honor of Paul Radin,* edited by Stanley Diamond, pp. 393–407. New York: Columbia University Press.

80. Rowe, John H. 1982. "Inca Policies and Institutions Relating to the Cultural Unification of the Empire." In *The Inca and Aztec States 1400–1800*, edited by George Collier, Renato Rosaldo, and John Wirth, pp. 93–118. New York: Academic Press.

81. Costin, C. L. 1996. "Craft Production and Mobilization Strategies in the Inka Empire." In Wailes, B. (ed.), *Craft Specialization and Social Evolution: In Memory of V. Gordon Childe*, University Museum of Archaeology and Anthropology, University of Pennsylvania, Philadelphia, pp. 211–25.

82. D'Altroy, Terrence N. 2002. *The Incas.* Oxford: Blackwell, 89–90.

83. Levine, Terry Y. 1992. "Inka State Storage in Three Highland Regions: A Comparative Study." In *Inka Storage Systems*, edited by Terry Y. Levine, pp. 107-48. Norman and London: University of Oklahoma Press.

84. Niles, Susan A. 1999. *The Shape of lnca History: Narrative and Architecture in an Andean Empire.* Iowa City: University of Iowa Press.

85. D'Altroy, Terrence N. 2002. *The Incas*, 216–17.

86. Moore, Sally Falk. 1958. *Power and Property in Inca Peru.* Morningside Heights, NY: Columbia University Press.

87. Zuidema, R. Tom. 1990. *Inca Civilization in Cuzco.* Austin: University of Texas Press.

88. Zuidema, R. Tom. 1990. *Inca Civilization.*

89. Costin, Cathy Lynne. 1998. "Housewives, Chosen Women, Skilled Men: Cloth Production and Social Identity in the Late Prehispanic Andes." *Archaeological Papers of the American Anthropological Association* 8(1):123–41.

90. Julien, Catherine J. 1982. "Inka Decimal Administration in the Lake Titicaca Region." In *The Inca and Aztec States 1400–1800*, edited by George Collier, Renato Rosaldo, and John Wirth, pp. 119–51. New York. Academic Press.

91. Ascher, Marcia, and Robert A. Ascher. 1981. *Code of the Quipu: Study in Media, Mathematics, and Culture.* Ann Arbor: University of Michigan Press.

92. Moore, Jerry D. 2004. "The Social Basis of Sacred Spaces in the Prehispanic Andes: Ritual Landscapes of the Dead in Chimú and Inka Societies." *Journal of Archaeological Method and Theory* 11(1):33–124.

93. Urton, Gary. 1981. *At the Crossroads of the Earth and Sky: An Andean Cosmology.* Austin: University of Texas Press.

94. Zuidema, R. Tom. 1990. *Inca Civilization.*

95. Earls, John and Irene Silverblatt. 1978. "La Realidad Fisica y Social en la Cosmologia Andina." *Proceedings of the International Congress of Americanists* 42(4):299–325.

96. Bauer, Brian S. 1996. "Legitimization of the State in Inca Myth and Ritual." *American Anthropologist* 98(2):327–37.

97. Silverblatt, Irene. 1987. *Moon, Sun, and Witches: Gender Ideologies and Class in Inca and Colonial Peru.* Princeton, NJ: Princeton University Press.

98. Morris, Craig, and Donald E. Thompson. 1985. *Huanaco Pampa: An Inca City and Its Hinterland.* London: Thames & Hudson.

99. Orlove, Benjamin S. 1987. "Stability and Change in Highland Andean Dietary Patterns." In *Food and Evolution: Toward a Theory of Human Food Habits*, edited by Marvin Harris and Eric Ross, pp. 481–515. Philadelphia: Temple University Press.

100. D'Altroy, Terrence N., and Timothy K. Earle. 1985. "Staple Finance, Wealth Finance"; Isbell, William H. 1978. "Environmental Perturbations and the Origin of the Andean State." In *Social Anthropology: Beyond Subsistence and Dating*, edited by Charles Redman, Mary Jane Berman, Edward Curtin, William Langhorne, Jr., Nina Versaggi, and Jeffery Wanser, pp. 303–13. New York: Academic Press.

The Chinese Great Tradition

Figure 8.0.   Chinese junk, nineteenth century (Ratzel 1898:440).

PRONUNCIATION GUIDE*

THE FOLLOWING IS THE APPROXIMATE PRONUNCIATION OF A selection of Chinese words in chapter 8:

KEY

a = *a* in f*a*ther
j = *j* in *j*acket
ay = *ay* in d*ay*
ou = *ou* in *ou*ch
oo = *oo* in f*oo*d
e = *e* in b*e*d
i = i in b*i*t
ng = *ng* in si*ng*
ts, tz = no precise English equivalents
ee = *ee* in b*ee*t
• = Syllable division
/ = Stress
Zhoukoudian [tzoo • koo • dian/]

K'ung Fu tzu [koong • foo • tzoo]
Meng-tzu [meng • tzoo]
Hzun Tzu [tzen • tzoo]
kwei [goo • way]
Xinjiang [shin • jiang]
hsiao [shou]
t'ien-ming [tian • ming/]
Huang-ti [wang • dee/]
An-yang [an • iang]

Note on transcription: Officially, the government of the People's Republic of China uses the Pin-yin system to write Chinese words in the Roman alphabet, but over the years scholars have used various spellings for transcribing Chinese words into the Roman alphabet. This chapter follows the form used by the primary published sources consulted, even though these may vary from the official spellings. There are

263

also differences in pronunciation in different parts of China and between Taiwan and the People's Republic. The suggested pronunciations are generalized for English speakers and omit the vocal tones that would be crucial for native speakers. This makes some words unstressed.

LEARNING OBJECTIVES

After studying this chapter you should be able to do the following:

1. Compare the basic organization of Chinese civilization with the civilizations of ancient Mesopotamia, the Andes, and Hawaii, identifying parallel developments and points of contrast.
2. Explain how tribal leaders could use shamanism, clans, and lineages to transform tribes into chiefdoms and states and make themselves divine rulers.
3. Identify common patterns underlying the origin of chiefdoms and states in China, Mesopotamia, the Andes, and Hawaii.
4. Explain how religious, or moral, belief and practice helped the Chinese nobility integrate the empire, focusing specifically on the Confucian Great Tradition.
5. Distinguish between Great Tradition and Little Tradition cultures in China, referring to their respective distinctive features, and explain how and why each is reproduced. Relate each of these cultures to the hierarchy of urban places.
6. Describe how labor-intensive preindustrial Chinese agriculture was able to support 500 million people, making comparisons with capital-intensive U.S. production systems and the land-extensive shifting cultivation system in tribal Amazonia.
7. Describe the distribution of social power in village-level China in comparison with tribal villages and explain why Chinese poverty might be attributed to exploitation rather than overpopulation.
8. Describe the formation and structure of Chinese families and households and discuss how the dynamics of domestic life shape the relations between men and women, young and old.

In this chapter and chapter 9, we will examine the great cultural traditions of China, India, and Islam. All are important area-study specializations that anthropology shares with history and geography. Because these cultures continue to shape the lives of well over half of the contemporary world's peoples, understanding them is essential to understanding world cultures. Traditional China is the largest imperial state to survive into the twentieth century on a preindustrial

base. With a population that probably numbered 400 million people by 1850, China is a dramatic example of an empire based on moral authority and a super-intensive agricultural system using human labor. Yet it was also the largest early literate civilization, with cities and a monetary economy continuously in place for more than 2,000 years. Chinese villagers, as a tax-paying rural peasantry, provide a sharp contrast with the egalitarian, politically autonomous tribal villagers of Amazonia seen in chapter 2.

IMPERIAL CHINA AND THE MANDATE OF HEAVEN

In China, the elite-directed politicization process produced a village-state civilization, which began with the Shang dynasty, perhaps as early as 2000 BC, and continued with only minor change up to 1949, when the People's Republic was established. As with Andean civilization, under the village-state mode of production, the persistence of Chinese civilization required self-sufficient villagers to support the royal capital and the ruling class with their taxes, tribute, and labor. The villagers consented in the belief that the divine monarch would, in turn, keep the cosmos in order, thus ensuring the good life in the villages. Chinese cities were political and ceremonial centers where the elites and their retainers lived. They were sustained by the labor and surplus production extracted from the villages. People were encouraged to imagine that the Chinese state functioned like an enormous village based on patrilineages, ancestor worship, and kinship-based reciprocity. Village life revolved around subsistence farming, the performance of rituals centered on nature deities and patrilineal ancestors, and the daily obligations of kinship and community. The ritual observances and sacrifices by the villagers were mirrored by similar rituals conducted in the royal capital for the benefit of the entire kingdom. Rulers were divinely appointed and held power as a "mandate from heaven" as long as they promoted village welfare and maintained order in the kingdom.

"Chinese" is not a single language, although there was a proto-Chinese common ancestor language. The predominant Chinese languages are all classified as Sino-Tibetan and are spoken by more than a billion people. Sino-Tibetan includes 12 modern Chinese languages with more than a million speakers each and more than 275 other languages scattered throughout southern and eastern China, Tibet, the Himalayas, and Burma. Japanese, Korean, and Mongolian are different languages grouped in the Altaic language family, which also includes Turkish and Ainu. The long use of a common writing system by speakers of related languages that are mutually unintelligible has led to the unfortunate use of the term *dialect* to refer to what are actually distinct languages. Chinese written characters are logographic—they refer to entire words and can retain their meaning with different pronunciation, in different languages. According to linguists, dialects must be mutually intelligible variations of a single language.

In China, the term *Han* is applied to all speakers of Chinese languages. Standard Chinese, or Mandarin, is spoken in northern China, and official Chinese is based on the Beijing dialect. All Sino-Tibetan languages are based on monosyllable words, and most are tonal—that is, the tone of a syllable constitutes a phonemic distinction, which makes a meaning difference in words.

The Nature of Early Chinese Civilization

China is a vast subcontinental area of 3.6 million square miles (9.5 million km²), approximately the same size as the United States. In the south, China reaches into the tropics; in the north, it reaches the subarctic. Much of the eastern half of the country, including the Tibetan Plateau and the Xinjiang (Sinkiang) region, is mountainous, relatively barren, and inhospitable and will not be treated in this chapter. Eastern China is divided into a northern temperate zone and a southern subtropical zone, with a dividing line running midway between China's two great rivers, the Hwang Ho (Huang He), or Yellow River, in the north and the Ch'ang Chiang (Yangtze), or Long River, in the south (see figure 8.1). The great Chinese agrarian civilizations developed on the rich alluvial soils along the lower reaches of these two rivers, primarily in the relatively flat plains and lake areas of the North China Plain at elevations below 650 feet (200 m). The temperate Hwang Ho zone was the center of millet and wheat production, while the warmer and wetter Ch'ang Chiang tropical zone was the main rice-producing area. Collectively, these grains were the primary foods.

Marvin Harris characterized traditional China as an agromanagerial state resembling the Inca state. The Chinese **peasantry** was subject to large-scale conscript labor service but, in theory, received emergency aid from the state in times of scarcity. The peasantry was also subject to the local elite, who extracted taxes and rents. A contrast can be drawn between this type of peasantry and European **feudalism**, in which serfs were granted hereditary rights to use land in exchange for payment of rent and military service to local lords. Chinese peasants were potentially subject to exploitation by both local elites and the central government, although the peasant was allowed relative freedom to relocate and upward mobility was possible.

The institutionalization of ancestor worship by the Shang state, the earliest well-documented Chinese state, had important consequences that helped set the future direction of Chinese civilization. With **ancestor worship**, the king was the central religious figure who served as his own priest, and the kingdom was in effect a **theocracy**. All lineage heads also worshiped their ancestors, and the whole kingdom was integrated as a single great politico-religious family, leaving little room for conflicting loyalties. Ancestor worship, especially involving lavish mortuary gifts and human sacrifice, emphasized the permanence of the social hierarchy and kinship structure. There was no difference between the secular and the sacred, there was no ambiguity in the system, and everything was assumed to work as long as everyone followed their hierarchically structured kinship-ritual obligations. The virtual deification of the ruler in Chinese civilization closely resembled the status of rulers in the Ur III and Inca empires, as well as in the Hawaiian kingdom.

Ancestor worship was thus a "strategic custom" that provided the foundation for the later elaboration of the concept of *hsiao*, or **filial piety**. In Mesopotamia, by contrast, there was a distinct priesthood, although temple and palace were not always in harmony and the clan and lineage system was not institutionalized. Even though one can speak analytically of social classes in early China, the emic view of the social system was kinship based, and the dominant value was family harmony. This certainly must have minimized the potential for conflict that the grossly unequal flow of resources might otherwise have generated.

Wealth and power in the Chinese system derived from control of the labor force, as in Inca Peru. A vast conscript labor army was mobilized for the construction of the 1,400-mile (2,250 km) Great Wall along the northern boundary of China (see figure 8.2) during the Ch'in dynasty (approximately 215 BC). Significantly, the major river valleys run east and west and thus remain in broadly similar ecological zones, reducing the importance of trade and providing little incentive for the development of a merchant class. The Grand Canal, only one of many monumental water development projects, linked the Ch'ang Chiang in

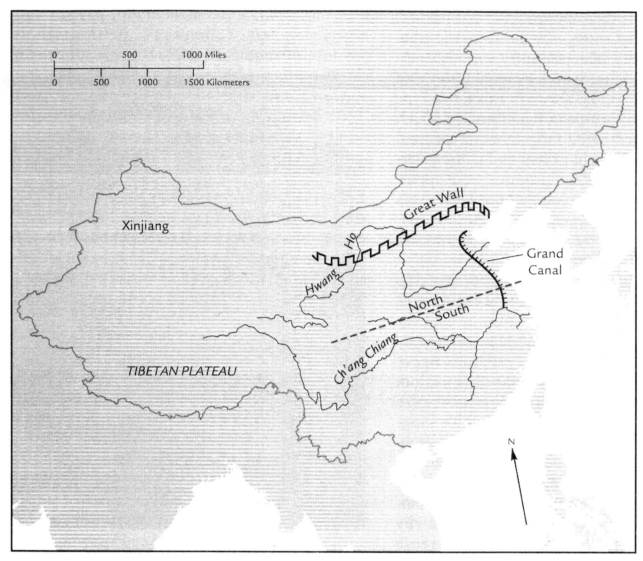

Figure 8.1. Map of the major rivers and regions of China.

the south with the Hwang Ho in the north by AD 610, providing a major boost to trade.

Chinese cities contained temples and palaces and were walled like Mesopotamian cities, but there were important differences. Chinese cities were intentionally designed to symbolize the emperor's central position in the universe. The city was a great square, aligned with the four cardinal directions, with the palace in the center, presumably aligned with the North Star on the earth's central axis. The world was literally thought to pivot about the emperor. In contrast to the Mesopotamian city-state, ancient Chinese cities were not economically self-sufficient, but depended on their immediate hinterlands for basic subsistence. They were not economic centers but were designed to reproduce the political and ideological infrastructure.

The imperial system of Chinese government was an expansion of the earlier Shang system, and it remained in place with variations in detail until 1911, when the last emperor was removed from power. Historians distinguish four stages in the development of Chinese government: Patrimonial (1766–221 BC), Meritocracy (221 BC–AD 220), Aristocracy (220–906 AD), and Gentry (960–1911 AD) (see table 8.1). Over the centuries, the political structure varied with cycles of civil war and conquest, with fluctuations in the strength of the central government versus regional kingdoms, and with shifts in the importance of local families. Important changes also occurred in the system of recruitment to political office. The patrimonial stage will be described in the next section using the Shang example. The rulers of the Chou dynasty, which overthrew

Figure 8.2.   The Great Wall of China in 1907 (Herbert Ponting).

Table 8.1.   Chinese Empires, 1766 BC—Present*

Modern China	1949–	People's Republic of China
(AD 1912–)	1912–1949	Republic of China
Gentry China (AD 960-1911)	1644–1911	Ch'ing dynasty: civil service exam abolished (1905); last Chinese monarchy
	1368–1644	Ming dynasty (Chinese rule)
	1272–1368	Yuan Dynasty (Mongol rule)
	960–1279	Sung dynasty: civil service exam established; invention of moveable type; Confucian scholar-officials
Aristocratic China (AD 220–906)	618–907	T'ang dynasty
	610	Great Canal Built
	265–420	Tsin dynasty
Meritocratic China) (221 BC–AD 220)	202 BC–AD 220	Han dynasty: paper invented (AD 105); Buddhism introduced (AD 65); Confucianism established as state orthodoxy
		Chin dynasty: imperial rule; hereditary rule abolished; written language standardized, Great Wall built
Patrimonial China (1766–221 BC)		Chou dynasty: iron; cavalry; mandate of heaven established; written laws; era of Confucious (551–479), Mencius (371–289), Hzun Tzu (298–238); followed by Warring States (403–221)

Sources: Chang (1986) and Dull (1990)

*This is not an exhaustive list of all Chinese kingdoms and empires. Only the most prominent are included, corresponding to the major phases in political development. Precise dates used by different authorities do not always agree, and there are gaps in the sequence and in the historically overlapping empires.

the Shang, elaborated the concept of the mandate of heaven (*t'ien-ming*) as the formal legitimization of dynastic rule. Chou kings called themselves "The Son of Heaven" to emphasize that their rule was a mandate from heaven. This led to the related concept of the "bad last emperor" because a dynasty could end only when the mandate of heaven was withdrawn due to the emperor's misconduct.

The Ch'in rulers, who ushered in imperial rule in 221 BC, called themselves *Huang-ti*, literally "august god" usually translated as "emperor," because their kings were not considered to be gods. The imperial bureaucracy under the Ch'in was territorially structured and more elaborate than the familial organization of the Shang, presumably because the former patrimonial system could not deal with the increased scale of empire. The emperor had three officials and nine ministers who ran the central government. The hinterland was divided into forty-two commanderies (*chun*), subdivided into prefectures (*hsien*); each territorial unit had an imperially appointed administrator, an inspector, and a police chief. Imperial officials were "outsiders," prohibited from operating within their home territories to minimize opportunities for corruption. Regional governments developed their own large bureaucracies with many positions that, in theory, were filled by local individuals who were promoted on the basis of merit; thus, this entire period was characterized as a meritocracy. The constant struggle against corruption led to the creation of provinces as a higher-level political unit, whose officials could oversee the commanderies.

During the aristocracy period, recruitment to the bureaucracy was dominated by membership in a nine-level hereditary hierarchy of social status. Recruitment during the gentry period was based on the examination system, which became highly elaborated and allowed more social mobility than under the aristocracy. Prospective bureaucrats took highly competitive examinations in the Confucian classics. There were three exam levels: provincial, national, and imperial (palace). The system was potentially open to anyone who could gain admission to the government schools. Only 2 to 3 percent passed their preliminary exams and were permitted to take the palace exam; after passing the palace exam, the person was rewarded with entry to elite or gentry status and a position in the bureaucracy. The examination system, which was ultimately controlled by the emperor, reduced the potential conflicts between local aristocratic families and the central government

and gave more people an interest in maintaining the system.

High Shamanism: The Emergence of the Shang Dynasty

The earliest Chinese states appeared by approximately 2000 to 1000 BC out of a Chinese co-tradition, or interaction sphere (see box 8.1). Like the Andean cultural tradition, the Chinese co-tradition contained elements that are still prominent features of Chinese culture and directly preceded the first Chinese urban civilizations. In the politicization process, towns became administrative and ritual centers, chiefs became kings who founded dynasties, simple writing systems were developed, and the production of crafts and specialized wealth objects was greatly expanded. This was the beginning of the period of initial Chinese civilization, which historians refer to as the Three Dynasties—the semimythical Hsia, the Shang, and Chou.

Shang (1766–1045 BC) is the earliest well-described civilization of early dynastic China, thanks to extensive excavations carried out since 1928 by Chinese archaeologists at An-yang, a major Shang center north of the Hwang Ho in Henan (Honan) province (see figure 8.3). An-yang was a sprawling urban complex centered on a palace-temple complex of elaborate wooden buildings constructed on low platforms of stamped earth. The center was surrounded by residential areas, cemeteries, and specialized workshops. The graves of nobles and commoners were clearly distinguished by the quality and abundance of grave goods. In addition, rank was indicated by the better quality of the dentition in higher-status individuals. This suggests that social stratification operated such that the nobility enjoyed better nutrition than commoners.

One of the most spectacular aspects of An-yang was the royal cemetery where eleven Shang kings and their consorts were buried. The royal tombs were wood-lined pits, up to 59 by 52 feet (18 by 16 m) at the top and 98 feet (30 m) deep, which were entered by four long excavated ramps oriented to the four compass directions. It is estimated that some 7,000 working days may have been required in their construction, but even more labor was invested in the treasure trove of bronze and jade grave goods.

Most royal tombs were looted over the centuries, but in 1976 an unlooted tomb belonging to Fu Hao, wife of a Shang king, was found to contain 440 bronzes, 590 jades, and many other bone, stone, ivory, and ceramic objects, along with 16 human sacrifices and 6 dogs. Similar to royal tombs at Ur, the An-yang

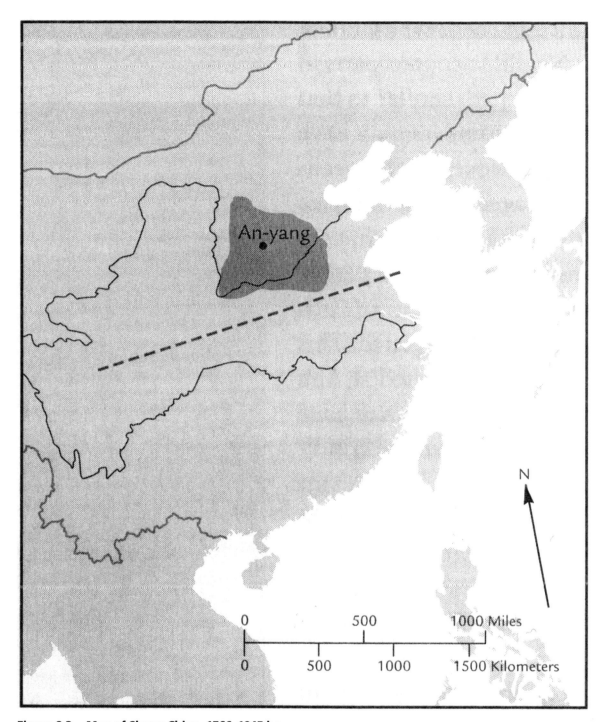

Figure 8.3. Map of Shang China, 1766–1045 bc.

royal burials and palace foundations were often accompanied by human and animal sacrifices. Whole chariots with horses still in harness were buried. One An-yang tomb contained 111 human skulls, and more than 600 people were sacrificed in the construction of a single Shang building. Such large-scale sacrifices clearly foreshadowed the recently uncovered 7,000-man life-size terra-cotta army buried with the first Ch'in emperor about 210 BC.

Historians sometimes imply that early Chinese states evolved directly from tribes, suggesting a certain inevitability and naturalness to the process. However, tribes are not miniature states waiting to grow. Aggrandizing leaders must first transform tribal societies into small chiefdoms by persuading people to make them rulers and to accept hereditary social ranks and unequal access to resources. The archaeological record suggests that in China, just as in Mesopotamia and the Andes, this politicization process occurred over a period of some 2,000 years in only a few places and under unique circumstances.

The elite-directed transformation of tribes into chiefdoms and chiefdoms into expansive kingdoms changed conditions in the neighboring tribal world. The new rulers transformed tribal societies under their control into **ethnic groups**, freezing their boundaries and imposing formal identities and cultural markers to make them easier to control. This imperial process changed formerly independent tribal peoples into peasants who retained distinctive linguistic or cultural characteristics. On the periphery of their territories, imperial rulers sometimes designated ethnically distinct "tribes" as political dependencies, allowing them to retain more autonomy than peasants. Such tribes were permitted to run their own village-level affairs, but they still paid taxes or tribute.

Even though Chinese urban civilization emerged some 1,500 years later than Sumerian city-states, urbanization in China apparently occurred independently of outside influences. There was no colonial expansion from Mesopotamia into China that might have led to the founding of urban centers, nor was there any obvious borrowing leading to the introduction of economic, religious, or political influences from Mesopotamia that might have indirectly stimulated cultural development. Borrowing can occur if the idea for some cultural trait, rather than its direct transfer, inspires its development in another culture.

The Chinese state was apparently constructed by political elites who gained control of the religious system and used it to increase their political power, creating self-reinforcing growth in wealth and power that allowed them to turn towns into cities and expand a complex chiefdom into a kingdom. This suggests that what people believed about the invisible world of the supernatural may have been more important politically than the technology that they used to make a living. Clearly, elites can use the superstructure of a culture to direct cultural growth and development.

The religious foundation of Chinese civilization can be called high shamanism because it was a direct elaboration of the shamanistic communication with spirits that characterizes tribal cultures. The official cosmologies of early dynastic China incorporated concepts of a stratified universe connected by a world tree, animal intermediaries, and transformations. The critical difference, however, was that unlike Amazonian or Australian shamanism, Chinese high shamanism involved highly exclusive communication with specific ancestors and deities who were sources of wisdom and supporters of the social hierarchy. Communication with the ancestors was by means of **scapulimancy**, which was conducted by full-time ritual specialists (see box 8.2).

This interpretation rejects theories of state formation that rely on economic determinants as prime movers. Early Chinese kings may not have gained their positions merely because they controlled irrigation systems, trade, or the means of production, or because certain social classes gained control over strategic subsistence resources. No significant change in Chinese agriculture preceded state formation. Bronze was an important technological innovation, but it was used to manufacture ritual paraphernalia, weapons, and chariots, which provided both religious and military support for elite political power. Early Chinese leaders succeeded in turning themselves into rulers by their skillful manipulation of both ideological and material systems.

Table 8.2. Prehistoric and Early Historic China

BC	
2000–1000	Early Chinese States
	Writing 1400 BC
	Shang Dynasty (1766–1045 BC)
3000–2000	Lung-shan culture, social stratification, complex chiefdoms, towns, metallurgy, ancestor cult
5000–3000	Yang-shao Culture, clans, lineages, ranking, simple chiefdoms
7000–5000	Regional Neolithic Cultures, early farming villages, ceramics
BP	
12,000–9000	Epipaleolithic, foragers, modern climate
50,000–12,000	Upper Paleolithic, modern *Homo sapiens*
200,000–50,000	Middle Paleolithic, archaic *Homo sapiens*
1 million to 200,000	Lower Paleolithic, *Homo erectus* in Zhoukoudian caves

Source: Chang (1986).

BOX 8.1. THE PREHISTORIC ORIGINS OF CHINESE CIVILIZATION

China is famous for the site of Zhoukoudian (Chou-k'ou-tien), west of Beijing (Peking), where fossils of the early hominid *Homo erectus*, dating to the Lower Paleolithic at approximately 1 million to 200,000 BP (before the present), were discovered in the 1930s. *Homo erectus* began to look more like *Homo sapiens* beginning about 200,000 years ago (see table 8.2), and fully modern peoples were clearly present by at least 25,000 BP. The pre-Neolithic of China is not well known, but this Late Pleistocene–Early Holocene period from about 12,000 to 9000 BP seems to mirror some of the general trends seen in other parts of the world, with foraging peoples steadily intensifying their subsistence activities. This trend is suggested, for example, by the appearance of microlithic tools— small, thin pieces of sharp stone, often a fragment of a long blade, which may be mounted on a shaft.

Wild rice and millet, which became the foundation of Chinese civilization, are spread through a wide zone from the Ganges region of India to southern China. Millet, which includes several grasses producing small round seeds, was being cultivated in the Hwang Ho river basin by 6000 BC, and rice in the lower Ch'ang Chiang region by 5000 BC, only a few centuries after their Neolithic counterparts in the Near East. Domestication in East Asia may have followed a path similar to that of the Near East.

The wild ancestral rices and millets may have expanded during favorable climatic conditions in the Early Holocene. The availability of very rich and predictable resources may have encouraged mobile foragers to sedentarize, which resulted in gradual population growth. Subtle climatic changes might have threatened the natural supply of the wild grains and encouraged people to turn to intentional cultivation, selecting plants that produced larger, more numerous seeds that ripened at the same time and stuck together when harvested. This is the same process that probably occurred in the Middle East, as illustrated at Abu Hureya (see table 7.1). Domestication may have occurred independently in China, at the limits of the natural range, where conditions would have been marginal and selection pressures most severe.

Early farming villages developed into seven regional cultures scattered throughout northern and southwestern China. These apparently were tribal-scale, basically egalitarian societies, with a wide range of domesticates, including millet, pigs, dogs, chickens, and water buffalo. People used stone sickles, mortars and pestles, and ceramics, including a three-legged pot, or *ting*, which later became such a prominent shape in bronze. The period from approximately 5000 to 4000 BC was characterized by steadily increasing cultural complexity, growing diversification, and emerging social ranking, as in the Mesopotamian and Andean regions. Status differences in burials appear in the Yang-shao culture in the lower Hwang Ho plain, suggesting that by 4000 to 2000 BC, simple chiefdoms had emerged. The larger mobilization of labor implied by the monumental constructions and craft specialization in Lung-shan and later Shang cultures suggests the transformation of simple chiefdoms into complex chiefdoms or small kingdoms. The expanding regional cultures had begun to influence one another such that a pan-Chinese culture could be distinguished on the basis of shared art styles, burial practices, and inferred common religious beliefs involving shamanism and ancestor worship. The best example of this period is the Lung-shan culture (3000–2000 BC), which showed the first bronze work, divination based on scapulimancy (divination using animal bones), elaborate burials, craft specialization, and large villages fortified with walls of stamped earth.

BOX 8.2. EARLY CHINESE SCAPULIMANCY

The basic technique of divination by scapulimancy involves interpreting the pattern of cracks that develops in a heated piece of flat bone, such as a scapula or turtle plastron (lower shell). In Shang China, scapulimancy was used to guide the conduct of official business in the royal court and was carried out by specialists at the request of the king. A royal representative would submit an official yes-or-no question to the diviner—for example, asking whether a proposed military campaign would be successful. The diviner would then apply heat to a specially polished, grooved, and notched bone, usually a turtle plastron or water buffalo scapula. The preparation helped direct the cracking into a center-line crack with intersecting side cracks. The angle of the side cracks and other details were then interpreted by an official prognosticator, who came up with an answer to the question. Each piece of cracked bone was inscribed by an official archivist with signs and pictographic characters, recording the date, name of the inquirer, question, answer, and final outcome. These bones were then archived for future reference. Some 100,000 inscribed oracle bones have been recovered from An-yang, and they have provided detailed insights into the organization of Shang society.

Shang Society

At the center of the Shang social hierarchy was the king, who was a member of the royal lineage (*wang tsu*) within the ruling clan (*tsu*), a patrilineal descent group that was not strictly exogamous. In many ways, the Shang system shows striking parallels to the organization of the Inca royal *ayllus*, but the differences are obvious enough that no direct connections need be posited. The Shang royal lineage was apparently divided into ten ritual units named after the celestial signs naming the ten days of the week and structuring the ritual calendar. These units were arranged in two groups between which the kingship alternated according to specific rules of succession, with the alternate group serving as the king's councilors. The royal court contained the king's many wives or consorts, princes, and at least twenty categories of titled officials, such as priest, prime minister, and diviner. The court and its dependents must have been large, because individual kings are known to have had up to 64 wives and 120 diviners.

The political power of Shang rulers is shown by the standing armies of up to 10,000 men that they commanded, and there are reports of some 30,000 war captives being taken in a single campaign. The army was organized into 100-man foot companies, with three companies to a regiment, and chariot companies of 5 chariots and 15 men, with 5 companies to a squadron. Troops were armed with bows, bronze halberds, knives, and shields. Rural towns were also organized as militia units and could supply thousands more troops if needed. Military force was an important means of expanding the state and maintaining internal order.

Law, in its formal sense (see box 8.3), supported the Shang social hierarchy, as in ancient Sumer, although no Shang law codes survive. Early historical texts referring to this period and fragmentary Shang records indicate that a well-developed court system must have existed. Subordinates were obligated to obey their rulers, and lawbreakers were harshly punished by various forms of shackling, mutilation, and execution. Rulers were obligated not to be too oppressive; if they failed, they faced supernatural punishments such as natural disasters or overthrow by a rival.

The underlying religious basis of the Shang state was the assumption that the king was the exclusive channel, via his personal ancestors, to *Ti*, the high god, who was responsible for the welfare of the entire population and the fertility of nature. The king was a key node in a supernatural communication network.

He called himself "I, The One Man" or "I, The Unique One," assuming absolute power as the parental authority over the whole land. By means of his diviners and through proper ritual, prayer, and sacrifice, the king could persuade his dead ancestors to appeal to the high god on behalf of the whole community.

The status and prestige of Shang royalty was further affirmed by the symbols of royalty: banners, battle axes, and bronze pots of particular size and shape, bearing specific decorations and inscriptions. Royal objects were often decorated with stylized animals such as tigers, which reinforced the king's religious role, because animals also served as supernatural messengers in Shang mythology. The parallels between Shang use of the tiger as a symbol of power and the jaguar at Chavín are striking.

The Shang state, like the Inca empire, was divided into four quarters, oriented to the compass directions. Away from the capital, which was the political, economic, and ceremonial center, the hinterland population lived in walled towns (*yi*), ruled by lords. The king claimed formal title to the entire kingdom and was responsible for its welfare, but the lords personally managed it to maintain and increase the power of the royal lineage. New towns were centrally planned and built as a unit by ranked lords to whom the king granted a clan name, town land, a title, ancestor tablets, and appropriate ritual paraphernalia. The townspeople constituted the working class or peasantry (*ch'ung-jen*) and were organized into ranked patrilineages (*tsu*). Because numerous pictographic lineage names depict various economic activities, lin-

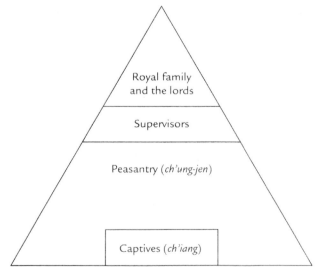

Figure 8.4. Social hierarchy of the Shang state (redrafted from Chang 1980:231, Figure 60).

eages may have been occupationally specialized. War captives (*ch'iang*) were at the very bottom of the social pyramid (see figure 8.4) and served as laborers; they also were probably the primary source of human sacrifices, because divination records list more than 7,400 such victims.

Modern Chinese scholars, following Marxist terminology, often refer to Shang as a slave society, whereas Western writers refer to a "free" peasantry. Probably only the war captives were slaves in a formal sense, but the bulk of the population enjoyed few of the benefits of their own labor. Even their semisubterranean housing symbolically separated them from the elite, who resided on stamped-earth platforms.

It is difficult to see what benefits, other than protection, the peasantry derived from the Shang state. Goods and services flowed to the center to support the army and the royal court, although some wealth returned as rewards to the lords ruling the towns. Writing was not concerned with recording economic transactions but dealt only with divination records and the identification of clans and lineages. There was no market system or trader class. Kinship obligations and religious duty were the primary foundations of the social structure, which basically resembled a large Hawaiian chiefdom.

BOX 8.3. THE LAW AND THE STATE

Law, if broadly defined as social control, is a universal. However, significant differences exist between social control in tribal societies—where basic equality and low population density reduce internal conflict to levels that kinship roles can easily manage—and social control in politically organized societies. Imperial societies face more difficulties. Anthropologist Leopold Pospisil identifies four attributes of law:

1. Authority: the ability to enforce a decision
2. Intention: the assumption that legal decisions will be applied universally
3. Obligation: specific rights and duties for different categories of people
4. Sanction: punishment for lawbreakers

These attributes can be recognized in the conflict-resolution mechanisms of some tribal societies. Law as a formal concept, however, is most appropriately applied to larger-scale, ranked-and-stratified societies and especially to politically organized states, where it serves a critical social-control function. States have courts, judges, and formally codified laws, which may be written. The authority of a king comes from his executioners, the palace guard, and the standing army. Legal codes specify what a ruler can demand of his subordinate subjects and what the subjects can expect from their rulers.

Confucianism and Liturgical Government

Confucianism is a Western label for what the Chinese themselves referred to as *fu-chia*, "family of scholars." It is a scholarly tradition and moral order, based on the humanistic teachings of Confucius (K'ung-Fu-tzu, 551–479 BC). Confucianism was not a religion as such, but it became a virtual state cult because it advocated filial piety and perpetuation of the ritual and political traditions of the Chou dynasty, which was at the core of Chinese civilization.

Confucianism taught that social order was based on virtue that came from ritual performance, beginning with household-level ancestor worship and moving up the hierarchy to the emperor. Confucius—whose teachings were preserved in the "Analects"—and other major teachers who followed, such as Mencius (Meng-tzu, 371–289 BC) and Hzun Tzu (298–238 BC), sought to promote practical ideals of good government, citizenship, and domestic life that would preserve a stable system of social inequality.

Confucianism was institutionalized by 124 BC with the creation of an imperial university focused on the five classics:

1. The *I Ching*, "Book of Change," is concerned with divination according to the principles of Confucian ethics and *yin-yang* complementary oppositions.
2. The *Shu Ching*, "Book of Documents," spells out the ideals of statecraft to be followed by the "Sage King" and all bureaucrats.
3. The *Shih Ching*, "Book of Songs," contains Confucian poetry.
4. The *Li Chi*, "Book of Rites," specifies the formal duties and rituals between social classes, kin, and husbands and wives.
5. The *Ch'un-ch'iu*, "Spring and Autumn Annals," deals with dynastic history.

Confucianism constituted the Chinese Great Tradition—elite culture, or high culture—because it was propagated by the literate elite and was directly involved with official ritual and the maintenance of the bureaucracy. Under Confucian ideals, which remained important into modern times, Chinese society was divided into a class system that was very similar to that of Shang times, but increased population resulted in more extreme social inequality.

The Confucian Great Tradition represented the power of the emperor in the form of great palaces, temples, rituals, literature, and artworks, which collectively must have inspired feelings of awe and subordination in the commoners. This elite culture, together with the literate and institutionalized elements of Taoism and Buddhism, receives most attention from Western historians and students of comparative religion, art, and literature. However, commoners, who constituted 98 percent of the population, were only passive participants in the Great Tradition; they also maintained their own **Little Tradition**, or popular cul-

ture. (The Chinese Little Tradition will be examined in the section on village life.)

By the end of the Ch'ing dynasty, under the Manchu rulers (AD 1644–1911), some 700 people belonged to the emperor's clan at the top of the hierarchy (see figures 8.5 and 8.6). Perhaps 40,000 more were part of the formal administrative bureaucracy. Beneath this group were four social classes: (1) scholars (*shih*), (2) merchants (*shang*), (3) artisans (*kung*), and (4) farmers (*nung*). The 7.5 million or so scholar-bureaucrats were part of the privileged elite (*kwei*) gentry (see figure 8.7), who controlled local affairs and enjoyed many special privileges.

The elite were set apart by special dress and their rigid adherence to Confucian ideals, linguistic forms, and ritual. In all, elites and their families may have

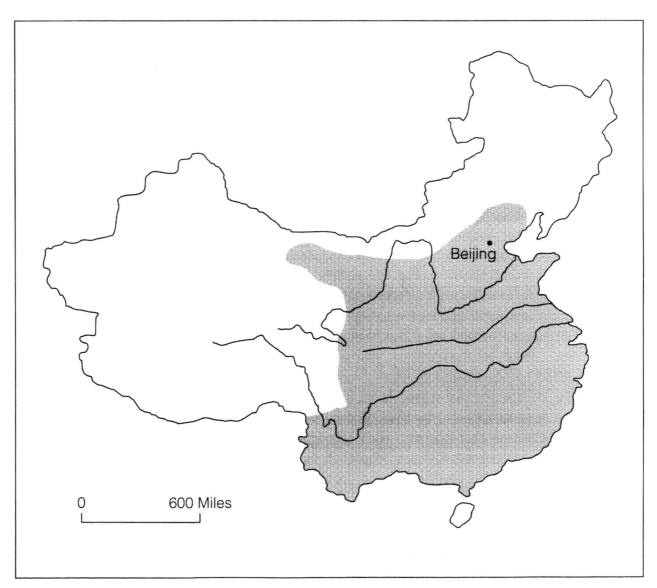

Figure 8.5. Map of Ch'ing China, 1900.

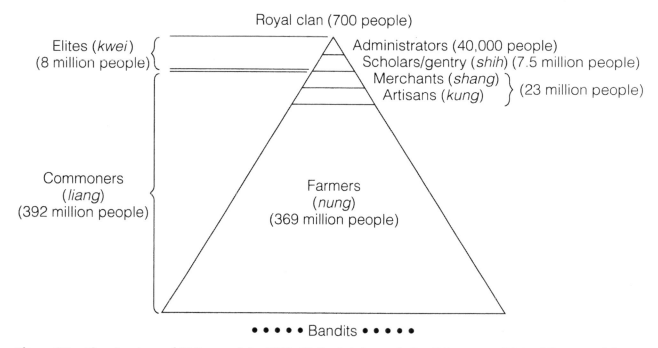

Royal clan (700 people)

Elites (*kwei*)
(8 million people)

Administrators (40,000 people)
Scholars/gentry (*shih*) (7.5 million people)
Merchants (*shang*)
Artisans (*kung*) } (23 million people)

Commoners
(*liang*)
(392 million people)

Farmers
(*nung*)
(369 million people)

• • • • • Bandits • • • • •

Figure 8.6.   The structure of Ch'ing society, 1900. Of the total population 7.7 percent (30.8 million people) was urban and 92.3 percent (369.2 million people) was rural.

Figure 8.7.   Mandarin, administrative official, Ch'ing China 1890s (Ratzel 1898:465).

totaled 8 million by 1900, perhaps less than 2 percent of the total population. Some authorities distinguish between three elite subgroups: (1) the upper gentry, who were entitled to formal offices in the bureaucracy, (2) scholars who did not qualify for high office, and (3) nonscholars who derived elite status from independent economic or political power.

The bulk of the population, which may have grown to some 400 million by the mid-nineteenth century, constituted the commoners (*Liang*), who were primarily farmers with very small landholdings. At the very bottom were outcasts, such as bandits and prostitutes.

Confucian concepts of formal ritual and etiquette, or *li*, regulated social conduct and helped people feel good about their social station. The Chinese system can be called **liturgical government**, or "culturalism," because Confucianism created a form of moral nationalism that held the empire together in the absence of overt political or military force. The emperor occupied the ritual center of the world, where he held lavish state rituals and established a formal ritual calendar, like the Inca emperor. The emperor lived a leisurely life of conspicuous consumption, defining and legitimizing the cultural ideal for the elite. In this view, which was probably accurate only during certain historical periods, the emperor was a politically weak figurehead who supported himself from local tribute, the imperial monopoly on the Grand Canal connecting north and south China, the salt tax, and foreign trade. The emperor's primary political role was to award scholarly degrees and official appointments and to maintain overall peace and security.

The local nobility and elite had virtually full political and economic autonomy in the countryside. Because they earned only token salaries, they supported themselves by extracting taxes and rents from the peasantry. The provincial elite returned little material support to the center but acknowledged the superior status of the imperial court by following the centrally issued ritual calendar and by observing the *kowtow* (*k'ou-t'ou*), or ritual prostration. Whenever an official received a message from the emperor, the official was required to bow to his knees three times, rapping his forehead against the floor three times for each bow. This was a small cost to pay to support a high culture that quieted the peasantry with the sayings of Mencius and Confucius that "inequalities are in the nature of things" (Mencius) and that one should "seek no happiness that does not pertain to your lot in life" (Confucius).

The *Li Chi*, "*Book of Rites*"

The Confucian classic, the *Li Chi*, was compiled during the Han dynasty in the first century BC by Confucian scholars. It specified details of dress, diet, ritual, and interaction between all ranks, offices, and kinship categories. The Inca state was no doubt guided by a similar cultural code; however, in the Inca case, the details were part of the oral tradition and were not compiled in a formal book. The *Li Chi* provides a remarkable inside view of the cultural minutiae of the Chinese Great Tradition. For example, for state rituals during the first month of spring, the *Li Chi* specifies the alignment of stars; the day names to be used; the deities, animals, musical notes, numbers, and tastes; the temple room in which sacrifices are to be offered by the emperor; the bells on the royal carriage; the type of horse drawing the carriage; the color of flags on the carriage; the color of the emperor's robes; and the type of jade ornaments on his cap. According to the *Li Chi*, the emperor is also supposed to eat mutton and wheat from vessels carved to represent sprouting plants, during the first month of spring.

In excruciating detail, the *Li Chi* prescribes deference behavior between officials of different rank. For example:

> All (officers) in attendance on the ruler let the sash hang down till their feet seemed to tread on the lower edge (of their skirt). Their chins projected like the eaves of a house, and their hands were clasped before them low down. Their eyes were directed downwards, and their ears were higher than their eyes. They saw (the ruler) from his girdle up to his collar. They listened to him with their ears turned to the left.

The respective contributions of individuals, families, officials, and the emperor to harmony are described as follows:

> When the four limbs are all well proportioned, and the skin is smooth and full, the individual is in good condition. When there is generous affection between father and son, harmony between brothers, and happy union between husband and wife, the family is in good condition. When the great ministers are observant of the laws, the smaller ministers pure, officers and their duties kept in their regular relations and the ruler and his ministers are correctly helpful to one another, the state is in good condition. When the son of Heaven [the emperor] moves in his virtue as a chariot, with music as his driver, while all the princes conduct their mutual intercourse according to the rules of propriety [*Li*], the great officers maintain the

order between them according to the laws, inferior officers complete one another by their good faith, and the common people guard one another with a spirit of harmony, all under the sky is in good condition. All this produces what we call (the state of) great mutual consideration (and harmony).

When everyone does their duty, the living are fed, the dead are properly buried, and the ancestral spirits are taken care of.

Taoism and Buddhism

Taoism and Buddhism are other important religious and philosophical systems that were part of the Chinese Great Tradition. Both had literate components and shared many elements with Confucianism, but they did not enjoy the official support the state gave Confucianism.

Most prominently, Taoism shares with Confucianism a concern with the *tao*, or "way," which could be identified with the "way of heaven" and all the cosmic forces, as well as with one's social and ritual duty. However, unlike Confucianism, which is strongly secular, Taoism is a mystical religious system that appealed to disaffected commoners and contained messianic elements that sometimes mobilized the peasantry to oppose the established political order. Taoism traces its origins to Lao-tzu (Lao-tze), a religious sage and contemporary of Confucius, who wrote the primary sacred text of Taoism, the *Tao-te Ching*. As a formal religious institution, Taoism has its saints and divinities, diverse sects and schools, and is represented in temples throughout China. There are full-time Taoist priests, who are celibate and live in monasteries. Taoist thought has been an important influence on both Confucianism and folk religion.

Buddhism reached China from India by AD 65, during the Han dynasty, and simply added another literate temple-monastic system and enriched the Chinese pantheon. It ultimately shaped the Taoist and Confucianist traditions and was absorbed into the folk religion, adding concepts of hell, sin, karma, and judgment.

DAILY LIFE IN VILLAGE CHINA

Farmers of Forty Centuries

U.S. Department of Agriculture soil scientist and agriculture professor F. H. King visited China and Japan during the first decade of the twentieth century to learn how these "farmers of forty centuries" could support dense populations and still maintain soil fertility after so many years of permanent agriculture. King found that Chinese farmlands were being cultivated so intensively that they directly supported 1,783 people, 212 cattle or oxen, and 399 pigs per 1 square mile (2.6 km^2), nearly thirty times the comparable human density for the United States at that time. He attributed the success of Chinese agriculture to favorable climate and soils and choice of crops, along with labor-intensive multicropping, intertilling, and terracing and highly efficient use of water and organic fertilizer. He estimated that some 200,000 miles (321,800 km) of major canals supported rice cultivation. Soil fertility was maintained by composting, reclamation of canal mud, manuring, and extensive application of night soil, or human waste. Soil and subsoil were sometimes carried to the village to be mixed with compost and then returned to the field. King credited the Chinese with judiciously rotating legumes in their gardens to improve fertility, even though Western scientists failed to understand their nitrogen-fixing role until 1888. Most of all, King was impressed with the Chinese economy of resource use:

> Almost every foot of land is made to contribute material for food, fuel or fabric. Everything which can be made edible serves as food for man or domestic animals. Whatever cannot be eaten or worn is used for fuel. The wastes of the body, of fuel and of fabric worn beyond other use are taken back to the field; before doing so they are housed against waste from weather, compounded with intelligence and forethought and patiently labored with through one, three or even six months, to bring them into the most efficient form to serve as manure for the soil or as feed for the crop.

Prerevolutionary China's 500 million people were supported by very small farms, usually of less than 5 acres (2 hectares), which were concentrated on just 8 percent of the land. The Chinese agricultural strategy was to apply human labor intensively to the lands that would yield the greatest return per acre. Chinese agriculture was a capital-maintaining, labor-absorbing, intensive hand-gardening system, in which the real crop was human beings. People were produced in the smallest possible space at the lowest energy cost.

In parts of southwest China where the population is low, rice is grown by shifting cultivation in clearings in forested uplands. Rice seeds can also be broadcast onto plowed fields, but the highest yields are obtained when seedlings are grown in nurseries and transplanted by hand into specially prepared diked fields. This is very intensive and highly skilled work. Carefully regulated irrigated flows of river water maintain a delicate ecosystem with the essential nutrients, fungi, and bacteria that produce maximum rice yields. Although transplanted rice brings the highest returns, it requires large, precisely timed labor inputs for uprooting seedlings, replanting, and harvest and thus is impractical unless population is high and landholdings small.

I observed intensive rice replanting in the Philippines by wage laborers on vast commercial estates using chemical inputs, as well as by tribal Ifugao villagers on steep hillsides. The Philippine Ifugao fully appreciated the ecological complexity of their terraced paddy system. Given an appropriate labor force and small landholdings, villagers do not consider capital-intensive technological innovations such as mechanization to be an advantage. Thus, not surprisingly, virtually all of the 77 farm implements described in traditional Chinese agricultural manuals published since AD 1313 were still in use in mid-twentieth-century China. The productivity of labor-intensive Chinese agriculture is remarkable. In 1940, Chinese researchers investigated a village of 611 people, which they called Luts'un, in central Yunnan province in south China. They found that when multicropped, a standard 2,688-square-foot (250-m²) unit of land (called a *kung*) produced 821 pounds (372 kg) of rice and beans per year, yielding approximately 1.147 million kilocalories of food. This assumed good-quality land and an input of 152 hours of human labor (see table 8.3). This is more than 60 times the per-acre productivity from industrially grown American rice in 1975, which required enormous inputs of chemical fertilizers, pesticides, and fossil fuels. The Chinese production system yielded a return of 50 kilocalories of food energy for each kilo-

calorie of human labor expended, whereas the American rice was grown at an energy deficit because of the energy cost of the fossil fuels expended.

The Chinese subsistence system is effective because it makes limited use of draft animals or animal protein. The Chinese diet is typically vegetarian, with only 2 to 3 percent of the caloric intake derived from meat. Only chickens, ducks, and pigs, which are scavengers, are raised to be consumed. They can also be fed rice hulls and bean stalks, whereas large draft animals are costly to feed, especially if valuable cropland is devoted to raising animal food. In some areas, fish ponds were also a significant source of food.

Immiseration, Overpopulation, and Exploitation

With periodic wars and famines, the population of China fluctuated between 30 and 60 million people during most of the first millennium AD, jumping to 100 million by AD 1100 and then moving steadily upward (see figure 8.8). The most dramatic change was the fivefold increase that began after 1400, during the Ming dynasty, and population approached 500 million by the end of the Ch'ing dynasty in 1911. By 1975, China's population reached 800 million, and, by 1990, it exceeded 1 billion. Several factors have been proposed to explain the Ming-Ch'ing increases, including a prolonged period of peace and stability; improvements in health, such as the development of smallpox vaccinations in the sixteenth century; the introduction of new food crops from the Americas; and a global warming trend that improved agricultural conditions.

Although population growth had fundamentally changed the scale of Chinese society by 1900, the culture remained basically the same, and many observers argued that the Chinese peasantry was undergoing a

Table 8.3. The Productivity of Chinese Intensive Agriculture (kcal/kung/year), Luts'un, Kunming, 1940.

	Picuals	kg/ year	kcal/ kg	Total kcal
Rice, hulled	3.8	192	3600	691,200
Broad beans	2.6	130	3380	439,400
Green beans	1.0	50	320	16,000

Total kcal produced: 1,146,600
Input: 20.3 days x 7.5 hours x 1 50 kcal = 22,837
Output-input ratio: 50.2 to 1
Comparison with U.S. Rice

	Production kg/ Acre	kcal/ Acre
U.S., 1975 Hulled rice	828	298,080
Luts'un, 1940 Multicrop	5952	18,345,600

Source: Fei and Chang (1945:70, Table 12).

Notes: The caloric value of "waste" by-products such as bean stalks, rice hulls, and straw, which are used as animal feeds, are not included. 1 *picual* = 50.1 kg; 1 *kung* = 250 m2 of land, 40 *kung* = 1 hectare, 16 *kung* = 1 acre; 1 *kung* of labor = 1 person day of labor, 7.5 hours; 1 hour of labor = 150 kcal expended.

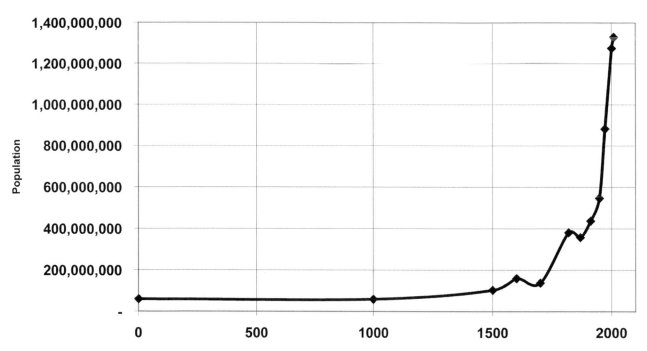

Figure 8.8. Chinese population growth, AD 100–2000 (data from Maddison 2003).

steady Malthusian **immiseration**, or impoverishment. The English demographer Thomas Malthus (1766–1834) theorized in his famous *Essay on the Principle of Population*[42] that populations naturally increased faster than their food supply and were limited by the misery that ensued when poverty set in. However, the Chinese case demonstrates that cultural factors significantly shape how Malthusian pressures are felt. By 1900, China's population was ten times larger than during the 2,000-year period between 1000 BC and AD 1000, when the basic cultural system of a stratified, agrarian state was established, with a ranked bureaucracy extracting taxes, rents, and labor from the peasantry. Large-scale migration out of the lower Hwang Ho and Ch'ang Chiang floodplains, as well as further agricultural intensification during the Ch'ing dynasty, helped the standard of living keep up with population growth. Pioneer expansion into the forested and hilly autonomous tribal areas of south and central China and into Taiwan and Manchuria accounted for a significant portion of the population increase. Large-scale deforestation and erosion accompanied this expansion, resulting in drastic changes in the Chinese landscape. Farmers tended to cultivate smaller plots more intensively. Maize, potatoes, and sweet potatoes from the New World complemented existing crops

and certainly increased productivity. The fragmentation of plots was accelerated by the Chinese practice of giving each son an equal division of the family land. There were also incentives for population growth. Patriliny and ancestor worship provided strong cultural reasons for having sons; indeed, Confucian ideals stressed the importance of maintaining the lineage. Furthermore, agricultural intensification depended on greater and greater inputs of human labor, so there was continuous demand for labor.

It is difficult to demonstrate the extent to which conditions for the peasantry deteriorated significantly with population increase. Per-capita economic productivity may have peaked during the Sung dynasty (AD 1000) and no significant change occurred in the basic standard of living until after 1900, despite population increase. However, a steady reduction in the urban proportion of the population and the increasing fragmentation of land suggests that overpopulation was also a factor. Population growth may have prevented an early industrial revolution in China, even though China in AD 1000 was technologically more advanced than Europe, because there was no incentive to produce labor-saving machinery.

Historian Lloyd Eastman suggested that immiseration was a myth because the lot of the peasantry had always been poor, although conditions reached a low during the political and economic upheavals of the 1930s and 1940s. However, the fact that the population continued to increase suggests that, contrary to Malthusian predictions, conditions did not become absolutely intolerable. Perhaps the most important factor underlying the pervasive impoverishment of the peasantry was the operation of a highly nonegalitarian market economy in which most of the population were subsistence farmers. The class structure in which a small elite controlled most of the best farmland kept the poorest classes at a permanent disadvantage. Peasants paid rent even to use "communally" owned clan land, and privately owned plots were often only tiny inheritances. Cash cropping to pay for land was risky and could undercut subsistence production.

The extent of social inequality at the household level in village China by 1940 is clearly shown in the data collected by Chinese sociologist and anthropologist Hsiao-Tung Fei and Chih-I Chang, which revealed three social classes in the village of Luts'un in Yunnan Province. At the top was a landowning leisured class that managed its land to produce enough subsistence and cash crops to ensure a minimum standard of living for the least effort. Men in this group often refused to engage in any agricultural labor and spent their time relaxing and smoking. The "middle" class was composed of owner-tenants who had to rent additional land to farm in order to produce a slim subsistence margin. At the bottom was the landless class—those who had to survive by hiring out their labor and purchasing basic necessities. In Luts'un, 41 percent of the farmland was owned by 15 percent of the households, and 31 percent of the households were completely landless. Nearly half of these non-landowning households were too poor to even rent land. The distribution of rich and poor in Luts'un was the opposite of that seen among East African cattle herders and mirrored the inequalities in the imperial society, but with a much smaller gap between rich and poor.

Energetics analysis (comparing annual input and output ratios and energy flow patterns between a modest landowning household in Luts'un village and a landless household) dramatically illustrates the physical dimensions of this social stratification. The sample households differed in size, with five individuals in the landholding family and only two in the landless household. The landowning household controlled only 27 *kung* (1.6 acres [0.65 hectares]), which placed it in the lower range of the landowning class, but it still

enjoyed a comfortable standard of living. Using the caloric value of rice as a cash equivalent showed that the landed household had a potential per-capita food consumption five times that of the landless household. On a per-capita basis, it also consumed more than four times the goods and produced at more than twice the energy efficiency of the landless household. The wealthy household had enough savings to last it for one year and was able to support pigs with its garden waste. The poor household was able to purchase only enough rice to meet its minimal caloric requirements and had difficulty meeting its protein needs. There was little left over for housing, clothing, fuel, or medical needs. Significantly, the poor household paid enough in rent and taxes to support two additional people, and this was actually more than was paid by the wealthy household. Inequality of this magnitude would have been intolerable in an unstratified tribal village.

It would seem appropriate to call the Chinese system exploitative, at least by late Ch'ing times, if exploitation is defined as the unjust or improper use of a person for someone else's benefit. Exploitation can be said to exist if the lower class is deprived of basic necessities relative to the upper class and if the upper class derives luxuries from the lower class yet refuses to redistribute its wealth. By this definition, exploitation was probably a frequent social problem in Chinese civilization. Confucian teaching explicitly condemned such abuse of the peasantry because it was not good government, and Buddhist and Taoist sages spoke against it. However, inequities of wealth and power were inherent features of the Chinese state. Whether the Chinese peasantry conceived of themselves as an oppressed social class in an emic sense is another matter. From a social scientist's etic perspective, social classes existed in China for at least 4,000 years, but the powerful ideology of ancestor cults and Confucianism made such inequality seem part of the natural order of things. Furthermore, the examination system always held open the possibility of upward mobility.

The Chinese Village System

The daily life of the Chinese peasantry was centered on the highly self-sufficient village, which probably contained an average of four hundred to five hundred people, approximately the same number as in Australian "tribes" or the largest Amazonian interfluvial village communities. Unlike these tribal societies, which maintained essentially horizontal interaction links with structurally similar neighbors, however, Chinese villages were the lowest rural units in an organizational hierarchy ultimately linking them to the imperial center. This system of social, economic, ritual, and political ties linking the literate elites of the Great Tradition and the peasantry of the Little Tradition has been called the **folk-urban continuum**. Cultural elements of the Great Tradition are most prominent in the urban capitals and decline steadily as one moves toward smaller towns and villages, where the Little Tradition becomes strongest.

American anthropologist G. William Skinner, inspired by his fieldwork in Sichuan Province in 1949, found that Chinese villages group themselves around local centers, which he called standard market towns, in order to most efficiently exchange their produce for the limited range of goods and services that they cannot produce themselves. Villagers were usually self-sufficient in food, but they purchased such items as lamp oil, candles, incense, needles, soap, and matches and occasionally made use of blacksmiths, coffin makers, medical practitioners, scribes, and ritual specialists.

An average of eighteen villages were arranged about a standard market town within an area of some 19 square miles (50 km²), such that the most distant village was only about 3 miles (5 km) from the center, although where population density was low, the most remote villagers might need to walk 5 miles (8 km) to town (see figure 8.9a). Markets were held in adjacent market towns according to a regular schedule, following the lunar calendar that divides the month into three ten-day "weeks." A typical cycle meant that a market would be held in the same town every five days; thus, an itinerant peddler or specialist could visit a different market every day and thereby greatly increase his potential customers. This system made it possible to efficiently sustain a very large and dense rural population without a costly and fuel-intensive transportation technology such as developed in industrial Europe and North America.

Skinner argued that the villages using a standard market town constituted the basic unit of the Chinese Little Tradition, or folk society. These 7,000 or so people formed a relatively discrete social network that regularly interacted on market days and was united by ties of kinship and marriage. They thought of themselves as a group; shared details of dress, ritual, and dialect; and sometimes even used their own system of weights and measures. The market town was where the villagers paid their rents and taxes; it also contained religious shrines and teahouses where the members of secret societies and mutual aid societies

could meet. With its varied specialized functions, the market town often served as the power base of a single large lineage or clan whose various members might be localized in villages within the market district.

Typically six standard market towns were grouped in hexagonal territories around an intermediate market town where the local gentry conducted much of their business (see figure 8.9b). Intermediate market towns were often enclosed by walls and contained a temple to an urban deity. They might serve an overlapping area of 135 square miles (350 km²) containing 50,000 people and were connected, in turn, with a central market town, where the lowest-level officials of the official bureaucracy were located. People maintaining connections between intermediate or central market towns likely were literate elites, whereas most peasants never left their local market districts.

In theory, Chinese social organization was based on the patrilineal *tsu*, usually translated as either "clan" or "lineage." These genealogically defined units were segmented, localized, property-holding groups, with a specific surname and clan temples or halls, where tablets dedicated to specific clan ancestors were kept. Villages or towns might be dominated by a single clan, with lineage segments occupying specific blocks. There might also be written genealogies of remarkable depth. For example, a village of 1,100 people examined in Guangdong (Kwangtung) province in 1957 contained members of two clans. The dominant clan preserved ancestor tablets back 42 generations to the founding of the village in AD 1091.

There are conflicting interpretations of how Chinese descent groups were organized and how they functioned. Chinese American anthropologist Francis Hsu probably presented an incomplete picture when he described the "clan" as a large extended family, which forms a warm, peaceful, mutually self-contained unit. British social anthropologist Maurice Freedman called the same descent group a "lineage" and stressed that it was characterized by both internal conflict and harmony, similar to the Nuer system of segmentary opposition. Freedman speculated that Chinese lineages may have gained special importance as landholding groups when lineage members cooperated in the development of local irrigation systems for wet-rice agriculture or formed self-defense groups on the frontiers of pioneer settlement.

Village Cosmology and the Little Tradition

In their daily lives, the commoners directly perpetuated shamanistic cultural traditions that were rooted

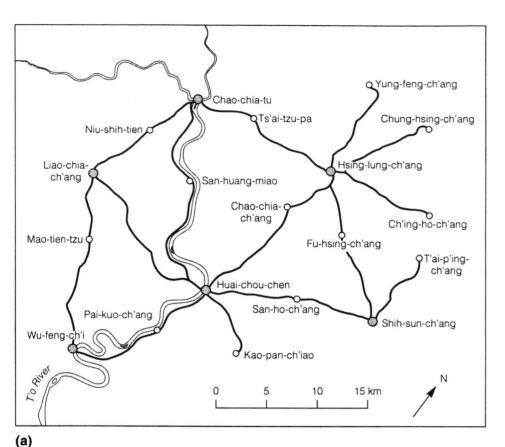

(a)

Figure 8.9. Chinese market towns groups about higher-level central places. (a) Map view of towns and the road network; (b) a diagrammatic view on a hexagonal grid (numbers represent market days in 10-day weeks). Note that (a) and (b) show the same urban places (Skinner 1964).

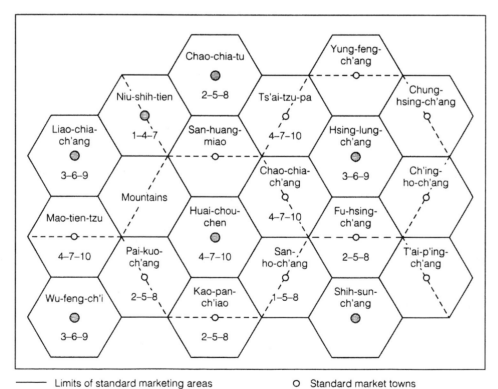

——— Limits of standard marketing areas

– – – Limits of intermediate marketing areas

▬▬▬ Roads connecting standard markets to intermediate markets

○ Standard market towns

◉ Higher-level central places

(b)

in the Neolithic past, underlying both the Great and Little Traditions. Commoners practiced a folk religion that drew freely on elements from formal Confucianism, Taoism, and Buddhism. Part-time Taoist priests, who did not live in the monasteries, were often called on as ritual specialists to perform at marriages, funerals, and curing ceremonies. The most prominent cultural elements shared by elites and commoners included the basic family system, with its emphasis on patrilineal descent lines and the ancestor cult, and basic cosmological traditions. The lowest-level deity, who operated at the household level, was the stove, or kitchen, god, who symbolized the domestic unity of the family. The stove god represented the bureaucracy and could report directly to the god symbolizing the emperor in the supernatural bureaucracy.

Complementary opposition, a prominent element in Australian and Amazonian cosmologies, was also a basic feature of Chinese popular culture. Complementarity was represented in Chinese cosmology by the yin-yang concept, symbolized in figure 8.10. Yin is female, passive, dark, and cool and is associated with earth, winter, valleys, tigers, and the color blue. Yang is male, light, and hot, and is associated with heaven, summer, mountains, dragons, and the color orange. The yin-yang concept was formalized by the Great Tradition during the early dynasties and combined with other philosophical features such as the concept of the five elements—metal, wood, water, fire, and earth—which were connected in a transformation cycle emphasizing balance, harmony, change, and continuity. According to five-element philosophy, "Water produces Wood but overcomes Fire. Fire produces Earth but overcomes Metal. Metal produces Water but overcomes Wood. Wood produces Fire but overcomes Earth. Earth produces Metal but overcomes Water."

The five elements were correlated with colors, directions, musical notes, and periods of Chinese history to produce an elaborate, often occult, cosmology. Color symbolism has also been important in Chinese popular culture. White, considered the color of mourning, was associated with the west, and the east was blue-green. Red was auspicious and south, black was north, and yellow was associated with the emperor.

This popular belief system has sometimes been called a correlative cosmology because it provided a framework that helped elites and commoners alike structure their daily lives in proper alignment with the cosmic forces to guarantee prosperity. Concern for proper alignments was reflected in the layout of cities,

Figure 8.10. Yin-yang.

temples, tombs, and houses; in the timing of ritual events; in the selection of mates; and in the seating of guests. Specialists in geomancy (divination by examining the spatial relationships of lines and figures) took cosmic forces into account when they studied the topographic details of a particular locality to select the most auspicious location for houses and graves. Correlative cosmology also influenced popular medicine, diet, and astrology.

Domestic Life and the Role of Women

Given the patrilineal descent system, the ideal Chinese nuclear family would produce many sons who would bring their wives to live in their father's house, or at least to his village. This would increase the strength of the lineage and ensure its perpetuation. Wealthy families could also add new members by adoption. Maurice Freedman described two broad types of Chinese families by size. The ideal was a large family containing two or more married sons, often called a joint family. The small family was either a nuclear family with no married sons or a stem family with only a single married son. Joint families were likely to be relatively wealthy, and they could form large lineage segments, whereas small families were usually poor members of disappearing lineages. The male members of Chinese families, large or small, held joint property, which was usually divided equally.

Western observers often regard the position of women in Chinese society negatively. Sons were said to be preferred over daughters, and women did not own lineage property. Favoring sons over daughters meant that in imperial China infant girls would be more likely to die from neglect or infanticide than boys. Furthermore, a child bride was dominated by her mother-in-law. Such domination, which reinforced the control of the extended family by the elders, was reflected in the common practice of adopting a girl into the family for the son to marry. Marriages were often arranged, and even though monogamy was the pattern, concubinage occurred, divorce was difficult, and widow remarriage was discouraged. Upon marriage, a woman was virtually absorbed into her husband's family. Marriage was so essential for women that if they died unmarried, their spirits could be married later in a pattern reminiscent of Nuer ghost marriage.

Foot-binding produced small, stunted feet, leaving many women virtually crippled. This practice demonstrated a man's affluence because it meant that his wife did not do heavy domestic work (see figure 8.11). But foot-binding was apparently not limited to the elite. It was thought to make women more attractive, but it also supported the ideal of wifely virtue by making it more difficult for women to venture unattended from the home.

This picture of female subordination is incomplete. Chinese women bring a sizable endowment of domestic articles and personal wealth with them when they marry. A woman can also manage her husband's share of the family estate, and she owns her private earnings. Although new daughters-in-laws may be treated harshly, they will become mothers-in-law in turn. As a wife, a woman has important responsibilities in domestic rituals, and her tablet will rest in her husband's ancestor hall (see box 8.4).

Figure 8.11. Chinese woman and child, nineteenth-century Ch'ing Dynasty. The woman's feet are contracted due to foot-binding (Ratzel 1898:466).

BOX 8.4. THE MEANING OF CHINESE KINSHIP TERMS

Chinese kinship terminology is complex because of the great diversity of terms that can be employed, but careful linguistic analysis reveals an orderly system that reflects the organization of Chinese society. In his study of the kinship terms used in Guangdong province by male speakers of Toishan, a Cantonese dialect of south China, John McCoy listed sixty-nine different terms used in indirect reference to kin and some fifty-three terms used in direct address. Table 8.4 presents a simplified list of thirty-five selected terms drawn from this list in Mandarin, but representing only terms used by males for five generations of consanguineal kin, excluding affines. The Chinese terms appear in column 2 in phonemic linguistic notation. The terms are also written using Chinese characters to represent each syllable. Column 1 describes the terms using the abbreviated primary kin terms introduced in chapter 3 (two new abbreviations are O, which means "older," and Y, which means "younger").

The genealogical distribution of the kin terms is diagrammed in figure 8.12, which is keyed to the kin term numbers used in table 8.4. Close inspection shows the importance of the male descent line and relative age, which is a very ancient pattern in Chinese culture. For example, FB's children (numbers 8, 9, 10, and 11) are terminologically distinguished from all other cousins because they could share surnames as members of ego's patrilineal descent group, the *tsu*, which existed during the Shang dynasty nearly 4,000 years ago. Cross-cousins were not distinguished from parallel cousins, and no cousins were typically considered marriageable. Mates normally had different surnames and were unrelated, and probably even unacquainted.

Older or younger age relative to ego is distinguished for everyone in ego's generation and for male siblings of ego's male lineal kin in higher generations. Concern with relative age reflects the increased ceremonial responsibilities of older siblings in carrying out the duties of *hsiao*, filial piety, and the preferential treatment that they might receive in many areas, including inheritance. Lineal relatives, who are ego's direct ancestors and descendants, are distinguished from all collateral relatives, who are off to the side. This distinction is important because it is lineal kin who must care for the elderly, play specific roles in mourning, and conduct ancestor rituals, all expressions of *hsiao*. Thus, an understanding of the meaning of Chinese kinship shows how important Chinese cultural patterns are enacted at the domestic level.

The House of Lim:
Chinese Marriage, Family, and Kinship

The intimate realities of a Chinese joint family and its stresses and strains as a common domestic unit are sensitively documented in a remarkable ethnography, *The House of Lim*, by Margery Wolf (1968), wife of anthropologist Arthur Wolf, and herself an anthropologist. The Wolfs lived for two years (1959–1960) with the Lim family (a pseudonym) while they studied daily life in a small farming village they called Peihotien on the Tamsui (Ta-han) River in northern Taiwan, fifteen miles southwest of Taipei. The Lim family was part of a large patrilineage whose Hokkien-speaking ancestors had migrated to Taiwan from Fukien province in adjacent mainland south China about 1770.

The House of Lim was the wealthiest family in the village. The Lims had realized the Chinese ideal with their three-generation joint family of fourteen people living as a single domestic unit, under one roof, with one kitchen. The household occupied a walled compound enclosing a large rectangular brick house with a central courtyard. The Lim family jointly owned the house, five acres of farmland, a small cement-bag factory, and a dozen pigs. They worked together, sharing their common economic resources under the general management of the senior male of the Lim patrilineage, Lim Chieng-cua. The joint family contained two branches (see figure 8.13):

1. Lim Chieng-cua, his wife, Chui-ieng, and their six unmarried children.
2. Lim A-bok, Lim Chieng-cua's deceased brother's son, with A-bok's wife, A-ki; their two unmarried children; his mother, Lim A-pou; and his younger unmarried brother.

Lim A-bok managed the farm while his mother took care of the pigs. The two wives, Lim Chui-ieng and A-ki, shared the cooking on a five-day rotation. Everything seemed to run smoothly in the family, but beneath the surface there was considerable tension between the two branches of the family, between spouses, and between parents and children. Many interpersonal problems seemed related to the practice of adoptive and arranged marriages. The family head, Lim Chieng-cua, had refused to marry his foster sister and then agreed to a marriage with Chui-ieng, arranged by her foster parents. Chui-ieng was not happy with her marriage, especially when her husband took on a mistress. She berated him and threatened to leave, and he violently assaulted her. One of the

Table 8.4.   Chinese Kinship Terminological System (Mandarin language)

O = older; Y = younger
B = brother; Z = sister
F = father; M = mother
S = son; D= daughter

Description		Chinese Term
1. F	父亲	Fu Qing [fù·tsīng]
2. FOB	伯父	Bo Fu [bó·fù]
3. FYB	叔父	Shu Fu [shū·fù]
6. FZ	姑母	Gu Mu [gū·mǔ]
8. FBOS	堂兄	Tang Xiong [táng·shōng]
9. FBYS	堂弟	Tang Di [táng·dì]
10. FBOD	堂姐	Tang Jie [táng·jěi]
11. FBYD	堂妹	Tang Mei [táng·mèi]
12. FZOS, MZOS, MBOS	表兄	Biao Xiong [bǐao·shōng]
13. FZYS, MBYS, MZYS	表弟	Biao Di [bǐao·dì]
14. FZOD, MBOD, MZYD	表姐	Biao Jie [bǐao·jěi]
15. FZYD, MBYD, MZOD	表妹	Biao Mei [bǐao·mèi]
16. FF	祖父	Zu Fu [tzǔ·fù]
17. FM	祖母	Zu Mu [tzǔ·mǔ]
18. FFOB	伯祖父	Bo Zu Fu [bó·tzǔ·fù]
19. FFYB	叔祖父	Shu Zu Fu [shū·tzǔ·fù]
22. FFZ	姑祖母	Go Zu Mu [gū·zǔ·mǔ]
24. M	母亲	Mu Qing [mǔ·tsīng]
25. MB	祖父	Jiu Fu [jìu·fù]
27. MZ	姨母	Yi Mu [yí·mǔ]
38. MF	外祖父	Wai Zu Fu [waì·tzǔ·fù]
39. MM	外祖母	Wai Zu Mu [waì·tzǔ·mǔ]
40. MFOB	外伯祖父	Wai Bo Zu Fu [waì·bó·tzǔ·fù]
41. MFYB	外伯祖母	Wai Shu Zu Fu [waì·shū·tzǔ·fù]
44. MFZ	外姑祖母	Wai Gu Zu Mu [waì·gū·tzǔ·mǔ]
46. OB	家兄	Jia Xiong [jiā·shōng]
47. YB	胞弟	Bao Di [bāo·dì]
50. BS	姪	Zhi [tzí]
51. BD	姪女	Zhi Nu [tzí·nǔ]
52. OZ	家姐	Jia Jie [jiā·jěi]
53. YZ	胞妹	Bao Mei [bāo·mèi]
56. ZS	甥子	Sun Zi [sūn·tzǐ]
57. ZD	甥女	Sun Nu [sūn·nǔ]
58. S	子	Zi [tzí]
62. D	女儿	Nu Er [nǔ·é]

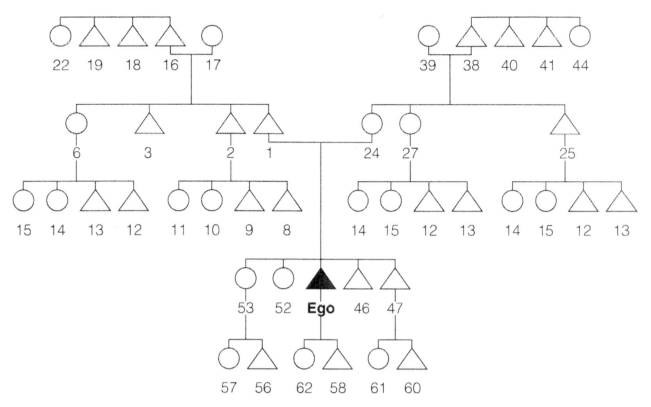

Figure 8.12. A Chinese kinship system.

family's adopted daughters turned to prostitution after she was given to another family but remained unmarried.

Lim A-pou had been adopted into the family as an infant, but her foster brother took a second wife after marrying her. Lim A-pou was considered a "little daughter-in-law" (*sim-pua*), because she was selected to later marry her foster brother. Her husband's new wife was a love match. *Sim-pua* marriages were not prestigious, but they were very practical because they saved expensive bride-wealth expenses. They accounted for nearly half the marriages in Peihotien, but this practice has now completely disappeared in Taiwan. The preference for sons over daughters is a strong incentive for giving away daughters in such adoptions. In China, where patrilineages are so important, sons are the best old-age insurance. Furthermore, giving away infant daughters saves the expense of raising a "useless" daughter, who would require a dowry. One woman bluntly told Margery Wolf, "Why should I want so many daughters? It is useless to raise your own daughters. I'd just have to give them away when they were grown, so when someone asked for them as infants I gave them away. Think of all the rice I saved."

The downside of such arrangements is that marrying someone with whom you have grown up does not make for a healthy marriage. Arthur Wolf's (1995) later analysis of the Chinese material seems to confirm Edward Westermark's theory in his *History of Human Marriage* that people who are raised together from infancy are likely to develop a sexual aversion to one another. Such aversion is especially likely in the Chinese case in which the couple actually called each other "brother" and "sister" before they married. Wolf found that Chinese marriages to adopted daughters showed lower fertility and higher adultery and divorce rates than other marriages.

The obvious insecurity of the women of the Lim household was reflected in frequent bickering between them, especially over workloads and the allocation of economic resources. Shortly after the Wolfs completed their fieldwork, the Lim family divided their property and set up a separate stove and kitchen for Lim A-bok and his branch of the family. The two households continued to live in the same house and worshiped at the Lim family altar in the guest hall where the ancestral tablet was kept, but they no longer formed a joint family.

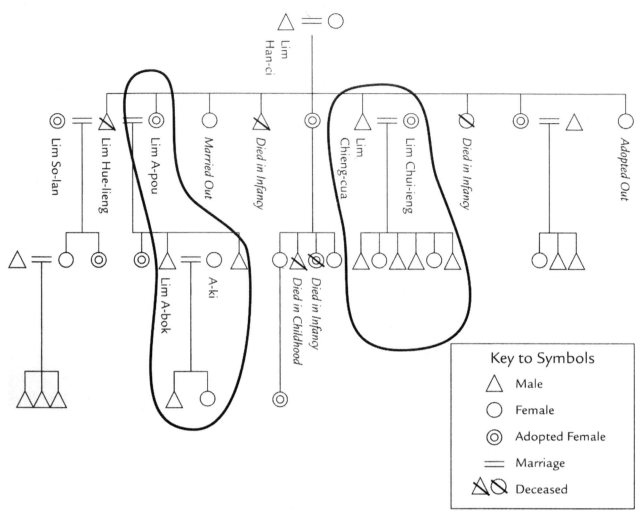

Figure 8.13. Two branches of the House of Lim in a Taiwanese village, 14 people living under one roof and sharing one kitchen (Wolf 1968).

SUMMARY

The Chinese Great Tradition began to develop some 7,000 years ago as a gradual transformation of the domestic-scale Neolithic farming cultures that had developed in the great river valleys of China 2,000 years earlier. Their foraging ancestors can be traced to at least 15,000 BP in the same region. Many of the distinctive features of Chinese civilization were in place by the time of the Shang dynasty, which began nearly 4,000 years ago and continued with only minor modifications until the last emperor was overthrown in 1911. Chinese civilization provides an important perspective on the debate over state origins because, in this case, control of religion by the political elite seems to have played a critical role in both the origin and long-term continuity of the state system. Chinese emperors were not deities, but they ruled with the mandate of heaven, and the political order has been described as a liturgical government based on moral authority backed by military force. Ancestor worship and the associated concept of filial piety were key elements in this system, especially at the domestic level. The entire ideology was expressed in a complex correlative cosmology based on complementary oppositions such as *yin-yang* and symbolism drawn from the five elements, which were correlated with colors, music, compass directions, and calendrical rituals.

Chinese agriculture was a gardening system powered by human labor on small family farms, operating within a highly efficient village system that provided basic subsistence needs to a very large and dense rural population at a minimal energy cost. This labor-intensive system is a significant contrast to the industrial-farming, fossil-fuel system described for the United States in chapter 11.

Chinese culture tended to encourage large families and population growth, but the intensely hierarchical system kept living standards extremely low for most of the population. Chinese domestic life was structured around the patrilineage and extended family, which were dominated by men. The importance of males, relative age, and the patrilineage is reflected in Chinese kinship terminology.

STUDY QUESTIONS

1. Identify, define, or discuss the following Chinese ideological concepts: Confucianism, Taoism, five classics, five elements, filial piety, *li*, mandate of heaven, august god, *yin-yang*, stove god, ancestor tablet, and *kowtow*.

2. Discuss the following political concepts within the Chinese context: meritocracy, patrimonial, aristocracy, and gentry.

3. Discuss the following aspects of subsistence intensification using Chinese examples: multicropping, intertillage, permanent agriculture, labor intensive, capital intensive, and population density.

4. How does the Chinese state fit within the various theories of the origin of the state?

5. Discuss problems with the concepts of exploitation, immiseration, and Malthusian overpopulation, using Chinese material.

6. Discuss the role of ancestor worship as a central integrating device in Chinese culture.

7. Show how the components of descent line, relative age, lineal and collateral, sex, and generation are significant in Chinese kinship terminological systems.

SUGGESTED READING

Chang, Kwang-Chih. 1986. *The Archaeology of Ancient China*, 4th ed. New Haven, CT: Yale University Press. An authoritative overview of Chinese prehistory.

Ropp, Paul S. 1990. *Heritage of China: Contemporary Perspectives on Chinese Civilization*. Berkeley: University of California Press. An interdisciplinary collection of articles on China including such topics as Confucianism, the origin of Chinese civilization, and the development of government, economy, and family.

Stover, Leon N., and Takeko Stover. 1976. *China: An Anthropological Perspective*. Pacific Palisades, CA: Goodyear. A wide-ranging analysis of Chinese culture.

Wheatley, Paul. 1971. *The Pivot of the Four Quarters: A Preliminary Enquiry into the Origins and Character of the Ancient Chinese City*. Chicago: Aldine. Examines the physical organization of Chinese cities through time in relation to worldview and cosmology.

GLOSSARY TERMS

Peasantry Village farmers who provide most of their own subsistence but who must pay taxes and are politically and often, to some extent, economically dependent on the central state government.

Feudalism A political system in which village farmers occupy lands owned by local lords to whom they owe loyalty, rent, and service.

Ancestor worship A religious system based on reverence for specific ancestors and sometimes involving shrines, rituals, and sacrifice.

Theocracy State government based on religious authority or divine guidance. The Chinese emperor was the highest civil and religious leader.

Filial piety *Hsiao*, the ritual obligation of children to respect their ancestors, and especially the duty of sons to care for shrines of their patrilineal ancestors.

Ethnic group A dependent, culturally distinct population that forms part of a larger state or empire and that was formerly autonomous.

Scapulimancy Divination by interpreting the pattern of cracks formed in heated animals' scapula or turtle shells.

Little Tradition Ritual beliefs and practices followed by nonliterate commoners, especially rural villagers who are part of a larger state-level society

Liturgical government The use of ritually prescribed interpersonal relations and religious, moral authority as a primary means of social control in a state-level society.

Immiseration Malthusian impoverishment, a declining standard of living attributed to continuous population growth on a limited-resource base.

Folk-urban continuum Robert Redfield's concept of a gradual distinction between the Little Tradition culture of rural commoners and the Great Tradition culture of the urban elites in a political-scale culture.

NOTES

1. Lewis, M. Paul, ed. 2009. *Ethnologue: Languages of the World*. 16th ed. Dallas, TX: SIL International.

2. Ruhlen, Merritt. 1987. *A Guide to the World's Languages*, vol. 1, *Classification*. Stanford, CA: Stanford University Press.

3. Harris, Marvin. 1988. *Culture, People, Nature: An Introduction to General Anthropology*, 5th ed. New York: Harper & Row.

4. Keightly, David N. 1990. "Early Civilization in China: Reflections on How It Became Chinese." In *Heritage of China: Contemporary Perspectives on Chinese Civilization*, edited by Paul Ropp, pp. 15–54. Berkeley: University of California Press.

5. Keightly, David N. 1990. "Early Civilization in China."

6. Wheatley, Paul. 1971. *The Pivot of the Four Quarters: A Preliminary Enquiry into the Origins and Character of the Ancient Chinese City.* Chicago: Aldine; Wright, Arthur F. 1977. "The Cosmology of the Chinese City." In *The City in Late Imperial China*, edited by G. William Skinner, pp. 33–73. Stanford, CA: Stanford University Press.

7. Dull, Jack L. 1990. "The Evolution of Government in China." In *Heritage of China: Contemporary Perspectives on Chinese Civilization*, edited by Paul Ropp, pp. 55–85. Berkeley: University of California Press.

8. Chang, Kwang-Chih. 1980. *Shang Civilization.* New Haven, CT, and London: Yale University Press.

9. Fried, Morton H. 1983. "Tribe to State or State to Tribe in Ancient China." In *The Origins of Chinese Civilization*, edited by D. N. Keightley, pp. 467–93. Berkeley: University of California Press.

10. Chang, Kwang-Chih. 1986. *Archaeology of Ancient China*, 4th ed. New Haven, CT: Yale University Press.

11. Chang, Kwang-Chih. 1980. *Shang Civilization.*

12. Wheatley, Paul. 1971. *The Pivot of the Four Quarters.*

13. Chang, Kwang-Chih. 1983. *Art, Myth, and Ritual: The Path to Political Authority in Ancient China.* Cambridge, MA: Harvard University Press; Chang, Kwang-Chih. 1986. *Archaeology of Ancient China*, 4th ed. New Haven, CT: Yale University Press.

14. Chang, Kwang-Chih. 1983. *Art, Myth, and Ritual*; Chang, Kwang-Chih. 1986. *Archaeology of Ancient China.*

15. Bellwood, Peter S. 1985. *Prehistory of the Indo-Malaysian Archipelago.* New York and Sydney: Academic.

16. Chang, T. T. 1983. "The Origin and Early Culture of the Cereal Grains and Food Legumes." In *The Origins of Chinese Civilization*, edited by D. N. Keightley, pp. 65–94. Berkeley: University of California Press.

17. Chang, Kwang-Chih. 1986. *Archaeology of Ancient China.*

18. Chang, Kwang-Chih. 1980. *Shang Civilization.*

19. Chang, Kwang-Chih. 1980. *Shang Civilization.*

20. Chang, Kwang-Chih. 1980. *Shang Civilization.*

21. Chang, Kwang-Chih. 1980. *Shang Civilization.*

22. Hoebel, E. Adamson. 1968. *The Law of Primitive Man.* New York: Atheneum.

23. Posposil, Leopold. 1972. *The Ethnology of Law.* Addison-Wesley Module in Anthropology, no. 12. Reading, MA: Addison-Wesley.

24. Wei-Ming, Tu. "The Confucian Tradition in Chinese History." *In Heritage of China: Contemporary Perspectives on Chinese Civilization*, edited by Paul Ropp, pp. 112–37. Berkeley: University of California Press.

25. Stover, Leon N., and Takeko Kawai Stover. 1976. *China: An Anthropological Perspective.* Pacific Palisades, CA: Goodyear.

26. Michael, Franz. 1964. "State and Society in Nineteenth-Century China." In *Modern China*, edited by Albert Feuerwerker, pp. 57–69. Englewood Cliffs, NJ: Prentice-Hall; Wolf, Eric R. 1969. *Peasant Wars of the Twentieth Century.* New York: Harper & Row.

27. Eastman, Lloyd E. 1988. *Family, Fields, and Ancestors: Constancy and Change in China's Social and Economic History, 1550–1949.* New York: Oxford University Press.

28. Stover, Leon N., and Takeko Kawai Stover. 1976. *China.*

29. Stover, Leon N., and Takeko Kawai Stover. 1976. *China*, 166, 170.

30. Legge, James. 1967. *Li Chi: Book of Rites.* 2 vols. New Hyde Park, NY: University Books.

31. Legge, James. 1967. *Li Chi: Book of Rites*, vol. 2:17 (Bk. 11, sec. 3, pt. l).

32. Legge, James. 1967. *Li Chi: Book of Rites*, vol. 1:390–91 (Bk. 7, sec. 13).

33. King, Franklin Hiram. 1911. *Farmers of' Forty Centuries or Permanent Agriculture in China, Korea and Japan.* Madison, WI: Mrs. F. H. King.

34. King, Franklin Hiram. 1911. *Farmers of' Forty Centuries*, 13.

35. Stover, Leon N., and Takeko Kawai Stover. 1976. China.

36. Hanks, Lucien M. 1972. *Rice and Men: Agricultural Ecology in Southeast Asia.* Chicago: Aldine.

37. Perkins, Dwight H. 1969. *Agricultural Development in China 1368–1968.* Chicago: Aldine.

38. Fei, Hsiao-Tung and Chih-I Chang. 1945. *Earthbound China: A Study of Rural Economy in Yunnan.* Chicago: University of Chicago Press.

39. Stover, Leon N. and Takeko Kawai Stover. 1976. *China.*

40. Eastman, Lloyd E. 1988. *Family, Fields, and Ancestors.*

41. Eastman, Lloyd E. 1988. *Family, Fields, and Ancestors.*

42. Malthus, Thomas R. [1798, 1807] 1895. *An Essay on the Principle of Population.* New York: Macmillan.

43. Feuerwerker, Albert. 1990. "Chinese Economic History in Comparative Perspective." In *Heritage of China: Contemporary Perspectives on Chinese Civilization*, edited by Paul Ropp, pp. 224–41. Berkeley: University of California Press.

44. Chao, Kang. 1986. *Man and Land in Chinese History: An Economic Analysis.* Stanford, CA: Stanford University Press.

45. Chao, Kang. 1986. *Man and Land in Chinese History.*

46. Eastman, Lloyd E. 1988. *Family, Fields, and Ancestors.*

47. Fei, Hsiao-Tung and Chih-I Chang. 1945. *Earthbound China.*

48. Bodley, John H. 1981b. "Inequality: An Energetic Approach." In *Social Inequality: Comparative and Developmental Approaches*, edited by Gerald Berreman, pp. 183–97. New York: Academic Press.

49. Harris, Marvin. 1988. *Culture, People, Nature.*

50. Redfield, Robert. 1941. *The Folk Culture of Yucatan.* Chicago: University of Chicago Press.

51. Skinner, G. William. 1964. "Marketing and Social Structure in Rural China (Part 1)." *Journal of Asian Studies* 24(l):3-43; Hammel, E. A. 2009. *George William*

Skinner 1925–2008. Biographical Memoir. Washington, DC: National Academy of Sciences

52. Freedman, Maurice. 1966. *Chinese Lineage and Society: Fukien and Kwangtung.* London School of Economics, Monographs on Social Anthropology, no. 33. London: Athlone Press.

53. Hsu, Francis L. K. 1963. *Clan, Caste, and Club.* Princeton, NJ: Van Nostrand.

54. Freedman, Maurice. 1966. *Chinese Lineage and Society.*

55. Wolf, Arthur P. 1974. "Gods, Ghosts, and Ancestors." *Religion and Ritual in Chinese Society*, edited by Arthur P. Wolf, pp. 131–82. Stanford, CA: Stanford University Press.

56. Chai, Ch'u, and Winberg Chai. 1967. "Introduction." In *Li Chi: Book of Rites*, vol. 1, translated by James Legge, pp. xxiii–lxxxiv. New Hyde Park, NY: University Books, lxviii.

57. Rawski, Evelyn S. 1987. "Popular Culture in China." In *Tradition and Creativity: Essays on East Asian Civilization*, edited by Ching-I Tu, pp. 41–65. New Brunswick, NJ, and Oxford, Eng.: Transaction Books.

58. Freedman, Maurice. 1966. *Chinese Lineage and Society.*

59. Wolf, Arthur P. 1968. "Adopt a Daughter-in-Law, Marry a Sister: A Chinese Solution to the Problem of the Incest Taboo." *American Anthropologist* 70(5):864–74.

60. Ebrey, Patricia. 1990. "Women, Marriage, and the Family in Chinese History." In *Heritage of China: Contemporary Perspectives on Chinese Civilization*, edited by Paul Ropp, pp. 197–223. Berkeley: University of California Press.

61. Freedman, Maurice. 1979. *The Study of Chinese Society.* Stanford, CA: Stanford University Press.

62. McCoy, John. 1970. "Chinese Kin Terms of Reference and Address." In *Family and Kinship in Chinese Society*, edited by Maurice Freedman, pp. 209–26. Stanford, CA: Stanford University Press.

63. Wolf, Margery. 1968. *The House of Lim: A Study of a Chinese Farm Family.* New York: Appleton-Century-Crofts.

64. Wolf, Margery. 1968. *The House of Lim*, 40.

65. Westermark, Edward. 1922. *The History of Human Marriage*, 5th ed. New York: Allerton Book Co.

CHAPTER 9

Hinduism and Islam in South Asia

Figure 9.0. Siva in the ring of fire.

PRONUNCIATION GUIDE

MOST OF THE HINDU WORDS IN THIS CHAPTER ARE FROM Sanskrit. Their approximate pronunciations for English speakers are as follows:

KEY

a = *a* in f*a*ther
o = *o* in g*o*
e = *a* in f*a*te
ee = *ee* in b*ee*
j = *j* in joke
ch = *ch* in *ch*arm
sh = *sh* in *sh*e
oo = *oo* in f*oo*d
ai = *i* in *i*ce
d = softer than in English
t = softer than in English
• = Syllable division
/ = Stress
Kshatriya [sha / tree • ya]
jajmani [jaj • ma / nee]
Vaisya [vai / shya]
Harijan [ha • ree / jan]
Sudra [shoo / dra]
Siva [shee / va]
jati [ja / tee]
kacha [ka / cha]
varna [var / na]
pakka [pa / ka]

darsan [dar • shan/]
Arthasastra [ar • ta • sha / stra]

LEARNING OBJECTIVES

After studying this chapter you should be able to do the following:

1. Explain the relationship between language, Great Tradition, and political organization in South Asia and neighboring geographic regions and make specific cultural comparisons between Hinduism, Buddhism, and Islam.
2. Compare the major stages of South Asian cultural development in comparison with developments in Mesopotamia, China, and the Andean region.
3. Outline the major cultural organizational features of Hindu kingdoms and empires in comparison with Mesopotamia, China, and the Andean region.
4. Make specific comparisons between ancient Hindu social organization, gender relations, and religious belief and practice and these cultural features in other ancient civilizations and contemporary national societies.
5. Compare the rank distribution of social power in the Thai kingdom and Akbar's empire, considering the household differences from top to bottom.
6. Outline the defining features of the Hindu caste system and describe how food, marriage, and service transactions encode caste identity, explaining how Hindu cosmology and ritual practice support the rank order of Hindu society.
7. Compare the Islamic and Hindu Great Traditions, referring to their origin and development, and how they structure society and shape the practices of daily life.
8. Describe the status of women in South Asia, referring to underlying cultural understandings and basic practices in both Hindu and Muslim traditions.

One-third of the contemporary world's people identify themselves as either Hindus or Muslims. These two Great Traditions arose independently more than 1,000 years ago and are culturally distinct, but both are centered on formal religions with sacred texts. These religions provide charters for a hierarchically organized society and regulate the smallest details of daily life, including family structure, gender relations, and diet. Europeans, as members of the Judeo-Christian Great Tradition, have been both fascinated and repulsed by Hindus and Muslims for centuries, but they have consistently misunderstood them. In this chapter, we focus primarily on classical Hindu civilization, especially the relationship between religion and society, and show how the ancient culture is reflected in modern India. The South Asian culture area is emphasized because it is the homeland of the Hindu Great Tradition and because Muslims and Hindus have coexisted here for eight hundred years. This area is examined again in chapter 12 in relation to contemporary issues of poverty and economic development.

THE SOUTH ASIAN CULTURE AREA

Languages, Geography, and Prehistory of South Asia

The South Asian culture area covers modern Pakistan, India, Nepal, Bhutan, Bangladesh, Burma, and Sri Lanka. It is a complex mix of languages and culture types, with more than 1 billion people occupying an area less than two-thirds the size of the United States. South Asia is centered on the Indian subcontinent and is predominantly a Hindu and Muslim region, with important Buddhist elements as well as many coexisting tribal cultures.

Most South Asian languages belong to one of three major language groups: Indo-European, Dravidian, and Sino-Tibetan (see figure 9.1). India alone recognizes fifteen official languages, including four of

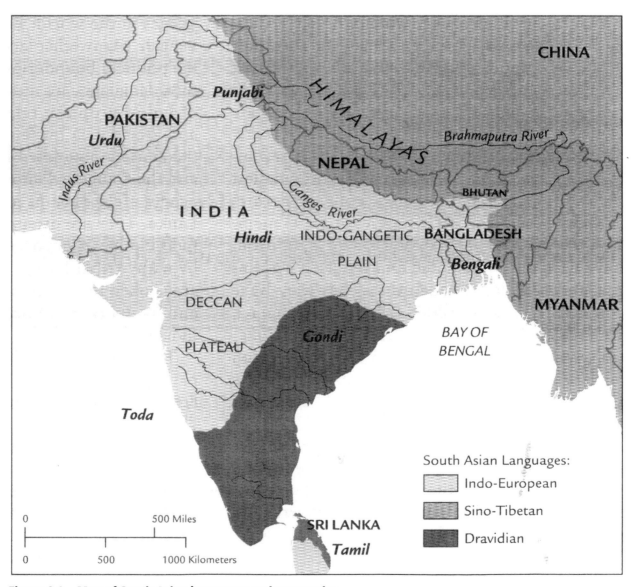

Figure 9.1. Map of South Asian languages and geography.

the twelve most populous languages in the world: English, Hindi, Urdu, and Bengali. Many other languages are spoken within the political boundaries of the country. The last three languages are members of the Indic branch of Indo-European, related to ancient Sanskrit, and are spoken by some 700 million people in the densely populated Indus Valley of Pakistan and the Gangetic Plain of India. Dravidian languages are spoken in southeastern India and Sri Lanka. They are presumed to have preceded the Indo-European languages in India and are spoken by many tribal groups. Sino-Tibetan languages are spoken in the Himalayan region, in Burma, and by many tribal peoples in extreme eastern India and Bangladesh.

The cultural Great Tradition with which people identify may be associated with a particular language. In the 1990s there were perhaps 60 million Buddhists in South Asia, primarily in India, Burma, and Sri Lanka, and some 350 million in all of Asia[1] (see figure 9.2a). South Asian Buddhists are most likely to be speakers of Dravidian or Sino-Tibetan languages. Furthermore, many Dravidian and Sino-Tibetan peoples are tribal peoples who do not identify with any Great Tradition. The largest cultural group in South Asia is composed of some 755 million Hindus centered in India, Bangladesh, and Nepal, who are primarily speakers of Indic languages. At its peak, the Hindu Great Tradition expanded into Southeast Asia as far as Java and Bali in what is now Indonesia (see figure 9.2b). In 2009 there were more than 450 million Muslims in Pakistan, Bangladesh, and India.[2] South Asian Muslims are predominantly speakers of Urdu and Bengali. There are more than a billion Muslims worldwide, including some 170 million in Malaysia and Indonesia and more than 200 million in Africa and the Middle East (see figure 9.2c). The Islamic Great Tradition, although originated by speakers of Arabic, a Semitic language, is now practiced by more Indic speakers in South Asia than Arabic speakers in the Middle East. Furthermore, because not all Arab speakers are Muslim, the common stereotype that equates Muslim with Arab is quite misleading (compare figures 9.2c and 9.2d).

The South Asian subcontinent (see figure 9.1) extends more than 2,000 miles (3,218 km) east to west and north to south, encompassing many sharply

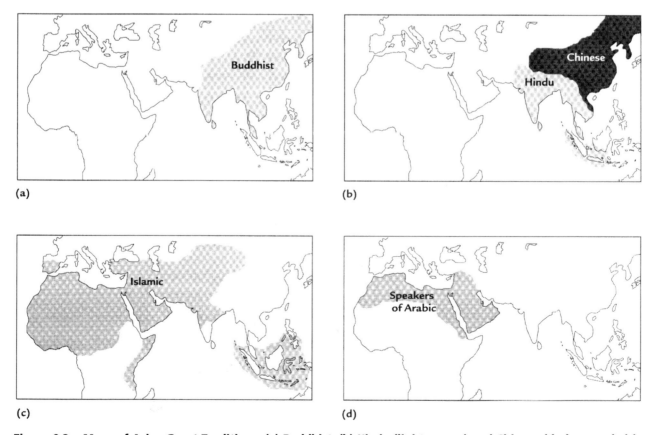

(a)

(b)

(c)

(d)

Figure 9.2.   Maps of Asian Great Traditions: (a) Buddhist; (b) Hindu (light screen) and Chinese (dark screen); (c) Islamic, and; (d) speakers of Arabic.

different environments. Because of this diverse expanse, cultures of very different scale have been able to interact with one another over the millennia while retaining their essential autonomy. South and central India lie within the tropics, while north India extends well into the temperate zones. Tropical rain forest is found along a narrow coastal strip of western India, Sri Lanka, and the hill tribe areas of Bangladesh, eastern India, and Burma. Much of southern India is an arid upland dominated by the Deccan Plateau, which was not conducive to intensive agriculture and sheltered many Dravidian-speaking tribal peoples.

India is separated from China and Central Asia by the Himalayan–Hindu Kush mountains, which form the southern boundary of the vast Tibetan Plateau and contain the world's highest mountains and the largest permanent snowfields outside the polar regions. The 1,500-mile (2,414-km) east-west trend of the massive Himalayan range creates an enormous rain shadow to the north and funnels tropical monsoonal rain from Southeast Asia onto the rich soils of the low Gangetic Plain, making it a highly productive agricultural zone. The Himalayas are the source of the Indus, the Ganges, and the Brahmaputra rivers, which annually carry tons of fertile Himalayan soil to the Indo-Gangetic Plain. The Indus Valley, where Indian civilization began, lies on the opposite end

of the Iranian plateau from Mesopotamia, which it ecologically resembles. The Indus Valley is an arid alluvial plain, bordered by mountains. The Indus, like the Euphrates, is a silt-laden, down-cutting river, ideally suited to floodplain agriculture yet frequently changing course.

Significant changes in the South Asian environment may have affected cultural development in ways that are still not understood. Changes in sea level and alluvial deposition on the floodplain have altered the area of prime agricultural lands. The Himalayas are still being pushed up by the northward-moving Indian continental plate colliding with the Eurasian plate, and this has happened rapidly enough to modify regional climate during the period of human occupation. Since the Lower Paleolithic, in some areas of India the climate has been both wetter and drier than at present.[3]

South Asia is not as well known archaeologically as the Near East, but cultural developments seem to have followed a similar pattern in both areas. The Lower Paleolithic is well represented by Acheulean hand axes and choppers found throughout India (see table 9.1). The Middle Paleolithic flake tools and Upper Paleolithic blade tools are also well represented. Archaeologists working in South Asia refer to cultures based on microlithic tools, foraging, fishing, and no-

Table 9.1. History and Prehistory of South Asia, 1 Million BP to AD 1971

Post-Colonial	
1971	Pakistan and Bangladesh partitioned
1947	India and Pakistan partitioned
1947	Indian independence
British Colonialism	
1818–1947	British Empire of India
1757–1947	British rule Bengal
1600–1873	British East India Company
Muslim India 1192-1818	
1526–1761	Mughal Empire
1556–1605	Akbar the Great
Classic Hindu India 600 BC – AD 1192	
350–100 BC	Mauryan Empire (Arthasastra, Dharma Sastra, Code of Manu)
563–483	Buddha (Siddhartha Gautama), founder of Buddhism
900–300	Upanishads compiled
Vedic India 1600–600 BC	
1600	Indo-European migrations
Harappan Civilization 2600–1900 BC cities, writing, temples, trade	
Chiefdoms 4600–3500 BC	
Neolithic India 8000–5500 BP Domestic wheat, barley, livestock	
Mesolithic 12,000–8000 BP Foraging, hunting, early domesticates	
Upper Paleolithic 18,000 BP Blade tools	
Middle Paleolithic 200,000 BP Flake and core tools	
Lower Paleolithic 1 million BP Acheulean hand axes and choppers	

Source: Allchin and Allchin (1982) for prehistory.

madic herding as Mesolithic. This adaptation began during the Early Holocene, about 12,000 to 8000 BP, and continued in various parts of the subcontinent into the twentieth century.

The South Asian Neolithic also went through a pre-ceramic phase of initial farming villages at about the same time as in the Near East (10,000–7000 BP) and a full-ceramic Neolithic (7000–5500 BP), which includes paint-decorated pottery. Because the earliest South Asian farming villages are known from the Indus region and the eastern edge of the Iranian plateau in Baluchistan, it is inferred that developments here were perhaps part of the same process that occurred in the Near East, especially given the similarities in ecological setting.

EARLY HINDU CIVILIZATION

Origin of the Hindu Kingdom

Harappa, the earliest South Asian civilization, may have arisen independently in the Indus Valley (see box 9.1). A clear break seems to have occurred between Harappa and the later Hindu civilization centered on the Gangetic Plain, which is attributed primarily to Indo-European-speaking Aryan pastoralists.

Sometime around 1600 BC, Indo-European-speaking peoples apparently moved from the Iranian plateau to the Indus plains. These were the Aryans, who were probably seminomadic pastoral people, speaking an early form of Sanskrit and organized in chiefdoms. These Aryans should not be confused with the imaginary north European "Aryan" super-race of Hitler's Nazi Germany and neo-Nazi racist political ideology. The Aryans of ancient Asia and the Neolithic settlers of Europe may well have had common ancestors in Southwest Asia some 8,500 years ago and may belong to the Indo-European language family, but otherwise they were different peoples.

The Aryans portrayed in the ancient Veda Hindu texts were cattle herders probably organized as warrior chiefdoms, who fought with the earlier, presumably Dravidian-speaking, peoples whom they encountered. Some historians believe that the Aryans may have contributed to the collapse of the Harappan civilization, but this is difficult to establish. The Aryans settled initially in the Punjab and between the Indus and Ganges rivers, the region that was identified in the Vedic texts as Brahmavarta, the Aryan heartland. They then expanded steadily eastward into the fertile Gangetic Plain, such that by 600 BC they effectively occupied the entire region and were becoming increasingly

sedentary and stratified. Over the next four centuries, classical Indian civilization became fully established, with cities, writing, states, empires, and the Great Traditions of Hinduism and Buddhism that continue to shape Indian culture to the present day (see table 9.1).

Hindu civilization has its roots in the religious hymns and verses preserved in the Vedas, especially the four Samhita Vedas compiled as oral texts between 1500 and 1000 BC. Pre-Aryan peoples, including members of the Harappan civilization, certainly contributed to what was, in effect, a second period of state formation, urbanization, and civilization in South Asia. The rise of early Hindu civilization between approximately 600 and 200 BC seems to have been primarily a political process that does not easily fit the Mesopotamian, Andean, or Chinese models of state origin examined previously. Hindu civilization developed after the Aryan invaders conquered the earlier tribal residents of the Ganges region and incorporated them into larger-scale centralized polities, whose rulers then began to war against one another. Because the Ganges, as an incised river, was a difficult source of irrigation water, early Gangetic states were not hydraulic societies; that is, they were not directed by rulers who also controlled irrigation works. Furthermore, because significant increases in population density took place only after political centralization, neither population pressure nor environmental circumscription could have been important causes of state formation. However, because Hindu civilization incorporated some elements of Harappan civilization and may also have been indirectly stimulated by contacts with Mesopotamian and Persian civilizations, it should not be considered an example of strictly pristine state development.

In his investigation of the development of Indian civilization, archaeologist George Erdosy focused on urbanization in the central Ganges region, viewing "the containers of those institutions that are required for the maintenance of increasingly complex and inegalitarian societies."[4]

Tribal societies did not need cities because small villages were self-regulating. Cities were places where the instruments of social control could themselves be developed and controlled, such that their appearance signals the arrival of state-level organization.

Erdosy surveyed settlement patterns at intervals covering the period from 1000 BC to AD 300, looking for changes in the size, distribution, and function of settlements that might serve as clues to changes in cultural complexity. During the first 400 years up to

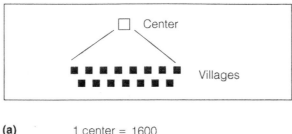

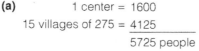

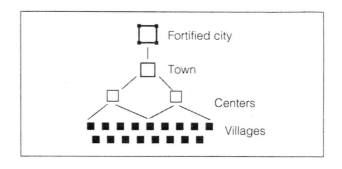

(a)

1 center = 1600
15 villages of 275 = 4125

5725 people

(b)

1 fortified city = 8000
1 town = 1920
2 centers of 1000 = 2000
17 villages of 240 = 4080

16,000 people

Figure 9.3. Settlement patterns, Ganges Plain: (a) chiefdoms (1000–600 BC and (b) early states (600–350 BC).

600 BC only two types of settlements could be distinguished: (1) numerous small villages of perhaps 275 people and (2) a small center of 1,600 people, which was in a position to control the flow of imported mineral resources. Even in the absence of clear archaeological evidence of rank, this two-level settlement hierarchy suggests that simple tribal chiefdoms existed at this time on the Ganges Plain (see figure 9.3a), but the institutions of social control must have been primarily religious and relatively unspecialized.

After 600 BC, an obvious change in political organization occurred, perhaps as high-ranking Aryans sought to enhance their control in the region. Elites apparently constructed a functionally diversified, four-level settlement hierarchy, which may have been a small kingdom (see figure 9.3b). The largest settlement within the study area became a small fortified city of perhaps 8,000 people. It contained material evidence of formal administrative, economic, and religious functions, in the form of coins, beads, sculptures, and iron slag. After 350 BC, the Ganges Valley settlement hierarchy, as archaeologically detected, successively revealed the presence of the kingdoms and empires of early classic Hindu civilization, which have also left their own historical record.

Hindu rulers merged political and religious power in their persons and were the center of a "circle of kings."[5] This was a radiating network of kings, little kings, and lords, all ranked relative to each other, and linked in a chain of personal **patron**-client relationships reaching to the village level. Each ruler commanded his own *chakra* (circle of power). This was a personal imperium, a fluctuating entourage of clients, kin, affines, dependents, or servants, all of whom were individually linked to the ruler by ties of patronage, but may not have been otherwise related to each other.[6] These elite imperia crosscut other social categories based on ethnicity, kinship, religion, or **caste** and made it possible for rulers to create and manipulate society and culture to their personal advantage, although rulers vied with each other for the loyalty of their followers and dependents. Operating as patrons, kings gave gifts and offered protection to lesser lords in exchange for loyalty and tribute. Lesser lords cultivated similar patron-client relations with villagers, offering them protection from oppressive taxation but still extracting their labor and produce. Similar patron-client relations were also acted out between people and the gods in temples and between husband and wife in households. Throughout, loyalty, devotion, or worship was expressed by means of gifts of food, goods, or service. This very personal use of power meant that individual rulers and dynasties could easily remain in control whether the Great Tradition was predominantly Hindu, Muslim, or Buddhist.

Kings were invariably insecure because they were seldom powerful enough to command unquestioned authority throughout their realms. Therefore they portrayed themselves as divine and channeled much of their resources into staging dramatic ritual performances to demonstrate their power. They represented the kingdom as a *mandala* (circle model of the Hindu universe), with concentric rings centered on Mount Meru, the axis of the world and center of the universe in Hindu mythology. Hindu kings might claim the title *cakravarti*, "world ruler," and their power was symbolized by the chakra shown in representations of the Hindu god Vishnu. Behind the legitimizing ideological framework lay military power, control over land, control over people, and a revenue-collecting bureaucracy.

The first Hindu rulers used invasion and conquest to construct their kingdoms, but power-seeking individuals quickly spread Hindu circles of kings throughout Southeast Asia into tribal areas occupied by Dravidian-, Sino-Tibetan-, and Austronesian-speaking peoples. However, chiefdoms and kingdoms were not irreversible social formations. In upland areas where shifting cultivation was practiced, often only fragile chiefdoms could be constructed, and then only temporarily. For example, in twentieth century Sino-Tibetan-speaking Burma, an enterprising tribal headman could, with effort and under the right circumstances, turn himself into a chief, local lord, or small king and form a small, fortified temple center.[7] Transformation from headman to chief required an especially productive resource base, skillful manipulation of marriage exchanges, and the ability to sponsor large feasts, ritually sacrifice cattle, support an expanded household, and build a network of supporters. Such success was a conspicuous demonstration of personal merit, potency, or spiritual virtue like Polynesian *mana*, except that in the Burmese case power could be achieved.[8] A chief might then become a client-vassal to a Hindu-Buddhist king who occupied a larger, walled center with a temple and palace. In addition to the Hindu kingdoms in South Asia, between AD 500 and 1400 perhaps a hundred small temple centers and some twenty-four large centers were formed in Southeast Asia.[9]

BOX 9.1. HARAPPAN CIVILIZATION: THE EARLIEST SOUTH ASIAN STATE

After 3500 BC, people had begun to develop the agricultural potential of the Indus floodplain, and the settled population began to increase. Between 2800 and 2500 BC, small, walled urban sites were constructed, and the presence of a highly uniform ceramic style over a wide area, together with further evidence of long-distance trade, indicate that a socioeconomic interaction network had developed. Over the next several centuries (approximately 2500 to 1500 BC), Harappan civilization flourished throughout the Indus region. This was the earliest state-level culture in South Asia.

Harappa, at the upper end of the Indus floodplain, and Mohenjo-Daro, in the lower, were major urban centers, both built according to a similar plan. Mohenjo-Daro may have had a population of 35,000 people. It contained an elevated, brick-walled citadel with a large ritual bath, grain storehouses, and probably a temple. Near the citadel was a separate, lower, and much larger grid cluster of brick buildings, which were residences and workshops. Houses had bathrooms complete with drains that emptied into what appeared to be a public sewer system. The diversity of house plans and the presence of single-room barracks suggest differences in social class or wealth, but no royal tombs have been found, and the Harappan elite remain anonymous, suggesting that this was a significantly different sociocultural system from those that followed.

The Harappans produced finely crafted utilitarian objects in bronze and copper, as well as jewelry and beads in gold, silver, and semiprecious stones. Because the floodplain lacked mineral resources, they maintained extensive trade contacts throughout India and as far as Central Asia and Mesopotamia. Standardized sets of weights and measures and numerous incised seals, resembling those from Mesopotamia but bearing unique Harappan markings, are further indications of the importance of trade. The Harappan language may be Dravidian, and a unique Harappan script appears to be a writing system, although it has never been successfully deciphered.[10] Terra-cotta figurines and inscriptions of earth mothers, horned men, bulls, composite animals, and human-animals have been interpreted to be cult objects and forerunners of important Hindu deities such as Siva and Parvati. The Harappan civilization apparently collapsed completely around 1500 BC for reasons that are not well understood.

Kautilya's Hindu Kingdom: An Emic Political Model, 250 BC

The ideal organization of the early Hindu state is precisely detailed in Kautilya's Arthasastra,[11] a written manual on ancient Indian statecraft. The Arthasastra is attributed to Kautilya, a minister in the Mauryan empire in 250 BC but was probably written by several people in the early centuries AD. It is a composite treatise on political science for kings and aspiring kings, written with candor, cynicism, and insight. As a manual for public administrators, it resembles the Confucian classics, but instead of professional ethics and ritual, the Arthasastra advocates the use of coercive power backed by the army, the police, the courts, and covert state security agents. The Arthasastra may be taken as a portrayal of the ideal structure and function of a hypothetical Indian kingdom during the early centuries of classic Hindu civilization. As an emic view, composed by elite political professionals, it may not be an accurate picture of any specific kingdom, and the ideal rules may not have been followed. However, the general system as described provides a useful model for comparison with the organization of tribes and other state systems.

The Arthasastra offers insider views on the use of state power for the king's personal advantage. It is filled with practical advice on palace intrigue—complete with how-to examples of the use of spies, sex, poison, and deception for political assassination—and ways to test the loyalty of government officials. In the Arthasastra, religion was simply another self-conscious tool of statecraft. Kings were advised to use

rituals and pilgrimages as excuses to raise revenue. It was even proposed that omens, such as spirits speaking in trees, be deliberately staged to stir up fear so that people would increase their religious donations.

The difference between political rulers in Indian kingdoms such as this and tribal leaders who might also use deception and treachery to personal advantage was simply that tribal cultures limited political power. Tribal leaders did not have standing armies, police forces, and secret agents at their disposal. They could not personally control the availability of basic subsistence goods to thousands of households. Tribal peoples feared and avoided those who abused their limited powers and thereby denied them control. Peasant villagers living in a world of rival kingdoms were pawns for the ruling kings, who tried to keep the levy just below the point at which disaffected villagers would join an enemy kingdom.

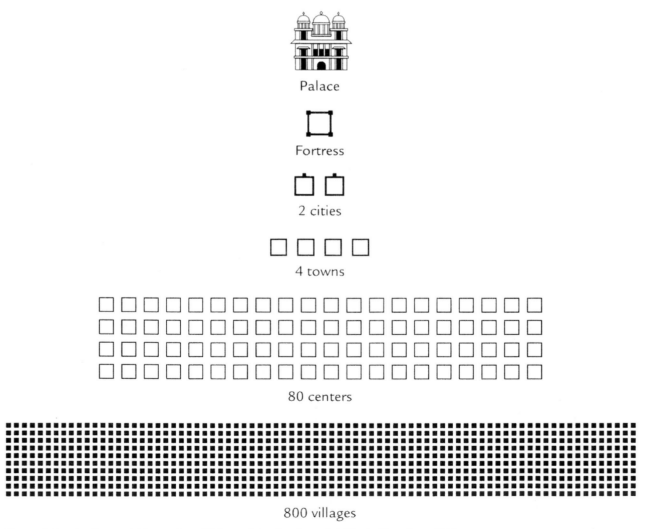

Figure 9.4. Settlement hierarchy within an idealized model Hindu kingdom, 250 BC.

In 500 BC there were some eighteen large kingdoms in northern India centered on the Gangetic Plain.[12] According to the Arthasastra, an ideally organized kingdom would have been divided into four districts, each containing eight hundred villages dominated by a fortified city, with two smaller cities, four towns, and eighty small local centers hierarchically arranged to facilitate administration and the flow of revenue. The government officials in two cities would have administrative responsibility for four hundred villages each, officials in four towns would control two hundred villages each, and some eighty local centers would each be responsible for very specific census taking, tax collecting, and police work in ten villages within the district (see figure 9.4). Such an arrangement closely corresponds to the archaeological record and suggests that a kingdom might have contained some 1.6 million people, with perhaps 143,000 people, 9 percent of the total population, living in cities of 2,000 people or more (see table 9.2).

A kingdom of 1.6 million people would have been much more amenable to management by direct political power than the 50 to 500 million people living in the vast Chinese empire, or the later Hindu-Muslim Mughal Empire. Mughal, also spelled Mogul, refers to the Mongol origin of the first Muslim dynasty in India. Traditional China and early Hindu India make an interesting comparison because they were both preindustrial, agrarian civilizations, yet there were significant cultural differences. As shown in chapter 8, China relied primarily on ethical principles, ritual, moral authority, and patrilineal descent groups to maintain social order. Hindu India, in contrast, used the moral authority of religion to support an endogamous caste system and relied on coercive political authority to a significant degree. Although patrilineage, clan,

and filial piety were primary integrating principles in China, and caste was primary in India, diverse forms of lineage and clan were also important in many areas of village India. Military power backed up the moral order in both cultural systems. In India, kings built a succession of empires that peaked with Akbar the Great's (1542–1605) empire of 110 million people. Akbar's empire was so large that military mobilization was a dominant preoccupation and absorbed much of the imperial social product.

The territory of an Indian kingdom was relatively small. The total population of 1.6 million required total territory of approximately 34,749 square miles (90,000 km²), 186 miles (300 km) on a side. In comparison, the 500 million people of the Chinese empire at its height were spread over a territory of 3.4 million square miles (9 million km²). It is not surprising that Chinese civilization came to rely so heavily on moral authority.

The approximate social composition of a hypothetical Hindu kingdom suggests that a surprisingly small elite maintained absolute power. There may have been fewer than 150 salaried elites in the top administrative ranks, barely 50,000 retainers, bureaucrats, specialists, and merchants who paid taxes in cash, and perhaps 275,000 farm householders. Most of the population, probably about 85 percent, lived in farm households, which supplied basic subsistence for the other 15 percent. State-supported craft specialists did produce consumer goods for the villagers, but much of their production directly supported the state.

The Arthasastra gives a detailed picture of the revenue system and basic administrative structure of the Hindu kingdom. State-controlled wealth was concentrated in the capital and in district fortresses. An underground royal treasury vault contained gold,

Table 9.2. Population of Model Hindu Kingdom, 350 BC

Number per District	Population in Each*	Total
Fortified City (1)	20,000	20,000
Cities (2)	3,500	7,000
Towns (4)	2,000	8,000
Centers (80)	1,000	80,000
Villages (800)	350	280,000

Total District Population
4 Districts = 1,580,000
Capital city = 35,000
Kingdom total = 1,615,000
Urban population (cities over 2000 people) = 143,000 (8.8%)

Sources: Erdosy (1988) and Kautilya's Arthasastra (Shamasastry 1960).

*The Arthasastra states that villages ranged in size from 100 to 500 families. Erdosy estimates 3.5 persons per family and average villages of 240 people, assuming 160 people per hectare of archaeological site. Thus, villages of 350 people represent the lower range for the Arthasastra figures but are higher than predicted archaeologically.

jewelry, coins, and precious textiles. Special storehouses held grain and other products, which were collected as taxes in kind or produced on crown land. Farmers paid an average grain tax of 16 percent, which was raised to 25 to 33 percent under emergency conditions. There were also village taxes, temple taxes, gate taxes, sales taxes, income taxes, tolls, fines, and excise taxes of various sorts. Some villagers submitted to corvée labor or military inscription in place of the grain tax.

Although there were no vast canal systems or irrigation works in ancient India, large armies were mobilized for frequent wars, and royal construction projects and defensive works required large labor forces. For example, estimates that construction of the 49-foot (15-m)-tall earthen ramparts stretching for 3.7 miles (6 km) around a fortified city would have engaged 20,000 workmen for 250 days.[13]

The state regulated commercial activities, mining, forestry, herding, and craft production to extract the maximum feasible revenue (see figure 9.5). Even prostitutes were licensed and they paid a monthly income tax. The supply of marketable consumer goods was centrally controlled. Only the Brahmans, who formed the religious elite, and frontier villages and state-supported colonization projects were exempt from taxes. A collector general attached to the royal palace was responsible for all revenue collection received from district and village tax collectors. There was also a high-ranking tax commissioner and a tax inspector, who used covert means to monitor the flow of revenue. Detailed bookkeeping was carried out at all levels, and all government expenses were further monitored by the central accounts office.

Many diverse functions were carried out in the fortified city, especially if it was also the capital. As described in the Arthasastra, the city was divided into twelve major sections, where specific categories of people were expected to live and where specific activities and buildings were to be located (see figure 9.6). Each of the four varna, or "colors," representing the four ranks of Vedic society—Brahman, Kshatriya, Vaisya, and Sudra—was assigned specific quarters within the city, grouped together with appropriately ranked economic activities. These social categories will be discussed in more detail in the later section dealing with caste.

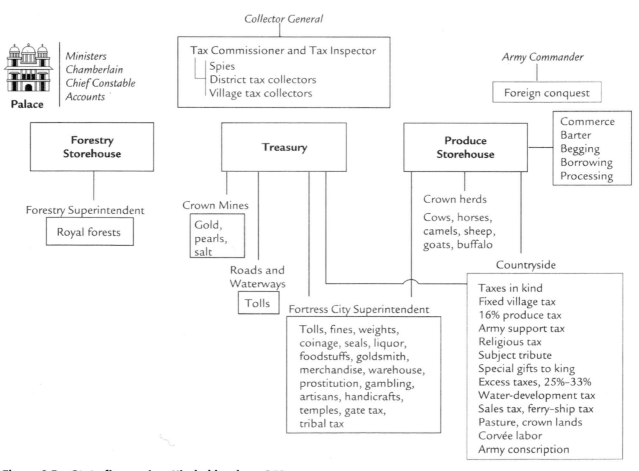

Figure 9.5. State finance in a Hindu kingdom, 250 BC.

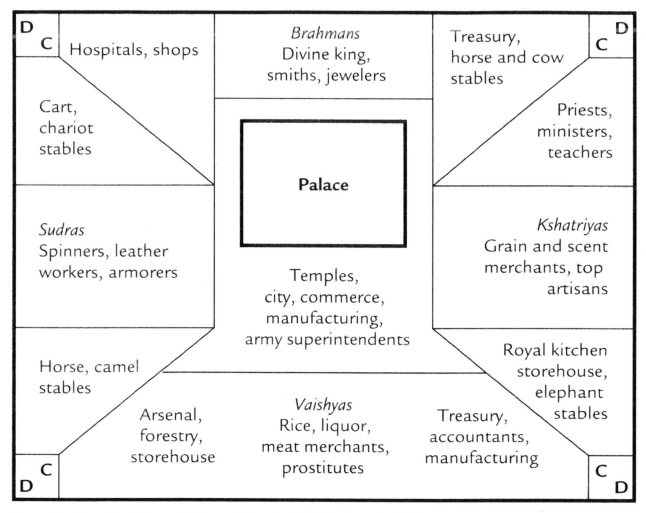

Figure 9.6. Functional diversification within a fortified Hindu capital, 250 BC.

The *varna* were the early form of the caste system. During this early period of Hindu civilization, they were already associated with endogamy, relative purity, and occupation. For example, the Sudra, in the lowest-ranked *varna*, were assigned to the city's west quarter, where leather working, an especially spiritually polluting activity, was carried out. The royal palace occupied one-ninth of the city and was to be located just north of city center, opening onto the sections occupied by Brahmans, jewelers, and the divine king. Merchants and high-ranking specialist crafts were located in the east quarter together with government ministers and the Kshatriya.

Law in the Hindu Kingdom

The legal system in the Hindu kingdom upheld the authority of the state and the *varna* social system, which gave ritual priority and economic advantage to the upper ranks. Furthermore, fines imposed by the court were a source of state revenue and enforced the

tax system. Law was based on tradition, or customary law, and on *dharma*, or sacred religious law, which resembled *li* in the Chinese system. Both *dharma* and *li* referred to duty, morality, and proper conduct; however, where *li* emphasized duty to emperor, ancestors, and family, *dharma* laid out different moral requirements for each *varna* and for individuals at different stages of the life cycle. Furthermore, the Hindu king was clearly a political ruler.

All law in the Hindu kingdom was ultimately vested in the king, who was assisted by his political ministers and priestly authorities on *dharma*. According to the secular authors of the Arthasasra, the king's traditional law had legal priority over *dharma*, and the king was expected to use the state's power and physical punishment to "maintain both this world and the next."[14]

Laws were explicitly designed to support the *varna* system and provided a quantified measure of the relative worth of each rank. For example, one could be fined for causing a Brahman to violate one of his food taboos, and a Sudra could be burned alive for committing adultery with a Brahman woman. Brahmans were generally immune from taxes, fines, and punishments. The fine for selling a Brahman child into slavery was four times as severe as when the victim was a Sudra. The sons of a Brahman woman were to inherit four shares of their Brahman father's estate, but only one share if their mother was a Sudra. Twenty-four different terms existed to describe the conditions of birth according to the *varna* of the parents. The caste system itself was generated by the legal classification and rank ordering of all the logically possible types of marriage between people in different *varna* categories.[15]

There was a broad, three-level scale for fines in pana, the basic monetary unit, ranging from under 100 to 1,000 pana. According to the government's salary scale, the highest officials were paid 24,000 to 48,000 pana a year, midrange officials earned 1,000 to 12,000 pana, and the lowest retainers earned just 60 pana. Those unable to pay fines could substitute an equal number of lashes or body parts according to a scale of equivalent values. A thumb was worth 54 pana; a right hand, 400 pana; and both eyes, 800 pana.

Verbal abuse or insults were scaled according to whether they were true, false, or sarcastic. For example, calling a blind man "blind" was true abuse, but telling a blind man that he had beautiful eyes was false abuse. Generally, the fine was doubled if the victim

was in a superior *varna* and halved if the victim was inferior (see table 9.3). More precise rank distinctions could also be made if one's profession was insulted, with the severity of the fine increasing by three for each increase in the victim's relative rank and decreasing by two for lower-level ranks.

The legal severity of physical assault was measured along a graduated scale of violence taking into account both the objects used and the body areas struck. The Hindu scale added relative rank. Throwing mud on a low-ranking person's feet was a minor offense (0.5 pana), whereas throwing feces on a high-ranking person's face was a very serious offense (96 pana). The most serious cases involved extreme differences in rank. Although striking with a hand or leg was normally a moderate offense, the Arthasastra declared "that limb of a Shudra with which he strikes a Brahmin shall be cut off."[16]

To convince people of the "omniscient power of the state," the Arthasastra advocated routine use of undercover agents, entrapment, arrest on suspicion, torture to elicit confessions, severe punishment, and public display of criminals. Workers who failed to produce on time or who fled their workshops were fined. Theft of a minor commodity from a home or shop was punished with public humiliation, but theft of an object of one-fourth the value from the government could bring banishment. Taking any govern-

Table 9.3. Legal Fines (in panas) for Verbal Abuse, Insult, and Assault in Relation to varna in the Hindu Kingdom, 350 BC

Verbal Abuse	Victim's Rank		
	Equal	Superior	Inferior
Valid	12+	6	0.5
False	12+	12	3
Sarcasm	12+	24	6

Insulter	Victim's Rank			
	Brahman	Kshatriya	Vaisya	Sudra
Brahman	12	10	8	6
Kshatriya	15	12	10	8
Vaisya	18	15	12	10
Sudra	21	18	15	12

Assault	Below Navel*		Above Navel		Head	
	Inferior†	Superior†	Inferior	Superior	Inferior	Superior
Throwing mud	0.5	6	3	12	6	24
Spitting	3	12	6	24	12	48
Throwing feces	6	24	12	48	24	96

Source: Shamasastry (1960 [Arthasastra]).

*Target

†Rank

ment property worth more than eight pana, spreading rumors, letting out prisoners, or using government documents without authorization could mean death. Insulting the king was punished by cutting out the offender's tongue. The most severe punishment, burning alive, was reserved for those spreading disorder in the countryside.

Power and Scale in the Thai Kingdom and the Mughal Empire

Remarkably, the distribution of social power by rank that can be inferred from Kautilya's model kingdom corresponds closely to the ethnographically documented power structure of the Hindu-Buddhist Thai kingdom in 1851 under the Chakri dynasty (1782–1932), and the much larger Hindu-Muslim Mughal Empire in 1605. These examples demonstrate the power-concentrating effects of growth in the scale of society and also show that similar social structures can be supported by diverse ideological systems.

Growth in scale produced an astounding concentration of power for Akbar, the Mughal emperor. The 110 million subjects commanded by Akbar were two orders of magnitude more numerous than the 4 million commanded by the Thai king, and the 1.6 million in the early Hindu kingdom. These scale differences were reflected in the size of ruler households and the magnificence of their lifestyles.

The social distance from top to bottom in these societies was staggering but not fundamentally different from that seen in Ur III, the Inca Empire, and imperial China. For example, in 1851 the Thai kingdom was divided into three broad but finely ranked social classes: nobles, commoners, and slaves (see table 9.4). The king assigned every household head a *sakdina* (dignity) rank from 5 to 100,000 *sakdina*, whereas his own *sakdina* was "infinite."[17] Each *sakdina* was worth 0.4 acres of cultivable land, the amount a water buffalo could plow in a day. Ninety-five percent of the households were at the maintenance level or below with an average of 25 or fewer *sakdina*, but 50 percent were objectively poor with only 10 *sakdina* or less, making them vulnerable to servitude. In contrast, the *sakdina* of the ordinary elite ranged from 400 to 5,000, and on the average may have supported households of 50 persons. At the top, King Mongkut (see figure 9.7) maintained a personal household of 9,000 wives, concubines, slaves, and retainers in a 100-hectare (247-acre) walled palace compound, at the center of a city of 50,000 people. Mongkut officially produced 82 children from 35 mothers. Life in the Thai royal court and harem was described in detail by the Englishwoman Anna Leonowens,[18] who spent six years as a tutor in Mongkut's palace.

The Thai kingdom was large enough that in addition to the royal dynasty, other high-ranking elites were able to perpetuate their personal imperia as dynasties. For example, just four nonroyal families were able to maintain cross-generational control over the six top ministries. One family held power from 1782 to 1886.[19]

Akbar's empire was so large that in 1605 he in effect commanded 20 percent of the world's people.[20] If Akbar's empire is counted together with the empire of his contemporary, the emperor of Ming China, then just two men commanded half of the world's people at

Table 9.4. Thai Households by Class, Rank, Title, and Imperial Chakri Dynasty, 1782–1932

Classes	Titles	Sakdina Ranks	Households	Dependents	Imperia
Nobles 0.2%	Universal Monarch Lord Buddha, Great Ruler, Lord of the Land, Lord of Life	infinite	1	225,000	Super-Elite 0.2%
	Royal Family and Top Officials, Crown Prince, Prince	Range 100,000–5000	500	Average 500	
	Nobles, Lesser Royalty	Range 5000–400	1000	50	Elite 5%
Commoners 75%	Petty Officials	Range 50–300	36,000	7	Maintenance 45%
	Labor Supervisors	25	120,000	0	
	Freemen	15	242,500		
	King's Men, Servants	10	200,000		Poor 50%
	Poor, Beggars	5	200,000		
Slaves 25%	Slaves, Bond Slaves, Criminals, Captives				

Sources: A. Rabibhadana (1969), Poumisak (1987), H.G. Quaritcha Wales (1934).

Note: Perhaps another 100,000 people were living as monks.

Figure 9.7. Thai King Mongkut, reign 1851–1868 (Ratzel 1898:427).

that time. They converted their social power into extraordinary personal luxury. The quantitative details of Mughal India during Akbar's reign are thoroughly documented in a text, the *Ain-i-Akbari* compiled in the 1590s by one of Akbar's ministers, Abu Fazl.[21] The record shows that at least 18 percent of the empire's national product of R 650 million (R = rupees, 1 rupee = 11 grams of silver) was appropriated by Akbar and his top 1,672 nobles.[22] This R 108 million financed the government and elite luxuries. Akbar's annual expenditure on his personal household was approximately R 20 million, or 3 percent of the empire's total annual product. This may seem like a small amount, but given that an average villager household subsisted annually on the equivalent of R 20, Akbar's personal consumption was a million times greater than minimum subsistence. About two-thirds of government income was used to support the military establishment, including the maintenance of Akbar's personal guard of 90,000 men, but a great deal was spent on extravagant luxury. Akbar maintained a harem of 5,000 women, and on

hunting expeditions traveled with an entourage of more than 2,000 men, 500 camels, and 100 elephants. This suggests that this was a practical ceiling for the size of harems and personal households, but palaces could be multiplied, and treasure could also be expended on art, monumental constructions, and other displays. In 1570 Akbar commanded the construction of the lavish city of Fatehpur-Sikri, as an entirely new walled royal capital and palace complex, complete with harems, audience halls, mosques, residences, gardens, waterworks, and tombs.[23] The city was an architectural splendor, but Akbar and his elite clients only occupied it from 1572 to 1588, when it was completely abandoned.

HINDU IDEOLOGY, SOCIETY, AND CULTURE

Caste and Orthodox Hinduism: The Brahman View of Dharma

Hindu civilization is most widely known for its caste system with its emphasis on hierarchy and on ritual **purity** and ritual or spiritual pollution, which continues to be a major fact of life in India. The caste system assumed its basic form in the Hindu kingdoms during the last centuries BC, as described in the preceding section. The term *caste* is an English version of the Spanish and Portuguese word *casta*, meaning "race," "breed," or "family." The corresponding Indian term is *jati*, "birth" or "breed," which emphasizes that caste membership is assigned by birth; each caste is ideally an endogamous group. At its most general level, caste has been defined as a society "made up of birth-ascribed groups which are hierarchically ordered and culturally distinct. The hierarchy entails differential evaluation, rewards, and association."[24]

By this definition, caste could also describe race relations in the United States in the 1950s[25] and the positions of blacksmiths in East Africa. French anthropologist Louis Dumont[26] took a more intellectualist approach, describing Indian caste as an ideological system of categories based on (1) hierarchically ordered social groups, (2) detailed rules of separation, and (3) a division of labor. The four *varna*—Brahman, Kshatriya, Vaisya, and Sudra—can be considered the most general castes, but castes are continuously segmented into many localized subcastes, which form finely ranked regional systems. The members of subcastes claim descent from a common founder and identify an original group specialty—such as herding, farming, blacksmithing, or weaving—even though it may not always be practiced.

Many scholars view caste as the defining symbol of Hindu society, but this is an incomplete understanding. What we know about "traditional" Hindu society and culture, including how we understand caste, is a product of centuries of conquest and empire building, and the selective transmission and creation of cultural knowledge. Hindu society is based on a continually evolving moral system that has been under construction for centuries (see figure 9.8). A tiny elite of Hindu intellectuals first recorded its features in ancient Sanskrit texts, but over the centuries various political and economic rulers, as well as ordinary people, have continually reshaped the Hindu cultural system into a tool for their self-interest. However, in this cultural process the elites, because of their dominant position, have been most influential and have been able to define the system's boundaries. This is the exercise of **cultural hegemony**. Most recently, from 1757 to 1947 British colonial rulers were the dominant influences on Hindu society. In asserting their rule over a vast and diverse society, they used laws, maps, and the census, backed by military and economic power, in ways that made caste the dominant social fact of Indian society. In the process they deposed Indian political rulers and transformed the caste system.[27] Before British rule, as the previous discussion of Kautilya's Hindu kingdom shows, kings, as political rulers, were the dominant agents in society, not the Brahman priests.

The caste system is supported by Hindu ideology. Modern Hinduism is a complex blend of beliefs and practices originating in the Vedic period and carried on in a formal, "Great Tradition" way by Brahman priests who follow rituals based on the sacred Vedic texts. A central feature of Hinduism is belief in *samsara*, an endless cycle of death and rebirth experienced by the human soul. This is reincarnation, or transmigration of the soul, and is closely connected with the concept of *karma*, the belief that what a person did in a previous existence determines the conditions of one's future existence. This explains one's position in the caste system and holds out the possibility of being reborn in a higher caste. It also focuses attention on the importance of following proper ritual behavior, which is the only means of finding salvation from *samsara*. The city of Varanasi (Benares) on the Ganges (see figure 9.9) is not only a central holy city, and sacred pilgrimage site for all Hindus, but those who die here may escape the *samsara* cycle of rebirth. For Brahmans, ritual purity as prescribed in the Veda is also required for approaching the supreme lord Brahman. Ritual pollution, or impurity, is caused by any behavior proscribed by the Vedic texts and requires ritual purification.

Caste organization and related concepts of ritual purity have a significant bearing on aspects of Hindu marriage and family life. Caste endogamy, the requirement that one marry within the caste, helps define caste boundaries, but subcastes are often further subdivided into exogamous lineages and clans. Marriage between different subcastes is often characterized by **hypergamy**, in which low-rank women marry equal- or higher-ranked men. This practice may severely limit choices for women in high-ranked subcastes, whereas down-marrying men (**hypogamy**) are unlikely to experience difficulty.

Marriage is one of the most important Hindu rituals. It involves great expenditure by the bride's family and extreme concern for ritual purity and status. Normally all marriages are arranged by the families of the prospective bride and groom. Chastity is a ritual requirement, especially for the highest castes, and is related to infant marriage, prohibition on divorce

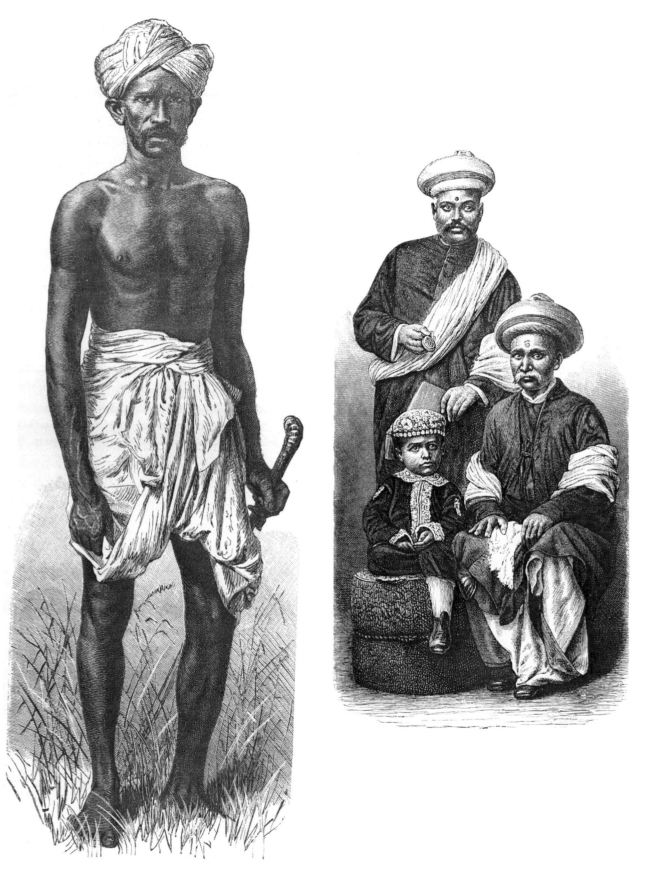

Figure 9.8. **Hindu types, nineteenth century India, A. laborer; B. merchants; C. ascetic (Ratzel 1898:357, 372, 529, respectively).**

Figure 9.8. (Continued)

and widow remarriage, and the practice of *sati*, or widow self-immolation, in which a "virtuous woman" throws herself on her husband's funeral pyre to be transformed into a goddess. Many of these practices are followed only by the strictest Brahman subcastes, which adhere to the severest requirements for ritual purity. It must also be stressed that marriages did not always conform to the expected patterns, but when they didn't, a loss of ritual status could occur.

Dumont[28] maintained that the three basic aspects of caste—hierarchy, separation, and division of labor—can all be reduced to the single principle of the opposition of pure and impure. The pure are defined as superior, and impure castes are impure because of their association with impure occupational specialties. **Impurity** for Hindus means a loss of status and is caused by association with "polluting" organic products and biological events such as birth, puberty, menses, and death. In tribal societies, such events may put individuals temporarily at supernatural risk, but Hindu ideology permanently associates particular social groups with impure biological events or organic products. The Hindu system is a logical reversal of the practice common in chiefdoms in which the chief is considered to be endowed with sacred power (*mana*), which makes him dangerously *tabu* to lower-ranked individuals, but in India it is lower-ranked individuals who endanger higher ranks.

The most extreme form of pollution could be transmitted by mere physical contact. This kind of impurity applied to members of the lowest Sudra castes, who were handlers of dead animals and human waste. They might also eat meat, including beef. Europeans called them untouchables, because any contact with such persons required some form of ritual purification, such as sprinkling with water. In India, untouchables are sometimes called Harijans, or "God's children," or "exterior castes." They are exterior because they are often excluded from many public activities due to their ritual disabilities. Untouchability was officially declared illegal by the Indian constitution of 1949 and by Pakistan's constitution of 1953, but it continues to be an important social phenomenon.

The mythical charter for caste is found in the *Purusha* myth, an account of creation contained in the Dharma Shastra of Manu[29] (see also box 9.2). According to this account, Lord Brahma, the creator god, "for the prosperity of the worlds" created the four *varna*—Brahman, Kshatriya, Vaisya, and Sudra—from his mouth, arms, thigh, and feet, respectively.[30] Separate duties were assigned by the creator to each *varna*. The Brahmans were the "Lords of Creation" and the perpetual incarnation of *dharma* (sacred law). They were the priests, teachers, sacrificers, and receivers of gifts, who, because of their "superiority and eminence of birth" were entitled to "whatever exists in the universe."[31] The Kshatriya were to be protectors of the people and took political roles as rulers and warriors. The Vaisya were responsible for cattle herding, farming, and trade. The Sudra were to serve the

Figure 9.9. Varanasi, or Benares, India, Hindu sacred city on the Ganges, late nineteenth century (Stoddard 1892:405).

top three *varna*, "without grudging." Similarly, only the top three were allowed to participate in a series of initiation rites that allowed them to be considered "twice-born," and only the twice-born could request the Brahman priests to perform sacrifices.

There are thousands of castes throughout modern India, and many different ways of grouping and ranking them. It is common, particularly in census-taking, to group them by *varna* ranks, but caste clusters, castes, and subcastes may be distinguished.

Hindu building manuals prescribe a physical layout of house and temple that supports the caste system and the social hierarchy. Figure 9.10 shows the formal architectural plan of a Brahman's house in South India based on a sixth-century text, which outlined a model for domestic houses that was still followed in the twentieth century.[32] Rooms are aligned with the cosmos, including the cardinal directions. The house literally

builds on the body of a mythic Foundation Man, who supports Brahma, the primordial solar creator god, Brahma's twelve attendants, the enlighteners, and an outer array of gods and demons, each associated with particular human concerns such as birth, death, illness, and ancestors. The sun rotates from east to west, and the north-south axis is associated with birth and death cycles respectively. The arrangement of the deities in concentric rings of one, four, eight, and thirty-two portrays a rank order that naturalizes hierarchy. This rank order is also reflected in the sequential order of domestic space with the atrium as the center of the house, and the rooms, the veranda, the compound, and the outside ranked in descending order of exclusivity. The rooms of the house are also functionally aligned with the Foundation Man so that the kitchen corresponds with his mouth, his genitals with the bedroom, and his impure left hand with the latrine.

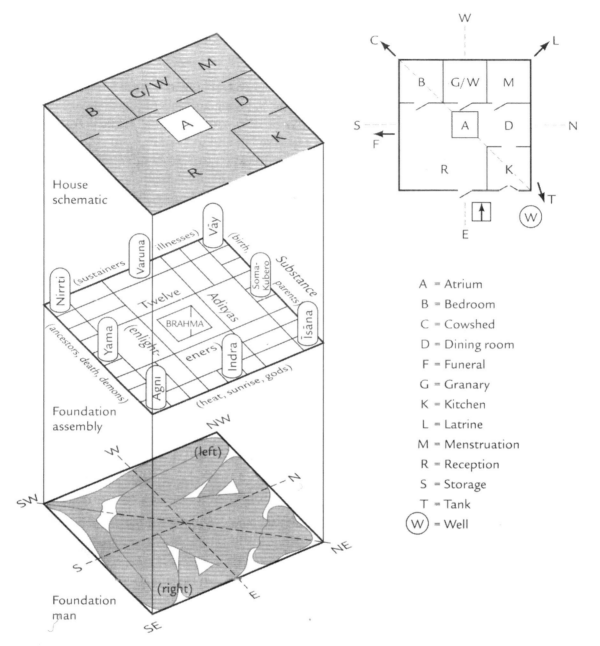

Figure 9.10. South Indian Brahman house layout with supporting gods and Foundation Man (re-drafted from Moore 1989, Figures 1 and 3).

A = Atrium
B = Bedroom
C = Cowshed
D = Dining room
F = Funeral
G = Granary
K = Kitchen
L = Latrine
M = Menstruation
R = Reception
S = Storage
T = Tank
(W) = Well

BOX 9.2. THE PURUSHA MYTH: A MYTHIC CHARTER FOR *VARNA* AND CASTE

"But in order to protect this universe, He, the most resplendent one, assigned separate (duties and) occupations to those who sprang from his mouth, arms, thighs, and feet.

To Brahmans he assigned teaching and studying (the Veda), sacrificing for their own benefit and for others, giving and accepting (of alms).

The Kshatriya he commanded to protect the people, to bestow gifts, to offer sacrifices, to study (the Veda), and to abstain from attaching himself to sensual pleasures.

The Vaisya to tend cattle, to bestow gifts, to offer sacrifices, to study (the Veda), to trade, to lend money, and to cultivate land.

One occupation only the lord prescribed to the Sudra, to serve meekly even these (other) three castes."
—Code of Manu[33]

Food, Eating, and Caste in Hindu Culture

Caste membership may be defined in a very general way by occupational specialty and by endogamy, but food rules are also very important. Certain caste groups are distinguished by strict vegetarianism, avoidance of domestic pigs and fowl, abstinence from alcohol, or the eating of pork or beef. At the village level, caste membership is also defined by the commensal hierarchy, according to which castes give or accept specific categories of food or water from each other or smoke together.[34]

Hindu intellectuals made ideas about food a central element in their esoteric cosmological texts. The food circulation model presented in figure 9.11 was abstracted from ancient texts and contemporary ethnographic observation by Indian anthropologist Ravindra Khare.[35] It is remarkably similar to the Andean cosmology (see figure 7.16). There is an explicit flow of energy and materials and a hierarchical structure in both cosmologies. Hindu cosmology distinguishes material and spiritual existence and assumes a three-ranked cosmos with a natural base, divided into organic and inorganic sectors; a human level in the middle, distinguishing individual and social group; and a supernatural level at the top, distinguishing human ancestors and gods. This resembles the familiar anthropological analytic framework of infrastructure, structure, and superstructure.

Food moves through the Hindu cosmos in four interconnected cycles, each more inclusive, as follows: (1) through the body of an individual person; (2) ritual exchanges between individuals and groups; (3) symbiotic and spiritual links between the gods, people, and nature; (4) from primordial material to spiritual order. The physical and cultural existence of food is variously degraded, regenerated, and degenerated in these cycles from inorganic to organic, from pure to impure, and from impure back to pure. As a natural category "food" may exist as food (*anna*), leftover garbage (*jutha*), or excrement (*git*). In the supernatural order food offered to the gods becomes *prasad* and can be eaten by everyone, but other forms of food necessarily encode social status and rank.

If village-level food transactions are viewed as a ranking game, then an individual player may win a point, or dominate, in any transaction between unequal partners in which he gives food to the other player, but loses points when he receives food.[36] The act of giving food can establish dominance, whereas receiving can establish subordination. Relative caste ranking in a community is the net score (wins minus losses) from a series of such transactions. Raw foodstuffs, *sidha*, such as grain, flour, and sugar are given back and forth among the members of all castes, except the very lowest castes, such as hunters and sweepers, who can receive from everyone but can only give to each other. Cooked foods are either *kacha*, which is commonly rice boiled in water, or *pakka*, which is fried in oil. *Kacha* foods are highly restricted by purity rules, and the way in which they are distributed makes fine distinctions in rank between givers and receivers. For example, anthropologist McKim Marriot[37] was able to sort the 166 families and 24 castes in a North Indian village into 12 ranks based on their *pakka*, *kacha*, and garbage transaction scores.

Within their households, orthodox Brahman Hindus make an important ritual distinction between cooking and serving areas and maintain separate storage areas for uncooked and cooked food.[38] The storage area is inside the house near the worship area, or in the pure end of the house as shown in figure 9.10, and must be kept far from the impure waste disposal area. The cooking area is compared to the most sacred area of a temple. It is an exclusive space where only the cook is allowed. The serving area is less exclusive. The serving and eating area may itself be subdivided into three ranked subzones by degree of purity and exclusiveness. The cooking and serving areas become impure when eating is over, and leftovers and cooking vessels must be cleaned in a separate washing place. Members of the lowest caste deal with the final waste, but a higher caste does the washing. The food area is ritually cleaned by low-caste workers twice a day after each of the two daily meals. All visible specks of dirt must be removed from floor, hearth, utensils, or furniture, and the wall freshly plastered with cow dung to return these areas to their original high rank. The important point is that the high-caste person requires the services of a lower-caste person to restore his own high ritual status. The cook must be either a Brahman or the highest-ranking person in the household, and in a state of ritual purity. Purification requires complete bathing in water and wearing freshly hand-washed clothing.

Kacha and *pakka* foods must be kept separate, because *pakka* foods become *kacha* when they come in contact with *kacha* food. A cook may not taste food as he cooks because that would make it "eaten" food, thereby polluting the entire meal. Food is polluted by contact with saliva. Offering food to the deity and keeping the fire going help it retain its pure state. Men eat before women, and a husband eats separately from

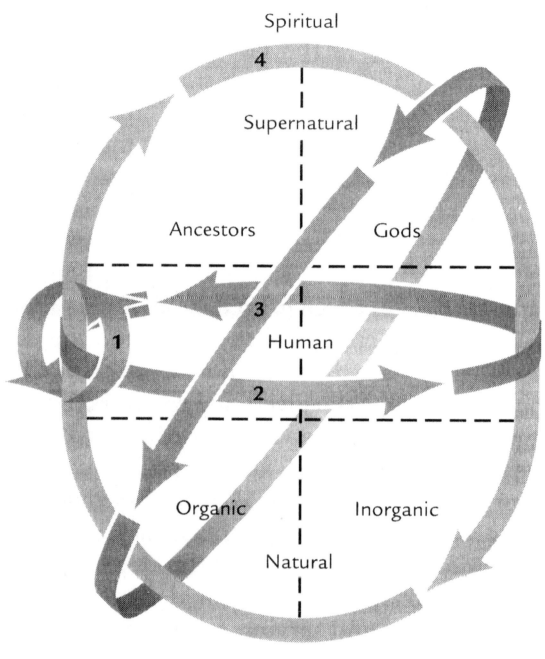

Spiritual

4

Supernatural

Ancestors   Gods

3

Human

2

Organic   Inorganic

Natural

Material

1 = Minimal (individual cycle)

2 = Primary (social-ritual cycle)

3 = Secondary (cosmographic cycle)

4 = Maximal (primordial cycle)

Figure 9.11.   A Hindu cosmology based on food cycles (redrafted from Khare 1976:136).

his wife. In preparation for his meal, a senior Brahman would be ritually purified by bathing and would wear only a hand-washed loincloth and sandals. He would wash his hands and feet, gargle, and sprinkle water on his head before seating himself on the floor in the eating area, on a spot where water had been sprinkled. Women servers would be veiled in his presence. Before eating, he would offer a food sacrifice to the fire, then he would eat in silence, and after eating he would touch the empty plate three times, thanking the food god. Then he would again wash his hands and feet, because eating makes one impure. He might leave food on his plate for his wife.

Village-Level Caste and Exploitation

From 1954 to 1956, anthropologist Adrian Mayer[39] studied caste relations in the village of Ramkheri in the Malwa district of Madhya Pradesh in central India. Ramkheri was a relatively large village with 912 people belonging to 27 different castes. The castes were grouped by mutual consent into 5 groups and 11 ranks, with the Brahmans at the top and five untouchable castes at the bottom. Groups of castes at a similar rank tended to be localized in distinct quarters of the village. An interdependent division of labor, called the *jajmani* system, operated between the castes, with certain castes, such as barber, carpenter, blacksmith, potter, tanner-shoemaker, and sweeper, providing community-wide services. For example, the sweeper caste was responsible for cleaning latrines and disposing of dead animals—highly polluting functions that benefited everyone. In exchange for their services, caste members received foodstuffs according to a regular schedule. Some caste members, such as farmers and tailors who sold their products in town, were paid in cash for their goods by their fellow villagers.

All castes could draw water from the village well except the Harijan, who used their own wells and even washed their clothes and bathed at a separate place in the stream. The Harijan were expected to avoid the village temple and stood in the background during community meetings.

In the case of Ramkheri the caste system had obvious implications for social stratification. The high-caste individuals owned more and tended to be more prosperous than low-caste people. However, wealth differences were not extreme and people partly attributed them to expectations about relative occupational abilities. The economic advantages enjoyed by the upper castes were to some extent offset by the mutual advantages provided by the caste division of labor, and

people appeared to accept their traditional occupations as a religious duty. Basic Hindu beliefs in *karma* and reincarnation support such acceptance by implying that one's karma (deeds or action) in life reflects previous existences and shapes one's future lives. The next life might be more pleasant.

Researchers in other areas described more extreme wealth inequities between castes. For example, Gerald Berreman,[40] who worked in the Himalayan foothills of Uttar Pradesh in 1957 and 1958, found that the Rajput and Brahmans enjoyed what has been called "decisive dominance"[41] in the region. From 1966 to 1968 the highest castes in the Kangra district of Himachal Pradesh received the best education, owned the most land, and held the best jobs.[42]

The conspicuous inequality inherent in the caste system has led Western observers to focus on its economic component and to see caste as an exaggerated form of social stratification and rank, perhaps designed by the Brahmans for their own benefit. Dumont[43] acknowledged that there is an important material dimension to caste but suggested that exclusive emphasis on this aspect is ethnocentric and obscures the native view in which caste forms a rational intellectual system. Dumont argued that it is most useful to examine caste as a "state of mind." He did not claim that mental facts cause the caste system—rather, they make it intelligible.

British anthropologist J. H. Hutton,[44] in his classic study of caste, identified the functionalist advantages of caste at several levels. He argued that it provides individuals with employment, a pattern for living, and personal security. The individual castes also function as self-reproducing corporate groups. They provide for themselves many services that the state might otherwise be required to supply. Hutton further argued that the caste system contributes to Indian national stability by creating a "plural society" capable of absorbing diverse groups into a single cohesive whole. Hutton was also critical of the inequities of caste—especially the disadvantages that women suffered under it—but as a functionalist, he cautiously concluded that it is too central to Hindu culture for reform-minded government administrators to attack directly.

The Hindu caste system is an extreme form of institutionalized inequality, which, as Berreman[45] argued, arose in the process of state building by the Aryan invaders of India. Many castes are historically known to have been distinct tribal groups that were absorbed into expanding Hindu kingdoms. In the process, the hierarchical ranking of kin within tribal societies was replaced by the hierarchical ranking of castes within the state system, which was actually an incipient form of social stratification. The new ranking system helped to secure the advantageous position of the political elites by making the former tribal groups dependent and divided against themselves.

Regardless of how it may be described in intellectualist or functionalist terms, or how it may be understood emically, the caste system is a form of oppression and exploitation that benefits certain elite groups at the expense of other groups. Ultimately, it is political power that perpetuates the system. As Berreman observed, "Poverty and oppression, whether rationalized by criteria of race, ethnicity, caste, or class, are endured not because people agree on their legitimacy, but because they are enforced by those who benefit from them."[46]

Hindu Aesthetics:
Divine Image and the Religious Power of Art

The caste system, with all its inequities, is closely identified with and supported by the Hindu religion. However, beyond the belief in spiritual reincarnation, Hinduism also provides important emotional compensations for those wishing to escape the very real material inequities of caste. As monotheists, Christians and Muslims have great difficulty understanding the Hindu religion because, from a Christian viewpoint, it is based on the worship of "idols." Furthermore, the prominence of erotic themes in Hindu religious art blurs the Western distinction between the sacred and the profane, thus making Hinduism appear very profane. Closer inspection of Hinduism shows that it contains an aesthetic system that makes culturally distinctive assumptions about art, worship, and the relationship between secular and sacred. Hinduism uses religious art as a powerful tool for helping individuals at all levels of the social hierarchy to experience a feeling of contact with an ultimate, eternal reality that transcends their daily mortal concerns. Christianity and Islam may accomplish the same objectives through different means.

Two key Hindu concepts, *rasa* and *darsan*, draw attention to some of the most important contrasts between Western and Hindu notions of religion and art. Anthropologist Richard L. Anderson[47] notes that early Hindu philosophers felt that art was an important enough component of Hinduism to be considered a "fifth veda" on a par with the principal sacred texts, but open to everyone, regardless of their *varna* level. Art in the Hindu context refers first to drama, poetry, music, and dance, all of which emphasize a temporal dimension, and second, to painting, sculpture, and architecture, which are relatively static. According to classical Hindu scholars, art is supposed to be an unconscious vehicle for moral improvement and pleasure, which are assumed to be mutually reinforcing.

Rasa refers to the emotional pleasure that the experience of art can provide. Hindu art is thought to be pleasurable because it helps people attain the most important goals of the Hindu good life: righteousness, spirituality, prosperity, and pleasure.[48] It is this linking of pleasure with religion that offends some Christians, who at the same time would readily acknowledge that doing "good" should make one feel good. The Hindu concept of good merges the "sacred" goals of righteousness and spirituality with the "profane" goals of material prosperity and sensual pleasure. Thus, for Hindus, there is no contradiction in erotic religious art. The religious use of sensuality is even more obvious in Tantrism, which is a Hindu and Buddhist sect that uses food and ritualized sex as a form of religious meditation.

Rasa refers to the fleeting peak experience that art can inspire, as distinguished from religious meditation, which also has an important role in Hinduism. In a more mundane sense, *rasa* also refers to culinary flavor, spice, or relish. Scholarly definitions of *rasa* identify eight universal human emotions—happiness, pride, laughter, sorrow, anger, disgust, fear, and wonder—which may be experienced as *rasa*. Some Hindu authorities add tranquility as a ninth *rasa* emotion. Thus, religious art uses culturally specific symbols to manipulate emotion to help people feel good. As Anderson explains, art in the service of religion can sweep us away, transporting our spirits from the tedious cares and anxieties that besiege our daily lives. It provides a means whereby we can transcend the sensory world around us and escape to a state of superior pleasure, practical betterment, and, ultimately, spiritual bliss.[49]

Although Hinduism assumes the existence of one ultimate divine reality, it encourages great diversity in how this reality is culturally expressed and approached. Christianity, in contrast, is a very exclusive religion and recognizes relatively few images of divinity, such as the Father, Son, Holy Ghost, and the Virgin Mary.

Darsan refers to religious "seeing." For Hindus, viewing an image of the divine is in itself a form of worship or devotion.[50] It is expressed in pilgrimages to sacred places, in the special reverence for Hindu holy persons, and in the attention given to religious art, sculpture, temples, and shrines. Religious seeing is a two-way process. The Hindu deity must "give" its image, and the observer must receive it. Hindu polytheism is expressed in a vast variety of religious images, which may be called icons when they take on a definite form—for example, as a representational painting or sculpture (see box 9.3). Often Hindu icons combine animal and human shapes with multiple arms, heads, or eyes to indicate different aspects of the deity. They are aniconic images when they are nonrepresentational, "formless" shapes, such as colored stones or a flame. Hindu religious images are not empty idols to Hindus; they are simply different forms or manifestations of the divine. Divine images are divine, and they focus the mind on the divine. Hindu devotion is expressed through the offering of humble gestures, flowers, food, and water or other special gifts, chants, and hymns to the divine images (see figures 9.12 and 9.13).

Figure 9.12. Worship at a Hindu Temple in "Little India" in Singapore (Victor Bloomfield).

Figure 9.13. Brahman priest making offerings at a Hindu Temple in "Little India" in Singapore (Victor Bloomfield).

As in Amazonia, Hindu supernatural practices are based on metaphors, chains of association, and complex multiple meanings for the same symbols. Sex, fertility, and eroticism are especially prominent themes in Hindu representations of the deities Siva, his wife Parvati, and their children, Ganesh and Murukan.[51] In Hindu iconography Siva is represented by a round-topped, phallic-shaped stone column (*linga, linkam*) with an iconographic vulva (*yoni*) at its base representing the goddess *Sakti* (power, or female power), or *Parvati*. The combined *linga* and *yoni* represent the union of male and female as the basis of existence. Active gods are incomplete without female energy. This is similar to Australian and Amazonian concepts of complementary opposition. Siva's first son, Ganesh, is depicted with an elephant head because he was generated directly by Parvati. Siva beheaded him out of jealousy, and Ganesh took on the elephant head. Siva's second son, Murukan, was conceived in the normal way.

Temple worship is conspicuously a "rite of hospitality" for the deities and enacts routine household duties that wives are expected to perform for husbands and guests.[52] In south India, Tamil Hindus are devotees of androgynous deities representing gender balance and complementarity in marriage. Reenactments of divine weddings are prominent features of Hindu temple ritual. This affirms the belief that marriage as a combination of male and female principles is a source of social power and helps define the social order. For example, every year the temple in Kalugumalai, in Tamil Nadu, south India, celebrates Siva's son Murukan's marriages with two very different daughters of Vishnu, each contributing to Murukan's multiple identity. In November local people celebrate Murukan's marriage with Vishnu's daughter Amutavalli. This connects Murukan with divine power, whereas in February they celebrate Murukan's marriage with Suntaravalli (Valli), who is associated with local tribes, forest, and agriculture. Significantly Tamils believe both of these marriages to be appropriate cross-cousin marriages, because for Murukan, Amutavalli and Suntaravalli are MBDs, daughters of his mother Parvati's brother Vishnu.

Daily Hindu temple liturgical practice involves six daily worship services (*puja*), each involving unction (anointing as a symbol of consecration), decoration, food-offering, and lamp-showing centered on divine couples who have their own connubial bedrooms in the temple. In these rituals divinities are represented either as separate entities or united as couples. These services give people opportunities to view images or "take darshan" of the divine at propitious times. The seven phases in the Kalugumalai temple are bedroom lamp-offering at 5:30 a.m., holy adorning at 6:00, festival worship at 8:00, the daily festival and the royal endowment at 11:00, the noon service, a lamp-showing at 6 p.m., and a "midnight service" and bedroom worship at 8:30.

BOX 9.3. SIVA ICONOGRAPHY

Siva, or Shiva, the "Auspicious One," is one of the most prominent Hindu deities and illustrates the complexity of Hindu polytheism and iconography. Siva incorporates many universal complementary oppositions and ambiguities. He is a creator and a destroyer, a sensuous ascetic, benevolent and vengeful. He may be portrayed with multiple faces, three eyes, and four arms and sometimes as both male and female. He is often portrayed as a dancing figure in a ring of fire (see figure 9.14). Diana Eck provides a concise exegesis of this image:

> The flaming circle in which he dances is the circle of creation and destruction called *samsara* (the earthly round of birth and death) or *maya* (the illusory world). The Lord who dances in the circle of this changing world holds in two of his hands the drum of creation and the fire of destruction. He displays his strength by crushing the bewildered demon underfoot. Simultaneously, he shows his mercy by raising his palm to the worshiper in the "fear-not" gesture and, with another hand, by pointing to his upraised foot, where the worshiper may take refuge. It is a wild dance, for the coils of his ascetic's hair are flying in both directions, and yet the facial countenance of the Lord is utterly peaceful and his limbs in complete balance. Around one arm twines the naga, the ancient serpent which he has incorporated into his sphere of power and wears now as an ornament. In his hair sits the mermaid River Ganga, who landed first on Siva's hair when she fell from heaven to earth. Such an image as the dancing Siva engages the eye and extends one's vision of the nature of this god, using simple, subtle, and commonly understood gestures and emblems.[53]

Controversy over the Sacred Cow

Cattle sacrifice, which was central to the ritual system, was a monopoly of the Brahman priests during the Vedic period in India. As Hinduism and the caste system developed, cattle were treated as deities and became an important feature of the ritual purity complex. The five products of the cow—fresh milk, sour milk, butter, urine, and dung—were important purifying agents, whereas the consumption of a cow's flesh and leather working were polluting. According to the Dharma Sastra, cows were not to be disturbed or injured. The Arthasastra was blunt: "Whoever hurts or causes another to hurt, or steals or causes another to steal, a cow, should be slain."[54] Under the influence of the *ahimsa* doctrine of nonviolence toward people and all animals, promoted by the Jains (adherents of Jainism, a major Hindu sect) and Buddhists since the sixth century BC, this reverence for cows was carried to the point that special templelike homes were maintained to care for aged and abandoned cattle. The sacred status of the cow was increased by the arrival of the beef-eating Muslims and the British because cow reverence

Figure 9.14. Siva in the form of Nataraja, the Lord of Dance, in a ring of fire.

became a conspicuous marker of Hindu culture (see figure 9.15). The Indian Sacred Cow Complex was the center of a theoretical debate between anthropologists, economists, and geographers over whether Indians keep too many cows for primarily religious reasons.

Anthropologist Marvin Harris[55] argued that practical economic choices by poor farmers were more important determinants of cattle practices in India than strictly religious considerations.

Harris was responding to numerous assessments by Indian public officials and development experts that Indians wastefully maintained vast numbers of useless cows because of irrational religious beliefs. Much of the criticism was over the poor quality of many of the animals and the quantity of fodder that they consumed. Harris challenged this interpretation, arguing that it was based on irrelevant market-economy cash accounting. He emphasized that the relationship between people and cows in India was more likely to be symbiotic. Cattle subsist on the by-products of the grain production system, which they in turn help sustain. He suggested that ecological pressures encouraged the maintenance of seemingly unproductive cattle, as well as the ideology of *ahimsa*, which supports the practice.

Figure 9.15. A sacred cow in Mysore, India (Victor Bloomfield).

Harris maintained that the most important contribution of Indian cattle was their support of the grain-based subsistence system as draft animals and through the production of dung for fuel and fertilizer. Bullocks pulling plows and carts help produce and transport the grain that supplies 80 percent of the calories people consume. For most peasant families, tractors would be prohibitively expensive to purchase and operate, and a pair of bullocks is an absolute necessity. There appears to be an actual shortage of traction animals during periods of intense plowing activity, which is determined by the annual cycle of monsoon rains. Furthermore, Harris argued, up to half of the cow dung may be used as a domestic cooking fuel, while the remainder serves as fertilizer. Considering the volume of energy involved in a country as densely populated as India, this resource would be very costly to replace with commercially produced fossil fuels. Harris concluded that it should be obvious that without major technical and environmental innovations or drastic population cuts, India could not tolerate a large beef-producing industry. This suggests that insofar as the beef-eating taboo helps discourage growth of beef-producing industries, it is part of an ecological adjustment that maximizes rather than minimizes the calorie and protein output of the productive process.[56]

The Cattle Complex of India resembles the East African Cattle Complex in that in both cultures cattle play a central role in the material infrastructure, the social structure, and the ideological superstructure, but there are important cultural contrasts. Indian cattle are managed primarily to produce male traction animals, yet the direct production of animal protein remains an important secondary outcome. At 413 pounds (187 kg) of milk a year, average milk production of Indian cattle is less than half that of East African cattle (1,606 lb [728 kg]) and 8 percent of an intensively managed U.S. dairy cow (5,000 lb [2,265 kg]). However, even this relatively low production rate represents a significant contribution to the animal-protein intake of the Indian population. It is also important to remember that beef is consumed in India by Muslims, Christians, and members of the untouchable castes who can afford it, and cattle are an important source of leather, which is produced by the untouchables.

Harris agreed that cattle can be environmentally destructive and are part of the problem of increased human pressure on resources. But he still argued that poorly fed, relatively inefficient cattle can nevertheless be advantageous to individual poor farmers. Indian cattle are malnourished during the dry season, but when their services as draft animals are most required they rebound when grazing improves with the monsoons. Like their East African counterparts they tolerate drought conditions better than larger breeds, and they rebound more quickly. Free-ranging cattle feed themselves at public expense and no doubt in some cases, at the expense of wealthy farmers and landlords; thus, they may play a role in wealth redistribution where great economic inequality exists.

The origin of the Sacred Cow Complex has been debated. Harris[57] proposed that it may have begun in the Ganges Valley by 1000 BC when population pressure resulted in decreased farm size and made cattle more valuable as draft animals. The religious taboo on killing cattle thus came about so that people would not be tempted to slaughter them for food and thereby threaten their agricultural system. Simoons[58] argued that the ban on killing cattle may have been proposed by the early Hindu kingdoms to secure a surplus for the expanding urban centers, thus benefiting the elite rather than the peasants. This is in agreement with Harris's view that the prohibition on cattle killing was part of an "imperial cult" that supported the elite and is not incompatible with the view that the ban also benefited the peasants.

At the village level, there is evidence for rational herd-management practices by farmers as well as decision making based on religious principles.[59] People do say that they protect cows as an act of worship, and there is no reason to doubt their sincerity. At the same time from an etic point of view, Indians selectively starve unwanted calves, while emically they claim that all calves must be protected.[60]

On balance, the controversy has drawn attention to the economic value of seemingly useless cows, but it also demonstrates the difficulty of positively determining why people do what they do. The sacred cow case does affirm the importance of religious belief. For example, many low-caste groups have stopped eating beef in order to avoid the ritual stigma of pollution and thereby enhance their social standing.[61] The relationships between belief and actions are complex, and the best analysis would take a holistic ethnographic approach.

The Buddhist Alternative

Buddhism is a system of religious philosophy and practice that offers a radical alternative to both Hinduism and Islam. It is a sociocultural system whose supreme object is for an individual to become a Buddha, or to gain enlightenment. In Buddhism it is most heroic to work as a *Bodhisattva* "to bring about the welfare of all sentient beings."[62] Buddhism was founded in South Asia by the teachings of Siddhartha Gautama, "The Buddha" (563–400 BC) in north India during the foundations of the Hindu Great Tradition. Buddhism spread as the very opposite of military and commercial conquest. Buddhism shares important cosmological elements with Hinduism, especially the concept of *karma* and *samsara*, the cycle of reincarnation, and a diverse pantheon of deities. The crucial difference is Buddism's emphasis on fostering a lifestyle devoted to personal enlightenment and altruism, and the absence of caste.

At the core of Buddhism are the Four Noble Truths, the Eightfold Noble Path, and the Three Jewels. The Noble Truths are that the world is full of suffering caused by bad *karma*, things done in one's life and their consequences, in present and past lives. Suffering can be ended and peace or *nirvana* obtained by following the Eightfold Noble Path of correct understanding, analysis, speech, action, livelihood, effort, mindfulness, and meditation, which leads to enlightenment. The Three Jewels are the Buddha, representing the ideal of an enlightened body; *Dharma*, consisting of texts of the Buddha's teachings; and the *Sangha*, the spiritual community of Buddhists and the monastic orders. The *Sangha* includes diverse schools of thought and systems, practices, and practitioners, as well as ranked grades of merit and wisdom on the path to enlightenment.[63] Significantly the concept of *chakra*, which for Hindus refers to rulers in a circle of political power, is for Buddhists a wheel representing the Buddha's teachings, the *dharmachakra*, in which the spokes symbolize the Eightfold Noble Path.

Tibet provides a remarkable example of elite-directed change in which the ruler rejected imperialist expansion in favor of intellectual and spiritual development. Tibetan emperor Songzen Gambo (King Songtsen Gampo) adopted Buddhism in 630 AD, making Tibet a pacifist kingdom and a center for Buddhist learning and practice. Songzen Gambo designed Llasa as his capital city and sacred landscape, building Jokhang Temple at its center. Unlike Inca temples with their straight *ceque* lines focused on astronomical alignments, Tibetan temples are *mandalas* focused on the central sacred space. The center is surrounded by *koras*, circular paths that pilgrims follow in a clockwise circumambulation.[64] In 1642 Buddhist spiritual leaders, the Dalai Lamas, gained full control over the political rulers and Tibet became a uniquely pacifist

monastic kingdom dedicated to promoting spiritual enlightenment. The Dalai Lamas disarmed the military and required the former aristocracy to support themselves from their own estates rather than from government funds. This unprecedented experiment continued for more than 300 years until the Chinese invasion in 1951.[65]

Bhutan, located in the Himalayas east of Nepal between India and China, was the last independent Buddhist kingdom at the beginning of the twenty-first century. The kingdom remained largely isolated from the commercial world until late in the twentieth century. Buddhist principles are strongly represented in the Bhutan's "Middle Path" for sustainable development initiated in 1990, which rejects the Western concept of economic growth measured by gross domestic product in favor of "gross domestic happiness." The Middle Path seeks to overcome "delusions arising from ignorance, aggression, and the desire for consumption and acquisition."[66] In 1999 King Jigme Singye Wangchuck began a series of reforms to convert Bhutan into a more democratic constitutional monarchy.

WOMEN IN SOUTH ASIA

South Asian women, whether under Hindu or Islamic Great Traditions, are clearly at a cultural disadvantage in comparison with men. This disadvantage is based on myth and religious ideology recorded in sacred texts and is expressed in ritual and physical separation between men and women, whereby men take leadership roles and enjoy relatively greater freedom outside the household. In this section, we will review the cultural-historical background of Islam to facilitate comparison with the Hindu Great Tradition. Then we will consider the position of women under both cultural traditions.

The Islamic Great Tradition

Striking parallels exist between the rise of Islam as an expansive state system and the development of Hindu civilization. Both cases are examples of secondary state formation from a pastoral tribal base in response to the influence of preexisting states. In both cases, a complex interethnic conquest state was integrated by means of a literate Great Tradition ideological system. It is remarkable that both traditions came to coexist in India even though the two systems were incompatible on fundamental issues of belief.

In contrast to Hinduism, the details of the founding of Islam are well known. Islam is a revealed religion, transmitted in Arabic directly by Allah to his messenger, the Prophet Muhammad (AD 570–632). God's message is recorded as sacred scripture in the *Qur'an* (Koran) and is augmented by the *hadith*, or traditions surrounding the Prophet. Islam, which in Arabic means "surrender," refers to the need of the Muslim (believer) to surrender to the will of Allah, the one God. The fundamental articles of faith are encompassed by the Five Pillars of Islam:

1. Recitation of the Shahadah, confession of faith: "There is no God but Allah and Muhammad is his Prophet"
2. The performance of five daily prayers
3. The giving of alms (*zakkat*)
4. Observance of the fast of Ramadan
5. Pilgrimage to Mecca (the *hajj*)

Muhammad was a member of the Quraysh, a sedentarized north Arabian Bedouin tribe that controlled the Red Sea trade from Mecca, which was already an important ritual center. Muhammad's religious visions began around AD 610; by the time of his death in 632, he had succeeded in uniting all the Bedouin tribes of Arabia into a religious state based on the new faith. The pre-Islamic Bedouin tribes were relatively egalitarian, patrilineal segmentary systems, led by popularly supported "chiefs" or *shaykhs* (sheiks), who led raids, settled disputes, and enjoyed some prestige but were still considered "first among equals." An essential element in this tribe-to-state transformation was the replacement of tribal and kinship loyalties with membership in the *Ummah*, the Islamic community, which created a united front by suppressing the blood feud that had characterized intertribal relations throughout Arabia.[67]

The *Ummah* was a nascent religious state, united by common belief and military opposition to unbelieving outsiders as expressed in the *jihad*, or holy war. Under Islam, the Prophet Muhammad was accepted as the divinely appointed head of state. However, Muhammad did not specify how his successor, the caliph, was to be selected. Conflict over the succession resulted in a sectarian split between the Sunnites, who believed they were following the *Sunnah* (the Prophet's collected sayings) in selecting the caliph, and the Shi'ites, who favored keeping the *imam* (foremost of the community) in the Prophet's closest line of descent and recognized their own line of *imams*. The caliph or *imam*, as the leader of the Islamic state and chief defender of the faith, was expected to lead prayers at the Friday service in the mosque. He was also responsible for settling disputes, collecting taxes, and organizing the jihad against unbelievers.

After the death of Muhammad, a period of rapid military expansion began that brought the Mesopotamian region and much of Persia, Egypt, and North Africa under Islamic control by AD 700. Next, Muslims entered Spain and began to raid northern India. Conquest was a major source of state revenue, whether directly as battlefield booty or as tribute or tax in agricultural production. During the expansion of Islam, unbelievers with literate sacred scriptures—such as Jews, Christians, and, by extension, Hindus—were granted protection as peoples of the book as long as they acknowledged Islamic political authority and paid their taxes. Small Islamic kingdoms, or sultanates, were established in India by 1200, and from 1526 to 1761, the Islamic Mughal empire ruled over most of the Indian subcontinent. Although the Mughal rulers generally tolerated Hindu practices, there were many areas of conflict between the two Great Traditions, as illustrated by the modern partitioning of British India into Muslim Pakistan and Hindu India in 1947.

The Islamic state was based on the *sharia*, which, like *tao* in Chinese, means "path" or "road." *Sharia*, like the Hindu concept of *dharma*, is God's law as outlined in the Koran and the *Sunnah* or the *hadith* accepted by the Shi'ites.[68] Islamic law is a detailed prescription for all areas of life, specifying whether individual acts are required, forbidden, recommended, disapproved, or permitted. Islam, like Hinduism, constitutes a complete social system and has had a profound influence over preexisting cultural practices whenever Islamic states have been established.

Women in Islamic Society

Any discussion of Islamic social practices must begin with a careful disclaimer acknowledging the great diversity of practices in specific countries and regions, at different historical times, between urban and village settings, and between different social classes. Furthermore, the Koran itself is interpreted in many different ways. However, certain principles do stand out. According to fundamentalist Islamic interpretations, women are generally viewed as morally and legally inferior to men. They are to be protected by their husbands and close male kin and are to stay out of public life. In several respects, in comparison with men, Muslim women are at a legal disadvantage by many interpretations of Islamic law. Daughters inherit less than sons. Women are permitted only one spouse at a time, whereas men may have up to four wives as long as they can provide for them and treat them fairly. Muslim women are expected to marry only other Muslims, whereas men may marry unbelieving peoples of the book. It is more difficult for a woman to obtain a divorce. Furthermore, modesty and male honor often require female seclusion (discussed in detail in the following section).

Many observers stress that Koranic law actually represented an improvement in the position of women over the common practice of pre-Islamic times. Women's rights in marriage, divorce, inheritance, and property ownership are specified in ways that no doubt increased their security.

A modern expression of Islamic gender roles is a common tendency toward gender segregation in education and employment. Labor migration by men for extended periods, leaving wives to maintain the household, is a common pattern. Women are less likely to work outside the home than men, and when they are employed as professionals, women tend to work with other women as teachers or doctors. Both high-status and low-status positions in the complementary occupational pairs—such as doctor-nurse, principal-teacher, executive-secretary, which are commonly seen as male-female sets in Western industrial countries—are more likely to be filled by men in Islamic countries.[69]

When they address Western audiences, and especially Western feminists, Muslim female social scientists often stress that many of the cultural patterns that Western women take as evidence of Islamic oppression of women are misunderstood in ways that perpetuate the view that Muslim women are passive and ignorant, if not inferior. For example, Westerners usually describe the harem entirely in male terms, as an institution for confining and controlling women to provide men with secure sexual access to multiple wives.[70] The harem system does segregate women from men; Islamic women themselves, however, recognize that such segregation need not be oppressive in itself. Ahmed notes that the word *harem* is derived from the Arabic word *haram*, meaning "forbidden." She suggests that it is women who forbid males to enter exclusively female space. The harem is a gathering place for women where they can freely discuss and ridicule men and the world of men. It is also a place where a feminist critique of Islamic society can take place. Many Western women, isolated in nuclear families,

do not enjoy such freedom. Thus, although Islamic women are in many ways discriminated against by their societies, seeing specific Islamic social institutions in entirely negative terms can be misleading. According to Ahmed, "…to believe that segregated societies are by definition more oppressive to women, or that women secluded from the company of men are women deprived, is only to allow ourselves to be servilely obedient to the constructs of men, Western or Middle Eastern."[71] It must be remembered, however, that the harem is part of a larger Islamic society, which is controlled primarily by men.

Female Seclusion: The Purdah System

The practice of purdah, the veiling and seclusion of women, is a conspicuous South Asian cultural pattern, shared by Hindus and Muslims alike, and is related to the institutionalization of gender inequality shared by both cultures. Purdah means "curtain" or "veil" in Urdu and Hindi and refers to the physical separation of the living spaces used by men and women, as well as the actual veiling of a woman's face and body. This is a South Asian variation of the harem of the Arab Islamic world. The concept of purdah is also commonly extended to refer to types of avoidance or deference behavior practiced by women, including not looking at or speaking to certain people. Adherence to purdah restrictions is related to specific factors such as employment, education, social class, politics, and religion. Some Muslim sects have abolished or intensified seclusion by decree. Western observers often denounce purdah as another example of male oppression, but like the harem, it plays an important functional role in the culture and is supported by many of the women who practice it.

In the strictest form of purdah, a woman must remain completely within the confines of her home throughout her adult life. Within a large house, there may be women's rooms and entrances that outside men cannot use, and special screens and partitions may be set up to hide women from view. In some cases, seclusion of women extends to otherwise public buildings and public transportation. Although there is considerable variation in the degree to which veiling is practiced, in extreme form, a Muslim woman in purdah can leave the seclusion of her home only when wearing the *burqa*, a full length garment covering head and body.

Purdah is based on the interconnected principles of separate worlds for men and women, and symbolic shelter for women.[72] The principle of separate worlds is expressed in a sharp division of labor and workplace and in the corresponding economic interdependence between men and women. The principle of symbolic shelter is founded in the belief that women are especially vulnerable in a hostile outside world and therefore must be kept sheltered at home. The outside danger from which women need protection is the threat of uncontrolled sexual and aggressive impulses. The underlying assumption seems to be that people need close external supervision to control themselves; thus, purdah restrictions physically remove women from possible harm. Hindus and Muslims may view the dangers to women somewhat differently, with Hindu women seen as potential temptresses and Muslim women seen as potential victims, but either way they need to be protected. The dependency of women and supremacy of men are as deeply rooted in Hindu culture as they are in Islam. In certain details, the Hindu version of purdah has been influenced by Islamic traditions, but the principles of symbolic sanctuary existed prior to Islam in India. For example, Manu, in the Dharma Sastra, declared the following laws for women:

> No act is to be done according to (her) own will by a young girl, a young woman, or even by an old woman, though in (their own) houses. In her childhood (a girl) should be under the will of her father; in (her) youth, of (her) husband; her husband being dead, of her sons; a woman should never enjoy her own will. She must never wish separation of her self from her father, husband, or sons, for by separation from them a woman would make both families contemptible. She must always be cheerful and clever in household business, with the furniture well cleaned, and with not a free hand in expenditure. But him to whom her father gives her, or (her) brother with the father's consent, she must obey alive, and dead must not disregard.[73]

Another important dimension of symbolic shelter is that women are "status demonstrators" for their husbands.[74] The Muslim concept of *izzat*, family "honor" or "pride," extends to the modesty and virtue of a man's wife, sister, and daughter. Of course, the reverse is not the case; that is, a woman's status is not determined by the virtue of her husband, brother, or father. This is the famous double standard that also has a long history in Western civilization. The observance of purdah is an expression of modesty, social solidarity, and family respectability. The importance

of feminine virtue is emphatically demonstrated by the ideal of Sita, the heroine of the Ramayana, one of the best-known Hindu myths (see box 9.4).

Anthropologist Manisha Roy,[75] a Bengali woman, has carefully documented how the experience of growing up in the Hindu extended family creates culturally conditioned expectations for women that are often unfulfilled. The popular Hindu myths, which stress the ideals of romantic love and self-sacrificing devotion to the husband, conflict with the realities of arranged Hindu marriages and generate psychological frustration for women. A woman's husband often turns out to be an emotionally remote protector who is close to his wife only when he relates to her as mother of his children. Upper-class, urban Bengali women are able to find some compensation for the frustrations in their domestic lives by developing a long-term relationship as a devoted disciple of a guru outside the extended family, but this is only possible after their children are grown.

There are significant differences between the way Muslim and Hindu women in South Asia practice purdah. For example, Muslim women are secluded from all outside men, whereas Hindu women are secluded from all male affines, especially from their husband's kinsmen.[76] The Hindu pattern has been described in detail by Doranne Jacobson based on her research in the Bhopal region of central India.[77] In this area, a Hindu woman remains fully veiled before virtually all male affines in her husband's joint family. She must also be partially veiled before many of the senior women in her husband's joint family. However, when she visits her natal village, she is virtually free of purdah restrictions.

Before examining the possible functions of purdah, it is important to consider the emic view. Women who practice purdah often attribute their adherence to feelings of shame, shyness, or embarrassment, and they relate it to parallel concerns for honor and respect. Their enculturation, especially through internalization of the heroic role models provided by mythic figures such as Sita, makes it an internal response that does not require outside sanctions. As Jacobson reports, "Most secluded women, too, pride themselves on their strict observance of purdah."[78] This emic view supports the symbolic sanctuary interpretation, but women also recognize that purdah can be a marker of elite status because only economically well-off households could afford to observe it fully.

Many functions of purdah have been proposed, and it seems clear that it does not represent a simple conspiracy of males to oppress women. Purdah also restricts men and imposes responsibilities on them. It creates dependency between men and women because a woman who cannot leave her home must rely on her husband, children, or servants to perform outside errands, such as shopping. A man, in turn, might not do domestic chores such as cooking and cleaning. It has been suggested that Hindus might use purdah to reduce the danger of female ritual pollution and to safeguard the purity of caste endogamy.[79] The most direct function of purdah is that it helps sustain the integrity of the patrilineal extended or joint family, which is the most viable minimal social unit in stratified state societies based on plow agriculture.[80] This system requires careful control of small parcels of land and support from neighboring families and seems to work best with unambiguous lines of authority, a strict division of labor, and a maximum of domestic tranquility.

Purdah imposes social distance between men and women and intensifies their respective role differences. Purdah also minimizes the possibility for potentially disruptive incidents of adultery, both within and outside the extended family, and supports the common pattern of arranged marriages. Unmarried girls who are secluded in their homes are unlikely to find lovers to marry who might undermine established community alliance networks. In Muslim societies, marriage may be arranged between patrilateral parallel cousins (a man marries FBD), which helps to concentrate lineage resources and furthers a woman's seclusion by making even her affines relatively close kin.

In Jacobson's view, purdah has played a vital cultural role:

> However inimical such a system may be to the ideals of Westerners, urban-educated South Asians, or even to the preferences of a certain number of veiled women themselves, there can be no doubt that arrangements of this kind have allowed hundreds of millions of people to live—and sometimes even to prosper—over the course of several centuries in various corners of the earth. It should also be acknowledged that for many fortunate women, sequestered life in bustling and affectionate family units has provided security and satisfaction. Only as alternative family structures become economically feasible or necessary are male-dominated societies undergoing alteration in the direction of allowing females to assert their individuality in any but limited circumstances.[81]

BOX 9.4. THE RAMAYANA: A HINDU MYTHIC CHARTER FOR FEMININE VIRTUE

The Ramayana is one of the most popular Hindu myths, dating to 300 BC, during the early classic period of Hindu civilization. This epic romance is a part of the cultural identity of all Hindus. It is frequently recited in dramatic performances and is required reading in Indian schools. It presents a compelling role model of the ideal Hindu wife.

Briefly stated, the Ramayana (the Romance of Rama) tells the story of Rama, an incarnation of Vishnu, who weds the beautiful Sita, the heroine, after passing a heroic test. However, he is cheated out of his place as heir to his father's throne and banished to a fourteen-year exile in the forest. Out of devotion to her husband, Sita follows her husband into exile, even though he urges her to stay behind. Later, Sita is treacherously abducted by an evil king who wants to marry her, but she rejects his advances and is imprisoned. Meanwhile, her husband, Rama, recruits an army and rescues her, but he suspects that Sita was unfaithful to him during her imprisonment and forces her to pass an ordeal by fire to prove her loyalty before accepting her back. Rama takes his rightful place on the throne of his kingdom with Sita as queen. When his subjects gossip that Sita really was unfaithful after all, Rama sends her away again to the forest, where she raises his twin sons. When Sita sends his grown sons back to him, he invites her to return but insists that she again prove her virtue. She has, of course, been completely faithful and totally devoted to him throughout her ordeal, but this time she accepts his rejection and asks the earth to swallow her up. This is a fitting gesture because in the myth she was born from the earth.

Bride Burning: Dowry Deaths in Modern Hindu India

In recent decades, Indian newspapers have increasingly reported on new brides who were burned to death in unexplained grease fires in their kitchens. It is generally understood that in these cases, the bride has been murdered by her husband after he has extorted as much dowry as possible from her family. The murderer is then free to seek more dowry "gifts" from a new bride.

In their analysis of this problem, anthropologists Linda Stone and Caroline James[82] estimated in the 1990s that 2,000 or more dowry deaths were occurring every year in India. Stone and James suggest that some of the causes of this violence against women are found both in traditional Hindu culture and in recent changes related to global commercial culture. Hindu culture provides many incentives for a woman's family to arrange marriage for their daughters and to give large dowries. In traditional India, it was not acceptable for a woman to be unmarried, even if widowed, as the traditional custom of *sati* demonstrated. Divorce is seen as dishonoring the family. Furthermore, with the cultural ideal of hypergamy, a Hindu bride and her parents are considered to be gifts from social inferiors. This places them in a subservient position relative to the groom's family, making them vulnerable to harassment and demands for higher dowry payments. Dowry payments reflect the reduced economic value of women in cultures in which plow agriculture, which is a male domain, is the dominant economic activity. Dowry payments are also associated with private land ownership and wage labor in agrarian civilizations. Bride-wealth is more common in tribal cultures, such as in East Africa, where women are valued for both their subsistence and their reproductive roles.

The emergence of a consumption-based middle class in modern India has inflated dowry payments. Traditionally, the Hindu dowry involved household articles that were produced directly by the bride's family. Modern dowry payments may include large amounts of cash and expensive consumer goods such as televisions and refrigerators that are beyond the financial means of many middle-class Indians. It is significant that bride burning is primarily an urban, middle-class phenomenon. Frustrated consumer aspirations are a powerful motivation for these murders.

A women named "Sita," who survived an attempted bride burning, told Caroline James that she brought a lavish dowry of $8,000 along with five hundred saris, jewelry, a television, a freezer, furniture, and kitchenware, but this was not enough to please her husband's family. Sita overheard her mother-in-law telling her husband, "Leave this woman and we will get another one; at least the other party will give us more and better dowry than what these people have given us. What her parents have given us is nothing. Moreover, this girl is ugly, and she is dark."[83] Sita woke up one night to find that her husband had doused her with kerosene, but she escaped when he couldn't find a match.

Stone and James note that in traditional Hindu India, women were not likely to be subjected to such violence because female fertility was highly valued as the means of perpetuating the patrilineage. A woman's ability to produce sons gave her significant domestic power and security. It is probably not a coincidence that bride burnings have emerged just as fertility rates in India have begun to decline, especially in urban areas, where children are more likely to be an economic burden. The vulnerability of women is further increased in the modern urban setting because, relative to men, they can contribute little to household income in the wage economy. The status of women is higher in tribal cultures than in traditional agrarian civilizations, especially when the commercial culture transforms domestic economies.

SUMMARY

The Hindu civilization of South Asia is a literate Great Tradition with significant cultural continuity over the past 3,000 years. The earliest South Asian Neolithic cultures were probably participants in the domestication process that occurred throughout Southwest Asia during the Early Holocene period. The Harappan civilization of the Indus Valley was the earliest South Asian state and probably had some connections with Mesopotamia. Hindu civilization arose in the Ganges region after the collapse of the Harappan civilization. Hindu culture apparently drew on some Harappan cultural elements but was primarily derived from the Indo-European-speaking Aryans who invaded South Asia from the west about 1600 BC.

The early Hindu kingdoms were a by-product of the Aryan conquest and the incorporation of the preexisting tribal cultures of the subcontinent. Classical Hindu kingdoms, as described in the Arthasastra, were organized around a complex government bureaucracy based on secular political power backed by a formal legal system with fines and physical punishments for offenders. It also relied on a religious system that divided society into four ranked groups, or *varna*. The dominant structure of Hindu society up to the present time is the caste system, which assigns everyone to a ritually ranked endogamous occupational group. This generates great social inequality, but it is justified and supported by Hindu religious beliefs that emphasize religious duty, the hope of reincarnation at a higher level, and the opportunity for people at all social levels to enjoy transcendental contact with the divine. Hindu religious beliefs also provide ritual protection for cows, which are an important source of fuel, food, and traction power for poor people who might otherwise have great difficulty supporting themselves.

Women are placed in inferior positions relative to men by both the Islamic and Hindu Great Traditions. These cultures rigidly separate men's and women's worlds in a way that supports the continuity of male-dominated extended families. Men occupy dominant roles in both their own families and the larger society. Women gain greater power as they grow older, and they benefit in certain ways from culturally prescribed separation. But women in modern India have been increasingly the targets of violence. Bride burning is related to the demand for high dowries and the difficulty women have contributing financially in a male-dominated wage economy.

STUDY QUESTIONS

1. Discuss the cultural significance of the following South Asian language groups: Indo-European, Dravidian, Sino-Tibetan, Hindi, Bengali, and Urdu.
2. Describe the basic social structure of the early Hindu kingdom. How did early Hindu kingdoms use direct political power to maintain and extend the state?
3. Compare and contrast the organization of the state in China and Hindu India.
4. How did the Hindu legal system reflect the inequalities of Hindu society?
5. Describe the basic structural features of the Hindu caste system, distinguishing it from class and clan.
6. In what way was ritual purity a central feature of Hindu culture?
7. Distinguish between *varna*, *jati*, Brahman, Kshatriya, Vaisya, and Sudra. Discuss the economic correlates of caste and weigh the arguments that it served positive social functions or was exploitive.
8. In what ways does the Hindu Sacred Cow Complex have positive adaptive functions? What are the arguments for the religious explanations of the Sacred Cow Complex?
9. Describe the position of women according to fundamentalist Islamic principles.
10. Distinguish between the Islamic and Hindu cultural context of purdah, referring to the principles of separate worlds and symbolic shelter. What are the functionalist explanations of purdah?
11. Contrast the basic features of Islam and Hinduism, placing each system in its appropriate cultural-historical context.
12. Discuss how bride burning is related to modern Indian economics and the status of women.
13. In what respect does Buddhism offer an alternative to both Hinduism and Islam?

SUGGESTED READING

Allchin, Bridget, and F. Raymond Allchin. 1982. *The Rise of Civilization in India and Pakistan.* Cambridge, Eng.: Cambridge University Press. An archaeological overview of South Asian prehistory and the early development of Harappan and Hindu civilization.

Basham, A. L. 1954. *The Wonder That Was India: A Survey of the Culture of the Indian Sub-Continent before the Coming of the Muslims.* London: Sidgwick & Jackson. A widely respected basic textbook on South Asian history and culture.

Eck, Diana L. 1985. *Darsan: Seeing the Divine Image in India.* Chambersburg, PA: Anima Books. An in-depth treatment of the visual aspects of Hindu religion.

Papanek, Hanna, and Gail Minault (Eds.). 1982. *Separate Worlds: Studies of Purdah in South Asia.* Delhi: Chanakya Publications. An interdisciplinary collection of papers on the seclusion of women in South Asia.

Tyler, Stephen A. 1986. *India: An Anthropological Perspective.* Prospect Heights, IL: Waveland Press. An anthropological overview of many aspects of Indian culture with an emphasis on linguistic and cognitive categories.

GLOSSARY TERMS

Patron A Spanish term for someone who extends credits or goods to a client who is kept in a debt relationship.

Caste An endogamous, ranked, occupationally defined group, known as *jati* in India, and based on differences in ritual purity and impurity.

Purity Ritually superior status; a category in logical opposition to impurity.

Cultural hegemony Preponderant influence, or authority, by an elite in the production and reproduction of a society's moral order and associated cultural beliefs, symbols, and practices.

Hypergamy Marriage to someone of higher rank. For example, Hindu women may marry men of a higher subcaste.

Hypogamy Marriage to someone of lower rank.

Impurity Low ritual status attributed to association or contact with polluting biological events or products.

NOTES

1. This estimate is for 1998 from the United States National Intelligence Council (NIC). 2000. *Global Trends 2015: A Dialogue about the Future with Nongovernment Experts.* http://infowar.net/cia/publications/globaltrends 2015/) based on figures from the *Encyclopedia Britannica World Book*, 1999.
2. CIA World Factbook, https://www.cia.gov/library/publications/the-world-factbook/index.html (accessed July 25, 2009).
3. Allchin, Bridget, and F. Raymond Allchin. 1982. *The Rise of Civilization in India and Pakistan.* Cambridge, Eng.: Cambridge University Press.
4. Erdosy, George. 1988. *Urbanization in Early Historic India.* BAR International Series 430. Oxford, Eng.: Oxford University Press, 5.

5. Hagesteijn, Renee. 1989. *Circles of Kings: Political Dynamics in Early Continental Southeast Asia.* Verhandelingen van het Koninklijk Instituut Voor Taal-, Land- en Volkenkunde No. 138. Dordrecht, Holland: Foris Publications.

6. Hanks, Lucien M. 1975. "The Thai Social Order as Entourage and Circle." In *Change and Persistence in Thai Society,* edited by G. William Skinner and A. Thomas Kirsch, pp. 197–218. Ithaca and London: Cornell University Press.

7. Leach, Edmund. 1964. *Political Systems of Highland Burma: A Study of Kachin Social Structure.* London School of Economics Monographs on Social Anthropology No. 44. London: The Athlone Press, University of London.

8. Kirsch, A. Thomas. 1973. *Feasting and Social Oscillation: Religion and Society in Upland Southeast Asia.* Data Paper: Number 92, Southeast Asia Program, Department of Asian Studies, Cornell University, Ithaca, NY.

9. Hagesteijn, Renee. 1989. *Circles of Kings.*

10. Rao, Rajesh P. N., Nisha Yadav, Mayank N. Vahia, Hrishikesh Joglekar, R. Adhikari, and Iravatham Mahadevan. 2009. "Entropic Evidence for Linguistic Structure in the Indus Script." *Science* 29 May 2009 324: 1165.

11. Shamasastry, R. (translator). 1960. *Kautilya's Arthasastra.* Mysore, India: Mysore.

12. Erdosy, George. 1988. *Urbanization in Early Historic India.*

13. Erdosy, George. 1988. *Urbanization in Early Historic India.*

14. Shamasastry, R. (translator). 1960. *Kautilya's Arthasastra,* book 3, chap. 1.

15. Tambiah, Stanley Jeyaraja. 1985. *Culture, Thought, and Social Action: An Anthropological Perspective.* Cambridge, MA, and London: Harvard University Press.

16. Shamasastry, R. (translator). 1960. *Kautilya's Arthasastra,* book 3, chap. 19.

17. Bodley, John H. 2003. *The Power of Scale: A Global History Approach.* Armonk, NY: M. E. Sharpe, 37–44.

18. Leonowens, Anna Harriette. 1870. *The English Governess at the Siamese Court: Being Recollections of Six Years in the Royal Palace at Bangkok.* Boston: Fields, Osgood; Leonowens, Anna Harriette. 1953. *Siamese Harem Life.* New York: Dutton.

19. Wyatt, David K. 1968. "Family Politics in Nineteenth Century Thailand." *Journal of Southeast Asian History* 9(2):208–28.

20. Goldsmith, Raymond. 1987. *Premodern Financial Systems: A Historical Comparative Study.* Cambridge: Cambridge University Press, 94–122.

21. Blochmann, H. (translator). 1939. The *Aini Akbari by Abu Fazl'Allami.* 2nd ed. Calcutta: Royal Asiatic Society of Bengal.

22. Goldsmith, Raymond. 1987. *Premodern Financial Systems,* 106–107.

23. Brand, Michael, and Glenn D. Lowry. 1987. *Fatehpur-Sikri.* Bombay: Marg Publications.

24. Berreman, Gerald D. 1979. *Caste and Other Inequities: Essays on Inequality.* Meerut, Uttar Pradesh, India: Ved Prakash Vatuk, Folklore Institute, 73.

25. Berreman, Gerald D. 1960. "Caste in India and the United States." *American Journal of Sociology* 66:120–27.

26. Dumont, Louis. 1970. *Homo Hierarchicus: An Essay on the Caste System.* Chicago: University of Chicago Press.

27. Cohn, Bernard. 1996. *Colonialism and Its Forms of Knowledge.* Princeton: Princeton University Press; Dirks, Nicholas B. 1989. "The Original Caste: Power, History and Hierarchy in South Asia." *Contributions to Indian Sociology* 23(l):59–77; Dirks, Nicholas B. 2001. *Castes of Mind: Colonialism and the Making of Modern India.* Princeton and Oxford: Princeton University Press.

28. Dumont, Louis. 1970. *Homo Hierarchicus.*

29. Buhler, G. 1886. "The Laws of Manu." In *The Sacred Books of the East,* edited by F. M. Muller. Oxford, Eng.: Clarendon Press; Burnell, Arthur Coke, and Edward W. Hopkins, eds. 1884. *The Ordinances of Manu.* London: Trubner.

30. Buhler, G. 1886. "The Laws of Manu," 1:31.

31. Buhler, G. 1886. "The Laws of Manu," 1:88–100.

32. Moore, Melinda A. 1989. "The Kerala House as a Hindu Cosmos." *Contributions to Indian Sociology* 23(1):169–202.

33. Buhler, G. 1886. "The Laws of Manu." In *The Sacred Books of the East,* edited by F. M. Muller. Oxford, Eng.: Clarendon Press, Manu 1:87–91.

34. Mayer, Adrian C. 1970. *Caste and Kinship in Central India: A Village and Its Region.* Berkeley and Los Angeles: University of California Press.

35. Khare, R. S. 1976a. *Culture and Reality: Essays on the Hindu System of Managing Foods.* Simla: Indian Institute of Advanced Study; Khare, R. S. 1976b. *The Hindu Hearth and Home.* New Delhi: Vikas Publishing.

36. Marriot, McKim. 1968. "Caste Ranking and Food Transactions: A Matrix Analysis." In Milton Singer, and Bernard S. Cohn, eds. *Structure and Change in Indian Society.* pp. 133–71. New York: Viking Fund Publications in Anthropology.

37. Marriot, McKim. 1968. "Caste Ranking and Food Transactions: A Matrix Analysis."

38. Khare, R. S. 1976a. *Culture and Reality.*

39. Mayer, Adrian C. 1970. *Caste and Kinship in Central India.*

40. Berreman, Gerald D. 1979. *Caste and Other Inequities: Essays on Inequality.* Meerut, Uttar Pradesh, India: Ved Prakash Vatuk, Folklore Institute.

41. Srinivas, M. N. 1959. "The Dominant Caste in Rampura." *American Anthropologist* 61(1):1–16.

42. Parry, Jonathan. 1979. *Caste and Kinship in Kangra.* London: Routledge & Kegan Paul.

43. Dumont, Louis. 1970. *Homo Hierarchicus.*

44. Hutton, J. H. 1963. *Caste in India: Its Nature, Function, and Origins.* 4th ed. London: Oxford University Press.

45. Berreman, Gerald D. 1979. *Caste and Other Inequities.*

46. Berreman, Gerald D. 1979. *Caste and Other Inequities,* 221.

47. Anderson, Richard L. 1990. *Calliope's Sisters: A Comparative Study of Philosophies of Art.* New York: Prentice-Hall.

48. Anderson, Richard L. 1990. *Calliope's Sisters.*

49. Anderson, Richard L. 1990. *Calliope's Sister,* 171–72.

50. Eck, Diana L. 1985. *Darsan: Seeing the Divine Image in India.* Chambersburg, PA: Anima Books.

51. Good, Anthony. 2000. "Congealing Divinity: Time, Worship and Kinship in South Indian Hinduism." *Journal of the Royal Anthropological Institute* 6:273–92.

52. Good, Anthony. 2000. "Congealing Divinity."

53. Eck, Diana L. 1985. *Darsan,* 41.

54. Shamasastry, R. (translator). 1960. *Kautilya's Arthasastra,* book 2, chap. 29.

55. Harris, Marvin. 1965. "The Myth of the Sacred Cow." In *Man, Culture, and Animals,* edited by A. P. Vayda and A. Leeds, pp. 217–28. Washington, DC: American Association for the Advancement of Science; Harris, Marvin. 1966. "The Cultural Ecology of India's Sacred Cattle." *Current Anthropology* 7(1):51–59.

56. Harris, Marvin. 1966. "The Cultural Ecology of India's Sacred Cattle," 57.

57. Harris, Marvin. 1966. "The Cultural Ecology of India's Sacred Cattle."

58. Simoons, Frederick. 1979. "Questions in the Sacred Cow Controversy." *Current Anthropology* 20(3):467–76.

59. Freed, Stanley A., and Ruth S. Freed. 1981. "Sacred Cows and Water Buffalo in India: The Uses of Ethnography." *Current Anthropology* 22(5):483–90.

60. Harris, Marvin. 1988. *Culture, People, Nature: An Introduction to General Anthropology.* 5th ed. New York: Harper & Row.

61. Simoons, Frederick. 1979. "Questions in the Sacred Cow Controversy."

62. Coleman, Graham. 1994. *A Handbook of Tibetan Culture: A Guide to Tibetan Centres and Resources throughout the World.* Boston: Shambhala, 285.

63. Coleman, Graham. 1994. *A Handbook of Tibetan Culture;* Thurman, Robert A. F. 1995. *Essential Tibetan Buddhism.* Edison, NJ: Castle Books, Book Sales, Inc.

64. Larsen, Knud, and Amund Sinding-Larsen. 2001. *The Lhasa Atlas: Traditional Tibetan Architecture and Townscape.* Boston: Shambhala, 43.

65. Thurman, Robert A. F. 1995. *Essential Tibetan Buddhism,* 40.

66. Bhutan, National Environment Commission. 1998. *The Middle Path: National Environment Strategy for Butan.* Royal Government of Bhutan, 19.

67. Lewis, Bernard. 1960. *The Arabs in History.* New York: Harper Torchbooks.

68. Levy, Reuben. 1962. *The Social Structure of Islam.* London: Cambridge University Press.

69. Papanek, Hanna. 1982. "Purdah: Separate Worlds and Symbolic Shelter." In *Separate Worlds: Studies of Purdah in South Asia,* edited by Hanna Papanek and Gail Minault, pp. 3–53. Delhi: Chanakya.

70. Ahmed, Leila. 1982. "Western Ethnocentrism and Perceptions of the Harem." *Feminist Studies* 8(3):521–34.

71. Ahmed, Leila. 1982. "Western Ethnocentrism and Perceptions of the Harem," 531.

72. Papanek, Hanna. 1982. "Purdah."

73. Burnell, Arthur Coke, and Edward W. Hopkins, eds. 1884. *The Ordinances of Manu.* London: Trubner, 130–31.

74. Papanek, Hanna. 1982. "Purdah."

75. Roy, Manisha. 1975. *Bengali Women.* Chicago and London: University of Chicago Press.

76. Papanek, Hanna. 1982. "Purdah"; Vatuk, Sylvia. 1982. "Purdah Revisited: A Comparison of Hindu and Muslim Interpretations of the Cultural Meaning of Purdah in South Asia." In *Separate Worlds: Studies of Purdah in South Asia,* edited by Hanna Papanek and Gail Minault, pp. 54–78. Delhi: Chanakya.

77. Jacobson, Doranne. 1982. "Purdah and the Hindu Family in Central India." In *Separate Worlds: Studies of Purdah in South Asia,* edited by Hanna Papanek and Gail Minault, pp. 81–109. Delhi: Chanakya Publications.

78. Jacobson, Doranne. 1982. "Purdah and the Hindu Family," 96–97.

79. Yalman, Nur. 1963. "On the Purity of Women in the Castes of Ceylon and Malabar." *Journal of the Royal Anthropological Institute* 93:25–58.

80. Boserup, Ester. 1970. *Women's Role in Economic Development.* London: Allen & Unwin; Jacobson, Doranne. 1982. "Purdah and the Hindu Family."

81. Jacobson, Doranne. 1982. "Purdah and the Hindu Family," 84–85.

82. Stone, Linda, and Caroline James. 1995. "Dowry, Bride-Burning, and Female Power in India." *Women's Studies International Forum* 18(2):125–34.

83. Stone, Linda, and Caroline James. 1995. "Dowry, Bride-Burning, and Female Power," 128.

Part Three

THE COMMERCIAL WORLD: GLOBAL CAPITALISM

THE COMMERCIAL WORLD IS ONLY A FEW CENTURIES OLD, YET at a global level it has transformed human societies, cultures, and the physical world much more dramatically and more rapidly than all ancient empires in the imperial world. Commercialization is a radical, revolutionary cultural process. The commercial world makes the success of business corporations and the accumulation of financial wealth more important human objectives than the need to maintain governments and households. The following chapters show that this massive cultural transformation has occurred in a way that is fundamentally similar to the construction of the imperial world. A very small number of elite decision makers designed the specific capitalist cultural institutions, including the financial system of banks and stock markets, giant multinational corporations, and the fiscal-military state that allowed the wealthiest investors to shape the entire world according to their needs. More financial capital has accumulated in proportionately fewer hands than at any time in the past. The human problem with these cultural developments is that in absolute numbers, the commercial world has generated more poverty, illness, and human suffering in a shorter time than any past civilizations. The process of accumulating financial wealth has also drawn down natural capital stored in ecosystems and in fossil fuels at a rate that threatens the long-term sustainability of the commercial world as a system.

Chapter 10 examines the distinctive cultural features of capitalism and the history of its European origins, as well as its impact on ordinary people, focusing on England. Chapter 11 examines the development of capitalism, democracy, corporate business, and factory food production systems in the United States, looking at both wealth and poverty. Chapter 12 looks at the impact of capitalist development on ecosystems and the biosphere, as well as its impact on the non-elite of the world. The objective is to assess the limits of commercial growth in a finite world characterized by great social inequality.

CHAPTER 10

The Capitalist World System

Figure 10.0.   Oil pumping unit and drilling rig, Texas. The switch to nonrenewable fossil-fuel energy sources was crucial to the creation of the commercial world (U.S. Department of Energy, Energy Information Administration, Annual Energy Review 2009).

LEARNING OBJECTIVES

AFTER STUDYING THIS CHAPTER YOU SHOULD BE ABLE TO DO the following:

1. Describe the differences in per-capita and total energy use in the tribal, imperial, and commercial worlds. Explain how these differences are related to size of population and their significance for human well-being and cultural sustainability.

2. Describe the distinctive features of capitalism as a world system and mode of production and distribution, in comparison with tribal and pre-capitalist systems.

3. Describe the distinctive features of capitalism as ideology and cosmology in comparison with tribal and pre-capitalist systems, identifying points at which capitalist belief may conflict with reality.

4. Identify the crucial elite-directed cultural processes and the unique historical circumstances that produced capitalism and the commercial world.

5. Describe the increase in English poverty as the commercial world was developed, identifying the

key causal factors, and make comparisons with household well-being in the tribal and imperial worlds.

6. Describe the evidence for elite direction in the development of the British colonial empire.
7. Describe the evidence for elite direction in the development of the postcolonial global commercial order since 1945.

In this chapter and chapters 11 and 12, we look at cultural developments in the modern world as it has been shaped by commercially driven increases in the speed and volume of production and distribution associated with modern technology and by related changes in the organization of social power. This is all about what we call economic growth, its causes and effects. Throughout the imperial world, economic power was controlled by political rulers; however, under the right set of circumstances it became possible for entrepreneurs to build great commercial imperia that pushed beyond the limits of political power. In addition to the persistent problem of collapse, the most important problem with the ancient imperial world from the perspective of power-seeking individuals was that there were severe limitations on the absolute number of power positions in the political hierarchy. It also became increasingly difficult for aspiring individuals to gain entry to the upper ranks of power or to gain positions of power for their family members.

After the fall of the Western Roman Empire in AD 476 the initial foundations of the commercial world were gradually constructed by a handful of European merchants, financiers, and investors during the five centuries between approximately AD 1000 and 1600. Shortly thereafter, and well before the new technologies of the Industrial Revolution had gained momentum, various economic elites quickly put in place virtually all of the crucial institutional structures of modern capitalism including banks, business corporations, stock exchanges, and insurance companies. These financial institutions worked together as the heart of a global commercial system and could operate independently of any particular government. The individuals who constructed the commercial world had no grand vision, and they could not have foreseen the consequences of their actions. They simply took advantage of the opportunities that they found. They expanded their personal economic power, concentrating the benefits of growth, and shifted the costs to society at large much as political rulers had done earlier.

Almost overnight, commercial interests became the primary influence on political systems, as well as on the daily life and well-being of people throughout the world. In this commercialization process, world population increased nearly sixfold, from some 800 million people in 1750 to 6.8 billion by 2010,[1] while per-capita rates of resource consumption soared to unprecedented levels in the industrial centers. A few people became fabulously wealthy, a comfortably well-off middle class emerged in Western Europe and its offshoots, and millions of people worldwide sank into poverty. All societies and cultures are now interconnected within a single economically stratified global system of nation-states dominated by the directors of giant corporations, finance managers, financiers, and investors. Everyone is now dependent on the quixotic flow of finance capital. These dramatic cultural changes present a major challenge for anthropologists and other social scientists seeking to understand how and why they occurred and to improve their effects on people. Technological changes, especially the adoption of mechanized mass production and the use of fossil fuels, were crucial factors in this transformation, but decision making by the human agents that directed these technologies and the underlying cultural changes were even more fundamental causes of this remarkable process.

Many people identify free-market capitalism with human freedom, democracy, economic growth, and material prosperity. However, capitalism evolved and flourished in the absence of democracy, and it was not originally designed to produce either prosperity or freedom for the mass of humanity. Freedom and democracy are a very recent, and not a necessary, historical convergence. They may be only indirectly related to capitalism. It is unfortunately possible that a continuation of economic growth as presently defined may ultimately undermine freedom, democracy, and prosperity. The cultural transformations that produce growth in the scale of societies and economies are humanly directed; they are not inevitable and may not be "progressive" in the sense of benefiting humanity as a whole.

This chapter examines specific human-directed cultural changes that increased the scale of European societies and produced a commercially organized world system, arguing that these changes were neither natural nor inevitable. This view contrasts sharply with popular explanations for the "inevitability" of cultural development as due to (1) natural population growth, (2) natural technological progress, and (3) natural economic progress. Given the relative stability of human population within tribal cultures and its sudden expansion under politically organized cultures, population growth is likely to be a culturally mediated process, not a natural constant. Furthermore, technology and economic organization clearly are cultural, not natural, phenomena.

In a popular book on the global economy, economist Lester Thurow[2] used the geological principles of plate tectonics to explain how economic forces shape the world. This reflects common beliefs in the irresistible force of markets but ignores human agency. A major assumption in this book is that economic growth is not a "natural" process. Rather, growth is a culture process and the result of many individual decision makers seeking greater economic power in particular places.

Many of those who now design and direct commercial technology also maintain that technological change is natural. For example, Microsoft founder Bill Gates insists, "No one gets to vote on whether technology is going to change our lives. No one can stop productive change in the long run because the market inexorably embraces it. ... I believe that because progress will come no matter what, we need to make the best of it—not try to forestall it."[3]

Individual decision makers use specific cultural institutions and cultural processes to promote or limit growth, and they guide cultural development in particular directions. In previous chapters, we saw that political rulers used population growth, technology, and economic organization to increase the scale of society, and thereby to enlarge their own social power. The disadvantage of this kind of directed culture change is that decision makers cannot know what the total consequences will be or how many will ultimately suffer or benefit. Gates speaks optimistically of the revolutionary, even "seismic" effects of computer technology, assuring us that computers will change every aspect of our lives. But he acknowledges some unanswered, and troublesome, questions when he asks, "What will happen to our jobs? . . . Will the gulf between the haves and the have-nots widen irreparably?"[4] These are serious questions, because since AD 1600, commercially directed technological change plunged millions into poverty even as it elevated a few to great wealth and power.

The contemporary world is fundamentally different from everything that preceded it because it is dominated by commercialization, a new, untested cultural process that now supersedes both politicization and humanization. Politicization, the process that produces and maintains centralized political power, has become a subordinate cultural process in the commercial world, maintaining the conditions that support economic growth in support of the commercialization process. The world's dominant national and international institutions primarily are concerned with promoting perpetual growth in the accumulation of financial capital and in the flow of money as a measure of commercial production, exchange, and consumption of goods and services.

This overwhelming focus on the accumulation and concentration of wealth, as an end in itself, is an extremely unusual cultural development. Neither concentrated wealth nor poverty exists in most tribal cultures, where production occurs at the household level to meet the needs that households define. Only in more complex tribal societies is there any cultural incentive for one household to accumulate more than any other or to produce beyond immediate needs. In ancient Mesopotamia, the Andes, imperial China, and Hindu India, wealth was used to maintain the politicization process—wealth accumulation was not an end in itself. In ancient civilizations, surplus production was extracted from the peasants to finance temples, irrigation works, and fortifications. Wealth maintained the infrastructure of state power, and wealth objects verified political rank, rewarded loyalty, and were buried in royal tombs and in mummy cults.

The infrequent rise and regular collapse of ancient states and empires suggest that they were not the most reliable human adaptations. Commercial culture is only a few centuries old, but it has already transformed and destabilized the world in unusual ways. Its cultural superiority remains to be demonstrated. After examining the dominant features of this remarkable cultural transformation, this chapter presents ethnohistoric data on European cosmology, feudalism, peasant farming systems, specific mercantile capitalists, and the London poor in order to trace the development of commercialization.

The Paradox of Growth

Economic growth is the dominant ideological feature of the contemporary commercial world. It is the primary goal of governments, businesses, and many nongovernmental organizations and is the principal justification for countless policies and actions. It is so firmly established in cultural belief and practice that its supremacy goes unchallenged, yet its real effects on humanity and the world are not well understood. This is remarkable from an anthropological perspective, because the concepts of "economy" and "economic growth" are very recent cultural inventions that paradoxically have only a partial connection to the realities of the physical world, although the human actions undertaken in their name have had vast consequences. We imagine the economy to be a thing that can grow in much the way that people in the tribal and imperial worlds thought of natural forces as objects or personified them as beings. The critical problem is that economies are cultural constructions, and by itself economic growth has not been universally beneficial to humanity and has produced many negative effects.

What Is Growth? What Economists
Measure and Why It Matters

Popular discourse on "the economy" in the capitalist centers of the contemporary commercial world focuses on **gross domestic product** (GDP) and "the market" as measured by the price of money (interest rates) and indices of corporate stock prices such as the Dow Jones Industrial Averages. **Gross national product** (GNP) or gross national income (GNI) is also commonly used to measure the size of an economy. GNI measures the value produced within a country as well as money returned to investors from their investments in other countries, less money that flows out to foreign investors. In considering GDP or GNI figures it is important to also note what currency is used, whether it is adjusted for inflation, and whether it is in global market exchange values or in **purchasing power parity**, which adjusts for the value of the currency in relation to a set of basic goods in the country. The difference between "domestic" and "national" in GDP and GNP matters because it calls attention to the role of capital, rather than flows of money, and to where the owners of capital are located. In regard to the distribution of social power the difference between *flow* of income and *accumulation* of capital as wealth is as important as the difference between GDP per capita, which is an average, versus the actual distribution of either income or wealth to people by percentiles of population, or the median, which is the middle point when everyone is ranked from richest to poorest. A single-minded public focus on GDP and GDP per capita masks all of these issues.

GDP, GNI, and stock market averages are very powerful symbols that were newly constructed in the twentieth century. Much of the power of these economic symbols is that published figures on GDP and stock prices influence human perceptions, which in turn influence GDP and stock prices. The reflexive quality of these dominant institutional and ideological features of the culturally constructed market economy is a reality that challenges economic theories of rational markets. Economic theories and theorists are also part of this popular discourse and are the basis of much current political ideology and national and international political decision making.[5] GDP and the market also have enormous human consequences, even though their empirical bases are not commonly understood.

GDP is the annual flow of money in a country measured either as income or consumption. Governments and economists usually depict these as a national aggregate or as a per-capita national average. In most contemporary monetary systems money is intangible. It is a means of exchange with no intrinsic value and now exists mostly as digital information in accounts. Money measures rights and obligations between people and is a primary source of social power. Money flows as income, but it also accumulates as wealth, or financial capital, which is a major source of social power and is often more inequitably distributed than flows of income. It is also important to recognize that there are other important forms of capital, such as natural capital, human capital, and cultural capital, which also accumulate as stocks rather than flows, but they are usually ignored in national economic discourse.

Economists use the national flow measures of GDP and GDP per capita to rank countries by economic performance. Such rankings reveal inequities in the distribution of income between countries, but the focus on GDP also obscures the often very large inequities in the distribution of both income and wealth between individuals, households, cities, and regions within countries. What matters most for the system is the quantity and distribution of the underlying stock of elite-managed wealth that directs the flow of money.

GDP and aggregate national measures of wealth (assets) and debt (liabilities) are part of the United Nations System of National Accounts (SNA), which began in 1953 and has been periodically revised up to the 2008 SNA. This is the international standard system of national government economic accounting and is used by the United Nations International Monetary Fund (IMF) and World Bank, as well as the European Union (EU) and the Organization for Economic Cooperation and Development (OECD). The "gross" part of GDP means that it does not measure the depreciation or loss of capital that accompanies production.

If economic sustainability were the most important concern, net domestic product (NDP) would be the preferred standard measure. As noted above, domestic product is the value of goods and services produced *within* a country, whereas national product includes the return on domestic capital for goods and services produced in other countries. However, capitalists and their wealth are so mobile that it can often be difficult to know what "domestic capital" means.

Two Thousand Years of World Economic Growth to AD 2001

The most comprehensive recent overview of the broad sweep of historical development of the global commercial economy was prepared by economist Angus Maddison[6] for the OECD. The OECD was formed in 1961 by twenty primarily Western European countries and the United States with the goal of promoting policies that would "achieve the highest sustainable economic growth and employment and a rising standard of living in Member countries ... and thus to contribute to the development of the world economy."[7] Maddison tracked economic growth over the 2,000 years from the year AD 1 to 2001 measured as

GDP in 1990 international Geary-Khamis PPP dollars pegged to the equivalent of a dollar's worth of goods purchased in the United States in 1990. PPP dollars are presumed to be more useful than the fluctuating value of international currencies on global exchange markets. The baseline minimum per-capita income in 1 AD was taken to be $400 (in Eastern Europe, North and Central Asia, New World) and the highest was only $450 (India, China, Western Europe). In 1 AD an estimated 75 percent of the global economy was in India and China.

Maddison shows the global economy growing a dramatic 362-fold from $102 billion in AD 1 to $37 trillion in 2001 (see figure 10.1). Over the same period global population grew only 27-fold from 230 million to 6 billion. This meant that GDP per capita increased 13-fold from $445 to $6,049 (see figure 10.2), suggesting that real progress had occurred. The reality of global poverty and environmental degradation was obscured by these measures, because GDP focuses on income not wealth, does not take into account the actual distribution of income, and does not account for all forms of capital, including the difference between tangible and intangible capital.

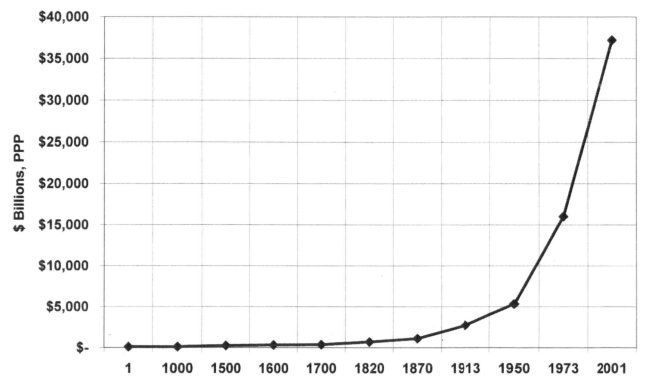

Figure 10.1. World GDP AD 1–2001 (data from Maddison 2003).

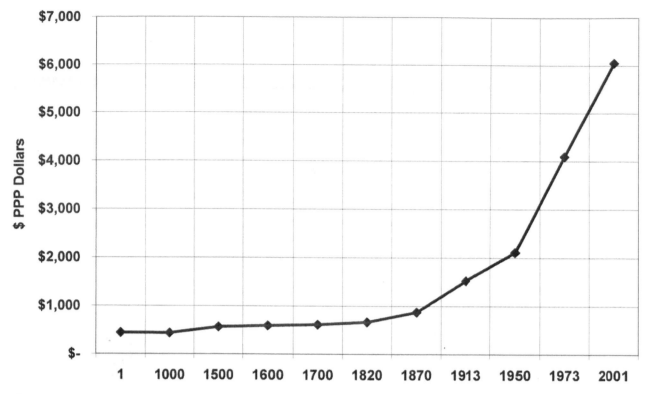

Figure 10.2. World GDP/Capita AD **1–2001 (data from Maddison 2003).**

Maddison's data shows a dramatic shift in the regional distribution of economic activity from over the past two millennia. Two thousand years ago 75 percent of global GDP was in Asia, primarily China and India, and Western Europe accounted for a mere 11 percent (see figure 10.3). Western Europe and its outliers in North America and Australia reached their maximum share of the global economy at 57 percent in 1950, when Asia's share had dropped to just 15 percent. By 2001 the Asian share, including Japan, had risen to 38 percent, and Western Europe had dropped to 45 percent. Africa was at its lowest with just 3 percent. If economic activity reflects the distribution of human benefit, it is very inequitably distributed. The paradox of economic growth is its bias toward increasing production and maximizing wealth accumulation and its apparent failure to distribute benefits in a way that maximizes human well-being.

Discovering the Economy

Economic growth could not be measured until the concept of national accounts was developed. This reminds us that the "economy" as a concept and economic calculations were from the very beginning closely tied to government policy and how it could be used to foster capital accumulation. The economy is

about commercial interests, and these interests can be seen to drive political practice and government policy.

The first national economic accounts that resemble modern accounting methods appeared in late seventeenth-century England to support government policies. Pioneer English economist and author of *Political Arithmetik* William Petty[8] (1623–1687) estimated the value of the standing stock (capital) of the land, buildings, money, and movable property including livestock, business inventories, farm equipment, and people of England and Wales at £667 million in 1665 and the annual "yield" or the national income at £40 million ($5 billion in 1990 Geary-Khamis PPP dollars). National income was thus an annual return of approximately 6 percent of the value of the nation's capital or national wealth. Petty estimated that nearly two-thirds (£25 million) of the £40 million annual income was produced by labor, with the balance (£15 million) as property income from rents, agriculture, and commerce. He estimated the English population at 6 million people, half of whom were workers earning an average of about £8 per year. Based on worker earnings capitalized over 17 years, Petty estimated the value of each person at £70 ($9,270 in 1990 $GK). He used these per-capita values to demonstrate the value of government-supported public health measures to

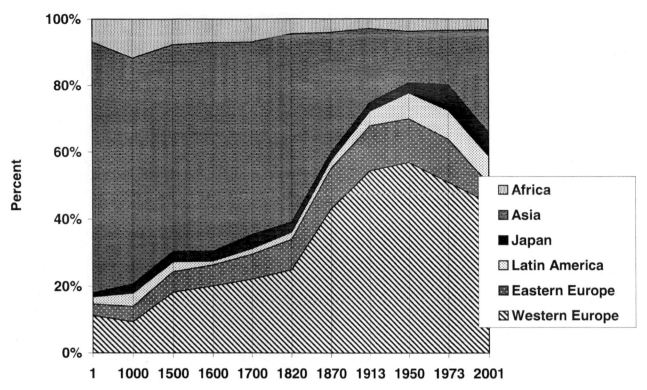

Figure 10.3. Regional distribution of world GDP, AD 1–2001 (data from Maddison 2003).

reduce deaths from the plague. Petty estimated government expenses at £1 million, which were raised by a tax of about 2.5 percent on all forms of income. Over half of the government's ordinary expenditures were military, and Petty suggested that if people just worked 14 more days a year and reduced their consumption by 5 percent, military expenditures could be doubled.

Petty himself was concerned with economic distribution as well as production and recognized that civil wars could occur because "the Wealth of the Nation is in too few men's hands, and that no certain means are provided to keep all men from a necessity either to beg, or steal, or be souldiers [sic] ... [and] allowing Luxury in some, whilst others [needlessly] starve."[9]

A major conceptual breakthrough, materializing the "economy" as a physical thing that could be readily visualized as an object in time and space, came a century later with the publication of William Playfair's *Commercial and Political Atlas*, which first appeared in 1785, at the very dawn of the industrial age. Playfair (1759–1823) was a Scottish engineer who became interested in economics. His Atlas included a simple graph of English imports and exports from 1700 to 1782. The years were measured on the horizontal axis, and the economic values were measured in millions of pounds sterling on the vertical axis. This was the

first such graph ever published (see figure 10.4 for an example of Playfair's economic graphs). The third edition of his Atlas included "The Statistical Breviary: Shewing on a principle entirely new, The Resources of every State and Kingdom in Europe" in which he published the first known pie graphs.

Even though Playfair's innovative graphs allowed people to see economic growth, Playfair himself had doubts about its benefits and thought that the most dramatic growth had already occurred. He also realized that future growth was not unlimited: "It is impossible to behold this rapid progress without concluding that it must come in time to a point which it cannot pass, as nothing is infinite; ... though it may be a question admitting of discussion, whether wealth, and what is commonly called commercial prosperity, is any real advantage to a nation, there can be no question that the loss of it, after having once enjoyed its possession, is a very severe misfortune."[10]

He also observed that "all is well enough" with nations that "never were rich."

Energy, Materials, and Growth

The elite-directed cultural innovations and social transformations that produced the commercial world have led to vast, almost inconceivable, increases in energy consumption. In the pre-capitalist imperial

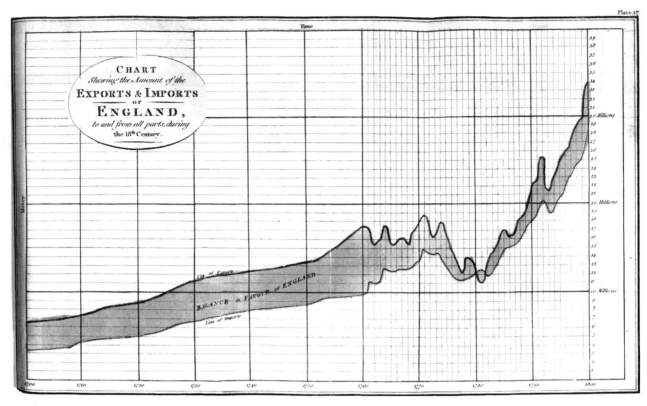

Figure 10.4. William Playfair's 1801 "Chart shewing the amount of the exports and imports of England to and from all parts during the 18th century" (Playfair, William. 1801. *The Commercial and Political Atlas and Statistical Breviary***).**

world, elites generated their social power from the relatively limited number of subjects that they could tax, whereas in the commercial world economic elites accumulate power by skimming profits from a growing volume of market transactions limited only by the availability of energy and materials, the scale of markets, and the human capacity to produce and consume. The revolutionary nature of the global transformation of production and consumption that accompanied commercialization can be readily seen in the changes in per-capita energy consumption in different cultures over time (see figure 10.5). Foragers drew their energy only from food and firewood for an estimated 5,000 kilocalories per capita per day. Tribal villagers using domesticated animals raised their daily per-capita total to perhaps 12,000 kilocalories. In the imperial world, this level increased only modestly with the gradual addition of water and wind power to support urbanization. By AD 1400, on the eve of the revolutionary transformations brought about by the commercialization process, the additional use of small amounts of coal may have raised daily energy consumption in England to 26,000 kilocalories per capita.[11] However, by 1875, with commercialization

well underway, increasing urbanization and industrialization fueled by expanded use of coal brought the English average to 77,000 kilocalories. The addition of fossil fuels can appropriately be called the **fuel revolution.** An even more revolutionary change in per-capita energy consumption was brought about during the twentieth century by the addition of petroleum, natural gas, and hydroelectric power. American per-capita consumption of commercial energy may have peaked at 245,000 in 1999 and had declined to about 225,000 by 2008.[12] Except for tribals, these figures do not include the kilocalorie value of food consumed.

Significantly, in 2000 the global average per-capita energy consumption of 45,000 kilocalories remained lower than England in 1875 and much lower than the average in the United States. This was because global population had grown so large, and very high energy use was so concentrated in the wealthiest countries. The increased per-capita energy consumption that accompanied commercialization also supported a human demographic revolution, which dramatically elevated *aggregate* energy costs. Global energy consumption of primary energy (coal, natural gas, petroleum, electricity, geothermal, solar, and wind)

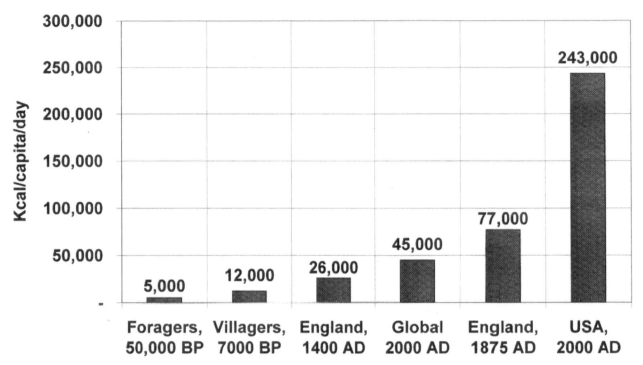

Figure 10.5. **Per capita daily energy consumption by cultures (kcal/capita/day), 50,000 BV–2000 AD (Cook 1971:136, U.S. Department of Energy 2003).**

reached 122 quadrillion kilocalories (484 quadrillion BTUs) annually by the year 2007.[13] These numbers are so large that they can only be displayed on a log scale (see figure 10.6). Even one quadrillion (1,000 trillion) is an inconceivably large number, but 100 quadrillion (10^{17}) is four powers of 10 greater than the aggregate of the modest 14.6 trillion kilocalories consumed annually in the forager world.

Remarkably, 85 percent of global energy consumption in the year 2000 was in the form of nonrenewable fossil fuels, and 45 percent of fossil fuel energy was in the form of petroleum. One country, the United States, consumed 25 percent of total global energy. This degree of energy inequality and dependency on unevenly distributed nonrenewable fossil fuels creates enormous stresses in the global system. Increased consumption combined with population growth has totally transformed the relationship between human groups, and between humans and the physical and biological world of nature. Within a single century of growth fueled by fossil fuels, the commercial world has suddenly placed human sustainability in doubt for the first time in the past 200,000 years of human existence.

Global population in the pre-capitalist imperial world had apparently reached a threshold at about 360 million people in the thirteenth century AD.[14] Rather than continuing to grow, population actually declined somewhat as unfavorable weather, plagues, and social and economic turmoil impacted the most densely settled areas of the world. This was similar to the environmental crisis produced by postglacial global warming in the early Holocene that contributed to the Neolithic and the formation of the first chiefdoms and city-states. However, given historical circumstances in Europe by AD 1400, these multiple crises created unique opportunities for economic elites to promote commercialization and accumulate wealth.

In a few centuries after 1400 the weakness of political rulers during times of social and economic turmoil gave merchants, financiers, and large landowners a free hand, allowing them to expand their influence over markets and making it possible for them to create personal power networks that connected sources of political and religious power. Economic elites were also wealthy enough to be insulated from economic crises and were able to take advantage of new economic opportunities as they arose. At the same time elite-directed changes in the organization of production forced vast numbers of people into economic dependency in crowded cities. The unprecedented combination of economic growth, poverty, and urbanization for the first time caused population to increase at exponential rates. Population growth created abundant cheap labor and larger markets. Global

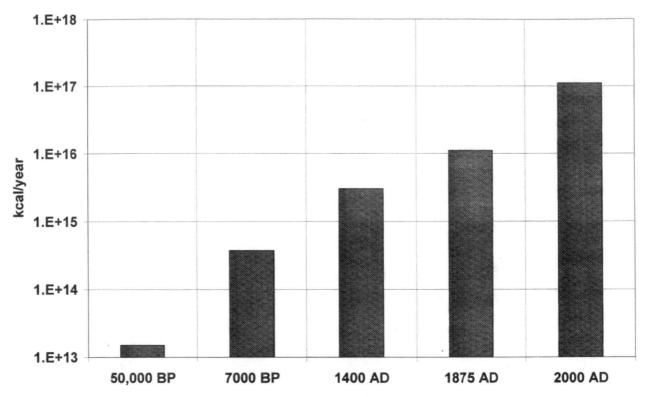

Figure 10.6. Global aggregate annual energy consumption (kcal/year), 50,000 BP–200 AD (Data from Cook 1971:136, U.S. Department of Energy 2003).

population suddenly passed the billion mark by about 1804, with intercontinental commercial transfers of food and materials drawing on preindustrial agricultural technology. Rapidly accelerating growth since then saw global population double to 2 billion within 123 years by 1927, and double again to 4 billion within 47 years by 1974 (see figure 10.7).

Population growth in the commercial world has been directly subsidized by the burning of fossil fuels. For example, in the year 2000, most of the world's 6 billion people were heavily dependent on food produced by large-scale factory farms. In addition to petroleum products farm machinery consumed, factory farms were consuming some 130 million metric tons of synthetically manufactured ammonia fertilizer (NH_3) produced at a cost of a quadrillion kilocalories of natural gas. Of course, primary agricultural production is only a small part of the energy cost of food in the commercial world.

The dramatic increases in energy consumption in the commercial world are paralleled by similar increases in the flow of materials. It is estimated that the per-capita weight of raw material consumed per year (exclusive of water and air)—food, wood, fodder, fossil fuels, minerals, metals, and plastics—quadrupled from one metric ton in the tribal world to four in the

pre-capitalist imperial world, and reached an average of nearly 20 tons in the industrialized nations by the late twentieth century.[15] People in industrial societies use an estimated 60 times more water per capita than tribal foragers.[16] Estimates for the city of Ann Arbor, Michigan, in 1997 showed an annual per-capita inflow of materials of nearly 30 tons, excluding tap water.[17] This figure includes direct and indirect material flows, counting all materials that contribute to the well-being of the residents of Ann Arbor, including manufacturing processes outside of Ann Arbor. Most of the weight is in food and construction materials. Remarkably, nearly 40 percent of the weight of food was in beverages, and nearly half of that weight was in carbonated soft drinks. Only about 3 tons of these material inputs actually passed through wholesale and retail businesses to end consumers.

The increased flow of materials consumed by commercial societies can also be measured in the proportion of global biological production that humans appropriate. When measured as ecological footprint, treating fossil fuels as a current biological product, humans have exceeded the annual biological production since 1987 and reached 122 percent by 2001.[18] A much more conservative approach suggests that humans are appropriating approximately 24 percent

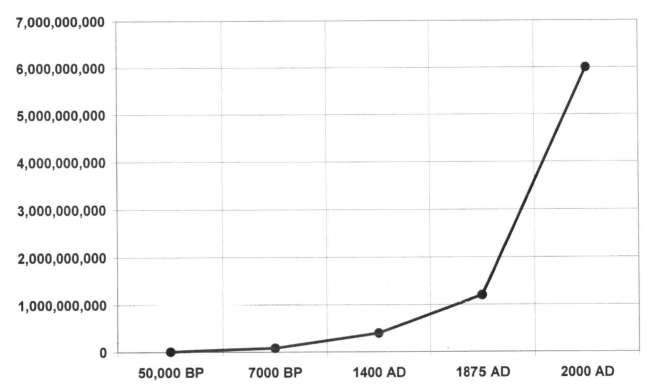

Figure 10.7. Global population, 50,000 BP–2000 AD.

of potential net primary productivity.[19] This considers biomass harvested from forest, pastures, and cropland; human-caused fires, urbanization, and land use practices; and taking into account increased biological productivity from energy-intensive factory farming, but not counting fossil fuels as current product. No matter how the physical impact of the commercial world is measured, it is dramatically greater than any previous cultural worlds.

Human Needs and Culture Scale: Flipping the Social Pyramid

By definition, tribal cultures were the only cultures to focus exclusively on satisfying basic human needs. Every household had access to the subsistence resources it needed and controlled its own production and consumption. Every household was, in effect, guaranteed what anthropologist Paul Radin called the "irreducible minimum," an inalienable right to "adequate food, shelter and clothing."[20] In the imperial world, the politicization process took some decision-making power and control away from households and communities; however, human labor power continued to be important and labor still was required to fulfill the needs of most people. Enormous differences in social power, wealth, and status separated the social classes in ancient civilizations. The lower classes were certainly exploited, but relatively few people, usually outsiders, were enslaved and sacrificed. Most people were able to maintain viable households.

In the commercialization process, everything that people need for their well-being has been converted into a commodity to be sold for profit. State power is used to encourage people to become wage laborers—producing, purchasing, and consuming commodities rather than pursuing noncommercial subsistence activities. The inherent problem with this system is that millions of people no longer have access to basic subsistence resources and cannot earn a sufficient wage to purchase a decent living. Thus, millions are unable to provide for such basic needs as food, shelter, clean water, and pure air. Infant mortality rates soar, and malnutrition is now common. This kind of poverty makes the commercial world seem inhumane relative to both imperial and tribal worlds. From a global perspective two millennia of economic growth has not changed the overall distribution of social power. In the commercial world, just as in the imperial world, only a few are wealthy and powerful. Elite-directed growth has flipped the social pyramid in comparison with the tribal world (see figure 10.8).

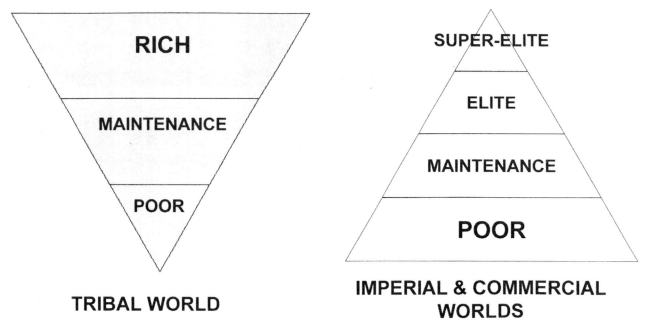

Figure 10.8. Flipping the social pyramid: the distribution of social power in tribal, imperial, and commercial worlds.

THE CULTURE OF CAPITALISM

Anthropological Economics:
Production and Exchange

The modern capitalist economy is radically different from all previous systems of production and exchange. The distinctive features of capitalism created the global political economy. The concept of political economy used in this book emphasizes the fact that economics cannot be separated from politics. This means that the commercial world is as much about a social structure that is maintained by political power as it is about a material infrastructure and an ideological superstructure. Capitalism as presently constituted is a particular property regime and an unequal distribution of wealth that is ultimately enforced by the coercive power of government. Capitalist economic organization uses social inequality to promote wealth accumulation and political expansion on a scale unequaled in human history.

The concept of an economy existing apart from the rest of society began as a uniquely European cultural construction. All societies have cultural systems of production and distribution, but only Europeans came to believe that human well-being depended on having a growing economy. In tribal societies what Europeans call "the economy" is embedded within everyday household activities. It is helpful for comparative purposes to distinguish three different systems of

production and distribution: kin ordered, tributary, and capitalist.[21]

Kin-ordered production characterizes the tribal cultures treated in chapters 2 through 4. In these systems, kinship constitutes the culturally defined social categories around which productive activities are organized. Relationships between individuals established by marriage or family connections, real or fictive, determine the form of food-producing and -sharing groups. In all social systems that are ordered exclusively by kinship, production is primarily for direct consumption, or **use value**, rather than for **exchange value**. Small Pacific Island chiefdoms such as Tikopia have ranked descent groups, but production and distribution continue to be primarily based on kinship. However, large Pacific chiefdoms and the Hawaiian kingdom are tributary political economies in which the rulers command a significant portion of both production and distribution.

Tributary production characterizes the ancient civilizations described in chapters 7 through 9. In these systems, the commoners, or peasantry, produced their own food, while the rulers supported themselves by extracting "surplus" production as tribute. Surplus extraction was exploitation whenever it reduced the security of the producers or lowered their standard of living. Title to land was often claimed by the state, but it was political power and ideology that compelled the peasantry to turn over surplus production to the state. The structure of surplus extraction was maintained by placing primary producers in subordinate status positions relative to the nonfood-producing elites. Much of the accumulated wealth went into maintaining status differences by means of the conspicuous display of luxury goods or the construction of awe-inspiring temples and funerary ritual. Bureaucratically organized tribute extraction often existed alongside long-distance, market-oriented exchange systems managed by merchants or traders. Developed market systems helped rulers acquire exotic luxury goods, but a fully commercialized distribution system would have undermined the status structure that supported the tribute system and would, in theory, have transformed it into a **capitalist production** mode.

Western Cosmology and the Industrial Revolution

Marshall Sahlins[22] points out that Judeo-Christian cosmology is apparently unique among cultural traditions because it attributes the evil in the world to a human act of free will, as recounted in the Book of Genesis. Western cosmology assumes that because of their original sin in the Garden of Eden, humans are inherently evil, and human misery is the natural punishment for this evil human nature. This gloomy cosmology derives from religious beliefs, but the underlying assumptions about human nature and economic scarcity seem to have permeated Western scientific and secular thought.

The European Enlightenment, which made riches a desirable goal, represented a change in thought that kept the underlying belief in original sin and human inadequacy intact. Material progress was assumed to be natural, although this view overlooked the contradiction that progress also increased human needs, leaving people perpetually unsatisfied. Commerce, industrial technology, and the science of economics are all seemingly designed to help people reduce, but never overcome, the inevitable scarcity that insatiable human nature implies. What Sahlins calls the industrial revelation is the sad realization that "in the world's richest societies, the subjective experience of lack increases in proportion to the objective output of wealth."[23] In effect, economic growth must impoverish.

In Western cosmology, people are driven by natural law to seek pleasure and avoid pain. Society itself is thought to be the product of selfish individuals seeking self-satisfaction, just as the "laws" of market supply and demand, or "free trade," will give us the best distribution of economic goods. As we have seen in previous chapters, this view of human existence is strikingly different from the belief of tribal peoples that life is good and that they can provide for all of their material and emotional needs through their own efforts. Liberated and empowered by their culture, tribal peoples maximize individual freedom and personal autonomy and do not view society as a coercive force. By contrast, Western philosophers from Bishop Augustine to Thomas Hobbes, as well as many modern sociologists and anthropologists, consider society to be a coercive power structure. This view equates society with government and treats it as a natural response to a selfish, and thus dangerous, human nature. Sahlins even argues that the "invisible hand" theorized by Adam Smith (discussed later in the chapter) and the functionalism of anthropology and sociology can be derived from the understanding of Divine Providence found in medieval cosmology, in which whatever happens is God's, or society's, plan and will result in collective good. This natural law of the Enlightenment philosophers provided the foundation for economics, natural science, political science, and national constitutions.

The notion of a spiritual soul existing apart from the physical body is virtually a human universal, but only Westerners see body and soul in conflict. Medieval philosophers extended the mind/body dualism to humans and nature. They situated humans midway between animals and gods in a hierarchical "chain of being," giving humans the mortal bodies of animals and godlike intellects. Judeo-Christian beliefs that humans have dominion over nature prepared the way for capitalism by making it easy to objectify nature and treat natural objects as commodities. Such dualism and universal commodification is quite alien to virtually all other cultures, where even the concept of nature as distinct from the supernatural does not exist. The outcome of this Western cosmology of evil humanity, natural scarcity, insatiable wants, human separation from nature, and presumably perfect markets based on free trade, is that people are persuaded to believe that their culture evolved naturally to meet our human needs, not that it was designed by particular people to meet their particular needs.

Capitalism is by definition an ideology that gives priority to the "free market" and makes economic growth and perpetual capital accumulation the most important human objective. In addition to thinking of capitalism as a belief system, commercialization (the production and maintenance of private profit-making business enterprise) is the dominant cultural process, and economic elites draw their social power from commercial transactions.

Under capitalism as a system of commercial production and exchange, land, labor, technology, money, raw materials, and goods and services are commodities to be bought and sold for a profit. The emergence of a monetary market for labor is a key distinguishing feature of capitalism, because wage labor reduced the self-sufficiency of the household far more decisively than did tribute systems. Political economist and theorist Karl Marx (1818–1883) argued that the labor market emerged historically when capitalists separated the peasantry from their land and other resources that constituted their means of production, thus compelling the peasantry to sell their labor to secure basic subsistence. Laborers came to constitute a social class characterized by their separation from the means of production. Land and tools became **capital**, which only a few owned, and basic products became **commodities** to be marketed. As a social class, capitalists, or the owners of capital, made a profit by appropriating surplus production above the costs of labor and capital. In this mode of production, the capitalist seeks to accumulate a surplus to increase profit. The surplus can be increased by depressing the wage of the laborers and by raising the level of technology. The interest of capitalists to increase their profits by keeping the labor wage low is opposed to the interest of laborers to increase their own share of the products of their labor. Individual capitalists also compete with one another to increase their profits. This incentive to increase profits, as well as the contradiction of interests between social classes, encourages economic elites to use their influence on political rulers to increase their social power. Elites lobby for government policies that direct public finance into infrastructure improvements and social institutions that will favor the development of capital-intensive technologies, increased production, and the expansion of markets. Capitalists also tend to favor expansionist foreign policies that will gain them access to new sources of labor, markets, raw materials, and land to further their personal goals of wealth accumulation.

The Greek concept of economy described by the ancient philosopher Aristotle (384–322 BC) illustrates the contrasts between the imperial and commercial worlds. The Greeks took economy to mean household economy (*oikonomia*). They did not think of "the economy" as something separate from daily life. They imagined a stable, **embedded economy**, much as in the tribal world, and they were not concerned with promoting economic growth. They tolerated, but stigmatized, merchants who engaged in moneymaking (*chrematistike*), on the assumption that they sought unjust profits from unequal exchange. Greek society

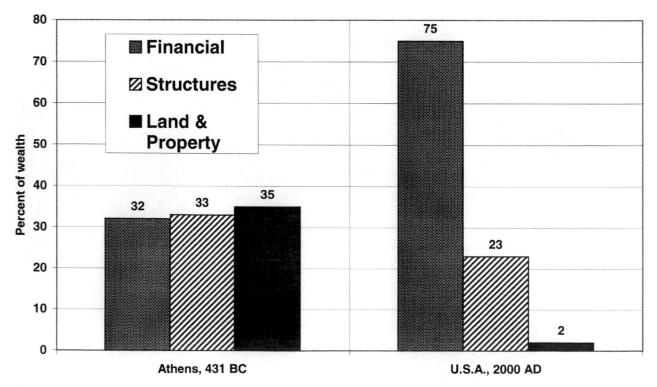

Figure 10.9. The composition of national wealth in ancient Greece and the United States.

was to be composed ideally of relatively equal citizens. Wealth accumulation was suspect because it could lead to wasteful luxury and impropriety, but it could be a source of honor if devoted to public interests. In the ancient city-state of Attica (Athens), two-thirds of all wealth was in buildings (33 percent) and coins (32 percent). The remainder was in farmland (22 percent), slaves (7 percent), and livestock and movable goods (6 percent).[24] Slightly more than half of all Athenian wealth was in public hands. Equally remarkable, most public wealth was economically unproductive, and nearly one-fourth of this was in religious buildings and cult objects. In comparison, in the United States in the year 2000, most wealth was in financial assets (75 percent) and structures (23 percent), and land and all movable assets together were only 2 percent of the total (see figure 10.9). In 1995, all U.S. governments—federal, state, and local—held only 11 percent of national wealth.

Aristotle advocated a production and exchange system that, in theory, was remarkably reminiscent of the "original affluent society" of foragers.[25] Aristotle felt that human wants were limited and that economic scarcity was not a problem. This ideal represents a view that is in direct opposition to the modern definition of a **disembodied economy**, which assumes limited means and unlimited wants. Aristotle's ideal city-state assumed a small community based on reciprocal exchange, self-sufficiency, and social justice, (except, of course, for slaves). In this system, individuals were not supposed to make a profit at their neighbors' expense because this would lead to inequality that would threaten community solidarity. Aristotle accepted money as a medium of exchange but argued that too much market trade would undermine the good life, and he considered wealth accumulation to be contrary to natural law.

The commercial world is obviously superior at wealth building. In 431 BC, the total wealth of Attica could be estimated at the equivalent of a mere $807 million, or $2,522 per capita in a population of 320,000 people. This is based on converting the minimum annual household subsistence value of 275 Greek drachma into the equivalent of $1,500, treated as universal income units for comparative purposes. In 2008 the aggregate wealth of the United States was $170 trillion.[26] This was an astounding six orders of magnitude greater than Greek wealth. Wealth was

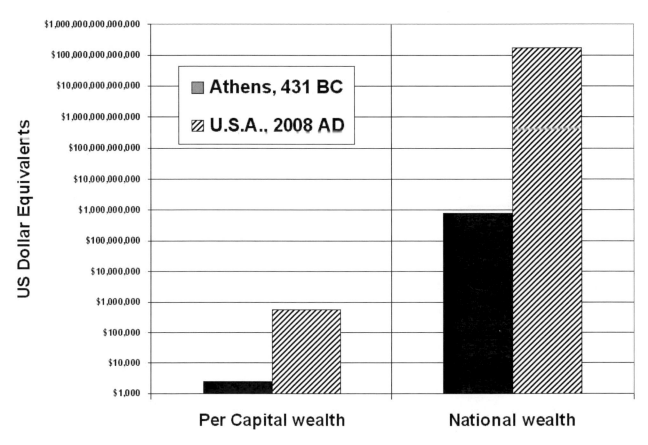

Figure 10.10. National and per capita wealth in ancient Greece and the United States.

much greater in the United States, both in absolute quantity and in the amount per capita. U.S. per-capita wealth was about $560,000 for 304 million people (see figure 10.10). Furthermore, even though private wealth was highly concentrated in both cultures, the vast volume of total American wealth, as well as the greater proportion that was privately held, meant that America's wealthiest controlled vastly more absolute power than the wealthiest Greeks. Even more importantly, as capitalists, wealthy Americans use their wealth to produce more wealth.

Earlier noncapitalist societies did not institutionalize private property and had no organized markets for land, labor, and money. Production and trade were directed by political rulers, and people became wealthy because of their political power. Furthermore, people lacked the concept of economic freedom and were bound to their occupations. In contrast, "...the capitalist employee has the legal right to work or not work as he or she chooses..." as well as the right to buy up farmland and turn it into a more profitable shopping center.[27]

Economists Heilbroner and Thurow consider capitalism to be "utterly alien" and a "volcanic disruption" in comparison to the "tradition and command" systems that preceded it. In their view, there were no "factors of production" in pre-capitalist societies, because "labor, land, and capital were not commodities for sale." Instead, these factors "...are the creations of a process of historic change, a change that divorced labor from social life, that created real estate out of ancestral land, and that made treasure into capital. Capitalism is the outcome of a revolutionary change—a change in laws, attitudes, and social relationships as deep and far-reaching as any in history."[28]

Immanuel Wallerstein on the Inequality and Instability of Capitalism

According to sociologist Immanuel Wallerstein,[29] the emergence of capitalism in sixteenth-century Europe led to a uniquely organized global world economy by the early twentieth century. Capitalism succeeded as a social system because it proved to be a more effective means of appropriating surplus production than the earlier tributary empires. Empires that used coercion to extract surplus were expensive to maintain and very fragile. Earlier noncapitalist states were, in effect, "homeostatic systems," in that they tended to rise and fall within certain limits set by their unstable political organization. In comparison with tribal cultures, the early states and empires functioned at a much higher density and total size, but they were still limited in absolute scale.

In the capitalist **world system**, expansion to the limits of the globe becomes theoretically possible because the system can function without a global political authority. Individual states are needed only to maintain internal order, to enforce contracts, and to encourage the international market economy. The key to capitalist expansion was that the market economy provided incentives for technological improvements that increased productivity, while a world division of labor allowed costs and benefits to be unequally distributed.

The emerging capitalist world system was a multilayered economic hierarchy divided into a European core, a southern European semiperiphery, and an eastern European and New World periphery. Each zone was defined by distinctive geography, political organization, economic production, and its form of labor control, but the zones were all linked to the center by **unequal exchanges** that contributed to **capital accumulation** in the **core**. The exploited lower classes were concentrated in the **periphery** and semiperiphery, where they were coerced to work as slaves and serfs for European managers. Conditions were somewhat less coercive for the tenant farmers in the semiperiphery. In the core, laborers worked for wages and small farmers worked their own land, while merchants and industrialists profited enormously from their privileged positions as the prime beneficiaries of the unequal exchange.

It is important to note the distinctions between world and globe in this context. The world system initially did not encompass the globe; it began in Europe and expanded outward. The system originated in an economic crisis that undermined European feudalism by 1450 and encouraged capital accumulation at the expense of the peasantry. Expansion was spurred on by the gold and silver extracted as booty from the New World, and the system consolidated between 1640 and 1815. The Industrial Revolution, utilizing coal as a new energy base, facilitated further expansion.

Wallerstein[30] lists six destabilizing realities that characterize the modern world system:

1. A hierarchical division of labor
2. Periodic expansion and incorporation
3. Continuous accumulation
4. Continuous progress
5. Polarization of individuals and groups
6. The impossibility of perpetual growth

These characteristics imply critical contradictions in the system and have generated particular ideologies that tend to obscure the realities and help keep the system functioning.

The global division of labor integrates the world into a single production system based on exploitation and inequalities that paradoxically are supported by ideologies that stress universal values of peace and world order. Racist ideologies are also used to justify the disadvantaged position of peripheral groups, with economic rewards apportioned differentially according to the intrinsic merit and ability of different groups.

Since 1450, the world system has gone through cycles of expansion marked by the steady incorporation of external cultural groups into the periphery. This trend has been supported by the ideology calling for all peoples to be assimilated into a universal Western culture, on the assumption that other cultures were simply incapable of "advance" on their own.

Continuous capital accumulation is made easier when workers are persuaded by an ideology that extols the virtues of hard work and competitiveness to overcome inequality. German social scientist Max Weber (1864–1920) was the first to point out that extreme Calvinist forms of Protestantism encouraged capital accumulation, in his famous book *The Protestant Ethic and the Spirit of Capitalism* (1904–1905).[31] According to Weber, German Calvinists believed that continuous hard work and self-denial were the best way to demonstrate that one was predestined for salvation. Such a belief was a religious endorsement for precisely the behavior that the new economic elite needed.

Capitalism tends to polarize people by steadily widening the gap between rich and poor. However, such a reality is destabilizing. It is therefore culturally denied by the world system's dominant myth of the rising standard of living, which ignores population increase, health problems, onerous workloads, and negative environmental impacts, all clear indicators of a declining living standard. Core elites also exhort the periphery to greater "development" efforts, while implying that failure to achieve development must be due to racial or cultural inferiority.

The human problems that perpetual economic expansion creates are highlighted by the existence of Kondratieff waves, or K-waves, of expansion and collapse, named after their discovery by Russian economist Nikolai Kondratiev in the 1920s.[32] These cyclical phenomena are also known as "long waves" and "price waves." They are long boom-and-bust episodes that seem to characterize market systems and have been identified in ancient empires, and in medieval Europe, as well as in the modern world system.[33] Waves resemble business cycles, but waves are longer, wider in scope, and less predictable. Waves begin with decades of prosperity, with economic growth, low interest rates, low prices, increased profits for investors, and higher wages for workers. Prosperity is followed by decades of high prices, unemployment, increased poverty, and hardship. Kondratiev identified three long waves between 1790 and 1925, accurately predicting the global economic depression of the 1930s. Theorists believe that military expenditures and wars may exert an important influence on wave phenomena,[34] but in the commercial world waves are too vast and complex to attribute to a single cause, or a single human decision maker.

Elites clearly have further concentrated their social power by moving beyond the constraints of nationally based political economies and creating transnational commercial empires based on capitalist market exchanges. This shift to transnational commercial empires has enormous significance for humanity. Commercially organized, globally integrated cultures are important because (1) they are reducing cultural diversity at an unprecedented scale, (2) they increased the number of poor, and (3) they may be ultimately limited by the integrity of the biosphere itself or by the human ability to tolerate mass impoverishment.

THE EUROPEAN ORIGINS OF CAPITALISM

Modernity and Postmodernity

The historical period that historians and social theorists call **modern** is a middle phase in the development of the commercial world in which the politicization and imperial expansion driven by military conquest were still important processes shaping the world, even as commercial elites succeeding in shifting the apparent goal of empire building toward capital accumulation, away from the production and maintenance of political power, which was the primary objective of political rulers in the pre-capitalist imperial world. The "modern" commercial world was an international system of sovereign nation-states characterized by industrial production, capitalist market economies, Enlightenment philosophy, and special forms of social control.

A commercial world **nation** is a society with a common territory, culture, history, and shared identity distinguishing it from other nations. A state is the government over a territory, and a **nation-state** combines nation and state in a common territory. Sovereignty refers to the authority of a superior government. There are many ways that nations and states might be combined. In the early modern commercial world the *sovereign* was the supreme ruler in the person of the king, prince, duke, or president, rather than a deity. The earliest visual representation of the transcendent power of the sovereign state is Thomas Hobbes's 1651 image of the Leviathan in the figure of a gigantic man emerging from the landscape wearing a crown and holding a sword and staff, his arms and body composed of hundreds of small human figures.[35]

In a formal sense the "modern" international system of nation-states began in Europe with the 1648 peace treaties of Westphalia ending the Thirty Years' War between Catholics and Protestants and recognizing sovereign states with their sovereign rulers. The Peace of Westphalia allowed each European state to designate a dominant national religion, which helped distinguish them as nations. Unlike tribal societies, modern nations are **imagined communities**[36] because they are too large for people to know each other face to face; instead people must imagine a common connection, or shared identity. Originally this imagination process was facilitated by the spread of literacy and print media, but now electronic media makes it possible for imagined communities to be detached from territory.

Construction of the core financial institutions of the modern market economy, such as banks and securities markets in Europe, allowed elites to expand the capitalist system before 1700, prior to industrialization that is customarily described as beginning with the application of steam power to machinery in Britain in the 1780s. Modernity is also considered to be the last phase of colonial conquest in which Africa, much of Asia, the Pacific region, and nearly all of the tribal world were brought under European political and economic control.

Ideologically, modern societies were shaped by the scientific and philosophical thought of the Enlightenment and the institutions that it encouraged. Reason and rationalism came to replace the authority of religion and the supernatural and supported the English (1688), American (1775–1783), French (1789–1799), and Haitian Revolutions (1791–1804), leading to the widespread establishment of constitutional representative democracies. The scientific revolution pioneered by Galileo Galilei (1564–1642), René Descartes (1596–1650), and Sir Isaac Newton (1643–1727),

among others, was quickly institutionalized and gave capitalist elites the technical means to dramatically accelerate the flow of energy and materials and their accumulation of wealth.

French social philosopher Michel Foucault[37] has characterized modern society as a **disciplinary society** in which individuals are controlled by disciplinary institutions including police, courts, prisons, welfare, charities, schools, and the practices of everyday life. These institutions carry their own thought-shaping logics that work against resistance by uncooperative people. Disciplinary institutions are in effect omniscient and work by forcing individuals to police themselves because they believe they are always being observed. As a visible metaphor for the disciplinary society, Foucault cited Jeremy Bentham's 1791 plan for a Panopticon,[38] a round, multilevel prison in which a single invisible observer in a central tower could watch every prisoner. This contrasts with earlier forms of control that Foucault called monarchical punishment, which relied on brutal public executions and terror and is characteristic of imperial world societies. Disciplinary societies use a form of power that Foucault calls **biopower**, because such power is directed at control over all of human life, including people's minds and bodies. In modern society biopower was directed primarily at individuals by means of institutions. Modern disciplinary society is elite directed toward perpetual capital accumulation. Marxists describe this process as the entire society being "subsumed," or brought under the control of capital and government. This means that more and more areas of life move from the domestic or the public to the commercial and government sectors. For example, most modern people must work for wages that they exchange for basic subsistence and consumer durables.

After World War II elite decision makers transformed the condition of modernity into **postmodernity**, a period in which finance capital and decision making by capitalists came to dominate the world, and the global market replaced colonialism as the most important form of elite wealth accumulation. There are various labels for this shift, with some theorists speaking of Late Capitalism,[39] but the term *postmodern* has gained wide acceptance. A "postmodern" society has also been called postindustrial, referring to the shift from the dominance of factory manufacturing toward service industries, especially electronic information technologies and other knowledge-based technical services.[40] Capital, or wealth itself, becomes increasingly immaterial, or not physically real. This shift means that **immaterial production**, work involving the use of language, symbols, and communication networks that shapes thoughts, emotions, and behavior, assumes a crucial role in the entire postmodern sociocultural system. The advertising industry and the mass media generally are prime examples of immaterial production.

The postmodern commercial world is, of course, conspicuously characterized by its global economy, which was fully in place by the beginning of the twenty-first century. Economic globalization superseded the division of the early modern world system into a capitalist center and colonial peripheries, and it also makes obsolete the common political designations of First (the United States and allies), Second (the former Soviet Union and its allies), and Third (neutral countries) worlds during the Cold War.

Perhaps the most critical defining feature of postmodernity is the emergence of what social theorists Michael Hardt and Antonio Negri[41] call **biopolitical production**. In this process commercial elites use the immaterial production of information technologies and electronic communication systems to combine economic, political, and ideological dimensions of sociocultural systems to produce social reality by means of biopower. This is an elaboration of the process that Italian philosopher Antonio Gramsci[42] (1891–1937) called cultural hegemony. Postmodern societies are **societies of control**, based on highly refined uses of technology to implement biopower more effectively than modern disciplinary institutions. This means that people internalize the cultural logic of their societies in all aspects of their lives, in their minds and bodies. They do not need to be visibly coerced but will want to work for wages and become consumers of commercial products seemingly of their own free will.

The United States is an example of a modern factory-based industrial state where elites developed three "isms" that refined modern capitalism in the decades before World War II, preparing the foundation for the transition to postmodernism: Taylorism, Fordism, and Keynesianism. **Taylorism** applies the principles of "scientific management" of workers developed by American mechanical engineer Frederick Winslow Taylor (1856–1915) to increase labor efficiency.[43] **Fordism** is pioneer auto manufacturer Henry Ford's (1863–1947) principles of assembly-line mass production combined with high enough wages to allow workers to buy the products they produced, which was a foundation of consumer culture. **Keynesianism** follows the progressivist economic principles advocated by British economist John Maynard Keynes[44] calling for government intervention in the economy to flatten market fluctuations and to sustain consumer income and expenditure by means of welfare assistance and public work projects. These three "isms" became ideological models for capitalist "modernization" and spread to much of the world.

Why Commercial Imperialism?:
Guns, Germs, and Steel or Elite Direction

On the eve of Papua New Guinea independence in 1972, Yali, a New Guinea politician, asked Jared Diamond, "Why is it that you white people developed so much cargo and brought it to New Guinea, but we black people had little cargo of our own?" "Cargo" is Melanesian pidgin for industrially manufactured commercial goods arriving in ships and planes. Cargo meant steel axes, knives, and metal cooking pots that clearly improved daily life, but Yali's question was not superficially materialist. It reflected the materialist bias of commercialism, but this was also a question about power inequalities in the contemporary world. Diamond thought Yali was asking a "how" question—how technically did Europeans and Americans come to be materially so much richer than New Guinea peoples? He rephrases this as "How did European societies, but not other societies, first conquer and now still dominate the world?" Diamond's well-known answer is the material effects of *Guns, Germs, and Steel.*[45] In his book Diamond focuses on whole societies and technologies, not individuals, and he argues that prior geographical advantages put some societies on upward trajectories and are the ultimate explanation for present inequalities of global wealth and power. Diamond appropriately rejects racist explanations and disavows ethnocentric comparisons between tribes and industrial civilization, acknowledging that "progress" may not always be "good." He also disavows historical inevitability; nevertheless, his explanation is incomplete.

The combined effects of guns, germs, and steel certainly helped Europeans conquer the world, making millions of tribal peoples "victims of progress," but it would be a mistake to see biological circumstances and technology as sufficient explanations for the historical, perhaps temporary, rise of Europeans to global dominance. Diamond imagines humanity at a 13,000 BP "starting line" of a race to see which society could become the most imperialistic. This is at once a deceptive view, because in reality, throughout history the big winners in the imperial and commercial world are not whole societies, but only the top 0.5 percent of households who direct and most benefit from conquest. The losers, including many individuals in winning societies, are exterminated, enslaved, and impoverished. This makes these cultural worlds fundamentally inhuman, especially given how frequently great political and commercial empires rise and fall. It is equally plausible and much more useful to see the goal of human development to be a continuous humanization process, in which people use open and overlapping sociocultural networks as tools to maintain and reproduce humanity. This is sustainable development, the opposite of imperialism.

Diamond identifies many of the geographic preconditions that made possible the technological, organizational, and ideological innovations that allowed a few aggrandizers to transform the tribal world into the contemporary commercial world in sequential developments spanning the last 13,000 years. Framing his answer geographically calls attention to how the shape and position of continents determined which plants and animals could have been most readily domesticated, where intensive farming could be practiced most productively, and where cities, kingdoms, and empires could best be created and sustained. These circumstances alone do not explain the rise of the commercial world. Instead, we can ask the philosophical *why* question: why are some peoples unable to prevent aggrandizing individuals from expanding their personal empires at other people's expense? It is easy to think of whole societies in competition, anonymously moving ahead on different trajectories, but the idea of societies and economies can be illusory ideological tools. Inequalities are now human problems for the majority of humanity, but only a relatively few individuals have gained primary decision-making power over the allocation of energy and materials, enabling them to construct the cultural foundations of the commercial world.

Commercialization under the Feudal Monarchs

The roots of the commercialization process were present in the rudimentary markets, trade structures, monetary systems, and craft specialization found in most ancient agrarian civilizations, but political rulers jealously regulated commercial activities to safeguard their personal power. It was in Europe in the centuries after the collapse of the Roman Empire that merchants and commerce gradually became the dominant forces in cultural development. How this vast cultural change came about is an intriguing anthropological problem, because under the politicization process virtually all resources were officially controlled by church and state, a rigid social hierarchy became entrenched, and an apparent ceiling on economic growth was reached. The established hereditary rulers were ambivalent about the rising commercial elite; they sought both to restrict their activities and to form alliances with them, establishing a pattern that still continues. The crucial point is that merchants gradually became the driving force of cultural development.

The Domesday Survey of England, conducted in 1086 for William the Conqueror shortly after the Norman Conquest, provides an excellent baseline for measuring the astounding cultural transformations eventually brought about by commercialization. Designed for tax purposes, the great Domesday Book[46] enumerated every manor in the country and all the plows, land, and cattle and ranked all adult males by social category. The survey dramatically reveals a remarkable concentration of social power and shows the limits of power under preindustrial technology with little commercial activity. More than 90 percent of the perhaps 2 million inhabitants were farm laborers living on the manors and dependent villages scattered over the countryside. A hierarchy of centrally placed market towns existed, but the peasantry produced most of their own food and manufactured domestic consumer goods by working part-time as independent millers, iron smiths, potters, and weavers in the household, village, or manor. Only 12,000 people lived in London, the largest city. Overseas trade and much of the industrial activity centered on supplying luxury goods to the hereditary nobility, who probably numbered fewer than 40,000 people, counting men, women, and children—about 2 percent of the population (see table 10.1). Political power and land ownership remained in the hands of the king and nobles. Forty percent of the land was controlled by thirty-two great landlords under Royal Charter, and much of the other productive land was held in manors under other subtenants. All landlords served as the king's representatives.

The bulk of the English population were serfs (unfree peasants), who held use rights to small subsistence parcels in return for working two to three days per week for the lord of the manor and who provided various additional services, taxes, and payments. These small holdings were worked cooperatively under the open-field system, which allowed the serfs to retain enough of the advantages of domestic-scale life to make serfdom bearable (see box 10.1). Almost 10 percent of the population were chattel slaves. Except for the nobles and a few wealthy burghers (towns-

Table 10.1. Norman England Imperia by Wealth, Income, and Social Class, 1086

Class	Rank	Households	Population	Wealth	Income	Imperia% population
Aristocracy	King	1	5	£17,650	£20,000	Super-Elite 0.06%
	Barons	10	50	£1,500	£1,500	
	Magnates	171	855	£115	£130	
	Lords	900	4,500	£20	£8	Elite 2%
	Subtenants	6,000	30,000	£2	£2	
Commoners	Burghers	24,000	120,000	£1	£0.3	Maintenance 8%
	Free peasants	38,511	192,555	£0.25	£0.22	
	Unfree peasants	236,568	1,182,840	£0.05	£0.2	Poor 90%
Totals		306,161	1,530,805			100%

Sources: Data from Snooks 1993; Roberts and Roberts 1980; Bodley 2003.

men) and clergy, most people had little control over the conditions that influenced their daily lives. Over the next 300 years, the bulk of the peasantry experienced steadily declining living standards, but conditions improved for the few landlords and merchants who gained access to the growing international market in wool. The English population increased threefold to some 6 million, with perhaps 15 percent living in the expanding urban centers.[47]

The manorial system had obvious limits, because a feudal land baron could effectively control only so many manors, but money was an inherently expandable form of wealth. Economic growth during this period is demonstrated by the dramatic forty-four-fold increase in the supply of royal coinage in circulation in medieval England—from £25,000 in 1086 to £1,100,000 by 1320. Under constant promotion by the emerging merchant class, money steadily replaced barter exchange, greatly facilitated government finance, and made trade much more profitable. However, the serfs could barely participate in this kind of economic activity, because they did not control sufficient productive land. Small farmers were being forced below a comfortable subsistence level at the same time that money to pay taxes and buy essentials was becoming critical for survival. Under the existing social structure, modest technological improvements barely increased total agricultural production and brought few benefits to the peasants. Land that could have generated adequate subsistence was devoted to the production of wool for export and was held in vast hunting preserves, horse pastures, and forests as a private luxury. By the fourteenth century, the social system was in crisis. Then disastrous famines and a series of plagues known as the Black Death reduced the population almost to the Domesday level.

Growth in medieval England clearly produced great wealth (see box 10.2). However, the proportion of the

wealth holders at the top of the feudal hierarchy probably did not increase as economic growth occurred. Rather, the scale of society and the total amount of extractable wealth increased, making those at the top even more powerful. Most of the newly wealthy merchants were probably already members of the upper class, whose numbers may have increased by 80,000 in this era. Before the Black Death struck in 1349, there were 3.6 million more impoverished peasants than at the time of the Norman Conquest. In the absence of culture change to produce a more equitable power structure, the growth in scale associated with commercialization left more people in England poor than wealthy.

BOX 10.1. THE OPEN-FIELD SYSTEM

For landlords, industrialists, and merchants to gain the labor and raw materials necessary to increase their wealth, they had to force the self-sufficient European peasantry out of the open field system of land use that had sustained them for millennia. Egalitarian peasant communities that relied on cooperative plow agriculture used the open-field system primarily to meet their subsistence needs, not to produce marketable surpluses.[48] This system helped individual farmers minimize the risk of crop failure in an unpredictable natural environment, where politics were uncertain and access to markets was limited.[49] It was easier for farmers to plow cooperatively, especially when not every farmer owned plows and full draft teams.

The open-field system produced a patchwork of individually held strips of land, each roughly an acre in area and representing one day's work for a single plow team. Each farmer held use rights from his landlord to a virgate, a collection of perhaps thirty acres of land scattered in strips throughout the manor (see figure 10.11). This would be sufficient to allow him to cultivate half to meet the annual subsistence needs of his household and keep half fallow to maintain soil fertility. A farmer's holdings were in scattered strips because this distribution made plowing most equitable and ensured that each farmer would have land of equal quality and distance from the village. The patchwork effect resulted because fields were plowed in blocks of furlongs (parallel plow strips), and the contour of the land determined the direction of plowing. As long as the cultivated area remained unfenced, it was open for common grazing after harvest. Every household also had access to common pastures, meadows, and woodlands beyond the cultivated fields for hunting, grazing, and gathering wood and materials.

The essentially tribal open-field system predated the Romans and operated in various forms throughout medieval Europe, but it was incompatible with the demands of large-scale commercial agriculture. By the fifteenth century, English landlords began to find feudal tenure and the open-field system ill suited to the new opportunities presented by the emerging urban and international markets. Landowners increasingly fenced their holdings in order to raise great herds of sheep to supply the growing urban market for wool. In the process, self-sufficient tenants and smallholders were driven off the land. A second wave of enclosures in the eighteenth century was prompted by the adoption of new crops and more intensive production systems.

BOX 10.2. RICHARD FITZALAN: MEDIEVAL ENGLAND'S RICHEST LORD

The level of wealth and luxury that the emerging commercial system could support at the top of the social pyramid is illustrated by an enterprising fourteenth-century nobleman, Richard Fitzalan, the earl of Arundel and Surrey, then the richest private person in England. When he died in 1376, Fitzalan had amassed capital of £72,245 in cash, property, and credits—three times the sum in circulation in 1086.[50] Fitzalan owned multiple residences, vast estates, and 25,000 sheep. His fortune came from the sale of wool, metals, and livestock; from overseas investments; from loans to the king and other nobles; and from political favors. He was a capitalist who used his money to make money. We can put Fitzalan's wealth and this early phase of commercialization in perspective. At the beginning of the politicization process in southern England in 3000 BC, the most powerful Neolithic chiefdom might have been able to mobilize the 1,200 people a year to build a megalithic monument. By contrast, even as a private citizen,

Fitzalan could support more than twice that number from his annual income and more than ten times more from accumulated capital. His annual landed income alone was sufficient to support 2,857 manor servants at the high grain prices of that time. And his total capital would have allowed him to hire 15,451 annual laborers.

The Financial Revolution and the Fiscal-Military State

Mass-production industrial technology did not have a major influence until the 1800s, but the basic institutional structures of capitalism, including joint stock corporations, securities trading, and investment banking were firmly in place in Europe prior to 1700. Less-savory cultural features such as monopoly, bribery, and market manipulation were also commonplace. In medieval Europe before the emergence of capitalism, commercial activities were strictly regulated by church and state in ways that discouraged the accumulation of money by private individuals. Prices were often fixed at what was considered to be a "just price." Moneylenders and the wealthy were looked down on, and there were sumptuary laws restricting luxury and gambling, as well as laws against usury (charging exorbitant interest rates). Profit-generating practices such as monopolies and reselling at a higher price were forbidden as "offenses against public trade." Money itself existed only as a relatively fixed supply of coins, and there were no banks. As merchants steadily increased interregional trade and rulers began to wage longer and more expensive military campaigns, they began to adopt more flexible ways of conceptualizing and handling money. Money is symbolic as well as "real." Its primary function is to store obligations between people. It exists both as numbers recorded in accounts and in the form of circulating coin and currency. And money can exist in the imagination. Credit (from the Latin *credere*, "to believe") is based on belief in return payment and makes it possible to multiply and manipulate money in truly amazing ways. The concept of credit was a simple extension of the concept of contract, based on the distinction between possessions in hand and possessions one was due to receive. When credit, interest charges, banking, and paper money and securities all became culturally acceptable, a *financial revolution* occurred that made capitalism possible. This cultural transformation was as significant as the Neolithic revolution.

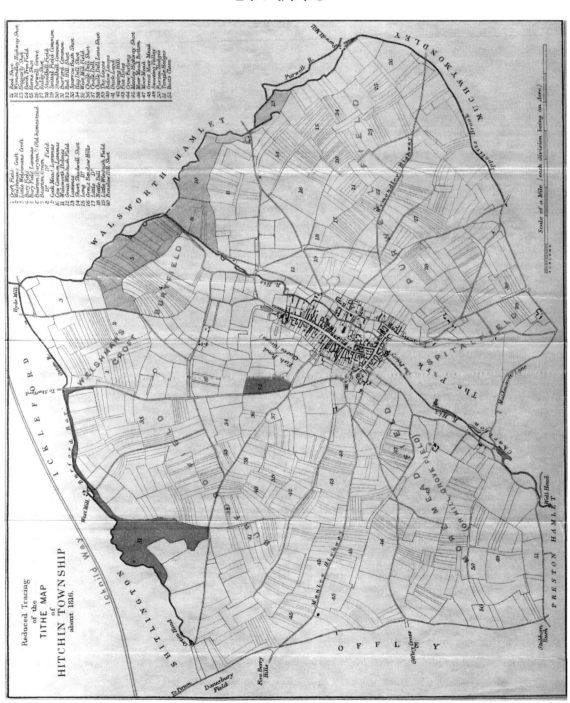

Figure 10.11. The open-fields system of the village of Hitchin in 1816, showing individually held strips of land. The village is at the crossroads in the center, and the numbers refer to place names (Seebohm, 1905).

The Amsterdam Exchange Bank, founded in 1609, was perhaps the first major bank, and it was followed shortly by the Amsterdam Stock Exchange. The first bank notes, the forerunners of modern paper money and checks, were issued by the Bank of Stockholm in 1661. Paper bills of exchange and bank notes greatly facilitated international trade, government and commercial finance, and capital investment. Economic growth quickly accelerated when enterprising bankers discovered they could lend out more money than they actually held in deposit. Finance capital is at the heart of capitalism, and money as a cultural symbol makes infinite economic growth seem deceptively possible, inevitable, and natural.

The system evolved as a small network of individuals managed to accumulate wealth by acting within triangles connecting governments, militaries, and financial institutions. Political rulers borrowed from the wealthy for military expenditures, and bankers sold the bonds back to the wealthy. This encouraged an arms race, but the investors, bankers, and military contractors all benefited, and they shifted the cost to taxpayers. The investors were also the politicians who borrowed the funds, and sometimes they were also the bankers. This arrangement created the "fiscal-military state" and promoted economic growth.[51]

The financial revolution suddenly gave the wealthy a powerful means of influencing the course of cultural development to personal advantage. The popular wisdom that money is power is correct, but successful financiers did not need to be personally wealthy. Credit and the newly created financial institutions allowed them to magnify their own power by using other people's money. Capitalism didn't just happen. Economic historians attribute the emergence of capitalism to rising consumer demand, but market demand came from people who could use money, not from the mass of the European population struggling to maintain themselves. The "demand" was for palaces, mansions, luxury goods, and military power to satisfy the aristocracy and to support their dependent servants, artisans, soldiers, and courtiers. The wealthy also demanded profitable new investments. These were the financial demands that created exciting opportunities for the most powerful merchants and financiers, who came to manage enormous accumulations of capital. A few prominent families such as the Fuggers in Augsburg (1367–1641), the Medici in Florence (1434–1737), and the Rothschilds in Frankfurt (1770–) were the principal financial architects of European capitalism (see box 10.3). These families, together with the own-

ers and directors of a handful of banks and trading companies, such as the Bank of Amsterdam, the Bank of England (see figure 10.12), the British East India Company, and the Dutch East India Company, were the driving forces behind the accumulation, exchange, and marketing of money that began to increase the scale of culture and transform the world long before the Industrial Revolution.

BOX 10.3. FUGGERS AND ROTHSCHILDS: BUSINESS FAMILY SUCCESS STORIES

The most successful early European capitalists accumulated great fortunes by forming family-owned business enterprises based on kinship and strategic marriage alliances. These corporate lineages became commercial dynasties that paralleled and were often intertwined with political dynasties.[52]

The German Catholic Fugger family created what became the richest and most influential business of the time. The Fugger enterprise began as a simple family-owned cotton and textile business in Augsburg, Bavaria, in 1367. The business expanded into the overseas spice trade and eventually grew into a distinctly modern, diversified mining, trading, and banking business with branches and property throughout Europe. By the third generation in 1485, four Fugger brothers operated the company offices in Rome and Florence in Italy, in Innsbruck in Austria, and at their Augsburg headquarters. The Fuggers cultivated the patronage of the most powerful civil and religious rulers of the time and profitably financed wars and political intrigues, buying elections and offices, and loaning money to create profitable supporters. After 1500, the Fugger company gained monopolistic control over copper and silver mines and smelters in Austria and Hungary, which were then Europe's principal source for these metals. Benefiting from Spain's conquests in the New World, they developed mining interests in Peru and became involved in the African slave trade. By 1546, their fortune had grown to more than 5 million guilders. If converted to wheat at prevailing prices, this would have been sufficient to support 521,477 persons for a year—a thirty-fold increase in social power over Richard Fitzalan's record in 1376. The Fuggers' lucrative monopoly and behind-the-scenes manipulations of church and state generated labor unrest, peasant revolts, and protests from other merchants; eventually led to nationalization of their mining interests; and contributed to the Protestant Reformation.

Much like the Fuggers, the Rothschild family rose from humble beginnings in the Jewish ghetto in

Figure 10.12.   Bank of England, London in the late nineteenth century (Stoddard 1892).

Frankfurt in 1744 to create an international banking dynasty operated by brothers from offices in Frankfurt, London, Paris, Vienna, and Naples by the 1820s. The family married carefully to increase their power, sometimes practicing cross-cousin marriage to keep their growing power and influence intact. Like the Fuggers, they maintained alliances with the most powerful political figures of the time and were able to control an enormous flow of finance capital in the most profitable way. By the end of the tumultuous nineteenth century, the Rothschilds had accumulated the world's largest private fortune. Their descendants are now billionaire financiers.

European Marriage and Family

The system of kinship and marriage in medieval Europe was severely constrained by economic inequality. While European civilization was still predominantly agrarian, people needed access to individual landholdings before they could marry and establish a new household. Given the manorial system, land was in extremely short supply, and even a peasant's right to rent tiny parcels was a crucial inheritance to be safeguarded. Land rights were normally transmitted by inheritance to men, whereas women received a dowry of movable property or money upon marriage. This meant that men might not be able to marry until they were over twenty-five. It also meant that many men and women could never marry, and they instead joined the religious monasteries as celibate monks or nuns.

European marriage was characterized by class endogamy, in which the bride's dowry and the groom's inheritance had to be a good "match" for a marriage to take place, because inheritance and dowry served as rough measures of social standing. This meant that parents usually arranged marriages for their children within their own class, but at the same time people tried to marry up.[53] Dowry thus helped the upper class keep their wealth intact. Dowry also made monogamy the preferred European form of marriage, because of the impossibility of sorting out multiple dowries within a single household. The European emphasis on female premarital chastity, chaperones, and arranged marriage may also be related to the importance of preventing lower-class men from marrying higher-class women and thereby diluting the family estate.[54]

Most European households were based on the small nuclear family, with peasant households averaging only 4.5 persons. On the manors, there were many single-person households, which would be unthinkable in the tribal world. Except among the very wealthy, there were no corporate descent groups, because impoverished peasants had too few resources to form a meaningful corporate estate. In this respect, European peasants were far poorer than people in most tribal societies, where everyone had access to an abundance of physical, social, and spiritual resources. In contrast to the peasants, the few upper-class Europeans often maintained large extended families and large households with many family members and domestic servants. As an extreme example, the French king Louis XIV (reigned 1643–1715) maintained a household of 500 personal attendants. Family and kin were important to the aristocracy because they had vast corporate estates and wealth to pass on to the next generation. The English dukes, marquises, earls, viscounts, and barons needed extensive genealogies to keep track of their complex kinship networks and inherited titles.

GROWTH AND POVERTY UNDER THE BRITISH EMPIRE

The Industrial Revolution and the Culture of Consumption

The most outstanding physical transformations accompanying the modern world system were dramatic increases in population and resource consumption, which began in England between 1760 and 1830. Immediately prior to the Industrial Revolution, world population growth was relatively slow, with a doubling time of approximately 250 years. However, with industrialization well established, the European population doubled in just 80 years after 1850, while the European population of the United States, Canada, Australia, and Argentina tripled between 1851 and 1900, thanks in part to large-scale immigration. Between 1851 and 1900, some 35 million people left Europe.[55]

This growth in population was accompanied by a shift in consumption patterns that marked a radical break with the relative stability of the imperial world. Capitalist economic growth requires continuous per-capita increases in consumption, which would inevitably deplete resources, at least in the core countries. For example, by 1850 England was unable to satisfy its needs for grain, wood, fibers, and hides from within its immediate borders. Newly industrializing countries initially secured more resources by expanding trade networks and colonial territories to draw resources from other parts of the world. Equally important was the switch in energy resources from the renewable, solar-driven fuels, such as wood, wind, and water, and a reliance on traction animals and human labor, which had characterized ancient civilizations, to the use of nonrenewable fossil fuels, such as coal, to power industrial machines. Many earlier civilizations utilized a complex division of labor, assembly-line mass-production techniques, and a wide variety of simple machines; however, their reliance on renewable energy sources was compatible with relatively stable consumption patterns.

Coal fueled the factories, ships, and trains of Western Europe and North America in the nineteenth century and prepared the way for the age of oil. In the short run, use of fossil fuels allowed the industrial, capitalist world system to consume global resources at unsustainable levels, subsidizing otherwise impossible growth. Industrial civilization is unique in human history as a culture of consumption.[56] In such a culture, economy, society, and belief systems are geared to "nonsustainable levels of resource consumption, and to continual, ever-higher elevation of those levels on a per-capita basis."[57] Biologically, this is overconsumption, as ecologist Howard Odum explained:

> In the industrial system with man living off a fuel, he manages all his affairs with industrial machinery, all parts of which are metabolically consumers. . . . This system of man has consumption in excess of production. The products of respiration—carbon dioxide, metabolic water, and mineralized inorganic wastes—are discharged in rates in excess of their incorporation into organic matter by photosynthesis. If the industrialized urban system were enclosed in a chamber with only the air above it at the time, it would quickly exhaust its oxygen, be stifled with waste, and destroy itself since it does not have the recycling pattern of the agrarian system.[58]

This biological imbalance in its urban centers and the pressure to increase consumption force the industrial civilization to be a global system because it would have difficulty sustaining itself in any other way.

The label *Industrial Revolution* that historians apply to this great cultural transformation overemphasizes the role of technological factors; but, as with the Neolithic, more than technology changed. It was not simply the inventive genius of a particular people that caused the Industrial Revolution. It was cultural changes in social organization and ideological systems that called forth technological innovation.

British historian T. S. Ashton argued that organizational and technological changes, rather than population growth, accelerated production during the Industrial Revolution in England.[59] Increased production was initiated by organizational changes that brought more land into production and facilitated the adoption of technological changes, such as new crops and cropping systems. Like Adam Smith, Ashton argued that social inequality, perhaps even "injustice," was the key that encouraged the accumulation of capital that funded the technological innovations of the Industrial Revolution: "It is generally recognized that more saving takes place in communities in which the distribution of wealth is uneven than in those in which it approaches more closely to modern conceptions of what is just."[60]

Technological innovations are not chance discoveries. They involve repeated trial and error and are often based on combinations of previous inventions. This is a panhuman process, but it is accelerated by specific cultural conditions. Invention was especially encouraged by specialization and the complex division of labor that emerged with the first states, but the unprecedented pressures for perpetual economic growth in the emerging capitalist world system set in motion the positive feedback between technical innovation and capital accumulation that became the Industrial Revolution. Increasing the flow of materials also called for a **Chemical Revolution** in which factory-produced chemicals replaced natural products and processes.[61] For example, chemical bleach replaced solar bleaching in the textile industry. Coal distillation products accelerated production in malting, smelting, metallurgy, dying, fertilizer, and coal gas. Sulfuric acid was required for numerous industrial processes, and the level of its production became a measure of industrial progress.[62]

Historians identify the **enclosure movement** as an important organizational change leading to the Industrial Revolution. In Europe during the seventeenth and eighteenth centuries, the shift from village self-sufficiency to market-oriented agriculture was accompanied by the transformation of open communal pastures and woodlands into numerous enclosed, privately controlled plots dedicated to the production of wool, meat, and hides.

Many historians urge us not to dwell on the fate of the formerly self-sufficient villagers who were forced off the land and impoverished by the enclosure process, which was supported by government decree. These peoples were surely being victimized by industrial progress. But according to the ideology of capitalism, we should focus on "the constructive activities that were being carried on inside the fences."[63] Dispossession increased agricultural productivity while reducing the rural population in order to raise the *national* standard of living. Those who were pushed off the land were considered to be "free to devote themselves to other activities," which in reality meant they could either become vagrants or accept poorly paid jobs in the newly appearing industrial factories in the cities.

The enclosure movement was only the beginning of a series of vast cultural disruptions that ultimately spread throughout the globe as the capitalist world system continued to expand. In the following section, we examine the second phase of this expansion process, using the production, distribution, and consumption of sugar as a specific case study.

Sugar, Slavery, and the World System

As European entrepreneurs began to accumulate capital, they were well positioned to take advantage of the opportunities opened to them by new trade routes to Asia and the Americas. The infrastructure for British overseas commercial empires was formed in the few decades from 1575 to 1630 by a total of about 6,000 investors who formed 33 London-based joint stock companies to seek overseas profits. In a given year only some 2,500 investors, mostly wealthy merchants, landed aristocrats, and members of Parliament, were involved. Perhaps only a hundred men served as directors. These individuals funded the Virginia and Massachusetts colonies in North America, the British East India Company, and various colonies and outposts in Africa, Eastern Europe, and elsewhere.[64] Their decisions created modern colonialism and ultimately transformed the world.

Refined sugar, or sucrose, played a major role in the rise of British colonialism and the modern world system, contributing to the accumulation of capital and helping the English lower class adjust to their changed life conditions.[65] During the Industrial Revolution, sugar was transformed from a rare European luxury before 1750 to a household necessity by 1850. In this process, the English subsistence system changed from its traditional reliance on a local, inexpensively produced complex carbohydrate, primarily wheat, to a system in which an imported, energy-intensive simple carbohydrate, sucrose, became a virtual staple food for the lower and middle classes.

Sugarcane is a tropical plant that was probably domesticated in Melanesia by 8000 BC for its sweet sap. By 400 BC it was being grown in India, where the earliest processed sugar is known to have been prepared by at least AD 500. Muslims spread sugarcane growing and sugar processing throughout the Mediterranean region by AD 1000. In medieval Europe, sugar was treated as a spice and had many medicinal uses but was too scarce to be available to any but the wealthiest. Sugar was used in the royal court to prepare edible decorative works of art, which served as symbols of power and status. Such objects were a special expression of power because they could be conspicuously consumed as a valuable on a ritual occasion. By 1500, sugar decorations were an important part of ritual feasts throughout the upper classes, and within 200 years such use had become common even among the middle classes as sugar became more readily available.

During the early phase of capitalist development in England, from approximately 1650 to 1750, sugar was the single most important product imported from its colonies. Produced by slave labor on plantations in the British West Indies, sugar supported a major trade triangle that contributed to the accumulation of profits in the capitalist core. Shipments of manufactured goods, such as cloth, tools, and iron shackles, moved from England to Africa; slaves were carried from Africa to the West Indies; and sugar was shipped from the West Indies to England, where it was further refined (see figure 10.13). Thus, sugar helped generate direct profits while providing a market for manufactured goods. In the process, millions of African slaves were forced to work 12-hour days, often while supplying their own provisions. After slavery was abolished in the British colonies in the 1830s, perhaps 50 million Asians, primarily from India, were carried to sugar-producing areas as contract laborers during the nineteenth century. The number of individuals who profited handsomely from the sugar trade was very small. For example in 1688 there were only some 2,000 capitalist merchants in England,[66] and in 1812 some

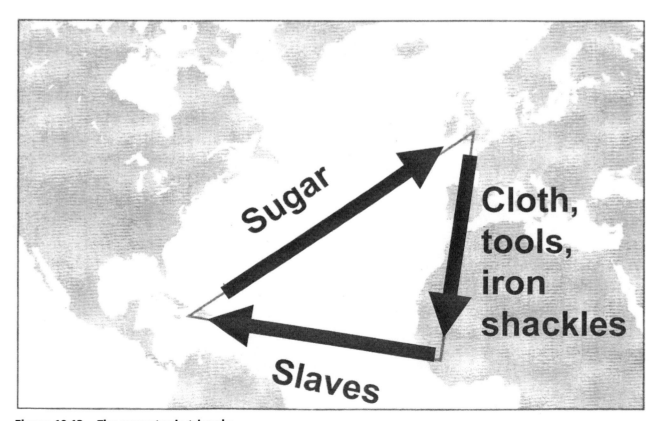

Figure 10.13. The sugar trade triangle.

3,500 eminent merchants and bankers.[67] Between 1735 and 1784 just 4 prominent, interconnected, London-based merchant families and their 19 associates maintained business properties and operations at every point in the sugar trade triangle.[68] One of these men, Richard Oswald, "exported" some 13,000 slaves from his station in Sierra Leone to his Caribbean sugar plantations and was also a major investor in the British East India Company. When Oswald died in 1784, he left a personal estate of £500,000, more than 10,000 times the prevailing annual subsistence wage.

Perhaps as important as sugar's role in the trade triangle was the energy boost and comfort it gave to the English working class who supplied the human energy for the Industrial Revolution. The large-scale introduction of energy-dense processed sugar to the diet at this time was the beginning of the unhealthy "nutrition transition" implicated in many lifestyle diseases afflicting people in the contemporary commercial world.[69] Sugar was especially appealing because it was quickly metabolized and absorbed, yet it provided "empty" calories, lacking in minerals and vitamins, and left people craving more. Sugar's crucial role in industrialization developed gradually as the plantation system expanded to make sugar more available and as sugar proved to be an ideal complement to the tropical "drug foods" such as tea, coffee, and chocolate, which began to reach England in the seventeenth century. These are all bitter, calorie-free, stimulating drinks that are sweetened by the addition of sugar. Tea had been imported from China by an English trading monopoly beginning in 1660, but it became the most popular English drink after tea plantations were established in British India by 1840. In combination with sugar from the British West Indies, tea from British India became cheaper than beer as a stimulating drink for the English working class.

As anthropologist Sydney Mintz[70] explains, sugar consumption by the English working poor grew in stages. It was used first with tea and then in rich puddings, which by the nineteenth century became a dessert course to end a meal. Sugar was combined with wheat flour in sweetened baked goods; by the end of the century, bread and jam became a meal, especially in households in which both parents were employed. At the national level, per-capita sugar consumption tripled from approximately 30 pounds (14 kg) per year in 1800 to approximately 90 pounds (41 kg) per year by 1900. By the 1970s, per-capita consumption seems to have peaked at about 115 pounds (52 kg). As a proportion of total caloric consumption, sugar rose from 2 to 14 percent over the course of the nineteenth century. Such an increase was possible because the price of sugar in England decreased by 50 percent between 1840 and 1870. Sugar became a relatively cheap source of calories and tended to supplement and replace more expensive grains, fruits, vegetables, meat, and dairy products.

The per-capita consumption figures mask the important role that sugar played in the diet of the working poor because actual rates varied by class and by age and sex within households. By 1850, sugar consumption by the English working class exceeded that of the upper class. Increased sugar intake was accompanied by a decline in bread consumption, from which some historians infer that more meat must have been eaten and nutrition improved. However, in most lower-class households, the working man ate the meat while his wife and children were left with the sugar as empty calories and were thereby systematically malnourished. This was justified by the householders because the husband had to remain in top physical condition to be an effective worker. This nutritional inequality, however, must have elevated infant mortality rates.

Sugar was especially important in the capitalist transformation of the world system because its capacity to stimulate perpetually increasing consumer demand neatly supported the endless-growth ideals of capitalism. Sugar became the first great consumer product. It was a substance of which people never seemed to get enough, and it proved that basic human needs could be culturally redefined and expanded as an instrument of national policy. Pre-capitalist economic theory held that most wage laborers were "target workers" who worked only long enough to satisfy their fixed needs. Alcohol consumption was potentially elastic, but alcoholics made poor workers. Sugar, on the other hand, made for contented workers.

England was converted into a nation of sugar eaters, at least in part because such a change served the interests of individuals who were in a position to exercise political power.[71] Many of the early West Indian sugarcane planters were themselves members of Parliament; along with the investors who supported them and those in slaving, shipping, refining, and marketing, who benefited from sugar, they formed a significant interest group that influenced government policy. It is not surprising that sugar was issued to the inmates of English poorhouses or that a half-pint of rum made from West Indian molasses became an official daily ration of the British Navy in 1731 (an amount that was soon raised to a pint a day). The

British government gained revenues from the sugar trade and indirectly subsidized the Caribbean planters by helping keep prices high. By the 1850s, the government shifted in favor of a free-trade policy to reduce the price of sugar and thereby increase the supply, thus making it more widely available.

Poverty and the Invisible Hand of the Market

Adam Smith (1723–1790), Scottish philosopher, political economist, and founding father of capitalism, presented an insightful and remarkably frank, emic view of how the early capitalist market economy was theoretically expected to work. In his famous book *Wealth of Nations* (1776), Smith identified labor specialization and private ownership of land, together with the related emergence of landlords, manufacturers, laborers, rent, and profit, as the fundamental elements of a market, or "commercial," economy. In this system, landlords received their share of production as rent and advanced part to laborers as wages for their maintenance. Labor specialization in manufacturing required that manufacturers accumulate stock or capital, but it permitted dramatic increases in production. Wealth inequality helped make the system work.

Smith felt that most laborers "naturally" needed masters to maintain them between harvests and to carry out productive tasks. The relative poverty of laborers gave manufacturers and landlords a strategic advantage in any disputes over wages. Even though they were ultimately dependent on their laborers, most manufacturers and landlords, with their larger stockpiles of wealth, could last more than one year if the laborers stopped working to enforce a demand for increased wages. Smith estimated that most laborers would not have enough stores to hold out more than one week without their wages.

Smith argued that as long as government did not intervene unduly, economic competition caused by people's natural desire for self-improvement would maintain orderly economic growth, as if by an **invisible hand**. Smith advocated that workers receive the lowest wage "which is consistent with common humanity."[72] This minimum wage would be determined by the short-run maintenance needs of individual workers combined with approximately double that amount to provide enough for workers to reproduce. Smith did not quantify this amount precisely, but he assumed that a worker would support a wife and four children, only two of which would reach adulthood. According to Smith, a direct feedback operated between increasing demand for labor during times of economic growth and an increase in the labor supply, because wages would necessarily go up, which would mean that the poor could better support their children so that more would grow up to become workers. If there were too many workers, wages would go down, and the ensuing poverty would increase infant mortality, thereby reducing the number of workers and sending wages back up.

Smith thought that improved wages would increase production, because it would give workers hope and make them work harder. Thus, continuous economic growth (the "progressive state") seemed to be the most desirable condition, as Smith explained:

> It is in the progressive state, while the society is advancing to the further acquisition ... that the condition of the labouring poor, of the great body of the people, seems to be the happiest and the most comfortable. It is hard in the stationary, and miserable in the declining state. The progressive state is in reality the cheerful and the hearty state to all the different orders of the society. The stationary is dull; the declining, melancholy.[73]

As the industrial era began, despite Smith's optimistic view of the invisible hand, England's lower class was desperately squeezed between declining agrarian living standards in the countryside and abysmally low wages in the towns and cities. The growing money economy had already made poverty such a serious social problem that long before Smith's time, severe compulsion was required to force people to find employment, even at wages that would not provide adequate subsistence. Family life disintegrated when households could not support children and elders, and the state was forced to deal with the problem. The first poor laws, in 1531–1536, called for compulsory almsgiving and made willful unemployment a crime punishable by forced labor, mutilation, and death. Later creative variations called for whipping, burning, branding, slavery, hard labor in chains, and then death for repeat offenders. Reforms in 1601 called for placing paupers, such as widows and those physically unable to work, in poorhouses, while the children of the poor were to be apprenticed to masters in workhouses. But modest welfare subsidies intended to bring the working poor up to a subsistence level only encouraged employers to offer substandard wages.

The absolute increase in poverty in England from 1086 to 1812 is clear evidence that the economic growth process was directed by elites who were more concerned with elevating production and accumulating capital for their own benefit than in building the commonwealth to benefit society as a whole. Table 10.2 shows that both between 1086 and 1688 and between 1688 and 1812 the number of poor households increased at a faster rate than either maintenance or elite households. This negative social outcome came about because political rulers directed public funds into the military and infrastructure improvements to support commerce, rather than into public education, public health, or meaningful social welfare. At the same time the barriers to upward mobility were formidable for anyone not fortunate enough to be born wealthy or to marry wealth.[74] The poor were forced to spend most of their meager incomes on food, clothing, and housing, and had nothing to invest. Wages for English workers gradually increased over the centuries,[75] but material conditions remained bleak, and during hard economic times between 1760 and 1800 and between 1830 and 1860 the average height of the poor actually shrank due to poor nutrition in childhood.[76]

By the 1830s, conditions among the working class in England had deteriorated so badly that the government took further measures in an effort to minimize the damage. Officially, 1.4 million people, nearly 10 percent of the population, were receiving relief under the poor laws. But this was an incomplete reckoning of poverty, and the assistance provided was woefully inadequate. A massive report presented to Parliament in 1842 by social reformer Edwin Chadwick[77] showed unequivocally that the poor were being forced to live in crowded and unsanitary conditions that contributed to contagious disease, high mortality, high fertility, and reduced life expectancy. For example, in Liverpool in 1840, health conditions were poor for everyone, but Chadwick found that laborers died at an average age of fifteen, whereas upper-class people died at thirty-five. More people were dying from poverty than in England's many wars. Chadwick viewed this costly and unnecessary loss of life as a public health problem and advocated better sewage drainage and administrative changes. But many others called for

drastic social reforms. The working poor understood that their basic problem was inadequate and irregular wages and the loss of control over their subsistence resources brought about by unbalanced industrialization. The Luddites who destroyed textile machines in 1811–1816 and the farm workers who rioted against the new threshing machines in the 1830s were not opposed to technological progress as such; they simply did not want to surrender their economic autonomy.[78]

The London Poor

By the 1840s, immigration and internal growth had swelled the population of metropolitan London to more than 2 million people, but employment opportunities remained inadequate. The human degradation that accompanied London's rapid industrial development was most vividly portrayed by novelist Charles Dickens,[79] journalist Henry Mayhew,[80] and shipping magnate turned sociologist Charles Booth.[81] Mayhew's pioneer ethnographic work was explicitly anthropological. Mayhew viewed the existence of such poverty in the midst of wealthy London as a "national disgrace." He was incensed that the British public knew more about distant tribes than they knew about the poorest Londoners, who were not even counted in the national census. He wanted "to give the rich a more intimate knowledge of the sufferings, and frequent heroism under those sufferings, of the poor." Mayhew spent years observing life on the streets of London and collecting life stories and personal accounts of hundreds of street folk, which he carefully recorded in their own words.

Most of Mayhew's ethnographic work was devoted to London's working poor, who comprised a ragged assortment of some 50,000 self-employed street vendors, refuse collectors, performers, artisans, vermin exterminators, and manual laborers. The street vendors, or costermongers, survived by selling everything from fresh produce and flowers to old books, dog collars, live birds, secondhand clothes, and old glassware. Mayhew found the costermongers to be hardworking and honest, and he admired their resourcefulness.

Table 10.2. English Households Ranked by Imperia, 1086–1812

	Norman England, 1086	Stuart England, 1688	Georgian England, 1812
Super-Elite	182	187	4,937
Elite	6,900	31,400	128,824
Maintenance	24,000	480,000	1,021,395
Poor	275,079	879,000	2,413,625

Sources: Colquhoun 1815, King 1936, Roberts and Roberts 1980, Snooks 1993.

Children sold things on the street as soon as they could walk and talk; most children went unschooled and might be informally married by age fourteen. Costermongers had minimal economic reserves, but those who were fortunate and extremely careful with their meager funds might have precariously comfortable lives. Others lived in squalor and struggled to survive.

Because of their economic marginality, many costermongers were too poor to buy the carts, donkeys, and miscellaneous equipment needed for their work. Their low and erratic income made them easy prey for those immediately higher in the economic hierarchy. Annual rent for a simple handcart was more than twice the cart's value. At those rates, enterprising small-scale capitalists turned a modest investment in handcarts into a profitable business. One man amassed an economic empire of 150 handcarts, which he rented to the costermongers at exorbitant weekly rates for a tidy return. Hard-pressed costermongers were also an easy target for unscrupulous moneylenders and pawnshop owners. Interest rates were so outrageous that costermongers were forced to pay £65 to borrow £25 during the year to buy their stock. Costermongers lived in specific neighborhoods and supported each other, even holding raffles to raise money for those in most distress. In good times, the average annual income of costermongers could provide a minimum living, but if a few days of bad weather depressed sales, thousands would face starvation. The lives of many of the street people were unbelievably bleak (see box 10.4).

At the end of the nineteenth century, England's political leaders still lacked a clear picture of the scale of the country's social problems (see box 10.5). London's population had now grown to 5 million people, and radical reformers claimed that 25 percent were impoverished. Successful London businessman Charles Booth thought this figure was an exaggeration, and in 1886, following Mayhew's lead, he set out to systematically count London's poor. Funding his own research, he picked the northeast quarter of the city, where nearly a million people lived, and

spent the next seventeen years methodically mapping income levels, occupations, and housing conditions—street by street, house by house, even room by room. To precisely identify the truly poor, he sorted his data along different dimensions using an eight-level scale, ranked A to H and color coded, black to yellow, by living standard. At the bottom of the scale in Class A, coded black, were semi-criminals, loafers, and occasional laborers, with minimal family life. On a Class A street, Booth found 200 households, containing probably 1,000 people, living in 40 four-story houses in a 2-acre (4.8 hectares) section of London near the British Museum. Entire families were crowded into single 8-by-8-foot, vermin-infested rooms. Fifty people shared a single outside toilet and water tap, drawing from a cistern. Most of these people found occasional work as market porters and costermongers, or they were unemployed. The "very poor" in Class B were characterized by "casual labour, hand-to-mouth existence, [and] chronic want." The "poor" in Classes C and D could find seasonal or poorly paid work, which was "barely sufficient for decent independent life." Members of all "poor" classes lived in crowded housing with two or more persons per room and were at or below a poverty level of 21 shillings of weekly income. Working-class people in Classes E and F were regularly employed and "fairly" paid, and Booth considered them to be "comfortable." At the upper end, Class G, "well-to-do" families had one or two servants. In Class H were "wealthy" families, with three or more servants and living in houses valued at £100 or more. In his final analysis, Booth discovered that more than 30 percent of London's population were poor by his own definition (see table 10.3). The radical reformers actually had underestimated the problem. The 1.2 million poor living in London in 1890 exceeded the entire population of the city in 1801, suggesting that a century of growth had produced an unusual sort of progress. The 18,000 wealthy constituted the top 0.5 percent of London society.

Table 10.3. Living Standards and Social Classes in London, 1890

Living Standard	Class	Income	Housing	Number	Percentage
Poor	A (lowest)	Occasional	Very crowded	37,610	0.89
Poor	B (very poor)	Casual	Very crowded	316,834	7.53
Poor	C-D (poor)	Ill-paid	Crowded	938,293	22.29
Comfortable	E-F (working class)	Fairly paid	–	2,166,503	51.47
Well-to-do	G (middle class)	–	–	732,124	17.39
Wealthy	H (upper class)	–	–	17,806	0.45
Totals				4,209,170	100.0

Source: Booth (1892-1903).

London's poverty in the 1890s was related to social conditions in the countryside. Rural land ownership had become so concentrated that an official inquiry was held in 1875, and for the first time the government published the names and holdings of all major landowners in a "New Domesday Book."[82] There were some 24 million people in England and Wales in 1875, in 4.8 million households; but fewer than 14,000 large landowners, who represented only 0.28 percent of all households, held nearly 75 percent of the land. This land tenure system distinctly resembled the Norman system of the original Domesday Survey. Ninety-five percent of households held less than 0.5 percent of all individually owned land. The smallholders represented 15 percent of the population, but their properties averaged less than a quarter acre each, certainly not enough to sustain a farm family.

BOX 10.4. MUD-LARKS, BONE-GRUBBERS, AND A COSTER LAD'S STORY

Henry Mayhew thought that the most degraded workers in London were the collectors who wandered the streets searching for marketable refuse, such as cigar butts, bits of metal, rags, rope, lumps of coal, and bone and dog feces used in industrial production. Three pounds of bone fragments were worth a penny, and a good bone-grubber (see figure 10.14) could gather six pence (half a shilling)'s worth in a day—only a third of the ten shillings that a costermonger might earn per day. Apples sold at six for a penny, and a four-pound loaf of bread cost four pence. Fortunate bone-grubbers would spend two pence of their meager earnings on the most wretched lodging and have four pence left to spend on a little sugar, coffee, and a quarter loaf of bread. Mayhew interviewed other unusual collectors including old-wood gatherers, dredgers, sewer hunters, and mud-larks. He thought the condition of the latter was the most deplorable—they were reduced to scavenging trash from the river mud at low tide. He described them as follows:

Among the mud-larks may be seen many old women, and it is indeed pitiable to behold them, especially during the winter, bent nearly double with age and infirmity, paddling and groping among the wet mud for small pieces of coal, chips of wood, or any sort of refuse washed up by the tide. These women always have with them an old basket or an old tin kettle, in which they put whatever they chance to find. It usually takes them a whole tide to fill this receptacle, but when filled, it is as much as the feeble old creatures are able to carry home.[83]

Mayhew[84] recorded the following life history from a sixteen-year-old coster lad. This illustrates the physical and emotional stress that misfortune caused economically marginalized families in nineteenth-century London:

Father I've heard tell died when I was three and brother only a year old. It was worse luck for us! . . . Mother used to be up and out very early washing in families—anything for a living. She was a good mother to us. We was left at home with the key of the room and some bread and butter for dinner. Afore she got into work—and it was a goodish long time—we was shocking hard up, and she pawned nigh everything. Sometimes, when we hadn't no grub at all, the other lads, perhaps, would give us some bread and butter, but often our stomachs used to ache with the hunger, and we would cry when we was werry far gone. She used to be at work from six in the morning till ten o'clock at night, which was a long time for a child's belly to hold out again, and when it was dark we would go and lie down on the bed and try and sleep until she came home with the food. I was eight year old then.

A man as know'd mother, said to her, "Your boy's got nothing to do, let him come along with me and yarn a few ha'pence," and so I became a coster. He gave me 4d. [pence] a morning and my breakfast.

BOX 10.5. MARX AND ENGELS: THE COMMUNIST MANIFESTO

Social revolutionaries Karl Marx (1818–1883) and Friedrich Engels (1820–1895) were both living in London and directly experienced the wretched social conditions described by Mayhew. Engels's book *The Condition of the Working-Class in England: From Personal Observation and Authentic Sources* was published in 1845 to inspire a social revolution.[85] Marx and Engels coauthored their famous *Communist Manifesto*[86] in London in 1848. They conceptualized the human problems of commercialization as a class struggle between "two great hostile camps"—the bourgeoisie (capitalists) and the proletariat (workers).

Their solution called for "the forcible overthrow of all existing social conditions," declaring in the famous last lines of the Manifesto: "Let the ruling classes tremble at a Communistic revolution. The proletarians have nothing to lose but their chains. They have a world to win. WORKING MEN OF ALL COUNTRIES UNITE!"

More specifically, Marx and Engels advocated worker control of government; the abolition of private property; government control of production, communication, and transportation; free education; and the elimination of social classes. Even though they considered material conditions to be the primary influences on social order, they believed that intellectual elites, like themselves, could organize the masses to purposively transform society. In order to achieve these goals quickly, they were willing to replace one form of totalitarian political power with another. They were also overly optimistic about the possibility of eliminating social classes and considered further economic growth, or material progress, to be a solution rather than a problem in itself. Consequently, they did not solve the problem of how to more equitably distribute social power in very large-scale social systems. However, they clearly understood the importance of political economy, and they recognized the human problems of the commercialization process. Marxist political ideology has certainly shaped the course of modern history, but simply placing commerce under state control does not solve all problems of scale and power, as the experience of the former Soviet Union demonstrated.

The British Commercial Imperial Order

By 1878, a political hierarchy in the global system was clearly established. More than half the world's land area was claimed by just four giant states and their related territories: Britain, Russia, China, and the United States. Together with seven other colonial countries, these major states held claims over two-thirds of the world.[87] Most of Africa was still under the control of traditional kingdoms, chiefdoms, and tribal systems. Minor independent modern states had emerged in Latin America, but vast areas were still occupied by autonomous tribal groups.

Beginning in the 1880s, the leaders of the major colonial powers scrambled to extend their political control over Africa and the Pacific, and by 1913 more than three-fourths of the world's land area was controlled by just thirteen countries. Throughout the modern colonial period from 1800 to 1945, a single power,

Great Britain, remained dominant. At its height in the 1930s, the British Empire spanned the globe, encompassing roughly one-fourth of the world's land area and population (see figure 10.15). The British Empire was primarily a loose federation held together by diverse political connections and the common British origin and English language of the ruling elites in each political unit.

In most of the colonies, a very small minority of European colonists enjoyed a privileged status over the majority native population, who were held in a structurally inferior position. Coercive military power was used to establish and maintain administrative control, but the common objective was the capitalist development of productive resources, growing markets, and the expansion of trade, not the extraction of tribute as in ancient empires.

For example, in 1750 fewer than 1,000 shareholders received nearly 90 percent of the profits from the British East India Company, and the 49 largest shareholders received one-fourth of the total annual profits.[88] Much like the Mughal Empire, but headquartered in London, the East India Company was a vast empire with a chief official and 14 corporate directors commanding 63,000 employees, 160,000 troops, and 40 million native workers.[89]

During the early period of British colonialism, the commercial elite, backed by the military power of the British navy, expanded their personal fortunes by plundering Great Tradition civilizations and the tribal world. Conquest provided revenue to the Crown as well as to private investors. In fact English piracy on Spanish shipments of gold and silver stolen from the Inca and Aztecs provided the highest return on investment. However, when captured territories had to be administered and policed, and roads and other infrastructure had to be built and maintained, the costs of colonialism quickly became a net loss for all but the very largest private investors.[90] The privileged economic elite promptly "socialized" the costs of colonialism by shifting them to the conquered peoples and through taxes to the British citizenry at large. The balance sheet shows that during the peak of imperial expansion from 1860 to 1912, the primary wealth benefits flowed to a tiny segment of the British elite composed of some 200,000 top shareholders: the bankers, military officers, government officials, members of Parliament, and largest property owners. Thus, the real beneficiaries were the top 0.6 super-elite percent of 33 million British citizens.[91]

Figure 10.14. The London bone-grubber (engraving from Beard Daguerrotype in Mayhew 1860–61).

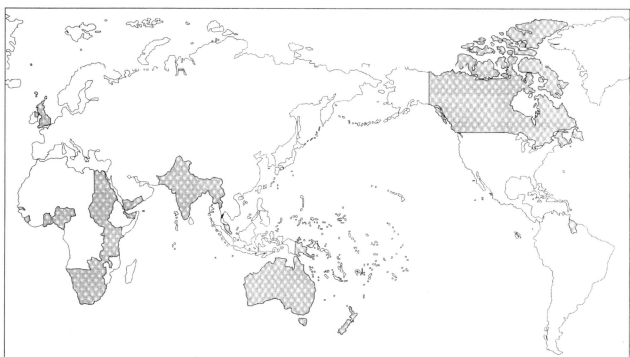

Figure 10.15. British colonies, territories, and dominions in the 1930s.

Investors extended their commercial enterprises far beyond the boundaries of the British Empire just as under the current postcolonial globalization process in the twenty-first century. The wealth of British capitalists grew so large that they could dominate markets and take advantage of investment opportunities everywhere in what had become an informal global empire centered in London. For example, by 1900 one man, Charles Morrison, a London financier and top landowner, personally controlled 10 percent of British investments in Argentina, which soon grew to £480 million.[92] At his death in 1909 Morrison left an estate valued at £10.9 million, and was one of 30 British multimillionaires at the time.[93]

Paradoxically, from the perspective of the ideology of benevolent growth and free markets that define the rise of the commercial world at the height of the British Empire, as many as 50 million people may have needlessly starved to death in famines that swept the "developing" tropical and subtropical world from 1879 to 1902.[94] This astonishing human tragedy occurred even as these areas were being integrated into the global economy, and their labor and products were contributing to the accumulation of capital in the global "core" of London. The famines resulted from a series of droughts related to the El Niño climate effects, but the mass deaths from starvation, especially in India and China, were a result of colonialist intervention that undermined the capacity of local food systems in the process of incorporating them into the global market.[95] Food was available in the stricken areas, it was just not accessible to people who were priced out of the market. Mass deaths occurred because government officials, who believed in "free markets," were unwilling to make food available to starving people, even as "the market" was extracting grain from impoverished areas to the wealthy centers where people could buy it.

Organization of the Twenty-First-Century Global Market

Colonialism was a costly system of economic growth subsidized by governments and taxpayers. It has now been totally superseded by a decentralized global market organized through an international system of financial institutions and regulatory bodies. Commercialization's triumph over the politicization process produced a world dominated by wealthy investors and the transnational corporations that they own and direct.

The Commercial World as Empire

According to Hardt and Negri[96] the postmodern world is now in the process of transformation into a single all-encompassing Empire, fundamentally different from the modern world that preceded it, and totally different theoretical tools are needed to understand it. Sovereign nation-states are no longer the center of empires as they were under modernism. Under postmodern conditions there is one Empire encompassing the entire world, but with no center and no outside boundaries as between colonizers and colonized, because all societies and nations are part of the Empire. In the Empire, human emotions and mentalities are shaped by much more than familiar social institutions. In contrast to the modern world system, the postmodern Empire is an inclusive system that ignores as irrelevant racial, gender, and cultural differences. Inclusion makes it possible to reach a formal, legal consensus, or legitimize what the Empire defines as universally good and true. Nonpolitical cultural differences are welcomed and are used to manage the workforce.

The "modern" form of industrialization required production to be concentrated in factories in a few centers, but the postmodern information economy, dominated by the service sector, encourages the dispersal or decentralization of production sites. Assembly lines can be replaced by production networks. This is called the "deterritorialization of production" and is especially important for immaterial labor. Significantly, such production networks are horizontal rather than hierarchical structures; however, they are likely to make central control stronger and thus weaken the bargaining power of labor. Network production also favors the growth and power of business services, especially financial services, which are concentrated in global cities.

The Empire is constantly changing but not totally formless. Writing at the end of the twentieth century, Hardt and Negri describe the Empire as a hybrid form of government, reflecting elements of monarchy, aristocracy, and democracy from the Classical and Renaissance traditions, as well as executive, legislative, and representative functions of government from the modern liberal view.[97] In concrete terms, the Empire is a three-tiered pyramid of command and control, with the top-tier monarchical layer providing unity and continuity (see figure 10.16). The top tier has three sublayers with the United States at the very top holding a virtual monopoly of military power with The Bomb as the ultimate symbol of destructive power.

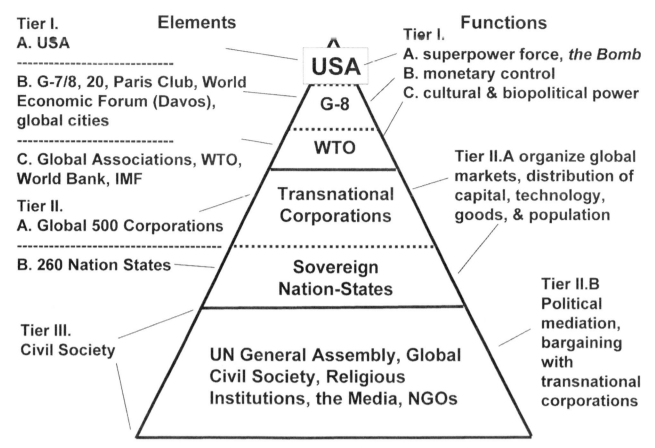

Figure 10.16. The Postmodern Commercial World as Empire as viewed by Michael Hardt and Antonio Negri (2000:309–314).

The second top-tier sublayer is composed of informal international elite organizations such as the G-8, the Paris Club, and the World Economic Forum, followed by more formal global institutions such as the World Trade Organization. All of the top-tier elements function to control the global monetary system as well as exercising cultural and biopolitical power over the entire Empire. Tier II governs as an aristocracy and consists of the largest global business corporations and the remaining somewhat-sovereign nation-states of the world. This aristocracy organizes markets and the distribution of capital, technology, goods, and people. The lowest tier is civil society representing the world's people, whom Hardt and Negri call "the Multitude," and corresponds to a potentially democratic form of government. It consists of the United Nations General Assembly, nongovernmental organizations, various religious organizations, and the media. Civil society is how the mass of people negotiate with political power and global business corporations.

The Empire is a dynamic network with no single center. It changes in response to resistance from the Multitude. This is a hopeful model of the global system, because even though the positive aspects of monarchy, aristocracy, and democracy often descend into their negative counterparts of tyranny, oligarchy, and ochlocracy (mob rule), the rapidly evolving communication system has the potential to change the Empire from inside by changing perceptions, emotions, and mentalities. This suggests that the ideological superstructure, rather than the material infrastructure, is the key to cultural transformation and sociocultural sustainability.

A key problem of life in a postmodern society of control dominated by biopolitical, technologically based immaterial production is that reality for people could effectively become "one-dimensional."[98] A single cultural rationality—for example, belief in the desirability of elevating material consumption and perpetual economic growth—could totally dominate the world, causing very negative consequences. German sociologist Herbert Marcuse warned of just such an outcome, and the evidence presented in chapter 12 suggests that this is in fact happening. At the same time, the prevailing economic theory makes self-interested individuals the basis of the economy, even as private business absorbs the commonwealth of public property, thereby further undermining community.

New Global Institutions: United Nations, World Bank, International Monetary Fund, World Trade Organization

The institutional foundation of the new economic world order was the United Nations system, the World Bank (International Bank for Reconstruction and Development), and the International Monetary Fund (IMF). This social structure did not just happen. It was not the only possible form of world order, and it was not inevitable. It was created by a handful of progressivist elite planners near the end of World War II in 1944–1945. A total of perhaps a hundred advisors worked out the details, with help from the Council on Foreign Relations, a private American policy-planning group, funded in part by the Rockefeller and Carnegie foundations.[99] These planners were not un–self-interested. They were also advisors and officials at the highest level of the Roosevelt Administration, and they were owners and managers of the largest American corporations, including the largest investment banks such as J. P. Morgan and Company.[100] The new global institutional structures these planners designed facilitated the ascendancy of the **financialization** process, but they were guided by a populist, humanitarian ideology. Following British economist John Maynard Keynes and American "New Deal" economists, they believed that the World Bank and the IMF would stabilize currency flows, make loans to governments for development purposes, and manage the global economy to promote commerce, prevent depressions, create employment, and distribute income to people to meet basic needs.

In practice, the new world order favored the financial elite and helped ensure their global access to investment opportunities, while promoting American-centered economic growth. It was no accident that the president of the World Bank must always be an American and that the American dollar is the standard international currency. In 2010 there were 186 member nations in the IMF, but just nine nations, headed by the United States, were the fund's largest financial contributors and controlled more than half of its voting power.[101]

The flow of finance capital is now more important in commerce than the flow of actual goods and services.[102] By the early 1990s as much as 90 percent of the world's commercial transactions by value involved stocks, bonds, and commodity futures.[103] The importance of financial capital is also reflected in the fact that by the year 2000, as noted above, 75 percent of American wealth was financial. The global market economy is "free" in that it is subject to less and less control by any national government or international political institutions. Centrally planned national economies, such as the former Soviet Union, have all but disappeared. International trade agreements, such as the GATT (General Agreement on Tariffs and Trade) and NAFTA (North American Free Trade Agreement), have greatly reduced national barriers to commerce such that commodities and finance capital now flow easily across borders. Virtually all of the world's people are part of a single commercial network, which is ultimately dependent on computerized financial transactions taking place in a few organized markets in the richest countries.

The rapid proliferation of consumer credit and credit cards also reflects the increasing importance of the financialization process. This process rapidly shifts wealth to financial elites, who already control large sums of finance capital, because by taking advantage of the power of scale, they can realize handsome returns from very large financial exchanges with small profit margins.

Directing the Global 500: Elite Networks at the Top

The world's largest publicly traded corporations dominate the global economy to a remarkable degree. For example, in 2009, the 500 largest companies listed in the *Fortune* Global 500 had annual revenues of more than $20 trillion, which was more than a third of global gross domestic product (GDP).[104] This degree of concentrated market power is astounding in a world in which there are some 60 million business companies, including 55,000 that are publicly traded.[105] At the very top the ten largest corporations had combined revenues of some $3 trillion, which was more than 5 percent of global GDP, and more than the combined GDPs of 130 countries. In 2009 the world was in the midst of the largest financial crisis since the Great Depression, but even so, the two largest companies—both oil companies, Royal Dutch Shell and Exxon-Mobil—made $71 billion. Given the world's current reliance on petroleum, it is not surprising that seven of the top ten were oil companies and one was a car manufacturer (Toyota). The other two were Walmart, the world's largest retailer, and ING, a financial services corporation. Shell Oil was the largest corporation in the world, with $458 billion in revenues.

In 2005 Shell had exploration and production operations in some forty countries.[106] Thirteen of Shell's board members were also directors of twenty-two other Global 500 corporations, giving them combined control over more than $1 trillion in revenues. At that time, this revenue flow was comparable to the GDP of Russia, a country of 143 million people. Shell's directors were most represented on the boards of some of the world's largest financial corporations, reflecting the close connections between financial flows and energy flows. One Shell director was also on the board of Rio Tinto, which, as we will see in chapter 13, owned the mining corporations that were developing major uranium and bauxite mines in the heart of some of the most vital remote areas of aboriginal groups in Australia. Shell's "vision" of its role was to meet the world's growing demand for energy, which it believed would be primarily centered on oil and gas for decades to come. The company saw itself as dedicated to sustainable development and to protecting the environment and communities. Shell and other large corporations are having a massive impact on the world. Their directors are well connected with other corporate leaders, and together they are among the elite directors of global growth, even though they are largely unknown to most people and are not democratically elected.

Global corporations themselves are organized in networks that link cities throughout the world to corporate headquarters that are clustered in a few "global cities." Work by urban specialists has added considerably to our understanding of the commercial structure of the world system. Sociologist Saskia Sassens[107] developed the **global city** concept to help understand the process of economic globalization. A global city is shaped by the special needs of multinational corporations to operate globally. The global city concept is closely related to Manuel Castells's concepts of the informational city, **information society**, and network society,[108] which together define the "Information Age" in which information networks are the basic form of social organization. Computer-based information technology has facilitated the construction of network organizational structures on a scale never before possible. These new organizational forms are transforming the world.

Global cities are command centers. They are locations of the headquarters of companies that provide essential services for the world's largest corporations. Researchers associated with the Globalization

and World Cities Research Network (GaWC)[109] have ranked cities by their level of integration into the world city network. World cities are cities that have "advanced producer firms," which are businesses that provide the special services, technical skills, and information that make it possible for other corporations to conduct international business. Advanced producer firms make globalization possible and include financial services such as banking, insurance, accounting, legal services, and business consulting. The network of global cities is formed by the connections between corporate headquarters and branches in different cities, such that the more offices a city has, and the more important the office, the more important a given city is in the global network. The original analysis used 100 service firms (18 accounting firms, 16 law firms, 23 banking and finance firms, 15 advertisers, 11 insurance firms, and 17 management consultancy firms) and 315 cities, based on data for the year 2000. New York and London are the world's most globally connected cities. For example, London was headquarters for 27 of the 100 advanced producer firms listed, and these firms were represented by branches in 283 countries around the world (see figure 10.17).

What is remarkable about these findings is the extent to which decision-making power is concentrated in a few individuals located in few centers. GaWC researchers conducted a new assessment of global cities in the first half of 2008, right before the global financial crisis.[110] The emphasis was on the apparent financial "command and control" functions based on the distribution of headquarters and branch offices of 75 major financial service firms in 526 cities across the world. The importance of each city was measured using scores on the *Forbes* financial command index (FCI) combining revenues, profits, and assets for the top 75 financial firms. A city with a financial firm in the top 5 would score 10, and a firm ranked 56 to 75 would score 2. New York had the top score and was treated as 100 percent. Only 35 cities even made it into the ranking, and 29 of these were located in Europe or North America. The top five financial command centers by FCI score were New York (100), London (60), Zurich (37), Paris (35), and Toronto (30). GaWC researchers also ranked cities by a Business Command Index based on the rankings of their corporate headquarters on the *Forbes* Global 2000 list of corporations. The rankings were again very concentrated with the top five ranked as follows: Tokyo (100), New York (70), London (68), Paris (53), and Houston (25). The surprising appearance of Houston in the top 5 is due

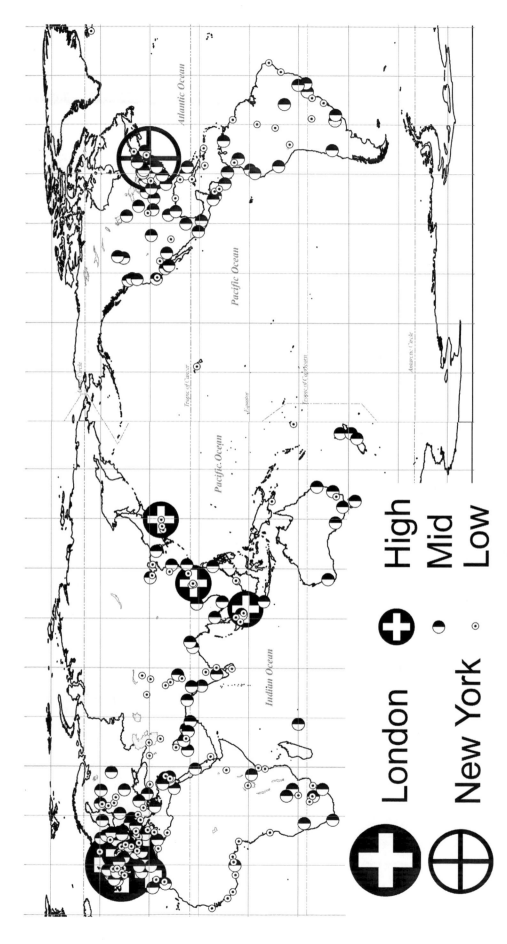

Figure 10.17. London's global reach, 2000 (data from Taylor, P. J. 2001). Global Network Service Connectivities for 315 Cities in 2000. (*GaWC Bulletin No. 23*). *Geographical Analysis* 33(2):181-194, www.lboro.ac.uk/gawc/datasets/da12.html.

to its place as the command center for global oil and gas.

The role of advanced producer firms in the network of global cities can be illustrated by the example of the advertising company McCannWorldGroup, which had operations in 154 cites. It was headquartered in New York, had major branches in Copenhagen, Lisbon, London, Oslo, Paris, São Paulo, and Toronto, in addition to 26 branch offices and 121 minor offices. The company management team consisted of just 27 people. McCann's service is "creating demand" for the products of leading brands in some ten countries worldwide. Its revenues were over $2 billion in 2007. Among the well-known global companies that McCann represented were Exxon-Mobil, General Motors, Microsoft, Coca-Cola, and MasterCard.

In a sense, the prime beneficiaries of the global flow of finance capital were the approximately 10 million high-net-worth individuals (HNWI), primarily European and American multimillionaires with investable assets of more than a million dollars.[111] At their peak in 2007, before the 2008 global market collapse, the world's HNWI held over $40 trillion. Their wealth represented approximately two thirds of the $65 trillion in global market capitalization (the value of all of the corporations listed on the world's stock exchanges). The HNWIs literally owned the corporate commercial world, although they represented a mere 0.15 percent of the world's population. Their wealth was also growing at 7.7 percent a year, in effect producing annual income of more than $3 trillion, for an average of $313,390 per HNWI.

The prominence of financial wealth in the global economy means that as individuals the poor have become virtually irrelevant, even though in the aggregate they constitute an important market for certain low-cost consumer goods. The World Bank estimated that in 2002 at the bottom of the global hierarchy, there were 2.5 to 3 billion people in the world living on less than $2 a day. This suggests that at that time nearly half of the world's people received less than 7 percent of global income and owned a much smaller proportion of the world's wealth. This means that most of the world's people had very little ability to influence the decisions that shaped their daily lives. The transnational corporations that dominate the economic sphere of the global system have become enormously powerful. For example, by 2002, Walmart was the world's largest corporation, with revenues of $245 billion. It operated 4,688 stores throughout the United States and in nine other countries, employing more than a million people.[112] At that time only eighteen countries had higher gross national incomes than Walmart's revenues. The largest individual owners of Walmart were five members of the founder's family, who each held personal fortunes of $16.5 billion, each ranking as the world's seventh largest fortune, worth in the aggregate more than $82 billion.

The level of social inequality produced by the global economy is difficult to comprehend. As economic growth accelerated during the 1990s, the number of global billionaires soared from 101 in 1993[113] to 476 in 2002.[114] Total global billionaire wealth increased from $451 billion to more than $1.4 trillion. This was equivalent to 4.4 percent of global income in 2001. Measured as income produced by a predictable 7 percent return on their $1.4 trillion in capital, these 476 individuals could expect to earn an aggregate of more than $98 billion in income a year. Only 36 countries had higher gross national incomes in 2001. Billionaire income of $98 billion would have been sufficient to raise 134 million people (about the population of Bangladesh in 2001) above the World Bank's designation of extreme poverty of $730 per person per year ($2 per day per person). It would even have elevated more than 5 million American four-person families above the official U.S. poverty level of $18,556 per year.

Nearly half of global billionaires in 2002 were Americans, and together with the billionaires in the other G-8 nations (the "Group of Eight" with the world's largest economies: Canada, France, Germany, Italy, Japan, United Kingdom, United States, and Russia), they accounted for 75 percent of global billionaires (see table 10.4). There were only two billionaires in Africa.

There is a clear trend throughout human history for the few hundred super-elite individuals at the top of every society to increase their wealth in step with growth in social income. Figure 10.18 demonstrates this trend by plotting average super-elite wealth by the size of social income for ten different societies, assuming that average minimum household subsistence in the imperial and early commercial worlds equals $1,500. The difference in scale of super-elite income and absolute size of social income for different societies is so great that these data must be shown on a log scale. Significantly, in the societies represented, super-elite wealth and size of economy are strongly correlated and can be graphed as a straight line. These findings are further evidence for elite direction in cultural growth and confirm the folk wisdom that the rich get richer. The Asháninka are shown as the

Table 10.4. Global Distribution of Billionaires and Billionaire Fortunes, 2002

	Number of Billionaires	Percent of Billionaires	Aggregate $ Billions	Percent of Wealth
United States	222	47	702	50
Other G-8	132	28	376	27
European	39	8	117	8
Asia-Pacific	39	8	90	6
Latin America	22	5	48	3
Middle East	20	4	64	5
Africa	2	0	4	0

Data Source: Forbes Magazine, March 17, 2003.

smallest society with the smallest super-elite wealth, even though in tribal societies the wealth difference between super-elite and "poor" households is insignificant in comparison to the inequalities of the imperial and commercial worlds. Asháninka household wealth is counted as $8,500 rather than $1,500 to reflect their social equality and greater access to natural resources.

The new global elite use their wealth to maintain a dominant influence in the world, or cultural hegemony, which maintains consumerism as a primary cultural ideal for the non-elite majority. Commercial advertisers shape people's beliefs and the smallest details of their behavior through the mass media. For example, in the early 1990s Coca-Cola—arguably the world's most successful brand—marketed its soft drinks to 20 percent of the world's people. In 1992–1993 it had sales of more than $13 billion. Coca-Cola spent $392 million in the United States to persuade people to drink an average of 37 gallons of Coke products per capita per year, producing sales of $4.3 billion.[115] It is not surprising that in 1998, Warren Buffett, at that time a principal Coca-Cola shareholder and corporate director, was perhaps the third-richest individual in the world, with a personal net worth estimated at $33 billion.

When the postcolonial era of national economic growth slowed in the 1980s, political economists promoted "New Growth Theory" favoring an even more

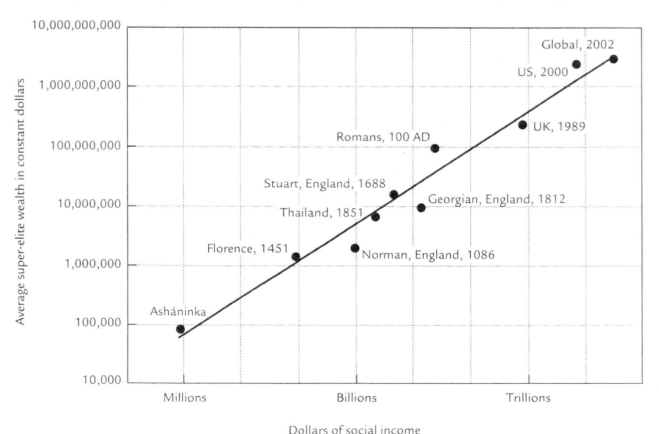

Figure 10.18. Super-elite wealth by social income in ten societies, 100 AD to 2002 AD.

globally integrated economy based on small and weak governments, minimal regulation of commerce, and removal of all trade barriers.[116] This new commercially organized world economic order is directed by a loose network of economic planners who occupy key positions in newly created international economic institutions, such as the International Monetary Fund, the World Bank, and the World Trade Organization, and on the boards of the world's largest corporations. The promotion of economic growth is the single objective of this new global-scale power elite, but the planners are often divided over key policy approaches and conflicting interests.

SUMMARY

Capitalism is a commercial system of production and exchange that treats land, labor, technology, money, raw materials, and goods and services as commodities to be bought and sold for a profit. This cultural system is totally unique and has transformed the world. The wealthy elite who most benefit from the capitalist market economy have used industrial production based on fossil fuel energy sources, colonialism, and unequal exchange to integrate the diverse societies and cultures of the world into a single global economic system. An ideology of continuous economic expansion and high rates of consumption are central features of this system that are derived from more fundamental European beliefs in natural scarcity, insatiable wants, and a dualism between mind and body, humans and nature.

During the early stages of commercialization in medieval England, the number of poor actually increased. Capitalism required a financial revolution that made money the dominant means of organizing social power. The most successful mercantile capitalists used kinship and marriage to organize their far-flung business enterprises and transmit their growing commercial estates from generation to generation. Early economic theorists such as Adam Smith assumed that capitalist development directed by self-seeking entrepreneurs would ultimately benefit everyone. However, ethnographic data collected in nineteenth-century London showed that unrestrained economic growth produced enormous poverty and serious public health problems.

The global process of sugar production and consumption illustrated the early expansion of the global system. Commercially driven colonial empires, exemplified by the British empire at its peak, controlled much of the world during the first half of the nineteenth century. Since the breakdown of the colonial system after World War II, many supranational political and economic institutions, such as the United Nations and the World Bank, have assumed formal leadership of the global system. But the policies of these institutions are influenced by powerful nations and by giant multinational corporations that benefit from the global structure of inequality. A new cultural process, financialization, controlled by the wealthiest individuals and financial institutions, is emerging as the dominant force in the world.

The next chapter will examine the United States as an example of one of the most dominant national cultures in the present global system. Chapter 13 will explore the problem of poverty in the countries that are "peripheral" to the wealthy industrial core.

STUDY QUESTIONS

1. Define the following concepts: embedded economy, kin-ordered production, culture of consumption, mode of production, capitalist production, tributary production.
2. Distinguish between a market and nonmarket economy.
3. Define a capitalist political economy and explain how it differs from the economic systems of ancient states.
4. Describe the structure of the global commercial economy as a world system.
5. What are the principal ideological features of the capitalist world system? Draw illustrations from Adam Smith and modern economists.
6. Discuss the specific changes in cultural organization that accompanied the Industrial Revolution in England. Refer to the role of technology, population, capital accumulation, inequality, and the enclosure movement.
7. What is the evidence for the argument that more people were impoverished than enriched by the cultural transformations that swept England between 1086 and 1890?
8. How were European economic conditions from 1086 to 1890 reflected in household organization and in kinship and marriage patterns?
9. What features of European cosmology and ideology supported capitalism?
10. Explain how dietary change (sugar and tea) in England was related to the Industrial Revolution and the expanding world system.
11. Describe the political and economic structure of modern colonialism in contrast to the empires of the past. Make specific comparisons between the Inca empire in the Andean world and the British empire in the modern world.

SUGGESTED READING

Bodley, John H. 2003. *The Power of Scale: A Global History Approach*. Armonk, NY: M. E. Sharpe.

Crosby, Alfred W. 1986. *Biological Imperialism: The Biological Expansion of Europe, 900–1900*. Cambridge, Eng.: Cambridge University Press. Discussion by a historian of the biological consequences of European colonialism on ecosystems and people throughout the world.

Ferguson, Niall. 2003. *Empire: How Britain Made the Modern World*. London: Allen Lane, Penguin.

Smith, Adam. 1776. *An Inquiry into the Nature and Causes of the Wealth of Nations*. Vol. 1. London: Strahan and Cadell. The classic formulation of the key features of the early capitalist economy.

Wallerstein, Immanuel. 1974. *The Modern World-System: Capitalist Agriculture and the Origins of the European World-Economy in the Sixteenth Century*. New York: Academic Press. The pioneer statement of world system theory.

Wolf, Eric R. 1982. *Europe and the People without History*. Berkeley: University of California Press. An anthropological treatment of European expansion since 1400, focusing on the political economy and showing how the capitalist system incorporated tributary and kin-based systems.

GLOSSARY TERMS

Gross domestic product (GDP) The total output of goods and services produced within a country, by monetary value.

Gross national product (GNP) The total output of a country's goods and services, by monetary value, that also includes net gains from foreign investments or activities.

Purchasing power parity (PPP) Monetary value adjusted for the value of the currency in relation to a set of basic goods in the country.

Fuel revolution The large-scale adoption of fossil fuels such as coal and oil.

Kin-ordered production A mode of production organized at the domestic or kinship level and producing primarily for domestic use rather than exchange.

Use value The value of goods produced for domestic consumption, usually within a kin-ordered mode of production.

Exchange value The value of goods when used as commodities.

Tributary production A mode of production in which products are extracted as surplus from a self-supporting peasantry and used to support the state.

Capitalist production A mode of production in which a few people control the means of production and purchase the labor of those who could not otherwise support themselves.

Capital Marx's term for land and tools as the means of production; also refers generally to accumulated wealth used for productive purposes.

Commodities Basic goods that are produced for their exchange value in a market economy to generate profit to be accumulated as capital.

Embedded economy An economy that can only be observed and understood within the context of the social, political, and religious systems of the culture.

Disembodied economy The concept of an economy as something that can be understood apart from the rest of society and culture, especially with a capitalist mode of production.

World system An international hierarchy of diverse societies and cultures integrated into a single economic system based on unequal exchange that allows wealth to accumulate in the core.

Unequal exchange Market-based exchanges in which one party is consistently able to accumulate a disproportionate share of the profit or wealth.

Capital accumulation Expansion of wealth and the means of production that can be devoted to further production.

Core The wealthy industrial countries at the center of the world system where the recipients of unequal exchange reside.

Periphery Capital-poor areas that supply raw materials and labor to the core; this area was integrated into the early capitalist world system through conquest and coercion.

Modern An international system of nation-states with industrial production and market economies.

Nation A people with a common culture and identity in an international system.

Nation-state A territory in which the government and the nation coincide.

Imagined communities Large communities where cultural identity is established by communication technologies including literacy, printing, and electronic networks.

Disciplinary society Modern society where individuals are controlled by disciplinary institutions including police, courts, prisons, welfare, charities, schools, and the practices of everyday life.

Biopower Foucault's concept of social power directed at control over all of human life, including people's minds and bodies.

Postmodernity Societies of control in which financial elites are the dominant decision makers; immaterial production and communication technologies are central features.

Immaterial production Language, symbols, computer software, information technologies, and communication networks.

Biopolitical production The human outcome of immaterial production used to control information and shape thoughts, emotions, and behavior through the media and advertising.

Societies of control Biopower is exercised by communication technologies.

Taylorism "Scientific management" of workers developed by American mechanical engineer Frederick Winslow Taylor to increase labor efficiency.

Fordism Henry Ford's principles of assembly-line mass production combined with high enough wages to allow workers to buy the products they produced, which was a foundation of consumer culture.

Keynesianism Keynes's policy of government intervention in the economy to sustain consumer income and expenditure by means of welfare assistance and public work projects.

Chemical Revolution Factory-produced chemicals replace natural products and processes.

Enclosure movement The transformation in seventeenth- and eighteenth-century Europe of open communal pastures and woodlands into enclosed, privately controlled properties, replacing village self-sufficiency with market-oriented agriculture and forcing people to become wage laborers in newly industrializing cities.

Invisible hand The capitalist belief that market forces, operating through supply and demand, will lead to continuous economic growth and benefit everyone.

Financialization A cultural process involving the flow of finance capital, money, and securities, rather than the actual production and distribution of goods and services.

Global city A city that serves as an important hub within a network of cities supporting financial and information services.

Information society A society organized within an electronic network of digital information supported by computers and communication technologies.

NOTES

1. U.S. Census Bureau. 2010. U.S. and World Population Clocks. www.census.gov/main/www/popclock.html (accessed Feb. 4, 2010).

2. Thurow, Lester C. 1996. *The Future of Capitalism: How Today's Economic Forces Shape Tomorrow's World*. New York: Morrow.

3. Gates, Bill, with Nathan Myhrvold and Peter Rinearson. 1996. *The Road Ahead*. 2nd ed. New York and London: Penguin Books, 11.

4. Gates. 1996. *The Road Ahead*, 10, 313.

5. Fox, Justin. 2009. *The Myth of the Rational Market: A History of Risk, Reward, and Delusion on Wall Street*. New York: HarperCollins; Soros, George. 2008. *The New Paradigm for Financial Markets: The Credit Crisis of 2008 and What It Means*. New York: PublicAffairs, Perseus Books Group.

6. Maddison, Angus. 2003. *The World Economy: Historical Statistics*. OECD: Development Centre Studies, Paris; Maddison, Angus. 2007. *Contours of the World Economy, 1–2030: Essays in Macro-Economic History*. Oxford: Oxford University Press.

7. OECD Convention, Article 1. www.oecd.org/document/7/0,3343,en_2649_201185_1915847_1_1_1_1,00.html.

8. Petty, William. 1899. [1676]. *Political Arithmetick*. In Hull, Charles Henry. 1899. *The Economic Writings of Sir William Petty Together with the Observations Upon the Bills of Mortality*, pp. 233–313, vol. 1. Cambridge: Cambridge University Press.

9. Petty, William.1899. [1662]. A Treatise of Taxes and Contributions. In Hull, Charles Henry. 1899. *The Economic Writings of Sir William Petty Together with the Observations Upon the Bills of Mortality*, pp. 1–97, vol. 1. Cambridge: Cambridge University Press.

10. Playfair, William. 2005. [1801]. *The Commercial and Political Atlas and Statistical Breviary* (Howard Wainer and Ian Spence, eds). 3rd ed. Cambridge: Cambridge University Press, 2.

11. Cook, Earl. 1971. "The Flow of Energy in an Industrial Society." *Scientific American* 224(3): 134–44, 136.

12. U.S. Energy Information Administration. 2009. *Annual Energy Review*. Table 1.1. Primary Energy Overview, 1949–2008. www.eia.doe.gov/emeu/aer/overview.html (accessed Feb. 5, 2010).

13. U.S. Energy Information Administration. 2009. *Annual Energy Review*. Table 11.3. World Primary Energy Consumption by Region, 1997–2007. www.eia.doe.gov/emeu/aer/overview.html (accessed Feb. 5, 2010).

14. McEvedy, Colin, and Richard Jones. 1978. *Atlas of World Population History*. Middlesex, England, and New York: Penguin Books.

15. Fischer-Kowalski, Marina, and Helmut Haberl. 1998. "Sustainable Development: Socio-Economic Metabolism and Colonization of Nature." *International Social Science Journal* 50(158): 573–87.

16. Fischer-Kowalski, "Sustainable Development," 578.

17. Garvin, Lewis, Natalie Henry, Melissa Vernon. 2000. *Community Materials Flow Analysis: A Case Study of*

Ann Arbor, Michigan. University of Michigan Center for Sustainable Systems. Report CSS00-02. Table 5.4 Total Material Inputs Per Capita for Ann Arbor; Wernick, Iddo K., and Ausubel, Jesse H. 1995. "National Material Flows and the Environment." *Annual Review of Energy and the Environment.* 20:463–92.

18. Loh, Jonathan, and Mathis Wackernagel. 2004. *Living Planet Report.* Gland, Switzerland: WWF-World Wide Fund for Nature.

19. Haberl, Helmut, K. Hennz Erb, Fridolin Krausmann, Veronika Gaube, Alberte Bondeau, Christoph Plutzar, Simone Gingrich, Wolfgang Lucht, and Marina Fischer-Kowalski. 2007. "Quantifying and Mapping the Human Appropriation of Net Primary Production in Earth's Terrestrial Ecosystems. *Proceedings of the National Academy of Sciences, PNAS* 104(31):12942–47.

20. Radin, Paul. 1971. *The World of Primitive Man.* New York: Dutton, 106.

21. World, Eric R. 1982. *Europe and the People without History.* Berkeley: University of California Press.

22. Sahlins, Marshall. 1996. "The Sadness of Sweetness: The Native Anthropology of Western Cosmology." *Current Anthropology* 37(3):395–428.

23. Sahlins. 1996. "Sadness of Sweetness," 401.

24. Goldsmith, Raymond. 1987. *Premodern Financial Systems: A Historical Comparative Study.* Cambridge: Cambridge University Press, 16–33.

25. Sahlins, Marshall. 1968. "Notes on the Original Affluent Society." In *Man the Hunter,* edited by Richard B. Lee and Irven DeVore, 85–89. Chicago: Aldine.

26. U.S. Bureau of Economic Analysis. 2009. *Fixed Asset Tables.* www.bea.gov/national/FA2004/SelectTable.asp (accessed Sept. 2009); U.S. Federal Reserve. 2009. Flow of Funds Accounts of the United States. Tables F101-F109 Financial Assets 1946-2008. www.federalreserve.gov/datadownload (accessed Sept. 2009).

27. Heilbroner, Robert, and Lester C. Thurow. 1987. *Economics Explained.* Englewood Cliffs, NJ: Prentice-Hall, 12–14.

28. Heilbroner and Thurow, *Economics Explained,* 15–16.

29. Wallerstein, Immanuel. 1974. *The Modern World-System: Capitalist Agriculture and the Origins of the European World-Economy in the Sixteenth Century.* New York: Academic Press.

30. Wallerstein, Immanuel. 1990. "Culture as the Ideological Battleground of the Modern World-System." *Theory, Culture and Society* 7:31–55.

31. Weber, Max. 1930. *The Protestant Ethic and the Spirit of Capitalism.* New York: Scribner.

32. Kondratiev, Nikolai. 1984. *The Long Wave Cycle.* New York: Richardson and Snyder; Mager, Nathan H. 1987. *The Kondratieff Waves.* New York: Praeger. Stoken, Dick. 1993. *The Great Cycle: Predicting and Profiting from Crowd Behavior, the Kondratieff Wave, and Long-Term Cycles.* Chicago: Probus.

33. Fischer, David Hackett. 1996. *The Great Wave: Price Revolutions and the Rhythm of History.* New York: Oxford University Press.

34. Goldstein, Joshua A. 1988. *Long Waves: Prosperity and War in the Modern Age.* New Haven, CT, and London: Yale University Press.

35. Hobbes, Thomas. Original 1651. *Leviathan; or, the Matter, Form and Power of a Commonwealth, Ecclesiastical and Civil.*

36. Anderson, Benedict. 1983. *Imagined Communities: Reflections on the Origin and Spread of Nationalism.* London: Verso.

37. Foucault, Michel. 1977. *Discipline and Punish: The Birth of the Prison.* New York: Pantheon Books.

38. Bentham, Jeremy. 1791. *The Works of Jeremy Bentham,* vol. IV, pp. 172–73.

39. Mandel, Ernest. 1999. *Late Capitalism.* London: Verso; Jameson, Fredric. 1991. *Postmodernism, or, the Cultural Logic of Late Capitalism.* Durham: Duke University Press.

40. Touraine, Alain. 1971. *The Post-Industrial Society: Tomorrow's Social History. Classes, Conflicts and Culture in the Programmed Society.* New York: Random House; Bell, Daniel. 1973. *The Coming of Post-Industrial Society: a Venture in Social Forecasting.* New York: Basic Books.

41. Hardt, Michael, and Antonio Negri. 2000. *Empire.* Cambridge: Harvard University Press.

42. Gramsci, Antonio. 1992. *Prison Notebooks.* New York: Columbia University Press.

43. Taylor, Frederick Winslow. 1911. *The Principles of Scientific Management.* New York: Harper.

44. Keynes, John Maynard. 1936. *The General Theory of Employment, Interest and Money.* London: Macmillan.

45. Diamond, Jared. 1999. *Guns, Germs, and Steel: The Fates of Human Societies.* New York and London: W. W. Norton.

46. United Kingdom, National Archives. *Domesday Book.* www.nationalarchives.gov.uk/documentsonline/domesday.asp.

47. Miller, Edward, and John Hatcher. 1995. *Medieval England: Towns, Commerce and Crafts 1086–1348.* London and New York: Longman.

48. Orwin, C. S., and C. S. Orwin. 1967. *The Open Fields.* Oxford, Eng.: Clarendon Press; Seebohm, Frederic. 1905. *The English Village Community Examined in Its Relations to the Manorial and Tribal Systems and to the Common or Open Field System of Husbandry: An Essay in Economic History.* London: Longmans, Green.

49. McCloskey, Donald N. 1976. "English Open Fields as Behavior Towards Risk." *Research in Economic History* 1:124–170; Townsend, Robert M. 1993. *The Medieval Village Economy. Study of the Pareto Mapping in General Equilibrium Models.* Princeton, NJ: Princeton University Press.

50. Given-Wilson, C. 1991. "Wealth and Credit, Public and Private: The Earls of Arundel 1306–1397." *The English Historical Review* 418:1–26.

51. Brewer, John. 1989. *The Sinews of Power: War, Money and the English State, 1688–1783*. New York: Alfred A. Knopf; Carruthers, Bruce G. 1996. *City of Capital: Politics and Markets in the English Financial Revolution*. Princeton, NJ: Princeton University Press.

52. Ehrenberg, Richard. 1928. *Capital and Finance in the Age of the Renaissance: A Study of the Fuggers and Their Connections*. New York: Harcourt, Brace; Flynn, John T. 1941. *Men of Wealth: The Story of Twelve Significant Fortunes from the Renaissance to the Present Day*. New York: Simon and Schuster.

53. Goody, Jack. 1976. *Production and Reproduction: A Comparative Study of the Domestic Domain*. Cambridge: Cambridge University Press, 14–25.

54. Stone, Linda. 1997. *Kinship and Gender: An Introduction*. Boulder, CO: Westview Press, 229–234.

55. Woodruff, William. 1966. *The Impact of Western Man*. London: Macmillan.

56. Bodley, John H. 2008. *Anthropology and Contemporary Human Problems*. 5th ed. Lanham, MD: AltaMira Press, 95–98.

57. Bodley, John II. *Anthropology and Contemporary Human Problems*. 3rd ed. Mountain View, CA: Mayfield, 65.

58. Odum, Howard T. 1971. *Environment, Power, and Society*. New York: Wiley Inter-Science, 17.

59. Ashton, T. S. 1969. *The Industrial Revolution 1760–1830*. London: Oxford University Press.

60. Ashton. 1969. *The Industrial Revolution*, 7.

61. Clow, Archibald, and Nan L. Clow. 1952. *The Chemical Revolution: A Contribution to Social Technology*. London: The Batchworth Press.

62. Atkins, Peter. 2003. *Atkins' Molecules*. 2nd ed. Cambridge: Cambridge University Press.

63. Ashton, *The Industrial Revolution*, 20.

64. Rabb, Theodore K. 1967. *Enterprise and Empire: Merchant and Gentry Investment in the Expansion of England, 1575–1630*. Cambridge, MA: Harvard University Press.

65. Mintz, Sidney W. 1985. *Sweetness and Power: The Place of Sugar in Modern History*. New York: Viking Press/ Penguin Books.

66. King, Gregory. 1936. *Two Tracts*. Edited by Jacob H. Hollander (original edition 1696). Baltimore: The Johns Hopkins Press.

67. Colquhoun, Patrick. 1815. *A Treatise on the Wealth, Power, and Resources of the British Empire*. London: Joseph Mawman.

68. Hancock, David. 1995. *Citizens of the World: London Merchants and the Integration of the British Atlantic Community, 1735–1785*. Cambridge: Cambridge University Press.

69. Popkin, Barry M. 1998. "The Nutrition Transition and Its Health Implications in Lower-Income Countries." *Public Health Nutrition* 1(1): 5–21; WHO, World Health Organization. 2003. *Diet, Nutrition and the Prevention of Chronic Diseases*. Report of a Joint WHO/FAO Expert Consultation. WHO Technical Report Series 916. Geneva: WHO.

70. Mintz, Sidney W. 1985. *Sweetness and Power*.

71. Mintz, Sidney W. 1985. *Sweetness and Power*.

72. Smith, Adam. 1776. *An Inquiry into the Nature and Causes of the Wealth of Nations*, vol. 1. London: Strahan and Cadell., Book One, Chapter 8.

73. Smith, Adam. 1776. *Wealth of Nations*, book 1, Chapter 8.

74. Earle, Peter. 1989. *The Making of the English Middle Class: Business, Society and Family Life in London 1660–1730*. Berkeley and Los Angeles: University of California Press.

75. Lindert, Peter H., and Jeffrey G. Williamson. 1982. "Revising England's Social Tables 1688-1812." *Explorations in Economic History* 19:385–408; Lindert, Peter H., and Jeffrey G. Williamson. 1983. "Reinterpreting Britain's Social Tables, 1688–1913." *Explorations in Economic History* 20:94–109.

76. Komlos, John. 1998. "Shrinking in a Growing Economy? The Mystery of Physical Stature during the Industrial Revolution." *The Journal of Economic History* 58(3):779–802.

77. Chadwick, Sir Edwin. 1842. *Report . . . on an Inquiry Into the Sanitary Conditions of the Labouring Population of Great Britain*. London: W. Clowes and Sons.

78. Noble, David F. 1993. *Progress without People: In Defense of Luddism*. Chicago: Keen.

79. Dickens, Charles. (1852–1853) 1953. *Bleak House*. Garden City, NY: The Literary Guild of America.

80. Mayhew, Henry, 1861–62. *London Labour and the London Poor*. 4 vols. London: Griffin, Bohn. (Reprinted 1968. New York: Dover.)

81. Booth, Charles. 1892–1903. *Life and Labour of the People in London*. London and New York: Macmillan.

82. Bateman, John. 1883. *The Great Landowners of Great Britain and Ireland*. 4th ed. London: Harrison.

83. Mayhew, Henry, 1861–62. *London Labour and the London Poor*. 4 vols. London: Griffin, Bohn. (Reprinted 1968. New York: Dover), vol. 2, p. 155.

84. Mayhew, 1861–62. *London Poor*, vol. 1, p. 39.

85. Engels, Friedrich. 1973. *The Condition of the Working Class in England*. Moscow: Progress.

86. Marx, Karl, and Friedrich Engels. 1967. *The Communist Manifesto*. London: Penguin Books.

87. Clark, Grover. 1936. *The Balance Sheets of Imperialism: Facts and Figures on Colonies*. New York: Columbia University Press.

88. Dickson, P. G. M. 1967. *The Financial Revolution in England: A Study in the Development of Public Credit 1685–1756*. London: Macmillan.

89. Colquhoun, Patrick. 1815. *A Treatise on the Wealth, Power, and Resources of the British Empire*.

90. Clark, Grover. 1936. *The Balance Sheets of Imperialism.*

91. Davis, Lance E., and Robert A. Huttenback. 1986. *Mammon and the Pursuit of Empire: the Political Economy of British Imperialism, 1860–1912.* Cambridge: Cambridge University Press.

92. Cain, P. J., and A. G. Hopkins. 1993. *British Imperialism: Innovation and Expansion 1688–1914.* London Longman, 290.

93. Rubinstein, W. D. 1981. *Men of Property: The Very Wealthy in Britain Since the Industrial Revolution.* New Brunswick, NJ: Rutgers University Press, 41–44.

94. Davis, Mike. 2001. *Late Victorian Holocausts: El Niño Famines and the Making of the Third World.* London and New York: Verso.

95. Polanyi, Karl. 1944. *The Great Transformation.* Boston, 159–60.

96. There are three books in Hardt and Negri's Empire series: Hardt, Michael, and Antonio Negri. 2000. *Empire.* Cambridge: Harvard University Press; 2004. *Multitude: War and Democracy in the Age of Empire.* New York: Penguin Books; and 2009. *Commonwealth.* Cambridge, MA: Belknap Press, Harvard University Press.

97. Hardt and Negri. 2000:309–14.

98. Marcuse, Herbert. 1964. *One-Dimensional Man: Studies in the Ideology of Advanced Industrial Society.* Boston: Beacon Press.

99. Domhoff, G. William. 1990. *The Power Elite and the State.* New York: Aldine de Gruyter, 113–44.

100. Shoup, Laurence H., and William Minter. 1980. "Shaping a New World Order: The Council on Foreign Relations' Blueprint for World Hegemony." In *Trilateralism: The Trilateral Commission and Elite Planning for World Management,* edited by Holly Sklar, pp. 135–56. Boston: South End Press.

101. International Monetary Fund (IMF), website. www.imf.org/external/np/sec/memdir/members.htm.

102. Phillips, Kevin. 1994. *Arrogant Capital: Washington, Wall Street, and the Frustration of American Politics.* Boston: Little, Brown.

103. Barnet, Richard J., and John Cavanagh. 1994. *Global Dreams: Imperial Corporations and the New World Order.* New York: Simon and Schuster.

104. *Fortune* magazine. 2009. *Global 500.* (July 20, 2008). http://money.cnn.com/magazines/fortune/global500/2009/full_list/; International Monetary Fund (IMF). 2009. *World Economic Outlook Database October 2009.* www.imf.org/external/ns/cs.aspx?id=28 (accessed Feb. 2010). Global GDP in current U.S. dollars of $57.2 trillion estimated for 2009, exchange rate dollars.

105. Bureau van Dijk. *Orbis: A World of Company Information.* www.bvdep.com/en/ORBIS.html (accessed Dec. 2009).

106. Royal Dutch Shell, Annual Report 2009. www.shell.com/home/content/investor/financial_information/annual_reports/2006/dir_2006_annualreport.html.

107. Sassen, Saskia. 1991. *The Global City: New York, London, Tokyo.* Princeton, NJ: Princeton University Press.

108. Castells, Manuel. 1989. *The Informational City: Information Technology, Economic Restructuring, and the Urban-Regional Process.* Oxford: Blackwell; Castells, Manuel. 2000. *The Rise of the Network Society: The Information Age: Economy, Society and Culture,* vol. 1, 2nd ed. Oxford: Blackwell; Arsenault, Amelia H. H. and Manuel Castells. 2008. "The Structure and Dynamics of Global Multi-Media Business Networks." *International Journal of Communication* 2:707–48. http://ijoc.org/ojs/index.php/ijoc/article/view/298.

109. Taylor, P. J., G. Catalano, and D. R. F. Walker. 2002. "Measurement of the World City Network." *Urban Studies* 39(13):2367–76; Data Set 11: Taylor, P. J. and G. Catalano. World City Network: The Basic Data. www.lboro.ac.uk/gawc/datasets/da11.html

110. Taylor, P. J., P. Ni, B. Derudder, M. Hoyler, J. Hugan, F. Lu, K. Pain, F. Witlox, X. Yang, D. Bassens, and W. Shen. 2009. "The way we were: Command-and-control centres in the global space-economy on the even of the 2008 geo-economic transition." *Environment and Planning A* 41(1):7–12.

111. Capgemini. 2008. *World Wealth Report 2008.* Capgemini, Merrill Lynch.

112. Walmart. 2003. *Annual Report, 2003.* Bentonville, AK.

113. Rogers, Alison. 1993. "Billionaires: The World's 101 Richest People." *Fortune,* June 28, pp. 36–66.

114. Kroll, Luisa, and Lea Goldman. 2003. "Billionaires: Survival of the Richest." *Forbes,* March 17, 2003.

115. Huey, John. 1993. "The World's Best Brand." *Fortune,* May 31, pp. 44–54.

116. Beach, William W., and Gareth Davis. 1998. "The Institutional Setting of Economic Growth." In 1998 *Index of Economic Freedom,* edited by Bryan T. Johnson, Kim R. Holmes, and Melanie Kirkpatrick, pp. 1–10. Washington, DC, and New York: The Heritage Foundation and Dow Jones and Co.

CHAPTER 11

The United States: An American Plutocracy

Figure 11.0. U.S. Statue of Liberty, late nineteenth century (Stoddard 1892).

LEARNING OBJECTIVES

AFTER STUDYING THIS CHAPTER YOU SHOULD BE ABLE TO DO the following:

1. Describe the distinctive features of U.S. cosmology or ideology in comparison with tribal and imperial cosmologies.
2. Distinguish between progressivist and neoconservative political ideologies in the United States and explain the shift from one to the other.
3. Evaluate the extent to which the realities of U.S. society reflect the ideals of the culture.
4. Make specific comparisons between Chinese and U.S. culture, referring to family life, economic practices, and core values.
5. Identify the distinctive, scale-related features of large business corporations and describe the role of elite decision makers in making them dominant features of U.S. culture.

6. Describe the social structure of early U.S. textile factories, explaining the distribution of costs and benefits to households.
7. Describe the social structure and physical infrastructure of U.S. factory-farming food production systems in comparison with tribal and Great Tradition systems. Analyze the human costs and benefits of these systems.
8. Evaluate the importance of material conditions, cultural symbolism, and intentional human decision making in shaping cultural patterns of consumption in the United States.
9. Evaluate the process of growth in the United States as related to the distribution of social power and human costs and benefits. Evaluate the evidence for elite direction.

Thanks to the enormous success of both its ideological and material culture, the United States is often a model for the rest of the world and is certainly an appropriate anthropological subject. For many, the United States represents the ideals of freedom, democracy, equality, and material abundance. Its size and economic power give it enormous influence; this means that even such seemingly trivial matters as the American food preference for beef can have a profound impact on peoples in distant parts of the globe. Furthermore, its economic success makes the United States a critical source of stress in the global ecosystem. In the year 2000, Americans made up less than 5 percent of the world's population but consumed nearly 25 percent of the world's commercial energy.

Attempting to understand a country as large and complex as the United States is a formidable task, one that has engaged anthropologists and other social scientists for a long time. It requires American anthropologists to ask basic questions about their own culture and its place in the world. This chapter focuses on aspects of American culture that offer the strongest contrasts with tribal cultures and the tribute-based civilizations discussed in chapters 7 through 9. In the first section, we examine the unique cosmological and ideological features of American culture, highlighting Americans' beliefs about their political system and the proper relationship between business, government, and households. A contrast will be drawn between the American emphasis on individualism and the Chinese emphasis on kinship and family, based on the perspective of a Chinese-American anthropologist. This section also examines the historical context behind America's most sacred texts—the Declaration of Independence and the Constitution. Next, we focus specifically on the commercialization process by examining the organizational and technological changes behind the evolution of business enterprise and the rise of the giant corporation in nineteenth-century America. Ethnohistorical case studies of a Pennsylvania textile mill village, twentieth-century factory farming, and the cattle industry will illustrate the impact of commercialization on various aspects of American culture. Finally, we draw on a variety of American ethnographic materials to evaluate the human risks and rewards of the growth process itself.

AMERICAN CULTURAL IDEALS VERSUS REALITY

The United States is the world's fourth-largest nation by land area, after Russia, Canada, and China. By 2002, when the United States had grown to approximately 288 million people, America ranked as the third largest national population in the world, after China and India. America is large enough to support great cultural diversity and is truly a complex culture. By the year 2000 the United States was a highly urbanized country. Approximately 80 percent of the population, 224 million people, were living in 256 metropolitan areas of 100,000 people or more. Forty-nine metropolitan areas contained a million people or more.

As an object of anthropological investigation, the United States is unique among all the cultures examined so far in the great wealth of information available. Federal, state, and local governments have continuously generated vast volumes of statistical material covering all aspects of American life. Newspapers, films, and books abound and constitute a cultural record of unprecedented detail. The challenge for cultural anthropologists is to sift and sort through the existing data to reach useful conclusions about this complex culture. The analysis that follows draws on statistical data from national, county, and city levels to offer a more precise and ethnographically realistic picture for cross-cultural comparison.

AN AMERICAN PROFILE: PATCHWORK NATION

America had the world's largest economy at $14 trillion in 2008, which was about one-fourth of world GDP. In 2007 the United States was responsible for about 20 percent of global carbon dioxide emissions from energy consumption, reflecting its consumption of 21 percent of the world's primary energy.[1] America also dominated global market capitalization and had the world's largest corporations, the largest military expenditures, and the largest number of the world's billionaires, but it ranked only thirteenth on the United Nations Human Development Index in 2009 and was only nineteenth best on the 2009 Failed State Index, which placed it in the "needs watching" category.

Beneath the global statistical comparisons, the United States is an extremely diverse nation. The diversity of American communities helps explain why it has become difficult to find a national consensus, particularly in times of economic crises. America is so diverse that it has been called a "Patchwork Nation" in a recent analysis.[2] To understand voter behavior, political scientist James G. Gimbel found that it was useful to sort America's 3,142 counties into just twelve categories based on a series of social and economic characteristics. The twelve national "patches" in descending order by population size were labeled Monied Burbs; Boom Towns; Industrial Metropolis; Service Worker Centers; Immigration Nation; Evangelical Epicenters; Minority Central; Campus and Careers; Emptying Nests; Military Bastions; Tractor Country; and Mormon Outposts. Each of these patches seems to represent a community of people who share enough of the same values, culture, and experiences that they are likely to vote in predictable ways.

The largest patch by population was the Monied Burb counties, which counted nearly 69 million people in 2006, approximately 23 percent of the population. They were scattered across the country but most densely represented in the urban northeast and California. Monied Burbs had median household incomes of $51,234 and highly educated people with little cultural diversity, and they tended to vote Democratic. Boom Towns were scattered throughout the country and covered about 20 percent of the population, with fast-growing economies that were severely impacted by the downturn spawned by the financial crisis. Boom Town populations grew twice as fast as the national average between 1996 and 2006, and they voted Republican in 2008 by a small but firm margin. The Industrial Metropolis patch consisted of higher-than-average-income, dense urban centers that tended to vote Democratic. Collectively Monied Burbs, Boom Towns, and Industrial Metropolises were 60 percent of the population. Most people in these community types were likely to share an interest in economic growth but were politically diverse. People living in Evangelical Epicenters and Mormon Outposts might have a political consensus on several very contentious cultural issues, yet together they constitute only just over 5 percent of the population.

Utopian Capitalism: An American Cosmology

Looking beyond the obvious cultural diversity of America, it is possible to identify a common cosmology that characterizes what most Americans believe about their culture. Americans may be political liberals or conservatives, Catholic or Protestant or Jewish. But a consistent cosmology crosscuts these differences and reveals a dominant worldview that is remarkably different from the worldviews found in both tribal cultures and the ancient agrarian civilizations we examined in earlier chapters. The most striking contrast is that in American culture, the economy is supreme, and all things are considered to be commodities to be regulated by the free market. There are three sectors to this economy: (1) business enterprises (the primary employers of labor and capital and the producers of products); (2) government (which taxes, spends, issues, and borrows money); and (3) individual households (which supply labor, own money, invest, and consume products).

The emphasis that Americans place on economic growth, and their belief that the world is defined by material scarcity, reflects the broader European cosmology discussed in chapter 10. But this worldview is combined with the contradictory belief that production and consumption must forever expand. This conceptualization of the world is cross-culturally unusual, and it leaves isolated households remarkably vulnerable to autonomous economic forces that are assumed to be beyond the control of individuals. Most Americans believe in the supernatural, but specific religious beliefs are overshadowed by the overarching European belief that the economy is a physical thing that must grow to ensure everyone's well-being. Business corporations have an important place in the American cosmology, but except for the very wealthiest families, there are no corporate kinship groups, and the isolated nuclear family replaces the extended family that is so prominent in noncommercial cultures. In comparison with Australian aboriginal and Amazonian cultures, the position of nature in the American cosmology is remarkable. Americans view nature as a part of the environment, which is separate from and often in conflict with humanity and the economy.

The autonomous market is believed to produce the culture as a whole, and as the driving force behind the economy, it has the same hallowed status. Like the economy, the market is conceived of as an entity quite apart from any physical marketplace, and a free market is assumed to work to benefit humans and society at large, as Adam Smith imagined. Although many Americans realize that particular markets may be dominated by giant corporations or controlled by government regulations, in many people's minds the market is equated with consumer demand and is thus thought to represent what people want as expressed by what they choose to buy. Americans assume that markets are natural, and they make them the mysterious arbiters of societal well-being that call into being such diverse products as wholesome food, cars, cigarettes, and land mines.

Americans believe that their cultural universe is both unique and superior, because it is thought to maximize personal liberty and economic freedom. This is America's great strength. In this system of Utopian capitalism, prosperity will be assured as long as individuals are free to buy and sell and to create and produce goods for the "free market." The self-serving actions of free people will produce continuous economic growth and material progress, which will ultimately benefit everyone. Many believe that the only threats to this system are government interference with the free market, restrictions on individual liberty and private property rights, and reductions in individual incentive for economic activity through rewarding undeserving people with unearned material benefits. This grand view of the structure of American society and the functioning of the "free enterprise" system was clearly described by Dwight Eisenhower, who served as president from 1952 to 1960 during a period of especially rapid economic growth:

> The economy of the American people has served this nation faithfully and well. . . . It has afforded not only material comfort, but the resources to provide a challenging life of the mind and of the spirit. . . . Our economy has grown strong because our people have made jobs for each other and have not relied on the government to try to do it for them. Our economy is the result of millions of decisions we all make every day about producing, earning, saving, investing and

spending. Both our individual prosperity, and our nation's prosperity, rest directly on the decisions all of us are making.[3]

In his 2002 National Security Strategy President George W. Bush called American political and economic freedom universal human values. President Bush made extending these values of freedom to the world America's "great mission" that justified an expansive American foreign policy, declaring: "These values of freedom are right and true for every person, in every society—and the duty of protecting these values against their enemies is the common calling of freedom loving people across the globe and across the ages. . . . Freedom is the non-negotiable demand of human dignity; the birthright of every person—in every civilization."[4]

In line with this emphasis on liberty and freedom is the belief that there is no hereditary aristocracy in America and that social class is unimportant, because everyone can rise to any economic level by their own intelligence, hard work, and creative energy. Public education makes prosperity available to everyone who truly wants to succeed. In this respect, wealth is an indirect measure of an individual's personal worth, and poverty indicates personal failure or irresponsibility. American society and culture are thought to reflect the interests of a broad middle class, whose members direct the economy and democratically elect the government. The economy itself is believed to be created and directed by the independent action of individual decision makers who make rational economic choices, freely choosing to buy or not buy commercial products that appear on the market. The ultimate measure of well-being in American culture is the rate of economic growth—this is the single concern that unites political conservatives, liberals, and radicals. Americans believe that only growth will create employment opportunities and make it possible for everyone to raise their standard of living.

Americans conceptually divide their society into two broad sectors: (1) the public sector, composed of the government, and (2) the private sector, composed of individuals and business corporations. The government is expected to provide military defense, public education, and highways and to enforce contracts and protect private property; the government also promotes economic growth by following optimum monetary, tax, and spending policies. Business corporations provide jobs, products, and profits that benefit everyone, and they are owned by everyone (in the form of stock market shares) in a "people's capitalism." Individuals are employees and consumers. The entire system functions properly as long as government does not become too large and does not interfere with the freedom of business, and as long as individuals take full responsibility for their lives. Americans generally believe themselves to be free of racial, ethnic, or religious prejudices, assuming that distinctions between people of all nationalities will tend to disappear in the American "melting pot."

Throughout much of the twentieth century the prevailing American political ideology was "progressivism." Elites who followed progressive ideology designed the United Nations and related institutions as discussed in chapter 10. Domestically, progressivists believed that government should build public infrastructure and promote public education and social welfare programs to benefit society at large. They also thought that government should intervene in the economy to keep employment high, keep wages and prices in balance, and promote economic growth. Progressivists sought a just alliance between workers and capitalists and favored the formation of labor unions to counterbalance the power of large corporations. This was called a demand-side economic policy, because it sought higher wages for workers and redistributed tax revenues downward to households so that people could buy industrial products. The progressivist approach is well represented in the works of economists John Maynard Keynes[5] and John Kenneth Galbraith.[6] It produced a rise in the proportion of national income received by the American middle class that peaked in 1960 and a related decline in the proportion received by the top 20 percent of households.

A change away from progressivist ideology began when America's economic elite became alarmed by a "crisis of capitalism" that occurred in the late 1960s and throughout the 1970s. This was a series of social and economic crises that included the Vietnam War, the youth counterculture, the peace movement, labor unrest, and social movements for civil rights, consumer rights, and environmental protection. All of this coincided with government scandals such as the Pentagon Papers in 1971 and Watergate in 1972–73, the American withdrawal from Vietnam in 1973, a slowing of economic growth, increased inflation, stagnant stock prices, and a decline in corporate profits. All of these problems were related to a sudden massive increase in oil prices by the Organization of Petroleum Exporting Countries, the international oil cartel. The American elite responded by shifting toward a more conservative political ideology. Policy now emphasized "supply-side economics," or increasing production rather than consumer purchasing power, and federal revenues shifted toward corporations and large private investors, even as government regulation of commerce was reduced. This meant the ascendency of "New Growth" economic theory referred to in chapter 10 and is often identified with the writings of economists Friedrich A. Hayek[7] and Milton Friedman.[8] Since the 1990s this approach has been called political neoconservatism and neoliberal, "free market" economics and has been used to promote economic globalization. Corporate directors began moving manufacturing production to cheaper, more manageable labor overseas, and they invested heavily in computerization. All of these changes shifted wealth and income away from the lower and middle classes to the highest ranks of society.[9]

Cosmologies are cultural constructions that may not accurately reflect the practical realities in particular societies. The existence of factional disagreements in America over the proper balance of power between business and government suggests that the harmony implied in America's basic cosmology may not always exist. American beliefs about wealth and power are ambiguous, because wealth is highly desired but the wealthy are both envied and distrusted. America is believed to be a democracy in which everyone has an equal vote, but wealth inequality obviously gives some people more economic power than others, and this can become political power. The degree to which American cosmology corresponds with historical and ethnographic reality will be explored in the following sections.

America from a Chinese Perspective

Chinese anthropologist Francis Hsu grew up in China and lived for many years in the United States and analyzed its culture. Hsu is a psychological anthropologist, interested in socialization, values, and personality. His deep familiarity with both Chinese and American culture allows him to make very insightful comparisons between the two cultures and provides an effective balance to the materialist bias of many American anthropologists. Hsu[10]argues that many of the key differences in economic life and class structure between Chinese and American culture can be attributed to what he considers to be the American core value of individual self-reliance versus the Chinese pattern of family dependence and filial piety. The emphasis that Americans place on self-reliance

is represented by the ideal of the rugged individualist and a corresponding fear of dependence. For example, American children are socialized to value privacy, independence, and self-expression, and American parents are not supposed to interfere in the domestic lives of their adult children.

The Chinese emphasis on kinship and continuity of patrilineage highlights the virtues of dependency. Chinese children are socialized within families that include at least three generations and in-laws. They are cared for by a variety of elders. There is little individual privacy within a Chinese household, but individuals are always surrounded by many people who can be called on for physical and emotional support. There is little cultural incentive for an individual to pursue perpetual economic profit. An individual's primary responsibility is to parents and extended family, not self. Indeed, it is a source of pride for an aging Chinese parent to be taken care of by a child. By contrast, in the United States one is expected to make it alone, and accepting economic aid from one's children might even be considered embarrassing.

Realistically, humans do depend on other people for many of their needs, and according to Hsu, culturally denying such dependence can generate psychological problems. Hsu maintains that the American ideal of self-reliance is likely to create emotional insecurity, which helps explain other seemingly contradictory American characteristics, such as racial and religious intolerance coexisting with an expressed belief in equality. Hsu suggests that personal insecurity drives Americans to accumulate material wealth to compensate and to demonstrate their self-worth. This not only makes Americans enormously competitive and intolerant of others but also serves the imperatives of a growth-centered capitalist economy. In contrast, the Chinese plow their earnings into family ceremonies, such as funerals, birthdays, and ancestor shrines, confident that they will be taken care of by their descendants.

The realities of American life pose some problems for Hsu's theory of self-reliance as a core value. The poorest classes in the United States likely survive by sharing with kin. Furthermore, the importance of inherited wealth and the existence of economically based kinship groups among the American elite suggests that extended-family dependency relations can be compatible with capitalist accumulation.

The role that Hsu ascribes to the American value of self-reliance fits well with the view that commercialization and profit making are the dominant cultural processes in commercially organized cultures. Chinese civilization was created by a politicization process that does not require perpetual economic expansion. In support of this interpretation, Hsu observes that the small wealthy class in preindustrial China was composed of government bureaucrats, not merchants, and modern China was very slow to industrialize until recently. He also notes that most large Chinese cities are political capitals, whereas most large U.S. cities are commercial centers. American acquisitiveness generated economic growth and a relatively large middle class. This is not to argue that American values in themselves shaped the rest of American culture, but it suggests that values and personality are functionally connected to other economic and social variables.

A Mythic Framework: Founders and Sacred Texts

America's cosmology is supported by a mythic history and by the functional equivalent of sacred texts in the form of the Declaration of Independence, the Constitution, and the written commentary in the Federalist Papers, all produced by the "Founding Fathers." The fifty-six men who signed the Declaration of Independence appealed directly to natural law with their lofty affirmation: "We hold these Truths to be self-evident, that all Men are created equal, that they are endowed by their Creator with certain unalienable Rights, that among these are Life, Liberty, and the Pursuit of Happiness."

The Constitution, the legal framework for the federal government of the United States, was drafted in 1787 in the name of "We, the People." The purpose of the new government was to "establish Justice, insure domestic Tranquility, provide for the common defence, promote the general Welfare, and secure the Blessings of Liberty to ourselves and our Posterity."

Many popular beliefs about America's founding are contradicted by the historical record.[11] The sentiments of the patriots of 1776 could have produced a loose federation of small-scale agrarian nations with high levels of local autonomy and individual freedom. There was no popular consensus that economic growth through the development of manufacturing and finance capital was a desirable goal or that a strong federal government was needed to protect business enterprise. On the contrary, many, including Thomas Jefferson, third U.S. president and author of the Declaration of Independence, and James Madison, fourth president and often called the Father of the Constitution, feared that unregulated commercial growth and subsequent wealth inequality would undermine democracy.

Those favoring a strong federal government did so for several reasons. Alexander Hamilton, first secretary of the treasury, wanted a strong banking and tariff system to promote industrialization and a powerful navy to protect international commerce. The Federalist argument that a strong federal government was needed to protect business and promote growth was the opposite of New Growth neoliberal theory that identifies "big government" with growth-dampening regulations that would inhibit the "free market." However, protectionism made sense for those in the newly independent country who wanted to promote U.S. industrialization.

The Founding Fathers were idealistic statesmen, but the Constitution was not approved by popular vote. Historians have concluded that perhaps only 160,000 people, about 5 percent of the population, selected the delegates who attended the constitutional conventions in the various states, which in turn ratified the Constitution. Only free adult males could vote, and some states required them to be property holders or to have certain levels of wealth. Historian Charles Beard[12] maintained that the Constitution was an economic document, drafted and promoted by a small, consolidated group interested in protecting their personal, national-, and even international-level economic interests. The fifty-five men who drafted the Constitution were large landholders, merchants, and professionals, not poor farmers (see box 11.1). More than half held government securities, nineteen were slave owners, and ten held bank shares. Although their personal economic interests often conflicted, they were all relatively wealthy men with significant economic power, and the document they produced did favor economic growth.

The Founding Fathers made a clear distinction between worthy, property-holding citizens and the property-less. Property-less people were considered to be too dependent to be informed citizens, and thus were assumed to be unfit to hold office or to vote. The founders feared that popular democracy might lead to social disorder if an "overbearing majority" gained power and sought wealth redistribution. As a result, the Senate was designed as a "natural aristocracy" to balance the potential excesses of the more democratic House of Representatives. In the view of some historians, the social ideology of the Federalists who assumed power in 1787 was not radically different from the elitist beliefs of the older European landed and wealthy aristocracy. Only the inherited titles were absent in America. However, the Constitution is an evolving, dynamic charter, and it produced an intricately balanced political system that can represent the democratic wishes of all the people.

The U.S. Constitution is a radical document. It expanded on the ideological transformations produced by the English Revolution of 1688 overturning belief in the "Divine Right of Kings" to rule, which had supported absolute monarchs throughout the imperial world for millennia. The idea that governments were established by "the people" to meet their needs was radical, but even more radical were the American ideals of human freedom as defined in the Bill of Rights adopted in 1791 to guarantee individual freedom of religion, speech, and press, and various other civil rights. The idea that individuals were entitled to equality of opportunity was also a radical break with the fundamentals of the precommercial imperial world.

BOX 11.1. ROBERT MORRIS: PRINCE OF MERCHANTS, PATRIOT FINANCIER

A brief ethnographic sketch of the personal business interests of Robert Morris (1734–1806), considered the most prominent and powerful merchant and financier of the time, illustrates the extent of individual commercial power in preindustrial America and demonstrates how closely commercial power was linked with political power. This case study strongly suggests that commercial elites created America's political structure. Robert Morris was a politically active Philadelphia merchant, signer of the Declaration of Independence, and member of the Continental Congress, who handled the financial aspects of the Revolutionary War and the Continental Congress, helped draft the Constitution, and served on the Pennsylvania legislature and in the U.S. Senate. He was variously described by his contemporaries as a prince of merchants, patriot financier, and great man. He is still revered as a Founding Father, and his personal power certainly helped determine the course of cultural development in America.

Morris's economic interests were remarkably diverse and included manufacturing, shipping, and banking and finance; speculation in commodities, currency, land, and government securities; and trade with England, France, the West Indies, and India.[13] Morris personally financed strategic troop movements during the Revolution, organized and was the largest shareholder in the original Bank of North America in Philadelphia, and organized and financed the first American trade expeditions to China. The key to his profit making was arbitrage, buying low in one market and selling high in another market. He

also secured handsome commissions from brokering large government transactions, such as when he helped the French provision their American military expeditionary forces during the Revolution. He was an important member of nine major business partnerships and maintained numerous short-term partnerships, including business connections with at least five other delegates to the 1787 Constitutional Convention. For a time he owned millions of acres of undeveloped western land that was still controlled by Native Americans, and he brokered land purchases for European investors. He attempted to gain a monopoly over the tobacco trade with Europe, and he quickly bought up speculative property in Washington, DC, as soon as the site was selected for the new national capital.

Politically, Morris was closely aligned with Alexander Hamilton and other prominent Federalists who favored a strong federal government. He was a firm believer in free trade, maintaining that commerce should be "free as air to place it in the most advantageous state to mankind." Like Adam Smith, Morris praised the invisible hand, and he could imagine no conflict between his public and private life. Speaking of American entrepreneurs in general, he said, "Their own interest and the publick [sic] good goes hand in hand and they need no other prompter or tutor."[14] However, he felt that only entrepreneurs themselves could be arbiters of the public good, and only they could define the proper balance of power between public and private. Morris's commercial vision certainly shaped America at a crucial moment in its history, but reckless speculation drove him into personal bankruptcy, and he was sent to debtors' prison in 1798, where he remained for three and a half years.

THE CONSTRUCTION OF CORPORATE AMERICA

The Founding Fathers on the Business of Politics

America is too large and too unequal to be a pure democracy. Instead, it is a representative democracy with officeholders elected by political subdivisions. American politics is largely a struggle between diverse commercial-interest groups competing against one another to obtain favorable government policies. The competition is played out through national-level political parties. The Founding Fathers explicitly understood many of the economic conflicts inherent in a large-scale, commercially organized culture. The Constitution set the ground rules for an ongoing political struggle but could not resolve the underlying social conflicts because it ignored the reality of social class.

Madison enumerated "a landed interest, a manufacturing interest, a mercantile interest, a moneyed interest, and many lesser interests," but not a household interest, as necessary features of civilized nations. Madison foresaw that it would necessarily be the business of government to protect property and legislate a balance between these unavoidably conflicting commercial interests through the operation of factions and party politics. Setting the tone for the next two centuries, Hamilton defined the primary objective of politics and government as the promotion of commerce and effectively rejected the possibility that there could be any significant class divisions in American society that would not be solved by economic growth. Anticipating the emergence of export-dependent agriculture, he argued that there was no conflict between mercantile and agrarian interests, because increased trade would benefit both.[15] He rejected political representation by social class as "visionary." He believed that artisans and laborers would prefer to give their votes to merchants as their "natural representatives," patrons, and friends, who would have more "influence and weight" in deliberative assemblies.

Madison knew that elected legislators would not be totally impartial, but he felt that pluralism, the great diversity of interests, would prevent the abuse of political power. Hamilton thought that the poorest tenants and wealthiest landlords were "perfectly united" on the issue of keeping taxes low, and thus there was no class conflict between them. He assumed that the poorest and wealthiest would have an equal chance of being elected, because voters would simply elect whomever they were most confident with. However, Hamilton correctly expected government to be composed of landholders, merchants, and lawyers.[16]

A simply binary political party system developed during the nineteenth century out of the original contrast between Jefferson's and Hamilton's visions for America. Jefferson's ideal of an agrarian nation became identified with slavery, western expansion, property rights, farmers, and labor and evolved in stages into the modern Democratic Party. Hamilton's Federalists promoted wage labor over slavery and favored industrialization, a national banking system, and large-scale capitalism; by 1854, they had evolved into the modern Republican Party. This means that historically the Democratic Party was politically conservative, and the Republican Party was liberal. The meanings have now reversed, just as the meaning of "big government" has changed from its original pro-business identification to its current anti-business image in many people's thinking.

Corporate America, 1790–1920

Twentieth-first-century America is dominated by those who own, direct, and manage a few hundred giant commercial corporations. Relative to ordinary humans, giant business corporations have the qualities of deities with superhuman form, immortality, and omnipotence. They are cultural constructions that have virtually taken the role of divine kings, but with computers adding omniscience to their powers. This may seem perfectly natural and inevitable, but nevertheless, corporate power of this scope and magnitude was a human creation and is not inevitable, and it is not the only way to organize commercial life. Corporate America was created by a handful of elites who purposefully used their political and economic power to design the legal and institutional structures to allow them to increase the scale of business organizations and amass greater amounts of wealth (see table 11.1).

Table 11.1. Stages in the Construction of Corporate America, 1790–1990

Date	Development	Characteristics
1790–1850	Traditional business firms	Generalized mercantile partnerships Single-unit enterprises
1850–1900	Transportation, communication, and fuel revolutions	Multiunit enterprises Executive hierarchies Railroad empires
1850–1890	The Production and Distribution Revolution	High-volume throughput Vertically integrated production Emergence of wholesalers and mass market retailers
1880–1917	Modern industrial corporations	Vertical integration of mass production and mass marketing Multidivision, multinational enterprises, Oligopolies, and Monopolies
1960–present	Conglomerates	Corporate mergers in unrelated industries

Source: Based on Chandler (1977).

They simultaneously constructed a national society and national-scale markets. This corporatization process disempowered millions of small farmers and merchants living in small towns and villages and totally changed their daily lives, even though they resisted vigorously.

In 1790, perhaps fewer than 2,000 people (approximately the top 0.5 percent of households) were wealthy enough to dominate the fledgling commercial economy and significantly influence political decisions and major cultural developments. America's leaders chose maximum growth by combining Jefferson's vision of agrarian expansion with Hamilton's commercial industrialization approach. This was the best way for the wealthiest to expand their wealth, but it also opened new opportunities for European immigrants who were denied all hope of improving their living standards by hereditary aristocracies in their homelands.

After 1787, America's new political economy especially favored increased commercial activity. Over the next century, the nation's territory was tripled by a policy of military conquest that reduced the population of Native Americans by 95 percent. The U.S. Navy protected American shipping. The rural poor and impoverished European immigrants offered a steady labor force. Under these conditions, it suddenly became enormously rewarding for elites to develop new methods of production and new technology to speed the flow of goods. It would be deceptively easy to attribute corporatization to the seemingly natural and inevitable effects of new technology. However, the steamships, railroads, and factory production systems that sustained large-scale business corporations were as much social organizational changes as technological changes.[17] They were called into being and effectively owned and controlled by a few people. An equally plausible but different form of ownership and control would have produced a very different human outcome. Corporations, as designed by wealthy investors, were given the unique form of "socialized property."[18] The vast scale of corporations and the minute division of ownership among thousands and even millions of small owners allowed the corporate elite to concentrate power and socialize the costs. That means that they amassed the primary benefits and others paid the costs. When ownership is widely dispersed, the few beneficial owners of a large corporation, those owning 5 percent or more of the shares, can dominate the board of directors, control the company, and receive a disproportionate share of the profits. The more-

numerous small owners and society at large share the risks but do not hold enough power individually to enjoy significant benefits. The multitude of owners and workers are also so dispersed and diversified that they would have difficulty organizing to press their interests. Large owners can further socialize costs by using their political power to gain public subsidies for their businesses, even as they are insulated from catastrophic failures that can wipe out lower-level managers, employees, and small shareholders.

The corporatization process unfolded quickly from 1810 to 1850 under the direction of a handful of merchants, investors, and intellectuals, based primarily in New England and the Northeast, who created a national American commercial culture.[19] They designed and directed a small number of elite colleges that trained the leaders, who in turn created and ran the public schools and colleges, trusts and endowments, charities, banks, insurance companies, and factories that transformed America from a rural agrarian to a national commercial society organized by giant corporations.

How few were involved in this process is illustrated by twelve investors, the Boston Associates, who initiated the factory system of textile production in America in 1813.[20] By 1845, a network of just seventy-seven associates controlled $12 million in capital and held nine companies, with factories, dormitories, towns, waterworks, real estate investments, banks, and railroads. One associate had interests in twelve companies, a railroad, two banks, and an insurance company. Another prominent entrepreneur, John Jacob Astor (1763–1848), became America's first millionaire business tycoon by using his political influence to build a personal empire in the western fur trade, New York real estate development, and trade with China. By 1845 there were 715 super-elite individuals in the country holding $100,000 or more in property in Boston, Brooklyn, New York, and Philadelphia. They used their wealth and influence to make themselves the primary human agents of culture change in America.[21]

As it developed, corporatization depended on permissive federal and state legislation and was supported by court decisions friendly to big business. For example, in 1819 U.S. Supreme Court justice John Marshall ruled that business corporations could make contracts, own property, extend charters indefinitely, and bring suit in federal court. This made corporate business a new form of private property. Many pro-big-business jurists and chief justices were trained by

Chief Justice Joseph Story and associates at Harvard Law School from 1829 to 1845, which was supported from 1805 to 1846 by just twenty-nine wealthy donors.[22] By the 1880s large corporations were winning court challenges to state laws that restricted access to local markets to protect small businesses.[23] This allowed retail chain stores and door-to-door salesmen for national manufacturers to overpower local producers and merchants. Giant meat processors could then ship meat throughout the country, overruling local and state health laws. This created a national-scale market for beef. In 1886 the Supreme Court made corporations "legal individuals" with rights of "due process" and "equal protection" under the Fourteenth Amendment, giving corporations rights to own other corporations. Later court decisions even gave corporations rights of "free speech," even though their legal omnipotence gives them vastly greater powers and a much louder voice than ordinary citizens.

Railroads were the key to the scale increases in commerce. Demand from national and international investors for railroad securities contributed to the rise of powerful New York investment banks and brokerage houses. As railroads became complex systems, operational problems were solved when their top managers created a hierarchy of middle managers and lower-level supervisors. This required all the features of a modern business corporation, including organizational charts, formal titles, job descriptions, lines of authority, regular written reports, performance evaluations, and new accounting procedures. By the 1850s, the largest railroads were already being consolidated into the first giant holding companies—corporations that owned other corporations—by a few superwealthy stock speculators seeking to limit competition. American railroads soon became the largest business enterprises in the world. For example, in the 1890s, the Pennsylvania Railroad employed 110,000 workers, nearly three times the size of the U.S. military, and it took in more than a third of the revenue of the federal government.[24]

Mass production of consumer goods is relatively easy, as long as energy and raw materials can be secured. The problem for commercial elites was how to promote mass distribution and consumption of their products. They created the first advertising agencies in the 1850s, and by the 1880s advertising was being used to market mass-produced consumer goods such as cigarettes and breakfast foods. Brands, patents, and trademarks soon became crucial new forms of property, used to control production and distribution in the national market and to create customer loyalty for particular corporations. Early in the twentieth century new advertising campaigns were designed to persuade people of the moral legitimacy of giant corporations. For example, in the 1920s Bruce Barton's campaign on behalf of General Motors portrayed the company as one big family and the country as its neighborhood. In effect, advertisers attempted to create the corporate soul, just as the courts created the corporate body.[25]

By the 1880s, giant, vertically integrated, multifunctional, multiunit, and often multinational business enterprises, controlled by a managerial class of corporate executives, dominated the American economy. These corporate giants created **oligopolies**, which allowed commercial bureaucrats to coordinate production and distribution decisions, effectively replacing the invisible hand of the market.[26] The objective was to increase the volume, speed, and efficiency of commercial transactions to reduce costs and generate a higher return on investments or to reduce competition by controlling markets. Large-scale business enterprises succeeded because they brought many formerly competing enterprises within a single organizational structure, thereby internalizing their diverse production, buying, and selling decisions within a single management hierarchy. Administrative coordination was the key. These institutional changes increased productivity and profits, because top managers could allocate resources more efficiently than could the managers of smaller firms competing in a decentralized marketplace with imperfect supply-and-demand information. The greatest transformation of corporate America occurred between 1898 and 1905, when the volume of the stock market suddenly expanded from tens of millions to billions of dollars.[27]

Rockdale: An American Industrial Village, 1825–1865

Anthropologist Anthony F. C. Wallace[28] produced a remarkable historical ethnography of the small textile-producing community of Rockdale in southeastern Pennsylvania during the four decades from 1825 to 1865. He spent eight years poring over public records, newspapers, biographies, letters, and memorabilia to construct a richly detailed picture of the people of Rockdale. His study illuminates the difficult human problems that the new machine technology and the factory system produced as it developed under early American industrial capitalism. In the 1820s, capitalist manufacturers intent on establishing new textile mills began buying up small, abandoned flour, paper, and lumber mills in the Rockdale district, southwest of Philadelphia. Their enterprises benefited from the federal government's policy of placing high tariffs on imported goods, rather than taxing domestic manufacturers, to encourage American manufacturing and to raise revenue. By 1850, there were 2,000 people living in 351 households in seven small hamlets along Chester Creek. Each hamlet was centered on a water-powered cotton mill, which provided the primary employment. Three local families, referred to by Wallace as Lords of the Valley, owned most of the land and mills in Rockdale and determined the overall pattern of life.

Altogether, some twelve families of manufacturers, merchants, and gentlemen farmers sat at the top of the social hierarchy, forming a tightly integrated economic class. They lived in comfortable, well-appointed, hilltop stone mansions. The men agreed on their pro-business politics; traveled regularly to Boston, New York, Washington, and nearby Philadelphia; and vacationed with their families at beach resorts. The wives and daughters of Rockdale's elite formed a close-knit sisterhood that included elites in neighboring communities. These women were well educated, well read, intellectually active, and musically and artistically accomplished. They had the leisure time to correspond and visit each other frequently, and write diaries and poetry. Beneath this elite group was a "middle-class" assortment of 150 professionals, teachers, ministers, and artisans; and beneath them were 162 mill-worker families, who lived very modestly. Workers lived in inexpensive tenements at the bottom of the hill near the mill. The low residential position of workers also reflected their low social, intellectual, and emotional standing as a depressed class in the minds of upper-class people. For example, Sophie Du Pont, a member of the nearby Du Pont industrialist family and member of Rockdale high society, expressed amazement in her diary that working-class women could be emotionally distressed by sick children. People in that "class of life" were not expected to be particularly sensitive.

The economic distance between top and bottom in the hierarchy was enormous. The minimum capital cost of a mill and its machinery was approximately $12,000 to $35,000, which was far beyond the means of all but the wealthy. A typical mill-worker family could earn about $250 a year and might bring in another $175 from boarders, for a total of $425. Basic household subsistence expenditures for food, fuel, and rent were $300, leaving $125 for clothing and all other expenses. This meant that with a stringent savings program, within a few years a healthy family might accumulate the $200 needed to move west and buy a small farm, but they could not hope to buy a textile mill. Most of the mill workers hoped their jobs would be temporary. Many of them were recent immigrants from England and Ireland, where workers were clearly not as well off.

Relations between owners and workers were generally satisfactory; however, there remained an intrinsic conflict of interest, which eventually led to an open clash. The top four mill owners determined everyone's quality of life, because they could hire and fire workers at will, set wages and hours, buy new machines that displaced workers, and determine health and safety conditions. Profits were always more important than the security and well-being of worker households. Owners hired workers as a specified number of "hands" supplied by household units. Many children, including some younger than ten, routinely worked in the factories, although they were probably better off than children in comparable British mills (see figure 11.1). The Rockdale owners considered mistreatment to be simply a poor personnel management practice, not a violation of worker rights, as mill owner John Crozier testified in 1837: "When factories were first established in this vicinity, severe whipping was often practiced, but it was found not to be the best mode of management, and has been, in a great degree, abandoned."[29]

The fourteen-hour workday ran by the bell from 5 a.m. to 7 p.m., with breaks for breakfast and dinner. The six-day workweek thus ran eighty-four hours, excluding breaks. The mills were hot and poorly ventilated, and the air was thick with cotton-fiber dust that gave workers chronic coughs. The work was so exhausting that young children sometimes fell asleep on the job. It was publicly acknowledged that factory conditions were mentally, morally, and physically unhealthy for children and less than ideal for adults. However, rather than calling for fundamental changes in the way factories were operated, religious reformers wanted the workers to improve themselves by attending Sunday school and becoming more responsible parents. The owners knew that working children did not have time for regular schooling, and many workers were illiterate. In principle, the Rockdale mill owners supported legislation that would shorten working hours and prohibit hiring workers younger than twelve. But they refused to institute such social reforms, arguing that their mills would be

Figure 11.1. "A little spinner in the Mollohan Mills, Newberry, S.C. She was tending her 'sides' like a veteran, but after I took the photo, the overseer came up and said in an apologetic tone that was pathetic, 'She just happened in.' Then a moment later he repeated the information. The mills appear to be full of youngsters that 'just happened in,' or 'are helping sister' (Dec. 3, 08. Witness Sara R. Hine. Location: Newberry, South Carolina) (U.S. National Archives and Records Administration).

economically uncompetitive unless all states had such laws. They blamed widows and lazy fathers and the absence of public assistance for child labor, not low wages. They recommended night school for working children. However, there were many female-headed households with small children in Rockdale, and many families were too poor to put their children in school. Obviously, the mills did not create a healthy social environment, but Crozier defended the economic necessity of child labor with impeccable functionalist logic, declaring: "The work of children cannot be shortened, without also abridging that of adults, as the labor of one is connected with that of the other, being part of a system, which, if broken in upon, destroys a connecting link in the chain of operations."[30]

For their part, Rockdale textile workers organized a labor union in 1836 and walked off their jobs in 1836 and again in 1842, demanding shorter hours and better pay. When the organizers were fired, strikers retaliated by destroying property. Later, some were fined

and jailed. The commercial elite quickly aligned themselves with the religious establishment to denounce labor unions as anti-Christian, un-American, and immoral. Social reform became a Christian enterprise, but it did not threaten the established capitalist order.

The Rise of Factory Farming

The industrialization of farming and the general commercialization of the food system, which was well under way in Europe and America by the mid-twentieth century, must rank as a cultural transformation as significant as the domestication of plants and animals during the Neolithic. This great change is a continuation of the broad trend toward subsistence intensification that has accompanied each increase in the scale of human culture—more food is produced at greater energy cost and ecosystem degradation. This characterization may seem counterintuitive, but the true costs of industrialization have been masked by the cultural accounting system that only emphasizes human labor and monetary cost. In an industrial culture such as the United States, farms are operated like factories. Often the emphasis is on a single crop that is mass-produced at the lowest possible monetary cost for the maximum cash return. Economic imperatives compel the farmer to use labor-saving machinery to reduce costs and to employ chemical pesticides and fertilizers to increase production.

When viewed from a long-term cultural ecological perspective, this **factory farming** raises troubling questions for the long-term viability of industrial civilization. As ecologist Howard Odum[31] observed, the factory farm replaces self-maintaining biological processes, which are fueled by renewable solar energy, with urban-based cultural processes that require vast **energy subsidies** in the form of nonrenewable fossil fuels. Factory farming simplifies natural ecosystems, making them less stable while extracting a larger energy share for human consumption. An obvious problem with this system is that it also rapidly depletes fossil fuels and soils and thus cannot be sustained indefinitely. The American sociocultural system's 85

percent dependence on fossil fuels is well illustrated by figure 11.2, which also shows that two-thirds of America's energy is from petroleum and natural gas, which are critical for food production.[32] It is astonishing to recognize that more than half of the total energy that Americans consume does not do useful work because one-fourth is wasted in electricity production and transmission and another fourth is wasted heat in the transportation system.

Because it requires relatively few farm laborers and produces very high per-acre yields, factory farming appears deceptively productive. In 1970, when viewed at the national level, each kilocalorie of American farm labor returned 210 kilocalories of food—four times the yield of intensive Chinese rice farming. However, when the full energy costs of production were calculated—including fuel, electricity, fertilizer, and farm machinery—2 kilocalories of energy were expended to produce 1 kilocalorie of food energy.[33]

Such **deficit production** is only possible when subsidized by vast inputs of solar energy stored in nonrenewable fossil fuels. Furthermore, when food

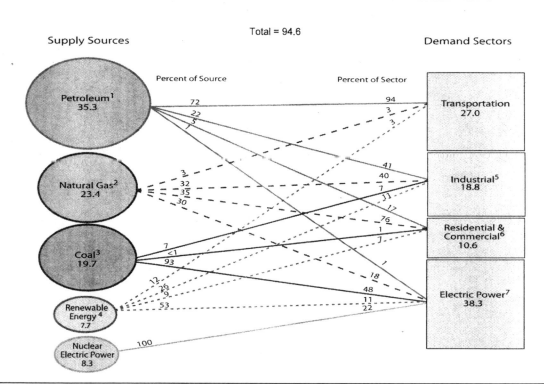

[1] Does not include biofuels that have been blended with petroleum—biofuels are included in "Renewable Energy."
[2] Excludes supplemental gaseous fuels.
[3] Includes less than 0.1 quadrillion Btu of coal coke net exports.
[4] Conventional hydroelectric power, geothermal, solar/PV, wind, and biomass.
[5] Includes industrial combined-heat-and-power (CHP) and industrial electricity-only plants.
[6] Includes commercial combined-heat-and-power (CHP) and commercial electricity-only plants.
[7] Electricity-only and combined-heat-and-power (CHP) plants whose primary business is to sell electricity, or electricity and heat, to the public.

Note: Sum of components may not equal total due to independent rounding.
Sources: U.S. Energy Information Administration, *Annual Energy Review 2009*, Tables 1.3, 2.1b-2.1f, 10.3, and 10.4.

Figure 11.2. United States primary energy flow by source and sector (quadrillion Btu), 2009 (U.S. Energy Information Administration, Annual Energy Review 2009, Figure 2.0).

Table 11.2. Energy Use in the U.S. Food System (in 1012 kcal), 1940 and 1970

	1940	1970
Farm production*	124.5	526.1
Food processing†	285.8	841.9
Distribution‡	275.2	804.0
Totals	685.5	2172.0

Source: Steinhart and Steinhart (1974).

*Farm production includes fuel, electricity, fertilizer, and irrigation and the costs of producing agricultural steel, farm machinery, and tractors.

†Processing includes production, machinery, packaging, transport fuel, and trucks and trailers.

‡Distribution includes commercial and domestic refrigeration and cooking.

production costs are calculated to include the costs of industrial processing and marketing, which necessarily precede domestic consumption in a highly urbanized society, then a minimum of 8 to 12 kilocalories were expended in the production of 1 kilocalorie of food (see table 11.2). Even this figure underestimates the actual energy costs of the American food production system because it does not include all transport costs, especially the use of private automobiles in trips to the grocery store, or the costs of advertising commercialized food products and disposing of the trash by-products. A more realistic total would probably approach 20 kilocalories expended for each 1 consumed.

U.S. farm production was not fully industrialized until fossil fuel–powered farm machinery and agricultural chemicals became widely used after 1940 (see figure 11.3). The social corollary of these technological changes was a decline in the rural population. The number of individual farms actually declined, but those that remained became much larger than before.

In America's large-scale subsistence system the food chain from farmer to consumer quickly became so complex that it drove up the price of food. Even by the 1920s there were so many steps between producer and consumer that the farmer received only 28 cents of the consumer's dollar spent on bread.[34] In 1949 a congressional committee documented the complexity of the wheat-to-bread network (see figure 11.4). They found that increased scale and complexity was accompanied by a greater concentration of economic power, as large food manufacturers and retailers bought up their suppliers and competitors and fought to expand their market and increase the "value" of food.[35] By the 1990s the farmer's average share of the food dollar had dropped to about 20 cents.

When viewed as a material flow by weight, it becomes apparent that an enormous quantity of grain is feed to livestock and poultry in the American food system. It is estimated that approximately 1.6 trillion tons of material in grain, hay, fruits, and vegetables flowed into the food system, but only 15 percent of this was actually consumed by people (see figure 11.5).[36] Sixty percent was expended by animals. Clearly America's heavy reliance on meat, poultry, and dairy products is very costly in energy and materials, especially when large-scale production systems require intensive feeding.

Wheat for Topsoil: Erosion and Plenty in Whitman County

The impact of farm industrialization at the local level can be illustrated using Census Bureau statistics for Whitman County in eastern Washington. Whitman County is the heart of the Palouse region, an area of steep, dunelike hills composed of deep loess soils, which were deposited by the wind 100,000 years ago (see figure 11.6). Climate and soil conditions in the Palouse are ideally suited for dry farming and help make Whitman County one of the world's leading wheat-producing regions. **Monocrop farming** of wheat was well under way in the Palouse by the 1880s.

According to Census Bureau figures, 27,000 people lived in rural Whitman County in 1910. Approximately 75 percent of the cash value of farm production was in grain. There were some 3,000 farms, averaging 383 acres (155 hectares). The primary farm production inputs were human labor and horses. Because much of the feed for the 38,000 horses and mules was grown locally, the county enjoyed a high degree of energy self-sufficiency.

By 1987, the switch to industrialization in Palouse farming was strikingly apparent in Census Bureau data that showed a drastic reduction in human labor inputs, the virtual disappearance of horses, and an enormous increase in fossil fuels and chemical fertilizers (see figure 11.7). Yields of wheat per acre suddenly doubled and tripled. Between 1910 and 1940,

Figure 11.3. The transition from animal traction to mechanized farming in the United States occurred between approximately 1910 and 1940 (John Deere Corporation).

approximately 30 bushels were produced per acre, but by 1987, yields averaged 69 bushels and sometimes reached 100. Such increases resulted from the use of newly developed "miracle grains," selectively bred to take maximum advantage of agricultural chemicals and machinery. This energy-intensive production system became known as the **Green Revolution** and was widely exported to the developing world in the 1970s and 1980s.

The social and environmental consequences of the technological changes in Palouse wheat farming were equally striking. As the demand for labor declined, by 1987 the total rural population had shrunk to less than half of what it had been in 1910. More significantly, the number of farms declined even more steeply, while total farm acreage remained approximately the same. This meant that individual farms tripled in size. Land became concentrated in fewer and fewer hands, such

that 15 percent of the farms came to control 46 percent of the land.

The most ominous change was the steady loss of soil due to erosion caused by deep cultivation of steep slopes with heavy machinery. The U.S. Department of Agriculture (USDA) began an annual program to monitor the problem in 1939. In 1978, the USDA issued a report documenting the total loss of topsoil from 10 percent of the land and estimating that annual soil losses averaged 14 tons (13 metric tons) of soil per acre. This means that each metric ton of wheat produced costs 13.5 metric tons of topsoil. This kind of factory farming is truly mining the soil and cannot continue indefinitely. More recently there have been experiments with no-till wheat farming to reduce the erosion, but the escalating cost of fuel and chemical inputs may ultimately push the system toward greater sustainability.

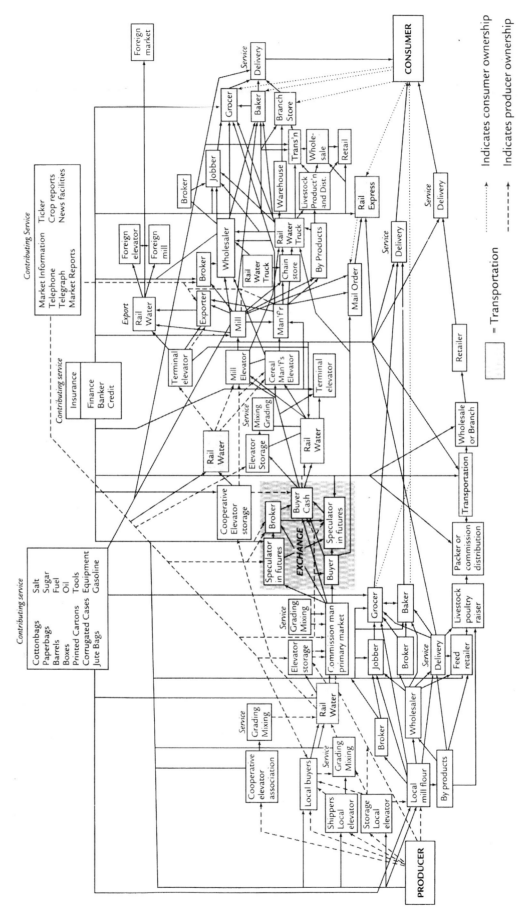

Figure 11.4. Chart showing the manufacturing and distribution of bread from wheat (U.S. House Committee on the Judiciary 1949, *Study of Monopoly Power*).

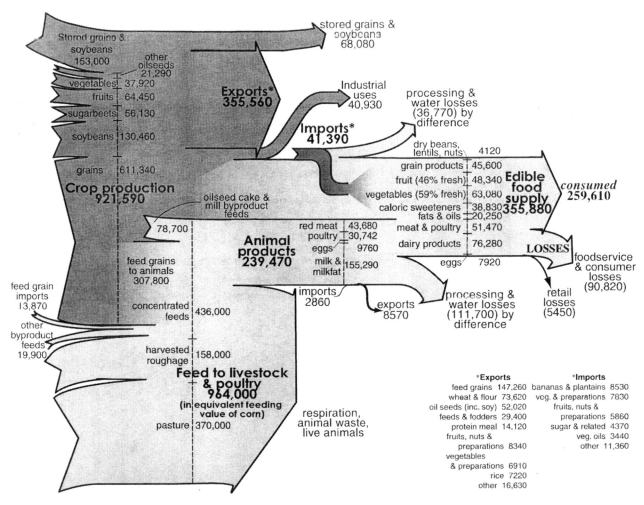

Figure 11.5. **The flow of materials in the American food system (flows in million pounds), 1995 (Heller, Martin C. and Gregory A. Keoleian. 2000.** *Life Cycle-based Sustainability Indicators for Assessment of the U.S. Food System.* **Figure 3, p. 37. Report No CSS00-04 Center for Sustainable Systems. University of Michigan. Ann Arbor, MI).**

Why would any culture institutionalize such a short-sighted technological system? This is a cultural problem that can best be understood by considering the dominant cultural role played by the economic elite in the United States. The logic of competitive commercial production aimed primarily at generating a cash profit forces U.S. producers to steadily accelerate output in order to gain economies of scale. Accelerated output is facilitated by technological innovation and by the concentration of economic control by a wealthy few. The concentration of economic power leads, in turn, to more social inequality and many other long-term costs.

The American Cattle Complex: Good to Sell

One can easily make the case that a Cattle Complex exists in America just as in East Africa. But the contrasts between the two cattle systems highlight the role of economic elites in shaping commercial-scale industrial cultures. Cattle are significant in American culture not only because they are "good to eat" but more importantly, as anthropologist Marvin Harris[37] emphasizes, because cattle are "good to sell."

The commercial elites who dominate the American cattle industry have used the most intensive production techniques to maximize the scale of their operations for the highest possible economic returns. Remarkably few people are the beneficial owners of the nation's beef. For example, the 1997 Census of Agriculture shows that the top 10 percent of farms and ranches owned half of the beef cattle in the United States, with the 212 largest farms having 2,500 cattle or more, averaging herds of nearly 8,000.[38] Herd size followed the power law distribution, suggesting that the 10 largest herds may have averaged as many as 200,000 head of cattle. A single ranch of this gigantic size would provide some 10,000 American ranch households with median-size herds of 20 animals, or

Figure 11.6. Active soil erosion on a cultivated wheat field in Whitman County, Washington. Note the soil slumping on the steep hillside in the upper background (U.S. Department of Agriculture).

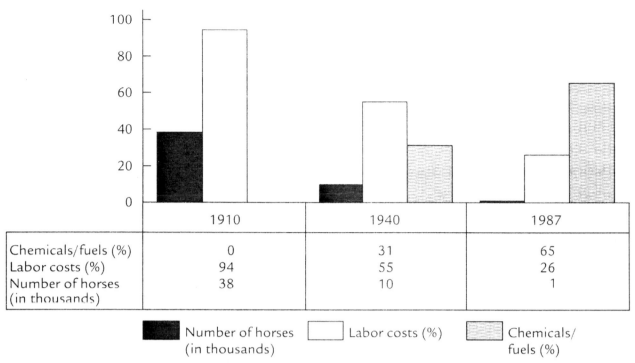

	1910	1940	1987
Chemicals/fuels (%)	0	31	65
Labor costs (%)	94	55	26
Number of horses (in thousands)	38	10	1

Number of horses (in thousands)   Labor costs (%)   Chemicals/ fuels (%)

Figure 11.7. Palouse farm inputs, 1910–1987.

would support some 30,000 East African cattle herder households. One of the largest ranches in the country, the King Ranch in Texas, covers 825,000 acres, more than 1,000 square miles, but with an intensive feeding program, even a relatively small-acreage ranch could support an enormous herd. For example, the Harris Ranch in California's San Joaquin Valley boasts an 800-acre feedlot with an annual capacity of 250,000 animals. This is vastly more animals than flowed annually through Emperor Ur-Nammu's livestock distribution center in ancient Nippur. The advantage of scale is reflected in market share, with the largest corporately owned cattle ranches receiving the largest share of the cattle market. The top 2 percent, 20,000 ranches, accounted for 50 percent of the $113 billion in cattle sales in 1997.[39]

Beef processing was also highly concentrated. Just three giant corporations, Tyson, Excel, and ConAgra, accounted for 62 percent of the cattle slaughtered and processed commercially in the United States.[40] In 2002, one company, Tyson Foods, claimed to be the number-one supplier of fresh, ground, and processed beef to U.S. retail grocers and food services and to Japan. Tyson also dominated poultry and pork processing, and, with $23 billion in sales, accounted for some 20 percent of the meat processing market.[41] In 2001 Tyson's 300 plants and 120,000 employees were processing an average of 196,881 head of beef, 42.5 million chickens, and 338,288 pigs every week. This

would be nearly 6 million pounds of beef per year and would supply 90 million Americans with their annual per-capita consumption of 65 pounds of beef. Tyson also claimed to be the number-one supplier of chicken to China and Russia, and frozen chicken to military commissaries. The principal beneficial owners of the company were members of the Tyson family and their close business partners. An enterprise of this scale is certainly profitable. Board chairman and CEO John Tyson received an annual salary and bonuses of more than $4.5 million. This degree of control, by so few, over all aspects of such a major element of subsistence is a remarkable cultural arrangement that certainly has no parallel in any domestic-scale cultures or ancient civilizations.

The scale of production shapes how cattle are handled, categorized, graded, slaughtered, and butchered and how the meat is named, packed, and distributed. In the tribal cultures of East Africa, cows are highly personalized, and slaughtering is a public and ritual act. The meat is distributed according to kinship relationships and is consumed immediately. In the United States, market cattle and meat are depersonalized commodities, the production of which is left entirely to specialists; few people have more than a vague idea of how their meat gets to them.

The production process is designed to move the animal to full slaughter weight as quickly as possible—usually within twenty-four months, although milk-fed calves may be slaughtered as veal at under three months. Calves may receive appetite stimulants and ear-implanted hormones to speed their growth. They are weaned at six to nine months, either to be returned to the range as "stockers" to grow further or to be vaccinated and sold to feedlots as "feeders" to be "finished" for slaughter. At the feedlot, cattle may receive more vaccinations and growth-hormone implants and are fattened on a weight-gain diet of grain, molasses, beef fat and by-products, and plant protein supplements, laced with antibiotics, vitamins, and growth steroids.[42]

The entire production process is regulated by federal and state laws. Live cattle are sorted by federal inspectors into classes by sex condition—steer, bullock, bull, cow, and heifer—and into grades—prime, choice, select, standard, commercial, utility, cutter, and canner. Regulations specify every detail of the slaughtering process, even prescribing the rate (in head per hour) at which inspectors can examine specific parts of animals. Such detailed regulation and classification are necessary to ensure quality standards when animals move rapidly through a complex chain of buyers and sellers, each seeking to maximize monetary return.

Economies of scale are a major factor in slaughtering. Larger plants, using highly specialized technology, were able to increase the hourly kill-and-butcher rate from 100 head per hour during the 1970s to 300 to 350 head per hour in the 1980s, thereby reducing the unit price of processing by 25 percent.[43] Faster butcher rates required a multitude of mechanized tools such as dehorners, dehiders, carcass splitters, brisket opener saws, bone saws, and primal cut saws. Further meat-processing operations use mechanical trimmers, dicers, massagers, tumblers, grinders, collagen films, patty machines, and vacuum stuffers. Meat cutting is a highly intensive, technical occupation in which the demand for increased efficiency produces a high rate of injuries in the workers.

Virtually every part of the animal finds some use. A beef carcass is split and quartered and then quickly reduced to six to ten primal and subprimal cuts for wholesale. Numerous other edible by-products include gelatin, marshmallows, and canned meat. Inedible by-products include leather, buttons, and soap from beef tallow, as well as pet foods and animal feeds. A wide range of pharmaceuticals such as insulin, estrogen, and thyroid extract are also derived from cattle.

Large-scale factory meat production also produces low-wage jobs, impoverished communities, and en-vironmental damage.[44] The scale and complexity of this form of subsistence and the speed of production also increase the risk of contamination. For example, in 2002 ConAgra voluntarily recalled some 19 million pounds of ground beef produced by its giant slaughterhouse in Greeley, Colorado, because of contamination by harmful E. coli bacteria.[45] Because it operated in a cultural system that socializes costs and maximizes economic returns, ConAgra officials were not required to publicly disclose all of the retail outlets that received their meat. Pressure from corporate lobbyists and generous political donations have encouraged lax enforcement of health regulations and self-inspection by producers, even as government regulatory agencies are underfunded and often staffed by former industry employees.[46]

The Cultural Construction of Consumption

Anthropologist Marvin Harris[47] argues that cultural preferences for specific meats are largely determined by utilitarian, ecological, and economic factors. He attributes the American preference for beef to the forced removal of bison and Native Americans from the Great Plains in the 1870s and their replacement by cattle. The ranchers were, in turn, displaced by grain farmers, and cattle had to be grazed on the arid lands and in the logged-over forests further west. The real boom for beef, according to Harris, came after World War II when large numbers of American women began to work outside the home and fast-food dining on hamburgers suddenly opened a vast new market for beef. The key to the success of hamburger, which legally must be all beef, is that it can contain added beef fat, up to 30 percent. The added fat helps bind the meat when it is cooked. Thus, hamburger can be ground from relatively tough, range-fed steers, combined with the abundant fat trimmed from feedlot-fattened beef, which otherwise supply tender, marbled, and very expensive cuts of meat.

Utilitarian interpretations of cultural practices are helpful, but they imply that cultural development unfolds naturally and inevitably, suggesting that change will be adaptive and progressive. This leaves out both the cultural meanings in people's heads and the elite decision makers who expend massive resources on advertising to create these meanings. Rejecting economic **utilitarianism**, Marshall Sahlins reminds us that what people consume, as well as our concepts of economic scarcity, and by extension poverty, are all cultural constructions. In his famous statement on foragers as "the original affluent society," Sahlins observed that tribal foragers easily satisfy their wants by desiring little, whereas for Americans,

> scarcity is the peculiar obsession of a business economy, the calculable condition of all who participate in it. The market makes freely available a dazzling array of products, all these "good things" within a man's reach—but never his grasp, for one never has enough to buy everything. To exist in a market economy is to live out a double tragedy, beginning in inadequacy and ending in deprivation. All economic activity starts from a position of shortage . . . one's resources are insufficient to the possible uses and satisfactions.[48]

Scarcity or poverty is thus not strictly a technological problem, and it is not inherent in nature; it is a cultural creation that is most elaborated by commercial-scale, industrial cultures. According to anthropologist Jules Henry,[49] the dependence of American culture on the deliberate creation of needs for goods and services constituted a "psychic revolution" with far-reaching impacts on human thought and behavior.

Sahlins[50] offered a cultural symbolic analysis of American food practices suggesting that in American culture, because of its long cultural association with virility and strength, beef, and especially steak, has a central place in the diet. Pork takes second place as a less preferred meat, while eating dogs or horses is virtually taboo.

Sahlins observed that in American culture, cattle and pigs form a structured set in opposition to horses and dogs (see figure 11.8). Cattle and pigs are treated as unnamed objects and are eaten, whereas dogs and horses are named subjects and are not eaten. Dogs and horses are seen as more "human"—both are talked to and petted, and dogs may live in the house and be buried upon death. Eating dogs would be like eating kin and implies cannibalism. Horses are more like servants, and eating them is only slightly less taboo. Pork is less preferred than beef, in part because pigs scavenge human food and are thus closer to people than cattle, such that eating pigs would be slightly cannibalistic.

A further cultural code of edibility is imposed on beef itself. Meat is culturally distinguished as the most edible part of the animal, in opposition to "innards" such as heart, tongue, and liver, which, like pork, imply cannibalism. Cuts of beef are subdivided into dozens of named categories and products, each priced according to its culturally defined desirability, such that eating a given cut reinforces one's social rank. Sahlins[51] stressed that pricing and desirability are not obviously related to supply and nutritional quality, because liver is highly nutritious and relatively scarce, yet is much cheaper than steak, which is more abundant per animal.

The use of cultural products to encode social differences among categories of people resembles the use of animal species as totems to distinguish cultural groups in tribal cultures. However, this analysis focuses on "cultural intention," suggesting that the cultural system operates independently of human intention. In reality, what Americans eat, and what they believe they should eat, can be intentionally changed. American food practices did change dramatically between 1940 and 2000 in response to decision making, advertising, marketing, and political lobbying by the corporate directors of the food industry. Corporate concentration in the "fast food" industry also shaped American eating patterns.[52] In 1940 Americans were primarily pork eaters, by 1960 they were beef eaters, but by 2000 Americans had become chicken eaters, eating more poultry than beef by weight.[53] Between 1940 and 2000 Americans actually increased their daily consumption of protein, fats, carbohydrates, and total calories by an average of 16 percent. Apparent annual per-capita consumption of refined sugar and corn syrup increased nearly 40 percent from 107 to 148 pounds. Soft drink consumption soared from 35 to 49 gallons between 1980 and 2000. These dietary changes are clearly related to official figures at that time showing more than half of the population overweight and over 20 percent obese.[54] Figures for 2008 showed adult obesity rates had increased to 33.8 percent of the population.[55]

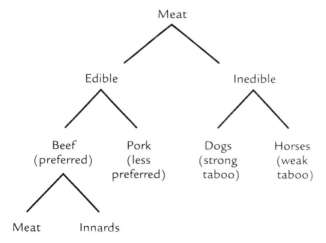

Figure 11.8. The cultural structure of meat edibility in the United States (based on Sahlins 1976b).

Changes of this magnitude in the practices of millions of people do not result from a nondirected, symbolically encoded cultural intention. American food practices are clearly influenced by the elite-directed drive to increase the scale of food production, marketing, and consumption. Much of this marketing is directed specifically at children and young people, who influence a significant share of household expenditures. In 2002 the directors of five candy and soft drink companies and four fast-food giants spent a total of $6.5 billion on advertising, persuading people to eat more calories, more sugar and fat, and more trans-fatty acids known to elevate harmful cholesterol levels. This advertising spending is aimed at the top, "use sparingly," end of the official Food Guide Pyramid issued by the United States Department of Agriculture in 2000 as a guide to daily food choices (see figure 11.9). The food pyramid was a compromise between food industry lobbyists who wanted to encourage consumption of all food commodities and independent nutritionists who wanted people to eat less of certain foods for their health.[56] The pyramid phrase "use sparingly" is certainly not the same as "eat less." Other food pyramids are possible.[57]

GROWTH, SCALE, AND POWER IN AMERICA

Growth is such a dominant element in American culture that it is important to closely examine its relationship to increases in culture scale and changes in the distribution of social power. This section uses broad ethnohistorical data for the country as a whole since 1776, as well as more detailed ethnography from New York City and the Palouse region of eastern Washington, to examine the social realities of 200 years of growth in the world's most successful commercial culture.

Growth in America: Wealth and Opportunity, 1776–1997

After his nine-month visit in 1831–1832, French political scientist Alexis de Tocqueville (1835–1840)

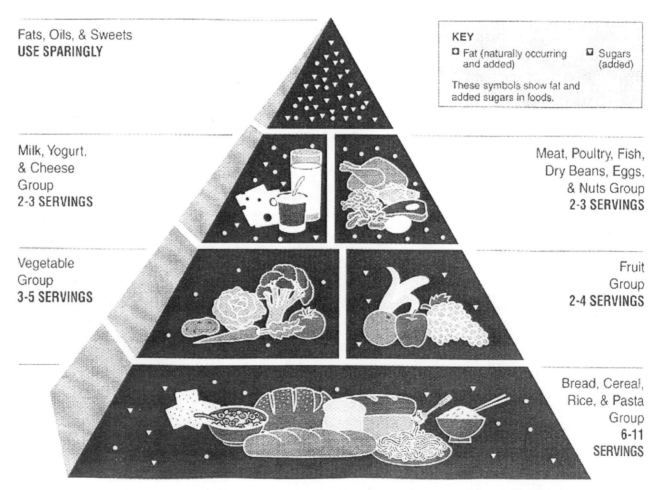

Figure 11.9. Food guide pyramid: a guide to daily food choices, 2000 (U.S. Department of Agriculture / U.S. Department of Health and Human Services).

described America as an egalitarian democracy, with a large middle class and few very rich or very poor. In his view, abundant resources, technological innovation, and hard work created equal economic opportunity in America. More recent observers point to the increasing numbers of wealthy as evidence of the benefits of American economic freedom, supporting the hope that economic growth makes it possible for everyone to become wealthy.[58] However, three independent lines of evidence—probate estate records, census data, and tax assessments—suggest that for much of American history, social and economic reality seldom matched the widespread belief that growth made America a land of equal opportunity.

To estimate the distribution of wealth and income in the thirteen colonies immediately prior to the American Revolution of 1776, historian Alice Hanson Jones[59] used detailed probate inventories of movable property and real estate in personal estates for 1773–1775, supplemented with tax lists, newspaper accounts, records of deeds and land grants, and church and town records of baptisms, marriages, and burials. Her findings suggest that the distribution of monetary income in 1776 was as top-heavy as in 1994, when the top 5 percent of households received 20 percent of national household income, the middle 20 percent received 15 percent, and the bottom 20 percent received only 4 percent.

Remarkably, historian Lee Soltow's[60] analysis of the distribution of property ownership recorded in the U.S. Census for 1798, 1850, 1860, and 1870 shows that political independence and a century of economic growth had no significant impact on the distribution of wealth in America. Soltow found extensive inequality in America throughout the nineteenth century. Perhaps half of American households owned no land. Soltow found such a strong correlation between wealth concentration and support for the Constitution that he concluded that it would not have been ratified by a popular vote because the poor saw no advantages in a strong federal government.

Other historians have used tax assessment data to examine the distribution of wealth in New York City during the nineteenth century, when especially rapid urban growth occurred.[61] Pessen documented very rapid wealth concentration during the first half of the century. In 1845, the top 1 percent held half of all wealth in property, and the top 4 percent owned an incredible 81 percent, including shares in New York's emerging corporate businesses (primarily banks and insurance companies). During this time, New York

City's wealth grew faster than its population. Per-capita wealth actually quadrupled, but the rich got much richer.

Careful analysis of the family connections of the economic elite showed conclusively that nineteenth-century New York was not a city of equal opportunity, because one needed inherited social status and wealth to prosper. The nineteenth-century New York economic elite proved to be closely integrated by kinship and marriage connections and were even forming marriage alliances with the European aristocracy. In 1898, 42 percent of New York's 1,368 millionaires were related by blood or marriage.[62] Ninety-five percent of New York's wealthiest individuals were born into already-wealthy families; only 2 percent started out poor. The wealthy proved to be very secure, with most holding their wealth intact during their lifetimes and successfully passing it on to the next generation, even through severe economic downturns.

Even though wealth was heavily concentrated at the very top of the social hierarchy in nineteenth-century America, there was still significant upward mobility in comparison with the virtually frozen hierarchy in Europe. Low-income American households were able to move up the economic ladder, but much of their increase was a function of aging within the domestic cycle and very gradual accumulation of small savings. Soltow[63] estimated that in 1870, 43 percent of adult males were poor, because they held total estates worth less than $100. Perhaps 52 percent of Americans were middle class, in the sense that they held at least $100 in property. Fewer than 10 percent were wealthy.

According to contemporary observers, in the 1850s accumulated wealth of $60,000, which would have generated an annual income of $3,000, was sufficient to provide the good life: "a comfortable house—servants, a good table—wine—a horse—books—'country quarters'—a plentiful wardrobe—the ability to exercise hospitality."[64] Only the top 0.5 percent of the urban population were in this category. If mid-nineteenth-century wealth accumulations of a mere $60,000 made one quite comfortable, it is understandable that $150,000 was considered to be a very substantial fortune, yet Soltow[65] estimated that there were already 41 American millionaires in 1860, 545 in 1870, and, as we have seen, 1,368 in New York City alone by 1898.

By 1890, small farms were being rapidly replaced by giant farms, and small businesses by giant corporations. With the closing of the frontier and the rise of manufacturing, about half the population had become urban, and most people needed income-producing jobs to survive. There were perhaps 25 million new poor who were unable to produce enough income to comfortably meet basic needs. During the twentieth century, further growth produced even more poverty.

Economic Elites and Urban Poverty, New York City, 1863–1914

All of the social stresses generated by rapid growth occurred in New York City during the nineteenth century, making this city an ideal place to examine scale and power issues. A remarkable geography of power had emerged in New York City by 1845, with city government, party politics, corporate finance, and massive private wealth situated side by side (see box 11.2). On the lower end of Manhattan Island stood City Hall, immediately flanked on the East River side by Tammany Hall and on the Hudson River side by the residence of John Jacob Astor, then richest man in the country. The New York Stock Exchange was located half a mile to the south in the Wall Street financial district. By 1890, New York had become, after London, the largest and the wealthiest city in the world. Home of the Statue of Liberty, it was the primary port of entry for immigrants. It handled more than half of all U.S. international trade and provided headquarters for America's largest corporations. With 2.5 million people, New York was the nation's largest urban center, with the greatest ethnic and religious diversity. Perhaps most importantly from our perspective, it also had the most powerful economic elites and the worst urban slums in the country.

In 1890, New York's economic elites probably consisted of fewer than 2,500 very wealthy individuals, representing no more than 0.5 percent of the city's households. The elite were a diverse lot, representing Anglo-American Protestants, German Christians, and German Jews. Many elites were members of aristocratic merchant and landholding families, while others were newly rich bankers, corporate entrepreneurs, and professionals. Members of these distinct elite groups sometimes had conflicting political and economic interests and belonged to different social, professional, and commercial associations. But they also were integrated by kinship and marriage ties, and all benefited from the tremendous economic growth that was occurring, especially in railroads, banking, oil, and manufacturing.

The wealthiest of the city's 200 or so most prominent citizens was John D. Rockefeller (1839–1937), who was personally worth perhaps $200 million in the 1890s. J. P. Morgan (1837–1913) probably ranked second, with an estate valued at $77.6 million in 1913. It is important to distinguish the personal wealth of these superwealthy from their actual social, political, and economic power, which was represented by the total assets of the corporations they controlled and the foundations they endowed.

Rockefeller and Morgan were at the top of a web of interlocking financial imperia centered in New York. In 1904 investment analyst John Moody approvingly described the Rockefeller-Morgan "family tree" as an interconnected alliance of trusts that dominated the financial, commercial, and industrial interests of the country (see figure 11.10). Trusts were the early form of holding companies. They were giant companies that owned other companies. Moody thought such concentrated power was good, inevitable, and a "law of nature." He argued, "[N]o amount of blind public opposition or restrictive legislation can prevent this constant change from small scale to large scale."[66] Even more emphatically, he declared, "The modern trust is the natural outcome or evolution of society conditions and ethical standards which are recognized and established among men today as being necessary elements in the development of civilization."[67]

Hearings held in Washington, DC, in 1912–1913 by the House Subcommittee on Banking and Currency, the Pujo Committee, provided a rare glimpse of the financial power of J. P. Morgan. Summaries of this material by Supreme Court Justice Louis Brandeis (1914) showed that as an investment banker operating through J. P. Morgan & Co., Morgan stood at the top of a complex web of commercial relationships. Through the directors of companies in which he held controlling interests, Morgan exerted direct and indirect influence over 34 large banks and trust companies, 10 insurance companies, 32 transportation systems, 12 public utilities, and 135 other corporations, with combined assets of $45 billion. His power was such that he virtually dominated all sectors of the national economy.

Morgan had effectively gained control over other people's money, such that he could assemble vast transfers of capital between "his" corporations and extract hefty commissions in the process. Decisions that he and his associates made influenced employment conditions and the well-being of millions of low-paid working people throughout the country. Morgan's economic focus was national and international. He had little interest in or influence over New York's domestic issues, although he was president of a

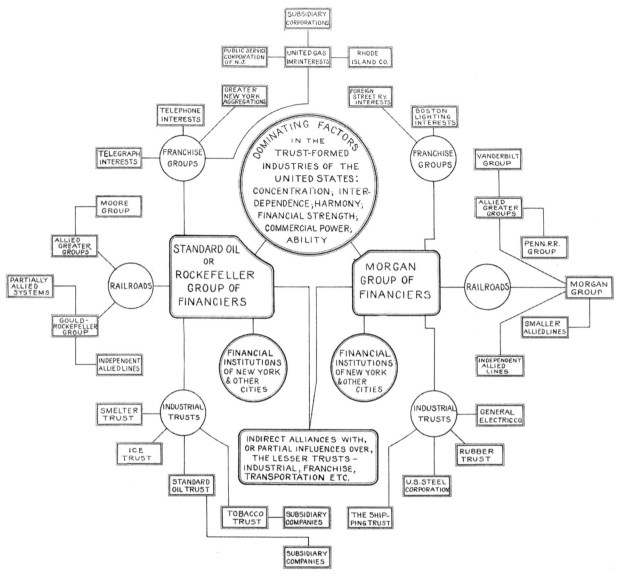

Figure 11.10. **The interlocking Rockefeller-Morgan commercial imperia of industrial trusts and financial institutions in 1904 (Moody 1904).**

prominent New York social club. As a principal owner of Manhattan's elevated railway line, Morgan unsuccessfully resisted the city's plans to build a publicly financed subway system. New York's elites were so divided on public policy that it was difficult for even one of the most powerful economic elites to impose his will everywhere.

Immigration caused the population of metropolitan New York to more than double between 1850 and 1880, and again between 1880 and 1910, providing a rental bonanza for slum landlords. There was enormous pressure on housing, and the large landowners responded by replacing single-family houses built on narrow lots with tenements housing three or more families, which would yield higher rents but at a much-reduced quality of life for the residents. The costs and benefits in this development process were clear. The New York housing market was a free-market paradise, with no pesky building codes requiring fire escapes and the like to interfere with developers' "natural" desire to maximize profits. The result was shoddy, even dangerous construction and unhealthy, overpriced housing for most of the city's people, who were overwhelmingly poor. Social reformers condemned crowded living conditions as conducive to immorality among the poor. It took a series of cholera outbreaks, centered in the tenements, to enable reform-minded physicians to persuade the city to establish a

Metropolitan Board of Health in 1866. The government was forced to grudgingly acknowledge that inferior housing was a public health problem.

Journalist photographer Jacob Riis vividly portrayed conditions in New York's crowded tenements in *How the Other Half Lives*.[68] Riis succeeded in arousing public indignation that spurred the government to action. Investigators for the New York State Tenement House Commission found in 1900 that 2.3 million people, approximately 70 percent of the population of metropolitan New York, lived in crowded, unsanitary tenements.[69] The average floor space in these small apartments approximated 4.7 square meters per person. This figure almost precisely matched the 4.6 square meters (10 by 10 feet) of floor space that Charles Booth (1892–1903) had used to identify the residences of the London poor. Remarkably, this was about half the floor space enjoyed by a typical Asháninka household. Furthermore, it was much less than the 6 to 10 square meters of floor space per person that seems to represent a cross-cultural constant for all precommercial cultures.[70]

In Ward 10, the Jewish quarter, a forty-five-block area on Manhattan's Lower East Side, 76,000 people were living in three- to seven-story tenements, with as many as 200 people to a house (see figure 11.11). Buildings were dark and poorly ventilated, and many had only a single outside water tap and pit toilet for all families. Sometimes hallway water-closet toilets were situated on each floor to be shared by two to four families. There were no baths or showers. Not surprisingly, over one five-year period, there were thirty-two cases of tuberculosis and thirteen cases of diphtheria in one sample block jammed with 2,781 people, and 660 families requested public assistance.

These wretched living conditions made turn-of-the-century New York a center of labor unrest and union and socialist activism that eventually resulted in small increases in wages and acceptance of the eight-hour workday. Building codes were also gradually modified. The elites were often divided on what policies the city should pursue, which made it possible for working-class people to influence events with their votes. Some elites favored a form of "municipal socialism" in which tax dollars and private investment would improve the commercial prospects of the city by developing better public transit systems, public education, public health and housing, municipal government, and cultural institutions.[71] The largest economic elites were reluctant to support reforms because they were suspicious of government involvement in the "free market," did not want their taxes to increase, and had much broader economic interests than in the city itself. Others blamed the city's problems on socialists, anarchists, immorality, and ethnic and religious diversity.

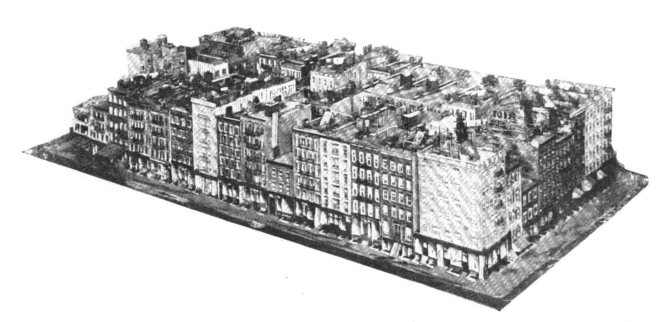

Figure 11.11. Model of a representative block in Ward 10, in Manhattan's Lower East Side, 1900 (DeForest, Robert W. and Lawrence Veiller 1903).

Social Power, Personal Imperia, and Family in the United States, 1980–2003

In the last decades of the twentieth century, social power became even more concentrated in America as neoliberal economic policies made it easier for investors to seek the highest returns on financial capital.

America has become a global economic and military superpower, but unlike societies in the ancient imperial world, it is not a totalitarian system. No single person, not the president, not the richest person, and not the CEO of the largest corporation commands the entire system. America is also not run by a small, secret, conspiratorial group. Rather, America is a heterarchy with economic, political, ideological, and military power divided into multiple hierarchies controlled by various, often shifting elites. In 2003 political power in the United States was commanded nationally by 630 top officials in the federal government, including the president, cabinet secretaries, Supreme Court justices, senators and representatives, and the directors of government agencies. Although the country is a formal democracy, only 51 percent of eligible voters voted in the 2000 presidential election. Federal expenditures were $2 trillion, and federal financial wealth and property were worth some $7 trillion. The president also commanded the vastly powerful American military, with a $408 billion budget and 2.6 million active and reserve military personnel, many posted all over the world. The American military budget exceeded the expenditures of the next twenty-nine countries ranked by troop strength, suggesting that some Americans seek global military supremacy.[73] The United States had more than 1,100 long-range ballistic missiles, including intercontinental and submarine launched, and 315 strategic bombers, capable of delivering some 3,500 nuclear warheads virtually anywhere in the world. These nuclear weapons of mass destruction were backed by massive, technologically superior conventional forces, giving America's military leaders the ability to project overwhelming military power or threats of violent force worldwide at will.

The American economy in 2002 was approximately $10 trillion in gross domestic product (GDP), the market value of all the goods and services produced in the United States. This was roughly one-third of global GDP. The degree to which economic power was concentrated in the hands of the directors and beneficial owners of commercial business corporations is indicated by the $7.4 trillion in revenues flowing through the 500 largest publicly traded corporations in 2001, which was more than 40 percent of all corporate revenues. Fortune 500 companies owned $19 trillion in assets. The 400 wealthiest American individuals in 2000 were collectively worth $946 billion. These 400 were the richest plutocrats in the American plutocracy. By 2007, just before the financial collapse, the 400 wealthiest had increased their wealth to

$1.5 trillion.[74] As plutocrats, those who commanded great personal wealth or the collective assets of giant corporations were able to shape the culture by their decisions to invest in certain activities or to produce certain products.

Ideological power is the ability to influence what people know and believe. In America this power resides with the directors of media corporations, the religious institutions, government agencies, educational institutions, foundations, and various nonprofit organizations, as well as, perhaps most importantly, with those who directed $243 billion in national advertising in 2000. National advertising expenditures were more than half of the amount spent on all public education from kindergarten through high school. Forty percent of national advertising was expended by the top 100 advertisers, and nearly half was for television ads. The commercial broadcast media draws virtually all of its revenue from advertising. This means that radio and television are primarily marketing tools. The emphasis on television advertising is understandable, with Americans over eighteen on the average watching thirty-five hours per week. The American media was concentrated in fewer than twenty corporations controlling most of the television, radio, publishing, music, and film in the country.[75] This meant that a very small number of people determined what Americans watched, read, and heard, and the primary message was that consumption of certain brands brings happiness. Advertising manipulates individual self-interest and is less concerned with the interests of society, because society is not a market. The other role of the mass media is "manufacturing consent," or persuading people to believe that the existing culture is the best possible way of life and that those in charge are making the right decisions.[76]

When any power elite uses the media primarily to sell products, the media becomes an unreliable source of information about the real world. Reliance on television is especially problematic because it is more likely to offer highly selective, emotional images and contrived events rather than objective, in-depth information that can be intellectually interpreted.[77]

America is too large and complex for one person to rule, but individual elites can move between power hierarchies, commanding personal imperia that crosscut different power domains. They can use their personal connections to enormous advantage. This is not different from the personal networks of power that exist in all societies. However, because America is such a large-scale system, with so much concentrated power,

the potential for unintended negative consequences of misguided decision making is very high. Conflicts of interest and corruption are also part of the system. Furthermore, elites do not always follow the rules.[78] The problem is that mistakes by even well-intended super elites commanding a superpower can affect the entire world.

Giant commercial corporations now dominate American life. Corporations are given the same rights as individuals, but unlike individuals and sole-proprietorship businesses, corporations can live forever and grow ever more powerful. Corporations also are not limited to particular places, and they can project their commercial power throughout the world. Furthermore, corporate structure and limited liability makes it difficult to hold corporations responsible for the total costs of their activities, even when they are criminal.

The scale of giant corporations can be illustrated by Philip Morris, the fourteenth-largest industrial corporation in the world in 1991 and seventh-largest in the United States. Philip Morris sold a staggering $50 billion worth of products in 1993, an amount far exceeding the national budgets of many countries. As a huge conglomerate, Philip Morris contained some 222 operating companies, subsidiaries, units, and divisions in the United States and forty-two other countries. From top to bottom, there were at least four major organizational levels, such that the corporation, with its 210,000 employees worldwide, was structurally as complex as a political state. Philip Morris produced hundreds of food items. The company has had an enormous impact on American life through its employment practices, its choice of plant locations, and the health effects of the products it markets.

By 2002 Philip Morris's directors had restructured the company into a giant conglomerate composed of Philip Morris USA, Philip Morris International, Kraft Foods, and Philip Morris Capital Corporation, all under the new parent company name of Altria. The company had expanded its global reach and shed 44,000 employees since 1993, but its revenue had risen to $80 billion.

Thomas R. Dye[79] and a team of graduate students at Florida State University painstakingly compiled and sorted biographical data on elites and concluded that 5,778 individuals controlled America's giant corporations, the federal government, the news media, and the primary cultural institutions in the early 1980s. Some of these people were elected officials, but many are completely unknown outside the networks of power. Similarly, a very small number of owners and managers exercise real power over American business. My investigation of Securities and Exchange Commission filings in 1994 revealed that a mere ten people helped direct thirty-seven American companies whose combined assets of $2 trillion represented nearly 10 percent of all corporate assets in the country. One individual directed five companies with $549 billion in total assets, or 2.5 percent of the national total. In 1995, a mere 600 people directed America's fifty largest companies, accounting for 16 percent of the country's business revenues and exceeding the combined revenues of all noncorporate businesses and nonprofit organizations. This change in the scale of business enterprise transforms commercial life in small American communities, making participation in markets difficult for many small-business owners. Concentrated wealth of this magnitude gives enormous freedom to a privileged few to produce and direct the economic processes that shape our future.

The Carlyle Group, a private equity corporation based in Washington, DC, is a good example of how super-elite personal imperia work in America and globally. In 2003 Carlyle's directors managed $17.5 billion in investments, primarily in private business and real estate throughout the world. Its principal investors were a few hundred high-net-worth individuals, with $5 million or more to invest, including members of America's 400 wealthiest. Carlyle has been characterized as an "iron triangle," because it conducts business by exploiting connections between powerful individuals who have held high-ranking positions in the American military, the federal government, and private corporations, including important defense contractors.[80] Along with CEOs from major corporations, among Carlyle's senior officers and advisors in 2003 were former U.S. secretaries of state and defense, a former director of the Federal Office of Management and Budget, and former chairmen of the U.S. Federal Communications Commission and the Securities and Exchange Commission. Since its founding in 1987, the Carlyle group has included among its members and advisors former president George W. Bush, former U.K. prime minister John Major, and former U.S. secretary of state Colin Powell. Carlyle associates play multiple roles as investors, corporate officers, and often as former or future government officials. This is much like the "fiscal-military state" under early European capitalism and creates wealth by capitalizing on personal connections and insider knowledge that crosscuts power domains.

Anthropologist Marvin Harris[81] attributed increased crime and family breakdowns to the rise of oligopoly in American business and the related shift from industrial production to services and information. These economic processes accelerated in the United States during the 1980s and 1990s, as changes in tax laws, deregulation of financial institutions, and the removal of global trade barriers prompted giant corporations to increase their financial power through leveraged buyouts and downsizing. This vast transformation, which has been called **deindustrialization**,[82] parallels the social disruptions caused by the Industrial Revolution. Deindustrialization caused millions of American workers to lose their manufacturing jobs and forced them to take low-paying, in-person service jobs. At the same time, as the economy grew, financial markets soared and the privileged few—wealthy investors and corporate executives—prospered. Upper-middle-class professionals may use "assertive mating"—marrying another well-paid professional— to double their income and join the financial elites.[83] Meanwhile, downsized production workers and service workers can gamble on the lottery.

Giant corporations, because of their size, can eliminate competition and control markets to such an extent that locally owned businesses may have difficulty surviving. Large corporations also derive a significant proportion of their profits from buying and selling smaller corporations rather than directly from production, and this reduces their long-term commitment to consumers, employees, or the local communities where their factories are located.

The increasing financial power of giant corporations is associated with a loss of power and control in local communities. Anthropologist James Toth,[84] who conducted ethnographic research on a small Pennsylvania town, found that the deindustrialization process reduced economic decision making by local businesspeople. Small businesses, local manufacturing plants, and independent contractors were being replaced by subsidiary electronics firms, shopping malls, banks, and realty agencies controlled by conglomerates headquartered in other cities, other states, and even other countries. This process drained financial capital from the local community.

Anthropologist Katherine Newman[85] estimates that 10.6 million Americans lost their jobs to corporate downsizing between 1981 and 1992. To assess the impact of this process, she gathered life histories and conducted intensive interviews with hundreds of Americans, including members of sixty families in a suburban New Jersey community. Newman found that many middle-class people who were experiencing declining living standards felt that the American Dream of continuous economic progress was passing them by. They accepted this as evidence of personal failure, rather than attributing it to larger economic forces. Anthropologist June Nash[86] found the same passive acceptance of economic misfortune among the 5,000 workers in Massachusetts who were laid off when General Electric moved their plant to Canada in 1986. Displaced workers may find lower-paying jobs, but they are often forced to sell their homes, and their households experience the stress of downward mobility.

The vast changes in American business have directly impacted family life. Few married women worked outside of the home in the 1890s, but since 1965 the declining value of wages has forced many women to seek employment in an effort to maintain a constant standard of living. Economic stresses are reflected in higher divorce rates and an increase in single-parent households. Furthermore, careful, large-scale statistical studies have demonstrated a direct relationship between income level and stability and mortality.[87] Differences in social class mean that in contemporary America, just as in nineteenth-century London and New York, well-paid professionals and managers live longer than laborers. Government reports have consistently shown that poor children are unlikely to see doctors or be vaccinated, and poor adults are more likely to be in poor health, to lack health insurance, and to die from chronic diseases.[88] Medical researcher Richard G. Wilkinson[89] argues that a high level of social inequality raises mortality at lower social levels, because inequality reduces social cohesion and increases stress. This connection between social cohesion, stress, and health is strongly supported by a thirty-year longitudinal study of health in Roseto, Pennsylvania, an Italian American village of

1,500 people, from approximately 1960 to 1990.[90] The Roseto villagers were the descendants of immigrants who came to Pennsylvania in the 1880s. Researchers found that as long as their family and clan structure remained strong, the villagers were almost completely free from heart attacks. The incidence of heart attacks increased sharply when they began to lose social cohesion in the mid-1960s, even though other risk factors did not significantly change.

Americans are reluctant to talk about social class, but researchers such as Ferdinand Lundberg,[91] C. Wright Mills,[92] and G. William Domhoff[93] have concluded that a very small upper class, perhaps the top 0.5 percent of the country, enjoys a disproportionate share of the benefits of the American economy and has a disproportionate influence over events. Indeed, in 1998, the $727 billion in combined wealth held by the 400 richest Americans was more than sixty times the wealth held by all the colonists in 1774, on the eve of the American Revolution.[94] Many of the wealthiest Americans know one another and may interact socially, but they no longer form a cohesive, self-conscious social class. They share a common interest in perpetuating economic growth but may disagree on details of political policy.

In my own analysis of the well-being of American households in 1998,[95] I found that the top 8 percent, about 6 million households, were elites and super-elites with incomes of $100,000 or more and net worths ranging into the millions and billions of dollars (see table 11.3). They were America's capitalists. They owned approximately half of the personal wealth in the country, especially income-generating property and financial assets, from which they received unearned income, and the luxury of saving and investing. Other households were producer-consumers. They were dependent on wages and salaries from their employers for their livelihoods but had little power to influence their conditions of employment. The median

Table 11.3. American Households by Economic Class, Power, and Imperia, 1998

Classes	Economic Type	Income Range	Net Worth	Households	Portfolio	Imperia
Capitalist 8%	Directors	$1 million+	$millions–$billions	0.4 million	$millions–$trillions	Super-Elite 0.5%
	Owners	$100,000–$999,999	$100,000–$millions	5.6 million	$millions	Elite 8%
Producer-Consumer 92%	High Consumers skilled wage & salary, small entrepreneurs	$10,000–$99,999	Median $60,000	55.8 million	none	Maintenance 79%
	Low Consumers Unskilled wage-earners	<$10,000	Median $3,600	8.9 million		Poor 13%

net worth of the middle 79 percent of the population who were maintenance level was only $60,000. Most children could not inherit a significant estate. Upward mobility was difficult for producer-consumers, because, as in early modern England, even middle-income households were forced to spend most of their income on maintenance. An Asháninka visiting America in 1998 would have been amazed by the level of social inequality. He would also have been surprised to discover that more than 10 percent of American adults lived alone in single-person households; 18 percent of family households had no husband present.

The distribution of social power in America clearly seems to be the result of elite-directed growth processes. This interpretation is supported by ethnographic research on the well-being of households in eastern Washington State showing an association between growth in the size of urban places and increasing concentration of property ownership and poverty (see box 11.3).

BOX 11.3. PROPERTY, GROWTH, AND POWER IN THE PALOUSE, 1997

I examined the well-being of households in different-sized communities in the Palouse region of eastern Washington State to test whether wealth-producing growth, and the resulting increases in population and economic value, produced more poor households.[96] I also wondered if there would be local-level evidence that growth was directed by the people who most benefited from increases in community scale.

Rather than relying on census data on income, intrusive survey questionnaires, or official definitions of poverty, I used publicly available property assessments to measure the well-being of Palouse households. I inferred that households owning property assessed at less than $10,000 would be too poor to easily meet their basic needs. Households owning $10,000 or more but less than $75,000 in property could maintain themselves comfortably but would have difficulty saving. Households with $75,000 or more in property would be able to save, invest, and steadily increase their economic level.

By carefully sorting through computerized data from the county assessors, I found that individuals owned nearly $10 billion worth of urban property in the Palouse. This was sufficient to put every household comfortably above the maintenance level, but instead the top 20 percent of owner-residents actually owned nearly 70 percent of all individually owned property. Many of the wealthiest property owners did

not even live in the Palouse. Incredibly, the top three owners held more property than all 10,200 people who lived in the twenty smallest towns.

Most significantly, community scale proved to be the best predictor of household well-being. More households were better off in small urban places with fewer than 2,500 people. The average value of property ownership increased with community scale, but the wealthiest households gained disproportionately, and there was an enormous increase in the absolute number of poor households in larger towns. There were proportionately more maintenance-level households and more home ownership in the smallest villages. There were few poor villagers, and they were better off than the poor in larger places. The communities that grew the least showed the least wealth concentration, and large property owners appeared to have less influence on municipal government. Property elites who generated wealth from the higher property values that accompanied urban growth needed progrowth municipal policies to expand city boundaries and change zoning restrictions. Not surprisingly, the communities that had grown the most proved to be places where big property owners were the most represented in the municipal government.

These findings suggest that in this case, wealth-promoting government policies were designed by the wealthy to serve the needs of the wealthy. Growth appeared to work against the interests of a significant number of households because elevated property values priced low-income households out of the housing market.

The Rockefeller Dynasty

The remarkable Rockefeller family (see figures 11.12 and 11.13) illustrates the extent to which wealth can be amassed in a commercial culture, be transmitted across four generations, and be used to exert enormous cultural, political, and commercial influence in the United States and in the world. The patriarch of the family, John D. Rockefeller (1839–1937), founded the Standard Oil Company in 1870 and gained monopolistic control over the American petroleum industry. The government dissolved the Standard Oil trust in 1911, but John D. Sr. had already become fabulously wealthy. In 1913, he established the Rockefeller Foundation with an endowment of $100 million "to promote the well-being of mankind throughout the world." Through the foundation and other charitable organizations, the family promoted worldwide

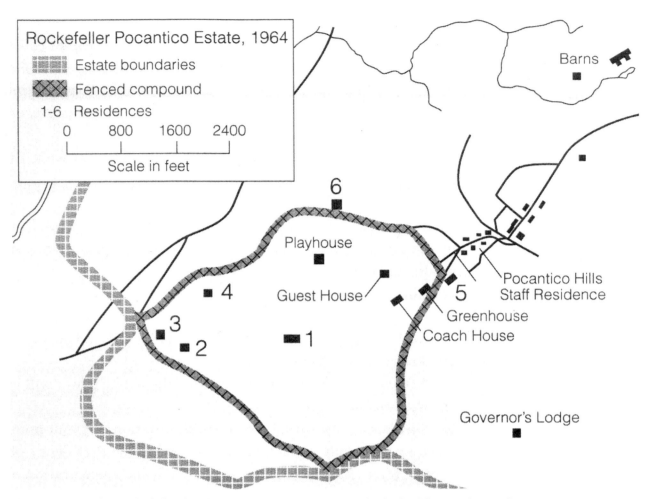

Figure 11.12. The Rockefeller family estate at Pocantico, 1964 (redrafted from Pyle 1964).

public health, Christian missions, technical research, and public education (including anthropology) on an unprecedented scale. By the 1930s, John D. Sr. had controlling interests over a vast financial empire consisting of stockholdings and directorships in some 287 companies, with assets estimated at over $20 billion at that time.[97]

The Rockefeller family's personal estate has been wisely stewarded by the family and has grown significantly over the years. In 1998, *Fortune* magazine estimated the family's combined wealth at $8 billion.[98] The Rockefeller Foundation was the nation's tenth-largest foundation with assets of $2.7 billion, and the Rockefeller Brothers Fund was worth $409 million.[99] The family's interests were long centered in Chase Manhattan Bank, the International Basic Economy Corporation, and the Rockefeller Center in New York. But their interests were dispersed in a complex web of national and international financial holdings and properties that included mines in Chile and oil and supermarkets throughout Latin America.

John D. Sr. and John D. Jr. maintained residences in Manhattan, New Jersey, Maine, and Florida, and Nelson owned huge ranches in Venezuela and Brazil. But most members of the family lived on the 3,600-acre Pocantico estate, 25 miles north of downtown Manhattan (see figures 11.12 and 11.13). This vast estate was carefully consolidated in various family trust funds, many of them managed through a family corporation, Rockefeller Family and Associates, headquartered in Rockefeller Center. Rockefeller family members were influential in building the World Trade Center and donated the property for the United Nations building. The Rockefellers also have been leaders in nature conservation and the arts, and their public policy interests have been fostered through support for conferences and organizations such as the Council on Foreign Relations.

The Rockefellers generally did not hold political offices, although Nelson served as governor of New York from 1958 to 1970 and as vice president of the United States from 1974 to 1977. Nelson's brother Winthrop

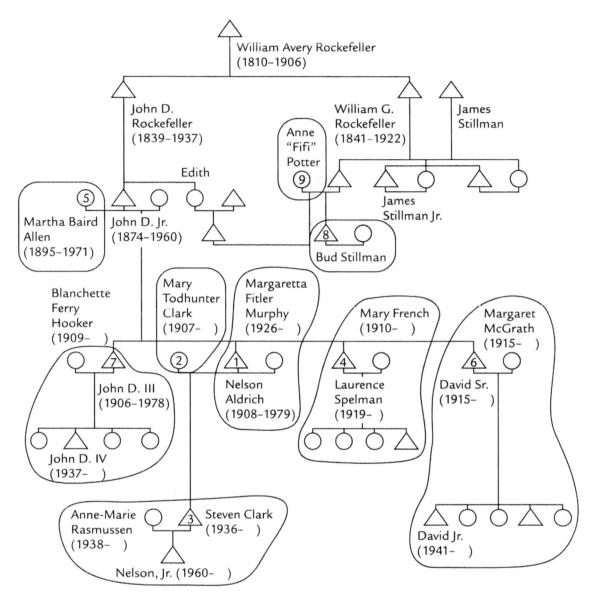

Figure 11-13. The Rockefeller Family genealogy and household groups in 1964. Numbers correspond to houses shown in Figure 11.12. Households numbered 5–9 were located within or adjacent to the Poncantico Estate, but outside the fenced compound.

served as governor of Arkansas from 1967 to 1971 and as lieutenant governor in 1998. John D. IV was a U.S. senator and governor of West Virginia. Many close associates of the family, including Henry Kissinger, Walt Rostow, and Dean Rusk, served in high-level appointments in the federal government.

SUMMARY

America is unquestionably the dominant economic and political-military power in the global system and is viewed by its own citizens as an ideal cultural model for the entire world. However, certain aspects of the culture raise important questions about its effectiveness in providing for the health and well-being, social

cohesion, and stability for all of its citizens. The American cultural ideal of individualism contrasts sharply with the Chinese emphasis on kinship, which is more representative of tribal cultures. Individualism can make life less secure for Americans.

Economic growth is a crucial feature of America's cosmology. Continuous economic growth can make it more difficult for any culture to maintain a balance with natural resources and ecosystems. Ethnohistoric examples from the nation's founding through the nineteenth century reveal the contradictions between the concentrated social power produced by growth in economic and social scale and the American emphasis on democracy, economic freedom, and equal opportunity. The key cultural transformation, which provided the real foundation of American culture, was in the evolution of business into ever-larger-scale organizational forms that were capable of taking full commercial advantage of industrial technology.

The ethnographic example of the industrial village of Rockdale, Pennsylvania, from 1825 to 1865 illustrates the social inequality that sustained America's commercial development. The ethnographic examples of factory farming and cattle raising show how the commercialization and industrialization of food production and consumption transformed the organization of American life. Inequality in the distribution of economic power is perhaps the greatest threat to social cohesion and cultural continuity in America. Inequality in the United States involves differential access to status and prestige, productive resources, income, and economic and political power generally. The existence of this kind of inequality is an objective contradiction in a country that enjoys formal democracy and a high degree of personal freedom. American culture demonstrates that the human problem of social inequality, which seems to be an intrinsic feature of states, is not necessarily solved by capitalist market economies and continuous economic expansion. It is important to understand the cultural significance of inequality in America and the way in which production and consumption is carried out, because at a global level the wealthiest industrial nations occupy the top of an international hierarchy of nations in which most of humanity is desperately impoverished.

STUDY QUESTIONS

1. Discuss the cultural ecological features of factory farming in comparison with less-intensive subsistence systems. Refer to monocrop, Green Revolution, energy input-output ratios, energy subsidy, social consequences, stability, and ecosystem degradation.
2. How is economic and social power distributed in the United States?
3. In what sense is it legitimate to speak of a Cattle Complex in the United States? Make specific comparisons between the role of cattle in the United States and their role in an East African cattle culture. Briefly describe the pathway that American cattle follow as commodities from production to consumption.
4. Using the American beef industry as an example, show how market forces influence specific production and processing practices and promote inequality and social conflict.

5. Discuss how the realities of American society reflect American cosmology.
6. Use the Rockdale case study to illustrate the human impact of industrial development and wage labor.
7. What economic interests did the Founding Fathers represent? Were these interests reflected in the American Constitution?
8. To what extent is it reasonable to speak of social class in America? What are the correlates of social class?
9. Use New York City in 1890 to illustrate the urban problems of particular forms of growth.
10. To what extent is American growth from 1790 to the present related to the distribution of social power?
11. What cultural ecological factors contributed to the importance of beef in the United States, and how do these factors compare with the influence of symbolic and ideological factors over dietary practices?
12. Describe how scarcity and consumption are culturally constructed in America.

SUGGESTED READING

Devita, Philip R., and James D. Armstrong. 1993. *Distant Mirrors: America as a Foreign Culture*. Belmont, CA: Wadsworth. Interpretations of American culture and descriptions of their experiences as outsiders by fourteen foreign scholars, primarily anthropologists.

Domhoff, G. William. 1998. *Who Rules America?: Power and Politics in the Year 2000*. Mountain View, CA: Mayfield. An updated version of Domhoff's 1967 book about elite domination of the American political economy.

Hsu, Francis L. K. 1981. *Americans and Chinese: Passage to Difference*. Honolulu: The University Press of Hawaii. A comparative analysis of American and Chinese culture by a Chinese psychological anthropologist.

Phillips, Kevin. 2002. *Wealth and Democracy: A Political History of the American Rich*. New York: Broadway Books. This is a detailed historical overview and critical analysis of wealth concentration in America since 1776, by a leading authority on political and economic issues.

Spradley, James P., and Michael A. Rynkiewich. 1975. *The Nacirema: Readings on American Culture*. Boston: Little, Brown. A collection of ethnographically based studies of diverse aspects of American culture.

GLOSSARY TERMS

Oligopoly Concentrated economic power when a few sellers can control a market with many buyers by controlling the price and availability of goods.

Factory farming Commercial agriculture based on fossil fuel energy subsidies, mechanization, pesticides, chemical fertilizers, and large-scale mono-cropping.

Energy subsidy The use of fossil fuels to increase food production above the rate that could be sustained through use of renewable energy sources.

Deficit production The situation in which more calories are expended in food production than are produced for human food.

Monocrop farming A system of growing one plant species, sometimes only a single variety, often in very large continuous stands.

Green Revolution Dramatic increases in agricultural production from use of hybrid grains that produce high yields in return for high inputs of chemical fertilizers and pesticides.

Utilitarianism The use of economic profit, direct material advantage, or physical welfare, such as food and shelter, as an explanation for cultural practices.

Deindustrialization The replacement of factory employment with service sector employment in formerly industrial countries as production jobs are moved to low-wage countries.

NOTES

1. U.S. Energy Information Administration. 2009. International Energy Statistics. Total Primary Energy Consumption (Quadrillion Btu), Table: Total Carbon Dioxide Emissions from the Consumption of Energy (Million Metric Tons) www.eia.doe.gov/emeu/international/contents.html.
2. Chinni, Dante. 2008. "About the Patchwork Nation Project." *Christian Science Monitor.* http://patchworknation.csmonitor.com/about/ (accessed March 2010); Gimpel, James G., and Jason E. Schuknecht. 2003. *Patchwork Nation: Sectionalism and Political Change in American Politics.* Ann Arbor: University of Michigan Press.
3. Wall Street 20th Century. 1960. *A Republication of the Yale Daily News' Wall Street 1955.* New Haven, CT: Yale Daily News, 7.
4. Bush, President George W. 2002. *The National Security Strategy of the United States of America* (September).
5. Keynes, John Maynard. 1936. *The General Theory of Employment, Interest and Money.* London: Macmillan.
6. Galbraith, John Kenneth. 1952. *American Capitalism: The Concept of Countervailing Power.* Boston, Houghton Mifflin; Galbraith, John Kenneth. 1958. *The Affluent Society.* Boston: Houghton Mifflin; Galbraith, John Kenneth. 1967. *The New Industrial State.* Boston: Houghton Mifflin.
7. Hayek, Frederick. 1944. *The Road to Serfdom.* Chicago: University of Chicago Press.
8. Friedman, Milton. 1962. *Capitalism and Freedom,* with the assistance of Rose D. Friedman. Chicago: University of Chicago Press.
9. Phillips, Kevin. 1990. *The Politics of Rich and Poor: Wealth and the American Electorate in the Reagan Aftermath.* New York: Random House; Phillips, Kevin. 2002. *Wealth and Democracy: A Political History of the American Rich.* New York: Broadway Books.
10. Hsu, Francis L. K., ed. 1972. "American Core Value and National Character." In *Psychological Anthropology,* pp. 240–62. Cambridge, MA: Schenkman; Hsu, Francis L. K. 1981. *Americans and Chinese: Passage to Difference.* Honolulu: University Press of Hawaii.
11. McDonald, Forrest. 1958. *We the People: The Economic Origins of the Constitution.* Chicago: University of Chicago Press; McDonald, Forrest. 1979. *E. Pluribus Unum: The Formation of the American Republic,* 2nd ed. Indianapolis, IN: Liberty Press; McDonald, Forrest. 1985. *Novus Ordo Seclorum: The Intellectual Origins of the Constitution.* Lawrence: University Press of Kansas.
12. Beard, Charles A. 1913. *An Economic Interpretation of the Constitution of the United States.* New York: Macmillan.
13. Beard, Charles A. 1913. *An Economic Interpretation of the Constitution of the United States.* New York: Macmillan; McDonald, Forrest. 1958. *We the People: The Economic Origins of the Constitution.* Chicago: University of Chicago Press; Ver Steeg, Clarence L. 1954. *Robert Morris Revolutionary Financier.* Philadelphia: University of Pennsylvania Press.
14. Ver Steeg, 1954. *Robert Morris,* 38.
15. Hamilton, Alexander. *Federalist Papers* No. 12.
16. Hamilton, Alexander. *Federalist Papers* No. 35.
17. Noble. 1977. *America by Design: Science, Technology, and the Rise of Corporate Capitalism.* New York: Alfred A. Knopf.
18. Roy, William G. 1997. *Socializing Capital: The Rise of the Large Industrial Corporation in America.* Princeton, NJ: Princeton University Press; Zeitland, Maurice. 1989. *The Large Corporation and Contemporary Classes.* New Brunswick, NJ: Rutgers University Press.
19. Hall, Peter Dobkin. 1982. *The Organization of American Culture, 1700–1900: Private Institutions, Elites, and the Origins of American Nationality,* New York: New York University Press.
20. Dalzell Jr., Robert F. 1987. *Enterprising Elite: The Boston Associates and the World They Made.* Cambridge, MA, and London: Harvard University Press.
21. Pessen, Edward. 1973. *Riches, Class, and Power before the Civil War.* Lexington, MA: Heath.
22. Hall, 1982. *The Organization of American Culture*; Newmyer, R. Kent. 1987. "Harvard Law School, New England Legal Culture, and the Antebellum Origins of American Jurisprudence." *The Journal of American History* 74(3):814–35.
23. McCurdy, Charles W. 1978. "American Law and the Marketing Structure of the Large Corporation, 1875–1890." *The Journal of Economic History* 38(3):631–49.

24. Chandler, Alfred D. Jr. 1977. *The Visible Hand: The Managerial Revolution in American Business.* Cambridge, MA, and London: The Belknap Press of Harvard University Press.

25. Marchand, Roland. 1998. *Creating the Corporate Soul: The Rise of Public Relations and Corporate Imagery in American Big Business.* Berkeley: University of California Press.

26. Chandler, 1977. *The Visible Hand.*

27. Roy, 1997. *Socializing Capital.*

28. Wallace, Anthony F. C. 1978. *Rockdale: The Growth of an American Village in the Early Industrial Revolution.* New York: Knopf.

29. Wallace, 1978, Rockdale, 180.

30. Wallace, 1978, Rockdale, 328.

31. Odum, Howard T. 1971. *Environment, Power, and Society.* New York: Wiley Inter-Science.

32. Whitesides, George M., and George W. Crabtree. 2007. "Don't Forget Long-Term Fundamental Research in Energy." *Science* 315 (9 February): 796–98.

33. Steinhart, John S., and Carol E. Steinhart. 1974. "Energy Use in the U.S. Food System." *Science* 184 (4134):307–16.

34. Borsodi, Ralph. 1929. *The Distribution Age: A Study of the Economy of Modern Distribution.* New York: D. Appleton, 55.

35. United States House Committee on the Judiciary. 1949. *Study of Monopoly Power. Hearings before the Subcommittee on Study of Monopoly Power of the Committee on the Judiciary, House of Representatives, Eighty-First Congress.* First Session. Serial No. 14, Pt. 1. Washington, DC: U.S. Government Printing Office.

36. Heller, Martin C., and Gregory A. Keoleian. 2000. *Life Cycle-Based Sustainability Indicators for Assessment of the U.S. Food System.* Report No CSS00-04 Center for Sustainable Systems. University of Michigan. Ann Arbor, MI.

37. Harris, Marvin. 1985. *Good to Eat: Riddles of Food and Culture.* New York: Simon & Schuster.

38. United States, Department of Agriculture. (USDA) 1997 *Census of Agriculture.* Table 28.

39. United States, Department of Agriculture. (USDA) 1997 *Census of Agriculture.* Table 45.

40. Tyson Foods. 2001. Investor Fact Book. Springdale, AK, 2.

41. United States, Department of Commerce, Bureau of the Census. 2001. *Statistical Abstract of the United States: 1990.* Washington, DC: Government Printing Office, Table 974; Tyson Foods. Tyson Annual Report 2002. Springdale, AK.

42. Thomas, Verl M. 1986. *Beef Cattle Production: An Integrated Approach.* Philadelphia: Lea Febiger.

43. Pietraszek, Greg. 1990. "Cattlemen Face Future Competition with Confidence." *National Provisioner* 202(12):5–8.

44. Olsson, Karen. 2002. "The Shame of Meatpacking." *The Nation* 275 (8):11–16; Schlosser, Eric. 2001. *Fast Food Nation: The Dark Side of the All-American Meal.* Boston: Houghton Mifflin; Stull, Donald D., and Michael J. Broadway. 2003. *Slaughterhouse Blues: The Meat and Poultry Industry in North America.* Belmont, CA: Wadsworth/Thomson Learning.

45. Schlosser, Eric. 2002. "Bad Meat: The Scandal of Our Food Safety System." *The Nation* 275(8):6–7.

46. Drew, Christopher, Elizabeth Becker, and Sandra Blakeslee. 2003. "Despite Mad-Cow Warnings, Industry Resisted Safeguards." *New York Times,* Dec. 28.

47. Harris, 1985. *Good to Eat.*

48. Sahlins, Marshall. 1968. "Notes on the Original Affluent Society" In *Man the Hunter,* edited by Richard Lee and Irven DeVore, pp. 85–89. Chicago: Aldine, 86.

49. Henry, Jules. 1963. *Culture Against Man.* New York: Random House.

50. Sahlins, Marshall. 1976b. *Culture and Practical Reason.* Chicago and London: University of Chicago Press.

51. Sahlins, Marshall. 1976b. *Culture and Practical Reason.*

52. Ritzer, George. 2000. *The McDonaldization of Society.* Thousand Oaks, CA: Pine Forge Press.

53. United States Statistical Abstract, 2002, Table 195.

54. Statistical Abstract, 2002, Table 190.

55. Flegal, Katherine M., Margaret D. Carroll, Cynthia L. Ogden, and Lester R. Curtin. 2010. "Prevalence and Trends in Obesity among U.S. Adults, 1999–2008. *JAMA (Journal of the American Medical Association)* 303(3):235–41.

56. Nestle, Marion. 2002. *Food Politics: How the Food Industry Influences Nutrition and Health.* Berkeley: University of California Press.

57. Willet, Walter C. 2001. *Eat, Drink, and Be Healthy.* New York: Simon & Schuster.

58. Gilder, George. 1981. *Wealth and Poverty.* New York: Basic Books.

59. Jones, Alice Hanson. 1977. *American Colonial Wealth: Documents and Methods.* 3 vols. New York: Arno Press; Jones, Alice Hanson. 1980. *Wealth of a Nation to Be: The American Colonies on the Eve of the Revolution.* New York: Columbia University Press.

60. Soltow, Lee. 1975. *Men and Wealth in the United States 1850–1870.* New Haven, CT, and London: Yale University Press.

61. Jaher, Frederic Cople. 1972. "Nineteenth-Century Elites in Boston and New York." *Journal of Social History* 6(1):32–77; Jaher, Frederic Cople. 1982. *The Urban Establishment: Upper Strata in Boston, New York, Charleston, Chicago, and Los Angeles.* Urbana: University of Illinois Press; Pessen, Edward. 1971. "The Egalitarian Myth and the American Social Reality: Wealth, Mobility, and Equality in the 'Era of the Common Man.'" *The American Historical Review* 76(4):989–1034; Pessen, Edward. 1973. *Riches, Class, and Power before the Civil War.* Lexington, MA: Heath.

62. Jaher, 1982. *The Urban Establishment*, 255.

63. Soltow, 1975. *Men and Wealth*, 53,

64. Cited in Pessen, 1971. "The Egalitarian Myth," 997.

65. Soltow, 1975. *Men and Wealth*, 112.

66. Moody, John. 1904. *The Truth about the Trusts: A Description and Analysis of the American Trust Movement*. New York: Moody Publishing, 44.

67. Moody, 1904. *The Truth about the Trusts*, 44.

68. Riis, Jacob A. 1904. *How the Other Half Lives: Studies Among the Tenements of New York*. New York: Scribner.

69. DeForest, Robert W., and Lawrence Veiller. 1903. *The Tenement House Problem: Including the Report of the New York State Tenement House Commission of 1900*. 2 vols. New York: Macmillan.

70. Brown, Barton McCaul. 1987. "Population Estimation from Floor Area: A Restudy of 'Naroll's Constant.'" *Behavior Science Research* 21(1–4):1–49; Naroll, Raoul. 1962. "Floor Area and Settlement Population." *American Antiquity* 27(4):587–89.

71. Hammack, David C. 1982. *Power and Society: Greater New York at the Turn of the Century*. New York: Russell Sage Foundation, 56.

72. Gronowicz, Anthony. 1998. *Race and Class Politics in New York City before the Civil War*. Boston: Northeastern University Press.

73. Mann, Michael. 2003. *Incoherent Empire*. London: Verso; Myers, Richard B. 2003. "Shift to a Global Perspective." *Naval War College Review* 56(4):9–17.

74. Miller, Matthew. 2007. "The *Forbes* 400." *Forbes*. www.forbes.com/2007/09/19/richest-americans-forbes-lists-richlist07-cx_mm_0920rich_land.html.

75. McChesney, Robert W. 2000. *Rich Media, Poor Democracy: Communication Politics in Dubious Times*. New York: The New Press.

76. Herman, Edward S., and Noam Chomsky. 2002. *Manufacturing Consent: The Political Economy of the Mass Media*. New York: Pantheon.

77. Mander, Jerry. 1978. *Four Arguments for the Elimination of Television*. New York: Quill; Boorstin, Daniel J. 1985. *The Image: A Guide to Pseudo-Events in America*. New York: Atheneum.

78. Simon, David R. 1999. *Elite Deviance*. 6th ed. Boston: Allyn & Bacon.

79. Dye, Thomas R. 1983. *Who's Running America? The Reagan Years*. Englewood Cliffs, NJ: Prentice-Hall.

80. Briody, Dan. 2003. *The Iron Triangle: Inside the Secret World of the Carlyle Group*. Hoboken, NJ: John Wiley.

81. Harris, Marvin. 1981. *America Now: The Anthropology of a Changing Culture*. New York: Simon & Schuster.

82. Bluestone, Barry, and Bennett Harrison. 1982. *The Deindustrialization of America*. New York: Basic Books.

83. Lasch, Christopher. 1995. *The Revolt of the Elites and the Betrayal of Democracy*. New York: Norton.

84. Toth, James. 1992. "Doubts about Growth: The Town of Carlisle in Transition." *Urban Anthropology* 21(1):2–44.

85. Newman, Katherine S. 1988. *Falling from Grace: The Experience of Downward Mobility in the American Middle Class*. New York: Free Press; Newman, Katherine S. 1993. *Declining Fortunes: The Withering of the American Dream*. New York: Basic Books.

86. Nash, June. 1989. *From Tank Town to High Tech: The Clash of Community and Industrial Cycles*. Albany: State University of New York Press; Nash, June. 1994. "Global Integration and Subsistence Insecurity." *American Anthropologist* 96(1):7–30.

87. Gregorio, David I., Stephen J. Walsh, and Deborah Paturzo. 1997. "The Effects of Occupation-Based Social Position on Mortality in a Large American Cohort." *American Journal of Public Health* 87(9):1472–75.

88. National Center for Health Statistics. 1998. *Health, United States, 1998*. Washington, DC: U.S. Government Printing Office.

89. Wilkinson, Richard G. 1996. *Unhealthy Societies: The Afflictions of Inequality*. London and New York: Routledge; Wilkinson, Richard G. 1997. "Comment: Income, Inequality, and Social Cohesion." *American Journal of Public Health* 87(9):1504–6.

90. Wolf, Steward, and John G. Bruhn. 1993. *The Power of Clan: The Influence of Human Relationships on Heart Disease*. New Brunswick, NJ, and London: Transaction Books.

91. Lundberg, Ferdinand. 1939. *America's 60 Families*. New York: Halcyon House; Lundberg, Ferdinand. 1968. *The Rich and the Super-Rich: A Study of Money Power Today*. New York: L. Stuart.

92. Mills, C. Wright. 1956. *The Power Elite*. New York: Oxford University Press.

93. Domhoff, G. William. 1967. *Who Rules America?* Englewood Cliffs, NJ: Prentice-Hall; Domhoff, G. William. 1983. *Who Rules America Now? A View for the '80s*. Englewood Cliffs, NJ: Prentice-Hall.

94. Jones, Alice Hanson. 1980. *Wealth of a Nation to Be: The American Colonies on the Eve of the Revolution*. New York: Columbia University Press; Table 3.1.

95. Bodley, John H. 2003. *The Power of Scale: A Global History Approach*. Armonk, NY: M. E. Sharpe, 46–53.

96. Bodley, John H. 1999. "Socio-Economic Growth, Culture Scale, and Household Well-Being: A Test of the Power-Elite Hypothesis." *Current Anthropology* 40(5):595–620.

97. Colby, Gerard, and Charlotte Dennett. 1995. *Thy Will Be Done: The Conquest of the Amazon: Nelson Rockefeller in the Age of Oil*. New York: HarperCollins, HarperPerennial; Collier, Peter, and David Horowitz. 1976. *The Rockefellers: An American Dynasty*. New York: Holt, Rinehart & Winston; Rochester, Ann. 1936. *Rulers of America: A Study of Finance Capital*. New York: International, 56.

98. Gorham, Kafka, and Neelakantan. 1998. "The *Forbes* 400: The Richest People in America." *Forbes* 162(8):165–428.

99. Foundation Directory. 1998, vol. 20. New York: Columbia University Press: xi.

CHAPTER 12

An Unsustainable Global System

Figure 12.0. Singapore high rise hotel towers under construction at casino complex, 2009 (Tom Bodley).

LEARNING OBJECTIVES

AFTER STUDYING THIS CHAPTER YOU SHOULD BE ABLE TO DO the following:

1. Understand the difference between making predictions about the future and using trend projection and simulated futures for policy development.
2. Understand the magnitude of the human impact on the physical and biological environment marking the Anthropocene and the Great Acceleration.
3. Understand how intergovernmental organizations such as the World Bank and the United Nations Development Program rank countries by their economies and by human development.
4. Explain why poverty may be considered a distribution problem rather than a production problem.
5. Describe the ethnographic realities of daily life in the impoverished world based on examples from Brazil and Bangladesh, identifying the political and economic factors that create these conditions.
6. Describe the human consequences of the Green Revolution in Bangladesh.
7. Describe the different approaches that the United Nations and its specialized agencies, such as the World Bank, have taken toward global poverty since 1945. Assess their effectiveness.
8. Describe the ideological assumptions of Utopian capitalism and test its predictions of progress against the evidence.
9. Understand the sustainability of sociocultural systems in reference to the humanization process as well as social and environmental sustainability.

The primary global problems of the contemporary commercial world can be reduced to three issues: environment, poverty, and conflict. Global warming, the degradation of natural resources, destruction of natural ecosystems, and loss of biodiversity are the obvious environmental problems. Hundreds of millions of people are malnourished or have unmet material needs. Some 200 million were killed by governments during the twentieth century, either in armed conflicts or by genocides and internal political violence. Some governments are so corrupt or underfinanced that they are not functional. These are problems of sociocultural systems that have grown too large and too complex to be successfully managed. Social power has become so concentrated that entire societies can not maintain a sustainable balance with natural resources or provide people with enough social support to successfully maintain their families and reproduce people and culture. This means that politicization and commercialization processes have overwhelmed the humanization process. In this respect, dysfunctional sociocultural systems can become dehumanizing. The present chapter will consider the extent to which this

419

might be the case. Chapters in part IV will consider how this situation can be changed to construct a sustainable national society and global system.

During the decades following World War II, the disparity in material welfare between the wealthy industrial nations and the rest of the world steadily widened, as did the gap between rich and poor within individual countries. Even as decolonization and technological progress proceeded, increasing millions of people throughout the world came to live in absolute poverty. By 1980, an estimated 730 million people (excluding China) were living on diets considered inadequate by international standards and had extremely limited access to material resources. By the late 1980s, dramatic increases in poverty were occurring throughout the world. Real living standards plunged while public spending for social services declined as many countries found themselves deeply in debt to First World lenders. When the new millennium began, 1.2 billion people were thought to be living in extreme poverty. That was roughly the entire population of the world in 1850. Nearly a billion urban people did not have access to basic sanitation. Viewed objectively, this would not seem to be an adaptive form of cultural evolution and lends more credibility to the theory that economic globalization is elite directed.

Development, as it has been practiced throughout most of the twentieth century, has systematically undermined the self-maintenance abilities of rural communities, leaving them highly vulnerable to outside exploitation. Nearly half of the global population was urbanized, but the lives of most were totally dependent on sources of employment and material resources that they did not control. The primary ideological justification for elite-directed economic growth was that it would ultimately improve everyone's lives, but the outcome of decades of development suggests that a fundamental reassessment of the entire issue is required.

This chapter begins with a close look at the Anthropocene. This is the visible cumulative global impact of human activities on the earth's natural system. The question is to assess the extent to which humans have undermined the natural processes that sustain our societies and cultures. The next section examines the international development establishment since 1945, focusing on the United Nations (UN) and related agencies and the United States. We examine the complex structure of development at the global level, considering the flow of resources, costs, and benefits and show why development often works against the interests of local communities. This section also examines the human realities of impoverishment using case material from Brazil and Bangladesh, where communities have been impoverished by technologically based development programs that leave grossly unequal power structures in place. Next, we discuss diverse anthropological perspectives on development, peasantries, and poverty. The final section considers the possibility of system collapse, which would constitute definitive evidence of nonsustainability.

LIMITS TO GROWTH

The 1972 *Limits to Growth* book, sponsored by the Club of Rome think tank, was the first major attempt to forecast broad trends between population and economic growth for a popular audience using computer simulations of the sustainability of the global system.[1] This work looked at broad patterns from 1900 to 1970 and projected trends to 2100, showing graphically that the global system as then constituted was unsustainable (see figure 12.1). The authors did not predict collapse, but they showed how it could occur if economic growth based on ever-increasing flows of energy and material and population growth could not be sustained for 200 years. Unlimited growth itself was the problem. This view, of course, conflicted with the prevailing paradigm of perpetual growth and capital accumulation promoted by the global elite, and the authors were falsely vilified and personally attacked. Criticism continued even though their findings were repeatedly verified in detail by many other studies.[2] It needs to be stressed that the Limits to Growth does not refer to limits set by any specific natural resources. It considers the interaction of the many factors—social, biological, and material—that make continuous growth impossible, and in this respect it remains a background for this chapter.

One of the strongest scientific forecasts of looming unsustainability, which came 20 years after *Limits to Growth*, was the 1992 Union of Concerned Scientists' "World Scientists' Warning to Humanity." In this strongly worded public statement some 1,700 senior scientists from all over the world, including five anthropologists, most of the living Nobel laureates in science, and the president of the American Association for the Advancement of Science declared:

> If not checked, many of our current practices put at serious risk the future that we wish for human society and the plant and animal kingdoms, and may so alter the living world that it will be unable to sustain life in the manner that we know. Fundamental changes

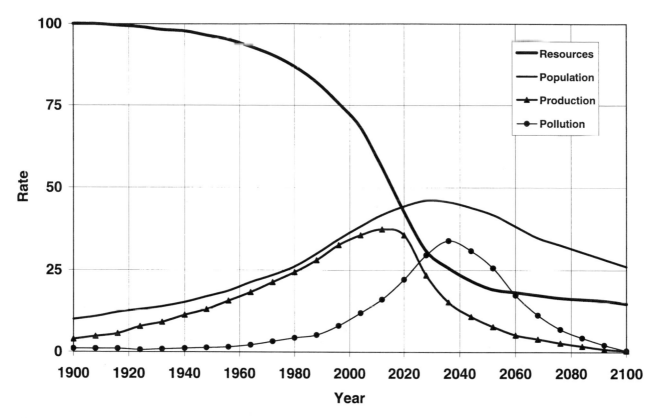

Figure 12.1. Graph of potential global system collapse. According to this famous computer projection from the 1972 *Limits to Growth* study, if historical trends in population and economic growth continued with no change, the global commercial culture would collapse well before 2100 (redrafted from Meadows et al. 1972:124).

are urgent if we are to avoid the collision our present course will bring about. . . . The greatest peril is to become trapped in spirals of environmental decline, poverty, and unrest, leading to social, economic and environmental collapse.[3]

They warned that action was needed within ten to twenty years to avoid the prospects for humanity being "immeasurably diminished." They described an unsustainable global society and environment, which now seems to be directly confronting us, and they issued a call for action. Their central message was that high levels of energy and material consumption alongside of great injustice and inequality do not constitute a sustainable global society. The following sections review some of the evidence for unsustainability.

THE ANTHROPOCENE: HUMANITY'S GLOBAL FOOTPRINT

Discovering the Anthropocene

In 2000 Dutch atmospheric chemist Paul Crutzen, who won the Nobel Prize for his work on ozone depletion, and marine biologist Paul Stoermer published

a brief overview of the recent evidence of the global-scale impact of humans on the physical world and atmosphere and concluded that humans had produced a new geological epoch they called the Anthropocene.[4] The Anthropocene began just two centuries ago and marks the end of the Holocene, which began with the end of the last glacial advances 10,000 to 12,000 years ago. Most of human biological evolution apparently occurred during the prior Pleistocene epoch, which began some 2.5 million years ago. Crutzen and Stoermer noted the astounding tenfold expansion of human numbers in just three centuries from 1700 to 2000; the parallel expansion in per-capita resource consumption; growth of the global herd of domestic cattle to 1.4 billion animals; and a tenfold increase in urbanization over the past century. They noted that humanity was depleting in a matter of centuries fossil fuels that nature had produced over hundreds of millions of years, and in the process people were pumping sulfur dioxide into the atmosphere at twice the rate of all natural resources. Sulfur dioxide produces sulfuric acid, which falls as acid rain and damages plants and marine animals and erodes buildings and monuments.

Humans are now producing synthetic nitrogen at a higher rate than plants. Humans produce more nitric oxide than nature, causing air pollution. We use more than half of all freshwater and have physically altered much of the landscape, causing a massive increase in the background rate of plant and animal extinctions. Humans have physically altered geochemical cycles in freshwater lakes and rivers in ways that leave traces in sediments produced by aquatic organisms and are taking 25 to 35 percent of marine biological production from the oceans. As noted in chapter 10, humans are also taking at least 25 percent of terrestrial biological product, and our global ecological footprint may have reached 122 percent of nature's potential production by 2001, when the biological equivalent of our fossil fuel use is counted. Estimates for 2007 showed the global footprint at 150 percent of nature's biocapacity.[5] The most visible human impacts on the earth may, of course, be climate change from emissions of greenhouse gases such as carbon dioxide (CO_2).

Crutzen and Stoermer selected the late eighteenth century to mark the beginning of the Anthropocene, because that is when sudden increases in anthropogenic greenhouse gases first appear in glacial ice cores. This is also the beginning of the "fossil-fuel revolution," the "Industrial Revolution," steam engines, and not coincidentally, the invention of the first graphs showing economic growth. Other geological researchers have also endorsed the concept of the Anthropocene.[6] They concur with the criteria listed by Crutzen and Stoermer and point to a sudden increase in the overall rate of anthropogenic denudation of the earth by increased erosion and sedimentation, which leave highly visible physical markers. They also suggest that a date of approximately 1800 AD could be accepted as the beginning of the Anthropocene. People are now quite literally moving more earth in a year than nature. The concept of the Anthropocene matters because it calls attention to the enormous magnitude of the impact on nature of human in the commercial world and the unsustainability of the commercial world as presently constituted.

During the 1980s, a sequence of environmental events occurred that made it difficult for even the most optimistic planners to deny the possibility that the commercial culture would need to make major adjustments to ensure its long-term survival. In 1982, German scientists announced that acid rain caused by industrial pollution was destroying European forests. In 1985, British scientists reported a thinning in the ozone layer over Antarctica, which was attributed to release of chlorofluorocarbons used in refrigerants and as propellants in spray cans. In 1986, world population passed the 5-billion mark; the Soviet nuclear reactor at Chernobyl exploded, spewing radiation worldwide; and an article in the British science journal *Nature* reported measurable evidence that global warming was taking place due to elevated levels of CO_2, the greenhouse effect.[7] Negative feedbacks of the sort predicted by the *Limits to Growth* model were taking place.

Anthropogenic Biomes: Transformed Nature

Humans have now become such a force in nature that biogeographers have recently acknowledged that the categorization and mapping of natural biomes and ecozones are no longer reliable guides for understanding the contemporary world. Natural biomes such as tropical forest, deciduous forest, coniferous forest, grassland, desert, and arctic and alpine tundra have in many cases become conspicuously "unnatural." In the tribal world people modified and managed otherwise-natural ecosystems, often taking advantage of natural ecosystem cycles to increase biological productivity, but since the beginning of the Anthropocene, human activities have completely degraded or replaced natural ecosystems that had formerly been relatively stable for millennia even with humans as part of the system. The Anthropocene marks an age in which humans have in effect created their own biomes in which they are the dominant agents. This new situation seriously threatens the sustainability of the biosphere that humans ultimately depend on.

Geographers Ellis and Ramankutty[8] have classified and mapped eighteen distinctly *Anthropocenic biomes* and just three Wildland biomes for the world, based on their analysis of human population, land use, and land cover using data from satellite imagery allowing the entire world to be mapped at a resolution of cells at the equator measuring approximately 6 x 6 miles (9 x 9 km). "Wild" areas were cells showing no visible human presence, whereas settlements, crops, or pastures were visible in anthropogenic areas, which could be sorted by density as dense, residential (>10 persons/km²), populated (>1 person/km²), and remote (<1 person/km²). Their analysis identified five major anthropogenic biomes: Dense Settlements; Villages; Croplands; Rangelands; and Forested; and one natural biome: Wildlands. Collectively, anthropogenic biomes covered more than 75 percent of the unglaciated terrestrial globe, 80 percent of forested lands, and accounted for an astounding 90 percent of terrestrial biological production. This means that although humans may not consume more than 25 percent of terrestrial nature's product, we direct 90 percent of nature's product. Furthermore, 45 percent of the earth's net primary biological product was produced in areas with a human density of more than ten persons per square kilometer.

Anthropogenic biomes for the entire world can be viewed in Google Earth and Google Maps.[9] For example, the Asháninka territory is entirely within the Wild Forests Wildland biome, indicated areas where human impact is not readily apparent from space, and Remote Forests and Populated Forests Anthropogenic biomes, where the human presence is visible, but their impact minor. Similar global maps have been produced measuring human influence on a single dimension.[10] "Last of the Wild" maps produced by the Wildlife Conservation Society and the Center for International Earth Science Information Network at Columbia University are at a finer resolution than the Anthropogenic biome map and use a scale of 1 to 100 to represent percent of human influence from least to most. A value of 1 on the human influence index indicates the wildest area of a natural biome. A score of 10 or below indicated "Wild" areas. Human influence visible from satellites included land transformation; human access by roads, rivers, and coastlines; and the electrical grid, measured by visible nighttime lights. This analysis showed a more pervasive human presence than the Anthropogenic biome map. The human footprint was visible on 83 percent of the land and on 98 percent of areas where rice, wheat, or maize could be grown.

A close inspection of these maps consistently shows that existing self-sufficient tribal groups and many indigenous peoples live in the areas of least human influence, or the lightest human footprints. These maps clearly settle the question of whether or not tribal peoples are more "in tune" with nature than peoples operating fully within the contemporary commercial world. Most tribal peoples tread lightly on the earth.

Anthropogenic Climate Change

Human-induced changes in global climate, which most experts conclude are now under way, are an ominous indication that critical natural thresholds have already been crossed. Global warming is probably the single most dramatic and far-reaching environmental impact of industrial development. The natural cycles of the past 2 million years would suggest that the world is more than halfway through an interglacial period and should be cooling, but instead the world has actually warmed over the past 100 years. The greenhouse effect, which has been recognized as a theoretical possibility since the nineteenth century, assumes that increased atmospheric CO_2 gas from the burning of fossil fuels (see figure 12.2) would heat the earth like the glass of a greenhouse by trapping solar heat near the earth's surface. Evidence that human activities were impacting global climate was presented at the first UN-sponsored World Climate Conference in 1979, but it was nearly a decade before a full institutional response began. However, further proof of the greenhouse effect continued to emerge. Precise measurements showed an increase of nearly 8 percent in atmospheric CO_2 between 1958 and 1984,[11] and CO_2 gas bubbles trapped in Antarctic ice showed relative stability over the previous 10,000 years.[12]

Carbon is stored in natural "sinks," or reservoirs, either as organic matter, especially in forest biomass, or in coal and oil, or in the ocean. In the natural carbon cycle, CO_2 is taken up by plants during photosynthesis. It is also stored chemically in the ocean. Carbon is released back into the atmosphere as CO_2 by respiration, decomposition, and other chemical and biological processes. Large-scale human burning of fossil fuels and forests imbalances the cycle by withdrawing carbon from storage faster than it can be reabsorbed by the forests and oceans.

In the 1980s, CO_2 was considered to be responsible for more than half of the predicted global warming, while other less common but more active greenhouse gases such as methane, chlorofluorocarbons (CFCs), and nitrous oxide contributed the remainder. Although methane is produced naturally as swamp gas and by termites, significant quantities are also produced by fermentation in rice paddies and in the digestive tracts of domestic cattle.[13] CFCs are a commercial product that chemists synthesized in the 1920s. Their ability to destroy the ozone that screens the earth from ultraviolet radiation has been suspected since 1974.[14]

It is impossible to predict with absolute confidence how much warming will occur; however, the Intergovernmental Panel on Climate Change (IPCC), established in 1988 by the World Meteorological Organization and the UN Environment Program, has produced the most comprehensive overview of the problem available. The IPCC issued its first report in 1991 and its Fourth Assessment Report in 2007.[15] Each assessment report is based on years of work by hundreds of scientists and contributions from dozens of research institutes from throughout the world.

Figure 12.2. The amount of emissions in the atmosphere rose by 8 percent between 1958 and 1984. Emission such as from this diesel-burning truck contributed to this increase (U.S. Environmental Protection Agency 2010 EPA 454/R-09-002, p. 26).

They are backed up by numerous special reports and technical papers. The Fifth Assessment Report is due in 2014.

IPCC researchers organized their effort in three working groups to examine respectively the scientific aspects of climate change, its impacts, and possible responses. The IPCC's findings show unmistakable evidence of global warming caused by human activities. The Fourth Assessment strengthened the conclusion that anthropogenic greenhouse gases were "very likely" the cause, and later research continues to confirm these conclusions.[16] Burning of fossil fuels and land development have caused atmospheric concentrations of CO_2, the principal greenhouse gas, to increase by more than 38 percent from 280 ppm (parts per million) in 1750 to 388 ppm by the year 2010.[17] Global CO_2 remained relatively constant over the thousand years before 1750, when global commercial development began to expand dramatically. Average global surface temperature increased by 0.6°C (1°F) during the twentieth century. Warming in the Northern Hemisphere was greater than in any century during the last thousand years, and the 1990s were the warmest decade of the millennium. It appears that climate change is already causing social and economic damage from floods, droughts, and other severe weather events. Glaciers are retreating, Arctic ice is thinning, permafrost is melting, winter snow cover is declining, northern rivers and lakes are thawing two weeks earlier than a century ago, growing seasons are increasing, and plant and animal distributions, flowering, and breeding seasons are changing. Global mean sea level increased at one to two millimeters annually during the twentieth century, for a total of some six inches. Sea level rise is caused by expansion of the ocean as it warms as well as by water added from melting glaciers and ice fields.

Anthropogenic climate change is barely detectable in the geological climate record until about AD 1850, when the effects of industrial development begin to be clearly visible. Since about 1960, human effects on greenhouse gases and climate have increased steadily in step with economic globalization and accelerated burning of fossil fuels and deforestation. Between 1960 and 2010 atmospheric CO_2 increased 21 percent from 317 to 388 ppm. In 2007 a 450-ppm atmospheric CO_2 threshold was proposed to meet the 1.7°C stabilization target, but new research quickly made this threshold seem far too high. By 2009 it seemed clear to many researchers that atmospheric CO_2 should not be allowed to rise above 350 ppm, and an emergency climate stabilization program was needed.[18] Several authorities[19] have urged that only a very rapid total abandonment of fossil fuels, or "decarbonization," would prevent atmospheric greenhouse gases from exceeding a "tipping point" that, if continued, would lead to a "point of no return" in which negative impacts would be beyond human control. Serious negative effects on alpine glaciers, polar ice sheets, the ocean, and coral reefs were already readily apparent in 2008 when CO_2 levels reached 385 ppm.

The projected effects of climate change are illustrated in color plate 12 and are discussed in the last section of this chapter.

Collapse of Marine Fisheries and Ecosystems

One of the more serious side effects of the global greenhouse process is acidification of the ocean caused by the increasing absorption of CO_2. John E. Veron, one of the world's leading authorities on corals and especially Australia's Great Barrier Reef, has made the case that global warming is bleaching and killing coral reefs worldwide on an unprecedented scale and speed due to warming ocean temperatures and acidification.[20] From a geological perspective, Veron compares the ongoing loss of coral reefs to similar die-offs that that occurred at least five times in the past, beginning at the end of the Ordovician some 434 million years ago, and most recently at the beginning of the Cenozoic some 65 million years ago. Each of these episodes was associated with mass extinctions of plants and animals, causing major shifts in biological evolution. Coral reefs and many other marine organisms, including plankton, live in calcium carbonate skeletons and are uniquely sensitive to acid levels, with available calcium declining as acid levels increase. Coral reefs and marine plankton are crucial parts of marine ecosystem, leading Veron to warn that we may be experiencing the beginning of the sixth episode of mass extinctions. Other researchers are reporting very rapid declines in reef calcification in the Great Barrier Reef and support Veron's warning: "There is little doubt that coral reefs are under unprecedented pressure worldwide because of climate change, changes in water quality from terrestrial runoff, and overexploitation."[21] The problem with the present event is that it is occurring much faster than at any time in the past, and organisms will have difficulty adapting by natural selection to a suddenly more acidic ocean. The loss of coral reefs is already a source of major concern for many Pacific Island peoples whose livelihood immediately depends on marine ecosystems.

The world's oceans account for nearly half of global biological production (net primary production, NPP), but until exploitation by commercial world peoples began, humans had relatively little measurable impact on the oceans. It is assumed that many of the earliest human colonists of the continents outside of Africa first exploited the rich marine shellfish of coastal areas and only later moved inland to hunt and fish and domesticate plants and animals. The transition from freshwater fishing to dependence on marine fisheries is documented for England at about 1000 AD, and this may have involved extensive trade with Norwegian fishermen.[22] Global-scale fishing did not expand dramatically until 1960, when the highly productive North Atlantic and North Pacific fishing grounds were fully developed, and commercial fishing moved to the Southern Hemisphere. In 1965 Swedish food scientist and ecologist Georg Borgstrom called attention to the importance of marine fisheries as a seemingly easy source of protein for expanding global population. Borgstrom called marine fisheries "ghost acres" because they replaced agricultural land that would otherwise be devoted to raising livestock. He estimated that Japan was already gaining the equivalent of six times its agricultural land from the sea.[23] Allowing for El Niño–related collapses of the Peruvian anchoveta fisheries and overreporting by Chinese fisheries, global commercial fisheries appear to have been in decline since 1988, but unreliability of reporting casts doubt on official figures.[24] By 2000 it seemed clear that the world's major global fisheries were fully fished, and fishermen were moving down the food chain, taking smaller and smaller fish.[25] The outlook was not good, as two Canadian fisheries researchers concluded in 2001: "The present trends of overfishing, wide-scale disruption of coastal habitats and the rapid expansion of non-sustainable acquaculture enterprises … threaten the world's food security."[26] Research by another team of marine biologists and ecologists showed fisheries in Europe, North America, and Australia remained relatively stable from 1000 AD to 1800, after which fisheries collapsed and extinctions began to occur. A close view of fishery trends from 1950 to 2003 in sixty-four large marine ecosystems worldwide showed such dramatic declines in population numbers and biodiversity and such slow recoveries that researchers projected a complete global collapse of fisheries by 2048 if drastic protection measures were not adopted.[27]

Very large, commercially valuable fisheries, such as the Atlantic cod, that had been exploited for centuries plummeted after reaching a peak in the late 1960s, and the bluefin tuna is currently in trouble. Ecological "fishprint" data by nations for 2003 show that most nations are overfishing based on the biocapacity of the marine areas within their EEZs (exclusive economic zones).[28] The fishprint is especially important because it accounts for all the biological production required to produce fish. As much as 1,500 tons of biomass goes into the production of one ton of large carnivorous fish such as salmon and the bluefin tuna at the top of the food chain. Some countries were seriously out of balance with their own marine resources. Japan, for example, was taking an estimated seven times its available marine bioproductivity by drawing fish from other waters and relying on global trade. Global fishprint data suggest that the world was taking 157 percent of global marine biocapacity in 2003, which explains the observed fishery collapses. This is significantly higher than the 122 percent of terrestrial biocapacity for the world in 2001 noted previously.

The worldwide decline or stabilization in fisheries was accompanied by a rise in aquaculture, which rose steeply between 1987 and 1997, and by 2000 farmed fish and shellfish accounted for about one-fourth of all human fish consumption (not counting fish meal fed to animals, including farmed fish).[29] Pacific Island peoples sometimes practiced sustainable aquaculture as part of their precommercial self-sufficient food systems, but the scale of some important new forms of aquaculture today may prove unsustainable. The paradox of fish farming as an obvious further step in subsistence intensification is that fish farming of carnivorous species, such as salmon, may damage local marine habitats; also, they are fed fish meal and oil from wild stocks, which may further accelerate the decline of wild fisheries. Many fish farms actually consume two to five times more fish protein than they produce. This is an energy subsidy that characterizes many aspects of high-energy commercial food systems, as noted in previous chapters.

The first detailed mapping of marine ecoregions was published in 2007,[30] in response to the obvious urgency of constructing a globally coordinated system of strategically selected marine-protected areas to save as much biodiversity as possible. The map divided the world's oceans and seas into 12 Realms, 62 Provinces, and 232 Ecoregions. This was followed by a detailed map of human impacts on the global marine ecosystems, which can be viewed online.[31] Every square kilometer of ocean was assigned a numerical score for the estimated effects of seventeen "anthropogenic drivers" of ecological change—including pollution from fertilizer and pesticide runoff, population density, different kinds of fishing, oil rigs, invasive species, shipping, changes in sea surface temperature, and ocean acidification—and assessed for twenty specific marine ecosystems such as coral reefs, seagrass, rocky reefs, mangroves, and pelagic (open ocean) waters. The impact scores were then merged into a single score and the value for each square kilometer was displayed on a six-level rank scale from very low to very high impact. Some degree of human impact was detected on every square kilometer of ocean, and more than a third (41 percent) showed medium high to very high impacts. As expected, coastal ecosystems were hit the hardest, and global warming had the most widespread impacts. Nearly half of all coral reefs were found to have medium high to very high human impacts. Less than 4 percent of the ocean was low impact, and these were largely in polar regions. However, the recent expansion of the international fishing fleet operating out of the Falkland Islands is beginning to tap Antarctic waters, which may represent the world's last great reservoir of marine protein.

The depletion of ocean fisheries and the rise of aquaculture is apparently not a response to the need to feed hungry people in the "developing" world. China, with its booming economy, takes a large share of global fish consumption that is attributed to the developing world, but even so, per-capita fish consumption is higher in developed countries and the net balance of trade in fish products is also toward developed countries.[32] Real social inequity is apparent in the consumption of fish and may be driving some of the shift to aquaculture, especially for shrimp and salmon. Exports of fish products exceeded the value of such familiar agricultural products as rice, coffee, sugar, tea, bananas, and meat from the developing world by 2001. Much of the consumer demand for farmed shrimp and salmon is from the corporate restaurant chains and large supermarkets in North America and Europe. Large corporations also control much of the production and distribution of farmed products and contract with fishing trawlers for their catch of wild fish.

Sustainability or Collapse? Perspectives on Humanity and Nature

The Millennium Ecosystems Assessment commissioned by UN Secretary-General Kofi Annan in 2001 was a definitive statement demonstrating that the present global system was having an unsustainable impact on the environment.[33] The goal of the assessment was to provide guidance to UN programs concerned with sustainable development. Some 1,360 experts worked on the $25 million project over four years, producing a multivolume report in 2005. The assessment is backed up by a detailed worldwide accounting of the status of nature, and of nature's ability to provide services to people such as nutrient cycling; soil formation; biological production of food; fiber, and fuel; provision of freshwater; and regulation of climate, watersheds, and disease. The assessment dramatically verified the pioneer *Limits to Growth* study and anticipated the *Great Acceleration* concept (see below) by declaring that the past fifty years have had the most extreme impacts of any time in human history.

The assessment board issued its conclusions in a separate volume, *Living beyond Our Means*, with a "stark warning" that "human activity is putting such strain on the natural functions of Earth that the ability of the planet's ecosystems to sustain future generations can no longer be taken for granted."[34] They found that nearly two-thirds of natural services were in decline worldwide, and that we were "on the edge of a massive wave of species extinctions. . . ." All of this would make it harder to meet human needs.

In 2005 a group of some forty top social and natural scientists initiated a new comprehensive project, IHOPE (Integrated History and Future of People on Earth). This project takes the long view of the interaction between people and nature, looking at blocks of time at scales of tens of millennia, millennia, centuries, decades, and years. The goal is to understand where we are now, how we got here, and our prospects for the future. Participants included several prominent anthropologists and archaeologists, as well as ecologists, ecological economists, and systems and complexity experts, including D. L. Meadows, one of the original authors of the Limits to Growth study. The IHOPE project divided the team by time scales, with each group treating the world. Land use is represented by the fraction of land in forest, cropland, and land in the three largest polities, which peaks in 1925 with Russia, France and its colonies, and the British Empire in the aggregate holding over 50 percent of the land area.

The findings of the Millennium Ecosystems Assessment team are confirmed and extended backward in time by the IHOPE project, which presents an integrated environmental-human history of the world for the past 100,000 years up to 2006, highlighting the remarkable recency of the Great Acceleration of human impacts on the environment. Their findings show that past, presumably natural, climate events shaped sociocultural systems, probably contributing to the rise of capitalism, but in a matter of decades since the beginning of the Great Acceleration human impacts on otherwise natural systems have become dramatically apparent. This clearly corresponds with the rise of atmospheric CO_2 and methane and increasing temperature anomalies, including rising temperatures and increased withdrawals of freshwater, all coinciding with dramatic increases in human population and economic product. Major technological events such as domestication, ceramics, sedentism, farming, writing, iron, paper, windmills, printing, mechanical loom, industrialization, the internal combustion engine, television, the Internet, and the Google search engine correlate with important social and political events, such as the shift from tribal sociocultural systems (the tribal world) to cities and politically centralized civilizations and empires beginning about 5,000 years before present. All of these events occur closer and closer together as we move toward the present. The start of the Great Acceleration is shown to have begun just fifty years ago, following the end of World War II, based on the status of several crucial "indicators" of the human-environment system including gross world product, human population in billions, and water withdrawals.

Jared Diamond,[35] in writing about the collapse of civilizations, argues that "societies" choose to succeed or fail, and stresses the relationship between population and environment as crucial ecological causes of collapse. He lists eight categories of historically observed ecological causes: deforestation and habitat destruction; soil problems; water management problems; overhunting; overfishing; effects of introduced species on native species; human population growth; and increased per-capita impact of people.[36] He later adds four more problems: human-caused climate change, buildup of toxic chemicals, energy shortages, and the full utilization of the earth's photosynthetic capacity. The problem with this analysis is that Diamond looks at societies as if everyone had the power to make crucial decisions, "to choose to succeed or fail," and sees social and political collapse as inevitable outcomes of people fighting over resources. He does not apply a concept of different types of societies by scale and their organization of social power.

In contrast with Diamond's view, the perspective of Fekri Hassan,[37] archaeologist and member of the IHOPE project, is more in agreement with the scale and power perspective advocated in the present text. Hassan sees the sustainability problem as an "inherent contradiction" in complex societies in which population growth and resource depletion arise from the tendency of the managerial elite of these complex systems to expand productivity and economic growth at the expense of most people. The elite use their physical powers of coercion as well as their hegemonic power to shape people's beliefs and win their consent to their growth projects. This is, in effect, "elite-directed growth," and the process leaves people out. Hassan specifically points to the historically recent rise of multinational corporations and large powerful international political and social institutions that promote ideologies and cultural practices that undermine the legitimacy of governments and leave people feeling hopeless. The Great Acceleration and the information technologies that have accompanied it have clearly amplified the alienation of people who feel left out by the great disparities of wealth and power, leading Hassan to warn that social and political collapse seems likely to occur before environment collapse as people lose hope that their governments will be able to address the multiple problems they face. Human social and psychological factors play a large part in this dynamic, because global marketers present the acquisition of material commodities as crucial determinants of self-worth, but this is in a world where great income and wealth inequalities keep desired commodities out of reach of millions. This failure of the global system to meet rising expectations makes the sense of injustice greater. The problem cannot be reduced to a "clash of civilizations," "overpopulation," or conflict between competing nations. In the postcolonial world people everywhere understandably want education and employment, and they want social equality, social justice, material prosperity, and peace.

Along with the present author, Hassan traces the contradictions and sustainability problems of governments to a process in which "disparity in wealth and power between those who were affiliated with the seat of power and the people led to persuasive and coercive control strategies and created a source for disjunction and discontent between the rich and the poor. This remains one of the main ills of our own times."[38]

The social power disparity problem has been in effect over the past 5,000 years. From this perspective new technologies are not simply technologies, they are "power technologies" that are designed by the elite to maintain consent and control with appeals to a divine mandate, or the belief that the elite really want to serve

Table 12.1. Failed States Ranking, 2009

Status	Score	Nations	People	Percent Nations	Percent People
Alert	90-120	38	1,219,485,054	21	18
Warning	60-89	93	4,332,154,389	53	65
Monitoring	30-59	33	978,228,458	19	15
Sustainable	0-29	13	124,307,645	7	2
Totals		*177*	*6,654,175,546*	*100*	*100*

the people and promote everyone's welfare. Religious beliefs and practices or political ideologies must persuade the non-elite that their well-being depends on elite decision makers to maintain a favorable balance with nature, the social order, or protection from enemies. In the present world, with the overwhelming presence of advertising and information as well as the dominance of financial and industrial elites, the legitimacy of the modern nation-state, which assumes to create a national identity from its necessarily diverse peoples, is being increasingly challenged. The ideals of human rights and democracy are contradicted by the realities of global poverty and powerlessness, and this is perhaps the central contradiction of the commercial world as propelled by the Great Acceleration. The almost inescapable conclusion is that the global system can not be sustained indefinitely as presently constructed.

POVERTY AND POWER IN A WORLD OF FAILING SOCIETIES

In addition to the shocking figures of human poverty in the world, perhaps the most definitive evidence of the unsustainability of present sociopolitical systems is contained in the annual indices of Failed States produced by the Fund for Peace since 2005. The Failed State Index[39] used twelve indicators to measure the economic, social, and political effectiveness of the governments of 177 UN member countries representing 6.6 billion people (99.4 percent of the world's population). The twelve indicators are demographic pressures; the presence of refugees and internally displaced persons; group grievances; human flight (people fleeing the country); uneven economic development; economic decline; delegitimization of the state; poor public services, poor human rights; inadequate security apparatus; factionalized elite; and intervention by outside powers. Each country was given a score of 0 to 10 on each indicator, with 0 for no problem, or most stable, to 10 for worst case, or least stable based on a careful reading of the best available evidence. Countries scoring 90 and above were ranked in the Red Alert or critical category; 60 to 89.9 is the

Warning Zone; and 30 to 59.9 is the Monitoring Zone; under 30 is considered Sustainable. These alert categories are estimates of vulnerability to collapse. The government of a failing state is becoming nonfunctional, and it is losing control of its territory and its legitimacy to govern. The remarkable finding is that only thirteen countries with 124 million people, 2 percent of the total population of UN member countries, were ranked sustainable (see table 12.1). Nearly half of the sustainable states were prosperous small Scandinavian or "Nordic" countries.

Extreme poverty is the most obvious indicator of a failure of the overall sociocultural system to provide people with the ability to meet their needs. The evidence for this kind of failure is clear. Some have concluded that social inequality and poverty are defining features of capitalism, resulting from the frequent unwillingness of individuals to take responsibility for their lives. There is no doubt that there are many cases of particular individuals who have managed to succeed by overcoming extreme obstacles, but it is also apparent that the societies with the most sustainable governments, the best measures of human development, and the most sustainable relationship with the environment are also those societies where wealth and opportunities are more equitably distributed.

Economic Ranks and the Human Development Index

There are two widely cited measures of how many people are "poor": (1) The World Bank's economic ranks for countries; and (2) The UN Human Development Index for countries. In 2009 from a purely economic perspective the World Bank sorted countries into four economic ranks by 2008 annual gross national income (GNI) per capita: Low ($975 or less); Lower Middle ($976–$3,855); Upper Middle ($3,856–$11,905); and High ($11,906+). GNI is gross domestic product (GDP) plus income received from abroad. At that time 4.6 billion people, 70 percent of the world's population, were living in Lower Middle and Low income-level countries, and only 1 billion were in High Income countries (see table 12.2). It is important

Table 12.2. The Distribution of Countries and People by the World Bank Economic Ranks, 2008

	Numbers		Percent	
	Countries	People	Countries	People
High Income	66	1,045,531,495	32	16
Upper Middle Income	46	948,454,299	22	4
Lower Middle Income	54	3,701,064,681	26	55
Low Income	43	974,022,882	21	15
Totals	209	6,669,073,357	100	100

to keep in mind that such figures are per capita, or averages. They say nothing about how income is actually distributed in a country or how it is used. In countries with high inequality and large expenditures contributing to economic growth, but not to tangible benefits for most people, GNI per-capita figures may grossly underestimate the extent of poverty.

The UN Human Development Index (HDI)[40] is the most widely used international composite measure of human well-being. The HDI uses a single value to represent three dimensions of human development: (1) life expectancy at birth as a measure of a "long and healthy life"; (2) knowledge, giving two-thirds weight to the adult literacy rate and one-third to level of school enrollments; and (3) GDP per capita (PPP US$) with the goal of attaining "a decent standard of living." The GDP index tries to measure all the things that make for a good life beyond a long and healthy life and knowledge. It uses a log scale with a range of $100 to $40,000 to reflect the reality that improvements in living standard level off quickly as income increases and do not expand indefinitely. Built into these measures is the assumption that it is possible to reach sufficiency. Infinite improvement is not required to meet the goal of human development. The HDI is skewed toward material measure of well-being to the extent that life expectancy and GDP measure material things, and literacy is of course a very incomplete measure of nonmaterial things such as knowledge, cultural, spiritual, and moral well-being that contribute to human development. Although it is incomplete, the HDI is an improvement over the World Bank's economic ranks.

All three HDI measures, high life expectancy, knowledge, and a decent living standard are equally weighted and are averaged to produce a single number on a scale from 0 to 1.00. The four HDI ranks are Very High (0.9–1); High (0.8–0.89); Medium (0.5–0.79); Low (0.49 and lower). The 2009 HDI index, which uses data from 2007, shows values for 182 countries ranging from Niger with a low of 0.34 to Norway, a Small Nation, with the highest value of 0.971. Only thirty-eight countries were ranked as very high human development with indices of 0.9 or higher (see table 12.3). This meant that 987 million were residents of these Very High HDI countries, but not all residents actually enjoyed the implied benefits of that rank. Adding the High to Very High list of countries brings the total of residents of reasonably well-off countries to 1.9 billion people, which is less than 30 percent of global population. This leaves 4.6 billion in the Medium and Low category of countries that are not doing so well for their people.

The World Bank economic rankings and the HDI can be related to each other by correlating per-capita income with the HDI for individual countries (see figure 12.3). It is apparent that virtually all High Income countries are also Very High HDI countries, and a small number of Upper Middle Income countries also make it into the Very High HDI rank. This means that it is possible for a country to do really well on

Table 12.3. The Distribution of Countries and People by the UN Human Development Index (HDI), 2009

Number HDI Rank	Percent Countries	People	Countries	People
Very High	38	987,517,353	21	15
High	45	913,467,436	25	14
Medium	75	4,312,834,471	41	65
Low	24	374,308,061	13	6
Totals	182	6,588,127,320	100	100

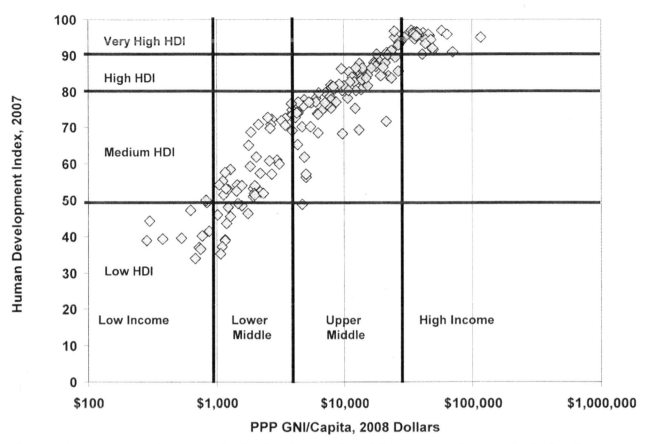

Figure 12.3. Human Development Index (HDI) and economic rank for 182 countries, 2007 (United Nations Development Program. 2009. *Human Development Report 2009 Overcoming Barriers: Human Mobility and Development***).**

a somewhat lower income. Many Upper Middle Income countries have High HDIs, but all Low Income countries are also Low HDI countries. This shows that below a GNI per capita of about $1,000, absolute levels of income really do matter, but the wide variation in countries in the range of income distribution shows that many variables other than income per capita are very important determinants of the human outcome of economic activity. Chapter 14 will show that the scale of a country's population is a crucial variable.

Scale Subsidies versus Human Well-Being

Looking at global problems from a power and scale perspective suggests that both social and environmental problems result from a dysfunctional positive feedback loop between concentrated social power and scale and complexity, which is perpetuated by elite-directed decision making. When elites can successfully promote growth in the scale of society or the economy in such a way that they can gain the largest share of the benefits and make others share the costs, they will be able to concentrate social power and promote more growth. Growth increases scale and complexity and

necessarily comes at a cost. The social costs of growth include increased bureaucracy, more specialization, conflict, and poverty. The costs of growth are scale subsidies, which refer to the extra cost of making things larger, especially including having larger markets and a larger economy. Perhaps the most obvious scale subsidy is the use of fossil fuels in production and distribution. But other scale subsidies include national and international advertising and maintaining large defense establishments.

A useful composite measure of scale subsidies is the gap between what in the United States is called the genuine progress indicator (GPI)[41] and in the United Kingdom the measure of domestic progress (MDP)[42] and the GDP. For example, American GDP increased fivefold between 1950 and 2002, but "genuine progress" remained virtually flat (see figure 12.4). GDI is here measured by counting the things that actually benefited households, such as the services of consumer durables, services of highways and streets, and personal consumption, but discounting the cost of things such as crime, commuting, auto accidents, and unemployment. The widening gap between genuine

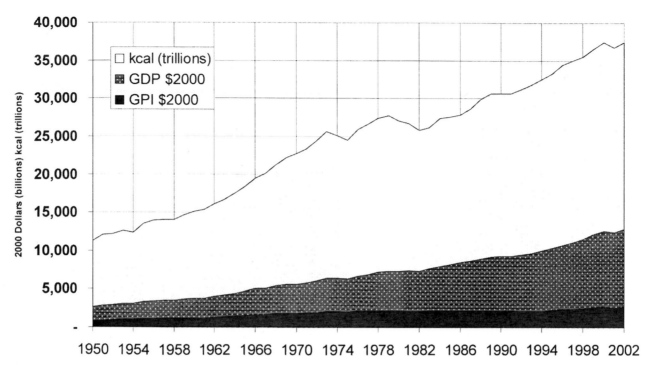

Figure 12.4. United States Genuine Progress Indicator, Gross Domestic Product, and Energy Consumption, 1950 to 2002 (data from Venetoulis, Jason and Cliff Cobb. 2004. *The Genuine Progress Indicator 1950-2002 (2004 Update).*

progress and GDP had become so great by 2002 that only 27 percent of GDP was considered to be progress. The gap itself could be considered a growth subsidy. In the United Kingdom GDP tripled over the same time, but just as in America, domestic progress remained flat. These examples mean that most of the money flowing through these national economies did not directly benefit people and households.

Other indications of the gap between economic growth and household well-being are readily apparent. Larger markets for basic subsistence help to produce a larger economy, but food is likely to be more expensive in a national-scale market where urban populations are separated from agricultural producers who grow their food. For example, in the United States, marketing costs for food processing, packaging, advertising and distribution, and wholesaling, which are reflected in retail prices, take an amazingly large and growing proportion of a dollar consumers spend for food. In 1980 marketing already took nearly 70 percent of the food dollar, but by 1999 the proportion spent on marketing had risen to more than 80 percent.[43] National-scale marketing also means large corporate businesses that extract income from local markets, whereas when people buy their food directly from local producers, their money is more likely to remain in their community.

The growth subsidy is also seen in the relatively flat trajectory of median household income in the United States, which grew by only about 20 percent in constant dollars between 1975 and 2008, whereas GDP per capita doubled over the same period. Median income actually dropped from its 1999 peak by $2,284 (4 percent) and showed fairly large downswings. Median household income is a measure of the economic position of the middle class, and this shows that growth in GDP was not paralleled by improvement for most people. This gap also appears in the declining proportion of their share in aggregate income received by the middle quintile (20 percent) of American households. In 1967 the middle received 17 percent of income, which was close to a perfectly equitable 20 percent, but by 2007 their share had dropped to 14.8 percent, even as the share of the top 20 percent rose from under 44 percent in 1967 to over 50 percent in 2006.[44] This means that income shifted to the upper ranks of society. All income groups except the top twenty actually saw their shares drop from 1967 to 2006, even as the economy measured by GDP soared. Even in the wealthiest country in the world, the benefits of growth were not being widely shared during a period of remarkable economic growth. This unequal distribution resulted from specific changes in public policies that shifted income and wealth to the upper ranks of society.

Perhaps the most significant evidence of a disconnect between growth and the physical well-being of most people in the United States is the difference in distribution and growth trajectories between tangible and financial assets during the deindustrialization and globalization process between 1982 and 2008. Tangible assets (or fixed reproducible wealth) refers to the total value of equipment such as machines and cars, houses and apartments, commercial buildings, durable consumer goods such as stoves and refrigerators, and physical infrastructure such as roads, airports, and rail networks. A critical issue is that tangible assets provide real services to people and produce the physical goods that people use and consume, whereas financial assets are only indirectly connected to physical things. Some critical tangible assets such as homes, cars, and durable consumer goods are widely distributed in society and directly improve the quality of daily life for millions of people. In 2007 87 percent of American families owned a vehicle, and 68 percent owned a primary residence.[45] For example, more than a third of the $40 trillion in tangible assets in the United States in 2007 was in the value of private residences and durable consumer goods.[46] These tangible things matter, and even though they depreciate over time and require continuous investment for their maintenance, they are much less volatile than financial assets, as evidenced by the fact that under the impact of the global financial crisis of 2007–2010 (and beyond) the value of financial assets declined much more steeply than tangible assets.

Globalization, liberalization of trade, and deregulation of the financial sector all helped double the American flow of dollars through the economy from about $6 trillion to over $13 trillion in constant dollars during this period, but paradoxically did not significantly increase the tangible wealth of most Americans. Enormous amounts of wealth accumulated as GDP surged, but remarkably this wealth accumulation was accompanied by a curiously widening gap between tangible and financial assets. This gap helps to explain the increasing global dominance of wealthy investors and the financial sector generally, as well as the continuing impoverishment of much of the world. Between 1945 and 1980 total wealth accumulation soared in the United States, suddenly increasing more than ten-fold from about $14 trillion in 1945 to more than $170 trillion in constant 2005 dollars by 2008 (see figure 12.5).[47]

This remarkable accumulation of wealth was a striking benefit of global economic development during this period, but these benefits were not broadly distributed, either in the United States or in the world. The really dramatic separation between accumulations of tangible and financial assets in the United States began after 1980, when government leaders at the center of the global economy adopted policies to promote faster economic growth by liberalizing trade, by deregulating financial institutions and businesses generally, and by rewarding wealthy investors with tax incentives. Previously, the value of American

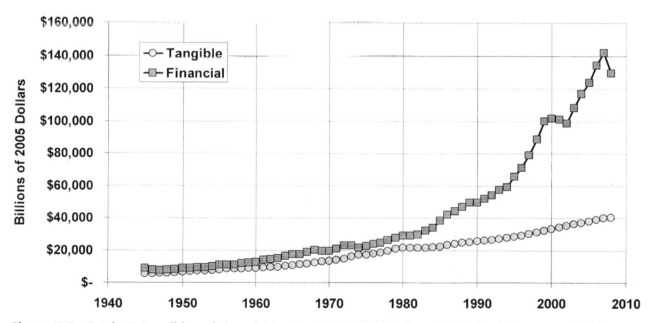

Figure 12.5. Total U.S. Tangible and Financial Assets, 1945–2008 (data from U.S. Federal Reserve and U.S. Bureau of Economic Analysis).

tangible assets and financial capital (the total value of cash, stocks, and bonds) had remained relatively close together, with financial wealth values usually only slightly higher than tangible wealth values. This suddenly began to change after 1980 when the accumulation of financial assets began a steep upward trajectory, reaching from $7 trillion to over $100 trillion by 2007. The disproportionate growth in financial assets is important because financial assets are much more concentrated in the top ranks of American society than income. The top 20 percent of households held $18 trillion in financial assets, or about 72 percent of the total financial assets held by households in 2007, whereas the top 20 percent received only about 50 percent of annual income flows.[48] Because economic growth was primarily in financial assets, this expansion effectively redistributed wealth upward, giving a smaller proportion of society greater control over economic decision making, both in the United States and globally.

The boom in financial wealth was especially prominent in the United States, but it had parallels in other rich nations and caused a massive transfer of wealth and power to a relatively tiny number of people. This wealth transfer is seen in the sudden global rise in the number of high-net-worth individuals (HNWI, or individuals with at least a million dollars in investable assets) in the world and in the value of their financial assets. In 1998 there were fewer than 6 million HNWIs in the world, with a total wealth accumulation of $21 trillion, but at the peak in 2007 there were more than 10 million with $40 trillion. These 10 million wealthy individuals were the prime beneficiaries of global economic growth since 1980, but if HNWIs and their families represented 50 million people, they were less than 1 percent of the global population. This was neither an equitable nor humane distribution of benefits, and it will be costly and difficult to sustain.

Although per-capita wealth for global HNWIs was about $4 million in 2007, their wealth was actually skewed toward the top ranks of even these wealthiest people, with the 946 billionaires at the top holding $3.4 trillion and averaging $3.6 billion each.[49] The wealthiest individual was worth over $50 billion.

The volatility of financial wealth and its disconnect from tangible wealth is demonstrated by the disappearance of nearly $8 trillion in HNWI financial wealth during the global financial crisis of 2008. When the financialization process dominates an economy, the investment process may become especially susceptible to bubble effects, and the system can resemble a casino where investors simply run up the prices of financial assets by gambling and juggling their portfolios in ways that are only remotely related to real assets or human well-being. The sudden disappearance of trillions of dollars of financial wealth had little immediate impact on tangible wealth and demonstrated that wealthy investors and unregulated markets do not always make the best decisions over the allocation of capital. That such boom-and-bust cycles can exist at the top of a global system where so many are desperately poor is a reminder that distribution of all forms of capital, rather than "production" of financial wealth, is what matters most for people in the real world.

The Failed Promise of Growth, 1960–2000

During the second half of the twentieth century, the previous era of colonialism was replaced by a new era of international development. New international agencies, many of them formed in the aftermath of World War II, together with governments, philanthropic foundations, and private agencies, jointly engaged in a massive effort to improve public health and increase economic productivity. The assumption was that such development would raise living standards and reduce poverty throughout the world, but the reality was that the number of poor actually increased. Development failed to achieve its stated goals because poverty was treated primarily as a technical problem rather than a cultural problem of scale and power. The cultural belief in the certain benefits of economic development had its roots in the recommendations of various economic specialists and planners who produced influential books beginning in 1960 predicting a Utopian future in a fully commercialized world. But these Utopian visions were flawed by a narrow view of human cultural history and by a focus on inadequate measures of economic growth and the distribution of costs and benefits. To better understand what went wrong, it will be helpful to examine the thinking behind international development efforts and to compare the reality of global poverty with the predictions.

The UN is the most prominent international organization concerned with global development issues. The UN Charter, which was formally adopted in 1945 by fifty-one nations, specifies that the promotion of "social progress and better standards of living" and "economic and social advancement of all peoples" are among the principal aims of the UN. Over the years since its founding, the UN has focused on a changing series of development issues and has proposed a

Table 12.4. UN Development Issues and Strategies, 1950–2015

Decade	Issues	Strategies
1950–1959	Disease	Public health programs
	Poverty	Public education
	Ignorance	Technology transfer
		Promotion of economic growth
1960–1969	Population	Integrated economic and social growth
	Urban growth	UN Development Decade
	Income inequality	
1970–1979	Social equity	Second UN Development Decade
	Global disparity	Unified economic-social-political approach
	Human environment	
1980–1989	Foreign debt	Third Development Decade
	Energy cost	Human development
	Economic downturn	Popular participation
		Grassroots development
		Appropriate technology
		International development cooperation
1990–1999	Poverty	Labor-intensive development
		Human-capital improvement
2000–2015	Millennium Development Goals	Eradicate extreme hunger and poverty
		Achieve universal primary education
		Promote gender equality and empower women
		Reduce child mortality
		Improve maternal health
		Combat HIV/AIDS, malaria and other diseases
		Ensure environmental sustainability
		Develop a global partnership for development

Sources: United Nations (1952, 1963, 1975), UNDP (2003), and World Bank (1988, 1989, 1990, 1991).

variety of development strategies (see table 12.4). To formulate and implement its development effort, the UN has also constructed an elaborate institutional framework of specialized agencies, councils, commissions, funds, and programs, each chartered by formal resolutions.

By the end of World War II, it was obvious to world leaders that much of the world was seriously impoverished. Vast numbers of people in many countries were living under conditions that were intolerable from a humanitarian perspective. Furthermore, because impoverished peoples made poor producers and consumers in the global economy and were potential sources of political instability, it was in their "enlightened self-interest" for wealthy industrialized countries to attempt to alleviate world poverty. War-caused impoverishment could be solved by reconstruction, but most authorities assumed that global poverty was caused by a vicious cycle of disease, ignorance, and poverty and would be eliminated by the transfer of industrial technology and education from rich to poor countries. In 1948, the UN began the international campaign to improve the human condition by issuing the Universal Declaration of Human Rights, which stated, "Everyone has the right to a standard of living

adequate for the health and well-being of himself and of his family, including food, clothing, housing and medical care."[50] This was a truly revolutionary document, comparable to the American Declaration of Independence and the U.S. Bill of Rights in its support of human freedom.

Experts were initially optimistic that development could be achieved, reflecting the general belief in technological progress of the time. In 1967, Hudson Institute futurists Herman Kahn and Anthony Wiener published their predictions for a "surprise-free" world by the year 2000,[51] assuming a continuation of what they called the "multifold trend" of technological progress and economic growth that they felt characterized Western civilization. Their multifold trend is what I here have called the commercialization process. They traced it back to the eleventh and twelfth centuries—precisely where we began in chapter 10 with our examination of the rise of money and markets in medieval Europe. Kahn and Wiener were convinced that unrestricted economic growth was benefiting and would continue to benefit the world. Kahn[52] specifically posed this prospect of continuous growth in direct opposition to "doomsday" trend forecasting in *Limits to Growth* and similar works that followed. The

Hudson Institute, a think tank founded by Kahn, continues to fight against the view that continuous growth might not be possible. The Hudson Institute's website includes the statement that "In the 1970s, Hudson's scholars helped turn the world away from the no-growth policies of the Club of Rome...."[53]

Kahn and Wiener optimistically expected that for at least the next thirty years, every nation would follow what they imagined to be the natural progression of development stages from takeoff, through maturity, to the high mass consumption outlined so elegantly in MIT economist Walt Rostow's influential 1960 book *The Process of Economic Growth*.[54] Rostow conceived of economic takeoff as a watershed event in which the "forces making for economic progress . . . [would] come to dominate the society" and overcome the "old blocks and resistances to steady growth."[55] As advisor to presidents Kennedy and Johnson, Rostow had a Utopian vision of unlimited growth that supported the thinking and interests of America's top intellectual, political, and economic leaders. In reality, of course, many of these people themselves constituted the "forces making for economic progress" that directed the global flow of finance capital.

In line with Rostow's view, the Hudson Institute futurists expected world population to double and the global economy to increase more than fivefold by the year 2000. They predicted that 25 percent of the world's population would bask in the luxury of "postindustrial" societies by the end of the century, while the rest of the world steadily grew to maturity and mass consumption. Kahn and Wiener expected growth to dramatically improve economic conditions in the less-developed nations, although the absolute gap between rich and poor would increase.

The Hudson Institute futurists were correct in their prediction that the global economy would increase fivefold by the year 2000 and global population would double, but they were wrong about how the human benefits of this growth would be distributed. By the year 2000 poverty was much more prevalent and wealth far more concentrated than expected. Where did they and other elite planners go wrong? A serious shortcoming of Utopian projections was their focus on gross national product (GNP) or gross domestic product (GDP). These macroeconomic statistics and their income equivalents are far removed from real people. They measure only values priced by the market. They typically leave out "services" performed in the household or exchanges between kin that do not involve money. They also do not include nega-

tive "externalities" that impoverish people, such as activities that deplete natural resources or damage communities, because these things are outside of the market. Even when presented as per capita to account for differences in population between nations, until 1990 these measures did not consider the actual distribution of income to people by rank within different countries or differences between income ranks at the global level. Aggregate measures made it possible to be optimistic about the benefits of economic growth, because they obscured the reality that a larger economy, measured as more products or more total income, often benefits only a few people unless policy measures override the trend toward wealth concentration.

Wealth versus Income: How Maldistribution Impoverished the World

The real issue is how the distribution of wealth and income relates to human well-being. Beginning with its 1990 World Development Report, the World Bank for the first time began to measure in detail the extent of global poverty by establishing poverty lines of $275 per person per year in 1985 PPP dollars for extreme poverty (purchasing power parity, an adjustment for price differences between countries) and $370 as an upper poverty line. PPP dollars tend to inflate the value of local commodities, and the World Bank's poverty lines were "arbitrary," but even so the $370 PPP poverty line produced the "staggering" and "shameful" figure of more than 1 billion impoverished people for 1985.[56] My own estimate[57] of global household well-being used a generalized version of the World Bank's estimates of the percentile distribution of income in different countries available as of 1995[58] applied to global population and income in 1965 and 1997. I used $2,500 as the global poverty line to more realistically reflect the living standard prevailing in the high-income nations that most benefit from global economic growth. It seemed reasonable to uniformly apply a single, high, but still modest threshold for economic prosperity, given that the economic elite treat capital and labor as part of a single pool within a single world economy. Poverty creates human suffering, and human suffering is not culturally relative. I used $12,500 as the line between maintenance-level people and the global elite, assuming that at this level people would be able to accumulate wealth by saving and investing. My figures expand the concept of poverty by attempting to include all those who must borrow to meet basic needs and are unable to own land or their own homes, together with the World Bank's "absolute poor," within a single "poor" category. Using these consistent categories, and adjusting for inflation, it is possible to ask whether economic globalization since 1965 produced more wealth than poverty in the world.

My calculations for 1997 show more than 4 billion (70 percent) poor people, 1.23 billion (25 percent) maintenance-level people, and 300 million (5 percent) growth-level people (see table 12.5). The figures also show a decline in the *proportion* who were poor by this new standard, but their actual numbers increased much more dramatically than the World Bank's categories suggest. By 1997, there were 260 million new individuals with growth-level incomes worldwide, but this increase was more than overshadowed by a new cohort of 1.25 billion poor. The wealthiest 5 percent of the world's population enjoyed 40 percent of global income. The 25 percent of maintenance-level people in the global "middle class" also had more than their share with 40 percent of the wealth, whereas the 70 percent of the world who were poor were left with less than 20 percent of global income. Clearly, if we accept this global standard of economic well-being, growth since 1965 impoverished more people than it enriched.

The realities of global wealth and income distribution in the world show clearly why poverty is such a problem and why ending poverty will require a redistribution process rather than simply continuing to increase production. The common focus on income per capita in discussions of development issues unfortunately diverts attention from wealth itself and how it is distributed. However, many of the earlier estimates of global poverty were very crude. Reliable information on wealth and income for the entire world was hard to find, and it is still often out of date. The first detailed estimates of the world distribution

of income were published in 2002 by World Bank economist Branko Milanovic.[59] This work was based on surveys that counted the income that people in 216 countries actually received as reported in very detailed household-level income surveys conducted throughout the world. The survey represented some 84 percent of the world's people and 93 percent of GDP as reported in 1988 and 1993. Milanovic found that income was much more skewed toward the top than previous official estimates had suggested. In 1993 the bottom 20 percent of the global population received about 2 percent of total income, whereas the top 20 percent received 73 percent, and the global middle 20 percent received only 6 percent (see figure 12.6). This seems to support my earlier assessments. In the tribal world, where relative equality prevailed, there would be no ranking by income—each 20 percent of households would receive 20 percent of income. It was remarkable that in the commercial world over the five years between 1988 and 1993, those in the bottom 80 percent of global society actually lost income share, whereas the top 20 percent gained nearly five percentage points. Income was being redistributed upward to those least in need.

Wealth really needs to be at the center of the discussion, because a poor distribution of wealth is a cause of poverty, and likewise income poverty reflects wealth poverty. Remarkably, it was not until 2006 that a group of researchers at the World Institute for Development Economics Research (WIDER) at the United Nations University (UNU) based in Helsinki, Finland, developed a country-by-country estimate of the distribution of household wealth, or net worth in both tangible and financial assets. The WIDER study[60] used the best, often very recent, household balance sheet data then available for 38 countries and imputed

Table 12.5. The Global Distribution of Population and Income, by Level of Household Well-Being, 1965 and 1997

1965	Poor	Maintenance	Elite	Totals
Persons	2,800,000,000	450,000,000	50,000,000	3,300,000,000
$ Income/capita	521	5378	16,800	1430
Percent persons	85	14	1	100
Percent income	31	51	18	100
1997	Poor	Maintenance	Elite	Totals
Persons	4,060,000,000	1,460,000,000	310,000,000	5,830,000,000
$ Income/capita	919	5637	24,903	3376
Percent persons	70	25	5	100
Percent income	19	42	39	100

Sources: Information Please Almanac Atlas and Yearbook 1967, United Nations (1968a, 1968b: Table 7B); World Almanac and Book of Facts 1998, World Bank (1995).

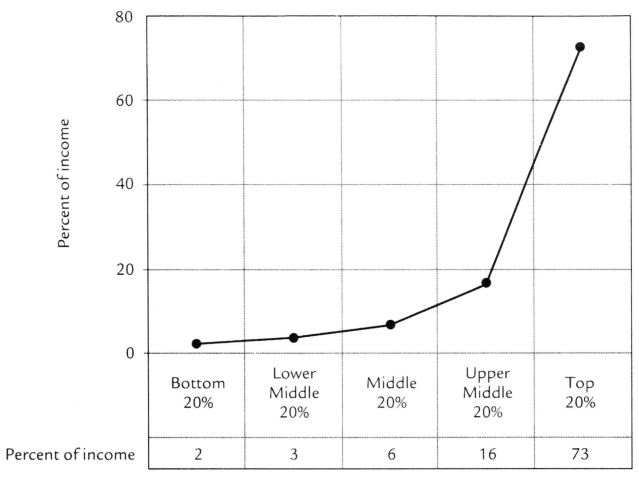

Percent of income	Bottom 20%	Lower Middle 20%	Middle 20%	Upper Middle 20%	Top 20%
	2	3	6	16	73

Figure 12.6. Percent distribution of global per capita income by quntile, 1993 (data from Milanovic 2002).

wealth distributions for another 112 countries, also using regression curves and regional and income class averages. This resulted in a sample of 150 countries covering 95 percent of global population in 2000 and suggested that households held about $125 trillion in wealth. This excludes wealth held by governments and corporations. They found that wealth was much more concentrated than income. Milanovic found that the top 10 percent received about 50 percent of global income in 1993, but the WIDER study showed that the top 10 percent held an astounding 85 percent of the wealth by using exchange rate values rather than PPP dollars to call attention to the role of concentrated wealth in global investment. This distribution is so extreme that the lower ranks are only visible on a log scale (see figure 12.7).

The WIDER household wealth study showed that the bottom 50 percent of the world collectively held barely 1 percent of the wealth, whereas the top 1 percent had 40 percent. Such wealth concentration is so grotesque that it immediately invites comparison with the degree of concentrated wealth in the United States, the world's wealthiest country. The wealthiest 400 Americans had more personal wealth than the poorest 2.5 billion people. The six wealthiest Americans had combined net worths of $172 billion, which exceeded all household net worth in Bangladesh. The wealthiest American was financially worth more than 675 million people in 81 poor countries. The 2.6 million HNWI Americans constituted 30 percent of the world's HNWIs in 2005. This tiny proportion of the global population has benefited most from economic globalization, whereas even in America, one of the world's richest countries, poverty still abounds.

Global Plutonomy and the Stock Market Backbone

In 2005, shortly before the downturn in the global financial system, three global financial equity strategists working for a research division of Citigroup issued an amazing emic view of the world from inside a gigantic, self-proclaimed global financial conglomerate.[61] In this case "equity" refers not to social justice,

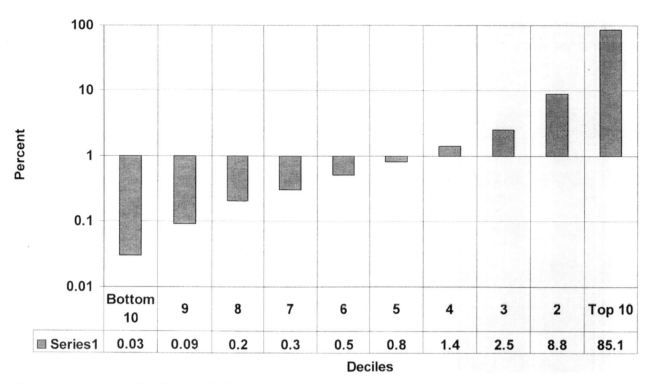

	Bottom 10	9	8	7	6	5	4	3	2	Top 10
▪ Series1	0.03	0.09	0.2	0.3	0.5	0.8	1.4	2.5	8.8	85.1

Deciles

Figure 12.7. Percent distribution of global household wealth by decile, 2000 (Davies, Sandstrom, Shorrocks, and Wolff. 2006. *The World Distribution of Household Wealth.* **World Institute for Development Economics Research).**

but to the market value of shares in large corporations that are traded in the world's stock markets. At that time Citigroup was the largest financial services corporation in the United States, and the eighth largest corporation in the country, with revenues of more than $131 billion. It helped define the network of global cities and was also the world's fourteenth-largest publicly traded corporation and second-largest global financial corporation, with 200 million accounts in more than 100 countries and reported assets of $1.5 trillion. Its assets actually peaked at over $2 trillion in 2007 before the global financial crisis, in which it lost more than $300 billion, causing the federal government to "bail out" the "too big to fail" company with massive loan guarantees, an infusion of cash, and by buying up 36 percent of Citigroup's shares.

Citigroup's equity strategists looked at the distribution of wealth in the world through the eyes of stock-portfolio advisors. They concluded, apparently correctly, that the world was divided into a small bloc of Anglo-Saxon countries that were plutonomies (singular), "economies powered by the wealthy," and the rest of the world, which was in effect irrelevant. In their view the United States, the United Kingdom, and Canada were the primary plutonomies, and their investors were largely responsible for the recent surge of worldwide wealth accumulation.

Japan and Europe, except for Italy, were viewed as an "egalitarian bloc" of rich countries that were too egalitarian to be effective drivers of wealth. The rest of the world was too irrelevant to matter to a stock broker. Furthermore, trade imbalances, low savings, and high government debt in the plutonomies were not a problem, because "the earth is being held up by the muscular arms of its entrepreneur-plutocrats, like it or not."[62] The world was a **Plutocracy**. It was ruled by the rich. This analysis did actually reflect the realities of the distribution of market capitalization in the world at that time—at least as it existed before the global financial crisis.

Market capitalzation is the key variable for global investors. Global market capitalization refers to the value of all the shares of corporations listed in all the stock exchanges across the world. These values of course fluctuate minute by minute as investors buy and sell stocks, but according to the World Bank's estimates for 2007,[63] there were $65 trillion in current U.S. dollars in the 112 countries where all the stock markets in the world were located. There were 71 countries with no stock markets, but that were home to more than 700 million people who represented over 10 percent of global population. Most of these people and countries were probably not owners of corporate stocks, like the 80 percent of Americans who owned no stocks directly.

The world organized as a plutonomy means that growth is directed by and its benefits are consumed by a wealthy few. This is my scale and power hypothesis of elite-directed growth concentrating benefits and socializing costs. The simplest definition of plutonomy is rule by the rich. Citigroup strategists assumed that plutonomies were created by productive new technologies, "creating financial innovations," friendly and cooperative governments, and the globalization process itself. They expected to see even more wealth inequality in the world, because rich and educated people would be best able to exploit the new opportunities. They were not worried about global imbalances and cheered on the growth of plutonomy, even as they noted that as wealth became more concentrated, most households found it difficult to save. This was evidence that as the rich got richer, the rest got poorer. Citigroup strategists had a novel natural explanation for the rise of plutonomy—it was largely produced by new immigrants to the Anglo-Saxon countries who self-selected for immigration because they were genetically predisposed to higher levels of the brain chemical dopamine, which rewards risk-taking with pleasure. This was old-fashioned Social Darwinist, genetic determinism with no supporting evidence.

A different view of the unequal distribution of wealth and power in the global system was produced by physicists and systems design analysts Glattfelder and Battiston, working in Switzerland. Like the global cities researchers described in chapter 10, these researchers looked at the network of owners behind global corporations and found concentrated power and control. They demonstrated in 2009 that most of the world's large shareholder-owned corporations were effectively controlled by a very small number of institutional owners who make up the "backbone" of the global stock market in each country.[64] They defined the backbone as "the smallest set of the most powerful shareholders that collectively are potentially able to control a predefined fraction of the market in terms of value."[65] Their major findings were that a small elite of controlling shareholders appeared in country after country, and that worldwide the dominant control was in the American financial sector. This is the reality behind the view presented by the Citigroup researchers discussed above.

Glattfelder and Battiston analyzed more than half a million ties between corporations by examining the pattern of shareholding for 24,877 corporations and 106,141 owners who were not also owned (individuals, families, cooperatives, associations, foundations,

public authorities, and so on), using data from 2007 in the ORBIS[66] database. The size of corporations was based on their market capitalization, which is share value times number of shares for each company. Their cross-national sample covered all stock exchanges in forty-eight countries, which collectively covered about 85 percent of global market capitalization in 2007. They looked systematically at the network of ownership to identify specific owners in each national market who were the most important shareholders by voting power relative to other shareholders in each national market.

There are significant cross-national differences in ownership patterns. English-speaking countries have the highest frequency of "widely held" corporations, those owned by many shareholders, but nevertheless, at the national level control was highly concentrated. In the more egalitarian European countries and Japan, where a few owners may have concentrated control over a few companies, there is less concentrated control at the national level. For example, American corporations are owned by many shareholders as is well known, but relatively few owners have enough shares to control any single company. Glattfelder and Battiston ranked owners by cumulative ability to own 50 percent or more of a company, or to be a member of the smallest coalition that owned 80 percent of more of a company, considering the value of the companies owned. Counting all of the most powerful owners in each of the forty-eight national markets, they discovered ten owners that appeared in the backbone of twelve or more countries.

The top ten backbone owners (Capital Group Companies; Fidelity Management; Barclays PLC; Franklin Resources; AXA Insurance; JP Morgan Chase; Dimensional Fund Advisors; Merrill Lynch; Wellington Management; and UBS) were not widely known outside of the investor world, but their owner-managers were among the financial "masters of the universe." Collectively they managed $15 trillion in assets, which was approximately one-fourth of the $65 trillion in all of the world's stock markets. Top-ten backbone owners were all financial companies, including investment management companies, investment banks, and insurance companies. Other giant corporations, such as Exxon-Mobil and Ford, have many shareholders but are not themselves in the backbone as owners. Two individual leaders of backbone companies also had management roles in Shell, which became the world's largest corporation in 2009. Individual persons seldom appeared in the backbone as owners, with a few exceptions such as billionaires Warren Buffett and Bill Gates, who appeared in the American backbone as number 9 and 26 respectively.

The backbone itself represents the financialization process in action and the concentrated power of the financial sector in the global economy. At least in America, the recent rise of the financial sector reflects a cultural shift away from the previous postwar dominant belief that everyone's well-being ultimately depended on the success of giant manufacturing corporations such as General Motors. After 1980 many people were apparently persuaded to believe that everyone's success depended on the success of the financial sector symbolized by "Wall Street."[67]

The power and control of the backbone owners goes beyond control over the largest corporations and the largest accumulations of financial capital in the world. Backbone power also extends to political influence over the American federal government by means of the mutually beneficial positive-feedback relationship between political and economic elites, which is a well-understood phenomenon in much of the commercial world. Many individuals associated with top-ten backbone owners also participated in the famous "revolving door" process in the United States in which individuals hold important positions in federal government and large corporations at different times (see figure 12.8). For example, Fidelity Management, number two of the backbone power holders with a leadership position in thirty-two countries, had two former associates take positions as commerce secretary (2001), treasury secretary, (2004), energy secretary (2005), and defense secretary (2006) in the American federal government. Fidelity is itself a privately held corporation owned by American billionaire Ned Johnson. Most American government officials are also HNWIs and global investors. Not surprisingly, the largest personal stockholdings of members of Congress and the executive branch were in the financial services sector, where they held up to $1.5 billion. Fifty-two members of Congress held shares in JP Morgan,[68] which was in the backbone of nineteen countries, and held $2 trillion in corporate shares worldwide. Lucrative contracts, tax breaks, and subsidies flow from the political elite to the economic elite, who return political support, campaign contributions, lobbyists, favors, and bribes. From 2000 through 2009 the financial services sector contributed more than $1.2 billion to state-level political campaigns and another $1.1 billion to federal campaigns and $3 billion to federal lobbying.

Simon Johnson, former chief economist at the International Monetary Fund, shows that the global financial crisis of 2008 was at least in part a result of a rapid expansion of the American financial sector since 1980. From 1948 to 1985 profits in the financial sector did not exceed 16 percent of domestic corporate profits, but after 2000 it reached 41 percent. Professionals working in the financial sector saw their compensation soar from about average for all sectors to 181 percent of average by 2007.[69] In addition to the plutonomies, sovereign funds and private equity funds are other important blocks of concentrated financial power in the global system that contribute to the financialization process and help to accelerate further concentration of wealth. Poverty is the other side of plutonomy, as the following sections show.

Daily Reality in the Impoverished World: Infant Mortality in Brazil

National-level statistics show that for job-dependent people, low wages and underemployment produce malnutrition, high infant mortality, and wretched living conditions on a vast scale. However, the impersonal statistics diminish the human reality. A close look at real people, households, and communities gives a more complete view of the impoverishment produced by elite-directed growth in the commercial world. The harsh reality is that when the quest for economic growth and wealth accumulation dominates the humanization process, children may be deprived of food, their most urgent human need. By contrast, tribal cultures placed human needs first and guaranteed food security to everyone.

During the 1980s, anthropologist Nancy Scheper-Hughes[70] conducted extensive research on women living in a northeast Brazilian squatter town, which she called Bom Jesus. The growth of giant sugar plantations in this region since the 1950s had pushed subsistence farmers off their lands, forcing them to survive on inadequate wages. During the 1980s, men who worked in the sugarcane fields were paid the legal minimum of $10 a week, while women received $5. At the same time, a family of four required $40 a week to meet their minimum food needs, because even the most basic foods, such as beans, could no longer be grown locally. As a result, sugar workers and their families had to adapt to a situation of chronic malnutrition. Babies were dying, just as Adam Smith[71] had predicted in 1776, but unfortunately wages were not improving because Brazil's poor had little political or economic power.

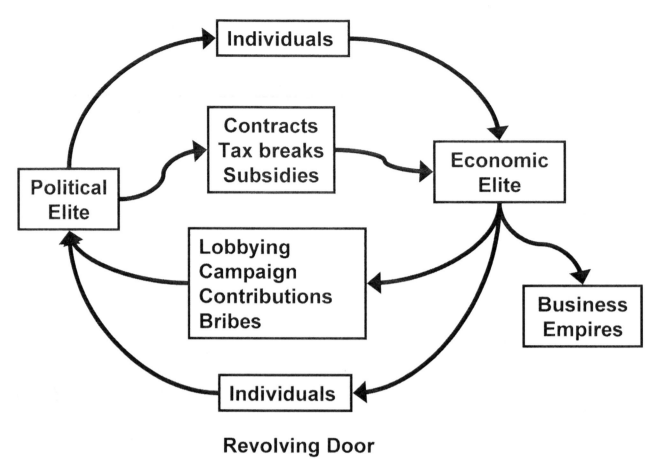

Figure 12.8. The revolving door: plutonomy and plutocracy in action.

The impoverished sugarcane workers were surviving on an average of 1,500 calories a day, virtually concentration camp rations. Regional statistics showed that 80 percent of the population, some 30 million people, constituted an impoverished underclass. Surprisingly, Scheper-Hughes found that people were actually able to survive under these conditions, even though two-thirds of their children were clinically undernourished and one-fourth were nutritionally dwarfed by their starvation diets. Women experienced high rates of miscarriage, and many of their babies were born underweight. Most disturbing was Scheper-Hughes's discovery that in 1987, infants in the community of Bom Jesus were dying at the rate of 211 per 1,000. By 1998 this figure was exceeded only by national-level infant mortality rates in five African countries—Malawi, Mali, Mozambique, Niger, and Sierra Leone—with figures ranging from 213 to 283. This compared with a low of five in Japan, Sweden, and Switzerland. The reality of this human cost of social inequality is partially buried in the regional statistic showing an aggregate infant mortality rate for northeast Brazil of 116 per 1,000. This is still a very high rate, but even this figure is obscured by Brazil's national-level statistic of just 57 infant deaths per 1,000 in 1993. The same obfuscation occurs with statistics that use per-capita GNP as the primary measure of economic growth and prosperity. Indeed, Brazil has experienced an economic miracle. In 1971, its total GNP was just $421 per capita; by 1993, it had reached $2,930 per capita. In 2003 the World Bank ranked Brazil as an upper-middle income nation with a per-capita GNP of $3,070, even though, based on 1997 figures, the bank estimated that 8 million Brazilians were living in "extreme poverty," with the equivalent of less than $1 a day per capita, and 28 million were "poor," with less than $2 a day per capita. The Bom Jesus household of four was living on 54 cents per capita per day.

Low wages put Brazilian working families in a terrible dilemma. Anthropologists Daniel Gross and Barbara Underwood[72] investigated sisal plantation workers in the same region. They found that sisal workers, like sugarcane workers, were forced to buy the cheapest high-calorie food and systematically starve their children to give their working men enough food energy to keep them in the fields.

Protein-calorie deficiency diseases, such as kwashiorkor and marasmus, cause a wasting away of body tissues and have dramatic effects on children.[73] Malnutrition is also known to damage the developing brain during early infancy,[74] and it can inhibit a child's intellectual ability by making the child less active. Fortunately, new research suggests that some of these effects are reversible if malnourished children can be given adequate nutrition early enough.[75]

Real detective work is required to measure the actual human cost of poverty. Scheper-Hughes visited the local cemetery and obtained the handwritten birth and death records from the registry books in Bom Jesus to learn how many babies were dying. She also collected full reproductive histories from 100 women and found that an average older (postmenopausal) woman had seen 4.7 of her children die. During the worst conditions, the infant mortality rate in Bom Jesus soared to 493 per 1,000 in 1 year.

The women of Bom Jesus certainly understood the general nature of their impoverishment. As one woman declared, "Our children die because we are poor and hungry."[76] However, similar to laid-off factory workers in the United States, the poor of Bom Jesus blamed themselves. They treated their own poor health as a problem of "nerves," which could be treated with tranquilizers and vitamins purchased at the pharmacy. Scheper-Hughes is emphatic about the real causes of sickness and death in Bom Jesus:

> I do not want to quibble over words, but what I have been seeing on the Alto de Cruzeiro [the slum in Bom Jesus] for two and a half decades is more than "malnutrition," and it is politically as well as economically caused, although in the absence of overt political strife or war. Adults, it is true, might be described as "chronically undernourished," in a weakened and debilitated state, prone to infections and opportunistic diseases. But it is overt hunger and starvation that one sees in babies and small children, the victims of a "famine" that is endemic, relentless, and political-economic in origin.[77]

The global financialization process itself has intensified the human costs of impoverishment. The Brazilian government borrowed heavily to finance economic growth and cut expenditures on public health in 1985 to help make its loan payments.

Medical anthropologist Paul Farmer is both a physician and an anthropologist and has worked among the poorest peoples in Haiti since 1983. He found conditions in Haiti as extreme as in the Brazilian northeast. National figures showed 65 percent of the Haitian people as officially poor in 1987. Haitians worked on coffee plantations for seven to fifteen cents per day and faced an epidemic of tuberculosis and AIDS, as well as hunger, rape, and political torture.[78] Historically, Haitian poverty was preceded by the extermination of the Amerindians by Spanish invaders in the sixteenth century, followed by the importation of African slaves by the English and French in the eighteenth-century trade triangle, and finally by repeated episodes of political violence and rule by tyrannical dictators in the twentieth century.

Farmer describes the everyday condition of the Haitian poor as structural violence. This means that poverty involves more than economic deprivation, and it calls attention to the inequities of social power that cause this kind of preventable human suffering. Structural violence means that relatively more powerful individuals are socially and culturally able to violate the most fundamental of human social, economic, civil, and political rights of less-powerful individuals and communities, resulting in human suffering, loss of human dignity, torture, rape, disease, malnutrition, vulnerability, and death. Structural violence includes the infrastructural dimensions of inadequate income and insufficient resources as well as the tyrannical use of state political and military power to oppress poor people; the inhumane use of concentrated economic power by economic elites; and superstructural forms of oppression based on race, gender, and ethnicity. Structural violence is produced by dangerous concentrations of social power, which throughout human history have been the predictable outcome of elite-directed growth.

The scale of structural violence in the twentieth century was unprecedented. Political rulers caused the deaths of perhaps as many as 200 million people through direct violence in wars, genocidal massacres, and internal repression, disproportionately targeting the poor and powerless. This was more than the entire population of the world a mere 1,500 years ago.[79] The Nazis killed some 21 million civilians between 1933 and 1945, and the Soviets some 62 million between 1917 and 1987.[80] This level of violence was made possible by the availability of fossil fuels and new armaments produced by giant commercial corporations.

Land and Food in Impoverished Bangladesh

The following pair of quotes encapsulate the way impoverishment was experienced by many south Asian villages and identify the commercial processes involved:

"Between 1933 and 1960 the village became poorer, and was polarized into two groups of households, one owning insufficient land to support an average household, and another owning a sufficient or excessive amount of it."[81]

"Thus, international systems of production and finance are changing the ways that the rich and poor [of Bangladesh] eat and lead their lives."[82]

Bangladesh, formerly East Pakistan (1947–1971), is a primarily Muslim nation centered on the Ganges-Brahmaputra delta region known as East Bengal, in the northeast corner of the Indian subcontinent at the head of the Bay of Bengal. In 1990, the World Bank listed Bangladesh as one of the world's poorest nations, fifth from the bottom with a per-capita GNP of $170.[83]

Given such precarious economic conditions, it is not surprising that several hundred thousand people died in famines in Bangladesh in 1974. In 1996 one-third of the Bangladeshi population was officially below the national poverty line, but by international standards 35 million people were living in extreme poverty on less than $1 per capita per day, and 95 million were poor at less than $2 per capita per day—this is more than the entire population of the Neolithic tribal world. Fifty-six percent of children under five were malnourished. Nearly half of adult men and 70 percent of women were illiterate and thus disadvantaged in a commercial world. Nevertheless, the economy was growing at 5 percent a year, and by 2001 Bangladesh had more than doubled its per-capita GDP to $360. Bangladesh remained in the low-income global rank of nations even though it had received enormous amounts of development aid from international lenders and assistance from nongovernmental organizations, including $13.8 billion in official development and from 1982 to 1988 and 4.6 million tons of food aid from the United States from 1985 to 1988. The Bangladesh experience suggests that economic growth and development assistance may not reduce poverty when the structure of social inequality remains unchanged.

As part of the UN-sponsored Millennium Development Goals, the government of Bangladesh published a Poverty Reduction Strategy Program in 2003 calling for "eradicating hunger, chronic food insecurity, and extreme destitution. . . ." The government wanted to cut in half the absolute number of poor, achieve universal primary education for boys and girls, eliminate gender disparity in education, gain large reductions in infant mortality, child malnutrition, and maternal mortality, make reproductive health services available to everyone, reduce or eliminate social violence, and prevent environmental degradation.[84] These were admirable goals, but the "Pro-Poor" growth measures advocated by planners included more intensive rice production, biotechnology, more information technology, increased **foreign direct investment**, and "reforming" state-owned enterprises, including utilities, by privatization. These elite-directed measures were in line with the New Growth, **neoliberal economic** policies prevailing among globalization planners in the United States. Such measures would further increase scale and seem unlikely to transform the underlying cultural structures of inequality.

To better understand poverty in Bangladesh it will be helpful to review its historical development. Under the Muslim rulers of the Mughal Empire (sixteenth to eighteenth centuries), East Bengal supported a prosperous cotton industry. The peasantry collectively controlled the land and remained economically self-sufficient, although they had to pay taxes to the *zamindars*, the title of local elites who were the appointed agents of the Muslim state. Shortly after the British completed their conquest of the region in 1765, they legally recognized the *zamindar* tax collectors as the rural landowners. Turning the *zamindars* into landlords, as well as tax collectors, amplified village-level inequalities. However, by giving the *zamindars* more power, it also made it easier for the new British rulers to maintain political stability and ensured a steady flow of taxes and profits for the shareholders of the British East India Company. The British also suppressed the indigenous cotton industry and converted the peasantry into agricultural laborers for the production of jute as an export crop to supply British-owned mills in Calcutta and England.

Thus, preexisting social structures created by state authority laid the foundation for the profound impoverishment of Bangladesh in the twentieth century. Despite various changes in the central government and apparent reforms in land laws, rural elites have tenaciously maintained their grip over the best agricultural land in Bangladesh. Their favored social standing, which ultimately was supported by the state, permitted them to benefit at the expense of their less-favored fellow villagers when agricultural development programs became important during the 1970s. Thus, Bangladesh demonstrates that the incorporation of a regional state into the global system can increase internal inequality and reduce the quality of life for much of the population. This is shown clearly in the large number of Bangladeshi citizens who immigrate overseas to find employment (see figure 12.9).

The impoverishment process in Bangladesh is well documented at the village level in some two dozen modern ethnographic studies.[85] A representative case is Goborgari, a single village described by the Dutch researcher Willem Van Schendel (1981).[86]

Goborgari is a Bengali-speaking, mixed Hindu and Muslim village situated on a level alluvial plain north of the Ganges and west of the Brahmaputra River in northern Bangladesh. Goborgari was primarily settled by immigrants during the nineteenth and early twentieth centuries. A government survey showed that in 1933 Goborgari was a small village of nineteen relatively egalitarian and self-sufficient farming households. There were no landless households and few large landholders, and the average acreage per household stood at approximately 4.3 acres (1.7 hectares), which was adequate for basic needs. The situation had changed dramatically by 1977. The population had increased from 30 people to 392. Total acreage increased, and cultivation was greatly intensified with irrigation and with double, even triple, cropping, but most people were impoverished (see table 12.6).

It might appear that natural population increase was the primary cause of impoverishment in Goborgari, but a closer look shows that this was not the case. Much of the growth of Goborgari since 1933 was because landless villagers moved in from other areas. More importantly, even with a tenfold population increase, subsistence resources still would have been marginally adequate if land were equitably distributed. If Goborgari had been organized as an egalitarian society, land resources and the risks of food production would have been shared equally. The primary crop in Goborgari by 1977 was the newly introduced Green Revolution (HYV, high-yield variety) of rice, which increased production by a third. The problem with the new HYV rice, which was promoted by government extension agents, was that it required access to land and high levels of water and chemicals. Despite these technological improvements, the village was still relatively impoverished in comparison with earlier conditions. Average household acreage dropped to 1.5 acres (0.6 hectare), which was insufficient to meet basic household needs. Thirty-two percent of households were suddenly landless, and the richest 10 percent of households owned 46 percent of the land. A full 63 percent of households were below the 2-acre line, which was the minimal acreage needed to produce what villagers considered to be a "moderately contented living" derived from full-time farming. It is likely that all households in 1933 were self-sufficient in rice, although there is no available figure. It is known

Figure 12.9. Bangladeshi migrant workers at a construction site in Singapore, 2009 (Tom Bodley).

Table 12.6. Change in a Developing Bangladeshi Village, Goborgari, 1933 and 1977.

	1933	1977
Population	30	392
Households	19	75
Average household size	1.5	5.2
Average acres/household	4.3	1.5
Households landless (5)	0	32
Land owned by richest 10% of households (%)	10	46
Households not self-sufficient in rice	n.d.	60%

Source: Van Schendel (1981). N.d. = no data.

that inequality was minimal, and no households were landless.

The land situation was more complex than the facts of legal ownership suggest because land quality and productivity varied and land fragmentation made cultivation difficult. An average household might own 1.5 acres (0.6 hectare) in six and one-half separate pieces. A significant amount of land was also either mortgaged or sharecropped under an arrangement in which the sharecropper could keep half of the production. Holding a mortgage or rights to sharecrop a given piece of land gave a degree of control over "unowned" land and made it considerably more difficult to assess the actual degree of poverty and inequality in the village. Virtually as critical as control over land was ownership of a plow and team of draft animals, yet only 33 percent of households owned a full team. A farmer who did not own a team could not sharecrop, and hiring a team to plow one's own land meant reduced yields and increased expenses. To a limited extent, sharecropping gave the poorest villagers a chance to make up their deficiencies; nevertheless, 60 percent of all households were not self-sufficient in rice. They could not produce enough rice to meet their minimal nutritional requirements and were even farther from producing a marketable surplus to help meet their physical needs for moderately contented living by local standards.

Because agricultural self-sufficiency was out of reach of two-thirds of the villagers, they were forced to supplement their incomes with seasonal part-time labor, with petty—and sometimes illegal—business operations, and with whatever irregular and poorly paid service employment they could find. Under these conditions, most villagers faced continual economic emergencies and scarcity, and serious poverty and inequality appeared to be steadily increasing. These conditions closely resembled the circumstances that faced English peasants during the enclosure movement and compelled millions of Bangladeshi to migrate to the cities in search of wage employment.

When he attempted to estimate the actual economic status of Goborgari households, Van Schendel found that cash values were inadequate to cover all of the significant economic exchanges that took place in the village and the varying requirements of individual households. Instead, Van Schendel used a four-point scale based on the villagers' own estimates of monthly household maintenance requirements and standard of living. Villagers implicitly recognized at

Table 12.7. Household Economic Categories in Goborgari, 1977

Category*	Households		Population	
	(no.)	(%)	(no.)	(%)
A: Substandard	15	20	74	19
B: Low	32	43	147	38
C: Moderate	16	21	90	23
D: Comfortable	12	16	81	20

Source: Van Schendel (1981).

*Etic categories distinguished by Van Schendel: (A) Substandard: virtually landless, tattered clothing, hungry; income insufficient for year. (B) Low: plow less than 2 acres, basic annual food and clothing. (C) Moderate: more than 2 acres, 1–3 months' surplus. (D) Comfortable: metal-roofed house, tube well, expensive clothes, bicycle, wristwatches, as status symbols; surplus of 3 months or more. Native economic categories within Goborgari: (1) Chhotolok: laborers, cannot produce rice. (2) Moidhom: sharecroppers, must also buy rice. (3) Dewani: eat rice they produce; wealthy landowners in other villages. (4) Mashari: wealthy, owners of 10–25 acres. (5) Adhoni: very wealthy, owners of more than 25 acres.

least four standards of living within the village, which Van Schendel labeled A (substandard), B (low), C (moderate), and D (comfortable) (see table 12.7), according to a household's ability to produce sufficient rice for its total annual needs. The poorest 20 percent of households (category A) often went hungry and could not afford respectable clothing. The top 16 percent of households (category D) enjoyed an annual surplus that would allow them to maintain their modest comforts and simple luxuries for more than three months beyond a given agricultural year. Households in the two middle categories existed on a very narrow margin.

The economic position of the village as a whole could be affected by war, famine, and fluctuations in the price of cash crops. Upward or downward mobility of individual households was determined by a variety of specific factors. Where the margin of economic viability is narrow, illness, a single poor crop, an expensive wedding or funeral, a robbery, or litigation can push a household into extreme poverty.

The local rural elite were wealthy landowners who could live relatively comfortably, even though in comparison with the national-level urban elite they did not appear wealthy. The rural elite were heavily dependent on the labor of sharecroppers who worked their land, and they made significant profit from lending money to the chronically indebted peasantry at exorbitant rates. The rural elite thus had a vested interest in maintaining the long-established peasant landholding system, which was defined by a large, high-density agrarian population, living under very marginal conditions. The system's basic features—especially landless laborers, sharecroppers, mortgages, and high rates of indebtedness—severely inhibit upward mobility.

Bangladesh and the Green Revolution

The Green Revolution refers to the use of institutionalized agricultural research, large-scale capital resources, and energy-intensive technology to increase per-acre food productivity in the developing world. This approach to agricultural development began in 1943 when the Rockefeller Foundation funded a special project in cooperation with the Mexican government to improve the yield of grain crops by selective breeding. By the early 1960s, the program had successfully produced a dwarf hybrid wheat capable of tripling yields. In 1966, the Mexican research center became an international agricultural research institute known as CIMMYT (International Center for the Improvement of Wheat and Maize). By 1977, after an

intensively funded international campaign, Mexican dwarf HYV wheat was being grown on half of the wheatland throughout the developing world and was replacing many indigenously produced varieties and other crops.[87] CIMMYT became a model for a dozen other similar centers, which spread throughout the developing world under the sponsorship of CGIAR (Consultative Group on International Agricultural Research).

The HYV grains are often presented as the primary factors behind the large per-acre yields of the Green Revolution; however, these production increases were won at a cost. The local crops that the new plants replaced were produced by many generations of local people to fit local environmental conditions and the requirements of small-scale, self-sufficient production techniques. The new plants have been called high-response varieties to emphasize that they depend on expensive inputs.[88] The "miracle grains" are extremely demanding plants. They only produce high yields under optimum conditions. They require a specific amount of water and large quantities of chemical fertilizer. They are also vulnerable to disease and pests because they are a genetic monocrop; thus, successful production also requires generous applications of chemical pesticides. They are often dwarf forms because a short stock is needed to support the heavy head of grain, but this leaves the plants more vulnerable to flooding and means that they cannot be grown in many otherwise-favorable areas. The special requirements of the new varieties mean that only the largest farmers with the best land and the best connections with the government can take advantage of the new technology and can afford the risk of occasional crop failure.[89]

Joining the Green Revolution means that small farmers are linked to a complex global political economy in which the seeds they plant, the tools they use, and the most critical factors affecting their security, such as land, marketing, wages, and credits, are all removed from effective village control. Ultimately, the fate of "developing" rural villagers is determined by the heads of governments, banks, corporations, foundations, and other international development agencies, all operating through many interconnected bureaucracies. Under the Green Revolution, village-level agricultural production is connected to global-level institutions, by way of national-level institutions, through a series of unequal exchanges, or inputs and outputs, in which power is concentrated at the top at each level and costs and benefits are unevenly distributed.

Figure 12.10 illustrates the three levels—global, national, and village—at which the Green Revolution is organized and lists some of the exchanges between levels. Although the avowed public purpose of this kind of agricultural development is "to help poor peasants feed themselves," at the global level it can be seen that important political and economic benefits accrue to the elites of the donor nations. Many elites at the national level also derive important benefits in the form of food surpluses, land, profits, cheap labor, bribes, and votes. National elites, including government officials at all levels in the bureaucracy and the wealthy in private enterprises (who are often also in government), control the technological and financial inputs, as well as the natural resources of land and water, that make the HYVs produce. In exchange, the developing countries have accepted an increasing burden of debt to international donors and often find that they must submit to specific conditions in order to keep up their payments. Thus, a form of international debt peonage has become part of the development process. Ironically, at the village level, the local elite repeat the unequal exchanges of higher levels, such that the majority of the rural population becomes impoverished, not nourished and empowered, by the Green Revolution.

Impoverishment was one of the unintended secondary outcomes that accompanied increased production as the Green Revolution reached the village level (see figure 12.10). This occurred as part of an interconnected process in which the new technology was linked to increased debt and landlessness and reduced nutrition in the villages. Nutrition declined because the monocrop HYVs replaced other food crops, while declining incomes made it more difficult for no-longer self-sufficient villagers to buy food. At the national level, land values increased along with grain hoarding by speculators, while grain prices fell. Many rural people forfeited their small landholdings when they were unable to pay off their debts. Increased mechanization reduced the demand for farm labor, and wages fell, driving many people to seek low-paying jobs in the cities. Elites at every level benefited from all of this while the total level of poverty increased.[90] Arguably, this growth process produced unintended structural violence.

Green Revolution impoverishment is well illustrated in Bangladesh. The local elite used their political connections to gain control of the tube wells required for irrigating the HYV crops. They also "cultivated" the government extension agents with bribes to make sure that the seeds, expertise, chemicals, and machinery came to them first. The elite dominated village agricultural cooperatives and effectively controlled whatever technological inputs reached the lower-class small landholders and sharecroppers. Skillful manipulation of their political and economic advantages helped the local elite to systematically appropriate the land of less-fortunate fellow villagers, while extracting their labor and grain. The landless laborers at the bottom of the village hierarchy had only their labor to exchange for inadequate wages.

Wheat steadily displaced rice and other crops as a primary food staple in Bangladesh because HYV wheat proved more suitable in Bangladesh than HYV rice. This crop change, however, has also had unexpected cultural consequences.[91] The traditional Bangladeshi diet consists of rice, lentils, fish, and vegetables. As inexpensive HYV wheat became widely available, it became the dominant food. The poor, who can afford little else, were forced to abandon their preferred foods and eat wheat three meals a day even though this meant a decline in the caloric and nutritional quality of their diet. Culturally, rice remained the most important food and was considered the essential element of a meal, whereas wheat was treated as a foreign snack food and was understandably associated with disease by villagers.

Some development experts have argued that the expansion of wheat production in Bangladesh benefits women because many women, who were formerly employed as rice hullers but were displaced by machines, may now find employment harvesting and threshing wheat. However, this work is taken only by the poorest women because it violates *purdah* restrictions, is very heavy and difficult work, and must take place during the hottest time of year.

BEYOND THE THRESHOLD: SPECTERS OF SOCIOCULTURAL COLLAPSE

Global Warming: Impacts, Adaptations, and Vulnerability

The effects of anthropogenic climate change on people, the environment, and human activities are examined in detail in Working Group II of the IPCC's Fourth Assessment Report (AR4), which was released in 2007 (see figure 12.11).[92] The Fourth Assessment is considerably grimmer than the Third Assessment Report (TAR), which was issued in 2001.[93] The AR4

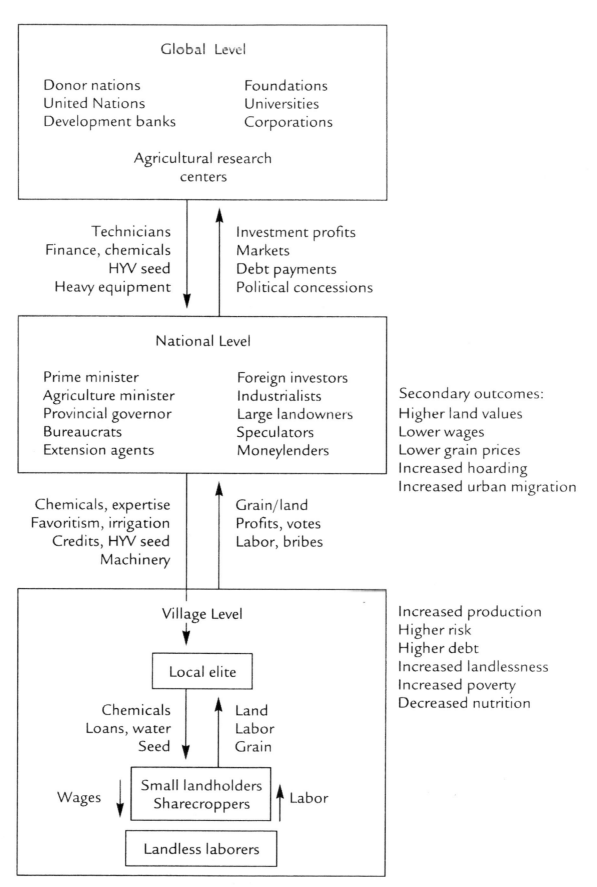

Figure 12.10. Input-output structure of the Green Revolution.

Key impacts as a function of increasing global average temperature change

(Impacts will vary by extent of adaptation, rate of temperature change, and socio-economic pathway)

† Significant is defined here as more than 40%.
‡ Based on average rate of sea level rise of 4.2 mm/year from 2000 to 2080.

Figure 12.11. The Intergovernmental Panel on Climate Change highlighted scientific consensus on the possible effects of climate change impacts in their Fourth Assessment Report in 2007. IPCC Figure SPM.2. Illustrative examples of global impacts projected for climate changes (and sea level and atmospheric carbon dioxide where relevant) associated with different amounts of increase in global average surface temperature in the 21st century [T20.8]. The black lines link impacts, dotted arrows indicate impacts continuing with increasing temperature. Entries are placed so that the left-hand side of the text indicates the approximate onset of a given impact. Quantitative entries for water stress and flooding represent the additional impacts of climate change relative to the conditions projected across the range of Special Report on Emissions Scenarios (SRES) scenarios A1Fl, A2, B1 and B2 (see Endbox 3). Adaptation to climate change is not included in these estimations. All entries are from published studies recorded in the chapters of the Assessment. Sources are given in the right-hand column of the Table. Confidence levels for all statements are high. (IPCC. 2007. *Summary for Policymakers.* **In:** *Climate Change 2007: Impacts, Adaptation and Vulnerability. Contribution of Working Group II to the Fourth Assessment Report of the Intergovernmental Panel on Climate Change.* **Parry, M. L. O.F. Canziani, J. P. Palutikof, P. J. van der Linden, and C. E. Hansen (editors). Cambridge, UK: Cambridge University Press.)**

report concludes that the effects of climate change over the twenty-first century will have "predominately negative consequences" for humans in much of the world. The group report has "high confidence" that changes due to global warming have already been ob-

served since 1970 in snow, ice, and frozen ground, including the formation or enlargement of glacial lakes, more avalanches, increased spring run-off, and earlier arrival of spring in temperate areas. Ironically, the developed countries in the mid- and high-latitude re-

450   CHAPTER 12

gions that were largely responsible for global warming may see some improvements in agricultural and forest production if temperature increases are in moderate ranges, whereas the relatively poor countries at lower latitudes will experience the most severe impacts. All projected climate change impacts are sensitive to the degree of global warming that actually occurs, and as warming increases, negative impacts will occur everywhere. Small differences in temperature can have very large effects, but there are many unknowns. Really massive impacts or "singular events" are more likely to occur beyond 2100 when catastrophic sea-level rises would follow the complete melting of the Greenland and West Antarctic ice sheets.

According to the report, climate change will at least initially disturb the distribution of freshwater in contradictory ways in different regions of the world. Some regions will be 10 to 40 percent wetter, others 10 to 30 percent drier than normal, and these changes can have profoundly negative impacts for societies dependent on irrigation agriculture or pastoral nomadism. Peoples living in High Mountain areas such as the Andes and Himalayas are likely to be threatened by avalanches and outburst floods from glacial melt water, followed by diminished water supplies. As mountain glaciers melt, supplies of freshwater that currently support a billion people in the world's great river valleys will shrink. Larger areas are likely to be impacted by droughts. East African pastoralists may be overwhelmed by abnormally severe droughts. A third of Amazonia's tropical rain forest could be turned into savanna, and massive species extinctions could occur by 2050. Large parts of the Kakadu and Arnhem Land in the Northern Territory of Australia could be flooded by saltwater. Pacific Islanders may see their islands and reefs eroding away by rising sea levels, increasingly severe storms, and a more acidic ocean, even as marine fisheries and ecosystems collapse. Terrestrial ecosystems that have already been under severe stress from human activities will be stressed even further by climate change–related flooding, drought, fires, insects, and ocean acidification.

The report anticipates that many plants and animals will face further risks of extinction, and global biological product could decline after about 2050, which could amplify global warming as burned plants release more carbon into the atmosphere. Under some conditions there may initially be small increases in agricultural productivity at mid and high latitudes, but productivity is expected to fall at lower latitudes, nearer to the equator. Declining biodiversity will further reduce ecosystem services that maintain freshwater and food for people as well as fiber and forest products. All of these impacts will amplify the economic impoverishment that much of the world already experiences as a result of existing inequalities of wealth and income.

Coastal systems, low-lying areas, river deltas, and especially the world's great mega-deltas such as the Nile, the Mekong, and the Ganges-Brahmaputra in Bangladesh and India, where millions of people live, are all highly vulnerable to sea-level rise caused by global warming.[94] Global warming–related sea-level rise and storm surges will be added to the current human impact on these areas caused by urban development and the loss of the annual deposits of river-borne sediments that are now trapped behind dams. These sediments would otherwise counteract the natural submergence and erosion that affects deltas. A special problem of these areas is that the very dense populations living here have only limited possibilities for moving inland to avoid flooding, because adjacent areas have limited agricultural potential and are already occupied. Many of the delta populations most exposed are also the poorest and have the fewest resources to either protect themselves or recover from damage. The impact of recent storms on vulnerable delta regions is illustrated by the example of Hurricane Katrina, which hit New Orleans and the Mississippi Delta in 2005. Katrina killed some 1,800 people and caused more than $100 billion in property and economic damage, but it also destroyed protective islands, wetlands that supported migratory waterfowl, and marine fisheries.

The expected health effects of climate change are complex but are expected to on balance be negative. Fewer people will obviously die from exposure to cold, but malnutrition is expected to increase, along with deaths from storms and fires, and from the expanded ranges of many diseases. Again, people in the poorest countries will be most vulnerable.

The IPCC studies have consistently used a set of scenarios called the SRES (Special Report on Emissions Scenarios),[95] global storylines that project greenhouse gas emissions under four different assumptions about how global development might occur. The four possible futures are defined by the intersection of two axes represented whether development emphasizes (A) economic growth or (B) environmental protection and social equity, and whether development is primarily (1) global or (2) regional. As one might expect, the A1 and A2 scenarios, which make global economic growth the primary objective of development, also consistently produce the most global warming and negative impacts. Projections for A scenarios maximizing economic growth lead to complete disaster by 2100, not unlike the *Limits to Growth* projections. As global mean temperatures reach 3°C above preindustrial levels, natural ecosystems collapse, and major extinctions occur worldwide. There would also be massive social and economic disruptions. Only the B scenarios offer any prospect that temperature rise might stabilize at lower than 3°C, where only 20 to 30 percent of species are "committed to extinction." Either way, the human costs of climate change are enormous, and we are forced to conclude that if economic growth requires ever-increasing flows of energy and materials, such growth will continue to produce an unsustainable global system.

Lights Out: Peak Oil and the Olduvai Hypothesis

The most immediately critical unsustainable aspect of the present global system is its heavy dependence on fossil fuels. As noted in chapter 10, fossil fuels were the basis of the growth of the commercial world, and they made possible the huge increase in per-capita energy consumption levels that anthropologist Leslie White used to define cultural evolutionary progress. Petroleum is the most desirable fossil fuel because by weight it contains twice the energy of hard coal, and it is relatively easy to transport by pipelines. About half of the world's commercial energy is currently in petroleum and natural gas. Petroleum literally fueled the massive increase in the global economy, in material flows, and in population that occurred during the twentieth century. Petroleum also made the commercial world's central myth of perpetual growth seem possible. However, two physical realities show that perpetual growth based on petroleum and other fossil fuels is not sustainable.

Fossil fuels create a double bind for humanity because we need them in two critical areas where their continued use is not sustainable: coal for generating electricity and petroleum for transportation. Previous sections have repeatedly shown that fossil fuels are the leading cause of global warming, which is the primary long-term sustainability problem for the commercial world in the twenty-first century. If the countries with the largest economies continue to burn massive amounts of abundantly available coal to produce electricity, this will contribute even more to the carbon emissions that cause global warming. Petroleum also produces unacceptable carbon emissions, although

at somewhat lower rates than coal, but the supply of easily available petroleum is much more limited than coal and will soon decline. Either use of fossil fuel is unsustainable. There are uncertainties over when global warming will have catastrophic effects, or when petroleum will become too costly to extract and burn in significant quantities. Either way, the limits of the present episode of growth will almost certainly occur during the twenty-first century, causing massive cultural transformations.

The concept of **peak oil** refers to the point at which half of the world supply of oil will have been exhausted, and supplies will begin to decline. This does not mean that oil will be totally gone, it will just steadily become more costly. The actual pathway of the decline will be greatly affected by the political and economic choices that people make. The decline of oil production was foreseen well in advance, but the warnings were disregarded by elite decision makers. In 1949, the same year that Leslie White published his energy-based law of cultural evolution, M. King Hubbert, an oil geologist working for Shell Oil, pointed out in an article in *Science* that when viewed from a millennial perspective, the age of fossil fuel energy would be a small blip, "rising sharply from zero to a maximum, and almost as sharply declining, and thus representing but a moment in the total of human history."[96] Hubbert felt that on the upside of the production curve we were experiencing events that were "the most abnormal and anomalous in the history of the world." The colorful history of the upward curve of petroleum development is well described by oil business consultant Daniel Yergin.[97] On the downside, Hubbert predicted that the world would soon return to a stable population using solar energy. In 1969 he estimated based on rates of discovery that the halfway point in global petroleum consumption would occur around the year 2000, assuming a total supply of 2.1 trillion barrels (see figure 12.12). This would mean that 80 percent of all the oil that existed would be consumed within about 60 years from about 1965 to 2025.[98] The age of oil would bracket the rapid rise of "globalization" and would be followed by a sharp period of tumultuous decline.

Hubbert's forecasts have proven remarkably accurate, even though it continues to be very difficult to obtain reliable figures on oil production and known reserves from key governments and corporations. In 1998 oil geologist Colin J. Campbell suggested that Hubbert's Peak would most likely occur during the first decade of the twenty-first century.[99] Campbell

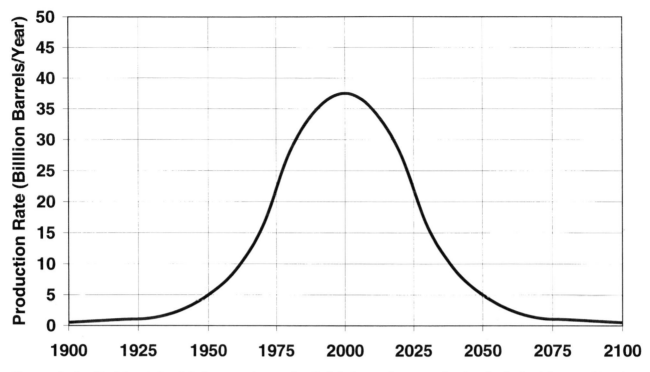

Figure 12.12. "Hubbert's Peak," the complete cycle of global petroleum production (redrafted from Hubbert).

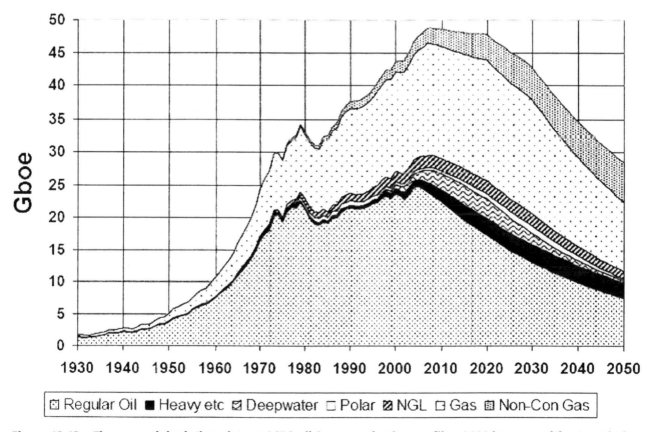

☐ Regular Oil ■ Heavy etc ☒ Deepwater ☐ Polar ▨ NGL ☐ Gas ▣ Non-Con Gas

Figure 12.13. The general depletion picture: ASPO oil & gas production profiles, 2008 base case (The Association for the Study of Peak Oil and Gas (ASPO) Newsletter No. 100. April 2009, Compiled by C.J. Campbell).

founded the Association for the Study of Peak Oil (ASPO), a network of scientists and organizations, to examine the problem.[100] In 2009 Campbell estimated that regular oil production had actually peaked in 2005 and that all forms of oil and gas would peak in 2008. By 2100 total production would be 2.4 trillion barrels of oil equivalent, only somewhat higher than Hubbert had estimated.[101] Figure 12.13 shows ASPO's projection of the global oil and gas production curve as of 2009. Another estimate places the peak of regular petroleum and natural gas liquid at between 2009 and 2021.[102] Some authorities prefer to speak of an "undulating plateau" by 2035[103] rather than a "dramatic peak" by 2010, but there is a broad consensus among petroleum experts that the supply of oil is not infinite and will eventually fail to meet demand. It is also clear that the costly extraction of unconventional forms of petroleum (heavy oil, tar sands, oil shales, polar oil, deepwater oil, and natural gas) will do little to delay the decline.[104]

The reality that petroleum is not an infinite resource means that the global system as presently constituted is not sustainable, but it does not mean that the transition to sustainability will be catastrophic as some have warned. For example, electrical engineer Richard C. Duncan sees a downslope from a fossil fuel peak of about 20 years, followed by a 20-year steep plunge off the cliff, which would mirror the upward curve of energy consumption in the opposite direction. He warns that the effects of declines in fossil fuels relative to demand will have their greatest impact on electricity production, not transportation. He points out that electricity is critical for urban life in the industrial world for the crucial functions of communication, computation, and control.[105] Duncan forecasts that electrical grids could began failing by 2012 and permanent blackouts would occur thereafter. Duncan declared: "If the grids are lost, then Industrial Civilization is paralyzed—no industry, no commerce, no jobs, no food." It would be "lights out" for civilization, a population die-off and back to the Stone Age in Olduvai Gorge for the survivors.[106] More optimistic forecasts speak of "The Long Emergency,"[107] or even a "Prosperous Way Down." Modern cities can adapt, but big changes will be needed.[108]

An energy crisis will of course also be an opportunity to shift to more energy-efficient consumption patterns and to truly sustainable sources of energy. This transition process may also be modeled after small-scale societies and small nations that can focus more directly and more efficiently on the humanization process, rather than building ever larger and more complex economies to accumulate greater masses of concentrated financial wealth. Part IV will explore these possibilities.

SUMMARY

Since the 1950s, poverty has been conceptualized as a development or modernization problem. Development planners assumed that people were poor because they were underdeveloped, and they were underdeveloped because they were technologically backward and culturally conservative. Hoping to reduce poverty, the developed countries optimistically financed the transfer of agricultural technologies, dam and highway construction, and other large-scale developments designed to promote economic growth throughout the world. Unfortunately, these efforts have not significantly reduced poverty.

Initially, anthropologists enthusiastically endorsed this development model and worked in small communities to identify the cultural barriers to economic progress. It became apparent, however, that traditional cultures were not the primary cause of poverty. National and international efforts to raise GNP in many cases actually further impoverished local communities by promoting debt and dependency and intensified internal inequalities that reduced access to basic resources. Anthropological data also show that many cultural traits, which development planners may consider to be causes of poverty, are rational coping mechanisms to conditions of extreme deprivation. Similarly, overpopulation cannot be a sole cause of poverty. Although population growth has certainly intensified poverty, the relationship is complex. Poverty and the development process itself have both fostered population growth.

The scale and power approach suggests that poverty will not be solved by increasing the scale of production or making everyone dependent on global market exchanges. The evidence presented in previous chapters showed that poverty was essentially absent in autonomous tribal cultures but was first created by the inequality inherent in the social ranking of political-scale cultures. Poverty was further intensified by the process of colonialism and the global system of stratification that emerged with commercialization. To be effective, development efforts designed to reduce poverty must deal with the inequalities of wealth and power that exist at all levels of the global system.

1. How did UN experts conceptualize the problem of global poverty in 1950? What specific indicators of underdevelopment did they refer to? What was the vicious cycle? What solutions did they call for?

2. In what sense can it be said that poverty has increased since 1950? Refer to poverty indicators, absolute numbers of impoverished people, and GNP rankings between nations.

3. Describe the official charter and the institutional basis for the UN's approach to development, referring to the following: UN Charter, Universal Declaration of Human Rights, and the World Bank.

4. Describe how the issues and strategies of the UN's approach to development have changed in the decades since 1950.

5. Define underdevelopment and poverty, discussing the conceptual and cultural problems that limit the usefulness of your definitions.

6. What is sustainability and how has it been defined? How can it be measured?

7. What is peak oil? Why is it significant for sustainability?

8. Discuss how colonialism, social structure, population growth, and technological advance were related to poverty in Bangladesh at both national and village levels.

9. Describe village social structure in Bangladesh, emphasizing access to land, labor, technology, food, and cash income in relation to standard of living.

10. What is meant by structural violence, and what does it add to the understanding of poverty?

11. In what sense can the global system be considered a plutonomy and a plutocracy? Why does it matter?

SUGGESTED READING

Hartmann, Betsy, and James K. Boyce. 1983. *A Quiet Violence: View from a Bangladesh Village.* San Francisco: Institute for Food and Development Policy. A detailed case study of development in Bangladesh, which expands on the coverage provided in this chapter.

Lappe, Frances Moore, Joseph Collins, and David Kinley. 1981. *Aid as Obstacle: Twenty Questions about Our Foreign Aid and the Hungry.* San Francisco: Institute for Food and Development Policy. Classic discussion of the problem of food aid.

Stiglitz, Joseph E. 2002. *Globalization and its Discontents.* New York: W. W. Norton. A critique of globalization and development policy by a former World Bank economist.

UNDP (United Nations Development Program). 2003. *Human Development Report. Millennium Development Goals: A Compact among Nations to End Human Poverty.* New York: Oxford University Press. Update on the UNDP's efforts to eradicate poverty.

World Bank. (annual). *World Development Report.* A basic source on economic current development issues and global poverty.

GLOSSARY TERMS

Anthropocene The age beginning about 1800 AD when human activites became geologically visible in biological, chemical, and physical processes on the earth.

Anthropogenic biomes Geographic regions defined by the density of human population, form of settlement, and land use.

Great acceleration The dramatic increase in human population and technology since 1945 that greatly amplified the human impacts on nature that have been apparent since 1800 with the Anthropocene.

Plutonomy An economy managed and directed by the wealthy.

Plutocracy Rule by the rich.

Market capitalization The collective market value of all the stocks issued by all the corporations listed in a particular market.

Structural violence Human suffering that is the direct result of social and cultural structures that enable more powerful individuals to violate the basic human rights of less powerful individuals.

High-yield variety High-yield plant varieties, especially wheat and rice developed by selective breeding as part of the Green Revolution.

Peak oil The point at which half of all extractable oil has been extracted and output begins to decline, because of increasing cost and difficulty of extraction.

NOTES

1. Costanza, Robert, Lisa J. Graumlich, and Will Steffen, eds. 2007. *Sustainability or Collapse? An Integrated History and Future of People on Earth.* Cambridge, MA, and London: The MIT Press; Costanza, Robert, Lisa Graumlich, Will Steffen, Carole Crumley, John Dearing, Kathy Hibbard, Rik Leemans, Charles Redman and David Schimel. 2007. "Sustainability or Collapse: What Can We Learn from Integrating the History of Humans and the Rest of Nature?" *Ambio* 36(2):522–27; Meadows, Donella H., Dennis L. Meadows, Jorgen Randers, and William W. Behrens III. 1972. *The Limits to Growth.* New York: Universe.

2. Meadows, Donella H., Dennis L. Meadows, and Jorgen Randers. 1992. *Beyond the Limits: Confronting Global Collapse, Envisioning a Sustainable Future.* Post Mills, VT: Chelsea Green Publishing Co.; Meadows, Donella, Jorgen Randers, and Dennis Meadows. 2004. *Limits to Growth: The 30-Year Update.* White River Jct., VT: Chelsea Green Publishing; Meadows, Dennis L. 2007. "Evaluating Past Forecasts: Reflections on One Critique of the Limits to Growth." In Costanza, Graumlich, and Steffen, eds. 2007. *Sustainability or Collapse? An Integrated History and Future of People on Earth*, pp. 399–415. Cambridge, MA and London: The MIT Press.

3. Union of Concerned Scientists. 1992. World Scientists' Warning to Humanity. www.ucsusa.org/ucs/about/1992-world-scientists-warning-to-humanity.html

4. Crutzen, Paul J., and Eugene F. Stoermer. 2000. "The 'Anthropocene.'" *IGBP Newsletter* No. 41: 17–18. The International Geosphere-Biosphere Programme (IGBP): A Study of Global Change of the International Council for Science (ICSU).

5. Pollard, Duncan (editor). 2010. *Living Planet Report 2010: Biodiversity, Biocapacity and Development.* Gland, Switzerland: WWF International.

6. Zalasiewicz, Jan, et al. 2008. "Are We Now Living in the Anthropocene?" *GSA Today* 18(2):4–8. Geological Society of America.

7. Jones, P. D., T. M. L. Wigley, and P. B. Wright. 1986. "Global Temperature Variations Between 1861 and 1984." *Nature* 322(6078):430–34.

8. Ellis, Erle C., and Navin Ramankutty. 2008. "Putting People in the Map: Anthropogenic Biomes of the World." *Frontiers in Ecology and the Environment* 6(8):439–47.

9. Ellis, Erle C., and Navin Ramankutty. 2008. "Anthropogenic Biome Maps." *The Encyclopedia of Earth.* www.eoearth.org/article/Anthropogenic_biome_maps (accessed Feb. 2010).

10. Center for International Earth Science Information Network (CIESIN). 2010. *Last of the Wild, Version Two.* sedac.ciesin.columbia.edu/wildareas/ (accessed Feb. 2010); Sanderson, E. W., M. Jaiteh, M. A. Levy, K. H. Redform, A. V. Wannebo, and G. Woolmer. 2002. "The Human Footprint and the Last of the Wild." *BioScience* 52(10); 891–904.

11. Landsberg, Helmut E. 1989. "Where Do We Stand with the CO2 Greenhouse Effect Problem?" In *Global Climate Change: Human and Natural Influences*, edited by S. Fred Singer, pp. 87–89. New York: Paragon House.

12. Graedel, Thomas E., and Paul J. Crutzen. 1989. "The Changing Atmosphere." *Scientific American* 261(3):58–68.

13. Cicerone, Ralph J. 1989. "Methane in the Atmosphere." In *Global Climate Change: Human and Natural Influences*, edited by S. Fred Singer, pp. 91–112. New York: Paragon House.

14. Rowland, F. Sherwood. 1989. "Chlorofluorocarbons, Stratospheric Ozone, and the Antarctic 'Ozone Hole.'" In *Global Climate Change: Human and Natural Influences*, edited by S. Fred Singer, pp. 113–55. New York: Paragon House.

15. IPCC (Intergovernmental Panel on Climate Change). 2007. *Climate Change 2007: The Physical Science Basis, Summary for Policymakers. Contribution of Working Group I to the Fourth Assessment Report of the Intergovernmental Pattern on Climate Change.* www.ipcc.ch/publications_and_data/publications_and_data_reports.htm#1 (accessed Feb. 2010).

16. Rosenzweig, Cynthia, et al. 2008. "Attributing Physical and Biological Impacts to Anthropogenic Climate Change." *Nature* 453(15 May): 353–58.

17. National Oceanic and Atmospheric Administration (NOAA). 2010. *Trends in Atmospheric Carbon Dioxide (Global).* Earth System Research Laboratory. www.esrl.noaa.gov/gmd/ccgg/trends/#global (accessed Feb. 2010).

18. Baer, Paul, Tom Athanasiou, Sivan Kartha, and Eric Kemp-Benedict. 2008. The Greenhouse Development Rights Framework: "The Right to Development in a Climate Constrained World." Heinrich Böll Foundation, Christian Aid, EcoEquity, and the Stockholm Environment Institute. http://gdrights.org/2009/02/16/second-edition-of-the-greenhouse-development-rights/; Baer, Paul, Tom Athanasiou, and Sivan Kartha. 2009. "A 350 ppm Emergency Pathway: A Greenhouse Development Rights Brief." Ecoequity and Stockholm Environment Institute. http://gdrights.org/2009/10/25/a-350-ppm-emergency-pathway/.

19. Meinshausen, Malte, Nicolai Meinshausen, William Hare, Sarah C. B. Raper, Katja Frieler, Reto Knutti, David J. Frame, and Myles R. Allen. 2009. "Greenhouse-Gas Emission Targets for Limiting Global Warming to 2°C." *Nature* 458(30 April):1158–62. nature08017.

20. Veron, John Edward Norwood. 2008. "Mass Extinctions and Ocean Acidification: Biological Constraints on Geological Dilemmas." *Coral Reefs* 27:459–72; Veron, John Edward Norwood. 2008. *A Reef in Time: the Great Barrier Reef from Beginning to End.* Cambridge, MA: Belknap Press of Harvard University Press.

21. De'ath, Glenn, Janice M. Lough, Katharina E. Fabricius. 2009. "Declining Coral Calcification on the Great Barrier Reef." *Science* 323(2 January): 116–19.

22. Pauly, Daniel. 2004. "Much Rowing for Fish." *Nature* 432 (16 December): 813–14.

23. Borgstrom, Georg. 1965. *The Hungry Planet.* New York: Macmillan.

24. Watson, Reg, and Daniel Pauly. 2001. "Systematic Distortions in World Fisheries Catch Trends." *Nature* 414 (29 November): 534–36; FAO, Fisheries and Aquaculture Department. 2009. *The State of World Fisheries and Aquaculture 2008.* Rome: Food and Agriculture Organization of the United Nations.

25. Naylor, Rosamond L., Rebecca J. Goldburg, Jurgenne H. Primavera, Nils Kautsky, Malcolm C. M. Beveridge, Jason Clay, Carl Folke, Jane Lubchenco, Harold Mooney, and Max Troell. 2000. "Effect of Aquaculture on World Fish Supplies." *Nature* 405 (29 June): 1017–24.

26. Watson and Pauly, 2001. ". . . World Fisheries Catch Trends," 536.

27. Worm, Boris, et al. 2006. "Impacts of Biodiversity Loss on Ocean Ecosystem Services." *Science* 314 (3 November)):787–90.

28. Talberth, John, Karen Wolowicz, Jason Venetoulis, Michel Gelobter, Paul Boyle, and Bill Mott. 2006. *The Ecological Fishprint of Nations: Measuring Humanity's Impact on Marine Ecosystems.* Oakland, CA: Redefining Progress.

29. Naylor, et al. 2000. "Effect of Aquaculture." 1017–24.

30. Spalding, Mark D. 2007. "Marine Ecoregions of the World: A Bioregionalization of Coastal and Shelf Areas." *BioScience* 57(7):573–83.

31. Halpern, Benjamin S. et al. 2008. "A Global Map of Human Impact on Marine Ecosystems." *Science* 319 (15 February): 948–52; Halpern, Benjamin S., Kimberly A. Selkoe, Fiorenza Micheli, and Carrie V. Kappel. 2007. "Evaluating and Ranking the Vulnerability of Global Marine Ecosystems to Anthropogenic Threats." *Conservation Biology* 21(5):1301–15; National Center for Ecological Analysis and Synthesis. 2010. "A Global Map of Human Impacts to Marine Ecosystems." Website access for Google Earth viewing: www.nceas.ucsb.edu/globalmarine (accessed Feb. 2010); for interactive map visit http://globalmarine.nceas.ucsb.edu/ (accessed Feb. 2010).

32. Wilkinson, John. 2006. "Fish: A Global Value Chain Driven onto the Rocks." *Sociologia Ruralis* 46(2): 139–53; FAO. 2009. *The State of World Fisheries and Aquaculture 2008.*

33. Millennium Ecosystem Assessment. 2005. *Ecosystems and Human Well-being: Synthesis.* Washington, DC: Island Press; Millennium Ecosystem Assessment. 2005. *Living Beyond Our Means: Natural Assets and Human Well-Being. Statement from the Board.* Technical Volume. Washington, DC: Island Press. www.maweb.org/en/Products.BoardStatement.aspx.

34. Millennium Ecosystem Assessment. 2005. *Living Beyond Our Means: Natural Assets and Human Well-Being. Statement from the Board.* Technical Volume. Washington, DC: Island Press, 5. www.maweb.org/en/Products.BoardStatement.aspx.

35. Diamond, Jared 2005. *Collapse: How Societies Choose to Fail or Succeed.* New York: Viking.

36. Diamond, 2005. *Collapse,* 6.

37. Hassan, Fekri. 2007. "The Lie of History: Nation-States and the Contradictions of Complex Societies. In Costanza, Graumlich, and Steffen, eds. 2007. *Sustainability or Collapse? An Integrated History and Future of People on Earth,* pp. 169-196. Cambridge, MA and London: The MIT Press.

38. Hassan, 2007. "The Lie of History," 176.

39. Fund for Peace. 2010. *Failed State Index 2009.* www.fundforpeace.org/web/index.php?option=com_content&task=view&id=99&Itemid=140 (accessed March 2010).

40. United Nations Development Program. 2009. *Human Development Report 2009: Overcoming Barriers: Human Mobility and Development.* New York: Palgrave Macmillan. http://hdr.undp.org/en/reports/global/hdr2009/.

41. Venetoulis, Jason, and Cliff Cobb. 2004. *The Genuine Progress Indicator 1950–2002 (2004 Update).* Oakland, CA: Redefining Progress. www.rprogress.org/projects/gpi/.

42. New Economics Foundation. 2004. *Chasing Progress: Beyond Measuring Economic Growth.* London, 2, Figure. www.neweconomics.org.

43. Elitzak, Howard. 2000. "Food Marketing Costs: A 1990's Retrospective." *Food Review* 23(3): 27–30.

44. U.S. Census Bureau. 2009. *The 2010 Statistical Abstract of the United States: 2010.* 129th ed. Washington, DC. Table 678. Share of Aggregate Income Received by Each Fifth and Top 5 Percent of Households. www.census.gov/compendia/statab/2010/tables/10s0678.xls#Notes!A1 (accessed Feb. 2010).

45. Bucks, Brian K., Arthur B. Kennickell, Traci L. Mach, and Kevin B. Moore. 2009. "Changes in U.S. Family Finances from 2004 to 2007: Evidence from the Survey of Consumer Finances." *Federal Reserve Bulletin* (February): A1–A56.

46. U.S. Bureau of Economic Analysis. 2009. *Fixed Assets Accounts Tables.* Table 9.1. Real Net Stock of Fixed Assets and Consumer Durable Goods. www.bea.gov/National/FA2004/ (accessed Feb. 2010).

47. U.S. Federal Reserve. 2009. Flow of Funds Accounts of the United States. Z.1 Statistical Release, Tables F 100-107. (released Sept. 17, 2009). www.federalreserve.gov/datadownload/Choose.aspx?rel=Z.1; U.S. Bureau of Economic Analysis. Table 1. Current-Cost Net Stock of Fixed Reproducible Tangible Wealth., 1929–95. www.bea.gov/scb/account_articles/national/0597niw/table1.htm.

48. Bucks et al. 2009. "Changes in U.S. Family Finances from 2004 to 2007."

49. Capgemini. 2001. *World Wealth Report 2001.* www.us.capgemini.com/worldwealthreport08/wwr_archives.asp; Capgemini. 2009. *World Wealth Report 2009.* www.capgemini.com/insights-and-resources/by-publication/2009_world_wealth_report/.

50. United Nations, Department of Social Affairs. 1952. *Preliminary Report on the World Situation: With Special Reference to Standards of Living,* E/CN.5/267/rev.l. New York: United Nations, 22.

51. Kahn, Herman, and Anthony J. Wiener. 1967. *The Year 2000: A Framework for Speculation on the Next Thirty-Three Years.* New York: Macmillan.

52. Kahn, Herman. 1982. "The Coming Boom: Economic, Political, and Social." New York: Simon and Schuster; Simon, Julian L. and Herman Kahn. 1984. *The Resourceful Earth: A Response to Global 2000.* Oxford and New York: Blackwell.

53. Hudson Institute. 2010. Mission Statement. www.hudson.org/learn/index.cfm?fuseaction=mission_statement (accessed March 2010).

54. Rostow, W. W. 1960. *The Process of Economic Growth.* New York: Norton.

55. Rostow, 1960, *The Process of Economic Growth,* 7.

56. World Bank. 1990. *World Development Report.* New York: Oxford University Press, 1.

57. Bodley, John H. 2000. *Cultural Anthropology: Tribes, States, and the Global System.* 3rd ed. Mountain View, CA: Mayfield Publishing, 376–88.

58. World Bank. 1995. *World Development Report.* New York: Oxford University Press, Table 30.

59. Milanovic, Branko. 2002. "True World Income Distribution, 1988 and 1993: First Calculations Based on Household Surveys Alone." *The Economic Journal* 112(476):51–92.

60. Davies, James B., Susanna Sandstrom, Anthony Shorrocks, and Edward N. Wolff. 2006. *The World Distribution of Household Wealth.* World Institute for Development Economics Research.

61. Kapur, Ajay, Niallo Macleod, Narendra Singh. 2005. *Plutonomy: Buying Luxury, Explaining Global Imbalances. Citigroup Global Markets.* www.scribd.com/doc/6674234/Citigroup-Oct-16-2005-Plutonomy-Report-Part-1.

62. Kapur et al. 2005. *Plutonomy,* 2.

63. World Bank. 2009. "Market Capitalization of Listed Companies (current US$)" *World Development Indicators, Online Databases.* http://web.worldbank.org/WBSITE/EXTERNAL/DATASTATISTICS/0,,contentMDK:20398986~menuPK:64133163~pagePK:64133150~piPK:64133175~theSitePK:239419,00.html (accessed Oct. 2009).

64. Glattfelder, J. B., and S. Battiston. 2009. "The Backbone of Complex Networks of Corporations: Who Is Controlling Whom?" *Physical Review E* 80(1):1–33.

65. Glattfelder, J. B., and S. Battiston. 2009. "The Backbone . . ." 15.

66. Bureau van Dijk. *Orbis: A World of Company Information.* www.bvdep.com/en/ORBIS.html.

67. Johnson, Simon. 2009. "The Quiet Coup." *The Atlantic* (May). www.theatlantic.com/magazine/archive/2009/05/the-quiet-coup/7364/.

68. Open Secrets. 2009. Personal Finance: Most Popular Investments, Top Sectors, 2007. www.opensecrets.org/pfds/index.php (accessed Sept. 2009).

69. Johnson, 2009. "The Quiet Coup."

70. Scheper-Hughes, Nancy. 1992. *Death without Weeping: The Violence of Everyday Life in Brazil.* Berkeley: University of California Press.

71. Smith, Adam. 1776. *An Inquiry into the Nature and Causes of the Wealth of Nations,* vol. 1. London: Strahan and Cadell.

72. Gross, Daniel R., and Barbara A. Underwood. 1971. "Technological Change and Caloric Costs: Sisal Agriculture." *American Anthropologist* 73(2):725–40.

73. Towell, Hugh C. 1954. "Kwashiorkor." *Scientific American* 191(6):46–50.

74. Montagu, Ashley. 1972. "Sociogenic Brain Damage." *American Anthropologist* 74(5):1045–61.

75. Brown, J. Larry, and Ernesto Pollitt. 1996. "Malnutrition, Poverty and Intellectual Development." *Scientific American* 274(2):38–43.

76. Scheper-Hughes, 1992. *Death without Weeping,* 313.

77. Scheper-Hughes, 1992. *Death without Weeping,* 146.

78. Farmer, Paul. 1994. *The Uses of Haiti.* Monroe, Maine: Common Courage Press; Farmer, Paul. 2001. *Infections and Inequalities: The Modern Plagues.* Berkeley: University of California Press; Farmer, Paul. 2003. *Pathologies of Power: Health, Human Rights, and the New War on the Poor.* Berkeley: University of California Press.

79. Rummel, R. J. 1997. *Death by Government.* New Brunswick, NJ: Transaction.

80. Rummel, R. J. 1997. *Death by Government.* 4, 70.

81. Van Schendel, Wiliem. 1981. *Peasant Mobility: The Odds of Life in Rural Bangladesh.* Assen: Van Gorcum, 82.

82. Lindenbaum, Shirley. 1987. "Loaves and Fishes in Bangladesh." In *Food and Evolution: Toward a Theory of Human Food Habits,* edited by Marvin Harris and Eric Ross, 427–43. Philadelphia: Temple University Press, 436.

83. World Bank 1988–1995. World Development Reports.

84. Bangladesh, Ministry of Finance. 2003. *Bangladesh: A National Strategy for Economic Growth, Poverty Reduction and Social Development,* 7–8.

85. For example, see: Hartmann, Betsy, and James K. Boyce. 1983. *A Quiet Violence: View from a Bangladesh Village.* San Francisco: Institute for Food and Development Policy; Jansen, Eirik G. 1986. *Rural Bangladesh: Competition for Scarce Resources.* Oslo: Universitetsforlaget, Norwegian University Press; Van Schendel, Willem. 1981. *Peasant Mobility: The Odds of Life in Rural Bangladesh.* Assen: Van Gorcum.

86. Van Schendel, 1981. *Peasant Mobility.*

87. CGIAR (Consultative Group on International Agricultural Research). 1980. *Consultative Group on International Development.* Washington, DC: CGIAR.

88. Palmer, Ingrid. 1972. *Science and Agricultural Production.* Geneva: UN Research Institute for Social Development.

89. Lappe, Frances Moore, Joseph Collins, and Carry Fowler. 1979. *Food First: Beyond the Myth of Scarcity* New York: Ballantine Books.

90. Lappe, Collins, and Fowler, 1979, *Food First.*

91. Lindenbaum, Shirley. 1987. "Loaves and Fishes in Bangladesh." In *Food and Evolution: Toward a Theory of Human Food Habits,* edited by Marvin Harris and Eric Ross, 427–43. Philadelphia: Temple University Press.

92. IPCC. 2007. *Climate Change 2007: Impacts, Adaptation and Vulnerability. Contribution of Working Group II to the Fourth Assessment Report of the Intergovernmental Panel on Climate Change.* Parry, M.L., O.F. Canziani, J. P. Palutikof, P. J. van der Linden, and C. E. Hanson (eds). Cambridge, UK, and New York: Cambridge University Press. www.ipcc.ch/publications_and_data/ar4/wg2/en/contents.html.

93. IPCC, 2001b. *Climate Change 2001: Synthesis Report.* Contribution of Working Groups I, II, and III to the Third Assessment Report of the Intergovernmental Panel on Climate Change, edited by R. T. Watson, and the Core Writing Team. Cambridge, UK, and New York: Cambridge University Press.

94. Nicholls, R. J., P. P. Wong, V. R. Burkett, J. O. Codignotto, J. E. Hay, R. F. McLean, S. Ragoonaden, and C. D. Woodroffe. 2007. "Coastal Systems and Low-Lying Areas." In *Climate Change 2007: Impacts, Adaptation and Vulnerability. Contribution of Working Group II to the Fourth Assessment Report of the Intergovernmental Panel on Climate Change.* Parry, M. L., O. F. Canziani, J. P. Palutikof, P. J. van der Linden, and C. E. Hanson (eds). Cambridge, UK, and New York: Cambridge University Press, Chapter 6, pp. 315–56; Ericson, J. P., C. J. Vorosmarty, S. L. Dingman, L. G. Ward and M. Meybeck. 2006. "Effective Sea-Level Rise and Deltas: Causes of Change and Human Dimension Implications." *Global Planet Change* 50: 63–82.

95. Nakicenovic, Nebojsa, and Robert Swart, eds. 2000. *Special Report on Emissions Scenarios: A Special Report of Working Group III of the Intergovernmental Panel on Climate Change.* Cambridge and New York: Cambridge University Press.

96. Hubbert, M. King. 1949. "Energy from Fossil Fuels." *Science* (Feb. 4) 109(2823): 103–109.

97. Yergin, Daniel. 1991. *The Prize: The Epic Quest for Oil, Money and Power.* New York: Simon and Schuster.

98. Hubbert, M. King. 1969. "Energy Resources." In *Resources and Man,* edited by National Academy of Sciences, pp. 157–242. San Francisco: Freeman.

99. Campbell, Colin J., and Jean H. Laherrère. 1998. "The End of Cheap Oil." *Scientific American* (March): 78–83.

100. ASPO, Association for the Study of Peak Oil and Gas. Website www.peakoil.net/ (accessed March 2010).

101. ASPO. Association for the Study of Peak Oil. 2009. Newsletter No. 100. (April) www.aspo-ireland.org/index.cfm/page/newsletter.

102. Maggio, G. G. Cacciola. 2009. "A Variant of the Hubbert Curve for World Oil Production Forecasts." *Energy Policy* 37:4761–70.

103. Jackson, Peter. 2009. *The Future of Global Oil Supply: Understanding the Building Blocks.* Cambridge Energy Research Associates (CERA). www.cera.com/aspx/cda/client/report/report.aspx?KID=5&CID=10720.

104. Mohr, S. H., G. M. Evans. 2010. "Long Term Prediction of Unconventional Oil Production." *Energy Policy* 38:265–76.

105. Duncan, Richard C. 2001. "World Energy Production, Population Growth, and the Road to the Olduvai Gorge." *Population and Environment* 22(5):503–22.

106. Duncan, 2001. "Olduvai Gorge," 518–19.

107. Kunstler, James Howard. 2005. *The Long Emergency: Surviving the End of Oil, Climate Change, and Other Converging Catastrophes of the Twenty-First Century.* New York: Grove Press; Odum, Howard T., and Elisabeth C. Odum. 2001. *A Prosperous Way Down: Principles and Policies.* Boulder, CO: University Press of Colorado.

108. Newman, Peter. 2007. "Beyond Peak Oil: Will Our Cities Collapse?" *Journal of Urban Technology* 14(2):15–30.

Part Four

BUILDING A SUSTAINABLE WORLD: LOCAL TO GLOBAL

THE CHAPTERS IN PART IV WILL FIRST CONSIDER IN CHAPTER 13 how peoples from the tribal world were impacted by the invasion of their territories by commercial world peoples to extract resources from tribal territories. Many tribal peoples died in this invasion, and they lost control over much of their territory, but by mobilizing politically in self-defense and appealing to the newly developed international human rights standards, many tribal peoples successfully redefined themselves as indigenous peoples and are demonstrating that small-scale societies can achieve social and environmental sustainability within the contemporary commercial world. Chapter 14 explores the place of small nations in the commercial world and their potential for serving as models for sustainability. These are governments; most are independent nations, often former colonies, all of which have populations of fewer than 10 million people. Small nations, because they are small, and because they are often remote from the financial and economic centers of the global economy, are ideally situated to develop truly sustainable sociocultural systems that can maximize the humanization process. The final chapter examines the most recent futurist thinking and scenarios that consider how sustainable systems can be achieved at global and national levels. It also shows that many working models of social sustainability already exist.

CHAPTER 13

Tribes to Nations: Progress of the Victims

Figure 13.0. An Asháninka man in the Gran Pajonal in 1969. He is now represented by OAGP, the Gran Pajonal Asháninka Organization, which belonged to ORAU, the Regional Organization of the Indigenous Peoples of AIDESEP-Ucayali.

LEARNING OBJECTIVES

After studying this chapter you should be able to do the following:

1. Explain the political significance of the term *indigenous peoples* and discuss the problem of labeling such peoples.
2. Evaluate realist and idealist policy approaches to indigenous peoples by analyzing their human impact.
3. Describe the process of colonial expansion into tribal territories and its negative consequences, using specific examples from Australia and Amazonia.
4. Describe and evaluate the diverse approaches that anthropologists have used in the attempt to understand and influence public policy on indigenous peoples' confrontation with the commercial world.

5. Describe and evaluate the diverse approaches that international organizations have adopted in regard to indigenous peoples' confrontation with the commercial world.
6. Explain what cultural autonomy means for indigenous peoples and why it would be desirable.
7. Understand the contemporary situation of indigenous peoples in the Peruvian Amazon and aboriginal areas of Australia.

Indigenous peoples are members of formerly independent tribal societies who are engaged in a contemporary struggle for autonomy and survival in a world dominated by national governments and commercial elites. Previous chapters detailed the cultural background of these peoples as they existed under independent conditions (see chapters 2 through 4). In this chapter, we examine the conceptual, philosophical, and political issues involved in defining the place of indigenous peoples within the global system. First, we discuss the complexities of devising a nonethnocentric concept of indigenous peoples. Next, we review the genocide and ethnocide that they suffered along the frontiers of national expansion, and we briefly examine the great humanitarian policy debate carried on by anthropologists, missionaries, and government officials since the 1830s over how states should relate to tribal peoples and their cultures. This debate finally ended when indigenous peoples fought for cultural autonomy by forming their own organizations and gained formal recognition of their claims in the United Nations Declaration on the Rights of Indigenous Peoples adopted by 144 nations in the UN General Assembly in 2007. Indigenous peoples are engaging the commercial world both economically and politically in ways that show that sustainable development can be achieved by small-scale societies.

To maintain maximum cultural context, we discuss these complex issues using extended case studies drawn from Amazonia (see chapter 2) and Australia (see chapter 3).

INDIGENOUS PEOPLES AND THE GLOBAL SYSTEM

Identity Politics and the Politics of Labels

The labels that one employs in any discussion of "indigenous peoples" are a critical matter because use of any specific label implies a particular understanding of what indigenous people are like and how they should be treated. Choice of labels may also be an expression of political domination or superiority. For example, use of such labels as "Stone Age tribe" implies that an indigenous group is an anachronism, perhaps lost or at least in the wrong time and place. A "Stone Age tribe" may also be seen as especially weak, childlike, helpless, and naive. However, peoples living in "voluntary isolation" carries no negative connotations, and they may be even seen to be making a brave and principled choice. In the interests of cross-cultural understanding, anthropologists generally prefer to use the self-selected terms that specific cultural groups apply to themselves.

As threatened tribal peoples became politically involved in self-defense movements early in the 1970s, many native leaders gradually adopted the term *indigenous* as a self-designation to use in pressing their claims in international forums such as the United Nations. Within the political arena, *indigenous* refers to the original inhabitants of a region and is posed in opposition to the colonists, usurpers, and intruders who came later in search of new resources to exploit. As a political category, indigenous people includes members of peasant groups and ethnic communities who have been absorbed by states but who still strongly identify with their cultural heritage and claim special rights to territory and resources on that basis.

In reference to most areas of the world, *indigenous* is an appropriate label for international discourse. However, if priority of residence in a territory is considered the most critical aspect of the concept of **indigenous peoples**, then the term *indigenous* must be applied cautiously in specific areas, because indigenous peoples have sometimes displaced or absorbed other, more indigenous inhabitants. Archaeological evidence would be needed to sort out the details of settlement priority in some areas of Africa and South America. In general, however, the priority of indigenous groups relative to modern invaders connected with modern states and global culture is obvious.

Indigenous does not distinguish between people living in tribal cultures or in political-scale chiefdoms or who were incorporated as peasants into states and empires. However, it is adherence to such tribal traits as community-level resource management, high levels of local self-sufficiency, and relative social equality that makes indigenous peoples so distinctive. It is also these traits that generate conflict with larger-scale cultures that seek to extinguish local control systems and create dependency in order to extract resources. Indigenous peoples are likely to resist any external pressures for change that undermine their autonomy, yet their small size and lack of political organization make them especially vulnerable to outside intervention and give them special claims before the international community. The term *indigenous* is often preferable to similar terms such as *native*, which in some settings carries negative connotations because of its use by colonial powers. In other areas, *native* may be a self-designation used interchangeably with *indigenous*. *Indigenous*, now a self-appellation, has no negative connotations for the people who use it. This usage calls attention to both cultural uniqueness and the political oppression, or at least the disadvantage that indigenous peoples must often endure from the larger-scale cultures surrounding them.

Colonizing peoples also used generic labels such as *Indian* or *Aborigine* in much the same way as the term *native*, to refer to original inhabitants. Indigenous peoples may themselves also use these terms, but in this case, a negative connotation is not implied.

Historically, anthropologists have used the terms *savage*, *primitive*, *uncivilized*, and *preliterate* to call attention to cultural differences. These terms have sometimes enjoyed a certain scientific respectability, but they have not successfully avoided the popular negative connotation of backwardness. Some writers used *primitive* in the sense of "primary" or "original" and emphasized positive cultural features,[1] but anthropologists have now abandoned the term.

Tribal is sometimes used synonymously with *indigenous* and is an acceptable self-designation in many areas of the world. In this chapter, *tribal* will refer to indigenous groups that maintain significant degrees of independence. However, the term is usually avoided in Africa because in nationalist political circles, tribal may be used pejoratively to imply backwardness and ethnic division. Many anthropologists also reject the term on historical grounds, because tribes, as political divisions, were created by colonial administrators. Furthermore, as was shown in earlier chapters, tribal cultures were not organized into discrete polities under centralized leadership. *Tribe* is also used to refer to a stage in cultural evolution, and missionaries often use the term to mean "ethnic group."

The problem of terminology also applies to labels given to specific cultural groups. Ethnic group names that find their way into the anthropological and popular literature may have originated as pejorative labels applied by neighbors who despised the group in question. For example, the term *Eskimo* is an outsider term applied to people who call themselves *Inuit*. Other names, like tribes, may be artificial creations of colonial governments.

Indigenous people self-identify as members of small-scale cultures and consider themselves to be the original inhabitants of the territories they occupy. In 2006, there were an estimated 350 million indigenous peoples scattered throughout the world,[2] often in remote areas containing valuable natural resources (see figure 13.1). They are aware of the advantages of their cultural heritage in comparison with life in the larger-scale systems surrounding them.

Because indigenous people claim a territorial base and a history of independence, they resemble politically organized states and sometimes call themselves nations. Geographer Bernard Nietschmann[3] adopted the term *nations* in place of *tribes* to refer to indigenous people, pointing out that nations have a common territory, language, and culture, in contrast to modern states that are often composed of diverse ethnic groups. Many newly independent states were created out of former colonies with little regard for the integrity of the indigenous peoples, which they incorporated and turned into internal colonies as their territories were thrown open for development.

Since the beginning of European colonial expansion, authorities on international law maintained that indigenous peoples held legitimate group rights to political sovereignty and territory that could be taken from them only by treaty or military conquest. Tribal groups were considered to be autonomous sovereign nations. Of course, tribal nations were often militarily weaker than the colonial powers that invaded their territories and were often easily defeated in war, but the important, internationally acknowledged legal point was that a formal written document had to define the relationship between the invading power and the tribal nation. Such a document would specify the details of land ownership and the degree of independence that the indigenous group might enjoy. This left room for the abuses of ethnocide, genocide, and ecocide that accompanied colonialism and sparked the great debate over humanitarian policy. At the same time, failure to sign treaties, as was the case in Australia, deferred the question of specific rights and provided a basis for modern negotiations. Former agreements may also be renegotiated in reference to the higher international standards of conduct toward indigenous peoples that have steadily evolved along with the emergence of the global system.

Ethnocide, Genocide, and Ecocide and the Humanitarian Response

During the first, preindustrial phase of capitalist expansion, which was under way by 1450, several European powers, such as Spain, Portugal, England, and France, gained political domination over large areas in North and South America, the Caribbean, and the islands of the eastern Atlantic. This was the beginning of a colonial process of conquest and incorporation that continued into the twentieth century.

Historian Alfred Crosby[4] notes that the Guanches, the original inhabitants of the Canary Islands in the Atlantic 200 miles (322 km) off the northwest coast of Africa, were perhaps the first tribal societies to be conquered by the advancing Europeans. The Guanches, who numbered some 80,000, appear to have been egalitarian village farmers with no metal tools. They resisted successive waves of French, Portuguese, and Spanish invaders from 1402 until the Spaniards gained full control of the islands in 1496.

The Guanches who survived the conquest were dispossessed, exiled, and enslaved. Their culture was destroyed, and by 1540, the Guanches had virtually disappeared as a people. The Spaniards stripped the forests and sold the timber and other resources of the Canaries. They replaced the native flora and fauna with European species and established sugarcane plantations based on slave labor. Deforestation initiated flooding and erosion and then caused the local climate to become arid. All of the negative impacts of colonial expansion—**ethnocide, genocide,** and **ecocide**—were under way in the Canaries when Christopher Columbus passed through in 1492 on his first crossing of the Atlantic.

In 1800, at the beginning of the Industrial Revolution, preindustrial states still existed in China, Japan, and Africa, and traditional kingdoms and chiefdoms in India, the Middle East, and the Pacific still retained considerable autonomy and in some cases were expanding. The great Western colonial powers had made claims over 55 percent of the world's land area but exercised effective control over only 33 percent of the world.[5] Approximately half the world was still controlled by relatively autonomous and largely self-sufficient tribal cultures, containing perhaps 200 million

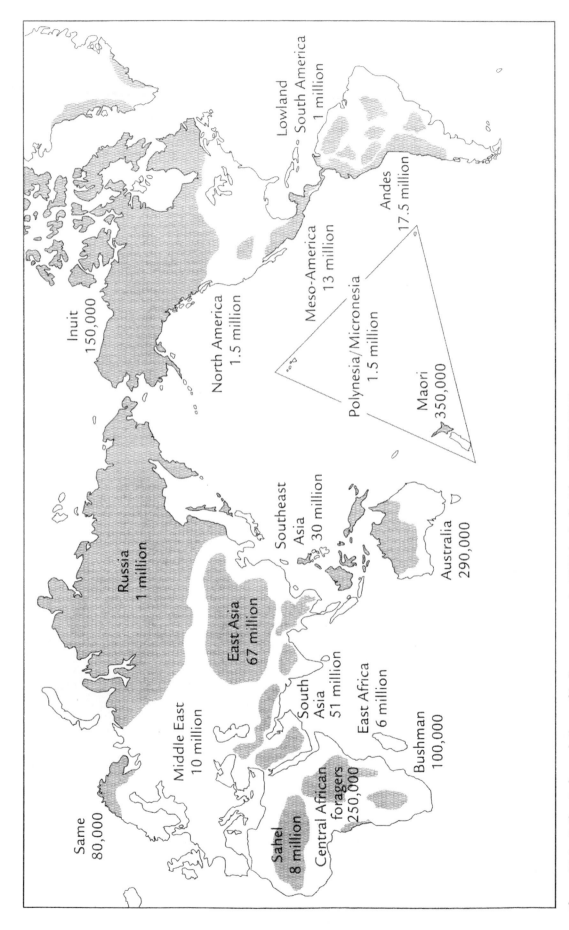

Figure 13.1. Estimated populations of indigenous people, 2001 (redrafted from IWGIA 2001).

people, roughly 20 percent of the global population (see figure 13.2). Over the next 150 years, virtually all tribal territory was conquered by colonizing industrial states, and perhaps 50 million tribal peoples died. This process created the modern world system, but at an enormous cost in the ethnocide, genocide, and ecocide suffered by the peoples and territories forcibly incorporated by the new global system.

Incorporation, in this context, means that natural resources and/or human labor begin to flow into the world system from formerly "external" areas. From the viewpoint of the peoples and cultures being incorporated, incorporation sets in motion a process of demographic disruption and destroys political and economic autonomy. Demographic disruption first appears as drastic depopulation when people are enslaved and killed by invaders and when they die from newly introduced diseases to which they have little immunity. Mortality is increased when culturally established support networks are interrupted and food systems disturbed. Epidemic diseases that make everyone sick at the same time can be devastating in a tribal society.

Much of the increased mortality occurred as a direct result of violence perpetrated against tribal peoples during their conquest by outsiders. In rare cases, governments followed a policy of deliberate genocide in an effort to totally exterminate a tribal population, and many government officials organized military campaigns against tribal groups. The largest tribal loss of life probably resulted from the actions of individual colonists who sought to profit from tribal territories before governments established formal political control. On the **uncontrolled frontier**, colonial governments, as a matter of policy, allowed their citizens to systematically kill and exploit tribal peoples[6] (see figure 13.3). Where tribal peoples were not needed as a source of labor, they were classified as "nonhuman" savages and were killed with impunity to remove them from the land.

Increased mortality is a special threat to the survival of tribal cultures that rely on fertility-limiting cultural practices to maintain their small, low-density, low-growth populations. Many of these groups simply disappeared when the frontier overtook them, and only their territories remained to be incorporated.

The loss of political autonomy by tribal peoples occurs when state governments gain enough power over a tribal territory to prevent tribal groups from acting in their own defense to expel outsiders. This can occur following military conquest, or it can be accomplished by formal treaty signing or some less formal process by which government control is extended over a formerly autonomous tribal area. In most cases, the relative difference in power between tribal cultures and states is so extreme that the state can impose control over a tribal territory virtually at will, although it can be a costly and time-consuming process.

State political control usually is symbolized by the appointment of political authorities and the introduction of a police force. State functions such as taxation, military recruitment, and census taking usually follow, along with the imposition of a legal system, courts, and jails. Administrative issues to be dealt with by colonial officials concerned specifying the differential rights of the native population and the colonizing population to land and other natural resources. Special regulations defined the conditions under which natives would be employed and how native culture could be expressed.

The loss of economic autonomy is fostered by political conquest because tribal groups must maintain control over their subsistence resources in order to remain self-sufficient. Drastic depopulation can reduce the economic viability of a tribal group, but competition with colonists over resources, especially when the tribal land base is reduced by government decree, is often the decisive factor. Any factors that undermined the traditional subsistence base would push tribal peoples toward participation in the market economy, whether as poorly paid wage laborers or **cash croppers**.

Tribal peoples also have a desire to secure some of the manufactured goods, such as metal tools and factory clothing, produced by the world system's industrial centers. However, the "pull" forces in themselves were insufficient to compel tribal peoples into large-scale participation in the market economy without a strong "push." Whenever their subsistence economy remained strong, tribal peoples were often poorly motivated target workers, and colonial administrators resorted to legal measures such as special taxes and planting laws to force reluctant tribal groups into the market economy. Once initiated, involvement in the market economy can become self-reinforcing because wage labor leaves little time for subsistence activities and cash cropping can degrade the local ecosystem and reduce its potential for subsistence production.

The cost of industrial expansion was minimized or ignored by the economists and politicians who championed growth with "differential benefits" for the colonized and the colonizers, but anthropologists

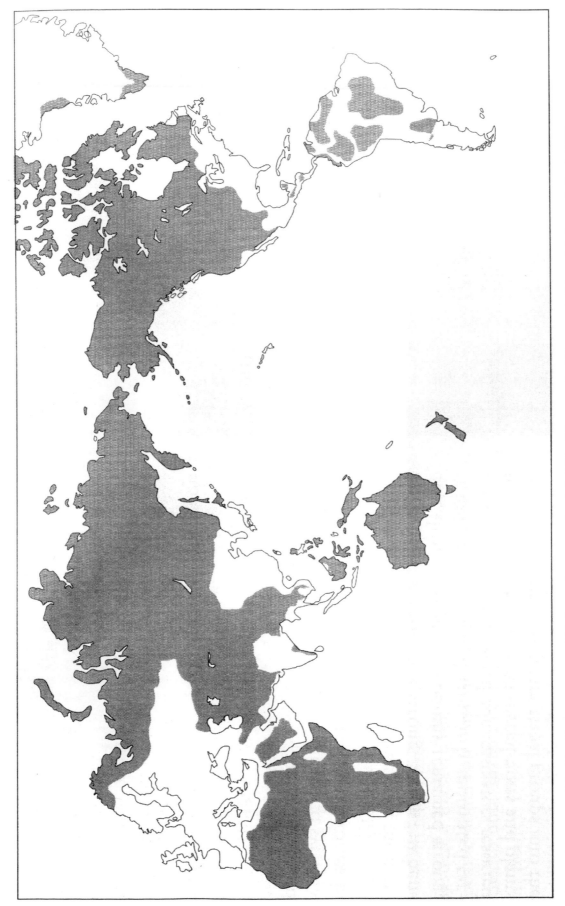

Figure 13.2. Areas inhabited by autonomous tribal peoples, approximately 200 million people (20 percent of the global population), 1800.

Figure 13.3. Contemporary engraving of an attack against Australian Aborigines. The uncontrolled frontier phase of capitalist expansion often involved direct physical violence against indigenous peoples (Karl Lumholtz. 1889. *Among Cannibals*. New York: Charles Scribners).

who conducted fieldwork on the colonial frontiers observed the devastation firsthand and often attempted to minimize it.

Throughout their expanding colonial empire, the British used military force against resisting indigenous peoples, but they consistently drew up formal treaties to legalize the transfer of political authority and tribal lands to Europeans. British policy in Australia was a striking exception because the presence of the Aborigines as mobile foragers was never legally acknowledged and no treaties were signed. Nineteenth-century British humanitarians lead by Thomas Fowell Buxton persuaded Parliament to ban slavery in the empire in 1833. They followed this success with the formation of a Select Committee to formulate official policies to protect the rights of tribal peoples and to ensure their just treatment.[7] In 1836 the humanitarians formed the Aborigines Protection Society (APS). They worked for the "advancement" of "uncivilized tribes" and sought to reduce the human suffering, but they did not oppose British imperialism in general. The APS was still active in 1919 after World War I, when the victors were dismembering Germany's colonies. The APS recognized that, ideally, this would be the time to grant full political sovereignty to existing tribal nations and grant self-determination to detribalized groups. However, the APS rejected tribal independence because it would have threatened the colonial system, even though it was obvious that "protection and uplift" policies had not prevented massive depopulation of tribal areas. These policy debates, which ultimately determined the fate of countless tribal groups, were permeated with paternalistic, racist, and demeaning language. Tribal peoples were variously referred to as backward races, subject races, and child races. Under the mandate system, established by the League of Nations Covenant in 1919 to administer former German colonies, tribal peoples were called "peoples not yet able to stand by themselves under the strenuous conditions of the modern world." They were to be administered according to the principle that "the well-being and development of such peoples form a sacred trust of civilization."[8]

In a short period of time in the 1920s and 1930s, applied anthropology became institutionalized in the British Empire, and like the earlier humanitarians, many anthropologists thought their work would help tribal peoples adapt to colonial conditions but did not question the legitimacy or the arrogance of colonialism (see figure 13.4). In 1921, A. R. Radcliffe-Brown was appointed to an anthropology professorship in South Africa, where he became a popular lecturer on the "native problem." Radcliffe-Brown stressed that understanding the "laws" of cultural development would give administrators "control over the social forces." More specifically, in 1923 he argued that knowing ". . . the functions of native institutions . . . can afford great help to the missionary or the public servant who is engaged in dealing with the practical problems of the adjustment of the native civilization to the new conditions that have resulted from our occupation of the country."[9]

Applied anthropologists did not expect to be too directly involved in policy making, for that was to be left to administrators. Aside from standard functionalist analysis, the major object of research for applied anthropologists was **acculturation**, or culture change;[10] both of these were ethically neutral concepts that masked the harsh political realities of imperialism.

Acculturation studies inventoried highly visible changes such as the adoption by tribal peoples of European clothing, crops, implements, language, and Christianity and the corresponding abandonment of traditional cultural features. The loss of political and economic autonomy was not usually examined as acculturation. In reality, firsthand contact meant conquest and dispossession of native peoples by colonial soldiers and settlers. Acculturation was forced culture change and was primarily an unequal process in which tribal peoples were subordinated and exploited. However, applied anthropologists in the service of the empire could hardly be expected to draw attention to the negative side of imperialism.

The real native problem that perplexed colonial administrators was how to keep the natives from resorting to armed resistance while settlers were depriving them of their lands and how to turn them into docile taxpayers and willing and effective laborers on their former lands. Culture change was supposed to be slow to avoid detribalization, which would make control more difficult and could lead to depopulation and labor shortages.

The primary recommendation from applied anthropologists was for administrators to use **indirect rule** to maintain political control. This meant using local native chiefs to serve as government agents and intermediaries and creating them when they did not already exist. **Direct rule** by European officers was culturally insensitive and prohibitively expensive.

Bronislaw Malinowski, a prominent British functionalist, was emphatic on the advantages of indirect,

Figure 13.4. Cecil Rhodes, prime minister of Britain's Cape Colony in southern Africa, astride the African continent. This 1892 political cartoon symbolizes the arrogance of European colonialism (*Punch, or the London Charivari* 1892 Vol. 103 December 10, p. 266).

or dependent, rule in a 1919 article: "In fact, if we define dependent rule as the control of Natives through the medium of their own organization, it is clear that only dependent rule can succeed. For the government of any race consists rather in implanting in them ideas of right, of law and order, and making them obey such ideas.[11]

The decolonization era, which began with the founding of the UN in 1945, was also the beginning of a gradual shift away from the paternalistic and ethnocentric bias of even the most humanitarian of colonial policies toward indigenous peoples. The UN and affiliated organizations such as the International Labour Organization provided an international framework within which the concept of human rights was steadily expanded to include indigenous peoples as cultural groups and to legitimize their struggle for self-determination. The extension of fundamental human rights to indigenous peoples has been a slow and difficult process requiring decisive participation by indigenous peoples themselves.

UN Declaration on the Rights of Indigenous Peoples

The position of indigenous people in the commercial world began to improve as soon as the international community elaborated on the concept of human rights, especially after World War II. From the perspective of indigenous peoples the early institutionalization of international development under the UN system represented a direct continuation of the old colonialism under new leadership. The UN Charter[12] provided an opening for indigenous rights, but it still contained ethnocentric thinking. Article 1 of the charter proclaimed support for "the principle of equal rights and self-determination of peoples," but it did not define peoples. Furthermore, the only provisions in the charter specifically applicable to indigenous peoples were in Chapters XI–XIII, describing the international trusteeship system. The Declaration Regarding Non-Self-Governing Territories in Article 73 ethnocentrically speaks of "territories whose peoples have not yet attained a full measure of self-government." This language was obviously ethnocentric when applied to Pacific Islanders with functioning chiefdoms, but it was equally patronizing to call small-scale cultures "non-self-governing" when they clearly managed their own internal affairs without formal government. Many "non-self-governing territories" were already under the League of Nations mandate system, and the framers of the UN Charter borrowed from the League of Nations Covenant when they referred to a "sacred trust" to promote "the well-being of the inhabitants of these territories." There are demeaning references to "stages of advancement" and "constructive measures of development," which were direct carryovers from the "protection and uplift" civilizing policies of the colonial era.

Fortunately, additional international covenants helped expand the concept of human rights, providing a framework on which indigenous political leaders could build. For example, Article 22 of the 1948 UN Universal Declaration of Human Rights[13] states that everyone is entitled to the realization of the "cultural rights indispensable for his dignity and the free development of his personality." This was amplified by Article 26 of the UN International Covenant on Civil and Political Rights,[14] adopted by the UN General Assembly in 1966: "In those states in which ethnic, religious or linguistic minorities exist, persons belonging to such minorities shall not be denied the right, in community with the other members of their group, to enjoy their own culture, to profess and practice their own religion or to use their own language." This is a significant statement because it refers specifically to the human rights of cultural groups as group rights, whereas most earlier international declarations have referred to individual human rights.

The first attempt to write an international convention devoted entirely to the relationship between indigenous peoples and governments was undertaken by the International Labour Organization (ILO) in 1946 in cooperation with the UN, UNESCO, Food and Agricultural Organization, and World Health Organization. Anthropologists were directly involved in this historic eleven-year effort, which culminated in 1957 when the General Conference of the ILO adopted "Convention (No. 107) concerning the protection and integration of indigenous and other tribal and semi-tribal populations in independent countries."[15]

ILO Convention 107 was a curiously ambiguous document that attempted to raise a new standard for the rights of indigenous peoples but fell short of its goal because it failed to incorporate the viewpoint of indigenous peoples themselves. Convention 107 made a strong statement in support of the human rights of tribal individuals while endorsing government programs that directly undermined tribal cultures. The key contradiction is found in Article 7, which stated, "These populations shall be allowed to retain their own customs and institutions where these are not incompatible with the national legal system or the objectives of integration programmes."

Indigenous peoples were excluded from the discussions that led to Convention 107, and the anthropologists who served on the "panel of experts" accepted the prevailing ethnocentric belief of policy makers that tribals would inevitably be assimilated, or integrated into national societies, and that this would ultimately be beneficial for them. Successfully integrated tribal groups would "identify themselves with the values of technologically advanced societies." This positive outcome mirrored the "benefits of civilization" approach advocated by the nineteenth-century humanitarians and was equally prone to failure, because it did not take into account the views of the people themselves.

Like the anthropologists who identified the obstacles to economic progress in peasant cultures, the ILO experts recognized that successfully adapted indigenous groups might resist imposed **integration**. The committee found that "isolated" tribal peoples were healthy and self-sufficient, yet this was called "an undesirable state of segregation" because it perpetuated tribal culture, thereby blocking successful integration.[16] Committee chair Ernest Beaglehole was explicit on his authority as an anthropologist in implementing culture change programs on behalf of other people: "The anthropologist, through his detailed knowledge of indigenous life, can note the areas of resistance, blockage and susceptibility to change, so that local patterns will be circumvented or utilised in order to reduce friction and resistance."[17]

Because force was not supposed to be employed in helping tribal groups realize their "inexorable destiny," the central problem for planners was "how to produce a shift from the satisfactions that indigenous forest dwellers find in their own societies to the satisfactions normally found in modern society."[18] Today this sounds shockingly arrogant and blatantly ethnocentric, but in the 1950s applied anthropology and international development had barely emerged from the colonial era.

The whole relationship between tribal peoples, governments, and international organizations began to change in the 1960s and 1970s, when tribals, now as indigenous peoples, began to form political organizations throughout the world to press their demands for full control over their traditional lands and communities. Indigenous organizations emerged at local, national, and international levels. Indigenous organizations were and are supported by various religious, environmentalist, humanitarian, and human rights groups in many countries. International organizations such as Cultural Survival, IWGIA (the International Work Group for Indigenous Affairs), and Survival International, which are directed by anthropologists, have played important support roles for indigenous organizations by raising funds and by helping them establish national and international contacts where their views can be expressed.

In the 1980s the ILO set out to revise the now outmoded ILO 107. This time international nongovernmental organizations and indigenous representatives were allowed observer status. Experts suggested that the new convention should grant indigenous peoples the right to "participation and consultation" in development projects carried out on their territories, but they still wanted to call indigenous peoples "populations," rather than "peoples," because being people implied a cultural and territorial identity. They wanted to avoid the possibility that tribal "peoples" might demand self-determination as a human right. When the final deliberations appeared to be supporting the old integrationist approach, the Australian aboriginal delegation withdrew in protest. Delivering an impassioned speech, aboriginal representative Geoff Clarke declared:

We define our rights in terms of self-determination. We are not looking to dismember your States and

you know it. But we do insist on the right to control our territories, our resources, the organisation of our societies, our own decision-making institutions, and the maintenance of our own cultures and ways of life. . . . Do you think that we are unaware of the actual meaning of words like consultation, participation and collaboration? Would you be satisfied with "consultation" as a guarantee for your rights? Unless governments are obligated to obtain our consent, we remain vulnerable to legislative and executive whims that inevitably will result in further dispossession and social disintegration of our peoples. The victims are always the first to know how the system operates.[19]

A final revision of ILO 107 was approved by the ILO in 1989 as Convention 169. The new convention did eliminate most of the ethnocentric language, but the contradictory emphasis on integration remained. The term *people* was introduced but was avowed to have no legal significance. Over the objections of indigenous leaders, governments retained responsibility for development and policy making over indigenous territories, with indigenous peoples relegated to "participation" and "cooperation." There were references to respect for indigenous culture and recognition of land rights, but the qualifications and escape clauses were so numerous that in many respects, less real protection was provided than in the original covenant. Not surprisingly, the new convention was widely rejected by indigenous peoples.[20]

Decades of persistent political struggle were required before international recognition of the rights of tribal peoples could be fully accomplished. Indigenous political organizations presented their viewpoints on indigenous rights before a variety of UN human rights forums, beginning in 1977 when more than fifty indigenous leaders were invited to attend the International Conference on Discrimination against Indigenous Populations in the Americas, organized in Geneva by the special UN Committee on Human Rights. Similar conferences followed, and in 1982 a special Working Group on Indigenous Peoples (WGIP) was established by the UN Subcommission on the Prevention of Discrimination and Protection of Minorities, of the UN Economic and Social Council Commission on Human Rights. The WGIP was directed to draft a Universal Declaration of Indigenous Rights for final adoption by the UN General Assembly in 1992. In this case, many indigenous groups were directly involved in the proceedings and in the drafting of the declaration. Indigenous peoples wanted international endorsements of their rights to self-determination, as well as a clear condemnation of genocide, ethnocide, and ecocide. The UN Human Rights Commission finally approved a draft of the Universal Declaration in 1994, with the expectation that it would be adopted by the UN General Assembly during the International Decade of the World's Indigenous Peoples 1995–2004. The UN established a special organization within the UN Economic and Social Council, the Permanent Forum on Indigenous Issues in 2000, but the Declaration on the Rights of Indigenous Peoples was not finally adopted by the UN General Assembly until 2007, when 144 nations voted for adoption, eleven abstained, and four nations—Australia, Canada, New Zealand, and the United States—voted against.

The final resolution included forty-six articles and is extremely comprehensive.[21] The first twelve articles enumerate specific rights in broad terms, whereas later articles elaborate in greater detail. The preamble affirmed that all peoples have the right to be different and recognized that indigenous peoples had "suffered from historic injustices" caused by "their colonization and dispossession of their lands, territories, and resources," which prevented them from developing autonomously. The enumerated rights "are equally guaranteed to male and female" (Article 44). Among the specific rights listed are the following. Article 3 specifically endorsed the rights of indigenous peoples to self-determination, and "to freely determine their political status and freely pursue their economic, social, and cultural development." This means the right to run their own local affairs, as well as to participate in the political, economic, social, and cultural life of the state, including citizenship (Articles 4, 5, and 6). They have the right to be free of genocide, forced assimilation (ethnocide), forced removal from their territories (Article 10), or forced removal of children from their families (Article 7). They are free to maintain their integrity as distinct peoples with their own lands and resources (Article 8) and have the right to belong to "an indigenous community or nation" (Article 9). The declaration also includes the right to revitalize, own, and practice their religious, ceremonial, and cultural knowledge and traditions; the right to the repatriation of human remains, such as skeletons in museum collections; the return of cultural properties, such as ceremonial objects (Articles 11, 12, 13); and to control their own educational institutions (Article 14).

In response to the problem of ecocide several articles strengthen indigenous ownership and control over the environment and natural resources within indigenous territories. Another crucial right was to control cultural and intellectual property, including genetic resources (Article 31). This is especially important in a commercial world where giant agricultural and pharmaceutical companies patent genetic material and restrict their availability to generate revenue. Indigenous peoples collectively own their cultivated plant varieties but do not typically turn ownership into a commercial advantage.[22]

The rights recognized in this declaration represent a significant departure from the ethnocentric uplift and limited protectionism of the colonial era. They also represent a clear repudiation of the forced-integration policies that were called "inevitable" by many authorities during the modern era of economic development. These new indigenous rights, if they are fully and effectively implemented by the international community, will provide a firm basis for the coexistence of indigenous peoples within the global system. However, as the draft declaration declares in Article 43, "The rights recognized herein constitute the minimum standards for the survival, dignity and the well-being of the indigenous peoples of the world."

The following case studies from the Peruvian Amazon and Australia show how the situation of indigenous peoples can be dramatically improved when they are empowered to exercise their basic human rights as peoples.

AMAZONIA: RESILIENT TRIBES

Historically, the European invasion of Amazonia nearly annihilated the indigenous populations. In 1500, when Amazonia was first claimed by Europeans, there may have been as many as 6.8 million native residents,[23] but by 1970 the population had declined by nearly 90 percent to less than 1 million. ILO expert committee member and anthropologist Darcy Ribeiro[24] reported that in Brazil more than one-third of the indigenous groups known to exist in 1900 were extinct by 1957, the year Convention 107 was adopted. In 1968, the year I began my dissertation research with the Asháninka, the Brazilian government revealed that officials of its Indian Protection Service had conspired with wealthy landowners to remove indigenous people from their lands using machine guns, dynamite, poison, and disease. Thousands must have died in an extermination process that rivaled the worst abuses of the early colonial period. Native dispossession and deaths were accelerated when construction of the trans-Amazon highway system began in 1970, followed by large-scale colonization, agricultural development, mining, and hydroelectric projects.[25]

Indigenous peoples in the Ecuadoran and Peruvian Amazon were unable to prevent multinational oil corporations from prospecting and development within their territories. This has caused such destructive pollution to the fragile rain forest ecosystem that Ecuadoran indigenous groups brought suit against Chevron Texaco in 2003 claiming up to $1 billion in damages. As of early 2010 this lawsuit was still under litigation.

The Asháninka versus Global Development: Local to Global Struggle

The Asháninka of eastern Peru, who were introduced in the first two chapters, provide a useful case study of how many tribal Amazonian peoples have gained control over their territories and cultures by means of political mobilization, and in spite of seemingly overwhelming global forces. In the 1960s, some 21,000 Asháninka, who at that time were called Campa by outsiders, were still the principal occupants of their vast homeland in the forested eastern foothills of the Andes in central Peru. They were highly self-sufficient and only minimally involved with the market economy. Their first contacts with Europeans occurred in the 1500s, and over the next two centuries, Franciscan missionaries gradually established outposts throughout the region and imposed their own culture change program. However, the Asháninka resented Franciscan disapproval of polygyny and other restrictions on their freedom. They destroyed the missions in 1742 and enjoyed complete independence for more than 100 years, demonstrating that the integration process was in fact reversible, not inevitable.

The situation began to change in the 1870s when the Republic of Peru turned to Amazonia as a frontier of national expansion. Asháninka territory was critical to government planning because it controlled the river pathways to the Amazon, but explorers and missionaries entering the area were frequently met with a rain of Asháninka arrows. Military force and gift giving eventually overcame most Asháninka resistance and cleared the way for colonists. A regional economic boom began after the Pichis Trail was successfully opened in 1891 as a mule road through the Asháninka homeland to a navigable point on the Pichis River, and a huge tract of Asháninka land was deeded to an English company for a coffee plantation. This development activity caused many Asháninka to experience all the negative aspects of the uncontrolled frontier and led to further hostilities. In 1913–1914, frustrated Asháninka warriors armed themselves with guns and attacked missions and outposts in the Pichis Valley, killing 150 settlers before they in turn were scattered by troops.

After these events, the government took little interest in the region until the 1960s. Small groups of fully independent Asháninka dominated the remote areas, while the more accessible riverine zones were only lightly settled by outsiders who established missions, small cattle ranches, and farms, following successive economic waves of rubber and lumber extraction. The Asháninka still maintained a viable culture after more than 400 years of colonial intrusion. But their future was increasingly threatened by a shift in government policy that began in 1960 with the *Plan Peruvia*, a development program that selected some 45,000 square miles (116,550 km^2) in Amazonia, including most of the Asháninka area, for long-term economic development. A special unit, the Office for the Evaluation of Natural Resources (ONERN) was established with United States Agency for International Development (USAID) funds to evaluate the natural resources in the zone and to formulate a detailed development proposal without regard for the indigenous inhabitants. Military engineer units, supported by U.S. military assistance programs, began constructing a network of "penetration" highways that would provide the primary infrastructure for the project.

In 1965, Peruvian president Fernando Belaunde-Terry[26] announced a definitive economic "conquest" of Amazonia. Ignoring the native population, he characterized the region as underpopulated and underexploited and promised that developing Amazonia would solve the overpopulation, poverty, food shortages, and land scarcity of the Andean and coastal zones. Indeed, Peru's population had tripled since 1900 and exceeded 10 million by 1965. However, the real issue was inequality, not population growth, because the Inca empire had supported an even larger population without invading Amazonia. The government's development program was simply an accelerated eastward extension of the national market economy, which had already generated Andean poverty and was now impoverishing native Amazonians. The new, multi-million-dollar program was eventually cofinanced by USAID, the UN Development Programme, the World Bank, and the Inter-American Development Bank. The project contributed to a vast increase in Peru's external public debt, from $856 million in 1970 to $12.4 billion by 1988. This debt arrangement helped make Peru a poor client state and made the fate of the Amazonians and their forest ecosystem ultimately linked to management decisions made at the global level.

My own investigations[27] in the region between 1965 and 1969 suggested that when Belaunde-Terry's project began, some 2,500 Asháninka in this central area still remained fully self-sufficient, whereas many others were drawn into exploitive **debt bondage** with patrons who offered cheap merchandise in exchange for labor (see figures 13.5 and 13.6). Many Asháninka had already joined Protestant mission communities and were establishing a marginal and precarious niche in the expanding regional market economy. These new mission communities did not control an adequate land base and were quickly depleting local subsistence resources, increasing their dependence on purchased goods. This placed the Asháninka at an enormous disadvantage in economic competition with the wealthier and more sophisticated colonists who were invading their lands.

At first the Asháninka were largely ignored by development planners. For example, air-photo maps posted in planning offices had "empty wasteland" printed over plainly visible Asháninka garden plots. In the Tambo-Pajonal planning unit, a 5,500-square-mile (14,245-km²) roadless area occupied by 4,000 Asháninka, plans called for 560 miles (901 km) of roads and the introduction of 145,000 settlers.[28] There were legal provisions for granting limited land titles to the Asháninka in accord with the general principles of Convention 107 but no provision for those who preferred not to be integrated into the national economy on terms dictated by others. Because these events coincided with the widely publicized Brazilian massacres, many anthropologists began making public statements on indigenous rights. The 39th Americanist Congress, assembled in Lima, Peru, in 1970, issued "recommendations" condemning ethnocide and calling threatened Amazonian communities "oppressed peoples" in need of "national liberation." In 1971, Stefano Varese, a Peruvian anthropologist who had also worked with the Asháninka, joined with Darcy Ribeiro and nine other anthropologists to draft the Declaration of Barbados.[29] They stated that native lands were being treated as **internal colonies**, and they called on governments, the missions, anthropologists, and especially the indigenous peoples themselves to work for their liberation. Varese,[30] optimistic that Peru's new approach to agrarian reform would reduce the exploitation and dependency of forest peoples, proposed that special government teams encourage native groups to mobilize politically in their own defense.

Figure 13.5.   A newly recruited Asháninka labor crew destined to work for a patron, being interviewed by the author in 1969.

Figure 13.6. Asháninka shaman processing sheets of raw rubber for sale at a mission station in the Peruvian Amazon. Missionaries sometimes displaced exploitive patrons by offering isolated indigenous groups access to markets.

Political mobilization was the key to cultural survival, and it was carried out by the people themselves.

The Cultural Autonomy Alternative

In 1972 I also ventured into advocacy anthropology by publicly proposing that the government demarcate the entire interfluvial upland zone between the Pachitea and Ucayli Rivers and along the Ene, Perene, and Tambo Rivers as inviolable "Asháninka Land" (see figure 13.7). Development by outsiders would have been permanently prohibited in this vast 29,000-square-mile (75,110-km^2) territory, which encompassed much of the traditional Asháninka homeland.[31] This was a realistic proposal given the ONERN studies showing that most of this area was considered unsuitable for commercial agriculture, contained no important mineral resources, and was best maintained as a protected watershed. In lowland areas where integration was already under way, I recommended that very large reserves be established on the best agricultural soils to give market-oriented Asháninka a competitive advantage. Later I called this approach the **cultural autonomy** alternative because it would allow tribal cultures the opportunity to maintain their independence. It specified three key points:

1. National governments and international organizations must recognize and support tribal rights to their traditional land, cultural autonomy, and full local sovereignty.

2. The responsibility for initiating outside contacts must rest with the tribal people themselves: outside influences may not have free access to tribal areas.
3. Industrial states must not compete with tribal societies for their resources.[32]

More than 30 years later, the principle of cultural autonomy was at last fully incorporated in the 2007 UN Declaration of Indigenous Rights and is especially represented in articles 5 and 6.

Article 5: "Indigenous peoples, in exercising their right to self-determination, have the right to autonomy or self-government in matters relating to their internal and local affairs. . . ." Article 6: "Indigenous peoples have the right to own, use, develop and control the lands, territories and resources that they possess by reason of traditional ownership or other traditional

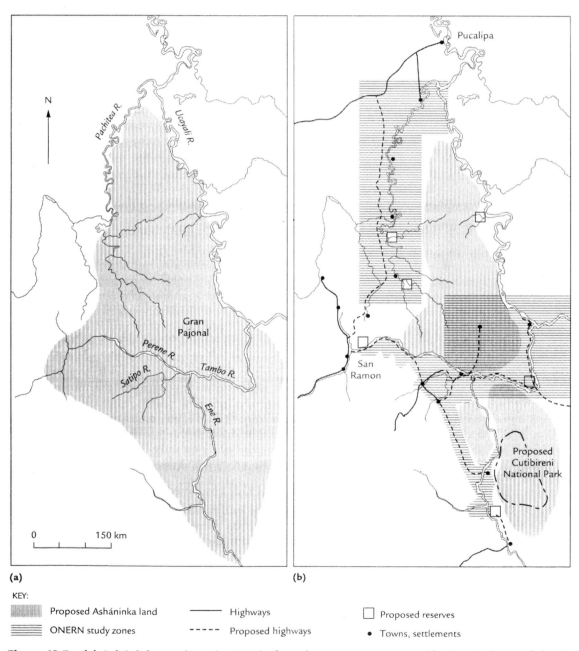

KEY:

▨ Proposed Asháninka land	—— Highways	☐ Proposed reserves
☰ ONERN study zones	- - - - Proposed highways	• Towns, settlements

Figure 13.7. **(a) Asháninka territory in 1850 before the most recent wave if colonization and development by outsiders; (b) the Asháninka cultural autonomy alternative proposed by Bodley in 1972, shown in relation to new colonization and economic development zones.**

occupation or use . . . States shall give legal recognition and protection to these lands, territories and resources. Such recognition shall be conducted with due respect to the customs, traditions and land tenure systems of the indigenous peoples concerned."[33]

Some limited aspects of cultural autonomy were coincidentally incorporated in the Manu National Park, a 5,800-square-mile (15,022-km²) environmental sanctuary established in the southern Peruvian Amazon in 1973. Park officials allowed independent tribal groups already living within the park, such as the Matsigenka, to remain undisturbed as long as they did not exploit park resources for commercial purposes.[34] Formation of the Manu Park was the first of many important alliances between indigenous peoples and national and international environmental conservationists. Both groups want to protect the rain forest, but what eventually brought real change was the political mobilization of the indigenous peoples themselves.

The institutional momentum for large-scale development was still too strong in 1972 for the government to grant the cultural autonomy that I advocated for the Asháninka. However, the situation was already beginning to change after President Belaunde was overthrown by a military coup in 1968 and the new government instituted reforms that opened the way for greater recognition to indigenous peoples. The Yanesha, or Amuesha as they were known to outsiders, close linguistic relatives of the Asháninka, immediately organized a Congress of Amuesha Communites.[35] In 1974 the Peruvian government passed a new law, the Law of Native Communities, that allowed indigenous groups to organize and claim legal titles to their community lands. This was a crucial opportunity for indigenous peoples to gain formal control over their resources and to construct cultural autonomy on their own terms. Cultural autonomy unfolded gradually in the central Peruvian Amazon with indigenous peoples working together with government and intergovernment agencies and forming alliances with nongovernmental organizations, such as IWGIA.

The construction of federated, or interethnic, organizations was a powerful step in the political mobilization of indigenous peoples in the Peruvian Amazon. In the northern Peruvian Amazon the Jibaroan-speaking peoples convened a general assembly in 1977 and formed the Aguaruna and Huambisa Council (CAH). Miqueas Mishari, an Asháninka leader, founded the Center for Native Communities of the Peruvian Central Forest (CECONSEC) in 1978.[36] In 1980 CECON-SEC and CAH combined to form the Inter-Ethnic Association for the Development of the Peruvian Rainforest (AIDESEP),[37] together with the Federation of Native Communities of the Ucayali, the Amuesha Congress, and other groups from across the Peruvian Amazon. Significantly, AIDESEP brought together indigenous groups from different language families with different cultures, many of whom had been enemies, but they all shared the urgent need for self-defense. AIDESEP leaders adopted the term *development*, but it was clear that development would be on their own terms. They refused to allow their territories to be treated as empty spaces open to invasions by rubber gatherers, miners, merchants, wood cutters, and oil companies, and they did not want paternalistic outside institutions and organizations to integrate them into the national society only at the service of commerce. The first president of AIDESEP, Evaristo Nugkuag, an Aguaruna, explained, ". . . we, the indigenous peoples, decided to fight for a solution to these problems with our own resources, maintaining ecological equilibrium, as is traditional, and developing the knowledge of our ancestors to survive and grow."

AIDESEP is a crucial organization because it links local communities with the international level. By 2008 AIDESEP represented 350,000 indigenous peoples living in 1,350 communities from sixteen language families. There were 57 ethnic federations grouped into six regional organizations. AIDESEP is itself a member of the Coordinating Body for the Indigenous Organizations of the Amazon Basin, which is a network of representative indigenous organizations from all Amazonian countries, and is itself a member of the International Alliance of Indigenous and Tribal Peoples of Tropical Forests, which is recognized by UN agencies. This means that the most isolated indigenous groups can press human rights claims through UN agencies.

The speed and magnitude of change is remarkable, as illustrated by the experience of Chonkiri's group, which I met in the Gran Pajonal in 1969 as described in chapter 1. By 1985 these formerly very isolated peoples had become the officially registered Native Community of Shumahuani with 358 people holding legal title to nearly 50 square kilometers of territory. The community became a member of the Gran Pajonal Ashéninka Organization, which belonged to the Regional Organization of the Indigenous Peoples of AIDESEP-Ucayali. This network of organization gave them a global-level voice that would have been unimaginable only a few decades earlier (see figure 13.8).

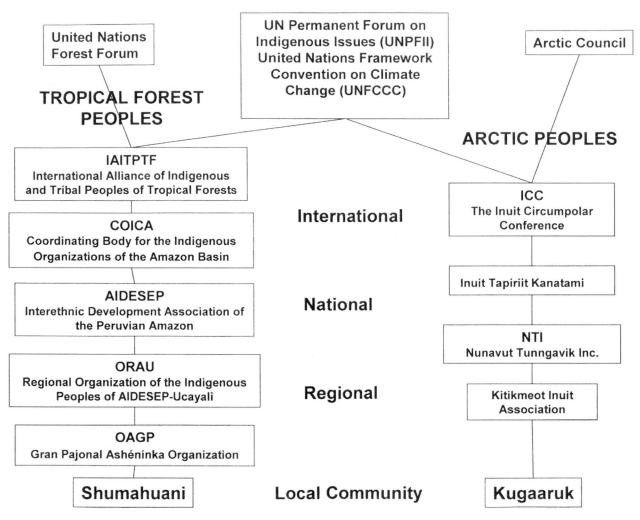

Figure 13.8. Local to global hierarchy of indigenous political organizations.

This organization hierarchy parallels those formed by other indigenous groups, such as the Inuit peoples in the Arctic as also shown in figure 13.8.

Since 1980 the indigenous peoples of the Peruvian Amazon have been engaged in almost continuous political struggle to defend their lands and communities. In 1980, even as AIDESEP was formed, the government actually began to implement a massive development project to bring 150,000 agricultural colonists into the Pichis-Palcazu Valleys, traditionally an indigenous heartland for Arawak-speaking peoples, and create a city of 20,000 people. No territory was deeded to the 12,000 resident Asháninka and Yanesha for them to control as cultural groups, and less than half the fifty-one scattered indigenous communities were given discrete village titles. This left the original inhabitants either landless or with fragmented blocks of land that were inadequate for traditional subsis-

tence activities or long-term commercial agriculture.[38] Protests by a coalition of native organizations, religious and human rights groups, and anthropologists brought only token reforms represented by village land titles, community development advisors, and agricultural credits that fostered debt,[39] but much more dramatic changes soon unfolded.

The Pichis-Palcazu project no doubt helped catalyze indigenous opposition and led to counterproposals. Anthropologist Richard Chase Smith[40] proposed a development plan that would have allowed significant autonomy for the Yanesha (Amuesha), western neighbors of the Asháninka, while protecting their vulnerable rain forest environment. Smith recommended creation of a 1,200-square-mile (3,108-km²) zone, divided into three blocks to include contiguous communal reserves, deeded to specific Yanesha communities to protect natural resources for their exclusive use;

tribal territory for all Yanesha as a cultural group; and a national park as an environmental preserve. Smith's plan was initially approved by the Peruvian Ministry of Agriculture but was tabled by 1980 in favor of the World Bank–funded program. Later the government and the international lenders took a very similar pro–cultural autonomy, pro–environmental conservation approach in partnership with indigenous peoples and nongovernmental organizations.

Initially, the World Bank, which provided $46 million for the Pichis Valley Project and cosponsored many similar projects that deprived indigenous groups of their resources and autonomy, responded to critics by issuing a position paper arguing that with "interim safeguards" it was possible to promote large development projects and still defend tribal people.[41] The bank's report advocated support for a limited form of "cultural autonomy…until the tribe adapts sufficiently," suggesting that they were not yet ready to consider cultural autonomy as a permanent policy. Anthropologists Sally Swenson and Jeremy Narby, who investigated conditions in the Pichis Valley in the mid-1980s, observed that development policies at international, national, and regional levels needed to be changed if indigenous groups like the Asháninka were to benefit from development. They urged that indigenous political organizations be allowed to participate directly in planning affecting them and declared, "A more appropriate approach would discourage colonization and place priority on the participation in development by current inhabitants; recognize native rights to, and title land sufficient for, subsistence and commercial production; and recognize the rationality of current native land use, incorporating native knowledge of the rainforest environment into development."[42]

Political violence compounded problems for the Asháninka, but their ability to mobilize under their own leaders helped them maintain control and assert an entirely new level of autonomy relative to Peruvian national society. In 1984 the Shining Path Maoist guerrillas attacked Asháninka in the Ene region and began invading the Gran Pajonal.[43] In 1989 the Tupac Amaru Revolutionary Movement Marxist-Leninist guerrillas abducted and presumably killed the leader of the Pichis Valley Asháninka. Even as these events occurred, the Asháninka in the Upper Ucayali were gaining strength. In 1987 they formed the Indigenous Organization of the Atalaya Region (OIRA), bringing together more than a hundred Asháninka communities affiliated with AIDESEP. In 1988, the Atalaya Asháninka denounced the debt-bondage patron system before a special multiagency government commission. Next, with the help of IWGIA and funds from the Danish government development agency DANIDA, they secured legal titles for 113 Asháninka communities in the region.[44] They demarcated their own territories to reflect their subsistence requirements, creating contiguous territories to block out patrons and other colonists. By 1994 coalitions of Asháninka from the Pichis, Pajonal, and Ucayali had regained control of the entire region. Many of the colonists had withdrawn after being compensated for their holdings. The Asháninka were proudly reasserting their culture. An Asháninka man, dressed in *cushma* and face paint, told IWGIA's Andrew Gray how he felt about their new autonomy: "We have no problems with colonists. There are no patrons or 'colonos.' Just Asháninka. We wanted titles for our lands and to work in the fields, harvest *yuca* [manioc], sow rice, pineapple. That is why we need land. In the future I want to live quietly. We in our community want to live in peace, drinking our *masato* [manioc beer]. We hunt animals throughout our land. We have a school now too. We think that our organization OIRA helps us and we are very pleased.[45]

When the system of indigenous organizations was firmly established, it became possible for these new organizations to form working relationships with government agencies and supportive nongovernmental organizations. At this time the Peruvian government moved to formally institutionalize sustainable development and invited participation by environmental nongovernmental organizations. The 1993 Peruvian Constitution declares in Article 68 that "the State is obligated to promote the conservation of biological diversity and of natural protected areas." Article 69 specifies that the State will promote sustainable development of Amazonia with adequate legislation. This was implemented in 1997 by the establishment of the National System for Natural Protected Areas under the direction of the National Institute of Natural Resources.

In 1996 with the passage of the Law of Protected Natural Areas (Ley de Areas Naturales Protegidas, Ley No. 26834) it became possible for the government to establish specific protected natural areas whose natural condition would be "maintained in perpetuity" to conserve biological diversity as well as associated cultural values as part of the national patrimony. As of 2006 nine different categories of Protected Areas were recognized, including National Parks, Communal Reserves, and Reserved Zones that especially affected indigenous peoples in the Amazon. Protected Areas could also be surrounded by designated buffer zones to guarantee the conservation of the Protected Area itself. Communal Reserves are designed to conserve natural resources for the benefit of neighboring rural populations. Any commercial development of the resources must be according to management plans carried out by the beneficiaries themselves.

Much of the vast region that I had proposed in 1972 be designated "Asháninka Land" was eventually incorporated into Peru's system of Protected Natural Areas. The El Sira Communal Reserve was established in 2001 to protect the Sira Range between the Ucayali and Pichis-Pachitea Rivers for the benefit of all the indigenous people living in the region (see figure 13.9). Comprising more than 6,000 square kilometers, the El Sira Reserve is the largest of four reserves established for the Arawak-speaking Asháninka, Asheninka (the self-identity of the Gran Pajonal Asháninka, who speak a distinct language), Yanesha, and Matsigenka peoples by 2004. The Asháninka and Matsigenka Communal Reserves immediately south of the El Sira were situated on either side of the Otishi National Park, which protected the Vilcabamba range. Altogether, these reserves, the park, and the San Carlos Protected Forest comprise more than 15,000 square kilometers.

Creating this system was an enormous effort involving many organizations and funding from many sources. IWGIA carried out some of the original planning for El Sira beginning in the early 1990s. The World Bank and the UN Global Environmental Facility with 10 percent matching funds from the Peruvian government contributed some $2 million to fund the El Sira project over five years. The communal reserves are to be managed according to master plans developed by the indigenous peoples themselves with technical support from nonprofit, nongovernmental organizations including the Instituto de Bien Común[46] and the Center for Development of the Indigenous Amazon.[47] These nongovernmental organizations have also supported the land titling projects for many years. The master plans will detail how specific areas can be used sustainably to benefit local people. Some 14,750 indigenous people were living within the El Sira buffer zone, and some 25,000 to 30,000 people in 400 communities were living in the region.[48] These protected areas adjoined and sometimes overlapped with titled community lands, and in combination create a truly remarkable system for protecting peoples, their societies and cultures, and the natural ecosystems that sustain them.

In 1995 the Asháninka community of Marankiari Bajo on the Perene River incorporated itself as CIAMB, Comunidad Indigena Asháninka Marankiari Bajo (Indigenous Asháninka Community). The community counted 1,027 inhabitants and 246 families in 1997 and began maintaining a website in 1999. CIAMB proudly proclaimed itself to be an "autonomous and independent communal organization." The Marankiari community received a three-year grant from the Inter-American Foundation in 2002 of $180,670 to expand agro-ecological production and marketing through agricultural and forest-based crop diversification, irrigation, and improved harvest and post-harvest practices and to increase the community's capacity for locally controlled economic development through title to land, the creation of household and community enterprises, and training in strategic planning and management (PU-510). CIAMB also received a three-year grant from the Inter-American Foundation (PU-553) for $228,450 in 2009 "to expand its program in agriculture and business development by offering training and technical assistance to eight neighboring Asháninka communities."[49] A supplemental grant of $86,200 in 2006 (PU-510-A4) helped CIAMB "continue training and technical assistance in organic agriculture for 120 indigenous farm families and will assist eight indigenous communities in promoting their heritage through ecotourism activities."

In 2009 indigenous groups in the northern Peruvian Amazon blocked roads and occupied oil terminals in protest over new laws that would open indigenous lands to developers in spite of their opposition. The government sent in police forces to forcibly put down the protests. The police used gunfire and tear gas, and more than a hundred people were killed or injured, including twenty-three police officers. The Asháninka blocked a major highway in the central region to show their support, and the president of AIDESEP was forced to seek political asylum in Nicaragua.

Peoples in Voluntary Isolation

One of my original intentions when I began my fieldwork in the Peruvian Amazon was to visit tribal peoples who were living fully independently with no direct permanent contact with the commercial world. In a few cases I sent my Asháninka assistants to check on the status of isolated groups, in order not to disturb them by my presence. These people were actively avoiding any face-to-face contact with nonindigenous outsiders because of their justifiable fears for their

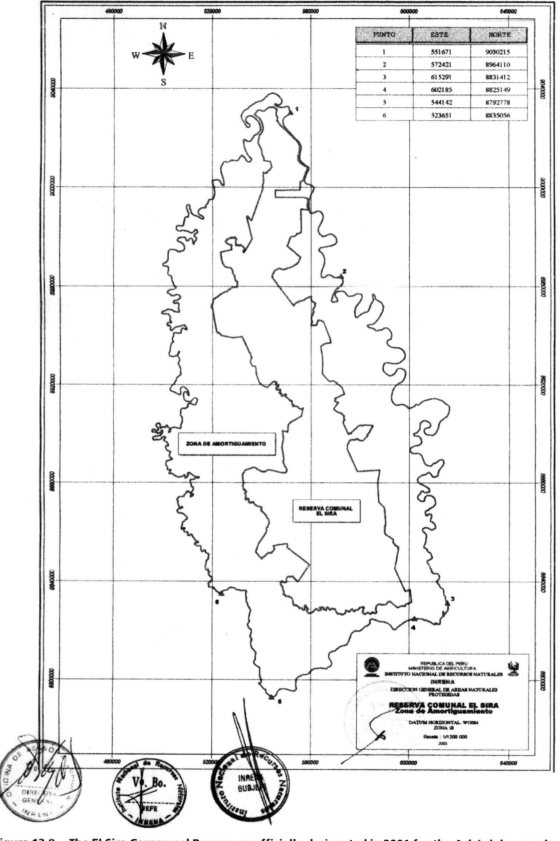

PUNTO	ESTE	NORTE
1	551671	9030215
2	572421	8964110
3	615291	8831412
4	602185	8825149
5	544142	8792778
6	523651	8835056

ZONA DE AMORTIGUAMIENTO

RESERVA COMUNAL
EL SIRA

REPUBLICA DEL PERU
MINISTERIO DE AGRICULTURA
INSTITUTO NACIONAL DE RECURSOS NATURALES
INRENA
DIRECCION GENERAL DE AREAS NATURALES
PROTEGIDAS

RESERVA COMUNAL EL SIRA
Zona de Amortiguamiento

DATUM HORIZONTAL: WGS84
ZONA 18

Escala : 1/1 200 000
2001

Figure 13.9. The El Sira Communal Reserve as officially designated in 2001 for the Asháninka people. The central area is the reserve proper, the surrounding area is the buffer zone (Resolución Jefatural No. 304-2001-INRENA).

lives and the continued existence of their societies and cultures. They knew that direct contact with outsiders caused fatal illnesses, and they knew that outsiders were often violent invaders.

Until very recently most anthropologists believed that it was neither "realistic" nor possible for tribal peoples to maintain their independent existence because there would be no way to prevent outsiders from invading their territories. The **realist** perspective was that autonomous tribals and their cultures were inevitably doomed to disappear. Furthermore, many believed that tribals would freely abandon their independent way of life in exchange for the "benefits of civilization." Anthropologists Robert Murphy and Julian Steward even suggested that it was a very predictable "acculturative factor" that tribals would almost inevitably be integrated into global society by their desire for industrially manufactured goods.[50] In contrast those advocating an **idealist** position argued that tribal peoples should have their basic human right to **self-determination** respected, allowing them to freely choose to remain autonomous.

The inevitability argument is proving to be wrong, because national and international ideologies and political practices have changed. Direct interaction between outsiders and isolated tribals on an uncontrolled frontier has indeed typically been destructive as discussed above, but the crucial variable is the effective emergence of human rights in international society and their application to indigenous peoples. Combined work by anthropologists, environmentalists, and the international human rights community has changed political realities in the twenty-first century to make tribal survival possible. In 2004 the International Union for the Conservation of Nature (IUCN)'s World Conservation Congress passed a landmark resolution calling for a coordinated effort to "develop and implement proposals aimed at protecting the lands and territories of indigenous groups living in **voluntary isolation**" especially in the Amazon region[51] The resolution affirmed as a basic principle that isolated tribal peoples had a right to the protection of their lives, natural resources, and territories, and stated that "indigenous peoples living in voluntary isolation have the right to freely decide to remain isolated, maintain their cultural values, and to freely decide if, when and how they wish to integrate into national society." Shortly thereafter UN human rights agencies and the governments of Bolivia, Ecuador, and Peru recognized "peoples in voluntary isolation" as a category deserving protection.[52] This is an enor-

mously important endorsement of the principle of cultural autonomy for tribal peoples, and if backed up by effective protection policies on the part of governments, fully autonomous tribal peoples will be able to maintain themselves into the foreseeable future. However, developing and implementing protective legislation has been a difficult political process.[53]

Brazil now recognizes sixty-eight groups of "isolated Indians" and USAID has provided financial support to the National Indian Foundation and a Brazilian nongovernmental organization, the Center for Indigenist Work, to help protect these isolated groups.[54] Isolated tribal peoples also have the support of their more integrated indigenous relatives. In 2007 eleven local, regional, and national indigenous organizations in South America with support from IWGIA and the UN High Commissioner for Human Rights formally established the International Indigenous Committee for the Protection of Peoples in Isolation and Initial Contact in the Amazon, the Gran Chaco, and Eastern Paraguay.[55] Their objective is to protect the ways of life and well-being of isolated indigenous peoples and those in initial stages of contact by keeping a close watch on the actions of governments and corporations that might affect them, and by forming alliances with international organizations. This is political struggle in which indigenous organizations and their allies often find themselves pitted against giant multinational energy companies.

In the Peruvian Amazon as of 2009 fourteen ethnolinguistic groups were known to be intentionally avoiding contact with outsiders, including Asháninka, relatives of the Matsigenka, and several other Arawak- and Panoan-speaking groups. There may be 5,000 to 10,000 peoples in this category in Peru, and the government has reserved some 28,000 square kilometers for their protection.[56] Indigenous organizations in Peru such as AIDESEP have been among the most forceful advocates for the protection of these isolated peoples. Unfortunately, many protected areas and especially those for isolated peoples also overlap with lumber and petroleum concessions, and it has proven politically difficult to protect them.

AUSTRALIAN ABORIGINES

The experience of Australian Aborigines further demonstrates how the political fate of tribal groups often is determined by government policies, which in turn are shaped by the demands of varied special-interest groups exercising political power. In Australia, as in Amazonia, anthropologists have often played a role in shaping and supporting government policies toward indigenous peoples.

The European invasion of Australia began in 1788 with the founding of Port Jackson, now Sydney, as a penal colony. Because the Aborigines were not settled farming peoples and had no chiefs, colonial administrators declared Australia to be an "empty wasteland" and dispensed with treaty signing. The Aborigines were granted no legal existence and no official claim to their land. As elsewhere, genocide and ethnocide followed the Australian frontiers of European settlement. Except where Aborigines were useful as labor, they were systematically eliminated by poison, disease, and shooting as if they were wild animals. Tasmania's aboriginal population was reduced from 5,000 to 111 within 30 years. In western Victoria, 4,000 aborigines were reduced to 213 within 40 years, and 10 years later no one remained who could reliably describe the culture.[57] Witnesses before the Select Committee in the 1830s reported "many deeds of murder and violence" committed by settlers on the Australian frontier. This situation persisted well into the twentieth century. In the Northern Territory in 1901, "It was notorious, that the blackfellows were shot down like crows and that no notice was taken."[58]

Appeals by the APS led to the establishment of aboriginal reserves and protectors of natives in Australia by 1850. These actions did not prevent the wholesale extinction of Aborigines in many areas of Australia, but they did demonstrate that such injustice was officially disapproved. Aboriginal reserves at this time were not considered to be aboriginal lands where Aborigines could live independently; instead, they served a dual protection and "uplift" role. Reserves were to contain mission schools and farms where Aborigines would learn civilized skills.

The fact, which no one disputed, was that Aborigines were facing extinction as a result of frontier violence and dispossession. By contrast, from 1788 to 1880, the European population increased to 3 million. And by 1920, there were 5 million Europeans and barely 60,000 Aborigines, a mere 20 percent of the widely accepted estimate of 300,000 for the pre-European population. All authorities anticipated a continuing decline in the aboriginal population, and many predicted their total extinction. Everyone agreed that the European invasion was responsible, but the government still followed the inadequate "protection and uplift" approach devised by the House of Commons Select Committee and the APS in the 1830s.

By 1880, the sparsely settled Northern Territory, which contained 17 percent of Australia's land area, had become the last great frontier. There were fewer than 700 Europeans throughout the territory's 500,000 square miles (1.3 million km²) stretching from the desert center of Australia to the tropical north coast. This vast, seemingly inhospitable region was the ancestral homeland of unknown thousands of Aborigines still living independently. European Australians saw the territory as a great pastoral frontier, and there was still no national policy permitting the Aborigines to defend themselves, their resources, and their culture against the final invasion that was just beginning.

The government encouraged immigration into the territory to promote economic development, fully aware that the Aborigines would be victimized. To minimize the damage, humanitarians recommended federal control of all Aborigines by a permanent Native Commission and urged the formation of reserves on which Aborigines could be preserved and "uplifted" by working for cattle ranchers.[59] A committee of the Australasian Association for the Advancement of Science, which included pioneer Central Australian ethnographers Baldwin Spencer and Francis Gillen, emphasized that Aborigines were "a valuable labor asset" in the pastoral economy as a justification for a preservation policy. There was no attempt to protect aboriginal culture, except in museums, or to defend aboriginal political autonomy; instead, the emphasis was on "the well-being and preservation of the native race," presumably as units of labor.[60] However, even these modest ameliorative proposals were ineffective.

By 1920, there were some 4,000 Europeans and 600,000 cattle in the Northern Territory, steadily advancing against an aboriginal population estimated at 17,000, who faced a grim future. A mere 30,000 square miles (77,770 km²), barely 6 percent of the territory, had been designated for aboriginal reserves, even though the Aborigines were still the majority population, outnumbering Europeans more than four to one. The reserves contained cattle stations and missions where the Aborigines were to be "civilized," just as the APS envisioned in the nineteenth century.

Reserves, Assimilation, and Land Rights

As the situation for Aborigines in the Northern Territory became increasingly desperate, Australian anthropologist Frederic Wood Jones issued a stinging condemnation of the established policy of limited protectionism and uplift.[61] In an emotional presidential address to the anthropology section of the Australasian Association for the Advancement of Science in 1926, Wood Jones declared that "civilizing" the

Aborigine, whether on missions or cattle stations, meant extermination. Using missionary reports, he showed that the Aborigines in the best condition were those most remote from civilization. Missionized Aborigines were unhealthy and ill-housed and continued to die. Arguing that the missions were a form of humanitarian euthanasia that had failed in every sense, Wood Jones concluded, "I fail to see any sort of justification for a belief that salvation for the Australian native can ever lie in this direction."[62]

Wood Jones was just as critical of the government effort to provide welfare to the Aborigines on the fringes of civilization. He suggested that it was a form of conscience money that served to hide the fact that aboriginals were being dispossessed. He also challenged the belief that the Aborigine could be converted to cheap labor for the pastoral stations. He pointed out that although individuals might become successful station hands, they did not reproduce to replace themselves. There seemed to be no substitute for the traditional independent life. The existing reserves were "fictions and frauds" because they existed only on paper and were revoked whenever outside economic interests demanded entry. The government would not allow Aborigines to live in what would be called "voluntary isolation" in twenty-first-century Amazonia.

The first real change in policy began after Melbourne anthropologist Donald Thomson proposed in a 1938 report[63] that the government declare Arnhem Land, in the far north of the Northern Territory, to be a reserve where Aborigines could live independently according to their own culture as Wood Jones had advocated. Some 1,500 Aborigines were still living independently in Arnhem Land, and when five Japanese fishermen and a policeman were killed on the reserve, the government commissioned Thomson to contact the Aborigines in Arnhem Land, find out what happened, and try to make peace. Thomson was trained in functionalist applied anthropology by Radcliffe-Brown at Sydney, but he was also a close associate of Wood Jones. Thomson's sympathies were clearly with the Aborigines. He concluded that the killings were self-defense, and he recommended that Arnhem Land be made an absolutely inviolable reserve, with missionaries and ranchers excluded, to allow the Aborigines freedom to maintain their nomadic settlement pattern, culture, and social structure. This was perhaps the first time such a cultural autonomy policy was seriously proposed for Australia.

This approach was soundly rejected by Sydney anthropologist A. P. Elkin, who believed that Aborigines would inevitably abandon their independent tribal life and be assimilated into a settled existence within Australian national society. Trained by Radcliffe-Brown and Malinowski in functionalist applied anthropology, Elkin was a leading expert on aboriginal culture. He also shared Radcliffe-Brown's belief that Aborigines, even if they did not disappear as a people, would have their cultures destroyed.[64]

As an anthropologist, Elkin clearly understood the centrality of totemism in aboriginal culture. But he considered totemism to be an obsolete and ignorant belief. He wanted to persuade Aborigines that ". . . their own spiritual life and the future of natural species is not bound up with the integrity of particular spots on the earth's surface."[65] In fact the Aborigines were right on this very critical issue. Totemism was not a matter of tribal ignorance that the Aborigines needed to abandon. The spiritual life of Aborigines and the future of their natural resources are inextricably linked to the ultimate integrity of their sacred sites, but it was nearly forty years before government policy grudgingly came to acknowledge this point with the Northern Territory Land Rights Act of 1971. Accepting the validity of the totemic system would have meant also acknowledging the legitimacy of the aboriginal claim to full control over their land, resources, and political and economic independence.

Elkin opposed any aboriginal claim to the land that would stand in the way of outside development interests, especially if aboriginal land contained gold or otherwise proved to be especially valuable. Elkin's policy approach was probably related to his position in the Sydney anthropology department, which he began to chair in 1934. The department developed an applied program under Radcliffe-Brown's earlier direction and with Rockefeller Foundation grants. The Sydney program was designed to support the Australian government's colonial development policies in its territories in New Guinea, the Pacific, and Australia. Elkin emphatically disassociated his department from any support for aboriginal autonomy, declaring: "It should be stated quite clearly and definitely that anthropologists connected with the Department in the University of Sydney have no desire to preserve any of the aboriginal tribes of Australia or of the islands in their pristine condition as 'museum specimens' for the purpose of investigation; this charge is too often made against anthropologists . . . for change is coming, and anthropologists, like all good members of a 'higher' and trustee race, are concerned with the task of raising primitive races in the cultural scale."[66]

In the twenty-first century this statement sounds outrageously racist and ethnocentric, but it reflected what seemed to be a realistic view of the future of indigenous peoples, assuming no change in the political and ideological order of the commercial world. Of course, cultural autonomy policies need not turn indigenous peoples into "museum specimens" and do not assume that indigenous cultures are static, or changeless. The point is that cultural autonomy acknowledges the human right of any people to determine how their culture develops. The real issue was not the existence of culture change, but the political independence of tribal peoples, their ownership of territory and resources, and whether outsiders should be allowed to dictate the kind of changes that occur on tribal land.

The alternative to cultural autonomy was the official government policy of **assimilation** for Aborigines, which was clearly defined in 1952 by Paul Hasluck, minister of territories, as follows: "A policy of assimilation means, to my mind, that we expect that, in the course of time, all persons of aboriginal blood or mixed-blood in Australia will live in the same manner as white Australians do, that they will have full citizenship, and that they will, of their own desire, participate in all the activities of the Australian community."[67]

Although Australia amended its Constitution in 1967 to allow the government to legislate for Aborigines and to allow Aborigines to be counted in the census, the government continued to reject aboriginal self-determination and land rights into the 1970s when politically active aboriginal organizations began to publicly demand legal ownership of traditional lands. The protest began in 1971 when the government rejected aboriginal claims of ownership to the Arnhem Land Reserve. The aboriginal landowners wanted to protect their sacred sites by preventing a multinational mining company from strip mining bauxite inside the reserve. By 1973, the protest began to take on international dimensions, and the government appointed an Aboriginal Land Rights Commission to find a solution. The result was the Aboriginal Land Rights (Northern Territory) Act of 1976 (ALRA), which provided a legal mechanism for aboriginal communities to gain title to their traditional lands. This was a major victory for Aborigines, although the act provided only limited protection from outside development and was later weakened by amendments. The real significance of the act was that it meant that the government was finally acknowledging the legitimacy of aboriginal culture and the right of Aborigines to maintain themselves as independent communities.

The preamble to the Aboriginal and Torres Strait Islander Act of 2005[68] was a remarkable acknowledgment by the Australian Parliament that "Aboriginal Persons and Torres Strait Islanders" are descendants of people who were the original inhabitants of Australia before Europeans arrived. Furthermore, the act acknowledged that aboriginals were "dispossessed of their lands, largely without compensation," and that aboriginals needed equitable compensation and reconciliation for this injustice. According to the preamble to the Act, it defined new policies to help Aborigines overcome the disadvantages they had suffered and help them enjoy their culture, and to "increase their economic status, promote their social well-being and improve the provision of community services. . . ." The 2005 act included special provisions intended to promote "self-management and self-sufficiency" and created three new national government entities: the Indigenous Land Corporation, the Aboriginal and Torres Strait Islander Land Account, and Indigenous Business Australia, a restructured Aboriginal and Torres Strait Islander Commercial Development Corporation, originally created in 1988. Five of the seven directors of the Indigenous Land Corporations, including the chair, must be indigenous.

The 2006 census estimated the total indigenous population of Australia as 517,174, including some 47,000 Torres Strait Islanders. Over half of all indigenous peoples in the country were living in the major cities and adjacent areas, whereas about 82,000 people or 15 percent of indigenous peoples were living in "very remote" areas. This is the most remote of the census bureau's five remoteness categories measured as distance from or access to major cities. The very remote category geographically covers most of Australia but is only occupied by about 1 percent of the total population. About 37,000 people, nearly half of the remote-area aboriginal population, were in the Northern Territory, and they constituted well more than half of the Northern Territory aboriginal population of 66,581. The total aboriginal population was just under a third of the total population of the Northern Territory,[69] but Aborigines owned most of the rural land.

The Political Economy of the Northern Territory

The contemporary situation of aboriginal peoples in the Northern Territory has evolved quite differently from in the Peruvian Amazon. The crucial variable was the series of legislative acts mentioned above, as well as the more recent political decentralization policy mandated by Local Government Act 2008. The vast size and sparse population of the Northern Territory, covering an area of 1.3 million square kilometers, which is the size of France, Italy, and Spain combined, with a total population of only 210,000 people in 2006 makes decentralizing very appealing. Decentralization replaced the earlier system of fifty-five Community Councils with eleven new shires, or local governments including most of the population outside of the larger municipalities. The problem for Aborigines was that this change abolished existing aboriginal community councils, which were already functioning as effective local governments. The new shires are subdivided into wards, which did not always take into account aboriginal cultural areas and languages. Arnhem Land, where the largest aboriginal population lives, is covered by two shires, East and West Arnhem Land. The government's stated objective in the reorganization was to improve the provision of government services to widely scattered, culturally diverse communities.[70] In this case decentralization makes for more efficient central coordination, but it is not clear that it will give formerly isolated communities a more effective voice in decision making, or whether it will improve people's daily lives.

Successful indigenous governance seems to require legitimacy, power, resources, and accountability on the part of government institutions and officials.[71] However, understanding how indigenous governing organizations have developed requires an understanding of actions by the larger governments that encompass them. Indigenous forms of government are "contested and negotiated" between all parties. The Australian federal, state, and territorial governments are the dominant powers in finance and have the means of direct coercion. These governments also have the power to create indigenous organizations and fund them, but indigenous peoples and their organizations are not passive, and the governing situation is extremely dynamic. These complex issues were explored in detail by the Indigenous Community Governance Project (ICGP) conducted by anthropologists in partnership with the Centre for Aboriginal Economic Policy Research at the Australian National University and Reconciliation Australia. Reconciliation Australia is a nonprofit nongovernmental organization formed in 2000 that seeks "to eliminate the glaring gap in life expectancy between Indigenous and non-Indigenous

children." The life expectancy of indigenous children is said to be seventeen years shorter than that of nonindigenous children in Australia. Reconciliation Australia's board of directors and staff include both indigenous and nonindigenous members, and it receives financial support from government and major corporations, including BHP Billiton, the world's largest mining company.

The ICGP project adopted the following working definition of governance: ". . . the evolving processes, relationships, institutions and structures by which a group of people, community or society organize themselves collectively to achieve the things that matter to them."

A close look at West Arnhem Shire shows how Aborigines are affected by the new political economy of the Northern Territory. This shire is home to many of the peoples described in some of the best-known modern ethnographic research in Australia, including peoples who provided the model for the concept of "the original affluent society."[72] There were an estimated 6,591 people living in West Arnhem Shire in 2006, which is divided into four wards, each composed of numerous named communities (see figure 13.10). The shire head office is in Jabiru, a village of about 1,100 people in Kakadu Ward, near the Kakadu National Park and the Ranger uranium mine. The largest aboriginal population in the shire is immediately east of Kakadu in Maningrida Ward, which is home to some 4,000 Aborigines. The major settlement of Maningrida was the largest aboriginal community in the territory in 2006, with some 2,700 residents speaking ten different languages. Maningrida provided basic services to more than thirty outstations, or aboriginal homelands communities. A Northern Territory government study of Maningrida[73] set out to identify "economic gaps" to be overcome by government and the private sector to promote economic growth, but this process saw little importance in the outstations where Aborigines were living and caring for their countries. There are certainly difficulties with providing education, health care, and employment and with operating community stores to supply basic goods and financial services to Aborigines in small communities and outstations; however, most of these people were also self-provisioning by hunting and fishing and were not totally dependent on store-bought food. The Bawinanga Corporation described below has been remarkably successful at meeting the needs of people in Maningrida Ward.

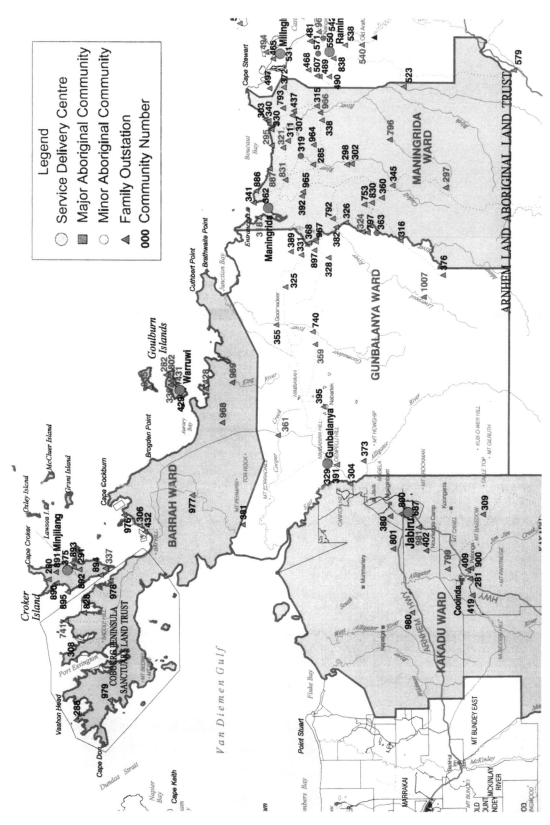

Figure 13.10. Aboriginal Service Delivery Centers, Communities, and Family Outstations in West Arnhem Shire, by Wards 2006 (Northern Territory Government, Department of Planning and Infrastructure).

Caring for Country: Natural Protected Areas and the WALFA Project

Indigenous people have now regained control over about 20 percent of the land area of Australia, and they have formed networks of indigenous organizations to restore and to again sustainably manage their territories. Indigenous lands and waters are threatened by overgrazing, feral animals and weeds, uncontrolled bushfires, erosion, and climate change. Before their basic human rights as indigenous peoples and citizens were recognized, many indigenous landowners were moving off their lands and into settlements to obtain basic services such as health care and education. As a result, they were also abandoning their careful burning practices, and with the land depopulated and unmanaged, disastrous wildfires resulted. Wildfires that are too hot and too extensive are very destructive. They contribute to global warming by releasing massive amounts of carbon dioxide, and they destroy natural vegetation and wildlife habitat, causing erosion, which damages aquatic ecosystems. As indigenous peoples reoccupy their lands by returning to indigenous communities and outstations, they are better able to care for their countries and preserve and transmit the knowledge of country that is retained by the oldest residents.

Aborigines have used fire to increase the natural productivity of the landscape for millennia, and these practices have a key role in environmental protection today. The West Arnhem Land Fire Abatement Project (WALFA) under way since 2006 is a good example of contemporary environmental restoration and resource management being carried out by indigenous peoples. The WALFA project was an outgrowth of efforts to control destructive fires begun by indigenous landowners in 1998, working with the Northern Land Council (NLC) in a 28,000-square-kilometer region in Arnhem Land. This tropical savanna area has pronounced wet and dry seasons during which grass grows luxuriantly and then turns tinder dry. In traditionally caring for this land, Aborigines burned savanna patches early in the dry season, setting small, cool fires, thereby avoiding large, destructive fires that would otherwise occur near the end of the dry season, killing trees and continuing to burn uncontrollably. Small fires create firebreaks, promote the growth of new grass, make travel and hunting easier, and improve wildlife habitat.

The WALFA project is funded by an agreement between ConocoPhillips, the Northern Territory government, and the NLC, in which ConocoPhillips contributes about US$15 million over seventeen years for aboriginal fire management. The WALFA project is intended to reduce carbon emissions in the region by at least 100,000 tonnes per year, nearly 2 million tonnes over the life of the project, and allows ConocoPhillips to offset carbon emissions from its new liquid natural gas (LNG) terminal near Darwin. Carbon abatement was a government requirement for granting a development permit for the LNG terminal. ConocoPhillips pays the Northern Territory government A$1 million (US$905,000) per year, based on an assumed value of A$10 per tonne of carbon abatement. Four different indigenous communities teamed up with the NLC to provide teams of rangers to carry out the burning project and thereby satisfy the conditions of ConocoPhillips's development permit. The NLC manages the finances and coordinates the project with the aboriginal communities. WALFA creates training and paid employment for many Aborigines in a very remote area and gives them an important reason for valuing their traditional environmental knowledge. Additional funds for the aboriginal rangers come from the Community Development Employment Projects program through the national Department of Families, Housing, Community Services and Indigenous Affairs.

The WALFA project also creates a remarkable link between the well-being of remote-area Aborigines, global climate, global corporations, global billionaires, and the 40 million people of the Tokyo metropolitan area. The Darwin ConocoPhillips LNG plant connects the 4 trillion cubic feet of natural gas from the Bayu-Undan field in the Timor Sea with Tokyo Electric Company's thermal electric power plants and Tokyo Gas Company's natural gas distribution system in Tokyo. Tokyo Electric and Tokyo Gas are also part owners of the gas field, pipeline, and refinery. Tokyo Electric is the largest company in Japan and the primary supplier of Tokyo's electricity. Tokyo gas is the primary natural gas supplier to Tokyo and several other Japanese cities. ConocoPhillips is the world's fourth-largest oil and gas refiner and the seventh-largest company in *Fortune*'s Global 500, with revenues of $230 billion in 2008. American billionaire Warren Buffett is one of its beneficial owners with a 5.7 percent share.

Following WALFA's success the North Australian Indigenous Land and Sea Management Alliance, an aboriginal organization formed by the Balkanu–Cape York Development Corporation, the Kimberly Land Council, and the NLC developed four major new carbon abatement projects across northern Australia.

Part of the indigenous environmental protection work is supported directly by the national government through the Indigenous Protected Area (IPA) program, which is part of the national Caring for Our Country program and follows IUCN (International Union for the Conservation of Nature) guidelines for natural ecosystems managed for sustainable use.[74] Protected areas are intended to "conserve healthy ecosystems that sustain human life." This is the kind of resource use indigenous peoples have been practicing for a very long time, which is why many of their territories now qualify for such designation. Several such areas were established in the Arnhem Land region between 2001 and 2009 to protect some 10,000 square kilometers of land, and hundreds of miles of coastline, including Laynhapuy; Anindilyakwa; the Groote Eylandt Archipelago; Dhimurru; Djelk; and Warddeken. There are thirty-three indigenous rangers, including eight women, working to protect Djelk. The Djelk rangers also train future rangers in the Maningrida High School. The government planned to spend more than US$45 million from 2009–2010 to develop and support IPAs, including over US$6 million in Arnhem Land.

In reality by living on their countries, Aborigines are providing services to Australian society, as well as to global society, in the form of environmental sustainability that benefits everyone. Many of the services that aboriginal land management provides are natural services from healthy natural ecosystems such as carbon storage, soil production, freshwater, and biodiversity. Aborigines "living on country" are also maintaining and reproducing healthy people, which saves governments health care and public health costs, and they maintain and produce aboriginal culture, which certainly has value to Australia and the world. It is also important for government to help Aborigines protect their natural resources, because Aborigines who live on country continue to derive a significant portion of their subsistence from hunting, gathering, and fishing. The market replacement value of securing these foods for small populations living in remote areas would be very high.

Unfortunately, Australian governments have not always acknowledged these benefits and have been slow to support them by providing services to Aborigines and investing in the aboriginal estate. The government's recent development of IPAs and the Working on Country program is a helpful move toward investment in the aboriginal estate.

The Northern Land Council and the Mining Industry

Anthropologist Jon Altman describes how indigenous Australians operate in a "hybrid economy" that includes overlapping state, market, and customary elements with both capitalist and kinship-based modes of production and distribution.[75] This description seems to apply well to indigenous peoples operating in many parts of the commercial world today, but it is often difficult for nonindigenous peoples to understand because they want them to be culturally "authentic." For example, land rights legislation requires Aborigines to prove their "authentic" connections to land in terms of customary cultural patterns. This imposes an unrealistic concept of a tribal culture frozen in time, even as it denies them full ownership of their territorial resources in the market economy. The authenticity requirement also creates internal conflicts because it locks out many urban indigenous Australians who have no land rights. "Real" indigenous people live in an "intercultural" world, just as in practice their economic life is both capitalist and kin-based. The ALRA called for the establishment of land trusts to hold title to aboriginal land, and an Aboriginal Benefits Account to administer royalties paid by mineral developers. The benefits account is administered by the Australian Department of Families, Housing, Community Services and Indigenous Affairs in Canberra. ALRA also called for Land Councils to mediate between aboriginal landowners identified by customary law and mining corporations seeking access to their lands. The needs of the mining industry are crucial elements in land rights legislation.

In 2009 Australia's gross domestic product was approximately a trillion U.S. dollars, putting it in the upper tier of global economies as fifteenth largest. Mining constituted about 10 percent of the economy. From 2001 to 2006 Australia experienced a mining boom in which the value of mining exports rose to over A$100 billion, with much of this expansion linked to economic growth in China and India. This boom produced A$63 billion in profits for the mining industry and A$7 billion in revenues for Australian governments in 2008.

Much of the mining occurs on aboriginal lands, but unfortunately aboriginal legal titles do not include ownership of the minerals. Paradoxically, Aborigines are land rich, owning 20 percent of Australia, but are "dirt poor" because they receive relatively little from their lands. It is generally recognized that Aborigines and their communities have received relatively small benefits from the mining boom. However, even though they do not own mineral rights, under land rights legislation they have been able to negotiate to a limited extent the terms of consent with mineral developers, before mining can take place on aboriginal lands.

Although government seems committed to "closing the gap" in income, employment, and commercial opportunities between Aborigines and the national society, "improvement" as measured by access to employment and significant cash incomes has been small for most remote Aborigines. In dealing with indigenous peoples in remote communities, it may be more useful to measure improvements in the lives and livelihoods of people, rather than focusing narrowly on income and employment. The challenge for Aborigines is that mining companies, government, and aboriginal communities and their organizations all need to work together if mining development is to actually benefit all parties. However, governments and corporations have their own conflicting interests, because both also receive financial returns from the mining enterprise. Aborigines initially resist mining development on the lands either to stop such development completely or to bargain for the best return they can get. When mining proceeds, they must cooperate with the mining company and actually minimize costs and maximize benefits, but many people still oppose the project, or realize few benefits, and this creates stress and conflict within the community. The relative distribution of power between the three actors (government, business, and indigenous peoples) is grossly unequal when measured in revenue flows, and the two most powerful actors (government and business) are likely to be allies in opposition to the weakest. There are many unresolved issues here. For example, should government or multinational corporations provide development services to indigenous communities? A central question is how can fair shares from development activities be allocated, and who decides?

The NLC describes its vision as "A Territory in which the land rights of every Traditional Owner are legally recognized and in which Aboriginal people benefit economically, socially and culturally from the secure possession of their lands and seas."[76] The council is in effect a government representing the interests of some 30,000 Aborigines, living in some 200 communities (see figure 13.11). The NLC is concerned with all aspects of aboriginal land, coastal areas, and islands within the northern part of the Northern Territory. NLC works with aboriginal land owners, consulting with them on requests by outside interests to develop resources on aboriginal land. It handles entry permits and helps people establish legal claims to land and protect and manage their resources. Its primary responsibility is to consult with aboriginal people to obtain their approval for any use of their lands by outsiders. During the 2008–2009 fiscal year the council administered a budget of over US$25 million. The NLC maintains an Anthropology Branch that keeps track of land ownership claims and identifies and protects sacred sites. The council has a staff of 120 and employs a chief executive through a head office in Darwin and eight regional offices. The full council has 78 elected members and meets twice a year. There are seven regional councils that are open to everyone and meet four times a year. There is a women's committee attached to the full council to make sure that women are involved in council business. In addition to the secretariat, corporate services, and the legal departments, there are departments for anthropology, resource management, and regional development. The anthropology department has native title, land interests, and mapping as special functions.

Seven major mining companies were operating in the Northern Territory in 2010. The two largest working in Arnhem Land were the Alcan Gove Mine, which extracts and processes bauxite for aluminum, and the Ranger Mine in Kakadu National Park, which mines uranium. Gove was the development project that originally touched off the aboriginal protests that led to the Land Rights Act. These two companies are situated at opposite sides of Arnhem Land, but they are connected through a chain of corporate ownership to the global mineral resource giant Rio Tinto Group. Rio Tinto is a dual British and Australian corporation, headquartered in London and Melbourne, with combined revenues of over US$54 billion in 2008 and total shareholder stock value of US$30 billion. In 2007 Rio Tinto acquired Alcan, the Canadian aluminum company that owned the mines and refineries operating at Gove in Arnhem Land. The Rio Tinto Group now supplies iron, copper, and aluminum, the key metals that supply China's growth. In 2009 China's largest metals company, Chinalco, which is owned by the Chinese government, acquired a 12 percent share of Rio Tinto, making it the largest owner. Chinalco borrowed from Alcoa, the world's largest aluminum producer, to buy into Rio Tinto. This means that the Aborigines living in "very remote" outstations in Arnhem Land receive a tiny share of the benefits from the activities of these giant global corporations, mediated through the NLC.

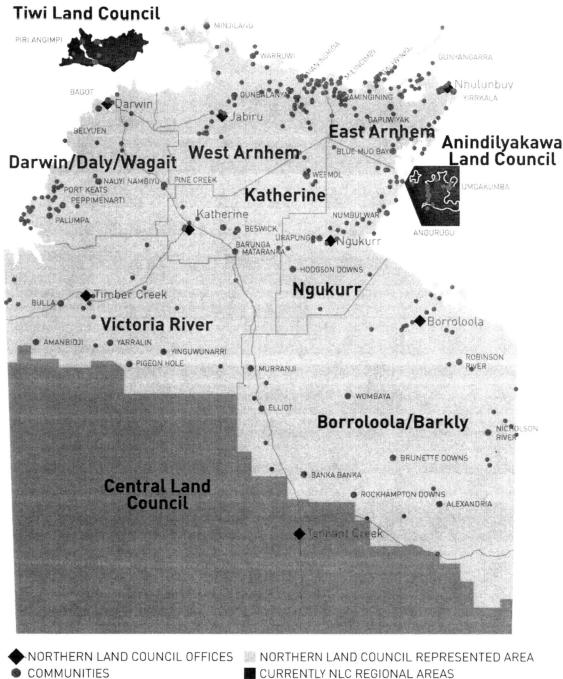

Figure 13.11. Northern Land Council communities and regional offices (Northern Land Council. 2009.
Annual Report **2008-2009. Map 1).**

Bawinanga Aboriginal Corporation:
Growth Hubs or Outstations?

The Corporations (Aboriginal and Torres Strait Islander) Act 2006[77] specifies in detail how indigenous corporations must be organized in Australia and requires that they register with a special government agency, the Registrar of Indigenous Corporations, and meet specific financial reporting rules. This does not

mean that the national society is totally imposing external forms on aboriginal culture, because Aborigines are able to organize their affairs by using both systems, as will be shown below. As of 2009 there were more than 2,700 indigenous corporations in the country. Most were in remote areas, where they provided social and public services for which they received significant public funds. Significantly, in view of the often-perceived male bias in aboriginal culture, where the gender of corporate directors was reported, nearly a third were women. Indigenous corporations were small, and nearly half had incomes of under A$25,000 and assets of under A$100,000. The largest had incomes and assets of tens of millions in Australian dollars.

The Bawinanga Aboriginal Corporation (BAC) in the community of Maningrida in West Arnhem Shire is the second-largest aboriginal corporation in Australia, with assets of nearly US$14 million and revenue of US$78 million in 2008.[78] It was incorporated in 1979 initially as an outstation resource agency to provide support for people living in outstations on their clan lands and soon expanded into a wide range of activities. But it soon took on additional welfare and economic development functions. The name *Bawinanga* combines parts of the names of three language groups in the region, **Ba**rada, Gun**win**ggu, and Ramba**rranga**.[79] At first BAC was federally funded by the Department of Aboriginal Affairs, and from 1980 to 2005 its chief executive was a *balanda* (non-aboriginal) man. In 1997 BAC began to administer the federal Community Development Employment Projects (CDEP) funds flowing into the region, and its annual revenues began to exceed A$10 million. By 2007 it employed a staff of more than 50, primarily non-aboriginals, and administered CDEP support for some 500 aboriginals.

The distinctive feature of BAC is that it is an indigenously owned and directed community corporation that operates businesses and promotes community development and the general welfare. It aims "to promote, in all its endeavours, the common good and mutual benefit of its members through fair, equitable and representative action and enterprise." BAC membership is open to all adult aboriginal persons who are permanent residents of, or who have "traditional rights, affiliations and interests" in Maningrida and the outstations that it serves. The first objective of the corporation is "to promote the maintenance of language, culture and traditional practice." There are no membership fees and no dividends paid.

In 2009 BAC reported a regular staff of 45 and 246 registered members, serving 800 "clients" in 32 outstations. BAC functions include agriculture, forestry, fishing, manufacturing, municipal services, construction, wholesale trade, shops, accommodation, cafés, restaurants, transport and storage, communication services, housing, education, health and community services, art services, personal and other services, employment and training, and land management. Its activities are organized in several business segments including the BAC Housing and Welding Shop; the Balmarrk Supermarket; BAC Outdoors for hardware and merchandise; a Buildings Activities for construction; a financial services division for banking; Good

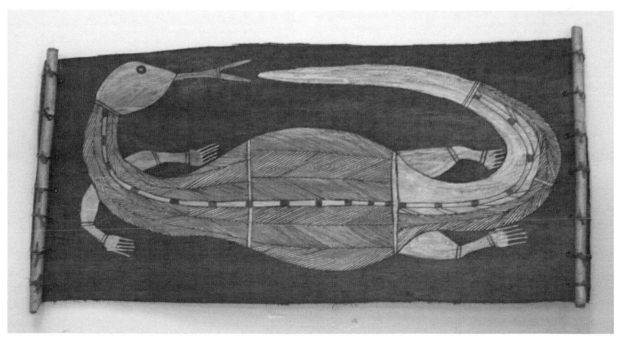

Figure 13.12. Aboriginal Bark Painting of Goanna Lizard, Artist B. Nibegoo, Gunwinggu Tribe, Oenpelli, Arnhem Land 1988.

Food Kitchen preparing take-out foods; Maningrida Arts and Culture division, selling local art works nationally and internationally; a road construction and maintenance division; a workshop for vehicle maintenance; as well as a wide range of other activities. Figure 13.12 illustrates the distinctive Arnhem Land aboriginal art style that is reaching outside markets.

The Aborigines have succeeded in governing the Bawinanga Corporation by combining the informal, open discussion characteristic of small, face-to-face, domestically based societies with the formality of legally chartered corporate institutions required by the federal government. In effect this is an intercultural blend of small- and large-scale cultural structures that must satisfy both Australian legal requirements and the expectations of Aborigines in the "very remote" Maningrida settlement and the linguistically and culturally diverse Aborigines living in outstations dispersed over a vast territory.

BAC is governed by an all-aboriginal ten- to fifteen-person executive committee elected annually by the members representing different language groups and outstations. Elected members include a "neo-elite" who understand the *balanda* world and a "customary elite" who are especially knowledgeable about local aboriginal culture and local affairs. A few executive members are elites in both respects, and elites of whatever sort were likely to serve as leaders in multiple organizations. The annual election means that the executive leadership changes frequently, and it reduces the possibility of a single cultural group dominating the organization. There were few Aborigines qualified by prior training, English fluency, and business experience to manage such a complex organization, but whoever receives the most votes becomes executive committee chair. The executive chair is a prized salaried position and comes with access to a motor vehicle, but it is consistently rotated among the different language groups. In this way the potential for abuse of executive power is severely limited. BAC's senior managers are more stable and more experienced, but they are *balanda* (non-aboriginal). This senior management adds an element of stability to the entire organization. They try to stay current with the interpersonal details of community life in a way that would be difficult in a larger-scale society. They help the executive committee mediate between national and customary law, and they offer a level of neutrality between different aboriginal language groups. The legal requirements of BAC as a formal corporation mean that the Aboriginal Executive Committee members must avoid conflicts of interest, but at the same time they do represent the interests of their close kin, clans, language groups, and outstation residents. Finding a successful balance between formal corporate practice and kinship-based customary practice has been improved by government-supported opportunities for aboriginal leaders to gain training in business practices and for the non-aboriginal staff to gain training in aboriginal culture. Balance is also achieved by frequent elections and by executive committee members operating in both formal and informal meetings and involving others to participate as observers and in informal discussions, as would be customary practice.

The apparent success of BAC and Maningrida generally has caused people to begin moving from outstations back to Maningrida, and some members are concerned that Maningrida itself may become too big, which would undermine some of its original goals of supporting outstations. A more critical problem has been BAC's continued reliance on funding from the Australian government. BAC receives funding from several commonwealth programs including CDEP, an employment program, and the Community Housing and Infrastructure Program, both of which became part of the commonwealth's Department of Family and Community Services. There has been considerable confusion and disarray in aboriginal policy that began with the abolition of the Aboriginal and Torres Strait Islander Commission, the threatened abolition of CDEP, and the declaration of a state of emergency in the Northern Territory in 2007 that brought in direct federal intervention in local affairs. Most of these policy changes were modified after a new federal government was elected in late 2007.

The Noongar Nation

In 2006 a federal judge ruled that when European settlement began in 1829, the Noongar people represented a single community in what became the metro area of Perth, because they shared laws and customs over their land and water, even though they did not have a central authority. The Noongar people in the southwest corner of Western Australia were organized around totemic clan estates, as elsewhere, but throughout the region they spoke closely related languages, and they considered themselves collectively to be a distinct group. This corner of Australia is a biologically rich environment compared with much of desert Australia. Aboriginal groups here were larger than in drier areas, and bands sometimes formed larger groups. As European settlers spread across aboriginal territories, the Noongar people retained their corporate identity and their attachment to their lands, but they gradually moved into settlements in search of employment, adopted English as a common language, and turned their bands and local groups into bilateral or cognatic descent groups resembling European families and family lines. Noongar families were often of mixed ancestry with European fathers and Noongar mothers. There are now some 400 Noongar family lines averaging some 250 people and with subfamilies of 40 or more people where most social interaction occurs. Families retain connections with particular towns, or "runs" of towns, which comprise their family "countries." In response to new federal legislation that opened the land claims process to more parts of the country, in 1995 the Noongar people formed the Noongar Land Council to represent them in negotiations for gaining title to their 78 existing land claims scattered across southwest Australia. The council was a representative body with four Noongar drawn from each of twelve electoral wards. By 1998, in order to facilitate the claim process, the council consolidated their claims into just six claims.

The Noongar Land Council created a new organization in 2002, the South West Aboriginal Land and Sea Council (SWALSC), which under its new constitution won official acceptance as a native title representative body for the purposes of land claims. The SWALSC divided the territory into fourteen wards, each with four representatives, producing a full council of fifty-six persons. SWALSC boundaries were aligned with Western Australia's existing Shire boundaries. SWALSC held a series of meetings with local people in six regional working groups and collected genealogies connecting some 400 families to 99 apical ancestors that were in turn connected to specific territories.

SUMMARY

Since the policy debate began over how states should deal with tribal peoples, only two basic positions have been argued. A fundamental philosophical conflict exists between the realists, who advocate policies to help indigenous people adjust to the "inevitable" changes brought by colonialism or postcolonial national integration and economic development, and the idealists, who oppose the state-sponsored invasion of indigenous territories by colonists or externally imposed development projects. This philosophical split has obvious political implications for indigenous peoples. If the realists set national and international policies, indigenous peoples are likely to disappear as distinct cultural groups, whereas the idealist position will foster indigenous self-determination that will make cultural survival possible.

Virtually all tribal cultures that anthropologists have described ethnographically have been adversely affected by the commercial world. Our discussion of these cultures in chapters 2 through 5 largely ignored this possibility by treating tribal cultures as if they existed only within tribal worlds. However, more complex cultures clearly have varied impacts on smaller-scale cultures. In chapters 6 through 9, we pointed out that ancient kingdoms and empires often absorbed tribal societies or forced them to organize into states in their own defense. In the modern era, industrial civilization has exerted an enormous economic and political influence in drawing tribal cultures into the emerging global system.

Throughout the nineteenth and the first half of the twentieth century, the realist policy approach of adjustment and integration clearly dominated. However, since World War II, a more evolved international concept of human rights, fostered by the UN system, has for the first time created conditions under which indigenous peoples themselves could develop their own formal political organizations and promote their own idealist perspective. This has given them the opportunity to directly shape international standards for the interaction between small-scale cultures and the larger state- and global-level forces surrounding them.

Very recently the political mobilization of indigenous peoples has been greatly facilitated by their ability to take advantage of digital information technologies to form international networks of indigenous organizations and supporting nongovernmental organizations. Indigenous people made significant gains in gaining control over their territories and cultural autonomy, and are demonstrating to the world that they can successfully satisfy their basic needs while at the same time protecting their natural resources. They are also helping reduce the threat of global warming by following traditional resource management practices. The new UN Declaration of the Rights of Indigenous Peoples was adopted by the UN General Assembly in 2007 and has made it easier for tribal peoples living in "voluntary isolation" to maintain their cultural autonomy.

STUDY QUESTIONS

1. Distinguish between the realist and the idealist positions on policy toward indigenous peoples. Refer

to specific examples, organizations, individuals, policies, or international conventions.

2. Define indigenous people. Differentiate between indigenous people and indigenous population. What are the limitations of the term *indigenous*? In what sense is *indigenous people* a political concept?

3. Why are the terms *tribal* and *primitive* sometimes avoided by anthropologists?

4. What features of small-scale cultures can be identified with indigenous peoples?

5. In what sense can indigenous peoples be referred to as nations?

6. Describe the philosophical position and the policy recommendations of the Select Committee and the Aborigines Protection Society. How were they actually applied?

7. In what way did colonial policy toward Australian Aborigines depart from standard British practice? How do you account for this?

8. What is the current relationship between aboriginal peoples and mining corporations and oil and gas companies operating in the Northern Territory?

9. In what way could the League of Nations mandate system, the UN Charter, and ILO Convention 107 be said to endorse ethnocentric policies that might be used to undermine the human rights of indigenous peoples?

10. What UN declarations or covenants provide a basis for the human rights of indigenous peoples?

11. Distinguish between the human rights of individuals and those of groups.

12. What were the assumptions of the anthropologists involved in drafting ILO Convention 107? How were they expressed in the convention?

13. Describe how Peru's economic development policies affected the Asháninka and their neighbors. What alternative policies were proposed?

14. What is meant by *internal colonialism*? Use examples from Australia and Peru.

15. What are the most important human rights that indigenous peoples themselves define as the minimum conditions for their survival?

16. What is the significance of "Peoples in Voluntary Isolation" in Amazonia?

SUGGESTED READING

Bodley, John H. 1988. *Tribal Peoples and Development Issues: A Global Overview*. Mountain View, CA: Mayfield. An edited collection of materials including case studies, policy positions, assessments, and recommendations on indigenous peoples and development issues throughout the world from the nineteenth century to 1988.

Bodley, John H. 2008. *Victims of Progress*, 5th ed. Lanham, MD: AltaMira Press. Examines the official policies and underlying motives that have shaped the interaction between indigenous peoples and members of commercial-scale culture, since the early nineteenth century; includes many case studies drawn from throughout the world.

Davis, Shelton H. 1977. *Victims of the Miracle: Development and the Indians of Brazil*. Cambridge, Eng.: Cambridge University Press. A critical analysis of the Brazilian government's development policies in the Amazon region and their impact on the native peoples.

GLOSSARY TERMS

Indigenous peoples The original inhabitants of a territory who seek to maintain political control over their resources and the cultural heritage.

Ethnocide The forced destruction of a cultural system.

Genocide The extermination of a human population.

Ecocide The degradation of an ecosystem.

Cash cropping The raising of crops for market sale rather than for domestic consumption.

Uncontrolled frontier A tribal territory that is invaded by colonists from a state-organized society but where the government chooses not to regulate the actions of the colonists.

Acculturation The concept used by colonial applied anthropologists to describe the changes in tribal culture that accompanied European conquest but that minimized the role of coercion and the loss of tribal autonomy.

Indirect rule The situation in which European colonial administrators appointed local natives to serve as mediating officials, or chiefs, to help them control local communities.

Direct rule The use of European colonial administrators to control a native community at the local level.

Integration The absorption of a formerly autonomous people into a dominant state society, with the possible retention of ethnic identity.

Assimilation Ethnocide without genocide; the loss of distinctive cultural identity as a population surrenders its autonomy and is absorbed into a dominant society and culture.

Debt bondage An exploitive economic relationship that is managed to keep individuals in virtually perpetual indebtedness.

Internal colony A territory within a state containing an indigenous population that is denied the right of self-determination.

Cultural autonomy Self-determination by a cultural group.

Realist A policy position that maintains that indigenous peoples must surrender their political and economic autonomy and be integrated into dominant state societies.

Idealist A policy position that advocates cultural autonomy for indigenous peoples as a basic human right.

Self-determination The right of any people to freely determine their own cultural, political, and economic future.

Voluntary isolation Official designation for tribal peoples who have chosen to actively avoid contact with outsiders, thereby maintaining their self-determination and exercising cultural autonomy.

NOTES

1. Bodley, John H. 1975. *Victims of Progress*. Menlo Park, CA: Cummings; 1976. *Anthropology and Contemporary Human Problems*. Menlo Park, CA: Cummings; Diamond, Stanley. 1968. "The Search for the Primitive." In *The Concept of the Primitive*, edited by Ashley Montagu, pp. 99–147. New York: Free Press.
2. IWGIA (International Work Group for Indigenous Affairs), 2007, Annual Report 2006. Copenhagen: IWGIA. www.iwgia.org/sw17779.asp.
3. Nietschmann, Bernard. 1988. "Third World Colonial Expansion: Indonesia, Disguised Invasion of Indigenous Nations." *Tribal Peoples and Development Issues: A Global Overview*, edited by John H. Bodley, pp. 191–207. Mountain View, CA: Mayfield.
4. Crosby, Alfred W. 1986. *Biological Imperialism: The Biological Expansion of Europe, 900–1900*. Cambridge, Eng.: Cambridge University Press.
5. Clark, Grover. 1936. *The Balance Sheets of Imperialism: Facts and Figures on Colonies*. New York: Columbia University Press.
6. Bodley, John H. 2008. *Victims of Progress*. 5th ed. Lanham, MD: AltaMira Press.
7. United Kingdom, House of Commons. 1837. *Report from the Select Committee on Aborigines (British Settlements)*. Imperial Blue Book, no. 7,425. British Parliamentary Papers (an excerpt appears in Bodley, John H. 1988a. *Tribal Peoples and Development Issues: A Global Overview*. Mountain View, CA: Mayfield, pp. 63–69).
8. Covenant of the League of Nations, Article 22. The Avalon Project, Lillian Goldman Law Library, Yale Law School. http://avalon.law.yale.edu/20th_century/leagcov.asp#art22.
9. Radcliffe-Brown, A.R. 1958. "Presidential Address to Section E. South African Association for the Advancement of Science, July 1928." In *Method in Social Anthropology: Selected Essays by A. R. Radcliffe-Brown*, edited by M. N. Srinivas. Chicago: University of Chicago Press, p. 32.
10. Redfield, Robert, Ralph Linton, and Melville J. Herskovits. 1936. "Memorandum for the Study of Acculturation." *American Anthropologist* 38(1):149–52.
11. Malinowski, Bronislaw. 1929. "Practical Anthropology." *Africa* 2(1):22–38, p. 23.
12. United Nations. 1945. Charter of the United Nations. www.un.org/en/documents/charter/index.shtml (accessed January 2010).
13. United Nations. 1948. The Universal Declaration of Human Rights. www.un.org/en/documents/udhr/ (accessed January 2010).
14. United Nations. 1966. United Nations International Covenant on Civil and Political Rights. www.hrweb.org/legal/cpr.html (accessed January 2010).
15. International Labour Organization. 1957. *C107 Indigenous and Tribal Populations Convention, 1957*. www.ilo.org/ilolex/cgi-lex/convde.pl?C107 (accessed January 2010).
16. (ILR 1954:424) ILR (International Labour Review). 1954. "Reports and Enquiries: The Second Session of the ILO Committee of Experts on Indigenous Labour." *International Labour Review* 70(5):418–41, 424.
17. Beaglehole, Ernest. 1954. "Cultural Factors in Economic and Social Change." *International Labour Review* 69(5):415–32.
18. Beaglehole, 1954. "Cultural Factors . . ." 424.
19. IWGIA (International Work Group for Indigenous Affairs). 1989. *Yearbook 1988: Indigenous Peoples and Human Rights*. 184–85. Copenhagen: IWGIA.
20. Gray, Andrew. 1990. "The ILO Meeting at the UN, Geneva, June 1989: Report on International Labour Organisation Revision of Convention 107." IWGIA Yearbook 1989, 173–91. Copenhagen: IWGIA.
21. United Nations. Permanent Forum on Indigenous Issues (UNPFII). 2010. *United Nations Declaration on the Rights of Indigenous Peoples*. UN General Assembly Resolution 61/295. Sept. 13. www.un.org/esa/socdev/unpfii/en/drip.html (accessed January 2010).
22. Cleveland, David A., and Stephen C. Murray. 1997. "The World's Crop Genetic Resources and the Rights of Indigenous Farmers." *Current Anthropology* 38(4):477–515.
23. Denevan, William. 1976. *The Native Population of the Americas in 1492*. Madison: University of Wisconsin Press.
24. Ribeiro, Darcy. 1957. *Culturas e Linguas Indigenas do Brasil*. Seprata de Educação e Ciencias Soçais. No. 6. Rio de Janeiro: Centro Brasileiro de Pesquisas Educaçionais.
25. Davis, Shelton H. 1977. *Victims of the Miracle: Development and the Indians of Brazil*. Cambridge, Eng.: Cambridge University Press.
26. Belaunde-Terry, Fernando. 1965. *Peru's Own Conquest*. Lima: American Studies Press.

27. (Bodley 1970,1972b) Bodley, John H. 1970. *Campa Socio-Economic Adaptation*. Ph.D. Dissertation, University of Oregon. Ann Arbor, MI: University Microfilms, Bodley, John H. 1972b. *Tribal Survival in the Amazon: The Campa Case*. IWGIA (International Work Group for Indigenous Affairs) Document, no. 5. Copenhagen: IWGIA.

28. ONERN (Oficina Nacional de Evaluación e Integración de los Recursos Naturales). 1968. *Inventario, Evaluación e Integración de los Recursos Naturales de la Zona del Rio Tambo-Gran Pajonal*. Lima: ONERN.

29. Bodley, John H. 1990. *Victims of Progress*. 3rd ed. Mountain View, CA: Mayfield.

30. Varese, Stefano. 1972. "Inter-Ethnic Relations in the Selva of Peru." In *The Situation of the Indian in South America*, edited by W. Dostal, pp. 115–39. Geneva: World Council of Churches.

31. Bodley, John H. 1972b. *Tribal Survival in the Amazon*.

32. Bodley, John H. 1975. *Victims of Progress*. 1st ed., 169; reprinted in Bodley, John H. 2008. Victims of Progress, 5th ed., 293–94.

33. UNPFII. 2010. *United Nations Declaration on the Rights of Indigenous Peoples*. www.un.org/esa/socdev/unpfii/en/drip.html.

34. D'Ans, André-Marcel. 1972. "Les Tribus Indigènes du Parc National du Manu." Proceedings of the 39th *International Americanists Congress* 4:95–100, D'Ans, André-Marcel. 1981. "Encounter in Peru." In *Is God an American? An Anthropological Perspective on the Missionary Work of the Summer Institute of Linguistics*. Edited by Søren Hvalkof and Peter Aaby, pp. 145–62. Copenhagen and London: IWGIA and Survival International.

35. Smith, Richard Chase. 1985. "A Search for Unity within Diversity: Peasant Unions, Ethnic Federations, and Indianist Movements in the Andean Republics." In *Native Peoples and Economic Development: Six Case Studies from Latin America*, Theodore Macdonald Jr., ed., pp. 5–38. Cultural Survival Occasional Paper 16, p. 16.

36. AIDESEP. 2005. "La Voz de los Apus." AIDESEP. Voz Indígena No. 27, 6-15; CECONSEC (Central de Comunidades Nativas de la Selva Central del Peru). FECONAU (Federación de Comunidades Nativas del Ucayali), el CAH, (Consejo Aguaruna Huambisa), and el Congreso Amuesha.

37. AIDESEP, Asociación Interétnica de Dessarrollo de la Selva Peruana. www.aidesep.org.pe/.

38. Swenson, Sally and Jeremy Narby. 1986. "The Pichis-Palcazu Special Project in Peru: A Consortium of International Lenders." *Cultural Survival Quarterly* 10(1):19–24.

39. Amazonia Indigena. 1981. "Pronunciamiento Sobre el Projecto Especial Pichis-Palcazu." *Amazonia Indigena* 1(3):3–5.

40. Smith, Richard Chase. 1977. *The Amuesha-Yanachaga Project, Peru: Ecology and Ethnicity in the Central Jungles of Peru*. Survival International Document 3. London: Survival International.

41. Goodland, Robert. 1982. *Tribal Peoples and Economic Development: Human Ecological Considerations*. Washington, DC: International Bank for Reconstruction and Development/World Bank.

42. Swenson and Narby 1986. "The Pichis-Palcazu Special Project . . ." :24.

43. Gorriti, Gustavo. 1990. "Terror in the Andes: The Flight of the Ashaninkas. *New York Times Magazine,* Dec. 2, Section 6: 40-48, 65–72; Weber, Hanne. 1998. "The Salt of the Montana: Interpreting Indigenous Activism in the Rain Forest." *Cultural Anthropology* 13(3):382–413.

44. Gray, Andrew. n.d. *Freedom and Territory: Slavery in the Peruvian Amazon*. Unpublished Manuscript; Hvalkof, Søren Hvalkof. 1990. "Inscription and Titling of Native Commuinities in the Ucayali Department." In *Supervision Report on Land Titling Project, Peruvian Amazon.* Report to IWGIA, Copenhagen.

45. Gray, Andrew. n.d. *Freedom and Territory*, 24.

46. Instituto de Bien Común. www.ibcperu.org/ (accessed January 2010); Smigh, Richard Chase, Margarita Benavides, Mario Pariona, and Ermeto Tuesta. 2003. "Mapping the Past and the Future: Geomatics and Indigenous Territories in the Peruvian Amazon. Human Organization 62(4):357–68.

47. CEDIA, Centro para el Desarrollo del Indígena Amazónico. www.cedia.org.pe/index.php (accessed January 2010).

48. Benavides, Margarita. 2005. "Conservación, Derechos Indígas y Poder en la Gestión de los Bienes Communes: El Caso de la Reserve Communal El Sira en la Amazonía Peruana." Originally presented at the Inter national Association for the Study of the Commons." Global Meeting, Oaxaca City, Mexico. 2004. www .ibcperu.org/doc/isis/5316.pdf, (accessed January 2010); ParksWatch. 2003. *Profile of Protected Area: Peru El Sira Communal Reserve*. www.parkswatch.org/park-profiles/pdf/escr_eng.pdf (accessed January 2010).

49. Inter-American Foundation. 2009. Peru: Award by Year. www.iaf.gov/grants/awards_year_en.asp?country_id=17&gr_year=2009.

50. Murphy, Robert, and Julian Steward. 1956. "Trappers and Trappers: Parallel Processes in Acculturation." *Economic Development and Culture Change* 4:335–55.

51. UCN, International Union for the Conservation of Nature. 2004. *Indigenous Peoples Living in Voluntary Isolation and Conservation of Nature in the Amazon Region and Chaco*. RES 3.056. www.iucn.org/congress/2004/members/Individual_Res_Rec_Eng/wcc3_res_056.pdf.

52. Stavenhagen, Rodolfo. 2006. *Report of the Special Rapporteur on the Situation of Human Rights and Fundamental Freedoms of Indigenous People.* Addendum. Mission to Ecuador. Human Rights Council. A/HRC/4/32/Add.2 28 December, 23. http://daccessdds.un.org/doc/UNDOC/GEN/G07/100/29/PDF/G0710029.pdf?OpenElement; United Nations, Permanent Forum on Indigenous Issues. 2007. *Report on the Sixth Session* (14-25 May 2007). Economic and Social Council Official Records, Supplement No. 23. E/2007/43 E/C.19/2007/12, Articles 39-42.

53. Gamboa Balbín, César. 2006. "Legal Status of Territorial Reserves for the Protection of Isolated Indigenous Peoples in Peru." The Field Museum. *Rapid Biological Inventory No. 17. Peru: Sierra del Divisor.* Pp. 210–16. http://fm2.fieldmuseum.org/rbi/results_per17.asp (accessed January 2010); Monteferri, Bruno, Elisa Canziani, Juan Luis Dammert, and José Carlos Silva. 2009. Conservación, Industrias Extractivas y Reservas Indígenas: El Proceso de Categorización de la Zona Reservada Sierra del Divisor. Cuaderno de Investigacin No. 2. Lima: Sociedad de Derecho Ambiental. www.spda.org.pe/portal/ver-publicacion.php?id=134.

54. USAID, Brazil. 2010. *Ethno-Environmental Protection of Isolated Peoples in the Brazilian Amazon.* http://brazil.usaid.gov/en/node/101 (accessed January 2010). FUNAI (Fundação Nacional do Índio), CTI (Centro de Trabalho Indigenista).

55. CIPIACI (Comité Indígena Internacional para la Protección da los Pueblos en Aislamiento y Contacto Inicial de la Amazonía, el Gran Chaco, y la Regió Oriental de Paraguay). www.cipiaci.org/home.htm (accessed January 2010).

56. Instituto de Bien Común. 2009. www.ibcperu.org/presentacion/indigenas-aislamiento.php.

57. Corris, Peter. 1968. Aborigines and Europeans in Western Victoria. Occasional Papers in Aboriginal Studies, no. 12, Ethnohistory Series, no. 1. Canberra: Australian Institute of Aboriginal Studies.

58. Price, A. G. 1950. *White Settlers and Native Peoples.* London: Cambridge University Press, 107–108.

59. Lefroy, Archdeacon. 1912. *The Future of Australian Aborigines.* Report of the Thirteenth Meeting of the Australasian Association for the Advancement of Science, Sydney, pp. 453–54.

60. ANZAAS (Australia and New Zealand Association for the Advancement of Science). 1914. "Welfare of Aborigines Committee." Report of the Fourteenth Meeting of the Australasian Association for the Advancement of Science, 450–52.

61. Wood Jones, Frederic. 1928. "The Claims of the Australian Aborigine." *Report of the Eighteenth Australasian Association for the Advancement of Science* 18:497–519.

62. Wood Jones, Frederic. 1928. "The Claims of the Australian Aborigine," 497–519.

63. Thomson, Donald F. 1938. *Recommendations of Policy in Native Affairs in the Northern Territory of Australia,* no. 56.-F.2945. Canberra: Parliament of the Commonwealth of Australia.

64. Elkin, A. P. 1934. "Anthropology and the Future of the Australian Aborigines." *Oceania* 5(1):1–18.

65. Elkin, 1934, Anthropology and the Future of the Australian . . . ,:7.

66. Elkin, 1934, Anthropology and the Future of the Australian . . . ,:3.

67. Hasluck, Paul M. 1953. "The Future of the Australian Aborigine." Twenty-Ninth Meeting of the Australian and New Zealand Association for the Advancement of Science, Sydney. *Australian and New Zealand Association for the Advancement of Science* 29:155–65, 163.

68. Aboriginal and Torres Strait Islander Act, 2005. www.austlii.edu.au/au/legis/cth/consol_act/aatsia2005359.txt.

69. Australian Bureau of Statistics. 2008. 4713.0.55.001—Population Characteristics, Aboriginal and Torres Strait Islander Australians, Australia, 2006.

70. Northern Territory, Department of Housing, Local Government and Regional Services. 2008. *Local Government Regional Management Plan, Northern Region.* www.dlgh.nt.gov.au/__data/assets/pdf_file/0016/41506/NORTHERN_REGION_RMP_Aug_08.pdf.

71. Dodson, Mark. 2008. "Foreword" In Hunt, Janet, Diane Smith, Stephanie Garling, and Will Sanders, eds. *Contested Governance: Culture, Power and Institutions in Indigenous Australia.*, pp. xvii-xx. Centre for Aboriginal Economic Policy Research. Research Monograph. No. 29. Canberra: Australia National University E Press, p. xviii. http://epress.anu.edu.au/caepr_series/no_29/pdf/whole_book.pdf. Dodson is here citing comments by Dr. Neil Sterritt, a Gitxsan leader from Canada, as well as findings of the Harvard Project on American Indian Economic Development.

72. Especially well-known published works by Jon Altman, Les Hiatt, Betty Meehan, and Marshall Sahlins, but many other anthropologists have done important work in this area as well. Much recent work is available online from the Centre for Aboriginal Economic Policy Research as monography, www.anu.edu.au/caepr/mono.php, and topical papers, www.anu.edu.au/caepr/topical.php.

73. Northern Territory Government. 2008. *Maningrida Study.* Department of Business, Economic and Regional Development (DBERD). www.nt.gov.au/d/Content/File/p/rd/Mngrda%20Study-08_04.pdf.

74. Australia, Department of the Environment, Water, Heritage and the Arts. www.environment.gov.au/indigenous/index.html.

75. Altman, Jon. 2009. "Contestations over Development." In Altman, Jon, and David Martin, eds. *Power, Culture, Economy: Indigenous Australians and Min-*

ing, pp. 1–15. Centre for Aboriginal Economic Policy Research. Canberra: Australia National University E Press. http://epress.anu.edu.au/caepr series/no_30/pdf/whole_book.pdf; Altman, Jon. 2009. "Indigenous Communities, Miners and the State in Australia." In Altman, Jon and David Martin, eds. *Power, Culture, Economy: Indigenous Australians and Mining*, pp. 17–49. Centre for Aboriginal Economic Policy Research. Canberra: Australia National University E Press.

76. Northern Land Council. 2009. *Annual Report 2008–2009*. www.nlc.org.au/html/wht_pub.html.

77. Corporations (Aboriginal and Torres Strait Islander Act) 2006. www.comlaw.gov.au/ComLaw/Management.nsf/lookupindexpagesbyid/IP200626899?OpenDocument.

78. Australia, Office of the Registrar of Indigenous Corporations. 2009. *Yearbook 2008–09*, p. 16, Table 4. www.orac.gov.au/html/publications/Yearbooks/Yearbook2008-09_72dpi_104pp.pdf; Bawinanga Aboriginal Corporation website www.bawinanga.com.au/index.htm (accessed January 2010).

79. Altman, Jon. 2008. "Different Governance for Difference: The Bawinanga Aboriginal Corporation." In Hunt, Janet, Diane Smith, Stephanie Garling, and Will Sanders, eds. *Contested Governance: Culture, Power and Institutions in Indigenous Australia.*, pp. 177–203. Centre for Aboriginal Economic Policy Research. Research Monograph. No. 29. Canberra: Australia National University E Press.

CHAPTER 14

Small Nations Solving Global Problems

Figure 14.0. Parliament building (on left) in Rouseau, the capital city of the Commonwealth of Dominica.

LEARNING OBJECTIVES

AFTER STUDYING THIS CHAPTER YOU SHOULD BE ABLE TO DO the following:

1. List the defining features of a small nation.
2. Explain why small nations are well suited for sustainability.
3. Make specific comparisons between small and large nations on several dimensions related to sustainability and human well-being.
4. Explain why Pacific Island small nations are especially concerned about global warming.
5. Understand how income, wealth, and social power are distributed in at least one small nation and relate this distribution to sustainability.

6. Explain how human well-being and sustainability are measured cross-nationally.

From an anthropological power and scale perspective it can be seen that the fate of humanity is strongly influenced by three variables deeply rooted in human nature and culture: (1) the scale at which people organize their sociocultural systems; (2) how people control other people, and (3) how we use culture to deceive each other about what is really happening. Peoples who live in **small nations** with small-scale sociocultural systems can more easily limit the power of their leaders, because they may retain the power to act in their own self-interest, thereby maximizing

503

their personal freedom and minimizing the dangers of system failure. Peoples in small nations can also more clearly understand the practical realities of the physical world and are more likely to live within the limits that nature imposes, because they directly experience the effects of their practices. Peoples who allow their systems to grow continuously, who allow their leaders to become rulers, and who allow themselves to be deceived about the realities of their society and the physical world have produced unsustainable imperialist and commercial worlds.

Fully two-thirds of the world's politically independent states are small nations, each with fewer then 10 million people, yet in total, the people in small nations constitute barely 5 percent of global population. The reality is that these few people have for decades been quietly developing practical solutions to global problems that can successfully prevent, reduce, or mitigate problems of environment, poverty, and conflict within their own territories. At the other extreme, the 5 percent of the world's people who are the top individual wealth holders and primary decision makers have left the world a disaster zone on the brink of catastrophe. Leaders of large nations, especially the global superpowers, and the global elite in general have directed the global economy and most enjoyed its benefits, but they have failed to solve the most crucial global problems that confront all of humanity. Many small-nation solutions are already in place and they are working, but they will ultimately fail if large nations and the dominant decision makers continue to mishandle the world. Small-nation solutions are not yet widely recognized by world leaders, because small nations are small, because the present world leaders view them as peripheral to the global system, and because small nation solutions are a major departure from the prevailing path of elite-directed economic globalization. Given the state of the world, it is time to consider dramatic alternatives. Small nations are models that larger nations can follow, because they work where large nations have failed.

DOMINICA: NATURE ISLAND OF THE CARIBBEAN

Although I had long been concerned with scale as a crucial sociocultural variable, most of my field research had focused on the scale extremes looking at either tribal societies or America and the global system. That changed when I visited the very small Caribbean micronation of Dominica in 2007 at the invitation of Robert and Marsha Quinlan, who were running a cultural anthropology field school in Dominica and who

had conducted village-level medical and ethnographic research there since 1993.[1] My primary interest was in viewing Dominica as a total national system in its larger setting.

Dominica is a small volcanic island in the Windward Islands of the Lesser Antilles in the Eastern Caribbean, situated within sight of the French islands of Guadeloupe and Martinique (see figures 14.1 and 14.2). It is about 30 miles long and 12 air miles wide at the widest points, but volcanic peaks reaching to nearly 5,000 feet dominate the rugged and heavily forested interior, and there are very few tourist-class beaches. The island is justly famous for having the best-preserved tropical forest in the Eastern Caribbean and still supports two endemic, critically endangered wild parrot species, one of which, the Imperial parrot, *Amazona imperialis*, is featured on Dominica's coat of arms. At the time of my visit the total population was estimated at about 72,000 people, including 2,000 indigenous Caribs.

Dominica was originally settled by indigenous peoples from South America, and when Columbus visited in 1493 Dominica was occupied by village gardeners and fishing peoples known as Kalinago and speaking Arawak and Carib languages with their closest relatives in greater Amazonia. Dominica was later visited by Spanish, English, and French adventurers, missionaries, and colonists, and for a time it was treated as a neutral territory and remained in Kalinago control. By the 1780s the British were fully in control and established a plantation economy variously based on coffee or sugar and imported African slave labor. The British made Dominica a colony in 1805. Slavery was officially abolished in 1834, and although settlers attempted to maintain large estates, the former slave population successfully gained control over the government and the land. The Commonwealth of Dominica has been a politically independent state since gaining independence from Britain in 1978.[2]

Dominica's Successful Small Economy and Small Government

Dominica is especially interesting because it ranked number 4 in the **Happy Planet Index** (HPI) in 2006.[3] The HPI is a composite measure of human well-being developed by the London-based New Economics Foundation. An advantage of the HPI is that it combines subjective, survey-based measures of personal satisfaction with life, or self-reported happiness, with the objective measure of average life expectancy to produce a measure of happy life years (HLY). The

Figure 14.1.   Fishing village of Scotts Head at the south tip of Dominica, 2007.

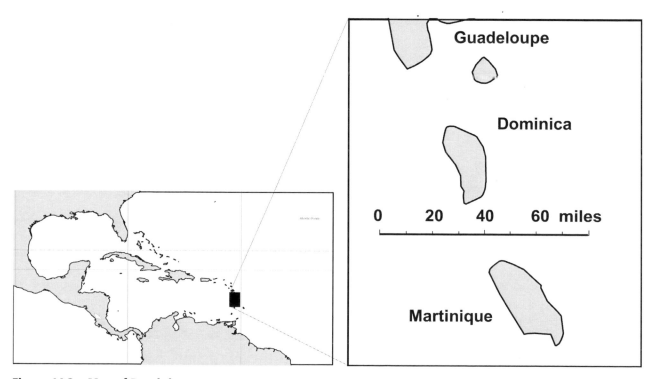

Figure 14.2.   Map of Dominica.

HLY measure is then factored together with the per-capita ecological footprint to produce a single index number to reflect life satisfaction and the consumption demand on nature that is required to support it. Significantly Dominica ranked number four out of 179 nations. This was due to Dominica's high reported life satisfaction as well as its high life expectancy of 76 years. This was amplified by a very low per-capita ecological footprint of under 2 global hectares, compared with the average American footprint, which approaches 10 global hectares.

Dominica also ranks "high" on the United Nations **Human Development Index** (HDI), which takes into account health, education, and income distribution. What was remarkable about these very positive scores was that Dominica has a very small economy and is ranked by the World Bank as only an "upper middle"–income country with a purchasing power parity (PPP) income of just $8,296 per capita in 2007. It is a relatively underdeveloped country. If exchange rate gross domestic product (GDP) is used, per-capita GDP drops to just $3,854. The PPP value gives Domi-nica credit for low prices for locally produced basic goods and indirectly for its strong subsistence economy, but when Dominicans engage in global trade, the exchange rate is to their disadvantage.

Although its local businesses are small (see figure 14.3), Dominica is certainly not unconnected to the global economy. The country has no stock market and thus no market capitalization ranking, but four publicly traded businesses were headquartered in Dominica: Dominica Coconut Products Ltd., Dominica Electricity Services, the National Bank of Dominica Ltd., and Dominica Brewery and Beverages Ltd. These were listed on the Eastern Caribbean Securities Exchange on the island nation of Saint Kitts. The largest commercial bank in the country had assets of US$246 million, producing revenues of nearly US$22 million in 2007. Dominica is a member of the Organization of Eastern Caribbean States, and its currency, the Eastern Caribbean dollar, is shared with seven other Eastern Caribbean island governments linked by the Eastern Caribbean Bank with total assets of US$892 million in 2009.

Figure 14.3.   Dominican small business. A roadside cassava (manioc) bread bakery, baker, and vendor in the Carib Reserve, 2007.

The development paradox of Dominica is that in spite of their high rankings for human well-being, according to a special report published by the Caribbean Development Bank in 2003, 29 percent of households and 39 percent of the population were officially "income poor" measured against a poverty-line income of US$1,260 per adult per year.[4] Fifteen percent were considered "indigent" or "very poor" with incomes under US$740. The bank report elaborated on the apparent paradox, noting that the people themselves, "…speak of good infrastructure, housing and natural environment, adequate supplies of water, excellent access to health and education, and a tradition of well integrated, self-supporting communities. Many strongly decry the idea that they are poor indicating a clear lack of correlation, in this instance, between income poverty and well-being."[5]

Furthermore, the report noted that the country was a democracy; there was little crime, no human rights abuses, children were educated, food plentiful, water clean, health good overall. Conditions sounded quite good. There were health clinics throughout the country with no access problems; free contraception; mass immunizations; and a low incidence or nonexistence of poverty-linked health problems. The report also found that most people owned their own homes, and they noted, "Traditional healthy diets of ground provisions and fish continue to be popular and there is little evidence of obesity or malnutrition." Nearly 90 percent of those considered "poor" owned their own homes, and nearly half owned televisions and phones; a third of those who were officially "not poor" owned vehicles.

My own observations verified these upbeat descriptions, with some qualifications. I found Dominicans to be healthy, self-confident people, who seemed in control of their lives. Only about twelve men in the capital were considered to be "homeless." One of these homeless men told me he lost his job in New York and sometimes slept in the city park. Many Dominicans lived abroad and sent remittances to home. Nevertheless, local businesses were thriving. There were virtually no fast-food franchises and no shopping malls. The farmers' market and street vendors were the major suppliers of fresh produce in the capital, and the entire island was a nation of small business owners and small farmers and fishermen. Rural families are strongly matrifocal, and women have an important role in the subsistence economy. Women also market their produce to other islands.

I thought that perhaps part of Dominica's success might be found in the country's founding documents and spent most of one morning in the capital city locating a print copy of the 1978 Dominican Constitution as amended through 1984. The Preamble connected human rights and economic rights, social justice, and belief in God, declaring: "Whereas the People of Dominica (a) have affirmed that the Commonwealth of Dominica is founded upon principles that acknowledge the supremacy of God, faith in fundamental human rights and freedoms, the position of the family in a society of free men and free institutions, the dignity of the human person, and the equal and inalienable rights with which all members of the human family are endowed by their Creator."

Part (b) of the preamble is so important that I quote it in full:

> [Dominica is founded on principles that] (b). respect the principles of social justice and therefore believe that the operation of the economic system should result in so distributing the material resources of the community as to subserve the common good, that there should be adequate means of livelihood for all, that labour should not be exploited or forced by economic necessity to operate in inhumane conditions but that there should be opportunity for advancement on the basis of recognition of merit, ability and integrity.

Clearly, Dominican people are very conscious of how their economic system is organized, and they want it to be fair and to serve human interests. That economic rights and social justice were so strong is perhaps not surprising for a government controlled by the descendants of freed slaves. Governments have a major presence on the island, and people are very politically engaged. There are ten local parish governments ranging in size from about 1,500 to just over 10,000 people, in addition to three urban councils, the Carib Council, and thirty-seven village councils. Rousseau, the capital and largest city, has fewer than 20,000 people. There is a president and prime minister and a thirty-member House of Assembly. There are four political parties.

Dominica and Kauai Comparisons

A small nation like Dominica demonstrates that it matters how an economy is organized, and that if well distributed, even very small financial flows through households, businesses, and government can meet human needs and serve the public interest. A careful comparison between Dominica and the Hawaiian island county of Kauai highlights some crucial differences. I make this comparison because I visited Kauai in 2004 and was immediately impressed by the differences when I reached Dominica. Both islands are superficially very similar and are ideal for a controlled comparison. Both are tropical islands with small land areas and small populations of similar magnitudes (see table 14.1). Both have indigenous populations and similar histories of conquest, plantations, and economies with the introduction of imported laborers. Both consider the development of nature tourism to be important development goals. The big contrast is that as part of the United States, Kauai has a highly developed commercial economy. Both islands have high life expectancy, but Kauai ranks 150th in the HPI because of its high environmental footprint, reflecting its large, energy-intensive economy. Kauai has a $2 billion economy, measured as total personal income, in comparison with Dominica's PPP GDP of under $1 billion, or $279 million in exchange rate dollars. Given their respective populations, this gives Kauai a per-capita income three to eight times greater than Dominica's. The annual budgets of each government are approximately the same, but on Dominica it represents 25 percent of the PPP GDP, or two-thirds of the exchange rate GDP, whereas on Kauai it is only 8 percent of total personal income. This means that the private commercial economy is much more important on Kauai.

Paradoxically, even though Kauai has a highly developed economy, a baseline report on Kauai in 2000 found that more than a third of Kauai households were not making a living wage, allowing them to qualify as "economically needy."[6] This is about the same level of official poverty as in Dominica, but the crucial difference was that Dominicans had access to land and were maintaining a viable subsistence economy. Much of Kauai's agricultural land was in large, privately held properties. The outlying seventy-square-mile island of Niihau is owned by two families. The effects of Kauai's historic plantation era have not disappeared, whereas Dominica effectively redistributed its land to

its residents. Development on Kauai has not benefited everyone.

Given the prevailing high property values and low wages, fewer than half of Kauai's households were homeowners in 2000.[7] Many housing units were second homes for nonresidents, or were rented to tourists. This means that how money and resources are actually distributed in a regional economy may be more important than total income and wealth. Growth appears to be less important than the actual distribution of ownership and benefits. For example, although tourism is important in the economies of both islands, in Dominica hotels are primarily small and locally owned. The largest hotel has only 70 rooms. In contrast, there are many large hotels on Kauai, and the largest are likely to be owned by very large corporations. For example, the Sheraton Kauai Resort on the south coast of Kauai has 394 rooms and is owned by Starwood Hotels and Resorts Worldwide, headquartered in New York. Starwood owned 53 hotels with 18,000 rooms worldwide, and produced total revenues of nearly $6 billion in 2007. Its Kauai Resort produced an estimated $50 million in revenue, given its average returns per room. Starwood's largest owner was Fidelity Management and Research (FMR). This connects Kauai with the global plutonomy. FMR was the second-largest owner-manager in the global stock market backbone discussed in chapter 12, was dominant in 32 national stock markets, and managed global assets of $1 trillion. It was itself privately owned and run by American billionaire Ned Johnson.

The size and ownership of retail establishments on each island also showed significant contrasts. For example, Dominica's largest retailer had revenues of just $20 million and was locally owned. The Walmart on Kauai produced estimated revenues of $40 million, but 40 percent of its profits went to the five billionaire Walton families living in Arkansas, Texas, and Wyoming. Walmart's largest institutional owner was again FMR, and it received nearly 3 percent of Walmart's profits. It is likely that very little of Walmart profit would have gone to Kauai residents, and many of

Table 14.1. Dominica & Kauai Comparisons, Area, Population, Economy, Government Budgets, 2007

	Area Miles 2	Population	Economy	$ Per Capita	Government Budget	Government % of GDP
Dominica						
GDP (PPP)	291	72,386	$712,100,000	9,838	$185,000,000	26
GDP (Ex)	291	72,386	$279,000,000	3,854	$185,000,000	66
Kauai, 2007	622	62,800	$2,093,500,000	33,336	$171,092,934	8

Walmart's Kauai employees were likely among those receiving subliving wages. These are significant cultural differences that represent very different ways of organizing a commercial system.

SMALL-NATION WORLD: CROSS-NATIONAL PERSPECTIVES

The nations of the world can be ranked for analytic purposes into seven orders of magnitude by population size from small to large as follows: (1) nano-states of a few thousand people; (2) micro-states with tens of thousands; (3) mini-states with hundreds of thousands; (4) small states with a few million; (5) large states with tens of millions; (6) mega-states with hundreds of millions; and finally (7) giga-states with billions of people.

For general reference, the first four ranks can conveniently be merged as small nations, and the large-, mega-, and giga-states can all be called large nations. In 2007 more than a third of the world's 6.6 billion people were crowded into just two giga-states, China and India, both inheritors of ancient imperial world great cultural traditions. Nine more mega-states in descending order, the United States, Indonesia, Brazil, Pakistan, Bangladesh, the Russian Federation, Nigeria, Japan, and Mexico added a billion and a half more people, such that just eleven giga- and mega-states contained more than 4 billion people, 60 percent of the world (see figure 14.4). Placing 4 billion people under the leadership for just eleven governments greatly narrowed the possibilities for sociocultural system innovation to implement sustainable development at a time when global systems seemed to be approaching scale limits of many sorts. Small nations numbered just over 400 million people, comparable to world population in AD 1200, but they lived in some 181 societies in diverse territories scattered across the globe, often in peripheral places that had little strategic or material value to the large-nation world (see figure 14.5). Their relative obscurity made it possible for each small nation to be its own unique experiment in sustainable-development problem solving, relatively free of the political and ideological conflicts of larger nations.

Small Nations as a Cultural Type

Small nations are so numerous and so diverse that any useful cross-national investigation requires some system of classification into types that might prove meaningful for producing and maintaining human well-being and sustainability. By definition for our purposes small nations have: (1) fewer than 10 million people; (2) a territorial jurisdiction; (3) a functional sociocultural system; (4) consensus decision making; and (5) the power to manage their own internal affairs.

As appropriate for specific problems, they can also be distinguished by degree of political autonomy; by scale of total economy; by isolation, or travel time from global cities; by per-capita income level; by degree of integration with the global economy; and by degree of cultural homogeneity.

Some small nations are fully independent states, some are highly autonomous subunits of larger nations, or they enjoy varying degrees of free association with larger states. Small nations are adapted to local conditions, but in every successful case small nations have a territory, a functional sociocultural system, consensus decision making, and the power to manage their own affairs. The U.S. government's National Geospatial-Intelligence Agency lists 270 "Countries, Dependencies, and Areas of Special Sovereignty," but only 192 of these are considered "states" and the 78 nonstates include several uninhabited islands.[8] Taking a somewhat broader view, the UN Population Division publishes population figures on 228 "countries or areas." The World Bank ranks only 210 "economies," and the World Almanac listed only 194 "nations" in 2007. My own expanded list of 260 "nations" includes 79 large nations and 181 small nations (see table 14.2). This small-nation count is expanded with a sample of partly autonomous subnational "nations" such as Corsica off France; the Basque Country, Catalonia, and Galicia in Spain; Scotland and Wales in the United Kingdom; and the indigenous nations of Nunavut in Canada and Kuna Yala in Panama. Many more subnational indigenous nations could of course be included. For example the U.S. Census lists 756 Indian Reservations, Pueblos, Rancherias, Communities, and Colonies, and there are some 600 Canadian "First Nations," but I have not included any of these internal nations in my list of 181 small nations.

Figure 14.5 shows how these 181 small nations are distributed across the world. They are clustered in Europe, Africa, Central America and the Caribbean, and the Pacific, but there are also several small-nation islands in the Pacific and Indian Ocean. The map uses transparent circular outlines to strip away the 79 large nations that contain 94 percent of the world's people and that effectively overshadow small nations. Many European small nations exist in the midst of some of the largest nations in the world, whereas others such

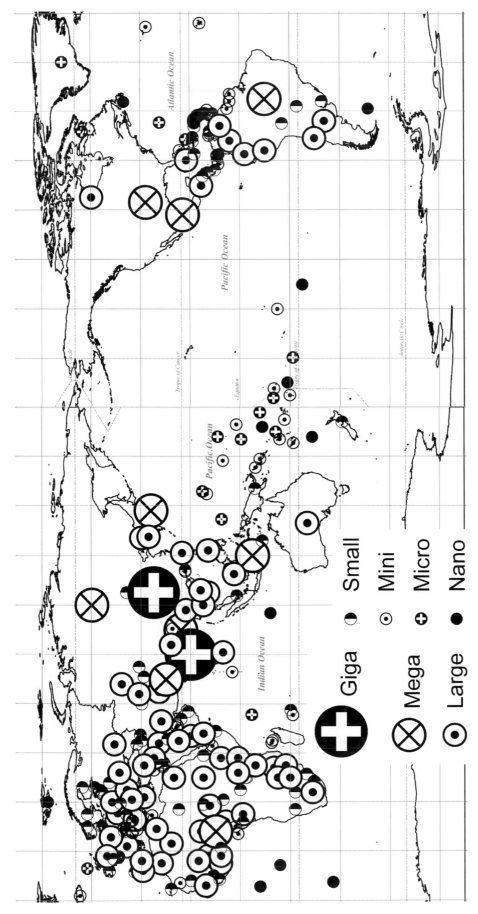

Figure 14.4. Map of 260 countries and 6.6 billion people in the commercial world by population scale, 2007.

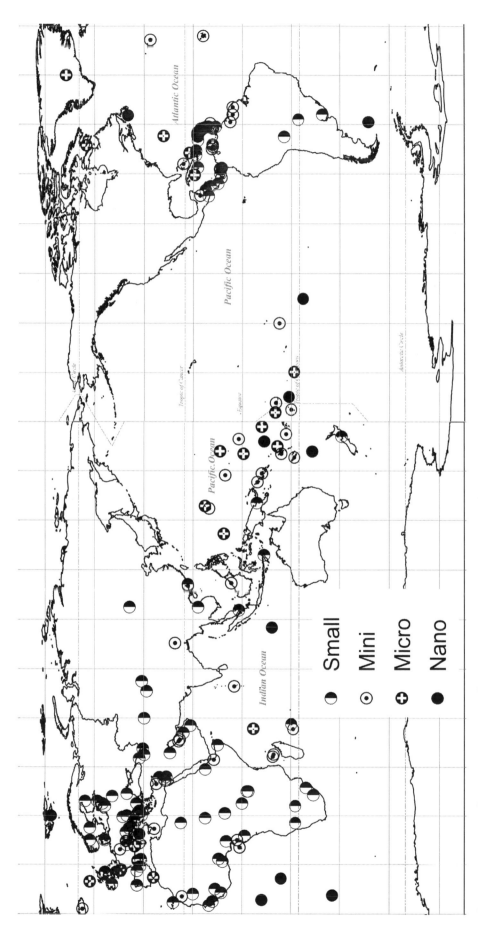

Figure 14.5.   Map of 181 small nations of the world, with 424 million people, 2007.

Table 14.2. 260 Nations by Scale Ranks, 2007

Scale	Nations		Population	Average Size	Percent Nations	Percent Population
79 Large Nations 30%	Giga	2	2,451,718,042	1,225,859,021		37
	Mega	9	1,553,578,155	172,619,795	3	23
	Large	68	2,199,049,958	32,338,970	26	33
181 Small Nations 70%	Small	84	405,492,470	4,827,291	32	6
	Mini	47	17,212,559	366,225	18	0
	Micro	33	1,524,784	46,206	13	0
	Nano	17	59,388	3,493	7	0
		260	6,628,635,356	00	100	100

as the nanoscale nation of Saint Helena, which is 1,200 miles from the African mainland and has no airport, are among the places most remote from global economic centers.

The small-nation concept used here is based on scale theory and therefore uses a strict population-size limit, but otherwise the definition of small nation is intentionally kept open and flexible, because the purpose is to consider the human problem-solving possibilities offered by a maximum range of socio-cultural diversity. For example, maintaining a limited-dependency arrangement with a larger nation, or joining an association or federation of nations, can be a huge financial advantage. Many small nations have no military establishments, because they face no military threats, or they rely on defense agreements with other nations for emergencies.

Small nations differ from large nations in structure in important ways; because they are small, they have small economies, and because they are also democratic, wealth and power are likely to be less concentrated in small nations than in larger nations. In the late 1950s American economist Simon Kuznets (1901–1985), who helped introduce the use of gross national product (GNP) for national economic accounting, examined small nations as separate experiments in economic growth, defining small as a population of 10 million or less.[9] He conjectured that small nations would have less-diversified economies, smaller land areas, and fewer natural resources than large nations with larger economies. He noted that small national economies are limited by their small domestic markets in relation to the efficiency scales of production units for certain industries, and could not, for example, support automotive or aircraft manufacturing industries. Likewise, they are likely to be more dependent on foreign trade than larger nations, and they will have fewer trading partners. Kuznets argued that in small nations it would be more efficient for

service industries requiring direct face-to-face interaction, such as public administration, business services, education, and construction, to be carried out domestically, so they would not be disadvantaged by their small size. The needs of national defense, assuming international anarchy, might be unbearably costly for very small nations, thus encouraging them to form defensive alliances with other nations.

An overview of contemporary small nations shows many of the patterns that Kuznets predicted. Government functions often dominate small-nation economies, and the provision of infrastructure and social services are often the primary functions of their governments. There are police, judges, and courts but often no armies, or only very small defense establishments, no defense industries, and no weapons of mass destruction. In the smallest small nations there may be few for-profit, corporately organized businesses, or large business partnerships. Instead, government-owned business enterprises, small businesses, or co-operatively owned businesses are often prominent. There may be no stock exchanges, little national advertising, no chemical or plastics industries, and no heavy industries, but communications and transportation infrastructures may be well developed. As noted above, small nations often score well on indices of human well-being and may have little visible poverty, even when they have low per-capita incomes, demonstrating that economic growth measured as GDP is not the only development path.

National economies can be ranked by size of economy from nano-economies measured in tens of millions of dollars to giga-economies with over 10 trillion PPP dollars. Small economies would be economies of under $100 billion and would correspond to small nations by population. Generally, larger populations have larger economies, and not surprisingly 75 percent of countries with small economies are also small nations, and only 10 small nations have large economies. So the question is, can a small nation also have a small economy and still produce a decent standard of living? In fact, the Human Development Report for 2005 listed 36 small nations with small economies and high HDIs. This shows that neither national populations nor economies need to grow large for people to have good lives. The next question is, what is the relationship between size of population and economy and sustainability?

There are many kinds of small nations, and not all are successful. We will look for the successes to find out what sociocultural systems can best work for people, but unsustainable small nations can also be illuminating, because the specific reasons for failure may be very clear. Small nations cross-cut the world's major languages, cultural traditions, value systems, and income levels and thereby demonstrate that global problems can be solved in many different ways. Indigenous-people small nations such as Nunavut and the Kuna draw inspiration from their tribal world heritage, whereas other small nations such as Bhutan, Tonga, and Tuvalu have their sociocultural roots in Great Tradition civilizations, kingdoms, and chiefdoms rooted in the imperial world. These examples, together with existing European small nations developed in the center of the contemporary commercial world, such as Switzerland and Norway, provide opportunities for exemplary ethnographic case studies.

Small nations are small-scale sociocultural systems that people have designed and organized to operate in the contemporary commercial world to solve local problems and to engage with neighboring nations, regions, and the international community to solve global problems. Small nations are small populations of fewer than 10 million people living in self-governing or autonomous political jurisdictions. Most are fully independent nation-states, but a few are formal dependencies, overseas territories, or otherwise legally associated with larger states. In some cases it is useful to also treat internal subunits of large states, such as cities, states, counties, or Indian tribal nations of the United States, as small nations. The important detail is that small nations are bounded territories within which people share a common cultural identity and interact as a society with a charter, or constitution, a judicial system, and formal political authorities. Small nations are likely to be highly democratic, but they include a wide range of formal political structures from federations to republics and constitutional monarchies, and they have national congresses, assemblies, or parliaments, often blending older tribal, chiefdom,

or kingdom political forms with modern democratic electoral practices.

Small nations are well suited to match the scale of their national economies with the productivity of their natural capital, which many theorists feel is a requirement for socioecological sustainability. Sustainable nations also need to equitably distribute their resources and opportunities across generations, and there needs to be a broad social consensus on the desirability of both equity and environmental sustainability. This highlights the importance of ideology, or cultural superstructure, and the role of metaphors, illusions, and delusions. Successful nations can not risk following the dictates of delusional growth ideologies that place them out of balance with the physical world. In a small-nation world a high quality of life can be supported by a national emphasis on services, like education, and by promoting technological efficiency rather than expanding material consumption. Also important is the ability for people to carry out sociocultural system transformations as they become necessary. Many of the small nations examined here are actively engaged in consensus-based system transformation in response to specific problems. This makes them ideal models for understanding how change can be internally generated.

Small nations, because they are small, are likely to have less concentrated social power than larger nations, which means that decision making would be expected to be more democratic. Wealth and income should be more equitably distributed. This suggests that there would be less incentive for elite-directed growth and explicitly progrowth policies and growth subsidies. Small nations are already solving global problems, they just happen to be operating on the peripheries of the mass media, and few people in the world of large nations hear about them.

Small nations offer real alternatives to the negative global scenarios of "barbarization," cycles of fear, or security regimes that some futurists now consider to be plausible outcomes of failing institutions, energy shortages, and collapsing ecosystems. The small-nations approach turns sixty years of failed international development work on its head by proposing that the largest nations, largest economies, and largest corporations are the worst models for the cultural patterns that can really improve the human condition. This chapter spotlights successful small nations scattered around the world to find some of the best working models of sustainable sociocultural systems and shows how these diverse small nations can be the building blocks of a transformed global system that will literally save the world. Many successful features of small nations are already being adopted piecemeal by communities within larger nations, and these cultural models will spread quickly as their benefits are more widely recognized. What must happen next is that oversize nations will need to transform themselves into small nations.

Growth Limits and Social Justice: The U.K. Overseas Territory of Saint Helena

There are certainly many pathways to sociocultural sustainability, but small nations, because they are small, have high potential for realizing the Eco-Social future identified by the European Union Terra-2000 project as the best pathway to building a sustainable sociocultural system.[10] The Eco-Social future imagines a society that achieves sustainability by maximizing social equity, or justice, while at the same time shifting away from economic growth based on ever-increasing flows of energy and materials to a stable economy that emphasizes knowledge, education, and information. Such a society would limit growth and promote social justice as a matter of public policy, and the entire sociocultural system would reflect that value orientation. Scale theory suggests that the necessary consensus for successfully producing and maintaining an Eco-Social society could most easily be reached in a small-scale society where there are few interest groups that might be in conflict. Growth limits are related to social justice in a small nation because when people realize that in a circumscribed environment the flow of energy and materials can not be endlessly expanded, they will need to shift attention away from material production and focus instead on achieving an optimum distribution of wealth, income, goods, and services.

Most small nations have either very small, often sharply circumscribed territories, especially if they are islands, or they have few, often precarious, natural resources. This means that there are often severe limits to economic growth, and maximum levels of production were often historically reached long ago. When populations are small, social justice is often by necessity in the forefront of political decision making. There is little wealth to be controlled, and with few people in the nation, people are likely to readily agree on the desirability of putting in place effective safety nets and maintaining an "irreducible minimum" to keep people from falling into material destitution. From this perspective small nations can work out solutions to the problem of how best to allocate re-

sources to people and live within physical limits of a territory. This is of course a central problem that confronts the entire world.

The island nation of Saint Helena is a good example of a nano-scale small nation confronting the limits to growth imposed by a severely circumscribed remote South Atlantic island setting (see figure 14.6). In 2009 there were only about 4,000 "Saints" resident on this rugged island of 47 square miles. Saint Helena was initially colonized by the British East India Company in the 1600s. It became a Crown Colony in 1834, a British Dependent Territory in 1981, and a British Overseas Territory in 2002. In 2002 all islanders became British citizens by Act of Parliament, but Saint Helena is effectively self-governing, with its own constitution, a formal governor appointed by the queen, a five-member executive council, and a twelve-member elected legislative council. The legal system is based on English common law. There are no political parties, but the political system is highly democratic and every adult resident can vote and run for office. The Constitution of 2009 contains a strong endorsement of basic human rights and political self-determination.

In addition to the island of Saint Helena, the United Kingdom treats two other South Atlantic island communities as dependencies of Saint Helena, although each also has its own constitution and government—Ascension Island and Tristan da Cunha. Ascension Island, 750 miles to the northwest, has about 1,100 resident Saints, and a few hundred other people associated with U.K. and U.S. military bases and communication facilities.[11] Tristan da Cunha, 1,500 miles south of Saint Helena, is home to a single village community of 264 people. Tristan da Cunha justifiably claims to be the most isolated community in the world. It is also one of the most intentionally egalitarian small nations. The settlement was established in 1817 by William Glass, a British soldier who with three companions signed an agreement to form the community based on the principle of "no one superior over another" and communal land ownership. Subsistence continues to be based on livestock and poultry, fishing, and potato farming. The community remains highly self-sufficient in food and committed to egalitarian principles. Sheep and cattle are owned by individual households, but grazing patterns are controlled by the government, and their numbers are strictly limited both to prevent overgrazing, and "to prevent better off families accumulating wealth."[12] Until recently the government was able to finance social services including education and health care by

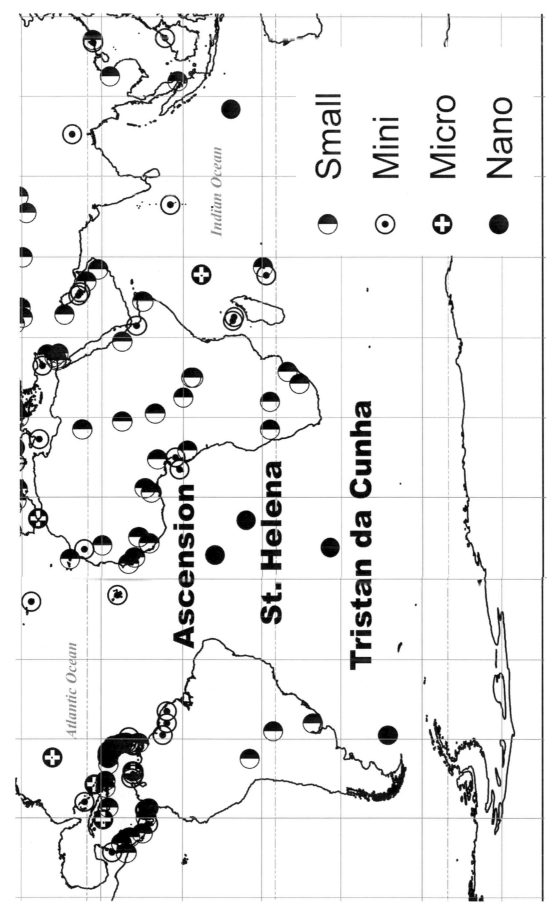

Figure 14.6. Maps of Saint Helena, Ascencion, and Tristan da Cunha.

revenues from overseas sales of rock lobsters, postage stamps, and handcrafts such as knit goods.

Although the main island of Saint Helena is internally self-governing, it is far from economic self-sufficiency in energy and materials, manufactured products, or government finance. Some 17,000 tons of goods valued at US$27 million were imported from the United Kingdom and South Africa in 2005. This is the equivalent of some 4 tons of material and $16,400 per capita. Food and fuel constituted nearly 45 percent of imports from the United Kingdom by weight, but only 7 percent by dollar value. However, as fuel prices climb in the future, the cost of all imports will increase steeply. A trivial 77 tons of goods worth $1.4 million were exported to the United Kingdom, but this did not balance the inflow, and an enormous trade deficit remained.[13] The Saint Helena government was able to cover only about half of its 2005 regular operating budget of US$20 million with domestic revenues from taxes, customs duties, and fees. The shortfall was made up by a $10.5 million grant-in-aid from the U.K. government. The Saint Helena government received an additional subsidy of $8 million from the United Kingdom to cover the island's shipping costs and technical assistance, bringing total government expenditures to about $28 million or $7,000 per capita. These budget imbalances add perspective to the island's 2005 GDP figures of $18 million, or $4,500 per capita. GNP of $22.7 million, or $5,800 per capita yields a higher figure because it includes some $4 million in remittances sent home by Saints working overseas. Saint Helena would be ranked as lower middle income by the World Bank, but its total economy is too small for the bank to count.

In comparison with other nations Saint Helena is a conspicuous outlier with its high life expectancy of 78 years and low income. Its infant mortality rate was 5.6 per 1,000 live births in 2005, which was better than the U.S. rate of 6.8. Its literacy rate of 98 percent was comparable with most high-income nations. These positive human outcomes may be related to the country's wide distribution of wealth and income, with high levels of public-sector control over capital and the distribution of benefits. Social power seems to be widely dispersed, and people seem to actually benefit from most of the money that flows through the economy. This is a real contrast with some large-scale countries such as the United States and the United Kingdom, where large parts of GDP actually reflect negative effects on people. More than half (58 percent) of economic consumption in Saint Helena was in the public sector, and much of the government's regular operating expenditure directly benefited the public in the form of public health, social security, education, and wages and pensions to government employees for a total of nearly $3,000 per capita. Other government expenditures on environment and public works and other social services add another $1,400 per capita to human well-being.

A close comparison between the U.K. Overseas Territory of Saint Helena and other small nations will help explain how Saint Helena, like Dominica, has maintained a high quality of life for its citizens with a very low per-capita GDP or personal income. Like Saint Helena, the U.S. states of Washington and Hawaii, the Hawaiian island county of Kauai, and the Commonwealth of Dominica all have adult life expectancies above 77 years, yet the American small nations have economies and GDP per capita that are orders of magnitude larger than Saint Helena (see table 14.3). There are also striking differences in the distribution of personal income and wealth between the State of Washington and Saint Helena. Washington is of course famous for being the home of Bill Gates, cofounder of Microsoft and one of the world's richest private individuals, with a net worth of $53 billion in 2006. At that time there were a total of four Microsoft billionaires in Washington, with a combined net worth of $83 billion. Sampling by the Internal Revenue Service in 2004 suggested that there were at least 50 Washington residents with an average net worth of over $3 billion, and some 6,000 with millionaire incomes in 1999.[14]

The distribution of income and wealth on Saint Helena is very different. The Saints' sociocultural system effectively maintains a low ceiling on earned incomes, and the high level of government ownership of capital also limits individual accumulation of unearned income, helping to keep wealth widely distributed. Most of the 200 businesses on the island are small, and the largest employs only 200 people. The government owns the only bank in the country and holds a 63 percent share of Solomon and Company, the largest private business on the island. Solomon and Company operates a dozen retail outlets, as well as a bakery, three fuel service stations, auto repair, shipping, insurance, and the bulk fuel storage facility that supplies all diesel fuel to the government-owned electric power station. The company also develops and sells land and maintains a farm and livestock operation. Between the bank and Solomon and Company, the citizens of Saint Helena in effect own and enjoy

Table 14.3. Life Expectancy for Five Small Nations: Washington State, Hawaii, Kauai County, Dominica, and St. Helena, by Scale of Population and Economy

	Life Expectancy	Population	GDP	GDP/Capita
Washington State	79.4	6,396,000	$289,070,000,000	$45,195
Hawaii	81.7	1,285,000	$59,131,000,000	$46,016
Kauai*	81.7	61,950	$1,950,248,000	$31,481
Dominica	75.5	72,500	$313,522,222	$4,324
St. Helena, UKOT	76.4	4,072	$20,258,920	$4,975

*BEA Personal Income, Life Expectancy as for State of Hawaii

UKOT = United Kingdom Overseas Territory

the benefits of $10 million in net assets, or $6,700 in wealth per household.

Wide public ownership of wealth makes it feasible for the government to maintain a social safety net that minimizes the effects of poverty. The low per-capita GDP of $4,500 is paralleled by a modest, almost flat personal income distribution with a very small spread from top to bottom. For example, a household expenditure survey in 2004 suggested that households in the top 5 percent income rank were able to spend annually an average of about $46,000 and the bottom 8 percent about $2,940. Middle incomes' consumption expenditures ranged from $6,500 to just under $20,000. The deputy chief secretary, a "super-scale" rank near the top of the government income scale, earns only about $25,000 a year. This is not the "natural" log-normal distribution that would otherwise be expected of the income distribution in most large nations. Saint Helena's incomes are less skewed in part because most (53 percent) of the 2,028 employees on the island are working for the government, and government pay scales strive for equity.

A careful inspection of figure 14.7 shows the difference in income distribution between Saint Helena and Washington State in 2004. Notice that the top ranks of Saint Helena incomes correspond to the bottom ranks in Washington. This of course reflects the very small absolute size of Saint Helena's economy. What really matters is the very different slopes of the lines that graph the two distributions (Saint Helena, -0.43; Washington, -0.97), and the much weaker R^2 correlation between income and rank for Saint Helena (0.18) versus 0.96 for Washington, where the distribution corresponds almost perfectly to the "natural" log-normal distribution. The 0.18 R^2 value shows that on Saint Helena income rank and size of income are only weakly related, and the -0.43 slope means that income is more equitably distributed. Washington's income slope of -0.97 corresponds almost precisely to the -1.00 slope defined by the distribution of power

in the Inca bureaucracy, which follows the predicted "natural" log-normal distribution. This implies that the political economy in Washington effectively puts no limits on the top end of the income scale and makes no cultural adjustment for the power-concentrating effects of growth. This is what we would expect to see if growth was an elite-directed process, and it is clear evidence that in Saint Helena the process is more egalitarian.

Helena receives no foreign direct investment and no portfolio investment; it has no stock market and no publicized level of market capitalization. It has no shopping malls, no fast-food franchises, no giant resort hotels, and no military. It is perhaps not surprising that taking care of people is a prime function of government, judging by how expenditures are allocated. It is also the case that here, in a very real sense, *the people are* the government. Scale limits also mean that there is no university, and the general hospital can not treat all medical conditions. Saint Helena is small, but there is still a business elite that is well-represented in the government, a chamber of commerce, and a government supported Saint Helena Development Agency. There is also an elite-directed development discourse on Saint Helena that lobbied hard for the U.K. government to fund construction of a long runway and airport on the island that would be large enough to accommodate 737 passenger jets. The objective is to market Saint Helena as a "nature island" with a historic and cultural heritage, just as Dominica and Kauai.

The government vision is for "...a prosperous, peaceful and democratic society for all achieved through sustainable economic environmental and social development leading to a healthy and eventually financially independent Saint Helena."[15] The hope is that 10,000 new tourists would be arriving within five years of the airport's completion and tourism would soon expand to 20,000. It was hoped that increased tourism dollars and new investment would make it

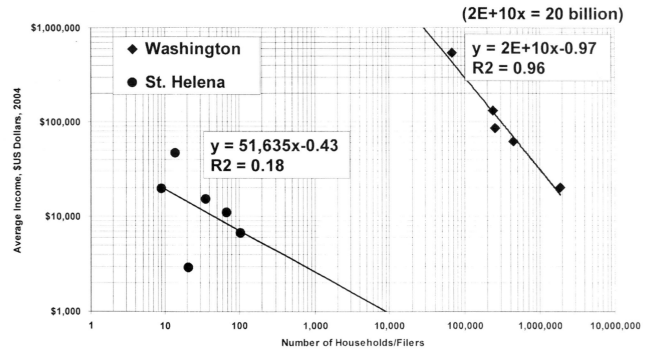

Figure 14.7. Income distribution ranks, Washington State and UK Overseas Territory of St. Helena, 2004.

possible for the country to be financially independent by 2025. The resident population could then expand to over 6,000, because new employment opportunities would reverse the labor immigration and restore the demographic imbalances.[16] However, the global economic downturn of 2008 caused the United Kingdom to put Saint Helena's airport project on hold.

Small to Nano: Small Nations Maximizing Well-Being

Small nations are already in the forefront of the widely forecast shift from what development specialists call industrial-materialist-modernist conditions, which still characterize much of the commercial world where survival values and traditional values predominate, to the much-heralded postindustrial, **postmaterialist** world, where self-expression and rational secular values predominate. Political scientist Ronald Inglehart describes this "culture shift" or "silent revolution" as the "human development sequence" in which contemporary societies move away from authoritarian systems toward personal autonomy, gender equity, and democracy.[17]

In the postmaterialist world the hope of futurists is that democratic decision making would challenge elite-directed growth, and the satisfaction of social and self-actualization needs would become more im-

portant for people than concern for meeting their now-satisfied physiological needs for subsistence and physical security. In the postmaterialist world national societies would be less concerned with economic growth and maintaining strong militaries or large police forces. The shift away from economic growth represents a new emphasis on social needs and individual self-actualization needs, including aesthetic needs for making urban places and local communities beautiful places to live rather than just places for commerce, and for restoring and safeguarding the natural environment. Self-actualization gives a high priority to intellectual needs for information, knowledge, and education, all of which are likely to reduce consumption of energy and materials. Social and self-actualization values are represented by actions supportive of feelings of belonging and self-esteem, and all of these are likely to be reflected in high life expectancy, low infant mortality, and high scores on the HDI.

The expectation is that peoples experiencing this shift to a postmaterialist world will feel physically and materially secure, and they will in fact enjoy higher levels of personal autonomy. Many small nations seem to already be postmaterialist, and many others are moving in that direction. Thirty-four of the 80 countries in Inglehart's World Values Survey[18] are small nations. They are concentrated in the secular pole of the traditional-secular dimension regardless of income level, and they are slanted toward self-expression over survival values (see figure 14.8). This shows that small nations of all income levels are likely to have secular-rational values, and most also have high self-expression values even in combination with traditional values and middle incomes. Small nations are strong evidence that a large economy and high consumption is not the only pathway to personal well-being, but basic needs do need to be satisfied.

The success of small nations with small economies may be understood by the seemingly counterintuitive findings of social psychologists that placing a high value on material acquisition and consumption beyond basic material needs, as in American corporate capitalism, may actually reduce an individual's subjective and actual well-being.[19] To the extent that people in small nations minimize the ideological, institutional, and behavioral structures of capitalism that are closely linked with a counterproductive emphasis on materialist values, they may succeed in achieving genuinely sustainable development. Strongly internalized materialist values and the institutionalization of advertising, extremely hierarchical wage scales, and

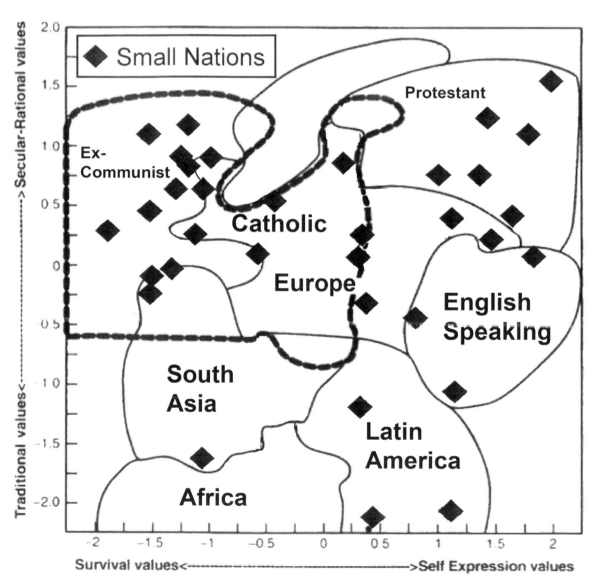

Figure 14.8. Values dimensions of 34 small nations in the world values survey, by major cultural zones (redrafted and modified from Inglehart and Welzel. 2005. *Modernization, Cultural Change and Democracy: The Human Development Sequence.* **New York and Cambridge: Cambridge University Press.** (Figure 2.4, page 63).

excessive pursuit of corporate profit are shown to conflict with values and goals for caring for others, maintaining close personal ties, and feelings of personal well-being, satisfaction, and control over one's life.[20]

There are at least two capitalist commercial world paths to well-being based on different ideological beliefs, institutionalized cultural practices, and different sets of values and individual goals (see figure 14.9). American corporate capitalism with its emphasis on economic growth and materialist consumerism has been shown to produce measurably low levels of well-being. The path more favored by successful small nations, which emphasizes cooperation, altruism, community relationships, and personal autonomy, leads to high levels of well-being.[21]

Beyond food and shelter, the basic necessities for human well-being and optimum health include an individual's feelings that they are competent to do what is needed, that they are connected to others by kinship and friendship, and that they have personal autonomy, freedom, and self-direction. The satisfaction of all basic needs is presumably linked to individual well-being through the specific motivations and behaviors that lead to need satisfaction. When motivation is culturally operationalized through strongly internalized materialist values for self-interest, competition, high consumption, and economic growth, corresponding values for cooperation, altruism, community, and strong interpersonal relationships may be suppressed, and basic needs may go unmet.

The ethnographic data suggests that small nations may be better able than larger nations to achieve a consensus on maintaining the values and institutions that most produce human well-being. If we take the World Bank's 2008 sample of 209 nations as the universe of nations, and use life expectancy (LE) at birth as a measure of how well a nation meets the basic needs of its citizens, then small nations clearly come out ahead of most larger nations (see table 14.4). More than two-thirds (85) of the 127 nations with LEs of 70 years or higher are small nations. This means that small nations significantly raise the world's average life expectancy. Stated differently, if we lived in a world of large nations, then fewer than half (47 percent) of the nations would have life expectancies of more than 70 years, whereas in a small nation world about two-thirds would be over 70 years.

High life expectancy in a nation is strongly associated with social equality, which in turn is strongly associated with small nations. For example in 2005, all but 2 of the 16 most egalitarian (Gini scores under 0.3) of 126 countries had life expectancies of 70 years or higher, and two-thirds of the 16 most egalitarian countries were small nations. Gini scores are calculated so that index values can range from 1.0, where in theory one person would have all the income, to 0, where everyone received exactly the same income. The small nation of Denmark was the most egalitarian country with a Gini score of 0.258, and Namibia was the least egalitarian with a score of 0.645. Ten of the 14

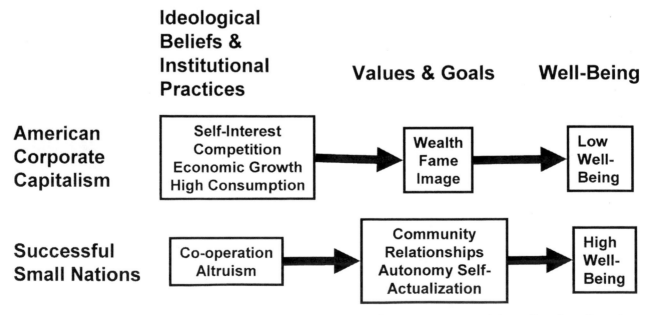

Figure 14.9. Two paths to well-being: American corporate capitalism versus successful small nations (based on Kasser et al 2007).

Table 14.4. Life Expectancy of 209 Nations by Scale, 2008 (World Bank)

| | Number of Nations by Life Expectancy | | | |
	<70	70+	80+	Total
Large	37	42	8	79
Small	44	86	29	130
Total	82	127	37	209

| | Percent of Nations by Life Expectancy | | | |
	<70	70+	80+	Total
Large	18	20	4	38
Small	21	41	14	62
Total	39	61		100

most egalitarian high-life-expectancy countries were small nations. Income equality does not require high per-capita incomes. Two-thirds (11) of the 16 most egalitarian nations were small nations, and their per-capita incomes ranged from Denmark with $41,420 per capita to the Ukraine with only $6,848 per capita. Nano-nations like Saint Helena and Tristan da Cunha are off the UN and World Bank charts, but they are among the best examples of very small nations with high social equality and human well-being but small economies and low incomes.

Small nations again rise to the top in the HDI. Most (60 percent) of the 38 countries ranked as very high human development were small nations (see table 14.5). The six micronations, the smallest of small nations, did best of all with one-third in the very high human development rank. Fewer than one-fourth of mega-nations ranked very high. Twelve countries, including seven small nations, ranked higher than the United States, and many of these achieved their high ranks with lower per-capita GDPs than the United States.

Managing the Environment and Natural Resources

Small nations can also be ranked on how well they manage their environments and natural resources and on overall environmental sustainability. The Yale Center for Environmental Law and Policy and the Center for International Earth Science Information Networks working in collaboration with the World Economic Forum and the European Commission's Joint Research Centre in 2008 produced an Environmental Performance Index (EPI) for the governments of 149 countries.[22] The EPI considers twenty-five indicators measuring government effectiveness on two important policy objectives: (1) Environmental Health, managing air pollution, protecting drinking water, and generally reducing mortality caused by poor environmental conditions; and (2) Ecosystem Vitality, considering policies directed at reducing the effects of air and water pollution and stress on the environment, maintaining productive natural resources, and confronting climate change.

The government with the best overall environmental performance was a small nation, Switzerland, with a rank of 96 out of 100, measuring percent of environmental goals met. The top eight governments were all small nations, and all but six of the top twenty countries with scores of 85 and above were overwhelmingly (70 percent) small nations. In general, environmental performance is strongly correlated with per-capita GDP, suggesting that it is better to have a relatively large commercial economy. At first glance the data seems to support that conclusion; however, a closer look shows that small-scale countries can perform at the top, even with small economies and low incomes. Nearly all of the top 20 on overall environmental performance were high-income countries with GDP per

Table 14.5. UN Human Development Index for 182 Nations by Scale, 2007

| Countries | Large Nations | | | Small Nations | | | |
	Giga	Mega	Large	Small	Mini	Micro	#
Very High	0	2	13	15	6	2	38
High	0	3	14	19	5	4	45
Medium	2	4	26	27	16	0	75
Low	0	0	12	12	0	0	24
	2	9	65	73	27	6	182

| Percent | Large Nations | | | Small Nations | | | |
Countries	Giga	Mega	Large	Small	Mini	Micro	%
Very High	–	1	7	8	3	1	21
High	–	2	8	10	3	2	25
Medium	1	2	14	15	9	–	41
Low	–	–	7	7	–	–	13
	1	5	36	40	15	3	100

capita above $12,000. However, Costa Rica was a small nation outlier in the top group with its upper middle income under $10,000 and a performance of 90.

The environmental performance database covers more countries for ecosystem vitality measures, and this allows more small nations to appear in the sample, where they can show even more clearly the distinct advantages of small-scale sociocultural systems for effective resource management. Overall ecosystem-vitality rankings for 154 countries showed that the top 7 countries meeting 87 percent or more of their ecosystem goals were all small nations: Laos, Switzerland, Congo, Costa Rica, Bhutan, Norway, and Sweden, and they ranged in income from Congo with a low of $1,159 per capita to Norway with $32,775. These rankings demonstrate again that a country does not need to be financially rich or large in population to take care of its natural environment.

Small nations absolutely excel at maintaining productive natural resources and having effective government policies to safeguard forests and prevent overfishing and degradation of agricultural soils and rangelands. This is an area where most countries do poorly, and only 25 percent of 214 countries were achieving 90 percent or more of their resource management goals. Most remarkably, 50 out of the 55 countries in the 90 percent rank for natural resource productivity were small nations. You could confidently predict that any country that is successfully managing its natural resources is a small nation. As the population scale of a country goes down, success at maintaining natural resource productivity goes up. This is not about population density, because there is no correlation between density and effectiveness of resource management policies. Many highly effective resource management countries are small nations with very high population densities. The issue is that people in small nations are better able to reach a consensus about their resource management goals and to make and implement effective policy decisions. Small nations were overwhelmingly represented at the very top, with 11 small nations achieving 100 percent of their goals, and 34 of the top 35 countries ranking at 95 percent or higher were small nations.

The cross-national data also shows that small nations do very well at maintaining a healthy environment for people. Only 67 countries (fewer than half of the 168 countries with adequate data) achieve 90 percent or more of their policy goals for managing the environment to protect public health. Again, small nations were well represented at the very top. Ten of the 14 countries with scores of 99 percent were European small nations: Ireland, Sweden, San Marino, Iceland, Finland, Norway, Denmark, Luxembourg, Slovakia, and New Zealand. All five micronations from Europe and the Caribbean—Andorra, San Marino, Antigua, Dominica, and Saint Kitts–were in the 90 percent and above rank, along with eight mini-nations. Significantly, eight small nations in the 90 percent rank and above had incomes under $10,000 per capita, showing that small nations can maintain public health even with small economies.

Population Growth and Economy

As noted above, from 1960 to 2008 global population more than doubled, but at the same time the total global economy increased more than fivefold from $7 trillion to nearly $37 trillion in constant 2000 US dollars. This enormous economic boom created huge pressures on the global environment, precipitating the present crisis of global warming, species extinctions, and resource depletion, but it also further amplified global poverty and social injustice. The reality is that one country, the United States, with less than 5 percent of global population, enjoyed nearly 30 percent of the gain in absolute dollars, adding $6.7 trillion to its total economy. Just seven giga, mega, and large countries, the United States, Japan, China, the United Kingdom, France, and Italy, with 31 percent of global population, gained $16 trillion, more than 70 percent of the increase. As we have seen, much of this new economic activity and income was concentrated in a handful of global cities, in the global financial, media, and information sectors and for associated managers, owners, and investors. Consequently, many small nations on the fringes of the global economy were bypassed by the benefits of this growth, even as some small nations benefited enormously.

On the average small nations (136 percent) actually grew at a somewhat higher rate than large nations (124 percent), but growth was very uneven and the averages were distorted by a few countries that experienced very high rates of growth. For example, China (giga), Korea (large), Botswana and Singapore (small), and Equatorial Guinea (mini) all grew more than 1,000 percent. Forty small nations can be considered low-growth nations, because they grew at 25 percent or less from 1960 to 2008, and more than half of these grew less than 1 percent or actually declined. The fact that low or no economic growth did not prevent some small nations from maintaining high life expectancies demonstrates that basic human needs can be effectively satisfied under very diverse sociocultural arrangements. There were actually 16 low economic-growth small nations with life expectancies of 70 years or higher, yet more than half also had GDPs per capita that were well below the $10,000 threshold typically associated with high life expectancies. For example, the micronation Marshall Islands, which grew at only 17 percent over 48 years and had low GDP per capita of under $2,000, and mini-nation Vanuatu, which grew at under 1 percent, both had life expectancies over 70 years. The highest life expectancy for a low-growth small nation was micro-state San Marino with life expectancy of 81 years and an economic growth rate under 4 percent. In San Marino's case GDP per capita was a very high $30,000 plus, but clearly GDP is not the sole requirement for high human well-being.

Between 1960 and 2008 thirty-eight small nations grew into large nations, but growth over the same period by mega-nations added 2.2 billion people to global population, and produced 2 giga-nations. Mega-nation expansion was the equivalent of creating 440 new small nations. The environmental cost of this population growth was amplified by the growth in global GDP per capita, which increased by 2.5 compared with population increase of 2.2 from 1960 to 1980.

Global population more than doubled from 3 billion to 6.6 billion from 1960 to 2008. Ninety-five percent of this increase can be attributed to the growth of large nations, and 60 percent to the ten largest. Average rates of increase over that 28-year period for all small nations (small, mini, and micro, 158 percent) were lower than for all large nations (giga, mega, and large, 179 percent).[23] There were twenty low-growth small nations with rates of increase of 25 percent or less, but only ten large nations were in this low-growth category. Of course there are more small nations in the world than large, but this makes greater diversity possible. Low-growth small nations represent a wide range of per-capita GDP levels and included three wealthy countries with above $10,000 GDP per capita.

Small Nations Ending Poverty and Meeting Climate Change Goals

Effective climate change policies are perhaps the most critical component of ecosystem vitality. The EPI measures this by estimating the percentage that each country has reached per-capita carbon emissions of 2.24 metric tons per year, zero grams of carbon per kWh of electricity, and .85 tons of carbon per US$1000 of industrial GDP output. The assumption is that in

combination these goals would reflect a 50 percent reduction in global greenhouse gas emissions by 2050. As of 2005 most countries were doing very poorly on climate policy. Fewer than 12 percent of countries were within 90 percent of the goal, but more than half at 90 percent or above were small nations.

The use of fossil fuels is of course a critical climate change policy issue, and small nations show how much diversity is possible in the energy sector. They demonstrate that fossil fuel use can be reduced while keeping human well-being and income levels high. The UN Intergovernmental Panel on Climate Change (IPCC) Fourth Assessment Report shows that fossil fuel use contributed more than half of the greenhouse gases causing global warming.[24] The enormous acceleration of fossil fuel–related CO_2 emissions since 1970 can be attributed to four crucial factors: (1) carbon intensity, the amount of CO_2 emitted per unit of energy production; (2) energy intensity, energy used per unit of GDP; (3) GDP per capita; and (4) population.[25] Improvements in carbon and energy intensity have not offset the increases in population and GDP per capita. Small nations are crucial because their populations have remained small in absolute numbers, even as on average they have grown at rates similar to larger nations'.

The 1992 UN Framework Convention on Climate Change commits the nations of the world to stabilizing atmospheric greenhouse gases at a level that would prevent "dangerous anthropogenic interference with the climate system" (article 2). There has been agreement that global temperatures should not rise more than 1.7 to 2°C (3 to 3.6°F) above preindustrial levels, but there is less certainty how much CO_2 in the atmosphere constitutes "dangerous interference."[26]

According to recent climate models that speak carefully of probabilities, the "very likely" probability of remaining below 2°C and thus avoiding dangerous climate change impacts would require cumulative CO_2 emissions of just 500 Gt from 2000 to 2049, when carbon balance with zero emissions would be achieved.[27] A cumulative total of 1,000 Gt is "likely," but not "very likely," to keep the world below the 2°C safety threshold, suggesting that if a small risk of catastrophic failure is assumed, then the necessary cultural changes may be more achievable. It is also "likely" that cumulative emissions are already so high that long-term climate stabilization over centuries may require that carbon emission remain at near-zero levels indefinitely into the future,[28] which means that drastic sociocultural changes will be needed to assure sustainability. Between 2000 and 2006 the commercial world had already burned through 234 Gt, and at that rate within 25 years will exceed the 1,000 Gt cumulative total, long before the 2050 target date for stabilization.

The problem with setting severe restrictions on carbon emissions is that most development authorities believe that improving living standards to meet human needs in the impoverished world will require poor countries to increase their energy use, which will put them in conflict with global efforts to reduce carbon emissions. The real question is how best to prevent "dangerous" anthropogenic climate change and at the same time assure that every nation can achieve sustainable development. In order to resolve this apparent dilemma, the Greenhouse Development Rights (GDR) framework developed by the Stockholm Environment Institute and Ecoequity[29] set a target development threshold at of $7,500 PPP GDP per capita per year, which is well above the World Bank's "extreme poverty" line of $1 or $2 per capita per day (<$1,000/year). A $7,500 "development threshold" is also higher than the World Bank's global "poverty" line of about $16 PPP per capita ($5,800/year). A threshold of $7,500 is intended to be above basic subsistence needs and would allow a country to achieve its **Millennium Development Goals (MDGs)** and achieve a high HDI. This is what I have elsewhere called a "maintenance level" to meet basic needs with a comfortable security margin, but it would not cover high levels of consumption, luxury, or "affluence," such as has characterized "developed" consumer cultures in high-income nations. Countries below the development threshold have done little to cause global warming and would not be expected to sacrifice to reduce carbon emissions. The GDR framework provides a basis for calculating the capacity of high-income countries to reduce emissions and continue to meet the basic needs of their citizens.

It is possible to imagine the magnitude of cultural changes that will be needed and to identify the kinds of already-developed cultural systems that meet the challenge and can serve as models for other countries. According to the U.S. Energy Information Administration (EIA), in 2006 the global average carbon emissions were just under 6 metric tons per capita.[30] If we assume a stationary global economy and population of 6.5 billion people in 2007, the average global emission rate would need to be 0.92 metric tons per capita to achieve the target cumulative emissions of 500 Gt by 2050. The somewhat riskier 1,000-Gt target could be achieved with a global per-capita emission rate that did not exceed 2.6 metric tons. The 2007 global aver-age rate of just under 5 tons per capita was already fivefold too high for the 0.92 target. The United States at 20 tons per capita was more than twentyfold over that target, but it was also far above the $7,500 well-being threshold.

The good news is that nearly half of the 207 countries in the EIA database are already below the 2.6-ton "likely safe" per-capita emission threshold, and nearly a third were at or below the 0.92 "very likely" safe level. The bad news is that most of these on-target countries were not on target for various important measures of human well-being. However, there were 19 small nations, including Dominica and Saint Helena, that were below the 2.6-ton carbon line and also had life expectancies of 70 years or higher (see figure 14.10).

Seven small nations have overcome poverty and responded effectively to the global warming threat. These very successful small nations include two Latin American countries, Costa Rica and Uruguay, and four Caribbean nations, Santa Lucia, Saint Vincent and Grenadines, Dominica, and Turks and Caicos Islands, together with Cape Verde in the Atlantic off West Africa. These seven small nations were all above the $7,500 line; had carbon emissions below 2.6 tons per capita; had high life expectancies; and, where reported, did well on the HDI (see table 14.6). One of these very successful countries, the Caribbean micronation of Dominica, was also among a group of twenty low-growth small nations whose populations had growth less than 25 percent from 1960 to 2008. Nicaragua, a Latin American small nation in the group of 19, experienced low economic growth from 1960 to 2008 and had a low GDP per capita of $3,760, but still achieved an over-70-years life expectancy and was even below the "likely safe" 0.92 emission target. Small nations demonstrate that it is feasible to lift people out of poverty, maintain high living standards, and respond to the climate change challenge.

Decentralized Power and Perpetual Peace

Small nations conform remarkably well to the conditions for "perpetual peace" among nations proposed by German Enlightenment philosopher Immanuel Kant (1724–1804) in 1795.[31] In the first place Kant imagined that peace treaties between nations would not be truces, or merely temporary pauses in an ongoing conflict. He also maintained that states were territorially based moral persons based on a social contract and could not be treated as property to be bought and sold or acquired by marriage. Likewise, citizens could not be hired out as mercenaries to fight foreign wars.

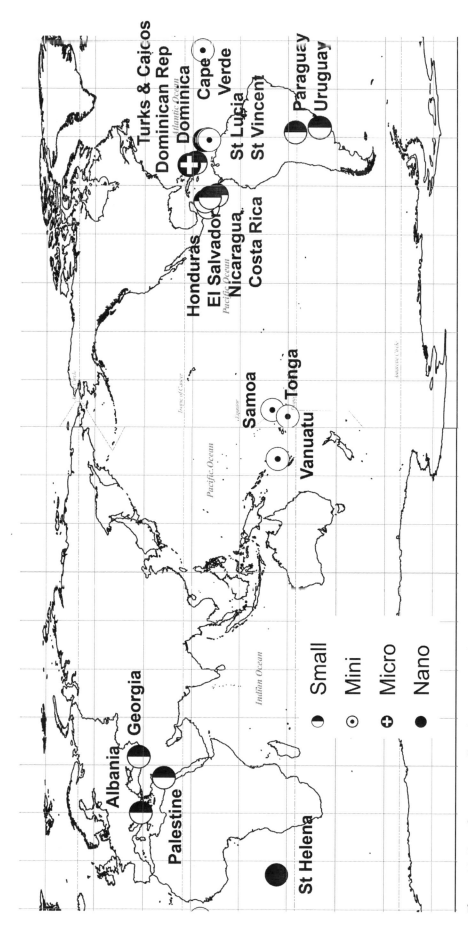

Figure 14.10. Nineteen small nations meeting (2.6 ton/capita) carbon goals with high life expectancies, 2007.

Table 14.6. Seven Small Nations Meeting (2.6 ton/capita) Carbon Goals while Ending Poverty and Achieving High Life Expectancy and High Human Development Index, 2007

Country	Scale	GDP/ Caita	Carbon Emissions tons/capita)	Human Development Index (HDI)		Life Exp.
Costa Rica	4,137,370	$12,772	1.65	85	High	79
Uruguay	3,460,610	$10,396	2.17	87	High	76
Cape Verde	24,400	$7,497	0.69	71	Medium	71
Saint Lucia	158,870	$10,014	2.42	82	High	74
Saint Vincent/ Grenadines	105,310	$9,553	1.89	77	Medium	72
Dominica	72,380	$9,120	1.65	81	High	76
Turks and Caicos Islands	21,760	$11,500	0.64			75

Kant advocated the complete abolition of standing armies, arguing that they produced costly arms races and that their very existence constituted a constant threat to other states. He also felt that recruitment into standing armies was a violation of "the rights of mankind in their own person" because it made people into tools and machines. When Kant was writing at the dawn of industrialization and capitalist expansion, many European states were experiencing a steep increase in trade and state revenues were also rising, but military expenditures to support frequent wars were climbing so rapidly that states borrowed extensively to finance their military expenditures. Such borrowing of course helped create some of Europe's greatest private fortunes, as noted in chapter 10. Kant's perpetual peace plan contained an implied critique of such unlimited capitalist accumulation and perpetual economic growth because he recognized that money was a more dependable weapon than armies or alliances. The "accumulation of treasure" by states in itself constituted an implied military threat.

The World Bank's 2008 figures on military expenditures by 191 nations[32] support Kant's contention that absolute size of a national economy is strongly correlated with the size and power of standing armies. These 191 countries spent more than $1.5 trillion on their militaries, but these expenditures were highly concentrated, with over half in just three nations: the United States, China, and Russia. Indeed having a large economy was a key to supporting a large military, because few nations were able to devote more than 5 percent of their GDP to their militaries, and even the United States, the largest spender, only devoted 4.2 percent of GDP to its military. It was striking that 23 small-nation "dropouts" had total military expenditures far smaller than would be expected from the size of their economies. Only one large nation, Nigeria, had smaller military expenditures than ex-

pected. Ninety-two of 191 nations of all scales spent $100 or more per capita on their militaries, and several highly militarized small nations such as Qatar, Oman, Israel, Kuwait, Singapore, and Brunei along with the United States and a large nation, Saudi Arabia, had military burdens that exceeded $1,000 per capita. Many small nations, such as Andorra, Antigua and Barbuda, Channel Islands, Costa Rica, Iceland, Isle of Man, Kiribati, Palau, Samoa, Saint Kitts and Nevis, Saint Lucia, Saint Vincent and the Grenadines, and Vanuatu either had military expenditures of less than US$1 per day, had no militaries, or they maintained only very small police establishments for public order.

The upside of low military expenditures is a "peace dividend" that makes it possible to devote more state money to public health, education, infrastructure, and other social services that improve human well-being. This is reflected in the 41 small nations that spent less than $78 per capita on the militaries and had life expectancies of 70 years or more.

Kant was a scathing critic of the growing commercial financial system and institutions, arguing that "a credit system which grows beyond sight . . . constitutes a dangerous money power." He specifically cited the "ingenious" English system of commercial credit, which amplified industry and commerce, and allowed the British government to borrow from the wealthy to accumulate a larger "war treasure" than all other states. He declared that "to forbid this credit system must be a preliminary article of perpetual peace." In the present commercial world there is still a direct connection between state finance and militarization, although some nations may borrow just to maintain government operations and some receive direct military assistance from abroad.

The link between the financial sector of the global economy and military expenditures remains strong.

Nations that have the largest investments in financial corporations also have the largest military expenditures. For example, in 2009 the S&P BMI (Broad Market Index) showed a combined market capitalization (share value) of over $7 trillion in about a thousand financial companies located in 46 countries. Together these financial corporations accounted for nearly 20 percent of global market capitalization. The countries where these financial corporations were located also accounted for more than 85 percent of global military expenditures in 2008. Fewer than a quarter of the 46 BMI countries were small nations, and these were mostly European; they all had per-capita military expenditures of more than $100 per capita. The financial sectors of the overwhelming majority of small nations were too small to be included in the S&P index. Market capitalization itself is strongly correlated with economic scale and increases steeply in step with GDP. However, market capitalization is poorly correlated with population, and per-capita capitalization actually declines as population scale increases. This suggests that stock markets themselves are business subsidies for economic growth.

There is another important dimension of economic scale for peace. Small nations have economies that are too small to finance many important weapons systems. It is no surprise that only a handful of countries

have nuclear weapons, and all those that do also have very large economies, or they impose severe sacrifices on their citizens. Forty-four small nations had individual GDPs smaller than the $6 billion construction cost of a single American nuclear aircraft carrier in 2005. There were ten such ships in the U.S. Navy. One F-15 jet fighter cost $55 million, and a single M-1 Abrams tank cost more than $4 million, which was more than the entire military budget of Trinidad in 2008. The primary corporations that produce such costly military hardware have annual revenues of tens of billions of dollars, and their shares are held by investment corporations that manage hundreds of billions or trillions in financial assets. These giant corporations, the stock markets, and other financial service institutions that support them are all critical parts of the military-industrial complex that Kant considered a major obstacle to perpetual peace.

The apparent military scale subsidy can be estimated by establishing a baseline average military expenditure for an economy of less than $10 billion. There are 50 small nations with economies in this size range, and 36 of these spent less than $50 million on their militaries, averaging less than $15 million. This would not buy very much military hardware (see figure 14.11). Military expenditures increase rather steeply as economies grow larger, although the

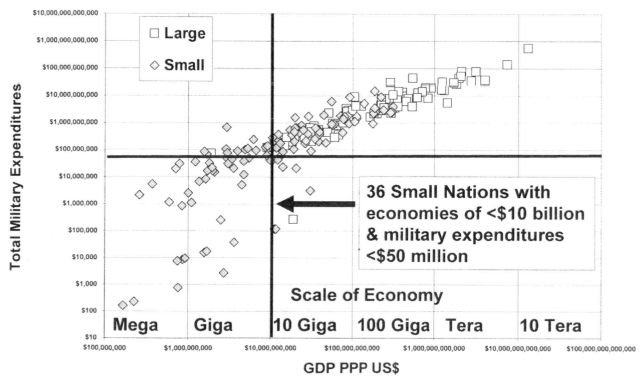

Figure 14.11.   Military expenditures for 191 countries by scale of society and GDP, 2008.

absolute amount of increase is of course much smaller for small economies. There is no obvious reason why military costs should increase in pace with economic growth, except perhaps for internal policing services as population increases, unless military expenditures actually take an increasing share of the economy, or military activities themselves facilitate economic growth. However, population scale is only weakly correlated with per-capita increases in military expenditures, and the rate of increase is low. This suggests that military expenditures are primarily a subsidy in support of economic growth.

In his definitive articles specifying the conditions of perpetual peace, Kant argued that peaceful states needed to be republics whose constitutions were adopted by consent of their citizens and contained separate legislative, executive, and administrative branches. Anticipating the UN and other international organizations, he declared that states need to be incorporated into federations with constitutions so that their relations can be legally regulated. This would not be a single world state dominating inferior subject states; rather states would be united in an international free federation forming a "league of nations" or a "league of peace." Kant imaged such an international federation expanding to incorporate the entire world.

SMALL ISLAND NATIONS AND SUSTAINABILTY

Sustainable development as a process has been the primary objective of international development since 1987, when the World Commission on Environment and Development, the Brundtland Commission, defined it as "…development that meets the needs of the present without compromising the ability of future generations to meet their own needs."[33] In 1992 at the UN Conference on the Environment and Development (UNCED), the Earth Summit held in Rio de Janeiro, the UN adopted Agenda 21 to implement sustainable development. At the same time the UN created a special Commission on Sustainable Development to monitor international progress toward sustainable development. The Rio Declaration, the consensus issued at the conclusion of the 1992 UNCED, affirmed that human well-being and social justice were the primary objectives of sustainable development. Principle 1 of the Rio Declaration stated: "Human beings are at the centre of concerns for sustainable development. They are entitled to a healthy and productive life in harmony with nature."[34] If fully implemented by the international community, this

first principle would restore the humanization process as the primary objective of sociocultural systems. The well-being of individuals and households would come ahead of the needs of government and commerce. The UN General Assembly further institutionalized the sustainable development process and the centrality of human well-being as international objectives by adopting the Millennium Goals in 2000, calling on nations to reduce poverty and improve health, education, and gender equity; make the benefits of globalization more equitably distributed by 2015; and stimulate "truly sustainable development."[35]

Small Island Developing States and Rising Sea Levels

Many small nations quietly gained their independence from colonial rule after 1950, but remained off the world political stage until 1989, when the IPCC issued its first report warning of the dangers of global warming. Recognizing their vulnerability to rising sea levels, small island nations began forging a political identity for self-defense by forming an action group at the Small States Conference on Sea Level Rise hosted by the Maldives in 1989. Their group became AOSIS, the Association of Small Island States, at the 1990 Second World Climate Conference, where they advocated for the creation of the UN Framework Convention on Climate Change (UNFCCC), which was adopted in 1992 and came into force for 194 nations in 1994. AOSIS representatives played a major role as an intergovernmental organization in the negotiations that lead to the adoption of the UNFCCC Kyoto Protocol in 1997. Facing the specter of being flooded into oblivion, small island nations understandably took an aggressive stance against the large greenhouse gas emitters. During negotiations in 1994 AOSIS proposed a target of a 20 percent reduction in greenhouse gases from the 1990 base by 2005, whereas the United States advocated simply returning to 1990 levels. AOSIS remains actively involved in post-Kyoto negotiations.

Small island developing states were singled out for special treatment in Chapter 17.G of *Agenda 21*, the UN global action plan for sustainable development in the twenty-first century drawn up at the 1992 UNCED, because they are remote from the economic and financial centers of the global economy, their land and freshwater resources are often limited, and they rely heavily on coastal areas, reefs, and fisheries.[36] Small island nations were also special because "their small size, limited resources, geographic dispersion and isolation from markets, place them at a disadvantage economically and prevent economies of scale" (Agenda 21, G 17.123). It was also recognized that small islands often had unique flora, fauna, and cultures. The plan stressed that small islands were especially vulnerable to sea-level rise and storms caused by global warming and advocated the creation of special action plans supported by international organizations to help small nations develop sustainably.

Small islands immediately see the effects of waste contamination and overuse of natural resources. Agenda 21 proposed that small island states would need perhaps $130 million in international assistance between 1993 and 2000 to provide necessary technical aid and to develop the human resources that sustainable management of marine and coastal resources would require.

Following the opening provided by Agenda 21, in 1994 AOSIS held a UN-sponsored Conference on the Sustainable Development of Small Island Developing States in Barbados that developed a detailed Programme of Action, putting climate change and sea-level rise first on the their list of concerns and proposing partnerships between governments, intergovernmental organizations, and nongovernmental organizations to help small island nations achieve sustainable development. The Barbados recommendations lead the UN to create a special Small Island Developing States (SIDS) unit in 1995 within the Department of Economic and Social Affairs, reporting to the UN Secretariat. Fifty-one nations with 59 million people were designated as SIDS, and all but one, Cuba, had fewer than 10 million people. In 2008 there were 39 AOSIS member countries representing 53 million people. From a larger anthropological perspective small nations need not be islands, and their territories need not be small. Their most important dimension is small population within which decision making and social action can be directed toward sustainable development and human well-being.

Small island nations and small nations generally are a special challenge for sustainable development because it may be difficult for them to gain economies of scale to support government and commercial activities. Small nations help show what institutional functions are really necessary to maintain a high quality of life in the commercial world. For example, public health and formal education are certainly necessities, but very small nations may have difficulty providing a hospital and equipping it with expensive diagnos-

tic equipment. Very small nations may not be able to provide postsecondary education to their citizens. Small governments are unlikely to maintain a military establishment, and they may have only a very small police force and limited legal system. They may have no central bank and currency, and government departments or ministries may have multiple functions. They may have only a very small private commercial sector, and the government may produce and distribute electricity, maintain telecommunications, and own and operate business enterprises to import, store, and distribute basic commodities rather than leaving this to private business.

In recent decades small nations have been quietly joining a vast network of nations, international organizations, and nongovernmental organizations that are dedicated to the spirit and practice of sustainable development. This "new global partnership"[37] is quite the opposite of the existing global commercial hierarchy of giant corporations, which are solely dedicated to accumulating financial capital for the benefit of a few institutional shareholders and high-net-worth individuals. The sustainability issues that confront small island nations are dramatically obvious, but they are not fundamentally different from the issues that confront all nations, and the international network solutions that are working for small island nations can work for all nations. Small islands require sustainable development based on international sharing and diffusing power and decision making, rather than concentrating power. Perhaps most importantly, the sustainable development network is about humanization, promoting human well-being, rather than simply accumulating financial capital. Sustainable development requires social justice and in this respect is a direct challenge to the single-minded GDP-growth model that dominated twentieth-century development. What is needed is not increased material production, but better distribution of existing global resources, knowledge, and skills, and a rapid transition to renewable energy sources. This is sustainable development that can be applied everywhere, but it is small nations that are showing the way. The sustainability challenge facing small island states was thought to be "particularly severe and complex," so what works here should work everywhere. Likewise, a major misstep, or the wrong development decision, can fairly quickly have catastrophic effects on a small island, just as global-scale reliance on fossil fuels can disastrously disturb global climate.

H. E. Tommy E. Remengesau Jr., president of the Republic of Palau, spelled out the global importance of the small island nation sustainable development project as follows:

> Ultimately, the success of the island nations in responding to and combating the maze of modern environment threats and dangers will stand as a litmus test for the rest of the world. If we fail this test in our small island communities, I can guarantee you, we will fail the test on a global level.
>
> For our sake, and for the sake of future generations, failure cannot be an option.[38]

In 1994, immediately following the Rio UNCED, the UN sponsored the first conference to implement Agenda 21. This was the special Global Conference on the Sustainable Development of Small Island Developing States to develop a specific implementation plan for SIDS.[39] Small nations became the pioneer test case for sustainable development. This globally significant conference was held in the Caribbean small island nation of Barbados and was attended by representatives of 125 countries and territories, 53 international commissions, UN bodies and programs, special agencies and organizations, and 89 nongovernmental organizations. This was a remarkable mobilization of human effort and resources. The Declaration of Barbados, adopted by the conference, affirmed that:

> The survival of small island developing States is firmly rooted in their human resources and cultural heritage, which are their most significant assets; those assets are under severe stress and all efforts must be taken to ensure the central position of people in the process of sustainable development. (Part One, I)
>
> There is an urgent need in small island developing States to address the constraints to sustainable development, including scarce land resources, which lead to difficult land and agriculture use decisions; limited fresh water; education and training needs; health and human settlement requirements; inordinate pressures on coastal and marine environment and resources; and limited means available to exploit natural resources on a sustainable basis. (Part One, VI)

The requirements for sustainable development on small islands of course also apply to large nations on the continents. According to the preamble of the Barbados Programme of Action adopted by the conference, islanders are clear about the tradeoffs between the material versus cultural dimensions of develop-

ment: "Sharing a common aspiration for economic development and improved living standards, small island developing States are determined that the pursuit of material benefits should not undermine social, religious and cultural values or cause any permanent harm to either their people or their land and marine resources, which have sustained island life for many centuries."[40]

The Barbados Declaration also stressed that small island nations are in a position to protect both the world's oceans and global biodiversity, which are critical resources for them, as well as for the entire global community. The conference acknowledged that SIDS will be among the first nations to suffer the effects of global warming, but they have contributed the least to the causes of global warming. SIDS are also dependent on international trade, but individually have limited capacity to influence the terms of trade in a global "free market" dominated by giant corporations and markets. The multiple vulnerabilities of SIDS are mirrored by the vulnerabilities of subnational regions and communities worldwide in the face of concentrated economic power that can dominate production and distribution everywhere.

In response to The Barbados Programme of Action in 2001 the UN established a special agency, the UN Office of the High Representative for the Least Developed Countries, Landlocked Developing Countries and the Small Island Developing States to report to the Secretary-General and coordinate and monitor UN activities in support of Agenda 21. A follow-up international conference held in Mauritius in 2005 reaffirmed the Barbados action plan and called for the establishment of a Global Island Partnership (GLISPA), which was established in 2006 as a program within the Convention on Biological Diversity. GLISPA networks 14 island nations with 35 international agencies and organizations and a dozen other governments, including large, wealthy nations such as Australia, the European Union, France, Germany, Italy, New Zealand, the United Kingdom, and the United States.[41] GLISPA is another addition to an expanding international network promoting sustainable development. This is a headless, nonhierarchical web, or heterarchy, in which even the UN Secretariat itself, although a crucial hub, is not the director. No single great economic power is in control. This is truly a newly evolving form of global organization.

The extensive international network that supports the sustainable development of small island nations includes the UN Environment Programme's (UNEP)

Regional Seas Program, which was begun in 1974.[42] Small nations are especially prominent in the Wider Caribbean Regional Sea and the Pacific Regional Sea. The Caribbean Regional Sea Programme includes some 25 small nations and overseas territories and is administered by UNEP through a regional coordinating unit in Jamaica. The South Pacific Regional Seas includes 21 SIDS as well as Australia, France, New Zealand, and the United States. It is coordinated by the South Pacific Regional Environment Programme (SPREP) headquartered in Western Samoa. The SPREP secretariat operated a 58-person staff in 2008.[43] In addition to nearly $1 million in contributions from member countries, dozens of international organizations, UN agencies, foundations, and governments contributed some $5 million toward SPREP's $7.7 million budget in 2008. No single donor dominated.

Pacific Islander Small Nations

In 2009 there were 22 small island countries and territories in the South Pacific with some 8 million people and a total economic product of about $23 billion. Only one country, Papua New Guinea, with a population of 5 million, had more than a million people. There were nine mini-nations with populations in the hundreds of thousands (Fiji, Solomon Islands, French Polynesia, New Caledonia, Vanuatu, Samoa, Guam, Federated States of Micronesia, and Tonga); and seven micronations with tens of thousands of people each (Kiribati, American Samoa, Northern Marianas, Marshall Islands, Palau, Cook Islands, and Wallis and Fatuna); and five nano-nations with fewer than 10,000 people each (Nauru, Tuvalu, Niue, Tokelau, and Pitcarin). The marginality of these nations in the global market economy was striking. There were only two stock markets in the entire region—in Fiji and Papua New Guinea.

Pacific Islander Mini-Nation: Republic of the Fiji Islands

Fiji is a cultural and economic center of the small-nation, small-island world of the South Pacific (see figure 14.12). Fiji shows that not all small nations have solved the sustainability problem, and their difficulties call attention to the importance of social justice and the distribution of crucial economic resources

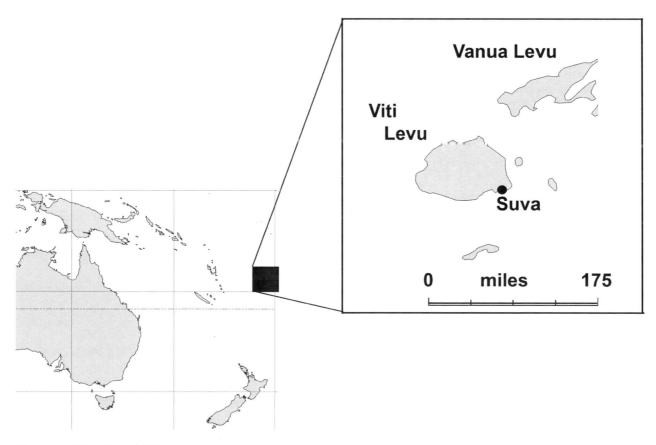

Figure 14.12. Map of Fiji.

for all nations. The Fiji example makes it clear that economic growth and a significant accumulation of capital is neither a necessary nor sufficient pathway to sustainability.

After Papua New Guinea, Fiji is the most populous Pacific Island nation. In 2007 just over half of its 837,000 people were indigenous Fijian Malayo-Polynesian–speaking Christians, and just over 40 percent were Indo-Fijians, predominantly Hindi-speaking, who were nearly 80 percent Hindu and 15 percent Muslim. Over half (52 percent) of the population was rural. Fiji's economy was $2.3 billion ($2,813 per capita) in exchange rate dollars, and $3.5 billion in PPP dollars ($4,180 per capita). This is a giga-scale economy ranking in size with Papua New Guinea, the American territory of Guam, and French Polynesia and New Caledonia, whereas all other small Pacific nations have mega-scale economies with GDPs of less than $1 billion. The critical human problem for Fiji is a poor distribution of material resources to people. This, in combination with a World Bank middle-level income, has produced seriously reduced living standards for many of its people.

Fiji is a member of the UN, was a founding member of the international Pacific Islands Forum, and has formal commitments with the World Trade Organization, the European Union, and the Commonwealth of Nations. The Fijian government endorses the UN MDGs in its development planning. It uses development guidelines and indicators issued by the World Bank, the International Monetary Fund, and the Organization for Economic Cooperation and Development. A regional office of the Secretariat of the Pacific Community is located in Fiji, as well as headquarters of the Pacific Power Association, the University of the South Pacific, the Pacific Islands Applied Geoscience Commission, and the Fiji School of Medicine.

In comparison with other small island nations, there is significant financial capital in Fiji, and much of it is coordinated by the South Pacific Stock Exchange located in Fiji itself. Fijian Holdings (FHL) is a domestic investment company that holds shares in 24 companies operating in Fiji, with total assets in 2009 of US$159 million and revenues of $113 million. FHL had 50 percent or more ownership of nine subsidiaries that included cement manufacturers, a tourism cruise line, property holding companies, financial service companies, a Fijian newspaper, an information technology company, and local retailers. This shows that foreign capital does not need to dominate investments in small countries, but there may still be important af-

filiations with global-scale corporations. FHL's affiliates were connected by ownership or working partnerships with some of the largest global corporations, such as Microsoft and Hewlett Packard, and the Australian food processing and marketing giant Goodman Fielder, whose revenues were $2.5 billion in 2009. FHL owned 10 percent of Goodman Fielder (Fiji) which produced ice cream, chicken products, and crispy snacks in Fiji. Goodman Fielder in turn was primarily owned by the world's largest banks and financial services companies, such as the National Australia Bank Group in Sydney, HSBC in London, and Morgan Chase and Citigroup in New York. This global network of owners and managers ultimately determined what many Fijians were eating and where they found employment. FHL's Goodman Fielder Fiji affiliate included a chicken-processing facility that annually processed 9 million chickens bearing the "Crest Is Best: The Healthy Alternative" logo for distribution throughout the Pacific region. Three million of those chickens were raised by 70 Fijian village farmers who grew their chickens in sheds housing 3,500 chickens each.[44]

The Fiji government played a major role in commercial business, owning and operating 11 public enterprises including airports; broadcasting; mahogany plantations and hardwood production; port facilities; shipyards; food processing; postal, telegram, and parcel service; rice mills; and mutual funds for small investors. Government ownership in effect made the public shareholders in some of the most important business enterprises in the country.

The Fijian financial capital market was thriving in 2008 in spite of the political turmoil in Fiji and in global financial markets. In addition to the stock exchange, four financial services companies provided investment advice, and there were more than a dozen stockbrokers or brokerage firms, and nearly two dozen licensed investment advisors.[45]

Capital markets on Fiji were relatively insulated from direct effects of the global financial crisis because most of their investors were domestic and because Fijian financial corporations avoided the complex financial instruments such as the collateralized debt obligations that proved so difficult for large-scale governments and businesses to mange. The global crisis did cause a decline in Fijian exports, in tourism revenues, and in remittances from overseas Fijian workers, and it led the Fijian central bank to devalue its currency in the foreign exchange market in 2009.

Sixteen corporations are listed on Fiji's South Pacific Stock Exchange. In 2008, 8 million shares worth some US$14 million were exchanged in this market, and total market capitalization was over US$500 million. In comparison, 3.5 billion shares moved daily on the New York Stock Exchange in 2008. Total market capitalization in the United States was nearly $12 trillion, which was more than five powers of ten greater than in Fiji. There was approximately US$1.5 billion in the Fijian bond market in 2008. Nearly 16,000 people invested in the mutual fund Unit Trust Market. There was no Securities and Exchange Commission in Fiji; instead the government created the Capital Markets Development Authority (CMDA) in 1996 to promote "fair, honest, and efficient" capital markets and increase investment by the public. The CMDA encourages the public to invest long term rather than engage in rapid trades to profit from short-term value fluctuation.

Fiji encapsulates the human rights problems of indigenous people; of colonialism and the arrival of new ethnic and religious groups; the injustices of the global market economy; and the new local and global stresses on the environment. In 1874–1879 the Fijian indigenous high chiefs accepted British colonial rule, and the British immediately introduced indentured laborers from India to work on the sugar plantations the colonists soon established. Much of the land remained under traditional tenure, and indigenous (Malayo-Polynesian–speaking) Fijians remained a dominant political presence. Fiji gained independence from Britain and became a republic in 1970. The Fijian Constitution, as amended in 1997, recognizes that Fiji is a multicultural society, "affirming the contributions of all communities to the well-being of that society, and the rich variety of their faiths, traditions, languages, and cultures" (Preamble). The constitution gives the English, Fijian, and Hindustani languages equal status. However, in spite of constitutional protections, poverty has increased, and life expectancy and the country's HDI have declined. Since 1987 the country has also experienced a series of military coups, most recently in 2006, followed by the suspension of the constitution, democratic institutions, and elections in 2009, and the consequent formal expulsion of the country from the Pacific Islands Forum and the British Commonwealth of Nations.

The Fijian Ministry of Finance Strategic Development Plan for 2007–2011[46] was the government's vision for "a peaceful, prosperous Fiji." It called for "multi-racial harmony" in which the "underprivileged" would not be left out. The plan assumed that sustained high levels of economic growth were essential for achieving "prosperity and decent living standards" for all segments of Fijian society, but reducing income and "opportunity" disparities was also an important objective. The government took direct responsibility for the well-being of the citizenry, declaring, "Government has a social responsibility to provide a safety net as well as to ensure the poor are equipped with a good education and are in good health, in order to benefit from income earning opportunities."[47] Central to the government's strategic plan are the eight-point MDGs: (1) eradicate extreme poverty and hunger; (2) achieve universal primary education; (3) promote gender equality and empower women; (4) reduce child mortality; (5) improve maternal health; (6) combat HIV/AIDS, malaria and other diseases; (7) ensure environmental sustainability; (8) develop a Global Partnership for Development.

The government treats the eight MDGs as "key performance indicators" to measure the effectiveness of policy. The key development challenge for the Fijian government is the reality that the country's HDI rank actually declined from 61st position in 1997 to 92nd out of 177 countries and an HDI score of 0.76 by 2005. This placed it in the medium HDI category, below very high and high, but above low. By 2007 Fiji's relative position had dropped to 108, and its HDI score had dropped to 0.74, based on average life expectancy at birth of 68.7 years, a GDP of only $4,304 PPP US$ per capita, and an education index of 0.86. The MDGs call for halving between 1990 and 2015 the proportion of people living on less than US$1 a day, and halving the number who are hungry.

Fiji's international development partnerships have primarily been with Australia (AusAID), New Zealand (NZAID), and the European Union, which especially provided aid for education and public health. Development loans have come from the Asian Development Bank to support water, sewage, and waste disposal projects.

Household economic surveys conducted in 2002 and 2003 showed that more than 34 percent of the population were below a basic needs poverty line, which was set at US$4,269. Poverty rates were higher in rural areas and among Indo-Fijians. At that time the income gap between the poverty line and the average income of poor households was US$1,386.

A more direct "participatory" assessment of poverty and hardship in which people were actually asked about their situation showed that many people were receiving public assistance, were living in crowded urban squatter settlements with inadequate utility service such as clean water, and felt that they had few employment opportunities. The poorest were predominantly rurals. Nearly two-thirds (61 percent) of rural indigenous Fijians were engaged in subsistence production, which was a significantly higher proportion than for rural Indo-Fijians (37 percent). This difference presumably reflected the fact that indigenous Fijians controlled most of the land. Poverty conditions were reflected by a surprisingly high proportion of underweight children, especially among the Indo-Fijian population (19 percent) versus only 5 percent for Fijian children, reflecting their low cash incomes and limited access to productive land.

The government was attempting to shore up its social safety net with a Family Assistance Allowance of up to US$381 annually, which would certainly not close the $1,366 average income gap for the poor. The Social Justice Act of 2001 established 29 affirmative action programs designed to benefit disadvantaged groups, but only two of these programs were specifically intended for the Indo-Fijian community. The National Integrated Poverty Eradication Programme Framework intended to reduce poverty by 5 percent a year with special projects for education, microfinance, and improvement of squatter settlements. Poverty was amplified by the structurally disadvantaged position of Indo-Fijians, rural-urban migration, the breakdown of tradition social support systems, and a shortage of well-paid employment.

Fiji: Managing Waste for Sustainability

Many Pacific islands have experienced severe environmental deterioration as their populations have increased, traditional resource management practices have declined, and consumption patterns have changed. Following the recommendations of the Barbados Declaration, in 1997 the SPREP brought together task forces representing twelve national Pacific Island nations including Fiji to adopted a Strategic Action Programme[48] to protect their international waters from environmental degradation. SPREP is headquartered in Samoa and is financed by Australia, New Zealand, the UN Development Program Global Environment Facility, and by contributions from 14 Pacific Island member states. SPREP's annual budget was only US$8.4 in 2010, which seems very modest to help 8 million people manage crucial marine resources directly affecting 500 inhabited islands scattered over an ocean covering one-sixth of the earth's surface. Much of the South Pacific is within the 200-mile Exclusive Economic Zone (EEZ) of one or another island

nation, and the SPREP action plan also encompasses waters within EEZs as well as the associated ecozones and watersheds. The reality is that threats to marine ecosystems are often transboundary. The SPREP Action Programme was concerned with three "imminent threats" to international waters in the Pacific region: (1) pollution of marine and freshwater (including groundwater) from land-based activities; (2) physical, ecological, and hydrological modification of critical habitats; and (3) unsustainable exploitation of living and nonliving resources use.[49]

The SPREP International Waters project assumed that the "root causes" of the environmental threats were problems of governance and understanding and could be solved by better resource management by government and local people that combined integrated coastal and watershed management and oceanic fisheries management, if decision makers had the appropriate information.

Waste generated by rural households was a major source of damage to marine ecosystems in Fiji. Survey research supported by the International Waters Project (IWP)[50] found that indigenous Fijians were producing an average of 134 kilograms of solid waste per capita annually, 94 kilograms of which was compostable vegetable material. They were discarding more than 10 kilograms of plastic every year. In contrast, Indo-Fijians were producing only 48 kilograms of compostable material from taro and manioc, presumably because they had less access to subsistence resources. About 15 percent of household waste could not be composted or recycled and would need to be disposed of in a landfill. At the time of the survey, most households were burning, burying, or simply dumping their waste, often in the mangroves or near the shore. Fewer than 10 percent were composting or feeding pigs with waste, or recycling nonvegetable wastes, but most Fijians were putting solid organic material back into the soil, rather than in landfills.

Indigenous Fijian villagers present a strikingly different solid waste profile than the average generated by American households in 2008.[51] Total municipal solid waste generated by Americans was 820 kilograms per capita per year, 492 kilograms (60 percent) of which was produced by households. The balance was from commercial businesses and institutions such as schools. Considering total household solid waste, Americans were disposing of more than three times as much as Fijian villagers. This might be taken as a measure of different levels of development, but levels of waste production also reflect different consumption patterns and overall lifestyles. Americans relied much more heavily on highly processed foods, shifting food-related waste to industrial factory farms and commercial processors, whereas rural Fijians relied heavily on food produced in their own gardens and processed in their households. If compostable vegetable material is excluded in the comparison, because it constituted 70 percent of Fijian solid waste, but only 26 percent for Americans, American household waste rises to nearly ten times greater than the Fijians, or 8 times more metal, 18 times more paper, and 6 times more plastic. In 2008 Americans were recovering or recycling about a third of their solid waste, but Fijians were working to increase their waste recovery.

Aside from the unsightliness of solid waste, the more serious pollution problem was from human and animal waste, sewage, and gray water. Following a workshop organized by the IWP, the village of Vunisinu, with 86 households and about 500 people in Rewa Province, launched a model waste management program to restore its dwindling marine resources. The people of Vunisinu were living well with abundant prawns, crabs, lobsters, and fish that they harvested from their adjacent mangroves, rivers, and ocean for household consumption or for sale. Years of pollution and wasteful fishing practices finally caused an alarming decline in the harvest. In 2003 workshops supported by the government and the IWP helped villagers turn things around. As Pita Vatucawaga explained, "It was only when we went on a field trip to see the dying coral reef that I realized that the depletion of our fisheries is also caused by leaks from our toilets, waste from our piggeries and our grey water. . . ."[52] With Vatucawaga directing the Village Environment Committee the village banned all waste dumping, began composting vegetable waste, and constructed composting toilets.[53] They encouraged recycling of solid waste and contracted with a private company to remove unrecoverable waste. Protecting the fish also meant stopping illegal poaching and use of dynamite, and banning nets with too fine a mesh. The reward was a visible improvement in their marine resources.

The Coral Reef Alliance (CORAL), a relatively small (budget of $1.6 million in 2008) California-based nongovernmental organization dedicated to protecting coral reefs worldwide, assisted Fijian peoples in managing their marine-protected areas. CORAL is guided by the realization that "when well-managed marine protected areas are supported by active local communities and defended against local threats, they not only recover, but also become resistant to large-scale stressors like climate change."[54] CORAL and the Fijians are also assisted by the Wildlife Conservation Society and the World Wide Fund for Nature, which are much larger international nongovernmental organizations. In 1997, the chiefs of the Kubulau district of Fiji created the Namena Marine Park and banned fishing in their waters to protect them from damage by commercial fishing. Eleven local villages are supporting a network of locally managed marine areas as protected sanctuaries within their 260-square-kilometer traditionally fished waters (qoliqoli), involving more than a dozen estuarine and reef areas, as well as a forest reserve.[55] Leadership by local chiefs and the respect that they held was crucial for the protected areas to work. As Josaia "Joe" Ramanatobue explained, "In the beginning it was very difficult; people didn't understand what we were trying to do. But now they are getting the picture. By protecting our reefs, we keep our reefs, and the money comes in. Today the reef is our main source of income. We fish for our own meals, but we also sell our catch at market. We use the reef every day to make a living."[56] The Namena marine reserve covers some 70 square kilometers of lagoon area surrounding the island of Namena and nearly 50 kilometers of barrier reef. The area is richly populated with corals, invertebrates, fish, sea birds, and sea turtles. An assessment of Namena Reef by the Planetary Coral Reef Foundation carried out in 2005 showed the management system seemed to be working well.[57]

Fiji's Energy Infrastructure

It is understandable that at the beginning of the twenty-first century the Fijian government was attempting to shift its energy system away from imported fossil fuels to local renewable sources. This effort reflected Fijian concerns with reducing carbon emissions as well as harsh economic realities. Like most Pacific Islands, Fiji has no local fossil fuel sources and was highly dependent on imported fuels for electric power generation and transportation. This made Fiji extremely vulnerable to global increases in oil prices, over which it had no control. All of Fiji's imported oil came from three multinational giants: Exxon Mobil, BP, and Total, the French oil company. Collectively these three companies had global revenues of more than a trillion dollars. Price jumps between 2000 and 2008 caused total Fijian expenditures on fuel to triple from nearly US$200 million to nearly $600 million in 2005 constant US dollars, whereas the total value of their imports less than doubled. This caused fuel costs to become more than a third of the value of all Fijian imports.[58] By 2008 Fijians were paying $649 per capita for imported fuel, which was 17 percent of their $3,800 GDP in PPP dollars per capita. In comparison, Americans in 2008 were paying nearly twice that ($1,209 per capita) for their fuel imports, but this was less than 3 percent of their much larger $43,781 GDP per capita. The cost of American fuel imports was only about one-fourth of total energy expenditures, because the United States used large amounts of its own coal, petroleum, and natural gas fuels, as well as hydroelectric and nuclear energy. If all U.S. expenditures on energy are counted, the per-capita figure for Americans would increase to about $3,860, based on 2006 figures, which would still be less than 10 percent of American GDP per capita. These figures dramatically illustrate the vulnerability of the Fijian energy system, and the wealth and energy intensity of the United States.

In 2007 more than half (52 percent) of Fiji's imported fuel was used for transportation.[59] Aviation took more than a third (35 percent), whereas vehicles used less than a fifth (18 percent). After transportation, the industrial manufacturing sector (38 percent) was the next-largest fossil fuel use, much of it for processing food products, sugar, and beverages. Residences and commercial establishments represented only about 3 percent of Fiji's fossil fuel consumption. In comparison, Americans used a third of their fossil fuels, mostly coal, for electricity production, and residential and commercial direct use of fossil fuels was about 14 percent. These differences are important because they mean that Fiji has real possibilities for maintaining a low emissions energy footprint if it can reduce its dependence on fossil fuels.

Most of the Fijian population, which lived on the two main islands of Viti Levu and Vanua Levu, obtained electric power from the government-owned Fiji Electricity Authority (FEA). These large islands have enough rainfall and elevation to support rivers favorable for hydropower production. In 2008 nearly two-thirds of Fiji's electricity was hydroelectric, whereas most of the remaining third is produced by diesel-fired generators.[60] In comparison, only 7 percent of electric power in the United States was hydroelectric, and nearly 70 percent was produced by thermal generators burning fossil fuels. The challenge facing Fiji's energy planners is reducing their dependence on ever-more-costly fossil fuels even as it extends power to the rural population, which in 2004 was about half of the total population, and only half of rural peoples had access to electricity.[61] FEA hopes to generate all its power based on fully renewable sources by 2011 with the help of independent power producers and was exploring all options, including wind; solar; biomass from sawmill, sugar mill, and copra waste; and small-scale hydroelectric. Biofuels based on sugar (bagasse) and coconuts may help phase out imported diesel fuel. The Fiji Sugar Corporation has already become energy self-sufficient by making use of what would otherwise be waste products of growing and processing sugarcane. Tropical biofuels can also be produced from manioc starch, molasses, and coconut oil. These alternative fuels may prove especially useful for Fiji's transport sector as global oil prices continue to rise. All new developments in rural areas were expected to be renewable, which realistically seemed to be the only feasible option for small islands.

FIJI Water and Fiji Sugar

Sugar was 25 percent of Fiji's $520 million in commodity exports in 2008. Fish were next at 14 percent, followed by bottled water (11 percent), garments (10 percent) and wood (8 percent).[62] The FIJI Water bottled water brand was developed by Canadian entrepreneur David Gilmour in 1998. Gilmour opened a bottling plant (originally Natural Waters of Viti Ltd.) on land that originally belonged to the Vatukaloko people, an indigenous group who resisted early British colonialism. The Vatukaloko were sitting on top of what proved to be an enormous aquifer. They attributed special powers to their water and made it part of their resistance movement. However, colonial authorities temporarily removed the Vatukaloko, and their lands were eventually sold to the Colonial Sugar Refining Corporation. Indigenous Fijians (*Itaukei*, "owners of the land") own 83 percent of Fiji's lands, which they will not sell, and they only allow Indo-Fijians or others to farm it on 20-year leases. Gilmour obtained a 99-year lease for his bottling plant from the government, because in 1973, after Fijian independence, the Vatukaloko homeland became the government-owned Yaquara Pastoral Company Ltd., a cattle ranch, and the government split off a portion for Gilmour. Some Vatukaloko people worked for FIJI Water, but in 2000 they seized the plant to assert their ownership claims to their land and water. Significantly, the Vatukaloko are asserting their claim as indigenous Fijian Itaukei, not on behalf of Fijian national society, but in opposition to both Indo-Fijian and European claims to indigenous Fijian property. Following capitalist forms introduced to Fiji by foreigners, the Vatukaloko even organized the Vatukaloko Investment Company to provide services to the foreign-owned bottling company. Gilmour sold FIJI Water in 2004 to Roll International, a privately held conglomerate with revenues of nearly $1 billion in 2007 that also dominates the production and distribution of citrus, almonds, and pistachios in the United States. Gilmour still owns the Fijian island of Wakaya, which he has converted into a luxury resort.

FIJI Water has been criticized for its claim that consumers who buy their bottled water are somehow helping the environment, even though the product must be packaged, shipped across the ocean, and marketed, and most consumers could safely satisfy their water requirements by simply drinking tap water.[63] The company had a careful audit of its carbon footprint carried out for a base year ending in 2007. They reported total emissions equivalent to 85,396 tonnes of CO_2 from all aspects of its operations. This represented only about 5 percent of Fiji's estimated emissions at that time. Over half of this came from the transport and manufacturing of packaging materials and the actual bottling operations. Transporting the product from the plant to the consumer took 43 percent. The company planned to be carbon neutral by 2010 by reducing emissions and by carbon offsets gained by protecting the rain forest in the Sovi Basin watershed for Suva and restoring the Yaqara Valley rain forest that protects FIJI Water's water supply. There is no doubt that the company is an important presence in Fiji. The actual value of FIJI Water may be much higher than the Fiji government export figures show. Elsewhere FIJI Water reported revenues of $150 million in 2008.[64] The company apparently negotiated a tax-free status with the government but reports that it donated $100,000 to a special Vatukaloko Trust Fund in 2007. FIJI Water hires nearly 350 Fijians and has an annual payroll of nearly $5 million. It also contributed $1.3 million to philanthropic projects in the country, such as schools, health clinics, and potable water.[65]

Anthropologist Martha Kaplan, who carried out fieldwork with the Vatukaloko people in 2002, points out that the success of the FIJI Water is due to a marketing strategy that associates the water with pristine nature: "natural artesian water"; purity: "untouched by man"; and health: "living water." Current labels also put consumers in touch with a pristine past by proclaiming that "FIJI Water fell as rain hundreds of years before the Industrial Revolution." Americans who drink it can feel virtuous because this water is perceived to be especially good for you, and a superior alternative to either high-calorie soft drinks, alcoholic beverages, or tap water, the purity of which some consumers do not trust because it is a government product and may even be fluorinated. Recent advertising also stresses that FIJI Water offsets its carbon footprint by teaming with Conservation International to protect Fijian rain forest. Steward Resnick, a principal owner and board chair of Roll International, is also a board member of Conservation International. In addition to its environmental credentials, FIJI Water conveys a special South Pacific natural exoticism because it is from a seemingly pristine Fijian ecosystem, but there one no Fijian culture or humanitarian issues. In contrast, Starbucks' Ethos Water dedicates part of its returns to "helping children get clean water."[66] According to Kaplan, by buying FIJI Water Americans are consuming an imagined nature, not unlike British imperialists who consumed refined, luxury commodities like sweetened tea.

Initially in the nineteenth century sugar production in Fiji was organized by an Australian company, the Colonial Sugar Refinery (CSR), which owned the sugarcane plantations and brought indentured laborers from India. As Carswell summarizes,[67] when indentured labor ended in 1920, CSR converted their laborers into smallholders on ten-acre (4.05 hectare) plots designed to support just a single cane-producing household presumably headed by a married man. Under strict cane-production contracts and wage and credit conditions dictated by the company, all household members—men, women, and children—necessarily became laborers. This was clearly an exploitative system, but it was not until 1969 that workers received a better return for their labor as a result of an official inquiry. The government bought out CSR in 1973. In 1996–1997, when Carswell conducted her field research, 22,500 smallholders were contracted to supply cane to the government's Fiji Sugar Corporation (FSC). At that time the cane production levels of most households were about half what was needed to meet basic needs, and half to 90 percent of their food was from subsistence crops. In 2007 the FSC still operated four sugar mills and seasonally employed up to 2,700 millworkers, but was losing money because of the huge decline in revenues caused by the EU's reduction of the trade subsidies that had supported Fiji's sugar prices for many years.

SUMMARY

Perhaps the most important conclusion about small nations is that high levels of human well-being can be achieved without growing a large nation, or a large economy, and even without a high per-capita income. This calls into question the commercial world's dominant ideological focus on economic growth as the primary goal of human endeavor. The success of small nations suggests that people in large nations could solve their own problems now by transforming themselves into small, more functional and more democratic nations and by adopting some of the crucial social and cultural changes already developed by small nations. Transformed large nations could join with successful small nations to build truly democratic international and planetary-scale institutions that would effectively address planetary-scale problems in a world of small nations. Technology by itself will not solve global problems, because they are primarily problems of scale, social power, and human perception and human action. Small nations show that it may be more important for societies to work to distribute social power and resources for optimum human benefit rather than continually increasing overall production in order to build larger economies. We have good models to follow; we just need to look beyond the existing superpowers. They are failed twentieth-century creations. By building new twenty-first-century social institutions and new, more effective sociocultural systems we can create a truly sustainable global system that will safely take our descendants into the next century and beyond. A small-nation world may be the best solution to global problems.

STUDY QUESTIONS

1. What is a small nation?
2. In what respects can Dominica be considered a successful small nation?
3. What are the most important differences between Dominica and Kauai that relate to sustainability and human well-being?
4. What proportion of the world's countries are small nations?
5. What proportion of the world's population lives in small nations?
6. Explain how Dominica and Saint Helena are able to maintain high life expectancies with small economies and low per-capita incomes.
7. What small nations have effectively eliminated poverty and succeeded in meeting climate change goals? How can their success be explained?
8. What small nations have maintained high levels of well-being without growing either their populations or their economies?
9. What special sustainability problems does Fiji confront?
10. How do small nations reduce the problem of military conflict?

SUGGESTED READINGS

Bodley, John H. 2003. *The Power of Scale: A Global History Approach.* Armonk, NY: M.E. Sharpe. Extended overview of the relationship between scale and concentrated social power in human history.

Bookchin, Murray. 1991. *The Ecology of Freedom: The Emergence and Dissolution of Hierarchy.* Montreal and New York: Black Rose Books. Advocates small federations, for social ecology, and libertarian municipalism.

Dahl, Robert A., and Edward R. Tufte. 1973. *Size and Democracy.* Stanford, CA: Stanford University Press. Sociological and political science perspective on scale of society.

Goetschel, Laurent. 1998. *Small States Inside and Outside the European Union: Interests and Policies.* Boston: Kluwer Academic Publishers. A political science perspective.

Sale, Kirkpatrick. 1980. *Human Scale.* New York: Coward, McCann and Geohegan. A useful discussion of the advantages of small-scale societies.

Kohr, Leopold. 1978. *The Breakdown of Nations.* New York: Dutton (originally published in 1957). The classic argument for why large nations are unsustainable.

Rapaport, Jacques, Ernest Muteba, and Joseph J. Therattil. 1971. *Small States and Territories: Status and Problems.* United Nations Institute for Training and Research. New York: ARNO Press. An early UN-sponsored study of small states.

Schumacher, E. F. 1973. *Small Is Beautiful: Economics As If People Mattered.* New York: Harper & Row.

GLOSSARY

Small nation A territorially organized sociocultural system in the commercial world with fewer than 10 million people.

Happy Planet Index A measure of a country's effectiveness at meeting human needs, based on life expectancy, subjective satisfaction with life, and the ecological footprint.

Human Development Index UN measure of sustainable development based on health, education, and income distribution.

Postmaterialist A sociocultural system where self-expression and rational secular values predominate, and people are less focused on material consumption.

Millennium Development Goals Eight-point set of development goals on poverty and health adopted by the UN in 2000.

Sustainable development UN Brundtland Commission official development goal since 1987, meeting the needs of the present without compromising the needs of future generations.

Small Island Developing States UN designation for countries that are especially vulnerable to environmental problems and global warming.

NOTES

1. Quinlan, Marsha B. 2004. *From the Bush: The Front Line of Health Care in a Caribbean Village*. Case Studies in Cultural Anthropology. Belmont, CA: Thomson Wadsworth.

2. Honeychurch, Lennox. 1975. *The Dominica Story: A History of the Island*. Oxford: Macmillan.

3. Marks, Nic, Saamah Abdallah, Andrew Simms, and Sam Thompson. 2006. *The Happy Planet Index: An Index of Human Well-Being and Environmental Impact*. London: New Economics Foundation. www.neweconomics.org/gen/z_sys_PublicationDetail.aspx?PID=225.

4. Halcrow Group Limited. 2003. *Dominica Country Poverty Assessment. Final Report*. Caribbean Development Bank, Government of the Commonwealth of Dominica.

5. Halcrow Group, 2003, *Dominica Country Poverty Assessment*, vi.

6. Kauai, County of. 2004. Kaua'i Economic Development Plan: Kaua'i's Comprehensive Economic Development Strategy (CEDS) Report 2005–2015. Office of Economic Development, Kauai Economic Development Board.

7. Kauai, 2004, Economic Development Plan, 38–40.

8. National Geospatial-Intelligence Agency. 2001. Geographic Names and FIPS 10 Digraph Codes: Countries, Dependencies, and Areas of Special Sovereignty. http://earth-info.nga.mil/gns/html/digraphs.htm.

9. Kuznets, S. 1960. Economic Growth of Small Nations. In Robinson, E.A.G., ed., *Economic Consequences of the Size of Nations*. Pp. 14–32. Proceedings of a Conference held by the International Economic Association. New York: St. Martin's Press.

10. Cave, Jonathan. 2003. *Towards a Sustainable Information Society*. TERRA 2000 IST-2000-26332, iii. www.terra-2000.org/htdocs/Terra-2002/index.htm.

11. Ascension Island Government, Official Website. www.ascension-island.gov.ac/aig/ascension-island-about.htm.

12. Tristan da Cunha Government Official Website. www.tristandc.com/economy.php.

13. DFID, UK Department for International Development 2009. A Review of Future Freight and Passenger Shipping Options for St Helena and Ascension Island. CNTR 07 8194, WSP Group. www.dfid.gov.uk/MediaRoom/Publications/?c=SH.

14. U.S. Internal Revenue Service, Statistics of Income. http://ftp.irs.gov/tastats/indtaxstats/article/0,,id=98123,00.html.

15. Government of Saint Helena. 2007. *St. Helena Sustainable Development Plan 2007/08–2009/10*. www.sainthelena.gov.sh/data/files/downloads/st_helena_sdp.pdf, 27.

16. Government of Saint Helena. 2007. *St. Helena Sustainable Development Plan 2007/08 2009/10*.

17. Inglehart, Ronald, and Christian Welzel. 2005. *Modernization, Culture Change, and Democracy: the Human Development Sequence*. New York: Cambridge University Press.

18. World Values Survey, www.worldvaluessurvey.org/organization/index.html.

19. Kasser, Tim, and Richard M. Ryan. 1993. "A Dark Side of the American Dream: Correlates of Financial Success as a Central Life Aspiration." *Journal of Personality and Social Psychology* 65(2):410–22; Kasser, Tim. 2002. *The High Price of Materialism*. Cambridge, MA: MIT Press.

20. Kasser, Tim, Steve Cohn, Allen D. Kanner, and Richard M. Ryan. 2007. "Some Costs of American Corporate Capitalism: A Psychological Exploration of Value and Goal Conflicts." *Psychological Inquiry* 18(1):1–22.

21. Kasser et al., 2007, "Costs of American Corporate Capitalism."

22. Esty, Daniel C., M. A. Levy, C. H. Kim, A. de Sherbinin, T. Srebotnjak, and V. Mara. 2008. *2008 Environmental Performance Index*. New Haven: Yale Center for Environmental Law and Policy. http://sedac.ciesin.columbia.edu/es/epi/downloads.html#summary.

23. These calculations are based on 29 large nations and 126 small nations from the World Bank online database, excluding from small nations three oil-rich countries United Arab Emirates, Qatar, and Kuwait whose resident population figures are distorted by extremely high number of immigrant laborers. http://ddp-ext.worldbank.org/ext/DDPQQ/member.do?method=getMembers&userid=1&queryId=6.

24. Metz, B., O. R. Davidson, P. R. Bosch, R. Dave, L. A. Meyer, eds. 2007. *Climate Change 2007: Mitigation of Climate Change. Contribution of Working Group III to the Fourth Assessment Report of the Intergovernmental Panel on Climate Change, 2007*. Cambridge, Eng. and New York: Cambridge University Press. www.ipcc.ch/publications_and_data/publications_ipcc_fourth_assessment_report_wg3_report_mitigation_of_climate_change.htm.

25. Kaya, Y. 1990. "Impact of Carbon Dioxide Emission Control on GNP Growth: Interpretation of Proposed Scenarios." Paper presented to the IPCC Energy and Industry Subgroup, Response Strategies Working Group, Paris. (cited in Metz et al. *Climate Change 2007*).

26. Hansen, James, et al. 2008. "Target Atmospheric CO2: Where Should Humanity Aim?" *The Open Atmospheric Science Journal* 2:217–31. www.bentham.org/open/articles.htm.

27. Meinshausen, Malte, Nicolai Meinshausen, William Hare, Sarah C. B. Raper, Katja Frieler, Reto Knutti, David J. Frame, and Myles R. Allen. 2009. "Greenhouse-Gas Emission Targets for Limiting Global Warming to 2oC." *Nature* 458(30 April):1158–62. nature08017.

28. Matthews, H. Damon. 2008. "Stabilizing Climate Requires Near-Zero Emissions." *Geophysical Research Letters* 35, L04705, doi:10.1029/2007GL032388, 208.

29. Baer, Paul, Tom Athanasiou, Sivan Kartha, and Eric Kemp-Benedict. 2008. *The Greenhouse Development Rights Framework: The Right to Development in a Climate Constrained World.* Heinrich Böll Foundation, Christian Aid, EcoEquity, and the Stockholm Environment Institute. http://gdrights.org/2009/02/16/second-edition-of-thegreenhouse-development-rights.

30. U.S. Energy Information Administration. 2009. "Total Carbon Emissions from the Consumption of Energy." www.eia.doe.gov/emeu/international/contents.html.

31. Kant, Immanuel. 1917 [1795]. *Perpetual Peace: A Philosophical Essay.* Edited and translated by M. Campbell Smith. London: Allen and Unwin.

32. World Bank, WDI Online. World Development Indicators. "Military Expenditure (% of GDP). http://ddp-ext.worldbank.org/ext/DDPQQ/member.do?method=get Members&userid=1&queryId=6 (accessed Nov. 2009).

33. WCED (World Commission on Environment and Development). 1987. *Our Common Future.* Oxford: Oxford University Press, 43.

34. United Nations Environment Programme. 1992. *Rio Declaration on Environment and Development.* www.unep.org/Documents.Multilingual/Default.asp?documentid=78&articleid=1163.

35. United Nations, Millennium Development Goals. 2009. www.un.org/millenniumgoals/.

36. United Nations. 1992. Agenda 21. Department of Economic and Social Affairs, Division for Sustainable Development, Chapter 17, Part G. Sustainable development of small islands, sections 123–36. www.un.org/esa/dsd/agenda21/res_agenda21_17.shtml.

37. UN General Assembly. 1994. Report of the Global Conference on the Sustainable Development of Small Island Developing States. A/CONF.167/9. Annex II Programme of Action for the Sustainable Development of Small Island Developing States, Preamble, Article 14. *www.sidsnet.org/docshare/other/BPOA.pdf.*

38. Global Island Partnership. 2008. GLISPA Brochure. www.cbd.int/island/glispa.shtml.

39. UN General Assembly. 1994. Report of the Global Conference on the Sustainable Development of Small Island Developing States.

40. UN General Assembly. 1994. Report of the Global Conference, Annex II Programme of Action for the Sustainable Development of Small Island Developing States, Preamble, Article 13.

41. Convention on Biological Diversity. 2009. Global Island Partnership. www.cbd.int/island/glispa.shtml.

42. United Nations Environment Programme (UNEP). 2009. Regional Seas Programme website., www.unep.org/regionalseas/programmes/default.asp.

43. Secretariat of the Pacific Regional Environment Programme (SREP). 2009. 2008 Annual Report of the Secretariat of the Pacific Regional Environment Programme. www.sprep.org/.

44. Fijilive. 2009. "Crest Chicken Eyes Local Feed Supply." Oct. 22, 2009. www.fijilive.com/news/2009/10/22/21058.Fijilive.

45. CMDA, Capital Markets Development Authority. 2008 Annual Report. www.cmda.com.fj/?page=cmdaAnnualReports.

46. Fiji, Ministry of Finance. 2007. *Strategic Development Plan 2007-2011.* www.mfnp.gov.fj.

47. Fiji, Ministry of Finance, *2007. Strategic Development Plan,* p. 3.

48. SPREP, South Pacific Regional Environment Programme. 1997. *Strategic Action Programme for International Waters of Pacific Islands.* www.iwlearn.net/iw-projects/sapsprep/reports/pacificislands_sap_1997.pdf/view.

49. SPREP. 1997. *Strategic Action Programme,* 5.

50. Lal, Padma, Margaret Tabunakawai, and Sandeep K. Singh. 2007. Economics of rural waste management in the Rewa Province and development of a rural solid waste management policy for Fiji. IWP-Pacific technical report (International Water Project) No. 57. Apia, Samoa: SPREP. www.sprep.org/publication/pub_detail.asp?id=574.

51. United States Environmental Protection Agency. 2009. Municipal Solid Waste Generation, Recycling, and Disposal in the United States, Detailed Tables and Figures for 2008, Table 1. www.epa.gov/osw/nonhaz/municipal/msw99.htm; SPREP, South Pacific Regional Environment Programme. n.d. "Pita Vatucawaqa: Protecting Fiji's rural communities from the impacts of human waste. www.sprep.org/iwp/IWPChamp/IWP-Fiji-Pita.htm.

52. Asian Development Bank. 2008. "Country Water Action: Fiji Islands Waste Threat Prompts Village Action." www.adb.org/Water/Actions/FIJ/Waste-Threat.asp.

53. SPREP, South Pacific Regional Environment Programme. 2005. "Romancing the Environment: Profile Pita Vatucawaqa." www.sprep.org/article/news_detail.asp?id=234.

54. Coral Reef Alliance, (CORAL). 2008. Building Healthy Coral Reef Communities: 2008 Annual Report, 1. www.coral.org/files/pdf/annualreports/2008annualreport.pdf.

55. Tu, Thomas, Paulo Kolikata, Sirilo Dulunaqio, Stacy Jupiter. 2009. *Integrating Ecosystem-Based Management Principles into the Fijian Context: A Case Study from Kubulau, Vanua Levu.* International Marine Conservation Congress: Making Marine Science Matter. May 17–24, 2009. Washington, D.C. http://www2.cedarcrest.edu/imcc/Program_Abstracts/data/20090522.html.

56. CORAL. 2008. Annual Report, 2.

57. Planetary Coral Reef Foundation. 2005. *Reef Report: Health of the Namena Reef.* www.pcrf.org/science/Namena/reefreport.html.

58. Singh, Anirudh. "The Sustainable Development of Fiji's Energy Infrastructure: A Status Report." *Pacific Economic Bulletin* 24(2):141–54; Fiji Islands Bureau of

Statistics, Economic Statistics, Overseas Merchandise Trade, Summary of Merchandise Trade Statistics. www.statsfiji.gov.fj/Economic/trade.htm (accessed January 7, 2010).

59. Singh, Fiji's Energy Infrastructure, Table 2; Fiji Islands Bureau of Statistics. 2008. Fiji Facts and Figures, As at 1st July 2008, p. 25. www.statsfiji.gov.fj/Economic/ecostats_index.htm.

60. Fiji Electricity Authority. 2008. FEA: Energizing Our Nation, Annual Report 2008. www.fea.com.fj/pages.cfm/about-fea/downloads/annual-reports.html.

61. Fiji Department of Energy. 2004. *National Energy Policy Document.* First Discussion Draft, p. 13. www.fiji.gov.fj/index.php?option=com_docman&task=doc_details&gid=78&Itemid=189.

62. Kaplan, Martha. 2005. "The *Hau* of Other Peoples' Gifts: Land Owning and Taking in Turn-of-the-Millennium Fiji." *Ethnohistory* 52(1):29–46; Kaplan, Martha.

2007. "Fijian Water in Fiji and New York: Local Politics and a Global Commodity." *Cultural Anthropology* 22(4):685–706; Fiji Islands Bureau of Statistics. 2009. *Key Statistics: Overseas Merchandise Trade.* Table 8.8. Exports by SITC. www.statsfiji.gov.fj/Economic/trade.htm.

63. Lenzer, Anna. 2009. "Fiji Water: Spin the Bottle." *Mother Jones.* September/October.

64. Carbon Disclosure Project. 2008. Fiji Water. www.cdproject.net/en-US/Results/Pages/Company-Responses.aspx?company=8190.

65. FIJI Water. 2009. *FIJI Water Responds to Mother Jones Article.* www.fijiwater.com/blog/2009/08/fiji-water-responds-to-mother-jones-article/.

66. Ethos Water website www.ethoswater.com/.

67. Carswell, Sue. 2003. "A Family Business: Women, Children and Smallholder Sugar Cane Farming in Fiji." *Asia Pacific Viewpoint* 44(2):131–48.

CHAPTER 15

Envisioning a Sustainable World

Figure 15.0. Newly constructed electric power generating windmills on the Thornton Bank, 28 km off shore, on the Belgian part of the North Sea (Source: Hans Hillewaert).

LEARNING OBJECTIVES

AFTER STUDYING THIS CHAPTER YOU SHOULD BE ABLE TO DO the following:

1. Critically evaluate power and scale solutions to the sustainability crisis, comparing them with other approaches.
2. Describe how the Nordic model contrasts with American corporate capitalism.

3. Describe how alternative forms of business organization can solve problems produced by corporations that are too large.
4. Describe what a sustainable planetary society might look like in the future.

The previous chapters in part IV examined how indigenous peoples and small nations at the margins of the global commercial world have been able to construct and maintain sustainable sociocultural systems that have both satisfied basic human needs and protected the natural environment. The primary conclusion from these small-scale societies is that social justice, democratic decision making, and equitable distribution of wealth and income are more important than economic growth by itself. The experience of indigenous people and small nations shows that development needs to focus on the satisfaction of real human needs, especially the needs for personal autonomy and self-actualization that healthy households and local communities can provide. In this final chapter the focus shifts to the prospects for large nations and wealthy highly developed nations to also construct sustainable systems. This approach reverses the first sixty years of international development work that was directed by elites in the developed world and instead considers how development might be directed by people who are not global elites. The question is to consider how the developed world can transform itself in positive ways by borrowing working models from small societies. It is time to ask how big economies and societies should be, if they are to be sustainable. This is an especially appropriate issue given that it is the developed world that produced the Great Acceleration in technology, production and consumption, and globalization that since 1950 has threatened the sustainability of the entire global system. At this time the future of humanity depends on how successfully people in the developed world transform their own societies and cultural systems in the next few decades.

TOWARD A SUSTAINABLE WORLD

Most global planners agree that significant cultural changes will be required if the global system is to remain intact through the end of the twenty-first century. This has been officially recognized since the much-cited 1987 report of the Brundtland Commission on environmental deterioration officially advocated sustainable development as a solution to global poverty and environmental deterioration.[1] The commission defined sustainable development as "development that meets the needs of the present without compromising the ability of future generations to meet their own needs." Sustainability is now a widely endorsed planning goal, as shown by frequent use of the expression "sustainable agriculture" and the oxymoron "sustainable economic growth." Institutionalized planning, however, still sets relatively short-term goals, often focused on single technologically defined issues such as global warming or food production. More fundamental problems, such as the need for a redistribution of political and economic power, are not being adequately addressed, even though the experience of small nations suggests that sustainability is a social scale and power problem. If progress is now equated with sustainability, the obvious failure of utopian capitalism to produce a demonstrably sustainable cultural system after 500 years of continuous growth suggests that increased scale and the more concentrated social power that growth produces may themselves be the primary obstacles to progress. Phrasing the sustainability problem in these terms opens the door to very exciting possibilities, because growth, scale, and power are cultural constructions that can be changed. People can gain control over the cultural processes that have produced instability. This final section discusses how social and economic scale relate to the distribution of power, examines the problems inherent in commercialization, and considers what cultural changes can produce, and have already produced, sustainable development in large nations and developed nations.

Global Crises and Cultural Response, 12,000 BC–AD 2050

The global crisis that humanity faces at the beginning of the twenty-first century is not entirely unprecedented. As detailed in previous chapters, humans have already transformed their cultures in response to four major global crises (see table 15.1). This demonstrates that we have an enormous capacity to adapt to new situations and shows that no particular cultural

development is inevitable or beyond human control. Other cultural worlds are possible.

Ten thousand years ago at the end of the last Ice Age, people faced a warming world and rising sea levels. They adapted in at least three different ways. Some, such as Australian Aborigines, kept their existing cultural system intact while gradually downscaling the size of their total population and of their territories. This option maintained the tribal world of mobile foragers. Others, such as Amazonian peoples and African cattle herders, opted to live in smaller territories and denser societies by adopting more-intensive food production systems and domestic technologies. This choice created the tribal world of Neolithic villagers. These tribal transformations were directed by everyone and must have happened so gradually that everyone benefited. A third option, which became possible under certain conditions, was to allow a few aggrandizing individuals to concentrate social power to permit survival for the majority, but at reduced levels of physical well-being and freedom. This decision ultimately created the imperial world of Pacific Island chiefdoms, the Ur-Nammu empire in ancient Mesopotamia, the Andean empires, and the Great Tradition civilizations in China and South Asia, but also produced many negative side effects for people and nature.

The chiefdoms, kingdoms, and empires of the imperial world went through repeated cycles of growth, collapse, and extinction, but these events did not become a global crisis until the cultures reached an effective growth ceiling during a period of deteriorating global climate. The European elite responded to the crisis of feudalism by concentrating economic power and ultimately creating the commercial world as a global capitalist system. Global capitalism allowed a few individuals and institutions to concentrate enormous levels of power, but by 1929 confronted its first crisis—a worldwide economic collapse, followed by massive social unrest and a destructive global war. The Euro-American elites responded by constructing a progressive global social order based on the ideals of human rights and social justice and capital- and fossil fuel–intensive economic growth. Unfortunately, in practice economic growth often overrode the ideals of human rights and justice.

By 1970 a second crisis of capitalism was under way as it became apparent to many people that the system was not working to benefit them as they expected and might not be sustainable. This time global elites responded by concentrating more power and

Table 15.1. Global Crises and Cultural Response, 12,000 BC – AD 2050

Agents	Decision	Outcome
I. Paleolithic Crisis: Post-Glacial Global Warming and Sea Level Rise, 12,000–5,000 BC		
Tribal Foragers	Downscale Society and Territory	Cultural Continuity of Mobile Forager World
Tribal Foragers	Intensify Subsistence Technology, Sedentarization	Creation of Neolithic Villager World
Aggrandizers, Political Elites	Concentrate Political Power, Urbanize, Conquer	Creation of Imperial World
II. Crisis of Feudalism: Scale Limits of Imperial World, AD 1300–1790		
European Elites	Depose Divine Monarchy, Concentrate Economic Power	Creation of Commercial World
	Promote: Colonialism, Capitalism, Democratic Regimes	
III. Crisis of Capitalism: Cyclical Economic Depressions and Wars, 1929–1950		
Euro-American Elites	Distribute Income Down	Creation of Progressive Global Order
	Promote: Decolonization, Energy- and Capital-Intensive Growth, Global Institutions, Human Rights	
IV. Crisis of Capitalism: Economic Downturn, Social Protest, 1970–1980		
Global Elites	Distribute Wealth & Income Up	Creation of Global Economy
	Promote: Multinational Corporations, Energy- & Capital-Intensive Development	
V. Sustainability Crisis: Environmental Degradation, Poverty, Social Protest, 1990–2050		
Global Citizens	Redistribute Social power, Downscale Societies	Creation of Sustainable Global Society
	Promote: Human Economic and Social Rights, Freedom, Social Equity, and Sustainability	

promoting even more intensive growth to create a larger, more integrated global economy. By 1990 with global warming beginning, global poverty unsolved, and social unrest and conflict increasing, including global terrorism and massive habitat destruction and extinctions, it was clear that the global system was not sustainable as constructed. The global financial crisis that began in 2007 demonstrated further instability in the commercial world.

Another major cultural transformation is required. The global warming crisis alone will force people to adjust over a very long period. Even if carbon dioxide emissions are stabilized and reduced by 2050, temperatures may take centuries to stabilize, and sea levels are expected to rise for millennia.

Power and Scale Solutions

Recognizing the dynamics of growth, scale, and power as the source of the present sustainability crisis calls attention to the solutions already developed by indigenous people and small nations. Elite-directed growth has created a succession of crises for humanity over the past 5,000 years. Societies and economies can-

not grow forever and survive in a finite world. Clearly, elite solutions have failed, because they have been self-interested and too narrowly focused to maintain viable societies. Likewise, concentrated social power has proven maladaptive, because it has given too few too much ability to transform the world.

Our first priority in achieving a sustainable global culture will be to gain universal acceptance for the principle that all of humanity, all citizens of the world, need to be decision makers and agents of cultural transformation. This will require full implementation of existing human rights conventions covering economic and social rights, as well as basic civil rights. Next, international institutions need to be reconstituted to fully protect human freedom, redistribute social power, and work for social justice in the global system. Effective international tribunals will be needed to hold individual and corporate tyrants responsible for human rights violations.

Redistributing social power to all citizens of the world will be a major undertaking. It will mean universalizing truly democratic political institutions at local, regional, national, and global levels. This would be facilitated in some cases by redistricting to down-scale political units in order to give citizens more effective control over elected officials and more influence in larger representative forums. The principles of democratic political order are already widely accepted but poorly practiced. Problems need to be addressed at the levels at which they occur. Military power can be downscaled by effective implementation of existing international arms conventions, especially those dealing with weapons of mass destruction. Great nations may also subdivide into several smaller nations, thereby reducing the threat of massive military power.

Redistributing ideological power will require full implementation of existing human rights applied to religious belief and practice. It will also require universal recognition of freedom of the press, speech, and assembly as incorporated in the American Bill of Rights and the European Union Charter of Fundamental Rights, and full application to all media. This may require limits on concentrated commercial ownership and control of the media, as well as limitations on commercial advertising.

Redistributing economic power will require a broader concept of wealth to include conventional financial and tangible forms of wealth, as well as natural capital, social and cultural capital, and human capital. Encouraging unlimited accumulation of private financial capital will not be the primary objective of the political economy in a sustainable world order. Different property regimes may be needed to preserve capital and meet human needs. Natural capital would not be freely available for short-term private benefits, because it would provide trillions of dollars in global services for such vital ecosystem services as climate regulation, water regulation, soil formation, and the

production of edible biomass and organic materials by ecosystems.[2] The GDP measure of income will need to be adjusted to account for perverse subsidies, and democratic public institutions will need to devise means to distribute income to meet the requirements of social justice and sustainability.

The objective of these cultural transformations would not only be to construct a sustainable global system but to create a world in which social units and institutions would be the best size to optimize human well-being, making it possible for people to enjoy "the good life" or the summum bonum, as defined by their particular culture. The summum bonum concept recognizes the individual need to maintain and reproduce a successful household, to socialize, to be prosperous and secure, and to enjoy expressive culture (see table 15.2). It is likely that all of these individual needs could be met within optimum-size societies having local communities of 500, towns of 5,000, regional urban centers of 50,000, and a metropolis of a few hundred thousand—all within a national society of up to 15 million.[3] As societies grow larger, individual needs are "socialized," becoming objectives of the whole society, such as economic growth or national glory. These are "post-optimum" objectives; socialization concentrates power and promotes further growth and quickly becomes a very costly and inefficient way to meet human needs. Many energy-intensive technologies can be considered "scale commodities," or "scale subsidies," because their primary function is to sustain post-optimum scale systems.

The concept of the summum bonum is closely related to the concept of Pareto optimality, identified by the Italian social philosopher and economists Vilfredo Pareto[4] (1848–1923), who also discovered the power

Table 15.2. Social Scale and the _Summum Bonum_

Individual Objectives	Organization, Institutions	Optimum Population Scale	Post-Optimum Socialized Objectives
HUMANIZATION Reproduction, maintenance	HOUSEHOLD	5–25 household	Social health
SOCIABILITY Companionship	VILLAGE Clubs, taverns	500 village, community	Social welfare
PROSPERITY Leisure & wealth	TOWN Factories, markets	5000 town, region	Economic growth GNP
SECURITY Security, peace, justice, defense	CITY Courts, city hall, armories	10,000–20,000 city, nation, absolute extended maximum 15 million	Military power empire
ESPRESSIVE CULTURE	METROPOLIS, STATE Theaters, churches, museums, galleries, universities	100,000–200,000 metropolis, nation, technological maximum 15 million	National glory

Source: Kohr (1977).

law distribution of income. Pareto optimality is the point at which economic growth should stop because no one can get ahead without pushing someone else down. This was the problem with most post-tribal world economic growth and can be understood as the cause of poverty and exploitation in both imperial and commercial worlds.

Toward a Multiscale Cultural World

We can create sustainable cultures. But this will require the construction of a world system composed of many independent regional cultures, each working to establish a humane balance between the cultural processes that sustain households and those that sustain communities, polities, and commercial activities. Domestically organized indigenous cultures could thrive in such a multiscale world while national polities also remained secure. The Basques of northern Spain have already shown that sustainable cultural systems can be designed that effectively integrate industrial technologies and commercialization within an existing nation-state (see box 15.1).

Designing sustainable cultures will require a localization process to diffuse social power by limiting growth and reducing the scale of both government and business enterprise. Localization built on existing local and regional governments would make democratic decision making by all adults a reality. It would also make it easier for workers to act as business owner-managers and for business profits to benefit local communities. Diffusing social power would allow local communities to regulate growth and scale by giving priority to the maintenance and reproduction of healthy households. The optimum balance between political and economic power could then be democratically established by each cultural community.

To make these changes, people in each region of the world need to be free to manage culture scale and social power in ways that are most sustainable in their particular cultural and natural settings. Truly sustainable development should demand nothing less, but this is precisely the opposite of the wealth-concentrating growth program being promoted by the experts at the World Trade Organization, the World Bank, and the International Monetary Fund, who make global commercial competitiveness the top priority. Unfortunately, dollars are not democratic. The poor do not have equal opportunity in this kind of world, and localities are pitted against each other. The next great cultural development must put the interests of all people first by letting local communities and

households set growth and development priorities. A useful guiding principle can be found in the concept of Pareto optimality, which is the ideal point at which development stops, that being when no one can get richer without making someone else poorer. Sustainable development policies could be most readily implemented by culturally homogeneous local communities, as is often the case with indigenous peoples. Large urban centers may also often have culturally distinct neighborhoods, but in many cases, locality rather than culture would necessarily be the basis of political mobilization. People in diverse communities and political constituencies may find a common ground in efforts to implement the humanitarian objectives enshrined in existing human rights charters, such as the United Nations Universal Declaration of Human Rights.

Our long-run self-interest demands that we diffuse social power and reduce the scale of culture to manageable human proportions. We can begin this essential evolutionary correction by moving now to construct public policies that will strengthen the political and economic powers of households, local and regional communities, and noncommercial institutional structures, including voluntary associations. We need to abandon the goal of perpetual economic growth as an end in itself and focus instead on the design of our cultural systems to truly democratize social power. We need to focus on allocation rather than production. The incentives for wealth concentration can be reduced by progressive tax laws that promote philanthropy. Corporate welfare can be channeled to small businesses. Corporations that misuse their power or engage in criminal conduct can be dechartered. The Tobin tax on international currency transactions can be implemented. Tax laws that reward mergers and speculative finance can be eliminated. Perhaps most importantly, we must deny anonymity to anyone with massive power. The public must have full information about power networks and the ways power is used.

The commercial culture's two unresolved, interconnected problems—impoverishing concentrations of social power and the impossibility of perpetual growth in a finite world—are both exaggerated by increases in scale. A more humane culture would use market forces to reward equitable and sustainable allocations of material prosperity. Democratic processes could bring both scale and power under control. Local and regional markets designed to draw on locally owned and managed resources could enhance every community's potential for self-reliance—much like tribal indigenous cultures that based their success on maintaining a permanent stake in particular places. Local residents would shift their finance capital out of remote mutual funds and foreign corporations into local enterprises in which investors have a direct, permanent stake. The efficiencies that local, small-scale enterprises gain by reducing the need for transportation costs, advertising, large CEO salaries, and ever-larger shareholder profits might offset the scale advantages that remote giant enterprises now enjoy. As energy costs rise and as the human costs of global business become more apparent, small-scale alternatives will become more attractive, and people will choose to bring their capital home. Many communities are already experimenting with local currencies and reviving regional produce markets. An energizing positive feedback will begin as citizens become increasingly disillusioned with remote and unresponsive political systems and turn to their own local and regional governments for solutions. Economic crises in the global system will only speed this inevitable cultural development process.

BOX 15.1. THE MONDRAGON COOPERATIVES

A successful, highly democratic, and economically just cultural system has been operating quietly in northern Spain since the 1950s.[5] Stubbornly independent Basques have created an integrated regional society of some 250,000 people, based on a system of numerous small-scale, worker-owned cooperatives centered on the town of Mondragon. Each Mondragon cooperative is limited in size to no more than 500 members, who each have an equal vote in management decisions. There are no giant, remotely owned corporations. The scale limit is crucial, because the Basques have learned that it is almost impossible for larger production units to remain truly democratic. Likewise, the pay scale normally increases by no more than a factor of six from top to bottom, which both rewards hard work and sets a ceiling on executive pay. Everyone shares in annual profits, and a proportion goes to support local community projects and the Basque cultural heritage.

The crucial principles of the Mondragon cooperative system is that workers and community are considered to be more important than capital, and workers are both owners and managers. Decision making is based on democratic principles.[6] The primacy of workers is reflected in the salary scale, which gave entry-level workers a livable wage of US$16,480 in 2005 and in which the highest income rank topped out at $98,880. Workers buy shares in their cooperative and receive annual dividends.

Mondragon cooperatives manufacture world-class computerized robots and a wide range of exported industrial goods and consumer durables. They also run their own consumer co-ops and cooperative banking, social insurance, education, and child care services that respond directly to the needs of local people. The Mondragon mission statement makes employment, community, equity, education, and environment the primary objectives, and Basque cultural autonomy is a key to their achievement. The Basques are a unique people who claim to be descendants of the Ice Age peoples who produced the great paintings on the cave walls at Lascaux and Altamira 30,000 years ago. In fact, their language and genetic roots do connect them with the most ancient Europeans. The Basques have learned that general welfare and domestic tranquility can best be achieved when everyone is allowed to manage the human, cultural, and natural resources that produce wealth.

This example shows how localization processes are actually being implemented in a particular region. The Basques are attempting to maintain high degrees of local cultural autonomy based on economic self-reliance. They are using industrial technology and capitalist economics within an integrated network of worker-owned, small-scale corporate business enterprises that strive to be highly democratic and egalitarian while supporting households and local communities.

By 2005 there were 108 cooperatives, 138 subsidiary companies, and 18 support organizations. There were 63,500 member shareowners and annual revenues of US$15 billion. The Mondragon cooperatives had become the seventh-largest business group in Spain, and it was the most prominent system of cooperatives in the world. By 2008 revenues had increased to $22 billion and total assets were US$18 billion. There are now affiliated cooperative corporations scattered throughout the world, all following the same cooperative principles.

Wealth Redistribution as Development in India

The only major alternative to the perpetual growth approach to development is wealth redistribution emphasizing social justice. Redistribution is a development process that would in effect return priority to the humanization goals championed by tribal cultures. Ideally, the satisfaction of basic human needs with maximum social equality would be the objective of this kind of development. This alternative is inherently difficult because it offers no immediate benefits to the wealthy and powerful; however, it has actually been tried in a few cases with some success, as the following examples show.

The state of Kerala in southwest India represents an unusual attempt at development directed by the poor to meet their needs. This was a social transformation process organized by poor farmers, workers, and tenants, who engaged in decades of political struggle to transform a cultural system that was dominated by inequities of caste and grossly concentrated wealth and power. This struggle for social justice, as analyzed by Richard Franke and Barbara Chasin,[7] has important implications for development theory. When Franke and Chasin assessed Kerala's economy in 1989, it had not grown significantly, as measured by per-capita GNP, and unemployment remained high. But the people's basic needs were being more effectively satisfied than in many countries where more economic growth had occurred. In fact, Kerala was the highest-ranked Indian state on the UN Human Development Index (HDI) and increased each decade from 0.5 in 1981, to 0.59 in 1991, and 0.63 in 2001, which was considered medium human development.[8]

According to Franke and Chasin, protests against caste injustices opened the way for a broad range of social reforms. The Kerala variant of the Hindu caste system required some of the most extreme and degrading forms of ritual separation in India. Lower-caste people were kept in perpetual servitude to higher-caste people while being denied access to marketplaces, temples, schools, and public roads. In a series of peaceful mass protests against these indignities during the 1920s and 1930s, low-caste people and their political supporters in the Indian Communist party used open violations of the taboos to win political reforms that eventually eased caste restrictions. "Eat-ins" were held in which higher-caste political organizers ate with untouchables in their homes, thus publicly violating the Hindu concepts of purity and pollution that sustained caste differences. Anti-caste movements eventually combined with labor movements and peasant unions, and together they succeeded in forcing the government to adopt wide-ranging political reforms that restructured society, redistributing wealth and power. These reform movements were conducted without resorting to armed violence, even though protesters were often murdered and imprisoned.

Before land reform was implemented in 1969, Kerala's agricultural land, the basic source of wealth and subsistence in the state, was controlled primarily by an upper class of Brahman landlords, who constituted about 2 percent of the population. The Brahmans owned both the irrigated rice fields and the plots where poor farmers built their house compounds and maintained small food-producing gardens. The landlords leased their land to a class of superior tenants, who often subleased to inferior tenants, who, if possible, hired untouchables to do the actual farmwork. Poor farmers were often perpetually in debt yet were forced to pay 50 to 94 percent of their gross harvest to landlords or face eviction. The land reform process turned former tenants into landowners while compensating the former landlords. Limits were also set on the size of landholdings.

Specific food distribution programs, some under way since early in the twentieth century, have included school lunch programs, free daily meal programs for infants and their mothers, and a system of ration shops selling basic foodstuffs to the poorest households at controlled prices. These programs appear to have had a significant effect. Regional food surveys in Kerala in the 1980s suggested that people were getting approximately 2,300 kilocalories per day. This was above the national average of 2,126 kilocalories and much more than the 1,500 kilocalories that the impoverished sugarcane workers in northeast Brazil were receiving, as discussed earlier. Childhood growth studies show that Kerala's young children are doing slightly better than the average for India, even though per-capita income is actually lower in Kerala.

Political reformers in Kerala regarded adequate housing, clean water, sanitation, and vaccinations as public health issues and campaigned for government programs to make these basic needs available to everyone. These goals have not been fully achieved, but the government has been successful in making health services, including doctors, primary health care centers, and hospitals, more available in Kerala than in other parts of India. The clearest measure of the overall success of this wealth redistribution effort can be seen in Kerala's figures for adult literacy (78 percent), life expectancy (68 years), and infant mortality (27 per 1,000 live births), which were significantly better than the Indian 1986 average of 43 percent, 57 years, and 86 per 1,000, respectively. Kerala's infant mortality rate of 27 was a spectacular achievement in comparison with the rate of 211 that Scheper-Hughes[9] found in Bom Jesus in the Brazilian northeast in 1987. Improvements in infant mortality, life expectancy, and education, together with government pension programs, have reduced the incentive to raise large families, particularly for poor farmers. When these social gains were combined with government-supported family-planning programs and general improvements in the status of women, birth rates declined significantly in comparison with the rest of India.

Conventional development programs emphasize economic opportunities for men and often adversely affect the economic contribution of women in the household. This is certainly the case in India and is a factor in the recent increase in bride burnings, as discussed in chapter 9. Thus, it is significant that the health status of women in Kerala is better than elsewhere in India. This improvement in the status of women is due in part to effective social support programs and has occurred despite high rates of female unemployment.

Kerala is a historically unique case, but it suggests that informed underclass groups can organize themselves and use democratic political processes to overcome the disadvantages imposed by the inequities of wealth and power. This kind of redistribution occurred in the absence of economic growth. In this post–Cold War world, it is also important to recognize that in many impoverished countries, leftist or socialist political organizations may be able to contribute positively to development, where externally financed and directed programs may have failed to meet the needs of the most impoverished classes.

Andean Development: The Vicos Experiment

The Cornell Peru Project conducted at the hacienda of Vicos in the Peruvian Andes from 1952 to 1963 is one of the best-known development anthropology projects.[10] This was a unique, long-term development effort, planned and directed by anthropologists as a **participant intervention** experiment in cultural change designed to empower the peasantry. Using research funds provided by the Carnegie Corporation of New York, the project codirectors—American anthropologist Allan Holmberg, then of Cornell University, and Peruvian anthropologist Mario Vazquez—rented the colonial-style hacienda of Vicos, where some 2,000 peasants lived as virtual serfs on a 60-square-mile (155-km²) estate. The anthropologists then used their position as managers of the hacienda to gradually turn political power back to the peasants and help them regain control over their ancestral land. This was a novel approach to development and was widely considered a success, but the key feature was the project's focus on social power and access to resources.

The **hacienda** system in the Peruvian Andes in 1952 was a continuation of colonial social structures created by the Spaniards following their conquest of the Inca empire in the sixteenth century. The original Spanish conquerors created great landed estates for themselves out of the best lands. These estates, or *encomiendas*, like European manors, included rights to extract labor and produce from the natives who were already residents on the land. After Peru became independent from Spain, the descendants of the conquerors retained their dominant position in Andean society, and many of the encomienda estates remained in place as vast haciendas and plantations.

The Andean haciendas were agricultural estates with a dominant landowner and a dependent labor force that produced primarily for subsistence and local markets.[11] In the twentieth century haciendas were often administered by absentee owners who intentionally kept the resident natives impoverished so that many would be forced to provide cheap labor. The hacienda was divided sharply into two classes that were each further stratified. Power was concentrated at the top with the *hacendado*, the Spanish owner, and his hired administrators. The *hacendado*, or *patron*, used his landholding to enhance his personal wealth and status and was supported in his power by regional and national political authorities and church officials.

Hacienda laborers, or *peones*, were Quechua-speaking indigenous peoples granted small subsistence holdings, often on marginal lands, and the landowners allowed them to graze their livestock on the estate. As rent, the *peones* were obligated to work three days a week for the hacienda, for which they received a token wage. They were also required to provide the hacienda free service and the labor of their animals on demand. The *peones* were treated as ignorant children by the patron and his managers. As serfs, they were expected to show exaggerated, hat-in-hand respect for those in charge. Uncooperative *peones* were subject to imprisonment and fines, although formerly they might have been beaten. Hacienda officials created support by dispensing small favors and sometimes acted as godparents to specific native families. Ritual coparenthood, the institution of *compradazgo*, established an informal alliance between families of different social ranks.

When the Vicos participant-intervention experiment began, the anthropologist-*patrons* immediately began to move the *peones* into administrative positions in the hacienda, replacing the former managers. Next they abolished free service and began to pay decent wages to their new native employees. Profits from agricultural production were returned to the community in the form of agricultural improvements and schooling. A formal group of community leaders was organized to participate directly in the planning of the entire project, and weekly meetings were held with all workers to discuss problems. In 1957, the project leaders petitioned the government for a decree of expropriation that would allow the natives to obtain full ownership of the hacienda. This action aroused the ire of the local elite, who accused the project of being a Communist plot, but after five years of persistent effort and the intervention of the U.S. ambassador and supportive officials within the Peruvian government, the Vicos hacienda was sold to its former serfs in 1962. The Cornell Peru Project terminated the next year. Holmberg attributed the apparent success of his experiment to its approach to political power: "The element of power proved to be the key that permitted the Cornell Peru Project to open the door to change; the devolution of power to the people of Vicos proved to be the mechanism that made the new system viable."[12]

The emphasis on changing the local power structure in Vicos was certainly innovative in development anthropology; in retrospect, however, it is difficult to precisely evaluate the long-term impact of the project. Surveys conducted up to 1964 showed measurable improvements in nutrition, education, and some indicators of material prosperity. The community did make some critical tradeoffs in its "modernization." Responding to the program's directives, they formed an agricultural cooperative organized along capitalist lines as a profit-making agricultural corporation. This move carried significant risks because it weakened or replaced many pre-Inca subsistence practices. To buy the land, the new Vicos corporation assumed a substantial long-term debt with the government for half of the total purchase price. Many Vicos families also assumed large individual debts with the Peruvian government's agricultural bank to pay for the expensive new agricultural inputs required for profitable market production.

Even the new production technology involved additional trade-offs, such as the adoption of hybrid high-yield potatoes, which were better suited for the national market. The new varieties proved to have many disadvantages for Andean communities.[13] The new potatoes are grown as a monocrop that requires exotic debt-producing inputs, and the crop must be sold on the national government-controlled market. By contrast, local communities control all the skills and other inputs required to produce and distribute native potatoes. Oxen and foot plows are locally produced and maintained. Unlike tractors, they require no imported fuel and are highly reliable. There are more than 2,000 varieties of traditional potatoes, each developed for special qualities of taste, storability, and hardiness under specific local conditions. These potatoes, greatly preferred by Andean people, are readily bartered and sold in the local markets.

Anthropologist Paul Doughty, who first visited Vicos in 1960, revisited in 1997 and provides an overview of the project's achievements and problems.[14] He found that the trend toward material prosperity was continuing; however, in 1996, the people of Vicos formally disbanded their agricultural cooperative and replaced it with more traditional forms of organization and access to land.

The Vicos project closely resembled Peru's later agrarian reform program of 1969, which also expropriated haciendas and promoted commercial agriculture. However, it is significant that although many Andean communities were eager to gain control over their lands under the new land reform program, they stubbornly and sometimes violently refused to form cooperatives and resisted agricultural "modernization." Their refusal to cooperate with the government program was not because the peasants were ignorant and backward. They simply did not want the government to become their new *patron*, and they rationally preferred their own forms of agricultural production.[15]

At the local level, the Andean system is based on barter of food products between communities, exchanges of labor based on *ayni* (simple reciprocity), and household ownership of widely dispersed plots. This form of land ownership is a distinctively kinship-based cultural pattern and assumes relative equality and self-sufficiency while it minimizes risk and makes effective use of local resources. In the Andean setting, small, intensively utilized plots, though disparaged by agricultural economists, can be highly productive. The national agrarian reform plan called for the peasants to be integrated into the national economy by means of agricultural cooperatives in debt to the government and dependent on the market economy. The advantage for the government of such an arrangement was that it gave it greater control over the peasantry and provided inexpensive food to support urban industrialization. This kind of rural development might make some farmers wealthy, but it brings substantial risks and means that local control systems and sustainability might be lost. These are especially critical issues today, now that global warming is causing Andean glaciers to melt, which could reduce irrigation water.

TRANSFORMING THE DEVELOPED WORLD

Governments, intergovernmental organizations, and businesses are now using many futurist scenarios and projections to guide their efforts to achieve sustainable development, but most of these projections accept perpetual growth as a given even far into the future. Much of this effort has focused on climate change, which is of course a major problem, but it is a symptom of the underlying problems of elite-directed growth, scale, and concentrated power that are not on the planning agenda. For example, the widely cited Special Report on Emissions Scenarios (SRES)[16] used by the UN Intergovernmental Panel on Climate Change to explore the effects on carbon emissions of different global futures assumes under the most optimistic high-technological economic globalization future (A1T) projects that the global economy would triple, reaching $187 trillion by 2050 and then nearly triple again to $550 trillion by 2100. Global gross domestic product (GDP) stood at $60 trillion in 2008, and the global environment and social system were already unsustainable, so it is difficult to imagine growth ever reaching these levels. The A1T world would see global population peak at 8.7 billion by 2050 and then decline to 7 billion by 2100. World average GDP per capita would soar from $6,023 in 2008 to $21,496 by 2050 and $77,948 by 2100. These projections do not consider the reality that in such a world, with the distribution of power remaining in its present "natural" power law form, the world would still be a plutonomy and a plutocracy, and it would be directed by a thousand trillionaire elite investors, rather than by a few million high-net-worth individuals as presently. The SRES scenarios do not consider the kind of sociocultural transformations that would change the distribution of wealth and power as required to produce genuine sustainability. This dimension of the sustainability problem is not on the agenda of intergovernmental organizations because it involves difficult political and ideological issues. The world of corporate business is working together with philanthropic foundations to solve the global warming problem, but again they approach it primarily as a technological problem, or a market design problem.[17]

This section will examine existing examples of the kinds of sociocultural structures in large wealthy nations that do work to distribute wealth and power in equitable ways that can serve as models of sustainable development that could be adopted more widely. Just as in the small nation examples, these are proven solutions that exist now. Solutions are right in front of us, but they are not being adopted widely enough because people do not recognize their reality. This suggests that the real problem is the elite use of self-interested deception, illusion, and delusion to alter majority perceptions. The problem lies in the way elites have used the cultural superstructure to promote power-concentrating growth. Greater transparency will help, but people also need to understand that there are many ways of organizing the commercial world.

Norway, Norden, and the Successful Nordic Model

Norway can be taken as an example of the most sustainable and successful country in the world. Norway is a small nation of 4.6 million people that stands out as a highly successful nation in regard to all the measures of quality of life, sustainability, and human development that we have considered (see figures 15.1 and 15.2). It ranked at the top of the HDI in 2009 and had increased steadily since 1980. In comparison, the United States ranked thirteenth in the HDI in 2009. In 2007 Norway's average life expectancy at birth was 80.5 years, and its GDP (PPP) was $53,433. Only 7 percent were living below 50 percent of the median income (compared with 17 percent below in the United States). Norway ranks second in the world, after Sweden, for gender empowerment (the United States ranked eighteenth), and women held 36 percent of the seats in Parliament (compared with 17 percent in the U.S. Congress). Norwegian women held 56 percent of ministerial rank positions (compared with 24 percent cabinet-rank women in the United States). Norway had a much more equitable income distribution than the United States, with the poorest Norwegians getting more and the richest less. The poorest 10 percent of Norwegians received nearly 4 percent of income, whereas the poorest 10 percent of Americans received less than 2 percent. The Norwegian top 10 percent received 23 percent, in comparison with nearly 30 percent going to the top 10 percent of Americans.

Norway is not exemplary on all sustainability measures. Although as a small nation, its total impact on the environment is low, it nevertheless has a relatively high per-capita ecological footprint, ranking eighth highest in the Living Planet Report for 2008, after the United Arab Emirates, United States, Kuwait, Denmark, Australia, New Zealand, and Canada.[18] However, Norway's per-capita annual carbon emissions of 9.1 tons were significantly lower than the U.S. at 19.9

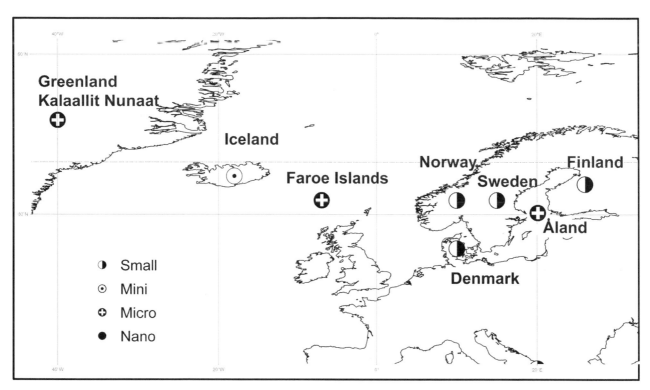

Figure 15.1. Map of Norden countries.

Figure 15.2. Fishing village, northwest Coast of Norway, 1997 (Victor Bloomfield).

in 2007.[19] Norway ranks sixth on the Environmental Performance Index, which represents achievement of policy goals, compared with the United States at 107th out of 154 countries. Sustainable development is officially a high priority for the Norwegian government.[20] The official sustainable development strategy of 2008 covers social development as well as environmental concerns, and it specifically takes into account the perspectives of the indigenous Saami people. Norway also accepts the conclusions of the 2006 U.K. government-commissioned Stern Review on the Economics of Climate Change[21] as a strong argument for urgent government-backed measures and international agreements to reduce carbon emissions. The Stern Review declared that from an economic perspective climate change "... is the greatest and widest-ranging market failure ever seen."[22] The Stern Review also concluded that the likely severity of future economic damage from climate change meant that taking significant action now to reduce carbon emissions would be cost effective in the long run. What is remarkable about the Norwegian government's acceptance of the urgency of action on climate change is that they were able to reach a consensus, whereas consensus has been difficult for the United States and China, the largest carbon-emitting nations.

The sustainability of Nordic countries can be attributed to important features of their sociocultural systems that contribute to a balance between social, political, and commercial sectors. The small size of their populations and economies probably makes balance more feasible. For example, a careful comparison between Sweden and the United States shows some significant scale-related differences.[23] The service sectors of Sweden and the United States are approximately the same size, but in the United States a much higher proportion is devoted to business services (nearly 34 percent versus 18 percent), whereas in Sweden, social services are proportionately larger (37 percent versus 26 percent). The higher labor cost of business in the United States may be due to scale subsidies required to support a very large-scale economy and market. Sweden has proportionately more teachers, professionals, and technicians than the United States, whereas the United States has more clerical workers and managers. Sweden also has a higher proportion of its employment in the state sector, which helps explain Sweden's larger proportion of professionals. State and professional workers are generally more autonomous as workers than those working under managers in large corporations. Autonomous workers are more likely to feel in control of the conditions of their daily life than workers who are simply employees.

The overall sociocultural features of the Nordic states may in part be a result of their specific historical situation in the modern evolution of the commercial world. Nordic states were never expansion imperialists, or colonial powers, but many people did emigrate to the United States during difficult economic times. Small economies in small countries face constraints on capital accumulation. The political struggle between capitalists and workers followed a more balanced pathway in the Nordic states than in the United States, which was due in part to other specific cultural historical differences. The economic philosophy behind the social welfare state has very deep roots in Scandinavia. Finns and Swedes claim Enlightenment philosopher and clergyman Anders Chydenius (1729–1803) as a free market advocate whose primary book, *The National Gain*[24] (1766), predated Adam Smith's *Wealth of Nations* by a decade but explicitly supported democratic human rights for everyone, including the poor.

Considering how Norway is organized and the distinctive features of its culture will help to illustrate what features might work in other countries. The earliest inhabitants of Norway were the ancestors of the fishing and reindeer-herding Saami people. Agriculturalists reached Norway about 6,000 years ago, and the Scandinavian kingdoms were established about 1,000 years ago. Norway became a self-governing territory under the Swedish monarchy in 1814 and became a fully independent constitutional monarchy in 1905. Norway is part of Norden, or the Nordic Council and Nordic Council of Ministers. Norden is an intergovernmental organization of eight small democratic countries in the north Atlantic and Baltic region. The Norden countries are three constitutional monarchies (Denmark, Norway, and Sweden), two republics (Iceland and Finland), and three self-governing territories (Greenland, or Kalaallit Nunaat; the Faroe Islands, associated with Denmark; and the island of Åland, an autonomous part of Finland). The 25 million people living in Norden are a culturally diverse cross-section of the northern hemisphere with speakers of three major unrelated language families—Eskimo-Aleut, Indo-European, and Uralic. Close relatives of these peoples and their languages live throughout northern Asia and Europe and North America and include arctic hunters and reindeer herders, along with descendants of the Vikings.

In 1995 two small Nordic nations, Norway and Iceland, joined with Liechtenstein and Switzerland to form the European Free Trade Association (EFTA).

These four nations are remarkably diverse. Liechtenstein has only 34,000 people and is a principality. Iceland, with only about 300,000 people, is perhaps the world's oldest democratic state. Switzerland is a confederation of 7.5 million people. The EFTA seeks to promote the economic integration of its members, which are already among the most successful nations in the world. After Norway, Iceland ranked number two and Switzerland number seven in the HDI for 2007 (Liechtenstein was not ranked). The EFTA involved trade agreements with some twenty other countries, often involving careful agreements on the country of origin for fish and agricultural products. There were sixty publicly traded companies in the EFTA countries ranking in the global 500 in 2006, and collectively EFTA ranked as the fourth-largest country in the world for the market capitalization of its publicly listed companies, after the United States, the European Union, and Japan.

Consensus may be the most crucial variable when costly long-range decision making must be carried out to avert long-term disaster. Nordic nations are more sustainable because they are small and culturally homogeneous enough that they can more easily maintain a consensus on basic values, especially on what sustainability means and how to achieve it. In a small nation such as Norway there will be fewer elites competing with each other, and wealth and power may be less concentrated than in larger nations, especially if there is consensus on the importance of human rights and social equality as in Norden. For example, a careful analysis of Norway's elites in 1967 found that there were only 894 elites including business (59 percent), politicians (20 percent), civil servants (12 percent) and labor (9 percent), out of a population of 3.7 million.[25] The business elite were the 527 directors and executives of the 122 largest corporations.

In 2008 Norway was a small nation of 4.7 million people with a $279 billion PPP gross national income (GNI) economy. Administratively it was organized into 19 counties, 431 municipalities, and 1,278 parishes. Seven major political parties (by rounded percentages in descending order Labour, 36; Progress, 22; Conservative, 14; Christian Democrat, 7; Centre, 7; Socialist Left, 9; and Liberal, 6) were represented in the 2005 national elections, but governing required the formation of a coalition. The Labour Party is the dominant party, and it maintains formal connection with organized labor unions.

Norway is heavily involved in the global capitalist economy, but it distributes decision making over capital in a way that decisions can be made democratically and the benefits can be distributed equitably. This is not incompatible with good business and market principles. In 2008 the Norwegian government was a significant shareholder in some 80 Norwegian companies, employing over 280,000 people, which was about 11 percent of the workforce, in addition to the high proportion of employees in government itself and public service institutions. The Norwegian state and municipal governments owned about 35 percent of the US$190 billion in share value listed on the Oslo Børs stock exchange in 2005. The Department of Ownership within the Ministry of Trade and Industry manages most of the government's interests in state-owned companies.

Among important Norwegian state-owned companies in 2008 were the government's 63 percent ownership of StatoilHydro, one of the world's largest oil and gas companies, with revenues of US$116 billion, making it the 36th-largest publicly traded company in the world. The government's interests in StatoilHydro were managed by the Norwegian Ministry of Petroleum and Energy. The Norwegian government also owned 100 percent of KBN, Kommunalbanken Norway, which provides loans to local and municipal governments. The government also owned a 34 percent share of DnB Nor, Norway's largest financial services, banking, insurance, and asset management company. DnB Nor had about US$270 billion in assets under management, which is a very large sum, but significantly less than the US$2 trillion managed by Citigroup, one of the largest U.S. financial services corporations. Cultural differences between Norway and the United States were also apparent in executive salaries. Significantly, the CEO of DnB received only US$700,000 in annual compensation, whereas the Citigroup CEO received some US$10 million.

Norges Bank, the Norwegian government's central bank, manages two large sovereign funds, the Government Pension Fund-Norway (*Folketrygdfondet*) and the Government Pension Fund-Global (*Statens pensjonsfond utland*). The *Folketrygdfondet* had about $28 billion invested in Norwegian companies in 2009, with the proceeds going to the national insurance pension fund. The *Statens pensjonsfond utland*, formerly called the Petroleum Fund of Norway, is managed by Norges Bank Investment Management under the Ministry of Finance and Norges Bank. This fund is derived from the government's share of revenues from StatoilHydro and oil and gas development generally.

The purpose of Norway's petroleum fund is "ensuring that a reasonable portion of the country's petroleum wealth benefits future generations." It is oil converted into financial wealth, and it must be managed to produce "a sound return in the long term, which is contingent on sustainable development in the economic, environmental and social sense."[26] Investments are made in foreign or "global" financial assets, not in Norwegian companies, and they are strictly controlled by ethical guidelines. These funds may not contribute to "unethical acts or omissions, such as violations of fundamental humanitarian principles, serious violations of human rights, gross corruption, or severe environmental damage." This means that companies that the fund invests in must follow the UN Global Compact and Organization for Economic Cooperation and Development Guidelines for Corporate Governance. The fund's ethical committee reviews investments and excludes companies in violation, especially manufacturers of banned military weapons such as cluster bombs, antipersonnel mines, and nuclear weapons, or those involved in military trade with illegitimate military dictatorships. They also will not invest in tobacco companies and have excluded Walmart for its labor practices, Monsanto for allowing child labor by companies in India that supply its genetically modified cotton seed, and the mining giant Rio Tinto for environmental damage.[27]

In 2009 Norway's petroleum fund was worth more than $450 billion, or about $220,000 per household, making it the largest pension fund in Europe and the fourth largest in the world. This fund is quite comparable in size to the $435 billion managed by TIAA-CREF, the retirement fund for 3.4 million American academics and professionals.

The Norwegian government's national budget was US$140 billion in 2008, or about US$30,000 per capita, and about half of its GNI. In comparison, the U.S. federal budget was $2.5 trillion in 2007, about $8,000 per capita and 18 percent of GNI. There were important differences in how these respective national governments allocated their expenditures. Norway transferred thousands, rather than hundreds of dollars per capita to local governments, with significantly more for social support, transportation, police and justice, and agriculture. Norway distributed much more in foreign aid per capita than the United States, but less for national defense (see figure 15.3). These differences reflect cultural differences as well as differences in scale and power.

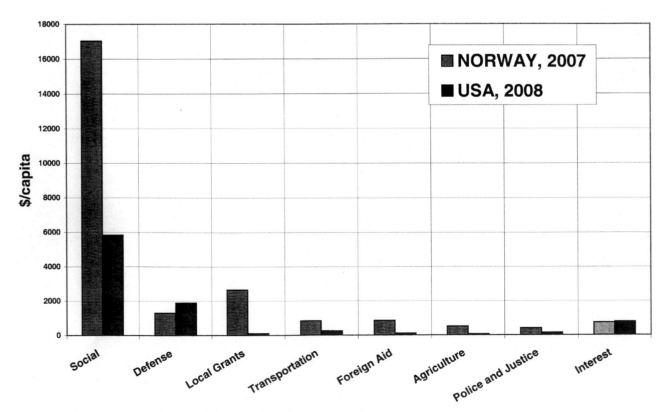

Figure 15.3. Government expenditures/capita of Norway and United States.

The World Values Survey for 2005–2008[28] also reveals interesting differences between Norway and the United States. Norwegians report much higher levels of health, satisfaction with life, and personal autonomy than Americans, whereas Americans report somewhat higher levels of freedom (see figure 15.4). Norwegians also show much more confidence in their justice system and parliament than Americans, but they have much lower confidence in their military.[29] More Norwegians also described themselves as feeling that they were a part of their local communities; more trusted the people in their neighborhood, and they did not consider water, sewage, and air quality to be serious problems (see figure 15.5).

The Nordic model is famous for enjoying peaceful labor relations, a fair income distribution, and social cohesion. Nordic countries have been able to grow their economies and keep the system sustainable in spite of high taxes and high levels of social equality and social security that critics warned would reduce incentives for workers to be productive. A central feature of the Nordic model is collective risk sharing.[30] The Nordic model is a welfare state that transfers income to households and publicly funds social services from income and consumption taxes. There is high public investment in child care and education, health care, retirement benefits and care for the elderly, infrastruc-

ture, and research and development. Labor unions are strong, wages are considered fair, and unemployment benefits are generous. This combination has produced economic efficiency and social equality and kept public corruption low, all at the same time. People seem to trust their government and public institutions, and this makes them willing to embrace aspects of "free enterprise" and globalization that benefit the economy. Some economists argue that the Nordic system is a "pro-growth" system in which the winners in the free market compensate the losers, and the economy continues to grow.[31] This is why some observers consider them to be good models for Agoria-type regional systems discussed in the following section. However, there is a long-term tendency for welfare costs to rise faster than GDP, and reforms will be needed to make the welfare state sustainable.

Alternative Forms of Business Organization

If corporate businesses that are too large and too powerful are a principal problem in the commercial world, then it is good news that many viable models of small businesses can solve these problems of scale. Businesses don't need to be superlarge, and they don't need to be multinational. They don't need to be giant monopolies or oligopolies. The alternatives are everywhere, and they are working; they just do not capture

Figure 15.4. Percent of Americans and Norwegians self-reporting as happy, healthy, satisfied with life, high levels of freedom and autonomy (data from *World Values Survey* 2005-2008).

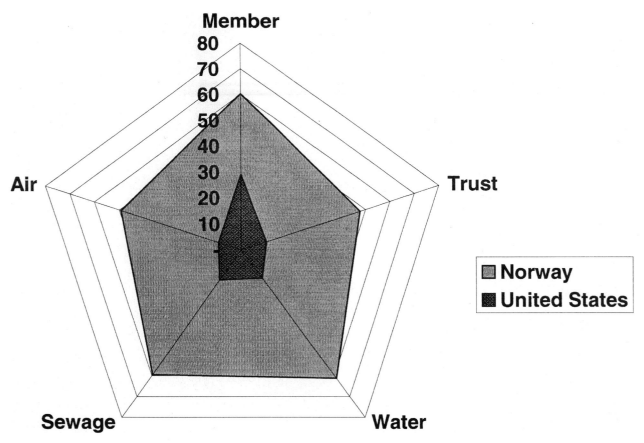

Figure 15.5. American and Norwegian perceptions of community well-being (data from World Values Survey 2005-2008).

popular attention because our attention is so focused on the giants. According to the U.S. Small Business Administration, most businesses (99.7 percent of all employer firms in 2008) in the United States are small businesses, defined as businesses with fewer than 500 employees.[32] Small businesses are like small nations. They are everywhere, but their importance is not commonly perceived.

In 2008 there were 29.6 million businesses in the United States, and 99.9 percent were small, with fewer than 500 employees. Most businesses were organized as sole proprietorships (23 million in 2007). There were 3 million partnerships and about 6 million corporations. Only about 18,000 businesses were large, and as we have seen only the top 500 or so were large enough to dominate our perceptions with their ownership of national brands and their role in national advertising. Small businesses employed more than half of all nongovernment employees in the country and accounted for 44 percent of the private payroll. Between 1993 and 2009 small business created 64 percent of the new jobs in the country. Small businesses also produced more than half of the private nonfarm

gross domestic product, 30 percent of exports, and per employee, they produced 13 times more patents than large businesses.

The corporate form of business is potentially a growth and scale problem, because as noted previously, corporations are by definition immortal. They can grow forever, whereas sole proprietorships exist only during the life of the proprietor, and partnerships dissolve when their members change. Nevertheless, the most common form of business corporation in the United States is the S corporation, and it is limited in scale and form. An S corporation, as defined by the Internal Revenue Service,[33] is a small business corporation. S corporations are owned by no more than 100 shareholder resident individual persons or families, or individually owned estates or trusts. S corporations cannot be owned by other corporations or by nonresident foreigners, but they may have wholly owned subsidiaries that cannot be treated as separate corporations. The advantage for shareholders is that S corporations are limited liability businesses, so a shareholder is risking only the value of his shares in the business. But the profits of S corporations are not taxed—only their shareholders are taxed on their share of the profits.

From a scale and power perspective the crucial advantage of S corporations is that they are themselves limited in size both by the number of their shareholders and by the fact that their shareholders must be real persons and not other corporations. Table 15.3 shows that the scale constraints on S corporations did limit size of assets, revenues, and profits. At the very top of the size ranks, the 14,312 largest S corporations in 2006, with revenues of $50 million or more, were still relatively small in comparison with the top corporations, whose growth was unlimited. The largest S corporations had average assets of only $75 million, revenues of only $144 million, and net income of $7.5 million.[34] Because there were few shareholders, these relatively small values still produced net income of $1.4 million per shareholder. In comparison, the 7,187 largest C corporations (not small S corporations) in the United States, those with revenues of $250 million or more, had average assets of $8 billion, revenues of $2.5 billion, and net income of $200 million in 2006.[35] The largest foreign-controlled domestic corporations, those with revenues of $50 million or more, averaged significantly larger in assets, revenue, and net income than S corporations of the same rank. This was probably because foreign corporations tended to be larger corporations, and it is thus not surprising that they accounted for 13 percent of total corporate revenues in 2006, even though they represented less than 0.06 percent of all corporations in the country.[36]

It is possible for a somewhat larger corporation to be organized in a way that its assets can be owned by a relatively small kinship-based group with a common culture and history. For example, Menasha Corporation is a privately held business headquartered in Neenah, Wisconsin, that owns four subsidiary companies that manufacture packaging materials.[37] It has operations in some twenty states, Canada, Mexico, and China. Menasha was founded by Elisha D. Smith, who purchased a wooden bucket manufacturing company in 1852 in Menasha, Wisconsin. In 2002 the 140

shareholders of the company were all descendants of Elisha Smith, but the family hired managers and laborers. Three of the nine members of the corporate board chair were descendants of Elisha Smith, including the board chair and the chair of the Smith Family Council. The seven Smith Family Council members were residents of the Midwest, New England, and the far West. The council coordinated family interests and worked to "uphold family values."

The family-held Menasha Corporation has certainly been successful. In 2008 its revenues were approaching a billion dollars, and the company had 3,084 employees. The details of Menasha's corporate profits and their distribution are not public information, but if profits were 5 percent of revenues, which was the average return for the largest American corporations in 2004, Menasha might have produced a net income of $46 million. Distributed evenly among 140 family owners, this would yield annual incomes of about $330,000 each, which would place them within the top 5 percent for American family incomes. This income level also suggests that these families would all be comfortable multimillionaires by wealth, but none of the principals of the family seem to appear in the lists of the American super-rich. The company also contributed $1.2 million to the Menasha Corporation Foundation, which gave out nearly $750,000 in grants and scholarships to schools and community organizations in 2008.[38] There was also a Menasha Corporation Employees Credit Union in Menasha with 1,174 members and $5 million in assets.[39]

Native American tribal governments are also interesting models of how corporate businesses can be owned and managed by a small related group with a shared culture for their mutual benefit. There are numerous other examples, including credit unions, cooperatives like the Mondragon example, and public utility districts.

The Great Transition to a Planetary Society

The Great Transition Initiative[40] is a global effort initiated by Paul Raskin of the Tellus Institute in 1995

Table 15. 3. Average Assets, Revenues, and Net Income of Largest U.S. Corporations, by Form of Organization, 2006

Form	Number	Revenue Rank	Assets	Revenue	Net Income
C	7,187				
		$250 Million+	$8 Billion	$2.5 Billion	$200 Million
S	14,312	$50 Million+	$75 Million	$144 Million	$7.5 Million
Foreign-Controlled	3,948	$50 Million+	$2 Billion	$923 Million	$49 Million

to facilitate the construction of sustainable communities and a sustainable global system by transforming people's beliefs and practices to promote human well-being and protect the environment. The **Great Transition** is a transition from the present world to a truly sustainable **planetary society**. This transition represents the magnitude of change that must occur.

In fictive retrospective scenarios, Raskin et al. imagined what the Great Transition planetary society would look like in 2068, a century after the Apollo 8 moon landings, and as fully developed by 2085. Planetary society is composed of hundreds of regions based on previously existing nations, states, or decentralized portions of former states. Many regions are bioregions defined by watershed or other natural areas. Regions may also be centered on cities or cultural groups. Cultural diversity is a fundamental characteristic of the regions, but they can be sorted into three types: **Agoria**, **Ecodemia**, and **Arcadia**.

Agoria evokes the classical Greek Athenian model of a market-centered city-state in which commercial life was not alienated from government. Regional agoria societies in many respects resemble standard early twentieth-century commercial world nation-states but with important differences. Some 4 billion people, about half the global population in 2085, live in Agoria regions organized around shareholder-owned corporations and private wealth, but corporate businesses are strictly regulated to bring them in line with the dominant values of society to maintain sustainability. The closest late-twentieth-century examples of Agoria regions would be the small nations such as Norway that followed the Nordic model discussed above.

About 2 billion people, one-fourth of global population, live in Ecodemia regions. Ecodemia stands for economic democracy and refers to societies in which corporate businesses are owned by the workers and many businesses are nonprofits, cooperatives, or owned by governments or communities. This is in effect the Mondragon cooperative model. These ownership arrangements reduce the incentive for growth, make environmental sustainability easier, and produce a more equitable distribution of costs and benefits. Under these conditions workers seek shorter working hours to have more free time. Time affluence rather than accumulation of financial capital is the dominant goal.

Arcadia regions are also about 2 billion people. They maintain many characteristics of tribal world societies, indigenous peoples, and some small nations. Arcadia regions emphasize face-to-face democratic decision making, economic self-reliance, and their connections with planetary society by means of communication and information technologies. Arcadian regions may also emphasize advanced technologies in sustainable agriculture and small-scale energy systems. Industries are artisanal and artistic and may include ecotourism and ethnic tourism. In comparison with other planetary society regions, Arcadian regions showed the highest levels of political participation, social cohesion, ecosystem preservation, and independence, but they have the lowest income, GDP, and time affluence levels.

It would be misleading to equate Agoria, Ecodemia, and Arcadia with twentieth-century capitalism, socialism, and anarchism respectively, but there are some parallels and obvious historical connections. The crucial differences are that there is no absolute poverty in Great Transition planetary regional societies. These societies will have effectively achieved the Millennium Development Goals. They are all sustainable, democratic, literate societies, and people consider themselves to be citizens of their local communities, their regionally autonomous societies, and of planetary society. Three crucial principles in the World Constitution support a political philosophy of "constrained pluralism," which is the foundation of planetary society: **irreducibility**, **subsidiarity**, and **heterogeneity**. Irreducibility refers to the reality that some issues such as global warming and universal human rights are planetary in nature because they affect everyone on the planet. Many other problems also require global-level decision making, such as management of ocean fisheries and marine pollution and protecting biodiversity, migratory birds, natural protected areas, and river basins. International peace and security is a global problem, as is the operation of global-scale markets, financial systems, communication systems, education, and science. Another way of recognizing irreducibility is the subsidiarity principle, which means that a managing body takes on a function only when a lower-level body is unable to perform it.

Heterogeneity makes allowances for regional and cultural diversity. Constrained pluralism can be worked out in many ways. For example, greenhouse gas limits may be set at a global level, with regional area allocations specified on a per-capita basis, but the details of how limits are met would be worked out in detail by local communities and subregions through democratic processes that would vary from place to place. The World Constitution specifies that everyone is entitled to "a decent standard of living," but how that is achieved is culturally defined in each region and subregion.

The planetary-level political system is based on the World Constitution and includes legislative, executive, and judicial branches of government. The legislative branch is based on a World Assembly of elected regional and world-at-large representatives. There are organized global-level political parties, continuous political activity, and protest movements at all levels, much of which is facilitated by global communications and information systems.

Planetary population is stable at about 8 billion, which is far below standard projections. This outcome was achieved by a combination of factors in comparison with conditions in 2000, including improved gender equity, improved education, improved availability of family planning practices, improved well-being, and greater overall social equity. At the same time the global economic product increases and average income triples. Economic growth of this magnitude is environmentally sustainable because it occurs at the same time that the global average ecological footprint shrinks. This reduction in footprint is made possible by a culturally directed change away from material consumption toward a "dematerialized" economy that emphasizes human services and information-based cultural products such as knowledge, arts, and crafts. This kind of economic activity requires much lower flows of energy and materials than a standard twentieth-century consumer culture. In many respects this is a lifestyle change characterized by a rejection of materialism and capital accumulation as an end in itself.

Raskin described the condition of his imagined planetary society in 2084 as follows: "The pursuit of money is giving way to the cultivation of skills, relationships, communities, and the life of the mind and spirit."[41] A dematerialized economy can also flourish with minimal use of fossil fuels. Global average incomes are of course not as high as in the United States in 2000, but actual human well-being, or "genuine progress" is better because a higher proportion of the economic product is actually beneficial. Furthermore, because income distribution is more equitable, the average is closer to the median, and the human outcome of a smaller average is better. Cultural differences also improve the global average because relatively low-income regions such as Arcadia are able to gain a higher human benefit from their economic product. At the same time regional pockets of extreme poverty are eliminated.

All Great Transition societies are more egalitarian than most twentieth-century commercial world societies. There are no superwealthy individuals, and poverty is almost entirely eliminated. These outcomes are achieved by means of a political consensus in favor of progressive income taxes that set limits for the highest incomes and inheritance taxes, making it more difficult for great wealth to be accumulated by a few families. Culturally variable measures in the different regions include guaranteed minimum incomes, full employment programs, or other means of income distribution, all based on the principle that everyone has a right to a decent standard of living. This of course is similar to the tribal concept of the irreducible minimum. These social justice policies help maintain an income balance in which the richest 10 percent receive only three to five times the income of the lowest 10 percent. In contrast, in the United States in 2000 the income of the top 10 percent was more than 16 times that of the lowest 10 percent. Achieving social security for everyone required decades of political struggle by women, indigenous peoples, and human rights activists against powerful entrenched elites. The political transformation was also accelerated by the rising costs of fossil fuels and the unmistakable deterioration of global environmental conditions, which was visible everywhere.

Economic globalization, measured as the volume of interregional trade, is lower than in 2000, because of the increased emphasis on local and regional economic production and increased transportation costs, as well as taxes on interregional trade and financial transactions designed to dampen the importance of global trade. Regions and communities have some discretion to limit external trade in the interests of their own culturally defined social and environmental goals, but not merely to make their products more globally competitive.

How the Great Transition Might Happen

Raskin et al. also described a fictional sequence of events that they imagined would culminate in the Great Transition by 2068. Events begin with a tumultuous phase of market euphoria from 1990 to 2015 that ends in crisis. In fact the recent intense phase of globalization began about 1980 and certainly stalled with the financial collapse of 2007–2010(+). Market euphoria was propelled by computerization, financialization, and the creation of a network of global cities. As Raskin suggests, this phase of market-driven growth proved to be unsustainable. The benefits were too narrowly distributed and remained tantalizingly out of reach for billions who were flooded with images of consumer lifestyles. Furthermore, the inability of pure materialism to deliver genuine satisfactions helped fuel protests even among many beneficiaries of growth. Antiglobalization movements began in the 1990s. Terrorism and the global war on terrorism initially diverted public attention from the obvious inability of market-driven globalization to deliver on its promises. Shortly after the events of 2001, elite policy makers in fact redefined their goals as "inclusive development," which meant economic growth designed to share benefits more widely and to specifically include the poor.[42] In their fictional retrospective, Raskin et al. imagine that these initial reform efforts were inadequate. In their futurist scenario inclusive development based on "market euphoria" failed to significantly reduce global poverty. The combined effects of the continuing collapse of ecosystems, the stress of global warming, and resource depletion set off a global economic crisis by 2015.

It is possible that reactions to the global financial crisis that began in 2007 will help initiate the transformations that Raskin's scenario attributed to a global economic crisis in 2015. Indeed, economists have in fact widely perceived the economic crisis of 2007 to be a failure of inadequately regulated markets and a challenge to the neoliberal economic philosophy of free-market growth that provided the ideological foundation for globalization.

The executive director and board chair of the Stockholm Environment Institute, which supports the Great Transition Initiative, argue that the "sophisticated financial castles in the air" that led to the global financial crisis also encouraged short-term consumption at the expense of natural capital and the future.[43] They saw a direct link between the financial system "meltdown" and the melting of the polar ice caps from global warming. Both crises could involve unsustainable borrowing against the future and long periods of incremental changes, leading to a sudden reduction in resilience and system upheaval.

In Raskin's retrospective scenario the economic crisis leads to a failed resort to authoritarian means by political conservatives to establish a "fortress world" to restore the faltering global order of market-driven growth. This only intensifies the antiglobalization movements and spurs governments to assert more control over the market, giant corporations, poverty alleviation, and environmental protection. In the real world the global civil-society-based movement for

change is represented by the well-organized protests against the World Trade Organization, such as the one that occurred in Seattle in 1999 and the Brazilian-based World Social Forum (WSF) network of antiglobalization organizations. The WSF organized around the theme "Another World Is Possible."[44] It began with a conference in Porto Alegre, Brazil, in 2001 as a counterpoint to the elite World Economic Forum held annually in Davos, Switzerland. Anthropologist Arturo Escobar points out that the WSF is indeed an alternative, nonhierarchical way to organize the world.[45]

Raskin imagines that the reform movements of 2015–2020 produce a new global order with stronger national governments and a stronger, more centralized international system with a World Union replacing the UN, a World Court, and World Regulatory Authority replacing the World Bank and the IMF. Serious efforts at establishing sustainable development are under way. Enforceable limits are imposed on carbon emissions; ocean fisheries and forests are protected; international currency flows are taxed; and benefits are redistributed to impoverished people. The World Court uses antitrust laws to break up the world's largest energy company. These efforts cause investment to be redirected and restored economic growth, but nevertheless the new order proves ungovernable and fails to produce sustainable development.

A new highly diverse civil society social movement emerges, the Coalition for a Great Transition, which is an outgrowth of the virtually universal access to the Internet put in place during the reform era of 2015–2020. One component of this imaginary coalition movement is the Yin-Yang Movement (YIN, Youth International Network, YANG, Youth Action for a New Globalization) organized by digitally sophisticated youth, many of them located in India and China. The Yin-Yang Movement helps bring about the Great Transition by 2025.

The central feature of these new social networks is that they connected numerous value-based organizations that help people replace their former consumption-based lifestyles with new values focused on "meaningful and fulfilling" lives. People mobilize their networked organizations and informational technologies to create an "accountability movement" to monitor and publicize the failures of giant corporations and ineffective governments. Public accountability compels corporations and governments to change, thereby forcing a transition to genuine sustainability. The transition causes "reindustrialization" to take place in which manufacturers vie with each other to achieve zero-impact production and fully recycle their products. Governments are forced to become more transparent, which encourages public involvement in policy development and decision making.

SUMMARY

The most fundamental issue facing humanity is this: How can a global commercial culture based on perpetual growth and inequality survive in a finite world? Truly successful cultural adaptation demands a long-term balance between available resources and consumption. In theory, there are measurable limits beyond which cultures cannot expand without degrading their resources and threatening their own existence. Industrial systems that rely primarily on fossil fuels will necessarily be a short-lived phenomenon lasting a few centuries at best. By contrast, cultural systems designed for lower levels of consumption can maintain a balance with renewable sources of solar energy and thus could exist for millions of years.

The ominous possibility exists that critical carrying-capacity limits may already have been exceeded, given the present structure of the commercial culture. Whether or not human-induced global warming is already under way, people now clearly have the capability to disrupt the life-support systems of the planet in a way that would have been inconceivable a mere 200 years ago. Food production systems are being strained in many areas of the world; unless distribution systems and consumption patterns can be modified, it is unlikely that even the most optimistic technological solutions will prevent Malthusian crises.

There are alternative solutions to create a more secure human future. Our comparative analysis of cultural systems from an anthropological culture-scale perspective suggests that an equitable and secure world needs to combine the best features of domestic-, political-, and commercial-scale cultural patterns. Social justice and preservation of the biosphere will require effective management by highly autonomous local communities, democratic regional governments, and fully representative global institutions.

STUDY QUESTIONS

1. Define the following terms and concepts related to Latin American and Andean peasantries: *patron, peones, compradazgo, hacienda, ayni*.
2. Describe the social structure of the Vicos hacienda when the Cornell Peru Project began in 1952. Explain how the participant intervention experiment was conducted and discuss the results.
3. Why did some Andean communities refuse to participate fully in Peru's agrarian reform program? Identify specific points of conflict, referring to production technologies, cooperatives, *ayni*, risk, debt, market economy, subsistence economy, and land ownership.
4. Distinguish between predominantly technological approaches to world problems and those that are more broadly cultural. Provide specific examples.
5. What is the argument in favor of wealth redistribution as a solution to sustainability problems?
6. Make specific comparisons between Norway as a "welfare state" and the United States, referring to basic values, culture, scale and power, and the organization of business.
7. What is the Great Transition and how would it solve sustainability problems?
8. Explain how the principles of irreducibility, subsidiarity, and heterogeneity might provide a basis for the constitution of a planetary society.
9. Describe the three regional variants of a sustainable planetary society—Agoria, Ecodemia, and Arcadia—and relate them to their real-world counterparts.
10. Discuss how the Great Transition to a sustainable world might occur, citing recent actual events.

SUGGESTED READING

Callenbach, Ernest. 1975, 2004. *Ecotopia*. Berkeley, CA: Heyday Books. A fictional futuristic account of Oregon, Washington, and Northern California forming an environmentally sustainable, independent, Arcadia-like nation.

Raskin, Paul, Tariq Banuri, Gilberto Gallopín, Pablo Gutman, Al Hammond, Robert Kates, and Rob Swart. 2002. *Great Transition: The Promise and Lure of the Times Ahead*. Global Scenario Group. Boston: Stockholm Environment Institute, Tellus Institute.

Raskin, Paul D. 2006. *The Great Transition Today: A Report from the Future*. GTI Paper Series 2 Frontiers of a Great Transition. Boston: Tellus Institute.

GLOSSARY

Participant intervention A form of culture change in which those in control become members of the system they seek to change.

Hacienda A Latin American agricultural estate with dependent laborers that produced for local rather than global markets and was designed to maintain the social status and lifestyle of the hacendado landowner.

Great Transition Change in cultural beliefs and practices that produce a truly sustainable global system.

Planetary society A hypothetical global social organization produced by a Great Transition.

Agoria A hypothetical regional society in the futuristic planetary society that emphasizes shareholder-owned commercial businesses and markets, as in the Nordic model.

Ecodemia A hypothetical regional society in the futuristic planetary society in which corporate businesses are owned by workers organized as a cooperative, as in the Mondragon model.

Arcadia A hypothetical regional society in the futuristic planetary society organized to maximize local self-reliance, autonomy, and ecosystem protection, as represented by many indigenous peoples and small nations.

Irreducibility Basic principle of planetary society recognizing that some problems are global in nature and require global decision-making authority.

Subsidiarity The principle that a managing body takes on a function only when a lower-level body is unable to perform it.

Heterogeneity Basic principle of planetary society that recognizes local, regional, and cultural diversity.

NOTES

1. WCED (World Commission on Environment and Development. 1987. *Our Common Future*. Oxford, Eng.: Oxford University Press, 43.

2. Costanza, Robert, et al. 1997. "The Value of the World's Ecosystem Services and Natural Capital." *Nature* 387(6630): 253–59.

3. Kohr, Leopold. 1978. *The Breakdown of Nations*. New York: Dutton.

4. Pareto, Vilfredo. 1971. *Manual of Political Economy*. Translated by Ann S. Schwier and Alfred N. Page. New York: A. M. Kelley.

5. Morrison, Roy. 1991. *We Build the Road as We Travel*. Philadelphia: New Society Publishers; Whyte, William Foote, and Kathleen King Whyte. 1988. *Making Mondragon: The Growth and Dynamics of the Worker Cooperative Complex*. Ithaca, NY: ILR Press.

6. Mondragon Corporation. 2008 Annual Report. www. mondragon-corporation.com/language/en-US/ENG/General-Information/Downloads.aspx.

7. Franke, Richard W., and Barbara H. Chasin. 1989. *Kerala: Radical Reform as Development in an Indian State*. Food First Development Report No. 6. San Francisco: The Institute for Food and Development Policy.

8. Roy, Hiranmoy, and Kaushik Bhattacharjee. 2009. Convergence of Human Development across Indian States. Munbai, India: Indira Gandhi Institute of Development Research. IGIDR Proceedings/Project Reports Series. www. igidr.ac.in/pdf/publication/PP-062-22.pdf.

9. Scheper-Hughes, Nancy. 1992. *Death without Weeping: The Violence of Everyday Life in Brazil*. Berkeley: University of California Press.

10. Dobyns, Henry F., Paul L. Doughty, and Harold D. Lasswell, eds. 1971. *Peasants, Power, and Applied Social Change: Vicos as a Model*. Beverly Hills, CA, and London: Sage. For history and more current background see also the Vicos Project website at Cornell University: http://courses.cit.cornell.edu/vicosperu/vicos-site/cornellperu_page_1.htm.

11. Miller, Solomon. 1967. "Hacienda to Plantation in Northern Peru: The Processes of Proletarianization of a Tenant Farmer Society." In *Contemporary Change in Traditional Societies*, vol. 3, *Mexican and Peruvian Communities*, edited by Julian Steward, pp. 133–225. Urbana: University of Illinois Press; Mintz, Sidney W., and Eric R. Wolf. 1957. "Haciendas and Plantations in Middle America and the Antilles." *Social and Economic Studies* 6:380–412.

12. Holmberg, Allan R. 1971. "The Role of Power in Changing Values and Institutions of Vicos." In Dobyns, Henry F., Paul L. Doughty, and Harold D. Lasswell, eds., *Peasants, Power, and Applied Social Change: Vicos as a Model*, pp. 33–63. Beverly Hills, CA, and London: Sage, 62.

13. Brush, Stephen B., Heath J. Carney, and Zosimo Huaman. 1981. "Dynamics of Andean Potato Agriculture." *Economic Botany* 35(1):70–88.

14. Doughty, Paul L. 2002. "Ending Serfdom in Peru: The Struggle for Land and Freedom in Vicos." In *Contemporary Cultures and Societies of Latin America*, edited by Dwight B. Heath. Prospect Heights, IL.: Waveland Press.

15. Hopkins, Diane E. 1985. "The Peruvian Agrarian Reform: Dissent from Below." *Human Organization* 44(1):18–32.

16. Nakicenovic, N., et al. (2000). *Special Report on Emissions Scenarios: A Special Report of Working Group III of the Intergovernmental Panel on Climate Change*, Cambridge University Press, Cambridge, U.K. www.grida.no/climate/ipcc/emission/index.htm.

17. California Environmental Associates. 2007. *Design to Win: Philanthropy's Role in the Fight Against Global Warming*. www.ceaconsulting.com/CaseStudyFiles/DesignToWin_FinalReport.pdf (accessed April 2010).

18. Hails, Chris, Sarah Humphrey, Jonathan Loh, Steven Goldfinger. 2008. *Living Planet Report 2008*. Gland, Switzerland: World Wide Fund for Nature.

19. U.S. Energy Information Administration. 2009. Annual Energy Review. Total Carbon Dioxide Emissions from the Consumption of Energy (Million Metric Tons). www.eia.doe.gov/emeu/international/contents.html.

20. Norway, Ministry of Finance. 2008. *Norway's Strategy for Sustainable Development*, published as part of the National Budget. R-0617E. www.regjeringen.no/upload/FIN/rapporter/R-0617E.pdf.

21. Great Britain, United Kingdom, Treasury. 2007. *The Economics of Climate Change*, Nicholas Stern, ed. Cambridge, UK and New York: Cambridge University Press. Also avail-

able: H.M. Treasury website: www.hm-treasury.gov.uk/ stern review report.htm.

22. Great Britain, 2007, *Economics of Climate Change*, Full Executive Summary, i.

23. Ahrne, Göran, and Erik Olin Wright. 1983. "Class in the United States and Sweden: A Comparison." *Acta Sociologica* 26(3/4), 211–35.

24. Chydenius, Anders. 1931. *The National Gain*. London: Ernest Benn Ltd. (original 1766).

25. Higley, John, G. Lowell Field, and Knut Grøholt. 1976. *Elite Structure and Ideology: A Theory with Applications to Norway*. New York: Columbia University Press.

26. Norway, Ministry of Finance. 2005. *The Government Pension Fund: The Ethnical Guidelines*. www.regjeringen.no/en/ dep/fin/Selected-topics/the-government-pension-fund/ responsible-investments/Guidelines-for-observation-and-exclusion-from-the-Government-Pension-Fund-Globals-investment-universe.html?id=594254 (accessed April 2010).

27. Norway, Ministry of Finance. 2008. *Council on Ethics, Government Pension Fund. Annual Report 2008*. www. regjeringen.no/en/sub/styrer-rad-utvalg/ethics_council/ annual-reports.html?id=458699.

28. Medrano, Jaime Diez. 2005. *WVS 2005 Codebook*, Variables 10, 11, 22, 46, 214. Data from online World Values Survey 2005–2008 www.worldvaluessurvey.org.

29. Medrano, *WVS 2005 Codebook*, Variables 132, 136, 137, 138, 140, 141. www.worldvaluessurvey.org.

30. Andersen, Torben M., Bengt HolmstrOm, Seppo Honkapohja, Sixten Korkman, Hans Tson Soderstrom, Juliana Vartiainen. 2007. *The Nordic Model: Embracing Globalization and Sharing Risks*. Research Institute of the Finish Economy (ETLA), Helsinki: Taloustieto Oy. http://www.etla.fi/Files/1892 the_nordic_model_complete.pdf.

31. Anderson, et al. 2007. *The Nordic Model*, 16–18.

32. U.S. Small Business Administration, Office of Advocacy. 2009. *Frequently Asked Questions*. (September). www.sba. gov/advo/stats/sbfaq.pdf (accessed Feb. 2010).

33. U.S. Internal Revenue Service (IRS). 2009. "S Corporations."www.irs.gov/businesses/small/article/0,,id=98263,00. html (accessed Feb. 2010).

34. U.S. Internal Revenue Service, (IRS). 2009. 2006 Corporation Returns—1120S Basic Tables. Table 4. S Corporation Returns: Total Receipts and Deductions, Portfolio Income, Rental Income, and Total Net Income, by Size Business Receipts and Sector. www.irs.gov/taxstats/bustaxstats/ article/0,,id=96405,00.html (accessed Feb. 2010).

35. U.S. Internal Revenue Service (IRS). 2009. 2006 Corporation Returns—Basic Tables. Returns of Active Corporations. Table 5. Selected Balance Sheet, Income Statement, and Tax Items, by Sector, by Size of Business Receipts. www.irs.gov/taxstats/article/0,,id=170691,00.html (accessed Feb. 2010).

36. Hobbs, James R. 2009. "Foreign-Controlled Domestic Corporations, 2006." *Statistics of Income Bulletin* Summer 2009, pp. 102–45.

37. Menasha Corporation. *Annual Report 2008: Staying the Course*. www.menasha.com/aboutUs/AnnualReports.html (accessed Feb. 2010). www.menasha.com/aboutUs/aboutUsFoundationannualreports.html (accessed Feb. 2010).

38. Menasha Corporation Foundation. 2008 Annual Report: Strengthening Communities. www.menasha.com/aboutUs/aboutUsFoundationannualreports.html (accessed Feb. 2010).

39. National Credit Union Administration. 2009. *Summary and Reports for Menasha Corporation Employees* [Credit Union] as of June 30, 2009. http://reports.ncua.gov/data/ cureports/index.cfm (accessed Feb. 2010).

40. Tellus Institute. 2005. *Great Transition Initiative: Visions and Pathways for a Hopeful Future*. GTI Brochure. www. gtinitiative.org/default.asp?action=42.

41. Raskin, 2006, *Great Transition Today*, 13.

42. Chibba, Michael. 2009. "Perspectives on Inclusive Development: Concepts, approaches and current issues." World Economics 9(4): 145–56.

43. Rockström, Johan and Lars Anell. 2008. "Statement from the Executive Director and the Chair of the Board." Annual Report 2008: Bridging Science and Policy. Stockholm Environment Institute, 4–5.

44. Sen, Jai, Anita Anand, Arturo Escobar, and PeterWaterman Escobar,Arturo, eds. 2003. *The World Social Forum: Challenging Empires*. New Delhi: Viveka Foundation. www. choike.org/nuevo_eng/informes/1557.html.

45. Escobar, Arturo. "Other Worlds Are (Already) Possible: Self-Organization, Complexity, and Post-Capitalist Cultures." In *The World Social Forum: Challenging Empires*, edited by Jai Sen, Anita Anand, Arturo Escobar, and PeterWaterman. pp. 349–58. New Delhi: Viveka Foundation. www.choike.org/nuevo_eng/informes/1557.html.

Glossary

Acculturation Culture change brought about by contact between peoples with different cultures. Usually refers to the loss of traditional culture when the members of tribal societies adopt cultural element of commercial-scale societies.

Acephalous A political system without central authority or permanent leaders.

Achieved status Social position based on a person's demonstrated personal abilities apart from social status ascribed at birth.

Affine A relative by marriage.

Age-class system A system in which individuals of similar age are placed in a named group and moved as a unit through the culturally defined stages of life. Specific rituals mark each change in age status.

Agoria A hypothetical regional society in the futuristic planetary society that emphasizes shareholder-owned commercial businesses and markets, as in the Nordic model.

Ambilocality (avunculocal residence) Where a couple resides near one set of parents or the other depending on circumstances.

Ancestor worship A religious system based on reverence for specific ancestors and sometimes involving shrines, rituals, and sacrifice.

Animism A belief in spirits that occupy plants, animals, and people. Spirits are supernatural and normally invisible but may transform into different forms. Animism is considered by cultural evolutionists to be the simplest and earliest form of religion.

Animistic thinking The soul concept used by tribal individuals as an intellectual explanation of life, death, and dream experiences, part of Edward B. Tylor's theory of animism as the origin of religion.

Anthropocene The age beginning about 1800 AD when human activites became geologically visible in biological, chemical, and physical processes on the earth.

Anthropogenic biomes Geographic regions defined by the density of human population, form of settlement, and land use.

Arcadia A hypothetical regional society in the futuristic planetary society organized to maximize local self-reliance, autonomy, and ecosystem protection, as represented by many indigenous peoples and small nations.

Aristocracy A political system in which a small, privileged elite rule. This is a rule by the "best."

Ascribed status The social status that one is born into; includes sex, birth order, lineage, clan affiliation, and connection with elite ancestors.

Assimilation Ethnocide without genocide; the loss of distinctive cultural identity as a population surrenders its autonomy and is absorbed into a dominant society and culture.

Avunculocal residence Where at marriage a man moves near his mother's brother, who is a member of his own matrilineage.

Band A group of twenty-five to fifty people who camp and forage together.

Bigman A self-made leader in a tribal society. His position is temporary, depending on personal ability and the consent of his followers.

Biopolitical production The human outcome of immaterial production used to control information and shape thoughts, emotions, and behavior through the media and advertising.

Biopower Michel Foucault's concept of social power directed at control over all of human life, including people's minds and bodies.

Bioproductivity The amount of new plant and animal material (biomass) produced annually in a given area.

Bride-service The cultural expectation that a newly married husband will perform certain tasks for his in-laws.

Bride-wealth Goods, often livestock, that are transferred from the family of the groom to the family of the bride to legitimize the marriage and the children of the couple.

Bureaucracy A centralized command and control social structure with officials arranged in an administrative hierarchy.

Capital Karl Marx's term for land and tools as the means of production; also refers generally to accumulated wealth used for productive purposes.

Capital accumulation Expansion of wealth and the means of production that can be devoted to further production.

Capitalist production A mode of production in which a few people control the means of production and purchase the labor of those who could not otherwise support themselves.

Carrying capacity The number of people who could, in theory, be supported indefinitely in a given environment with a given technology and culture.

Cash cropping The raising of crops for market sale rather than for domestic consumption.

Caste An endogamous, ranked, occupationally defined group, known as *jati* in India and based on differences in ritual purity and impurity.

Chemical Revolution Factory-produced chemicals replace natural products and processes.

Circumscription Robert Carneiro's explanation for the development of political centralization—that villagers may be forced to surrender their autonomy if they are unable to move away from authorities because of geographic barriers or neighboring societies.

City-states Politically organized societies based on the intensive exploitation of landless workers in the local area.

Clan A named group claiming descent from a common but often remote ancestor and sharing a joint estate.

Cognates Related words that are found in more than one language and that were derived from a common protolanguage.

Cognatic line A descent line that is traced to a common ancestor and that need not rely on exclusively male or female links.

Collective representations Ideas, or thoughts, and emotions common to a society as a whole, especially in reference to the supernatural.

Commercialization The cultural process of producing and maintaining private profit-making business enterprise as a means of accumulating capital, by co-opting the humanization and politicization processes.

Commercial scale Organized by impersonal market exchanges, commercial enterprises, contracts, and money, and potentially encompassing the entire world.

Commodities Basic goods that are produced for their exchange value in a market economy to generate profit to be accumulated as capital.

Complementary opposition A structural principle in which pairs of opposites, such as males and females, form a logical larger whole.

Consanguine A relative by culturally recognized descent from a common ancestor; sometimes called a "blood" relative.

Core The wealthy industrial countries at the center of the world system where the recipients of unequal exchange reside.

Cosmogony An ideological system that seeks to explain the origin of everything: people, nature, and the universe.

Cosmology An ideological system that explains the order and meaning of the universe and people's places within it.

Cross-cousin The son or daughter of someone in the category of mother's brother or father's sister.

Cultural autonomy Self-determination by a cultural group.

Cultural hegemony Preponderant influence, or authority, by an elite in the production and reproduction of a society's moral order and associated cultural beliefs, symbols, and practices.

Culture What people think, make, and do. Socially transmitted, often symbolic, information that shapes human behavior and that regulates human society so that people can successfully maintain themselves and reproduce. Culture has mental, behavioral, and material aspects; it is patterned and provides a model for proper behavior.

Debt bondage An exploitive economic relationship that is managed to keep individuals in virtually perpetual indebtedness.

Deferred exchange A form of trade in which gift giving is reciprocated with a return gift at a later time, thus providing an excuse for maintaining contacts and establishing alliances between potentially hostile groups.

Deficit production The situation in which more calories are expended in food production than are produced for human food.

Deindustrialization The replacement of factory employment with service sector employment in formerly industrial countries as production jobs are moved to low-wage countries.

Demand sharing Requesting food or other things from kin who are obligated to give.

Descent group A social group based on genealogical connections to a common ancestor.

Direct rule The use of European colonial administrators to control a native community at the local level.

Disciplinary society Modern society where individuals are controlled by disciplinary institutions including police, courts, prisons, welfare, charities, schools, and the practices of everyday life.

Disembodied economy The concept of an economy as something that can be understood apart from the rest of society and culture, especially with a capitalist mode of production.

Domestic mode of production Material production organized at the household level with distribution between households based on reciprocal sharing.

Domestic scale Characterized by small, kinship-based societies, often with only 500 people, in which households organize production and distribution.

Dunbar's number The number of individuals that can interact in a face-to-face social group, as limited by cognitive ability. Approximately 150 individuals for humans.

Ecocide The degradation of an ecosystem.

Ecodemia A hypothetical regional society in the futuristic planetary society in which corporate businesses are owned by workers organized as a cooperative, as in the Mondragon model.

Ecological footprint The amount of the biological product that people consume measured as the equivalent of the global average biological product per hectare.

Elite-directed growth When less than a majority, often a tiny percent of people, promote growth that concentrates benefits and socializes costs or disperses costs to society at large.

Embedded economy An economy that can only be observed and understood within the context of the social, political, and religious systems of the culture.

Emic Relating to cultural meanings derived from inside a given culture and presumed to be unique to that culture.

Enclosure movement The transformation in seventeenth- and eighteenth-century Europe of open communal pastures and woodlands into enclosed, privately controlled properties, replacing village self-sufficiency with market-oriented agriculture and forcing people to become wage laborers in newly industrializing cities.

Endogamy Marriage within a specified group.

Energy subsidy The use of fossil fuels to increase food production above the rate that could be sustained through use of renewable energy sources.

Estate Property held in common by a descent group, perhaps including territory, sacred sites, and ceremonies.

Ethnic group A dependent, culturally distinct population that forms part of a larger state or empire and that was formerly autonomous.

Ethnocide The forced destruction of a cultural system.

Ethnographic method Reliance on direct participant observation, key informants, and informal interviews as a data-collecting technique.

Ethnographic present An arbitrary time period when the process of culture change is ignored in order to describe a given culture as if it were a stable system.

Etic Relating to cultural meaning as translated for cross-cultural comparison.

Exchange value The value of goods when used as commodities.

Exogamy Marriage outside a culturally defined group.

Extended family A joint household based on a parent family and one or more families of its married children.

Factory farming Commercial agriculture based on fossil fuel energy subsidies, mechanization, pesticides, chemical fertilizers, and large-scale monocropping.

Feudalism A political system in which village farmers occupy lands owned by local lords to whom they owe loyalty, rent, and service.

Feuding Chronic intergroup conflict that exists between communities in the absence of centralized political authority. It may involve a cycle of revenge raids and killing that is difficult to break.

Filial piety *Hsiao*, the ritual obligation of children to respect their ancestors, and especially the duty of sons to care for shrines of their patrilineal ancestors.

Filiation A parent-child relationship link used as a basis for descent-group membership.

Financialization A cultural process involving the flow of finance capital, money, and securities, rather than the actual production and distribution of goods and services.

Folk-urban continuum Robert Redfield's concept of a gradual distinction between the Little Tradition culture of rural commoners and the Great Tradition culture of the urban elites in a political-scale culture.

Fordism Henry Ford's principles of assembly-line mass production combined with high enough wages to allow workers to buy the products they produced, which was a foundation of consumer culture.

Foreign direct investment When businesses headquartered in a given country buy productive assets in another country and retain control over them.

Forest fallow A system of cultivation in which soil nutrients are restored by allowing the forest to regrow.

Fraternal polyandry When a woman marries two or more men who are brothers.

Fuel revolution The large-scale adoption of fossil fuels such as coal and oil.

Genealogical method Method used to trace the marriage and family relationships among people as a basis for identifying cultural patterns in a community.

Generalized reciprocity The distribution of goods and services by direct sharing. It is assumed that in the long run giving and receiving balances out, but no accounts are maintained.

Genitor The biological father of a child.

Genocide The extermination of a human population.

Gerontocracy An age hierarchy that is controlled or dominated by the oldest age groups.

Global city A city that serves as an important hub within a network of cities supporting financial and information services.

Glottochronology A method of estimating the relative date at which related languages separated from a common ancestral language by calculating the percentage of cognates shared between the related languages.

Great acceleration The dramatic increase in human population and technology since 1945 that greatly amplified the human impacts on nature that have been apparent since 1800 with the Anthropocene.

Great Tradition The culture of the elite in a state-organized society with a tradition that is usually written and not fully shared by nonliterate, village-level commoners.

Great Transition Change in cultural beliefs and practices that produce a truly sustainable global system.

Green Revolution Dramatic increases in agricultural production from use of hybrid grains that produce high yields in return for high inputs of chemical fertilizers and pesticides.

Gross domestic product The total output of goods and services produced within a country, by monetary value.

Gross national product The total output of a country's goods and services, by monetary value, but also includes net gains from foreign investments or activities.

Hacienda A Latin American agricultural estate with dependent laborers that produced for local rather than global markets and was designed to maintain the social status and lifestyle of the hacendado landowner.

Happy Planet Index A measure of a country's effectiveness at meeting human needs, based on life expectancy, subjective satisfaction with life, and the ecological footprint.

Headman A political leader who coordinates group activities and is a village spokesman but who serves only with the consent of the community and has no coercive power.

Heterogeneity Basic principle of planetary society that recognizes local, regional, and cultural diversity.

High-yield variety High-yield plant varieties, especially wheat and rice developed by selective breeding as part of the Green Revolution.

Household A social unit that shares domestic activities such as food production, cooking, eating, and sleeping, often under one roof, and is usually based on the nuclear or extended family.

Human Development Index UN measure of sustainable development based on health, education, and income distribution.

Humanization The production and maintenance of human beings, human societies, and human cultures, based on social power organized at the household or domestic level.

Hypergamy Marriage to someone of higher rank. For example, Hindu women may marry men of a higher subcaste.

Hypogamy Marriage to someone of lower rank.

Idealist A policy position that advocates cultural autonomy for indigenous peoples as a basic human right.

Imagined communities Large communities where cultural identity is established by communication technologies including literacy, printing, and electronic networks.

Immaterial production Language, symbols, computer software, information technologies, and communication networks.

Immiseration Malthusian impoverishment, a declining standard of living attributed to continuous population growth on a limited-resource base.

Imperia, imperium (singular) An individual's personal power network, including everyone that one might command or call on for assistance, as well as the institutional structures that one might direct

Impurity Low ritual status attributed to association or contact with polluting biological events or products.

Inclusive fitness A biological concept referring to the degree to which individuals are successful in passing on a higher proportion of their genes to succeeding generations.

Indigenous peoples The original inhabitants of a territory, who seek to maintain political control over their resources and the cultural heritage.

Indirect rule The situation in which European colonial administrators appointed local natives to serve as mediating officials, or chiefs, to help them control local communities.

Information society A society organized within an electronic network of digital information supported by computers and communication technologies.

Integration The absorption of a formerly autonomous people into a dominant state society, with the possible retention of ethnic identity.

Internal colony A territory within a state containing an indigenous population that is denied the right of self-determination.

Invisible hand The capitalist belief that market forces, operating through supply and demand, will lead to continuous economic growth and benefit everyone.

Irreducibility Basic principle of planetary society recognizing that some problems are global in nature and require global decision-making authority.

Irreducible minimum The culturally defined standard of material needs for food, clothing, and shelter. In the tribal world this material standard is available to everyone.

Key informant A member of the host culture who helps the anthropologist learn about the culture.

Keynesianism Keynes's policy of government intervention in the economy to sustain consumer income and expenditure by means of welfare assistance and public work projects.

Kin-ordered production A mode of production organized at the domestic or kinship level and producing primarily for domestic use rather than exchange.

Kinship terminology An ego-centered system of terms that specifies genealogical relationships of consanguinity and affinity in reference to a given individual.

Law of participation The assumption that a thing can participate in or be part of two or more things at once.

Law of sympathy Sir James Frazer's explanation for the logic underlying magic, sorcery, and shamanism. He thought that tribal peoples believed that anything ever connected with a person, such as hair or blood, could be manipulated to influence that person.

Levirate A cultural pattern in which a woman marries a brother of her deceased husband.

Liminal phase An ambiguous phase of ritual transition in which one is on the threshold between two states.

Little Tradition Ritual beliefs and practices followed by nonliterate commoners, especially rural villagers who are part of a larger state-level society.

Liturgical government The use of ritually prescribed interpersonal relations and religious, moral authority as a primary means of social control in a state-level society.

Male supremacy complex A functionally interrelated series of presumably male-centered traits, including patrilocality, polygyny, inequitable sexual division of labor, male domination of headmanship and shamanism, and ritual subordination of women.

Mana An impersonal supernatural force thought to reside in particular people and objects. In the Pacific Islands *mana* is the basis of chiefly power.

Market capitalization The collective market value of all the stocks issued by all the corporations listed in a particular market.

Matrilocal residence Residence near the wife's kin, normally near her parents.

Millennium Development Goals Eight-point set of development goals on poverty and health adopted by the United Nations in 2000.

Modern An international system of nation-states with industrial production and market economies.

Moiety One part of a two-part social division.

Monocrop farming A system of growing one plant species, sometimes only a single variety, often in very large continuous stands.

Multilinear evolution Julian Steward's theory that, given similar conditions, cultures can develop independently along similar lines. For example, he argued that irrigation agriculture led to state organization several times.

Myth A narrative that recounts the activities of supernatural beings. Often acted out in ritual, myths encapsulate a culture's cosmology and cosmogony and provide justification for culturally prescribed behavior.

Mythical thought Claude Levi-Strauss's term for the thinking underlying myth and magic; logically similar to scientific thought but based on the science of the concrete and used to serve aesthetic purposes and to solve existential problems.

Nation A people with a common culture and identity in an international system.

Nation-state A territory in which the government and the nation coincide.

Natural symbols Inherent qualities of specific plants and animals used as signs or metaphors for issues that concern people.

Neoliberal economics Advocates government deregulation of commerce or nonintervention in the "free market" to promote economic growth.

Neolithic paradox Claude Levi-Strauss's term for the fact that tribal peoples invented all the major domestic technologies, such as cooking, textiles, and ceramics, that satisfied household needs but did not go on to invent metallurgy and writing, which served political ends.

Neolocal residence Where a newly married couple resides independently of either set of parents.

Nonmarket economy Goods and services distributed by direct exchange or reciprocity in the absence of markets and money.

Noumenal Relating to mental constructs, concepts, and things that people know through the mind rather than phenomena observed or perceived through the senses.

Nuclear family The primary family unit of mother, father, and dependent children.

Official development aid Aid that is donated by several countries and channeled through a single international agency such that it can be free of political favoritism.

Oligopoly Concentrated economic power when a few sellers can control a market with many buyers by controlling the price and availability of goods.

Participant intervention A form of culture change in which those in control become members of the system they seek to change.

Participant observation Field method in which the observer shares in community activities.

Pater The culturally legitimate, or sociological, father of a child.

Patrilineage A lineage based on descent traced through a line of men to a common male ancestor and sharing a joint estate.

Patrilocal band A theoretical form of band organization based on exogamy and patrilocal residence.

Patrilocality A cultural preference for a newly married couple to live near the husband's parents or patrilineal relatives.

Patron A Spanish term for someone who extends credits or goods to a client who is kept in a debt relationship.

Peak oil The point at which half of all extractable oil has been extracted and output begins to decline because of increasing cost and difficulty of extraction.

Peasantry Village farmers who provide most of their own subsistence but who must pay taxes and are politically and often, to some extent, economically dependent on the central state government.

Periphery Capital-poor areas that supply raw materials and labor to the core; this area was integrated into the early capitalist world system through conquest and coercion.

Phoneme The minimal unit of sound that carries meaning and is recognized as distinctive by the speakers of a given language.

Planetary society A hypothetical global social organization produced by a Great Transition change in cultural beliefs and practices that produce a truly sustainable global system.

Plutocracy Rule by the rich.

Plutonomy An economy managed and directed by the wealthy.

Political economy A cultural pattern in which centralized political authority intervenes in the production and distribution of goods and services.

Political scale Characterized by centrally organized societies with thousands or millions of members and energy-intensive production directed by political rulers.

Politicization The cultural process of producing and maintaining centralized political power by co-opting the humanization process.

Polyandry When a woman marries two or more men.

Polygyny A form of marriage in which a man may have more than one wife.

Polytheism A religious system based on belief in many gods or deities.

Postmaterialist A sociocultural system where self-expression and rational secular values predominate and people are less focused on material consumption.

Postmodernity Societies of control in which financial elites are the dominant decision makers; immaterial production and communication technologies are central features.

Primogeniture Preferential treatment to a couple's firstborn offspring or oldest surviving child; may be a basis for establishing social rank.

Purchasing power parity Monetary value adjusted for the value of the currency in relation to a set of basic goods in the country.

Purity Ritually superior status; a category in logical opposition to impurity

Rank Social position in a status hierarchy.

Realist A policy position that maintains that indigenous peoples must surrender their political and economic autonomy and be integrated into dominant state societies.

Redistribution A form of exchange in which goods, such as foodstuffs, are concentrated and then distributed under the control of a central political authority.

Rite of passage A ritual marking culturally significant changes in an individual's life cycle, such as birth, puberty, marriage, old age, and death.

Sapir-Whorf Hypothesis Suggests that one's view of the world is shaped by language, such that the speakers of different languages may live in different perceptual worlds.

Scale subsidy Social support in the form of taxes or tribute for activities that promote growth in scale or that maintain a larger-scale society when benefits are inequitably distributed.

Scapulimancy Divination by interpreting the pattern of cracks formed in heated animals' scapula or turtle shells.

Science of the concrete Claude Levi-Strauss's term for thought based on perceptions and signs, images, and events, as opposed to formal science based on concepts.

Section system A social division into four (sections) or eight (subsections) intermarrying, named groups, which summarize social relationships. Members of each group must marry only members of one other specific group.

Segmentary lineage system A tribal political system in which there are no permanent leaders, and instead individuals align with groups according to their assumed genealogical distance.

Self-determination The right of any people to freely determine their own cultural, political, and economic future.

Shaman A part-time religious specialist with special skills for dealing with the spirit world; may help his community by healing, by divination, and by directing supernatural powers against enemies.

Slash and burn A gardening technique in which forest is cleared and burned to enrich the soil for planting; a forest fallow system depending on forest regrowth. Also called swidden cultivation.

Small Island Developing States UN designation for countries that are especially vulnerable to environmental problems and global warming.

Small nation A territorially organized sociocultural system in the commercial world with fewer than ten million people.

Social class A group of people in a stratified society, such as elites and commoners who each share a similar level of access to resources, power, and privilege.

Social Darwinism A political philosophy that treats other societies as biologically and culturally inferior and therefore "unfit" for survival.

Social intelligence The cognitive ability to imagine what others are thinking.

Social power An individual's ability to get what he or she wants, even when others might object.

Social product The value of the aggregate annual production of a society, measured either as production or consumption.

Social status A position that an individual occupies within a social system; defined by age, sex, kinship relationships, or other cultural criteria and involving specific behavioral expectations.

Social stratification A ranking of social statuses such that the individuals of a society belong to different groups having differential access to resources, power, and privileges.

Societies of control Biopower is exercised by communication technologies.

Sororal polygyny When a man marries two or more women who are sisters.

Sororate When a man marries his deceased wife's sister.

Specialist An individual who provides goods and services to elites in hierarchically organized societies. Such a specialist does not produce his or her own food but is supported from the surplus that is politically extracted by central authorities.

Staple economy The state-controlled production, storage, and distribution of subsistence staples, such as potatoes and maize in the Inca case, to support nonfood-producing specialist groups and to provide emergency aid.

Structural violence Human suffering that is the direct result of social and cultural structures that enable more powerful individuals to violate the basic human rights of less powerful individuals.

Structuralism A theoretical approach that examines how people construct meaning by using contrasting relationships between symbols, much as languages create meaning by contrasting sounds (phonemes).

Structure The social, economic, and political organization of a culture, which is shaped by the technological base, or infrastructure, according to Marvin Harris's cultural materialist theory.

Subsidiarity The principle that a managing body takes on a function only when a lower-level body is unable to perform it.

Subsistence economy Production and distribution carried on at the local community and household levels, primarily for local consumption.

Subsistence intensification Technological innovations that produce more food from the same land area but often require increased effort.

Summum bonum The maximum human good, or the "good life" as culturally defined.

Superstructure The mental, ideological, or belief systems as expressed in the religion, myths, and rituals of a culture. According to Marvin Harris's cultural materialist theory, superstructure is shaped by the structure.

Surplus Subsistence production that exceeds the needs of the producer households and that is extracted by political leaders to support nonfood-producing specialists.

Sustainable development UN Brundtland Commission official development goal since 1987, meeting the needs of the present without compromising the needs of future generations.

Tabu Actions that are forbidden under the sanction of supernatural punishment. Tabus may be imposed by chiefs and are supported by chiefly *mana*.

Taylorism "Scientific management" of workers developed by American mechanical engineer Frederick Winslow Taylor to increase labor efficiency.

Theocracy State government based on religious authority or divine guidance. The Chinese emperor was the highest civil and religious leader.

Totem In Australia, specific animals, plants, natural phenomena, or other objects that originate in the Dreaming and are the spiritual progenitors of aboriginal descent groups. Elsewhere, it refers to any cultural association between specific natural objects and human social groups.

Transhumance Seasonal movements of livestock to different environmental zones often at different elevations or latitudes.

Tribe A politically autonomous, economically self-sufficient, territorially based society that can reproduce a distinct culture and language and form an in-marrying (endogamous) society.

Tributary production A mode of production in which products are extracted as surplus from a self-supporting peasantry and used to support the state.

Uncontrolled frontier A tribal territory that is invaded by colonists from a state-organized society but where the government chooses not to regulate the actions of the colonists.

Unequal exchange Market-based exchanges in which one party is consistently able to accumulate a disproportionate share of the profit or wealth.

Use value The value of goods produced for domestic consumption, usually within a kin-ordered mode of production.

Utilitarianism The use of economic profit, direct material advantage, or physical welfare, such as food and shelter, as an explanation for cultural practices.

Village-states Politically centralized societies based on an urban administrative and ceremonial center drawing their support from self-sufficient peasant villagers scattered over a vast region.

Voluntary isolation Official designation for tribal peoples who have chosen to actively avoid contact with outsiders, thereby maintaining their self-determination and exercising cultural autonomy.

Wealth economy The state-controlled production, storage, and distribution of wealth objects that support the status hierarchy.

World system An international hierarchy of diverse societies and cultures integrated into a single economic system based on unequal exchange that allows wealth to accumulate in the core.

Bibliography

Aaby, Peter. 1977. "What Are We Fighting For? 'Progress' or 'Cultural Autonomy'?" In *Cultural Imperialism and Cultural Identity,* edited by Carola Sanbacka, pp. 61–76. Transactions of the Finnish Anthropological Society, No. 2. Helsinki: Finnish Anthropological Society.

Aboriginal and Torres Strait Islander Act, 2005. www.austlii.edu.au/au/legis/cth/consol_act/aatsia2005359.txt.

Adams, Richard N. 1988. *The Eighth Day: Social Evolution as the Self-Organization of Energy.* Austin: University of Texas Press.

Adams, Robert McCormick. 1981. *Heartland of Cities: Surveys of Ancient Settlement and Land Use on the Central Floodplain of the Euphrates.* Chicago and London: University of Chicago Press.

Ahmed, Leila. 1982. "Western Ethnocentrism and Perceptions of the Harem." *Feminist Studies* 8(3):521–34.

Ahrne, Göran, and Erik Olin Wright. 1983. "Class in the United States and Sweden: A Comparison." *Acta Sociologica* 26(3/4), 211–35.

AIDESEP, Asociación Interétnica de Dessarrollo de la Selva Peruana. www.aidesep.org.pe.

AIDESEP. 2005. "La Voz de los Apus." Voz Indígena No. 27, 6-15; CECONSEC (Central de Comunidades Nativas de la Selva Central del Peru). FECONAU (Federación de Comunidades Nativas del Ucayali), el CAH (Consejo Aguaruna Huambisa), and el Congreso Amuesha.

Algaze, Guillermo. 2005. *The Uruk World System: The Dynamics of Expansion of Early Mesopotamian Civilization.* 2nd ed. Chicago: University of Chicago Press.

Alexander, Richard D. 1987. *The Biology of Moral Systems.* New York: Aldine De Gruyter.

Alkire, William H. 1965. *Lamotrek Atoll and Inter-Island Socioeconomic Ties.* Studies in Anthropology, no. 5. Urbana: University of Illinois Press.

Allchin, Bridget, and F. Raymond Allchin. 1982. *The Rise of Civilization in India and Pakistan.* Cambridge, Eng.: Cambridge University Press.

Allen, Harry. 2002. *The Hunter Gatherer Mode of Thought and Change in Aboriginal Northern Australia.* Presented at the Ninth International Conference on Hunting and Gathering Societies, Heriot-Watt University, Edinburgh, Scotland.

Altman, J. C. 1987. *Hunter-Gatherers Today: An Aboriginal Economy in North Australia.* Canberra: Australian Institute of Aboriginal Studies.

Altman, J. C. 2006. *In Search of an Outstations Policy for Indigenous Australians.* Working Paper No. 34. Centre for Aboriginal Economic Policy Research, 3, Tables 1 and 2.

Altman, Jon. 2008. "Different Governance for Difference: The Bawinanga Aboriginal Corporation." In Hunt, Janet, Diane Smith, Stephanie Garling, and Will Sanders, eds. *Contested Governance: Culture, Power and Institutions in Indigenous Australia.*, pp. 177–203. Centre for Aboriginal Economic Policy Research. Research Monograph. No. 29. Canberra: Australia National University E Press.

Altman, Jon. 2009. "Contestations over Development." In Altman, Jon, and David Martin, eds. *Power, Culture, Economy: Indigenous Australians and Mining,* pp. 1–15. Centre for Aboriginal Economic Policy Research. Canberra: Australia National University E Press. http://epress.anu.edu.au/caepr_series/no_30/pdf/whole_book.pdf.

Altman, Jon. 2009. "Indigenous Communities, Miners and the State in Australia." In Altman, Jon, and David Martin, eds. *Power, Culture, Economy: Indigenous Australians and Mining,* pp. 17–49. Centre for Aboriginal Economic Policy Research. Canberra: Australia National University E Press.

Altman, Jon, and David Martin, eds. *Power, Culture, Economy: Indigenous Australians and Mining.* Centre for Aboriginal Economic Policy Research. Canberra: Australia National University E Press.

Alva, Walter, and Christopher B. Donnan. 1993. *Royal Tombs of Sipan.* Los Angeles: Fowler Museum of Cultural History, University of California.

Amazonia Indigena. 1981. "Pronunciamiento Sobre el Projecto Especial Pichis-Palcazu." *Amazonia Indigena* 1(3):3–5.

Ambrose, Stanley H. 1984. "The Introduction of Pastoral Adaptations to the Highlands of East Africa." In *From Hunters to Farmers: The Causes and Consequences of Food Production in Africa,* edited by J. Desmond Clark and Steven Brandt, pp. 212–39. Berkeley: University of California Press.

American Anthropological Association. 1998. *Code of Ethics of the American Anthropological Association.* www.aaanet.org/committees/ethics/ethcode.htm (accessed April 25, 2009).

American Anthropological Association. *Race: Are We So Different?* www.understandingrace.org/humvar/index.html.

American Psychiatric Association (APA). 1980. *Diagnostic and Statistical Manual of Mental Disorders,* 3rd ed. Washington, DC: American Psychiatric Association.

American Psychiatric Association (APA). 2000. *Diagnostic and Statistical Manual IV.* Text Revision (DSM-IV-TR).

Andersen, Torben M., Bengt Holmstrom, Seppo Honkapohja, Sixten Korkman, Hans Tson Soderstrom, Juliana Vartiainen. 2007. *The Nordic Model: Embracing Globalization and Sharing Risks.* Research Institute of the Finish Economy (ETLA), Helsinki: Taloustieto Oy. www.etla.fi/Files/1892 the_nordic_model_complete.pdf.

Anderson, Benedict. 1983. *Imagined Communities: Reflections on the Origin and Spread of Nationalism.* London: Verso.

Anderson, Richard L. 1990. *Calliope's Sisters: A Comparative Study of Philosophies of Art.* New York: Prentice-Hall.

ANZAAS (Australia and New Zealand Association for the Advancement of Science). 1914. "Welfare of Aborigines Committee." Report of the Fourteenth Meeting of the Australasian Association for the Advancement of Science, 450–52.

Aristotle. *The Politics.* 1323al4.

Arsenault, Amelia H. H., and Manuel Castells. 2008. "The Structure and Dynamics of Global Multi-Media Business Networks." *International Journal of Communication* 2:707–748. http://ijoc.org/ojs/index.php/ijoc/article/view/298.

Ascension Island Government, Official Website. www.ascension-island.gov.ac/aig/ascension-island-about.htm.

Ascher, Marcia, and Robert A. Ascher. 1981. *Code of the Quipu: Study in Media, Mathematics, and Culture.* Ann Arbor: University of Michigan Press.

Ashton, T. S. 1969. *The Industrial Revolution 1760–1830.* London: Oxford University Press.

Asian Development Bank. 2008. "Country Water Action: Fiji Islands Waste Threat Prompts Village Action." www.adb.org/Water/Actions/FIJ/Waste-Threat.asp.

ASPO. Association for the Study of Peak Oil. 2009. Newsletter No. 100. (April) www.aspo-ireland.org/index.cfm/page/newsletter.

ASPO, Association for the Study of Peak Oil & Gas. Website www.peakoil.net (accessed March 2010).

Atkins, Peter. 2003. *Atkins' Molecules.* 2nd ed. Cambridge: Cambridge University Press.

Australia, Department of the Environment, Water, Heritage and the Arts. www.environment.gov.au/indigenous/index.html.

Australia, Director of National Parks. 2005. Welcome to Aboriginal Land: Uluru-Kata Tjuta National Park Visitor Guide and Maps. Canberra: Department of the Environment, Water, Heritage and the Arts. www.environment.gov.au/parks/publications/uluru/visitor-guide.html (accessed July 13, 2009).

Australia, Director of National Parks. 2009. *Uluru-Kata Tjuta National Park. Draft Management Plan 2009-2019.* Canberra: Department of the Environment, Water, Heritage and the Arts. www.environment.gov.au/parks/publications/uluru/draft-plan.html (accessed July 13, 2009).

Australia, Office of the Registrar of Indigenous Corporations. 2009. *Yearbook 2008–09,* p. 16, Table 4. www.orac.gov.au/html/publications/Yearbooks/Yearbook2008-09_72dpi_104pp.pdf.

Australian Bureau of Statistics. 2007. *Population Distribution, Aboriginal and Torres Strait Islander Australians, 2006.* Cat no. 4705.0. www.abs.gov.au/AUSSTATS/abs@.nsf/DetailsPage/4705.02006?OpenDocument.

Australian Bureau of Statistics. 2008. 4713.0.55.001 – Population Characteristics, Aboriginal and Torres Strait Islander Australians, Australia, 2006.

Baer, Paul, Tom Athanasiou, and Sivan Kartha. 2009. "A 350 ppm Emergency Pathway: A Greenhouse Development Rights Brief." Ecoequity and Stockholm Environment Institute. http://gdrights.org/2009/10/25/a-350-ppm-emergency-pathway.

Baer, Paul, Tom Athanasiou, Sivan Kartha, and Eric Kemp-Benedict. 2008. *The Greenhouse Development Rights Framework: The Right to Development in a Climate Constrained World.* Heinrich Böll Foundation, Christian Aid, EcoEquity, and the Stockholm Environment Institute. http://gdrights.org/2009/02/16/second-edition-of-the-greenhouse-development-rights.

Bailey, Robert C., G. Head, M. Jenike, B. Own, R. Rechtman, and E. Zechenter. 1989. "Hunting and Gathering in Tropical Rain Forest: Is It Possible?" *American Anthropologist* 91(1):59–82.

Bangladesh, Ministry of Finance. 2003. *Bangladesh: A National Strategy for Economic Growth, Poverty Reduction and Social Development.*

Barnard, Alan. 2002. "The Foraging Mode of Thought." In *Self and Other-Images of Hunter-Gatherers,* edited by Henry Stewart, Alan Barnard, and Keiichi Omura, pp. 1–24. Senri Ethnological Studies No. 60. Osaka: National Museum of Ethnology.

Barnet, Richard J., and John Cavanagh. 1994. *Global Dreams: Imperial Corporations and the New World Order.* New York: Simon & Schuster.

Bateman, John. 1883. *The Great Landowners of Great Britain and Ireland.* 4th ed. London: Harrison.

Bauer, Brian S. 1996. "Legitimization of the State in Inca Myth and Ritual." *American Anthropologist* 98(2): 327–37.

Bauer, Brian S. 1998. *The Sacred Landscape of the Inca: The Cusco Ceque System.* Austin: University of Texas Press.

Bawinanga Aboriginal Corporation website www.bawinanga.com.au/index.htm (accessed January 2010).

Beach, William W., and Gareth Davis. 1998. "The Institutional Setting of Economic Growth." In 1998 *Index of Economic Freedom,* edited by Bryan T. Johnson, Kim R.

Holmes, and Melanie Kirkpatrick, pp. 1–10. Washington, DC, and New York: The Heritage Foundation and Dow Jones & Co.

Beaglehole, Ernest. 1954. "Cultural Factors in Economic and Social Change." *International Labour Review* 69(5):415–32.

Beard, Charles A. 1913. *An Economic Interpretation of the Constitution of the United States.* New York: Macmillan.

Beckwith, Martha Warren. 1951. *The Kumulipo: A Hawaiian Creation Chant.* Chicago: University of Chicago Press.

Behrens, Clifford A. 1984. *Shipibo Ecology and Economy: A Mathematical Approach to Understanding Human Adaptation.* Doctoral Dissertation. Los Angeles: University of California.

Behrens, Clifford A. 1986. "Shipibo Food Categorization and Preference: Relationships between Indigenous and Western Dietary Concepts." *American Anthropologist* 88(3):647–58.

Beidelman, T. O. 1966. "The Ox and Nuer Sacrifice: Sonu Freudian Hypothesesa Nuer Symbolism." *Man* 1(4): 453–67.

Beidelman, T. O. 1971. "Nuer Priest and Prophets: Charisma, Authority, and Power Among the Nuer." In T. O. Beidelman, ed. *The Translation of Culture: Essays to E. E. Evans-Pritchard,* pp. 375–415. London: Tavistock.

Belaunde-Terry, Fernando. 1965. *Peru's Own Conquest.* Lima: American Studies Press.

Bell, Daniel. 1973. *The Coming of Post-Industrial Society: A Venture in Social Forecasting.* New York: Basic Books.

Bell, Diane. 1983. *Daughters of the Dreaming.* Sydney: McPhee Gribble/Allen & Unwin.

Bell, Diane. 1987. "Aboriginal Women and the Religious Experience." In *Traditional Aboriginal Society: A Reader,* edited by W. H. Edwards, pp. 237–56. South Melbourne: Macmillan.

Bellwood, Peter S. 1985. *Prehistory of the Indo Malaysian Archipelago.* New York and Sydney: Academic.

Benavides, Margarita. 2005. "Conservación, Derechos Indígas y Poder en la Gestión de los Bienes Communes: El Caso de la Reserve Communal El Sira en la Amazonía Peruana." Originally presented at the International Association for the Study of the Commons." Global Meeting, Oaxaca City, Mexico. 2004. www.ibcperu.org/doc/isis/5316.pdf (accessed January 2010).

Benedict, Ruth. 1934. *Patterns of Culture.* Boston: Houghton Mifflin.

Bentham, Jeremy. 1791. *The Works of Jeremy Bentham,* vol. 4, pp. 172–73.

Bergman, Roland W. 1974. *Shipibo Subsistence in the Upper Amazon Rainforest.* Ph.D. dissertation, Department of Geography, University of Wisconsin-Madison. Ann Arbor, MI: University Microfilms.

Berlin, Brent, and Paul Kay. 1969. *Basic Color Terms: Their Universality and Evolution.* Berkeley and Los Angeles: University of California Press.

Bernardi, Bernardo. 1985. *Age Class Systems: Social Institutions and Polities Based on Age.* Cambridge, Eng.: Cambridge University Press.

Berreman, Gerald D. 1960. "Caste in India and the United States." *American Journal of Sociology* 66:120–27.

Berreman, Gerald D. 1979. *Caste and Other Inequities: Essays on Inequality.* Meerut, Uttar Pradesh, India: Ved Prakash Vatuk, Folklore Institute.

Betzig, Laura L. 1986. *Despotism and Differential Reproduction: A Darwinian View of History.* New York: Aldine.

Betzig, Laura L. 1993. "Sex, Succession, and Stratification in the First Six Civilizations: How Powerful Men Reproduced, Passed Power on to Their Sons, and Used Power to Defend Their Wealth, Women, and Children." In *Social Stratification and Socioeconomic Inequality,* edited by Lee Ellis, pp. 37–74. Westport, CT: Praeger.

Bhutan, National Environment Commission. 1998. *The Middle Path: National Environment Strategy for Butan.* Royal Government of Bhutan.

Binford, Lewis R. 2001. *Constructing Frames of Reference: An Analytic Method for Archaeological Theory Building Using Hunter-Gatherer and Environmental Data Sets.* Berkeley: University of California Press.

Bird-David, Nurit. 1992. "Beyond 'The Original Affluent Society': A Culturalist Reformulation." *Current Anthropology* 33(1):25–47.

Birdsell, Joseph B. 1957. "Some Population Problems Involving Pleistocene Man." *Cold Spring Harbor Symposium on Quantitative Biology* 22:47–70.

Birdsell, Joseph B. 1973. "A Basic Demographic Unit." *Current Anthropology* 14(4):337–50. Blochmann, H. (translator). 1939. *The Aini Akbari by Abu Fazl'Allami.* 2nd ed. Calcutta: Royal Asiatic Society of Bengal.

Bluestone, Barry, and Bennett Harrison. 1982. *The Deindustrialization of America.* New York: Basic Books.

Blundell, Valda. 1980. "Hunter Gatherer Territoriality: Ideology and Behavior in Northwest Australia." *Ethnohistory* 27(2):103–117.

Boas, Franz. 1911. *The Mind of Primitive Man.* New York: Macmillan.

Bocquet-Appel, Jean-Pierre, and Claude Masset. 1981. "Farewell to Paleodemography." *Journal of Human Evolution* 11:321–33.

Bodley, John H. 1970. "Campa Socio-Economic Adaptation." Ph.D. dissertation, University of Oregon. Ann Arbor, MI: University Microfilms.

Bodley, John H. 1972a. "A Transformative Movement Among the Campa of Eastern Peru." *Anthropos* 67:220–28.

Bodley, John H. 1972b. *Tribal Survival in the Amazon: The Campa Case.* IWGIA (International Work Group for Indigenous Affairs) Document no. 5. Copenhagen: IWGIA.

Bodley, John H. 1973. "Deferred Exchange Among the Campa Indians." *Anthropos* 68:589–96.

Bodley, John H. 1975. *Victims of Progress.* Menlo Park, CA: Cummings.

Bodley, John H. 1976. *Anthropology and Contemporary Human Problems.* Menlo Park, CA: Cummings.

Bodley, John H. 1981a. "Deferred Exchange Among the Campa: A Reconsideration." In *Networks of the Past: Regional Interaction in Archaeology,* edited by Peter Francis, F. J. Kense, and P. G. Duke, pp. 49–59. Calgary: University of Calgary Archaeological Association.

Bodley, John H. 1981b. "Inequality: An Energetic Approach." In *Social Inequality: Comparative and Developmental Approaches,* edited by Gerald Berreman, pp. 183–97. New York: Academic Press.

Bodley, John H. 1988. *Tribal Peoples and Development Issues: A Global Overview.* Mountain View, CA: Mayfield.

Bodley, John H. 1990. *Victims of Progress,* 3rd ed. Mountain View, CA: Mayfield.

Bodley, John H. 1992. "Anthropologist at Work: Inequality and Exploitation in the Peruvian Amazon." In *Discovering Anthropology,* by Daniel R. Gross, p. 483. Mountain View, CA: Mayfield Publishing.

Bodley, John H. 1993. "Human Rights, Development and the Environment in the Peruvian Amazon: The Asháninka Case." In *Who Pays the Price? Examining the Sociocultural Context of Environmental Crisis.* A Society for Applied Anthropology Report on Human Rights and the Environment Submitted to the United Nations Commission on Human Rights Subcommission for the Prevention of Discrimination and Protection of Minorities, edited by Barbara R. Johnston, pp. 158–62. Oklahoma City: Society for Applied Anthropology.

Bodley, John H. 1996. *Anthropology and Contemporary Human Problems,* 3rd ed. Mountain View, CA: Mayfield.

Bodley, John H. 1999. *Victims of Progress,* 4th ed. Mountain View, CA: Mayfield.

Bodley, John H. 1999. "Socio-Economic Growth, Culture Scale, and Household Well-Being: A Test of the Power-Elite Hypothesis." *Current Anthropology* 40(5):595–620.

Bodley, John H. 2000. *Cultural Anthropology: Tribes, States, and the Global System.* 3rd ed. Mountain View, CA: Mayfield Publishing, 376–88.

Bodley, John H. 2001. "Growth, Scale, and Power in Washington State." *Human Organization* 60(4):367–79.

Bodley, John H. 2003. *The Power of Scale: A Global History Approach.* Armonk, NY: M.E. Sharpe.

Bodley, John H. 2005. "The Rich Tribal World: Scale and Power Perspectives on Cultural Valuation," paper presented at the Annual Meeting of the Society for Applied Anthropology, Santa Fe, NM.

Bodley, John H. 2008. *Anthropology and Contemporary Human Problems.* 5th ed. Lanham, NY: Altamira Press.

Bodley, John H. 2008. *Victims of Progress.* 5th ed. Lanham, MD: AltaMira Press.

Bodley, John H., and Foley Benson. 1979. *Cultural Ecology of Amazonian Palms.* Reports of Investigations, no. 56. Laboratory of Anthropology, Washington State University.

Bolnick, Deborah A. (Weiss), Beth A. (Schultz) Shook, Lyle Campbell, and Ives Goddard. 2004. "Problematic Use of Greenberg's Linguistic Classification of Native American Genetic Variation." *American Journal of Human Genetics* 75:519–23.

Bookchin, Murray. 1991. *The Ecology of Freedom: The Emergence and Dissolution of Hierarchy.* Montreal and New York: Black Rose Books.

Boorstin, Daniel J. 1985. *The Image: A Guide to Pseudo-Events in America.* New York: Atheneum.

Booth, Charles. 1892–1903. *Life and Labour of the People in London.* London and New York: Macmillan.

Borsodi, Ralph. 1929. *The Distribution Age: A Study of the Economy of Modern Distribution.* New York: D. Appleton.

Boserup, Ester. 1970. *Women's Role in Economic Development.* London: Allen & Unwin.

Boster, J. 1983. "A Comparison of the Diversity of Jivaroan Gardens with that of the Tropical Forest." *Human Ecology* 11(1):47–68.

Bourliere, François, and M. Hadley. 1983. "Present-Day Savannas: An Overview." In *Ecosystems of the World 13: Tropical Savannas,* edited by Francois Bourliere, pp. 1–17. New York: Elsevier.

Bowdler, S. 1977. "The Coastal Colonisation of Australia" In *Sunda and Sahul: Prehistoric Studies in Southeast Asia, Melanesia and Australia,* edited by J. Allen, J. Golson, and R. Jones, pp. 205–246. London: Academic Press.

Boyd, Robert, and Peter J. Richerson. 1985. *Culture and the Evolutionary Process.* Chicago and London: University of Chicago Press.

Boyd, Robert, and Peter J. Richerson. 2005. *The Origin and Evolution of Cultures.* Oxford: Oxford University Press.

Boyer, Pascal. 2000. "Functional Origins of Religious Concepts: Ontological and Strategic Selection in Evolved Minds." *Journal of the Royal Anthropological Institute* 6:195–214.

Braidwood, Robert J. 1964. *Prehistoric Men,* 6th ed. Chicago: Chicago Natural History Museum.

Brand, Michael, and Glenn D. Lowry. 1987. *Fatehpur-Sikri.* Bombay: Marg Publications.

Brandeis, Louis D. 1914. *Other People's Money and How the Bankers Use It.* New York: Frederick A. Stokes.

Brewer, John. 1989. *The Sinews of Power: War, Money and the English State, 1688–1783.* New York: Alfred A. Knopf.

Briody, Dan. 2003. *The Iron Triangle: Inside the Secret World of the Carlyle Group.* Hoboken, NJ: John Wiley.

Broch-Due, Vigdis. 2000. "The Fertility of Houses and Herds: Producing Kinship and Gender among Turkana Pastoralists." In Hodgson, Dorothy L., ed. *Rethinking Pastoralism in Africa: Gender, Culture and the Myth of the Patriarchal Pastoralist,* pp. 165–85. Oxford: James Currey; Athens, OH: Ohio University Press.

Brown, Barton McCaul. 1987. "Population Estimation from Floor Area: A Restudy of 'Naroll's Constant.'" *Behavior Science Research* 21(1–4):1–49.

Brown, Cecil H. 1977. "Folk Botanical Life-Forms: Their Universality and Growth." *American Anthropologist* 79(2):317–42.

Brown, Cecil H. 1979a. "Folk Zoological Life-Forms: Their Universality and Growth." *American Anthropologist* 81(4): 791–817.

Brown, Cecil H. 1979B. "Growth and Development of Folk Botanical Life Forms in the Mayan Language Family." *American Anthropologist* 6(2):366–85.

Brown, J. Larry, and Ernesto Pollitt. 1996. "Malnutrition, Poverty and Intellectual Development." *Scientific American* 274(2):38–43.

Brown, Michael F. 1984. "The Role of Words in Aguaruna Hunting Magic." *American Ethnologist* 11(3):545–58.

Brush, Stephen B., Heath J. Carney, and Zosimo Huaman. 1981. "Dynamics of Andean Potato Agriculture." *Economic Botany* 35(1):70–88.

Bucks, Brian K., Arthur B. Kennickell, Traci L. Mach, and Kevin B. Moore. 2009. "Changes in U.S. Family Finances from 2004 to 2007: Evidence from the Survey of Consumer Finances." *Federal Reserve Bulletin* (Feburary): A1–A56.

Buhler, G. 1886. "The Laws of Manu." In *The Sacred Books of the East*, edited by F. M. Muller. Oxford, Eng.: Clarendon Press.

Bunsen, C. C. J. 1854. *Outlines of the Philosophy of Universal History Applied to Language and Religion*. 2 vols. London: Longman.

Burbank, Victoria Katherine. 1994. *Fighting Women: Anger and Aggression in Aboriginal Australia*. Berkeley: University of California Press.

Bureau van Dijk. *Orbis: A World of Company Information.* www.bvdep.com/en/ORBIS.html (accessed Dec. 2009).

Burger, Richard L. 1992. *Chavin and the Origins of Andean Civilization*. London: Thames and Hudson.

Burnell, Arthur Coke, and Edward W. Hopkins, eds. 1884. *The Ordinances of Manu*. London: Trubner.

Burton, John W. 1980. "Women and Men in Marriage: Some Atuot Texts (Southern Sudan)." *Anthropos* 75:710–720.

Burton, John W. 1981. "Ethnicity on the Hoof: On the Economics of Nuer Identity." *Ethnology* 20(2):157–62.

Bush, M. B., M. R. Silman, C. McMichael, and S. Saatchi. 2008. "Fire, Climate Change and Biodiversity in Amazonia: A Late-Holocene Perspective." *Philosophical Transactions of the* Royal Society B 363:1795–1802.

Bush, President George W. 2002. *The National Security Strategy of the United States of America* (September).

Cain, P. J., and A. G. Hopkins. 1993. *British Imperialism: Innovation and Expansion 1688–1914*. London and New York: London.

California Environmental Associates. 2007. *Design to Win: Philanthropy's Role in the Fight Against Global Warming.* www.ceaconsulting.com/CaseStudyFiles/DesignToWin_FinalReport.pdf (accessed April 2010).

Callenbach, Ernest. 1975, 2004. *Ecotopia*. Berkeley, CA: Heyday Books.

Campbell, Colin J., and Jean H. Laherrère. 1998. "The End of Cheap Oil." *Scientific American* (March): 78–83.

Cannon, Walter B. 1942. "'Voodoo Death." *American Anthropologist* 44(2):169–81.

Capgemini. 2001. *World Wealth Report 2001.* www.us.capgemini.com/worldwealthreport08/wwr_archives.asp.

Capgemini. 2008. *World Wealth Report 2008*. Capgemini, Merrill Lynch.

Capgemini. 2009. *World Wealth Report 2009*. www.capgemini.com/insights-and-resources/by-publication/2009_world_wealth_report.

Carbon Disclosure Project. 2008. FIJI Water. www.cdproject.net/en-US/Results/Pages/Company-Responses.aspx?company=8190.

Carneiro, Robert L. 1960. "Slash-and-Burn Agriculture: A Closer Look at Its Implications for Settlement Patterns." In *Men and Cultures: Selected Papers of the International Congress of Anthropological and Ethnological Sciences*, edited by A. Wallace, pp. 229–34. Philadelphia: University of Pennsylvania Press.

Carneiro, Robert L. 1967. "On the Relationship between Size of Population and Complexity of Social Organization." *Southwestern Journal of Anthropology* 23(3):234–43.

Carneiro, Robert L. 1970. "A Theory of the Origin of the State." *Science* 169:733–38.

Carneiro, Robert L. 1978a. "The Knowledge and Use of Rain Forest Trees by the Kuikuru Indians of Central Brazil." In *The Nature and Status of Ethnobotany*. Anthropological Papers, no. 67, edited by R. Ford, pp. 210–216. Ann Arbor: Museum of Anthropology, University of Michigan.

Carneiro, Robert L. 1978b. "Political Expansion as an Expression of the Principle of Competitive Exclusion." In *Origins of the State: The Anthropology of Political Evolution*, edited by R. Cohen and E. R. Service, pp. 205–223. Philadelphia: Institute for the Study of Human Issues.

Carneiro, Robert L. 1981. "The Chiefdom: Precursor of the State." In *The Transition to Statehood in the New World*, edited by Grant Jones and Robert Kautz, pp. 37–79. Cambridge, Eng.: Cambridge University Press.

Carneiro, Robert L. 1983. "The Cultivation of Manioc among the Kuikuru of the Upper Xingu." In *Adaptive Responses of Native Amazonians*, edited by Raymond Hames and William Vickers, pp. 65–111. New York: Academic Press.

Carneiro, Robert L., and Stephen F. Tobias. 1963. "The Application of Scale Analysis to the Study of Cultural Evolution." *Transaction of the New York Academy of Sciences* (ser. 2) 26:196–207.

Carruthers, Bruce G. 1996. *City of Capital: Politics and Markets in the English Financial Revolution*. Princeton, NJ: Princeton University Press.

Carswell, Sue. 2003. "A Family Business: Women, Children and Smallholder Sugar Cane Farming in Fiji." *Asia Pacific Viewpoint* 44(2):131–48.

Castells, Manuel. 1989. *The Informational City: Information Technology, Economic Restructuring, and the Urban-Regional Process.* Oxford: Blackwell.

Castells, Manuel. 2000. *The Rise of the Network Society: The Information Age: Economy, Society and Culture,* vol. 1, 2nd ed. Oxford: Blackwell.

Cavalli-Sforza, Luigi Luca. 1991. "Genes, Peoples, and Languages." *Scientific American* 265(5):104–110.

Cavalli-Sforza, Luigi Luca, and Francesco Cavalli-Sforza. 1995. *The Great Human Diasporas: The History of Diversity and Evolution.* Reading, MA: Addison-Wesley.

Cavalli-Sforza, Luigi Luca, and M. Feldman. 1981. *Cultural Transmission and Evolution.* Princeton, NJ: Princeton University Press.

Cavalli-Sforza, Paola Menozzi, Alberto Piazza. 1994. *The History and Geography of Human Genes.* Princeton, NJ: Princeton University Press.

Cave, Jonathan. 2003. *Towards a Sustainable Information Society.* TERRA 2000 IST-2000-26332, iii. www.terra-2000.org/htdocs/Terra-2002/index.htm.

Cawte, John. 1974. *Medicine Is the Law. Studies in Psychiatric Anthropology of Australian Tribal Societies.* Honolulu: University Press of Hawaii.

Cawte, John E. 1976. "Malgri: A Culture-Bound Syndrome." *Culture-Bound Syndromes, Ethnopsychiatry, and Alternate Therapies.* Vol. 4 of *Mental Health Research in Asia and the Pacific,* edited by William Lebra, pp. 22–31. Honolulu: University Press of Hawaii.

CEDIA, Centro para el Desarrollo del Indígena Amazónico. www.cedia.org.pe/index.php (accessed January 2010).

Center for International Earth Science Information Network (CIESIN). 2010. *Last of the Wild, Version Two.* http://sedac.ciesin.columbia.edu/wildareas (accessed Feb. 2010).

Centre for Aboriginal Economic Policy Research. Monographs, www.anu.edu.au/caepr/mono.php, Topical Papers, www.anu.edu.au/caepr/topical.php.

CGIAR (Consultative Group on International Agricultural Research). 1980. *Consultative Group on International Development.* Washington, DC: CGIAR.

Chadwick, Sir Edwin. 1842. *Report. . . on an Inquiry Into the Sanitary Conditions of the Labouring Population of Great Britain.* London: W. Clowes and Sons.

Chagnon, Napoleon A. 1968a. *Yanomamo: The Fierce People.* New York: Holt, Rinehart & Winston.

Chagnon, Napoleon A. 1968b. "Yanomamo Social Organization and Warfare." In *War: The Anthropology of Armed Conflict and Aggression,* edited by Morton Fried, Marvin Harris, and Robert Murphy, pp. 109–159. Garden City, NY: Doubleday.

Chagnon, Napoleon A. 1979. "Is Reproductive Success Equal in Egalitarian Societies?" In *Evolutionary Biology and Human Social Behavior: An Anthropological Perspective,* edited by Napoleon Chagnon and William Irons, pp. 374–401. North Scituate, MA: Duxbury Press.

Chagnon, Napoleon A. 1983. *Yanomamo: The Fierce People,* 3rd ed. New York: Holt, Rinehart & Winston.

Chagnon, Napoleon A. 1988. "Life Histories, Blood Revenge, and Warfare in a Tribal Population." *Science* 239(4843): 985–92.

Chagnon, Napoleon A. 1992. *The Yanomamo,* 4th ed. New York: Holt, Rinehart & Winston.

Chai, Ch'u, and Winberg Chai. 1967. "Introduction." In *Li Chi: Book of Rites,* vol. 1. Translated by James Legge, pp. xxiii–lxxxiv. New Hyde Park, NY: University Books.

Chandler, Alfred D. Jr. 1977. *The Visible Hand: The Managerial Revolution in American Business.* Cambridge, MA, and London: The Belknap Press of Harvard University Press.

Chang, Kwang-Chih. 1980. *Shang Civilization.* New Haven, CT, and London: Yale University Press.

Chang, Kwang-Chih. 1983. *Art, Myth, and Ritual: The Path to Political Authority in Ancient China.* Cambridge, MA: Harvard University Press.

Chang, Kwang-Chih. 1986. *Archaeology of Ancient China,* 4th ed. New Haven, CT: Yale University Press.

Chang, T. T. 1983. "The Origin and Early Culture of the Cereal Grains and Food Legumes." In *The Origins of Chinese Civilization,* edited by D. N. Keightley, pp. 65–94. Berkeley: University of California Press.

Chao, Kang. 1986. *Man and Land in Chinese History: An Economic Analysis.* Stanford, CA: Stanford University Press.

Chibba, Michael. 2009. "Perspectives on Inclusive Development: Concepts, Approaches and Current Issues." *World Economics* 9(4): 145–56.

Chinni, Dante. 2008. "About the Patchwork Nation Project." *Christian Science Monitor.* http://patchworknation.csmonitor.com/about/ (accessed March 2010).

Chydenius, Anders. 1931. *The National Gain.* London: Ernest Benn Ltd. (original 1766).

CIA World Factbook, https://www.cia.gov/library/publications/the-world-factbook/index.html.

CIBA Foundation. 1977. *Health and Disease in Tribal Societies.* CIBA Foundation Symposium 49, pp. 49–67. Amsterdam: Elsevier/Excerpta Medica/North-Holland.

Cicerone, Ralph J. 1989. "Methane in the Atmosphere." In *Global Climate Change: Human and Natural Influences,* edited by S. Fred Singer, pp. 91–112. New York: Paragon House.

CIPIACI, (Comité Indígena Internacional para la Protección da los Pueblos en Aislamiento y Contacto Inicial de la Amazonía, el Gran Chaco, y la Regió Oriental de Paraguay). www.cipiaci.org/home.htm (accessed January 2010).

Clark, Grover. 1936. *The Balance Sheets of Imperialism: Facts and Figures on Colonies.* New York: Columbia University Press.

Clark, J. Desmond. 1984 "Prehistoric Cultural Continuity and Economic Change in the Central Sudan in the Early Holocene." In *From Hunters to Farmers: The Causes and Consequences of Food Production in Africa,* edited by J. Desmond Clark and Steven Brandt, pp. 113–26. Berkeley: University of California Press.

Clastres, Pierre. 1977. *Society against the State: The Leader as Servant and the Humane Uses of Power Among the Indians of the Americas.* New York: Urizen Books.

Cleave, T. L. 1974. *The Saccharine Disease.* Bristol, Eng.: John Wright.

Cleveland, David A., and Stephen C. Murray. 1997. "The World's Crop Genetic Resources and the Rights of Indigenous Farmers." *Current Anthropology* 38(4):477–515.

Clow, Archibald, and Nan L. Clow. 1952. *The Chemical Revolution: A Contribution to Social Technology.* London: The Batchworth Press.

CMDA, Capital Markets Development Authority. 2008 *Annual Report.* www.cmda.com.fj/?page=cmdaAnnual Reports.

Cohn, Bernard. 1996. *Colonialism and Its Forms of Knowledge.* Princeton: Princeton University Press.

Colby, Gerard, and Charlotte Dennett. 1995. *Thy Will Be Done: The Conquest of the Amazon: Nelson Rockefeller in the Age of Oil.* New York: HarperCollins, HarperPerennial.

Coleman, Graham. 1994. *A Handbook of Tibetan Culture: A Guide to Tibetan Centres and Resources throughout the World.* Boston: Shambhala.

Collier, Jane Fishburne. 1988. *Marriage and Inequality in Classless Societies.* Stanford, CA: Stanford University Press.

Collier, Peter, and David Horowitz. 1976. *The Rockefellers: An American Dynasty.* New York: Holt, Rinehart & Winston.

Colquhoun, Patrick. 1815. *A Treatise on the Wealth, Power, and Resources of the British Empire.* London: Joseph Mawman.

Convention on Biological Diversity. 2009. Global Island Partnership. www.cbd.int/island/glispa.shtml.

Cook, Earl. 1971. "The Flow of Energy in an Industrial Society." *Scientific American* 224(3):134–44.

Cook, Noble David. 1981. *Demographic Collapse: Indian Peru, 1520–1620.* Cambridge: Cambridge University Press.

Coral Reef Alliance (CORAL). 2008. *Building Healthy Coral Reef Communities: 2008 Annual Report,* 1. www.coral.org/files/pdf/annualreports/2008annualreport.pdf.

Cordy-Collins, Alana. 1978. "The Dual Divinity Concept in Chavin Art." *El Dorado* 3(2):1–31.

Corporations (Aboriginal and Torres Strait Islander Act) 2006. www.comlaw.gov.au/ComLaw/Management.nsf/lookupindexpagesbyid/IP200626899?OpenDocument.

Corris, Peter. 1968. *Aborigines and Europeans in Western Victoria.* Occasional Papers in Aboriginal Studies, no. 12, Ethnohistory Series, no. 1. Canberra: Australian Institute of Aboriginal Studies

Costanza, Robert, et al. 1997. "The Value of the World's Ecosystem Services and Natural Capital." *Nature* 387(6630): 253–59.

Costanza, Robert, Lisa J. Graumlich, and Will Steffen, eds. 2007. *Sustainability or Collapse? An Integrated History and Future of People on Earth.* Cambridge, MA, and London: The MIT Press.

Costanza, Robert, Lisa Graumlich, Will Steffen, Carole Crumley, John Dearing, Kathy Hibbard, Rik Leemans, Charles Redman, and David Schimel. 2007. "Sustainability or Collapse: What Can We Learn from Integrating the History of Humans and the Rest of Nature?" *Ambio* 36(2):522–27.

Costin, Cathy Lynne. 1996. "Craft Production and Mobilization Strategies in the Inka Empire." In Wailes, B. (ed.), *Craft Specialization and Social Evolution: In Memory of V. Gordon Childe,* University Museum of Archaeology and Anthropology, University of Pennsylvania, Philadelphia, pp. 211–25.

Costin, Cathy Lynne. 1998. "Housewives, Chosen Women, Skilled Men: Cloth Production and Social Identity in the Late Prehispanic Andes." *Archaeological Papers of the American Anthropological Association* 8(1):123–41.

Coughenour, M. B., J. E. Ellis, M. Swift, D. L. Coppock, K. Galvin, J. T. McCabe, and T. C. Hart. 1985. "Energy Extraction and Use in a Nomadic Pastoral Ecosystem." *Science* 230(4726):619–25.

Covenant of the League of Nations, Article 22. The Avalon Project, Lillian Goldman Law Library, Yale Law School. http://avalon.law.yale.edu/20th_century/leagcov. asp#art22.

Cowlishaw, Gillian. 1978. "Infanticide in Aboriginal Australia." *Oceania* 48(4):262–83.

Critical Ecosystem Partnership Fund. 2005. *Tropical Andes Hotspot: Vilcabamba-Amoró Conservation Corridor: Peru and Bolivia Briefing Book.* www.cepf.net/Documents/final. tropicalandes.**vilcabamba**amboro.**briefingbook**.pdf (accessed May 12, 2008).

Crosby, Alfred W. 1986. *Biological Imperialism: The Biological Expansion of Europe, 900–1900.* Cambridge, Eng.: Cambridge University Press.

Crumley, Carole L. 2001. "Communication, Holism, and the Evolution of Sociopolitical Complexity." In *From Leaders to Rulers,* edited by Jonathan Haas, pp. 19–33. New York: Kluwer Academic.

Crutzen, Paul J., and Eugene F. Stoermer. 2000. "The 'Anthropocene.'" *IGBP Newsletter* No. 41: 17–18. The International Geosphere-Biosphere Programme (IGBP): A Study of Global Change of the International Council for Science (ICSU).

Cumberland, Kenneth Brailey. 1956. *Southwest Pacific: A Geography of Australia, New Zealand and Their Pacific Neighborhoods.* London: Methuen.

D'Altroy, Terrence N. 2002. *The Incas*. Oxford: Blackwell.

D'Altroy, Terrence N., and Timothy K. Earle. 1985. "Staple Finance, Wealth Finance, and Storage in the Inka Political Economy." *Current Anthropology* 26(2):187–206.

Dalzell, Jr., Robert F. 1987. *Enterprising Elite: The Boston Associates and the World They Made*. Cambridge, MA, and London: Harvard University Press.

D'Ans, André-Marcel. 1972. Les Tribus Indigènes du Parc National du Manu." *Proceedings of the 39th International Americanists Congress* 4:95–100.

D'Ans, André-Marcel. 1981. "Encounter in Peru." In *Is God an American? An Anthropological Perspective on the Missionary Work of the Summer Institute of Linguistics*. Edited by Søren Hvalkof and Peter Aaby, pp. 145–62. Copenhagen and London: IWGIA and Survival International.

Davies, James B., Susanna Sandstrom, Anthony Shorrocks, and Edward N. Wolff. 2006. *The World Distribution of Household Wealth*. World Institute for Development Economics Research.

Davis, Lance E., and Robert A. Huttenback. 1986. *Mammon and the Pursuit of Empire: the Political Economy of British Imperialism, 1860–1912*. Cambridge: Cambridge University Press.

Davis, Mike. 2001. *Late Victorian Holocausts: El Niño Famines and the Making of the Third World*. London and New York: Verso.

Davis, Shelton H. 1977. *Victims of the Miracle: Development and the Indians of Brazil*. Cambridge, Eng.: Cambridge University Press.

Dawkins, Richard. 1989. *The Selfish Gene*. New York: Oxford University Press.

Day, Kent C. 1982. "Ciudedelas: Their Form and Function." In *Chan Chan: Andean Desert City*, edited by Michael Moseley and Kent C. Dean, pp. 55–66. Albuquerque: University of New Mexico Press.

De'ath, Glenn, Janice M. Lough, Katharina E. Fabricius. 2009. "Declining Coral Calcification on the Great Barrier Reef." *Science* 323(2 January): 116–19.

DeBoer, Warren R. 1974. "Ceramic Longevity and Archaeological Interpretation: An Example from the Upper Ucayali, Peru." *American Antiquity* 39(2):335–43.

DeBoer, Warren R., and Donald W. Lathrap. 1979. "The Making and Breaking of Shipibo-Conibo Ceramics." In Carol Kramer, ed., *Ethnoarchaeology: Implications of Ethnography for Archaeology*, pp. 102–138. New York: Columbia University Press.

DeForest, Robert W., and Lawrence Veiller. 1903. *The Tenement House Problem: Including the Report of the New York State Tenement House Commission of 1900*. 2 vols. New York: Macmillan.

Denevan, William. 1976. *The Native Population of the Americas in 1492*. Madison: University of Wisconsin Press.

Denevan, William M. 2002. *Cultivated Landscapes of Native Amazonia and the Andes*. Oxford, New York: Oxford University Press. 1976. *The Native Population of the Americas in 1492*. Madison: University of Wisconsin Press.

Dennett, Glenn, and John Connell. 1988. "Acculturation and Health in the Highlands of Papua New Guinea." *Current Anthropology* 29(2):273–99.

DFID, U.K. Department for International Development 2009. *A Review of Future Freight and Passenger Shipping Options for St. Helena and Ascension Island*. CNTR 07 8194, WSP Group. www.dfid.gov.uk/Media-Room/Publications/?c=SH.

Diakonoff, I. M. 1987. "Slave-Labour vs. Non-Slave Labour: The Problem of Definition." In *Labor in the Ancient Near East*, edited by Marvin A. Powell, pp. 1–3. American Oriental Series, vol. 68. New Haven, CT: American Oriental Society.

Diamond, Jared. 1997. *Guns, Germs, and Steel: The Fates of Human Societies*. New York and London: W. W. Norton & Co.

Diamond, Jared. 2005. *Collapse: How Societies Choose to Fail or Succeed*. New York: Viking.

Diamond, Stanley. 1968. "The Search for the Primitive." In *The Concept of the Primitive*, edited by Ashley Montagu, pp. 99–147. New York: Free Press.

Dickens, Charles. (1852–1853) 1953. *Bleak House*. Garden City, NY: The Literary Guild of America.

Dickson, F. P. 1981. *Australian Stone Hatchets: A Study in Design and Dynamics*. Sydney: Academic Press.

Dickson, P. G. M. 1967. *The Financial Revolution in England: A Study in the Development of Public Credit 1685–1756*. London: Macmillan.

Dirks, Nicholas B. 1989. "The Original Caste: Power, History and Hierarchy in South Asia." *Contributions to Indian Sociology* 23(1):59–77.

Dirks, Nicholas B. 2001. *Castes of Mind: Colonialism and the Making of Modern India*. Princeton and Oxford: Princeton University Press.

Divale, William, and Marvin Harris. 1976. "Population, Warfare and the Male Supremacist Complex." *American Anthropologist* 78(3):521–38.

Dobyns, Henry F., Paul L. Doughty, and Harold D. Lasswell, eds. 1971. *Peasants, Power, and Applied Social Change: Vicos As a Model*. Beverly Hills, CA, and London: Sage.

Dodson, Mark. 2008. "Foreword." In Hunt, Janet, Diane Smith, Stephanie Garling, and Will Sanders, eds. *Contested Governance: Culture, Power and Institutions in Indigenous Australia*. pp. xvii–xx. Centre for Aboriginal Economic Policy Research. Research Monograph No. 29. Canberra: Australia National University E Press http://epress.anu.edu.au/caepr_series/no_29/pdf/whole_book.pdf.

Dole, Gertrude. 1964. "Shamanism and Political Control Among the Kuikuru." In *Beitrage zur Volkerkunde Sudamerikas Festgabe fur Herbert Baldus zum 65. Geburtstag*, edited by Hans Becher, pp. 53–62. *Volkerkundliche Abhand-lungen*, vol. 1. Des Niedersachsischen Landesmuseum.

Dole, Gertrude. 1978. "The Use of Manioc Among the Kuikuru: Some Implications." In *The Nature and Status of Ethnobotany.* Anthropological Papers, no. 67, edited by R. Ford, pp. 217–47. Ann Arbor: Museum of Anthropology, University of Michigan.

Domhoff, G. William. 1967. *Who Rules America?* Englewood Cliffs, NJ: Prentice-Hall.

Domhoff, G. William. 1983. *Who Rules America Now? A View for the '80s.* Englewood Cliffs, NJ: Prentice-Hall.

Domhoff, G. William. 1990. *The Power Elite and the State.* New York: Aldine de Gruyter.

Doughty, Paul L. 2002. "Ending Serfdom in Peru: The Struggle for Land and Freedom in Vicos." In *Contemporary Cultures and Societies of Latin America,* edited by Dwight B. Heath. Prospect Heights, IL: Waveland Press.

Douglas, Mary. 1966. *Purity and Danger: An Analysis of Concepts of Pollution and Taboo.* New York: Praeger.

Dow, James. 1986. "Universal Aspects of Symbolic Healing: A Theoretical Synthesis." *American Anthropologist* 88(l):56–69.

Drew, Christopher, Elizabeth Becker, and Sandra Blakeslee. 2003. "Despite Mad-Cow Warnings, Industry Resisted Safeguards." *New York Times,* Dec. 28.

Drewnoski, Adam, and Barry M. Popkin. 1997. "The Nutrition Transition: New Trends in the Global Diet." *Nutrition Review* 55(2):31–43.

Driver, H. E. 1956. "An Integration of Functional Evolutionary, and Historical Theory by Means of Correlations." Indiana University Publications in Anthropology and Linguistics. Memoir 12.

Dull, Jack L. 1990. "The Evolution of Government in China." In *Heritage of China: Contemporary Perspectives on Chinese Civilization,* edited by Paul Ropp, pp. 55–85. Berkeley: University of California Press.

Dumont, Louis. 1970. *Homo Hierarchicus: An Essay on the Caste System.* Chicago: University of Chicago Press.

Dunbar, Robin I. 1993. "Neocortex Size as a Constraint on Group Size in Primates." *Journal of Human Evolution* 20:469–93.

Duncan, Richard C. 2001. "World Energy Production, Population Growth, and the Road to the Olduvai Gorge." *Population and Environment* 22(5):503–522.

Durham, William H. 1979. *Scarcity and Survival in Central America: Ecological Origins of the Soccer War.* Stanford, CA: Stanford University Press.

Durham, William H. 1991. *Coevolution: Genes, Culture, and Human Diversity.* Stanford, CA: Stanford University Press.

Durham, William H. 1995. "Political Ecology and Environmental Destruction in Latin America." In *The Social Causes of Environmental Destruction in Latin America,* edited by Michael Painter and William H. Durham, pp. 249–64. Ann Arbor: University of Michigan Press.

Dyson-Hudson, Rada, and Neville Dyson-Hudson. 1969. "Subsistence Herding in Uganda." *Scientific American* 220(2):76–89.

Earle, Peter. 1989. *The Making of the English Middle Class: Business, Society and Family Life in London 1660–1730.* Berkeley and Los Angeles: University of California Press.

Earle, Timothy. 1978. *Economic and Social Organization of a Complex Chiefdom: The Halelea District, Kaua'i, Hawaii.* Anthropological Papers, no. 63. Ann Arbor: Museum of Anthropology, University of Michigan.

Earle, Timothy. 1987. "Specialization and the Production of Wealth: Hawaiian Chiefdoms and the Inka Empire." In *Specialization, Exchange, and Complex Societies,* edited by Elizabeth Brumfiel and Timothy Earle, pp. 64–75. Cambridge, Eng.: Cambridge University Press.

Earle, Timothy K. 2001. "Institutionalization of Chiefdoms: Why Landscapes Are Built." In *From Leaders to Rulers,* edited by Jonathan Haas, pp. 105–124. New York: Kluwer Academic/Plenum.

Earls, John, and Irene Silverblatt. 1978. "La Realidad Fisica y Social en la Cosmologia Andina." *Proceedings of the International Congress of Americanists* 42(4):299–325.

Eastman, Lloyd E. 1988. *Family, Fields, and Ancestors: Constancy and Change in China's Social and Economic History, 1550–1949.* New York: Oxford University Press.

Eastwell, Harry D. 1982. "Voodoo Death and the Mechanisms for Dispatch of the Dying in East Arnhem, Australia." *American Anthropologist* 84(1):5–18.

Ebrey, Patricia. 1990. "Women, Marriage, and the Family in Chinese History." In *Heritage of China: Contemporary Perspectives on Chinese Civilization,* edited by Paul Ropp, pp. 197–223. Berkeley: University of California Press.

Eck, Diana L. 1985. *Darsan: Seeing the Divine Image in India.* Chambersburg, PA: Anima Books.

Edgerton, Robert B. 1992. *Sick Societies: Challenging the Myth of Primitive Harmony.* New York: Free Press.

eHRAF, Electronic Human Relations Area Files, website. www.yale.edu/hraf/collections.htm.

Ehrenberg, Richard. 1928. *Capital and Finance in the Age of the Renaissance: A Study of the Fuggers and Their Connections.* New York: Harcourt, Brace.

Eisenburg, J., and R. Thorington, Jr. 1973. "A Preliminary Analysis of a Neotropical Mammal Fauna." *Biotropica* 5(3):150–61.

Elitzak, Howard. 2000. "Food Marketing Costs: A 1990s Retrospective. *Food Review* 23(3): 27–30.

Elkin, A. P. 1934. "Anthropology and the Future of the Australian Aborigines." *Oceania* 5(1):1–18.

Ellis, Erle C., and Navin Ramankutty. 2008. "Putting People in the Map: Anthropogenic Biomes of the World." *Frontiers in Ecology and the Environment* 6(8):439–47.

Ellis, Erle C., and Navin Ramankutty. 2008. "Anthropogenic Biome Maps." *The Encyclopedia of Earth.* www.eoearth.org/article/Anthropogenic_biome_maps (accessed Feb. 2010).

Enard, Wolfgang, et al. 2002. "Molecular Evolution of FOXP2, A Gene Involved in Speech and Language." Author's *Nature* advance online publication, 14 August 2002 (doi:10.1038/nature01025).

Engels, Friedrich. 1973. *The Condition of the Working Class in England*. Moscow: Progress.

Erdosy, George. 1988. *Urbanization in Early Historic India*. BAR International Series 430. Oxford, Eng.: Oxford University Press.

Escobar, Arturo. "Other Worlds Are (Already) Possible: Self-Organization, Complexity, and Post-Capitalist Cultures." In *The World Social Forum: Challenging Empires*, edited by Jai Sen, Anita Anand, Arturo Escobar, and Peter Waterman. pp. 349–58. New Delhi: Viveka Foundation. www.choike.org/nuevo_eng/informes/1557.html.

Esty, Daniel C., M. A. Levy, C. H. Kim, A. de Sherbinin, T. Srebotnjak, and V. Mara. 2008. *2008 Environmental Performance Index*. New Haven: Yale Center for Environmental Law and Policy. http://sedac.ciesin.columbia.edu/es/epi/downloads.html#summary.

Ethos Water website www.ethoswater.com.

Evans-Pritchard, E. E. 1940. *The Nuer: A Description of the Modes of Livelihood and Political Institutions of a Nilotic People*. New York and Oxford, Eng.: Oxford University Press.

Evans-Pritchard, E. E. 1951. *Kinship and Marriage Among the Nuer*. Oxford, Eng.: Oxford University Press.

Evans-Pritchard, E. E. 1953. "The Nuer Conception of Spirit in Its Relation to the Social Order." *American Anthropologist* 55(2, pt. 1):201–214.

FAO. Fisheries and Aquaculture Department. 2009. *The State of World Fisheries and Aquaculture 2008*. Rome: Food and Agriculture Organization of the United Nations.

Farmer, Paul. 1994. *The Uses of Haiti*. Monroe, ME: Common Courage Press.

Farmer, Paul. 2001. *Infections and Inequalities: The Modern Plagues*. Berkeley: University of California Press.

Farmer, Paul. 2003. *Pathologies of Power: Health, Human Rights, and the New War on the Poor*. Berkeley: University of California Press.

Federalist Papers (Alexander Hamilton, James Madison, John Jay, papers No. 1–85, originally published 1787–1788, numerous editions have been republished).

Feher, Joseph. 1969. *Hawaii: A Pictorial History*. Bernice P. Bishop Museum Special Publication, no. 58. Honolulu: Bishop Museum Press.

Fei, Hsiao-Tung, and Chih-I Chang. 1945. *Earthbound China: A Study of Rural Economy in Yunnan*. Chicago: University of Chicago Press.

Ferguson, Niall. 2003. *Empire: How Britain Made the Modern World*. London: Allen Lane, Penguin.

Feuerwerker, Albert. 1990. "Chinese Economic History in Comparative Perspective." In *Heritage of China: Contemporary Perspectives on Chinese Civilization,* edited by Paul Ropp, pp. 224–41. Berkeley: University of California Press.

Fiji Department of Energy. 2004. *National Energy Policy Document*. First Discussion Draft. www.fiji.gov. fj/index.php?option=com_docman&task=doc_details&gid=78&Itemid=189.

Fiji Electricity Authority. 2008. *FEA: Energizing Our Nation, Annual Report 2008*. www.fea.com.fj/pages.cfm/about-fea/downloads/annual-reports.html.

Fiji, Ministry of Finance. 2007. *Strategic Development Plan 2007–2011*. www.mfnp.gov.fj.

Fiji Islands Bureau of Statistics, Economic Statistics, Overseas Merchandise Trade, Summary of Merchandise Trade Statistics. www.statsfiji.gov.fj/Economic/trade.htm (accessed January 7, 2010).

Fiji Islands Bureau of Statistics. 2008. *Fiji Facts and Figures, As at 1st July 2008*. www.statsfiji.gov.fj/Economic/ecostats_index.htm.

Fiji Islands Bureau of Statistics. 2009. *Key Statistics: Overseas Merchandise Trade*. Table 8.8. Exports by SITC. www.statsfiji.gov.fj/Economic/trade.htm.

Fijilive. 2009. "Crest Chicken Eyes Local Feed Supply." Oct. 22, 2009. www.fijilive.com/news/2009/10/22/21058. Fijilive.

FIJI Water. 2009. *FIJI Water Responds to Mother Jones Article*. www.fijiwater.com/blog/2009/08/fiji-water-responds-to-mother-jones-article/.

Firth, Raymond. 1957. *We the Tikopia: A Sociological Study of Kinship in Primitive Polynesia,* 2nd ed. New York: Barnes & Noble.

Firth, Raymond. 1967. "The Work of the Gods." In *Tikopia,* 2nd ed. London: Athlone Press.

Firth, Raymond. 1975. *Primitive Polynesian Economy*. New York: Norton.

Fischer, David Hackett. 1996. *The Great Wave: Price Revolutions and the Rhythm of History*. New York: Oxford University Press.

Fischer-Kowalski, Marina, and Helmut Haberl. 2002. "Sustainable Development: Socio-Economic Metabolism and Colonization of Nature." *International Social Science Journal* 50(158): 573–87.

Fittkau, E., and H. Klinge. 1973. "On Biomass and Trophic Structure of the Central Amazonian Rain Forest Ecosystem." *Biotropica* 5(1):2–14.

Fleck, David W., and John D. Harder. 2000. "Matses Indian Rainforest Habitat Classification and Mammalian Diversity in Amazonian Peru." *Journal of Ethnobiology* 20(1):1–36.

Flegal, Katherine M., Margaret D. Carroll, Cynthia L. Ogden, and Lester R. Curtin. 2010. "Prevalence and Trends in Obesity Among U.S. Adults, 1999–2008. *JAMA (Journal of the American Medical Association)* 303(3):235–41.

Fletcher, Roland. 1995. *The Limits of Settlement Growth: A Theoretical Outline*. Cambridge: Cambridge University Press.

Flood, Josephine. 1980. *The Moth Eaters*. Atlantic Highlands, NJ: Humanities Press.

Flood, Josephine. 1983. *Archaeology of the Dreamtime*. Honolulu: University of Hawaii Press.

Flowers, Nancy M. 1983. "Seasonal Factors in Subsistence, Nutrition, and Child Growth in a Central Brazilian Indian Community." In *Adaptive Responses of Native Amazonians*, edited by Raymond Hames and William Vickers, pp. 357–90. New York: Academic Press.

Flynn, John T. 1941. *Men of Wealth: The Story of Twelve Significant Fortunes from the Renaissance to the Present Day.* New York: Simon & Schuster.

Fortune Magazine. 2009. *Global 500.* July 20, 2008. http://money.cnn.com/magazines/fortune/global500/2009/full_list/.

Foucault, Michel. 1977. *Discipline and Punish: The Birth of the Prison.* New York: Pantheon Books.

Foundation Directory. 1998, vol. 20. New York: Columbia University Press.

Fouts, Roger S. 1994. "Transmission of a Human Gestural Language in a Chimpanzee Mother-Infant Relationship." In *The Ethological Roots of Culture*, edited by R. A. Gardner et al., pp. 257–70. Dordrecht, Boston, and London: Kluwer Academic.

Fox, Justin. 2009. *The Myth of the Rational Market: A History of Risk, Reward, and Delusion on Wall Street.* New York: HarperCollins.

Frangipane, Marcella. 2000. "The Development of Administration from Collective to Centralized Economies in the Mesopotamian World: The Transformation of an Institution from 'System-Serving' to 'Self-Serving.'" In G. Feinman and L. Manzanilla, eds. *Cultural Evolution: Contemporary Viewpoints*, pp. 215–32. Fundamental Issues in Archaeology. New York: Kluwer Academic/Plenum.

Frangipane, Marcella. 2007. "Different Types of Egalitarian Societies and the Development of Inequality in Early Mesopotamia." *World Archaeology* 39(2):151–76.

Franke, Richard W., and Barbara H. Chasin. 1989. *Kerala: Radical Reform as Development in an Indian State.* Food First Development Report No. 6. San Francisco: The Institute for Food and Development Policy.

Fratkin, Elliot. 1989. "Household Variation and Gender Inequality in Ariaal Pastoral Production: Results of a Stratified Time-Allocation Survey." *American Anthropologist* 91(2): 430–40.

Fratkin, Elliot. 1998. *Ariaal Pastoralists of Kenya: Surviving Drought and Development in Africa's Arid Lands.* Boston and London: Allyn & Bacon.

Fratkin, Elliot, and Eric Abella Roth. 1990 "Drought and Economic Differentiation Among Ariaal Pastoralists of Kenya." *Human Ecology* 18(4):385–402.

Frazer, Sir James. 1990 [1890] 1900. *The Golden Bough.* 3 vols. London: Macmillan.

Frazer, Sir James. 1910. *Totemism and Exogamy.* 4 vols. London: Macmillan.

Freed, Stanley A., and Ruth S. Freed. 1981. "Sacred Cows and Water Buffalo in India: The Uses of Ethnography." *Current Anthropology* 22(5):483–90.

Freedman, Maurice. 1966. *Chinese Lineage and Society: Fukien and Kwangtung.* London School of Economics, Monographs on Social Anthropology, no. 33. London: Athlone Press.

Freedman, Maurice. 1979. *The Study of Chinese Society.* Stanford, CA: Stanford University Press.

Fried, Morton H. 1983. "Tribe to State or State to Tribe in Ancient China." In *The Origins of Chinese Civilization*, edited by D. N. Keightley, pp. 467–93. Berkeley: University of California Press.

Friedman, Milton. 1962. *Capitalism and Freedom,* with the assistance of Rose D. Friedman. Chicago: University of Chicago Press.

FUNAI, (Fundação Nacional do Índio), CTI, (Centro de Trabalho Indigenista), www.funai.gov.br/.

Fund for Peace. 2010. *Failed State Index 2009.* www.fundforpeace.org/web/index.php?option=com_content&task=view&id=99&Itemid=140 (accessed March 2010).

Galaty, John G. 1982. "Being 'Maasai'; Being 'People-of-Cattle': Ethnic Shifters in East Africa." *American Ethnologist* 9(1):1–20.

Galbraith, John Kenneth. 1952. *American Capitalism: The Concept of Countervailing Power.* Boston, Houghton.

Galbraith, John Kenneth. 1958. *The Affluent Society.* Boston: Houghton Mifflin.

Galbraith, John Kenneth. 1967. *The New Industrial State.* Boston: Houghton Mifflin.

Gale, Fay, ed. 1983. *We Are Bosses Ourselves: The Status and Role of Aboriginal Women Today.* Canberra: Australian Institute of Aboriginal Studies.

Gallimore, R. and Howard, A. 1968. "The Hawaiian Life Style: Some Qualitative Considerations." In Gallimore, R., and Howard, A., eds. *Studies in a Hawaiian Community. Namakamaka O Nanakuli*, pp. 10–16. Pacific Anthropological Records No. 1. Honolulu: Department of Anthropology, B. P. Bishop Museum.

Gamboa Balbín, César. 2006. "Legal Status of Territorial Reserves for the Protection of Isolated Indigenous Peoples in Peru." The Field Museum. *Rapid Biological Inventory No. 17. Peru: Sierra del Divisor.* Pp. 210–216. http://fm2.fieldmuseum.org/rbi/results_per17.asp (accessed January 2010).

Gardner, R. Allen, and Beatrix T. Gardner. 1994a. "Development of Phrases in the Utterances of Children and Cross-Fostered Chimpanzees." In *The Ethological Roots of Culture*, edited by R. A. Gardner et al., pp. 223–55. Dordrecht, Boston, and London: Kluwer Academic Press.

Gardner, R. Allen, and Beatrix T. Gardner. 1994b. "Ethological Roots of Language." In *The Ethological Roots of Culture*, edited by R. A. Gardner et al., pp. 199–222. Dordrecht, Boston, and London: Kluwer Academic Press.

Garvin, Lewis, Natalie Henry, Melissa Vernon. 2000. *Community Materials Flow Analysis: A Case Study of Ann Arbor, Michigan.* University of Michigan Center for Sustainable Systems. Report CSS00-02.

Gates, Bill, with Nathan Myhrvold and Peter Rinearson. 1996. *The Road Ahead*, 2nd ed. New York and London: Penguin Books.

Gelb, I. J. 1965. "The Ancient Mesopotamian Ration System." *Journal of Near Eastern Studies* 24(3):230–43.

Gemini Consulting 1998. *World Wealth Report 1998*. New York: Gemini Consulting.

Gennep, Arnold L. van . 1909. *Les Rites de Passage*. Paris: E. Nourry.

Gilder, George. 1981. *Wealth and Poverty*. New York: Basic Books.

Gifford, E. W., and A. L. Kroeber. 1937. "Culture Element Distributions: IV. Pomo." *University of California Publications in American Archaeology and Ethnology* 37(4):117–254.

Gimpel, James G., Jason E. Schuknecht. 2003. *Patchwork Nation: Sectionalism and Political Change in American Politics*. Ann Arbor: University of Michigan Press.

Given-Wilson, C. 1991. "Wealth and Credit, Public and Private: The Earls of Arundel 1306–1397." *The English Historical Review* 418:1–26.

Gladwin, Thomas. 1970. *East Is a Big Bird*. Cambridge, MA: Harvard University Press.

Glattfelder, J. B., and S. Battiston. 2009. "The Backbone of Complex Networks of Corporations: Who Is Controlling Whom?" *Physical Review E* 80(1):1–33.

Global Island Partnership. 2008. GLISPA Brochure. www.cbd.int/island/glispa.shtml.

Gluckman, Max. 1956. *Custom and Conflict in Africa*. New York: Barnes & Noble.

Goetschel, Laurent. 1998. *Small States Inside and Outside the European Union: Interests and Policies*. Boston: Kluwer Academic Publishers. A political science perspective.

Goldman, Irving. 1970. *Ancient Polynesian Society*. Chicago and London: University of Chicago Press.

Goldschmidt, Walter. 1969. *Kambuya's Cattle*. Berkeley: University of California Press.

Goldsmith, Raymond. 1987. *Premodern Financial Systems: A Historical Comparative Study*. Cambridge: Cambridge University Press.

Good, Anthony. 2000. "Congealing Divinity: Time, Worship and Kinship in South Indian Hinduism." *Journal of the Royal Anthropological Institute* 6:273–92.

Goodall, J. 1986. *The Chimpanzees of Gomhe*. Cambridge, MA: Belknap Press.

Goodland, Robert. 1982. *Tribal Peoples and Economic Development: Human Ecological Considerations*. Washington, DC: International Bank for Reconstruction and Development/World Bank.

Goody, Jack. 1976. *Production and Reproduction: A Comparative Study of the Domestic Domain*. Cambridge, Eng.: Cambridge University Press.

Gordon, Raymond G. 2005. *Ethnologue: Languages of the World*. 15th ed. Dallas, TX: SIL International. Web version: www.ethnologue.com/home.asp.

Gorham, John, Pete Kafka, and Shailaja Neelakantan. 1998. "The Forbes 400: The Richest People in America." *Forbes* 162(8):165–428.

Gorriti, Gustavo. 1990. "Terror in the Andes: The Flight of the Ashaninkas." *New York Times Magazine*, Dec. 2, Section 6: 40–48, 65–72.

Gould, Richard A. 1969. "Subsistence Behavior Among the Western Desert Aborigines of Australia." *Oceania* 39(4): 253–73.

Gould, Richard A. 1969. *Yiwara: Foragers of the Australian Desert*. New York: Charles Scribner's Sons.

Gould, Richard A. 1970. *Spears and Spear-Throwers of the Western Desert Aborigines of Australia*. American Museum Novitates, no. 2403. New York: American Museum of Natural History.

Gould, Richard A. 1980. *Living Archaeology*. Cambridge, Eng.: Cambridge University Press.

Gould, Richard A. 1981. "Comparative Ecology of Food-Sharing in Australia and Northwest California." In *Omnivorous Primates: Gathering and Hunting in Human Evolution*, edited by Robert Harding and Geza Teleki, pp. 422–454. New York: Columbia University Press.

Goulding, Michael. 1980. *The Fishes and the Forest: Explorations in Amazonian Natural History*. Berkeley: University of California Press.

Government of Saint Helena. 2007. *St. Helena Sustainable Development Plan 2007/08–2009/10*. www.sainthelena.gov.sh/data/files/downloads/st_helena_sdp.pdf.

Gray, Andrew. n.d. *Freedom and Territory: Slavery in the Peruvian Amazon*. Unpublished Manuscript.

Gray, Andrew. 1990. "The ILO Meeting at the UN, Geneva, June 1989: Report on International Labour Organisation Revision of Convention 107." IWGIA Yearbook 1989, 173–91. Copenhagen: IWGIA.

Gray, J. Patrick. 1999. "A Corrected Ethnographic Atlas." *World Cultures* 10(1):24–85. http://worldcultures.org/.

Gray, J. Patrick. 1999. "Ethnographic Atlas Codebook. *World Cultures* 10(1):86–136. 1999. "A Corrected Ethnographic Atlas." *World Cultures* 10(1):24–28.

Great Britain, United Kingdom, Treasury. 2007. *The Economics of Climate Change* (Nicholas Stern, ed.). Cambridge, U.K., and New York: Cambridge University Press. Also available: H.M. Treasury website: www.hm-treasury.gov.uk/stern_review_report.htm.

Greenberg, Joseph H., and Merritt Ruhlen. 1992. "Linguistic Origins of Native Americans." *Scientific American* (November):94–99.

Gregorio, David I., Stephen J. Walsh, and Deborah Paturzo. 1997. "The Effects of Occupation-Based Social Position on Mortality in a Large American Cohort." *American Journal of Public Health* 87(9):1472–75.

Gronowicz, Anthony. 1998. *Race and Class Politics in New York City before the Civil War*. Boston: Northeastern University Press.

Gross, Daniel R. 1975. "Protein Capture and Cultural Development in the Amazon Basin." *American Anthropologist* 77(3):526–49.

Gross, Daniel R., and Barbara A. Underwood. 1971. "Technological Change and Caloric Costs: Sisal Agriculture." *American Anthropologist* 73(2):725–40.

Gudschinsky, Sarah C. 1956. "The ABC's of Lexicostatistics (Glottochronology)." *Word* 12:175–210.

Guglielmino, C. Viganotti, B. Hewlett, and L. L. Cavalli-Sforza. 1995. "Cultural Variation in Africa: Role of Mechanisms of Transmission and Adaptation." *Proceedings of the National Academy of Sciences* 92:7585–89.

Gulliver, P. H. 1955. *The Family Herds: A Study of Two Pastoral Tribes in East Africa, the Jie and Turkana.* London: Routledge & Kegan Paul.

Gunderson, Lance H., and C. S. Hilling, eds. 2002. *Panarchy: Understanding Transformations in Human and Natural Systems.* Washington, DC: Island Press.

Gunter, Chris, Ritu Dhand, Tanguy Chouard, Henry Gee, Jane Rees, and John Spiro. 2005. "The Chimpanzee Genome." *Nature* 4371 (September): p. 47.

Haberl, Helmut, K. Hennz Erb, Fridolin Krausmann, Veronika Gaube, Alberte Bondeau, Christoph Plutzar, Simone Gingrich, Wolfgang Lucht, and Marina Fischer-Kowalski. 2007. "Quantifying and Mapping the Human Appropriation of Net Primary Production in Earth's Terrestrial Ecosystems." *Proceedings of the National Academy of Sciences, PNAS* 104(31):12942–47.

Hagesteijn, Renee. 1989. *Circles of Kings: Political Dynamics in Early Continental Southeast Asia.* Verhandelingen van het Koninklijk Institut Voor Taal-, Land- en Volkenkunde No. 138. Dordrecht, Holland: Foris Publications.

Hails, Chris, Sarah Humphrey, Jonathan Loh, Steven Goldfinger. 2008. *Living Planet Report 2008.* Gland, Switzerland: World Wide Fund for Nature.

Halcrow Group Limited. 2003. *Dominica Country Poverty Assessment. Final Report.* Caribbean Development Bank, Government of the Commonwealth of Dominica.

Hall, Peter Dobkin. 1982. *The Organization of American Culture, 1700–1900: Private Institutions, Elites, and the Origins of American Nationality,* New York: New York University Press.

Hallpike, C. R. 1979. *The Foundations of Primitive Thought.* Oxford, Eng.: Clarendon Press.

Halpern, Benjamin S., et al. 2008. "A Global Map of Human Impact on Marine Ecosystems." *Science* 319 (15 February): 948–52.

Halpern, Benjamin S., Kimberly A. Selkoe, Fiorenza Micheli, and Carrie V. Kappel. 2007. "Evaluating and Ranking the Vulnerability of Global Marine Ecosystems to Anthropogenic Threats." *Conservation Biology* 21(5):1301–1315.

Hamilton, Alexander. *Federalist Papers* No. 12.

Hamilton, Alexander. *Federalist Papers* No. 35.

Hamilton, Annette. 1979. "A Comment on Arthur Hippler's Paper 'Culture and Personality Perspective of the Yolngu of Northeastern Arnhem Land: Part 1.'" *Mankind* 12(2):164–69.

Hammack, David C. 1982. *Power and Society: Greater New York at the Turn of the Century.* New York: Russell Sage Foundation.

Hammel, E. A. 2009. *George William Skinner 1925–2008.* Biographical Memoir. Washington, DC: National Academy of Sciences.

Hancock, David. 1995. *Citizens of the World: London Merchants and the Integration of the British Atlantic Community, 1735–1785.* Cambridge: Cambridge University Press.

Handy, E. S. C., and E. G. Handy. 1972. *The Native Planters in Old Hawaii: Their Life, Lore, and Environments.* Bernice P. Bishop Museum Bulletin. 233. Honolulu: Bishop Museum Press.

Hanks, Lucien M. 1972. *Rice and Men: Agricultural Ecology in Southeast Asia.* Chicago: Aldine.

Hanks, Lucien M. 1975. "The Thai Social Order as Entourage and Circle." In *Change and Persistence in Thai Society,* edited by G. William Skinner and A. Thomas Kirsch, pp. 197–218. Ithaca and London: Cornell University Press.

Hansen, James, et al. 2008. "Target Atmospheric CO2: Where Should Humanity Aim?" *The Open Atmospheric Science Journal* 2:217–31. www.bentham.org/open/articles.htm.

Hardin, Garrett. 1968. "The Tragedy of the Commons." *Science* 162(3859):1243–48.

Hardt, Michael, and Antonio Negri. 2000. *Empire.* Cambridge: Harvard University Press.

Hardt, Michael, and Antonio Negri. 2004. *Multitude: War and Democracy in the Age of Empire.* New York: Penguin Books.

Hardt, Michael, and Antonio Negri. 2009. *Commonwealth.* Cambridge, MA: Belknap Press, Harvard University Press.

Harner, M. J. 1980. *The Way of the Shaman.* New York: Harper & Row.

Harris, Marvin. 1965. "The Myth of the Sacred Cow." In *Man, Culture, and Animals,* edited by A. P. Vayda and A. Leeds, pp. 217–28. Washington, DC: American Association for the Advancement of Science.

Harris, Marvin. 1966. "The Cultural Ecology of India's Sacred Cattle." *Current Anthropology* 7(l):51–59.

Harris, Marvin. 1971a. "A Comment on Heston: An Approach to the Sacred Cow of India." *Current Anthropology* 12(2):199–201.

Harris, Marvin. 1971b. *Culture, Man, and Nature: An Introduction to General Anthropology.* New York: Crowell.

Harris, Marvin. 1974. *Cows, Pigs, Wars, and Witches: The Riddles of Culture.* New York: Random House.

Harris, Marvin. 1980. *Cultural Materialism: The Struggle for a Science of Culture.* New York: Random House/Vintage Books.

Harris, Marvin. 1981. *America Now: The Anthropology of a Changing Culture.* New York: Simon & Schuster.

Harris, Marvin. 1984. "A Cultural Materialist Theory of Band and Village Warfare: The Yanomamo Test." In *Warfare, Culture, and Environment,* edited by R. Brian Ferguson, pp. 111–140. New York: Academic Press.

Harris, Marvin. 1985. *Good to Eat: Riddles of Food and Culture.* New York: Simon & Schuster.

Harris, Marvin. 1988. *Culture, People, Nature: An Introduction to General Anthropology,* 5th ed. New York: Harper & Row.

Hartmann, Betsy, and James K. Boyce. 1983. *A Quiet Violence: View from a Bangladesh Village.* San Francisco: Institute for Food and Development Policy.

Hasluck, Paul M. 1953. "The Future of the Australian Aborigine." Twenty-Ninth Meeting of the Australian and New Zealand Association for the Advancement of Science, Sydney. *Australian and New Zealand Association for the Advancement of Science* 29:155–65.

Hassan, Fekri. 1981. *Demographic Archaeology.* New York: Academic Press.

Hassan, Fekri. 2007. "The Lie of History: Nation-States and the Contradictions of Complex Societies." In Costanza, Graumlich, and Steffen, eds. 2007. *Sustainability or Collapse? An Integrated History and Future of People on Earth,* pp. 169–96. Cambridge, MA and London: The MIT Press.

Hayden, Brian. 1977. "Stone Tool Functions in the Western Desert." In *Stone Tools as Cultural Markers: Change, Evolution and Complexity,* edited by R. V. S. Wright, pp. 178–88. Prehistory and Material Culture Series, no. 12. Canberra: Australian Institute of Aboriginal Studies.

Hayden, Brian. 1995. "Pathways to Power: Principles for Creating Socioeconomic Inequalities." In *Foundations of Social Inequality,* edited by T. Douglas Price and Gary M. Feinman, pp. 15–86. New York and London: Plenum Press.

Hayek, Frederich. 1944. *The Road to Serfdom.* Chicago: University of Chicago Press.

Headland, Thomas N., Kenneth L. Pike, and Marvin Harris. 1990. *Emics and Etics: The Insider/Outsider Debate.* Newbury Park, CA: Sage.

Heilbroner, Robert, and Lester C. Thurow. 1987. *Economics Explained.* Englewood Cliffs, NJ: Prentice-Hall.

Heller, Martin C., and Gregory A. Keoleian. 2000. *Life Cycle-Based Sustainability Indicators for Assessment of the U.S. Food System. Report No CSS00-04 Center for Sustainable Systems.* University of Michigan. Ann Arbor, MI.

Hemming, John. 1978. *Red Gold: The Conquest of the Brazilian Indians.* Cambridge, MA: Harvard University Press.

Heckenberger, Michael, et al. 2003. "Amazonia 1492: Pristine Forest or Cultural Parkland?" *Science* 301:1710–14.

Henry, Jules. 1963. *Culture against Man.* New York: Random House.

Herman, Edward S., and Noam Chomsky. 2002. *Manufacturing Consent: The Political Economy of the Mass Media.* New York: Pantheon.

Herskovits, Melville J. 1926. "The Cattle Complex in East Africa." *American Anthropologist* 28(l):230–72, 28(2):361–88, 28(3):494–528, 28(4):633–64.

Hewlett, Barry S., Annalisa De Silvestri, and C. Rosalba Guglielmino. 2002. "Semes and Genes in Africa." *Current Anthropology* 43(2):313–21.

Heyerdahl, Thor. 1952. *American Indians in the Pacific: The Theory Behind the Kon-Tiki Expedition.* London: Allen & Unwin.

Hiatt, L. R. 1984a. *Aboriginal Landowners: Contemporary Issues in the Determination of Traditional Aboriginal Land Ownership.* Oceania Monograph, no. 27. Sydney: University of Sydney.

Hiatt, L. R. 1984b. "Your Mother-in-Law Is Poison." *Man* 19(2):183–98.

Hiatt, L. R. 1987. "Aboriginal Political Life." In *Traditional Aboriginal Society,* edited by W. H. Edwards, pp. 174–88. South Melbourne: Macmillan.

Hiatt, L. R. 2002. *Edward Westermarck and the Origin of Moral Ideas.* Presented at the Ninth International Conference on Hunting and Gathering Societies, Heriot-Watt University, Edinburgh, Scotland.

Higley, John, G. Lowell Field, and Knut Grøholt. 1976. *Elite Structure and Ideology: A Theory with Applications to Norway.* New York: Columbia University Press.

Hill, Kim, and A. Magdalena Hurtado. 1996. *Ache Life History: The Ecology and Demography of a Foraging People.* New York: Aldine.

Hobbs, James R. 2009. "Foreign-Controlled Domestic Corporations, 2006." *Statistics of Income Bulletin* Summer 2009, pp. 102–45.

Hobbes, Thomas. 1907 [1651]. *Leviathan; or, The Matter, Form and Power of a Commonwealth, Ecclesiastical and Civil.* London: Routledge and Sons; New York: Dutton and Co.

Hodgson, Dorothy L., ed. 2000. "Introduction." In Hodgson, Dorothy L., ed. *Rethinking Pastoralism in Africa: Gender, Culture and the Myth of the Patriarchal Pastoralist,* pp. 1–28. Oxford: James Currey; Athens, OH: Ohio University Press.

Hoebel, E. Adamson. 1968. *The Law of Primitive Man.* New York: Atheneum.

Hole, Frank. 1994. "Environmental Instabilities and Urban Origins." In *Chiefdoms and Early States in the Near East,* G. Stein and M. S. Rothman, eds. pp. 121–52. Madison: Prehistory Press.

Holmberg, Allan R. 1971. "The Role of Power in Changing Values and Institutions of Vicos." In Dobyns, Henry F., Paul L. Doughty, and Harold D. Lasswell, eds. *Peasants, Power, and Applied Social Change: Vicos as a Model,* pp. 33–63. Beverly Hills, CA, and London: Sage.

Holmes, Rebecca. 1995. "Small Is Adaptive: Nutritional Anthropometry of Native Amazonians." In *Indigenous Peoples and the Future of Amazonia,* edited by Leslie E. Sponsel, pp. 121–48. Tucson and London: The University of Arizona Press.

Holtzman, Jon. 2002. "Politics and Gastropolitics: Gender and the Power of Food in Two African Pastoralist Societies." *JRAI* 8(2):259–78.

Homewood, K. M., and W. A. Rodgers. 1984. "Pastoralism and Conservation." *Human Ecology* 12(4):431–41.

Hommon, Robert J. 1986. "Social Evolution in Ancient Hawai'i." In *Island Societies: Archaeological Approaches to Evolution and Transformation,* edited by Patrick V. Kirch, pp. 55–68. Cambridge: Cambridge University Press.

Honychurch, Lennox. 1975. *The Dominica Story: A History of the Island.* Oxford: Macmillan.

Hopkins, Diane E. 1985. "The Peruvian Agrarian Reform: Dissent from Below." *Human Organization* 44(1):18–32.

Hornborg, Alf. 1988. "Dualism and Hierarchy in Lowland South America: Trajectories of Indigenous Social Organization." *Acta Universitatis Upsaliensis, Uppsala Studies in Cultural Anthropology* 9. Uppsala University, Uppsala, Sweden.

Hornborg, Alf. 2001. *The Power of the Machine: Global Inequalities of Economy, Technology, and Environment.* Walnut Creek, CA: Alta Mira Press.

Hornborg, Alf. 2002. *Beyond Universalism and Relativism.* Presented at the Ninth International Conference on Hunting and Gathering Societies, Heriot-Watt University, Edinburgh, Scotland.

Hornborg, Alf. 2005. "Ethnogenesis, Regional Integration, and Ecology in Prehistoric Amazonia." *Current Anthropology* 46(4):589–620.

House of Commons, see United Kingdom, House of Commons

Howard, Alan. 1967. "Polynesian Origins and Migrations: A Review of Two Centuries of Speculation and Theory." In *Polynesian Culture History: Essays in Honor of Kenneth P. Emory,* edited by Genevieve Highland, Roland Force, Alan Howard, Marion Kelly, and Yosihiko Sinoto, pp. 45–101. Bernice P. Bishop Museum Special Publication, no. 56. Honolulu: Bishop Museum Press.

Howard, Alan. 1968. "Adoption and Significance of Children to Hawaiian Families." In Gallimore, R., and Howard, A., eds. *Studies in a Hawaiian Community. Namakamaka O Nanakuli,* pp. 87–101. Pacific Anthropological Records No. 1. Honolulu: Department of Anthropology, B.P. Bishop Museum.

Hsu, Francis L. K. 1963. *Clan, Caste, and Club.* Princeton, NJ: Van Nostrand.

Hsu, Francis L. K., ed. 1972. "American Core Value and National Character." In *Psychological Anthropology,* pp. 240–62. Cambridge, MA: Schenkman.

Hsu, Francis L. K. 1981. *Americans and Chinese: Passage to Difference.* Honolulu: University Press of Hawaii.

Hubbert, M. King. 1969. "Energy Resources." In *Resources and Man,* edited by National Academy of Sciences, pp. 157–242. San Francisco: Freeman.

Hudson Institute. 2010. "Mission Statement." www.hudson.org/learn/index.cfm?fuseaction=mission_statement (accessed March 2010).

Huey, John. 1993. "The World's Best Brand." *Fortune,* May 31, pp. 44–54.

Hull, Charles Henry. 1899. *The Economic Writings of Sir William Petty Together with the Observations Upon the Bills of Mortality,* vol. 1. Cambridge: Cambridge University Press.

Hummel, Ralph P. 1987. *The Bureaucratic Experience.* New York: St. Martin's Press.

Hunt, Janet, Diane Smith, Stephanie Garling, and Will Sanders, eds. *Contested Governance: Culture, Power and Institutions in Indigenous Australia.* Centre for Aboriginal Economic Policy Research. Research Monograph. No. 29. Canberra: Australia National University E Press, p. xviii. http://epress.anu.edu.au/caepr_series/no_29/pdf/whole_book.pdf.

Hunt, R. C. 1991. "The Role of Bureaucracy in the Provisioning of Cities: A Framework for Analysis of the Ancient Near East." In *The Organization of Power: Aspects of Bureaucracy in the Ancient Near East,* edited by McGuire Gibson and Robert D. Biggs, pp. 59–100. Studies in Ancient Oriental Civilization, No. 46. The Oriental Institute of the University of Chicago.

Hutton, J. H. 1963. *Caste in India: Its Nature, Function, and Origins,* 4th ed. London: Oxford University Press.

Hvalkof, Søren Hvalkof. 1990. "Inscription and Titling of Native Communities in the Ucayali Department." In *Supervision Report on Land Titling Project, Peruvian Amazon.* Report to IWGIA, Copenhagen.

Hyslop, John. 1984. *The Inka Road System.* New York: Academic Press.

Ii, John Papa. 1983. *Fragments of Hawaiian History.* Bernice P. Bishop Museum Special Publication, no. 70. Honolulu: Bishop Museum Press.

ILR (International Labour Review). 1954. "Reports and Enquiries: The Second Session of the ILO Committee of Experts on Indigenous Labour." *International Labour Review* 70(5):418–41.

Ilyatjari, Nganyintja. 1983. "Women and Land Rights: The Pitjantjatjara Land Claims." In *We Are Bosses Ourselves: The Status and Role of Aboriginal Women Today,* edited by Fay Gale, pp. 55–61. Canberra: Australian Institute of Aboriginal Studies.

Information Please Almanac Atlas and Yearbook. 1967. 1966. New York: Simon & Schuster.

Inglehart, Ronald, and Christian Welzel. 2005. *Modernization, Culture Change, and Democracy: the Human Development Sequence.* New York: Cambridge University Press.

Initiative for the Integration of Regional Infrastructure in South America (IIRSA). http://iirsa.org/index_ENG.asp?CodIdioma=ENG (accessed May 7, 2009).

Instituto de Bien Común. www.ibcperu.org/ (accessed January 2010).

Instituto de Bien Común. 2009. www.ibcperu.org/presentacion/indigenas-aislamiento.php.

Inter-American Foundation. 2009. Peru: Award by Year. www.iaf.gov/grants/awards_year_en.asp?country_id=17&gr_year=2009.

International HapMap Consortium. 2003. "The International HapMap Project." *Nature* 426:789–96.

International Labour Organization. 1957. *C107 Indigenous and Tribal Populations Convention, 1957.* www.ilo.org/ilolex/cgi-lex/convde.pl?C107, accessed January 2010.

International Monetary Fund (IMF), website. www.imf.org/external/np/sec/memdir/members.htm.

International Monetary Fund (IMF). 2009. *World Economic Outlook Database October 2009.* www.imf.org/external/ns/cs.aspx?id=28 (accessed Feb. 2010).

IPCC. 2001a. *Climate Change 2001: Impacts, Adaptation, and Vulnerability.* Contribution of Working Group II to the Third Assessment Report of the Intergovernmental Panel on Climate Change, edited by James J. McCarthy, James J. Osvaldo, F. Canziani, Neil A. Leary, David J. Dokken, Kasey S. White. Cambridge, U.K., and New York: Cambridge University Press.

IPCC. 2001b. *Climate Change 2001: Synthesis Report.* Contribution of Working Groups I, II, and III to the Third Assessment Report of the Intergovernmental Panel on Climate Change, edited by R. T. Watson, and the Core Writing Team. Cambridge, U.K., and New York: Cambridge University Press.

IPCC. 2007. *Summary for Policymakers.* In *Climate Change 2007: Impacts, Adaptation and Vulnerability.* Contribution of Working Group II to the Fourth Assessment Report of the Intergovernmental Panel on Climate Change. Parry, M. L., O. F. Canziani, J. P. Palutikof, P. J. van der Linden, and C. E. Hansen, eds. Cambridge, U.K.: Cambridge University Press.

IPCC (Intergovernmental Panel on Climate Change). 2007. *Climate Change 2007: The Physical Science Basis, Summary for Policymakers.* Contribution of Working Group I to the Fourth Assessment Report of the Intergovernmental Pattern on Climate Change. www.ipcc.ch/publications_and_data/publications_and_data_reports.htm#1 (accessed Feb. 2010).

Irvine, S. H., and J. W. Berry, eds. 1988. *Human Abilities in Cultural Context.* Cambridge, Eng.: Cambridge University Press.

Isbell, William H. 1978. "Environmental Perturbations and the Origin of the Andean State." In *Social Anthropology: Beyond Subsistence and Dating,* edited by Charles Redman, Mary Jane Berman, Edward Curtin, William Langhorne Jr., Nina Versaggi, and Jeffery Wanser, pp. 303–13. New York: Academic Press.

IUCN, International Union for the Conservation of Nature. 2004. *Indigenous Peoples Living in Voluntary Isolation and Conservation of Nature in the Amazon Region and Chaco.* RES 3.056. www.iucn.org/congress/2004/members/Individual_Res_Rec_Eng/wcc3_res_056.pdf.

IWGIA (International Work Group for Indigenous Affairs). 1989. *IWGIA Yearbook 1988: Indigenous Peoples and Human Rights.* Copenhagen: IWGIA.

IWGIA (International Workgroup for Indigenous Affairs). 2001. The Indigenous World 2000/2001. Copenhagen: IWGIA.

IWGIA (International Work Group for Indigenous Affairs). 2007. Annual Report 2006. Copenhagen: IWGIA. www.iwgia.org/sw17779.asp.

Jackson, Peter. 2009. *The Future of Global Oil Supply: Understanding the Building Blocks.* Cambridge Energy Research Associates (CERA). www.cera.com/aspx/cda/client/report/report.aspx?KID=5&CID=10720.

Jacobsen, Thorkild. 1976. *The Treasures of Darkness: A History of Mesopotamian Religion.* New Haven, CT, and London: Yale University Press.

Jacobsen, Thorkild, and Robert McCAdams. 1958. "Salt and Silt in Ancient Mesopotamian Agriculture." *Science* 128 (3334):1251–58.

Jacobson, Doranne. 1982. "Purdah and the Hindu Family in Central India." In *Separate Worlds: Studies of Purdah in South Asia,* edited by Hanna Papanek and Gail Minault, pp. 81–109. Delhi: Chanakya Publications.

Jaher, Frederic Cople. 1972. "Nineteenth-Century Elites in Boston and New York." *Journal of Social History* 6(1):32–77.

Jaher, Frederic Cople. 1982. *The Urban Establishment: Upper Strata in Boston, New York, Charleston, Chicago, and Los Angeles.* Urbana: University of Illinois Press.

Jameson, Fredric. 1991. *Postmodernism, or, the Cultural Logic of Late Capitalism.* Durham: Duke University Press.

Jansen, Eirik G. 1986. *Rural Bangladesh: Competition for Scarce Resources.* Oslo: Universitetsforlaget, Norwegian University Press.

Johannes, Robert E. *Words of the Lagoon; Fishing and Marine Lore in the Palau District of Micronesia.* Berkeley: University of California Press.

Johns, C. H. W. 1926. *The Oldest Code of Laws in the World: The Code of Laws Promulgated by Hammurabi, King of Babylon b.c. 2285–2242.* Edinburgh: T. & T. Clark.

Johnson, Allen. 1975. "Time Allocation in a Machiguenga Community." *Ethnology* 14(3):301–310.

Johnson, Allen. 1983. "Machiguenga Gardens." In *Adaptive Responses of Native Amazonians,* edited by Raymond Hames and William Vickers, pp. 29–63. New York: Academic Press.

Johnson, Allen. 1985. "In Search of the Affluent Society." In *Anthropology: Contemporary Perspectives,* edited by David Hunter and Phillip Whitten, pp. 201–206. Boston: Little, Brown. (reprinted from *Human Nature,* September 1978).

Johnson, Allen. 2003. *Families of the Forest: The Matsigenka Indians of the Peruvian Amazon.* Berkeley: University of California Press.

Johnson, Allen, and Clifford A. Behrens. 1982. "Nutritional Criteria in Machiguenga Food Production Decisions: A Linear-Programming Analysis." *Human Ecology* 10(2):167–89.

Johnson, Bryan T., Kim R. Holmes, and Melandie Kirkpatrick, eds. 1998. *Index of Economic Freedom.* Washington, DC, and New York: The Heritage Foundation and Dow Jones.

Johnson, Simon. 2009. "The Quiet Coup." *The Atlantic* (May). www.theatlantic.com/magazine/archive/2009/05/the-quiet-coup/7364/.

Johnson, Gregory Alan. 1973. *Local Exchange and Early State Development in Southwestern Iran.* Anthropological Papers, no. 51. Ann Arbor: Museum of Anthropology, University of Michigan.

Jones, Alice Hanson. 1977. *American Colonial Wealth: Documents and Methods.* 3 vols. New York: Arno Press.

Jones, Alice Hanson. 1980. *Wealth of a Nation to Be: The American Colonies on the Eve of the Revolution.* New York: Columbia University Press.

Jones, Doug. 2003. "Kinship and Deep History: Exploring Connections between Culture Areas, Genes, and Languages." *American Anthropologist* 105(3):501–514.

Jones, P. D., T. M. L. Wigley, and P. B. Wright. 1986. "Global Temperature Variations Between 1861 and 1984." *Nature* 322(6078):430–34.

Jones, Rhys, and Betty Meehan. 1978. "Anbarra Concept of Colour." In *Australian Aboriginal Concepts*, edited by L. R. Hiatt, pp. 20–39. Canberra: Australian Institute of Aboriginal Studies.

Julien, Catherine J. 1982. "Inka Decimal Administration in the Lake Titicaca Region." In *The Inca and Aztec States 1400 1800*, edited by George Collier, Renato Rosaldo, and John Wirth, pp. 119–51. New York: Academic Press.

Kahn, Herman. 1982. *The Coming Boom: Economic, Political, and Social.* New York: Simon and Schuster.

Kahn, Herman, and Anthony J. Wiener. 1967. The Year 2000: *A Framework for Speculation on the Next Thirty-Three Years.* New York: Macmillan.

Kant, Immanuel. 1917 [1795]. *Perpetual Peace: A Philosophical Essay.* Edited and translated by M. Campbell Smith. London: Allen & Unwin.

Kaplan, David. 1960. "The Law of Cultural Dominance." In *Evolution and Culture*, edited by Marshall Sahlins and Elman Service, pp. 69–92. Ann Arbor: University of Michigan Press.

Kapur, Ajay, Niallo Macleod, Narendra Singh. 2005. *Plutonomy: Buying Luxury, Explaining Global Imbalances.* Citigroup Global Markets. www.scribd.com/doc/6674234/Citigroup-Oct-16-2005-Plutonomy-Report-Part-1.

Kaplan, Martha. 2005. "The *Hau* of Other Peopes' Gifts: Land Owning and Taking in Turn-of-the-Millennium Fiji." *Ethnohistory* 52(1):29–46.

Kaplan, Martha. 2007. "Fijian Water in Fiji and New York: Local Politics and a Global Commodity." *Cultural Anthropology* 22(4):685–706.

Kasser, Tim, and Richard M. Ryan. 1993. "A Dark Side of the American Dream: Correlates of Financial Success as a Central Life Aspiration." *Journal of Personality and Social Psychology* 65(2):410–22.

Kasser, Tim. 2002. *The High Price of Materialism.* Cambridge, MA: MIT Press.

Kasser, Tim, Steve Cohn, Allen D. Kanner, and Richard M. Ryan. 2007. "Some Costs of American Corporate Capitalism: A Psychological Exploration of Value and Goal Conflicts." *Psychological Inquiry* 18(1):1–22.

Kauai, County of. 2004. *Kaua'i Economic Development Plan: Kaua'i's Comprehensive Economic Development Strategy (CEDS) Report 2005–2015.* Office of Economic Development, Kauai'i Economic Development Board.

Kay, Paul, and Willett Kempton. 1984. "What Is the Sapir-Whorf Hypothesis?" *American Anthropologist* 86(l):65–79.

Kaya, Y. 1990. "Impact of Carbon Dioxide Emission Control on GNP Growth: Interpretation of Proposed Scenarios." Paper presented to the IPCC Energy and Industry Subgroup, Response Strategies Working Group, Paris. (cited in Metz, et al. *Climate Change 2007*, pp. 180–83).

Keeley, Lawrence H. 1996. *War Before Civilization.* New York and Oxford: Oxford University Press.

Keen, Ian. 2000. "A Bundle of Sticks: The Debate Over Yolngu Clans." *Journal of the Royal Anthropological Institute* 6(3):419–36.

Keightly, David N. 1990. "Early Civilization in China: Reflections on How It Became Chinese." In *Heritage of China: Contemporary Perspectives on Chinese Civilization*, edited by Paul Ropp, pp. 15–54. Berkeley: University of California Press.

Kemp, Barry J. 1989. *Ancient Egypt. Anatomy of a Civilization.* London and New York: Routledge.

Kenchington, Richard. 1985. "Coral Reef Ecosystems: A Sustainable Resource." *Nature and Resources* 21(2):18–27.

Keswani, Priscilla Schuster. 1996. "Hierarchies, Heterarchies, and Urbanization Processes: The View from Bronze Age Cyprus." *Journal of Mediterranean Archaeology* 9:211–50.

Keyfitz, Nathan. 1989. "The Growing Human Population." *Scientific American* 261(3):119–26.

Keynes, John Maynard. 1936. *The General Theory of Employment, Interest and Money.* London: Macmillan.

Khare, R. S. 1976a. *Culture and Reality: Essays on the Hindu System of Managing Foods.* Simla: Indian Institute of Advanced Study.

Khare, R. S. 1976b. *The Hindu Hearth and Home.* New Delhi: Vikas Publishing.

Killeen, Timothy J. 2007. *A Perfect Storm in the Amazon Wilderness: Development and Conservation in the Context of the Initiative for the Integration of the Regional*

Infrastructure of South America (IIRSA), 8, 12. AABS, Advances in Applied Biodiversity Science, No. 7. Arlington, Virginia: Conservation International. www.conservation. org/publications/Pages/perfect_storm.aspx (accessed April 27, 2009).

King, Franklin Hiram. 1911. *Farmers of Forty Centuries or Permanent Agriculture in China, Korea and Japan.* Madison, WI: Mrs. F. H. King.

King, Gregory. 1936. *Two Tracts,* edited by Jacob H. Hollander (original edition 1696). Baltimore: The Johns Hopkins Press.

Kirch, Patrick Vinton. 1984. *The Evolution of the Polynesian Chiefdoms.* Cambridge: Cambridge University Press.

Kirch, Patrick Vinton. 1985 *Feathered Gods and Fishhooks: An Introduction to Hawaiian Archaeology and Prehistory.* Honolulu: University of Hawaii Press.

Kirch, Patrick Vinton. 2000. *On the Road of the Winds: An Archaeological History of the Pacific Islands Before European Contact.* Berkeley: University of California Press.

Kirch, Patrick Vinton. 2001. "Polynesian Feasting in Ethnohistoric, Ethnographic, and Archaeological Contexts: A Comparison of Three Societies." In *Feasts: Archaeological and Ethnographic Perspectives on Food, Politics, and Power,* edited by Michael Dietler and Brian Hayden, pp. 168–84. Washington and London: Smithsonian Institution Press.

Kirch, Patrick Vinton, and Marshall Sahlins. 1992. *Anahulu: The Anthropology of History in the Kingdom of Hawaii,* vol. 1. Chicago: University of Chicago Press.

Kirch, Patrick Vinton, and Douglas E. Yen. 1982. *Tikopia: The Prehistory and Ecology of a Polynesian Outlier.* Bernice P. Bishop Museum, Bull. 238. Honolulu: Bishop Museum Press.

Kirsch, A. Thomas. 1973. *Feasting and Social Oscillation: Religion and Society in Upland Southeast Asia.* Data Paper: Number 92, Southeast Asia Program, Department of Asian Studies, Cornell University, Ithaca, NY.

Kirkbride, Mary, and Richard Grahn. 2008. *Survival of the Fittest: Pastoralism and Climate Change in East Africa.* Oxfam Briefing Paper 116, Oxfam International.

Klengel, Horst. 1987. "Non-Slave Labor in the Old Babylonian Period: The Basic Outlines." In *Labor in the Ancient Near East,* edited by Marvin A. Powell, pp. 159–66. American Oriental Series, vol. 68. New Haven, CT: American Oriental Society.

Klich, L. Z. 1988. "Aboriginal Cognition and Psychological Nescience." In *Human Abilities in Cultural Context,* edited by S. H. Irvine and J. W. Berry, pp. 427–52. Cambridge, Eng.: Cambridge University Press.

Knudson, Kenneth E. 1970. "Resource Fluctuation, Productivity, and Social Organization on Micronesian Coral Islands." Ph.D. dissertation, University of Oregon.

Kohr, Leopold. 1978. *The Breakdown of Nations.* New York: Dutton.

Komlos, John. 1998. "Shrinking in a Growing Economy? The Mystery of Physical Stature during the Industrial Revolution." *The Journal of Economic History* 58(3):779–802.

Kosse, Krisztina. 1990. "Group Size and Societal Complexity: Thresholds in the Long-Term Memory." *Journal of Anthropological Archaeology* 9(3):275–303.

Kramer, Samuel Noah. 1963. *The Sumerians: Their History, Culture, and Character.* Chicago: University of Chicago Press.

Kramer, Samuel Noah. 1967. *Cradle of Civilization.* New York: Time-Life Books.

Krantz, Grover S. 1978. *Interproximal Attrition and Modern Dental Crowding.* Occasional Papers in Method and Theory in California Archaeology, no. 2, pp. 35–41. Society for California Archaeology.

Krantz, Grover S. 1980. Climatic Races and Descent Groups. North Quincy, MA: Christopher.

Krech, Shepard, III. 1999. *The Ecological Indian: Myth and History.* New York: W. W. Norton and Co.

Kroeber, Alfred L.1948. *Anthropology.* New York: Harcourt, Brace & World.

Kroll, Luisa and Lea Goldman. 2003. "Billionaires: Survival of the Richest." *Forbes,* March 17, 2003.

Kunstler, James Howard. 2005. *The Long Emergency: Surviving the End of Oil, Climate Change, and Other Converging Catastrophes of the Twenty-First Century.* New York: Grove Press.

Kuper, Adam. 1982. "Lineage Theory: A Critical Retrospect." *Annual Review of Anthropology* 11:71–95.

Kuznets, S. 1960. "Economic Growth of Small Nations." In Robinson, E.A.G., ed. *Economic Consequences of the Size of Nations.* Pp. 14–32. Proceedings of a Conference held by the International Economic Association. New York: St. Martin's Press.

Larsen, Knud, and Amund Sinding-Larsen. 2001. *The Lhasa Atlas: Traditional Tibetan Architecture and Townscape.* Boston: Shambhala.

Lal, Padma, Margaret Tabunakawai, and Sandeep K. Singh. 2007. "Economics of Rural Waste Management in the Rewa Province and Development of a Rural Solid Waste Management Policy for Fiji." IWP-Pacific technical report (International Water Project) No. 57. Apia, Samoa: SPREP. www.sprep.org/publication/pub_detail.asp?id=574.

La Lone, Darrell E. 1982. "The Inca as a Nonmarket Economy: Supply on Command Versus Supply and Demand." In *Contexts for Prehistoric Exchange,* edited by Jonathon Ericson and Timothy K. Earle, pp. 291–316. New York: Academic Press.

Landsberg, Helmut E. 1989. "Where Do We Stand with the CO_2 Greenhouse Effect Problem?" In *Global Climate Change: Human and Natural Influences,* edited by S. Fred Singer, pp. 87–89. New York: Paragon House.

Lanning, Edward P. 1967. *Peru Before the Incas.* Englewood Cliffs, NJ: Prentice-Hall.

Lappe, Frances Moore, Joseph Collins, and Carry Fowler. 1979. *Food First: Beyond the Myth of Scarcity.* New York: Ballantine Books.

Larick, Roy. 1986. "Age Grading and Ethnicity in the Style of Loikop (Samburu) Spears." *World Archaeology* 18(2):269–83.

Larrick, James W., James A. Yost, Jon Kaplan, Garland King, and John Mayhall. 1979. "Patterns of Health and Disease Among the Waorani Indians of Eastern Ecuador." *Medical Anthropology* 3(2):147–89.

Lasch, Christopher. 1995. *The Revolt of the Elites and the Betrayal of Democracy.* New York: Norton.

Lathrap, Donald W. 1970. *The Upper Amazon.* New York: Praeger.

Leach, Edmund. 1964. *Political Systems of Highland Burma: A Study of Kachin Social Structure.* London School of Economics Monographs on Social Anthropology No. 44. London: The Athlone Press, University of London.

Leach, Jerry W. 1983. "Introduction." In Leach, Jerry W., and Edmund Leach, eds. *The Kula: New Perspectives on Massim Exchange*, pp. 1–26. Cambridge: Cambridge University Press.

Lee, Richard B. 1981. "Is There a Foraging Mode of Production?" *Canadian Journal of Anthropology* 2(1):13–19.

Lefroy, Archdeacon. 1912. *The Future of Australian Aborigines.* Report of the Thirteenth Meeting of the Australasian Association for the Advancement of Science, Sydney, pp. 453–54.

Legge, James. 1967. *Li Chi: Book of Rites.* 2 vols. New Hyde Park, NY: University Books.

Lenzer, Anna. 2009. "Fiji Water: Spin the Bottle." *Mother Jones.* September/October.

Leonowens, Anna Harriette. 1870. *The English Governess at the Siamese Court: Being Recollections of Six Years in the Royal Palace at Bangkok.* Boston: Fields, Osgood.

Leonowens, Anna Harriette. 1953. *Siamese Harem Life.* New York: Dutton.

Levine, Terry Y. 1992. "Inka State Storage in Three Highland Regions. A Comparative Study." In *Inka Storage Systems*, edited by Terry Y. Levine, pp. 107–48. Norman and London: University of Oklahoma Press.

Levison, M., R. G. Ward, and J. W. Webb. 1973. *The Settlement of Polynesia: A Computer Simulation.* Minneapolis: University of Minnesota Press.

Levi-Strauss, Claude. 1944. "The Social and Psychological Aspects of Chieftainship in a Primitive Tribe: The Nambikuara of Northwestern Matto Grosso." *Transactions of the New York Academy of Sciences* 7:16–32.

Levi-Strauss, Claude. [1949] 1969. *The Elementary Structures of Kinship.* Boston: Beacon Press.

Levi-Strauss, Claude. 1963. *Totemism.* Boston: Beacon Press.

Levi-Strauss, Claude. 1966. *The Savage Mind.* Chicago: University of Chicago Press.

Levi-Strauss, Claude. 1969. *The Raw and the Cooked: Introduction to a Science of Mythology 1.* New York: Harper & Row.

Levi-Strauss, Claude. 1973. *From Honey to Ashes: Introduction to a Science of Mythology 2.* New York: Harper & Row.

Levi-Strauss, Claude. 1978. *The Origin of Table Manners: Introduction to a Science of Mythology 3.* New York: Harper & Row.

Levy, Reuben. 1962. *The Social Structure of Islam.* London: Cambridge University Press.

Levy-Bruhl, Lucien [1922] 1923. *Primitive Mentality.* New York: Macmillan.

Levy-Bruhl, Lucien. 1926. *How Natives Think [Les Fonctions Mentales dans les Societes Inferieures].* New York: Knopf.

Lewis, Bernard. 1960. *The Arabs in History.* New York: Harper Torchbooks.

Lewis, D. 1976. "Observations on Route-Finding and Spatial Orientation Among the Aboriginal Peoples of the Western Desert Region of Central Australia." *Oceania* 46(4):249–82.

Lewis, M. Paul, ed. 2009. *Ethnologue: Languages of the World.* 16th ed. Dallas, TX: SIL International.

Li, Jun Z. 2008. "Worldwide Human Relationships Inferred from Genome-Wide Patterns of Variation." *Science* 319:1100–104.

Lindenbaum, Shirley. 1987. "Loaves and Fishes in Bangladesh." In *Food and Evolution: Toward a Theory of Human Food Habits,* edited by Marvin Harris and Eric Ross, pp. 427–43. Philadelphia: Temple University Press.

Lindert, Peter H., and Jeffrey G. Williamson. 1982. "Revising England's Social Tables 1688–1812." *Explorations in Economic History* 19:385–408.

Lindert, Peter H., and Jeffrey G. Williamson. 1983. "Reinterpreting Britain's Social Tables, 1688–1913." *Explorations in Economic History* 20:94–109.

Linnekin, Jocelyn. 1985. *Children of the Land: Exchange and Status in a Hawaiian Community.* New Brunswick, NJ: Rutgers University Press.

Linnekin, Jocelyn. 1990. *Sacred Queens and Women of Consequence; Rank, Gender, and Colonialism in the Hawaiian Islands.* Ann Arbor: University of Michigan Press.

Little, Michael A., and George E. B. Morren, Jr. 1976. *Ecology, Energetics, and Human Variability.* Dubuque, IA: Brown.

Lizot, Jacques. 1977. "Population, Resources and Warfare Among the Yanomami." *Man* 12(3/4):497–517.

Lobel, Phil S. 1978. "Gilbertese and Ellice Islander Names for Fishes and Other Organisms." *Micronesica* 14(2):177–97.

Loh, Jonathan, and Mathis Wackernagel. 2004. *Living Planet Report.* Gland, Switzerland: WWF-World Wide Fund for Nature.

Louandos, Harry. 1985. "Intensification and Australian Prehistory." In *Prehistoric Hunter-Gatherers: The Emergence of Cultural Complexity,* edited by Douglas Price and James A. Brown, pp. 385–423. New York: Academic Press.

Louandos, Harry. 1987. "Pleistocene Australia: Peopling a Continent." In *The Pleistocene Old World: Regional Perspectives,* edited by Olga Soffer, pp. 147–65. New York: Plenum.

Lozoff, Bettsy, and Gary M. Brittenham. 1977. "Field Methods for the Assessment of Health and Disease in Pre-Agricultural Societies." In *Health and Disease in Tribal Societies,* pp. 49–67. CIBA Foundation Symposium, no. 49. Amsterdam: Elsevier/Excerpta Medica/North-Holland.

Lundberg, Ferdinand. 1939. *America's 60 Families.* New York: Halcyon House.

Lundberg, Ferdinand. 1968. *The Rich and the Super-Rich: A Study of Money Power Today.* New York: L. Stuart.

Luten, Daniel B. 1974. "United States Requirements." In *Energy, the Environment, and Human Health,* edited by A. Finkel, pp. 17–33. Acton, MA: Publishing Sciences Group.

Maddison, Angus. 2001. *The World Economy: A Millennial Perspective.* Paris: Development Centre of the Organization for Economic Co-Operation and Development.

Maddison, Angus. 2003. *The World Economy: Historical Statistics.* OECD: Development Centre Studies, Paris.

Maddison, Angus. 2007. Contours *of the World Economy, 1–2030 AD: Essays in Macro-Economic History.* Oxford, U.K.: Oxford University Press.

Mager, Nathan H. 1987. *The Kondratieff Waves.* New York: Praeger.

Maggio, G. G. Cacciola. 2009. "A Variant of the Hubbert Curve for World Oil Production Forecasts." *Energy Policy* 37:4761–70.

Maisels, Charles Keith. 1990. *The Emergence of Civilization: from Hunting and Gathering to Agriculture, Cities, and the State in the Near East.* London and New York: Routledge.

Malinowski, Bronislaw. 1922. *Argonauts of the Western Pacific: An Account of Native Enterprise and Adventure in the Archipelagoes.* London: G. Routledge.

Malinowski, Bronislaw. 1926. *Crime and Custom in Savage Society.* New York: The Humanities Press.

Malinowski, Bronislaw. 1929. "Practical Anthropology." *Africa* 2(1):22–38.

Malinowski, Bronislaw. 1941. *The Sexual Life of Savages in North-Western Melanesia: An Ethnographic Account of Courtship, Marriage and Family Life among the Natives of Trobriand Islands, British New Guinea.* New York: Halcyon House.

Malinowski, B. 1944. *A Scientific Theory of Culture.* Chapel Hill: University of North Carolina Press.

Malinowski, Bronislaw. 1948. *Magic, Science, and Religion.* Boston: Beacon Press.

Malinowski, Bronislaw. 1965. *Coral Gardens and Their Magic.* 2 vols. Bloomington, IN: Indiana University Press.

Malo, David. 1951. *Hawaiian Antiquities,* 2nd ed. Bernice P. Bishop Museum Special Publication, no. 2. Honolulu: Bernice P. Bishop Museum.

Malthus, Thomas R. [1798, 1807] 1895. *An Essay on the Principle of Population.* New York: Macmillan.

Mandel, Ernest. 1999. *Late Capitalism.* London: Verso

Mander, Jerry. 1978. *Four Arguments for the Elimination of Television.* New York: Quill.

Mander, Jerry. 1996. "The Rules of Corporate Behavior." In *The Case Against the Global Economy and for a Turn Toward the Local,* edited by Jerry Mander and Edward Goldsmith, pp. 309–22. San Francisco: Sierra Club Books.

Manica, Andrea, Franck Prugnolle, and François Balloux. 2005. "Geography Is a Better Determinant of Human Genetic Differentiation Than Ethnicity." *Human Genetics* 118:366–77.

Mann, Michael. 1986. *The Sources of Social Power,* vol. 1, *A History of Power from the Beginning to* AD 1760. Cambridge, Eng.: Cambridge University Press.

Mann, Michael. 2003. *Incoherent Empire.* London: Verso.

Marchand, Roland. 1998. *Creating the Corporate Soul: The Rise of Public Relations and Corporate Imagery in American Big Business.* Berkeley: University of California Press.

Marcuse, Herbert. 1964. *One-Dimensional Man: Studies in the Ideology of Advanced Industrial Society.* Boston: Beacon Press.

Marks, Nic, and Saamah Abdallah, Andrew Simms, and Sam Thompson. 2006. *The Happy Planet Index: An Index of Human Well-Being and Environmental Impact.* London: New Economics Foundation. www.neweconomics.org/gen/z_sys_PublicationDetail.aspx?PID=225.

Marriot, McKim. 1968. "Caste Ranking and Food Transactions: A Matrix Analysis." In Milton Singer, and Bernard S. Cohn, eds. *Structure and Change in Indian Society.* pp. 133–71. New York: Viking Fund Publications in Anthropology.

Marx, Karl, and Friedrich Engels. 1967. *The Communist Manifesto.* London: Penguin Books.

Masai [sic] Women—the Masai of Kenya. 1974. Researcher and anthropologist, Melissa Llewellyn-Davies; producer and director, Chris. Disappearing World Series. Curling. Granada Television International. Chicago: Films Incorporated.

Maslow, Abraham H. 1954. *Motivation and Personality.* New York: Harper.

Matthews, H. Damon. 2008. "Stabilizing Climate Requires Near-Zero Emissions." *Geophysical Research Letters* 35, L04705, doi:10.1029/2007GL032388, 208.

Mayer, Adrian C. 1970. *Caste and Kinship in Central India: A Village and Its Region.* Berkeley and Los Angeles: University of California Press.

Mayhew, Henry, 1861–62. *London Labour and the London Poor.* 4 vols. London: Griffin, Bohn. (Reprinted 1968. New York: Dover.)

McArthur, Margaret. 1960. "Food Consumption and Dietary Levels of Groups of Aborigines Living on Naturally Occurring Foods." In *Records of the American-Australian Scientific Expedition to Arnhem Land.* Vol. 2 of *Anthropology and Nutrition,* edited by Charles Mountford, pp. 90–135. Melbourne: Melbourne University Press.

McCabe, J. Terrence. 1990. "Turkana Pastoralism: A Case against the Tragedy of the Commons." *Human Ecology* 18:81–103.

McCabe, J. Terrence. 2003. "Sustainability and Livelihood Diversification Among the Maasai of Northern Tanzania." *Human Organization* 62(2):100–111.

McCarthy, F. D., and Margaret McArthur. 1960. "The Food Quest and Time Factor in Aboriginal Economic Life." *Records of the American-Australian Scientific Expedition to Arnhem Land.* Vol. 2 of *Anthropology and Nutrition,* edited by Charles Mountford, pp. 145–94. Melbourne: Melbourne University Press.

McCay, Bonnie J., and James M. Acheson, eds. 1987. *The Question of the Commons: The Culture and Ecology of Communal Resources.* Tucson: University of Arizona Press.

McChesney, Robert W. 2000. *Rich Media, Poor Democracy: Communication Politics in Dubious Times.* New York: The New Press.

McCloskey, Donald N. 1976. "English Open Fields as Behavior Towards Risk." *Research in Economic History* 1:124–70.

McCorriston, Joy. 1997. "The Fiber Revolution: Textile Extensification, Alienation, and Social Stratification in Ancient Mesopotamia." *Current Anthropology* 38(4):517–49.

McCoy, John. 1970. "Chinese Kin Terms of Reference and Address." In *Family and Kinship in Chinese Society,* edited by Maurice Freedman, pp. 209–226. Stanford, CA: Stanford University Press.

McCurdy, Charles W. 1978. "American Law and the Marketing Structure of the Large Corporation, 1875–1890." *The Journal of Economic History* 38(3):631–49.

McDonald, Forrest. 1958. *We the People: The Economic Origins of the Constitution.* Chicago: University of Chicago Press.

McDonald, Forrest. 1979. *E. Pluribus Unum: The Formation of the American Republic,* 2nd ed. Indianapolis, IN: Liberty Press.

McDonald, Forrest. 1985. *Novus Ordo Seclorum. The Intellectual Origins of the Constitution.* Lawrence: University Press of Kansas.

McEvedy, Colin, and Richard Jones. 1978. *Atlas of World Population History.* Middlesex, Eng., and New York: Penguin Books.

McGrew, W. C. 1992. *Chimpanzee Material Culture.* Cambridge, Eng.: Cambridge University Press.

McNeil, William H. 1982. *The Pursuit of Power: Technology, Armed Force, and Society Since A.D. 100.* Chicago: The University of Chicago Press.

McNeil, William H. 1987. *A History of the Human Community: Prehistory to the Present.* Englewood Cliffs, NJ: Prentice-Hall.

Meadows, Dennis L. 2007. "Evaluating Past Forecasts: Reflections on One Critique of the Limits to Growth." In Costanza, Graumlich, and Steffen, eds. 2007. *Sustainability or Collapse? An Integrated History and Future of People on Earth,* pp. 399–415. Cambridge, MA, and London: The MIT Press.

Meadows, Donella H., Dennis L. Meadows, and Jorgen Randers. 1992. *Beyond the Limits: Confronting Global Collapse, Envisioning a Sustainable Future.* Post Mills, VT: Chelsea Green.

Meadows, Donella H., Dennis L. Meadows, Jorgen Randers, and William W. Behrens III. 1972. *The Limits to Growth.* New York: Universe.

Medrano, Jaime Diez. 2005. *WVS 2005 Codebook.* www.worldvaluessurvey.org/.

Meehan, Betty. 1982. "Ten Fish for One Man: Some Anbarra Attitudes Towards Food and Health." In *Body, Land and Spirit: Health and Healing in Aboriginal Society,* edited by Janice Reid, pp. 96–120. St. Lucia: University of Queensland Press.

Meggers, Betty J. 1954. "Environmental Limitation on the Development of Culture." *American Anthropologist* 56:801–24.

Meggers, Betty J. 1971. *Amazonia: Man and Culture in a Counterfeit Paradise.* Arlington Heights, IL: AHM.

Meggers, Betty J. 2007. "Sustainable Intensive Exploitation of Amazonia: Cultural, Environmental, and Geopolitical Perspectives." In Alf Hornborg and Carole L. Crumley, eds. *The World System and the Earth System: Global Socioenvironmental Change and Sustainability Since the Neolithic,* pp. 195–209. Walnut Creek, CA: Left Coast Press.

Meinshausen, Malte, Nicolai Meinshausen, William Hare, Sarah C. B. Raper, Katja Frieler, Reto Knutti, David J. Frame, and Myles R. Allen. 2009. "Greenhouse-Gas Emission Targets for Limiting Global Warming to 2°C." *Nature* 458(30 April):1158–62. nature08017.

Mellaart, J. 1967. *Çatal Hüyük: A Neolithic Town in Anatolia.* London: Thames & Hudson.

Menasha Corporation. *Annual Report 2008: Staying the Course.* www.menasha.com/aboutUs/AnnualReports.html (accessed Feb. 2010). www.menasha.com/aboutUsFoundationannualreports.html. (accessed Feb. 2010).

Menasha Corporation Foundation. 2008 *Annual Report: Strengthening Communities.* www.menasha.com/aboutUs/aboutUsFoundationannualreports.html. (accessed Feb. 2010).

Metz, B., O. R. Davidson, P. R. Bosch, R. Dave, L. A. Meyer, eds. 2007. *Climate Change 2007: Mitigation of Climate Change.* Contribution of Working Group III to the Fourth Assessment Report of the Intergovernmental Panel on Climate Change, 2007. Cambridge, U.K., and New York: Cambridge University Press. www.ipcc.ch/publications_and_data/publications_ipcc_fourth_assessment_report_wg3_report_mitigation_of_climate_change.htm.

Michael, Franz. 1964. "State and Society in Nineteenth-Century China." In *Modern China,* edited by Albert Feuerwerker, pp. 57–69. Englewood Cliffs, NJ: Prentice-Hall.

Milanovic, Branko. 2002. "True World Income Distribution, 1988 and 1993: First Calculations Based on Household Surveys Alone." *The Economic Journal* 112(476):51–92.

Millennium Ecosystem Assessment. 2005. *Ecosystems and Human Well-Being: Biodiversity Synthesis.* Washington, DC: World Resources Institute.

Millennium Ecosystem Assessment. 2005. *Ecosystems and Human Well-Being: Synthesis.* Washington, DC: Island Press; Millennium Ecosystem Assessment. 2005. *Living Beyond Our Means: Natural Assets and Human Well-Being. Statement from the Board.* Technical Volume. Washington, DC: Island Press. www.maweb.org/en/Products. BoardStatement.aspx.

Miller, Edward, and John Hatcher. 1995. *Medieval England: Towns, Commerce and Crafts 1086–1348.* London and New York: Longman.

Miller, Matthew. 2007. "The *Forbes* 400." *Forbes.* www. forbes.com/2007/09/19/richest-americans-forbes-lists-richlist07-cx_mm_0920rich_land.html.

Miller, Solomon. 1967. "Hacienda to Plantation in Northern Peru: The Processes of Proletarianization of a Tenant Farmer Society." In *Contemporary Change in Traditional Societies.* Vol. 3, *Mexican and Peruvian Communities,* edited by Julian Steward, pp. 133–225. Urbana: University of Illinois Press.

Mills, C. Wright. 1956. *The Power Elite.* New York: Oxford University Press.

Mintz, Sidney W. 1985. *Sweetness and Power: The Place of Sugar in Modern History.* New York: Viking Press/Penguin Books.

Mintz, Sidney W., and Eric R. Wolf. 1957. "Haciendas and Plantations in Middle America and the Antilles." *Social and Economic Studies* 6:380–412.

Mittermeier, Russell, Cristina Goettsch Mittermeier, Patricio Robles Gil, Gustavo Fonseca, Thomas Brooks, John Pilgrim, and William R. Konstant. 2003. *Wilderness: Earth's Last Wild Places.* Chicago: University of Chicago Place.

Mittermeier, Russell, Norman Myers, Cristina Goettsch Mittermeier. 2000. *Hotspots: Earth's Biologically Richest and Most Endangered Terrestrial Ecoregions.* Arlington, VA: Conservation International.

Mittermeier, Russell, Patricio Robles Gil, Michael Hoffman, John Pilgrim, Thomas Brooks, Cristina Goettsch Mittermeier, John Lamoreux, Gustavo A. B. da Fonseca, Peter A. Seligmann, Harrison Ford. 2005. *Hotspots Revisited: Earth's Biologically Richest and Most Endangered Terrestrial Ecoregions.* Arlington, VA: Conservation International.

Mohr, S. H., G. M. Evans. 2010. "Long Term Prediction of Unconventional Oil Production." *Energy Policy* 38:265–76.

Mondragon Corporation. 2008 *Annual Report.* www.mondragon-corporation.com/language/en-US/ENG/General-Information/Downloads.aspx.

Montagu, Ashley. 1972. "Sociogenic Brain Damage." *American Anthropologist* 74(5):1045–61.

Monteferri, Bruno, Elisa Canziani, Juan Luis Dammert, and José Carlos Silva. 2009. Conservación, Industrias Extractivas y Reservas Indígenas: El Proceso de Categorización de la Zona Reservada Sierra del Divisor. Cuaderno de Investigacin No. 2. Lima: Sociedad de Derecho Ambiental. www.spda.org.pe/portal/ver-publicacion.php?id=134.

Moody, John. 1904. *The Truth About the Trusts: A Description and Analysis of the American Trust Movement.* New York: Moody Publishing.

Moore, A. M. T., G. C. Hillman, and A. J. Legge. 2000. *Village on the Euphrates: From Foraging to Farming at Abu Hureyra.* New York: Oxford University Press.

Moore, Jerry D. 2004. "The Social Basis of Sacred Spaces in the Prehispanic Andes: Ritual Landscapes of the Dead in Chimú and Inka Societies." *Journal of Archaeological Method and Theory* 11(1):33–124.

Moore, Melinda A. 1989. "The Kerala House as a Hindu Cosmos." *Contributions to Indian Sociology* 23(1):169–202.

Moore, Sally Falk. 1958. *Power and Property in Inca Peru.* Morningside Heights, NY: Columbia University Press.

Morgan, Dan. 1979. *Merchants of Grain.* New York: Viking Press.

Morgan, Lewis Henry. 1877. *Ancient Society.* New York: Holt.

Morris, Craig and Donald E. Thompson. 1985. *Huanaco Pampa: An Inca City and Its Hinterland.* London: Thames & Hudson.

Morris, Ian. 1996. *Kakadu National Park Australia.* Steve Parish Natural History Guide. Fortitude Valley, Queensland: Steve Parish Publishing.

Morrison, Roy. 1991. *We Build the Road as We Travel.* Philadelphia: New Society Publishers.

Moseley, Michael Edward. 1975. *The Maritime Foundations of Andean Civilization.* Menlo Park, CA: Cummings.

Mountford, Charles P. 1965. *Ayers Rock: Its People, Their Beliefs, and Their Art.* Honolulu: East-West Center Press.

Munn, Nancy D. 1969. "The Effectiveness of Symbols in Murngin Rite and Ritual." In *Forms of Symbolic Action: Proceedings of the 1969 Annual Spring Meeting of the American Ethnological Society,* edited by Robert Spencer, pp. 178–207. Seattle and London: American Ethnological Society.

Munn, Nancy D. 1973. *Walbiri Iconography: Graphic Representation and Cultural Symbolism in a Central Australian Society.* Ithaca, NY, and London: Cornell University Press.

Murai, Mary, Florence Pen, and Carey D. Miller. 1958. *Some Tropical South Pacific Island Foods: Description, History, Use, Composition, and Nutritive Value.* Hawaii Agricultural Experiment Station, bull. 110. Honolulu: University of Hawaii Press.

Murdock, George P. 1949. *Social Structure.* New York: Macmillan.

Murdock, George P. 1967. *Ethnographic Atlas.* Pittsburgh: University of Pittsburgh Press.

Murdock, George P. 1973. "Measurement of Cultural Complexity." *American Anthropologist* 12(4):379–92

Murdock, George P. 1981. *Atlas of World Cultures.* Pittsburgh: University of Pittsburgh Press.

Murdock, George Peter. 1983. *Outline of World Cultures.* 6th ed. New Haven, CT: Human Relations Area Files.

Murdock, George P., and Caterina Provost. 1973. "Measurement of Cultural Complexity." *Ethnology* 12(4):379–92.

Murdock, George P., and Douglas R. White. 1969. "Standard Cross-Cultural Sample." *Ethnology* 8(4):329–69.

Murdock, George P., and Suzanne F. Wilson. 1972. "Settlement Patterns and Community Organization: Cross-Cultural Codes 3." *Ethnology* 11(3): 254–95.

Murdock, George Peter, et al. 2000. *Outline of Cultural Materials.* 5th ed. New Haven, CT: Human Relations Area Files.

Murphy, Robert, and Julian Steward. 1956. "Trappers and Trappers: Parallel Processes in Acculturation." *Economic Development and Culture Change* 4:335–55.

Murphy, Yolanda, and Robert F. Murphy. 1974. *Women of the Forest.* New York and London: Columbia University Press.

Murra, John V. 1960. "Rite and Crop in the Inca State." In *Culture in History: Essays in Honor of Paul Radin,* edited by Stanley Diamond, pp. 393–407. New York: Columbia University Press.

Murra, John V. "El Control Vertical de un Maximo de Pisos Ecologicos en la Economia de las Sociedades Andinas." In *Vista de la Provincia de Lean de Huanuco (IS62),* vol. 2. Edited by Inigo Ortiz de Zuniga, pp. 429–76. Huanuco, Peru: Universidad Hermillo Valdizan.

Myers, Fred R. 1980. "The Cultural Basis of Politics in Pintupi Life." *Mankind* 12(3):197–214.

Myers, Norman, and Jennifer Kent. 2001. *Perverse Subsidies: How Tax Dollars Can Undercut the Environment and the Economy.* Washington, DC: Island Press.

Myers, Norman, Russell A. Mittermeier, Christina G. Mittermeier, Gustavo A. B. da Fonseca, and Jennifer Kent. 2000. "Biodiversity Hotspots for Conservation Priorities." *Nature* 403, 24 February, 853–58.

Myers, Richard B. 2003. "Shift to a Global Perspective." *Naval War College Review* 56(4):9–17.

Myers, Thomas P., William M. Denevan, Antoinette Winklerprins, Antonio Porro. 2003. "Historical Perspectives on Amazonian Dark Earths." In J. Lehmann, et al, eds. *Amazonian Dark Earths: Origin, Properties, Management,* pp. 15–24. Netherlands: Kluwer Academic Publishers.

Naroll, Raoul. 1962. "Floor Area and Settlement Population." *American Antiquity* 27(4):587–89.

Nakicenovic, N., et al. (2000). *Special Report on Emissions Scenarios: A Special Report of Working Group III of the Intergovernmental Panel on Climate Change,* Cambridge University Press, Cambridge, U.K. www.grida.no/climate/ipcc/emission/index.htm.

Nash, June. 1989. *From Tank Town to High Tech: The Clash of Community and Industrial Cycles.* Albany: State University of New York Press.

Nash, June. 1994. "Global Integration and Subsistence Insecurity." *American Anthropologist* 96(1):7–30.

National Center for Health Statistics. 1998. *Health, United States, 1998.* Washington, DC: U.S. Government Printing Office.

National Credit Union Administration. 2009. *Summary and Reports for Menasha Corporation Employees* [Credit Union] as of June 30, 2009. http://reports.ncua.gov/data/cureports/index.cfm (accessed Feb. 2010).

National Geographic Society. 2010. *The Genographic Project.* https://genographic.nationalgeographic.com/genographic/index.html (accessed August 2010).

National Geospatial-Intelligence Agency. 2001. Geographic Names and FIPS 10 Digraph Codes: Countries, Dependencies, and Areas of Special Sovereignty. http://earth-info.nga.mil/gns/html/digraphs.htm.

National Oceanic and Atmospheric Administration (NOAA). 2010. *Trends in Atmospheric Carbon Dioxide (Global).* Earth System Research Laboratory. www.esrl.noaa.gov/gmd/ccgg/trends/#global (accessed Feb. 2010).

National Provisioner. 1990a. *National Provisioner* 202(2).

National Provisioner. 1990b. *National Provisioner* 202(9).

Naylor, Rosamond L., Rebecca J. Goldburg, Jurgenne H. Primavera, Nils Kautsky, Malcolm C. M. Beveridge, Jason Clay, Carl Folke, Jane Lubchenco, Harold Mooney, and Max Troell. 2000. "Effect of Aquaculture on World Fish Supplies." *Nature* 405 (29 June): 1017–24.

Neel, James V. 1970. "Lessons from a 'Primitive' People." *Science* 170(3960):815–22.

Nestle, Marion. 2002. *Food Politics: How the Food Industry Influences Nutrition and Health.* Berkeley: University of California Press.

New Economics Foundation. 2004. *Chasing Progress: Beyond Measuring Economic Growth.* London, 2, Figure. www.neweconomics.org.

Newman, Katherine S. 1988. *Falling from Grace: The Experience of Downward Mobility in the American Middle Class.* New York: Free Press.

Newman, Katherine S. 1993. *Declining Fortunes: The Withering of the American Dream.* New York: Basic Books.

Newman, Peter. 2007. "Beyond Peak Oil: Will Our Cities Collapse?" *Journal of Urban Technology* 14(2):15–30.

Newmyer, R. Kent. 1987. "Harvard Law School, New England Legal Culture, and the Antebellum Origins of American Jurisprudence." *The Journal of American History* 74(3): 814–35.

NIC (National Intelligence Council). 2000. *Global Trends 2015: A Dialogue about the Future with Nongovernment Experts.* NIC 2000–02. http://infowar.net/cia/publications/globaltrends2015/.

Nicholls, R. J., P. P. Wong, V. R. Burkett, J. O. Codignotto, J. E. Hay, R. F. McLean, S. Ragoonaden, and C. D. Woodroffe. 2007. "Coastal Systems and Low-Lying Areas." In *Climate Change 2007: Impacts, Adaptation and Vulnerability. Contribution of Working Group II to the Fourth*

Assessment Report of the Intergovernmental Panel on Climate Change. Parry, M. L., O. F. Canziani, J. P. Palutikof, P. J. van der Linden ,and C. E. Hanson (eds). Cambridge, U.K., and New York: Cambridge University Press, chapter 6, pp. 315–56.

Nietschmann, Bernard. 1988. "Third World Colonial Expansion: Indonesia, Disguised Invasion of Indigenous Nations." *Tribal Peoples and Development Issues: A Global Overview,* edited by John H. Bodley, pp. 191–207. Mountain View, CA: Mayfield.

Niles, Susan A. 1999. *The Shape of Inca History: Narrative and Architecture in an Andean Empire.* Iowa City: University of Iowa Press.

Nissen, Hans J. 1986. "The Archaic Texts from Uruk." *World Archaeology* 17(3):317–34.

Noble, David F. 1977. *America by Design: Science, Technology, and the Rise of Corporate Capitalism.* New York: Alfred A. Knopf.

Noble, David F. 1993. *Progress without People: In Defense of Luddism.* Chicago: Keen.

Noll, Richard. 1984. "The Context of Schizophrenia and Shamanism." *American Ethnologist* 11(1):191–92.

Northern Land Council. 2009. *Annual Report 2008–2009.* www.nlc.org.au/html/wht_pub.html.

Northern Territory, Department of Housing, Local Government and Regional Services. 2008. *Local Government Regional Management Plan, Northern Region.* www.dlgh.nt.gov.au/__data/assets/pdf_file/0016/41506/NORTHERN_REGION_RMP_Aug_08.pdf.

Northern Territory Government. 2008. *Maningrida Study.* Department of Business, Economic and Regional Development (DBERD). www.nt.gov.au/d/Content/File/p/rd/Mngrda%20Study-08_04.pdf.

Norway, Ministry of Finance. 2005. *The Government Pension Fund: The Ethical Guidelines.* www.regjeringen.no/en/dep/fin/Selected-topics/the-government-pension-fund/responsible-investments/Guidelines-for-observation-and-exclusion-from-the-Government-Pension-Fund-Globals-investment-universe.html?id=594254 accessed April 2010.

Norway, Ministry of Finance. 2008. *Council on Ethics, Government Pension Fund. Annual Report 2008.* www.regjeringen.no/en/sub/styrer-rad-utvalg/ethics_council/annual-reports.html?id=458699.

Norway, Ministry of Finance. 2008. *Norway's Strategy for Sustainable Development,* published as part of the National Budget. R-0617E. www.regjeringen.no/upload/FIN/rapporter/R-0617E.pdf.

Oates, Joan. 1993. "Trade and Power in the Fifth and Fourth Millennia BC: New Evidence from Northern Mesopotamia." *World Archaeology* 24(3):403–22.

Ocholla-Ayayo, A. B. C. 1979. "Marriage and Cattle Exchange Among the Nilotic Luo." *Paideuma* 25:173–93.

O'Connell, James F., and Kristen Hawkes. 1981. "Alyawara Plant Use and Optimal Foraging Theory." In *Hunter-Gatherer Foraging Strategies,* edited by B. Winterhalder and E. A. Smith, pp. 99–125. Chicago: University of Chicago Press.

Odum, Howard T. 1971. *Environment, Power, and Society.* New York: Wiley Inter-Science.

Odum, Howard T., and Elisabeth C. Odum. 2001. *A Prosperous Way Down: Principles and Policies.* Boulder, CO: University Press of Colorado.

Oliver, Douglas L. 1989. *Oceania: The Native Cultures of Australia and the Pacific Islands.* 2 vols. Honolulu: University of Hawaii Press.

Olsson, Karen. 2002. "The Shame of Meatpacking." *The Nation* 275 (8):11–16.

ONERN (Oficina Nacional de Evaluación e Integración de los Recursos Naturales). 1968. *Inventario, Evaluación e Integración de los Recursos Naturales de la Zona del Rio Tambo-Gran Pajonal.* Lima: ONERN.

Open Secrets. 2009. *Personal Finance: Most Popular Investments, Top Sectors, 2007.* www.opensecrets.org/pfds/index.php (accessed Sept. 2009).

Orlove, Benjamin S. 1987. "Stability and Change in Highland Andean Dietary Patterns." In *Food and Evolution: Toward a Theory of Human Food Habits,* edited by Marvin Harris and Eric Ross, pp. 481–515. Philadelphia: Temple University Press.

Ortner, Sherry B. 1996. *Making Gender: the Politics and Erotics of Culture.* Boston: Beacon Press.

Orwin, C. S., and C. S. Orwin. 1967. *The Open Fields.* Oxford, Eng.: Clarendon Press.

Palmer, Ingrid. 1972. *Science and Agricultural Production.* Geneva: UN Research Institute for Social Development.

Papanek, Hanna. 1982. "Purdah: Separate Worlds and Symbolic Shelter." In *Separate Worlds: Studies of Purdah in South Asia,* edited by Hanna Papanek and Gail Minault, pp. 3–53. Delhi: Chanakya.

Pareto, Vilfredo. 1971. *Manual of Political Economy.* Translated by Ann S. Schwier and Alfred N. Page. New York: A. M. Kelley.

ParksWatch. 2003. *Profile of Protected Area: Peru El Sira Communal Reserve.* www.parkswatch.org/parkprofiles/pdf/escr_eng.pdf (accessed January 2010).

Parry, Jonathan. 1979. *Caste and Kinship in Kangra.* London: Routledge & Kegan Paul.

Paulsen, Allison C. 1974. "The Thorny Oyster and the Voice of God: Spondylus and Strombus in Andean Prehistory." *American Antiquity* 39(4):597–607.

Pauly, Daniel. 2004. "Much Rowing for Fish." *Nature* 432 (16 December): 813–14.

Peregrine, Peter N. 2001. *Outline of Archaeological Traditions.* Human Relations Area Files.

Peregrine, Peter N. 2003. "Atlas of Cultural Evolution." *World Cultures* 14(1):2–75.

Perkins, Dwight H. 1969. *Agricultural Development in China 1368–1968.* Chicago: Aldine.

Perry, W. J. 1923. *The Children of the Sun.* London: Methuen.

Pessen, Edward. 1971. "The Egalitarian Myth and the American Social Reality: Wealth, Mobility, and Equality in the 'Era of the Common Man.'" *The American Historical Review* 76(4):989–1034.

Pessen, Edward. 1973. *Riches, Class, and Power before the Civil War*. Lexington, MA: Heath.

Peters, Larry G. and Douglass Price-Williams. 1980. "Towards an Experiential Analysis of Shamanism." *American Ethnologist* 7(3):397–418.

Peterson, Nicolas. 1986. *Australian Territorial Organization*. Oceania Monograph, no. 30. Sydney: University of Sydney.

Peterson, Nicolas. 1997. *Demand Sharing: Sociobiology and the Pressure for Generosity among Foragers*. In *Scholar and Sceptic: Australian Aboriginal Studies in Honour of L. R. Hiatt*, edited by F. Merlan, J. Morton, and A. Rumsey, pp. 171–90. Aboriginal Studies Press, Canberra.

Petty, William. 1899. [1662]. *A Treatise of Taxes and Contributions*. In Hull, Charles Henry. 1899. *The Economic Writings of Sir William Petty Together with the Observations Upon the Bills of Mortality*, pp. 1–97, vol. 1. Cambridge: Cambridge University Press.

Petty, William. 1899. [1664]. *Verbum Sapienti*. In Hull, Charles Henry. 1899. *The Economic Writings of Sir William Petty Together with the Observations Upon the Bills of Mortality*, pp. 99–120, vol. 1. Cambridge: Cambridge University Press.

Petty, William. 1899. [1672]. *The Political Anatomy of Ireland*. In Hull, Charles Henry. 1899. *The Economic Writings of Sir William Petty Together with the Observations Upon the Bills of Mortality*, pp. 121–231, vol. 1. Cambridge: Cambridge University Press.

Petty, William. 1899. [1676]. *Political Arithmetick*. In Hull, Charles Henry. 1899. *The Economic Writings of Sir William Petty Together with the Observations Upon the Bills of Mortality*, pp. 233–313, vol. 1. Cambridge: Cambridge University Press.

Phillips, Kevin. 1990. *The Politics of Rich and Poor: Wealth and the American Electorate in the Reagan Aftermath*. New York: Random House.

Phillips, Kevin. 1994. *Arrogant Capital: Washington, Wall Street, and the Frustration of American Politics*. Boston: Little, Brown.

Phillips, Kevin. 2002. *Wealth and Democracy: A Political History of the American Rich*. New York: Broadway Books.

Pietraszek, Greg. 1990. "Cattlemen Face Future Competition with Confidence." *National Provisioner* 202(12):5–8.

Pike, Kenneth. 1954. *Language in Relation to a Unified Theory of the Structure of Human Behavior*, vol. 1. The Hague: Mouton.

Pitman, Nigel C. A., John Terborgh, Miles R. Silman, and Percy Nuñez V. 1999. "Tree Species Distribution in an Upper Amazonian Forest." *Ecology* 80(8):2651–61.

Planetary Coral Reef Foundation. 2005. *Reef Report: Health of the Namena Reef*. www.pcrf.org/science/Namena/reefreport.html.

Playfair, William. 2005. [1801]. *The Commercial and Political Atlas and Statistical Breviary*. (Howard Wainer and Ian Spence, eds). 3rd ed. Cambridge: Cambridge University Press, 2.

Plog, Stephen. 1995. "Equality and Hierarchy: Holistic Approaches to Understanding Social Dynamics in the Pueblo Southwest." In *Foundations of Social Inequality*, edited by T. Douglas Price and Gary M. Feinman, pp. 189–206. New York and London: Plenum Press.

Polanyi, Karl. 1944. *The Great Transformation*. Boston.

Polanyi, Karl. 1977. *The Livelihood of Man*. New York: Academic Press.

Pollard, Duncan (editor). 2010. *Living Planet Report 2010: Biodiversity, biocapacity and development*. Gland, Switzerland: WWF International wwf.panda.org/about_our_earth/all_publications/living_planet_report/.

Popkin, Barry M. 1998. "The Nutrition Transition and its Health Implications in Lower-Income Countries." *Public Health Nutrition* 1(1):5–21.

Porteus, S. D. 1931. *The Psychology of a Primitive People*. London: E. Arnold.

Posposil, Leopold. 1972. *The Ethnology of Law*. Addison-Wesley Module in Anthropology, no. 12. Reading, MA: Addison-Wesley.

Poumisak, Jit (pseudonym Somsamai Srisudravarna). 1987. "The Real Face of Thai Saktina Today." In *Thai Radical Discourse: The Real Pace of Thai Feudalism Today*, editor and translator Craig J. Reynolds, pp. 43–148. Studies on Southeast Asia, Cornell University, Ithaca, NY.

Powell, H. A. 1960. "Competitive Leadership in Trobriand Political Organization." *Journal of the Royal Anthropological Institute* 90(1): 118–45.

Price, A. G. 1950. *White Settlers and Native Peoples*. London: Cambridge University Press.

Price, Weston Andrew. 1945. *Nutrition and Physical Degeneration: A Comparison of Primitive and Modern Diets and Their Effects*. Redlands, CA: Weston Price.

Pukui, Mary Kawena, and Samuel H. Elbert. 1986. *Hawaiian Dictionary*. Honolulu: University of Hawaii Press.

Pyle, Tom. 1964. *Pocantico: Fifty Years on the Rockefeller Domain*. New York: Duel, Sloan & Pearce.

Quilter, Jeffrey, and Terry Stocker. 1983. "Subsistence Economies and the Origins of Andean Complex Societies." *American Anthropologist* 85(3):545–62.

Quinlan, Marsha B. 2004. *From the Bush: The Front Line of Health Care in a Caribbean Village*. Case Studies in Cultural Anthropology. Belmont, CA: Thomson Wadsworth.

Rabb, Theodore K. 1967. *Enterprise and Empire: Merchant and Gentry Investment in the Expansion of England, 1575–1630*. Cambridge, MA: Harvard University Press.

Rabibhadana, Akin. 1969. *The Organization of Thai Society in the Early Bangkok Period, 1782–1873*. Data Paper:

Number 74, South East Asia Program, Department of Asian Studies. Cornell University, Ithaca, NY.

Radcliffe-Brown, A. R. 1913. "Three Tribes of Western Australia." *Journal of the Royal Anthropological Institute* 43: 143–95.

Radcliffe-Brown, A. R. 1918. "Notes on the Social Organization of Australian Tribes." *Journal of the Royal Anthropological Institute* 48:222–53.

Radcliffe-Brown, A. R. 1929. "The Sociological Theory of Totemism." Proceedings of the Fourth Pacific Science Congress. (Reprinted in *Structure and Function in Primitive Society,* edited by A. R. Radcliffe-Brown, pp. 117–32. New York: Free Press, 1965.)

Radcliffe-Brown, A. R. 1935. "On the Concept of Function in Social Science." *American Anthropologist* 37(3):394–402.

Radcliffe-Brown, A. R. 1941. "The Study of Kinship Systems." *Journal of the Royal Anthropological Institute.* (Reprinted in *Structure and Function in Primitive Society,* edited by A. R. Radcliffe-Brown, pp. 49–89. New York: Free Press, 1965.)

Radcliffe-Brown, A. R. 1958. Presidential Address to Section E. South African Association for the Advancement of Science, July 1928. (In *Method in Social Anthropology: Selected Essays by A. R. Radcliffe-Brown,* edited by M. N. Srinivas. Chicago: University of Chicago Press.)

Radin, Paul. 1971. *The World of Primitive Man.* New York: Dutton.

RAISG, Red Amazónica de Información Socioambiental Georeferenciada. 2009. *Amazonia 2009 Áreas Protegidas Territorios Indígenas.* www.raisg.socioambiental.org (accessed April 14, 2009).

Rao, Rajesh P. N., Nisha Yadav, Mayank N. Vahia, Hrishikesh Joglekar, R. Adhikari, and Iravatham Mahadevan. 2009. "Entropic Evidence for Linguistic Structure in the Indus Script." *Science* 29 May 2009, 324:1165.

Raskin, Paul, Tariq Banuri, Gilberto Gallopín, Pablo Gutman, Al Hammond, Robert Kates, and Rob Swart. 2002. *Great Transition: The Promise and Lure of the Times Ahead.* Global Scenario Group. Boston: Stockholm Environment Institute, Tellus Institute.

Raskin, Paul D. 2006. *The Great Transition Today: A Report from the Future.* GTI Paper Series 2, Frontiers of a Great Transition. Boston: Tellus Institute.

Rawski, Evelyn S. 1987. "Popular Culture in China." In *Tradition and Creativity: Essays on East Asian Civilization,* edited by Ching-I Tu, pp. 41–65. New Brunswick, NJ, and Oxford, Eng.: Transaction Books.

Raymond, J. Scott, Warren R. DeBoer, and Peter G. Roe. 1975. *Cumancaya: A Peruvian Ceramic Tradition.* Occasional Papers No. 2. Calgary, Alberta: Department of Archaeology, The University of Calgary.

Read, Dwight W. 2002. "A Multitrajectory, Competition Model of Emergent Complexity in Human Social Orga-

nization." *Proceedings of the National Academy of Sciences* Vol. 99, Supplement 3, 7251–56.

Redfield, Robert. 1941. *The Folk Culture of Yucatan.* Chicago: University of Chicago Press.

Redfield, Robert, Ralph Linton, and Melville J. Herskovits. 1936. "Memorandum for the Study of Acculturation." *American Anthropologist* 38(1):149–52.

Redman, Charles L. 1978a. "Mesopotamian Urban Ecology: The Systemic Context of the Emergence of Urbanism." In *Social Archaeology: Beyond Subsistence and Dating,* edited by Charles Redman, Mary Jane Berman, Edward Curtin, William Langhorne Jr., Nina Versaggi, and Jeffery Wanser, pp. 329–47. New York: Academic Press.

Redman, Charles L. 1978b. *The Rise of Civilization: From Early Farmers to Urban Society in the Ancient Near East.* San Francisco: Freeman.

Reichel-Dolmatoff, Gerardo. 1971. *Amazonian Cosmos: The Sexual and Religious Symbolism of the Tukano Indians.* Chicago: University of Chicago Press.

Reichel-Dolmatoff, Gerardo. 1976. "Cosmology as Ecological Analysis: A View from the Rain Forest." *Man* 11(3): 307–18.

Ribeiro, Darcy. 1957. *Culturas e Linguas Indigenas do Brasil.* Seprata de Educação e Ciencias Socais. No. 6. Rio de Janeiro: Centro Brasileiro de Pesquisas Educaçionais.

Richerson, Peter J., and Robert Boyd. 1999. "Complex Societies: The Evolutionary Origins of a Crude Superorganism." *Human Nature* 10(3):253–89.

Riis, Jacob A. 1904. *How the Other Half Lives: Studies Among the Tenements of New York.* New York: Scribner.

Ritzer, George. 2000. *The McDonaldization of Society.* Thousand Oaks, CA: Pine Forge Press.

Riviere, Peter. 1969. *Marriage Among the Trio: A Principle of Social Organization.* Oxford, Eng.: Clarendon Press.

Roberts, Clayton, and David Roberts. 1980. *A History of England: Prehistory to 1714,* vol. 1. Englewood Cliffs, NJ: Prentice-Hall.

Roberts, Richard G., Rhys Jones, and M. A. Smith. 1990. "Thermoluminescence Dating of a 50,000-Year-Old Human Occupation Site in Northern Australia." *Nature* 345:153–56.

Rochester, Ann. 1936. *Rulers of America: A Study of Finance Capital.* New York: International.

Rockström, Johan, and Lars Anell. 2008. "Statement from the Executive Director and the Chair of the Board." Annual Report 2008: Bridging Science and Policy. Stockholm Environment Institute, 4–5.

Roe, Peter G. 1980. "Art and Residence among the Shipibo Indians of Peru: A Study in Microacculturation." *American Anthropologist* 82(1):42–71.

Roe, Peter G. 1981. "Aboriginal Tourists and Artistic Exchange Between the Pisquibo and the Shipibo: 'Trade Ware in an Ethnographic Setting.'" In *Networks of the Past: Regional Interaction in Archaeology,* edited by Peter D. Francis, F. L. J. Kense, and P. G. Duke, pp. 61–84.

Roe, Peter G. 1982. *The Cosmic Zygote: Cosmology in the Amazon Basin.* New Brunswick, NJ: Rutgers University Press.

Rogers, Alison. 1993. "Billionaires: The World's 101 Richest People." *Fortune,* June 28, pp. 36–66.

Rosaldo, Michelle Zimbalist, and Louise Lamphere, eds. 1974. *Woman, Culture, and Society.* Stanford, CA: Stanford University Press.

Rosenberg, Noah A. 2002. "Genetic Structure of Human Populations." *Science* 298:2381–85.

Rosenzweig, Cynthia, et al. 2008. "Attributing Physical and Biological Impacts to Anthropogenic Climate Change." *Nature* 453(15 May): 353–58.

Rostow, W. W. 1960. *The Process of Economic Growth.* New York: Norton.

Rowe, John H. 1962. *Chavin Art: An Inquiry into Its Form and Meaning.* New York: The Museum of Primitive Art.

Rowe, John H. 1982. "Inca Policies and Institutions Relating to the Cultural Unification of the Empire." In *The Inca and Aztec States 1400–1800,* edited by George Collier, Renato Rosaldo, and John Wirth, pp. 93–118. New York: Academic Press.

Roy, Hiranmoy, and Kaushik Bhattacharjee. 2009. *Convergence of Human Development across Indian States.* Mumbai, India: Indira Gandhi Institute of Development Research. IGIDR Proceedings/Project Reports Series. www.igidr.ac.in/pdf/publication/PP-062-22.pdf.

Roy, Manisha. 1975. *Bengali Women.* Chicago and London: University of Chicago Press.

Roy, William G. 1997. *Socializing Capital: The Rise of the Large Industrial Corporation in America.* Princeton, NJ: Princeton University Press.

Royal Anthropological Institute of Great Britain and Ireland. 1951. *Notes and Queries on Anthropology.* 6th ed. London: Routledge and K. Paul.

Royal Dutch Shell, Annual Report 2009. www.shell.com/home/content/investor/financial_information/annual_reports/2006/dir_2006_annualreport.html.

Rubinstein, Don. 1978. "Native Place-Names and Geographic Systems of Fais, Caroline Islands." *Micronesica* 14(l):69–82.

Rubinstein, W. D. 1981. *Men of Property: The Very Wealthy in Britain Since the Industrial Revolution.* New Brunswick, NJ: Rutgers University Press.

Ruhlen, Merritt. 1987. *A Guide to the World's Languages,* vol. 1, *Classification.* Stanford, CA: Stanford University Press.

Rummel, R. J. 1997. *Death by Government.* New Brunswick, NJ: Transaction.

Ruttan, Lore M., and Monique Borgerhoff Mulder. 1999. "Are East African Pastoralists Truly Conservationists?" *Current Anthropology* 40(5):621–52.

Sahlins, Marshall. 1958. *Social Stratification in Polynesia.* Seattle: University of Washington Press.

Sahlins, Marshall. 1961. "The Segmentary Lineage: An Organization of Predatory Expansion." *American Anthropologist* 63(2, pt. l):322–45.

Sahlins, Marshall. 1963. "Poor Man, Rich Man, Big-Man, Chief: Political Types in Melanesia and Polynesia." *Comparative Studies in Society and History* 5:285–303.

Sahlins, Marshall. 1965. "On the Ideology and Composition of Descent Groups." *Man* 65 (July/August):104–107.

Sahlins, Marshall. 1968. "Notes on the Original Affluent Society" In *Man the Hunter,* edited by Richard Lee and Irven DeVore, pp. 85–89. Chicago: Aldine.

Sahlins, Marshall. 1972. *Stone Age Economics.* Chicago: Aldine.

Sahlins, Marshall. 1976a. "Colors and Cultures." *Semiotica* 16:1–22.

Sahlins, Marshall. 1976b. *Culture and Practical Reason.* Chicago and London: University of Chicago Press.

Sahlins, Marshall. 1976c. *The Use and Abuse of Biology. An Anthropological Critique of Sociobiology.* Ann Arbor: University of Michigan Press.

Sahlins, Marshall. 1985a. *Islands of History.* Chicago: University of Chicago Press.

Sahlins, Marshall. 1985b. "Hierarchy and Humanity in Polynesia." In *Transformations of Polynesian Culture,* edited by A. Hooper and J. Huntsman. Auckland: The Polynesian Society.

Sahlins, Marshall. 1992. "Historical Ethnography." In Kirch, Patrick Vinton, and Marshall Sahlins. *Anahulu: The Anthropology of History in the Kingdom of Hawaii,* vol. 1, pp. 1–243. Chicago: University of Chicago Press.

Sahlins, Marshall. 1996. "The Sadness of Sweetness: The Native Anthropology of Western Cosmology." *Current Anthropology* 37(3):395–428.

Sahlins, Marshall, and Elman Service (Eds.). 1960. *Evolution and Culture.* Ann Arbor: University of Michigan Press.

Sale, Kirkpatrick. 1980. *Human Scale.* New York: Coward, McCann & Geohegan.

Sandel, Michael J. 1998. *Liberalism and the Limits of Justice.* Cambridge, U.K., and New York: Cambridge University Press, xi.

Sanderson, E. W., M. Jaiteh, M. A. Levy, K. H. Redform, A. V. Wannebo, and G. Woolmer. 2002. "The Human Footprint and The Last of the Wild." *BioScience* 52(10); 891–904.

Schattenburg, Patricia. 1976. "Food and Cultivar Preservation in Micronesian Voyaging." Miscellaneous Work Papers. *University of Hawaii Pacific Islands Program* 1:25–51.

Scheper-Hughes, Nancy. 1992. *Death without Weeping: The Violence of Everyday Life in Brazil.* Berkeley: University of California Press.

Schlosser, Eric. 2001. *Fast Food Nation: The Dark Side of the All-American Meal.* Boston: Houghton Mifflin.

Schlosser, Eric. 2002. "Bad Meat: The Scandal of Our Food Safety System." *The Nation* 275(8):6–7.

Schneider, Harold K. 1979. *Livestock and Equality in East Africa: The Economic Basis for Social Structure.* Bloomington and London: Indiana University Press.

Schneider, Stephen H. 1989. "The Changing Climate." *Scientific American* 261(3):70–79.

Schumacher, E. F. 1973. *Small Is Beautiful: Economics as if People Mattered.* New York: Harper & Row.

Seebohm, Frederic. 1905. *The English Village Community Examined in Its Relations to the Manorial and Tribal Systems and to the Common or Open Field System of Husbandry: An Essay in Economic History.* London: Longmans, Green.

Secretariat of the Pacific Regional Environment Programme (SREP). 2009. *2008 Annual Report of the Secretariat of the Pacific Regional Environment Programme.* www.sprep.org/.

Sen, Amartya. 1981. *Poverty and Famines: An Essay on Entitlement and Deprivation.* Oxford, Eng.: Clarendon Press.

Sen, Jai, Anita Anand, Arturo Escobar, and Peter Waterman, eds. 2003. *The World Social Forum: Challenging Empires.* New Delhi: Viveka Foundation. www.choike.org/nuevo_eng/informes/1557.html.

Shamasastry, R. (translator). 1960. *Kautilya's Arthasastra.* Mysore, India: Mysore.

Shapiro, Warren. 1981. *Miwuyt Marriage: The Cultural Anthropology of Affinity in Northeast Arnhem Land.* Philadelphia: Institute for the Study of Human Issues.

Shepard Jr., Glenn H. 1998. "Psychoactive Plants and Ethnopsychiatric Medicines of the Matsigenka." *Journal of Psychoactive Drugs* 30(4):321–32.

Shepard Jr., Glenn. 1999. "Shamanism and Diversity: a Machiguenga Perspective." In Daryl Posey, ed. *Cultural and Spiritual Values of Biodiversity,* pp. 93–95. United Nations Nairobi, Kenya: Environment Programme.

Shepard Jr., Glenn H., Douglas W. Yu, Manuel Lizarralde, Mateo Italiano. 2001. "Rain Forest Habitat Classification Among the Matsigenka of the Peruvian Amazon." *Journal of Ethnobiology* 21(1):1–38.

Shoup, Laurence H., and William Minter. 1980. "Shaping a New World Order: The Council on Foreign Relations' Blueprint for World Hegemony." In *Trilateralism: The Trilateral Commission and Elite Planning for World Management,* edited by Holly Sklar, pp. 135–56. Boston: South End Press.

Silverblatt, Irene. 1987. *Moon, Sun, and Witches: Gender Ideologies and Class in Inca and Colonial Peru.* Princeton, NJ: Princeton University Press.

Silverman, Julian. 1967. "Shamans and Acute Schizophrenia." *American Anthropologist* 69(1):21–31.

Simon, David R. 1999. *Elite Deviance.* 6th ed. Boston: Allyn and Bacon.

Simon, Julian L., and Herman Kahn. 1984. *The Resourceful Earth: A Response to Global 2000.* Oxford and New York: Blackwell.

Simoons, Frederick. 1979. "Questions in the Sacred Cow Controversy." *Current Anthropology* 20(3):467–76.

Sindiga, Isaac. 1987. "Fertility Control and Population Growth Among the Maasai." *Human Ecology* 15(1):53–66.

Singh, Anirudh. "The Sustainable Development of Fiji's Energy Infrastructure: A Status Report." *Pacific Economic Bulletin* 24(2):141–54.

Siskind, Janet. 1973. *To Hunt in the Morning.* London: Oxford University Press.

Skinner, G. William. 1964. "Marketing and Social Structure in Rural China (Part 1)." *Journal of Asian Studies* 24(1):3–43.

Slurink, Pouwell. 1994. "Causes of Our Complete Dependence on Culture." In *The Ethological Roots of Culture,* edited by R. A. Gardner et al., pp. 461–474. Dordrecht, Boston, and London: Kluwer Academic Press.

Smith, Adam. 1776. *An Inquiry into the Nature and Causes of the Wealth of Nations,* vol. 1. London: Strahan & Cadell.

Smith, Andrew B. 1984. "Origins of the Neolithic in the Sahara" In *From Hunters to Farmers: The Causes and Consequences of Food Production in Africa,* edited by J. Desmond Clark and Steven Brandt, pp. 84–92. Berkeley: University of California Press.

Smith, E. A. 1988. "Risk and Uncertainty in the 'Original Affluent Society': Evolutionary Ecology of Resource-Sharing and Land Tenure." In *Hunters and Gatherers,* vol. 1, *History, Evolution, and Social Change,* edited by T. Ingold, D. Riches, and J. Woodburn, pp. 222–51. Berg, Oxford.

Smith, G. Elliot. 1928. *In the Beginning: The Origin of Civilization.* New York: Morrow.

Smith, Richard Chase. 1977. *The Amuesha-Yanachaga Project, Peru: Ecology and Ethnicity in the Central Jungle of Peru.* Survival International Document 3. London: Survival International.

Smith, Richard Chase. 1985. "A Search for Unity within Diversity: Peasant Unions, Ethnic Federations, and Indianist Movements in the Andean Republics." In *Native Peoples and Economic Development: Six Case Studies from Latin America,* Theodore Macdonald Jr., ed. pp. 5–38. Cultural Survival Occasional Paper 16.

Smith, Richard Chase, Margarita Benavides, Mario Pariona, and Ermeto Tuesta. 2003. "Mapping the Past and the Future: Geomatics and Indigenous Territories in the Peruvian Amazon. *Human Organization* 62(4):357–68.

Smith, Wilberforce. 1894. "The Teeth of Ten Sioux Indians." *Journal of the Royal Anthropological Institute* 24:109–16.

Snooks, Graeme Donald. 1993. *Economics without Time: A Science Blind to the Forces of Historical Change.* London: Macmillan Press.

Society for Applied Anthropology. "Ethical and Professional Responsibilities." www.sfaa.net/sfaaethic.html (accessed April 26, 2009).

Soltow, Lee. 1975. *Men and Wealth in the United States 1850 1870.* New Haven, CT, and London: Yale University Press.

Soltow, Lee. 1989. *Distribution of Wealth and Income in the United States in 1798.* Pittsburgh: University of Pittsburgh Press.

Soros, George. 2008. *The New Paradigm for Financial Markets: The Credit Crisis of 2008 and What It Means.* New York: PublicAffairs, Perseus Books Group.

Southall, Aidan. 1976. "Nuer and Dinka Are People: Ecology, Ethnicity and Logical Possibility." *Man* 11:463–91.

Spalding, Mark D. 2007. "Marine Ecoregions of the World: A Bioregionalization of Coastal and Shelf Areas." *BioScience* 57(7):573–83.

Spencer, Paul. 1965. *The Samburu: A Study of Gerontocracy in a Nomadic Tribe.* Berkeley: University of California Press.

Spencer, Paul. 1988. *The Maasai of Matapato: A Study of Rituals of Rebellion.* Bloomington and Indianapolis: Indiana University Press.

SPREP, South Pacific Regional Environment Programme. 1997. *Strategic Action Programme for International Waters of Pacific Islands.* www.iwlearn.net/iw-projects/sapsprep/reports/pacificislands_sap_1997.pdf/view.

SPREP, South Pacific Regional Environment Programme. 2005. "Romancing the Environment: Profile Pita Vatucawaqa." www.sprep.org/article/news_detail.asp?id=234.

Spradley, James P., and Michael A. Rynkiewich. 1975. *The Nacirema: Readings on American Culture.* Boston: Little, Brown.

SPREP, South Pacific Regional Environment Programme. n.d. "Pita Vatucawaqa: Protecting Fiji's Rural Communities from the Impacts of Human Waste." www.sprep.org/iwp/IWPChamp/IWPFiji-Pita.htm.

Srinivas, M. N. 1959. "The Dominant Caste in Rampura." *American Anthropologist* 61(1):1–16.

Stannard, David E. 1989. *Before the Horror: The Population of Hawai'i on the Eve of Western Contact.* Honolulu: Social Science Research Institute, University of Hawaii.

Statistical Abstract of the United States. *See* United States, Department of Commerce, Bureau of the Census.

Stavenhagen, Rodolfo. 2006. *Report of the Special Rapporteur on the Situation of Human Rights and Fundamental Freedoms of Indigenous People.* Addendum. Mission to Ecuador. Human Rights Council. A/HRC/4/32/Add.2 28 December, 23. http://daccessdds.un.org/doc/UNDOC/GEN/G07/100/29/PDF/G0710029.pdf?OpenElement.

Steadman, David W. 1995. "Prehistoric Extinctions of Pacific Island Birds: Biodiversity Meets Zooarchaeology." *Science* (Feb. 24)267:1123–31.

Stein, Gil. 1994. "Economy, Ritual, and Power in 'Ubaid Mesopotamia.'" In *Chiefdoms and Early States in the Near East: The Organizational Dynamics of Complexity,* edited by Gil Stein and Mitchell S. Rothman, pp. 35–46. Monographs in World Archaeology No. 18. Madison, WI: Prehistoric Press.

Steinhart, John S., and Carol E. Steinhart. 1974. "Energy Use in the U.S. Food System." *Science* 184 (4134):307–16.

Steinkeller, Piotr. 1991. "The Administrative and Economic Organization of the Ur III State: The Core and the Periphery." In *The Organization of Power: Aspects of Bureaucracy in the Ancient Near East,* edited by McGuire Gibson and Robert D. Biggs, pp. 15–33. Studies in Ancient Oriental Civilization, No. 46. The Oriental Institute of the University of Chicago.

Steward, Julian H. 1936. "The Economic and Social Basis of Primitive Bands." In *Essays in Anthropology in Honor of Alfred Louis Kroeber,* pp. 331–50. Berkeley: University California Press.

Steward, Julian H. 1949. "Cultural Causality and Law: A Trial Formulation of the Development of Early Civilization." *American Anthropologist* 51:1-27.

Stiglitz, Joseph E. 2002. *Globalization and its Discontents.* New York: W. W. Norton.

Stone, Elizabeth C. 1987. *Nippur Neighborhoods.* Studies in Ancient Oriental Civilization No. 44. Oriental Institute of the University of Chicago. Chicago, IL.

Stone, Linda. 1997. *Kinship and Gender: An Introduction.* Boulder, CO: Westview Press.

Stone, Linda, and Caroline James. 1995. "Dowry, Bride-Burning, and Female Power in India." *Women's Studies International Forum* 18(2):125–34.

Stover, Leon N., and Takeko Kawai Stover. 1976. *China: An Anthropological Perspective.* Pacific Palisades, CA: Goodyear.

Stull, Donald D., and Michael J. Broadway. 2003. *Slaughterhouse Blues: The Meat and Poultry Industry in North America.* Belmont, CA: Wadsworth/Thomson Learning.

Swanson, G. E. 1960. *The Birth of the Gods.* Ann Arbor. University of Michigan Press.

Swenson, Sally, and Jeremy Narby. 1986. "The Pichis-Palcazu Special Project in Peru: A Consortium of International Lenders." *Cultural Survival Quarterly* 10(1):19–24.

Sykes, Bryan. 2001. *The Seven Daughters of Eve.* New York: W.W. Norton. www.oxfordancestors.com/component/option,com_frontpage/Itemid,1/.

Talberth, John, Karen Wolowicz, Jason Venetoulis, Michel Gelobter, Paul Boyle, and Bill Mott. 2006. *The Ecological Fishprint of Nations: Measuring Humanity's Impact on Marine Ecosystems.* Oakland, CA: Redefining Progress.

Tambiah, Stanley Jeyaraja.1985. *Culture, Thought, and Social Action: An Anthropological Perspective.* Cambridge, MA, and London: Harvard University Press.

Taylor, Frederick Winslow. 1911. *The Principles of Scientific Management.* New York: Harper.

Tellus Institute. 2005. *Great Transition Initiative: Visions and Pathways for a Hopeful Future*. GTI Brochure. www.gtinitiative.org/default.asp?action=42.

Terborgh, John 1990. "An Overview of Research at Cocha Cashu Biological Station." In A. H. Gentry, ed., *Four Tropical Rainforests*, pp. 48–59. New Haven, CT: Yale University Press.

Thomas, Nicholas. 1989. "The Force of Ethnology." *Current Anthropology* 30(1):27–41.

Thomas, Verl M. 1986. *Beef Cattle Production: An Integrated Approach*. Philadelphia: Lea & Febiger.

Thomson, Donald F. 1938. *Recommendations of Policy in Native Affairs in the Northern Territory of Australia*, no. 56.-F.2945. Canberra: Parliament of the Commonwealth of Australia.

Thurman, Robert A. F. 1995. *Essential Tibetan Buddhism*. Edison, NJ: Castle Books, Book Sales, Inc.

Tierney, Patrick. 2000. *Darkness in El Dorado: How Scientists and Journalists Devastated the Amazon*. New York: Norton.

Tindale, Norman B. 1974. *Aboriginal Tribes of Australia: Their Terrain, Environmental Controls, Distribution, Limits, and Proper Names*. Berkeley: University of California Press.

Tindale, Norman B. 1981. "Desert Aborigines and the Southern Coastal Peoples: Some Comparisons." In *Ecological Bio-geography of Australia*, vol. 3, pt. 6. Edited by Allen Keast, pp. 1853–84. *Monographiae Biologicae*, vol. 41. The Hague: Dr. W. Junk.

Tishkoff, Sarah A., et al. 2007. "Convergent Adaptation of Human Lactase Persistence in Africa and Europe." *Nature Genetics* 39(1):31–40.

Tocqueville, Alexis de. 1835–40. *Democracy in America* (original *De la démocratie*), various editions.

Todd, Ian A. 1976. *Çatal Hüyük in Perspective*. Menlo Park, CA: Cummmgs.

Tomasello, Michael. 1994. "The Question of Chimpanzee Culture." In *Chimpanzee Culture*, edited by Richard W. Wrangham, Frans B. M. de Waal, and W. C. McGrew, pp. 301–17. Cambridge, MA: Harvard University Press.

Toth, James. 1992. "Doubts About Growth: The Town of Carlisle in Transition." *Urban Anthropology* 21(1):2–44.

Touraine, Alain. 1971. *The Post-Industrial Society: Tomorrow's Social History. Classes, Conflicts and Culture in the Programmed Society*. New York: Random House

Townsend, Robert M. 1993. *The Medieval Village Economy. Study of the Pareto Mapping in General Equilibrium Models*. Princeton, NJ: Princeton University Press.

Towell, Hugh C. 1954. "Kwashiorkor." *Scientific American* 191(6):46–50.

Tristan da Cunha Government Official Website. www.tristandc.com/economy.php.

Tu, Thomas, Paulo Kolikata, Sirilo Dulunaqio, Stacy Jupiter. 2009. *Integrating Ecosystem-Based Management Principles into the Fijian Context: A Case Study from Ku-bulau, Vanua Levu*. International Marine Conservation Congress: Making Marine Science Matter. May 17–24, 2009. Washington, DC. www2.cedarcrest.edu/imcc/Program_Abstracts/data/20090522.html.

Turner II, Christy G. 1989. "Teeth and Prehistory in Asia." *Scientific American* 260(2):88–96.

Tylor, Edward B. 1871. *Primitive Culture*. London: Murray.

Tylor, Edward B. 1875. "Anthropology." *Encyclopaedia Britannica*, vol. 1.

Tyson Foods. 2001. Investor Fact Book. Springdale, AR.

Tyson Foods. 2002. Tyson Annual Report 2002. Springdale, AR.

Underhill, Peter A. and Toomas Kivisild. 2007. "Use of Y Chromosome and Mitochondrial DNA Population Structure in Tracing Human Migrations." *Annual Review of Genetics* 41:53–64.

UNDP See United Nations Development Program.

United Kingdom, National Archives. *Domesday Book*. www.nationalarchives.gov.uk/documentsonline/domesday.asp.

United Kingdom, House of Commons. 1837. *Report from the Select Committee on Aborigines (British Settlements)*. Imperial Blue Book, no. 7, 425. British Parliamentary Papers (an excerpt appears in Bodley, John H. 1988a. *Tribal Peoples and Development Issues: A Global Overview*. Mountain View, CA: Mayfield, pp. 63–69).

United Nations. 1948. *Universal Declaration of Human Rights*. www.un.org/Overview/rights.html (accessed April 26, 2009).

United Nations. 1966. *United Nations International Covenant on Civil and Political Rights*. www.hrweb.org/legal/cpr.html, (accessed January 2010).

United Nations. 1968a. *Statistical Yearbook 1967*. New York: United Nations.

United Nations. 1968b. *Yearbook of National Accounts Statistics 1967*. New York: United Nations.

United Nations. 1992. *Agenda 21*. Department of Economic and Social Affairs, Division for Sustainable Development, Chapter 17, Part G. Sustainable Development of Small Islands, sections 123–136. www.un.org/esa/dsd/agenda21/res_agenda21_17.shtml.

United Nations, Department of Social Affairs. 1952. *Preliminary Report on the World Situation: With Special Reference to Standards of Living*, E/CN.5/267/rev.l. New York: United Nations.

United Nations Environment Programme (UNEP). 2009. Regional Seas Programme website, www.unep.org/regionalseas/programmes/default.asp.

UN General Assembly. 1994. *Report of the Global Conference on the Sustainable Development of Small Island Developing States*. A/CONF.167/9. Annex II Programme of Action for the Sustainable Development of Small Island Developing States, Preamble, Article 14. *www.sidsnet.org/docshare/other/BPOA.pdf*.

United Nations, WHO/FAO. United Nations, World Health Organization / Food and Agriculture Organization. 2003.

Joint WHO/FAO Expert Consultation on Diet, Nutrition and the Prevention of Chronic Diseases. WHO Technical Report Series 916. Geneva.

United Nations Development Program. 2003. *Human Development Report. Millennium Development Goals: A Compact among Nations to End Human Poverty.* New York: Oxford University Press.

United Nations Development Program. 2009. *Human Development Report 2009 Overcoming Barriers: Human Mobility and Development.* New York: Palgrave Macmillan. http://hdr.undp.org/en/reports/global/hdr2009/.

United Nations Environment Programme. 1992. *Rio Declaration on Environment and Development.* www.unep.org/Documents.Multilingual/Default.asp?documentid=78&articleid=1163.

United Nations, Permanent Forum on Indigenous Issues. 2007. *Report on the sixth session* (14-25 May 2007). Economic and Social Council Official Records, Supplement No. 23. E/2007/43 E/C.19/2007/12, Articles 39–42.

United Nations. Permanent Forum on Indigenous Issues (UNPFII). 2010. *United Nations Declaration on the Rights of Indigenous Peoples.* UN General Assembly Resolution 61/295. Sept. 13. www.un.org/esa/socdev/unpfii/en/drip.html (accessed January 2010).

United Nations Millennium Development Goals. www.un.org/millenniumgoals/ (accessed April 26, 2009).

United States, Bureau of Economic Analysis. 2009. *Fixed Asset Tables.* www.bea.gov/national/FA2004/SelectTable.asp (accessed Sept. 2009).

United States, Bureau of Economic Analysis. 2009. *Fixed Assets Accounts Tables.* www.bea.gov/National/FA2004/ (accessed Feb. 2010).

United States Congress. 1974. *Nomination of Nelson A. Rockefeller to Be Vice President of the United States.* Hearings Before the Committee on the Judiciary, House of Representatives, Ninety-Third Congress. Serial No. 45.

United States Environmental Protection Agency. 2009. *Municipal Solid Waste Generation, Recycling, and Disposal in the United States,* Detailed Tables and Figures for 2008, Table 1. www.epa.gov/osw/nonhaz/municipal/msw99.htm.

United States, Department of Agriculture. (USDA) 1997 *Census of Agriculture.* Table 28.

United States, Department of Commerce, Bureau of the Census. 2001. *Statistical Abstract of the United States: 1990.* Washington, DC: Government Printing Office.

United States, Department of Commerce, Census Bureau. 2009. *The 2010 Statistical Abstract of the United States: 2010.* 129th ed. Washington, DC. Table 678. Share of Aggregate Income Received by Each Fifth and Top 5 Percent of Households. www.census.gov/compendia/statab/2010/tables/10s0678.xls#Notes!A1 (accessed Feb. 2010).

United States, Energy Information Administration. 2009. *Annual Energy Review.* www.eia.doe.gov/emeu/aer/overview.html.

United States, Energy Information Administration. 2009. *International Energy Statistics.* www.eia.doe.gov/emeu/international/contents.html.

United States, Energy Information Administration. 2009. "Total Carbon Dioxide Emissions from the Consumption of Energy." www.eia.doe.gov/emeu/international/contents.html.

United States, Federal Reserve. 2009. Flow of Funds Accounts of the United States. Tables F101-F109 Financial Assets 1946-2008. www.federalreserve.gov/datadownload (accessed Sept. 2009).

United States House Committee on the Judiciary. 1949. *Study of Monopoly Power. Hearings Before the Subcommittee on Study of Monopoly Power of the Committee on the Judiciary, House of Representatives, Eighty-First Congress.* First Session. Serial No. 14, Pt. 1. Washington, DC: U.S. Government Printing Office.

United States, Internal Revenue Service, Statistics of Income. http://ftp.irs.gov/taxstats/indtaxstats/article/0,,id=98123,00.html.

United States Internal Revenue Service (IRS). 2009. "S Corporations." www.irs.gov/businesses/small/article/0,,id=98263,00.html (accessed Feb. 2010).

United States Internal Revenue Service (IRS). 2009. *2006 Corporation Returns – 1120S Basic Tables.* Table 4. S Corporation Returns: Total Receipts and Deductions, Portfolio Income, Rental Income, and Total Net Income, by Size Business Receipts and Sector. www.irs.gov/taxstats/bustaxstats/article/0,,id=96405,00.html (accessed Feb. 2010).

United States Internal Revenue Service (IRS). 2009. *2006 Corporation Returns – Basic Tables.* Returns of Active Corporations. Table 5. Selected Balance Sheet, Income Statement, and Tax Items, by Sector, by Size of Business Receipts. www.irs.gov/taxstats/article/0,,id=170691,00.html (accessed Feb. 2010).

United States Small Business Administration, Office of Advocacy. 2009. *Frequently Asked Questions.* (September). www.sba.gov/advo/stats/sbfaq.pdf (accessed Feb. 2010).

Union of Concerned Scientists. 1992. "World Scientists' Warning to Humanity." www.ucsusa.org/ucs/about/1992-world-scientists-warning-to-humanity.html.

Urton, Gary. 1981. *At the Crossroads of the Earth and Sky: An Andean Cosmology.* Austin: University of Texas Press.

U.S. See United States.

USAID, Brazil. 2010. *Ethno-Environmental Protection of Isolated Peoples in the Brazilian Amazon.* http://brazil.usaid.gov/en/node/101 (accessed January 2010).

Valeri, Valerio. 1985. *Kingship and Sacrifice: Ritual and Society in Ancient Hawaii.* Chicago: University of Chicago Press.

Van Schendel, Willem. 1981. *Peasant Mobility: The Odds of Life in Rural Bangladesh.* Assen: Van Gorcum.

Varese, Stefano. 1972. "Inter-Ethnic Relations in the Selva of Peru." In *The Situation of the Indian in South America,* edited by W. Dostal, pp. 115–39. Geneva: World Council of Churches.

Vatuk, Sylvia. 1982. "Purdah Revisited: A Comparison of Hindu and Muslim Interpretations of the Cultural Meaning of Purdah in South Asia." In *Separate Worlds: Studies of Purdah in South Asia*, edited by Hanna Papanek and Gail Minault, pp. 54–78. Delhi: Chanakya.

Vaughn, Kevin J. 2006. "Craft Production, Exchange, and Political Power in the Pre-Incaic Andes." *Journal of Archaeological Research* 14: 313–44.

Venetoulis, Jason, and Cliff Cobb. 2004. *The Genuine Progress Indicator 1950–2002 (2004 Update)*. Oakland, CA: Redefining Progress. www.rprogress.org/projects/gpi/.

Verdon, Michel. 1982. "Where Have All Their Lineages Gone? Cattle and Descent Among the Nuer." *American Anthropologist* 84(3):566–79.

Veron, John Edward Norwood. 2008. "Mass Extinctions and Ocean Acidification: Biological Constraints on Geological Dilemmas." *Coral Reefs* 27:459–72.

Veron, John Edward Norwood. 2008. *A Reef in Time: The Great Barrier Reef from Beginning to End*. Cambridge, MA: Belknap Press of Harvard University Press.

Ver Steeg, Clarence L. 1954. *Robert Morris Revolutionary Financier*. Philadelphia: University of Pennsylvania Press.

Viveiros de Castro, Eduardo. 2004. "Exchanging Perspectives: The Transformation of Objects into Subjects in Amerindian Ontologies." *Common Knowledge* 10(3):463–84.

Waal, Frans de. 1982. *Chimpanzee Politics: Power and Sex Among Apes*. London: Jonathan Cape.

Waetzoldt, Hartmut. 1987. "Compensation of Craft Workers and Officials in the Ur III Period." In *Labor in the Ancient Near East*, edited by Marvin A. Powell, pp. 117–41. American Oriental Series, vol. 68. New Haven, CT: American Oriental Society.

Wake, Charles Staniland. 1872. "The Mental Conditions of Primitive Man as Exemplified by the Australian Aborigine." *Journal of the Royal Anthropological Institute* 1:78–84.

Wales, H. G. Quaritch. 1934. *Ancient Siamese Government and Administration*. London: Bernard Quaritch.

Wallace, Anthony F. C. 1978. *Rockdale: The Growth of an American Village in the Early Industrial Revolution*. New York: Knopf.

Wallerstein, Immanuel. 1974. *The Modern World-System: Capitalist Agriculture and the Origins of the European World-Economy in the Sixteenth Century*. New York: Academic Press.

Wallerstein, Immanuel. 1990. "Culture as the Ideological Battleground of the Modern World-System." *Theory, Culture & Society* 7:31–55.

Wall Street 20th Century. 1960. *A Republication of the Yale Daily News' Wall Street 1955*. New Haven, CT: Yale Daily News.

Walmart. 2003. *Annual Report, 2003*. Bentonville, AR.

Walsh, J., and R. Gannon. 1967. *Time Is Short and the Water Rises*. Camden, NJ: Nelson.

Warner, W. L. 1958. *A Black Civilization*. New York: Harper.

Watson, Reg, and Daniel Pauly. 2001. "Systematic Distortions in World Fisheries Catch Trends." *Nature* 414 (29 November): 534–36

WCED (World Commission on Environment and Development). 1987. *Our Common Future*. Oxford, Eng.: Oxford University Press.

Weber, Hanne. 1998. "The Salt of the Montana: Interpreting Indigenous Activism in the Rain Forest." *Cultural Anthropology* 13(3):382–413.

Weber, Max. [1904–1905] 1930. *The Protestant Ethic and the Spirit of Capitalism*. New York: Scribner.

Weber, Max. 1968. *Economy and Society: An Outline of Interpretive Sociology*, edited by Guenther Roth and Claus Wittich. 3 vols. New York: Bedminster Press.

Wei-Ming, Tu. "The Confucian Tradition in Chinese History." In *Heritage of China: Contemporary Perspectives on Chinese Civilization*, edited by Paul Ropp, pp. 112–37. Berkeley: University of California Press.

Weiner, Annette B. 1988. *The Trobrianders of Papua New Guinea*. New York: Harcourt Brace Jovanovich.

Weiss, Gerald. 1975. *Campa Cosmology: The World of a Forest Tribe in South America*. Anthropological Papers, no. 52(5). New York: American Museum of Natural History.

Wells, Spencer. 2002. *The Journey of Man: A Genetic Odyssey*. Princeton and Oxford: Princeton University Press.

Weiss, Kenneth M. 1973. *Demographic models for anthropology*. Memoirs of the Society for American Archaeology No. 27. *American Antiquity* 38(2).

Werner, Dennis. 1983. "Why Do the Mekranoti Trek?" In *Adaptive Responses of Native Amazonians*, edited by Raymond Hames and William Vickers, pp. 225–38. New York: Academic Press.

Wernick, Iddo K., and Ausubel, Jesse H. 1995. "National Material Flows and the Environment." *Annual Review of Energy and the Environment*. 20:463–92.

Westermark, Edward. 1922. *The History of Human Marriage*, 5th ed. New York: Allerton Book Co.

Western, David, and Virginia Finch. 1986. "Cattle and Pastoralism: Survival and Production in Arid Lands." *Human Ecology* 14(l):77–94.

Wheatley, Paul. 1971. *The Pivot of the Four Quarters: A Preliminary Enquiry into the Origins and Character of the Ancient Chinese City*. Chicago: Aldine.

Wheeler, Jane C. 1984. "On the Origin and Early Development of Camelid Pastoralism in the Andes." In *Animals and Archaeology*, vol. 3. Edited by Juliet Clatton-Brock and Caroline Grigson, pp. 395–410. BAR International Series, no 202. Oxford, Eng.: BAR.

White, J. Peter, and James F. O'Connell. 1982. *Prehistory of Australia, New Guinea and Sahul*. New York: Academic Press.

White, Leslie A. 1949. *The Science of Culture*. New York: Grove Press.

Whitehead, Neil L. 2002. *Dark Shamans: Kanaimà and the Poetics of Violent Death*. Durham and London: Duke University Press.

Whitesides, George M. and George W. Crabtree. 2007. "Don't Forget Long-Term Fundamental Research in Energy." *Science* 315 (9 February): 796–98.

Whorf, Benjamin Lee. 1956. "Science and Linguistics." In *Language, Thought and Reality*, John B. Carroll, ed. Cambridge, MA: MIT.

Whyte, William Foote, and Kathleen King Whyte. 1988. *Making Mondragon: The Growth and Dynamics of the Worker Cooperative Complex*. Ithaca, NY: ILR Press.

Wilbert, Johannes. 1987. *Tobacco and Shamanism in South America*. New Haven and London: Yale University Press.

Wilkinson, John. 2006. "Fish: A Global Value Chain Driven onto the Rocks." *Sociologia Ruralis* 46(2): 139–53.

Wilkinson, Richard G. 1996. *Unhealthy Societies: The Afflictions of Inequality*. London and New York: Routledge.

Wilkinson, Richard G. 1997. "Comment: Income, Inequality, and Social Cohesion." *American Journal of Public Health* 87(9):1504–1506.

Willet, Walter C. 2001. *Eat, Drink, and Be Healthy*. New York: Simon & Schuster.

Williams, Nancy M. 1986. *The Yolngu and Their Land: A System of Land Tenure and the Fight for Its Recognition*. Stanford, CA: Stanford University Press.

Wilson, E. O. 1987. "The Arboreal Ant Fauna of Peruvian Amazon Forests: A first Assessment." *Biotropica* 19(3):245–51.

Wilson, Peter J. 1988. *The Domestication of the Human Species*. New Haven, CT, and London: Yale University Press.

Winter, Irene J. 1991. "Legitimation of Authority through Image and Legend: Seals Belonging to Officials in the Administrative Bureaucracy of the Ur III State." In *The Organization of Power: Aspects of Bureaucracy in the Ancient Near East*, edited by McGuire Gibson and Robert D. Biggs, pp. 59–100. Studies in Ancient Oriental Civilization, No. 46. The Oriental Institute of the University of Chicago.

Winterhalder, Bruce. 1993. "Work, Resources and Population in Foraging Societies." *Man* 28(2):321–40.

Wittfogel, Karl A. 1957. *Oriental Despotism: A Study of Total Power*. New Haven, CT: Yale University Press.

Wolf, Arthur P. 1968. "Adopt a Daughter-in-Law, Marry a Sister: A Chinese Solution to the Problem of the Incest Taboo." *American Anthropologist* 70(5):864–74.

Wolf, Arthur P. 1974. "Gods, Ghosts, and Ancestors." *Religion and Ritual in Chinese Society*, edited by Arthur P. Wolf, pp. 131–82. Stanford, CA: Stanford University Press.

Wolf, Arthur P. 1995. *Sexual Attraction and Childhood Association: A Chinese Brief for Edward Westermarck*. Stanford, CA: Stanford University Press.

Wolf, Eric R. 1969. *Peasant Wars of the Twentieth Century*. New York: Harper & Row.

Wolf, Eric R. 1982. *Europe and the People without History*. Berkeley: University of California Press.

Wolf, R. Eric. 1999. *Envisioning Power: Ideologies of Dominance and Crisis*. Berkeley: University of California Press.

Wolf, Margery. 1968. *The House of Lim: A Study of a Chinese Farm Family*. New York: Appleton-Century-Crofts.

Wolf, Steward, and John G. Bruhn. 1993. *The Power of Clan: The Influence of Human Relationships on Heart Disease*. New Brunswick, NJ, and London: Transaction Books.

Woodburn, James. 1982. "Egalitarian Societies." *Man* 17(3): 431–51.

Wood Jones, Frederic. 1928. "The Claims of the Australian Aborigine." *Report of the Eighteenth Australasian Association for the Advancement of Science* 18:497–519.

Woodruff, William. 1966. *The Impact of Western Man*. London: Macmillan.

Woolley, Sir Leonard. 1982. *Ur of the Chaldees*. London: Herbert Press.

Woolley, Sir Leonard and P. R. S. Moorey. 1982. *Ur of the Chaldees*. Ithaca, NY: Cornell University Press.

World Almanac and Book of Facts. 1998. Mahwah, NJ: World Almanac Books.

World Almanac and Book of Facts. 2004. New York: World Almanac Books.

World Bank, WDI Online. World Development Indicators. "Military Expenditure (% of GDP)." http://ddp-ext.worldbank.org/ext/DDPQQ/member.do?method=getMembers&userid=1&queryId=6 (accessed Nov 2009).

World Bank. 1988–1995. *World Development Report*. New York: Oxford University Press.

World Bank. 2001. *World Development Report 2000/2001: Attacking Poverty*. Oxford: Oxford University Press.

World Bank. 2002. *World Development Report 2003: Sustainable Development in a Dynamic World*. Oxford: Oxford University Press.

World Bank. 2009. "Market Capitalization of Listed Companies (Current US$)." *World Development Indicators, Online Databases*. http://web.worldbank.org/WBSITE/EXTERNAL/DATASTATISTICS/0,,contentMDK:20398986~menuPK:64133163~pagePK:64133150~piPK:64133175~theSitePK:239419,00.html (accessed Oct. 2009).

World Values Survey, www.worldvaluessurvey.org/organization/index.html.

Worm, Boris, et al. 2006. "Impacts of Biodiversity Loss on Ocean Ecosystem Services." *Science* 314(3 November):787–90.

Wright, Arthur F. 1977. "The Cosmology of the Chinese City." In *The City in Late Imperial China*, edited by G. William Skinner, pp. 33–73. Stanford, CA: Stanford University Press.

Wright, Erik Olin. 1997. *Class Counts: Comparative Studies in Class Analysis*. Cambridge: Cambridge University Press.

Wright, John W. 1990. *The Universal Almanac.* Kansas City, MO: Andrews & McMeel.

Wyatt, David K. 1968. "Family Politics in Nineteenth Century Thailand." *Journal of Southeast Asian History* 9(2):208–28.

Yalman, Nur. 1963. "On the Purity of Women in the Castes of Ceylon and Malabar." *Journal of the Royal Anthropological Institute* 93:25–58.

Yde, Jens. 1965. *Material Culture of the Waiwai.* Nationalmuseets Skrifter. Ethnografisk Roekke 1-. Copenhagen: National Museum.

Yengoyan, Aram A. 1981. "Infanticide and Birth Order: An Empirical Analysis of Preferential Female Infanticide Among Australian Aboriginal Populations." In *The Perception of Evolution: Essays Honoring Joseph B. Birdsell*, edited by Larry Mai, Eugenia Shanklin, and Robert Sussman, pp. 255–73. Anthropology UCLA, vol. 7, nos. 1 and 2. Los Angeles: Department of Anthropology, University of California.

Yergin, Daniel. 1991. *The Prize: The Epic Quest for Oil, Money & Power.* New York: Simon & Schuster.

Zalasiewicz, Jan, et al. 2008. "Are We Now Living in the Anthropocene?" *GSA Today* 18(2):4–8. Geological Society of America.

Zeder, Melinda A. "Of Kings and Shepherds: Specialized Animal Economy in Ur III Mesopotamia." In *Chiefdoms and Early States in the Near East: The Organizational Dynamics of Complexity*, edited by Gil Stein and Mitchell S. Rothman, pp. 175–91. Madison, WI: Prehistory Press.

Zeitland, Maurice. 1989. *The Large Corporation and Contemporary Classes.* New Brunswick, NJ: Rutgers University Press.

Zettler, Richard L. 1991. "Administration of the Temple of Inanna at Nippur Under the Third Dynasty of Ur: Archaeological and Documentary Evidence." In *The Organization of Power: Aspects of Bureaucracy in the Ancient Near East*, edited by McGuire Gibson and Robert D. Briggs, pp. 101–114. Studies in Ancient Oriental Civilization, No. 46. The Oriental Institute of the University of Chicago.

Zuidema, R. Tom. 1990. *Inca Civilization in Cuzco.* Austin: University of Texas Press.

Index

117–18; of Polynesia, 197–98; of Tukano, 58; of Turkana, 118–19; of U.S., 383–85; Western, 345

costermongers, 364

cousin marriage, 148, *152*

cousins. *See* cross-cousin; parallel cousins

credit, 354, 356; proliferation of, 370

croplands, 422

crop zones, 189

Crosby, Alfred, 465

cross-cousin, 40–41, 61, *89*, 148, 568

Crow kinship system, 154, *155*, 157

Crutzen, Paul, 421–22

cultural anthropology, 4, 21

cultural autonomy alternative, 477–82, *478*, 498, 568

cultural concepts, 11

cultural development, 222

cultural hegemony, 307, 327, 568

culturalism, 276

cultural processes, 10–11

cultural relativity, 18

cultural selection, 10

cultural structure, actual practice compared to, 13

Cultural Survival, 473

cultural transmission, 11, *11*

cultural understanding, as survival skill, 4

culture-bound syndromes, 166–67

culture, cultures, 4, 13, 19, 21; as biological organisms, 136; definitions of, 12, 22, 131, 134, 568; desert, 68–69; familiarity with, 8; genes and, 10; global distribution of, *135*; of Hindu civilization, 306–21; as means of survival, 10; nature and, 12; as possessed by women, 56; scale of, 130–31. *See also* material culture; nonmaterial culture

cuneiform, 230, 236–37, *237*

curacas, *44*, *249*, 251

Cushitic-speaking peoples, 103

cushmas, 4, 7–8, 36, 481

Cuzco, 244, 248

cylinder seals, 232–36, *233*

Danish government development agency, 481

darsan, 315–16

Dawkins, Richard, 134

debt bondage, 476, 498, 568

Deccan Plateau, *294*, 296

Declaration of Barbados, 476

Declaration of Independence, 382, 386

decolonization, 471

deferred exchanges, 54, 61, 568

deficit production, 393, 415, 568

deforestation, 26

deindustrialization, 409, 415, 568

delusion, 14

demand sharing, 86, 95, 568

democracy, 381, 387

Democratic Party, 388

demographic disruption, 467

Denmark, 520, *553*

dental disease, 172

dental health, of tribal cultures, 170–71

dependency, virtues of, 385

deregulation, 433

descent groups, *43*, 52, 61, 113–14, 281, 569; conical, 198; matrilineal, *40*; patrilineal, *40*

desertification, 105–6

deterritorialization of production, 368

development, 420, 454, 479, 543; failure of, 434

deviant behavior, 13

Devil's Lair, *70*

dharma, 303, 322; Brahman view of, 306–11

Dharma Sastra, 318, 324

diabetes, 172

Diamond, Jared, 19, 351–52, 428

Dickens, Charles, 363

diet, of tribal cultures, 170–71

differential benefits, 467, 470

diffusion, 136

digging stick, 82–84

dingo, 83

Dinka, 103, 115

direct participatory democracy, 219

direct rule, 470, 497, 569

disciplinary society, 350, 376, 569

discrimination, 15

disease, 6, 10, 331, *435*; protein-calorie deficiency, 443

disembodied economy, 347, 376, 569

divine guidance, 569

division of labor, global, 349

divorce, 123, 307, 309, 323

DNA molecule, 14

DnB Nor, 555

Domesday Survey of England, 352, 365

domestic livestock, *132*, 148, *149*; advantage of, 101; population density and, 101; variety of, 107. *See also* animal domestication

domestic mode of production, 86, 95, 569

domestic scale, 130, 174, 569

domestic sector, 113

Domhoff, G. William, 410

Dominica, *503*, 504–5, *505*, *506*, 516, 524; development paradox of, 507; GDP of, 506; Kauai compared to, 507–9, *508*; life expectancy on, *517*

Dominican Constitution, 507

Doughty, Paul, 551

Dow, James, 167

dowry, *153*, 357–58

dowry deaths, 325–26

Dravidian languages, 294–95

Dreaming. *See* Australian Dreaming

Dreamtime ancestors, 75

drinking and fighting complex, 51

ghost woman marriage, *110*

giga-economies, 512

giga-nations, *521*

giga-states, 509, *510*

Gillen, Francis, 485

Gilmour, David, 536

Gimbel, James G., 382

glaciers, 425

Gladwin, Thomas, 188

Glass, William, 514

global biological production, 426

global city, 371, 377, 570

global corporations, 371

global crises, cultural response to, 544–45, *545*

Global Island Partnership, 530

globalization, 433, 543, 561

Globalization and World Cities Research Network, 371

global market economy: Chonkiri and, 8; growth of, 337. *See also* market economy

global per capita income, *438*

global population, 1, 131, 334, 341, *343*, 523, 561

global system, 544; collapse, 420–21, *421*; indigenous peoples and, 464–74

global warming, 419, 448–52

glottochronology, 186, 212, 570

GNI. *See* gross national income

GNP. *See* gross national product

goats, 107

Goborgari, 445, *446*

gold, 245–47

Golden Bough, The (Frazer), 163

Gondi, *294*

government, 1, *18*; business of, 388; expenditures, *556*; of indigenous peoples, 488; liturgical, 273–76, 571; personal power over, 13; worker control of, *366*

Government Pension Fund-Global, 555

Government Pension Fund-Norway, 555

Gran Pajonal, 4

Gran Pajonal Asháninka Organization, *463*, *480*

grass seeds, as food source, 80–82

Gray, Andrew, 481

Great Acceleration, 427–28, 455, 543, 570

Great Barrier Reef, 425

Great Dividing Range, 69, 82

Great Tradition, 223, 257, 274, 298, 513, 570; Chinese, 273, 276–77, 283, 288; Hindu, 293–94, *295*, 321; Islamic, 295, *295*, 321–22; Judeo-Christian, 294

Great Transition Initiative, 559–60, 562, 563, 570

Great Wall of China, *267*

Greenberg, Joseph, 15

greenhouse effect, 423, 425

Green Revolution, 395, 415, 570; Bangladesh and, 447–48; input-output structures of, *449*

Gross, Daniel, 442–43

gross domestic product (GDP), 336, 370, 376, 407, 436, 570; of Australia, 491; of Dominica, 506; per capita, *338*; regional distribution of, *339*; of U.S., 431–32, *432*; world, *337*

gross national income (GNI), 336, 429, 555

gross national product (GNP), 336, 376, 436, 570; of Brazil, 442

group identity, 72

growth: under British Empire, 358–75; cost of, 431; creation of, 220; elite-directed, 130, 174, 569; failed promise of, 434–36; of global market economy, 337; paradox of, 335–36; unlimited, 420. *See also* economic growth

growth trajectories, 130–31

Guanches, 465

Guns, Germs, and Steel (Diamond), 19, 351

hacienda, 550, 563, 570

Hadza, 101

Haitians, poverty for, 443

Halaf peoples, 228

hamburger, 400

Hamilton, Alexander, 386, *387*, 388

Hammurabi, King, 236–37

haplogroups, 14

Happy Life Years, 504, 506

Happy Planet Index, 504, 538, 570

Harappa, 297, *299*, 326

Hardin, Garrett, 106

Hardt, Michael, 351, 368–69, *369*

harem, 323

harpy eagle, *57*, 58

Harris, Marvin, 17, 136, 319–20, 397, 400, 409

Hasluck, Paul, 487

Hassan, Fekri, 428

Hawaii, *221*, 516; deities, 205–6; homes in, 205; life expectancy on, *517*; nobility in, 209–10; oral and documentary history of, 203–4; reef zones of, 203; rituals of, 206; sacrificial consecration in, 206–7; social power distribution in, 204–5; Tikopia compared to, 203; wicker-work helmet, *209*

Hawaiian Kingdom: filiation in, 210; gender relations in, 208–9; polygyny in, 205, 210; social classes of, 208; social structure of, *204*, 211

Hawaiian kinship system, 48, 154, *155*, *211*

Hawaiians, Sahlins on, 199

Hayek, Friedrich A., 385

HDI. *See* Human Development Index

headman, 61, 570; authority of, 46, *46*; position of, 46; power of, 45–46; responsibilities of, 43, 45; skills of, 45–46. *See also* bigman

health, measurements of, 20–21

hearth-hold, 113

Henry, Jules, 401

herders, as capitalists, 117

Herskovits, Melville, 105
heterogeneity, 560, 564, 570
Heyerdahl, Thor, 184
Hiatt, L. R., *89*
hierarchy, *146*; age, 93; in Amazonia, 144; of Asháninka people, *146*; decimal-based, 251; in Hindu kingdom, *300*; of human needs, 20; of Matsigenka people, *146*; political, 225; ruler status, *222*; in Tikopia, *202*
high-net-worth individuals, 373, 434, 438
high shamanism, 270
high-yield variety (HYV), 445, 448, 455, 570
Himalayas, *294*, 296
Hindu ascetic, *309*
Hindu civilization, *308*; aesthetics of, 315–18; building specifications in, 310, *311*; cosmology of, *313*; culture of, 306–21; early, 297–306; eating in, 312–14; food cycles in, 312, *313*; food in, 312–14; functional diversification within, *303*; ideology of, 306–21; law in, 303–5; legal fines in, 303–4, *304*; marriage in, 307, 309; organization of, 299; population model of, *301*; settlement hierarchy in, *300*; social composition of, 301; society and, 306–21; state finance in, 301–2, *302*; theft in, 304–5. *See also* caste
Hindu Great Tradition, 293–94, *295*, 321
Hindu Kush mountains, 296
Hindu laborer, *308*
Hindu merchants, *308*
Hindu temple, *316*, *317*
History of Human Marriage (Westermark), 287
Hobbes, Thomas, 84, 345
Holmberg, Allan, 550–51
homicide, 115
Homo erectus, 14, *271*
homogeneity, 509
Homo sapiens, 10, 14, 75
horizontal transmission, 136
horses, *149*
horticulture, 33
household, 10, 32, 61, 570; Asháninka, *45*; size, 225; Thai, *305*; in U.S., *410*
household groups, 39
household structures, 9
House of Lim, The (Wolf, M.), 285
How the Other Half Lives (Riis), 406
Hsu, Francis, 385
huacas, 248, 252
Huanaco Pampa, 253–55, *255*
Hubbert, M. King, 452
Hubbert's Peak, 452, *453*
Human Development Index (HDI), 429, *430*, *431*, 506, 518, *521*, 538, 570; World Bank and, 430–31
humanization, 10–11, *11*, 17, 21–22, 136, 335, 570
Human Relations Area Files, 134
human sacrifice, 238, 269
humus, 189

hunter-gatherer societies, 144, 146
hunting, 50; of Asháninka, 39; virility and, 46
Hurricane Katrina, 451
Hutton, J. H., 314
Hwang Ho River, *266*
hypergamy, 307, 326, 327, 570
hypogamy, 307, 327
HYV. *See* high-yield variety

Iceland, *553*, 554–55
idealist, 484, 498, 570
ideals *v.* reality, 382
ideological power, 13, *13*, 408; redistribution of, 546
ideology, *18*, 513; of Hindu civilization, 306–21
ignorance, 435
illusion, 14
imagined communities, 350, 376, 570
imam, 322
immaterial production, 351, 377, 570
immediate-return systems, 92
immigration, 363, 405
Immigration Nation, 382
immiseration, 278–80, 289, 570
imperia (imperium), 13, 22, 193, 570–71; under British Empire, *363*; of Norman England, *353*; personal, 220, *221*, 407–11; of Ur III empire, *235*
imperial cultures, 4, 17, *18*, 20, *344*; cultural processes and subprocesses of, *11*; economic power in, 334; farming systems of, 33; inequality measures in, 137; irrigated agriculture and, 142; rulers in, *13*; size of, 219; social class in, *139*; tribal cultures compared to, 227
imperialism, 20
imperial subjects, 179
impurity, 309, 327, 571. *See also* purity
Inanna, Temple of, 233
Inca agricultural terraces, *256*
Inca empire, 240, *242*, 242–55, 475; peak of, 241
Inca people, 142, *221*, *254*; bureaucracy and, 249, 252; chosen women of, 248–51; complexity rating of, 143, *143*; copper blades of, *246*; cosmology of, 252–53; kinship and, 250–51; labor force organization of, *248*; Mesopotamia and, 257; rank of, 241
Inca rulers, distribution of, *249*
Inca trade, 39
incest avoidance, *89*, 117
inclusive fitness, 54, 61, 571
income: capital value of, 38; distribution, *437*; global per capita, *438*; U.S. median, 432; wealth compared to, 436–38. *See also* gross national income
incorporation, 467
increase ceremonies, 75
India, 296, 509; armies in, 302; official languages of, 294–95; political rulers in, 300; wealth redistribution in, 548–50
Indian, 464

plutocracy, *442*, 455, 572
plutocrats, 407–8
plutonomy, 438–41, *442*, 455, 572
political autonomy, 43
political centralization, 137
political complexity, *197*
political economy, 210, 212, 572
political hierarchy, 225
political power, 13, *13*; centralization of, 219
political scale, 130, 174, 572
political sector, 113
politicization, *11*, 17, 21, 22, 136, 219, 335, 343, 572; chiefdoms and, 196–97; China and, 386; commercialization and, 368; growth and, 196; tribal cultures and, 131
polity, *18*
polyandry, *151*, 210, 212, 572
polygyny, 45, 91, 95, *110*, 123, 148, *151*, 158, 572; in Hawaiian Kingdoms, 205, 210; incentive for, 46; pastoralism and, 119; sororal, 210, 212, 573
Polynesia, *183*; conical descent groups of, 198; cosmology of, 197–98; elite-directed cultural transformation in, 194–95; islands of, 182, 184; ranks in, 198
polytheism, 239, 258, *318*, 572
populated forests, 27
population, 137, *435*; Andean, 243; Asháninka, 10, 33; distribution, *437*; founder, 194; global, 1, 131, 334, 341, *343*, 523, 561; of indigenous peoples, *466*; low-density, 33; Matsigenka, 33
population density, 1, 34, 70; domestic livestock and, 101
population growth, 46, *46*, 131, 228, 341–42, 358, 522–23; in China, 278–79, *279*, 288; in Pacific Islands, 194; poverty and, 454; regulation of, 171; in tribal cultures, 171
Pospisil, Leopold, *273*
postmaterialist, 518, 538, 572
postmodernity, 350, 368, 376–77, 572
postpartum sex taboo, 168, 171
potatoes, 245–47
pottery, 19; Lapita, 185, *186*; of Shipibo, 50–51
poverty, 331, 343, 419, 429, *435*, 437, 454; under British Empire, 358–75; ending, 523–24; in Fiji, 533–34; in Haiti, 443; population growth and, 454; urban, 404–6
Poverty Reduction Strategy Program, 444
power, 13, 196; coercive, 218; concentration of, 195; decentralized, 524–28; desire for, 385; dominance and, 52–53; of headman, 45–46; in herding societies, 116–17; ranks, *222*; scale solutions and, 545–47; sugar and, 360. *See also* economic power; elite power; ideological power; military power; personal power networks; political power; social power
power-elite hypothesis, 131
Price, Weston, 171
primary tribal sections, *114*
primate social instincts, 193

Primitive Culture (Tylor), 12, 163
primogeniture, 198, 212, 572
private sector, 384
production, 1; by Asháninka, 36; biopolitical, 351, 377, 567; capitalist, 345, 376, 568; deficit, 393, 415, 568; deterritorialization of, 368; domestic mode of, 86, 95, 569; exchange and, 344–45; global biological, 426; global transformation of, 340; immaterial, 351, 377, 570; kin-ordered, 344, 376, 571; of manioc, 30, 32; mass, 390; net primary, 426; in small nations, 522; tributary, 344–45, 376, 574. *See also* food production
progress, meaning of, 19
proletariat, *365*
Prophet Muhammad, 322
prostration tabu, 206
protein-calorie deficiency diseases, 443
protein intake, of Amazonians, 34
Protestant Ethic and the Spirit of Capitalism, The (Weber), 349
Proto-Austronesian culture, 185
Proto-Austronesian language, *187*
prototribes, 193
psychopathology, shaman and, 165–66
public sector, 384
punishments, 250; social status and, 237
Punjabi, *294*
purchasing power parity, 336, 376, 436, 506, 572
purdah system, 323–25, 448
purity, 307, 309, 327, 573. *See also* impurity
Purusha myth, 309–10, *311*

quality of life, 196, 430, 560–61
Quinlan, Marsha and Robert, 504
quinoa, 243
quipu, 143, 248, *251–52*

race, cultural construction of, 14–15
racism, 19, 349
Radcliffe-Brown, A. R., 72, 134, 136, 161, 470
Radin, Paul, 343
raiding, 46, *46*, 53–54, 60, 115, 124; mortality and, 171–72
railroads, 390
Rainbow Serpent, 168
rain forest, 27; biological productivity of, 26; economic value of, 38
Rama, *325*
Ramanatobue, Josaia, 535
Ramayana, *325*
rangelands, 422
rank, 181, 212, 573; in Amazonia, 144; of Asháninka, 144; economic, *430*, *431*; of Inca peoples, 241; of Matsigenka, 144; in Mesopotamia, 234; in Polynesia, 198; power, *222*; social power and, 305
rank endogamy, 28, 144, *146*
rasa, 315

Raskin, Paul, 559–62
rationalism, 350
ration system, *236*
Ravenga, 200, *201*
realist, 484, 498, 573
reality testing, 14
reciprocal gift, *153*
reciprocity, 92, 220
Reconciliation Australia, 488
Redfield, Robert, 289, 569
redistribution, 198, 212, 573
Redman, Charles, 228
Regional Organization of the Indigenous Peoples of AIDESEP-Ucayali, *463*, 479, *480*
Registrar of Indigenous Corporations, 493
Reichel-Dolmatoff, Gerardo, 58
reindeer, *149*
reindustrialization, 562–63
religion, 237–39, 321–22. *See also* animism; animistic thinking
Rengifo, Manuel, 58
representative democracy, 219–20
reproduction, 58
Republican Party, 388
residence. *See* ambilocality; avunculocality; matrilocal residence; neolocal residence; patrilocality
resilience, foraging and, 71
resources, 1; consumption of, 131; depletion, 86; overuse, 529; regulation of, 75
respect, 8
revealed religion, 321–22
revenge killing, 60
Ribeiro, Darcy, 474, 476
rice, 277–78, 393; HYV, 445, 448
Riis, Jacob, 406
Rio Tinto Group, 492
rites of passage, *93*, 95, 573
ritualized combat, 46, *46*
ritualized rebellion against parents, 122
rivalry, 199
riverine environment, *29*; village size and, 46
Rockdale, Pennsylvania, 390–92, 414
Rockefeller, John D., 404, 411
Rockefeller dynasty, 411–13, *412, 413*
Rockefeller Foundation, 411–12, 486
Rockefeller-Morgan commercial imperia, *405*
Roe, Peter, 51, *57*, 58, *59*
Roseto villagers, 410
Rostow, Walt, 436
Rothschild family, 356, *356–57*
Roy, Manisha, 324
rulers, in imperial cultures, *13*
ruler status hierarchies, *222*
Russia, *226*

saccharine disease, 171
Sacred Cow Complex, 319–20. *See also* cattle; Cattle Complex
sacred flute myth, 52, 168
sacred sites, 75–76
sagina, 232, *233*
Saharan Pastoralism, *103*
Sahlins, Marshall, 84–86, 114, 136, 345, 400–401; on Hawaiians, 199
Sahul Shelf, 69, *70*
sailing, Pacific islanders, 185
Saint Helena, 514–18, *515, 517, 525*
Sakti, 317
Samhita Vedas, 297
samsara, 307, *318*, 321
sanction, *273*
Sandel, Michael, 20
Sapir, Edward, 15
Sapir-Whorf hypothesis, 14–15, 22, 573
Sargon the Great, *231*
Sassens, Saskia, 371
sati, 309, 326
Saudi Arabia, *226*
Savagery, 19, 464
scale solutions, power and, 545–47
scale subsidy, 235, 258, 431–34, 573
scale theory, 514
scapulimancy, 270, *271*, 289, 573
schemas, 134
Scheper-Hughes, Nancy, 441–43, 549
schizophrenia, 166
science of the concrete, 165, 174, 573
S corporation, 558–59, *559*
sea-level rise, 451
secondary tribal sections, *114*
section system, 88, *89*, 95, 573
sedentarization, 60, *230*
segmentary lineage system, 115, 125, 573
self-actualization, 518
self-determination, 484, 498, 573
self-immolation, 309
self-sacrifice, 12
seme, 134, 136
Semitic language, 295
serfs, 352–53
Service Worker Centers, 382
settlements: dense, 422; permanence of, 33; size of, 33, 46
sex, 317; in myth, 56
sexual antagonism, 56, 58
sexual competition, 46
shaman, 55, 61, 270, *477*, 573; jaguar, 59–60; psychopathology and, 165–66
shamanic paradox, 167
Shang China, *133, 269*; as slave society, 273
Shang Dynasty, 268–71; divisions of, 272–73

Shang society, *272*, 272–73
sharing, 7
sheep, 107, *149*
Shell Oil, 370–71, 440, 452
shifting cultivation, 30, *31*, 32, 146, 157, 277
Shipibo people, 28, *29*, 30, *31*, 46–51, 142, 143, *143*;
    Asháninka-Matsigenka people compared to, 38–39;
    big drinking ceremony, 51–52; fisherman's catch, 48,
    50; kinship terminology of, 154; material culture
    of, 50–51; pottery of, 50–51; preferred foods of,
    171
Shulgi, *231*
sibling-exchange marriage system, 41, *41*
Siddhartha Gautama, 321
Silverman, Julian, 166
sim-pua marriage, 287
Sino-Tibetan language, 264, 294–95
Sioux Indians, 170–71
El Sira Communal Reserve, 482, *483*
sisal workers, 442–43
sister-exchange, *153*, 154
Sita, 324, *325*
Siva, *299*, 317, *318*, *319*
Skinner, G. William, 281
slash and burn agriculture, 30, 61, 200, 573
slaughter weight, 399–400
slavery, 137, 304; occurrence of, *141*; sugar and, 359–62
slum landlords, 405
small economies, 512–13
small island developing states, 528–31, 539, 573
small nations, 503–4, *511*, *519*, *521*, 531, 538, 573; carbon
    goals for, *525*, *526*; as cultural type, 509–14; economy
    of, 512–13; life expectancy for, *517*, 520–21, *521*;
    national resource production in, 522; success of,
    519–20, *520*, 538; well-being of, 518–21
small states, 509, *510*
small stature, as adaptive response, 169
Small Tool Tradition, 83
Smith, Adam, 345, 359, 362, 375, 383, 554; on infant
    mortality, 441
Smith, Elisha D., 559
Smith, Richard Chase, 480–81
Smith, Wilberforce, 170–71
social cages, 219
social class distinctions, 137, *139*, *140*, 199, 212, 573; in
    China, 274; in London, *364*
social cohesion, 20–21
social Darwinism, 161, 174, 440, 573
social equity, *435*
social grooming, 11
social groupings, 12
social intelligence, 11, 22, 573
socialization, *11*
socially transmitted behavior, 10
social norms, 20

social power, 13, 22, 71, 130–31, 407–11, 573; civilization
    and, 218; concentration and dissipation of, 78, *223*;
    cultural organization of, *13*; diffusion of, 547; disparity,
    428–29; distribution of, 411; equitable distribution of,
    20; in Hawaii, 204–5; organization of, 21; rank and, 305;
    redistribution of, 545–46; types of, *13*; in Ur III, 232–36
social product, 234, 258, 573
social scale, 33, *546*
social solidarity, 16, *94*
social status, 198, 212, 573; acceptance of, 211–12;
    punishment and, 237
social stratification, 181, 199, 212, 228, 5*7*3
social structure, Australian Dreaming and, 71–75
social unit, family as, 10–11
societies of control, 351, 377, 573
society, *18*; Asháninka, 39–43; clan-based, 114; of control,
    377, 573; disciplinary, 350, 376, 569; Hindu civilization
    and, 306–21; hunter-gatherer, 144, 146; information,
    371, 377, 571; network, 371; Nuer, 109–13; Pacific
    Islands, 193–211; planetary, 560, 564, 572; scale of, *222*;
    Shang, *272*, 272–73
Society for Applied Anthropology Code of Ethics, 19
sociocultural growth, 130–31
sociocultural systems, 38–54, 70–71; evaluating, 18–21;
    functional organization of, 17–18
soil fertility: of Amazon basin, 33–34; in China, 277
Solomon and Company, 516
Soltow, Lee, 403
sororal polygyny, 210, 212, 573
sororate marriage, 210, 212, 573
soul: of animals, 55–56; concept of, 55, 59–60
South Alligator River, 69
South America, complexity in, 140–44
South Asia: environments of, 296; history of, *296*;
    languages of, *294*, 294–97; lithic tools of, 296–97;
    Neolithic, 297; prehistory of, 294–97, *296*; women in,
    321–27
South Asian culture area, 294–97
South Asian geography, *294*, 294–97
South Asian languages, *294*, 294–97
South West Aboriginal Land and Sea Council, 496
spear, 82–84, *85*
spear-thrower, 83, *83*
specialists, 205, 212, 244, 573
specialization, *11*, 17, 236
Special Report on Emissions Scenarios, SRES, 451–52, 552
speech: purpose of, 11; Tylor on, 11–12; use of, 10. *See also*
    languages
Spencer, Baldwin, 485
Spencer, Paul, 119
spirit beings, 56, 72
Spondylus shells, 244, *246*
SPREP, South Pacific Regional Environment Program, 534
Sri Lanka, 294, 296
Stages of Economic Growth, The (Rostow), 436

yam, 189, *190*
Yanesha (Amuesha), 479–80
Yanomami, *29*, 169
yin-yang, *283*, 288
Yin-Yang Movement, 562
Yolngu, 77
Yolngu land tenure system, 78

Youth Action for a New Globalization, 562
Youth International Network, 562

Zanzibar, 103
Zebu, 103
Zhoukoudian, *271*
Ziggurat of Ur, 237, *238*

About the Author

John H. Bodley (M.A., Ph.D. 1970, University of Oregon) is Regents Professor of anthropology at Washington State University where he has taught since 1970. His research interests include indigenous peoples, cultural ecology, and contemporary issues with an emphasis on complexity, scale, and power. Bodley conducted field research with the Asháninka, Conibo, and Shipibo indigenous groups in the Peruvian Amazon throughout his early career. He has visited other indigenous groups in Alaska, Australia, Ecuador, Guatemala, Mexico, and the Philippines. He has held visiting academic appointments at the University of Alaska, Fairbanks (1986), and the University of Uppsala, Sweden (1985). He was a visiting researcher at the International Work Group for Indigenous Affairs in Copenhagen (1980). In 1986, Dr. Bodley served on the Tasaday Commission for the University of the Philippines Department of Anthropology in Manila. He was a member (1991–1994) of the advisory subcommittee for the human rights section of the American Association for the Advancement of Science's Committee on Scientific Freedom and Responsibility. He is also the author of *The Power of Scale* (2003), *Anthropology and Contemporary Human Problems* (2008), and *Victims of Progress* (2008).